The Moneywise Guide to North America

This unique, traveller-centred guide first appeared in 1964 as the *Guide to the New World* and contained just 64 pages! Since then, tens of thousands of users and contributors later, it has become the most sought-after guidebook for the budget traveller who wants to see and experience all that the North American continent has to offer and do it on a shoestring!

The *Moneywise Guide* continues to be the only guidebook covering all three countries of North America in one sensible-size volume. It remains the only guide that covers not only all the usual cities and tourist areas of North America, but also those lesser-known cities, towns and communities which form natural waypoints on the major travel routes.

Ideal for the budget traveller, whether just passing through or staying a while, the *Moneywise Guide* will inform you, entertain you and above all, save you money.

Where to stay—budget accommodation tested, assessed and updated by the users, checked by the editors. Small downtown hostels, economy motels, YMCAs, youth hostels, bed and breakfasts, tourist homes, how to book a night and how to find them on the internet.

Where not to stay—'no-go' areas, seedy spots, and places to avoid.

Where to eat—the latest in 'mean cuisine' for those who still buy their meals with cash, not plastic.

What to see and do—the sights you'll want to see and the things you will want to do, from Disneyland to national parks, to museums and art galleries; to entertainment, sport, beaches, shopping – all across the continent. Hundreds of free attractions listed.

General information—the most comprehensive 'General' section of any guide to North America. How to get there to visit or to work, what to take, what to wear; visas, insurance and other paperwork; immigration, people and customs; climate and health; driving, hiking and other forms of low-budget travel plus where to get further information including access to the internet.

"One of the most invaluable things to me on my travels in the USA was this comprehensive and informative guide book. The book contains little gems of information that otherwise would remain unknown to travellers like me. I really wouldn't have been without it."

About the authors:

Anna Crew is British and works for BUNAC in Connecticut. She is the director of BUNAC'S camp counsellor programme, *Summer Camp USA*, and responsible for many of BUNAC's publications including the *Moneywise Guide*.

Nicholas Ludlow is also British and based in Washington DC. An inveterate traveller throughout North America and the world at large, Nick is a freelance writer and editor and specialist in the economics of developing countries. He is responsible for the Background Canada section this edition and the chapters on Alberta, British Columbia, the Territories, and Quebec.

Gokce Akkoclu from Izmir, Turkey, received her MBA in International Business from Baruch College in New York in 2005. Gok started writing short stories when she was 13. She has lived and stayed all over the US including California, Florida, Washington DC and New York.

Susan Brown lives in Maryland and has been (at various times) an English teacher, clinical social worker, and journal editor. In her free time, she is either travelling, up and down the coasts of the US, Canada, Mexico, Europe, Australia and New Zealand, or researching intriguing ideas for future trips.

Laurie Chamberlain was born in New York City and has travelled extensively across the US. She recently moved to Washington, DC where she is working in international development.

Melanie Gedge is studying Law at Cambridge University and intends to pursue a Masters' degree in the US. She has travelled extensively in North America, including a Gap Year at a High School in Virginia. Melanie speaks French and German, has a great interest in Trans-Atlantic relations, and hopes to pursue a legal career with an international aspect.

Laurel Schwartz is an undergraduate at the University of Pittsburgh.

Acknowledgements The editors thank the following for their assistance, contributions, and suggestions – Alan Anderson, Jill Bogard, Judith Britten, Jim Buck, Lorna and David Evans, Jo Haynes, Tony Harvey, Christine Herron, Philippa Howe-Ivain, Justin Johnson, Sarah Leavesley, Oliver and Val Ludlow, Normand Marceau, Joan Schwartz and Jacqueline and Peter Sinclair.

Last and very far from least, the editors thank the many readers who have sent in comments and contributions.

2006

MONEYWISE
GUIDE
to North America

The USA, Canada
and selected Mexico

EDITORS:
Anna Crew and Nicholas Ludlow

RESEARCH AND REVISION:

Gokce Akkoclu, Susan Brown, Laurie Chamberlain, Melanie Gedge,
Laurel Schwartz

THE MONEYWISE GUIDE TO NORTH AMERICA
36th Edition

© Copyright BUNAC 2006

Published by BUNAC Travel Services Ltd,
16 Bowling Green Lane, London EC1R 0QH

British Library Cataloguing in Publication Data
Moneywise Guide to North America: USA,
Canada, Mexico. – 36 ed
  I. Crew, Anna   II. Ludlow, Nicholas H.
  917.04
  ISBN: 0-9552350-0-6

General Editors: Anna L. Crew and Nicholas H. Ludlow.

Research and Revision: Gokce Akkoclu, Susan Brown, Laurie Chamberlain,
Melanie Gedge, Nicholas Ludlow and Laurel Schwartz

Cover design: Randak Design Consultants Limited, Glasgow, Scotland
Design and maps: Vera Brice; Randak Design Consultants Limited.

Printed and bound in Great Britain by The Bath Press, Lower Bristol Road,
Bath BA2 3BL.

Contents

THE FUTURE OF THIS GUIDE

Quoted comments throughout the *Guide* are genuine remarks made by users over the years. Comments from present readers, the more descriptive the better, are welcome for the next edition.

For brief comments and most importantly for correcting or adding information about accommodation, fares and so on, please use the **Amendment** slips at the back of the *Guide*. Hotel brochures, local bus schedules, maps and similar tidbits are gratefully received. Also welcome are longer accounts, so feel free to send in letters about your travels and any new places you may discover.

In all cases, please write only on one side of each sheet of paper. Thank you for your help and Happy Travels!

One of the most amazing things about travelling in North America is that the experience invariably turns out to be so different from what you had expected. Everyone thinks that they have a good idea of what the American continent is like. American technology, politics, media and entertainments daily make their mark around the world. More than ever, North America is the most publicised continent on earth.

But the projected image frequently hides, both from foreigners and North Americans themselves, a largely still undiscovered continent. The polyglot of peoples out of which Canada, the United States and Mexico are each differently formed can make Europe, for example, look comparatively homogeneous. Just a ride on the New York City or Toronto subways is enough to convince you of that.

Then there is the land itself. Coast to coast and north to south, the ever-changing landscape is little short of amazing. There are huge tracts of magnificent landscapes, unsettled and hardly explored: forests, glaciers, deserts and jungles; mountains, canyons, prairies, vast lakes and seashores; orchards in Oregon, farming valleys in Vermont, pre-Columbian Indian settlements, many of them unchanged and still inhabited, in Mexico and Arizona, totem poles in British Columbia, fishing villages in Nova Scotia.

Anchoring it all are the large cities, the hubs of North American life and culture: Los Angeles, an exploding star in the far west; San Francisco riding on a sea of hills; New York, a concrete canyon and focus of world attention after September, 2001; Washington DC, political heart of the nation; Chicago scraping the sky with the longest fingers in the world, Houston, a port and rocket centre; New Orleans blowing jazz across the Mississippi; Toronto and Montreal, modern, international and exciting – the new Canada; Québec only geographically in the New World, its soul still back across the Atlantic; Vancouver, Canada's golden gateway to the Pacific; and Mexico City a brilliant mosaic of Spanish and Aztec design. In between is the 'heartland', made up thousands of smaller cities, towns and communities, each with its own distinctive character and way of life.

The reality, variety and complexity of it all are more than a lifetime of sitting in front of a television set, or searching on the internet could even remotely convey to you. There is the excitement and discovery too of the instant, of the future, for in North America you feel you are reaching ahead and in the running to be where it matters. You've seen the movies, read the books; it's time to 'live' the dream for yourself.

About the *Moneywise Guide*

This is a guide to most of the usual and many of the unusual places in North America and should prove of service to anyone, but most of all to the moneywise traveller. North America can be an expensive continent if you let it, but its great variety offers places to eat and sleep and different ways of moving about to suit every pocket. With the help of this guide it can be a real bargain. Anyone who is happy about spending more money will easily find a $90 hotel bed and a $40 meal, in which case this guide is content with showing you the way to the Statue of Liberty or the Grand Canyon. For people really on a budget, this is also a guide to thousands of inexpensive places to rest your head, eat cheaply and well *and* get you to the Grand Canyon on a shoestring.

In separate sections this *Guide* covers the USA, Canada and parts of Mexico. General introductions precede the coverage of each country. Make a point of first reading these background chapters. Here you will find general information on each country, facts about visas, currency, health and other matters, money-saving tips on eating, accommodation and travel. *Note that much of the general travel information found in the US Background section will also be of value for travel to Canada and Mexico.*

Each country is then divided into regions, e.g. The Midwest, and in the case of the USA and Canada, states and provinces within each region follow *alphabetically*. There is an index at the back of the *Guide*.

Hotel and restaurant listings are the result of research and the first-hand experience of the *Guide*'s authors and its readers since the preceding edition. Please note therefore that comments in the book are based on personal opinion and your own individual experience and opinion may be different. Please don't hesitate to forward your comments and experiences to: *Moneywiseguide@bunacusa.org.*

Prices quoted are usually the lowest available. However, within the same month at the same hotel, one traveller might spend more on a room than another. This is usually because the rooms were of different standards, but never be afraid to question room rates or even to bargain over them. You should also allow for inflation when budgeting for the trip. It is therefore probably advisable to allow more for the overall cost of accommodation than the rates printed here would indicate. Similarly it should be remembered that all travel/vacation costs tend to rise each year in North America and so it is quite possible that prices will change after the *Guide* has gone to print. Apologies if this happens but note that all information in this book is correct at press time.

Please be aware that the maps in this *Guide* are only intended to give you a rough orientation—an artist's impression almost—when first arriving in the city. They are not, nor are they intended to be, fully comprehensive. If staying anywhere for any length of time, buy a good street map, though first see if you can get one free from the local tourist office.

Accommodation listing abbreviations: S = single; D = double; T = triple; Q = quad; XP = extra person in room; Bfast = breakfast; facs = facilities; AC = air conditioning; ess = essential; rec = recommended; nec = necessary.

1. USA

BACKGROUND

Before you go

Unless you plan to enter the USA under the *Visa Waiver Program*, which allows visitors to the US for less than 90 days to apply for entry permission on arrival, you must obtain an entry visa before departing. Check with your airline or travel agent about this and note that, although correct at the time of writing, the US Government may alter these provisions in the future. See *http://travel.state.gov* for the latest accurate information.

As a reader of this *Guide*, you will probably be on the *Exchange Visitor Visa (J) Programme*, which is for non-immigrant exchange visitors and obtainable only through an approved, sponsoring organisation. The terms are specific. J-1 participants can work, study, train, research or lecture, depending on individual programme conditions, for a specified period of time.

On entry to the US, immigration officials ask you the purpose of your visit and how long you plan to stay. If your visa permits you to work, say so. In answer to the question: How long do you plan to stay? Immigration officials are looking for proof of planning. As a reader of this *Guide*, you're probably on a budget anyway. Immigration officials want to know how you're going to manage. You need to show them things like your return ticket home; rail, air and bus passes; accommodation reservations; student or senior identification. If you plan to stay in campsites, hostels, guest houses or with friends, tell them. If you have credit cards, show them. Immigration officials will usually ask for the address of your first night's accommodation. They will also take a photo of you, and scan your fingerprints. *Be aware that the US Government is tightening up on all visa and US entry procedures. Allow plenty of time to apply for a visa and expect costs to increase.*

Customs permit foreign residents to bring in one litre of spirits or wine (provided you are 21 or over), 200 cigarettes or 100 cigars (not Havana) or two kg of tobacco or proportionate amounts of each , $100 worth of gifts provided you stay at least 72 hours and have not claimed the gift exemption in the previous six months, and your personal effects free of duty. You may not bring in fruits, dairy products or meats.

For additional details on visa, health and customs regulations, contact the nearest American embassy or consulate or visit *www.usembassy.org.uk*.

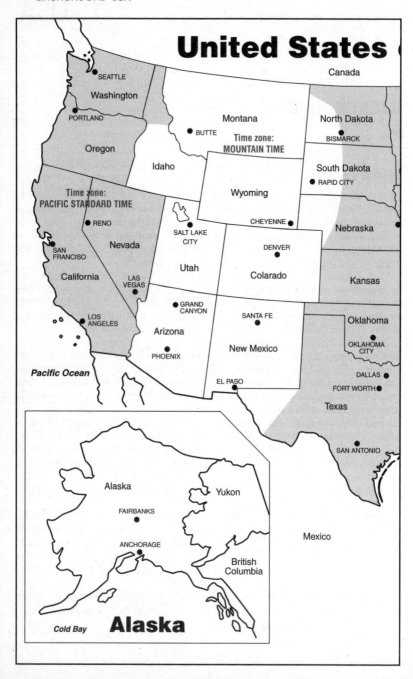

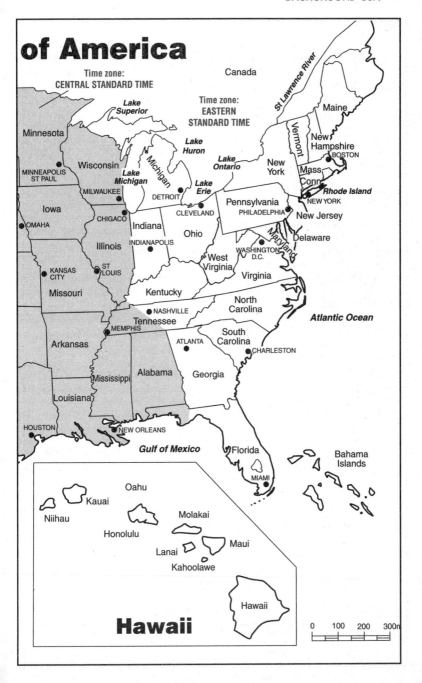

# of America

Time zone:
CENTRAL STANDARD TIME

Canada

Time zone:
EASTERN STANDARD TIME

St Lawrence River

Lake Superior

Maine

Lake Huron

Vermont

Minnesota

New Hampshire

● BOSTON

Lake Michigan

Michigan

Wisconsin

Lake Ontario

New York

Mass.

Conn.

Lake Erie

Rhode Island

MINNEAPOLIS ST PAUL ●

NEW YORK ●

MILWAUKEE ●

DETROIT

Pennsylvania

Iowa

CHIGACO ●

CLEVELAND ●

PHILADELPHIA ●

New Jersey

OMAHA ●

Indiana

Ohio

Delaware

Illinois

INDIANAPOLIS ●

WASHINGTON D.C. ●

Maryland

KANSAS CITY ●

ST LOUIS ●

West Virginia

Virginia

Missouri

Kentucky

North Carolina

NASHVILLE ●

Tennessee

MEMPHIS ●

Atlantic Ocean

Arkansas

South Carolina

ATLANTA ●

CHARLESTON ●

Mississippi

Alabama

Georgia

Louisiana

HOUSTON ●

NEW ORLEANS ●

Gulf of Mexico

● Florida

Bahama Islands

MIAMI ●

Oahu

Kauai

Molakai

Niihau

Honolulu

Lanai

Maui

Kahoolawe

Hawaii

Hawaii

0   100   200   300m

Temporary work

Doubtless many people do work in 'underground jobs' such as casual labour, fruit harvesting, farm work, restaurant work, etc., but if you are contemplating this you should be aware of the risks involved. The penalties you would be likely to incur include deportation, with the knowledge that you would have to face an extremely uphill task should you ever want to return to America again. You should also be aware that the terms of the recent Immigration Act mean that an employer hiring an illegal alien faces stiff penalties if caught. This of course acts as a deterrent should an employer be contemplating the possibility and lessens the chances of employment for someone without a work visa.

What to take and how to take it

Take as little as possible; choose clothes for their use in a variety of situations and when you have made your final selection, halve it! It is always a nuisance to have too much and anyway, if necessary, you can purchase what you need in America. American stores offer many shopping bargains for visitors. In particular, items like jeans, shirts, T-shirts and casual clothes are good buys in the US. Nation-wide department stores, such as *Hechts*, *Kohl's*, and *JC Penney* are well-known for their sales: Hint - they always have one!

  Laundromats are often open 24 hours a day. The cost of a wash is usually $1.50 (in quarters); drying machines usually take 25¢—just keep feeding in the quarters, total per load is about $1.25.

   Whatever luggage you take, make sure it's easy to handle. Getting on and off buses and trains, even just changing planes, can be an ordeal if your bags are too heavy or too many. The best solution is to take one hold-all, be it a suitcase or a backpack, and then a smaller bag which you can sling from your shoulder. When you have to check in your hold-all at the airport or bus station, you must keep all your documents, travellers' cheques and your paperback novel safely and conveniently by your side. It is also a good idea to keep a change of clothing in your shoulder bag in case your suitcase/backpack gets lost by an airline or bus company or your flight is delayed. Beware of lower weight limits for luggage on domestic flights.

  For extra security many travellers also wear a neck (or belt) wallet/pouch for passport, cash, travellers' cheques and other valuables. It is also a good idea to photocopy your passport and other important documents and keep the copies SEPARATE from the originals. Should you lose your passport you should immediately contact your nearest national consulate (British consulates are in Atlanta, Boston, Chicago, Houston, Los Angeles, New York, San Francisco, and Washington DC).

  Whether you are planning on driving in the USA or not, it is a good idea to bring your driver's license with you for use as photo ID. Taking your passport everywhere is sometimes risky, and a University student ID is not always recognised.

  Some tips: at bus stations in particular, make absolutely certain that your bag is going on your bus and that you get a check-in ticket for it. You would be amazed at the number of times bag and body go off in different directions. And if you're a backpacker just arrived in a big city, you can usually leave your pack at one of the museums for free and then skip off to look for a room or do a little sightseeing unencumbered.

Climate

Remember that you are not travelling over a country but across a vast continent and that the climate varies accordingly. Indoors, these differences are minimised by central heating and air conditioning. Temperatures approaching 90°F (32°C) day after day, sometimes accompanied by a suffocating humidity, are not unusual in the summer. Pollen counts can be high too in summer on the East Coast. New York, Washington DC, New Orleans and the Deep South can be particularly unpleasant. You can always check the current and projected future weather conditions for any city (or zip code) in North America on _www.weather.com_.

New England, the Northeast, Mid-Atlantic and Midwest. Cold in the winter, often very humid in the summer and as hot as anywhere else in America.

The Southwest. Warm to really hot throughout the year, and nearly always dry.

The Pacific States. Washington, Oregon and northern California have moderate climates: not too cold in the winter-though often wet, not too hot in the summer. San Francisco is often bathed in summer afternoon fogs. Southern California is warm to hot the year round, and nearly always dry.

The South. Hot with thunderstorm activity in summer, mild in winter though agreeably warm in Florida. Summer is also the hurricane season, which can be vicious.

The Mountains. In summer, days are warm but nights can be cold. Very cold throughout the winter.

The Deserts. Very hot and dry throughout the year, but can be cold at night.

Time zones: The continental US is divided into four time zones, Eastern Standard Time, Central Standard Time, Mountain Standard Time and Pacific Standard Time. Exact zone boundaries are shown on most road maps.

Noon EST= 11am CST =10am MST =9am PST. Standard time in Alaska is one hour earlier than PST (i.e. 9am PST=8am AST) and Hawaii is two hours earlier than PST (i.e. 9am PST=7am HST). Daylight Savings Time occurs widely though not universally throughout the United States; from the end of April to the end of October, clocks are put forward one hour. Carefully check air, rail and bus schedules in advance.

City temperatures (in Fahrenheit)		Jan-Feb	Mar-Apr	May-June	Jul-Aug	Sep-Oct	Nov-Dec
CHICAGO	Low	20°	35°	56°	67°	53°	28°
	High	34	51	74	83	69	42
	Average	27	43	65	75	61	35
DENVER	Low	18	29	58	43	43	22
	High	46	57	88	73	73	50
	Average	32	43	73	58	58	36
HONOLULU	Low	68	69	72	74	73	69
	High	74	75	80	84	83	79
	Average	71	72	76	79	78	74
HOUSTON	Low	48	58	71	75	67	50
	High	64	74	89	93	87	68
	Average	56	66	80	84	77	59
LAS VEGAS	Low	35	47	64	76	61	47
	High	57	73	84	102	87	61
	Average	46	60	79	89	74	54
LOS ANGELES	Low	46	50	57	62	59	49
	High	64	66	71	76	75	69
	Average	55	58	64	69	67	59
MIAMI	Low	59	64	72	75	73	61
	High	77	82	88	89	87	79
	Average	68	73	80	82	80	70
NEW ORLEANS	Low	49	59	71	76	68	52
	High	67	75	87	92	84	68
	Average	58	67	79	84	77	60
NEW YORK	Low	26	38	58	68	54	34
	High	40	54	76	84	72	44
	Average	33	46	67	76	63	39
SAN FRANCISCO	Low	43	46	51	54	52	45
	High	57	64	65	72	72	61
	Average	50	55	58	63	62	53
ST LOUIS	Low	24	38	58	67	52	30
	High	42	60	80	89	76	50
	Average	33	49	69	78	64	40
SEATTLE	Low	24	39	47	54	47	37
	High	46	55	69	76	65	49
	Average	35	47	58	65	56	43
WASHINGTON DC	Low	29	41	61	68	56	35
	High	45	61	79	86	74	51
	Average	37	51	70	77	65	43

GENERAL INFORMATION

Public holidays

New Year's Day (1 January)
Martin Luther King Jr Birthday (15 January)
Presidents Day (third Monday in February)
Memorial Day (last Monday in May)
Independence Day (4 July)
Labor Day (first Monday in September)
Columbus Day (second Monday in October)
Veterans' Day (11 November)
Thanksgiving (fourth Thursday in November)
Christmas (25 December)

Though many smaller shops and almost all businesses close on public holidays, many of the biggest stores and multiples will make a point of being open - often offering sales. Outside of cities, supermarkets are often open during at least part of a public holiday. On days of all primary and general elections all bars are closed. There are a few other public holidays that are not nationwide, e.g. Patriots Day in Massachusetts and Maine. Jewish New Year brings New York to a standstill.

The summer tourism and recreational season extends from Memorial Day to Labor Day. After Labor Day you can expect some hours or days of opening to be reduced, or some attractions to be closed altogether. The same may apply to related transport services. Unless otherwise specified, times and days of openings in this guide refer to the summer season. Outside this period, you should phone in advance.

Health and welfare

Unless you are coming from an infected area, in which case you must have proof of a smallpox vaccination, there are no **health requirements** for entry into the US. It is essential however, to be insured before leaving for the USA, and it's a good idea to get a dental check-up also. If you wear glasses or contact lenses take spares, or at least prescriptions.

There is no free or subsidised national health service in the United States for anyone under retirement age. For most people, therefore, medical, dental and hospital services have to be paid for and they can be expensive. However, the emergency room of any public hospital provides medical care to anyone who walks in the door (and is prepared for a long wait), and will often only charge those who have insurance or are otherwise able to pay, the government reimbursing them for the rest.

The 'emergency' doesn't have to be a car crash or the like-it can be a high fever or stomach pains, anything of a reasonably acute nature or which you feel needs immediate attention. Teaching hospitals-medical and dental-are other possible sources of free, or cheaper, treatment. Women may find help through the local women's centre.

Electricity

Voltage is 110-115V, 60 cycles AC. American plugs have two flat pins. You will not be able to use your home hairdryer, shaver or whatever, even if you have a dual voltage appliance, so try to get an adapter before you go. Because the voltage is lower in America, you may find your appliance does not run to its full capacity. It may be worth buying a cheap one when you arrive, simply for use during your stay.

Weights and measures

The US still uses feet and miles, pounds and gallons, Fahrenheit instead of Centigrade/Celsius, and it appears as though it will for some time to come. The only things that have gone metric are liquor and wine bottles, some gasoline pumps and the National Park Service. A conversion table is to be found in the Appendix.

Emergencies/Safety

Many towns and cities have '911' as the emergency telephone number for the police, fire, and ambulance services. Otherwise you dial '0' for the operator. The emergency number is always indicated on public telephones.

Yes, the USA can be a dangerous place, but then so can your own home town if you happen to be in the wrong place at the wrong time. In other words, chance or fate alone may determine what may or may not happen to you. This is not to say that you should not take reasonable, sensible, standard precautions to protect your safety.

Don't wander into parks or dark alleys alone or late at night; carry your valuables in a neck or waist pouch; don't leave your belongings unattended; stay in what you know to be safe areas of towns and cities - if it feels 'wrong', get out; don't hitchhike or drive alone; and stay alert to what is happening around you. Remember, although crime rates are high, most Americans never encounter crime in their daily lives.

Listed below are a few helplines and hotlines, should you or anyone travelling with you run into difficulties. The first thing to remember is, always consult your local telephone directory. Many states have their own 'information lines' or INR numbers (Info 'n' Referral). These lines may help you with anything from suicide prevention to health information, providing you with facts and referrals for counselling and support where needed.

Traveler's Aid can be found at major airports, bus and rail stations and will help in emergency situations. Traveler's Aid can also be found nationwide (check Yellow Pages, _www.yellowpages.com_) and specialise in helping people who are out-of-state get back to where they need to be.

National AIDS & STD Hotline, (800) 342-AIDS, 24 hours. Answers questions and gives out information as well as providing a referral service for testing and counselling where needed. (See also 'Health Agencies' in Yellow Pages.) _www.ashastd.org_ or _www.cdc.gov_.

(800) ALCOHOL, (800) 252-6465, 24 hours. Provides help and hotline referral for drug and alcohol problems.

National Drug & Alcohol Treatment Referral Hotline, (800) 662-HELP, 24 hours. Publications on drug or alcohol abuse and related issues. Referrals to local drug treatment or counselling centres.

Pregnancy Hotline, (800) 230-PLAN, 24 hours. Information for pregnant (or possibly pregnant) women, counselling and pregnancy testing.

Accessing Information

A multitude of resources exists in the US both to make your stay more informed and enjoyable and to help you out if you encounter problems. Among the most useful:

1. *Libraries.* One in every town, often open late hours and on weekends, libraries and librarians are a traveller's best friend. Besides reference works, atlases, and local guidebooks, most offer computer use/internet access (sometimes free) and wi-fi, transit schedules, local and other newspapers, magazines, free community newspapers, phone books, and brochures on helpful organizations. Librarians are unfailingly kind about answering questions and making phone enquiries for you. Libraries also have toilets, comfy chairs and often a social calendar of free evening events.

2. *Traveler's Aid.* Their kiosks are found at bus, train and plane terminals across the country- solid support if your trip runs into a snag.

3. *Chambers of Commerce and Visitors Bureaux.* Found almost everywhere, with lots of free materials, maps (although you usually have to purchase the really good maps) and advice. A drawback is that they are primarily member organisations; few of them will even recognize, much less recommend, non-member hotels, restaurants, etc. If driving, look out for state highway 'welcome stations'. They are a good source of free maps and local information and often provide free juice or coffee.

4. Many communities have a *volunteer clearinghouse phone service* designed to answer a variety of needs, from real emergencies to simple orientation. Usually listed in both the white and yellow pages of the phone book, and variously called Hotline, Helpline, Crisis Center, People's Switchboard, Community Switchboard, We Care, or some such. Their well-trained volunteers can steer you to the resources available in the community - free, cheap and not-so-cheap.

5. *Women's Centres and Senior Centres* provide the same kind of clearinghouse info and friendly support on a walk-in basis; you will find them in nearly every US town, listed in the phone book. You might also try the free clinics, which still exist in a number of big cities. Many of them operate hotlines, referral services, crash pad recommendations and other services besides free health care.

6. *Maps.* Find free ones from visitors' centres, roadside and other state tourism offices.

7. The Internet. There are two excellent Internet sites designed specifically for hostellers. The Internet Guide to Hostelling is an electronic magazine that offers a mountain of help to travellers. It has a worldwide hostel

guide, tips and tales from other budget travellers, info on special events and discounts. The guide can be accessed at www.hostels.com.

A second useful site for budget travellers is the Hostelling International-American Youth Hostels web page, which features information on HI-AYH hostels throughout America and provides links to other helpful travel organisations. Indeed, every HI-AYH hostel has a wealth of local information for bargain hunters. www.hiahy.org

Most states and cities have their own websites with helpful tourist information, as do many museums, parks, tour organisations, and bus and rail companies. We have listed helpful addresses throughout the book.

MONEY MATTERS

Dollars

Dollars and cents are of course the basic units of American money. The back of all denominations of dollar bills are green (hence 'greenbacks'). The commonly used coins are: one cent (penny), five cents (nickel), 10 cents (dime), and 25 cents (quarter). 'Always carry plenty of quarters when travelling. Very useful for phones, soda machines, laundry machines, etc.'

It's always useful to carry small change for things like exact-fare buses. However, keep the bulk of your money in **travellers' cheques** that can be purchased both in the US and abroad and should be in US dollar denominations. The best known cheques are those of American Express, so you will have the least difficulty cashing these, even in out of the way places. Thomas Cook travellers' cheques are also acceptable, especially as lost ones can be reclaimed at some Hertz Car Rental desks. Dollar denomination cheques can be used like regular money. There's no need to cash them at a bank: use them instead to pay for meals, supermarket purchases or whatever. Ten or 20 dollar cheques are accepted like this almost always and you'll be given change just as though you'd presented the cashier with dollar bills. Be prepared to show ID, usually your passport, when you cash your cheques.

Credit cards can be even more valuable than travellers' cheques as they are often used to guarantee room reservations over the phone and are accepted in lieu of a deposit when renting a car - indeed without a credit card you may be considered so untrustworthy that not only a deposit but your passport will be held as security too. Or, you may not be able to rent at all without a credit card. The major credit cards are VISA, MasterCard, Diners Club and American Express. If you hold a bank card (e.g. VISA), it could well be worthwhile increasing your credit limit for travel purposes- you should ask your bank manager. If you have a Switch or Delta card you can use it to withdraw cash from ATMs (cashpoints). There is a surcharge but convenience makes up for it - check with your bank on the surcharge amount and whether your card will work abroad. You may have difficulty using a British credit card on the internet or over the phone because the UK billing address may not be recognised.

Banks. Bank hours are usually 9am-3pm, Monday to Friday, although some branches, especially in big cities, have a longer day. Many banks stay open until 6pm on Fridays and some are open for limited hours on Saturdays.

If you receive a cheque, it is important to cash it in the same area - i.e. at a branch of the bank on which it is drawn. If you are paid by cheque then make sure that you change your pay check into travellers' cheques. Without a bank account to pay into, it will be impossible to cash it elsewhere - the American banking system is not as integrated as elsewhere in the world. Some form of photo identification (e.g. passport) is necessary when cashing a personal or company cheque. Some banks may not allow you to perform a transaction (cash cheques or get a money order) unless you have an account with them, or they may charge you for the service.

Tax. There is usually a three to nine percent sales tax on most items over 20¢ and meals over $1. This is never included in the stated price and varies from place to place according to whether you are being charged state or city sales tax. There is also a 'bed tax' in most cities that ranges from five to ten percent on hotel rooms. 'Bed tax' does not generally apply to bed and breakfast places. *Note that unless stated, accommodation rates in this Guide do not include tax.*

Tipping. It is customary in the US to tip the following: taxi drivers, waiters, chamber maids, hotel bellboys, airport luggage porters. Basically you should tip anyone who performs a service for you. Ten to 15 percent is the accepted amount, except for waiters, especially in cities, who will expect 15-20 percent. Some restaurants do include service in the menu price so make sure you don't tip them twice.

COMMUNICATIONS

Mail: Post offices are infrequent, but since the alternative is a commercial stamp machine that in the spirit of free enterprise sells stamps at a considerable profit, it is advisable to stock up at post offices when you can. As of going to press, first class letters within the US are 39¢; the air mail rate for post cards and aerogrammes to Europe is 75¢, and air mail letters up to 1 oz. cost 84¢. *www.usps.com*.

Mail within the US travels at a snail's pace: allow a week coast to coast or to Canada, and four days for any distance more than around the corner. For three-day (no guarantees!) delivery use Priority Mail, $3.85 for up to 1lb. For guaranteed overnight delivery you have to use Express Mail, UPS or FedEx. You must always include the ZIP code on a US address. To mail a letter without a ZIP code is to invite considerable delay, if not everlasting loss!

It is possible to have mail sent General Delivery (Poste Restante) for collection. The post office will usually keep it for 10 days before returning it to sender.

American post offices deal *only* with mail.

Telephone. Phones in North America are easy to use. All numbers have an area code (3 digits), and a telephone number (7 digits). Sometimes you do not need to dial the area code if you are within that dialing area; consult the local phone directory.   When calling from out-of-state in most areas of North America, you dial the whole number preceded by 1, or by 0 (zero) if you are making a collect call (reverse charges call, via the operator). For international calls, dial 011, the country code (44 for the UK) and then the phone number.

If you don't have a cell, look for pay phones in drug stores, gas stations, highway rest areas, in transport terminals and along the street. They have become harder to find as more and more Americans acquire cell phones. If you are not going to be in a rural area where there is no signal, it may be worthwhile considering buying a cell phone or bring your own from home with an international calling plan.

At a pay phone, before dialing, you insert the minimum amount of money as instructed (e.g. 50¢). When you have dialed the complete number, the operator will tell you how much to put in (if you dialed 1 first). If you dialed 0 first, a recorded message may ask you to 'please dial your card number or zero for an operator now'. Press 0, wait, and the operator will ask how he/she can help you. You then say: 'I'd like to make a collect call, please. My name is...'

Whenever the operator answers, your money is refunded to you. Don't forget to take it out of the machine! You may find that you are being spoken to by a recording which says something like 'Deposit 40 cents, please'. Obey the voice...

For directory enquiries call 411 or 555-1212 wherever you are and that will get you through to information for that state; if you want a number in another state, use that state's area code before you dial. To call New York information from out of state you would dial 1 (212) 555-1212.

One class of numbers, usually beginning with an 8, are for free calls anywhere in the country, or sometimes within a state or province – 800, 866, or 877. For information on (800) numbers, call 1 (800) 555-1212.

If calling at peak time, you may need to have ready up to $3.50 a minute in 25¢, 10¢ and 5¢ coins. The cheapest time to make a long distance call is between 11pm and 8am. Between 5pm and 11pm and at weekends is the next cheapest time; 8am-5pm is the most expensive time. Remember to allow for time zone differences when phoning.

If making calls from your hotel, remember that it is cheaper to use the phone in the hotel lobby rather than the one in your bedroom. It's always cheaper to dial direct and not through the operator. In many areas, local calls are free from private phones. If you make a pay call from a private phone you can get the operator to tell you how much the call will cost.

Phone cards are now very readily available in North America. However, the US-style phone cards work somewhat differently to those available in the UK, for example. They use a more complicated electronic system and are generally offered initially in $10 or $20 units but with the ability to 'top up' the card once the initial investment runs out.

Internet. The Internet brings you emails and the fantastic array of websites now available in the US – relevant sites are listed throughout this Guide.

Most city libraries have computers available for Internet access and wi-fi.

Some require you to have a library card, but many do not. In most libraries, there are a limited number of computers and users have a time limit, but access is often free. The Guide has listed public library information under *Internet Access* within each section.

To find out local wi-fi hotspots, check _www.wifinder.com_, _www.wififreespot.com_, _www.wi-fihotspotlist.com_ or _www.wifimaps.com_

If you have an e-mail account, there are a couple of ways to check your mail from any computer with Internet access. Most computers have Telnet, which gives you access to your university e-mail account. If Telnet is not available or doesn't work with your e-mail address, _www.mailstart.com_ works in basically the same way. Just enter your e-mail address and your password and it allows you to receive and send mail from your own account. Both Telnet and _www.mailstart.com_ tend to be slow, but they're both faster than regular mail.

Another option is opening a web-based e-mail account. Several websites offer free e-mail services (paid for by advertising) and you can set up an account in a matter of seconds. Yahoo! has e-mail (go to _www.yahoo.com_ and click on 'check e-mail.'), as does Hotmail (_www.hotmail.com_). You can also check your other e-mail accounts through Hotmail.

Once you have your e-mail account set up, you should be able to access your account from 'cybercafes' and wi-fi points which are located in most big cities in the US and Canada for an hourly or per minute rate. We've listed cybercafes in all the major cities, but this is a new, volatile industry and many cybercafes are short-lived. When possible, call ahead to make sure the cybercafe is still in business. There are a number of useful websites that list cyber cafes in the US and Canada, and worldwide, such as _www.cybercaptive.com_, _www.cybercafe.com_. Ironically, it is likely that you'll need access to a computer first before you can start searching for cyber cafes! Alternatively, search the good ol' fashioned *Yellow Pages*.

CULTURE

The American people

Keeping in mind the vastness of the United States and the knowledge that the area you are visiting covers an entire continent, it becomes a little easier to appreciate the diversity of the land and its people. America is an incredibly cosmopolitan society. Glance at the names in the telephone book of almost any town in America for evidence of this. Every nationality on earth, speaking scores of the world's languages, every creed, every race is represented here.

The only true native peoples of the USA, of course, are the Indians, who are thought to have arrived in America by way of the Bering Strait from Asia several thousands of years before the Pilgrim Fathers set foot in Massachusetts. Since the time of the European migration the lot of the 'Native American' has not been a happy one. Harried and hounded by the westward-moving white man, Native Americans were eventually pushed into reservations, inevitably on the poorest and most infertile land around.

In more recent times the position of the Native American has improved a little but there is still a long, long way to go. Having Indian blood is a matter of fierce pride and many Indians still harbour great resentment towards the white man. Be aware of this should you visit a reservation and be respectful towards the people and their laws and customs.

America may be cosmopolitan, but it's not yet a real melting pot. National groups tend to stick together-you will see bumper stickers reading 'Irish-American', 'Proud to be Polish' for instance. At the top of the social heap are still the WASPS (White Anglo-Saxon Protestants) represented by the British, Germans and Scandinavians, and followed by the Irish and other European groups. Next come Asians, who are most visible in California, where the first Chinese immigrants have been traced to 1421, then Blacks and Hispanics, the fastest-growing group in America. It is estimated that Hispanics will soon outnumber the Black-American population and become the largest minority group. In fact, the Census Bureau has predicted that by 2050 whites will comprise only 50% of the population. As immigration continues and fortunes around the world turn this way or that, so will American society continue to evolve and reflect new national groupings and social trends.

This constantly changing society, the moving frontier, is perhaps one of the roots of the violence present in American society. Where a nationwide sense of tradition is scarce, where the future is always being built anew, there is often a sense of rootlessness and self-doubt in which violence, crime, drug or alcohol dependency, and religious, political or social fads can easily flourish. There is a great deal of poverty in the land of opportunity, contrasting sharply with the material splendours of those who have it in abundance.

That is the down side. On the brighter side, American people are hospitable, kind and generous. Even the newest immigrants take great pride in their new land. Even before the terrorist attacks of 11th September 2001 had brought a national focus on unity, there was always a US flag flying, on private homes as well as on public buildings; allegiance to America was and is constantly recited and renewed. The USA remains on the whole an optimistic land, still reaching towards the future, trying to stay ahead, and proud of its role in the world. Americans tend to be demanding, enthusiastic; living hard, playing hard; conformist, yet individualistic; always expecting the best of everything.

Meeting people

Americans in their own country are naturally outgoing and friendly, more so when they detect a foreign accent. Your novelty value is particularly enhanced outside of the big cities, where curiosity and interest is generated amongst locals as soon as you open your mouth. Don't be surprised if you are invited to dinner, taken places and shown round the local sights. Staying at a private bed and breakfast is a prime way to mingle with Americans - the services you get and the friendliness you'll receive go far beyond the monetary exchange. State fairs and other such special events-rodeos, clambakes, New England autumn fairs, etc., are an essential slice of the American pie and another way of meeting people informally.

If you want a more organised approach for meeting Americans, we suggest a number of organisations within our listings and also the following (most of which require making advance arrangements):

1. **National Council for International Visitors** (NCIV), 1420 K St NW, Suite 800, Washington DC 20005, (202) 842-1414. Their *Membership Directory* can provide details of their members who may be able to offer assistance/information. Open 9am-5pm. *www.nciv.org*
2. Enquire at local **Chambers of Commerce** and **Visitors Bureau** about their 'Visit a local family' programmes, if any. Some of them are very active. Several also have volunteer language banks, if you're having difficulty communicating.
3. **Servas**. An organisation of approved hosts and travellers arranging homestays. Charges membership fee of $85 a year then requires a refundable deposit of $25 for 1-5 host lists. Guests then make their own contacts. US Servas, Inc., 11 John St, Rm 505, New York, NY 10038, (212) 267-0252, email: *info@usservas.org.* Open Mon-Fri 10am-4pm. *www.usservas.org.*

Media and Entertainment

In these days of cable and satellite TV it is not unusual to be able to tune into more than 60 channels on your set. Network television can be condescending, boring, total rubbish - an insult to the intelligence but, also has excellent and interesting programmes including old movies (squeezed in between commercials) and news coverage. The networks also offer reruns of old sitcoms, especially *Seinfeld,* which provide, besides a good laugh, an interesting look at bygone America, as well as the more well known contemporary American shows such as *The Sopranos* and *Curb Your Enthusiasm* available on HBO. Among the most recommended shows are *60 Minutes,* on CBS every Sunday night, and the nightly news of the three main networks – ABC, CBS and NBC.

Public TV is very important in the US. Most local public television channels have superb documentaries, and also show British imports such as *As Time Goes By, Coupling, Keeping up Appearances, Are You Being Served,* etc., and offer excellent current affairs, science, nature, and travel programs as well as live theatre, music, and mysteries. *History Detectives* is one of public TV's best shows. Public TV also offer news from the BBC (eg in Washington DC you can get the BBC's nightly news on three public TV stations – Channels 26, 32, and 56) as well as other programmes from the UK. Some cable companies also offer *BBC America.*

And there's even more **radio**. Here the overkill holds promise: in amongst the top 40 musical pop stations are first-rate classical, jazz, blues, bluegrass, country, gospel, R&B, progressive and regional music stations, as well as some solid all-news stations. Radio is also an excellent way of finding out about an area you're visiting or just driving through. Highly recommended are the local public radio stations at the lower end of the FM dial (eg 88.5 or 90.9 fm) with excellent morning, evening and weekend editions (Scott Simon), and other interesting programmes, including *Prairie Home Companion* broadcast live. Many of these emanate from National Public Radio (NPR, *www.npr.org*), the closest the US has to the BBC.

Every major city has **theatres**, and its own **orchestra** and **opera company**, with performances often to a very high standard. In this respect, Americans arguably enjoy a greater access to culture than Europeans with their more distinguished but more centralised cultural traditions. Many cities have dozens of Equity and non-Equity theatre companies. In most cities half price tickets are available from **Ticketplace.**

Hollywood still turns out more **movies** than anywhere else in the world except India, and with the decline of the studios there has been more free-lancing, more opportunity for outsiders with new ideas to hit the big screen. In writing, directing and acting, America easily holds its own as one of the four or five great film-making nations.

Often movies are cheaper before 6pm and some are $3-$6 at weekends. Free papers in every city are essential reading for entertainments/events, etc. If you're interested in concerts, plays, etc, one easy solution is to look up **Ticketmaster** in the local phone book. They are nation-wide agents, but have information on what's on in the particular city you're in, though they take a percentage on any tickets you buy from them. There are half-priced ticket agencies in most major cities.

The *New York Times* is one of the most respected of American **newspapers** and in content comes closest to being the country's national newspaper. The mammoth Sunday edition of the *Times* should keep you going at least until Thursday. There is, of course, an actual coast-to-coast, national newspaper - *USA Today*. Published weekdays across America, and using full colour throughout, it manages to a large extent to overcome the problems of time zones, and the diversity of life in the US. Among the best of the rest are the *Los Angeles Times*, the *Washington Post* and the *Wall Street Journal*. In general people still buy their local papers and all towns and cities have at least one. Wherever you are, of course, the local paper (perhaps free) is your best resource for local events as well as adding to your picture of American life.

Magazines proliferate, covering every conceivable interest and point of view. Sample the offerings on hot rods, sex, flying saucers, sport, computers, snowmobiles, collectibles and so on if you want to appreciate the American appetite for every sort of information. Some of the best writing is found in *The New Yorker*, the *Atlantic Monthly* - which grew out of the Transcendentalist and anti-slavery movements, the *Nation*, and *Esquire*. *Rolling Stone* is still the voice of pop, and there's always *Time* and *Newsweek* to read on the loo.

Last but not least there are the **comics**, including that whole stable of Marvel heroes (Captain America, Spiderman, The Hulk) who express the variety of American neuroses, or those old standbys from a more innocent, confident age, principally Superman and Scrooge McDuck.

Sport and Recreation

At times on your travels across America it may seem that every man, woman, child, and dog jogs, runs or otherwise 'keeps fit' at least four times a week. Certainly as a nation Americans tend towards the active, outdoors existence. After all they have the climate and the country to make it all possible. If it exists as a sport you will find it somewhere in America - yes, even rugby and croquet.

On the professional scene the biggies are American football and baseball. The baseball season runs from April through October and football starts at the end of the summer and finishes in January when finally overtaken by the weather. Try to go to a professional game in either sport - it's a real slice of American pie (baseball can be very slow but it is as much about beer, hot dogs and tailgating as it is about the game). There is a major league team in almost every large city. Soccer is starting to catch on in a big way, although it doesn't cause the same sort of frenzy as it does in Europe. There is a national league but the real strength of the game is at grassroots level. Basketball, ice hockey, tennis, horse/motor racing and wrestling, are other major spectator sports.

One interesting point about the US sports scene is the attention given nationally to the often near-professional college/university teams. This is especially the case with basketball and football where the college teams are often followed with an enthusiasm equal to that given to the pros.

Shopping

Major stores in out of town malls often have long opening hours, e.g. from 9am or 10am to 9pm or 10pm - on one, several or even all days of the week. Smaller shops in cities are sometimes open all night: you should have no trouble getting a meal or a drink, or shopping for food and other basics, 24 hours a day - though you'll pay more for the privilege.

Large American supermarkets and department stores can make their foreign equivalents look like they're suffering from war-time rationing. The variety of goods on offer - and at relatively low prices - is amazing. The

Clothing and Shoe sizes

Women's Clothes

American	2	4	6	8	10	12	14	16
British	6	8	10	12	14	16	18	20
Continental	36	38	40	42	44	46	48	50

Women's Shoes

American	5	6	7	8	9	10	11	12
British	3	4	5	6	7	8	9	10
Continental	36	37	38	39	40	41	42	43

Men's Suits—same as UK

Men's Shirts—same as UK

Men's Shoes

American	7	7.5	8	8.5	9.5	10	10.5	11
British	6	7	7.5	8	9	9.5	10	11
Continental	39	40	41	42	43	44	45	46

American consumer is a keen and well-practised shopper with an eye for a bargain, seldom in fact, buying anything that's not on sale. With over 15,000 malls nationwide, almost every town has at least one shopping mall on the outskirts where you can browse to your heart's content from about 10am to 9pm. Look for designer and brand name bargains in the proliferating outlet malls across America.

Good buys in the US include cameras, CDs, electronic goods, sound equipment, denims, winter clothes, and casual clothes, in particular western gear. Just how good a bargain will of course depend upon the exchange rate at the time of your visit. Even if it is not in your favour, if you do as all Americans do and shop only when the item you want is on sale, you will still be able to net some bargains.

Drinking

Although nation-wide Prohibition ended in the US in 1933, you will still find places in which you cannot get a drink at all, or where you cannot drink while standing, or must bring your own bottle - one anomaly after another. This is because each state decides whether it will be 'dry' or 'wet', and sometimes this is left to counties on an optional basis. You may notice some people on the street drinking out of paper bags. This is because in many cities it is illegal to *visibly* drink alcoholic beverages in public.

American mass-produced beer (which as a legacy of Prohibition has a relatively low alcohol content) is of the lager variety-Knickerbocker, Miller, Schaeffer, Budweiser, Pabst. Be sure to ask for micro-brewery beers, now standard fare at most bars and restaurants, and tending to eclipse the old standards. There are now scores of delicious and interesting micro-brews from honey-brown ale to raspberry wheat, made by at least 1,334 craft brewers all over the US. *www.beertown.org, www.beerme.com/breweries/us*

America is the home of the cocktail. Spirit concoctions are excellent and a major part of American ingenuity is devoted to thinking up new ones-and extraordinary names for them! Bars never close before midnight and sometimes stay open till 4am, or even 23 hours a day.

Try to sample local wines. New York and California turn out the best although many states, including Washington, Virginia, Michigan and even New Jersey also produce some decent varieties. Visit the growing number of wineries in these states too. You can locate almost any winery by state at *www.allamericanwineries.com* .

The minimum drinking age is now 21 in every state in the US. A strong anti-drink climate of opinion exists in the US at present and under-age drinking rules are strictly enforced. Someone under 21 may not be able to drink alcohol at all during their stay in the USA. You will need to carry photo ID when ordering a drink or buying liquor in a store just in case you are asked - even if you think you look much older than 21! War veterans have even been asked to show ID when ordering alcohol! Student cards, etc., are generally not acceptable as ID and even a passport is sometimes not enough. You can, however, obtain a US ID with your photo on it from any DMV (Department of Motor Vehicles) office (where drivers' licences are issued). Check the *Yellow Pages* for location.

Tobacco

Cigarettes are about $5 for a pack of 20, five big cigars for about the same price. Pipe tobacco is heavily flavoured - imported brands are better and not much more expensive. Unless you learnt to chew tobacco at the same time as you were breast-fed, forget it. Tobacco addicts should stock up on cartons at supermarkets for substantial savings.

Smoking is increasingly frowned upon and many restaurants and other public places now have 'non-smoking' sections. In New York City and California, the ban on smoking in restaurants, and most other public places, is total. Smoking is banned in all government buildings; post offices, libraries, banks, cinemas, subway stations, etc. and on all public transport, including Amtrak and Greyhound.

Drugs

A great deal has been written about the 'drug culture' of the US. The best advice is the obvious - stay away from it. Reject all advances made to you on the street, in bus terminals, airports, wherever. It is illegal to possess or sell narcotics and penalties can be severe.

ON THE ROAD

ACCOMMODATION Let's face facts: accommodation in North America is going to absorb at least one-third of your travel money. So how can you keep that figure to a minimum while enjoying your trip to the maximum?

1. *Learn your accommodation options.* You'll constantly hear about the visible and well-advertised options: chain hotels and motels, lodgings close to freeways and tourist attractions, National Park, YMCAs and youth hostels. But a wealth of inexpensive and almost invisible alternatives exist in North America. Examples: guest and tourist homes; bed and breakfast in private residences; farms and ranches; resorts and retreats; residence clubs, *casas de huespedes* and other pension-style lodgings; free campsites on Indian lands; non-hostel accommodations which honour hostel rates and philosophies; university-associated places to stay, many open to the general public; and self-catering digs, from apartments to rustic cabins to housekeeping/efficiency units in standard hotels/motels. (You will see lots of specific examples of these choices throughout this Guide.) Use the web, especially local town or state tourism sites and Craigs List, *www.craigslist.org*, to search for possible places to stay in any particular place and of any particular type.
2. *Choose a lodging that also gives you a taste of North America.* Want to stay in a New York City brownstone, a San Francisco painted Victorian, a Maui condo, a solar-heated A-frame near a ski slope? How about spending a few days on a Mississippi River houseboat or riding through Kansas prairies with a covered wagon train? Maybe you'd rather tent-camp in a Sioux tepee, explore a Mennonite farm, visit a Southern plantation, sleep in a gold miner's cabin, gain a few pounds at a Basque

boarding house, beachcomb near a lighthouse hostel or stay in a 400-year old Mexican mansion. It's all here. And by integrating your sleeping (and sometimes eating) arrangements with an offbeat experience, you'll receive double value. In the process, you'll get acquainted with everyday Americans from many walks of life.

3. ***Rent a room the way you shop for a car.*** If tourism is down and vacancy rates are up, you'll have added leverage and bargaining power. Use it! Don't be afraid to haggle - hotel/motel rates in the US are extremely fluid and based on what the market will bear. (Unlike Mexico, where they are government regulated.) Rooms within a building are never identical - ask to see the cheapest. It may be small, viewless or noisy. It may also suit your needs very well. If you're willing to share a bath, sleep in a dorm, or take a room without air-conditioning or TV, *say so*. 'Ask for a room that is out of service and then offer a price for the night. You may be lucky.'

4. ***Use impeccable timing.*** Plan ahead to take advantage of special offers and slow times. Do your travelling on weekends so you arrive to catch the midweek (Sunday through Thursday) rates. Alternatively, look for higher-priced hotels at your destination that offer low-cost weekend or 'getaway' packages - often very good value. If you can possibly swing it, travel in May or September: best weather, fewer crowds and significantly lower off-season prices. Another timing tip: the later in the evening it gets, the more likelihood you have of a reduced rate on a room. You may be tired and worried about a place to lay your weary head but remember: the hotel/motel owner is even more worried about filling that room, which goes on costing him money whether empty or full. But beware: in resort areas and big cities at peak holiday times, desirable accommodation fills by 4-5pm.

5. ***Always ask about discounts and special rates.*** You'd be amazed at the discount categories that exist in North America. Always check! Hotels/motels sometimes grant 'commercial rates' as a face-saving way to fill rooms, so it pays to flash your business card, if you have one, or student I.D. 'Being a British student was worth a $2 discount to many motel owners'. Being a *Moneywise Guide* holder sometimes gets you a better deal too!

6. ***Ask other travellers for accommodation leads.*** When travelling in the US most Americans tend to stay with families/friends, at chain motels/hotels, or in campgrounds or RVs (recreational vehicles). Thus they are often oblivious to the unsung lodging opportunities around them.

7. ***Double up. Better yet, triple up.*** US lodgings (with the exception of hostels, YMCAs and a few hotels/motels that give the lone traveller a break) have a Noah's Ark, two-by-two mentality. Your best bet is to travel with one or more companions. 'Five of us crammed into a $60 double room with owner's consent. Try any motel.'

8. ***Learn about local variants and accommodation nomenclature.*** Lodging traditions vary around North America. For instance, the best bargains in Hawaii are called hotel apartments - Honolulu is full of them. In Colorado, ski lodges with dorms (ask for 'hiker' or 'skier' rooms) are popular. San Francisco is a mecca for congenial residence clubs, which

offer weekly rates for room and board. Parts of the South and New England are full of small guest houses. In Canada, low-priced B&B digs are called 'tourist homes'. When you enter an area, ask the Visitors Centre or librarians, or look in the Yellow Pages; if there's a local variant, you should spot it. Second, learn what lodging descriptions really mean. In the US, the cheapest and simplest accommodation is variously described as 'economy', 'budget', 'no frills', 'rustic', 'basic' or 'European-style rooms'. The breakfast portion of bed and breakfast may vary from a continental roll-and-coffee to a full meal; ask. Unlike Europe, many US B&Bs offer (for a modest fee) other meals, transportation, tours and worthwhile goodies from free bike loans to use of libraries, saunas and tennis courts. Beware of lodging descriptions that include the words 'affordable', 'quaint', 'Old World charm' (evidently it costs a fortune to drag charm from the Old World to the New), and 'standard' or 'tourist class' (travel agents for mid-price range).

Hotels and Motels. Except for chains like Motel 6 and Super 8, motels tend to be regional in scope and with prices that vary from unit to unit and season to season. To be fair: many of them offer more for your money (e.g. pool, larger rooms, bath, phones, TV, etc.). See page 21 for a list of budget motel chains in the US.

Budget motels work out cheapest with three or more people. Unfortunately, they are often difficult to reach without a car, but do call to ask about bus connections, if any. As a rule, cheapie motels (chain or non-chain) provide better, cleaner and safer accommodation for the money than do cheap downtown hotels.

Finding a hotel with the ideal mix of low price and reasonable quality is an art. Besides the website suggestions in this Guide, you could try: (1) comparing notes with other travellers; (2) check out coupons especially in leaflets available at tourist information centres (3) check at the Travellers Aid kiosks in transit terminals. It's also wise to leave your luggage in a locker so you can check out your prospects. Ask to see rooms and don't settle for doors that don't lock or that have signs of forced entry, unclean linen, etc. If you are a woman alone, we strongly advise you to arrive in big cities during daylight hours.

YMCAs and YWCAs. Most YMCAs offering accommodation are located in the often run-down heart of big city downtowns. Y lodgings have no membership or age restrictions and the use of recreational facilities is often free. Most are co-ed.

The economics of desperation bring in a mixed clientele; that, coupled with the grimy streets outside and steadily rising prices make the YMCA less and less of a bargain, but an AYH card can help-many Ys give hostel rates. Contact the Y's Way, (212) 308-2899. _www.ymcanyc.org_. The women-only YWCAs are concentrated in the Northeast, the Midwest and Texas. They tend to be smaller, more cheerful and better bargains than their YMCA counterparts-if you can get in.

BUDGET MOTEL CHAINS IN THE US

Budget Host Inns, Budget Host International, 3607 Pioneer Parkway West, Arlington, TX 76013. 1-(800) 283-4678. *www.budgethost.com*

Choice Hotels, PO Box 1748, Minot, ND 85702. 1-(877) 424-6423. *www.hotelchoice.com*

Comfort Inns, contact Choice Hotels (above).

Days Inn, 1910 8th Avenue NE, PO Box 4090, Aberdeen, SD 57402-4090. 1-(800) 329-7466. *www.daysinn.com.*

Econo-Lodges of America, contact Choice Hotels (above)

Exel Inns, 4706 E Washington Avenue, Madison, WI 53704. 1-(800) 307-3935. *www.exelinns.com.*

First Interstate Inns, PO Box 760, Kimball, NE 69145. 1-(800) 426-7866. *www.1stinns.com*

Hampton Inn, 755 Crossover Lane, Building 2A, Memphis, TN 38117. 1-(800) 426-7866. *www.hamptoninn.com*

Hospitality International, 1726 Montreal Circle, Tucker, GA 30084. 1-(800) 251-1962. www.reservahost.com OR 1-(800) 547-4677 *www.bookroomsnow.com*

Knights Inn, PO Box 4090, Aberdeen, SD 57401. 1-(800) 843-5644. *www.knightsinn.com*

Motel 6, AEL Guest Relations, PO Box 1054, Geenville, TX 75403-1054. 1-(800) 466-8354. *www.motel6.com*

Quality Inns, contact Choice Hotels (above).

Red Roof Inns, 14651 Dallas Parkway, Suite 500, Dallas TX 75254. 1-(800)733-7663. *www.redroof.com*

Rodeway Inns, contact Choice Hotels (above).

Super 8 Motels, PO Box 4090, Aberdeen, SD 57402-4090. 1-(800) 800-8000. *www.super8.com*

Travelodge Forte Hotels, PO Box 4090, Aberdeen, SD 57402-4090. 1-(800) 578 7878. *www.travelodge.com*

Hostels. American Youth Hostels (AYH) has adopted the International Youth Hostel Federation blue triangle symbol and become Hostelling International-USA.
Members can make reservations through the International Booking Network (IBN), (202) 783-6161 or through the free 800 number: 1-800-909-4776. Refer to HI-USA *Handbook* for details on how this works. Most major USA gateway hostels are part of the network. *www.hiusa.org.*
All in all, the hostel situation in the USA is pretty good. If you belong to

an overseas Youth Hostel Association, you're entitled to use HI-USA and AAIH facilities. Overseas visitors who are not members in their own country must make use of the introductory pass most hostels offer so you can try it on a one-time basis. Get your pass stamped each time you use it, and after 6 times you become a 'guest member'-although you will not be entered onto the database, which may cause complications. Annual fees in the US to become a guest member are usually $18 (age 18-55). Write to HI-USA, Membership Dept, 8401 Colesville Road, Suite #600, Silver Spring, MD 20910, (301) 495 1240 or e-mail *members@hiusa.org*.

In addition to HI-affiliated hostels there are a growing number of independently run hostels in the US and Canada. The American Association of Independent Hostels (AAIH) has hostels, or else provides hostel-type (i.e. dorm) accommodation within large hotels in several cities. Aimed primarily at the young, international traveller, they are generally located in downtown areas near the bus terminal. There are many other smaller independents that seem to spring up like mushrooms, mostly in the large cities such as Los Angeles (a prime hostel spot) and New Orleans. In some cases they last one season and then disappear! So be careful.

The accommodation provided by independent hostels can be a bit of a mixed bag. Some are very good, but others aim simply to cram in as many people as possible regardless of standards of cleanliness, safety or sanitation. If you are on a budget, of course, you may feel you don't really have a choice. The majority of the hostels listed in this book have been recommended by previous users.

Another helpful resource is the *Hostel Handbook for the USA and Canada*, which provides information on both HI-USA and independent hostels. To order a guide, send a cheque or money order for $6 ($10 from outside the US) payable to Jim Williams at The Hostel Handbook, Dept: HHB, 722 Saint Nicholas Ave, NY, NY 10031 (212) 926-7030 or order online from *www.hostel-handbook.com*. Email: *editor@hostelhandbook.com*. For hostels in Canada, obtain the latest edition of *Hostels in Canada and Abroad (Les Auberges au Canada et a l'Etranger)* from *www.hihostels.ca* .

Hostelling in North America can be a good choice for the independent and budget conscious traveler as many offer special activities free or at low cost, from wilderness canoe or cycling trips to hot-tubbing. Reader comments show that US hostels are generally more relaxed and friendly than their European counterparts. 'I found youth hostels most convenient places to stay. Full of young people of all nationalities, the hostels were a nucleus of information and I met many travelling partners. Whilst not boasting of exceptional comforts, the hostels generally proved to be very good value and certainly took a lot out of the loneliness of travelling on one's own.'

Drawbacks? Uneven distribution make hiking or biking itineraries impractical, except for certain regions. Remote locales make it tough to use public transport to get to many of them. And hostel curfews and customs can cramp your style, particularly if you plan to do much urban or night-time sightseeing. 'Most US hostels insist on your having (or renting) a sheet sleeping bag.' 'On the whole American hostels were very good indeed.'

University-associated lodging. Many universities in the US and Canada offer on-campus housing in dorms and residence halls. They are usually available summer only (exceptions noted in listings); rates vary widely and definitely favour doubles and weekly stays; facilities often heavily booked; campuses can be far from city centres. It's always worth trying the local student union or campus housing office when in the vicinity.

You can also find off-campus residences, fraternity and sorority houses with summer space to rent, all of which tend to be looser, friendlier and cheaper than on-campus options. Fringe benefits: use of kitchen facilities (sometimes) and entree into the thirsty social life of local students, including the infamous TGs or kegger parties.

Camping. Camping provides the cheapest and one of the most enjoyable means of seeing the best parts of North America, the national and state parks and other preserves. Your choices are almost infinite. Campground facilities vary from fully developed sites with electricity, bunk-equipped cabins and hot showers to primitive sites where you're expected to bury your wastes and pack out your rubbish. Tent campers are advised to avoid RV-oriented campgrounds. They may offer a pool, laundromat, store and other amenities but the noise, asphalt and vehicle fumes sadly dilute the 'wilderness' experience. More expensive, private campgrounds can be good options too.

A number of readers have recommended KOA (Kampgrounds of America). In general, while their sites are not always the most scenic, their facilities are luxurious in camping terms. 'We used the KOA campgrounds the whole time-they have the best facilities available'. Check out the KOA website for info on reservations and site locations: _www.koakamp-grounds.com_. You can purchase the KOA Value Kard for $14; this allows a 10% reduction on the cost of a campsite, plus a "free" guide and road atlas. Sites cost $12-$20. For the hiking/biking camper, many state parks offer a few sites designated as 'hiker/biker' for 50¢-$1 per night on a first-come, first-served basis.

State park camping fees are indicated with the state listings. For further information, write to the National Park Service, 1849 C St, NW, Rm 7102, Washington DC 20240, or call (202) 208-4747. A $50 pass allows free entry to any park for 1 year (1-800) 365-2267. _www.nps.gov/parks.html_ Other excellent sources for campground info are the AAA books, Rand McNally's _Campground and Trailer Park Guide_ (17,000 US and Canada listings) and the tourism offices of each state.

You should be aware that the biggest drawback for the on-foot traveller is access. Ironic as it sounds, you really need a car to get to numerous camp-grounds and trailheads to backcountry camping, especially those sites located on National Forest or Bureau of Land Management property. Once you have wheels it is possible to zigzag your way across America camping in some of the loneliest, loveliest spots in the world. It might even be worth investigating hiring a camper vehicle (the dreaded RV) for an extended trip. For a group of three or more it could be worth the extra expense.

Native American campgrounds and other Indian-run lodging facilities are a great way to get acquainted with North America's first people. Most sites are located on reservation land which, if you remember your history, has traditionally been located about a million miles from nowhere. Although the whites did their best to fob off nothing but marginal lands on the Indians, what they ended up with is often superbly scenic. A car is nearly imperative as you'll find little public transport to and from reservation land.

Besides campgrounds, Native American-owned facilities range from simple motels to sumptuous resorts. Some offer traditional dancing, crafts and native food.

Tips: In the north, the camping season lasts from mid-May to mid-September or sooner, depending on weather. In the Rockies and other mountainous areas, temperatures drop dramatically in the evening, making warm clothing vital. In the warm dry southwest, you probably won't have to put up a tent, although you might want to exclude any unwelcome wildlife! At Yellowstone and other northern parks, you may encounter bears who roam the campground for food. Wear a bell! These bears are not interested in campers as nourishment and will not harm you as long as you leave them well alone. Do not leave food in the tent, in ice chests, on picnic tables or near your sleeping bag. Lock it in the trunk of your car, or use park-recommended 'bear cables'. Bring along a generous supply of insect repellent and calamine lotion to combat mosquito bites, chiggers (a maddening insect that burrows beneath your skin) and poison ivy/poison oak (glossy three-leafed plants).

Popular national and state parks get very crowded from Memorial Day through to Labor Day, making May and September the ideal months for visits. When possible, make advance reservations. To get the best site, try to arrive by 5pm or earlier. Beware that some campgrounds keep the 'No Vacancy' sign up all summer so always ask. At the most popular parks queuing all night for space is not unusual.

Bed and Breakfast. An old concept in Europe, B&B has crossed the Atlantic and hybridised in several directions. Most visible are the 'too cute to be true' B&B Inns, widely written about and gushed over and punitively expensive in most cases. Least visible but most moneywise are the private homes in the US, Canada and Mexico which only rent rooms through an agency intermediary. (This is partly for security reasons, partly because of US zoning laws.) Most agencies concentrate on a given city or state; you'll find their names and addresses under the appropriate listing. Booking procedures, type of breakfast, length of stay and other conditions vary from agency to agency. The common denominator is the need to book ahead. If in the US, this can often be handled with a phone call. Only rarely can you breeze into town and get same-day accommodation.

Is the lack of flexibility worth it? Most people think so. Foreign visitors who want to meet locals, see American homes and eat home cooking are particularly enthusiastic. Private home B&Bs are an inexpensive, warm and caring environment for women travellers on their own, too. Bonuses: many B&Bs serve meals other than breakfast and a large number are willing to pick up and deliver guests (sometimes for a small fee). Hosts often speak other languages, so make your needs known at booking time. Canadian B&Bs are called hospitality homes. In Mexico, the B&B programme is known as Posada Mexico.

Alternatively, if you are planning to do a lot of B&Bing you should consider buying one of the many books on the market, which list hundreds of guest houses or tourist homes on a national or regional basis. There are several B&B umbrella agencies that cover a number of states (and countries) and which cater to foreign and US travellers. They can book you into one B&B or work out a whole itinerary of B&Bs for you. Write for details and brochures. A few of the better known agencies:

1. **BB Explorer – Alaska, California, Hawaii, Idaho, Oregon & Washington** Check _www.bbexplorer.com_ Rates from $95 for doubles, most with full breakfast.
2. **Pacific B&B**, PO Box 46894, Seattle, WA 98146; (206) 784-0539/ (800) 684-2932. Rates from $60 for single/double (shared bath). Homes in Washington, Oregon and British Columbia. _www.seattlebedand-breakfast.com._ Email: _pacificb@nwlink.com._
3. **B&B League Ltd**, PO Box 9490, Washington DC 20016-9490. Phone: (202) 363-7767. Recommended primarily for travellers in pairs, since rates are S-$70-$140, D-$85-$160 plus $10 booking fee plus tax. Continental bfast. Makes rsvs for B&Bs in DC and surrounding area.

Like every other business in America, new organisations mushroom all the time, so it is always worth checking in the immediate vicinity (e.g. Yellow Pages) for local listings.

Other accommodation possibilities. If you're planning to bicycle around the US, it makes sense to contact **Adventure Cycling Association**, a national non-profit organisation, at 150 E Pine St, Missoula, Montana 59807. Tel: (406) 721-8719. They provide books and maps to help you. **Hostelling International** offers special tours for cyclists and of course accommodation. Many individual hostels arrange their own bike rental and tours.

Should you decide to (or be reduced to) crash out, it is a good idea to ask locally whether or not your chosen spot is safe. The local police, or students, are probably the best people to ask but it's not a good idea to just crash out by the side of the road or on the beach without checking first. Some readers have suggested highway rest areas as good sleeping places but sometimes this is not allowed and you should only do this if other people are clearly doing so already - never alone.

FOOD

To eat cheaply and well in America is easy once you realise that menu prices have more to do with restaurant decor and labour costs than with food quality. Everyone will quickly develop his or her own game plan depending on available funds and taste. However you should plan to get at least some of your meals from non-restaurant sources: supermarkets, open-air farmers markets, roadside stands and farms. Check the many menu sites now available in North America, such as *www.menupages.com* which has over 4,500 menus by type and neighbourhood in Manhattan and New York City.

When possible, avoid higher-priced outlets like 24-hour stores, bus station canteens, street vendors, beach stands, airport restaurants and liquor stores. 'Some convenience stores, especially 7-11s, have microwaves, so a hot stew can be eaten for the price of the can and if you are on the road this is generally also true of some gas stations.' Keep away from endless soft drinks; even at supermarkets, they're 75¢ and up, double that elsewhere. Accompany your dining-out meals with ice water or lower-priced multiple refills like coffee or tea. In general the food you buy and prepare yourself will always be the cheapest. At least one meal a day could fall into this category.

Wherever you are, check out the Happy Hour situation. States and cities with liberal liquor laws often honour a daily discount period (usually 4pm-7pm) with cheap drinks and free food, sometimes a stunning array of it. Fittingly, California is the Happy Hour paradise.

Regional and local specialities are usually wonderful, or at the very least a worthwhile cultural experience. As you work your way around the country, sample Key Lime pie, Virginia ham and redeye gravy, Chicago-style deep-dish pizza, California guacamole dip, Texas chili, Southern grits, biscuits, and boiled peanuts, Hawaiian poi and roast pig, Wisconsin bratwurst, Maryland crab cakes, and Navajo tacos. Large sandwiches (often with local nomenclature like grinder, submarine, po' boy, blimp, hero, hoagie, etc.) on rolls with meatballs, sausage, corned beef are available everywhere for a couple of dollars.

Coast to coast chains such as KFC and MacDonald's are always the same! The Taco Bell chain has been recommended for a good, filling, cheap vegetarian meal e.g. 89¢ for a bean burrito. And there's always pizza! For dessert, lots of the ice -cream parlours will give you free samples until you hit on the one you want most.

Wherever you eat, portions are invariably enormous - you'll soon understand why Americans invented the doggie bag for leftovers! 'Forget doggie bags - nobody objected to our ordering one portion and two plates and sharing portions still bigger than at home.'

'Nowhere have I found it difficult, and usually I've found it fun, hunting out a place to suit my quite small pocket. I do feel that discovering food, rather than following a map to it, is part of the holiday.'

TRAVEL

Once in the USA your thoughts will turn to how, as well as when and where, you would like to travel. The means you choose to travel around North America will depend on your budget, your time and your adventurousness amongst a number of other factors. Since there may be discounts available to travellers who buy their tickets outside North America, it is a good idea to give careful consideration to travel plans *before* you go. Also, when you buy your tickets outside the US, you save the sales tax. Basically, travel is like everything else in America - you have to shop around for the best buys. Never be afraid to ask for the cheapest fare. There are always variations and the clerk selling you a ticket is not necessarily about to offer you the cheapest one.

BUS Travelling long distances cross-country by bus has become a part of American mythology and for natives and overseas visitors alike, bus remains a popular method of cheap travel in North America. Despite competition from comparatively inexpensive air fares which has resulted in the cutting back of bus routes and facilities in recent times, the major nationwide company, Greyhound, and the many regional, smaller companies, have survived and will no doubt still be the chief means of inter-city transportation for most budget travellers to North America for the foreseeable future. **Greyhound's** central information number is (800) 231-2222, _www.greyhound.com_, or _www.discoverypass.com_. In the UK, call: 0870 1 600 599, or try STA Travel at _www.statravel.co.uk_.

It is possible to travel all over North America on Greyhound or on one of the many other bus lines. Bus terminals provide restaurants, ticket, baggage and parcel services, travel bureaux, restrooms and left-luggage lockers, although you should be aware that bus stations are often in the seediest areas of downtown and therefore not a place to actually plan on spending a lot of time. Periodic rest stops are made every three to four hours en route and if you are on a very tight budget you can save by travelling at nights and sleeping on the bus.

When travelling by bus from point A to point B, always ask about the cheapest available fare. Fare reductions are made and usually depend on the time of travel, how long away, when returning, etc. Look out for special promotional fares and when possible buy a round-trip ticket rather than a one-way fare. It can be a little cheaper. For example, 'We went R/T Washington DC – New York for $35 on Washington Deluxe including movies. One way is $20.'

Available to overseas visitors, before leaving for the USA, are the various Greyhound **Ameripasses**. Student rates for summer: 7-day Pass-$215, 10 days-$260, 15 days-$314, 21 days-$377, 30 days-$431, 45 days-$476 and 60 days-$575. NB. These are peak rates, valid 16th May to 30th September. The Ameripass is not valid for travel in Canada. However, Greyhound now has a **CanAm Pass** that allows unrestricted cross-border travel and is valid for Canada and the USA, as well as a **North America CanAm Pass** which includes selected areas of Mexico. For example, in peak season a 15-day North American pass is US $386, $422 for 21 days (with student ID). _For further information on Greyhound fares in Canada, please see the Background Canada section of this book._

In addition, Greyhound offers US regional passes. All USA passes are available at the Greyhound International office in New York City, Port Authority Bus Terminal. Remember that time on all the passes starts ticking away when you start your journey. The passes offer unlimited travel on Greyhound routes (and those of participating carriers) and represent excellent value for the cross-country traveller.

Tips. Whenever possible, take your bags on to the bus with you, otherwise get a check-in ticket; make sure they are labelled and checked to your final destination. Then watch them like a hawk - it is not uncommon for you and your bags to set off in different directions, and without the check-in ticket you may never get them back. If you have to put your bag underneath the bus it is recommended that at each stop en route to your destination you get off the bus and watch to make sure that your bag stays there and continues with you - on the same bus. 'If all lockers are taken, luggage can be stored for up to 24 hours for a small fee, in the bus depot luggage store.' And if you're a backpacker just arrived in a big city, you can usually leave your pack at one of the museums for free and then skip off to look for a room or do a little sightseeing unencumbered. 'Bus pass coupons have to be validated each time for further travel. As ticket lines can be very long, it's good to have your ticket stamped for the next journey as soon as you arrive.'

If planning to sleep on the bus, get a cheap inflatable pillow. It can make all the difference to your comfort, though some readers say a sleeping bag is better 'and doesn't puncture'. Malleable wax ear plugs are also a good idea for lighter sleepers. Always have a sweatshirt or pullover with you. Bus drivers seem to be impervious to cold. 'Even at 3am on a chill night the air conditioning is set to combat the climate of Death Valley.'

The bus passes often entitle you to discounts at station restaurants, nearby hotels and on various sightseeing tours. It's in fact cheaper to eat away from the stations, but you might not always have the time to do so.

Most bus routes are meant solely to get you from A to B; scenic considerations rarely come into it.

The Green Tortoise. A kind of alternative bus/tour combo designed to get the budget traveller across country cheaply, but in a fun, laid-back way. Time is not of the essence here. No effort is made to get there fast. The idea is to meander gently with the route changing at the request of the passengers. The coast to coast trips begin and end in either New York or Boston and San Francisco, depart 1-2 times a month, last 12-14 days and at present cost between $549-$649, plus $151-$171 for meals/park admission fees. Other tours are available - to Yosemite, the Grand Canyon, Mexico, Death Valley, Costa Rica, Alaska and New Orleans for Mardi Gras (usually in February).

Buses accommodate 28 to 44 people and have most of their seats removed and replaced by wooden platforms covered with foam rubber padding. They also have stoves and refrigerators. Often you can eat at scenic places such as a Louisiana bayou or the banks of the Rio Grande. Smoking is banned on the buses.

'A wonderful trip. I made many new and lasting friends and saw many places I might otherwise have missed.' 'Don't do it if you're an insomniac, a loner, need a shower more than once every three days, or a moaner.'

Reservations should be made through Green Tortoise, 494 Broadway, San Francisco CA 94133. Or for information phone: (800) TORTOISE (867-8647); when in the Bay area call (415) 956-7500. *www.greentortoise.com* Email: *tortoise@greentortoise.com*.

CAR. The car overwhelmingly remains the most popular form of travel and the vast system of super-highways - 'monuments to motion' - enables you to cover great distances. 'The National System of Interstate and Defence Highways is designed for maximum efficiency. For enjoyment, try state and country roads, even for a lengthy trip. The additional time spent will be more than compensated for by the increased intimacy with American culture and scenery.' 'Driving up the coast from LA to San Francisco was breathtaking; the views are priceless, well-worth it!'

For planning road trips, _www.mapquest.com_ is a highly useful source. It offers detailed driving directions, along with a list of hotels and information on area attractions for any given destination.

Buying a car. For a group of three or four it can be worthwhile buying a second-hand car. Try to buy and sell privately, utilising the notice boards of universities, and the local press.

Be sure to obtain a 'title' or, in states such as New York, a notarised bill of sale. If stopped by the police, proof of ownership will be required. (In some states it is illegal to drive without this.) Allow for a delay while the title comes through. If you buy from a dealer he can issue temporary licence plates on the spot.

You can have your car checked over at a gas station at a very low cost. If you have to buy new parts, get them at one of the nation-wide stores like Sears, or from major gas stations like Shell and Mobil. They will give you guarantees and have the advantage of being readily available all over the continent. Garages are efficient and friendly and if you are from out-of-state, will usually do repairs, however major, on the spot.

Prices of second-hand cars vary widely from place to place and tend to be higher on the West Coast. Prices fall in September when the next year's new cars come on to the market. Leave several days for selling your car and if possible try not to do it in New York. Remember that automatic cars are easier to sell. 'Two of us bought a large station wagon for $800 and drove it 12,000 miles in two months. We slept in it often, and sometimes ate in it too. We sold it back to the dealer we bought it from at half-price. Worst problems: two $50 repair bills and finding places to park.' 'We bought a car. It cost $400 among seven. I personally paid $50 and to travel 5000 miles it cost me $60 in gas. Well worth it and it gave us freedom to visit so many places.'

Insurance. You are strongly advised to take out at least third-party cover - full comprehensive coverage is preferable - as insurance claims can be very high and inadequate insurance can lead to financial ruin.

Insurance premiums are generally high, particularly for males under 25. Women are considered better risks and their premiums are lower. Premiums are lower if you are resident outside large urban areas. Allow time for your policy to come through.

In states where insurance is compulsory it is necessary to have it before you can register your car. 'We bought a car in Colorado and had trouble insuring it with an International Drivers' License. So be prepared to take a test and get a state license!'

Licences. All states and provinces of the US and Canada now officially recognise all European licences and those of Japan, Australia and New Zealand among others. However, an International Driving Licence is recommended since it provides you with an additional source of photographic ID. Also police are more familiar with them and this could save you time and embarrassment. However, don't forget to bring your *original* licence too, including the paper counterpart to the card. You may not be able to hire a car or get a drive-away without it. Although not a legal requirement, it's a good idea to have it done, particularly if your licence is not in English. You won't encounter many multi-lingual patrolmen along the way. You must always have your insurance certificate, car registration certificate and driving licence with you in the car. There is no grace period; you will simply be fined for driving without the legally required documents.

AAA membership. Benefits include: helping with car rental, hotel reservation, towing service, $5000 bail if arrested, excellent and free maps and regional guide books and a comprehensive information and advisory service. For example, the AAA will plan your journey for you, giving the quickest or most scenic routes, and provide detailed maps of the towns you will pass through.

Touring membership varies depending on where you join. In New York for example it costs $55 for the first year and $45 thereafter. Apply to: AAA, 1881 Broadway and 62nd St, New York 10023, (212)-586-1166, or to the Club in whichever state you happen to be. *www.aaa.com* There are also a few other motor clubs with similar benefits. Allstate Motor Club, (800) 347-8880, $48 annual fee, is one of the better known ones. *www.allstate.com.*

Gasoline. Depending on which part of the country you are in, expect to pay more than $2.50-3.50 a gallon. (The American gallon is one-fifth smaller than the imperial gallon used in Britain and Canada and is equivalent to 3.8 litres.) When driving in remote areas, always keep your tank topped up. Gas stations can be few and far between. Keep a reserve supply in a container for emergencies. Shop around and use self service pumps for the cheapest gas.

Automobile transporting companies - Driveaways. Americans change homes more often than any other people and may, for instance, live for a few years in New York and then move off to California. When they do move they sometimes put their car (or one of them) into the hands of an automobile transporting company which does no more than find someone like you to drive the car from A to B.

Most movements are from east to west, major starting points being New York, Detroit and Toronto. 'East-west is the easiest route to get; otherwise New York-Florida or New York-Atlanta. The cheapest way to travel bar hitching'. Even on the popular routes you may have to wait a couple of days for a car, particularly in summer.

Conditions regarding age limitation, time schedules, routing, gas and oil expenses, deposit, insurance and medical fitness vary considerably and should always be carefully checked. And another thing: 'The car trunk may be full of the owner's belongings, leaving no room for yours.' A fair example would be for a driver 21 years or over, with character references, to be charged about $300 deposit, refundable on safe delivery. 'A superb and cheap way of travelling. I went with three others in a van and it only cost us $70 each in gas to get from New York to San Francisco via the Grand Canyon.' 'Beware. We had a series of bad experiences. Each office acts independently and sometimes against what the same company's office elsewhere tells you.' 'You have to take a reasonably direct route, but the time limit (after which you are reported to the FBI) allows a fair amount of sightseeing. I was given nine days for the coast-to-coast trip and made it in six. It's certainly a great way to see America.'

'I drove a new Cadillac with only two thousand miles on the clock. It was air conditioned, everything electric - really unbelievable, and we slept in it at night. Good places to sleep are truck-stops run by Texaco, Union 76, etc. They have 24 hour restaurants and free showers, and the truckers themselves, though rough-looking, are often interesting people to talk to.' 'Try and have more than one driver in the car.'

'When asking for your deposit back and before handing the keys over, hold out for cash. American cheques are a bugger to cash.' And a word of warning: 'It is essential to check the car thoroughly for dents and scratches before taking it. We lost $135 because the owner complained about scratches and we could not prove they were there before we took it.'

The names of companies can be found in the Yellow Pages under 'Automobile and Truck Transporting'. It is a good idea to shop around, go to the office in person, and make sure you do not sign away your insurance rights - i.e. make sure you personally are covered and not just the vehicle. Try **Auto Driveaway**, 310 S Michigan Ave, Chicago, IL 60604, (800) 346-2277, _www.driveaway.com_ The addresses of some other companies are listed under many towns and cities below or check the web at: _www.movecars.com_

Rentals. The biggest national firms are Hertz, Avis, National, Budget, Thrifty and Dollar. The last two are generally cheaper, but even Hertz can offer some amazing deals. It's important to phone around. Always compare costs per day against costs per mile and other variations, such as unlimited mileage or so many miles free, within the context of your specific needs. Many rental companies offer discount rates to foreign visitors, though sometimes only when bookings are made abroad.

The renter must usually be 21 or over, sometimes over 25. If you don't have a credit card then a hefty cash deposit will be required, and for foreigners a passport may also have to be deposited as security. 'It's very difficult to rent a car without a major credit card, and in many cases it's not possible to leave a deposit.' 'Small companies generally ask drivers to be 25 or over; large companies usually accept drivers from 18 provided they have a major credit card.' 'Younger the driver, higher the surcharge-in some cases as high as $45 per day!'

Insurance is not usually included in the cost, or often it's only third-party. It's essential that you take out full coverage; the alternative may be a lifetime of paying off someone's massive hospital bills.

Enterprise and Alamo are also recommended. Then there are the companies renting out older cars, e.g. Rent-a-Wreck, Rent-a-Heap, Rent-a-Junk and Ugly Duckling. But they are not always the cheapest or most flexible, e.g. in some instances you must stay within a 50 or 100-mile radius of the point of rental. Worth checking out, though. 'Phone the national company number as well as the local agent's number. One may well offer a better deal than the other.'

'Ask a travel agent for good deals; I found them to be in the know.' 'It's a good idea to check with the airline you're travelling on for special arrangements. Sometimes these can only be booked before the flight.' 'Don't entertain a firm that charges for mileage and drop-off; there are plenty that don't.' 'If you want unlimited mileage you must usually go to a large company.' 'We found car rental easiest, most convenient and, for groups of three or more, the cheapest way of getting to see National Parks and other areas where transport, other than tours, is minimal.'

Road Tips. Traffic regulations, including speed limits, vary from state to state, so familiarise yourself with them in each. Many readers recommend buying the Rand McNally *Interstate Road Atlas*, useful even for non-drivers. Maps from gas stations cost around $3.

'Most truck drivers have CBs. When driving, follow the example they set. If they adhere to the speed limit it means they've picked up the police lurking in the locality.'

If you have a breakdown, raising the hood is the recognised distress signal. Also switch on your flashing warning lights.

Never pass a stopped and flashing school bus (they are usually yellow) no matter which side of the road it is on: it is not only against the law, but could easily result in death or injury to young children.

AIR. The vast distances of the North American continent have resulted in popularity and relative cheapness of domestic air travel, and there are usually some air travel bargains to be had. The best advice is to always double check on fares and routes. So if you plan to fly, check airline sites on the web and with travel agents, phone around the airlines and keep an eye on newspaper advertising - and always ask for the cheapest available fare. In particular, check the Sunday travel sections in major newspapers, and especially on the web at sites that specialize in finding you the lowest fares such as *www.expedia.com*,   *www.travelocity.com*,   *www.cheapticket.com*, *www.uniglobeonline.com*, or *www.vacationweb.com*. One airline or another is almost always offering cheap flights somewhere in North America!

Some other possibilities: night flights are sometimes cheaper than day flights; some airlines from time to time offer off-peak, cheaper, fares. In particular, try Jetblue, Spiritair, AirTran, Southwest, and US Airways. Other airlines make discounts if you travel on a flight making stops en route and, if planning to travel great distances, it may pay to investigate the air passes (see below). There may be considerable price competition on major routes such as New York to Florida and New York to the West Coast. Once again, the message is shop around!

Additionally there are the *Visit USA* bargains available only to non-US residents and offering incredible value for cross-country travel. The terms

RIDING SCENIC RAIL

North America, especially the Rockies, is full of scenic narrow gauge railways, where restored steam locomotives backtrack to bygone days. These are some of the more interesting rides:

Blue Ridge Scenic Railway (800) 934-1898, in Blue Ridge, Georgia is a 26 mile trip along the Toccoa River. 3½ hr r/t $22-28, rsvs rec. _www.brscenic.com_. **Cumbres & Toltec Scenic Railroad** in Antonito, CO, (888) 286-2737, is North America's highest narrow-gauge steam railroad. Full-day trip leaves at 10am, a 64-mile tour, $55-70. _www.cumbrestoltec.com_ **Grand Canyon Railway** (800) 843-8724, 2hr15min trip from Williams, Arizona, through the northern Arizona countryside to Grand Canyon National Park. Includes strolling musicians and western characters recreating turn-of-the-century train travel. Coach, $60 r/t. _www.thetrain.com_. **Great Smoky Mountain Railroad**, (800) 872-4681, Bryson City, NC. Trips through Nantahala Gorge, Fontana Lake, and along the Tennessee River. Hrs subject to change; $28-$40 for 4.5hr r/t with 1hr layover. _www.gsmr.com_.

Mt Washington Cog Railway, New Hampshire, (800) 922-8825. The world's first mountain climbing cog railway along a historic route, offering a highly scenic trip to the highest point in Northeast; 3 hr trip, $49. _www.thecog.com_. **Narrow Gauge Railroad**, Durango, CO, (888) 872-4607. Along Animas River Valley to Silverton. Old fashioned and spectacular. $60 r/t, 1-4 trips daily. _www.durangotrain.com_. **Pikes Peak Cog Railway**, Manitou Springs, CO, (719) 685-5401. Several 3 hr trips daily from Manitou Springs to Pikes Peak, the highest route in the US, $29. _www.cograilway.com_. **Roaring Camp & Big Trees Narrow-Gauge Railroad**, Felton, California, (831) 335-4484. Winds through the Rincon Valley of giant redwood trees and down the San Lorenzo River Gorge to the beach at Monterey Bay. 1hr trip, 10.30 am and 2.30 pm daily, $18 r/t. _www.roaringcamp.com_. **Skunk Train**, Ft Bragg, CA, (800) 866-1690. Half day $35. Scenic route through Redwoods. _www.skunktrain.com_. **Strasburg Railroad**, Strasburg, PA, (717) 687-7522. 45 min route through Amish country, $9.75 + upgrades. America's oldest short-line steam locomotive. _www.strasburgrailroad.com_.

and prices vary from airline to airline, but the principles are the same and the tickets have to be purchased BEFORE leaving for America.

Delta Airlines currently (_check for up-to-date information_) offers 'Discover America' coupons, which can be bought in conjunction with Delta or Air France trans-Atlantic flights. _www.delta.com_ **United Airlines** offers a similar deal-0845 84447777.

Northwest Airlines has several pass-type options, but only in conjunction with a transatlantic flight on Northwest or KLM. 'Visit USA' coupons are purchased with the transatlantic flight. When you begin using your coupons, there is a maximum stay of 60 days permitted. Call (800)447-4747. _www.nwa.com_. **America West** offers 'Visit USA' (VUSA) valid in conjunction with any air carrier. For info contact: (800)-292-9378. _www.americawest.com._

RAIL The railroads played a major role in the history of the United States, but over recent decades they've declined in service, increased in price, lost money and seen much of their former business go to cars and airlines. Part of the reason for this may have been the great number of competing railways and the inability of the individual companies to undertake the new investment necessary to improve service and efficiency. But in 1971 **Amtrak** was established. The railways remain privately owned but losses on passenger services are made up by government subsidy.

On long-haul Western routes, outdated equipment has been replaced by double-decker superliners, variously fitted up as lounges, dining cars (restaurant upstairs, kitchen below), sleeping cars (with bedrooms) and open-plan coaches. On shorter routes and generally in the East, cylinder-shaped 'Amcoaches' are used, their interiors like luxury airliners.

In the East, frequency, time-keeping and the large number of destinations served permit comparison with European railways. From Chicago westwards it is the trans-Siberian railway that comes to mind. There are only four east-west routes, but all except one operate daily. Delays are common. But for the traveller that should not matter: the scenery is often spectacular, the service is better than on any railway in the world, the seats recline and have foot rests, you can eat and drink well and inexpensively, and the company is congenial. The Western railways are the last stronghold of graceful travel in America and many readers have written in to praise Amtrak and the standard of its services. 'Ideal for the student traveller going from city to city.' 'Very comfortable.' 'The best way to see a wide variety of scenery. On occasions we felt less worn from 20 hours on a train than four hours on a bus.' 'A wonderful window on to the USA.'

A rundown on some of the more interesting routes:

The Empire Builder runs between Chicago and Seattle or Portland, Oregon via Milwaukee, Minneapolis/St Paul, Fargo in North Dakota, Glacier National Park and Spokane. Majestic scenery. Takes about 46 hours; operates daily.

The Coast Starlight, between Los Angeles and Seattle, offers superb coastal, forest and mountain scenery. 'Attracts many young people. A highly social train: spontaneous parties and lust.' Takes 35 hours; operates daily.

The California Zephyr, formerly operated by The Denver & Rio Grande Western Railroad, is now operated by Amtrak, daily. The train starts in Chicago; the journey between Denver and Salt Lake City takes 18 hours, almost all in daylight, and climbs 9000 feet over the Rockies for what is considered the greatest railway ride in America. It then runs on to San Francisco. Also special are the *Adirondack* between New York and Montréal, and the *Capitol Limited* between Washington DC and Chicago.

Amtrak passes for 15/30 days unlimited travel are available to overseas visitors outside the US and are available in some cities at the Amtrak station. Check first however. Current high season rates (28th May-1st Sept) are: $440/$550 nationwide (15/30 day).   Discounted fares are available to ISIC card holders on the North American Railpass between Canada and the USA. Once you have bought the pass you can make reservations by phoning 1-800-USA-RAIL. 'Excellent value, great way to travel. Trains spacious and comfortable. Staff friendly and helpful.' 'Disadvantages -

trains slow and often late.' 'It is essential to make reservations for the busy east coast routes to Florida.' 'One drawback is the early morning (4am!) arrival time at some mid-west stations.' 'Beware the out of town location of some stations. Taxis to downtown add expense.'

In Britain: **Trailfinders**, 020-7628-7628, are one of the agents that offer Amtrak tickets, although bear in mind that you may not be able to access the discounts advertised on the web page. _www.trailfinders.com._ **STA** offer student fares.   Check _www.statravel.co.uk._ In the US call (800) 872-7245, **Amtrak Vacations**, or look up some interesting routes on _www.amtrak.com._

BOATS. 'If you want to take a longer trip on the Mississippi, you can try to get on a towing boat. But you'll have to work hard. Look in the _Yellow Pages_ under "Towing-Marine".'

How about paddling your own canoe? The Appalachian Mountain Club publishes books of interest to canoeists and kayakers including: _AMC River Guide Maine; AMC River Guide Massachusetts, Connecticut and Rhode Island; AMC River Guide New Hampshire and Vermont, Sea Kayaking along the Mid Atlantic; Sea Kayaking along the New England Coast._ They're available by mail from AMC Books, 5 Joy Street, Boston MA 02108, or PO Box 298, route 16, NH 03581, (800) 262-4455 or online at _www.outdoors.org_.

The Chicagoland Canoe Base Inc, 4019 N Narragansett Avenue, Chicago IL 60634, (773) 777-1489, can provide you with all the information you need on canoes, kayaks, rafts, accessories, rentals, books and maps. _www.chicagoland-canoebase.com_.

HITCHHIKING. We strongly recommend that women, or even men, do not hitch alone, or even at all! However hitchhiking in the United States does happen and it can be 'good, simply due to the long rides'. So if you find yourself in a situation where you feel you must hitchhike, don't do it alone and be careful. Never accept a lift that you don't feel 100 percent comfortable about. 'A sure way of getting long rides in relative comfort and at speeds in excess of the general 55 mph limit is to ask for rides at truck stops. At Union 76 truck stops there will often be hundreds of trucks going to all parts of America. Just ask the drivers in the canteen. Truck stop directories can be obtained free at truck stops.'

Hitching by air is another, somewhat off-the-wall, possibility with the same warnings applying of course as for auto hitching. That is: be very careful, check out the plane and the pilot and if possible don't try to do it alone. America is dotted with thousands of _small airfields_ located outside most towns from which people fly in _small aircraft_ for pleasure or business. Those are the people you ask.   'Difficult across US/Canada border.' 'Air hitching is really difficult but saves so much time it's worth a try.' 'I walked into an air freight company office in San Francisco and got a free ride back to New York with the overnight packages.' Not a good idea to carry much luggage though - small light aircraft remember?

BICYCLE. There's a 4450-mile TransAmerica Trail stretching from Virginia to Oregon, covered by 12 maps available from the Adventure Cycling

Association, PO Box 8308, Missoula, Montana 59807, (406) 721-1776, email: *info@adventurecycling.org* or check out *www.adv-cycling.org* for more routes. In total there are 35,000 miles of mapped trails in the USA. Some hostels do bicycle tours; information is available from local regional offices and the hostels themselves.

A strong bicycle lock is advisable for security when parking in towns, plus a helmet (US drivers are not attuned to looking out for bikes). Bicycles are cheaper in the US than abroad. It's possible to ship a bike around the US with Amtrak or the bus companies provided it's dismantled and boxed. Bikes can sometimes be taken free on flights to and from the US as part of your baggage allowance and again must be boxed. The cost, if any, varies from airline to airline.

ON FOOT. Given the available time-and a stout pair or two of hiking boots-what better way can there be to find out about America and the American people than by walking across the continent! Like John Lees of Brighton, England, who in 1972 walked from City Hall, Los Angeles, to City Hall, New York, a distance of 2876 miles, in 53 days 12 hours 15 minutes, averaging 53.75 miles per day.

'When asking for directions, remember that most people think you are on wheels. I was directed to one place along a roadway that took me 15 minutes to negotiate in the boiling hot sun, an excursion I could have avoided by cutting - in one-third the time - through a leafy forest. Unfortunately, the guy I asked thought I was a Chevy, so I had to go the long way round.'

American Discovery Trail, opened at the end of 1999, is the United States' first coast-to-coast, nonmotorized trail. Covering over 6,800 miles, the trail starts at Cape Henlopen State Park on the Delaware Coast in the east and ends at Limantour Beach in Point Reyes National Seashore, about 45 miles north of San Francisco in the west. In between, this walking window on America passes through hundreds of small towns, larger centres like Kansas City, Denver and Cincinnati, along forest footpaths and urban walkways, by canals, up mountains and along river banks; all in all covering 15 states and accessing 14 National Parks.

For information, call the American Trail Discovery Society on: (800) 663-2387, or check out the website: *www.discoverytrail.org*

There's also the 2000 mile **Appalachian Trail**, *www.appalachian.org* which tracks that aged mountain range northward from Georgia to Maine, and the **Great Western Trail**, *www.gwt.org* that runs from the Mexican to the Canadian border along the Rocky Mountains.

A list of more than 31 hiking clubs along the east coast can be obtained by writing to the Appalachian Trail Conference, Box 807, Harpers Ferry WV 25425, (304) 535-6331, which manages the Appalachian Trail in conjunction with the National Park Service. They'll send you information about the trail, membership, etc. *www.appalachiantrail.org.* In the west there's the Sierra Club. They provide information about the **Pacific Crest Trail**, 2600 miles along the Pacific Coast from Canada to Mexico, but also offer backpack and camping advice as well as trips lasting 6-10 days. For details, contact 85 2nd St, 2nd floor, San Francisco CA 94105, (415) 977-5500, *www.sierraclub.org*.

NATIONAL PARKS. There are 41 national parks in the United States, all of which offer the visitor beautiful scenery; everything from fantastic seascapes, deep canyons, spectacular volcanoes, to pure lakes and craggy mountains. Many parks are somewhat off the beaten track and although the roadways in all are excellent, the parks are best seen more slowly on foot, by bicycle, horse, or canoe. Most offer camping facilities and some offer cabin or hotel accommodation.

Should you intend to use the National Park system extensively, purchase a National Park Pass on sale at all parks, or from the National Parks Foundation, 1849 C St, NW, Rm 7102, Washington DC 20240, or call (888) GO-PARKS. *www.nationalparks.org*. The pass costs $50 and gives you, and anyone accompanying you in a private vehicle, free entrance to all the parks for a year from first use. Otherwise paying individually may vary from free to $10 approx. Other activities such as camping, parking, or swimming, of course, cost extra. Also, visitors arriving before 7am sometimes get in free. Reservations for camping are essential in peak season; apply in advance to be sure of a pitch. For further information and reservations, look up *http://reservations.nps.gov.*

There are also numerous national seashores, monuments and forests, and other federally-administered preserves which should not be overlooked. In addition there are thousands of state parks across America, many of which provide facilities for swimming, camping, hiking, etc., for a modest entry fee. Almost all the national parks are included in this Guide. For more information write directly to the park, asking for details and brochures. A list of the major national parks in the US follows.

Acadia, Maine
Arches, Utah
Badlands, South Dakota
Big Bend, Texas
Bryce Canyon, Utah
Canyonlands, Utah
Carlsbad Caverns, New Mexico
Crater Lake, Oregon
Denali, Alaska
Everglades, Florida
Glacier, Montana
Grand Canyon, Arizona
Grand Teton, Wyoming
Great Basin, Nevada
Great Smoky Mountains, TN
Guadalupe Mountains, Texas
Haleakala, Maui, Hawaii
Hawaii Volcanoes, Hawaii
Hot Springs, Arkansas
Isle Royal, Michigan

Kings Canyon, California
Lassen Volcanic, California
Mammoth Cave, Kentucky
Mesa Verde, Colorado
Mount Rainier, Washington
National Reef, Utah
North Cascades, Washington
Olympic, Washington
Petrified Forest, Arizona
Platt, Oklahoma
Redwood, California
Rocky Mountain, Colorado
Sequoia, California
Shenandoah, Virginia
Theodore Roosevelt, ND
Virgin Islands, St John, VI
Voyageurs, Minnesota
Wind Cave, South Dakota
Yellowstone, WY/MT
Yosemite, California
Zion, Utah.

Tours with a difference. If young, on your own and looking for fun and adventure, one of the proliferation of alternative tours or treks would be worth considering. Typically they either load up a van full of young people and tour chunks of the country or else they operate a roughly scheduled service allowing the traveller to get off and on when they please. One of the longest running companies (so to speak) is **TrekAmerica,** which offers around 70 different itineraries from seven days to nine weeks, covering virtually every area of North America. During the summer season, a 14-day tour costs approximately $917-$1072 plus $7 per day for food. They fill up quickly, so reserve early. There is a 15% discount for all BUNAC members. Extras such as horseback riding and rafting are available at additional cost.

In Britain, contact TrekAmerica, Worldwide Reservations, 4 Waterperry Court, Middleton Road, Banbury, Oxon, OX16 4QB. Tel: 01295-256777. In the USA: TrekAmerica, PO Box 189 Rockaway, NJ 07866. (973) 983-1144 or (800) 221-0596. Email: *info@trekamerica.com* or check out *www.trekamerica.com*. 'An excellent way to see America if you don't mind camping and long drives. For a girl travelling on her own who didn't want to Greyhound or hitch, it enabled me to see a terrific amount in three weeks.'

For exploring the western national parks north to Alaska, south to Baja California, you could consider **Adventurebus**. All trips depart from Las Vegas and, for example, the 8-day trip costs about $825 which includes about 70% of the food costs. Take off 50% if you decide to take a second week. Adventurebus offers a discount to BUNAC members. Call: 1-888-737-5263/ (909) 797-7366, email: *info@adventureplanet.com* for info and reservations, or check them on the web at: *www.adventurebus.com*

Urban travel. Local city buses and subway systems generally offer good services throughout North America. Usually, a flat fare is used which can make short hops expensive but long rides very reasonable. Many cities have a transfer system allowing you to change from one bus line to another, or even from bus to subway, without paying extra. Robberies have meant that bus drivers will not carry any more money than is absolutely necessary, so you must always have the exact fare. Many systems have facilities to transport bikes.

Taxis can be pretty expensive unless shared. The ubiquitous Gray Line company ensures that nearly every city has its bus tour, and some have boat tours as well.

For further details, see under city headings throughout this Guide.

FURTHER READING

Fiction

The Awakening, Kate Chopin
Bonfire of the Vanities, Tom Wolfe
Catcher in the Rye, J. D. Salinger
The Color Purple, Alice Walker
Gone with the Wind, Margaret Mitchell
Glitz, Elmore Leonard
The Grapes of Wrath, John Steinbeck
The Great Gatsby, F. Scott Fitzgerald
Huckleberry Finn, Mark Twain
Lake Wobegon Days, Garrison Keiller
Main Street, Sinclair Lewis
A Month of Sundays, John Updike
Native Son, Richard Wright
Ninety-Two in the Shade, Thomas McGuane
On the Road, Jack Kerouac
O Pioneers! Willa Cather
Outcasts of Poker Flat, Bret Harte
The Scarlet Letter, Nathaniel Hawthorne
Southern Discomfort, Rita Mae Brown
Stepping Westward, Malcolm Bradbury
To Kill a Mockingbird, Harper Lee
USA, John Dos Passos

Other Works

Apple's America, R.W. Apple Jr.
Blue Highway: A Journey into America, William Least Halfmoon
Bury My Heart at Wounded Knee: an Indian History of the American West, Dee Brown
Fear and Loathing in Las Vegas, Hunter S. Thompson
New York Days, New York Nights, Stephen Brook
The Nine Nations of North America, Garreau
Old Glory, Johnathan Raban
The Lost Continent: Travels in Small Town America, and *A Walk in the Woods*, Bill Bryson
Undaunted Courage, Stephen E. Ambrose
Vagabonding in America, Ed Buryn (if you can get hold of it)
Walk West, David Jenkins

NEW ENGLAND

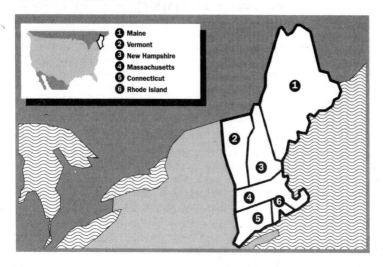

1 Maine
2 Vermont
3 New Hampshire
4 Massachusetts
5 Connecticut
6 Rhode Island

The upper north-east corner of the United States is sometimes called the nation's attic. One of the first areas in the New World to be colonised by Europeans, it is the old historical ties, more than any other, that bind these New England states together. It was here that American independence was born, embodied by such patriots as Paul Revere and Samuel Adams, and here that America's anti-slavery movement emerged, led by William Lloyd Garrison. The region's size does not match its great historical significance— its six states are together smaller than Oklahoma.

New England is a melting pot, spiced with a rich diversity gained from the British, Irish, Italians, French Canadians, Portuguese, Jews and many others who now make up the population. Cultural contrasts abound: contemporary, cosmopolitan Boston stands alongside peaceful country towns whose life centres on charming village greens—revered reminders of early American society. To 'Southerners', however, New Englanders are still Yankees. The northernmost actions in the Civil War took place in New England in 1864 in the form of carefully planned Confederate cross-border raids from Canada on Calais, in Maine, and in St. Albans, Vermont, the latter netting $208,000 from four banks, a fortune for the time.

This compact region offers a great variety of scenery, from the rugged White Mountains of New Hampshire to the rolling green hills of Vermont, Massachusetts and Connecticut. Lush green countryside becomes weatherbeaten and sun-bleached as it meets the Atlantic. Sometimes spectacular coastal roads stretch for miles, weaving around jagged points and hidden inlets.

Politically, New England is important; the world's first written 'constitution'—the Mayflower Compact—was signed by the Pilgrim Fathers here in 1620. The American Revolution was hatched in Boston, and in modern times, ex-President Bush and the Kennedys hail from the area.

Perhaps more than any other region, New England has been home to some of America's best known painters and writers. Norman Rockwell lived and worked in Vermont, Maxfield Parrish in New Hampshire. Quadruple Pulitzer prize winner Robert Frost, although he started his famous poem *The Road Not Taken* ("I took the one less traveled by") in England, where he knew Ezra Pound and Yeats, Frost finished it in New Hampshire. Frost owned several farmhouses at various times in New Hampshire and Vermont, taught at Harvard, Dartmouth, and Amherst, and read his poetry at President Kennedy's inauguration. He's buried in Bennington, Vermont.

The seasons are distinct in New England: a long, cold, winter followed by a short blossom-filled spring, a hot, often humid summer, and best of all, a glorious autumn when the leaves turn the hillsides gold, scarlet and amber.

Hard-core hikers may like to tackle the 2000-mile long **Appalachian Trail**—the longest marked trail in the world. Beginning north of Bangor in Maine it winds more than 2000 miles from Baxter State Park to the mountains of Georgia.

CONNECTICUT - The Nutmeg State

Connecticut is the third smallest state in the Union and is one of the most densely populated. Historically it has regarded itself as part of New England, although the area abutting New York State along Long Island Sound has far stronger ties with New York City than it has with **Burlington** or even **Hartford,** the state capital. **Greenwich, Stamford** and **Bridgeport** make up a significant commuter-belt and many people here look to the New York media for their news and entertainment.

The state divides itself into four regions, each with its own picturesque setting. Away from the shoreline beaches along Long Island Sound, Connecticut is a state of broad rivers, farms, forests, rolling hills and placid colonial villages. In particular, the **Litchfield Hills** in the North West region offer pretty scenery and have several excellent state parks good for camping and walking.

Since 1656 with the first public library, a bequest to New Haven, Connecticut has produced many originals: the submarine was invented here in 1776 and it is also the birthplace of the lollipop and the payphone. The insurance industry has its roots in Connecticut and the Constitution State is home to America's first law school. Some of the oldest university art collections in the US are at **Yale University**, in New Haven. For information visit: *www.ct.gov* and *www.ctbound.org*.

The telephone area code for south-western CT is 203, elsewhere it is 860.

HARTFORD   The state capital, is home to the nation's insurance industry, and thanks to the dark-suited image this presents, the city is not ordinarily known for its sparkling social scene. Recently, however efforts have been made to turn the city into a livelier regional attraction. **The Civic Center** and **State House Square** provide shopping, restaurants, and entertainment, and should be added to a list of more antique sights, such as **Mark Twain's**

House, _www.marktwainhouse.org_, the pre-World War One carousel in **Bushnell Park**, and, in the nearby suburbs of **Wethersfield** and **Farmington,** some of the oldest colonial houses in the US.

While here, pick up the _Hartford Courant_, _www.ctnow.com_, founded in 1764 and the newspaper with the oldest continuous name and circulation in the nation, possibly in the world. _www.enjoyhartford.com_ or _www.hartford.com_.

Accommodation

Most hotels downtown start at $50 for doubles. Try **Manchester** for cheaper deals.

Super 8 Motel, 57 W Service Rd, 246-8888/(800) 800-8000. From $54. Coffee and doughnut incl. _www.super8.com_.

Mark Twain Hostel, 131 Tremont St, 523-7255/(800) 909-4776 (code 124). Victorian house preserved in its natural state. Dorm from $15. Private rooms S-$48, D-$54, rsvs required. Kitchen, dining room, picnic area, bike storage, laundry. Friendly, enthusiastic staff, open 24 hrs, 365 days a year, check in 5pm-10pm. Tours available for Mark Twain House, only a block away. _www.hiayh.org_.

YMCA, 160 Jewel St, 522-4183. $20-25 per day, $133-168 weekly. Residents get free access to the gym, sauna and pool. Walking distance to Civic Center. _www.ghymca.org_. Downtown Hartford branch.

Food/Entertainment

City Steam Brewery Cafe, 942 Main St, 525-1600. Lunch $8-$15, dinner $10-$25. Very popular with the locals. Home to **Brew HaHa Comedy Club;** live comedy Thu $5, Fri-Sat $15. Daily 11.30am-midnight, Fri/Sat 'til 1am, Sun noon-10pm. _www.citysteam.com_.

Webster Theatre, 31 Webster St, in Barry Sq, off Maple Ave, 525-5553. Concert hall with 5 bars in a restored, art-deco style, 1930s movie theatre. Live bands, from rock to folk music. Cover varies. Call for details or visit _www.webstertheatre.com_.

Of Interest

Bushnell Park, adjacent State Capitol, 232-6710, America's first public park, designed in the late nineteenth century, has a 1914 carousel; you can ride one of its 48 horses or a chariot to the tunes of a Wurlitzer Band Organ for 50¢. April-Sep, Tue-Sun 11am-5pm. _www.bushnellpark.org_.

Monday Night Jazz Series, Bushnell Park, Jul-Aug, free concerts, start 6pm. Take a picnic and it makes for a lovely evening. Call 521-4388 for info.

Greater Hartford Festival of Jazz, Bushnell Park, (866) 943-JAZZ. Third weekend in July, free. Three days of concerts, local acts from the tri-state area and in the evenings. The national and international performers are Fri from 6pm, Sat-Sun from 4pm. Festival atmosphere with plenty of stalls and artisan booths. _www.hartfordjazz.com_.

Elizabeth Park Rose Garden, Prospect Ave, 231-9443. First municipal rose garden in the US. Nature walks, rock gardens, Pond House with auditorium. Daily dawn-dusk. _www.elizabethpark.org_.

Harriet Beecher Stowe House, Nook Farm, Forest St, 525-9317. This charming Victorian cottage was the home of HBS after the publication of _Uncle Tom's Cabin_, from 1873 to her death in 1896. Mon-Sat 9.30am-4.30pm, Sun from noon. Tours $8. _www.harrietbeecherstowe.org_.

Mark Twain House, 351 Farmington Ave, next door to Harriet Beecher Stowe House, 493-6411. Calling all lovers of American literature—MT, who was related on his mother's side to the Earl of Durham, lived here for almost 20 years, publishing _Huckleberry Finn_ and other major works from this quirky Victorian-Gothic style mansion. Summer: daily 9.30am-5.30pm, Sun from noon, last tour at 4.45pm. Closed Tuesdays, Jan-April. $12, $10 w/student ID, includes 1 hr tour of the house, entrance to the visitors centre and theatres. Bring a picnic to a free **'Twain by Twilight' concert** evening held in the grounds during summer. Call for dates and details. *www.marktwainhouse.org*.

New England Air Museum, Bradley International Airport, Windsor Locks, 14 miles from Hartford, 623-3305. Three huge display hangars and more than 80 aircraft from all periods of aviation history. Daily 10am-5pm, $8. *www.neam.org*.

Old State House, 800 Main St, 522-6766. Formerly the State Capitol, restored and refurbished back to its 1796 appearance. Free, self-guided tours. Information centre, Mon-Sat 10am-4pm. *www.ctosh.org*.

State Capitol, Capitol Ave and Trinity St, 240-0222, exit 48 off I-84. A dazzling Gothic monolith capped by a gold dome. Contains lots of Connecticut historical memorabilia. Be sure to see the dramatic Hall of Flags. Free tours available: hourly Mon-Fri 9.15am-2.15pm, Sat 10.15am-2.15pm (Apr-Oct only). *www.cga.state.ct.us/capitoltours*.

The Trash Museum, 211 Murphy Rd, 247-4280. Tours and interactive exhibits on solid waste management and recycling, including the 'Temple of Trash'. Summer hours: Wed-Fri 10am-4pm, free. *www.crra.org*.

Wadsworth Athenaeum Museum of Art, 600 Main St, 278-2670. One of New England's best art collections with 45,000 works; it is the country's oldest public art gallery. Renowned for its collection of *Hudson River School* landscape paintings—the largest in the world. Tue-Fri 11am-5pm, Sat-Sun from 10am, 'til 8pm on the first Thu of the month; $10, $5 w/student ID. *www.wadsworthatheneum.org*.

Information

Convention and Visitors Bureau, 31 Pratt St, 4th fl, 728-6789/(800) 446-7811. *www.enjoyhartford.com.*

Hartford Guides, 101 Pearl St, 522-0855. Goodwill ambassadors on duty in town, ready to serve the lost and the curious. Also run a hospitality van; free car service, e.g. refuelling and jumpstarts! Easily recognisable in red, white and blue uniforms. Mon-Fri 8am-9pm.

Internet Access

Hartford Public Library, 500 Main St, 543-8628. Free Internet access, 1 hr time limit. Mon-Thu 10am-8pm, Sat 9am-5pm.

Travel

Greyhound, 1 Union Pl, 247-3524/(800) 231-2222. NYC, 3 ½ hrs, Boston, 2 hrs.

Amtrak, 1 Union Pl, (800) 872-7245. NYC $36-$41, 3 hrs, Boston (change at New Haven), 3-4hrs, $60-$69.

Connecticut Transit Information Center, behind old State House, between Main & Market Sts, 525-9181, has info on public transport within the city (basic fare $1.25) and a map of downtown area. Mon-Fri 7am-6pm. *www.cttransit.com*.

NB. Only regular transport available from downtown to Bradley International Airport is via shuttle service from the Old State House, $1.25.

LITCHFIELD HILLS In the northwestern corner of the state, is an area of rolling hills, woods, rivers, streams and lakes. The town of Litchfield is a movieman's epitome of New England, with its white wooden churches, fine colonial houses, and of course, white picket fences. The town centre itself is a National Historic Site. Harriet Beecher Stowe and Ethan Allen were born here: the **Litchfield Historical Society**, 7 South St, 567-4501, has all the facts, with historical and art exhibits. *www.litchfieldhistoricalsociety.org*. Those of a judicial frame of mind may wish to stop at the **Tapping Reeve House and Law School**, 82 South St, 567-8919, America's first law school. April-Nov, Tue-Sat 11am-5pm, Sun 1pm-5pm. $5, $3 w/student ID, includes entrance to the **Litchfield History Museum**. Visit _www.ctwine.com_   for details on CT's wine trail, made up of 10 separate wineries; take 2-3 days to visit them all. **Haight Vineyard**, 29 Chestnut Hill, 567-4045/(800) 567-9463. Complimentary tasting and winery tours, all day every day. Mon-Sat 10.30am-5pm, Sun noon-5pm. _http://www.haightvineyards.com/_.

Hopkins Vineyard, 868-7954, in New Preston, is considered one of the most scenic vineyards in the east. Daily guided tours by appointment only, $8. The vineyard is open Mon-Sat 10am-5pm, Sun 11am-5pm. _www.hopkinsvineyard.com_.

Nearby is **Bantam Lake**, good for water sports, including ice yachting in winter. The **White Memorial Conservation Center**, 80 Whithall Rd, 567-0857, a free wildlife sanctuary and museum, $4, takes up about half of the lake's shoreline, with 35 miles of hiking trails. Museum: Mon-Sat 9am-5pm, Sun from noon. _www.whitememorialcc.org_.

Southwest of the lake via Rte 109 and Rte 47 is the village of **Washington**, another 'jewel of a colonial village', home to many artists and writers. The **Institute for American Indian Studies**, 38 Curtis Rd, 868-0518, is also here. Take Rte 47 to Rte 199. The Institute is home to a replicated Algonquian village complete with wigwams and a traditional longhouse, a walk trail and museum. Mon-Sat 10am-5pm, Sun from noon, $4.

Lime Rock Park, Lakeville, 435-5000/(800) RACE-LRP, for auto racing. Although 50 miles from Hartford, nestled in the scenic Berkshire Hills, the Park is a great day out if you can get there; you might even catch Paul Newman on the track! Bring a picnic and stay all day at the Labor Day weekend vintage car festival, or take a look behind the scenes at a professional road race. 10 public events are held, March-Nov. Amateur races about $15, full access weekend pass $35-$65, with free on-site camping. _www.limerock.com_.

The Litchfield Hills are a good area for walking and camping. Three of the nicer state parks where you can do both are **Housatonic Meadows, Lake Waramaug** and **Macedonia Brook**, none of which is far from Kent. For more information on parks, historic sites, accommodation and restaurants in the area contact **Litchfield Hills Visitors Bureau,** 567-4506. _www.litchfieldhills.com_. For camping permits in the State Parks write to the **Bureau of State Parks and Forests**, 79 Elm St, Hartford, 06106, 424-3200. Mon-Fri 8am-5pm. _dep.state.ct.us/_.

BRISTOL   As you meander through picturesque landscapes and tiny hamlets on your way to New Haven, stop off in Bristol, the one time clock-making capital of the US. Arrive at the **American Clock and Watch Museum**, 100 Maple St, 583-6070, in time to hear the midday chimes! A horologist's delight, brimming over with 2000 timepieces past and present, comic and stately, grand and miniature. April-Nov, daily 10am-5pm, $5. _www.clockmuseum.org_.

Step back in time and visit the **New England Carousel Museum**, 95 Riverside Ave, 585-5411, Mon-Sat 10am-5pm, Sun noon-5pm, $5. Some 300 carved horses, cats, elephants, chariots, etc., of intricate and occasionally bejewelled design. Daily guided tours include two hurdy gurdy organs, and a workshop restoring working carousel figures and parts. Magical. *www.thecarouselmuseum.org.*

Lake Compounce Theme Park, 822 Lake Ave, 583-3300, (exit 31 off I-84). Founded in 1846, this is the country's oldest running theme park. The World's only coaster built into a mountainside, Boulder Dash and New England's largest Sky Coaster, a 180 ft free fall at 70 mph, are 'fantastic fun-good laugh'. 'Some of the rides are really scary but the best part of the park is the Water Park. Cool off and definitely go on the Thunder Rapids'. Also paddleboats, mini-golf, Sky Ride and free shows. Mid-June thru mid-Aug, daily 11am-8pm, Fri & Sun 'til 9pm, Sat 'till 10pm. $32 all day rides, water park, shows and unlimited free soda. *www.lakecompounce.com*.
Visit *www.ci.bristol.ct.us* for more information on Bristol.

NEW HAVEN The city grew up around its harbour and **Yale University** (boola, boola). This Ivy League university celebrated its 300th anniversary in 2001 and is one of the best and oldest in the United States. Yale graduates include current and former presidents Bill Clinton, George Bush, and George W. Bush, as well as Senator Hillary Rodham Clinton.

Sadly, however, New Haven has failed to uphold its 19th-century reputation as one of America's most beautiful cities. While some areas are undergoing renovation, the nicest parts by far are still found on and around the **Green**. On the credit side, however, theatre and music thrive in New Haven, and there are numerous enjoyable bars, cafes, and restaurants visited by the student population.

Going east along Long Island Sound, you come to New London, from where you can catch a ferry to Long Island and Block Island. Further still, there's Mystic, en route to Newport, RI and the Massachusetts seacoast. *www.cityofnewhaven.com*.

The telephone area code for New Haven is 203.

Accommodation
Regal Inn, 1605 Whalley Ave, (Exit 59 off rte 15), 389-9504. $50-65.
Three Judges Motor Lodge, 1560 Whalley Ave, 389-2161. $55-70.

Food
The most popular restaurants in town are on **Wooster St,** in the Italian district.
Archie Moore's, 188 Willow St, ½ mile north of Peabody Museum, 773-9870. Named 'best watering hole in state', great buffalo wings, nachos, burgers, pasta, baseball on the tube, popular with grad students and locals. Appetizers $5-$8. Choice of 20 sandwiches, salads and hamburgers around $7.50. Daily 11.30am-1am.
Atticus Bookstore, 1082 Chapel St, 776-4040. Relaxing coffee shop in the Yale Center for British Art. Daily 7am-midnight.
Louie's Lunch, 263 Crown St, 562-5507. Lunches are good, and worth the wait at this reputed birthplace of the hamburger, $4 and up. 'Unique, antique, friendly atmosphere.' Lunch and dinner $4-$7. Tue & Wed 11am-4pm, Thu-Sat noon-2am.
Pepe's Pizzeria and the Spot, 157 Wooster St, 865-5762. Try their specials, clam and garlic, broccoli and sausage or invent your own! Mon, Wed, Thu 4pm-10pm, Fri-Sat 11.30am-11pm, Sun 2.30pm-10pm.
Thai Taste, 1151 Chapel St, 776-9802. Appetisers from $4, entrees from $7.50. Pad Thai a speciality. 'Extremely good.' Mon-Sat 11.30am-3pm & 5pm-10pm, Sun 5pm-10pm.

Of Interest

The Green, once a wild, swampy forest trodden by Indians, is now a shaded park. Despite encroaching modern buildings, the Green still retains much of its original flavour, flanked as it is on the north side by the impressive, ivy-clad halls of Yale. Mid-August, New Haven plays host to world tennis champions in the **International Pilot Penn Tennis Tournament,** The Connecticut Tennis Center, Yale University, I-95, exit 44. Call 776-7331/(888) 997-4568 for details of this prestigious annual event when the world's top players, such as Agassi and the Williams sisters compete. If you missed Wimbledon, this is a must! Tickets $5-$70; don't forget your strawberries! *www.pilotpentennis.com*.

Amistad Memorial, City Hall, 165 Church St. Statue depicting Senghe Pieh, leader of the Amistad revolt. Situated on the site of the jail where the captives were held. East **Rock Park,** East Rock Road, 946-6086. Spectacular view of Long Island Sound and the harbour, nature trails, bird sanctuary, picnic facilities. Open daily dawn-dusk.

Peabody Museum of Natural History, 170 Whitney Ave, 432-5050. Dinosaurs, wildlife dioramas and Connecticut flora and fauna. Mon-Sat 10am-5pm, Sun noon-5pm, $5 w/student ID. *www.peabody.yale.edu*.

Shore Line Trolley Museum, 17 River St, East Haven, 5 miles from New Haven, 467-6927.The oldest trolley museum in the United States, with nearly 100 vintage vehicles. Summer: daily 10.30am-4.30pm. Admission and 3-mile all day rides aboard a restored vintage trolley car, $6. *www.bera.org*.

Yale Center for British Art, 1080 Chapel St, 432-2800. Hogarth, Constable, Turner, Pre-Raphaelites and contemporary art, including the work of Damien Hirst. Most comprehensive collection of British works outside Britain. Tue-Sat 10am-5pm, Sun noon-5pm, closed Mon; free. Provides a fascinating and informative tour through the permanent collections. *www.yale.edu/ycba*.

Yale University, 432-2300. Free tours around the old spires and cobbled courtyards of the university, mostly built in the thirties, and meticulously designed to look effectively ancient, are available in summer. Mon-Fri 10.30am & 2pm, Sat & Sun 1.30pm, starting at Visitor's Center, 149 Elm St. Open daily 10am-4pm, S-Sun from 11am. Highlights include the Old Campus through **Phelps Gate** off College St, **Connecticut Hall** (the oldest building), the **Art of Architecture Building** designed by Paul Rudolph and the **Beinicke Rare Book Library.** *www.yale.edu/visitor*.

Yale University Art Gallery, 1111 Chapel St, 432-0600. Home to a collection of French Impressionists, an excellent assortment of contemporary American paintings; Hopper, Aitkins and Homer, and Van Gogh's Night Cafe. Tue-Sat 10am-5pm, Sun 1pm-6pm, free. *www.yale.edu/artgallery*

Entertainment

Try Thursday's *New Haven Advocate*. Free news, arts and entertainment weekly. *www.newhavenadvocate.com.*

Festivals. Enjoy free outdoor summer concerts: R&B, Jazz and ethnic bluegrass, Latin, rock, folk and Cajun, on the Green, June-Aug on Saturday evenings. Call the **Cultural Affairs Office,** 946-7821, for details or visit *www.newhavenjazz.com* for info on the **Jazz Fest.** Also catch the free, outdoors, Friday, **Flicks on the Green.** *www.filmfest.org*.

Toad's Place, 300 York St, 624-8623. Dance club and concert venue; the Rolling Stones once played here. Box office 11am-6pm Mon-Fri, or call Ticketmaster on 624-0033, concert tkts about $15. Sat night dance party, free w/student ID. *www.toadsplace.com*.

Look for current productions at the **Long Wharf Theater,** 222 Sergent Dr, 787-4282/(800) 782-8497. Season runs Oct-June. Closed Mon. Discount tkts available for students on day of performance. *www.longwharf.org*   The excellent **Yale Repertory Theater,** 1120 Chapel St, 432-1234, boasts Meryl Streep, Henry Winkler among others as alumni. Offers drama and comedy classics Sept-May. $20-$45, ½ price w/student ID. *www.yalerep.org*.

Information
Maps and guides from the **Yale Visitors' Center,** 149 Elm St, 432-2300. Mon-Fri 9am-4.30pm, Sat-Sun 11am-4pm. *www.yale.edu*
Greater New Haven Convention and Visitors Bureau, 59 Elm St, 777-8550/(800) 332-STAY. *www.newhavencvb.org.*

Internet Access
New Haven Free Public Library, 133 Elm St, across from the Green, 946-8130. Free Internet access w/picture ID. Hour limit. First come, first served basis. Mon 12pm-8pm, Tue-Wed 10am-6pm, Thu 'til 8pm, Fri 1pm-5pm. Closed Sat & Sun, July-Aug. *www.cityofnewhaven.com*.

Travel
Amtrak, 50 Union Ave, 773-6176/(800) 872-7245. Services to Penn Station, NYC. Newly renovated station but unsafe at night. NYC 1½ hrs ($36-$41), Boston 2½ ($48-$55). *www.amtrak.com*.
Metro-North Commuter Railroad, 50 Union Ave, (800) 638-7646/in NYC (212) 532-4900. Services to Grand Central, NYC. NYC $14 off-peak, $18.50 rush hour. *www.mta.nyc.ny.us*.
Connecticut Limousine Service, Sports Haven Complex, 600 Long Wharf Dr, (800) 472-5466. Frequent runs to JFK, Bradley, Newark and La Guardia Airports. One Way: $56 to JFK and LGA, $71 to Newark. Also runs from other CT towns and some hotels. 24 hr rsvs policy. Check out *www.ctlimo.com* for more details.
Greyhound, 50 Union Avenue, 772-2470/(800) 231-2222. One Way: NYC, approx 2 hrs, $20. Boston, approx 3 ½ hrs, $29. *www.greyhound.com*.

CONNECTICUT RIVER VALLEY The lower river valley, where river meets sea between New Haven and New London, is one of the state's loveliest, most unspoilt and peaceful areas. Once an important seafaring commercial centre, this is now an area for gentle sailing, pottering around the small towns, or watching the wildlife at **Selden Neck State Park** or on the salt marshes around **Old Lyme.** *Use area code* 860.

Accommodation
Unless you feel like treating yourself to a night at one of the expensive old inns here you will have to search out a motel or campground somewhere off I-95. Some worth trying are the **Heritage Motor Inn,** 1500 Boston Post Rd, exit 66 off I-95, 388-3743. $70-$130 for two, free local calls, outdoor pool, 6 miles from downtown Essex. *www.heritagemotorinn.com*. Also try **Liberty Inn,** 55 Springbrook Rd, exit 67/68 off I-95, 388-1777. $70-$100 for two, 1 mile from downtown Old Saybrook.

Of Interest
Essex: Main St is lined with the white clapboard homes of colonial sea captains. America's first warship, *Oliver Cromwell*, was built here. The **Connecticut River Museum**, 67 Main St, Steamboat Dock, 767-8269, tells the history of it all; open Tues-Sun 10am-5pm, $6, $5 w/student ID, visit *www.ctrivermuseum.org*.
Essex Steamtrain and Riverboat, Valley Railroad, Exit 3 off Rte 9, 767-0103/(800) 377-3987. Runs scenic 2 hr steam train and riverboat rides, daily10.30am-3pm in summer, past the **Gillette Castle** and **Goodspeed Opera House.** Prices: $16-$24. Closed winter except for special Xmas trains. Also visit the **Jazz Festival** at Valley Railroad in late June, (800) 348-0003. *www.essexsteamtrain.com*.
East Haddam: Gillette Castle State Park, across the river from Essex, off Rte 82,

526-2336. Once the estate of actor William Gillette who made his name playing Sherlock Holmes. The castle was built and furnished 1914-1919 in an arts and crafts style. 'Weird.' June-Oct, daily. Grounds: 8am-7pm, Castle: 10am-4.30pm, $5. Reach the Park by the **Chester-Hadlyme Ferry** 443-3856, for the trip across the Connecticut River and in service since 1769. The trip costs $3 for a car and driver, $1 per pedestrian.

Ivoryton: **Ivoryton Playhouse,** 103 N Main St, 767-8348, is where Katharine Hepburn 'found out what theatre was all about', _www.ivorytonplayhouse.com_. Prices vary from $10-$27.

Old Lyme: Florence Griswold Museum, 96 Lyme St, 434-5542, one-time boarding house and centre of the Old Lyme art colony. The bohemian antics of Miss Griswold and her fellow impressionists were considered somewhat shocking by the locals. You can see their work, Tue-Sat 10am-5pm, Sun 1pm-5pm. $7, $6 w/student ID. _www.flogris.org_.

Information
Connecticut River Valley & Shoreline Visitors Council, 393 Main St, Middletown, 347-0028/(800) 486-3346. _www.visitctrivershore.com_.

NEW LONDON AND MYSTIC   Off I-95, on the River Thames (pronounced as it looks), is the town of New London. This once important whaling port had the distinction of being burnt to the ground by Benedict Arnold and his troops in 1781. Today it is the home of **Connecticut College** and the **US Coast Guard Academy,** catch one of their free concerts at **Leamy Hall Auditorium,** 444-8444. _www.cga.edu_. There are some well-restored houses on **Star Street** and on **Green Street** is the **Dutch Tavern** once frequented by Eugene O'Neill. 'The best bar in the US; unique atmosphere.' Visit O'Neill's boyhood home, **Monte Cristo Cottage,** 325 Pequot Ave, 443-0051, named after the Count of Monte Cristo, his actor-father's most famous part. The house inspired sets for his comedy _Ah, Wilderness_ and for _Long Day's Journey Into Night_. Summer: Tue-Sat 10am-5pm, $5. The **Eugene O'Neill Theatre Center,** 305 Great Neck Rd, is located in **Waterford,** across the river and has many summer performances, 443-5378. _www.oneilltheatercenter.org_.

Another unique attraction of New London is Connecticut's only Underground Railway stop open to the public, the **Hempstead Houses,** 11 Hempstead St, 443-7949. Summer Thu-Sun noon-4pm, $4. For more attractions and details on New London visit _www.newlondon-ct.com_. Nearby in **Groton,** east across the Thames, on Rte 12 has **The Historic Ship** _Nautilus_ **& Submarine Force Museum,** 694-3174/(800) 343-0079. Here you can investigate WW2 paraphernalia and climb aboard the world's first nuclear-powered sub launched from the Electric Boatyard here in 1954. May-Oct: Daily 9am-5pm, Tues from 1pm, free. _www.ussnautilus.org_.

Mystic lies east of Groton on I-95, exit 90. A small town but major tourist destination. Why? Well, in 1988 a young Julia Roberts starred in a movie set and filmed in and around a pizzeria in the town of Mystic, the name, you guessed it - _Mystic Pizza_! Although too small to hold a Hollywood film crew, the restaurant was recreated authentically and you can dine in the familiar surroundings while eating tasty pizza at 56 W Main St, 536-3700 today, no rsvs necessary. A more traditional point of interest in town is **Marine Life Aquarium,** 572-5955. Whales, sea lions and seals. Summer: w/day

10am-5pm w/end 9am-6pm, last tkts sold 1 hr before closing, $20. *www.mysticaquarium.org*

The **Mystic Seaport,** 572-0711, is a re-created mid-19th century coastal village and maritime museum on Rte 27. Some of the fastest clipper ships were built in Mystic and the last of the wooden whaling ships; the *Charles W. Morgan* (which celebrated its 160th anniversary in 2001) awaits inspection. Daily 9am-5pm in summer, $17. Seasonal events include a lobster festival over Memorial Day weekend, and an October Chowderfest. *www.mysticseaport.org*.

Travel/Information

Cross Sound Ferry, New London Ferry Dock, exit 83/84 off I-95, 443-5281. Chartered ferry which crosses Long Island Sound from New London to Orient Point in Long Island. 1 hr 20 min crossing time, $18 round trip. A relaxing, picturesque way to cross the divide between NY and Connecticut. *www.longislandferry.com*.

Connecticut's Mystic & More Convention Bureau, 470 Bank St, New London, 444-2206/(800) TO-ENJOY. *www.mysticmore.com.* Telephone Area Code 860.

STAMFORD located in the coastal Fairfield County, 40 miles southwest of New Haven, is a 40 minute train ride away from Grand Central Station in New York City. Stamford has flourished and is now the eighth largest business center in the US. Growth and renovation continue on a waterfront area along the **Mill River,** that traverses downtown. *www.ci.stamford.ct.us*. The main hub of activity is located along **Bedford, Atlantic** and **Broad Sts.** The **Main Public Library,** at the junction of these streets at 1 Public Library Plaza, 964-1000, offers free internet access on a first come, first served basis, hour time limit. Mon-Thur 10am-9pm, Fri 'til 6pm, Sat 'til 5pm and Sun 1pm-5pm. *www.fergusonlibrary.org*.

The main **shopping district** is adjacent to the library's pretty building, housed in **Macy's Mall,** 151 Broad St, **Sak's Fifth Avenue,** 140 Atlantic St, and **Filenes,** 230 Tresser Blvd, department stores. 'The Malls have continuous sales and are definitely a good place to spend an afternoon.' The **Stamford Center for the Arts** has two facilities: the **Palace Theatre,** 61 Atlantic St, a restored historic theatre and the **Rich Forum,** 307 Atlantic St, a modern state of the art facility. Both have performances year round. Visit *www.onlyatsca.com* or call 325-4466 for details.

Food/Entertainment

All of Stamford is extremely accessible - you can walk everywhere. At nights you don't have to wander far to come across the local nightlife.

Tigin's Irish Pub, 353-8444, *www.tiginirishpub.com* and **The Temple Bar,** 708-9000 both along Bedford St, will make you feel very much at home with Irish themed interiors and live music at the weekends. Karaoke at the Temple on Mon. Also serve dinner 4pm-9pm daily, *www.thetemplebar.com*.

Ocean 211 for fresh seafood, 211 Summer St, 973-0494. Open: Mon-Fri noon-2.30; Mon-Thur 5.30pm-9.30pm; Fri-Sat 5.30pm-10.30pm. Lunch from $9 and dinner from $17.

Public transport is excellent in the area and it's only a short $1.25 fare ride to **Norwalk,** a picturesque town with shops, galleries, bars and clubs. Historic **South Norwalk (SoNo)** offers events and festivals during the summer: the **Harbor Splash!** has a dragon boat parade, cook-off and many performances, held June along Washington St, 846-8800. List of free concerts can be found at _www.internationalperformingarts.com_ or call (866) IPA-4ART. In nearby **Rowayton's** Pinkney Park, catch a free, open-air performance of **Shakespeare on the Sound**, 299-1300. Begins 7.30pm, throughout the summer, call for schedule. Take a blanket and picnic but arrive early for a good view. _www.shakespeareonthesound.org_. 'Friendly atmosphere and fantastic show.'

The **Norwalk Maritime Aquarium**, 10 N Water St, 852-0700, explores the marine life of Long Island Sound. Summer, daily, 10am-6pm, $10.50. CT's only **IMAX theatre**, $8.50. Combo tkt $16. _www.maritimeaquarium.org_. Nightspots are located along Washington St, between Main and Water St. Try **Liquid**, 112 Washington St, 866-0800, hot and sweaty, with two floors and good atmosphere. _www.liquidsono.com_. The **Rattlesnake Bar and Grille**, 15 N Main St, 852-1716, is a good place to mingle with college students; food served from 11.30am. For more exotic cuisine try **Habana's**, 70 N. Main St, 852-9790. 'Fantastic Cuban food and classy atmosphere', Sun-Thu 5pm-10pm, Fri-Sat 5pm-late.

Travel/Information
CT Transit, 26 Elm Court, Stamford, 327-7433. Basic fare on buses $1.25. _www.cttransit.com_.

MAINE - The Pine Tree State

As big as the other five New England states combined, Maine has a modest size population, similar to that of Rhode Island. In some areas the wildlife outnumbers the human inhabitants which means it is the perfect place to get away from it all. Maine offers a variety of spectacular environments and unspoiled natural wonders, from rugged coastline to mountains, clear lakes and breathtaking white water.

Especially recommended is the drive 'down east' (north-east) along the rocky coastline. On a straight line, the coast of Maine is 250 miles long, but all the bays, harbors and peninsulas lengthen the shoreline to some 2400 miles. Inland are acres of unexplored, moose-filled forests and huge lakes, remote and seldom visited, 2,500 in all. While here, look out for blueberry festivals, clambakes, and lobster picnics—the state annually harvests millions of pounds of fish and shellfish, and fertile farmlands mean Maine is also among the top spud producers in the US.

In addition to hiking, boating, and swimming, Maine offers great opportunities for biking and white water rafting. Thousands of miles of peaceful, scenic secondary roads—good for biking—wind through the interior and along the coast. Bike rentals are widely available, and two guidebooks list scenic routes and travel tips: 25 _Bicycle Tours in Maine_, by Howard Stone (Back Country Publications, PO Box 175, Woodstock, VT 05091), and _Bicycling_, by DeLorme Publishing Company. _www.bikemaine.org_.

White water rafting in Maine is an adventure not to be missed. You'll find both water and outfitters to be plentiful at **The Forks** (named for the confluence of the **Dead** and **Kennebec** Rivers in the upper Kennebec Valley) and the West Branch of the **Penobscot** between Moosehead Lake and Baxter State Park in the Katahdin/Moosehead Region. Several outfitters throughout the state organise kayaking tours; try: Loon Bay Kayaking, (888) 786-0676, _www.kayak1.com;_ Maine Sport Outfitters, (800) 722-0826, _www.mainesport.com;_ World Within Sea Kayaking, (207) 646-0455, *www.worldwithin.com*; Maine Island Kayak Co., (800) 796-2373, *www.maineislandkayak.com*.

For more information on camping and access rules write to the **Bureau of Parks and Lands**, Maine Department of Conservation, 22 State House Station, Augusta, 04333-0022, or call on (207) 287-3821. *www.maine.gov/doc* Camping fees are $15-$20 per site, $2 rsvs fee.

If all that exercise is not for you, then Maine has one other main attraction: **factory outlet stores** 'headquartered' in the Kittery area, one hour north of Boston, and south of Portland, exit 3 off I-95, call 1-888-KITTERY. There are real bargains to be found with products often having 20%-75% off. *www.thekitteryoutlets.com*, *www.state.me.us*, *www.visitmaine.com* and *www.mainerec.com*.

The telephone area code for Maine is 207.

SOUTH COAST If you're in a hurry to head 'down east', hop on I-95, but if you have the time to meander try coastal Rte 1. This winding road, which can be busy during the summer, provides easy access to a variety of seaside towns and attractions. *www.gatewaytomaine.org*.

Though actually beginning further south, the Maine section of Rte 1 begins in **Kittery**. Known historically for its shipbuilders, this town is buzzing with bargain hunters at the factory outlets mentioned above. *www.kittery.org* If relaxing on a long, sandy beach is more appealing, head for **Ogunquit** about 10 miles north. Centuries after the Indians named this 'beautiful place by the sea,' it is still an attractive and popular resort. Hear the sound of it at *www.ogunquit.com*

You'll find a quieter spot a few miles off Rte 1 on Rte 9 at the **Rachel Carson National Wildlife Refuge** in **Wells**, 646-9226. Here, solitude and rare birds among 1600 acres of shady wetlands combine to delight ornithologist and picnicker alike. *www.fws.gov/rachelcarson*.

Continuing up Rte 9 brings you to **Kennebunkport**, vacation residence of former president George Bush. Though beautifully maintained, this one-time ship-building village is sadly falling victim to 'quaint disease'. Avoid downtown at rush hour. *www.kennebunkport.org*

Try **Dixon's Campground**, 2 miles south of Ogunquit on **Cape Neddick**, 363-3626. Sites for two, $21-30, reservations recommended. *www.dixonscampground.com*.

PORTLAND The gateway to northeast Maine, Portland is the largest city (pop. 64,000) in a state where cities and towns are few and far between. Here the coast changes from long sections of beach to a hodgepodge of islands, bays and inlets. Portland had an early history of Indian massacres and British burnings. The city has recently been revitalised and restored and is now a commercial and cultural centre, as well as being home to the **University of Southern Maine**.

Take a ferry to one of the hundreds of islands in **Casco Bay**. Inland there is vast **Sebago Lake** for summer swimming, sailing, waterskiing and sunning. *www.visitportland.com*.

Accommodation
Pomegranate Inn, 49 Neal St, 772-1006. From $95 off season. B&B. Just a short walk

from the Midtown Arts District. *www.pomegranateinn.com*.

Inn at St. John, 939 Congress St, 773-6481. $55 upwards, shared bath, bfast included, 20 min walk from downtown. 'Excellent location opposite Greyhound.' 'Exceptionally clean and pleasant.' *www.innatstjohn.com*.

Portland-Days Inn, South Portland, 461 Maine Mall Road, 772-3450. Ave. $99. 10% discount w/student ID. Free bfast and local telephone calls. Free shuttle from airport and bus station. Call for reservations on 1-800-544-8313. *www.daysinn.com*.

Food
Check *www.foodinportland.com*

Great Lost Bear, 540 Forest Ave, 772-0300. Choose from over 100 items on the menu and 54 varieties of draft and bottled beer! Burgers and veggie specials $7-$12. Mon-Sat 11.30am-11.30pm, Sun noon-11.30pm. 'Best place to drink in Maine.' *www.greatlostbear.com*.

Silly's, 40 Washington Ave, 772-0360. Burgers, pizza, seafood, home-made ice-cream shakes. Try their famous Jamaican jerk chicken dinner, or their creative roll-up sandwiches,' $3.25 & upwards. Mon-Sat 11am-9.30pm, Sun 1pm—8pm.

Three Dollar Dewey's, 241 Commercial St, 772-3310. Pub-style eatery. 36 beers on tap, 50-plus bottle beers, three alarm chilli, lots of seafood and ethnic veggie dishes. Nothing on menu over $11.95. Mon-Sun 11.30am-1am.   *www.3dollardeweys.com*.

Of Interest
www.portlandlandmarks.org and www.portlandme.about.com.

For memorable boat trips and best views of the rugged coastline try **Casco Bay Lines** (America's oldest ferry service), CBITD Ferry Terminal, Commercial & Franklin Sts, 774-7871. Year round service to Peaks, Chebeague, Long, Great and Little Diamond and Cliff Islands. $6.25-$9.50. *www.cascobaylines.com*.

Farmers Market: sells local produce; some organic food. Mon-Sat 9am-7pm, Sun 10am-5pm, one block from Monument Square behind the library.

Henry Wadsworth Longfellow House, 489 Congress St, 772-1807. Was the poet's childhood home. May-Oct, Mon-Sat 10am-5pm, Sun noon-5pm, $7, $6 w/ student ID, includes tour. *www.mainehistory.org*.

Old Orchard Beach, south of Portland. 'Maine's answer to Blackpool. Large water slides, good beach. Lots of French Canadians frequent this place.' Biddeford/Saco Shuttle Bus, 282-5408, leaves Portland for Old Orchard Beach six times daily, from City Hall on Congress St., $1 o/w. *www.oldorchardbeachmaine.com*.

Higgins, **Crescent** and **Scarborough** beaches are also good, and Prout's Neck is where artist Winslow Homer did much of his painting.

Old Port Exchange, on the waterfront. Reconstructed in Victorian style with cobblestone streets, gas lamps, boutiques and restaurants. Favourite haunt for locals as well as visitors.

Portland Head Coastguard Station and Lighthouse, 799-2661, follow road to Cape Elizabeth south from Portland, off US 1. Commissioned by George Washington and built in 1791, Portland Head is Maine's oldest lighthouse. Small museum and picnic facilities, $2. 'Great views.' Daily 10am-4pm. *www.portlandheadlight.com*.

Portland Museum of Art, 7 Congress St, 773-ARTS. Painting, sculpture and decorative arts, including works by Homer and Wyeth. Daily 10am-5pm, Fri 'til 9pm, $8, $6 w/student ID, Fri 5-9pm free. *www.portlandmuseum.org*.

Information
Greater Portland Convention and Visitors Bureau, 245 Commercial St, 772-5800. Provides visitor's guide and area map. Daily 8am-5pm, Visitors Centre open also Sat 10am-5pm. *www.visitportland.com*.

Internet Access
JavaNet Cafe, 37 Exchange St, 773-2469. $8/hr.

Portland Main Library, 5 Monument Sq, 871-1700. Free Internet use, half hour time to 1 hr time limit. Mon, Wed & Fri 9am-6pm, Tue, Thu noon-9pm, Sat 9am-5pm. _www.portlandlibrary.com_.

Travel
Concord Trailways, Thompson Point Rd, (800) 639-3317. Boston (o/w $19, 2 hrs), Bangor (o/w $23, 2 hrs). _www.concordtrailways.com_.
Greyhound, St John & Congress Sts, 772-6587/(800) 231-2222. Be careful at night. Boston o/w $16.75. _www.greyhound.com_.

Continuing on up the coast will bring you to **Freeport**, a haven for over 100 factory outlets, chief of which is THE sporting and outdoor goods store, **L.L. Bean**. Open 365 days, 24 hrs, Bean's is a Mecca to middle America, and the pilgrims come here at all hours. 'It was really strange to be shopping at 3am.' _www.freeportusa.com_   has info about the town's outlets.

In case you're feeling overly verdant, there's relief just around the corner at the **Desert of Maine**, Desert Rd, Freeport, exit 19 off I-95, 865-6962. A natural phenomenon, $7.75 gets you a guided tour and tram rides (9am-5pm) through the dunes. Watch the unusual art of sand designing with the 100 different shades of sand in the desert. Acres and acres of sandy glacial remains create dunes up to 80 feet high. You have to feel it to believe it. If you don't have transportation from Freeport, call ahead and ask if the Desert of Maine Shuttle is coming into town. _www.desertofmaine.com_.

For accommodation, try **Delia B. Powers Winslow Memorial Park**, Rt 95 north, exit 17 (left at the Indian statue), 865-4198, 'the best campground, sea views and sunset'; sites $17-$19, without hook up.

MID-COAST   **Brunswick** is home to small, but lovely **Bowdoin College**, alma mater of writers Hawthorne and Longfellow and explorers Peary and MacMillan among others. The college hosts **Bowdoin Summer Music Festival** featuring nationally renowned artists and low-priced concerts, call 373-1400 for details, _www.summermusic.org_. Also on campus: the **Peary-MacMillan Arctic Museum** in Hubbard Hall, 725-3416. Polar exploration, ecology and Inuit culture, Tue-Sat 10am-5pm, Sun 2pm-5pm _www.academic.bowdoin.edu_; and the **Museum of Art** in the Walker Art Building, 725-3275, featuring Baskins as well as old masters and Greek and Roman artifacts, Tue-Sat 10am-5pm, Sun 2pm-5pm. _www.academic.bowdoin.edu_.

You can camp among the tall pines at **Thomas Point Beach** _www.thomaspointbeach.com_, off Rte 24, Cook's Corner, **Brunswick**, 5 miles from downtown, 725-6009. Sites $20, $5 electric. The park is the site of an annual **Bluegrass Festival** on Labor Day weekend, and in August it hosts the **Maine Highland Games** and the **Maine Crafts Fair**, which features folk arts, workshops and local foods, tkts $5-12. _www.mainecrafts.org._ **Brunswick Chamber of Commerce**, 725-8797, _www.midcoastmaine.com_.

Dipping off Rte 1 onto Rte 27 takes you into **Boothbay Harbor**, a bit touristy but a good taking off point for quiet, isolated **Monhegan Island**, _www.monhegan.com_, where cars are prohibited and artists take refuge. This is not an island for wild nights (no bars or discos in town), but if you're in the mood for rocky cliffs, ocean spray, and hiking amid 600 varieties of wildflowers it's worth the 1 hr ferry ride into **Muscongus Bay**. Call for exact times and schedule changes, 633-2284; rsvs recommended.

Getting back onto Rte 1 and continuing north you hit **Rockland**, which hosts an annual **Maine Lobster Festival** in early August, $7 entry, call 596-0376 for details. _www.mainelobsterfestival.com_. Generations of artists have found this coast an inspiration; Andrew Wyeth spent much of his life in nearby **Cushing**, and the **William A. Farnsworth Museum and Library** in Rockland, 596-6457, daily 9am-5pm, Wed 'til 7pm, $10, $8 w/student ID, has a large collection of paintings by the Wyeth family, _www.farnsworthmuseum.org_. Just north of Rockland is **Camden**. Picturesquely situated with a busy little harbour, the town has a Cornish-like charm despite the tourists. Even though the trash-trend emporia fast encroach, there are still genuine and attractive local craft shops. If it's not foggy, the observatory atop **Mount Battie** affords a spectacular view of Camden harbour, the sea and the surrounding hills. It's an enjoyable two-mile hike from the town.

Try camping at **Camden Hills State Park**, 1H miles north of town on Rte 1, 236-3109. Sites $20. Rsvs recommended, apply to the Park Bureau in Augusta, 287-3824, 14 days in advance (but arrive btwn 10am & 4pm and you'll probably get a pitch). Hot showers, stone fireplace and picnic table at each site, take-out store within walking distance. _www.stateparks.com/camden_hills.html_.

If you have your own transport, spend a few relaxing days at the beautiful wooded **Megunticook Campground By-The-Sea** between Camden and Rockland at Rockport on Rte 1, 594-2428. _www.campgroundbythesea.com_ Sites $30-$40 w/hook up, rsvs recommended in summer. Cabins can be hired ($49-$69) but call first. Small store, bathrooms and free showers, laundry and heated outdoor pool. Rent kayaks nearby.

Feeling adventurous? Contact **Maine Sport**, Rte 1 between Rockport and Camden, (800) 722-0826; ask about their guided kayaking trips. The Camden harbour trip ($35) takes 2 hrs. The Penobscot Bay day-trip ($65 incl. lunch) takes 4 hrs—try navigating a keowee! Equipment provided, no experience necessary, rsvs required. _www.mainesport.com_.

For energetic landlubbers, bikes are available to rent; from $18 full-day, includes helmet and lock, cheaper weekly rates available.

For tourist info on Rockport and Lincoln, contact **Camden Chamber of Commerce**, PO Box 919, Camden, Maine 04843, 236-4404, or visit _www.visitcamden.com_.

Take a highly-recommended detour off Rte 1, following State Road 166 to the charming town of **Castine**. _www.castine.me.us_ This is where Paul Revere, of 'Midnight Ride' fame, ended his undistinguished military career in the ill-fated naval battle against British troops in the **Penobscot Bay** in 1779, the second worst US naval disaster after Pearl Harbor. Revere was arrested for disobeying orders and abandoning the expedition—a court martial later acquitted him and he got by with just a censure. The **Castine Historical Society**, on the town commons, has exhibits about local history, 326-4118. _www.castinehistoricalsociety.org_.

Continue on your way to **Bar Harbor** via the coastal route, or else head inland where thousands of lakes make this a popular area for canoeists. **Moosehead Lake**, 40 miles long and 10 miles wide, is the largest.

ACADIA NATIONAL PARK / BAR HARBOR   The park encompasses a magnificent wild, rocky stretch of coast and its hinterland. Its granite hills sweep down into the Atlantic where the ocean has carved out numerous inlets, cliffs and caves. At every twist and turn of the roads around the coast a new and spectacular view of the sea becomes visible.

For the best view of all, it's an easy walk or drive to the summit of **Cadillac Mountain** (1530 ft), the highest place on the Atlantic coast north of Rio. Beneath the 'mountain' lie lakes, cranberry bogs, quiet spruce forests, and the Atlantic itself. The dramatic **Loop Road**, cars $10 per week, $5 pp, from the Park Visitor Center takes about 1½ -3 hrs (depending on the number of stops you make) and offers incredible views, *www.acadiamagic.com/CadillacMountain.html*. A stop right on the Loop, not to be missed, is tea and popovers ($7.50) at **Jordan Pond House**, 276-3316, *www.jordanpond.com*. The House is an easy drive from Seal or Bar Harbor and accessible by several hiking trails.

Bar Harbor is the most popular resort on the **Mount Desert Island** part of Acadia National Park. This was a town of fashionable summer homes owned by the wealthy until 1947 when a great fire destroyed most of them. More recently, chic boutiques and restaurants have moved in, forcing prices up. *www.barharbormaine.com*. Come and enjoy the **Bar Harbor Music Festival** in July and August or take in a whalewatching tour or an excursion on a working lobster boat. The less frequented **Isle au Haut** is the other half of Acadia; a good place for walking, it can be reached by ferry from Stonington on the southern tip of Deer Isle. *www.isleauhaut.net* and *www.isleauhaut.com*

Further inland lies **Bangor**, a good stopping off point before heading into the interior. With a name said to be derived from an old hymn tune, the town is socially about that exciting. *www.bgrme.org*. The best time to be there is during the **Bangor Fair**, one of the oldest in the country, held annually the first week in August, $6 entry, 947-5555. In early summer **harness racing** is held at Bass Park on Main St, 947-5555, free.

Accommodation
Anchorage Motel, 51 Mt. Desert St, 288-3959. May-Oct $59-129. Close to restaurants and shops. $49-129.

YWCA, 36 Mt Desert St, 288-5008. Downtown, close to amenities.Women only. Dorm $25/$70 weekly, S-$35/$95 weekly, D-$30 pp/$80 pp weekly. Linens provided. Rsvs recommended.

Camping. Within the park there are sites at **Black Woods**, 288-3338, and **Seawall**, 244-3600, July-Aug. Both areas require a park entrance permit and can be reached by car, Black Woods costs $20/night, Seawall $20/night with car, walk-ins $14. Seawall operates on a first-come, first-served basis, but rsvs are essential at Black Woods in peak season, apply two months in advance to be sure of a pitch. (800) 365-2267 is the number to reserve pitches in parks nation-wide—persevere, the line is always busy! There are also more expensive private campgrounds near the park.

Of Interest
Bike rentals are available from **Acadia Bike and Canoe,** 48 Cottage St, 288-5483,

bikes $15 half-day, $20 full-day, includes helmet and map, and organise kayaking trips $36 2½ hrs, $45 4hrs. _www.acadiabike.com_

Bar Harbor Whale Watch Co., 1 West St, Harbor Place, 288-9800, (888) 533-WALE. 3 hr tour costs $42, rsvs recommended. _www.barharbourwhales.com_ gives detailed information and photos of various cruises offered.

Information

Acadia Outdoors, 45 Main St, 288-2422. Sells camping gear. Daily 8am-10pm.

Chamber of Commerce, 93 Cottage St (in basement), 288-5103. 'Extremely helpful.' _www.barharbormaine.com._

Park Visitors Center, 288-3338, just off Rte 3 at Hulls Cove. Short film about the park shown every hour, offers audio cassette tours and all the information you'll need. Daily mid-Apr to June, Sept-Oct 8am-4.30pm, July-Aug 8am-6pm. _www.nps.gov/acad_

Travel

Bay Ferry to Yarmouth, Nova Scotia, (888) 249-7245. 3 hr crossing, leaves Thu-Tue 8am, 4pm, Wed 8am, mid-May to mid-Oct $58 pp, $99 car (+ fuel surcharge $20).

Greyhound/Vermont Transit run a shuttle to Ellsworth, 20 miles away, (under $10). Leaves every day at 8.50am, opposite the Villager Motel, 2071 Maine Street. Call (800) 522-8737. _www.vermonttransit.com._

THE APPALACHIAN TRAIL/BAXTER STATE PARK About 100 miles north of Bangor is **Baxter State Park**, where Mount **Katahdin** (5267 ft) marks the northern starting point of the Appalachian Trail. _www.mainelyhiking.com,www.mtkatahdin.com_. This is wild, remote country where moose out-number humans. (Best time to see a moose: early morning/late afternoon, late spring to early summer. Best place: near bogs and ponds, keep yourself unobtrusive.) The park can be reached via **Millinocket** on Rte 11 off I-95, or **Greenville**, a small lumber town, on Rte 15, at the southern end of Moosehead Lake. There are ten campgrounds in the park, $9 pp per night (min $18), only two of which are inaccessible by car. For all information on camping and for detailed area maps call in or write to the **Baxter State Park Headquarters**, 64 Balsam Drive, Millinocket, 04462. Tel: 723-5140, _www.baxterstateparkauthority.com_.

Just to the north of Baxter lies the **Allagash Wilderness Waterway**. This is a canoeist's paradise, a 100-mile-long stretch of lakes and rivers preserved in their primitive state to provide white-water and backwoods experience for the modern canoeist.

For $40/half-day, **Northwoods Outfitters** in Greenville, 695-3288, will provide a shuttle service, tour guide, and a canoe/kayak with paddle and life jacket. For a few days, a week or longer, explore the Moosehead Lake region, the largest undeveloped wilderness area in the eastern United States, by taking part in one of the many organised trips. Try the moose safari where you are guaranteed to catch a glimpse of the moose. Rsvs. recommended, _www.maineoutfitter.com_

If you are staying near Greenville, contact **Folsom's Air Service**, Greenville 695-2821, about their floatplane adventures; it costs $75 1 hr and $40 ½ hr to take in the local sights and the vast Moosehead Lake.

Information

Write to the **Appalachian Trail Conservancy**, P.O Box 807, Harper's Ferry, WV

25425, (304) 535-6331, _www.atconf.org_ ; or the **Appalachian Mountain Club**, 5 Joy St, Boston, MA 02108, (617) 523-0655, _www.outdoors.org_.

Moosehead Lake Chamber of Commerce, P.O Box 581, Greenville, ME 04441, 695-2702/ 888-876-2778. _www.mooseheadlake.org_.

MASSACHUSETTS - The Bay State

The Bay State is rivalled only by Virginia in the richness of its history. Massachusetts was the colony where the loudest and most open protests were raised against the British prior to 1777. After the initial skirmishes, the war moved to the other colonies, but Massachusetts contributed the largest number of troops.

Presidents John Adams, John Quincy Adams, John F. Kennedy and George Bush all came from Massachusetts, as did Daniel Webster; in the field of literature, Robert Frost, John Whittier, Emily Dickinson, Louisa May Alcott, Nathaniel Hawthorne (read _The Scarlet Letter_ for a look into Massachusetts' Puritan past), Henry David Thoreau, E.E. Cummings, Eugene O'Neill, John Updike, Robert Parker, James Carroll and Ralph Waldo Emerson were either born or came to live here.

Just to show that there is a lighter side to the Bay state, Massachusetts is also the birthplace of sewing machines, plastic pink flamingos, frozen food and roller skates.

Massachusetts takes its name from the Massachuset Indians who occupied the Bay Territory, including Boston, in the early 17th century. An annual Indian pow-wow is still held at Mashpee in July. _www.mass-vacation.com_.

The telephone area code for the eastern part of the State is 617, for mid-Massachusetts and the Cape it's 508, and in the west it's 413.

BOSTON Capital of Massachusetts and, undeniably, of New England, Boston is a proud Yankee city and seaport thick with reminders of its past. Bostonians are fiercely loyal, regarding their city as the hub of New England and revelling in its Colonial past. Boston was the spiritual heart of the Revolution, the birthplace of American commerce and industry, and leader of the new nation in the arts and education. These days, the original WASPs (White Anglo-Saxon Protestants) have been joined by successive generations of Blacks, Irish, Poles and Italians, and the city has developed a more cosmopolitan feel.

The city has always had its own unique character; for a glimpse into local culture watch Oscar-winning _Good Will Hunting_, a fairly adequate introduction to the 'real Boston'; or brush up on your Boston English ('pahk the cah in Hahvahd Yahd') at _www.boston-online.com/glossary_. George V. Higgins' _The Friends of Eddie Coyle_ follows a crook through the Boston Underworld, and for classics-lovers, there's always Henry James' _The Bostonians_.

Known as 'America's Walking City', Boston has a cosier feel to it than most major US cities, and also something of a European flavour. Within a comparatively small area you can stroll through 18th century cobbled streets, on the **Common** where the colonists grazed their cattle, down by the

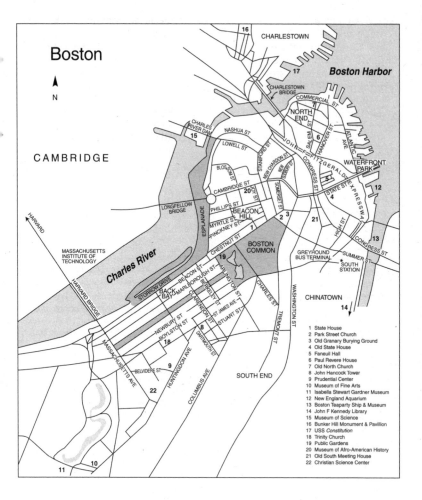

Boston

N

CAMBRIDGE

Charles River

MASSACHUSETTS
INSTITUTE OF
TECHNOLOGY

CHARLESTOWN

Boston Harbor

CHARLESTOWN
BRIDGE

COMMERCIAL ST

NORTH
END

CHARLES
RIVER DAM

NASHUA ST

LOWELL ST

WATERFRONT
PARK

STATE ST

LONGFELLOW
BRIDGE

CAMBRIDGE ST

ESPLANADE

PHILLIPS ST

BEACON
HILL

MYRTLE ST

PINCKNEY ST

CHESTNUT ST

BOSTON
COMMON

GREYHOUND
BUS TERMINAL

SOUTH
STATION

STORROW DRIVE

BEACON ST

BACK
BAY

MARLBOROUGH ST

BERKELEY ST

ARLINGTON ST

CHARLES ST

WASHINGTON ST

CHINATOWN

NEWBURY ST

CLARENDON ST

ST JAMES AVE

STUART ST

BOYLSTON ST

DARTMOUTH ST

TREMONT ST

HARVARD BRIDGE

MASSACHUSETTS AVE

BELVIDERE ST

HUNTINGDON AVE

COLUMBUS AVE

SOUTH END

1 State House
2 Park Street Church
3 Old Granary Burying Ground
4 Old State House
5 Faneuil Hall
6 Paul Revere House
7 Old North Church
8 John Hancock Tower
9 Prudential Center
10 Museum of Fine Arts
11 Isabella Stewart Gardner Museum
12 New England Aquarium
13 Boston Teaparty Ship & Museum
14 John F Kennedy Library
15 Museum of Science
16 Bunker Hill Monument & Pavillion
17 USS Constitution
18 Trinity Church
19 Public Gardens
20 Museum of Afro-American History
21 Old South Meeting House
22 Christian Science Center

harbour or river, or around such fine examples of modern architecture as in **Back Bay** or the impressive **Government Center**.

For all its historical associations, Boston is a city of youth and vitality. In addition to prestigious **Harvard** and **MIT**, there are 70 accredited colleges in Greater Boston, and many of the city's businesses and amenities cater to the young and diverse population, some of whom will be involved in the Democratic National Convention.

Boston acquired its nickname, 'the Athens of America', by the 19th century and continues to earn it as a centre for music, literature and the arts. At any time it is possible to see good theatre and modern dance or hear classical, jazz, folk and pop music. Sport too has its place. In summer, when the Boston Red Sox baseball team is battling it out in the race for the

American League title, the only place to be is at **Fenway Park**, eating Fenway franks, shelling peanuts, and drinking cold beer. In winter the mania transfers itself to basketball with the Celtics, football with the New England Patriots and ice hockey with the Boston Bruins.

One of the nation's finest examples of creative urban renewal is **Faneuil** (pronounced "Fan-Yul") **Hall Marketplace**. Once a rundown building on the blighted waterfront, its revitalisation became Boston's bicentennial gift to itself. It now houses over 100 shops, boutiques and food stalls along with many restaurants, as well as a highly popular comedy nightclub.

Boston is particularly convenient for visits to nearby Cambridge, Concord, Lexington, Salem and Gloucester. Further afield, the Berkshire Hills and sandy Cape Cod are unforgettable destinations for an expedition. *www.boston-online.com*.

The telephone area code for Boston and Cambridge is 617.

Accommodation
The Information Center at the Tremont St side of the Boston Common provides a list of low-cost accommodation. Budget chain hotels can be expensive in summer, but call, or check their websites, for details of special offers.

HI-Fenway, 575 Commonwealth St, 267-8599. Private ensuite $69 HI, twin private ensuite $34.50 HI. $3 more for non-HI. Linen/towels incl, laundry facs, 2 common rooms and bfast incl.

Beantown International Hostel, 222 Friend St, 723-0800. Dorm $25, kitchen, bar and restaurant. Linens included, towels $1. Close to Quincy Market and the Freedom Trail. Partnered to Irish Embassy Hostel.

Boston International Youth Hostel, 12 Hemenway St, 536-9455, in Back Bay. 24 hrs, check-in all day. Dorm $35 HI, $38 non-HI, private room $89 HI, $92 non-HI. Rsvs recommended, credit card required. Individual lockers in room, will sell locks. E-mail, $1/5mins. Govt issued photo ID req. 'Superb kitchen facilities. Very friendly staff.' 'Excellent hostel, launderette, clean, good value, maximum stay 14 days, take subway to Hynes Convention Center then 2 blocks.'

Greater Boston YMCA, 316 Huntington Ave, 927-8040. S-$46, D-$65, plus $5 cash key deposit; includes free use of pool and well equipped gym. Mixed reviews. 'Clean, friendly, safe.' 'Unpleasant clientele, be careful, seems to have a bad atmosphere.' *www.ymcaboston.org*.

Irish Embassy Hostel, 232 Friend St, 973-4841. Prices and facilities the same as Beantown International Hostel. 'Turn up early.' Mixed reports.

Longwood Inn, 123 Longwood Ave, Brookline, 566-8615. Green Line subway, downtown 10-15 mins. $79-$109. Kitchen, parking, TV and laundry. 'Clean and safe.' 'Old-fashioned style guest house.' *http://longwood-inn.com*.

Nolan House B&B, 10 G St, S Boston, 269-1550. $100. No credit cards. 'Full breakfast and large, comfortable room.' Rsvs required. *www.nolanhouse.com*.

YWCA, Berkeley Residence Club, 40 Berkeley St, 375-2524. Women only. S-$60, D-$90, $2 temp. membership, bfast incl. 'Very safe, clean, canteen, laundrette and roof-deck.' *www.ywcaboston.com*.

Housing Information
Central Reservation Services, 569-3800. Located in Logan Airport, has listings of hotels, guest houses, etc. Daily 8.30am-11.30pm. Free.

Matching Roommates, 24 hr info 1-(800) APT SHARE. If you're staying for the summer, it might be cheaper and safer to pay the $75 fee than advertise. Shared accommodation, short/long term Boston & suburbs. By appointment. "Very helpful." Founded in 1966. *www.matchingroommates.com*.

Food

In addition to clambakes and seafood, Boston is home to many diverse restaurants. Small family owned eating-places occupy every corner of the North End. Thai, Vietnamese and Polynesian foods are available in Chinatown, while the South End offers American Southwestern fare and cafes. Other nearby neighbourhoods tempt the hungry and the curious with Indian, Japanese, Mexican, Hungarian and Greek delights.

Cheers, 84 Beacon St, 227-9605, by the Public Garden. An English pub; burgers, sandwiches, etc., from $8-$15. Only the exterior has anything to do with *Cheers* (the series was filmed in LA), but at least you can imagine that Sam or Diane is going to walk in the door. 'Great wings!' 'Very disappointing.' Daily 11am-2am. *www.cheersboston.com*.

Charlie's Sandwich Shoppe, 429 Columbus Avenue (between Dartmouth and West Newton Streets), 536-7669. Strangers share tables at this old-time diner. Lunch for around $6-$9. Mon-Fri 6am-2.30pm, Sat 7.30am-1pm.

Country Life, 200 High St. (Financial dist., across from Rowes Wharf, Aquarium subway), 951-2534. 'Supreme veggie food.' 100% vegan. All you can eat lunch $7.30, dinner $8.40 (Sun, Tue, Weds, Thu), Sunday brunch $9.90. Mon-Fri 11.30am-3pm & 5pm-8pm, Sun 10am-3pm.

Durgin Park, 340 Faneuil Hall in Quincy Market, 227-2038. Known for its good food, great prices, long bar, and wisecracking waitresses. Family-style eating. Ribs, seafood; famous for its prime rib and great chowder. Go for lunch for the best buys. About $8/9. Mon-Sat 11.30am-10pm, Sun 'til 9pm. *www.durgin-park.com.*

The Purple Shamrock, 1 Union St, 227-2060. A favourite among sports fans, it has long been Boston's place to warm up and cool down for Boston Garden events. TV, live bands Fri/Sat (cover fee), supreme chowder and large beers. Serves food Mon-Fri 11.30am-9pm, bar closes at 1.30am. *www.thepurpleshamrock.com*.

Quincy Market, also known as **Faneuil Hall Marketplace**, complete with street performers and hordes of tourists, has plenty of food stalls of great variety: Chinese, Italian, Greek, health foods and of course, the requisite pizzas, burgers, doughnuts, etc. It also claims to sell more lobster items than anywhere else in the world. Take the green, blue or orange lines. Daily 10am 'til late evening, Sun from noon. *www.faneuilhallmarketplace.com*.

Sevens, 77 Charles St, 523-9074, 'Authentic British pub atmosphere; serves both local and imported beer. Friendly.' Mon-Sat 11.30am-1am, Sun noon-1am.

Of Interest

If you plan on being in Boston for more than a few days consider buying the **City Pass,** $39. The pass is valid for nine days from start of use and includes admission at the Museum of Science, New England Aquarium, Skywalk Observatory, Museum of Fine arts, Boston, Harvard Museum of Natural History and the JFK Library and Museum. It can be purchased at any site at the **Visitor Information Center** on Boston Common and at Prudential Plaza. *www.citypass.com*.

Back Bay, southwest of the common, is a lively, beautiful 19th century development project built on land reclaimed from the Charles River. In this area is **Trinity Church,** Copley Square, 536-0944. Daily 8am-6pm. Designed in 1877 by HH Richardson, this church is French Romanesque style on the outside. Inside its highly decorated walls and flamboyant mosaics give it more the feel and look of Greek Orthodox; $5 entrance, $5 guided tour. *www.trinityboston.org*.

Boston Common, 536-4100. Boston is the only large American city still to have its common, but the flower-filled Public Gardens have more to offer; enjoy gliding around the lagoon on the world-famous swan boats in summer. This is where Louis the Silent Cygnet serenaded passengers in E.B. White's *Trumpet of the Swan*. Both areas are unsafe at night.

Beacon Hill, especially Louisburg Square, is Boston's old residential section to which every visitor must make a pilgrimage. Louisa May Alcott, William Dean Howels, the Brahmin Literary Set and many other famous Bostonians lived here. *www.beaconhillonline.com*.

Black Heritage Trail, 742-5415, a guided walking tour that explores the history of 19th century Boston's African-American community. *www.nps.gov/boaf*. The 1.6 mile tour starts at Robert Gould Shaw and 54th Regiment Memorial, Beacon and Park Sts and ends up at the African Meeting House and campus of the Museum of Afro-American History, 46 Joy St, 725-0022, where the New England Anti-Slavery Society was founded by William Lloyd Garrison in 1832. Open daily 10am-4pm, Free, suggested donation $5. *www.afroammuseum.org/trail.htm*.

Christian Science Center, 175 Huntington Ave, 450-2000, world HQ of the Christian Science religion, is a conglomerate of stunning buildings including the Mother Church; the Publishing Society, which produces among other literature the highly respected *Christian Science Monitor*; and the Mapparium, a beautiful 40-foot stained glass, walk-thru globe with unusual acoustics. 'You walk *into* the world! Tremendous visual and sensory delight.' Church tours, 45 mins, Mon-Sat 10am-5pm, Wed 'til 4pm, Sun 11.30am-3pm, free. *www.tfccs.com.*

Faneuil Hall, Quincy Mkt, 242-5642. Built in 1742 and given to the city of Boston by Peter Faneuil. Known as the 'Cradle of Liberty', the hall was the scene of mass meetings during the pre-revolutionary period and it is where Samuel Adams urged for the country's independence from the British. Daily 9am-5pm. Don't leave without catching a glimpse of the weathervane in the form of a grasshopper that sits atop Faneuil Hall, placed there at the request of Peter Faneuil himself. 'Grasshopper' was the symbol of the Boston port; during the War of 1812 it was the password used to weed out spies: if you couldn't identify it as the symbol of Boston, you were in trouble. Special events are often held here so ring in advance.

The Freedom Trail is a walking tour through the heart of old Boston, beginning on Boston Common at the Visitors Center. On it you can visit nearly all Boston's associations with the American Revolution. The Trail is clearly marked by a path of red bricks set in the sidewalk; few visitors to Boston escape it. At 5 km, and offering a 3-4 hr walk, the Trail tends to be a tad dull, and unless you have a passionate interest in American revolutionary history, forget it. *www.thefreedomtrail.org*.

Institute of Contemporary Art, 955 Boylston St, 266-5152. Tue-Fri 12pm-5pm, Thu 'til 9pm, free after 5pm on Thu, Sat/Sun 11am-5pm. $7, $5 w/student ID. *www.icaboston.org*.

Isabella Stewart Gardner Museum, 280 The Fenway, 566-1401. Italianate villa built by the eccentric Mrs Gardner to house her art collection in 1903. It lost about a dozen pieces of fine works in a 1990 robbery but still has a lot to see, including the house itself. Retreat to the cool sanctuary of the Venetian courtyard. Tue-Sun, 11am-5pm, $10 weekdays, $11 w/ends, $5 w/student ID. 'Excellent.' *www.gardnermuseum.org*.

Literary Trail. *The Literary Trail of Greater Boston: A Tour of Sites in Boston (Susan Wilson)* suggests self-guided tours of sites relating to Boston writers, including the homes of Nathaniel Hawthorne, Henry Wadsworth Longfellow, Louisa May Alcott, and Henry David Thoreau. $12, available at area book stores or from the Boston History Collaborative, 650 Beacon St, 350-0358. The Boston History Collaborative also offers guided Literary Trail tours $30, $22 self-guided, incl literary trail book and tkts to the Gibson Hse, the Orchard Hse and the Concord Msm. *www.lit-trail.org.*

Museum of Fine Arts, 465 Huntington Ave, 267-9300. One of the finest art collections in the US, with outstanding Asiatic and 'marvellous Egyptian' sections. Also some fine American watercolours, wonderful Gaugins and Degas and the largest collection of Monets outside of France. Mon-Tue 10am-4.45pm, Wed-Fri 10am-9.45pm, Sat-Sun 10am-4.45pm. $15, $13 w/student ID. Wed 4pm-9.45pm voluntary contribution, 'Well worth the money; allow at least a whole day.' 'Inexpensive cafeteria.' _www.mfa.org_.

New England Holocaust Memorial, Congress Street, adjacent to Faneuil Hall, 457-8755. Six 54ft glass towers, etched with six million numbers, commemorate those who died in Nazi concentration camps during World War II. _www.nehm.org_.

Old Granary Burying Ground, on the location of a 17th century granary. An interesting graveyard with many 18th century heroes including Paul Revere, Sam Adams and John Hancock. A grave marked 'Mary Goose' is supposedly the final resting place of Mother Goose. Daily 9am-5pm.

Old North Church, Salem St, in the north end. Built 1723, the two lanterns gave Paul Revere the signal to ride. 'Perhaps the most historic church in the USA.' Daily 9am-5pm. _www.oldnorth.com_.

Old South Meeting House, Milk & Washington Sts, 482-6439, built 1729, was where Samuel Adams gave the signal that launched the Boston Tea Party in 1773. Open daily 9.30am-5pm, $5, $4 w/student ID. _www.oldsouthmeetinghouse.org_.

Old State House Museum, Washington & State Sts, 720-1713. Built 1713 as the seat of British colonial government; the Declaration of Independence was read from the East Balcony in 1776. Has an important display of Americana. Daily 9am-5pm, $5, $4 w/student ID. _www.bostonhistory.org_.

Old Town Trolley tour bus, 269-7010, goes everywhere of historical note; you get on and off and on again when you like (9am-last reboard at 4pm,), tkts $29, $26 w/student ID. Info and tkts available from the Trolley Stop Store at Charles and Boylston Sts, 422-0105. _www.trolleytours.com_. **National Park Service walking tours** leave from Visitors Center, 242-5642, at 15 State St, 90 mins; daily 10am-3pm—Old South Meeting House, Old State House, Paul Revere's house, Old North Church, and Faneuil Hall, free.

Park St Church, 523-3383, at Brimstone Corner, built 1809. Where _America_ was first sung, in 1832, and William Lloyd Garrison disclaimed against slavery for the first time in 1829. Tue-Sat 9.30am-3.30pm, free. _www.parkstreet.org_.

Paul Revere House, in the North End on the Freedom Trail, 523-2338. Paul Revere lived here from 1770 to 1780 and owned the house 'til 1800. His famous ride to inform the nation the British were about to attack began across the river in Charleston. The oldest building in downtown Boston; built 1670s. Daily 9.30am-5.15pm; $3, $2.50 w/student ID. _www.paulreverehouse.org_.

Prudential Center, 236-2300. A daring, $150 million urban renewal project of the 1960s, with apartments, offices, and countless shops. On the 50th floor is an observatory, SkyWalk, with a 360 degree viewing deck. Daily 10am-10pm, $9.50.

State House, 727-3676, with its large gold dome, is the seat of the Massachusetts State Government. Charles Bulfinch, greatest American architect of the late 18th century, designed the central part of the building. Look for the Sacred Cod over the entrance to the House of Representatives, pointing to the party in power. In 1933, a group of Harvard students stole the fish and the State House was thrown into turmoil—reps refused to conduct any business until the fish was found, four days later. Free guided tours Mon-Fri 10am-4pm. Enter on Beacon St.

On the Waterfront

Bay State Cruise Co, 748-1428, runs Summer Entertainment Cruises, with concerts and dances on board, Fri/Sat from Commonwealth Pier. Leaves at 8.30pm, returns 11.30pm. Rsvs required, must be over 21. $16-$20, admission only. Also, you can catch the **Provincetown Express** from here (Boston-Provincetown 90mins) May-Sept, 8am, 1pm & 5.30pm, $59 r/t, $38 o/w. _www.baystatecruises.com_.

Boston Tea Party Ship & Museum, Congress St Bridge, 338-1773. _Beaver II_, replica of ship whose dumped cargo brewed rebellion in 1773. 'A rip-off. Makes you feel proud to be British.' _www.bostonteapartyship.com_. Undergoing renovations until late 2006.

John F Kennedy Library and Museum, Columbia Point, overlooking harbour, 514-1600. Another IM Pei building, it houses mementoes and memorials to not only JFK but also his brother Robert. Daily 9am-5pm; $10, $8 w/student ID. Take T to U Mass then take free shuttle bus (runs every 20 mins). *www.jfklibrary.org*.

Museum of Science, on the Charles River Dam in Science Park, 723-2500. The $10 million large-screen theatre is worth a visit—so big it can project a life-size image of a whale. 'Could spend 2 days here and still not see it all.' Accept the robot challenge, and through interactive screens, control a robot over the Internet. Giant plasma screens in the *Current Science and Technology Center* deliver the latest scientific discoveries, as well as NASA coverage. Or you could create your own cyber fish at the virtual fish-tank. Daily 9am-7pm, Fri 'til 9pm; combo tkts to theatre, planetarium and museum $23, $15 for museum only. *www.mos.org*.

New England Aquarium, Central Wharf, off Atlantic Ave, 973-5200. One of Boston's most popular attractions; contains 2000 specimens in a 187,000 gallon tank. Sea lion shows daily, as well as 'Animal Interviews' with seals, penguins and sea otters. 'Excellent! Could spend the whole day there.' Open Mon-Thu 9am-6pm, Fri-Sun 'til 7pm, $15.95. *www.neaq.org* is great for landlubbers who want to try virtual whale-watching!

Whale-watching trips, 973-5281, organised by the Aquarium. April-Oct, $29, $23 w/student ID. Also qualifies for disc price entrance to Aquarium. Rsvs recommended.

USS Constitution, a frigate from the war of 1812, is the oldest commissioned war ship in the US Navy, preserved in Charleston Navy Yard, 242-0543. Open Tue-Sun 10am-4pm, free. Nearby is the **Bunker Hill Monument** commemorating the first set battle of the Revolution. The battle was actually fought on a different hill, but all the good stuff is here; Bunker Hill Pavilion, 241-7575; $3: An audio-visual programme, *The Whites of Their Eyes*, gives the background to the battle with dramatic effects (every ½hr, 9.30am-5pm). *www.historictours.com*.

Entertainment

For who, what, where and when, read the *Boston Phoenix, www.bostonphoenix.com,* or check the Thursday edition of the *Boston Globe's* Calendar section *www.boston.com/globe/calendar*. *Theater Mirror www.theatermirror.com* has play reviews and listings along with links to area theatres. The **Bostix booth** in Faneuil Hall, 482-2849, has half-price tickets on day of performance. Look for free jazz concerts in Copley Square, lunch-time in summer.

Symphony Hall, 301 Massachusetts Ave, 266-1492. Discount 'Rush' tickets—bought on day of performance. Home of the Boston Symphony and the Boston Pops. During the first week in July, the Pops, who were for many years led by John Williams of Star Wars music fame, and more currently Keith Lockhart, play at the Hatch Memorial Shell by the Charles River. The free outdoor concerts, including jazz, start at 8pm, so get there early if you want to get good places. 'Take a picnic, lots of fun.' *www.bso.org.*

Wang Center for the Performing Arts, 270 Tremont St, 482-9393. If you don't manage to 'catch a show' at this old vaudeville theatre make a visit anyway. The building is an historic landmark and the architecture is more than worth it; the lobby was used as the interior of Jack Nicholson's mansion in *The Witches of Eastwick*. See the world-renowned Boston Ballet here. Occasionally 'student rush' discounted tickets are available. *www.wangcenter.org*.

Friday Flicks at the Hatch Shell at sunset, Jul-Aug. Check the Department of Conservation and Recreation's web page for movie listings and other park events: *www.mass.gov/dcr/rec-act.htm*.

Tune into WGBH, the city's non-commercial TV channel and reputed to be one of the best in America. *www.wgbh.org.*

Sports

Boston's four professional sports teams inspire devotion in the city and in fans nationwide. In summer the Boston Red Sox play at historic **Fenway Park,** 267-1700, one of the most beautiful ball parks in the States. In fall and winter the New England Patriots play American football at **Foxboro,** (800) 543-1776, an easy train ride from South Station. 'A fantastic day out.' The **Boston Garden** is the home of both the Celtics for basketball, 523-3030, and the Bruins for ice-hockey, 624-1050. Call TicketMaster, 931-2000, to purchase tickets.

Beaches: Closest beach is **Revere.** 'Scruffy but only $1 (to Airport Station) on the Blue Line.' Further afield is Ipswich, only a short train ride away for a splash in the sea; orange line to North Station, then commuter rail, $4.25. For schedules and info call 722-3200.

Biking: A 14 mile loop follows both banks of the Charles River, from the Museum of Science to Watertown, and may be entered at any point on the Cambridge or Watertown sides. Or explore Boston's hidden places in Beacon Hill and along quaint side-streets in the North End and the Waterfront. Call **Back Bay Bikes and Boards,** 336 Newbury St, 247-2336. Rent a bike for $20, 24 hrs, $10, 2 hrs.

Canoeing: Charles River Canoe & Kayak, 965-5110, kiosk located on the bank of the river across Soldier's Field Rd from Harvard Stadium (head upstream from Elliot Bridge), Thu 4pm-8pm, Fri-Sun 1pm-8pm. Canoes $12 p/hr, $48 p/day, double kayaks $15 p/hr, $60 p/day.

Inline skating: 'Paths along both banks of the Charles River are good for novice rollerblading.' Start from Memorial Dr at Harvard on Sun, the rest of the time, skate along the Esplanade, which takes you along the river. Rent skates from **Blades, Board & Skate,** 349 Newbury St, 437-6300. Mon-Fri 11am-9pm, w/ends 11am-8pm, $15/day and $200 deposit on credit card. _www.blades.com._

Information

Boston Common Visitors Center, (the place to go for tourist info), the Common on Tremont St, 536-4100, daily 9am-5pm; and **Greater Boston Convention and Tourist Bureau,** west side of Prudential Plaza, 867-8389, daily 9am-6pm. For $1.50 you can purchase the _Official Guidebook to Boston_, 100-plus pages with numerous maps of city and discount coupons. _www.bostonusa.com._

National Park Service Visitor Center, 15 State St, 242-5642, centrally located. Has short slide show of Freedom Trail, books, pamphlets and brochures on Boston and surrounding areas. Free guided tours of the trail, from Old South Meeting to Old North Church, 10am-3pm. Office open daily 9am-5pm.

Internet Access

The Chelsea City Café, 173 Washington Ave, 889-9887. Internet access $8/hr. Accessible via commuter rail, get off at the Chelsea stop; you can also take the 111 bus from Haymarket. Check _www.chelseacity.com_ for opening times.

The Boston Public Library, 700 Bolyspon St, Copley Square. Internet time limit 15mins-1hr. Take the Green line to Copley Station. _www.bpl.org._

Travel

Amtrak, (800) 872-7245, South Station (Red Line, main station) and Back Bay Station (Green Line, Copley; Orange line, Back Bay). NYC ($64, 4 hrs).

Bonanza Bus Lines, South Station, (800) 556-3815, buses to New York ($37), Portsmouth ($17), Newport ($18).

Green Tortoise, (800) 227-4766. Camper bus touring company which offers interesting, economical 1-4 week trips all over North America. (Leave from Boston to west coast but no travel between east coast cities—see New York section for more details.) _www.greentortoise.com._

Greyhound, South Station, (800) 231-2222. NYC ($30, 5 hrs).

Logan Airport is across the bay only 3 miles from downtown: Blue Line T to

Airport station ($1) from where there's a free shuttle bus to the terminals, daily 5.30am-1am. Taxis from airport to downtown cost $10-$21. You can take **the water shuttle**, (800) 235-6426, from Logan, across the harbour, to Rowe's Wharf for $10. Leaves every 15/30 mins Mon-Fri 7am-6pm. 'A great way to see the city.'

Massachusetts Bay Transit Authority (MBTA), 222-3200, runs buses, trains and trolleys throughout Boston and surrounding towns. Flat fare subway $1, bus 75¢, free transfers. At the visitors centre, you can also buy the Boston Passport that provides unlimited travel on bus, trolley and subway lines: 1 day ($6), 3 days ($11) or 7 days ($18). Bus and subway services shut down around 12.30am-1am. MBTA also run a commuter rail system to Rockport and Salem.

Peter Pan Bus Line, South Station, (800) 237-8747, serves Massachusetts, New Hampshire, and Connecticut. For Maine/New Hampshire, try **Concord Trailways,** South Station, (800) 639-3317.

Plymouth & Brockton Bus Lines, South Station, 773-9401, to Plymouth ($9), Hyannis ($14) and Provincetown ($23). *www.p-b.com.*

CAMBRIDGE   Just across the river, Cambridge is often referred to as 'Boston's Left Bank'. Teeming with an eclectic collection of cafes, bookstores and boutiques, and nestled in the shadows of two of the world's premier educational institutions, **Harvard** and **Massachusetts Institute of Technology (MIT)**, the lively streets and bustling squares are home to a young, diverse population. The lifestyle of the students here sets the pace for both sides of the Charles River and **Harvard Square** is where it all happens. You will be amazed at the range of entertainment and activity to be found in such a small area.

Over one hundred restaurants and cafes will satisfy any craving and on warm summer evenings sidewalk entertainers fill the air with music. This "book Mecca" also has 25 bookstores dotted along brick pathways. For a cosier atmosphere head to one of the many blues bars and jazz clubs. For those interested in history there are some outstanding 19th century mansions and nine museums.

You can take the T to Harvard Square from Boston, but it's better to walk across **Harvard Bridge**, taking in the cityscapes, and the sailors, windsurfers and rowers on the Charles River below. *www.cambridge.ma.us* and *www.townonline.com/cambridge*   provide introductions to the city.

Accommodation

Cambridge is a 10 min T-ride from the heart of Boston where accommodation is more readily available. For choices, try **Bed & Breakfast in Cambridge & Greater Boston,** PO Box 626, Cambridge, Mass 02128, 720-1492/ (800) 888-0178. Rooms from $70-$135 in Cambridge, Boston, and Lexington.

Budget chain hotels: Before you call, check out the discounts available at the information booths off I-90, make rsvs from phones there to take advantage of the best deals.

Cambridge Bed and Muffin, 267 Putnam Ave, 576-3166. D-$88, shared bathroom. Includes bfast and linens/towels.

The Irving House at Harvard, 24 Irving Street, 547-4600. 5-10 mins from Harvard Yard and T, S-$85 w/shared bath, $115 w/private bath, D-$120 w/shared bath, $190 w/private bath. Bfast, free local calls, free parking, cable TV, laundry. *www.irvinghouse.com.*

Food

An array of ethnic restaurants and sidewalk cafes will tempt even the most adventurous palate. Pick up the free *Square Deal* newspaper for special offers at local eateries.

Border Cafe, 32 Church St, 864-6100. Super tasty Tex-Mex and Cajun cooking at this ever-popular hot spot. Fabby fajita dinners $9-$13, Mexican specials $6-$13. 'Good, authentic food.' Mon-Thu 11am-12.45am, Fri-Sat 11am-12.45am, Sun noon-12.45am.

Cafe of India, 52A Brattle St, Harvard Sq, 661-0683. Good, hearty Indian food. W/day lunch buffet $7.95, w/end $11.95, dinner $13-$19. Open Mon-Thu 11.30am-11pm, Fri 'til 12am, Sat 8am-12am, Sun 8am-11pm.

Shilla, 57 JFK St, Harvard Sq, 547-7971. Japanese and Korean food. Lunch $5.95-$7.95, dinner from $10.95. Fresh fish and 'friendly service'. Open Sun-Wed 11.30am-10.30pm, Thu-Sat 'til 1am.

Pizzeria Uno, 22 JFK St, Harvard Sq, 497-1530. Pizzas $6.39-$15.79, try their special Spinniccoli! 'Lively Italian restaurant. Good value.' Mon-Sun 11am-12.30am, Fri & Sat 'til 1am. *www.unos.com.*

Of Interest

Old Town Trolley Tours, 269-7010, daily 9am-5pm. Non-stop tours of Boston and Cambridge last 1 hr 45 mins, otherwise get off and on again when you like, $25, $23 w/student ID. *www.historictours.com*.

Harvard University, founded 1636, is the oldest university in North America. Massachusetts Hall (1720) is the oldest building still standing. The **Harvard University Visitors Information Center** is at 1350 Mass. Ave, 495-1573 (in the Holyoke Center). For guided walking tours and an information session on Harvard University, start at Byerly Hall, held Mon-Fri 11am & 3pm, Sat 3pm only, Sun 11am only; lasts 1½ hrs. Info sessions Mon-Fri 10am & 2pm, walks (90 mins-2hrs) Mon-Fri 11am & 3pm, Sat 11am, Info session (1hr) Mon-Fri 10am & 2pm, free. Walk from Harvard Square up Brattle St past Radcliffe, previously a women's college, now fully merged with Harvard, and Harvard Yard. *www.harvard.edu*

Then to **Longfellow's house**, 105 Brattle St, 876-4491, where the poet lived between 1837 and 1882. The house is furnished with Longfellow's furniture and books. In earlier times George Washington used this house as his HQ. Tours Wed-Sun 10am-4.30pm, $3. *www.nps.gov/long*.

Also in the campus area is the **Fogg Art Museum**, Quincy & Broadway Sts, 495-9400; which has the largest collection of Ingres outside of France, and works by Rembrandt, Monet, Renoir, Picasso and Rothko. Mon-Sat 10am-5pm, Sun 1pm-5pm, $6.50, $5 w/student ID, free Sat 10am-12pm. *www.artmuseums.harvard.edu.*

Le Corbusier's Carpenter Center of the Visual Arts, the **Houghton Library** (housing the Keats collection), and the **Harvard Museums of Natural History**, are all contained in one building with entrances at 11 Divinity & 26 Oxford St, and also include: **Peabody Museum of Archeology and Ethnology, Museum of Comparative Zoology, Botanical Museum** and **Mineralogical and Geological Museum**. 'It takes all day to see most of it. There's a spectacular collection of glass flowers in the Botanical Museum.' For info on all Harvard museums: 495-3045. All museums (except Fogg) open daily 9am-5pm; $7.50, $6 w/student ID. *www.artmuseums.harvard.edu/information.*

MIT tours, 253-4795, include a look at the lovely chapel designed by Eero Saarinen. Student conducted tours Mon-Fri begin at 10.45am & 2.45pm at the information centre, 77 Massachusetts Ave. 'It's probably just as worthwhile to get a map and wander around yourself.'

MIT Museum, 265 Massachusetts Avenue at Front Street (Building N52), 253-4444. Science and technology, architecture, and nautical exhibitions, plus the 'Hall of Hacks' documenting MIT students' pranks. Come here to learn about the weather balloon that exploded in a cloud of talcum powder on the playing field of the 1982 Harvard-Yale football game. Tue-Fri 10am-5pm, Sat/Sun noon-5pm, $5, $2 w/student ID. _web.mit.edu/museum._

Mt Auburn Cemetery on Mt Auburn St, contains the graves of Longfellow, James Lowell, Oliver Wendell Holmes and Mary Baker Eddy, founder of Christian Science. Both a cemetery and a park, with ponds, hills, footpaths, arboretum. 'Quiet relaxing place, great for bird watching in spring.'

Walking tours, pick up a self-guided tour map ($2) from the info booth in Harvard Sq and discover the historic sites of Cambridge and Harvard Yard for yourself.

Book Stores: It's not surprising, perhaps, that America's academic capital plays host to one of the world's largest concentrations of book stores. A few of the more intriguing shops:

Grolier Poetry Bookshop, 6 Plympton St, 547-4648, oldest continuously operating poetry bookshop in US, since 1927, more than 15,000 titles. Mon-Sat noon-6.30pm. _www.grolierpoetrybookshop.com._

Harvard Co-op, 1400 Mass Ave, 499-2000, books, posters, music, and more. Mon-Sat 9am-10pm, Sun Noon-7pm. _www.thecoop.com._ **MIT Coop**, 3 Cambridge Center.

Revolution Books, 1156 Mass. Ave, 492-5443, anything you could want by Marx, Lenin, Stalin, Mao, etc. Tues-Fri 2pm-8pm, Sat 12pm-8pm, Sun 2pm-6pm.

Entertainment

Watch the _Boston Phoenix_ for details of concerts and lectures. _The Harvard Gazette, Crimson_ and _Independent_ are also good, though the latter is not published in summer. The active music scene is closely tied to Harvard and MIT; summer is therefore quieter.

Cantab Lounge, 738 Mass. Ave, Central Sq, 354-2685. Packed out with locals enjoying Little Joe Cook and the Thrillers w/e, bluegrass etc. Cover varies. Open Mon-Wed 8am-1am, Thu-Sat 'til 2am, Sun noon-1am. _www.cantablounge.com._

John Harvard's Brew House, 33 Dunster St, 868-3585. Brewery restaurant serving good homemade ales, lagers and seasonal beers. Try a brewery sampler. Open Mon-Thu 11.30am-12.30am, Fri/Sat 'til 2am, Sun 'til 12am. _www.johnharvards.com._

Ryles Jazz Club, 212 Hampshire St, Inman Sq, 876-9330, Cover $10, Sun Brunch 10am-3pm. Not cheap, but good jazz. _www.rylesjazz.com._

TT The Bear's Place, 10 Brookline St, Central Sq, 492-0082, hard rock, beer. Live 'n loud! Live music 7 nights a week. 6pm-Midnight. Call 492-BEAR for concert information. _www.ttthebears.com._

LEXINGTON/CONCORD   Lexington and Concord are ideally situated for day trips from Boston, and are easily accessible by public transport or pedal power (you can bike up the **Minute Man Commuter Bike Trail** from Arlington). Known as the 'Birthplace of American Liberty', the towns share the distinction of being the site of the first skirmish in the American Revolution. Near Concord's Old North Bridge on 19 April 1775, local farmers took aim at advancing British redcoats and fired the 'shot heard round the world'.

The bridge is part of the **Minute Man National Historic Park**, (978) 369-6993; park rangers give excellent historical talks here on request. Battle re-enactments are staged throughout both towns in April to mark Patriot's Day (closest Monday to April 19), and a special 'Colonial Weekend' in early October. _www.nps.gov/mima._ The **Minute Man Visitor's Center**, provides free maps and a 25-minute multimedia production, _The Road to Revolution_, on the park's history, 9am, and every hr. Take route 128, exit 30B. Daily 9am-5pm.

Concord is also the home of the literary transcendentalist movement. Interestingly, all of the best-known transcendentalists—Ralph Waldo Emerson, Henry David Thoreau, Nathaniel Hawthorne, Amos Bronson Alcott and his daughter, Louisa May—at one point lived within blocks of each other in this tiny, pristine town. Also here is **Sleepy Hollow Cemetery**, (3 blocks from town) where some of them have been laid to rest. Not far away is Thoreau's **Walden Pond**.

The telephone area code for Concord is 978, Lexington is 781.

Accommodation
Accommodation here is limited and rather expensive. See Cambridge for local B&B options.
Col. Roger Brown House, 1694 Main St, Concord, 369-9119. D-w/private bath $120-$150. *www.colrogerbrown.com.*
Desiderata B&B, 189 Wood St, Lexington, 862-2824. $69-89, includes good bfast. No credit cards, rsvs req. *www.desideratabb.com.*
Battlegreen Motor Inn, 1720 Mass Ave, Lexington, 862-6100. $79-99, bfast incl. Rsvs rec. *www.battlegreeninn.com.*

Food
Bertucci's, 1777 Mass Ave, Lexington, 860-9000. Pizza, pasta, salads; $7-$11. *www.bertuccis.com.*
Concord Tea Cakes, 59 Commonwealth Ave, Concord, 369-7644. Home-made cakes, muffins, cookies and tea-time treats. *www.concordteacakes.com.*
Sally Ann Food Shop, 73 Main St, Concord, 369-4558. Soups, sandwiches and bakery takeouts at reasonable prices.

Of Interest
Hancock-Clarke House, 36 Hancock St, Lexington, 861-0928, is where Sam Adams and John Hancock were staying when Paul Revere came galloping by to warn them. Mid-April to Oct, daily 11 am-2pm, last tours 2pm). **Monroe Tavern**, 1332 Mass Ave, was HQ and hospital for British troops. One tour daily, 3pm. **Buckman Tavern**, 1 Bedford Street, was the gathering place for Minutemen and Militia members from Lexington, tours on half-hour 10am-4pm. $5 each building, or combo ticket all three for $10. Call 862-1703. *www.lexingtonhistory.org.*
Lexington Green, where it all happened two centuries ago, is lined with lovely Colonial houses; on the east side, facing the road by which the British approached, is the famous Minute Man Statue. Over in the southwest corner of the Green is the Revolutionary Monument erected in 1799 to commemorate the eight minute men killed here. Near the Green is Buckman Tavern, the oldest of the local hostelries and gathering place of the minutemen on drill nights.

Information/Travel
Concord Chamber of Commerce, 15 Walden St, 369-3120. Mon-Fri 9am-2pm. Visitors Centre is located at 58 Main St, open daily 9.30am-4.30pm *www.concordmachamber.org.*
Lexington Information Center, 862-1450, near Buckman Tavern at 1875 Mass Ave, has details and literature. Daily 9am-5pm. In summer guides give lectures on the Green.
To get there; take the commuter train from Boston's MBTA North Station, (617) 722-3200, to Concord, or the subway to Alewife in Cambridge, then the bus to Lexington. *www.lexingtonchamber.org.*

THE NORTH SHORE Meandering north on Hwy 1 your first port of call should be **Salem**. The **Witch House**, 310 Essex St, 744-8815, has tours ($7) of the judges' quarters, daily 10am-5pm, in what was the site of the famous witch trials in 1692 during which Puritan judges sent 19 suspected witches to the gallows and ordered a man to be crushed to death under millstones. _www.salemweb.com/witchhouse_. Arthur Miller uses the whole horrific series of events in his play, _The Crucible_, as a metaphor for McCarthy's communist 'witch hunts' in the 1950s.

The **Salem Witch Museum**, Washington Sq North, 744-1692, has an audio-visual programme with life-sized dioramas that tell the story of the witchcraft history. Exhibit examining phenomenon of witch hunting. Daily in summer 10am-5pm, Jul/Aug 'til 7pm, $6.50. 'Sensationalised for profit. History students prepare to be disappointed.' _www.salemwitchmuseum.com_ Even more so at the **Witch Dungeon**, 16 Lynde St, 741-3570. A witch trial is re-enacted for the audience's edification. Afterwards, visitors tour the lower dungeons. Daily 10am-5pm; $6. 'A rip-off. Lasts about 15 minutes and not very realistic.' _www.witchdungeon.com._

Nathaniel Hawthorne's birthplace—made famous in his novel—the _House of Seven Gables_, 54 Turner St, 744-0991, still stands complete with amazing secret stairways, hidden compartments and beautiful period gardens. Daily in summer 10am-5pm, summer extended 'til 7pm; $11. _www.7gables.org._

A prominent port in Colonial days, Salem is a veritable museum of American architecture of the 17th and 19th centuries. Chestnut Street is lined with the lovely homes of Salem clipper captains and owners.

On **Cape Ann**, about 30 miles north of Boston, lies **Gloucester**, a rugged port packed with fishing boats and seafood restaurants. This is the setting for Sebastian Junger's _Perfect Storm_ that sank the swordfishing boat _Andrea Gail_ on October 30, 1991; the bar featured in the book and movie is the Crow's Nest, 334 Main St, (978) 281-2965. _www.perfectstorm.org_. For whale watching call: 1-888-283-1776. _www.7seaswhalewatch.com._ Four miles north of Gloucester, off Rte 127A, is the typical fishing village of **Rockport**, now an artist colony and full of arty-crafty stores.

On your way north from here to New Hampshire and Maine, there's the small town of **Newburyport**. The High Street is adorned with splendid early American mansions. 'While you're here, go whale watching; from Hilton's Fishing Dock', with **Newburyport Whale Watch,** (800) 848-1111. $35 for $4^{1}/_{2}$ hrs, Tue-Sun 8.30am & 1.30pm. _www.welikewhales.com._
The telephone area code for Salem and the North Shore is 978.

PLYMOUTH   South of Boston, Plymouth marks the spot where the Pilgrims landed in 1620; the first Thanksgiving celebrations were held here in 1621. A few 17th-century houses still stand, and on Leyden St markers indicate where the very first houses stood. Moored by the Rock is _Mayflower II_, a full-size replica of the original. 'Worth a quick visit, but it's really for Americans.'

Today Plymouth County is known as **Cranberry Country**. Harvest in September is a colourful ritual; the dazzling crimson of America's native berry covers over 12,000 acres and seems to reach to the horizon. _www.townofplymouth.org._
The telephone area code for Plymouth is 508.

Accommodation

Guest houses are the cheapest option, but they become more coveted and expensive every year. Try looking in the area behind the Tourist Information Center.

Blue Anchor Motel, 7 Lincoln St, 746-9551. Rooms $60-$80.

In-Town B&B, 23 Pleasant St, 746-7412. $70-75, full bfast. Includes historical walking tour of Plymouth and afternoon tea, as well as off-street parking. Good location. 'Lovely people.'

Camping: Plymouth Rock KOA Kampground, Middleboro, 15 miles from Plymouth on Rte 105, just off US44, 947-6435. Laundromat, showers, pool, game room, food store. Sites $25-$35 for two, $47/$69 for a cabin. 'Friendly; great place.'

Food

There are many reasonably priced sub shops and good greasy spoons in Plymouth. Generally, the farther away from the water, the cheaper.

Cap'n Harry's Deli & Sandwich Shop, 170 Water St, 747-5699. Sandwiches from $5; try their Cajun turkey roll-ups. Daily 7am-2pm.

Of Interest

Pilgrim Hall Museum, 75 Court St, 746-1620. Personal possessions and records of the Pilgrims. Daily 9.30am-4.30pm, $6. _www.pilgrimhall.org._

Plimoth Plantation. Rte 3 & Warren Ave, 746-1622. Re-creates the 1627 Plymouth community, 3 miles south of town square. Daily 9am-5pm. Combo tkt: _Mayflower II_ and Plimoth Plantation $24, valid for two days. Both staffed by Americans dressed as Pilgrims speaking with 'English accents', pretending they are still in the 17th century. _www.plimoth.org._

Plimoth Rock, on the harbour, supposedly the site of the pilgrims' arrival in the New World. Good for a chuckle, but don't make a special trip for it. Moored on the adjacent pier is _Mayflower II_, 746-1622. The replica of the original, built in England and sailed to America in 1957. $8 (but see above).

Whale Watching, Captain John's Boats, (800) 242-AHOY. Three trips daily in summer, 9am, 11am, & 2pm, $30. _www.captjohn.com._

Information/Travel

Plymouth Information Center, 130 Water St, 747-7525. General information on historical attractions.

Plymouth & Brockton Bus Lines, 746-0378. Boston, $11, o/w. _www.p-b.com_ Take the short cut to Provincetown with **Capt John's Boats**, (800) 242-2469/746-2643, Town Wharf. **Express** ferry takes 1½ hrs from Plymouth to the tip of Cape Cod, $32, r/t.

CAPE COD A 65 mile-long hook jutting out into the Atlantic, the Cape is a narrow string of sand from where, atop a dune, you can gaze at the ocean on one side and Cape Cod Bay on the other. Known for its distinctive architectural style of gable-roofed houses, the Cape can be an icy cold and blustery spot out of season, but summers are warm and sunny with a refreshing tang of salt in the air.

The Cape, with no less than 77 beaches, is home to many scientists who come to study the ocean's mysteries. The **Woods Hole Oceanographic Institute**, at the southern point of the Cape, is the most famous research group here. Be sure to see the **National Marine Fisheries Service's Aquarium**, 495-2001, open Tue-Sat 11am-4pm, free, home to many rare New England species of sea life. _www.nefsc.noaa.gov/omi/aquarium._

At the other end of the Cape, near the north-east tip, is the **Wellfleet Bay Wildlife Sanctuary** in South Wellfleet, 349-2615, a 1000-acre area operated by the Massachusetts Audubon Society. The nature center is open daily 8.30am-5pm; the nature trails are open 8am 'til dusk, $5. *www.wellfleetbay.org.*

Although the Cape is an extremely popular summer resort, it is still possible to avoid the crowds and escape to deserted sand dunes or down beautiful, sandy New England lanes leading to the sea: simply avoid Hyannis and the coast south of Cape Cod National Seashore.

Hyannis and the surrounding area is the part of the Cape most exploited by tourism and free enterprise, but over in the lower Cape, small towns like Sandwich, Barnstaple, Catumet and Pocasset remain relatively quiet, even in the high season. After Labor Day you can have the whole Cape to yourself. (Well, sort of; Cape Codders let you know in no uncertain terms that it belongs to them. However, high unemployment in recent years means that the Cape's commercial community is depending on tourists more than ever for their livelihood.)

On the Cape you will come up against numerous private beaches, or public ones that extract heavy parking fees. The Chamber of Commerce booklet *Cape Cod Vacationer*, free and available everywhere, lists all beaches and their status and has other useful information. There is plenty of camping near Sandwich where there is also a free public beach. State run and private sites can also be found in Bourne, Brewster, and Truro. Near Brewster is Orleans—a favourite beach for surfers.

Aside from the tourist, the Cape's great source of revenue is the cranberry: Nearly a third of the US cranberry crop is produced here and in neighbouring Plymouth County (Wisconsin has overtaken Massachusetts as the main cranberry producer.)

The telephone area code for Cape Cod is 508.

Accommodation
Can be expensive, but there are several camping sites and also 3 youth hostels. For other listings, see Hyannis or Provincetown, or else consult *Yankee Magazine's Guide to New England* or the *Cape Cod Vacationer*.
Bed & Breakfast, Cape Cod, 225-3824. Reservation service; in-season rooms $85-$225 incl bfast, plus $10 one-time booking fee and 25% deposit. *www.bedandbreakfastcapecod.com.*
Mid-Cape Hostel, 75 Goody Hallet Dr, Eastham, 255-2785. Mid-May to mid-Sept; daily 8am-10pm. $20-22. Summer rsvs essential. 20 miles from Truro, ideal if you're working your way up the Cape.' 'Very strict.' *www.usahostels.org/cape*.
Camping: Be warned: 'Campsites are often full right up to Labor Day and you may need to drive right out to North Truro to find a vacancy.' Plan your summer Cape Cod accommodation as early as possible.
Shawme Crowell State Forest, 42 Maine St, Route 130, Sandwich, 888-0351. Sites $10-17 per night. Free hot showers, laundry facilities and grocery stores within a mile, incl free pass to Scuttet beach.

Travel
See also under **Hyannis**.
The Cape Cod Automated Travel Service, 771-6191, offers 24 hr comprehensive info on fares and schedules for transport to, from and within the area. *www.gocapecod.org/travinfo.htm.*
Bonanza Bus Lines, 59 Depot Ave (old train depot), Falmouth, 548-7588/(800) 556-3815. Boston $17, New York $51.

HYANNIS   The metropolis of the Cape, Hyannis is the main supply centre for the area and a busy summer resort. Main Street is an example of the typical all-American strip; for charm you want the outlying areas like Hyannisport and Craigville with its excellent beach for swimming.

More upper crust than most of the other Cape Cod towns, Hyannis is the home of wealthy trendies and is bathed in the aura of the Kennedy family sequestered in their Hyannisport compound.

Accommodation
Cascade Motor Lodge, 201 Main St, 775-9717. $74-165, very close to bus station. 'Had large, luxurious room with bathroom and double waterbed!' _www.cascademotorlodge.com._
Sea Beach Inn, 388 Sea St, 775-4612. $70-90. Bfast incl. Close to beaches and downtown.

Food
Hearth & Kettle, 132 Hyannis, 771-3000. Breakfast and lunch $7-$15, dinner $11-$21. Try a kettle of lobster chowder $4.99. Daily 7am-10pm.
Perry's, 546 Main St. 775-9711. Breakfast $7, sandwiches from $5, stacked sandwiches with fries $7. Daily 5am-3pm.

Information
Cape Cod Chamber of Commerce, Rtes 6 & 132, 362-3225/(888) 332-2732. Offers accommodation and entertainment information for the entire Cape area. Ask for _The Vacationer_ booklet, _Resort Directory_, and the _Current Events_ booklet. A good place to start learning about the Cape highlights. _www.capecodchamber.org._
Hyannis Area Chamber of Commerce, 1481 Rte 132, 775-2201.

Travel
Cape Cod Central Railroad, (888) 797-7245, Hyannis to Sandwich, Tue-Sun, $16 r/t. _www.capetrain.com._
Ferries: During the summer, boats leave frequently from Hyannis South St Dock for Nantucket, o/w is $14 (high-speed $27.50), cars $175. O/w from Woods Hole to Martha's Vineyard is $6, cars $57. Contact **Steamship Authority**, 477 8600 for schedule or visit _www.steamshipauthority.com._
Trips around the Hyannis Inner Harbour to gape at the Kennedy compound are also available for $12. Contact **Hy-Line Harbour Cruises**, on the Ocean St docks, 778 0404. Hy-Line give same-day discounts with coupons available at any Cape or Island hostel. Also has services to Nantucket and Martha's Vineyard _www.hy-linecruises.com._
Plymouth & Brockton Bus Lines, 17 Elm Ave, 746-0378. Provincetown $10, Boston $17. Logan Airport $22. _www.p-b.com._

PROVINCETOWN   P-town, as it's known locally, is at the very tip of the Cape, thus giving it its other nickname: Land's End. The Pilgrim Fathers' first landfall in North America was actually here. They stayed for four or five weeks before moving on to Plymouth. The town has made its name on tourism and fishing.

Provincetown has been a haven for artists since the 1870s. In 1899 Charles Hawthorne opened Provincetown's Cape Cod School of Art. Modernists dominated the scene from the 30s to the 50s—Jackson Pollock and Mark Rothko both lived here.

In summer the town is still jam-packed with artists, playwrights and craftsmen (including a very large gay community), now out-numbered by the tourists and hangers-on who come to watch them. All in all, the off-season population of around 4,000 swells to nearly 50,000 people! P-town is an attractive spot with old clapboard houses, narrow streets and miles of sandy beaches. Commercial St, appropriately named, is the main drag, so to speak.

In the summer months, it's a perpetual street fair. For a special evening's entertainment, take a beach taxi ride over the sand dunes. 'Nightlife is very limited if you are looking for "straight" bars and there are very few college age students around.' *www.provincetown.com*.

Accommodation

HI-Truro, 111 N Pamet Rd, 349-3889, 10 miles from Provincetown. $24, kitchen. Rsvs essential. Two minute walk to beach.

Joshua Paine Guest House, 15 Tremont St, in the west end (quiet, non-commercial part), 487-1551. June 15-Sept 15. $50-65. 'Friendly; nice place.'

The Outermost Hostel, 28 Winslow St, 487-4378. $22 per night. Dorm-style cabins, kitchen facilities, May-Oct. 'Good location.'

Food

Cafe Heaven, 199 Commercial St, 487-9639. Home-made muffins and granola for breakfast, over-stuffed sandwiches for $6-$9.

Clem and Ursie's Food Ghetto, 85 Shank Painter Rd, 487-2333. Inexpensive seafood, sea clam pot pie $6.99. *www.clemandursies.com*.

Surf Restaurant, 315A Commercial St on MacMillan Wharf, 487-1367. Eat on the deck overlooking the harbour. A drafthouse with jug band, washboard, and kazoos! Seafood menu $7-$28.

Of Interest

Art's Dune Tour, 487-1950, leaves from Commercial & Standish Sts. April-Nov. $18 for standard tour, $26 for sunset tour (need rsvs). From 10am throughout the day. Interesting ride out to the site of dune shacks once belonging to Tennessee Williams and Eugene O'Neill, then on to a cranberry bog before heading out to the ocean. *www.artsdunetours.com.*

Fine Arts Work Center, 24 Pearle St, 487-9960. Conducts a summer workshop for prominent writers and artists and offers weekly readings, lectures, slide shows, and exhibits. Gallery open Mon-Fri 9am-5pm. *www.fawc.org.*

Provincetown Art Association and Museum, 460 Commercial St, 487-1750. Daily noon-5pm, 8pm-10pm, $2. *www.paam.org.*

Provincetown Museum, at the base of the Pilgrim Monument, 487-1310. 'The Treasures of the pirate ship, *Whydah*. Artefacts from the ship of the pirate Samuel (Black Sam) Bellamy sunk in 1717 and identified in 1984.' Daily 9am-5pm, last admission 4.15pm; shorter winter hours. $7 admission to monument, museum and exhibit, $5 w/student ID. *www.pilgrim-monument.org.*

Whale Watching from MacMillan Wharf, $28 for 3 hrs at sea. Call Dolphin Fleet: (800) 826-9300, rsvs rec. 'Good, interesting commentary on board; we saw several whales, including one that swam under and around the boat; incredible and not to be missed.' *www.whalewatch.com.*

Information

Province Land's Visitors Center in Cape Cod National Seashore, 487-1256, off Race Point Road. Tour information, maps of seashore.

Provincetown Chamber of Commerce, 307 Commercial St, 487-3424. Offers maps and accommodation listings.

NANTUCKET 'The Little Grey Lady of the Sea', as the island is known, provided inspiration for Melville's *Moby Dick*. You will find yourself in another world as you step off the ferry: thirty miles off Cape Cod, the island retains a certain charm with its weather-worn (though meticulously preserved) houses, cranberry bogs and salt marshes. Lobster boats crowd the small harbour in the evenings, when they sell their catch to restauranteurs and passers-by.

On every side of the island there are miles of open sand beaches terrific for swimming, surfing, fishing and all-night bonfire parties. Rent a bike near the ferry port and follow the bike paths or explore the island on the narrow streets and winding lanes. The 10-mile scenic ride to the beaches at Siasconset on the east coast will whet your appetite for a dip in the ocean.

The cobblestoned Main Street of Nantucket town and fine Colonial homes testify to the past prosperity built on the blubber of hunted whales. Today the money flows in with the flood of 'off-islanders' in summer. It can be a crowded place then, but a lot of fun. For the pristine scene, come out of season when there's nobody there but the 'on-islanders', some of whom brag that they have never seen the mainland. _www.nantucket.com_.
The telephone area code for Nantucket is 508.

Accommodation
The island is generally a very expensive place to stay, and to maintain premium hotel rates any riffraff caught camping will be fined $50, i.e., what you would have paid for a bed. But all is not lost:

Nesbitt Inn, 21 Broad St, 228-2446 in centre of town. $75-95; Bfast incl. Rsvs req.

Robert B. Johnson Hostel, 31 Western Ave, Nantucket, 228-0433. 3 miles from ferry wharf. $19/22 HI/non-HI, linen $2. 2 mins to beach, 11pm curfew. Rsvs essential in summer.

Food
Check _www.clickcapecod.com_ for places to eat.

Captain Tobey's Chowder House, Straight Wharf, 228-0836. Winner of 'Best Chowder' award. Serves local seafood, daily early bird specials. 'Good seafood.' Pricey but worth it. $17-28.

Henry's, on Steamboat Wharf, 228-0123, has the biggest, and some say the best, sandwiches on the island, $3.95-$12. Daily 8am-10pm.

Of Interest
Whaling Museum, Broad St, 228-1736. In the 18th and early 19th centuries, Nantucket was the best known whaling place in America. You can recapture something of the flavour of those times here. Has a good scrimshaw collection. Mon-Sat 10am-5pm, Sun noon-5pm, $15, incl walking tour, lectures and entrance to Hadwen House. _www.nha.org._

Whale Watching. Call 1-800-WHALING for details. Daily 8.30am-12.30pm & 1.30pm-5.30pm, $38. Guarantee sighting or return visit. 'Saw more than 20 whales. Best part of our trip.' Rsvs rec. _www.yankeefleet.com._

Young's Bicycle Rental, 6 Broadstreet, 228-1151. $25 per 24 hrs. Mon-Sat 8.30am-6pm, Sun 9am-5.30pm. _www.youngsbicycleshop.com._

Entertainment
Check _www.clickcapecod.com_ for entertainment spots.

Gaslight Theatre, N Union St, 228-4435. Mainstream and art films, max. $10. _www.gaslighttheater.com._

The Muse, 44 Surfside Rd (1 mile out of town), 228-6873. Best live entertainment on the island: rock 'n roll, reggae, blues, cover up to $15. Don't miss the lip-synching contest on Sundays!

Rose and Crown, S Water Street, 228-2595. Good pub-grub from $4-$25, sandwiches and seafood. Live entertainment, karaoke, cover for bands around $5. 'Packed out but has a dance floor.'

Information
Chamber of Commerce, 48 Main St, 228-1700, maps, restaurant and accommodation information. _www.nantucketchamber.org._
Hub Board, Main St. Very useful for ads of jobs and rooms. 'We found two rooms from it on the first day.'
See under **Hyannis** for travel information.

MARTHA'S VINEYARD   Once you've experienced the 'Vineyard', as it is fondly called, you will never forget it. Just five miles off the Cape, New England's largest island boasts sandy beaches, pine forests, moorland, winding lanes and picturesque towns steeped in maritime history. It's a pleasure to visit at any time of year, although July and August are the most lively. In September, the island becomes a peaceful haven once again, basking in the warmth of Indian summers.

Surfing, swimming and sailing are the attractions, although ever-increasing prices exclude such sports to anyone other than the jet-set who take over the island in the summer. Bill and Hillary Clinton are currently among the island's most prominent visitors. Settle instead for a bicycle (rentals widely available) and pedal around Edgartown, the elegant yachting centre where you can admire the fine old houses of the whaling captains, or make the strenuous 20-mile-trip out to Gayhead to watch the setting sun do its light show against the dramatic coloured cliffs.

In summer it is possible to take a tour bus from the ferry terminals in Vineyard Haven and Oak Bluffs for a fascinating visit 'up-Island' (and 'down-Island'). While in Oak Bluffs, take a ride on the **Flying Horses Carousel**, the country's oldest platform carousel. Circuit Ave, 693-9481, $1.50.

If you long to ditch people for the gentler company of swans, lesser terns and mergansers, pay a visit to one of the Vineyard's three wildlife refuges: **Cedar Tree Neck** on the North Shore, 693-7233; **Long Point** on the South Shore, or **Wasque Point** on Chappaquiddick, 627-7689. Massachusetts Audubon Society run natural history tours to bird haven **Monomoy Islands**. 3hr tour $35, rsvs required, 349-2615. _www.massaudubon.org/-Nature_Connection/Sanctuaries/Wellfleet/index.php_

The island is dry (no alcohol sold) except for Edgartown and Oak Bluffs. _www.mvol.com_.

The telephone area code for Martha's Vineyard is 508.

Accommodation
Manter Memorial AYH, Edgartown Rd, 693-2665. 7.3 miles from ferry terminal. April-Nov 7am-10am, 5pm-10pm. $17-$27. Check-in 8am-9pm. Rsvs essential for summer; include SAE with first night deposit for confirmation. 'A long way from anywhere.' 'Friendly; excellent rooms.'
Camping: Martha's Vineyard Family Campground, 569 Edgartown Rd, 693-3772. Sites $42 for 2 ppl w/hook up, XP-$10. _www.campmvfc.com._

Food
The Black Dog Tavern, 21 Beach St, Vineyard Haven, 693-9223. Bfast/lunch $10-

$15, dinner $20-$40, very popular with both tourists and locals. Summer: daily 7am-8pm. _www.theblackdog.com._

Linda Jean's Restaurant, Circuit Ave, Oak Bluffs, 693-4093. Home cooking, breakfast $3-$5, lunch and dinner $5-$12, daily specials. Daily 7am-8pm.

90 Main Street Deli, 90 Main St, 693-0041. Gourmet sandwiches $4.75-$11.50, specials $6, salads and subs. Daily 6.30am-6pm.

Information/Travel Visitor Center, at Ferry terminal in Vineyard Haven, 693-0085. Accommodation lists, maps and employment information available. _www.mvy.com_. See under **Hyannis** for travel information.

NEW BEDFORD / FALL RIVER   On Rte 6 on the way from the Cape to Providence, RI, **New Bedford** was once the whaling capital of the world. It has recently been transformed from a dismal, rundown place to a cross between Mystic Seaport and Nantucket. There is a fascinating **whaling museum**, well worth visiting and known for its exceptional collections of scrimshaw, 18 Johnny Cake Hill, 997-0046, daily 9am-5pm, 'til 9pm Thursdays in Summer, free from 5pm-9pm; $10, $9 w/student ID. _www.whalingmuseum.org._ Scrimshaw, perfected by New England sailors in the 19th century, involves carving and etching the surface of the teeth or jawbone of the whale. Further west is the port town of **Fall River**, where the _Battleship Massachusetts_, 678-1100, veteran of WWII Pacific battles, is moored. Daily 9am-5pm, $10.

The telephone area code for New Bedford/Fall River is 508.

THE BERKSHIRE HILLS   Only about two and a half hours from NYC and Boston, Berkshire County is an ideal escape from the hustle of the city. The Green Mountains of Vermont in the north slope down to become the Berkshire Hills, a sub-range of the Appalachians that sneaks south to leafy Connecticut along the western border of Massachusetts.

A great area to venture off the beaten track, explore picturesque villages such as **Lenox** and **Stockbridge**, or hike in idyllic countryside on the trails around Mt Greylock (at 3491 feet the highest peak in the state) or the 80 miles of the Appalachian Trail that winds through Massachusetts. Drive along The Mohawk Trail and feast your eyes on panoramic views of this green and pleasant land.

Finish up in **Williamstown** (famous for its college), or make your stop in **Pittsfield**, the county seat of the Berkshires, and from here canoe the Housatonic, investigate the many theatrical and musical events on offer around Lenox, Lee and Stockbridge or simply soak up the local history. The free _Berkshire Eagle_ will keep you abreast of current happenings. _www.berkshires.org._

The telephone area code for the area is 413.

Accommodation
Berkshire Hills Motel, 1146 Cold Spring Rd, Rt 7, Williamstown, 458-3950/(800) 388-9677. Rooms from $89-$119-weekdays, $129-$159-weekends (June-Oct), bfast incl. Check in after 2pm. _www.berkshirehillsmotel.com._

Days Inn, 194 Pittsfield Lenox Rd, Massachusetts Turnpike, exit 2, on Rtes 7 & 20, 637-3560. Rooms ave $85. Bfast included, outdoor pool. Rsvs recommended. _www.daysinn.com._

Of Interest

Pittsfield was the birthplace of writer Herman Melville of *Moby Dick* fame. The **Atheneum** has a room devoted to his effects, and you can visit his house, **Arrowhead**, at the edge of Pittsfield on Holmes Road 442-1793. Daily 9.30am-5pm, last tour at 4pm; $10, $5 w/student ID. *www.mobydick.org.*

Hancock Shaker Village (5 miles West of Pittsfield), 443-0188. Earning their name from an early nickname 'Shaking Quakers', the Shakers originated in the late 18th century in Manchester, England and flourished for two centuries. Perhaps due to an avowal of celibacy, only one Shaker community remains, in Sabbathday Lake, Maine. Known for their simple yet exquisite architecture, furniture and handicrafts, the Hancock Shaker Village, founded in 1790, displays many fine examples of their craftsmanship. Alas the Shakers abandoned their village to the tourists in 1960. Daily in summer 9.30am-5pm, $15. 'Worth a visit.' *www.hancockshakervillage.org.*

The Mount, Plunkett St, Lenox, 637-1899. Designed and built in 1901 by the writer Edith Wharton, author of *Ethan Frome*, *The Age of Innocence* and *The Buccaneers*. Wharton's opulent mansion was a source of inspiration for her writings. In 2005 was being extensively restored. Summer: Daily 9am-5pm, $18, $9 w/student ID. *www.edithwharton.org.*

Norman Rockwell Museum, Rte 183, Stockbridge, 298-4100. The museum houses a vast collection of original works and the studio of America's favourite illustrator. Summer: daily 10am-5pm, Thu 'til 7pm $12.50, incl audio tour. *www.nrm.org.*

The **Tanglewood Music Festival** held in Lenox late June-Labor Day, is the summer home to the Boston Symphony Orchestra. Sit out on the lawns with a blanket and picnic. Tkts from $14-$20, for info call 637-1600. All kinds of music are performed, and many other fringe activities are available in the area. *www.bso.org.*

Jacob's Pillow Dance Festival, 243-0745, with ballet, jazz and contemporary dance, held at the Ted Shawn Theater off US 20 east of Lee, late June-August. North of Lee is the October State Forest, with the Appalachian Trail running through it. *www.jacobspillow.org.*

Information

Berkshire Visitors Bureau, 2 Berkshire Common, Pittsfield, 443-9186/(800) 237-5747. *www.berkshires.org*.

Mount Greylock Visitors Information Centre, Rockwell Rd, Lanesborough, 499-4262, have free maps of the trails.

Pittsfield Information Booth, S Street, 395-0105.

Travel

Amtrak's *Lake Shore Limited*, Boston-Chicago, stops here: Depot St between North & Center. Call (800) 872-7245. Boston-Pittsfield $15, 4 hrs, rsvs rec.

Berkshires Regional Transit Authority, 499-2782, covers the Berkshires from Great Barrington to Williamstown. Fares 75¢. *www.berkshireplanning.org*.

Bike Rentals, from Arcadian Shop, 637-3010, Pittsfield Rd, Lenox. 4 hrs $25, 8 hrs $35. *www.arcadina.com.*

NEW HAMPSHIRE - The Granite State

Many people consider the Granite State the most scenic state east of the Mississippi. The only state named after an English county, New Hampshire has a short but sandy Atlantic coastline, hundreds of lakes (the biggest is 72-square-mile **Lake Winnipesaukee**, the best known is nearby **Squam Lake** aka *Golden Pond*), the impressive White Mountain range, more than 60 covered wooden bridges and a 90 percent tree cover. The countryside, warm and green in the summer, seems to catch fire when the leaves change colour in the Fall Foliage Show. The long, cold, snowy winters make the state a popular and fashionable skiing centre.

Notice the granite walls everywhere. Built by the early settlers to enclose their fields, the walls remain even though most of the fields are forest again.

New Hampshire was the first state to declare its independence and also the first to adopt its own constitution. Nowadays it is regarded as a political barometer, the results of its early primary elections strongly influencing the country's choice of candidates in the presidential elections.

The state has attracted many artists and writers. South of Lebanon, in the artists' colony of **Cornish**, Maxfield Parrish lived, painted, and shared 55 years of his life with model Sue Lewin. He died there in 1966 at the age of 95. In the 1920s, the distinctive Parrish paintings adorned one out of every 4 American homes; his art can be seen at the **Cornish Colony Gallery** (Rte 12-A, 675 6000). The studios of one of America's significant sculptors, Augustus Saint-Gaudens can be seen at nearby **Saint-Gaudens National Historic Site** (Rt 3, 675 2175).

Cornish is also home to the reclusive writer J.D. Salinger, who does not like to be disturbed; and it was once the summer home of President Woodrow Wilson. The longest 2-span covered bridge in the US is the **Cornish-Windsor Bridge**, built in 1866. New Hampshire-born Dan Brown, the author of the *Da Vinci Code*, once taught English at the **Phillips Exeter Academy** and now lives in the Exeter area in the south-east of the State.

Poet Robert Frost also spent much of his life in New Hampshire. He wrote his first published poem, *The Butterfly*, there in the few months he was a freshman at **Dartmouth** in 1892, began poetry in earnest at his farm in **Derry** in the south of the state during 1901-1909, years he considered "the core of my writing" (**Robert Frost Farm Historic Site**, Rte 28, 432 3091), and spent another five years (1915-1920) near **Franconia** in the north of the state at **The Frost Place** (Ridge Road, 823 5510). His poem *New Hampshire* (1923, written in Vermont) declares: "She's one of the two best states in the Union. Vermont's the other…"

The inhabitants are mostly genuine, laconic Yankees, and the state motto 'Live Free or Die' reflects the tough Yankee spirit behind the Revolutionary War. New Hampshire's passion for freedom extends to shopping—the state has no sales tax, so you may want to check out the outlets while you're here.

Bus travel in the state is mainly by **Concord Trailways** *www.concordtrailways.com* which, with Vermont Transit, also serves Boston's Logan Airport. New Hampshire is served by two airports: Lebanon, near Hanover/Dartmouth (298-8878), and Manchester (624-6539). Check *www.visitnh.gov* before you visit.

The telephone area code for New Hampshire is 603.

PORTSMOUTH Its situation at the mouth of the Piscataqua River has always made Portsmouth a significant port and it was the state capital until 1808. The only seaport on the state's modest 18-mile coastline, the city has numerous old and well-preserved colonial homes. Nearby are several fine, sandy beaches, including those at Wallis Sands and Rye Harbor. *www.portcity.org.*

Accommodation/Food

Accommodation in town is invariably expensive, a better bet would be to try areas off US-1 instead. Also, try _www.sml.cornell.edu/shtml/s-hotels.htm_   for accommodation listings and _www.dininginnh.com_   for local eateries.

Comfort Inn at Yoken's, 1190 Lafayette Rd, on US-1, 433-3338/(800) 552-8484. Rooms average $110 in Summer, bfast incl, pool and exercise facs. _www.comfortinn.com_.

Pine Haven Motel, 183 Lafayette Rd, about 6 miles south of town on US-1, 964-8187. Prices: $39-109.

Portsmouth Brewery, 56 Market St, 431-1115. New Hampshire's original brewpub, lagers and ales brewed on the premises. Pizza and sandwiches $7-$10, dinner from $13. Rsvs required for brewery tours. Daily 11:30am-12:30am. _www.portsmouthbrewery.com_. A newer, craft brewery, named after a nearby island, is **Smuttynose Brewing**, 225 Heritage Ave 436 4026 _www.smuttynose.com_.

Muddy River Smokehouse, 21 Congress St, 430-9582. Serves BBQ and seafood. Lunch from $7, dinner from $11. Martini bar with over 20 different. Mon-Fri 11am-9.30pm, Sat-Sun 'til 10:30pm. _www.muddyriver.com_.

Of Interest

Isles of Shoals, just off-shore, and the supposed haunt of Blackbeard the Pirate. The **Isles of Shoals Steamship Company,** (800) 441-4620, offers a range of cruises and harbor tours, $24/32, _www.islesofshoals.com_.

John Paul Jones House, Middle & State Sts, 436-8420. Built 1758, house of the US Naval hero. Jones obtained the surrender of a British warship in 1779, as his own ship was sinking. Later, he became a Russian contra-admiral and died in Paris during the French Revolution. June to mid-Oct Mon-Sat 10am-4pm, Sun noon-4pm, $5. _www.seacoastnh.com/touring/jpjhouse.html._

Old Harbor Area, Bow & Ceres Sts, once the focus of the thriving seaport, is now an area of craft shops and eateries.

Strawbery Banke Museum, just off exit 7 of I-95 on the waterfront, 433-1100. From this settlement, starting in 1623, grew the town of Portsmouth. Tour historic homes and period gardens dating from 1695. Craft demonstrations and exhibits. May-Oct Mon-Sat 10am-5pm, Sun noon-5pm, $15. Nov-Apr reduced hours, $10. Walking tours are available in the winter months, visit _www.strawberybanke.org_ for details.

Water Country, off Exit 5 of I-95 on Rt. 1, 3 miles south of the traffic circle, 427-1111. New England's largest water park. $30, $20 after 3pm. Mid-June to Sept daily 10am-6pm, _www.watercountry.com_.

Information

Portsmouth Chamber of Commerce, 500 Market St, 436-3988.

CONCORD Situated on the banks of the Merrimack River, New Hampshire's financial and political centre is reputedly home to the fourth largest deliberative body in the world.

While much of the region's character is shaped by the state's three largest cities—Concord, Nashua and Manchester—the Merrimack Valley is surprisingly rural. If you're about to tour the state, this is a reasonably central place to start. Located on the main highway from Boston, it has long been the main thoroughfare to the lakes of central New Hampshire, the alpine-like White Mountains and further north still to Quebec, Canada.

Accommodation

Brick Tower Motor Inn, 414 S Main St, I-93 Exit 12S, 224-9565. $70-90, bfast incl. Large rooms, TV. Pool.

Camping: Sandy Beach Campground, 677 Clement Hill Rd, Contoocook, 746-

3591. Open May-Oct. Sites w/hook-up $35, rvs $40, free hot showers and electricity. Lake swimming. _www.sandybeach.org_.

Food
Durgin Lane Deli, 88 Washington St, 228-2000. American food. Sandwiches from $6. Mon-Fri 7am-5pm, Sat 'til 2pm. _www.durginlane.com_.

Capitol Grille Restaurant & Lounge, 1 Eagle Square, 228-6608. Standard American fare, Italian and seafood. Lunch $5-$8, dinner $8-$20, Sunday brunch $4-$7. Tue-Sat 11am-1am, Sun 10am-1am. _www.capitol-grille.com_.

Margarita's, 1 Bicentennial Sq, 224-2821. Eat Mexican food and massive Margaritas, behind bars at this atmospheric watering hole in the old police station. Food $8-$14. Mon-Thu 4pm-10pm, Fri-Sun 4pm-11pm for food, bar open 'til 1am. _www.margs.com_.

Of Interest
America's Stonehenge, 1-93, Exit 3, route 111, Mystery Hill, N Salem, 893-8300. July-Aug daily 9am-5pm. Sept-June reduced hrs. One of the largest and possibly the oldest stone-constructed sites in the country. $9, _www.stonehengeusa.com_.

Christa McAuliffe Planetarium, I-93 exit 15E, then exit 1 off of I-393, 271-STAR. 'Take an expedition through space,' land on Mars or explore the constellations in the night sky. Shows (last 1 hr) Mon-Sat 10am-5pm, Sun noon-5pm $8, $5 w/student ID, advance tkts recommended. _www.starhop.com._

Concord On Foot, a self-guided, downtown walking tour of over 50 historic sights including the State House, where the Hall of Flags is worth seeing. Call 224-2508 for details. Brochures, $2, are available from Chamber of Commerce.

Franklin Pierce Homestead, meeting of Rtes 9 and 31, Hillsborough, 478-3165. Restored home of President Franklin Pierce. July-Aug: Mon-Sat 10am-4pm, Sun 1pm-4pm, $3. June, Sept wkds only. _www.franklinpierce.ws/homestead._

Robert Frost Homestead, Rte 28, Derry (south on I-93 from Concord), 432-3091. Home of poet Robert Frost from 1901-1909. June-Sept Mon-Sat 10am-5pm, Sun noon-5pm, $2.50.

Information/Travel
New Hampshire Division of Travel and Tourism Development, 172 Pembroke Rd, 271-2665. _www.visitnh.gov_

Greater Concord Chamber of Commerce, 40 Commercial St, 224-2508. _www.concordnhchamber.com._

Concord Trailways, 228-3300. From Boston $13.50, 1 hr. _www.concordtrailways.com._

Internet Access
Concord Public Library, 45 Green St, 225-8670. Free Internet access, limit 30 mins. _www.onconcord.com/library_

THE WHITE MOUNTAINS   A popular destination year-round with hikers in summer and skiers in winter, the range is dominated by **Mount Washington**—at 6,288 ft the highest peak in the Northeast—where wind velocity has been recorded at 231 mph, the highest ever observed by man (in 1934)! Climbing the mountain is quite a feat, but it can be done in summer and the view is well worth the effort. Cairns mark paths, including the Appalachian trail. Be warned: the weather can be nasty, even in July and August; take warm clothing and seek local advice before setting off on a serious expedition.

Most visitors ride the amazing **Mt. Washington Cog Railway**, the world's first mountain cog railway (began operations 1869, four years before the first one in Switzerland): At the top, which is often above the clouds, six states and Canada are visible on a clear day. 278-5404/(800) 922-8825. Steam-powered locos chug carriages up an average 25 percent grade (steepest 37.4 percent) that defies gravity in the 3 hr round trip. Cost $49; discount available on 9am & 4pm trains. "Well worth it." _www.cograilway.com_ The auto (toll) road to the summit is $18 per car plus $7 pp. $24 pp for a tour, call 466-3988 for info.

Loon Mountain, 745-8111/(800) 229-LOON provides summer and winter activities, with scenic chair-lifts, an outdoor climbing wall, mountain bike trails, rollerblading, skateboarding and horse riding, _www.loonmtn.com_. **Ski Bretton Woods**, 278-5000, offers similar attractions. North Conway is the best area for equipment rentals. Bikes are available from **Loon Mountain Bike Center**, 745-8111, on Kancamagus Hwy, Lincoln; and **Joe Jones**, 356-9411, 2709 White Mtn Hwy, N Conway. While in N Conway take a ride on the **Conway Scenic Railroad**, 356-5251/(800) 232-5251. The ride to Crawford Notch carries you past some of the finest scenery on the east coast, 5 hrs, $38 r/t, rsvs strongly recommended, especially in fall. There are also shorter rides available 'over the river and through the woods,' 1 hr-1 hr 40 mins, $11.50-$18.50.

At the base of Mt Washington, along Rte 302, is the resort of **Bretton Woods** and the vast **Mt Washington Hotel**, an early railway destination and site of the 1944 conference that laid the groundwork for a post-war financial structure that created the World Bank and International Monetary Fund. Now it's a cosy ski resort, _www.brettonwoods.com_. About 20 miles north of Bretton Woods on Rte 2 is **Christie's Maple Farm**, (800) 788-2118, where you can visit the Maple Heritage Museum and an authentic working sugarhouse with the White Mountains and Presidential Mountains as a backdrop, May-Oct: daily 9am-5pm, by appointment at other times, free. _www.ChristiesMapleFarm.com._

Visit **Franconia Notch** and its 700-ft flume chasm with the **Old Man of the Mountain**, a natural stone profile rising at the north-west end. **Cannon Mountain** can be conquered by an aerial tramway. The **New England Ski Museum** is on Rte 3 in Franconia Notch State Park, 823-7177/ (800) 639-4181, _www.nesm.org_. Ancient skiing artifacts from New England and elsewhere. Daily noon-5pm, free. **The Frost Place**, Ridge Rd, Franconia off exit 38 of I-93, 823-5510, Robert Frost's farm is now a centre for poetry and the arts with a museum, nature-poetry trail, and resident poet; summer from 1pm-5pm (exc Tue), $4. _www.frostplace.org._

Cranmore and **Wildcat Mountains** to the south-east of Mt Washington are more sheltered than most, and have the best skiing facilities in the White Mountains.

If you head further north, be sure to catch the **Moose Festival** in the towns of Colebrook and Pittsburg. The annual August event includes street fairs, live music, hot-air balloon rides, and of course, moose calling contests and moose sighting tours. Call the North Country Chamber of Commerce, 237-8939, for more info, Tue & Fri 9am-noon, Thu & Sat 9am-11am, or visit _www.northcountrychamber.org_.

Accommodation

Hikers might consider staying at one or several of the **Appalachian Mountain Club's (AMC) 8 huts**, spaced a day's hike apart; from $77 pp AMC-members, $85 pp non-AMC, meals provided. Rsvs and deposit required. Call 466-2727 or write for brochure and to make rsvs at AMC Pinkham Notch Camp, P.O Box 298, Gorham, NH 03581. 'Clean, friendly and helpful. Hearty meals.' Visit _www.amc-nh.org_ or _www.outdoors.org_.

Highland Center at Crawford Notch, Rte 302, 466-2727, run by AMC. Shared room $57-69 members, $68-87 non-members. _www.outdoors.org/lodging/highland_.

Hikers Paradise at the Colonial Comfort Inn, 370 Main St, Gorham, (800) 470-4224. Co-ed dorm, $17 pp, kitchen area. Private rooms at the inn vary, ave $85. _www.hikersparadise.com._

HI-Conway, 36 Washington St, Conway 447-1001. Dorms $18-$21. Private rooms, $48 AYH, $51 non-AYH. Bfast and linens incl, BBQs. Kitchen and common area. Bikes available for guests. _www.conwayhostel.com._

Camping: campers may pitch their tents, for free (vehicles require a parking pass, $3 day, $5 week), anywhere below the tree line in the White Mountains National Forest, but there are strict rules for your safety and you are advised to read the Backcountry Camping Rules, call the **US Forest Service**, 528-8721 or visit _www.fs.fed.us/r9/white_.

Information

White Mountains Attractions Center, exit 32 off I-93 in N Woodstock, 745-8720/(800) FIND-MTS, can provide maps and accommodation brochures. _www.whitemtn.org_.

White Mountain National Forest Information, 466-2713. Crawford Notch State Park, 374-2272. Trail & weather info 24 hrs, 466-2725. Franconia Notch State Park, 823-5563. _www.fs.fed.us/r9/white_

LAKE WINNIPESAUKEE is New Hampshire's largest body of water. Set against a backdrop of tree-covered hills and the White Mountains to the North, it is a popular summer spot with a festival stage. Come here for sunning, swimming and sailing. **Center Harbor**, **Laconia**, **Wolfeboro** and **Meredith** are the main centres for accommodation and sightseeing. There are several campgrounds around the lake. _www.winnipesaukee.com_   North of the lake is Squam Lake, where _On Golden Pond_ was shot.

Winnipesaukee Scenic Railroad, 279-5253, operates 1 hour ($10) and 2 hour ($11) scenic trips along the lake shore between Meredith and Weirs Beach, daily in summer, _www.hoborr.com/winni.html_. **Cruise Lake Winnipesaukee**, 366-5531/(888) THE-MOUNT, offers scenic tours of the lake leaving from Weirs Beach, May-Oct 2½ hours, $20. _www.cruisenh.com_.

About 50 miles east of Laconia lies the small town of **Enfield**, where you can stay at **The Enfield Shaker Inn**, 632-4900/(866) 918-4900, centrepiece of the **Enfield Shaker Village**. Double rooms start from $105, bfast incl. _www.theshakerinn.com_.   There are no more Shakers in New Hampshire, but the village operates as a museum of Shaker history, 632-4346, June-Oct, Mon-Sat 10am-5pm, Sun from noon. $7, $3 w/student ID. _www.shakermuseum.org_.

RHODE ISLAND - The Ocean State

'Little Rhody' is the smallest state in the nation. With 400 miles of shoreline, it is dominated by the sea and Narragansett Bay, which cuts the state almost in half.

Founded by Roger Williams, who dissented from Massachusetts' Puritan theocracy, Rhode Island developed successfully by smuggling, slaving and whaling and for a while hesitated to sacrifice its post-Revolutionary War independence by joining the United States. Little Rhode Island is home to two of America's biggest music events—the **Newport Jazz and Folk Festivals**. _www.visitrhodeisland.com._

The area code for the entire state is 401.

PROVIDENCE   Founded by Roger Williams in 1636 and named for the act of God that he believed led him there. Rhode Island's state capital and New England's second largest city, Providence is enjoying a renaissance as a modern industrial city and port. A college town and home to the prestigious **Brown University**, Providence is fiercely proud of its success, its traditions and its historic past. Elegant Colonial homes and early nineteenth century commercial buildings survive on Benefit St, the 'mile of history'. Many of these are open to the public during the **Festival of Historic Houses** in May. _www.providencecvb.com._

Accommodation
Very expensive within Providence, try towns a little further away.
Super 8 North Attleboro/Providence, 787 S Washington, North Attleboro, MA, (508) 643-2900/(800) 800-8000. From $70, 20 mins away from Providence. _www.super8northattleboro.com_.
Warwick Hostel, 75 Shenandoah Road, Warwick, (401) 884-1311. 15 mins from Providence, public transport is good. Private rooms, $19/person, $2 linens. This is the only hostel in the Providence area and is a private home. Not affiliated with Hostelling International.

Food
Best Italian food can be found on Federal Hill, just 5 mins from downtown by trolley.
Meeting St Cafe, 220 Meeting St, on College Hill, 273-1066. Pastries, soups, salads, sandwiches, hormone-free burgers and steaks. Popular with students. Daily 7am-11pm.
Murphy's Bar and Deli, 55 Union St (behind the Biltmore), 621-8467. 'Mountain High' sandwiches (from $4) are as big as Rhode Island. Daily 11am-1am, Fri-Sat 11am-2am.
South Street Café and Bar, 54 South St, 454-5360, sandwiches $3.50-$7.50. Mon-Fri lunch 11am-4pm, bar 'til 1am, Fri 'til 2am, Sat noon-2am, Sun noon-1am.
Wes's Ribs, 38 Dike St, Olneyville Sq, 421-9090, dinner $7-$17.50. Sun-Thu 11.30am-2am, Fri-Sat 11.30am-4am. _www.wesribhouse.com._

Of Interest
Brown University, College Hill, 863-1000. A member of the Ivy League, here since 1764. Interesting libraries and exhibitions, visit the Annmary Brown Memorial with pre-16th century books and Renaissance through 20th century paintings. _www.brown.edu_. For tours, stop by the **Admissions Welcome Center**, 45 Prospect St, 863-2378, Mon-Fri 8.30am-4pm. Times and schedules vary; call or check the website.
Rhode Island School of Design (RISD), 224 Benefit St, contains a first-rate museum, 454-6500. 19th century French, including works by Monet, Renoir and Cezanne, and also modern Latin American painters, 18th century porcelains and oriental textiles, Egyptian collection and classical art; also the **Pendleton House**, faithfully furnished replica of an early Providence house, contains collections of

eighteenth and early nineteenth century decorative arts. Museum hrs: Tue-Sun 10am-5pm, third Thu of every month 'til 9pm, $8, $3 w/student ID. _www.risd.edu._
Roger Williams National Memorial, 282 N Main St, 521-7266, a 4.5 acre landscaped, urban park commemorating the state's founder. Open daily, 9am-4.30pm, free. _www.nps.gov/rowi_. Also, the **State House** is worth a visit, if only to see its amazing dome which is the fourth largest unsupported dome in the world (St. Peter's in Rome has the largest, with the Taj Mahal in third place). Inside is the 1663 charter granted by Charles II and a full-length Gilbert Stuart portrait of George Washington. Mon-Fri 9am-3pm, free. _www.state.ri.us._
Rhode Island Historical Society, 438-0463/331-8575, offers a range of guided walking tours, July-Oct daily, $12. _The Providence River Walk_ is a combination of boat ride and walking tour, beginning at the Visitors Information Center, 1 Sabin St, $14. Visit _www.rihs.org_ for more details.

Entertainment
The daily, 50¢ _Providence Journal_ has complete entertainment listings. Providence's nightlife is generally student-generated, though Thayer Street is always bustling and in summer the influx of tourists ensures a lively atmosphere.
Lupo's Heartbreak Hotel, 79 Washington St, 272-5876. White Stripes, The Dave Matthews Band, Counting Crows and Joan Baez have all performed here. Dance party every Thu night. Tkts range from $10-$45. _www.lupos.com._
The Met Cafe, 130 Union St, 861-2142, The original home of the blues in Providence, established in 1969. Up-and-coming modern bands, national touring acts, and blues legends all perform here. Cover ranges from $6-$15.
Providence Performing Arts Center, 220 Weybossett Street, 421-2997, an architectural jewel in the heart of the city. Broadway shows and popular musical entertainment. _www.ppacri.org._
The Cable Car Cinema, 204 S Main St, 272-3970, $8, Mon-Wed $6 w/student ID, and the **Avon Cinema**, 260 Thayer St, 421-3315, show good independent and art films, $9, matinees $6.50. _www.avoncinema.com._

Information/Travel
Providence Preservation Society, 21 Meeting St, 831-7440. 1772 publishing house. Plenty of info on historical Providence. Mon-Fri 8.30am-5pm. _www.ppsri.org._
Providence/Warwick Visitor Center, in the Convention Center Rotunda, 1 Sabin St, 751-1177/(800) 233-1636. 'Very helpful.' _www.goprovidence.com._
Amtrak, 100 Gaspee St, 727-7379/(800) 872-7245, Boston $14 o/w. _www.amtrak.com_.
Bonanza Bus Lines, 1 Bonanza Way (off I-95), 751-8800/(888) 751-8800. Services to Boston, New York and Logan Airport. Call or check the website for prices and schedules. _www.bonanzabus.com._
Greyhound, 1 Kennedy Plaza, 454-0790/(800) 231-2222. Boston $15, 1 hr. _www.greyhound.com_.
Rhode Island Public Transit Authority (RIPTA), 265 Melrose St, 781-9400. Fares throughout Rhode Island from $1.50. Fares for the _Providence Link_, a trolley service, $1.50. _www.ripta.com._
Internet Access: Providence Public Library, 225 Washington St, 455-8000. Free internet access, 2 hr limit. Rsvs required. Mon & Thu Noon-8pm, Tue & Wed 10am-6pm, Fri-Sat 9am-5.30pm. _www.provlib.org._

PAWTUCKET If you're in the mood for a side trip of historic and contemporary dimensions, make the short (5-10 minute) drive up I-95 to Pawtucket. **Slater Mill Historic Site**, Roosevelt Ave, 725-8638, features an 8-ton water wheel operating a 19th-century machine shop as well as exhibits of local history and fibre artists. Tours given daily 10.30am, 1pm and 3pm, $7. _www.slatermill.org._

Travelling east across town on Armistice Blvd takes you to **Slater Memorial Park**, 728-0500, ext.252, a fine place for a picnic and a tour through **Daggett House**, the Colonel's home built in 1645, which has an impressive collection of 17th and 18th century memorabilia. Open summer-December w/ends only, 2pm-5pm, $2. The park has no less than 9 baseball fields, tennis courts and a merry-go-round. Daily 8am-9pm. Wind down your day as the pitchers wind up at **McCoy Stadium**. Eat hot dogs, drink beer and watch the **AAA Pawtucket Red Sox** play their hearts out to make the major leagues. 724-7300 or _www.pawsox.com_ for ticket and schedule information.

NEWPORT   Thirty miles from Providence on Narragansett Bay, Newport is a lively summer resort and home to such enchanting events as the **Newport Bermuda Race**—a tall ships regatta—and the famous **Newport Folk and Jazz Festivals,** held in August. Check out _www.festivalproductions.net_ for details.

Although a rival of Boston and New York in Colonial times, Newport really came into its own only around the turn of the century when the town became the place for millionaires to build their summer 'cottages'. Many of these ridiculously ornate relics of the Gilded Age are now open to the public. Find them close to Newport's fabulous beach and on **Bellevue Avenue.**

The new **Americas Cup Avenue** has changed the feel of the waterfront. Somewhat sanitised bars and boutiques have appeared, but the twinkling lights of the harbour still make for a beautiful setting to sit and watch the world go by on summer evenings. _www.visitnewport.com._

Accommodation
Hotels here are above average in price and fill up quickly, especially in summer, so make plans for Newport as early as possible.
Gateway Visitor Center, 23 Americas Cup Ave, 849-8048/(800) 976-5122. Have some helpful accommodation listings. Daily 9am-5pm.
Bed and Breakfast Newport, 7 Park St, (800) 800-8765. Accommodations in B & Bs throughout the area, starting from $95, lower rates in winter. _www.bbnewport.com_
Burbank Rose, 111 Memorial Blvd W, 849-9457/(888) 297-5800. Downtown location, private baths, b/fast, summer D-$99-$199, Nov-May $59-$109. _www.burbankrose.com_
Seamen's Church Institute, 18 Market Square, 847-4260. Ave. $125/week. First come, first served with preference to seafaring folk, but 'if you're here and there's a vacancy, we'll take you.' Limited female accommodation. People start arriving in May for the summer.

Food
Anthony's Seafood, 963 Aquidneck Ave, Middletown, 848-5058. Casual, family dining. Inexpensive chicken and seafood, beer and wine. Lunch from $5, dinner from $10. Summer: Mon-Thu 11am-8pm, Fri-Sat 'til 8.30pm, Sun noon-7pm.
Dry Dock Seafood, 448 Thames St, 847-3974. Bring-your-own-booze. Inexpensive fish n' chips $7, lobster dinner $14. Daily 11am-10pm.

Of Interest
Beaches: Easton's Beach, Memorial Blvd, 846-1398. Includes amusements and a $1 carousel. Parking Mon-Fri $8, w/ends $10. **Fort Adams State Park**, Ocean Drive,

847-2400. Site of a 19th century fort, includes beach and fishing areas, along with soccer and rugby fields. Tours of the fort available, May-Oct daily, 10am-4pm, 841-0707. _www.riparks.com/fortadams.htm._ **Beavertail State Park**, Jamestown on Rte 138, 884-2010. Beach, hiking trails, picnicking and fishing, free. _www.riparks.com/beaverta.htm._

Belcourt Castle, Bellevue Ave, 849-1566, has a staggering collection of antiques and treasures from all over the world. Daily 10am-5pm. Guided tours $10, $7 w/student ID, ghost tours $15, Thu 5pm only but check in advance. Rsvs recommended. _www.belcourtcastle.com._

Cliffwalk, designated a National Recreation Trail, meanders for 3.5 miles along the Atlantic Ocean and offers views of the sea and several mansions. Maps available in the Gateway Visitors Center. A guided tour, $14 is available; call 847-0857. The Newport Historical Society also offers a guided walking tour of the Historic Hill area, May-Sept, Thurs-Sat 10am, $12. Call 846-0813 or visit _www.newporthistorical.com_ for more details.

Cruising by ship or sailboat around Narragansett Bay is a pleasant introduction. _Spirit of Newport,_ departing Bowens Ferry Landing, 2 Bowens Wharf, 849-3575, offers 1 hr narrated cruises of the Bay, $12, _www.bowenswharf.com;_ **Newport Sailing School & Cruises Ltd**, departing Goat Island, 848-2266, offer 1 hr ($22) & 2 hr ($40) cruises aboard 230' sloops. Pure sailing, no motors! Rsvs only. _www.newportsailing.com._ Viking Boat Cruises, depart Goat Island Marina, 847-6921, and offer 1 hr cruises, $12. _www.vikingtoursnewport.com._

The **Newport Preservation Society**, 424 Bellevue Ave, 847-1000, maintains 7 of Newport's mansions: The Breakers, Marble House, Rosecliff, Chateau-sur-Mer, Kingscote, Hunter House, and The Elms, plus Green Animals, a topiary garden. **The Breakers**, Cornelius Vanderbilt's villa, is unquestionably the most opulent. Marble House is thought to have been inspired by the Petit Trianon at Versailles. Rosecliff is where _The Great Gatsby_ was filmed. The Breakers is $15; other houses are $10. Combo tkts available. Open daily in summer, 10am-5pm. _www.newportmansions.org._

Other privately owned mansions of interest: Mrs Astor's Beechwood, 589 Bellevue Ave, 846-3772, is the most enjoyable to visit. Actors play Mrs Astor's servants and family, leading you as her personal guest through the historical recreation of the 1891 Astor household. Daily 10am-5pm, $15. Special evening events: every Tues, July-Sept, the Astor Speakeasy, $30 and the Murder Mystery evening, every Thurs, June-October. Reservations necessary. _www.astors-beechwood.com._

Newport Folk Festival. The folk festival of the sixties. Was revived by Ben and Jerry of ice cream fame and now sponsored by Apple and Eve (of juice fame), it once again provides a forum for top talent. Annual event at Fort Adams State Park over the 1st weekend in August. _www.newportfolk.com_.

JVC Jazz Festival Newport. The oldest—and considered by many to be the finest—jazz festival in the world. Held outdoors in mid-August. 'Expensive but worth it', tkts approx. $50/day.

Call 847-3700 or visit _www.festivalproductions.net_ for details of both events.

Block Island, 12 miles south of the mainland, a peaceful summer resort with wonderful beaches, first settled in 1661; classified by the Nature Conservancy as one of the '12 great places in the Western hemisphere'. Has two interesting restored lighthouses, one featuring a 19th century newspaper story that tallied the value of ships wrecked around the island as greater than that of the island itself. Check out _www.blockislandinfo.com_ for more details.

Ideal for biking (plenty of rentals from $20 p/day), try **Boat Basin Rentals**, the New Harbor, 466-5811. Day trips recommended since food and lodging prices tend to gouge the unwary; although **Maple Leaf Cottage**, Beacon Hill Rd, 466-2056, a farmhouse in the remote interior of the island, is worth a try; Ave. $110, includes bfast. Rsvs essential in summer. Also, try **Block Island Reservations**, (800) 825-6254, for help in reserving accommodation; no fee but a deposit (refundable) is required. Office hours (summer): daily 8am-9pm, visit *www.blockislandhotel.com*.

Block Island Holidays Inc. offer hotel packages from $149. This includes r/t ferry, 1 dinner, 1 lunch, a walking tour and is based on double occupancy. Call (800) 905-0590 or check *www.blockislandholidays.com* for more details.

Try lobster rolls at **Smugglers Cove**; Eli's homemade dessert; **Pizza Place** for pizza; and clam chowder at **Harbor Grille**. The **Block Island Ferry**, 783-4613, provides trips to the island from, Newport ($9 o/w) and Point Judith (Galilee) ($9.45 o/w). *www.blockislandferry.com.*

Information/Travel

Both the *Newport Life www.newportlifemagazine.com* and the monthly *Pineapple Post* have details of what's on in and around Newport.

Newport Chamber of Commerce, 45 Valley Rd, in Middletown, 5 min drive from Newport, 847-1600. 'Very helpful'. *www.newportchamber.com.*

Bonanza Bus Lines, 23 Americas Cup Ave, 846-1820/(888) 751-8800. Boston $17, 1 hr 30 mins. Visit the Newport Gateway Visitors Center here, 849-8048. Daily 9am-5pm. *www.bonanzabus.com*.

Block Island Chamber of Commerce, Old Harbor, is helpful—466-2982/(800) 383-BIRI. Summer: daily 9am-5pm. *www.blockislandchamber.com*

Internet Access Newport Public Library, 300 Spring St, 847-8720. Free Internet use, 1 hr limit—expect to wait for a computer. *www.newportlibraryri.org.*

VERMONT - The Green Mountain State

Vermont has always been known for its fiercely independent people, from Colonial days when it asserted its own independence by forming a republic. The state remained that way for 14 years, operating its own post office and minting its own money. It was the first state to outlaw slavery, in 1777. Vermonters have retained their spirit and protective sentiment—their motto is 'Freedom and Unity'. They cherish the beauty of their Green Mountains, banning billboards and imposing the toughest anti-pollution laws in the US. Montpelier is the only state capital not to have a McDonalds. The **Long Trail** runs 270 miles along the highest ridges of the Green Mountains: contact the **Green Mountain Club,** Waterbury Center, (802) 244-7037, for advice and books on hiking in Vermont, *www.greenmountainclub.org*.

Vermont is famous for maple syrup, Cheddar cheese, its 106 covered bridges, and its magnificent autumn foliage and winter ski trails. The autumn colours are at their best toward the end of September; this is also the time for **foliage festivals** and community get-togethers. March is the season for **syrup festivals,** but there are a number of museums open year-round devoted entirely to the history and manufacture of this state institution. On New Year's Eve in many Vermont towns, as in the rest of the US, there is a **First Night** celebration - large, varied, and usually snowy, with free performances of all kinds. The **St Johnsbury** event is one of the best. There are also numerous festivals in the State throughout the year, such as the **Ryegate (est 1761) Heritage Days** south of St. Johnsbury in mid-August. For details contact *bwatts@mail.crt.state.vt.us*, (802) 439-5647.

The state has many small, progressive schools and has always attracted artists, craftsmen and writers. The painter Norman Rockwell lived in Arlington. Rudyard Kipling wrote *The Jungle Book* and *Captains Courageous* in **Dummerston** where he received so much mail that a special post office was authorized for him in the home of neighbour Anna Waite in 1895-1896, the only such personal post office in the US before or since (the Waite postmark is now a prized philatelic rarity). The Pulitzer-showered poet Robert Frost lived at the **Homer Noble Farm** near Middlebury from 1939 to 1963. And the prodigious and alcoholic Nobel Prize winner Sinclair Lewis wrote *Dodsworth* at **Twin Farms** near **Woodstock**; he also wrote *Prodigal Parents* there after a stormy session with Marxist student "pipsqueaks" at nearby **Dartmouth**.

Among Vermont's notable native sons—Hiram Bingham, the famous missionary to the Sandwich Islands (now known as Hawaii), whose namesake grandson discovered Machu Picchu; President Calvin Coolidge, the laconic "Silent Cal" who made the first Presidential radio address in 1923 (born and sworn in at **Plymouth Notch** near Woodstock, now a state historic site); John Deere from Middlebury, who designed the first cast steel plough able to break the tough soil of the Great Plains in the 1850s and later established the famous tractor-maker Deere and Co.; John Dewey, the father of progressive education; Joseph Smith, founder of the Mormon Church, and Brigham Young, the "American Moses" who led the "Exodus" of some 16,000 Mormons to the "Promised Land" of Utah, where he founded Salt Lake City.

www.vtguides.com , *www.vermont.org*, and *www.vermontvacation.com*.
The area code for the entire area is 802.

BURLINGTON   This small city of approximately 39,000—a metropolis by Vermont standards—is set on the eastern shore of **Lake Champlain**, the beautiful 120-mile-long lake (the seventh largest in the US) that divides the New York Adirondacks from the Green Mountains of Vermont. Home of the **University of Vermont** and **State Agricultural College** (the first agricultural college in the US) and several other colleges, the city is crawling with young people. It became the first city in the US to elect a socialist mayor in 1981, and the town's economy boomed as a result.

Burlington hosts a number of festivals each year, the craziest of which has to be the 'Fools-a-Float' challenge each September. Pick up local rag *Seven Days* free, for all local area events, films, festivals, restaurants etc. *www.sevendaysvt.com*. The town also has an extensive underground mall, especially nice during long, cold winters.

Use Burlington as a base for some of Vermont's most interesting sites such as **St Albans**, 29 miles north up I-89 where there was famous Confederate Raid from Canada on the town in 1864; **Rokeby Museum**, about 18 miles south on Rte 7, near charming **Ferrisburg** and **Vergennes**, a restored 18th century farmhouse that was a stop on Vermont's Underground Railroad; **Richmond**, south off I-89, with its old Round Church; and delightful **Bristol**, with coffee shops and bookstores, about 25 miles southeast on Rte 116, originally granted to Admiral Sir George Pocock, who commanded the British fleet that took Havana from the Spanish and later married a descendant of Sir Francis Drake. *www.ci.burlington.vt.us.*

Accommodation

Allenholm Orchards Bed and Breakfast, 150 South St, South Hero, 20 miles from Burlington on Rte 2, 372-5566/(888) 721-5566. Stay on a working apple orchard on an island in Lake Champlain. Eat apple pie for breakfast! $100-155, rsvs recommended. *www.allenholm.com.*

Midtown Motel, 230 Main St, 862-9686. D-$68-95, with private bathroom. 15 mins walk from downtown.   *www.themidtownmotel.com*.

Mrs. Farrell's Home Hostel, 865-3730. Call between 4pm and 6pm. Open April-Oct, 31st. $17 AYH, $20 non-AYH. Linen $1. 1 private room $40 AYH, $43 non-AYH. Bicycles available, $3. Check-in by 5pm. Call ahead for reservations.

Tetreault House, 251 Staniford Rd, 862-2781. Rooms $50-125, bfast incl. 3 miles from downtown, located on lakefront, nr bicycle path, direct to downtown.

Food

Ben & Jerry's, 36 Church St, 862-9620. 'Best ice cream in the world,' according to *Time* magazine. A Vermont original; destined to reach the far ends of the earth. $3 for a factory tour. *www.benjerry.com.*

Five Spice Cafe, 175 Church St, 864-4045. Award-winning Asian food. Sumptuous feasts include their famous siumai, Evil Jungle Prince with chicken. Mon 5pm-9.30pm, Tue-Thu 11.30am-9.30pm, Fri/Sat 11.30am-10pm. *www.fivespicecafe.com.*

Greenstreets, 30 Main St, 862-4930. Standard American fare, deli sandwiches and gourmet dishes; waterfront location. Lunch $5-$7.50, dinner $12-$20. Extensive wine list and small selection of bottled beers. Occasional live music. Daily 8am-8.30pm. *www.greenstreetsrestaurant.com*.

Sweetwaters, 120 Church St, 864-9800. Award winning menu, located in Church St Marketplace. Live music on weekends and outdoor seating make a great combo! Daily 11.30-2am, Sat 'til 1am, Sun 'til midnight. *www.sweetwatersbistro.com.*

Of Interest

Boat tours of Lake Champlain aboard *Spirit of Ethan Allen*, 862-8300. A 500 passenger cruise ship. April-Oct, four daily cruises around the lake, $12.99, sunset trips $16.99. *www.soea.com*.

Church Street Marketplace, 863-1648, downtown. One of the most successful pedestrian malls in the country, a vibrant thoroughfare often compared to Boston's Faneuil Hall area. In summer the marketplace is crawling with street performers, musicians, and the Great Rondini, an escape artist. *www.churchstmarketplace.com.*

Ethan Allen Homestead Trust, off Rte 127 N, 865-4556. Restored 1787 farmhouse home of Ethan Allen, Revolutionary War hero. 200-acre park with picnicking, fishing, canoeing. May-Oct Mon-Sat 10am-5pm, Sun 1pm-5pm, $5. The Ethan Allen Monument in Greenmount Cemetry, Colchester Ave, marks the flamboyant military leader's grave. *www.ethanallenhomestead.org.*

Magic Hat Brewing Co, 5 Bartlett Bay Rd, South Burlington, 658-BREW. Free tours and samples; Wed-Fri 3.30pm-5pm, Sat 1pm-2.30pm. Store open daily, summer: 10am-7pm, also w/self-guided tours and sampling. *www.MagicHat.net*.

Shelburne Museum, 7 miles south on Hwy 7, 985-3346. Outdoor museum of early New England life. 45 acres of Americana, folk-art and architecture. Daily in summer, 10am-5pm, $18, $13 w/student ID, pass valid for two days. 'Worthwhile if you have a whole day.' *www.shelburnemuseum.org.*

Water sports are common in and around Burlington, try: **Waterfront Boat Rentals,** Perkins Pier, 864-4858. Kayaks $10/hr, $30 half-day; canoes $15/hr, $40 half-day. For more options visit *www.vermont.org*.

Ben & Jerry's Free Outdoor Movies, Hospitality Dept., 1280 Waterbury Stowe Rd, 882-1240 Ext. 2300. 'Classic' movies shown on Tuesdays, July-Aug, at dusk in Marketsquare, Church St. See Montpelier section. *www.benjerry.com.*

Internet access: Fletcher Free Library, 235 College St, 863-3403. Free internet use, ½ hr limit. No rsvs. Mon-Fri 8.30am-6pm, Wed 'til 9pm, Sat 9am-5.30pm, Sun noon-6pm. *www.fletcherfree.org.*

Information/Travel
Chamber of Commerce and Visitor Center, 60 Main St, 863-3489/(877) 686-5253. *www.vermont.org.*

Amtrak, 29 Railroad Ave. Essex Junction 879 7298. Served by daily *Vermonter* from New York and St Albans. Fares, schedule *www.amtrak.com/trains/vermonter.html* or (800-872 7245). From the Amtrak station take the CCTA bus, 25 mins to downtown Burlington. $1.25. *www.cctaride.org.*

Vermont Transit Daily services to and from Montreal, St. Albans, Middlebury/Rutland, Montpelier/White River Junction, Boston. Fares (800) 552-8737; schedules *www.vermonttransit.com*.

Burlington International Airport, Airport Drive, 863-1899. CCTA buses, 3 miles to town. *www.vermontairports.com.*

ST JOHNSBURY
The cultural and commercial "capital" of Vermont's Northeast Kingdom (where traffic jams consist of cows crossing at milking time and moose outnumber people in some townships), St Johnsbury flourished in the early 1800s when Vermont was the New Zealand of its day with six (mainly merino) sheep for every inhabitant, and later as a Victorian-era manufacturing centre. Much of the town is built on the fortune of the Fairbanks family that manufactured the platform scale.

President Coolidge learned Latin and Greek at the Academy here, and perched on Main Street above the banks of the Passumpsic River are two of the most fascinating museums in the state, and one of its few art movie houses, the **Catamount Arts Center**, 139 Eastern Avenue, 748 2600. *www.catamountarts.com* The town dates to 1790 when it was named in honour of Hector St. Jean de Crèvecoeur, the French Consul of the day, a warm supporter of the newly-independent America.

Of Interest
Fairbanks Museum and Planetarium, 1302 Main Street. 748-2372. New England's largest, must-see museum of natural history, founded in 1889 by Franklin Fairbanks, nephew of Thaddeus, the inventor of the platform scale. Has 165,000 exhibits of mounted birds, spine-chilling snakes, endangered species such as the gavial and hutia, mummies, etc., plus Vermont's heritage as "sheep heaven", and nine unique and amazingly colourful "Bug art" pictures created in the 1870s by Cheshire-born John Hampson. The "pictures" consist entirely of insects, 6,000 to 13,000 each, depicting George Washington, Old Glory, etc. $5 for museum, $3 for planetarium. *www.fairbanksmuseum.org*.

St Johnsbury Athenaeum, 1171 Main Street, 748 8291. National historic landmark, with library with over 45,000 volumes and art gallery, built in 1871 by Horace Fairbanks, the oldest art gallery in the US maintained in its original condition. The 100 plus piece collection features Albert Bierstadt's 1867 floor-to-ceiling vista *Domes of the Yosemite*. The *NY Times* lamented that the painting was "doomed to the obscurity of a Vermont town where it will astonish the natives." Also many stunning Hudson River School pieces, including *Under the Elms* by Hart (1872), *Girl Reading* by Lambdin (1872), and *Sunset of the Needles* by De Haas (1870). Mon-Fri 10am-5.30pm (Mon & Wed till 8pm), Sat 9.30am-4pm. Free. *www.stjathenaeum.org*

Maple Grove Museum and Gift Shop, 1006 Portland St 748-5141 Open daily. See how maple syrup is made and taste samples at America's oldest and largest maple factory. Factory tours. Sugarhouse open daily 8am-5pm (4pm Jan-May). $1 *www.maplegrove.com*.

Food

Elements Food & Spirit, 98 Mill St.-Ste. 1 748-8400. Good food, serves Green MountainBlue cheese, local Trout River ale on tap, carrot ginger soup, trout cakes" Daily 11.30-9pm. _www.elementsfood.com_.

Information/Travel

Northeast Kingdom Chamber of Commerce, 357 Western Ave, #2-748 3678 or (800) 639-6379. Has comprehensive guide to area restaurants, places of interest, and B & Bs. _www.nekchamber.com._

Vermont Transit Daily, service to and from White River Junction and Newport. Fares: In state, (800) 642-8737; schedules: _www.vermonttransit.com_.

ELSEWHERE IN THE N.E. KINGDOM   Cabot Visitor's Center, Cabot Village west of St J, 563-2231 and (800) 837-4261. See how Vermont cheddar has been made since 1919. Visitors Center open daily June-Oct 9am-5pm, Nov-May 9am-4pm $2. _www.cabotcheese.com_. **Old Stone House Museum**, 28 Old Stone House Road, Brownington, 754-2022. N of St J, W off 1-91 at Orleans, where Alexander Lucius Twilight, the nation's first African-American college graduate (from Middlebury, 1823) and state legislator, built his school in 1836. Wed-Sun 11am-5pm daily in July, August. Fri-Tue rest of year. $5, students $2. **Lake Willoughby,** n of St J, has a public swimming beach in a dramatic mountain setting. **Trout River Brewing Co,** Route 5, Lyndonville, north of St J, 626-9396 Tasting room Wed-Sun 11 am-6pm. _www.troutriverbrewing.com_.

MIDDLEBURY   This small, beautiful New England town bordering on the Green Mountains has miles of hiking trails—including the Long Trail East on Rte 125 that connects south with the Appalachian Trail—with overnight shelters and various state parks for camping. One of Vermont's nicest state parks is not far from Middlebury, on beautiful **Lake Dunmore**. The town is built around a village green and **Otter Creek**, Vermont's longest river flowing right through the middle of Middlebury that once powered mills and is now home to **Otter Creek Brewing Company** (793 Exchange Street, (800) 473-0727 Mon-Sat 10am-6pm, free tours and samples, including Wolaver's Certified Organic. _www.ottercreekbrewing.com_.

Picturesque, stone-built **Middlebury College**, founded in 1800, is famous for its excellent 'total-immersion' summer school of foreign languages, and gives a lively flavour to the town. It was the first college to graduate an African-American, in 1823. Middlebury was home to the first institution of higher learning for women in the US. It was also a centre for Merino sheep in the days, over 150 years ago, when a breeding ram cost the same as a house - $5,000. For info on festivals and other events, consult the free weekly paper _Seven Days_. _www.sevendaysvt.com_.

Accommodation

Accommodation in Middlebury itself is expensive but usually elegant and friendly. Call ahead as most have limited availability.

Priscilla's Victorian Inn, 52 South St, Middletown Springs, 235-2299, S of Middlebury. Large Victorian house with English gardens. Downtown, 40 mins from ski areas. Ave $95, incls bfast.

The Blue Spruce Motel, 2428 Rt 7, S, 388-4091, (800) 640-7671. Spacious rooms with beautiful mountain view. Cable, fridge, microwave., full bath. $65-$150.

Camping: Branbury State Park on east side of Lake Dunmore, 10 miles south of Middlebury on Rte 53, 247-5925. Swimming, fishing, boating, bath house. May-Oct, sites $16. Day rates for activities are $2.50.

Lake Dunmore Kampersville, south of E Middlebury on Rte 53, 352-4501. Sites from $22-$38. Laundry, pools, arcade, children's play area, daily activities, internet access. _www.kampersville.com_.

Greystone Motel, Rte 7 S, 388-4935, Modern rooms with cable, fridge, breakfast included.Room, $70-95._www.midvermont.com/lodging/greystone_.

Food

Fire and Ice, 26 Seymour St, 388-7166. Friendly. Seafood, steak, great salad bar. Locals, students, and travellers. Sandwiches $7, dinner entrees from $7-$29. Mon-Thurs 5pm-8.30pm, Fri-Sat noon-8:30pm, Sun 1pm-8.30pm. _www.fireandicerestaurant.com_.

Tully Marie Restaurant, 5 Bakery Lane, 388-4182. Outdoor dining. Seafood specials, steaks, pasta. Lunch $7, dinner $12, burgers, etc. 'til late, Sunday brunch $6. _www.tullyandmaries.com_.

Green Peppers, Shaw's Shopping Plaza, 388-3164. Pizza, pasta, subs, salads and calzones. 10:30am-10pm. $6-$20. _www.greenpeppersrestaurant.com_.

In nearby Vergennes, Vermont's oldest (1788) and smallest "city": **Eat Good Food**, Main St, "Good tapanade, fantastic chocolate mousse cake!" "Best value around."

Of Interest

Henry Sheldon Museum, 1 Park St, 388-2117. Oldest community museum in the US (opened in 1884), the museum provides a vivid portrayal of life in the 1800s when Middlebury was a wool mill town, including muslin dresses from 1828 and 1832, a total town inventory of 1876, and info on the local burial of a 4,000 year old Egyptian prince. Tue-Sat 10am-5pm. $5, $3.50 students with ID. _www.henrysheldonmuseum.org._

UVM Morgan Horse Farm, 74 Battell Dr, Weybridge, 2.5 mi off Rte 23N, 388-2011, where the first American breed of horse has been bred and trained since the 1870s. May-Oct, daily 9am-4pm.Tours $5. _www.uvm.edu/morgan_.

Vermont Folklife Center, 3 Court St, 388-4964. Packed with oral and physical history exhibits featuring the extraordinary gamut of New England roots. Summer gallery hours: Tues-Sat 11am-4pm, free. _www.vermontfolklifecenter.org._

Vermont State Craft Center at Frog Hollow, 1 Mill St, 388-3177 (800) 388-3177. Craft gallery featuring the work of over 300 Vermont craftspeople, studios open to the public. Summer gallery hours: Mon-Thu 9.30am-5.30pm, Fri & Sat 9.30am-6pm, Sun 11am-5pm. _www.froghollow.org._

Homer Noble Farm, off Rte 125 E of Middlebury, Robert Frost's home and comfortable screened-in writing cabin where he spent the summers from 1939 until his death in 1963, is 500 m up an unmarked stony track immediately to the left after the Robert Frost picnic area on the left. Free. Before the picnic spot, on the right is the mile-long **Robert Frost Wayside Area and Trail** marked with some of his better-known poems, best read with bug-spray at hand.

Vermont Soapworks, 616 Exchange St, 388-4302, _www.vermontsoap.com_. Watch as the master soapmakers make some of the mildest soaps in the world today. Mon-Fri 8am-4pm.

Information/Travel

Chamber of Commerce, 2 Court St, 388-7951 (800) 733-8376. _www.midvermont.com_.
Vermont Transit Daily service to and from Burlington and Albany. Fares: (800) 451-3292; schedules _www.vermonttransit.com._

MONTPELIER This smallest capital in the nation (of about 8,000 people) is also surely one of the most beautiful. The granite industry built Montpelier and nearby Barre. Today the economy is based mainly on the state government and the insurance business, though a granite revival is afoot. The town also holds the dubious distinction of being home to the largest number of lawyers per capita of any city in America.

Montpelier is a thriving centre for theatre, music, crafts and antiques, and boasts its own **Museum and Historical Society** (109 State St, 828-2291). 'New exhibit is Freedom and Unity, one ideal, many stories'. **Vermont Historical Society Library**, 60, Washington St, Barre, 479-8500, has a vast array of Vermont history books. _www.vermonthistory.org_.

If you want to get away from it all, wander the back roads and admire the scenery. 'Come here for a slice of 50s rural village community life!' _www.montpelier-vt.org_.

Accommodation

Econolodge, 101 Northfield St, ½ mile from downtown, 223-5258. $50-80. Cable TV, breakfast included.

Montpelier Guest Home, 138 North St, 229-0878. Ave. $50. Victorian house, 10 min walk to downtown, no smoking. 15% discount for stays of two days or more, excludes foliage season. 15% discount for cyclists. Spacious deck and lovely gardens. Free use of cross-country skis and snowshoes for those adventuring to nearby Hubbard Park in winter.

Vermonter Motel, Barre-Montpelier Rd, 3 miles from Montpelier and Barre, 476-8541. $50-60, XP-$4.

Food

Montpelier is home to the **New England Culinary Institute**, 250 Main St, 223-6324, so quality, low-priced restaurants abound. Sample culinary practice at the Institute. Tours and demonstrations at the Institute are available. _www.neci.edu_.

Coffee Corner, 83 Main Street, 229-9060. Diner with good food at reasonable prices. Bfast $6, lunch $7-$10. Read the hand-lettered messages tacked up by customers while you wait for your food. Daily 6am-3pm. _www.coffeecorner.com_.

Hunger Mountain Co-op, 623 Stonecutter's Way, 223-6910. Outskirts of Montpelier. Natural foodstore coop. 'Fantastic selection at great prices. Good place to stock up on food.' Daily 8am-8pm, _www.hungermtncoop.com_.

Julio's, 54 State St, 229-9348. Good Tex Mex food, $6.50-$14. 'The cheapest eats in town.' 11:30am-midnight, Weds til 1am.

Thrush Tavern, 107 State St, 223-2030. Lunch, dinner, seafood, burgers, steak sandwiches. Lunch $6, dinner $10-$15. Mon-Fri 11am-9:30pm, Sat 4pm-10pm.

Of Interest

Swimming/boating at Groton and Elmore lakes nearby.

Ben & Jerry's Ice Cream Factory, Nov-May 10am-5pm, June-Aug 9am-8pm, Sept-Oct 9am-6pm, frequent tours, $3. Ask about their interesting management philosophy. 'The only flavour graveyard I've ever seen!' See Burlington section. _www.benjerry.com/tourinfo._

Ben & Jerry's Free Outdoor Movies, See Burlington section.

Cold Hollow Cider Mill, Rte 100, Waterbury Center, 16 miles from Montpelier, 244-8771/ (800) 327-7537. Watch cider-making, drink free samples, and buy cider jelly and apple butter in the store. Mon-Sun 8am-6pm, free. _www.coldhollow.com._

Hubbard Park, 200 acres of woodland with seven miles of hiking and skiing trails, picnic areas, a small pond, a sledding hill, and an observation tower.

Rock of Ages Quarry, 773 Graniteville Road 225-7646, 10+ miles from town. Founded in 1885, painted by Norman Rockwell, uses high technology to extract and carve blocks of granite. Narrated, breathtaking shuttle tours of the world's largest active granite quarry, June-Oct, Mon-Fri, 9.15am-3pm, $4. _www.rockofages.com._

Vermont State House, 115 State St, 828-2228. Built in 1859 and newly restored, topped with a gold-leaf dome and adorned with intricately carved wood trim. Contains some stunning Civil War and other paintings. Free tours in summer and fall, Mon-Fri 10am-3.30pm, Sat 11am-2.30pm. _www.leg.state.vt.us_

Internet Access
Kellog-Hubbard Library, 135 Main St, 223-3338. Free Internet access, half-hour time limit. Call same day to reserve time slot. Mon-Thu 10am-8pm, Fri 'til 5.30pm, Sat 'til 1pm in summer, 'til 5.30pm rest of year.

Information/Travel
Montpelier Chamber of Commerce, Stewart Rd & Paine Turnpike, 229-5711. Mon-Fri 8.30am-5pm. _www.central-vt.com._

Visitor's Center, 134 State St, 828-5981. Open daily 8am-6pm. _www.vermontvacation.com._

Vermont Transit Daily service to and from Burlington and White River Junction. Fares 800 552-8737; schedules: _www.vermonttransit.com_.

Amtrak – _Vermonter_ daily from New York and Burlington/St Albans. Fares, schedule _www.amtrak.com/trains/vermonter.html_   or (800) 872-7245.

STOWE At the foot of Vermont's highest peak, Mt Mansfield (4393 ft), sits Stowe, one of New England's most popular resorts. Although predominately a skiing town, Stowe is gaining popularity in all seasons for its variety of outdoor activities—hiking, biking, canoeing and hang-gliding. It is also the home of the von Trapp Family, of _Sound of Music_ fame, who operate a lodge and ski touring centre.

Accommodation/Food/Of Interest
Stowe-Bound Lodge, 645 S Main St, Rt 100, 253-4515. Hostel and B&B located on a small organic farm. Hostel $20, B&B $30-$45, private bathroom, incl bfast. Can provide dinner for groups of around 15.

McCarthy's, Mountain Rd, half mile from centre of town, 253-8626. Sandwiches, grinders, soups, daily specials. 'Lots of home-made goodies.' Daily 6.30am-3pm.

Ye Olde England Inn/Mr Pickwick's Pub, 433 Mountain Rd, Rte 108, 253-7558. English-style pub with pints of ale. 'Great place.' Occasional music and an extensive wine and beer list. Daily, restaurant 7.30am-10pm, pub 11.30am-2am. 'friendly Brits run this establishment' _www.englandinn.com._

Stowe Mountain Resort, 5781 Mountain Rd, 253-3500 (800) 253-4754. Offers a range of summer and winter outdoor pursuits. Alpine Slide rides, trips on a gondola and a skate park, visit _www.stowe.com_   for more details.

Information/Travel
Stowe Chamber of Commerce, 51 Main St, 253-7321, (800) 467-8693. _www.gostowe.com._

Amtrak, At nearby Waterbury, _Vermonter_ daily from New York and Burlington/St Albans. Fares, schedule: _www.amtrak.com/trains/vermonter.html_.

TAKE ME OUT TO THE BALLGAME

Baseball may be even more American than apple pie. First played in modern form, it's said, by Abner Doubleday in Cooperstown, New York 1839, America's national sport is an inexpensive treat not to be missed. The pleasure of watching a game on a warm summers evening, beer and hot dog in hand, cannot be beaten. Along the way, brush up on your ballgame terms: steal; chopper; pickle; fly; bunt; line-drive; slider; ERA; LIPS; bottom-of-the-ninth; check-swing; and strikeout. These enhance the game, if understood!

Catch the action now, before every baseball team sells out to a corporate under-writer and commercialises their stadium names. There are two major leagues, the **National** and the **American**. Each is divided into three divisions and the champions of each meet in October at the end-of-season **World Series**. For a complete run-down on each team, current scoreboards, links to team sites and the basics of the game, visit _www.mlb.com_.

NATIONAL LEAGUE (est.1876)
East—Atlanta _Braves_, Florida _Marlins_, Washington _Nationals_, New York _Mets_, Philadelphia _Phillies_.
Central—Chicago _Cubs_, Cincinnati _Reds_, Houston _Astros_, Milwaukee _Brewers_, Pittsburgh _Pirates_, St Louis _Cardinals_.
West—Arizona _Diamondbacks_, Colorado _Rockies_, LA _Dodgers_, San Diego _Padres_, San Francisco _Giants_.

BALLPARKS of the National League:
EAST: **Atlanta Braves, Turner Field,** (404) 522-7630. AOL and Time Warner have signed this team from previous owner, TV mogul Ted Turner. You can see the Braves for just $1 if you buy tickets on game days. _http://atlanta.braves.mlb.com._
Florida Marlins, Dolphins Stadium, (305) 623-6100. In North Miami off the Florida Turnpike, where the Marlins beat the Cleveland Indians in the World Series in 1997 in only the 5th year of their existence. _http://florida.marlins.mlb.com._
Washington Nationals, RFK Stadium, (866) 800-1275. In memory of Senator Robert F Kennedy. Originally the home of the football team, the Washington Redskins, and baseball team, the Senators, the stadium has undergone renovation to house the Washington Nationals, previously the Montreal _Expos. http://washington.nationals.mlb.com._
New York Mets, Shea Stadium, (718) 507-METS. Where the Beatles played their first US gig, in August 1966. A 57,393 capacity stadium, in centerfield, a large apple rises out of a top hat after every Mets home run. It doesn't happen very often, although in 2000 the team made it to the World Series. _http://newyork.mets.mlb.com._
Philadelphia Phillies, Citizens Bank Park, (215) 463-5000. The new ballpark opened April 2004, seats 43,000, has bleacher seats on the roof and features the largest video display in the majors. _http://philadelphia.phillies.mlb.com._

CENTRAL: **Chicago Cubs, Wrigley Field,** (773) 404-CUBS. The second oldest ballpark in the league, but the most traditional; ivy-covered walls and hand-turned scoreboards. In 1988, Wrigley became the last ballpark to install lights. They had purchased lights in 1941 that were due to be installed that same year, however, plans changed when the Japanese bombed Pearl Harbor and the lights were donated to the war effort instead. Catch a game and join legendary Ronnie in shouting 'Go Cubs, Go Cubs.' _http://chicago.cubs.mlb.com._
Cincinnati Reds, Great American Ballpark, (513) 765-7096. The GABP opened March 2003 and has the longest escalator in the majors! You can seek autographs up to 45 mins prior to games along the railing between sections 113-111 and 133-135 or take a tour of the field and ballpark, $5. Or visit the Hall of Fame. _http://cincinnati.reds.mlb.com._
Houston Astros, Minute Maid Park, (713) 259-8000. This park replaces Houston's legendary Astrodome, called the 8th wonder of the world when it opened in 1965. The new grass, outdoor stadium is a 1st for Houston, as well as the 242 ft high, retractable roof. _http://houston.astros.mlb.com._
Milwaukee Brewers, Miller Park, (414) 902-4400. Maintains Milwaukee's reputa-tion for having the best stadium food and beverages, including bratwurst, barbecued chicken and steak with secret sauce. Hank Aaron wound up his career in the old

stadium here in 1976 with the major league lifetime home run record of 755. The new stadium features a state-of-the-art, fan-shaped convertible roof, which takes just 10 mins to open and close. *http://milwaukee.brewers.mlb.com.*
Pittsburgh Pirates, PNC Park, (412) 323-5000. Opened in 2001, its 38,000 seats and two-deck design provide an intimate setting, ensuring good views all round. *http://pittsburgh.pirates.mlb.com.*
St Louis Cardinals, Busch Stadium, (314) 421-3060. Opened in 1966, but a new stadium, of the same name, opens in 2006. The city has a passion for baseball, so joining the crowd at this 50,354 capacity ballpark is certainly an experience. *http://stlouis.cardinals.mlb.com.*

WEST: **Arizona Diamondbacks, Bank One Ballpark,** (602) 514-8400/(888) 777-4664. After being in existence only since 1998, the D-Backs claimed the title as 2001 World Champions, beating the phenomenal NY Yankees in the 9th innings of the 7th game. Their ultra-posh, $354 million, stadium beats the Arizona heat with poolside seats and an air-conditioning unit equivalent to that of 2,500 Arizona homes. *http://arizona.diamondbacks.mlb.com.*
Colorado Rockies, Coors Field, (303) 292-0200/(800) 388-ROCK. In the mile-high city, a horizontal row of upper deck seats marks the point where the ballpark elevation passes the mile-high mark. It's the highest facility in the majors. *http://colorado.rockies.mlb.com.*
Los Angeles Dodgers, Dodger Stadium, (323) 224-1500. Most palatial of the stadia, and probably the only one with as many celebrities in the bleachers as on the field. The 1988 World Series opened here, during which Kirk Gibson of LA hit a 2-run homer in the final inning with two outs, giving the Dodgers a 5-4 victory over the Oakland Athletics. *http://losangeles.dodgers.mlb.com.*
San Diego Padres, PETCO Park, (888) MY-PADRES. Baseball a la California, complete with sunny skies, warm temps, and fans in bathing suits tossing giant beach balls. Complete with garden terraces, picturesque views and palm trees to lure spectators in. *http://sandiego.padres.mlb.com.*
San Francisco Giants, SBC Park, (415) 972-2000. Completed in 2000, the 1st privately financed park since 1962, it has a 9 ft statue of baseball great, Willie Mays in the foyer, an 80 ft Coca-Cola bottle playground and mini P.B. Park behind left field. The right field short wall allows some home run balls to fall into the bay. *http://sanfrancisco.giants.mlb.com.*

AMERICAN LEAGUE (est.1900)
East—Baltimore *Orioles*, Boston *Red Sox*, New York *Yankees*, Tampa Bay *Devil Rays*, Toronto *Blue Jays*.
Central—Chicago *White Sox*, Cleveland *Indians*, Detroit *Tigers*, Kansas City *Royals*, Minnesota *Twins*.
West—Anaheim *Angels*, Oakland *Athletics*, Seattle *Mariners*, Texas *Rangers*.

BALLPARKS of the American League:
EAST: **Baltimore Orioles, Oriole Park, Camden Yards,** (888) 848-BIRD. The $110 million, 48,000-seat downtown ballpark opened in 1992. Only 4 blocks from Baltimore's inner harbour, it has a wonderful barbecue-soaked atmosphere. *http://baltimore.orioles.mlb.com.*
Boston Red Sox, Fenway Park, (617) 267-9440. The oldest ballpark in the major leagues and home of the 'Green Monster' in left field. The intimate atmosphere lets you be a part of the game like in the good ol' days. The Red Sox were the first team to win the World Series when it was established in 1903. *http://boston.redsox.mlb.com.*
New York Yankees, Yankee Stadium, (718) 293-4300. 26-time World Champs—most recently in 2000—so-called 'team of the century'—and wellspring of many baseball legends, including Yogi Berra who, once when a game was poorly attended, is reported to have said, 'if the people don't want to come out to the park, nobody's gonna stop them'. Fans voted unfriendliest by baseball players. The 1927 'Murderers' Row Team' included Lou Gehrig, Bob Meusel, Tony Lazzeri, and Babe Ruth who hit a home run every nine trips to the plate that year. Catch Yankees fans at their most partisan during a game with arch-rivals Boston Red Sox. If you can't make it, watch George's antic progress there on *Seinfeld*. A new stadium is planned for the 2009 season. *http://newyork.yankees.mlb.com.*

Tampa Bay Devil Rays, Tropicana Field, (888) 326-7297. The stadium was built ten years before professional baseball came to Tampa, with the long-unfulfilled promise that it would one day do so. Wander along the 900 ft tropical-theme ceramic mosaic walkways in this 1.1 million sq ft ballpark. *http://tampabay.devilrays.mlb.com.*

Toronto Blue Jays, Rogers Centre, (416) 341-1000. Opened in 1989 with the largest retractable roof in the world, Rogers Centre's popularity caused the park to break attendance records in its maiden season. The Blue Jays were also the first non-US world champions. They won in 1992 and again in 1993. *http://toronto.bluejays.mlb.com.*

CENTRAL: **Chicago Whitesox, US Cellular Field,** (312) 674-1000. Home of the current World Champions, the park was renamed in 2003, following the US Cellular merger, which has allowed for numerous renovations. The field is home to the craziest fans who staged 'Disco Sucks Night' in 1979 and the crazy organist, Nancy: a jokester who cranks out an appropriate song for every situation and player. Host to the 'Black Sox Scandal', the World Series was fixed here in 1919. 'Say it ain't so, Jo,' they asked of Jo Jackson, one of eight players involved. *http://chicago.whitesox.mlb.com.*

Cleveland Indians, Jacobs Field, (216) 420-4200. Opened 1994, Jacobs Field is part of the same downtown revival efforts that produced the Rock 'n' Roll Hall of Fame. A fan-friendly stadium, it has an intimate environment and great views. *http://cleveland.indians.mlb.com.*

Detroit Tigers, Comerica Park, (313) 962-4000. New for the 2000 season, Comerica replaced Tiger Stadium. The ballpark is now a blend of not only a great field but also theme park and museum. Ride a hand-painted tiger carousel, a 50 ft Ferris wheel and stroll through the "walk of fame" from the 1800s to present day. *http://detroit.tigers.mlb.com.*

Kansas City Royals, Kauffman Stadium, (816) 921-8000. More than one baseball player has conceded that this is their favourite away stadium. KC barbecue, baked beans and baseball make for a great game. The outfield is particularly beautiful, with waterfalls just beyond the home run barrier. *http://kansascity.royals.mlb.com.*

Minnesota Twins, Metrodrome, (612) 375-1366. Home to the twins for 18 years, efforts continue to build a new ballpark in which they can rival better-equipped teams. Their home was originally an American Football stadium and so is not at all well designed to cater to the baseball crowd. Plans for a new 42,000-seat ball field are underway, the new park to be "up-close, in the great outdoors and on natural grass," set to open in Rapid Park in 2009. *http://minnesota.twins.mlb.com.*

WEST: **Anaheim Angels, Angel Stadium,** (714) 634-2000. Renovated for the 1998 season, the left-center fence opens to a natural-looking venue with views of a rock pile and erupting geysers. 2002 World Champions with Garret Anderson in Left Field, selected to the All Star Team and named most valuable player (MVP) in 2003. *http://losangeles.angels.mlb.com*

Oakland Athletics, McAfee .Coliseum, (510) 638-4900. Here baseball combines with the finest sound and video system in the league to create baseball-rock. The aesthetics of the stadium leave something to be desired; its drab appearance earned it the nickname, 'The Oakland Mausoleum.' *http://oakland.athletics.mlb.com.*

Seattle Mariners, Safeco Field, (206) 346-4000. When Safeco opened in 1999, Seattle became the first baseball team to move from an indoor facility to an outdoor facility. *http://seattle.mariners.mlb.com.*

Texas Rangers, Ameriquest Field, Arlington, (817) 273-5222. About $190 million was spent on this ballpark, which opened in 1994. It has the feel of an old, inner city park situated amongst the mini-vans of a suburban parking lot. In summer, there are only night games played here—it's too hot during the day. *http://texas.rangers.mlb.com.*

THE NORTHEAST

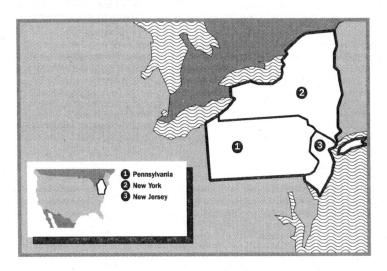

Through the Northeastern region runs most of the 400-mile strip of the megalopolis known as 'Boswash' (Boston to Washington); its sturdy backbone being Interstate 95. This rates as the USA's most crowded urban concentration, containing the nation's largest city, New York and heaviest industry. The region has been called the headquarters of Enterprise America for, from the time of the industrial revolution, much of the impetus for commercial and industrial expansion has stemmed from here.

You would be cheating yourself if during your tour of the Northeast you did not veer away from the monotony and dirty billboards of I-95 to visit the large tracts of unspoiled countryside within easy reach of the cities. Especially worth seeing are the mountainous Adirondacks in northern New York State and the rolling farmlands of western Pennsylvania, but there is greater variety still. In a region rich in historical and cultural associations, there is a wealth of places to visit and things to do. The climate varies as much as the geography. Winters are very cold and snow can be expected everywhere, while summers are marked by searing heat and sapping humidity.

NEW JERSEY - The Garden State

Sandwiched between industrial Pennsylvania and New York State, New Jersey, when first glimpsed after crossing the Hudson River from Manhattan, seems to be an incredible wasteland, a lunar cesspool difficult to miss. The New Jersey Turnpike (toll road) dominates the landscape – people in New Jersey don't ask where you're from, they ask, "what exit?" Riding the turnpike between New York and Delaware and seeing mile after mile of refinery pipes, gasoline storage tanks and smelly smokestacks, you may well ask yourself whatever happened to America the Beautiful!

What is hard to believe is that there really is some truth to the state's label, the Garden State. West from the New York suburbs and interstate highways that bisect the state lies the bucolic **Delaware River Valley** in a corner of the Appalachian Mountains. To the east lie a virginal pine forest called the **Pine Barrens** and the **Jersey Shore** along the Atlantic, 150 miles of sandy beaches and boardwalks. In the west and south, there are even 17 wineries whose bottles are offered at fine Manhattan restaurants. _www.newjerseywines.com_. From paved paths to muddy tracks, New Jersey has dozens of bike trails. _30 Bicycling Tours in New Jersey_, by Arline Zatz, is a useful book, available from the National Book Company, 800 Keystone Industrial Park, Scranton, Pennsylvania, 18512 (800) 233-4830.

www.state.nj.us/travel. _Area codes are: 201, 609, 908, 973, 732 and 865_

NEWARK In truth, this is one of America's most unpleasant cities, with a history of physical decay, political corruption, racial tension and plain old ugliness. 'Newark' may sound like a corruption of its affluent cousin New York; the name comes from puritan settlers who were searching for a 'new ark'. Although their vision has not quite been realised, Newark's airport has bolstered commercial redevelopment. The busy international airport has made Newark a frequent first and last stop in America for overseas travellers-and is as much as the traveller need ever see.

There is no reason to go into downtown Newark. Accommodation is available near the airport but it is on the expensive side. It's better to catch a bus into Manhattan and stay there. (See New York City section for further info.)

Information/Travel
Travelers Aid, Newark Liberty International Airport, (973) 623-5052, Terminal B, International Arrivals. Mon & Tue 10am-6pm, Wed-Fri 10am-10pm, Sat & Sun 2pm-10pm.
Greyhound, Penn Central Station, (973) 662-6740 /(800) 231-2222.
Olympia Trails Airport Express, (212) 964-6233/(908) 354-3330, $13 from Newark airport to midtown Manhattan, runs every 15-30 min.
Super Shuttle, (800) 258-3826, 24hrs $15-19 from Newark Airport to Manhattan hotel. _www.supershuttle.com_.

THE PALISADES are a 15-mile long line of granite cliffs rising as high as 500ft above the Hudson. The most impressive view is from the George Washington Bridge when riding over from Manhattan, but on the New Jersey side you can enjoy the Palisades Interstate Park with its picnic grounds and beautiful woods.

Just across the Hudson River from lower Manhattan is the gritty port town of **Hoboken**, famous as the place where _On The Waterfront_ was filmed and where Frank Sinatra was born. PATH commuter trains from New York will get you there, and as you pass through the station, marvel at its intricate marble construction. One of the better technological universities, **Stevens Institute**, also calls Hoboken home, as did an old Maxwell House coffee plant that was the largest in the world when it opened in 1939; now it's a condominium development with a pleasant waterfront Park. *www.maxwellplace.com*.

Two fine universities lie just off the New Jersey Turnpike (toll) south-west of Newark. New Brunswick is the home of **Rutgers University**, and 30 miles further on is **Princeton**, a beautiful New England town that ran away to New Jersey. Both Albert Einstein and Thomas Mann lived here, while F. Scott Fitzgerald and Eugene O'Neill are among the more luminous alumni of **Princeton University**. Free tours of the campus start at the Frist Campus Centre, (609) 258-3603, Mon-Sat 9.45am, 11am, 1pm, 3.30pm, Sun 1pm & 3.30pm. Highlights include Nassau Hall, built in 1756, where the Continental Congress met in 1783, and which was used as barracks during the Revolution by both American and British soldiers. *www.princeton.edu*. Fifteen miles west from Princeton is the point where General Washington crossed the Delaware River on a bone-chilling Christmas night in 1776 to deliver a special Christmas present to the British troops at Trenton. Eight days later he stormed the garrison at Princeton.

Food in Princeton
Chuck's Spring St Cafe, 16 Spring St, 921-0027. Daily 11am-9.30pm.
Small World Coffee, 14 Witherspoon St, 924-4377. Pastries and desserts, bfast and lunch at reasonable prices. Mon-Thu 6.30am-10pm, Fri and Sat 6.30am-11pm, Sun 7.30am-10pm. *www.smallworldcoffee.com.*

THE JERSEY SHORE begins south of Newark. Drive along the **Garden State Pkwy**, which follows the contour of the coast. Gritty **Asbury Park**, where it seems everyone works in a garage, is Bruce Springsteen country. Forty miles further south is the road to **Long Beach**. 'A great place to relax and enjoy sea, sun and sand. No usual boardwalk, but no usual commercialism.'

ATLANTIC CITY 'The playground of the world' was once the best loved seaside resort in America and the original model for the game of Monopoly, but Atlantic City saw its glamour wilt when better-off bathers made for hotter climes in the south and the west. The home of salt-water taffy (America's equivalent of Brighton Rock) and the Miss America contest, the town was revitalised in 1977 when casino gambling was legalised here. Funnily enough, the cheaper properties in the board game to this day remain slums, while Atlantic Avenue and Park Place are host to ritzy hotels.

With the arrival of the gambling resorts, a new game of monopoly has ensued (Donald Trump heading the list of players), with speculators raising entire city blocks in hopes of profit, and investors raising a dozen garish, neon-lit pleasure palaces. The result is an urban desert spotted with casinos and linked to the rest of the world by hundreds of buses bringing the hopeful from Philadelphia, New York and Washington. Special Amtrak trains, with connecting buses to the casinos, go there too.

To escape the crowds and gaudy *joie de vivre* of Atlantic City, go north to the **Island Beach State Park**, (732) 793-0506, a 10-mile strip of white sand.

For more info see *www.atlanticcitynj.com*.
The telephone area code for Atlantic City is 609.

Accommodation
Atlantic City is more expensive than the rest of the Jersey shore, especially during the summer season. If you're stranded and have to stay in town, try AmeriRoom **Reservations**, (800) 888-5825. Free reservation service for hotels and casinos throughout the city; pricey (from $100), but efficient.

Sunset Inn on the Bay, 1 mile from the Boardwalk, 344-2515, D $69.

Irish Pub Inn, 164 St. James Pl, 344-9063, Victorian style inn, weekday special $55 with private shower, $80 weekends; cheaper rates for shared bath. _www.theirish-pub.com_.

Camping is the cheapest alternative. **Evergreen Woods**, Hwy 575 & 561 Alternate S, 12 miles west of Atlantic City, 652-1577. Sites $29.75 for two XP-$3.50 w/full hook-up. Lakefront cabins sleep 4 for $55. Cottages sleep 4 for $44.

Food/Entertainment

Many of the casinos serve breakfast, lunch and dinner buffets that are often 'eat as much as you want'.

Tony's Baltimore Grill (Tony's to the locals), 2800 Iowa & Atlantic Ave, 345-5766. Cheap food in snug booths with your own personal juke-box. 'Pizzas are the best in city, especially topped with home-made sausage.' $6.60 up. Beer 1.25¢ a mug pint $2. Daily 24 hrs (kitchen open 11am-3pm). _www.baltimoregrill.com._

Irish Pub, 164 St James Pl, 344-9063, named the best bar in Atlantic City by Philadelphia Magazine. Lunch specials $1.95, dinner specials $5.95, most dishes under $10. Pub and food service open 24 hrs. _www.theirishpub.com._

Little Saigon, 2801 Arctic Ave & Iowa, 347-9119. Fresh Vietnamese cuisine.

White House Sub Shop & Deli, 2301 Arctic Ave, 345-1564. Sublime hoagie sandwiches, world-famous since 1946. $12-13, half-subs $6-7.

Of interest

Boardwalk Hall, 2301 Boardwalk, 348-7000. Although the largest in the world when built in 1929, seating 13,800 in the arena, it has been superceded. It houses the world's largest pipe organ. Watch the Miss America Pageant here mid-Sept. _www.boardwalkhall.com._

Lucy the Margate Elephant, 9200 Atlantic Ave., 823-6473. A building in the shape of an elephant, originally built of wood and tin in 1881. Tours $4, daily in summer, 10am-8pm, Sun till 5pm, in winter 10am-5pm Fri-Sun. _www.lucytheelephant.org_.

Renault Winery, 16 miles from Atlantic City on Breman Ave, off Rte 30, 965-2111. Tours of working winery that was built in 1864. Guide will show you bottling process, a museum and take you through a wine-tasting, $2. **Grape Stompin' Festival** at harvest time in September. Mon-Fri 11 am-4pm, Sat 'til 8pm, Sun noon-4pm. Get discount coupons at _www.renaultwinery.com_.

Information/Travel

Chamber of Commerce, 1125 Atlantic Ave, Suite 105, (888)-228-4748/345-5600/4524. Mon-Fri 9am-5pm. _www.atlanticcitychamber.com_.

Convention and Visitors Authority, 609-348-7272, 2300 Boardwalk. Open Mon-Wed 9.30am-5.30, Thu-Sun till 8pm. _www.atlanticcitynj.com_.

Many of the casinos run free or low-priced buses to Atlantic City from New York and Philadelphia. Check the Yellow Pages under 'Casinos' for information or look for billboard ads.

Greyhound, 1901 Atlantic Ave, 345-6617/(800) 231-2222. Also, **New Jersey Transit**, same location, (800) 582-5946 (in state only), (215) 569-3752.

Internet access

Atlantic City Free Public Library, 1 North Tennessee Avenue, 345-2269. Open Mon-Wed 10am-8pm, Thu-Sat 9am-5pm. Free, use ltd. to 1hr. _www.acpl.org_.

OCEAN CITY Eight miles south, teetotal cousin to hedonistic Atlantic City. Alcohol cannot be bought on the island but the summer workers who flock here every year can walk a sobering 2.3 miles across 9th St bridge to find importable drink on the mainland. Plenty of casual jobs in 'America's greatest family resort' make this a popular destination for BUNACers and others

who share the long, crowded beaches and lively nightlife. There is a wide choice of cheap rooms in boarding houses and old resort hotels, if you get there early enough (beginning of June if you're planning to stay.) Ocean City's 2.5 mile long boardwalk is known for its wacky contests and festivals, which reach a bizarre peak in July and August. *www.oceancityvacation.com*.
The telephone area code is 609.

Accommodation
Sandaway Inn, 8th and Ocean Ave, 399-2779, D $95 includes parking, beach tag.

Food
Blue Planet, 841 Ashbury Ave. at 9th St, 525-9999. Styled after a 50's American diner-don't forget your poodle skirts, pompadours and quarters for the jukebox! Open w/days 8am-9pm, w/ends 7am-9pm.

Of interest
Ocean City Boardwalk Art Show, over 150 artists, sculptors and photographers from the northeast display work for sale and compete for prizes. First w/end in August. Sponsored by the **Ocean City Arts Center**, who do other shows during the course of the summer, 399-7628. *www.oceancityartscenter.org*.
Miss Crustacean Hermit Crab Beauty Pageant, the world's only beauty pageant for hermit crabs. First week in Aug, 12th St beach. Free.

Information
Greater Ocean City Chamber of Commerce, Rte 52, 9th St Causeway, btwn Somers Point & Ocean City, 399-2629/(800)-BEACH-NJ, has info on beaches, hotels, restaurants. Open Mon-Sat 9am-5pm, Sun 10am-2pm.

WILDWOOD is a smaller, perhaps more wholesome, version of Atlantic City, practically at the tip of the southern peninsula of the state. The beach is 1000 ft wide in some places and there are 2 miles of boardwalk, six amusement parks, and plenty of wild nightlife. It's also a resort where families come for their traditional week by the sea. 'Lots of American students work here. Everyone works hard and plays hard. We had a fabulous time.' 'A fantastic place to spend the summer.'

Accommodation
'Accommodation easily found by walking around and asking. Wildwood Crest is the nicest area to live.'
24th Street Motel, 2401 Surf Ave, 522-8334. One-half block from Morey's Pier. D-$85; room for 4, $120. *www.24thstreetmotel.com.*
Holly Beach Hotel, 137 E Spicer Ave, 522-9033. S-$110-125, D-$85 pp inc. bfast. *www.hollybeach.com.*

Food/Entertainment
Recommended for its 'good food and atmosphere', is Big Ernie's on Atlantic Ave & Garfield, 522-8288. Open daily, 7am-10pm. Other suggestions include **The Hot Spot**, 3816 Boardwalk, 522-9777, open daily 9am-11pm and Kelly's Café, 4400 Atlantic Ave, 522-6817, 11.30am-midnight.

CAPE MAY Family-oriented Victorian beach resort where the houses date from the 1870-80s. The main attraction is the pristine beach where beach tags must be displayed if you plan to hit the sand; $4 or $13 weekly from beach vendors or the Beach Tag Office, 884-9520. More secluded beaches and gentle dunes are located at **Cape May Point**, take Cape Ave off Sunset

Blvd. At **Sunset Beach** you can join the hunt for the famous and elusive Cape May diamonds, milky stones which, when polished, glitter like precious gems.

For spectacular views of the coast walk for about 30 minutes from the town centre and climb the curling stairs of the old lighthouse, built in 1859, which stands just inside the entrance gates to **Cape May State Park**, $4. If you're heading south, you may want to take the **Cape May Ferry**, (800) 64-FERRY, to Lewes, Delaware. Frequent daily sailings, $25 car and driver ($8 p/car passenger), foot passengers $8 o/w, same-day r/t $15. Bikes $8 (summer prices). _www.capemaylewesferry.com._

The area code is 609.

Food: Cucina Rosa, 301 Washington St, 898-9800. Charming Italian bistro, dishes $19, daily except Wed 5pm-10pm. _www.cucinarosa.com_.

Of interest
The **East Creek Trail,** 7 mile long hiking trail path, with some cycle paths, in the **Belleplain State Forest**, Woodbine, which may be accessed from County Rte 550, 861-2404. _www.nj.gov/dep/parksandforests_.
Cape May Ghost Tour, candlelight walking ghost tour through the historic district. Meets at **Elaine's Dinner Theater**, 884-4358, $10. Rsvs rec.
www.elainesdinnertheater.com.
Bikes may be rented at **Village Bike Rentals**, Lafayette and Elmira Sts, opposite the Acme parking lot, 884-8500, $10 day, $35 week. Daily 7am-6pm.

Information: Welcome Center, 405 Lafayette St, 884-9562, has info on restaurants, accommodation, tours, etc. Mon-Sat 9am-4.30pm.

OCEAN GROVE Founded in 1869 by a group of Methodist lay leaders, this seashore resort boasts the largest assemblage of Victorian architecture in the country, for which it was entered into the National Register of Historic Places in 1976. When you get sick of the beach, stroll along the boardwalk or Main Ave to browse in the gift and antique shops, or take in one of the many arts and crafts shows. Every year, on the first Saturday after both Memorial and Labor Day, there are giant flea markets. Beach tags ($6 single, $11 w/end, $30 for 7 days) are sold at the Beach Office, Ocean and Embury Aves, 988-5533. _www.oceangrove.ws_.

The telephone area code is 732.

Accommodation
Albatross Hotel, 34 Ocean Pathway, 775-2085/(201) 709-6543. Was closed for renovations in 2005. E-mail for up-dates: _albatrosshotel@yahoo.com_.
The Quaker Inn, 39 Main Ave, 775-7525. D $55-80. Located 2 blocks from ocean.

Of interest/Information
Music events frequently take place at the **Ocean Grove Camp Association Auditorium** which holds 6,500, Saturdays through the summer. For more info. see _www.oceangrove.org_ or call (800) 773-0097.
Ocean Grove Tourist Information **(Chamber of Commerce)**, 45 Pilgrim Pathway, 774-1391. Open Mon-Sat 10am-4pm, Sun noon-4pm. _www.oceangrove.ws_.

DELAWARE WATER GAP Where the 'Garden State' comes into its own. Here the hills diverge dramatically to make way for the Delaware River and a national recreation area, which is a haven for outdoor enthusiasts, offering everything from swimming to rafting, canoeing to cross country skiing, hiking to biking. For information call the **National Recreation Area**, (570) 588-2451. _www.nps.gov/dewa_.

NEW YORK - The Empire State

Everything about New York State is big. It has the biggest industrial, commercial and population centre in the United States all rolled into one great metropolis, which together with the vast upstate area contributes mightily to the nation's manufacturing and agricultural output.

In Colonial times New York was one of the most sizeable chunks of land in North America, hence its nickname, the Empire State. Although New York State was technically discovered in 1524 by Giovanni da Verrazano sailing for France, Henry Hudson (an Englishman employed by the Dutch) sailed through the Lower Bay of New York in 1609, and on up the river which now bears his name. The river was later fought over by the British and the Dutch, whilst the Brits also wrested the Northern area from the French.

Peter Minuit governed the 300 strong Dutch Colony of New Amsterdam (renamed New York City by its conquerors in 1664) after buying Manhattan from the Indians for $25 worth of trinkets. Yet it says something about the vastness of the state, much of it still wilderness even today, that as late as 1700 the most formidable empire in New York was that of the Iroquois Confederacy of the Five Nations based in Syracuse and controlling the water routes to the coast and therefore trade. Their power was broken only in the middle of that century when the British defeated the Indians and their French allies at Ticonderoga, Niagara and Montréal.

The Empire State continues to be one of the leading political regions in America. What happens in New York always counts, whether it be in politics, finance, culture, entertainment, fashion or sport. _www.iloveny.com_.

NEW YORK CITY 'There are many apples on the tree, but when you pick New York City, you pick the Big Apple.' So said the jazz musicians of the 1930's, as fascinated by the lure and excitement of NYC as visitors are today. More than 8 million people now live and work in New York, the USA's largest city, home to the United Nations, and the business, entertainment and publishing capital of the nation.

It isn't possible within this book to give more than the briefest introduction to New York, so, if you plan to spend some time here, we recommend you buy one of the many available guides to NYC. Particularly useful are the free _NYC Visitor's Guides_ available from NYC & Co - Convention & Visitors Bureau (212-484-1200 or visit _www.nycvisit.com_), and for depth, the excellent _Gotham – A History of NYC to 1898_ by Edwin Burrows and Mike Wallace. (Washington Irving coined Gotham in his _Salmagundi_ papers in 1807, from a fabled village based on Gotham near Sherwood Forest.) For essential NYC spirit and humour, the ageless episodes of _Seinfeld_ are highly recommended, and for the soul and amazing cultural diversity of NYC, the documentary _Mad Hot Ballroom_ (2005). _www.paramountclassics.com/madhot_

The city comprises five boroughs, Brooklyn, the Bronx, Queens, Staten Island and Manhattan, but the greater metropolitan area stretches out into New Jersey and Connecticut. You're really talking about Manhattan when you say New York City - that long stretch of stone lying between the Hudson and East Rivers, the place where skyscrapers tower over an intense mish mash of social extremes. As Burrows and   Wallace point out, here is where NYC has defined the nation: Wall St supplied the capital, Ellis Island the manpower, Madison Ave the advertising, Broadway the entertainment, Fifth Ave the styles and social trends, the Village, alternative society.

New York's explosive variety and its appeal to so many different types of people make it an exciting, friendly, and pleasant place to visit. Chances are that whatever you are looking for, you will find, and so much more besides. In the words of President John F Kennedy, 'Other cities are nouns. New York is a verb.' New York offers the finest in theatre, cinema, music, museums, shopping, restaurants and general tourist attractions, as well as a riveting study in social contrast where you'll see bag ladies huddle over steam grates across the street from a row of limousines. Summers can be painfully hot and humid, and winters are bitterly cold and windy.

In the last decade, the Big Apple has gone through a renaissance. Controversial former Mayor Giuliani promised a safer, cleaner city when he was elected in 1993, and he did deliver-especially in Manhattan where assaults have plummeted, streets are no longer littered with trash, and new subway cars feature two types of electronic signboards. In 2004, under Mayor Michael Bloomberg, the FBI recognised New York as the safest big city in America. Visitors who use caution and common sense rarely have problems.

The housing boom of the nineties, which some said threatened the diversity in older neighbourhoods by driving up rents, continues. Some artistic and ethnic centers like SoHo and southern Harlem continue to be gentrified, as 'the Village' did, but new neighborhoods foster incredible diversity and the next generation of sparkling young artistic talent. Today, look to the Lower East Side and Williamsburg/Greenpoint across the East River for the next big thing in avant-garde art. Indeed, New York is one of the most vibrant, electric places in the country. The city's rebirth is perhaps most evident on a sunny Sunday afternoon in Central Park, when hoards of New Yorkers come out to bike, stroll, jog, play ball or just relax. Today, among Manhattan's nicest secrets are the tip-to-toe Westside parks, piers – especially Pier 45, and bike paths, and the East Village, quietly full of bistros and coffee shops, and the verdant Tompkins Sq. Park.

NYC can be filthy, sometimes dangerous, flashy, or funny, but it is always outrageous, alive, enthusiastic and, above all, resilient. In 2001, the people of the city, led by outgoing Republican Mayor Rudolph Giuliani and Governor George Pataki, showed the heroic depth of that resilience in the aftermath of the terrorist attack that demolished the 200,000 tons of the twin-tower World Trade Center on September 11th and changed the skyline of lower Manhattan forever. Since then life in New York has returned to mostly normal, amazing new glassy buildings are looming up everywhere, and more people than ever seem to be coming to live in the city.

Whatever your initial approach to Manhattan, when you see the skyline, even without the World Trade Center, day or night, you will experience an unforgettable feeling of intimidation, enchantment and awe. Welcome to the fastest-moving, most famous and fascinating city on earth, the city that really 'never sleeps'. _www.nycvisit.com._

The telephone area codes are 212, 917 and 646 for Manhattan, 718 for the Bronx, Brooklyn, Queens and Staten Island. For the following listings use 212 unless otherwise specified.

NEIGHBOURHOODS

THE BOROUGHS: QUEENS Most people know Queens just for its airports – Kennedy and La Guardia, but it's here that the US Open is played at the USTA National Tennis Center, the NY Mets play baseball at Shea Stadium, and Aqueduct and Belmont tracks host major races including one of the triple crown stakes _www.nyra.com_. Polyglot Queens was also home to many jazz greats - the **Queens Jazz Trail** visits the whereabouts of Louis Armstrong, Count Basie, Ella Fitzgerald, Dizzy Gillespie, Billie Holiday, Illinois Jacquet, Scott Joplin, Clark Terry, among others. **Flushing Town Hall** (718) 463-7700, provides a 3-hour tour 10am-1pm one Saturday a month led by historians and musicologists that includes a stop at the **Louis Armstrong Archives** at Queens College, which has 650 of his audiotapes. _www.flushingtownhall.com_. The **Louis Armstrong House Museum** opened in 2003 at 34-56 107th St, 10am-5pm Tue-Fri, Sat and Sun noon-5pm (#7 line to 103rd St). Armstrong said of his house: "...when one visits the Interior of the Armstrong's home, they see a whole lot of comfort, happiness, & the nicest things. Such as that Wall to Wall Bed". _www.satchmo.net_.

BROOKLYN The **Brooklyn Museum of Art** is repository of one of the world's largest Egyptian collections, including seven Egyptian galleries. **Prospect Park** in Brooklyn has a zoo and a 60-acre lake you can paddle across, and neighbours **Brooklyn Botanical Gardens**. Take the #2 or 3 trains to Grand Army Plaza, the F train to 7th Ave, or the S or Q trains to Prospect Park. _www.prospectpark.org_. **Coney Island** at the end of the W line features the famous Cyclone coaster; it's down from **Brighton Beach**, also known as Little Odessa for its sizeable Russian population. And of course, there's **Brooklyn Heights**, a neighbourhood of brick, brownstone and wooden houses overlooking New York harbour - New York as it was a century ago. You can walk here across the **Brooklyn Bridge**, a 121-year-old suspension bridge, from South Street Seaport in lower Manhattan, for a fine view of Manhattan along the local promenade. It's worth taking a stroll around **Park Slope**, known for its beautiful brownstones. And remember that Brooklyn is the birthplace of Woody Allen, Jerry Seinfeld, and Mae West!

THE BRONX The Bronx, north of Manhattan, is home to the great **Bronx Zoo** – the largest urban zoo in the US, with over 4000 animals. The Zoo, est. 1899, is home to the Wildlife Conservation Society. Reach it on the #2 or #5 uptown to Tremont Ave. _www.bronxzoo.com_. Nearby there's the 250-acre **NY Botanical Garden** with out-croppings, wetlands, ponds, a cascading waterfall, a 50-acre tract of the original forest that once covered New York City, and 48 gardens and plant collections. The Peggy Rockefeller Rose Garden has 2,700 rose plants with over 260 cultivated varieties _www.nybg.org_. Also in the Bronx is **Edgar Allen Poe's Cottage**, E Kingsbridge Road, Tel (718) 881-8900, his final home, 1846-49. Sat 10am-4pm, Sun 1-5pm. Take #4 or #5 to 138th/Grand Concourse.

STATEN ISLAND At the other end of Manhattan take a pleasant free 5-mile ferry trip to this other NY island, full of parks and historic sites including **Historic Richmond Town**, 441 Clarke Avenue, (718) 351-1611, a restored village area and museum with 27 buildings, some dating to the 1600s and 1800s. Guided tours and demonstrations of daily activities. _www.historicrichmondtown.org_. The monastery-like _Jacques Marchais Museum of Tibetan Art_, est. 1947, has the largest Tibetan art collection outside of Tibet. 338 Lighthouse Avenue (718) 987 3500. Open Wed-Sun 1pm-5pm, $5. *www.tibetanmuseum.com*.

MANHATTAN Manhattan itself is a collection of neighbourhoods, each as distinctive as the next.

Financial District This is the oldest part of the city, a maze of narrow winding canyons that stand where Peter Stuyvesant, Dutch governor, once erected his wall to keep the British colonists out. Hence, Wall Street. The **New York Stock Exchange** is here on Broad St, and the **American Stock Exchange** is on Trinity Place. George Washington was inaugurated first President of the United States at **Federal Hall**, Wall and Nassau Sts, in 1789. From South Ferry and Battery Park you can take the ferries to Staten Island, Ellis Island, and the Statue of Liberty, or start on a bike/walking path that stretches the length of west-side Manhattan. Here is where the 1350-ft twin towers of the **World Trade Center**, once the second tallest buildings in the world, stood until September 2001, now a poignant memorial site.

Battery Park City situated near Battery Park, and the unusual, round **Castle Clinton**, is literally a land-fill. Water was pumped out and the roads dropped to create this waterfront community. The district is a necropolis on Sundays, thus great for cycling or a picnic on the steps of City Hall. The thriving **South Street Seaport** area combines a museum, tall ships, a small shopping mall, and a cluster of seafood restaurants that collectively bear witness to New York's origins as a port.

Chinatown The public telephones are housed in miniature pagodas, and the local grocery shops are great for snow peas or bok choy (Chinese lettuce). Restaurants are good, plentiful and cheap. Chinese New Year is celebrated with the explosion of colour the first full moon of the first lunar month of the year (Jan/Feb). Mott and Canal are the major streets that house restaurants as well as small shops selling 'designer' goods. Be sure to stop by a bakery for unique pastries. There are also now other Chinatowns, in Flushing, Queens, and in Brooklyn, near Bensonhurst at U, and Sunset Park.

Little Italy Just north-west of Chinatown, in the area of Mulberry and Grand Sts, slowly being eclipsed by Chinatown. Good restaurants, bakeries and grocery shops, and a lively place in June with the Festival of St. Anthony, and again in September with the feast of San Gennaro, when you can eat lasagne, zeppoles, and cannolis, and buy large buttons that beckon, 'Kiss me, I'm Italian.' 'Perfect to people watch'

SoHo Formerly a warehouse and trading district, SoHo, the area south of Houston (pronounced HOW-ston) St, is now packed with upscale art studios amazingly alternating with chic uptown establishments such as Chanel, Prada, Eileen Fisher, and Sotheby's, each with limos double-parked back-to-back. Walk down W Broadway on a weekend and you'll find the sidewalks mobbed with visitors sharing the offbeat glitz. Here you'll also find Vosges Haut Chocolat that sells Naga Bars (sweet curry powder, coconut flakes and chocolate), Black Pearl Bars (Japanese ginger, wasabi, sesame seeds, chocolate), and Woolloomooloo Truffles, among other exotic delights.

Tribeca (stands for <u>tri</u>angle <u>be</u>low <u>ca</u>nal), the area between SoHo and Chambers Street, is a haven for up-and-coming artists and musicians. Their artwork, music and theatre fill the old industrial lofts with avant-garde American culture. Chic (yet affordable) restaurants and designer stores are opening all the time, and excellent cheap clothing and electronic stores abound. Tribeca is also home to a wealth of nice restaurants (buy your coffees and brunches here) and, as in SoHo, there are many cast-iron buildings, dating from the turn of the century. Movie star Robert De Niro moved here in 1982 and opened his own film centre and restaurant (TriBeCa Grill). Other celebrity residents include Dan Ackroyd, Bette Midler, Harvey Keitel and Naomi Campbell.

Lower East Side focussed on Orchard and Delancey Streets, has attracted waves of

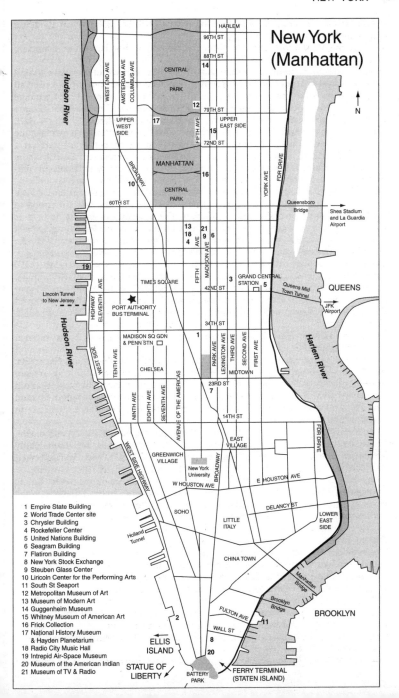

New York (Manhattan)

N

1 Empire State Building
2 World Trade Center site
3 Chrysler Building
4 Rockefeller Center
5 United Nations Building
6 Seagram Building
7 Flatiron Building
8 New York Stock Exchange
9 Steuben Glass Center
10 Lincoln Center for the Performing Arts
11 South St Seaport
12 Metropolitan Museum of Art
13 Museum of Modern Art
14 Guggenheim Museum
15 Whitney Museum of American Art
16 Frick Collection
17 National History Museum & Hayden Planetarium
18 Radio City Music Hall
19 Intrepid Air-Space Museum
20 Museum of the American Indian
21 Museum of TV & Radio

immigrants: Eastern European Jews in the early part of this century, Puerto Ricans and Haitians today. Some older Jews still remain and Sunday is their big market day, a good time to swoop in for bargains. Note that many stores are closed on Saturdays-the Jewish Sabbath. The Lower East Side is slowly growing more fashionable, with poor immigrants being chased out by galleries and restaurants. Visit the **Lower East Side Tenement Museum**, 90 Orchard St at Broome St, 431-0233, to experience immigrant life in this building where, between 1863 and 1935, over 7000 people, from over a score of countries, lived. Mon 11am-5.30pm, Tue-Fri 'til 6pm, Sat-Sun 10:45am-6pm, $13, students w/ID $11. _www.tenement.org_.

The East Village St Mark's Place and 2nd Ave. took the overflow from increasingly pricey Greenwich Village to become the hang-out for struggling avant-garde and iconoclastic artists, writers, and students including W.H. Auden, Lenny Bruce, William Burroughs, William de Kooning, Allen Ginsberg, Emma Goldman, Jimi Hendrix, Abbie Hoffman, Jack Kerouac, Madonna, Charlie Parker, Jackson Pollock, and Andy Warhol. Explore two oases of calm here: Leafy green **Tompkins Sq Park** at E 7th at Ave A with its weekend farmers' market and fountain dedicated to Temperance and Faith; and the **Liz Christy Community Garden** at Bowery & Houston, NYC's charming, arbor-filled original community garden dating to 1973, when Liz Christy and the Green Guerillas planted seeds that would sprout into the more than 700 such gardens in NYC today. (212) 594 2155 _www.greenguerillas.org_. The Bowery, formerly the Dutch Bouwerie, was once famous for its bums (that's American for derelict) but no longer: the E Village is experiencing a quiet, uncrowded renaissance, with bars and cafes pleasantly waiting at every corner, perhaps hang-outs for the cultural style-setters of the 21st century. The same can be said of **Williamsburg**, in Brooklyn, just one stop across the East River on the L train.

Greenwich Village: New York's original bohemian quarter and home of such figures as Edgar Allan Poe, E.E. Cummings, Eugene O'Neill, Dylan Thomas, and Calvin Trillin, the Village has evolved but, fortunately, not too much. Expensive plastic cafes now cater to tourists, but tree-lined 10th, 11th and 12th Sts remain peaceful, faced with brownstones of celebrities and the wealthy. **New York University** (NYU) overlooks the ever-lively and crowded **Washington Square**, with its version of the Arc de Triomphe and statue of Garibaldi. Listen here to casual guitar strumming and classical violin; watch jugglers and magicians; compare strategy with chess players. **Christopher Square** is the focus of New York's large gay community; close by at 15 Christopher St is the **Oscar Wilde Memorial Bookstore**, the oldest gay bookstore (since 1967), and the **Stonewall Pub**, that lent its name to one of the earliest gay street riots. Further towards the river, 120 Christopher is home since 1923 to delectable home-made **Li-Lac Chocolates**, 243-7374. But the little-known, real renaissance in the Village is on the Hudson, with new residential buildings, a 5-mile flower-filled west-side park, north-south bike path, and **Pier 45**, at W 10th St, that amazingly pokes a newly-mown meadow way across the Hudson - a perfect place to sojourn on a sunny afternoon. _www.hudsonriverpark.org_.

Chelsea Between 14th and 30th Sts, Chelsea is a vast, transforming stretch of warehouses and lofts on the West Side, north of the Village. At 14th St and 9th Ave, the once pungent meatpacking district has been transformed into a haven for fashion designers such as Diane von Furstenberg, Stella McCartney, and Alexander McQueen. Planned rezoning of the area between 10th and 11th Aves, W 16th St to W 30th St, will further encourage residential and commercial development, facilitate reuse of the High Line elevated rail line, and enhance the thriving art gallery district. Among the buildings planned is what the NY Times calls a "Ship of Glass," Frank Gehry's 9-story white glass cyberspace design for e-commerce as the **InterActive Corp HQ** (Expedia, Ticketmaster etc), on the West Side Highway near the Chelsea Piers. The crumbling remains of other docks where great transatlantic liners used to embark still line the Hudson; some cruise ships still leave from here(Piers 76, 81, 83 and 86). **The Flower District** remains dug in around 27th /28th St btw 6th and 7th Aves. To forget city grime, stroll along here among the ferns, tropical plants and examples of every imaginable flower in season, then wander to W 28th St, the original **Tin Pan Alley**.

Midtown This neighbourhood has seen some revitalization since the completion of the giant space-age **Jacob K Javits Convention Center.** Further uptown, around Herald Square and 34th St, things are bustling around the large department stores like **Macy's**, as well as inside the nine-storey Herald Center shopping mall. Just a block away in either direction stand the **Empire State Building** and revamped **Madison Square Garden**. The Garden is where sports events, exhibitions and pop concerts happen; beneath it is **Penn Station** where you can catch commuter trains out to Long Island, or Amtrak to Boston, Washington or Chicago. From W 34th St to 40st St around 7th Ave is the **Fabric District** - formerly the Garment District: small stores, big fashion names.

Theatre District The core of the Big Apple. East and West, btwn 42nd & 59th Sts, is the heart of the theatre, cinema, and shopping districts, and was once the centre of NYC's porn industry. Few vestiges of Midtown's former seedier self remain, though, now with new zoning laws, there has been an advanced invasion by Disney and other tamer businesses. **Times Square:** Once home to pimps and prostitutes as well as Broadway theatres; now Broadway and 42nd St is a blazing spectacle of the digital revolution, packed with sightseers gawking at amazing electronic ads and tickers in every direction. Amid a canyon of shiny bottle-green buildings, a huge Cadillac sticks its nose out at would-be consumers. Despite these larger distractions, street vendors seem to do well selling mementos of the experience. Well policed, Times Square doesn't seem dangerous, but be on guard - the action goes on all night. Nice places to cool the feet are the **'pocket parks'** hidden away in Midtown: 57th St E of 5th Ave, and 47th btwn 2nd & 3rd Aves.

Fifth Ave splits midtown down the middle, marking the border between the East side and the West side. **Rockefeller Center**, ablaze at night with its open-air Rink Bar and home to NBC, and **St Patrick's Cathedral** are here, and when Britain decides to pawn the crown jewels, they'll be on sale at **Tiffany's**, corner of 57th and Fifth. The swankiest shops in the city elbow for space along this justifiably famous street – Henry Bendel, Bulgari, Cartier, Bergdorf Goodman, Gucci, FAO Schwarz, Harry Winston...**The Trump Tower**, ritziest building in New York, packs five floors of astonishingly expensive boutiques around a rose marble waterfall and a Starbucks. 'You won't be able to afford anything, but definitely worth a look.' **The New York Public Library** that featured prominently in *The Day After Tomorrow* is at 42nd St. And the brotherhood of mankind fulminates daily in the **United Nations Building** on 44th St, by the East River. **Grand Central Station**, with trains to upstate New York and Connecticut, dominates E 42 St, a community in itself.

The Upper East Side The 60s, 70s and 80s in this area are among the most coveted addresses in New York. The vast **Metropolitan Museum of Art** and the spiralling **Guggenheim** anchor **Museum Mile** along 5th Ave. East 86th St is the heart of **Yorkville**, the German part of town, with beer and Gemutlichkeit on draught. Beginning at 96th St and running north to 145th is **East Harlem**, the largely Puerto Rican section called El Barrio. A sprinkling of Irish and Italian families remain, but Spanish dominates storefront signs.

The Upper West Side The intersection of Columbus and Broadway lies the cultural hub of Manhattan, **Lincoln Center**, which includes the **Metropolitan Opera House** and the **New York State Theatre**. At night it's pretty crowded; by summer's day it's a pleasant place to sit and eat ice cream. Around 72nd St and on Columbus Ave. is a young, semi-posh and lively neighbourhood with plenty of good value restaurants; on Central Park West is the impressive Dakota, the Victorian building where John Lennon lived and died. North on Central Park West is the **Natural History Museum**, and still further, in the Morningside Heights area, is **Columbia University** at Broadway & 116th St.

Harlem The centre of New York's black community stretches from the top end of Central Park to 155th, encompassing everything from fashionable residential rows, especially in the gentrifying southern section, to miserable tenements further north. A historic area, Harlem is over its 'stay out' reputation and attracts many visitors to landmark churches and soul/gospel/jazz venues such as the **Cotton Club** and famous **Apollo Theater** on 125th St, also known as Dr. Martin Luther King Jr Blvd. Former President **Bill Clinton** has his law office in Harlem and the **Magic Johnson Center** has helped revive the 125th St neighbourhood. Down a few blocks, amidst store front churches and elegant brownstones, modern and pleasant Settepani bakery/café is now at 196 Lenox Avenue at 120th St. The **Mount Morris Historic District** (the Marcus Garvey Park was built where 5th Ave stopped) is one of the most architecturally interesting parts of Harlem, with late 19th C buildings and revival in full swing.

One of the best, if expensive, ways to see the district is by guided tour (**Harlem Spirituals**, 757-0425, $45, Wed and Sun, $85 with brunch and show on Sun only *www.harlemspirituals.com* or **Grayline Harlem Gospel Tour**, 397-2600, $45, Sun only. Saturday walking tours are available inc. **Harlem Old and New**, at $25, *www.harlemmtmorris.org* 369-4241. Head for a tour that includes Sunday brunch if possible so you can try tongue-tingling Cajun cuisine and 'soul' food.

ACCOMMODATION

To find cheap accommodation try the classified ads in *The Village Voice* newspaper, which hits the stands Wed am. Shops near Columbia are sometimes good for sublets. Also try the NYU residence halls in the summer months (applications taken in Jan., call 998-4621) or see *www.nyu.edu/summer/housing* for more info).

New York Habitat, 307 7th Ave, Suite 306, New York, NY 10001, 255-8018 was named best sublet service in the city by *New York* Magazine. Finds accommodation in safe areas and according to budget. Fee: less than 30 days 35% of one month's rent, 30 days-3 months, 50%. Call in advance for the best deals. *www.nyhabitat.com*. 'NY Information Center at Penn Station has price info on all hotels in New York. Very useful if you don't want to stay at a hostel.' Single accommodation can be very expensive, but rates for D & T are less, so travel in herds where possible.

Big Apple Hostel, 119 W 45th St (btwn 6th & 7th Ave), 302-2603. $34.50-37.50 dorm, $91.50-96.50 for small private rm. 'Excellent location.'. Rsvs online at *www.bigapple-hostel.com.*

Carlton Arms Hotel, 160 E 25th St (at 3rd Ave), 679-0680. S-$70-85, D-$85-99, T-$110-120 Q-$130-140. Flamboyant artwork makes each room a shrine to downtown New York style. 'Check the room first!' *www.carltonarms.com*.

Chelsea International Hostel, 251 W 20th St, 647-0010. On a leafy street btwn 7th & 8th Aves. Dorm $28, private rooms $70, $10 key deposit. The linen, showers and toilets are clean, as are the single-sex dorms. Will lock-up bags until 12pm. Great location. 'We made some great international friends here.' 'Good self-catering facilities.' 'Rooms cramped and hot.' 'Be there by 1.30pm.' *www.chelseahostel.com*.

Chelsea Center, 313 W 29th St, 643-0214, $33 dorm style, bfast inc. Kitchen, showers. $5 key deposit. German, French & Spanish spoken. Check-in 8.30am-11pm. no curfew, rsvs required. 'Very cramped.' 'Safe, friendly, personal atmosphere.' Coed and women-only dorms. Annex on E 12 St in the East Village, call for information. *www.chelseacenterhostel.com*.

Chelsea Lodge, 318 W 20th St, btwn 8th & 9th Aves, 243-4499/(800) 373-1116. Small, clean, comfortable and friendly hotel conveniently located in the Chelsea district. S-$95, D-$110. *www.chelsealodge.com*.

Chelsea Star Hotel, 300 W 30th St at 8th Ave, (877) 827-NYNY/244-STAR. Dorms $30, S-$85, D-$99, T-$119, Q-$129. *www.chelseastar.com*.

Gershwin Hotel, 7 E 27th St, 545-8000. Mixed dorms $40, private room w/bath $99. Female-only dorms of nicer quality $45. Sundeck. Near Empire State Building. Check-in 3pm, Check-out 11am. 'Basic, but clean and good security.' 'Nice, friendly staff.' 'Slow check in and out.' *www.gershwinhotel.com*.

Habitat Hotel, 130 E 57th St, btwn Park and Lexington Aves, 753-8841. Excellent location, S-$75-95 depending on size and private bathrooms. 'Stylish modern hotel.' *www.habitatnewyork.com*.

International AYH-Hostel, 891 Amsterdam Ave, and 103rd, 932-2300. Take #1 or #9 subway to 103rd St and walk 1 block east. Largest hostel in the USA. Kitchen, garden, daily activities. 24 hrs, HI member. Dorms $29-$35 depending on number of beds in dorm. Rsvs rec. *www.hinewyork.org*.

International Student Center, 38 W 88th St, 787-7706. $30 dorm-style. Kitchen, linen provided. Foreigners aged 18-30 only. Check-in 10.30am, 7 nights max stay. 'Good safe area but dirty rooms.' *www.nystudentcenter.org*.

Jazz on the Park Hostel, 36 W 106 St, 932-1600. Dorm $27 and up, private room $75 inc. tax. Inc. light bfast. Social activities. 'Relatively new hostel'; 'very cramped rooms'; 'disorganised staff'. Mixed reports. *www.jazzonthepark.com*. Also has new second location, **Jazz on the Town**, at 307 E 14 St, 228-2780.

Madison Hotel, 62 Madison Ave, 532-7373. S-$94 D-$104, Q-$119. Call for special deals. Check-in after mid-day & before 11pm 'Good location, security and helpful staff.' *www.madison-hotel.com*.

Sugar Hill International Hostel, 722 St. Nicholas Ave., 926-7030. Run by author of the *Hostel Handbook* (see background USA section) keen to pass on knowledge of hostelling and NYC. Clean, spacious dorms $20-25. Private rooms $30 pp.'Very friendly staff, safe hostel (opposite 145th St subway stop),' for those who don't mind being uptown in Harlem. Check in 9am-10pm, 24 hr access. Lock-up, kitchen, and free internet access avail. Take A, B, C, or D train to 145th St. Rsvs required 7 days in advance. *www.sugarhillhostel.com*.

Seafarers & International House, 123 E 15th St, 677-4800, *www.sihnyc.org*, S-$75, D-$95 shared bath.

YMCA-Greenpoint (Brooklyn), 99 Meserole Ave. at Lorimer., (718) 389-3700. S-$43-58 D-$70, weekly rate- $350. Rooms inc use of pool and sauna. 10 min walk south on Lorimer and then Bedford Avenues and a 5 minute subway ride on the L train from the Bedford Ave. station will put you in the heart of Greenwich Village. *www.ymcanyc.org*.

YMCA-Vanderbilt, 224 E 47th St, 756-9600. Co-ed. S/D=$85 with shared bath. Three week advance rsvs required. Gym, pool. 'Great location-15 mins from Empire State & Times Square'. *www.ymcanyc.org*.

YMCA-West Side, 5 W 63rd St, 875-4282/4206. Co-ed. S or D$72-89 with shared bath. Check-in 2.30pm. Pool, cafe, gym, sauna, steam room, TV, AC. One week advance rsvs nec. 'Brilliant place.'

FOOD

A spirit of adventure will keep you well-fed in Manhattan. With thousands of multi-ethnic eateries serving everything from bagels to Bratwurst, borscht to baklava, do not resist the temptation to try it all! Food can be expensive but for a budget alternative, the all-American diner will provide endless coffee and pancakes drenched in maple syrup. Go to *www.menupages.com* for over 4,500 menus in the city, by location, neighbourhood, and cuisine, and 'hot menus.' Below you'll find some tried-and-true favourites as well as neighbourhood places.

For cheap, spicy **Indian food**, visit Madison Ave around 27th St, also E Sixth St btwn 1st & 2nd Aves and other nearby streets. The number of hole-in-the-wall restaurants here has exploded recently. Dinner for $6 isn't a fantasy.

HARLEM There are a few interesting eateries here, in general along Malcolm X Blvd (formerly Lenox Ave) btwn 116th & 126th Streets. **Bayou**, 308 Malcolm X Blvd, is a Creole restaurant patronized by Bill Clinton. **Native**, 161 Malcolm X Blvd & 118th St, is a fusion bistro-French-Moroccan-Caribbean restaurant. **Settepani Bakery**, 196 Lenox Ave at 120th St, (917) 492-4806, offers excellent coffee in huge cups, outdoor seating, alfresco dining, appetizers and light fare from bresaola to quiche $4.50-$9.50.

QUEENS is packed with ethnic restaurants, if you care to explore it - Greek, Turkish, Chinese, Romanian, etc., most easily accessible on the subway. The **New Post Coffee Shop** at 40-01 Queens Boulevard (718) 784-8980, serves great value diner-style breakfasts of all kinds, including eggs with Irish bacon and huevos rancheros, plus all day Mexican - a true NYC experience.

UPPER WEST SIDE, btwn 60th & 90th Sts and beyond has an endless succession of trendy restaurants. **Monks** in Seinfeld, aka **Tom's Restaurant**, is at 2880 Broadway at 112th street, 864-6137. Try **Victor's Cafe**, 236 W 52nd, 586-7714 for Cuban food. $16-33. **Metro Diner**, 2641 Broadway, 866-0800, for that first time visit to an all American diner, and just a short walk from the AYH hostel on Amsterdam Ave . **EJ's Luncheonette**, 447 Amsterdam at 81st, 873-3444, serves bargain burgers and breakfasts all day, including Buttermilk Belgian Waffles. Next door is a little pricier **Louie's Westside Café**, 441 Amsterdam, 877-1900, named after the last line in Casablanca, that has exquisite corned beef hash. **Hungarian Pastry Shop**, 1030 Amsterdam (btw 110 & 111th Sts), 866-4230 has selection of pastries and cookies-somewhere to read and relax. Also try next door, **P&W Sandwich Shop**, 1030 Amsterdam Ave. (110 & 111th St) 222-2245, for lunch. **Big Nick's**, 2175 77th and Broadway, 362-9238. Hamburgers, Greek food and pizza. Open 23 hrs, dinner from about $5; 'the best'. **Mughlai** at 320 Columbus Ave 724-6363 has excellent Indian cuisine at reasonable prices. **H&H Bagels**, 2239 Broadway, W 80th St, 595-8000, and also on the E Side at 1551 Second Ave. Traditional American bagels. Great bargain snacks to hold off mid-sightseeing starvation. Unadulterated plain or cinnamon raisin are best, 90¢ each. 24 hrs. **West End**, 2911 Broadway, btwn 113th & 114th Sts, 662-8830. Bar/restaurant popular with CU students. Dishes $6-10. Jazz brunch Sat & Sun. *www.thewestendnyc.com* . Daily 11am-4am.

UPPER EAST SIDE: Patsy's Pizzeria, 2287-91 First Ave. at 118th St, 534-9783. A branch of the famous Sinatra haunt, just as tasty and much cheaper (pizzas from $12.50). 'Does deliveries to the Yankees!' Open 11am-12pm.

UPPER MIDTOWN: Despite the moneyed aura of Midtown 5th Ave, this area tucks away plenty of small coffee shops and places with good value meals. The **Great American Health Bar**, 35 W 57th, 355-5177, has huge salads, sandwiches, and entrees, $6.45-$9.95. **Wolf's Deli** at 41 W 57th, 888-4100, has almost every kind of sandwich you can imagine and great breakfasts, starting at $6.95, such as 2 eggs, corned beef hash, with hash browns, juice, bread, and coffee, all for $7.70, enough to last you all day. **Carnegie Deli**, 7th Ave at 55th, 757-2245, has sandwiches large enough for two, from $11.95, all beef franks $5.50, and other Jewish specialities. Featured in Woody Allen's *Broadway Danny Rose*. The corned beef and pastrami are rated no.1 in the country. Also staggering cheesecake. *www.carnegiedeli.com*. **La Bonne Soupe** at 48 W 55th St, 586-7650, is French for "the good life, with health, wealth and happiness." *www.labonnesoupe.com*. The **Westway Diner** at 614 9th Ave btw 43rd and 44th west of Times Sq, 582-7661, is where Larry David and Jerry Seinfeld thought up the show about nothing.

CHINATOWN is a haven for good, inexpensive Chinese cooking. Walk along Mott, Bayard & Pell Sts, look for the restaurant where the most Chinese people are eating. Among Chinatown's edible delights suggested by the *New York Times* are **New Big Wong**, 67 Mott, 964-0540; **Chanoodle**, 79 Mulberry, 349-1495; **Congee**, 98 Bowery, 965-5028; and **Congee Village**, 100 Allen, 941-1818.

LITTLE ITALY, to the north of Chinatown, between Bowery and Broadway, has a number of good Italian restaurants, cafes and groceries. Mulberry & Lafayette Sts, south of Houston, are especially fertile territory. But Italian restaurants and cafes are almost everywhere in Manhattan these days, many of them invitingly spilling tables into the open air, tempting us with a glass of chianti or an expresso.

SOHO, south of Houston to Canal, has many interesting, though pricey Italian and French restaurants squeezed between galleries and fashion houses on Church St, W Broadway et al. For great taste and value try **Tennessee Mountain**, 143 Spring, 431-3993, which has a delicious beef chili ($6.95), pulled-pork barbeque platter ($12.95), slow-cooked pork ribs, etc., all prepared almost under your nose. (Other BBQ places to try in NYC, some using pure wood smoke: **Blue Smoke**, 116 East 27th Street, **Daisy May's BBQ USA** on 11th Ave, **Dallas BBQ** near NYU, **Pearson's Texas BBQ** on E 81st St; and **Virgil's** in Times Sq.).

The **EAST VILLAGE** is a world of fascinating and affordable polyglot bistros and cafes. **The Bowery Poetry Club Café and Bar** at 308 Bowery btw Bleecker & Houston, 614-0505, serves daily poetry, movies, and zany entertainment. Then sit out at **Cremcaffé**, 65 2nd Ave btw 3rd and 4th Sts, 674-5255 - Italian wine and coffee, pollo, ravioli, pizze, crostini, a pleasant oasis on weekends. **Elvie's**, 214 1st Ave at 13th, 473-7785, offers authentic Philippine cuisine from adobong manok o baboy to tinolang. **Mama's**, 200 E 3rd St, 777-4425, has home-cooked delights. **Miracle Grill**, 112 1st Ave (btw 6th&7th), 254-2353, offers bargain Cajun brunch at w/ends ($10/11 avg). **Odessa** 119 Ave A, 253-1482, home-cooked burgers, blintzes, kielbasa, piroghies, etc $3.25- 8.00. **Salt & Battery** 80 2nd Ave, 254-6610, is voted NYC's best fish and chip shop by NY Magazine. **SideWalk**, 94 Ave A at 6th, 253-8080 serves wraps, quesadillas, salads, pasta $4.95-7.95. **Two Boots**, 42 Ave A, 254-1919, has Cajun pizza. **Veselka**, 144 2nd Ave at 10th, 228-9682, is a 24 hr Ukrainian café, best Borscht in the city. **Le Zoccole Osteria** 95 Ave A at 6th, 260-6660, offers antipasti, insalate, paste, secondi piatti, and dolci $5.75-14.95. Along St Mark's Place are **Yaffa Café**, at #97, 677-9001, for 24 hr kitsch; **St Dymphna's** at #118, 254-6636, Irish/American pub food 10.30am-4am daily, and just north, is **Ess-A-Bagel**, 359 First Ave. at 21st St, 260-2252. Arguably the best bagel in the city, which means the best around, life preserver sized, it will keep you occupied for a while.

GREENWICH VILLAGE is full of pleasant restaurants and bars, but first visit **Chumley's** at 108 Bedford, otherwise unmarked, the only NYC speakeasy still in existence, est 1922, haunt of writers such as Cummings, Dos Passos, Lillian Hellman, Hemingway, Scott Fitzgerald, and Sinclair. Another literary landmark is the **White Horse Tavern**, 567 Hudson at 11th, 243-9260, dating to 1880, where Dylan Thomas died of drink, serves brunch, burgers, cottage pie, etc., for $4.75-$6.50. **Pepe Verde**, 559 Hudson at 11th, 255-2221, panini, insalate, antipasti, paste, bibite, $5.95-9.95, "No diet coke, no skim milk, no decaf coffee, only good food." Next door at 557 Hudson is **Da Andrea,** also ristorante italiano, 367-1979, $7-$18.50. Also at 11th and Hudson is **Ma Ma Buddha**, 929-7800, Chinese everything inc special diet and health menu, $1.75-12.95. **Tea and Sympathy**, 108 Greenwich Ave, 807-8329, satisfies English food cravings. Entrees $10-15. The best Spanish food in NYC is at the **Sevilla**, 62 Charles St, 929-3189, for over 60 years, (not far from the contrary intersection of W 10th and W 4th) _www.sevillarestaurantandbar.com_.

BETWEEN E & W VILLAGE Dallas BBQ, 21 University Place, 674-4450. Friendly, spacious student favourite, right across from NYU. Mobbed in the evenings. 'Great early bird specials.' $12.50 till 6.30pm exc. Sat. Filling bowl of home-made chili with corn-bread, $4. Veggie options. **El Cantinero**, 86 University Place, 255-9378. Authentic Mexican food. Fajitas a speciality. Entrees $6.50-10.95. Large garden. Has happy hour. Mon nights all-you-can-eat fixed price.

LOWER EAST SIDE: Katz's Delicatessen, 205 E Houston at Ludlow, 254-2246. NY institution since 1888, a noisy nosh hall filled with pix of famous customers, including President Clinton. At the long counter, sample the meat before deciding on which amazing sandwich (about $11.75). Mouth-watering chopped liver w/ onion on rye $8.45, pastrami on rye $10.95, each delicious and large enough for two. Katz's special potato pancakes, latkes, $6.75 with apple sauce or sour cream on the side. Draft, pitcher, and bottled beers. Open 8am till 10pm. **Russ & Daughters**, 179 E Houston, 475-4880, since 1914, the place in NYC for smoked fish – gaspe and nova salmon, whitefish, tuna, mackerel, roe, sable, herring fillets – in wine sauce and onions, mustard and dill, etc. A treat for picnics. *www.russanddaughters.com* For the dedicated, "It takes a Downtown knish to satisfy an Uptown craving" at **Yonah Schimmels's**, since 1910 at 137 E Houston, 477-2858, savory knishes $2, sweet cheese knishes, $2.50, blintzes $3. **Famous Ray's Pizza**, 319 6th Ave, 645-8404, and 11th St & 6th Ave, 243-2253. 'This is the best.' Regular cheese slice $2, large pie $13.50.

Smoking in Bars & Restaurants: Although New York banned smoking in most bars and restaurants in 2003, places where smoking in NYC is still possible include 'cigar bars' such as **Campbell Apartment** in **Grand Central Terminal**; **Circa Tabac**, 32 Watts Street; **Karma** at 51st Ave between 3rd and 4th Ave; **Lexington Bar and Books**, 1020 Lexington Ave between 72nd & 73rd; **Mezzo Mezzo** at 31-29 Ditmars Blvs; **Nat Sherman**, 500 5th Ave at 42nd Street; and the **Piano Bar at Jilly's**, 41 West 58th Street. Bars in NYC that allot part of their outdoor patios as smoking areas include: Aubette, 119 East 27th Street; **Bohemian Hall and Park**, 19-29 24th Ave, Astoria; **Cherry**, 120 East 39th Street; **Oscar Wilde**, 221 East 58th Street; **Porch**, 115 Avenue C (between 7th and 8th Street); and **Whiskey Blue**, 541 Lexington. Other restaurants have established separate sections for smokers, including: Bar None, 98 3rd Avenue; F. **Ille Ponte Ristorante**, 39 Desbrosses St at West Street; **Half King**, 505 West 23rd Street; **Heartland Brewery**, 244 East 51st Street; Les Halles 35 Union Square West; **Liquids**, 266 East 10th Street; and **Nublu**, 62 Avenue C.

OF INTEREST

There is so much to do and see in Manhattan alone and the atmosphere of this sprawling movie set will captivate, if not awe you.

Cathedral of St John the Divine, 1047 Amsterdam Ave & 112th St, 316-7540. The largest Gothic cathedral in the world, with an awe-inspiring vaulted roof that sweeps up as high as a 12-storey building. Otherwise known as St John the Unfinished. Work began in 1892, but was suspended in 1941 when America entered the war. Enthusiasm waned, funds dried up and Americans forgot how to build Gothic cathedrals. Recently work has begun again in a small way. 'Go and watch an angel being carved out of stone before your very eyes.' Tours Tue-Sat, 11am; Sun, 1pm, suggested donation $2, tour $3. Vertical tour to top of cathedral has been suspended due to fire. Check website for latest info. 'Weird, wonderful, memorable.' Also, don't miss the Peace Park and its amazing fountain right next door. *www.stjohndivine.org*.

Chrysler Building, 405 Lexington & 42nd St, 682-3070. An evocative landmark of the NYC night skyline, the famous Chrysler spire sits atop a building which typifies the art deco style inside and out. Built as a tribute to the great American automobile in the 1920s, some of its gargoyles are radiator grills. At 77 storeys, (1045 ft), it was the world's tallest building for one year until the Empire State Building snatched the record in 1931. No tours, although visible from the Empire State Building.

Chelsea Hotel, 222 W 23rd St, 243-3700. A hotel since 1905, and a haven for artists, writers and other fringe elements in NYC. Its history was transcribed in Nicole Burdette's play, Chelsea Walls. Expensive rates ($175-$485) now mean it's better just to look at the landmark where Thomas Wolfe, Dylan Thomas, Bob Dylan, and Jimmy Hendrix stayed amongst many others. *www.chelseahotel.com.*

Coney Island, (718) 372-0275, where generations of New Yorkers met, played, fell in love and screamed on the Cyclone roller-coaster (rides paid for individually in **Astroland**). The beach is crowded on w/ends and a bit dirty. *www.astroland.com* While here visit the **NY Aquarium**, (718) 265-3400/265-FISH. Daily 10am-6pm, last tkt 5pm, $11. See penguins, walrus, sea lions, sharks and Beluga whales. 'Fantastic.' Take F or D subway to W 8th St exit. Coney Island is directly opposite, a pedestrian bridge which leads to the Aquarium. While there, take the boardwalk to the amazing **Brighton Beach** where the Russians have really landed. *www.nyaquarium.com.*

Empire State Building, 5th Ave & 34th St, 736-3100; the tallest building in NYC. The view, night and day, is fantastic, but try the outdoor deck to really get the adrenaline buzzing. 'Go up at night, unforgettable views and less crowded.' Daily 9am-12midnight, last elevator to observation deck at 11.15pm $15. *www.esbnyc.com.*

Flatiron Building, 175 5th Ave & Broadway. The ornate wedge shaped building, built in 1901 was one of the first iron-framed buildings. Standing at 285 ft, it was the world's tallest building for 10 years. No tours.

Grand Central Station, 42nd St & Park Ave. Opened in 1913, it soon became a star of many movies. Take a look at the famously beautiful zodiac ceiling which depicts a Mediterranean winter sky with 2500 stars. Said to be backwards, it is actually seen from a point of view outside our solar system. Free tours avail. from Info booth on Grand Concourse, Wed 12.30pm, call 935-3960 for more info. Self-guided walking tours also available. *www.grandcentralterminal.com*.

Lincoln Center for the Performing Arts, Columbus Ave & 62nd-65th Sts, 875-5350. The first performing arts center of its kind in America, and the largest in the world, containing opera house, concert hall, theatre, exhibits and Juilliard School. 1 hr tour $12.50, $9 w/student ID, 10am-4.30pm. Schedule changes weekly so call for resv. *www.lincolncenter.org*. **The Metropolitan Opera House**, 769-7020 has its own 90 min backstage tours, Oct-June only, 3.30pm weekdays, Sun 10.30am, $10. Look for free concerts and other events early during the summer. *www.metoperafamily.org*.

NBC Television Studio Tours, 30 Rockefeller Plaza, on 49th St, btwn 5th & 6th Ave, 664-7174. Home to the famous *Saturday Night Live* show, tours last 1 hr 10. Daily, 9am-4.30pm, every 15 minutes, $10. First come, first served at tour desk, 49th St entrance. 'Fantastic, definitely the best tour I went on.'

New York Stock Exchange, 11 Wall St, 656-3000. Observation Gallery and Visitors Center have been closed indefinitely.

Radio City Music Hall, 1260 Ave of the Americas (6th at 50th St), 247-4777. Renovated art deco showtime palace, created by 30's impresario 'Roxy' Rothafel. Home to the world's largest movie sunset-inspired theatres, some two-ton chandeliers and 70 years of showbiz history. 1 hr tours every half hour, Mon-Sun 11am-3pm, $17. See the Great Stage and meet a Rockette. *www.radiocity.com*.

South Street Seaport, 748-8600. Historic waterfront district, just off Wall St, restored as it was 200 years ago. Now featuring a museum, and shopping mall with cheap fast-food outlets. Includes a craft centre and 19th century printing store. Several different tours and cruises offered daily. Summer hours, daily 10am-6pm. *www.southstseaport.com.*

Staten Island Ferry, (718) 815-2628/718-330-1234. Nobody should miss what is certainly the best travel bargain to be found anywhere. It's free!! Frequent departures from South Ferry at Battery Park, the tip of Manhattan. Passes close to the Statue of Liberty. Superb view of the Manhattan skyline, many people's favourite view of New York. 'Take the ferry at night for amazing views.' Operates 24 hrs daily. *www.siferry.com.*

Statue of Liberty National Monument on **Liberty Island**. Ferry info: 866-STATUE4. Take Circle Line ferry ($11.50 r/t) from Battery Park, goes via Ellis

Island. Daily every 1/2 hr. Reserve tix online at *www.statuereservations.com.* in advance to avoid queue. Security check prior to boarding. Consider going via NJ, from Liberty State Park - 75% of visitors leave from Manhattan. Great view of downtown and mushrooming New Jersey skyscrapers. Audio tour also available, $6. *www.nps.gov/stli/ www.circlelinedowntown.com.*

United Nations Building, 1st Ave & 46th St, 963-8687. 45-60 min tours every 20-30 min, 9.30am-4.45pm weekdays, Sat & Sun 10am-4.30pm $11.50, $7.50 w/student ID. *www.un.org/tours*

Woodlawn Cemetery, (718) 920-0500, the last stop on the subway (#2, 5 or 4) in the Bronx. The last stop for much of New York's high society, too. 400 landscaped acres of opulent mausolea and monuments to men who started from nothing and worked their way to a spot of turf at Woodlawn. Cast includes Westinghouse, Bat Masterson (associate of Wyatt Earp), Fiorello La Guardia, FW Woolworth, JC Penney, and A Bulova, the watch tycoon.

World Financial Center, Battery Park City, Hudson River & West St. Particularly relaxing (and free!) on a hot day is the **Winter Garden**, one of the most beautiful indoor spaces around, and a popular venue for free performances and recitals. Tall, elegant palm trees and AC, a superb view of the harbour and a flowing monumental staircase. Info: 945-0505. *www.worldfinancialcenter.com*.

World Trade Center Site - 'Ground Zero', Church, Vesey, West and Liberty Sts. Visitors view this enormous, poignant site from galleries between historical photos. Architect Daniel Libeskind has designed the controversial redevelopment of the 9/11 site. Spanish artist Santiago Calatrava has designed the new transit hub. *www.september11news.com* provides archived stories from news media.

MUSEUMS & ART GALLERIES

American Museum of Natural History, Central Pk W btwn 79th & 81st Sts, 769-5000. Vast natural history collection from all continents and seas. Especially strong on Africa and North America. Meet Tyrannosaurus Rex and Velociraptor in the newly renovated dinosaur halls. Daily 10am-5.45pm. Entry by donation, suggested $13, $10 w/student ID. In the same complex is the new **Hayden Planetarium**, a 50-foot blue sphere encased in the glass cube-structure of the **Rose Center for Earth and Space**, with new exhibits about meteorology and cosmology. Planetarium shows are $22, $16.50 w/student ID but that fee includes the rest of the museum. *www.amnh.org*.

The Brooklyn Museum of Art, 200 Eastern Parkway at Washington Ave (in Brooklyn, nr Prospect Park), (718) 638-5000. The museum specializes in ancient Egyptian and African art and was the first American museum to display African craftwork as art. The permanent collection includes one of the best American collections of work by Rodin as well as several by Winslow Homer and John Singer Sargent. Notoriety in the past few years has been the result of temporary collections of avant-garde work inc. two parts of a perfectly bisected pig floating in tanks of formaldehyde and images of the Virgin Mary that caused former Mayor Giuliani to threaten to withdraw funding. This publicity only served to increase attendance! Open Wed-Fri 10am-5pm, Sat-Sun 11am-6pm, first Sat of each month until 11pm except Sept. Suggested donations $8, $4 w/student ID. *www.brooklynmuseum.org.*

The Cloisters, Fort Tryon Park, off Henry Hudson Pkwy, call 923-3700 for bus and subway info. A branch of the Metropolitan Museum of Art devoted to medieval European art and architecture. On top of a hill overlooking the Hudson, the structure incorporates 5 different monasteries from the south of France built in the 11th and 12th centuries, brought across the Atlantic, and reassembled by the patronage of George Barnard and John D. Rockefeller Jr. It shelters magnificent medieval sculptures and the famed Unicorn Tapestries. Mar-Oct, Tue-Sun 9.30am-5.15pm; otherwise closes at 4.45pm. $15, $7 w/student ID (includes same-day admittance to Metropolitan Museum of Art). *www.metmuseum.org*.

Ellis Island Immigration Museum, via ferry from either Battery Park in lower Manhattan or Liberty State Park in NJ, via **Statue of Liberty**, r/t tickets $11.50. Open-decked boats every half-hour; lines for security check move relatively quickly. Best at 8.30am to avoid crowds. Admission free. Museum, of enormous significance for many Americans, tells poignant story of the 12 million immigrants who entered America via Ellis Island between 1892 and 1954 in 3 floors of self guided exhibits and audio/visual displays detailing the history of this processing station, including the 11-second medicals. 'Highly recommended.' An old Italian story quoted reads: "Well, I came to America because I heard the streets were paved with gold. When I got here, I found out three things: first, the streets weren't paved with gold; second, they weren't paved at all; and third, I was expected to pave them." A *Word Tree* highlights origins of ethnic Americanisms. Allow 3 hours. Audio tour narrated by Tom Brokaw is recommended, $6. 45 min. ranger-led tour free. (212) 363-3200. Open daily 9:30am-5pm. *www.ellisisland.com*, *www.nps.gov/elis/*
The Frick Collection, 1 E 70th St at 5th Ave, 288-0700. Walk into what was once Henry Frick's home, and there is a peaceful hush in the small courtyard. Walk round the rooms and see works by Titian, Velazquez, Whistler and a searing Rembrandt self-portrait; plus wonderful furniture and interiors. A small delight. Tue-Sat 10am-6pm, Fri till 9pm, Sun 1pm-6pm. $12, $5 w/student ID. 'Unsuspected highlight of New York.' *www.frick.org.*
Governors Island National Monument Ranger lead tours, 1.5 hours, free. They highlight two early 19th C fortifications. Star-shaped Fort Jay (1806-1809) is one of the best preserved and largest of its type in the US. Castle Williams (1807-1811) is a massive three-tier, 200-ft diameter masonry fort with 8-ft sandstone walls, unique casemated tiers, and 102 guns that made it a formidable seacoast defense. With its sister, Castle Clinton, the fort proved an effective deterrent to British forces attacking New York in the War of 1812. Tours Tue-Sat, 10am and 1pm, Free. Advance purchase required except on Sat. Info and tickets available from *www.nywatertaxi.com*. To register, call 514-8296. Access via 7-min ferry from Battery Maritime Building, Ferry Slip 7, in Lower Manhattan. *www.nps.gov/gois*
Solomon R. Guggenheim Museum, 1071 5th Ave at 89th St, 423-3500. After restoration the fantastic building is finally as architect Frank Lloyd Wright wished it. A spiral curls down taking you past exhibitions, contemporary and 20th Century art collections. Sat-Wed 10am-5.45pm, Fri till 8pm, $15, $10 w/student ID, *www.guggenheim.org.*
International Center of Photography, 1133 Avenue of the Americas at 43rd St, 857-0000. A prominent forum for up and coming photographers, a smaller collection allows space for rotating exhibitions - call for the current ones. Open Tue-Thu 10am-6pm, Fri 10am-8pm and Sat-Sun 10am-6pm, $10, $7 w/student ID. *www.icp.org.*
Intrepid Sea-Air-Space Museum, W 46th St & 12th Ave, Pier 86, 245-2533. Restored aircraft carrier with planes, replica submarine and space exhibit. Mon-Fri 10am-5pm (last admit 4pm), Sat-Sun 10am-6pm (last admit 5pm), $16.50, $12.50 w/student ID. *www.intrepidmuseum.org.*
Metropolitan Museum of Art, Central Park, 5th Ave & 82nd St, 879-5500. One of the world's greatest collections and the largest of its kind in the Western Hemisphere. There are over 2 million works tracing the evolution of art from pre-history to the present day, inc. the largest Egyptian art collection outside Cairo with 36,000 objects, including one of the original versions of the Book of the Dead and the actual *Temple of Dendur*. The Impressionist galleries are filled with Cezannes, Van Goghs, Bonnards, Matisses, etc. Particularly restful on a blistering summer's day is the Astor Court, modeled on a Ming scholar's retreat. Stone, flora and a miniature waterfall are arranged in a yin and yang relationship, installed by 27 Chinese craftsmen in 1980. 'Be prepared to be overwhelmed, mesmerised and

utterly amazed by how much there is here... allow plenty of time.' Tue, Wed, Thu, Sun 9.30am-5.30pm, Fri-Sat 9.30am-9pm, closed Mon. Suggested donation, $15, $7 w/student ID. *www.metmuseum.org.*

Museum of Modern Art, 11 W 53rd St, 708-9400. Newly renovated and expanded, this is the place to see Picasso, Monet, and just about any other modern painter you care to think of, plus superb photography. Open Sat-Thu 10am-5.30pm, Fri 'til 8pm, closed Tue & Wed; $20, $12 w/student ID, pay what you can Fri after 4pm. *www.moma.org.*

Museum of the American Indian, Smithsonian Institution, Alexander Hamilton US Customs House, 1 Bowling Green, nr Battery Park, 514-3700. One of the finest collections of native American artefacts in the world. Forerunner to the Museum of the American Indian now open on the Mall in Washington DC. Daily 10am-5pm, Thu 'til 8pm, free. 'A treasure house.' *www.nmai.si.edu*

Museum of TV and Radio, 25 W 52 St, btwn 5th & 6th Aves, 621-6800. The computer library here holds over 120,000 TV and radio programs, commercials for listening and viewing. Popular. Also special exhibits and screenings. Tue-Sun noon-6pm, Thu 'til 8pm. $10, $8 w/student ID. *www.mtr.org.*

Museum of the City of New York, 1220 5th Ave at 103rd St, 534-1672. Fascinating story of city's growth from a small Dutch community. Free, although donations suggested, $7, $5 w/student ID. Wed-Sun 10am-5pm, *www.mcny.org.*

Whitney Museum of American Art, 945 Madison Ave, at 75th St, 1(800)-WHITNEY for info, 1(877)-WHITNEY for tkts. Devoted exclusively to 20th-century American art. Wed-Thu 11am-6pm, Fri 1pm-9pm, 6-9pm pay what you can, Sat-Sun 11am-6pm; $12, $9.50 w/student ID. *www.whitney.org.*

Williamsburg Art and Historical Center, 135 Broadway (Brooklyn), (718) 486-7372. The organizational center of the blossoming art community in Williamsburg, a neigbourhood that was most recently warehouses and slums. Has rotating shows and theatricals ($3-10) in its 1867 gallery during the season (Fall-Spring) and has information all year round about smaller galleries in the area. Sat-Sun 12pm-6pm. Free. *www.wahcenter.org.*

TOURS

Tours really worth taking include the boat trips around Manhattan and the guided bus/foot tours of Harlem. Other than these, one of the best and cheapest ways to explore New York is on foot.

Circle Line, 809-0808. Zephyr Harbor Cruise-1 hr cruise up the Hudson and East Rivers, departs from South St Seaport daily, noon-7.30pm; Battery Park Harbor Cruise sails the lower Hudson and E Rivers,1.5 hours, $25; and *The Shark* speed boat gives 30 min thrill rides, $16, departs South St Seaport. 'Can get chilly.' 'Great value.' 'Breathtaking at night.' *www.circlelinedowntown.com*

Grayline Tours, 49 W45th St, 397-2600. Offers many different tours (including Harlem and Manhattan) daily. Depart from Number 1 Times Sq. See leaflets in hotel lobbies and tourist centres. The Grayline tours are probably not worth taking unless you're only in New York for a brief time-a 'hop on and off' tour starts at 9am. *www.coachusa.com/newyorksightseeing*. Grayline operates sightseeing aboard open-decked double-decker buses, half-day Downtown Loop or Uptown Loop $37, combination of four Loops $49 for 2 days. May-Oct daily 8.30am-5.30 pm, later hours in summer.

Harlem Your Way, 690-1687. Bus and walking tours of gospel churches and jazz venues, from $39. *www.harlemyourwaytours.com.*

Big Apple Greeter, 669-8159. Let a Big Apple Greeter volunteer welcome you to New York City! This is a free service where NYC residents volunteer their time to take you to places of interest and neighbourhoods that you would like to visit. Call 669-8159 or visit *www.bigapplegreeter.org* for rsvs.

ENTERTAINMENT

No other American city can offer such a variety of amusements. Entertainment, however, can be expensive for the stranger who does not know her or his way around. Broadway theatres, most night clubs and some cinemas will put a strain on modest budgets. At the same time, free entertainment abounds. Read the entertainment sections of the *New York Times,, New Yorker, Village Voice, Where Magazine, Seven Days, New York Magazine* for complete details of shows, jazz and cinemas. **NYC & Company** (formerly **New York Convention and Visitors Bureau**), 810 7th Ave at 53rd St, Times Square, 484-1200/1222, *www.nycvisit.com* provides excellent information regarding shows, events, and entertainment, and you can book through them too. There are free orchestral, pop, operatic concerts, dance groups, and theatrical performances in Central Park throughout the summer. Try to arrive at least 2 hrs before the performance to stake your claim. Also, look out for local street festivals.

Greenwich Village, SoHo, TriBeCa, East Village, and 'Alphabet City' are some of the most interesting entertainment areas. Good jazz and folk music, as well as eating places, can still be found among the many tourist traps in the Village. Go to the better places, even if there is an admission charge; you will find the best music. Beware of places that do not advertise an admission or cover charge but extract large sums for a required drink and offer inferior entertainment.

Jazz Check the *Village Voice, New York Magazine* and *Jazz Interactions* news sheet for all the gigs, or *www.gothamjazz.com*. Jazz remains one of New York City's biggest sounds and the action takes place all over town.

Apollo Theatre, 253 W 125th St, 531-5300, Box Office 531-5305, subway 125th St on 8th Ave line. Historic 1930s jazz cabaret and theatre that featured Duke Ellington, Louis Armstrong, and Ella Fitzgerald in its time. Now has shows from $37. Try the famous Wednesday Amateur nights, 7.30 pm, which gave so many their big break, for $18-$24. Book ahead at Ticketmaster, 307-7171. *Showtime at the Apollo* is televised here, admission free on Sunday mornings. Look for some of the biggest names in contemporary music. Be careful in Harlem at night.

Cajun, 129 8th Ave at 16th St, 691-6174. Come here for the classic New Orleans sound. 8pm-11pm live jazz every night (Fri/Sat 8.30pm-midnight). Jazz brunch on Sundays, $12.95, noon-4pm.

Blue Note, 131 W 3rd St, 475-8592. Serves food and hot jazz. 'Small, but attracts some big names.' 'Jazz capital of the world.' Cover charge varies depending on artist, $5 min drink (drinks from $6.25). *www.bluenotejazz.com/newyork*.

Ellen's Stardust Diner, 1650 Broadway (at 51st St), 956-5151 1950's themed diner singing waiters, *www.ellensstardustdiner.com*. Not to be missed is the **Iridium Jazz Club** 582-2121, located downstairs at this venue, which opens the week every Monday night with Les Paul and his trio, and jazz brunches on Sundays. Cover $30, 50% off for students w/ID for the second set only, Tue, Thu, and Sun.

The Lenox Lounge, 288 Malcolm X Blvd, 427-0253 a restored Art Deco Jazz club located in Harlem that serves lunch and dinner with live music at 9pm, 10.45pm and 12.30am. Cover ranges, free-$15, *www.lenoxlounge.com.*

Village Vanguard, 178 7th Ave S, 255-4037. Sleazy, unkempt, chaotic and cramped; the perfect jazz club, always worth going to, whoever's playing. Shows at 9pm & 11pm, Sat 12.30am as well. Admission $30 incl $10 drink min all nights. Mon is Big Band night. Student discount Sun-Thu, second set only, admission $20 incl. $4 drink credit. *www.villagevanguard.com.*

The elusive Woody Allen plays Dixieland Clarinet with the **New Orleans Jazz Band** on occasional Monday nights at the **Café Carlyle** under the hotel of the same name, 35 E 76 St, 744-1600. Cover $85. *www.thecarlyle.com.*

Rock, Pop and Indie

Arlene's Grocery, 95 Stanton St, 358-1633. Promotes an assortment of up-and-coming and established stars, always a good scene. Cover $7+, no cover Mon (karaoke night). *www.arlenes-grocery.net*.

Bowery Ballroom, 6 Delancey St, 533-2111. Open since 1998, still one of the best scenes for alternative music. Cover $8-15. *www.boweryballroom.com*.

Canal Room, 285 W Broadway, 941-8100. Live music, dancing, and celebrity sightings. *www.canalroom.com*.

CBGB, 315 Bowery at Bleecker, 982-4052/228-1577. Since 1973 has started new rock bands off on the route to fame and fortune. The Ramones, Blondie, and Talking Heads had their debuts here. Whilst still infamous, other clubs are now eclipsing its reputation. $20 cover. *www.cbgb.com*.

Crobar, 530 W 28 St, 736-9497. Huge dance floor, good house music, unpretentious atmosphere. Admission $25. *www.crobar.com.*

The Delancey, 168 Delancey St, 254-9920. Rooftop bar w/views of the Williamsburg Bridge, free bbq on Sun 6-8pm, bands and dj's every night. *www.thedelancey.com.*

Country/Western/Blues/Zydeco

Rodeo Bar/Albuquerque Eats, 375 3rd Ave at 27th St, 683-6500. Authentic Southwest cuisine with late night live country & western entertainment. Open daily 11:30am-2am or later.

A & M Roadhouse, 57 Murray Street bet Church and W Broadway, 385-9005. Blues and zydeco. Ribs, southern fare. Wed-Sun, shows 9:30 and 11:00pm. No cover. *www.amroadhouse.com*.

Swing Dance: Midsummer Night's Swing at the Lincoln Center, 875-5000. Take a 6.30pm lesson then dance the night away to the music of a live band, Wed-Sat, June-July. Learn to salsa, fox trot, swing or jitterbug, for a bargain $15 pp. Tickets Centercharge at 721-6500 or at the door. *www.lincolncenter.org.*

Comedy

In the past few years, led by New York City, the number of comedy clubs across America has exploded, . Since these clubs are popular, call at least a day before to reserve a table and check out prices.

Caroline's, 1626 Broadway btwn 49th & 50th Sts, 757-4100, light snacks offered as well as full menu of Mediterranean, American and Asian fusion cuisine. Two drink min and cover charge. 'The later the set, the better the comedy.' *www.carolines.com*.

New York Comedy Club, 241 E 24th St at 2nd Ave, 696-5233. Former stomping grounds of Chris Rock and Damon Wayans. Cover $10-$12, 2 drink minimum. Rsvs rec. Buy half-price tix online at *www.newyorkcomedyclub.com*.

Gotham Comedy Club, 34 W 22nd St btwn 5th & 6th Ave, 367-9000. Opened in 1996, Gotham is 'NYC's premier comedy venture'. Cover $10-16 + 2 drink min. *www.gothamcomedyclub.com*.

THEATRE

Broadway prices are high, but tickets go on sale at 25%-50% off ($3 service charge) on the day of performance at the **TKTS** booth, **47th St at Times Sq**. 'Be prepared for very long queues.' Wed & Sat matinee sales 10am-2pm, Sun 11am-closing, Mon-Sat evening sales 3pm-8pm. Get there at least 11/2 hrs in advance. Cash and travellers' cheques are accepted; credit cards are not. **Another TKTS location: South St Seaport**, open for eve. performance tix Mon-Fri 11am-6pm, Sat 'til 7pm, Sun 'til 4 pm; for matinees, buy tix a day in advance.

There is also always something interesting happening **'Off-Broadway'** and prices are lower. For **Off-off Broadway** dance, music, and theatre tickets go to **La MaMa**, 74 E 4th St, 475-7710, open noon-10 pm, same day tickets $15-20, cash or credit cards *www.lamama.org* and the Brooklyn Academy of Music (BAM), 30 Lafayette

Ave (718) 636-4111, _www.bam.org_. Both are always good for interesting and experimental theatre.

Read the _Village Voice_ for 'Off-off-Broadway' plays, discounts and the best theatre buys. Keep a look-out in hotels, drugstores, coffee shops, newsstands and Visitors Bureau in Times Square for 'Two Fers' (two tkts for the price of one). If you hang around outside a show that is not sold out, right before it begins you can bargain your way into very cheap theatre seats, but timing is critical. Standing room is often available at the most popular shows.

CINEMA

Movie houses around Times Square and along the Upper East Side start around $10. For both art house and mainstream movies, visit the **Loews Lincoln Square**, 1998 Broadway at 68th St, 336-5000/5020, a lavishly decorated monster of a movie house with twelve screens, plus an eight-storey-high IMAX theatre. Also worth a visit is the enormous screen at the **Ziegfeld**, 141 W 54th St, btwn 6th & 7th Aves, 765-7600, but for independent films and a more intimate atmosphere, try the Angelika, 18 W Houston at Mercer St, 995-2000. _www.angelikafilmcenter.com._ There are many other smaller and cheaper neighbourhood cinemas, however. Look them up under 'Other Movies' in the Village Voice, or in _Time Out New York_.

For a real New York summer experience catch a free Monday night movie at **Bryant Park**, W 42nd St east of 6th Ave, for info call 512-5700. Thousands take picnics and watch old classics under the stars. Pitch your site in the afternoon to be sure of a good view. 'A great atmosphere.' The Park is also a venue for music and dance throughout the summer, call 768-4242.

Info on tickets to TV shows being taped in Manhattan can often be obtained from the NYC & Company in Times Square. Or just call the TV stations.

SHOPPING

Department Stores: Macy's, 695-4400 (Broadway at 34th St). The world's largest, 2.1 million square ft over 10 floors with a half a million items _www.macys.com_.

Bloomingdale's, 705-2000 (Lexington Ave & 59th St), **Saks 5th Ave**, 611 5th Ave (b/t 49th and 50th Sts), 753-4000, and **Lord and Taylor**, 5th Ave, btwn E 38th & 39th Sts, 391-3344, the epitome of American Style.

F.A.O. Schwarz Fifth Ave, 767 5th Ave btwn 58th & 59th Sts, 644-9400. Magical toy store with several storeys of fantasy-fulfilling goods. Where actor Tom Hanks danced on a pavement-sized electric keyboard in Big. Worth a visit just to gawk at the amazing Lego and pedal-power Porsches that cost almost as much as the real thing. _www.fao.com_.

Book Stores: Strand Bookshop, 828 Broadway at 12th St, 473-1452. Huge second-hand bookstore. **Barnes and Noble**, 33 E 17th St, 253-0810, 675 6th Ave, 727-1227, and other locations all over the city. **Village Comics**, 214 Sullivan St, 777-2770, stocks a horde of back issues and Sci-Fi magazines. **Rizzoli Books**, 31 W 57th St btwn 5th & 6th Aves, 759-2424, for beautiful, coffee table books.

Records: J&R Music World, 31 Park Row, 238-9000. Enormous stocks of CDs and tapes. **Other Music**, 15 E 4th St, 477-8150. Specializes in anything outside the mainstream. **Tower Records**, 1961 Broadway at 66th St, 799-2500, and 692 Broadway at 4th St, 505-1500. **The Virgin Megastore** is at Times Square, 921-1020.

Clothing: **Orchard St Market**, Lower East Side, off **Canal St**, Sun mornings. 'Traditional Jewish street market, lots of bustle and colour.' For vintage classics visit **Screaming Mimi's**, 382 Lafayette St, btwn 4th & Great Jones Sts, 677-6464; or **Cheap Jacks**, 841 Broadway, b/t 13th and 14th Sts, 995-0403. If you yearn for a little designer number, take a look in the **Armani Exchange**, 568 Broadway nr Prince St, 431-6000, for his 'diffusion collection' - labels at more affordable prices. **St Marks** and **East Village** area for 'unique, cheap boutiques'.

Outlets: **Woodbury Commons,** 498 Red Apple Court, Central Valley, I-87,

Harriman, exit 16. (845) 928-7467, *www.premiumoutlets.com*. A mind-boggling massive collection of premium outlets, including Levi's, Timberland, Gap, J. Crew and every big name designer you can think of. Spend a full exhausting day there and you still won't cover it all! Gray Line buses from Port Authority Bus Terminal.
Markets: The Green Market, in Union Square (Mon, Wed, Fri, Sat 8am-6pm) is a not-to-be-missed experience. Fresh produce, pressed juices, home-baked pies, breads, cookies, fruit and flowers - wander amongst the bustling crowds, investigate the stalls and ask to taste, the stall holders are generally very willing. Listen out for interesting street musicians - jazz quartets frequently appear.
Flea Markets: Annexe Antique Fair & Flea Market, 6th Ave, btwn 25th & 26th Sts, 243-5343. Sat & Sun only. For quintessential East Village style on the cheap.

OUT OF DOORS

The Bronx Zoo, Fordham Rd & Southern Blvd, (718) 367-1010. Take the #5 or #2 to E 180th St. New York's biggest zoo. *www.bronxzoo.com*. There's also the 250-acre **NY Botanical Garden** nearby, with a tract of the original forest that once covered New York City, and 48 gardens and plant collections. Both worth visiting.
Central Park: A huge, rambling green oasis designed by Frederick Law Olmsted and Calvert Vaux out of swamp land and a shantytown, the Park has been open since 1876 and it's impossible to conceive of life in NY without it. Stretching for miles through the heart of Manhattan, the park extends from 59th to 110th St with ponds, gardens, 36 bridges, a zoo, and ever-winding paths designed to make you forget the city and lose yourself in thought.
On Sundays the streets in the park are blocked off and the park fills with New Yorkers boating, blading, cycling, jogging, walking, sailing, horse riding, skate boarding, playing baseball or reading the *Sunday NY Times*. (Bikes & blades are available to hire.) Others contemplate **Strawberry Fields**, the international garden of peace, W side btw 71st and 74th, named in memory of John Lennon who lived near the park. A mosaic there has the single word Imagine. Further north at 79th St, an imitation medieval castle, **Belvedere**, crowns Vista Rock with climbable turrets and spires.
The Literary Mall at 66th on the E side is a rather majestic promenade with a cathedral ceiling of rare American elms and a statue of Shakespeare. Look for the **Shakespeare Festival** and free concerts, plays and opera in the summer; ice-skating in the winter. Ask at the **Dairy** west of the zoo near 64th S 5th, (212) 794-6564, and Belvedere 772-0210, and other visitor centres for schedules of events. 'Extremely helpful staff.' Don't forget to clear out at night; the park is unsafe after sundown, except when there are public events. *www.centralpark.org*.
Central Park Zoo, 830 5th Ave at 64th, 861-6030. A compact collection of 100 species, with exquisite rainforest, arctic and other exhibits, Open daily in summer 10am-5pm, w/ends till 5.30pm, admission $6.
Prospect Park in Brooklyn. (718) 965-8951. Designed by Olmstead and Vaux, the architects of Central Park, and considered to be their masterpiece. The park features playgrounds, an ice rink, a carousel, and a boathouse along its 60-acre lake. Stand in the 90-acre **Long Meadow** in the centre of the park and you'll forget you're in New York-building restrictions in the surrounding neighbourhood prohibit tall buildings. Just across **Flatbush Avenue** is the **Brooklyn Botanical Garden**, 1000 Washington Ave, (718) 623-7200. Stroll through several unique climates encased in greenhouses, or take to the cherry tree esplanade, one of the largest displays outside of Japan. Open Tues-Fri 8am-4:30pm, w/end 10am-4:30pm, 'til 6pm in the summer. $5, $3 w/student ID. Free Tue, and Sat 10am-noon, *www.bbg.org*.
Rockefeller Center, 48th & 50th St, btwn 5th & 6th Aves, 632-3975. At Christmas the Rockefeller Plaza has a gigantic, sparkling tree, gossamer angels and a cold bite rising off the ice-rink. In summer it's a place to sit and enjoy free lunchtime concerts. Skating from Oct, 332-7654. Charges apply, skate hire avail. New in Fall 2005:

Top of the Rock, new 6-level observatory 67-70 floors above the city, spectacular views, reserve timed tix in advance. _www.rockefellercenter.com_.

The extensive Manhattan **waterfront** once dominated by shipping, warehouses, and industry in the first half of the 20th C, and by their ruins in the second, is now well along to being cleared for the public pleasure. Some of the more beautiful areas to stroll along include the Hudson waterfront and new **Piers 45 & 46 W of the Village** at W 10th St, and at the northern extreme of the island. 'Take the A train' to Dyckman St or 181st St and walk west for 5 minutes to happen upon the most rural scenes the city holds in store at **Dyckman Fields** or **Fort Washington Park**. Short of tearing down the Piers, some have been turned into recreation spaces!

Up and down **Hudson River Park**, the aquatic boundary to Chelsea, are tennis and volleyball courts, football fields, and many other modes of self-contained entertainment jutting out on ancient steel platforms. To the south, **Battery Park** is the most frequently trodden coastline on the island, but is very pleasant if short of time, and is the start of a bike-path up the West side.

Beaches: Coney Island and **Brighton Beach**, Brooklyn, reached by D Subway-both have interesting Russian communities. **Jones Beach**, by LIRR from Penn Station to Freeport, then local bus to beach.

SPORT

Chelsea Piers, W 23rd St on the Hudson River, 336-6666. Sports and entertainment complex inc in-line skating, basketball, roller hockey, soccer, golf range, ice-skating, shopping, eating, etc. Built in converted historic piers. _www.chelseapiers.com_.

Times Up! 802-8222. This direct-action environmental organization offers over 80 different events during the year including several free bicycle and skate tours of the city. Hordes assemble for their guided tour of Wall St area sights on summer evenings, but the most popular is **The Moonlight Ride** through Central Park, which takes place on the first Friday of every month at 10pm from Columbus Circle. Bring your own bike/blades. _www.times-up.org_.

Skating: Blades, Boards & Skate, 120 W 72nd St, 787-3911 (and other locations). In-line skates $20 all day, $200 deposit nec. Open 10am-8pm. **Skate Patrol**, 439-1234. In-line skating classes in Central Park, **Blades West**, 120 W 72nd St. Second and fourth w/end of every month, except holiday weekends. $20 pp. rsvs rec. _www.skatepatrol.org_.

Wollman Skating Rink, Central Park, 439-6900. One of NYC's most popular recreation facilities. Oct-Mar $8.50 w/days, $11 w/ends. In summer, May-Sep, turns into a Victorian-style family amusement park. $15 pass (unlimited rides). Nr 59th and 6th Ave. _www.wollmanskatingrink.com_.

Wollman Ice Rink, Prospect Park, Brooklyn. (718) 287-5252 Nov-March, ice-skating all day skate rental $5. Entrance $5. _www.prospectpark.org_.

SPECTATOR SPORTS

Like everything else in New York, the pro-sports following is enormous!

Baseball's regular season runs from April through the end of September-but don't expect New York's teams to stop there! The city went wild for weeks in October 2000 when the Yankees and Mets actually met in the 'subway series' world championships. The **Mets**, 2000 National League pennant winners, are at Shea Stadium in Queens, the Willets Point/Shea Stadium stop on the 7 line. Call (718) 507-8499 for tickets or visit _www.mets.com_.

The world champs for 4 of the years from 1996 to 2000 and current American League East title holders, the Yankees are at Yankee Stadium in the Bronx; take the 4 train to 116th St/Yankee Stadium. Call Ticketmaster, (212) 307-1212/(201) 507-8900/(800) 943-4327 or visit _www.yankees.com_.

Basketball, in season from October to April: the **Knicks** are at Madison Square

Garden, 7th Ave btwn 31st and 33rd Sts, take the subway to 34th St stations. Call (800) 4NBA-TIX for tkts. *www.nba.com/knicks*. The NJ Nets play across the Hudson in the Meadowlands. Call (800) 765-6387 for tickets. A shuttle from the Port Authority runs before and after the game, purchase tickets at the NJ Transit windows. *www.nba.com/nets*.

The Islanders ice hockey team plays at the Coliseum, and the **Rangers** skate in Madison Square Garden. Call Ticketmaster, (212) 307-7171, for both teams. For tennis devotees, the **US Open** takes place at Flushing Meadows, across from Shea Stadium, in Queens in early September. Call (800) 378-5318 for tickets. The **Jets** and **Giants** American football teams play at the Meadowlands in New Jersey, but don't sell individual tickets.

INFORMATION

NYC & Company (formerly New York Convention and Visitors Bureau), 810 7th Ave at 53rd St, Times Square, 484-1200/1222, (also downtown at the southern tip of City Hall Park, and in Harlem at 163 West 125th Street, just east of 7th Ave) provides excellent, useful information regarding shows, events, entertainment, museums, restaurants, and neighborhoods, and the Official NYC Guide, free, call 800/NYC-VISIT or 397-8222. Mon-Fri 8.30am-6pm, w/ends 9am-5pm. Free maps, including handy pocket subway map that links attractions to subway stops, list of current shows and attractions, pamphlets with walking tours of the city. *www.nycvisit.com.*

Times Square Visitors Center, 869-1890/768-1560, Suite 800, 1560 Broadway btwn 46th & 47th Sts. Daily 8am-8pm, free tours of Times Square at noon on Fridays. Long queues for 5 computers with free internet access until 7.45 pm, limit 10 minutes. *www.timessquarebid.org*.

Ephemera Press, 400 Third Ave, Brooklyn, (718) 254-9400, has excellent pictorial walking tour map/posters in colour of the East Village, Harlem, Queen's Jazz Trail, and Lower Manhattan, featuring all prominent landmarks and residents, with street addresses and historical notes. Avail online and at bookstores. *www.ephemerpress.com*.

Traveler's Aid, (718) 656-4870, JFK Airport, Terminal 6. Mon-Fri 10am-6pm, w/ends 11am-7pm.

Post Offices: there are dozens around the city but major ones are at 8th Ave at 33rd St (24 hrs) 330-3002, 340 W 42nd St, 502-0420, and 62nd St at Broadway.

INTERNET & WI-FI ACCESS

EasyInternetcafé, 234 West 42nd Street (b/t 7th and 8th Aves), 398-0775. World's largest internet café, with 648 computers. Open 7 days a week 7am-1am *www.easyeverything.com*.

Newsbar Internet at 107 University Place, 260-4192.

Mid-Manhattan Public Library, 455 5th Ave at 40th St, 340-0818, free, but half hr time limit. Open Mon, Wed, Thu 9am-9pm, Tue 11am-7pm, Fri & Sat 10am-6pm.

New York Public Library, 5th Ave from 40th to 42nd Sts, 930-0800. Free Internet use ltd to ½hr.

TRANSPORTATION WITHIN THE CITY

Subways: One of the largest subway systems in the world - 714 miles of track and 468 stations, the NY subway is one of the quickest, cheapest ways to get around all NYC boroughs and contrary to popular belief, generally safe, clean, full of friendly locals, clearly announced stops, and electronic destination signs. Many stations are full of beautifully tiled designs, i.e. the Natural History Museum stop on the A & B lines at 81st,. and you may be pleasantly entertained by strolling singers or mariachi bands. For info call Metropolitan Transit Authority (MTA) at (718) 330-1234, 24 hrs. *www.mta.info*.

Ticket booths distribute a free multilingual Subway Map (French, Spanish,

German, Italian, Japanese and Chinese) and another free larger version, The Map, with bus and ferry connections, inc MTA Railroads and LIRR out to neighbouring counties. **NYC & Co** (see above) has a dinky, pocket-size free subway map New York that links each major sight/site to a subway stop.

Basic fare: $2. Buy tokens or **MetroCards** at fare booths, vending machines or local stores. There are various options, all of which include free transfers for unlimited travel on the subway and local buses: **1-Day Fun Pass**, is $7; **7-Day MetroCard**, $24, or **30-Day MetroCard**, $76. You may also buy a **pay-per-ride MetroCard**, $10 on card gives a 20% bonus. Note that there are express and local trains; check the best to get there fastest. The system is complex but well marked; a venturesome spirit is a prerequisite. Women alone should avoid using the subway at night. 'Off-hour waiting areas,' visible to the clerks at all times, are marked by yellow signs which usually hang from the ceiling. There are information centres at Penn Station, Grand Central Station and Port Authority. **PATH** trains link several subway stops with points in New Jersey, fare $1.50.

Buses: (718) 330-1234. Over 4900 blue and white MTA buses will take you to just about anywhere within the five boroughs. Fare: $2 in exact change (no bills or pennies), token or MetroCard. Free transfers avail (use Metrocards). Exit buses from rear doors only.

Taxis: Only ride in the bright yellow taxis, others are impostors. 'Insist that the meter is put on, "private deals" don't work.' Learn the meaning of fear, as your certified driver squeezes the cab between two buses at 45 mph in traffic. Always tip the driver 15 percent, if you arrive alive! Expensive for one, but for three or four, economical over short distances.

Bikes: The cheapest way to travel, the city has 108 miles of bike lanes, 75 miles of off-road trails, and some 3,000 bike racks. The City Bicycle Master Plan sets out a 900 mile network. You can take your bike on the subway and bike across bridges. The city printed 200,000 New York City Cycling Maps in 2005, available at the Planning Dept Map & Bookstore, First Floor, 22 Reade Street, 720-3667, 10am-4 pm weekdays, or download from their website. For everything on bike paths, maps, network development plans, bike shops, bikes on bridges and transit, etc., go to *www.nyc.gov/html/dcp/html/bike/bm .html.*

Arriving in/leaving Manhattan

Buses: All inter-city bus lines, including **Greyhound**, (800) 231-2222, use the Port Authority Bus Terminal, 625 8th Ave & 41st St. Arrive at least one hour early to purchase tickets. It's worth shopping around; cheaper and faster travel can sometimes be found with **Peter Pan/Trailways**, (800) 237-8747. Ask at the information desk on street-level floor if confused about where to go - don't accept offers of help or directions from 'friendly' strangers who sidle up as you walk through the door unless you want hassle. Most will expect a tip for showing you the way and can be offensive if you say no. The inhabitants late at night can be a bit unsavoury. Be careful. **Green Tortoise**, (800) 227-4766. 14 day bus trips westbound to SF, LA for $549-$649 plus $151-$171 for food, May-Oct. (See USA Background for more details.)

Ivy Media Bus Bargains. There are many bus bargains out of Manhattan, for example $15/20 o/w 6 times daily to Washington DC from NYC Chinatown 88 E Broadway to DC Chinatown 610 I St via **Today Travel**, 964 6334 (DC 326-0892). NYC - **Boston Deluxe** o/w $15 twice daily, and to Washington DC **Washington Deluxe** (718) 387-7523 or (866) 287-6932 o/w $20 5 times daily, both pick up at 303 W 34th (Penn St), *www.washny.com*. For all these and many other services on both east and west coasts, check *www.ivymedia.com*.

Trains: Penn Station, 33rd St & 8th Ave, under Madison Sq Garden. Amtrak service, (800) 872-7245, btwn Boston, Washington, Chicago and towards Montréal and Toronto amongst other destinations. Also **Long Island Railroad**, (718) 217-5477, and **PATH**, (800) 234-7284, which operates in Manhattan and New Jersey, fare

$1.50. **New Jersey Transit** trains, (973) 762-5100, can take you to Princeton, Philadelphia and also to the AirTrain Newark link to Newark Airport.

Grand Central Station, 42nd St & Park Ave. Handles Metro-North Commuter Railroad (532-4900) to NY suburbs, Hudson River Valley and Connecticut.

Car Rides: For rides with college students, check the bulletin boards at NYU, Loeb Center, Washington Sq, or at the Columbia University Bookshop, near Columbia U. Hitchhiking is illegal on major roads in New York State, discouraged by police and highly dangerous. Single men or women absolutely mustn't do it. For maps, try the **American Automobile Association**, if you are a member, 1881 Broadway at 62nd St, 586-1166.

Airports: For general info on transportation to New York airports call (800) 247-7433. To and from all three airports, **Super Shuttle**, a fleet of blue mini vans: $13-$22 depending on route. 212-BLUEVAN; _www.supershuttle.com._

J. F. Kennedy Airport, (718) 244-4444. Allow at least 1½ hrs travel. There are three different routes that can be taken from JFK to Manhattan taking the **AirTrain**. Take the AirTrain from JFK to Howard Beach Station. From there take the 'A' train. Or take the AirTrain from JFK to Jamaica Station, and from there take the 'E' train to 53rd and Lexington Av. The AirTrain costs $5, the subway costs $2 for any trip.

The cheapest way to JFK: subway to Howard Beach, $2, then free shuttle bus to airport terminals. Otherwise: take the E/F subway trains to Union Turnpike/Kew Gardens, then catch the Q10 bus to JFK. Total cost $7 with MetroCard bus transfer, (718) 995-4700 for info. You can also take the Long Island Railroad from Penn Station to Jamaica, then the **NY Airport Service bus**, $5. Another quick, easy way: **NY Airport Service Bus** (718 875-8200), $13, o/w from 125 Park Ave near Grand Central Station and from Port Authority to JFK/La Guardia. _www.nyairport-service.com._

LaGuardia Airport, (718) 533-3400. Allow at least 1 hr travel. The cheapest way in and out: Q47 or Q33 bus to/from Roosevelt Ave/Jackson Heights station on the #7 and E lines to Manhattan. Going out take the N or W lines to Astoria-Ditmars Blvd, get a local cab beneath the station, $9. Easier: NY Airport Service Bus-$10, to 125 Park Ave near Grand Central Station and Port Authority. Also, bus M60 from 116th St and Broadway or 125th St direct for $2.

Newark Airport, (973) 961-6000. Allow at least 1 hr travel. Olympia Airport Express to Penn Station, Grand Central Station, or Port Authority, $11 o/w, (212) 964-6233. Also **AirTrain Newark** linking passengers to Amtrak and NJ Transit trains into Manhattan; $11.55 to Penn Station on NJ Transit.

LONG ISLAND

'The Island,' as New Yorkers call it, is a 150-mile-long glacial moraine, the terminal line of the last encroachment of the Ice Age. Extending eastwards from Manhattan, it includes the New York City boroughs of Brooklyn and Queens, and the built-up suburban county of Nassau, though more than half the length of the island is occupied by the more rural county of Suffolk.

Long Island Sound quietly laps against its North Shore where hills, headlands, fields and woods have been home to some of America's rich and famous. F. Scott Fitzgerald's Gatsby partied here, and **Sagamore Hill**, (516) 922-4788, outside of Oyster Bay, Nassau County, was the home of President Theodore Roosevelt. You may take a tour of what is described as "the summer White House of the President" for $5. _www.nps.gov/sahi._ In **Huntington**, further east, poet Walt Whitman spent his childhood (you can visit the house, 246 Old Walt Whitman Rd, (631) 427-5240, summer hrs Mon-Fri 11am-4pm, w/end noon-5pm. Tours $3, $2 w/student ID.

www.nysparks.com. Nearby, the Vanderbilts had an estate they connected to New York City with their own private motorway.

The South Shore, protected by **Fire Island**, receives a surprisingly gentle Atlantic breeze. The beaches here are generally flat and sandy. Except right out at the **Hamptons** (Southampton and East Hampton), this shoreline has always been less exclusive than the North Shore. Its magnificent beaches stretch in a virtually unbroken line 100 miles out from the city, attracting throngs of tourists.

All areas of Long Island are easily accessible from Manhattan via the Long Island Railroad from Penn Station, or via the Northern State and Southern State Parkways, and the Long Island Expressway, which at the city end is so often jammed with traffic that it's known as 'the longest parking lot in the world.' Eventually, though, it sweeps beyond the pandemonium towards the remoteness of Montauk Point's majestic lighthouse.

Long Island is fraught with social experiments, and **Jones Beach** is one of the nicest of them. With millions unemployed during the Depression, President Franklin Roosevelt found work for many and fun for more by developing this four-mile stretch of the South Shore into an excellent sandy beach. On a hot summer's weekend, especially the 4th of July, up to half a million people and their cars join the seagulls for a good splash in the sun and water. Go there during the week if you want more of the beach to yourself. The Long Island Railroad, (718) 217-5477/(516) 822-LIRR, offers train/bus service between the beach, at Freeport Station, and Manhattan, approx. $14 r/t, prices vary with times.

Fire Island, on a long sandbar further east than Jones Beach, is nicer yet. Not so much developed as preserved for its natural beauty and bird life, the area has been designated a National Seashore run by the National Park Service. This is an excellent place for swimming, surfing, sunbathing, fishing, cooking over an open grill and getting up to no good in the sand dunes. Take Long Island Railroad to Bay Shore, $19.50 r/t, then ferry, to Ocean Beach, $12.50 r/t.

Facing the calm waters of Gardiners Bay, **Sag Harbor**, a whaling port (1760 – 1850) that once had more tons of square-rigged commercial vessels than New York City, is now a pleasant town where John Steinbeck chose to end his days, and where those wealthy enough to own sailing boats moor them. The **Sag Harbor Whaling Museum**, (631) 725-0770, is at 200 Main St. Mon-Sat 10am-5pm, Sun 1pm-5pm, $5. *www.sagharborwhalingmuseum.org*.

There are in fact several such salty and tranquil spots at the end of the island, as well as an Indian Reservation. A few days wandering is well worth it. For more info, go to *www.nps.gov/fiis*.

Many of the place names on Long Island derive from the Indians who once lived here fishing, planting or hunting deer: the Wantaghs, Patchogues and Montauks were a few of the tribes. **Montauk Point** marks the eastern extremity of Long Island where a towering **lighthouse**, (631) 668-2544, built in 1792 by order of George Washington, looks over three sides of water and offers magnificent views of the rising sun. *www.montauklighthouse.com*.

Curiously enough, the oldest cattle ranch in the United States is also located out here: **Deep Hollow Ranch** in Montauk, (631) 668-2744, where visitors can go horseback riding. 'Birthplace of the American cowboy.' _www.deephollowranch.com_.

Accommodation
Camping: There are vast campsites scattered around the State Parks in Long Island. All advise rsvs at w/ends during the summer, tent sites $13-16. **Wildwood State Park** has campsites on Long Island Sound with path to the beach. Picnic area, baseball/volleyball courts. By train, take Long Island Railroad to Riverhead station, where you can catch a bus to the campsite. Info and rsvs avail. at _www.licamping.com_.

Information
Long Island Convention and Visitors Bureau, (631) 951-3440/(877)-FUN-ONLI. Offer a comprehensive, free Long Island travel guide and have information centres on the Southern State Pkwy btwn exits 13 & 14 and on Long Island Expressway btwn exits 52 & 53. _www.licvb.com_.

HUDSON RIVER VALLEY Though not the key to the Northwest Passage that many early explorers hoped it would be, the Hudson has gouged a considerable valley from the mountains of upstate New York past the chalk cliffs of the Palisades to the granite slab of Manhattan, and onwards even from there, forming a great underwater trench several hundred miles long out to the edge of the continental shelf.

Much of the scenery along the valley has a special beauty, in the 1820s inspiring the first American school of painting, the Hudson River School, whose painters shared the philosophies of transcendentalists of the time, embodying in idyllic landscapes the ideals about which their contemporaries Ralph Waldo Emerson, Henry Thoreau, and Walt Whitman wrote: "I sing...the body electric, a song of myself, a song of joys, a song of occupations, a song of prudence, a song of the answerer, a song of the broad-axe, a song of the rolling earth...". Among the leading painters in this genre were Albert Bierstad, Frederic Church, Thomas Cole, Asher Durand, Sanford Gifford, George Inness, John Kensett, and Thomas Moran. _www.pbs.org/wnet/ihas/icon/hudson.html_ The valley contains several historical towns such as **Tarrytown**, **West Point**, **Hyde Park** and **Ossining**, home of electrifying **Sing Sing State Prison**.

About 16 miles north of the George Washington Bridge on the eastern side of the Hudson, **Tarrytown** was the home of Rip Van Winkle creator, Washington Irving and the model for his story _The Legend of Sleepy Hollow_. His books, manuscripts and furniture are still here, in his house, **Sunnyside**, on West Sunnyside Lane, (914) 631-8200/591-8763. The creeper-covered, white brick cottage is open to visitors Apr-Dec, Wed-Mon 10am-5pm, $10. Both Irving and Andrew Carnegie, the American Steel magnate, are buried in **Sleepy Hollow Cemetery**.

Also worth a visit are two restored (with Rockefeller money) Dutch colonial manors, the **Philipsburg** and **Van Cortlandt Manors**. The Philipsburg Manor has a working grist mill. Entrance to each of the manors is $10. Tours of the **Rockefeller Estate** at **Kykuit**, (914) 631-9491, with its collections of art, sculpture (Henry Moore, Alexander Calder, etc.), carriages and classic cars, begin at Philipsburg Manor. Allow a day to see the estate. Also check the Matisse and Chagall windows at the nearby **Union Church**. For info call

(914) 631-8200, or see _www.hudsonvalley.org_. Reach the manors via all-day excursion with **NY Waterway Ferry** ($46-$64) or Metro-North Railroad, (212) 532-4900, from Grand Central (admission, r/t fare $32.25). **NY Waterway** also offers a 2 hour cruise along the Hudson, departing from Tarrytown ferry dock on W 38th at 12th Ave, May-Oct daily at 10am, 11am, 1pm, 2pm. $26. _www.nywaterway.com_.

West Point is the site of the **US Military Academy**, founded in 1802 to train military officers. The Academy is the _alma mater_ of such architects of victory as Robert E Lee, General Custer and William (Sue the Media) Westmoreland. Visitor Center, (845) 938-2638, daily 9am-4.45pm, 1 hour guided tours, $7. If you like brass bands and cadets walking in straight lines, this is the place for you. Museum and grounds open daily. _www.usma.edu_. Close by is the 5000-acre **Bear Mountain State Park**, good for hiking. Park office, (845) 786-2701. **Beaver Pond Campground** (845) 947-2792, tent sites $13-14, $9 registration fee, rsvs rec.

Hyde Park, a small village 80 miles north of New York City, lies on scenic Rte 9 overlooking the Hudson River. It was the home of President Franklin D Roosevelt and both he and Eleanor lie buried in the Rose Garden of the **FDR Library and Museum**, (845) 486-7770. Nearby is the **Frederick W Vanderbilt Mansion**, (845) 229-9115, a Beaux-Arts-style house set in 600 glorious acres, formerly country retreat of the industrialist/ philanthropist Vanderbilt. See how the big-time millionaires lived, daily 9am-5pm, $8. _www.nps.gov/vama_.

Near here is also the renowned headquarters campus of the **Culinary Institute of America (CIA)** at 1946 Campus Drive, Hyde Park (another campus is in Napa Valley, CA). Tours of the CIA are Mon 10am and 4pm, Wed and Thu 4pm. Call (845) 451-1588, _www.ciachef.edu_. Taste the cuisine of future master chefs at the CIA's five associated restaurants nearby—American Bounty, Apple Pie Bakery, Ristorante Caterina de' Medici, Escoffier, and St. Andrews (reservations essential). **Hyde Park Trail**, a hiking trail over 7 miles in length that snakes along the banks of the Hudson River, links historic sites such as the Roosevelt Home and the Vanderbilt Mansion.

Dia Museum (Riggio Galleries), 3 Beekman street, **Beacon**, (845) 440-0100, $7 for students, is a huge 240,000 sq ft of converted factory gallery space on 31 acres on the banks of the Hudson. Dia has an extensive but little seen collection of contemporary art with each gallery featuring a single artist, such as Dan Flavin, Gerhard Richter, and Andy Warhol. One gallery includes 72 canvases from Warhol's _Shadows_ series. _www.diaart.org_.

About 18 miles to the west of Hyde Park lies the small town of **New Paltz**, an excellent starting point for a trip to **Minnewaska State Park**, (845) 255-0752. The park offers two lakes for swimming and several hiking trails with excellent views of the Shawangunk Mountains.

Just a little further up the Hudson is the quaint, stockade city of **Kingston**, founded as a Dutch trading post in 1614. In 1777 it became the first state capital and you can visit the restored **Senate House**, (845) 338-2786, on Fair St, where the senators met before fleeing for their lives in the face of a British attack. April-Oct Wed-Sat 10am-5pm, Sun 1pm-5pm, $3.

There are several Colonial buildings in the area, including the **Old Dutch Church** on Main St.

Woodstock, a magic name from the 1960s, is nearby off Rte 28. Many an ageing hippie can be seen making a nostalgic pilgrimage to the village, which came to symbolise the Age of Aquarius youth movement after the rock concert to end all concerts in 1969. Imagine their surprise upon learning that the festival was actually held 57 miles south on Rte 17-B in the town of Bethel! Promoters intended to hold the festival in Woodstock but as its popularity grew they were forced to move it to a more spacious location. Today Woodstock is, as it has long been, an arts colony with lots of boutiques and summertime craft and theatrical festivals. Call the **Woodstock Chamber of Commerce**, open Thu-Mon 11am-6pm at 10 Rock City Rd, (845) 679-6234, for more info: _www.woodstockchamber.com_.

The **Catskill Mountains**, just to the west of Kingston, is an area of hills, streams, hiking paths and ski trails, and is reputedly the spot where Rip Van Winkle dozed off for 20 years. The Catskills used to be the place where wealthy New Yorkers took their holidays and there is just a touch of decay and nostalgia at the resorts, an air of having seen better days. The resorts still operate, but no longer cater to an Eastern European Jewish clientele (the old nickname for the area was the 'Borscht Belt'). The area remains a marvellous retreat for walking and getting away from it all. **Catskills Regional Tourist Office**, (800)697-2287. Also see _www.roundthebend.com/catskill_, an online guide to upstate NY.

ALBANY Capital of the State of New York and named after the Duke of York and Albany who later became James II of England. Not the greatest place for the casual visitor but downtown does have some interesting architecture in the shape of the Rockefeller Empire State Plaza, a massive shopping, office and cultural complex that cost a billion dollars to build.

Situated near the juncture of the Hudson and Mohawk Rivers, and on a line with the boundary between western Massachusetts and southern Vermont, the city is a convenient halting place before visiting these states, or before exploring the local New York attractions of Saratoga, Lake George and Ticonderoga, the Adirondacks and Ausable Chasm. _www.albany.org_.

The telephone area code is 518.

Accommodation
The most inexpensive accommodation during the summer is likely to be at the residence halls of the **College of St Rose**, 454-5171. Call ahead to see if a room is available.

America's Best Inn, 1600 Central Ave, 456-8982, avg. room D-$69.

Pine Haven B&B, 531 Western Ave, 482-1574. Family run 1896 Victorian house in safe neighbourhood. S-$69, D-$89 ($74 w/ shared bath), inc bfst. Single hostel rooms for $30 w/AYH card, exc bfst. 'Friendly; excellent breakfast!' _www.pinehavenbedandbreakfast.com_.

Of interest
Albany Institute of History and Art, 125 Washington Ave, 463-4478. Oldest museum in the state and one of the oldest in the country. Many Hudson River School and Colonial Albany paintings, sculpture, as well as ancient Egyptian art. Tue-Sat, 10am-5pm, Sun 12pm-5pm. $7, $5 w/student ID. _www.albanyinstitute.org_.

Gov. Nelson A. Rockefeller Empire State Plaza, btwn Madison & State Sts, 474-2418, centre of town. 12-building complex housing 30 state agencies and cultural facilities. The most striking feature of this ultra-brute-modern affair is the 42-storey state office tower with observation deck up top offering panoramas. Tours Mon-Fri at 11am and 1pm, free. _www.ogs.state.ny.us/curatorial/plaza_.

New York State Museum, Empire State Plaza, 474-5877. Geology, History, Native Americans and natural history. In the New York Metropolis Hall is a vast display of the NYC urbanisation process, including a 1940 subway car, 1929 Yellow Cab, 1930 Chinatown import-export shop and mock-up of Sesame Street stage set. Daily 9.30am-5pm. $2 sugg. donation. 'Superb.' _www.nysm.nysed.gov_.

Schuyler Mansion State Historic Site, 32 Catherine St, 434-0834. Built in 1762, home of Gen. Philip Schuyler, revolutionary luminary, it was the location of Schuyler's daughter, Betsy's marriage to Alexander Hamilton. Tours $4, $3 w/student ID. April-Oct Wed-Sun 11am-5pm. During summer months, open Tue. _www.nysparks.com/sites_.

State Capitol, northern end of Empire State Plaza, 474-2418. Free 1 hr tours, call for times. Begun in 1867, the building includes the Million Dollar Staircase, which took 14 years to complete. The carvers of the staircase reproduced in stone not only the famous, but also their family and friends. Also Senate and Assembly Chamber. _www.assembly.state.ny.us/tour_.

Information

Albany County Visitors Center, 25 Quackenbush Sq, (800) 258-3582/(518) 434-1217. Mon-Fri 9am-4pm, Sat-Sun 10am-4pm. _www.albany.org_.

Visitors Assistance, #106 on the Concourse, Empire State Plaza, 474-2418, 8.30am-5pm daily. Has information on free events taking place in the plaza.

Travel

Greyhound, 34 Hamilton St, 434-8461/(800) 231-2222.

Amtrak, Albany-Rensselaer station, 555 East St, (800) 872-7245/462-5763.

SARATOGA SPRINGS About 30 miles north of Albany, this favourite resort with its mineral springs bears a Mohawk name meaning 'place of swift water'. The waters, high in mineral content, are on tap at the Spa State Park. Abraham Lincoln's son, Bob, came here to celebrate his graduation from Harvard and found a town agog with its new racecourse. Now the nation's oldest thoroughbred racing track, the **Saratoga Race Course**, 584-6200, runs races every July-Sept. _www.nyra.com/saratoga_. Before you go, be sure to read **Damon Runyon's** (1880-1946) wonderful short stories, such as _The Snatching of Bookie Bob_ and _All Horse Players Die Broke_, on which _Guys and Dolls_ was based. During July-Sept, accommodation is more expensive and less available than at other times of the year. However, the **Saratoga Downtowner**, 413 Broadway, 584-6160, is a good deal at D-$89-$99 in summer(except during racing season), inc bfast, pool. **National Museum of Racing and Hall of Fame**, 584-0400, on Union Ave and Ludlow St, open Mon-Sat 10am-4pm, Sun 12-4pm. $7, $5 w/student ID. _www.racingmuseum.org_.

Saratoga Springs is also the summer home of the **New York City Ballet** in July, the **Philadelphia Orchestra** in August, and various transient rock and roll bands, all of which play at the outdoor **Saratoga Performing Arts Center**, 584-9330. Lawn seats cost $8-$40, depending on event. The Arts Center also hosts the **Saratoga Jazz Festival** in June. _www.spac.org_.

Saratoga claims to have more restaurants per capita than any other American town, so finding good food won't be hard. Finding cheap food may be harder, so to savour the essence of Saratoga cuisine, buy a bag of crisps called Saratoga Chips, which were invented here 100 years ago.

Saratoga County Tourism Dept, 28 Clinton St (800) 526-8970 Mon-Fri 9am-5pm. *www.saratoga.org*. *The telephone area code is 518.*

LAKE GEORGE Another 25 miles north of Saratoga Springs is the town of Lake George and the lake itself, running to Fort Ticonderoga where it constricts before opening out again as Lake Champlain.

Lake George is billed as the resort area with 'a million dollar beach', but that refers less to the shore's quality and more to how much it probably costs to clean the place up after the tourist hordes have been by. Best to keep going through the area and on to the Adirondack Park but, a reader writes: 'Lake George is lively and beautiful. Great locals, great beach, great entertainments'.

Fort Ticonderoga at the other end of the lake is accessible by road or by boat from Lake George town, and is of interest to those who would know the methods by which the British Empire grew great. Constructed by the French in 1755, the British waited just long enough for it to be made comfortable before taking it over in 1756. Perhaps requiring some repairs to be made, the British then let rebel Ethan Allen grab it in 1775, and when suitable again for officers and gentlemen, Burgoyne took it back in 1777. The Yanks got the place in the end and now conduct guided tours in summer for $12. Includes the museum and displays inside the fort where 'non-stop action' is promised. Call 585-2821 for information. Daily 9am-5pm mid-June to mid-Oct. There is a car ferry service from Ticonderoga to Vermont. *www.fort-ticonderoga.org*.

The telephone area code is 518.

THE ADIRONDACKS This 100+ year old state park encompasses the year round resort area of the Adirondack Mountains, an enormous expanse of mountains (including the state's highest peak, Mt. Marcy at 5344 ft), forests and lakes stretching thousands of square miles west of Lakes George and Champlain.

Lake Placid is the sporting centre of the area and hosted the original Winter Olympics in 1932. The games came back in 1980 and left behind an Olympic ski-jump platform which still offers the best view of the area. Call 523-2202, Wed-Sun 9am-4pm, $5. The landscape, with cross-country and downhill ski trails, large lakes and chairlifts is equally suitable for summer and winter excursions. 'Worth it for the view alone.' **Lake Placid Visitor Center**, 216 Main St, (800) 447-5224, Mon-Fri 8am-5pm, w/ends 9am-4pm. *www.lakeplacid.com*.

Angling fanatics can obtain fishing licences for the river from the **Town Hall** at 301 Main St (523-2162), or in local stores. $15 day pass, $25 seven days, $40 season pass. **Adirondacks Regional Information**, (800) 648-5239. Mon-Fri 8am-4.30pm.

The telephone area code is 518.

Accommodation: Lake Placid is generally expensive. Try the **Alpine Inn**, 2830 Wilmington Rd, 523-2180. Economy rooms (no view) from $66, others from $75.

Of interest
Ausable Chasm, 834-7454, on the western shores of Lake Champlain where the Ausable River has cut a vast canyon through the rock The tour by foot, raft and return bus costs $16 plus $8 extra for rafting or tubing. Lantern Tour is the only guided tour—starts at dusk, $18.57. Available mid-May-mid-Oct, daily 9.30am-5pm. 'Not worth the effort. Big tourist trap full of little English grannies.' Also has a big campground: $18-28 for full hookup, XP-$5. *www.ausablechasm.com*.
Blue Mountain Lake, about 40 miles south-west of Lake Placid en route to Utica and Syracuse. Lake and mountain scenery, and the **Adirondack Museum**, 1 mile north, 352-7311. Shows life in the Adirondacks since colonial times, with 1890 private railroad car, log hotel, 1932 Winter Olympics memorabilia. May-Oct, daily 10am-6pm, $14. 'Allow 4 hrs to see it all.' 'Excellent.' *www.adirondackmuseum.org*.
Lake Placid: John Brown Farm State Historic Site, 2 miles out of town on Rte 73; 523-3900. This is where he lies a'mouldering in the grave (see Harper's Ferry, West Virginia). Summer: Wed-Mon 10am-5pm. $2.

THE FINGER LAKES The Native Americans believed the Finger Lakes were formed when the Great Spirit reached out to bless the region and left behind the imprint of his hand. Their names – Canandaigua, Seneca, Cayuga, Keuka, and Skaneateles- still speak of this Indian legend. *www.fingerlakes.org* and *www.fingerlakes.net*.

Today, this scenic region of New York State is the oldest wine-producing district in the East, known especially for its crisp Rieslings, good sparkling wines as well as many varietals unique to the region. Over 80 wineries in the area produce over 100 million bottles of wine a year, and there are plenty of opportunities to sample the local product. **The Cayuga Wine Trail**, (800) 684-5217, will take you on a tipsy tour through 15 vineyards that sit on the lake's edge. *www.cayugawinetrail.com*. Also worth visiting are the wineries around Lake Seneca. *www.senecalakewine.com*. Both Belhurst and Red Newt *www.rednewt.com* have small bistros (lunch around $10-$20) in addition to wine-tasting facilities. Wagner Vineyards *www.wagnervineyards.com* is another reasonably-priced spot to have lunch, and offers tastings of its home-brewed beers as well as its wines. Hammondsport, *www.hammondsport.com* at the tip of Lake Keuka, *www.keukawinetrail.com* is a lovely place to spend the night and only ten minutes from one of the finest wineries in the region - Dr Konstantin Frank's *www.drfrankwines.com*.

Try the **Village Tavern** for rooms (from $79 for a double on weekdays, $99 w/ends) *www.villagetaverninn.com*. Call the **Finger Lakes Tourism Association**, (800) 548-4386, Mon-Fri 8am-4.30pm, for info. *www.fingerlakes.org* or *www.fingerlakeswinecountry.com*.

En route be sure to pitch up to the **National Baseball Hall of Fame** in the pleasant summer resort of **Cooperstown**. The Hall of Fame is open May-Sept 9am-9pm, 9am-5pm the rest of the year. (607) 547-7200, $14.50. *www.baseballhalloffame.org*. Not to be outdone, the **National Soccer Hall of Fame** has kicked off in nearby **Oneonta**. (607) 432-3351. 9am-7pm summer, 10am-5pm winter, $9. *www.soccerhall.org*.

Syracuse, to the east of the Finger Lakes, was the site Chief Hiawatha chose in about 1570 as the capital for the Iroquois Confederacy. Around the council fires of the longhouse met the Five Nations, which for two centuries dominated north-eastern North America. Salt first brought the Native

Americans and later the French and Americans to the shores of Lake Onondaga. Syracuse was founded in 1805 and for many years most of the salt used in America came from here. The **New York State Fair** is held annually in Syracuse from late August through Labor Day and high-ranking **Syracuse University** was founded here in 1870. **Downing International Hostel**, HI-USA, 535 Oak St, (315) 472-5788. $14 HI, $17 non-HI. Private rooms, $17-HI, $20 non-HI inc private bathroom. Check-in Sun-Thu 5pm-10pm, Fri & Sat till 11pm. Rsvs rec. 'Arrive early.' The place to eat: **Dinosaur Bar-B-Que**, 246 W Willow St, 476-4937. Honky-tonk ribs joint. 'Outstanding ribs.'

ITHACA As the bumper sticker saying goes 'Ithaca is gorges'. Situated at the southern end of **Cayuga Lake**, Ithaca has within its boundaries many deep river gorges and spectacular waterfalls as well as hills that rival those of San Francisco in their steepness.

Perched high atop a hill overlooking Cayuga Lake is Ivy-Leaguer **Cornell University**, _www.cornell.edu_ (on a campus considered by many to be the most beautiful in the US) and also in town is well-regarded liberal arts **Ithaca College**. This high concentration of students (24,000 or so) make the campus and town a fun, lively place to visit. _www.visitithaca.com_.

The telephone area code is 607.

Accommodation
Elmshade Guest House, 402 S Albany St, 273-1707, room $60-80. Inc. bfast.
Hillside Inn, 518 Stewart Ave, 272-9507, room $60-80. AC, cable TV, continental bfast. Free local calls, and parking. V. close to Cornell Uni. Rsvs rec.
Super 8 Motel, 400 S Meadow St, 273-8088. $89.
Camping: Buttermilk Falls State Park, 273-5761, 1 mile south on Rte 13, $13 per night. Rsvs on (800) 456-2267. _www.reserveamerica.com_.

Food/Entertainment
Cornell is reputed to have the best campus food in the US. **The Ivy Room, Willard Straight Hall**, is open to all, term-time only. Cornell also makes its own (very nice) ice cream. The **Collegetown area** on the edge of campus is also good for eating and is the place to be when the sun goes down. Try **The Nines**, 311 College Ave, 272-1888, for live bands, beer and cheap pizza and **Collegetown Bagels**, 415 College Ave, 273-0982, for 'cheap, yummy bagels'. Big student hang-out.
Ithaca Commons downtown has various inexpensive eateries and student bars, recommended is **The Haunt**, 702 Willow Ave, 275-3447, with live music on Sat. Open daily Tue-Fri 11am-1am, Sat from 3pm.
Hal's Delicatessen, 115 N Aurora St, 273-7765. Old fashioned, but cheap, filling sandwiches ($4) etc. 'Well fed for $5.' 6am-9pm daily.
Moosewood Restaurant, Seneca & Cayuga Sts, 273-9610. Famous vegetarian restaurant. The owners have written several very popular vegetarian cookbooks to be found on the kitchen shelf of every self-respecting US college student. Lunch $5-$7.50, dinner $11-$15. _www.moosewoodrestaurant.com_.

Of interest
Hiking and biking are the ways to get around the area. There is a 30-mile hiking trail which loops around Ithaca and this may be a good way to start.
Cornell University is on the northeast side of town and can be reached by local bus from downtown. Take a 75 min guided tour (254-4636) or just wander. Climb the **McGraw Tower** (162 steps) for a glorious view of the lake and hills. Further vistas

can be had from the **Herbert F. Johnson Museum of Art**, University and Central Aves, (255-6464). Designed by I M Pei and dubbed 'the sewing machine', the museum offers collections of Asian and modern; prints, paintings and drawings. Tue-Sun 10am-5pm. Free. _www.museum.cornell.edu._

Cornell Plantations: the campus covers some 4000 acres including the main campus buildings, experimental farms, nature trails, **Beebe Lake** and **Sapsucker Woods**, a bird sanctuary. Recommended are **The Plantations**, which comprise an arboretum, specialised plant collections in the botanical gardens, and a network of forest trails. Nice to wander and picnic. Off Judd Falls Rd; 255-2400. _www.plantations.cornell.edu._

There are several **wineries and cider makers** near Ithaca, all good for tours and tasting, i.e. **Six Mile Creek Vineyard** and **Bellwether Hard Cider** (part of the Cayuga Wine Trail).

Taughannock Falls State Park, 8 miles N on Rt 89, 387-6739. A mile-long glen with 400 ft walls and 215 ft high falls (higher than Niagara).

Buttermilk Falls State Park, south on Rte 13, 273-5761. Waterfalls and quiet pools are the main features. Good for swimming, hiking and a picnic, $7 park fee.

Information/Travel

Ithaca City Convention & Visitor Bureau, 904 East Shore Drive, (800) 284-8422/(607) 272-1313. _www.visitithaca.com._

Local Ithaca Transit (T-CAT), 277-RIDE, covers Ithaca, Tompkins County and Cornell campus. Fares $1.50-$3.

Greyhound, 710 W State & N Fulton Sts, 272-7930/(800) 231-2222.

Still within the Finger Lakes region is **Corning**, 50 miles southwest of Ithaca. Corningware and Steuben Glass originated here, and it's well worth spending several hours at the amazing **Corning Glass Museum**, watching glass being cut, moulded, blown into any shape for every conceivable use. For information phone 974-8271. Daily 9am-5pm, 'til 8pm Jul-Aug. $12, students with ID 10% discount. Midway between Ithaca and Corning is **Elmira**, where Mark Twain wrote _Huckleberry Finn_. Twain is buried here - in **Woodlawn Cemetery**.

North of Corning at the extremity of Seneca Lake is **Watkins Glen**, famous for a lovely park, motor racing and discount shopping. For info on international motor racing events phone 535-2421. Various car and go-kart meets are held throughout the summer. The small town of **Hammondsport**, at the southern end of Keuka Lake, has its own salute to another form of high speed travel - flying. This is the birthplace of pioneer aviator, **Glen H. Curtiss** and you can visit the aviation museum named after him here, 569-2160. _www.linkny.com/curtissmuseum._

Northeast of the Finger Lakes, on the shores of Lake Ontario, **Rochester** is a grimy, crowded city encircled by insipid flowery suburbs. But one mile east of downtown is the **George Eastman House**, (585) 271-3361, abode of the founder of Kodak and now the **International Museum of Photography**, 900 East Ave, sure to fascinate amateur and professional alike. Tue-Sat 10am-5pm, Thu 'til 8pm, Sun 1pm-5pm. $8, $5 w/student ID. _www.eastman-house.org._

The telephone area code for the whole region is 607.

NIAGARA FALLS
A traditional destination for honeymoon couples, including Marilyn Monroe in _Niagara_, in search of the awesome. Mere

tourists also flock to Niagara to see one of the most outstanding spectacles on the continent.

On the US side are the **American Falls** and the **Bridal Veil Falls** with a drop of 190 ft and a combined breadth of 1060 ft in a fairly straight line; the **Horseshoe Falls**, belonging half to the US and half to Canada, describe a deep curve 2200 ft long though with a slightly lower drop of 185 ft. About 1,500,000 gallons of water would normally plummet over the three falls each second, but the use of the river's waters to generate electricity reduces that flow by half in the summer and by three-quarters in the winter.

The Canadian side offers the better view (see Niagara Falls, Ontario), but it's more commercialised.

The telephone area code is 716.

Accommodation/Food

Coachman Motel, 523 3rd St, 285-2295. Rates vary, w/ends in summer are the most expensive times, 6 minute walk from the falls. Rooms $39-129. 'Very good location near falls.' 'Clean and comfortable, but quite noisy, rough area of town.'

Frontier Youth Hostel (HI-USA), 1101 Ferry Ave, corner of Memorial Pkwy, 282-3700. $14 HI, $18 non-HI. Rsvs rec. 'One of the friendliest and most helpful hostels in America; clean small dormitories; 20 mins from falls.' 'Very cramped.' Closed 10.30am-4pm. Check in 4pm-midnight.

Rainbow Guest House, 423 Rainbow Blvd S, 282-1135. D-$65-$125, inc 'wonderful breakfast'. Rsvs essential. Less than a 10 min walk from falls. 'Friendly and welcoming.' *www.rainbowhousebb.com*.

Econo-Lodge, 5919 Niagara Falls Blvd, 283-1100. Mon-Fri July-Aug, D-$79-139. TV, pool, rsvs advised. Taxi from Falls $6. 'Clean, bright and friendly ... some rooms have waterbeds.' 'Free coffee and donuts.' 'Very cheap for a group of 4/5 people.'

YMCA, 1317 Portage Rd, 285-8491. 'mat room,' (provide your own sleeping bag), co-ed, $10; mattress, private room $25 for men only, $20 key deposit sleeping hrs 10pm-6am. Exact change only for check-ins after 9pm. 'Wonderful showers, incredible security.' 30 min walk to the falls.

Food: 'Rainbow Blvd N, variety of quite cheap places to eat Chinese, Italian, American.'

Of interest

Beware of tours offered by various information centres charging anything up to $60, the ones listed below see the same sights. If you plan on spending a lot of time here, consider buying the **Passport to the Falls**, $24.50, which gives a 30% discount on all *local* attractions, including the **Observation tower**, the **Cave of the Winds**, **Festival Theater**, *Maid of the Mist*, and other attractions. The pass is sold in the Visitors Center. Call 278-1770 for more info. *www.niagarafallsstatepark.com*.

Aquarium of Niagara, 701 Whirlpool St, 285-3575. World's first inland oceanarium, using synthetic seawater. Sea lions in summer and sharks in winter; $7.50. Daily summer 9am-7pm, otherwise till 5pm. *www.aquariumofniagara.org*.

Cave of the Winds, 278-1730, on Goat Island is not really a cave. Don oilskins for a trip to the base of Bridal Veil Falls, $8. Daily 9am-10pm. 'A must do.'

Old Fort Niagara. About 6 miles north in **Fort Niagara State Park**, 745-7611. The fort saw service under three flags - British, French and American and contains some pre-revolutionary buildings. Displays of drill, musket firing, during summer. Mon-Sat 9am-6pm, shorter hrs during winter $8.50. *www.oldfortniagra.org*.

Prospect Point Observation Tower, 278-1796, $1. Deck overlooking falls adjacent to *Maid of the Mist*, daily 8.30-11pm.

Seeing the Falls. Walk from the US to Canada via the **Rainbow Bridge**. (716)-282-1500/1800-563-2557 Cost $2.50, and don't forget your passport. If you have a restricted visa, check in with the customs people on the US side to make sure you won't have any problems returning. On either side you can don oilskins for a trip on the *Maid of the Mist* **boat**, 284-8897, which will carry you within drenching distance of the falls. Cost $11.50, mid-Apr–mid-Oct, 9.15am-7.30pm. Boat leaves every 15 mins. 'Youth Hostel provides people staying there with a discount voucher.' 'Excellent.'

Niagara International Factory Outlets, 1900 Military Rd, 297-2022. Huge 'fabulous' mall stocked to the roof with discounted name brands.

Information

Niagara Falls Tourism & Convention Corp. 345 3rd St, Suite 605, 800-338-7890. Mon-Fri 8.30am-5pm. Ask about the festival of lights in Nov. *www.niagara-usa.com.*

Travel

Amtrak, 27th St & Lockport Rd, (800) 872-7245/683-8440. NB: station is two miles out of town.

Greyhound, 343 4th St, 282-1331, you can get Greyhound tkts and a city bus to Buffalo Greyhound Station for $3.60 (exact).

From/to Buffalo Niagara International Airport, 855-7211, #24P bus to downtown, $1.75, ask for 'punched' zone 2 transfer. Get off at Eagle St and catch #40 at Main and Church Sts to Falls. $.30 to enter bus w/transfer, pay $.60 more when you get off. *www.nfta.com*.

BUFFALO is known for its cold snowy winters. Its proximity to Niagara Falls and Canada and location on the Great Lakes and Erie Canal have made the city an important travel and communications centre. Buffalo's location is what also brings it all that snow – known as the 'lake effect'; on average, more than 93 inches a winter. However the astonishing 7 feet of snow which fell over Christmas week in 2001 beat all previous records by far.

To the visitor Buffalo offers several museums and art galleries, notably the **Albright-Knox Museum**, 1285 Elmwood Ave, (716) 882-8700, with a broad collection of modern artists from Renoir and Picasso to Warhol, Wed-Sun 11am-5pm, Fri 'til 10pm, $8 students w/ID. *www.albrightknox.org*. **The Michigan Street Baptist Church**, 511 Michigan Ave, 854-7976, built in 1845, was a legendary final stop on the **Underground Railroad**, providing refuge to escaping slaves before their final trip to Canada and freedom from the bounty hunters. Buffalo promotes its outstanding architecture, with six buildings designed by **Frank Lloyd Wright**, as well as a lively student life. Be sure to enjoy one other thing Buffalo is famous for-spicy chicken wings, $3 and up for 10 at many restaurants, especially along the Elmwood strip. *www.visitbuffaloniagara.com*.

The telephone area code is 716.

Accommodation

Buffalo Hostel International, 667 Main St, 852-5222. Members: $20 p/night May-Aug, non-members $22 per night. Kitchen, laundry. Open 8am-10am, 5pm-10pm. 'Clean, well-equipped.'

Oak Tree Inn, 3475 Union Rd, 681-2600, avg. room D-$85.

Food

Anchor Bar, 1047 Main & North Sts, 886-8920. Where the chicken wings originated. $8-$25.

Bocce Club, 630 Clinton St, b/t Fillmore and Jefferson, 856-7023. Best pizza in Buffalo. Open Mon-Sat 1pm-9.30pm.

Information/Travel

Convention and Tourism Division of Greater Buffalo, 617 Main St, 852-0511/(888) 228-3369. Will advise on accommodation. Mon-Fri 10am-4pm, winter 10am-2pm.

Buffalo Bus and Metro Information: 855-7300. _www.nfta.com_.

Amtrak, 75 Exchange St, at Washington St (800) 872-7245. Also Depew Station.

Greyhound, 181 Elliott St, (800) 231-2222/855-7531. Bus #40 to Falls, $1.75.

Buffalo Niagara Airport, see under Niagara above; _www.nfta.com/airport_.

PENNSYLVANIA - The Keystone State

The 'Keystone State' seemed at one time destined to become one of the most powerful states in the nation, bridging the gap between North and South. The Civil War, the worst armed conflict America has known, was fought here during the confederation's most northerly invasions. During the Industrial Revolution, Pennsylvania retained its prominence, with Pittsburgh as the steel-producing capital of the country. America's oil industry also took off to the north of Pittsburgh, later dominated by the wealthiest American of all time, John D. Rockefeller. Today, as industry has migrated south, Pennsylvania's economy and population have shifted. Although the state capital is Harrisburg, Pittsburgh and Philadelphia, the two major cities, are enjoying a renaissance and renewed economic growth, and tourism in all parts of the state is now second only to health services in contribution to Pennsylvania's economy.

Pennsylvania is known for its lush scenery: rolling hills; rich, meticulously cultivated farmlands; and the Appalachian Mountains, which provide good hunting, hiking, and camping. _www.visitpa.com, www.pennsylvania.com._

PHILADELPHIA   English Quaker William Penn founded Philadelphia in 1682, on New World land given to him by Charles II in payment for a debt. By the time of the American Revolution the city had become the second largest in the English-speaking world - it is currently the fourth largest city in the country. Both the Declaration of Independence and the Federal Constitution were signed here. For visitors interested in pursuing the Liberty Trail, Philadelphia rivals Boston in historical reminders.

In the early 1800s, when commercial and political power moved to New York City and Washington DC, Philadelphia's stature began to wane. The early 1900s were dreary for the city, which gained the nickname 'Filthydelphia' and became the brunt of jokes by W C Fields, who quipped that he 'spent a month in Philadelphia one day'. Asked by _Vanity Fair_ magazine what he would like to have on his tombstone, he replied: 'I'd rather be in Philadelphia'.

Today Philadelphians are having the last laugh. The city is once again an important manufacturing and cultural centre, and some glamour has returned – the result of an urban and riverside face lift. Although one of the country's oldest cities, Philadelphia has one of the youngest populations, in addition, there are numerous universities and colleges in the area, hence plenty of restaurants, bars, pubs and clubs; and the Italian Market and Chinatown provide a special ethnic flavour. The 'City of Brotherly Love' lives up to its nickname – *Conde Nast Traveler* magazine has ranked Philadelphia 'the friendliest and most honest' city in the country. Philadelphians refer to downtown as Center City. Most recently, it has become the venue for the poignant TV series *Cold Case*.

Valley Forge and the Pennsylvania Dutch Country lie just to the west, and New York City is only an hour and a half away. For further info see www.gophila.com and www.pcvb.org.

The telephone area code for the Philadelphia area is 215.

Accommodation
Major hotels in the city centre are worth checking for special offers which allow three or four people to take a double room for around $125, (e.g. **Holiday Inn Express**, 735-9300, $109-179).

Bank Street Hostel, 32 S Bank St, 922-0222. Dorm $20 HI member, $23 non-member, $2 for sheets (must use one). AC, laundry, kitchen, and videos shown daily at 9pm. Closed 11am-4.30pm. 12.30 am curfew, Fri & Sat 1am. Within walking distance of most major attractions. 'The perfect hostel.' No rsvs over the phone. www.bankstreethostel.com.

B&B Connection/B&B of Philadelphia, PO Box 21, Devon PA, 19333, (610) 687-3565 (in Philly) or (800) 448-3619 (out of Philly) email: bnb@bnbphiladelphia.com. Rooms in and around Philadelphia, some hosts fluent in European languages. From $45. Credit card nec. to make rsvs. Some hosts require a two night stay. Be sure to ask about cancellation fees. www.bnbphiladelphia.com.

Chamounix Mansion International Youth Hostel, 9250 Chamounix Dr, 878-3676. $15 AYH member, $18 non-member, plus 50% deposit for groups and $2 sheet rental. 'Excellent, but out of the way.' 'I cannot speak highly enough of this place.' Take #38 bus from Market St. Get off at Ford & Cranston, continue on Ford, left at Chamounix to the end. 'Take food with you.' www.philahostel.org.

Knights Inn, 2707 US Route 1, North I-276 exit 28, Trevose, 639-4900. Free cable movies. D-$65 The #14 bus South goes 10 miles into city center. www.sleepnrest.com.

Several fraternity houses at the **University of Pennsylvania** offer summer housing to transient students. Call 898-5263 for info.

Camping: West Chester KOA, in Embreville on Rte 162 (just west of West Chester), 45 miles from Philadelphia, (610) 486-0447, Rsvs (800) 562-1726. Inc. laundry, showers, store, swimming, fishing, miniature golf, daily van trips into Philadelphia with minimum of 4 people. Tent site $25-37; camper cabin, $50 for two. www.koa.com.

Food
The local specialities are 'hoagies,' cold subs of all kinds; 'Philly steaks', thin slices of steak on an Italian roll with onions, catsup, mayo, green peppers, cheese ... and you name it; and soft pretzels, gigantic twists of dough freckled with salt crystals, zigzagged with mustard. All these and many more are sold everywhere on the street, especially in neighbourhoods filled with fast food stalls.

The Bourse, 111 S Independence Mall East, 625-0300, certainly the most convenient collection of eateries, in the heart of the historical area - opposite the Liberty Bell. A restored building full of interesting shops and a large variety of food stalls, including a good one for your mandatory Philly cheesesteak. Closes at 6pm, Sun 11am-5pm.

Famous 4th St Delicatessen, 700 S 4th St, (4th & Bainbridge), 922-3274. Traditional, Kosher deli est. 1923. Often has free chocolate-chip cookies when sitting in. Daily 7.30am-6pm, Sun 'til 4pm.

Jim's Steaks, 400 South St, 928-1911. A local tradition, features mouth-watering Philly cheesesteaks, from $6, served cafeteria-style. Mon-Thu 10am-1am, Fri & Sat 'til 3am, Sun noon 'til 10pm.

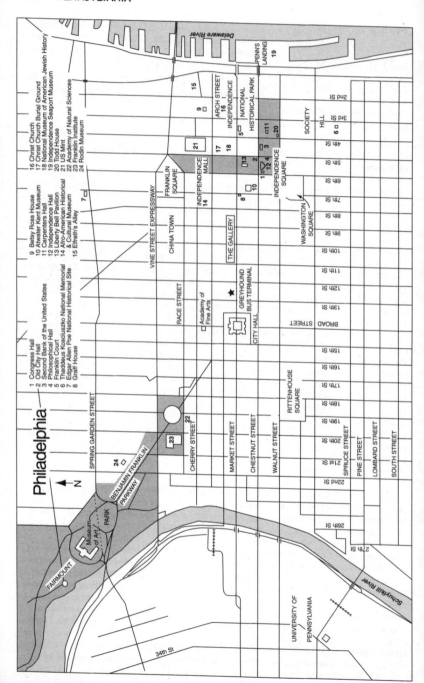

Philadelphia

◄—N

1 Congress Hall
2 Old City Hall
3 Second Bank of the United States
4 Philosophical Hall
5 Franklin Court
6 Thaddeus Kosciuszko National Memorial
7 Edgar Allen Poe National Historical Site
8 Graff House

9 Betsy Ross House
10 Atwater Kent Museum
11 Carpenters Hall
12 Independence Hall
13 Liberty Bell Pavilion
14 Afro-American Historical & Cultural Museum
15 Elfreth's Alley

16 Christ Church
17 Christ Church Burial Ground
18 National Museum of American Jewish History
19 Independence Seaport Museum
20 Todd House
21 US Mint
22 Academy of Natural Sciences
23 Franklin Institute
24 Rodin Museum

Reading Terminal Market, 12th & Arch Sts, 922-2317. Huge Farmers Market where you can satisfy your heart's desire – from Pennsylvania Dutch breakfasts to Southern Soul Food. Try 'shoo-fly pie', a heavy, molasses-packed Pennsylvania Dutch concoction brought by the Amish merchants themselves and 'the best blueberry pancakes ever!'. Mon-Sat 8am-6pm. *www.readingterminalmarket.org*.

Pat's King of Steaks, 1237 E Passyunk Ave, 468-1546. Claims the original cheesesteak and comes close to truthful, the most popular variety is the cheez wiz. Get the cheese fries and a cherry coke. *www.patskingofsteaks.com*.

Southeast China Restaurant, 1000 Arch St, 629-1888. In the centre of Chinatown. 'Good for vegetarians.' Lunch $5-$7, dinner $8-$16, Mon-Thu 11.30am-11pm, Fri & Sat till midnight, Sun noon-10pm.

Of interest

The best way to begin a tour of Philadelphia is to go first to **Independence Hall National Historical Park**, the four-block area near the Delaware River known as the 'Most Historic Square Mile in America'. *www.nps.gov/inde*. The park's **Visitors Center**, 3rd & Chestnut Sts, 965-2305/597-8974, distributes the *Visitors' Guide Map of Philadelphia* and other free maps and literature on the city and surrounding area. Open daily in summer, 9am-5pm, most buildings 9am-5pm, 9am-8pm in summer. Free. Tickets for tours at Visitors Center, free. *www.independencevisitorcenter.com*. The park includes:

Carpenters Hall, home of the first Continental Congress, 10am-4pm, Tues-Sun.

Independence Hall, Chestnut St btwn 5th & 6th Sts, where the Declaration of Independence was signed. 9am-5pm, timed and dated tickets; resv. Fee $.50 per ticket.

Liberty Bell Center, at Market St btwn 5th & 6th Sts. Exhibits history of the Bell, movie. The first Liberty Bell was manufactured by the Whitechapel Bell Foundry in east London, but arrived cracked in 1752, whereupon it was twice recast in Philadelphia in 1753.

Other sites administered by the park include:

Congress Hall, Chestnut & 6th Sts next door to Independence Hall, is where the legislature met when Philadelphia was the nation's capital, 1790-1800. 9am-5pm.

Declaration (Graff) House, 7th & Market Sts, is a reconstruction of the house where Thomas Jefferson drafted the Declaration of Independence. 9am-5pm.

Franklin Court, at Market btwn 3rd & 4th Sts. Interesting collection of buildings. A working print shop, showing Franklin's trade; a post office (daily 9am-5pm), where you can get your letters hand cancelled with a colonial-style stamp; an underground museum which features a diorama of Franklin's life and inventions; a phone bank (you can call up Thomas Jefferson and find out what he thought of Ben); and an archaeology exhibit in house dating to the 1780s that Franklin rented.

New Hall Military Museum, Chestnut between 3rd and 4th, displays formation of the army, navy, and marines during the revolutionary 1700s. 9am-5pm.

Old City Hall, 5th & Chestnut, was the first home of the US Supreme Court. Daily 9am-5pm.

Thaddeus Kosciuszko National Memorial, 3rd & Pine Sts, where Mr K, who helped the colonists win the revolution, stayed 1797-98. 9am-5pm.

Todd House, 4th & Walnut Sts. A house that figured prominently in Philadelphia society of the 1790s and the home of Dolley Todd, who later married James Madison. Sign up at the Visitors Center, 3rd St btwn Walnut & Chestnut Sts for a tour. 9am-5pm.

The park also includes **Gloria Dei (Old Swedes') Church**, built 1698-1700, the oldest church in Pennsylvania; and the **Deshler-Morris** House commandeered by British Commander Sir William Howe, during the Battle of Germantown in 1777. It was later known as the Germantown "White House" in the yellow fever epidemic of 1793, when Washington presided over cabinet meetings here with, among others, Thomas Jefferson and Alexander Hamilton.

Other historic sites close to the park include:

Afro-American Historical and Cultural Museum, 701 Arch St, at 7th St, 574-0380. Tue-Sat 10am-5pm, Sun noon-5pm, $8, $6 w/student ID. *www.aampmuseum.org*.

Atwater Kent Museum, 15 S 7th St btwn Market & Chestnut Sts, 685-4830. Depicts Philly's growth through the centuries. Wed-Sun 1pm-5pm; $5. *www.philadelphiahistory.org*.

Betsy Ross House, 239 Arch St, 686-1252. Betsy Ross is said to have put together the first American flag from strips of petticoats. Daily 10am-5pm, donations rec. $3, $2 students. *www.betsyrosshouse.org*. Near this house, off 2nd Ave is **Elfreth's Alley**, 574-0560. The oldest continuously occupied residential street in America, lined with Georgian and Federal homes. House at numbers 124 & 126 are museums, summer Mon-Sat 10am-5pm, Sun noon-5pm, $2. *www.elfrethsalley.org*.

Christ Church, on 2nd St just above Market St, 922-1695, Mon-Sat 9am-5pm. Franklin and six other signatories to the Declaration of Independence & Constitution are buried at Christ Church Burial Ground, 5th & Arch Sts. *www.christchurchphila.org*.

Italian Market, 9th St btwn Wharton and Christian Sts, the world's largest outdoor market with over 100 stores and street stalls. Lots of Italian and Vietnamese restaurants in the surrounding neighbourhood. *www.phillyitalianmarket.com*.

Mural Arts Program (MAP), 1729 Mount Vernon St, 685-0750. There are over 2000 wall murals throughout Philadelphia and you can download maps w/self-guided tours of some of the more interesting ones. Or take a guided trolley tour Wed and Sat 11am (2 hrs.), $15 for students. A great way to see Philly's neighbourhoods. Call ahead to check office hours. *www.muralarts.org*.

National Constitution Center, 525 Arch St. in Independence National Historical Park, 409-6600 or (866) 917-1787, tells story of the US Constitution through more than 100 interactive and multimedia exhibits, photographs, sculpture, text, film and artefacts. Daily 9.30am–5pm, 'til 6pm Sat. $7. *www.constitutioncenter.org*.

National Museum of American Jewish History, Independence Mall E, 55 N 5th St, 923-3811. Devoted to telling the American Jewish experience. Mon-Thu 10am-5pm, Fri 10am-3pm, Sun noon-5pm; $3 students. *www.nmajh.org*.

Penn's Landing, East of Columbus Blvd, btwn Market and South Sts, 923-8181. Revitalised waterfront area. Free concerts in summer. *www.pennslandingcorp.com*. Also here; **Independence Seaport Museum**, 211 S Columbus Blvd & Walnut St, 925-5439. Museum telling the story of the city's port and maritime history. Daily 10am-5pm, $8 inc tour of historic ships and working boat-building shop. *www.phillyseaport.org*.

Philosophical Hall, 150 S Independence Mall East, 440-3400, built in 1788/9 it is the home of the American Philosophical Society, founded by Benjamin Franklin in 1743. Exhibits focus on early days of Philly and the nation. Free admission. 10am-4pm Fri-Sun, 5pm-8pm Wed. *www.amphilsoc.org*.

Second Bank of the United States, 420 Chestnut St, (215) 965-2305, a beautiful Greek Revival building looking somewhat out of place here. Has an 'extraordinary' portrait collection depicting the main players in 18th Century development. Daily 11am-5pm.

Society Hill, colonial town houses around Spruce & 4th Sts. The name comes from the Free Society of Traders, a stock company connected to William Penn.

South Street, between 11th and Front Sts, largely a Jewish neighbourhood in the 1800s, now the street is lined with clothing, book, music and antique stores, sidewalk cafes and restaurants. South St's east end is known for its nightlife.

United States Mint, 5th & Arch Sts, 408-0114. Self-guided tours are offered first-come, first-served; 9am-3pm. *www.usmint.gov*.

Elsewhere in Philly: Academy of Natural Sciences, 1900 Benjamin Franklin Pkwy, at 19th St, 299-1000, big dinosaur exhibit and tropical butterflies. Mon-Fri 10am-4.30pm, w/ends 'til 5pm, $9 w/student ID. *www.acnatsci.org*.

Edgar Allen Poe National Historic Site, 532 N 7th St, 597-8780, where Poe lived when his short stories The Black Hat, Gold Bug, and Tell Tale Heart were published, 1843-1844. Wed-Sun 9am-5pm, free. *www.nps.gov/edal*.

Fairmount Park, west along Benjamin Franklin Pkwy towards the **Schuylkill** (pronounced 'Skoo-kill') **River**. 685-0000. A beautiful riverside park of nearly 9000 acres. Has no less than 100 baseball diamonds, 115 all weather tennis courts, and over 100 miles of walks, bike and bridle paths. Outdoor concerts. A 90 min ride on a recreated turn-of-the century trolley to see it all – Call **Trolleyworks** at 925-TOUR. *www.phila.gov/fairpark*. Within the park are several colonial mansions, and the Japanese house and gardens in the grounds of the **Horticultural Center**, 878-5097. Visitors required to wear socks and no shoes. May-Oct Tue-Fri 10am-4pm; Sat and Sun in summer 11am-5pm, $4, $3 w/student ID. *www.shofuso.com*.

Rodin Museum, 22nd St & Benjamin Franklin Pkwy, 763-8100. Somehow, they pried The Thinker and The Burghers of Calais away from the French. Tue-Sun 10am-5pm. Suggested donation, $3. *www.rodinmuseum.org*.

Philadelphia Museum of Art, in the centre of Fairmount Park, 763-8100, ranks as one of the world's greatest, with more than 500,000 works of art. See the arms & armour collection. Tue-Sun 10am-5pm, Fri 'til 8.45pm, $10, $7 w/student ID. Sun-pay what you wish. 'Worth every penny.' While you're here, look for the plaque on the museum steps marking the site where the famous 'Rocky' scene was filmed. *www.philamuseum.org*.

Philadelphia Zoo, 34th & Girard Sts, 243-1100, America's first, open daily 9.30am-5pm, $16.95. *www.phillyzoo.org*.

Franklin Institute Science Museum and newly-renovated **Fels Planetarium**, 222 N 20th St at Benjamin Pkwy, 448-1200/ (800) 285-0684. Worth a visit. Daily 9.30am-5pm. $13.75, combo ticket $18.75. Planetarium show 1.15pm daily, Mon-Fri; 12.15 and 2.15 Sat. Complex includes the **Mandel Future Center**, and the **Franklin Air Show** with 20+ interactive devices in three environments—aircraft hangar, midway and pilot training area, plus a newly restored 1911 Wright Model B Flyer. The complex also includes the **Tuttleman IMAX Theater**, one of the world's most modern cinemas with a 4-storey screen and 3D sound, $9. *www.fi.edu*.

Germantown, 6 miles northwest of Center City and originally settled by German folk. Many old houses and fine mansions, some of distinctive German design. Among the best is **Cliveden**, 6401 Germantown Ave, 848-1777, dating back to 1763. Thu-Sun noon-4pm, $8, $6 w/student ID. Closed in the winter until 1 April. *www.cliveden.org*.

Mummers Museum, 2nd & Washington Aves, 336-3050. Tue-Sat 9.30am-4.30pm, Sun 12pm-4.30pm, $3.50, students $2.50. Hypnotic and hilarious, the Mummers – a Philly original – are hard to explain; you just have to see. Their New Years Day parade is legend. They also hold outdoor string band concerts May-Sept Tue at 8pm. *www.riverfrontmummers.com/museum.htm*.

Mutter Museum, part of the College of Physicians of Philadelphia, 19 S 22nd St, 563-3737 ext. 242. This one is not for the weak of heart! A section of the Neo-Georgian style building is set apart as a scientific collection of physical oddities, truly the extremes of human existence. Showcased are the 'soap lady;' skeletons of a dwarf, normal man, and the tallest giant on display in the country side by side; plaster casts of various types of Siamese twins; preserved body parts, and wax models of real-life deformations and mutations. Absolutely fascinating, if you can handle it. Open daily, 10am-5pm, $10, $7 w/student ID. *www.collphyphil.org*.

Pennsylvania Academy of the Fine Arts, Broad & Cherry Sts, 972-7600. Nation's oldest art museum and school. Good collection of American art dating from 1750.

Tue-Sat 10am-5pm, Sun 11am-5pm. $5, $4 w/student ID. _www.pafa.org_.
University Museum of Archaeology/Anthropology, University of Pennsylvania Campus, 33rd & Spruce Sts, 898-4001. Outstanding archaeological exhibits ranging in geography from Mesopotamia to Alaska. Tue-Sat 10am-4.30pm. Also Sun 1pm-5pm after Labour Day; $8, $5 w/student ID. _www.upenn.edu/museum_.

Entertainment/Tours
Check the _Weekend_ section of the Friday _Philadelphia Inquirer_. Half price day of show tkts are available from **Upstages**, at 1412 Chestnut St, 569-9700. Phone lines: Mon-Fri 10am-6pm, Sat 10am-5pm, Sun noon-5pm.
Shampoo, 417 N 8th St, 928-6455. Unique club, cutting-edge dance music 9pm-2am, avant-garde art and stylish jazz lounge. Cover $7-$20 depending on night. _www.shampooonline.com_.
South St, from Front to 7th and from South to Market, the old city area, is the funky end of town, with many restaurants, pubs and clubs. The area around Walnut and 38th Sts is also good for pubs.
Haunted Philadelphia, 413-1997. Candlelit walking ghost tours of the Old City, 7.30pm Mon-Sat May-Oct. The tour meets at 6th and Chestnut Sts, lasts 1hr15min. $15, rsvs required. _www.ghosttour.com_.

Information
Visitors and Tourist Information Center, Independence National Park, 6th St & Market St, 636-1666. Daily in summer 8.30am-7pm.
Philadelphia Convention and Visitors Bureau, 1515 Market St, #2020, 636-3300. Mon-Fri 8am-5.30pm. _www.pcvb.org_.

Internet access
Central Library, 1901 Vine St at 19th St, 686-5322. Free Internet use, 1/2 hr limit. Mon-Wed 9am-9pm, Thu-Sat 'til 5pm.
Independence Branch Library, 18 S 7th St, 685-1633. Free, 1/2 hr limit. Mon-Wed noon-8pm, Tue, Thu, Fri 10am-5pm.

Travel
PHLASH buses, 474-5274, are purple buses, which run in a loop from Logan Circle through Center City, to waterfront, to South St and all major attractions. Bus stops are all along Benjamin Franklin Pkwy, Market St and Old City, marked by signs with PHLASH wings. $1 per ride or $4 all day. Buses run 10am-6pm, summer till 8pm. _www.gophila.com/phlash._
SEPTA, 580-4000, operates trains to suburbs from Market East Station, buses and street cars in the city. Base fare, $2, additional suburban zones $.50, transfer $.60. Tourist-friendly DayPass, $5.50 for unlimited travel on all city transit vehicles, plus o/w on the airport line, available at 30th St, Market East, and suburban Stations. _www.septa.org_.
Amtrak, for intercity trains, 30th St Station, 2955 Market St, (800) 872-7245. To and from NYC, DC, Boston. _www.amtrak.com_.
Greyhound, 1001 Filbert St at 10th St, 931-4075/(800) 231-2222. NYC, DC, $21 o/w.
Ivy Media Bus Bargains Check _www.ivymedia.com_ for low-cost bus bargains between Philadelphia and New York City and Washington DC.

VALLEY FORGE / BRANDYWINE RIVER VALLEY
Just south-east of Philadelphia, this is a region steeped in history and art. Valley Forge National Historical Park, (610) 783-1077, one of the nation's most solemn memorial grounds, is 20 miles west of Philadelphia. (Inquire at Welcome Center, Rt. 23 and N. Gulph Rd, about buses, tours.) General Washington hibernated here along with his half-starved troops through the bitter winter

of 1777-78. Loaded with Americana, including Washington's headquarters, cabins modelled after those in which the troops were billeted, and a few museums. _www.nps.gov/vafo_. Dogwoods blooming in spring enhance the pastoral air. For those more interested in shopping, check out the huge King of Prussia mall. You can get there from Center City, Philly by bus-route #125. For more info on the Valley Forge area check out _www.valleyforge.org_.

South of Valley Forge, the **Brandywine River Valley** has inspired three generations of Wyeths-NC, Andrew and Jamie-to produce a uniquely American brand of art. The **Brandywine River Museum** in **Chadds Ford**, (610) 388-2700, holds one of the world's largest collection of Wyeth paintings. Daily 9.30am-4.30pm, $8, $5 w/student ID. 'Highly recommended.' _www.brandywinemuseum.org_.

PENNSYLVANIA DUTCH COUNTRY While most of the original settlers of Lancaster County have long since been absorbed into modern society, the Amish and Mennonites have retained their traditional identities in this stretch of country west of Philadelphia. Eschewing electricity and modern machinery, the 'plain people' still speak a form of Low German ('Dutch' is a derivation from 'Deutsch,' the German word for 'German'). The women in their long dresses and small caps and the bearded menfolk in sombre black suits and broad-brimmed hats continue to live as simply as they did centuries before in southern Germany.

The Pennsylvania Dutch have always fascinated visitors, and the 1984 award-winning film _Witness_ only increased the interest. In order to really understand what you are seeing, try reading _Amish Life_, by John A. Hostetler, and _A Quiet Peaceable Life_, by John L. Ruth, which provide an excellent introduction to the area and its people; another highly informative book, recommended by the Amish people themselves, is _Twenty Most Asked Questions about the Amish and Mennonites_, by Merle Good, $6.95. All are available at the **Peoples Place**, Main Street, Intercourse, 768-7171 _Note_: Restrain your cameras; the people here consider photographs to be 'graven images'.

The area lies on Hwy 30, but to avoid an excess of tourists, take to the side roads. One good excursion is the 3 mile jaunt from **Paradise** to **Strasburg**, equally enjoyable on foot or via the old railroad. **Lancaster**, US capital-for-a-day (the day was 27 September, 1777), was a prominent city in the late 18th century; the well-preserved downtown reflects the town's colonial heritage. If you're looking for **Intercourse**, you'll find it signposted at the junction of Hwys 772 & 340 east of Lancaster.

Keep an eye out in late June and early July for the **Kutztown Folk Festival**: soap making, sauerkraut shredding, pewtering, square dancing and folklore sessions. 'The festival is a real hoe-down straw-in-the-hair fun affair.' Call (888) 674-6136 for details, $10. _www.kutztownfestival.com._

The telephone area code is 717.

Accommodation
Accommodation is relatively inexpensive here, but in summer prices rise and the best deals go quickly. The best places to stay are the farm homes: they're cheaper, serve hearty breakfasts, and you'll learn more about your hosts. For the best infor-

mation on accommodation, contact the **Mennonite Information Center**, (see below).

Days Inn East, 34 Rt. 896 N, Lancaster, 390-1800. North of the intersection with Rt. 30. D-$79 during summer months.

Country Acres Family Campground, 687-8014/ (866) 675 4745. 20 Leven Road, Gordonville, 5 min from Bird-in-Hand. Tent site $20, $27-36 w/hook-up. Cabins for $45/49, 2 night min. stay. Open 8am-8/9pm.Has complimentary 2-hour tour of PA Dutch Country _www.countryacrescampground.com_.

Food

Amish austerity does not extend to eating. Many restaurants in the area serve bountiful communal feasts of sausage, scrapple, pickles, beef, chow-chow, schnitz and knepp, noodles, homebaked bread, apple butter, funnel cakes and molasses shoo-fly pie.

Lancaster's Central Market, in Penn Square at King & Queen Sts, 291-4723, sells produce and goodies; it's one of the best places to see what Pennsylvania Dutch food is all about. Tue & Fri 6am-4pm & Sat 6am-2pm. _www.cityoflancasterpa.com_.

Of interest

Amish Village Inc., on Hwy 896, 7 miles south-east of Lancaster in Strasburg, 687-8511. See the Amish way of life, and tourists seeing the Amish way of life. Summer daily 9am-5pm, Sun opens at 10am. $6.50. _www.amishvillagestore.com_.

Ephrata Cloister, 12 miles north of Lancaster on Hwy 322, 733-6600, was founded and later forsaken by a German community of Seventh Day Baptists. Living as sisters and brothers, they stooped through low doorways to learn humility and walked down narrow hallways to assure themselves of the straight and narrow path. Many of their original structures of unpainted wood, now gloomy-grey with time, still stand. Mon-Sat 9am-5pm, Sun noon-5pm (last tour at 4pm), $7. _www.ephratacloister.org_.

Historical Lancaster Walking Tours, 100 S Queen St, 392-1776. Interesting walking tour of colonial Lancaster. 11/2 hr tours Mon-Sat at 1pm; extra 10am tour Mon, Tues, Fri, Sat, $7. Many special tours. _www.lancastercountyheritage.com/_

Landis Valley Farm Museum, in Lancaster, Landis Valley Rd on Hwy 272, 3 miles north of Lancaster, 569-0401. Museum village with the buildings, homes, trades and tools of three centuries. Mon-Sat 9am-5pm, Sun noon-5pm, $9. _www.landisvalleymuseum.org_.

People's Place, Main St, Intercourse, 768-7171. Summer, Mon-Sat 9.30am-7pm. Take the self-guided tour, 'Twenty Questions', $5. Award-winning 25 min slide documentary, Who are the Amish? $5, $8 combo ticket for tour and slide show. 'Worth every penny.' _www.thepeoplesplace.com_.

Railroad Museum of Pennsylvania, Rte 741 east of Strasburg, 687-8628. Historic locos and rolling stock. Mon-Sat 9am-5pm, Sun noon-5pm, closed Mon in winter, $7. _www.rrmuseumpa.org_.

Strasburg Railroad, Rte 741, 1 mile east of Lancaster on Rte 896 south, 687-7522. America's oldest short-line steam locomotive goes to and from Paradise, 45 min. Summer, daily 11am-7pm, $9.75. _www.strasburgrailroad.com_.

Information/Travel

Mennonite Information Center, 2209 Millstream Rd, 41/2 miles east of Lancaster off Rte 30, 299-0954. Go here first. Very helpful and friendly staff who can assist you in finding accommodation, tours and background on Mennonites and Amish. Informative introductory film of the area and people. The center also has the most non-commercial tour of the area, which is a treat in this overly exploited area. Here you can hire a local Mennonite guide (2 hr min.) for a fascinating country tour of homes, barns, factories, $36. 'Not to be missed.' _www.mennoniteinfoctr.com_.

Pennsylvania Dutch Convention and Visitors Bureau, 501 Greenfield Rd,

Lancaster, 299-8901. Brochures and maps. Summer, Mon-Sat 8am-6pm, Sun 9am-5pm. *www.padutchcountry.com*.
Amtrak, 53 McGovern Ave, Lancaster, (800) 872-7245.

READING Thirty miles from Lancaster. With over 300 factory outlets claiming "savings up to 75% and no sales tax on shoes or clothing", Reading is known as the 'Outlet Capital of the World'. *www.outletsonline.com/nercpa.htm* Besides deals on clothing, appliances, jewellery, and even chocolate, the town also boasts four wineries and a local brewery, an Apple Dumpling Festival, and several antique and farmers' markets. From Lancaster take US 222 north. Call the **Reading and Berks County Visitors Bureau**, 352 Penn St, (610) 375-4085/(800) 443-6610, Open Mon-Fri 9am-5pm, Sat 10am-2pm or check out *www.readingberkspa.com* for a free Visitors Guide and more information.

HARRISBURG The undistinguished capital of Pennsylvania has two outstanding features. Heading west, the landscape becomes beautiful, even dramatic, where the broad Susquehanna River cuts a gap through granite bluffs and green forests. The city itself is crowned with a stunning Italian Renaissance capitol dome modelled after St. Peter's in Rome (and built on graft; get the scandalous scoop from a local resident). Rockville Bridge, 4 miles west of Harrisburg, spanning the Susquehanna, is the longest and widest stone arch bridge in the world.

The Harrisburg area sprang to international attention in 1979 after the nuclear accident at nearby **Three Mile Island**, which brought into question the safety of nuclear reactors. The accident didn't scare away tourists, of course. Tourism, in fact, increased fourfold in the area.

Further north up the Susquehanna River lies the **Pine Creek Gorge**, otherwise called the Grand Canyon of Pennsylvania, and said to be one of the last and most extensive wilderness regions between New York and Chicago. This once industrial area has been reabsorbed into nature and, with its free-flowing river and creek-side track, is now a haven for hikers, bikers, canoeists and horseback riders alike. **Wellsboro** is the nearest town for the area and a good base for activities. Call **Pine Creek Outfitters**, (570) 724-3003, for more info. *www.pinecrk.com*.

In **Honesdale: The Purple Cow**, 375 Willow Ave (570) 253-0633, serves great shakes and ice cream, 'so many different flavours and toppings….wow….cheap huge great ice cream'. Mon-Thu noon-9pm, Fri-Sun till 10pm. **The Coffee Grinder**, 526 Main St (570) 253-2285 'Huge selection; good quality.' Mon-Sat 5am-9pm, Sun 6am-3pm.

East of Harrisburg, in **Hummelstown**, are the **Indian Echo Caves**, 566-8131, with impressive natural formations. Daily 9am-6pm in the summer; $10 for a 45 min guided tour. You can pan for gems at **Gem Mill Junction**, $5 a bag. *www.indianechocaverns.com*.

The telephone area code is 717.

HERSHEY A company town built in 1903 by a Mennonite candy bar magnate of the same name who came up with the inspired concept of milk chocolate. The air is thick with the aroma of chocolate and almonds; the two main streets are Chocolate and Cocoa Aves, and even the street lamps are shaped like Hershey's famous 'kisses'. A beautiful Spanish-style resort hotel, the Hotel Hershey, sits atop the town; luscious gardens surround it. Hershey's Chocolate World near the park entrance takes you on a free 15 minute ride from the cocoa bean to the candy shop (but not into the factory). But you never leave without spending money on chocolate (there are worse fates). Opens 9am, closing times vary, call 534-4900 or visit _www.chocolate-world.com_ for more info.

Also here is **Hershey Park**, 534-3900, a theme park with 70 rides and enough entertainment to keep you occupied all day. Daily, 10am-10pm in the summer, $39.95 for the day. Call (800) 437-7439 for info on Hershey, or check out _www.hersheypa.com_.

GETTYSBURG The quiet peaceful town that Gettysburg is today belies its history as the site of 51,000 casualties in 3 days in the most significant battle of the worst war America has ever known, the Civil War. On 3 July, 1863, General Robert E Lee was defeated here and the tide turned irrevocably against the South. Lincoln came later to give his famous Address at the dedication of the National Cemetery. The battlefield is now preserved as a national military park where visitors may follow the struggle of both sides on maps and displays. _www.gettysburg.com._

The telephone area code is 717.

Accommodation

Gettysburg has many 'Ma and Pa' motel/guest house operations, so with a little bit of searching you can find good, central, and relatively inexpensive accommodation even in the summer, the peak season.

Budget Host, 205 Steinwehr Ave, 334-3168, bus #15. D-$64 in summer. Pool, morning coffee, walk to all major attractions. For rsvs call (800) 729-6564.

North of Gettysburg: Ironmaster's Mansion Youth Hostel, 1212 Pine Grove Rd. on Rte 223 in Pine Grover Furnace State Park, 486-7575, $15 AYH members, $18 non-members, $2 sleeping sheet; rsvs recommended. Built in 1826, the building was an ironworks that manufactured cannonballs during the Revolutionary War. It was also part of the underground railway that sheltered escaped slaves. Open daily 7.30am-9.30am and 5pm-10pm. Appalachian Trail runs past front door; half hour to battlefield by car.

Round Top Campground, south on Rte 134, 334-9565. Showers, laundry, pool and mini-golf. Tent site $18 for two, XP-$4, $29.50 w/hook-up. _www.roundtopcamp.com_.

Of interest

Go directly to the **National Park Visitors Center**, 97 Taneytown Rd, on Business Rte 15, 334-1124, for complete introduction and information. Park staff are extremely knowledgeable and helpful. Here you can make arrangements for touring groups, for 1-6 people $40 for 2 hrs. You can hire a local licensed battlefield guide (AutoTour cassettes, $13.73 or $15.85 for the CD-tour is approx. 2 hrs, available from the **Wax Museum** in town, 334-6245). Here also you can see the Electric Map, showing troop movements during the battle; daily 8am-5pm, $4. **The Cyclorama** is closed for restoration until 2007-2008. _www.nps.gov/gett_.

A. **Lincoln's Place Theater**, 460 Baltimore St, 334-6049. Here James Getty, a Lincoln scholar and look-alike, gives an intimate talk in which he, as Lincoln, recounts memories, describes events and answers any question you could possibly have about the man. Not to be missed. 'Unbelievable!' Irregular show schedule, check both days and times when arriving; $7, $5.50 w/student ID. _www.gettysburg.com_.

Civil War Heritage Days, 334-6274 , last w/end in June-1st week in July. When the town comes out to commemorate the Battle of Gettsyburg with concerts, shows and fascinating, immense and stunning battle re-enactments involving thousands of 'troops'.
Eisenhower National Historic Site (take shuttle bus from Visitors Center), 338-9114, is a farm where the President retired and died. Daily 9am-4pm; $7, includes shuttle, admission and tour.

Information
National Park Visitors Center, 97 Taneytown Rd, on Business Rte 15, 334-1124. Daily 8am-5pm.
Gettysburg Convention & Visitor Bureau, 35 Carlisle St, 334-6274. Daily, 8.30am-5pm. Very helpful; has accommodation information. _www.gettysburgcvb.org_.

PITTSBURGH   When Rand McNally named Pittsburgh 'the nation's most liveable city' in 1985, everyone was surprised but the Pittsburghers, for they have always had fierce pride in their city. Famous for steel and home of much of the nation's industry, Pittsburgh coughed its way through the Industrial Revolution in a perpetual cloud of smoke. After World War II it began a clean-up campaign and in recent years has emerged, blinking, into the sunlight. And an amazing transformation it is: Pittsburgh's skyline of blast furnaces, open hearths, steel mills and primrose yellow bridges is imposing, and the city's air is reportedly now cleaner than that of any other American metropolis. There is some exciting architecture down at the Golden Triangle, where the Allegheny and Monongahela Rivers join to form the Ohio River. The dramatic view here was first seen in 1753 by George Washington, who was a British major at the time. Pittsburgh's terrain is an appealing mix of plateaux and hillsides, narrow valleys and rivers; with elevations ranging from 715 ft to 1240 ft; expect to do some climbing.
　As a bizarre footnote, the former nation of Czechoslovakia was founded in Pittsburgh, of all places. In 1918, the leaders of the Czechs and the Slovaks met in the Moose Club (now the Elks Club) at Penn & Scott Place to hammer out the Pittsburgh Agreement uniting these peoples. _www.visitpittsburgh.com._
　The telephone area code for Pittsburgh is 412.

Accommodation
Hotel and motel accommodation is expensive in the Pittsburgh area; if you have a car, you would do better to stay on the outskirts in the **Monroeville** and **Green Tree areas**. Wherever you stay in Pittsburgh, reservations are advisable.
Days Inn Harmarville, 6 Landings Dr, Rt 28 and PA Tpk, 828-5400. Comp. bkfst, D-$62.
Travel Inn, 100 Kisnow Dr. at I-79 & Steubenville Pike, 922-0120. S-$40, D-$49, $5 extra on w/ends.

Food
The local brew is **Iron City Beer**, available at any bar that knows it's in Pittsburgh.
Benkovitz Seafoods, 23rd & Smallman Sts, 263-3016. A market and one-time truckers' joint in the wholesale district, now moved up several pegs but keeping down its prices. Mon-Thu 9am-5pm, Fri 'til 5.30, Sat 8am-5pm..
Max's Allegheny Tavern, 537 Suismon St, 231-1899. 'North Side' hangout with German Sausage, schnitzel and a broad selection of beer. Mon-Thu 11am-11pm, Fri-Sat 11am-12am, Sun 9.30am-10pm, fancy brunch 'til 2pm on Sun.

Primanti Brothers, 9 outlets in Pittsburgh area. The 18th St location is open 24 hrs; 263-2142. Unique recipe grilled cheese sandwiches served with fries and coleslaw. $4.55. Also soup and chili.

Of interest

Pittsburgh culture was once severely neglected by the city's big-money steel magnates, who couldn't wait to get out of town to the refined air of Europe and New York's 5th Ave. The cultural life has picked up considerably since then, and Pittsburgh now boasts several fine museums and universities as well as the world-class Pittsburgh Symphony Orchestra.

Carnegie Library, 4400 Forbes Ave, Oakland, 622-3114 (as seen in Flashdance).

Carnegie Museums of Pittsburgh, _www.carnegiemuseums.org_, includes two internationally-known museums: the **Museum of Art**, 4400 Forbes Ave, Oakland, 622-3131, their strongest collection of American and European pieces from 1850's includes contemporary and French Impressionist masterpieces as well as decorative arts of the ancient world. The **Carnegie Museum of Natural History**, 622-3131, tells the story of the earth and man in hundreds of displays of arts, crafts and natural history, including minerals, gems and Egyptian mummies. An impressive herd of prehistoric dinosaurs towers over strange skeleton birds. The museums are open Tue-Sat 10am-5pm, Sun noon-5pm; $10 admission to both museums. Open Mondays Jul-Aug. Plus there's the **Andy Warhol Museum**, 117 Sandusky St, 237-8300, which is the largest single-artist, and Warhol museum in the world. Open Tue-Sun 10am-5pm, Fri 10am-10pm. $10, $6 w/student ID. _www.warhol.org_.

Carnegie Science Center, 1 Allegheny Ave, 237-3400, W of Heinz Field. This includes the **Henry J. Buhl Jr. Planetarium** with sky shows daily, and the **Omnimax Theater** with shows on the 79 ft domed ceiling drawing the audience into the action. $14 includes planetarium. IMAX only, $8. There are also tours around the **WW2 Requin** (meaning 'shark') submarine in front of the Center. Sun-Fri 10am-5pm, Sat 'til 7pm. _www.carnegiesciencecenter.org_.

Duquesne Incline, 1220 Grandview Ave, 381-1665, a vertical trolley from 1877 carries you 400 ft into the air for a bird's eye view of the city and its three rivers, daily till 12.45am. About $1.75 each way. _www.incline.cc_.

Fallingwater, south-east of Pittsburgh, (724) 329-8501. This futuristic home-over-a-waterfall is a paragon of Frank Lloyd Wright design. Take Hwy 51 South to Uniontown, Rte 40 East to Farmington, 381 North for 12 miles (through Ohio Pyle Park) to Fallingwater on left. Tours every half hour, Tue-Sun 10am-4pm, $13, w/ends $15. Rsvs nec. _www.paconserve.org/index-fw1.asp_.

Frick Museum, 7227 Reynolds St, Pt Breeze, 371-0600. French, Flemish Italian Renaissance paintings. Tue-Sun 10am-5pm, free. Free jazz and chamber concerts Oct-May, art at noon, offers free lectures on temporary exhibits. Also the immaculately restored **Clayton House**, call for rsvs. $10, $8 w/student ID.

Nationality Classrooms at University of Pittsburgh, in the Gothic masterpiece, the **Cathedral of Learning**, 624-6000. Impressive conglomeration of 26 classrooms in different international designs with authentic furnishings from all over the world. Mon-Sat 9am-2.30pm, Sun 11am-2.30pm, $3. _www.discover.pitt.edu/tour_.

Pittsburgh Zoo, Hill Rd, Highland Park, 665-3640. 77 acres of natural habitat, animals that include 32 species of endangered primates. A tropical rain forest exhibit has 90 primates and 150 species of tropical plants. The **PPG Aquarium** features state-of-the-art exhibits such as a crawl-through stingray tunnel, a two-story shark tank. and unique revolving tanks; exhibits include penguins, sharks, acific giant octopus, jellyfish, potbellied sea horses, an electric eel, and live coral. 9am-5pm, last admittance 4pm, $9 admission to both. _www.pittsburghzoo.com_ and _zoo.pgh.pa.us_.

White-Water Rafting on the **Youghiogheny River**. Day trips last 5-6 hrs and cost $34-$57 (peak summer prices). Inc. orientation, lunch and guide. Call **Laurel**

Highlands River Tours, (800) 472-3846, _www.laurelhighlands.com_, or **White Water Adventurers Inc**, (800) 992-7238, _www.wwaraft.com_ for more info. 'Spectacular.'

Entertainment
For students, **Oakland** is the place, although the **Shadyside** area still has its fair share of swing. Read _Rock Flash_ and _In Pittsburgh_ free from around town, to find out what's going on. Rock and pop concerts, ice shows, sports events at the **Mellon Arena**, Center and Bedford Aves, downtown at Washington Plaza, 642-1800. The arena has a vast, retractable, dome-shaped roof, home to the **Penguins** ice hockey team. _www.mellonarena.com_.

Heinz Field, 100 Art Rooney Ave, 323-1200, home to the American football team, the Pittsburgh Steelers.

Heinz Hall, 600 Penn Ave, downtown, 392-4900/642-2062 (info line). Elegant hall named after the ketchup king. Home to the Pittsburgh Symphony Orchestra. _www.pittsburghsymphony.org_.

PNC Park, 115 Federal St, 323-5000, home to the Pirates baseball team,. _www.pittsburghpirates.com_.

Information/Travel
Convention and Visitors Bureau, 425 Sixth Ave, 30th Floor, (800) 821-1888. Mon-Fri 8.30am-5.30pm. _www.visitpittsburgh.com_.

Amtrak, 1100 Liberty Ave & Grant St, near bus terminal, 471-6170/(800) 872-7245.

Greyhound, 55 11th & Liberty Ave, 392-6513/(800) 231-2222.

Internet access
Carnegie Library, 4400 Forbes Ave, 622-3114. Free, here and all branches.

TITUSVILLE The oil well business got off to a picturesque start out here in northwestern Pennsylvania. In 1859, Col Edwin Drake, right here in Titusville, sank the first oil well in the world. The site is now **Drake Well Memorial Park**, with a working reconstruction of the original rig and a museum containing photos and artefacts of the early boom days, (814) 827-2797, Mon-Sat 9am-5pm, Sun noon-5pm. $5. Daily 9am-dusk. _www.drakewell.org_. Nearby **Oil Creek State Park** stretches between Titusville and Oil City, btwn 11/2 -2 hrs north of Pittsburgh, call (814) 676-5915. _www.dcnr.state.pa.us_.

AMERICAN MUSIC—THE SOUND OF SURPRISE

BLUEGRASS: A uniquely American style of music, bluegrass can be thought of as a mix of folk music, country and blues with a hint of jazz thrown in. Invented in the 1930s by Bill Monroe and his Blue Grass Boys, bluegrass is heard today throughout the Midwest, South and in larger cities too. **The Birchmere** in **Alexandria, VA**, (703) 549-7500, presents a premier showcase of folk music, bluegrass and country. *www.birchmere.com*. **The Station Inn, Nashville, TN**, (615) 255-3307, plays bluegrass six nights a week. Live bands most evenings. *www.stationinn.com*.

For progressive style, hear the *New Grass Revival*. Most bluegrass action happens at some 400+ festivals across the country. For listings refer to *Bluegrass Unlimited*, PO BOX 771, Warrenton, VA 20188, (540) 349-8181/(800) 258-4727, *www.bluegrassmusic.com*.

BLUES: Legendary performer Memphis Slim described them best: "The blues ain't nothin' but a botheration on your mind." There are good local blues bands all over the US, but those in **Chicago** reign supreme. Pick up a copy of *The Reader* for info. Don't miss **B.L.U.E.S**, (773) 528-1012, with low-down blues and fresh acts; hot, smoky, and cramped. *www.chicagobluesbar.com*. Also try **Rosa's**, (773) 342-0452: small, not as well known, but great music. *www.rosaslounge.com*. Don't miss the free **Blues Fest** in early June, (312) 744-3315, *www.cityofchicago.org/specialevents*.

In **Washington DC** try **Madam's Organ**, (202) 667-5370. Raunchy live blues, jazz and an eclectic clientele. *www.madamsorgan.com*. **Oakland, CA**, is also filled with blues bars. The closely related mid 20th-century **R&B** tradition (which was early **Rock and Roll's** pappy), rooted in Bo Diddly, Jerry Lee Lewis, Chuck Berry, Carl Perkins and others, still survives at the **Rum Boogie Cafe**, (901) 528-0150, or catch blues legend B.B King at his own club, **B.B. King's Blues Club**, (901) 524-5464, *www.bbkingclubs.com/memphis/index.html*, both in **Memphis, TN**. Once a month you can catch Mr. Chuck Berry himself in the Duck Room at **Blueberry Hill, St Louis, MO**, (314) 727-0880, *www.blueberryhill.com*.

COUNTRY: Branson, MO, has become the new centre for country. With over 50 theatres featuring over 60 shows, Branson plays host to musical legends such as Andy Williams and the Osmond family, as well as to a bounty of country stars. **The Grand Palace**, (800) 884-4536, has been host to big names like Kenny Rogers and LeAnn Rimes, *www.thegrandpalace.com*. You can also catch performances on a regular basis by country greats such as **Moe Bandy**, (888) 3-BANDY-4, at their home theatres. The legendary **Broken Spoke, Austin, TX**, (512) 442-6189, once frequented by Willie Nelson and Ray Price, is one of the last honky-tonks, with the 'best country-fried steak in Texas!' Continues to showcase bands just on the verge of hitting the big time. *www.brokenspokeaustintx.com*. **Rodeo Bar**, (212) 683-6500, **NYC**, southwestern food, country and western entertainment, *www.rodeobar.com*.

Crazy Horse Saloon and Steakhouse, Irvine, CA, (714) 549-1512, is billed as the top country and western entertainment (and disco) spot; top names perform here.

You never know what legend will turn up next at the **Grand Ole Opry**, (615) 889-6611, in **Nashville, TN**. *www.opry.com*.

FOLK: Smithsonian Folklife Festival, Washington DC, late June/early July, has authentic folk and ethnic music and plenty of dancing. Excellent performers grace the back room of **McCabe's** guitar shop at weekends in **Santa Monica, CA**, (310) 828-4497, *www.mccabes.com*. Try the **New Orleans Jazz & Heritage Fest**, (504) 522-4786, for an eclectic mix of gospel, zydeco, progressive rock, jazz and more. Held late Apr-May, *www.nojazzfest.com*. **Newport Folk Festival**, held in August in **Newport, RI**, (401) 847-3700. Since 1959, a classic festival with a picturesque setting on Narragansett Bay. *www.festivalproductions.net/folk/fr-info.htm*. **Classical Music** festivals can range from surprisingly good local acts to the internationally renowned **Aspen Music Festival, Aspen, CO**, late June-Aug, 9 weeks, (970) 925-3254. *www.aspenmusicfestival.com*. As good as **Tanglewood Music Festival** in Lenox, **MA**, in terms of prestige and importance. Open rehearsals and other free events.

GOSPEL: Two million people fill the streets of Harlem during its massive week-long fest of gospel, rhythm & blues and jazz. *http://harlemdiscover.com/harlemjazz/index.htm*. To hear gospel at its best, go to church in **Detroit, Chicago** or **Harlem**. In **Washington DC**, superb, uplifting gospel music can be heard each Sunday at **St Augustine's Catholic Church**, 15th & V Sts NW, (202) 265-1470. *www.saintaugustine-dc.org*. For information on venues and on the gospel music industry itself, go to *www.gospelflava.com*.

JAZZ: There are good jazz clubs in most North American cities. **Preservation Hall** is the hub of **New Orleans** jazz, (504) 522-2841, *www.preservationhall.com*. In **Washington DC**, **Blues Alley**, (202) 337-4141, has attracted such greats as the late Dizzie Gillespie and Ahmad Jamal and recently Wynton Marsalis. *www.bluesalley.com*. There's no place like **New York City** for jazz: try **Blue Note**, (212) 475-8592, *www.bluenotejazz.com*. Downstairs in the **Time Cafe**, is the **Fez**, (212) 533-2680; The **Iridium Jazz Club**, (212) 582-2121, is home to jazz legends and rising stars, *www.iridiumjazzclub.com*; 'Village temple of jazz': the venerable **Village Vanguard**, (212) 255-4037, *www.villagevanguard.com*. Don't miss the **JVC Jazz Festival**, **NYC**, late June, (212) 501-1390. More than 40 events and 1000 performers at different locations including the Lincoln Center and Carnegie Hall. All the best including Ella Fitzgerald, Ray Charles and many others. *www.festivalproductions.net*. **The Baked Potato** near Universal Studios in **Los Angeles**, (818) 980-1615, has been a launch pad for jazz acts of the past 25 years, *www.thebakedpotato.com*. Other excellent festivals: **Chicago Jazz Fest** is exceptional, Labor Day weekend, (312) 744-3315, *www.cityofchicago.org/specialevents*; **Monterey, CA, Jazz Festival**, mid-September, (925) 275-9255, *www.montereyjazzfestival.org* and **Montreux-Atlanta Festival**, in Georgia, early Sept, (404) 817-6815, *www.atlantafestivals.com*. See magazines *Jazz Times* or *Downbeat* for the latest on the jazz scene nationwide.

ALTERNATIVE: Mostly big flashy nationwide tours or small underground movements, with no real established annual events, excepting **Locobazooka**, held in **Worcester, MA**, in mid-Sept, *www.locobazooka.com*. Eleven years old and each year it heralds the 'future of rock'. **The Vans Warped Tour** combines skateboarding and rock n' roll, creating a global event that hits most major US cities throughout the summer. *www.warpedtour.com*. Check local listings for the best modern rock shows in town. Info on all the above music genres, *www.sbgmusic.com/html/teacher/reference/styles.html*. For festival info, look at *www.festivalfinder.com*.

THE MID-ATLANTIC

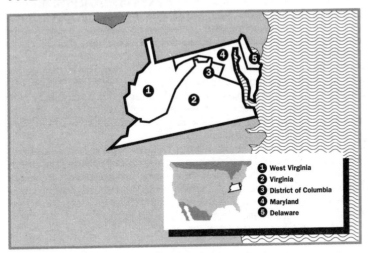

1. West Virginia
2. Virginia
3. District of Columbia
4. Maryland
5. Delaware

A visit to this region, where North meets South historically and climatically, reveals not only America's past, but the shape of her future. Centred around Washington DC, the area features politics, Colonial and Civil War history, legions of lawyers and an ever-increasing amount of federal research. The nation's governmental heart has spawned technology, research and information industries in neighbouring Maryland and Virginia, where there are such notable federal establishments as NASA's Goddard Space Flight Center (*www.nasa.gov/centers/goddard/home/index.html*), the National Security Agency at Fort Meade (*www.nsa.gov*), the National Institute of Health in Bethesda (*www.nih.gov*) and the Smithsonian Institution in Washington (*www.si.edu*). The I-270 'Technology Corridor' from Washington to Frederick now outpaces growth in California's 'Silicon Valley'.

The region has a varied and extreme climate (snowy in winter, almost monsoonal in July), brilliant springtime flora (azaleas, dogwoods, flowering cherries, followed by crepe myrtles) and its natural resources offer recreation in all seasons. You can sail, swim and fish on the Chesapeake Bay, or hike, raft and ski in the Appalachians of Virginia and West Virginia.

DELAWARE - The First State

This skinny triangle of a state should have been named, in all fairness, 'du Pont', given that it was built on the success of the du Pont empire. The family traces its roots in Delaware back 200 years to when Pierre Samuel du Pont de Nemours, a counsellor to Louis XVI at the time of the French Revolution, decided to visit his friend Thomas Jefferson and take an extended vacation in the US for health reasons. The state is instead named for the British Lord de La Warr, who never set foot on his namesake's soil.

Delawareans proudly call it the First State, as it was the first to ratify the US Constitution in 1787. Although small pockets in the south of the state were slave-holding areas, Delaware sided with the North in the Civil War and was a throughway along the 'underground railway,' a clandestine escape route from house cellar to house cellar that brought 3000 blacks to Northern freedom.

If you're like most travellers, you will probably only pass through the northern tip of the triangle—across the Delaware Memorial Bridge (the world's largest twin span bridge) and on to Baltimore, Philadelphia, or New York City. Between the state's northern metropolis, Wilmington, and the southerly Fenwick Island lie miles of sandy coastline. Great beaches offer a variety of sporting activities and cheap camping.

Flat coastal plain covers 94 per cent of Delaware's three counties (New Castle, Kent and Sussex). There's even a cypress swamp, the most northerly state-owned in the US. Ponds and tidy farms are sprinkled across the wooden backbone of the peninsula, which levels out towards the Maryland border. There's no sales tax in Delaware, so if you have any large purchases to make, do it here. _www.visitdelaware.com_ _www.destateparks.com/_.

The telephone area code for the entire state is 302.

WILMINGTON The 'Incorporation Capital of the World' due to its business-friendly operating climate and the fact that the majority of Fortune 500 corporations are incorporated here (as well as elsewhere in the state). It is also the spot where Eleuthere du Pont decided to build his powder mill in 1802. Wealth, labs, factories and eyesores followed, though the recent rebirth of the **Christina Riverfront** with its shops, bars and cafes (_www.riverfrontwilmington.com_), has revitalized the area. There are also several interesting historical relics to see before pushing on to Dover, 45 miles south.

Accommodation
Days Inn Wilmington, 5209 Concord Pike, 302 478-0300. From $75, check-in after 3pm, out 11am. Outdoor pool, continental bfast included and free coffee and tea 24 hrs. _www.daysinn.com_.
Super 8 Motel, 215 S DuPont Hwy, New Castle, 322-9480/(800) 800-8000. From $55, free coffee in morning. Check-in anytime, out 11am. _www.super8.com_.

Food
Kahunaville, 550 S. Madison St, Wilmington, 571-8402. The hot-spot on Wilmington's Riverfront, with a live DJ and acrobatic bartenders! The island flair spills out onto a massive riverfront deck and huge concert stage. Caribbean/American food, entrees $8.99-$13.99. Open daily 11:30am-1am. _www.kahunaville.com_.
Kelly's Logan House, 1701 Delaware Ave, Wilmington, 65-LOGAN. This classic Irish pub and restaurant has an extensive menu, entrees $6-$14. Live music and outdoor patio dining area. Open Mon-Sat 11am-1am. _www.loganhouse.com_.

Of interest
Brandywine Zoo, 5 N Park Dr, Brandywine Park, 571-7788. Exhibits of exotic species of animals from N and S America and Asia. Open daily 10am-4pm, free Nov-Mar, $5 Apr-Oct, _www.brandywinezoo.org/_.
Grand Opera House, 818 N Market St Mall, 652-5577/(800) 37-GRAND. Built in 1871 with an ornate cast iron facade, it now houses the Delaware Center for the Performing Arts, _www.grandopera.org_.

Hagley Museum, Barley Mill Rd & Brandywine Creek, 658-2400. 225-acre complex on the site of the original du Pont black powder works, with restored granite buildings amidst wooded hillsides and huge trees. Pleasant walks along the Brandywine. Exhibits, demonstrations and museum. Daily 9.30am-4.30pm. $11, $9 w/student ID. 'Very interesting and worthwhile.' *www.hagley.org*.

Longwood Gardens, 12 miles north of Wilmington at US 1 & Rte 52 near Kennett Square, PA, (610) 388-1000. Yet another du Pont hangout, formerly the country estate of industrial magnate Pierre S du Pont. Spectacular gardens open daily 9am-6pm, Tue, Thu & Sat 'til 10:15pm; conservatories 10am-6pm, Tue, Thu & Sat 'til 10:15pm. $14 (over 21), $6 (ages 16-20). Admission includes concerts and choreographed, illuminated fountain displays during the summer months (up to Aug 30th). 'Beautiful.' *www.longwoodgardens.org*.

New Castle, 6 miles south of Wilmington on Rte 9, is a small town full of atmosphere and Colonial-Republic architecture. Near Strand and Delaware Sts, William Penn entered his vast Colonial lands. Here, a round border separates the states of Pennsylvania and Delaware and the spire of the New Castle courthouse was used as the compass point to create this odd configuration.

The Rocks, waterfront park at the foot of 7th St, 1 block south of Church St. A monument marks the site of Fort Christina, built by the Swedish-Dutch expedition that landed here in 1638, making it the site of the first permanent settlement in the Delaware Valley.

Wilmington & Western Railroad, Greenbank Station, 2201 Newport Gap Pike (off Route 41), (800) 998-1930. Ride through historic red clay valleys on this turn-of-the-century steam train. W/ends only, 11/2 hr trip $7-10. Check schedule ahead of time. *www.wwrr.com*.

Winterthur Museum, 6 miles northwest on Rte 52, (800) 448-3883. Once the home of Henry Francis du Pont, Winterthur now houses one of the world's greatest antique collections—nearly 200 period rooms display American decorative arts from the 17th-19th centuries. General admission $15 ($13 w/student ID), tours cost an additional $10 or $20. Tue-Sun 10am-5pm, *www.winterthur.org*.

Information/Travel
Greater Wilmington Convention & Visitors Bureau, 100 W 10th St, Suite 20, 652-4088/(800) 422-1181, *www.visitwilmingtonde.com*.

Amtrak, Martin Luther King Jr Blvd & French St, 429-6529/(800) 872-7245, *www.amtrak.com*.

Greyhound, Wilmington Bus Station, 101 N French St, 655-6111/(800) 231-2222, *www.greyhound.com*.

DOVER One of the oldest state capitals in the nation, Dover was founded in 1683 when William Penn decided to build two key elements of civilised life—a prison and a courthouse—on the site.

Accommodation/Food
Dover Budget Inn, 1426 N DuPont Hwy, 734-4433. A 69-room motel with double rooms averaging $70 in summer. Cable TV, refrigerators, microwaves, swimming pool. Check-in after 2pm, out 11am. *www.doverbudgetinn.com/*.

Super Lodge, 246 N DuPont Hwy, 678-0160. TV, fridge in room. Approx. $50, check-out 11am.

Where Pigs Fly, US 13 at Loockerman St, 678-0586. Fantastic BBQ, everything under $15. Open Sun-Thur 11am-10pm, Fri-Sat 'til midnight. *wherepigsflyrestaurant.com*.

Of interest
Museum of Archaeology and Museum of Small Town Life, 316 S Governors Ave, 739-4266. Three galleries house fascinating range of Americana. Tue-Sat 10am-3:30pm, free. _www.destatemuseums.org_.
Legislative Hall, capitol building on Court St.
Old State House, the Green, 739-4266. Built in 1792, a fine example of American Georgian architecture with portraits of Delaware personalities inside. Mon-Sat 10am-4:30pm, Sun 1.30pm-4:30pm. Go to the visitor centre for tkts, free (donations accepted). _www.destatemuseums.org_.

Information/Travel
Dover Information Center, 406 Federal St, 739-4266. Information on accommodation, restaurants and museums. 'Very helpful.' Mon-Sat 8.30am-4.30pm, Sun 1.30pm-4.30pm, _www.destatemuseums.org_.
Kent County Tourism Convention and Visitors Bureau, 435 N DuPont Hwy, Dover, 734-1736/(800) 233-KENT, open Mon-Fri 8:30am-4pm, _www.visitdover.com_.
Greyhound, 1166 S Bay Rd, 734-1417. Mon-Fri 8am-8pm, Sat 9am-2pm, Sun 10am-2pm, _www.greyhound.com_.

THE DELAWARE COAST Much of the coastline follows Delaware Bay out towards the Atlantic, but even the southern shore is protected from the open ocean by Fenwick Island. **Lewes** (pronounced 'Lewis') in Sussex County is one of the earliest European settlements in the New World. First inhabited by the Dutch in 1631, visited by Captain Kidd in 1700, and bombarded by the British in 1813, Lewes is now the traditional home of pilots who guide ships up Delaware Bay and a charming town to explore by foot. The excellent **Zwaanendael Museum** (Kings Highway at Savannah) features maritime history, including the shipwrecked Brig DeBraak, whose artifacts were used as models in Master & Commander. Lewes is also the port for the ferry to Cape May, NJ, 645-6346/(800) 64-FERRY, _www.cape-maylewesferry.com_.

Further south past the WWII watch-towers along the 4-mile beaches, bike paths, and bird sanctuaries (where 141 species were spotted in 2003) of 4000-acre **Cape Henlopen Park**, is **Rehoboth Beach**, famous for its mile-long boardwalk and **Gordon Pond** trail, and popular with Washingtonians fleeing the capital's cruel summer heat. 'Rehoboth', Hebrew for 'enough room', will seem ironic to anyone visiting the body-blanketed beach on a hot weekend, but retains a pleasant small town atmosphere and is packed with good value, non-chain eateries. Nearby **Dewey Beach** and **Bethany Beach** are nearly as popular. _www.beach-net.com_, _www.visitsouthern-delaware.com_.

Accommodation
In **Rehoboth**, summer rates are very high. Try searching on foot away from the ocean or contact the **Chamber of Commerce**, 501 Rehoboth Ave, 227-2233/(800) 441-1329, for room listings. _www.beach-fun.com_.
Sandcastle Motel, 123 Second St, 227-0400. A short walk from the beach, heated indoor pool, sauna, free morning coffee. Summer $69-189. _www.thesand-castle motel.com_.
Camping: Near Lewes, Cape Henlopen State Park on Rte 9, 645-2103. Sites $27, $29 w/hook-up. **Big Oaks Family Campgrounds**, on Rte 1, 21/2 miles north of Rehoboth, 645-6838. Pool, store, shower facilities, sites from $35 for 2 people. Shuttle to beach for a small fee. _www.bigoakscamping.com_.

Food

In Lewes, **Lemon Tree Restaurant**, 416 E Savannah, (302) 645-0481 has the best value, juiciest burgers on the coast.

Rehoboth has several good value taverns – **Dogfish Head**, 320 Rehoboth Ave, 226-2739 (_www.dogfish.com_) brews own ales, has great five-ale sampler, delicious wood-grilled pizza, music after 10 pm; **Rams Head** at 15 Wilmington Ave, 227-0807, has crab pretzels, $9.95, _www.ramsheadtavern.com/_; **Arena's** 149 Rehoboth Ave, 227-1272, has chili and crab soup, salads, specials every day, global ales. **Adriatico**, 1st at Baltimore, 227-9255, Italian, Wed/Thu buy one entrée, get one free _www.rehoboth.com/adriatico/_; **Café Sole**, 44 BaltimoreAve, 227-7107, for affordable crab cakes and good-value lunch; **Crystal Diner**, 620 Rehoboth Ave, has the best-value breakfasts; **Grotto Pizza**, 36 Rehoboth Ave, 227-3575, has a huge variety of pizzas. _www.grottopizza.com_. **Go fish**, 24 Rehoboth Ave, 226-1044. A good old British-owned and run chippy! Lunch: 11am-4pm, dinner: 4pm-10:30pm daily, _www.gofishrehoboth.com_.

Of interest

Rehoboth Art League, set in historic grounds with **Homestead Mansion** (1743) 12 Dodds Lane, Henlopen Acres, 227-8408, open to public, has concerts, fine arts, crafts. _www.rehobothartleague.org/_.

Bob's Bike Rentals at 1st and Maryland Ave in Rehoboth Beach, 227-7966. $3.50-$4/hour, $9-10/day. Excellent biking, e.g. Gordon Pond trail.

Boat rentals, **Rehoboth Bay Marina** on Collins St in **Dewey**, 226-2012. Rents skiffs daily or half-daily. $75-140. Open daily 7am-6pm.

Concerts, at the bandstand on Rehoboth Ave. Summer–w/end (and some week-days) evenings at 8pm. Call 227-6181 for more info, or check out _www.cityofre-hoboth.com_.

Outlet Shopping: Rehoboth Outlets, 36470 Seaside Outlet Dr 1600, 226-9223. 20%-70% discounts, no sales tax. Over 140 stores including the GAP, J. Crew, Nike and Polo Ralph Lauren. Free shuttle downtown. Open Mon-Sat 9am-9pm, Sun 11am-7pm (Apr-Dec). _www.tangeroutlet.com/_.

Peppers, 1815 Ocean Outlets #3, 227-4608/(800) 998-FIRE. Largest collection of hot sauces in the world, with over 6,500 spicy concoctions gracing the walls of a 'hot sauce museum'. Sign a waiver before sampling the 'scorcher'! _www.peppers.com_.

Surfing, Surf Sessions, 10 South Carolina Ave on Fenwick Island, 539-2126. Offers surfing lessons, $40 first half-day, $15 every half-day thereafter. _www.atlanticbreezes.com/_.

Whale and Dolphin Watching, Fisherman's Wharf Cruises in Lewes, on the left by the drawbridge, 645-8862. 2-3 hour dolphin and whale cruises, check days; sunset cruises 6pm and 8pm daily mid-June-Aug, 6:30pm mid-Aug–Sept, $15. _www.fishlewes.com_.

Information

For what's going on where, pick up free copies of the _Beachcomber_, _Chesapeake Music Guide_, _Cape May-Lewes Traveller_, _Delmarva Quarterly_ and _S Delaware Explorer_.

Delaware State Tourism Bureau, 99 King's Hwy, (800) 441-8846, _www.visit-delaware.net_.

Rehoboth Beach-Dewey Chamber of Commerce: (302) 227-2233, _www.rehoboth.com._

Travel

Greyhound, 801 Rehoboth Ave, (800) 231-2222. Daily trips to DC ($38.50 o/w), Baltimore ($36.50 o/w) and Wilmington ($27 o/w), _www.greyhound.com_.

Jolly Trolley of Rehoboth, 227-1197, between Rehoboth boardwalk and South Dewey with stops throughout the area every 30 minutes, 8am-2am. _www.jollytrol-ley.com_.

Red Dart, 648-9001, every 30 min between Outlets and Rehoboth boardwalk. Free.
DART, (800) 553-3278, Delaware Transit System between Rehoboth, Lewes, Georgetown, Laurel and Milford. Rtes 206, 210, 212. $1.15. _www.dartfirststate.com/_.
Park 'n' Ride Transit System, 226-2001, along Rte 1 between Lewes and Dewey Beach with stops in Rehoboth, inc Outlets. $2.10 all day pass. _www.beachbus.com_.

DISTRICT OF COLUMBIA

WASHINGTON DC   Born of an idea and meticulously planned out by Frenchman Pierre L'Enfant in 1791, Washington is different from cities anywhere else in the US and yet its character is distinctly American. The ideals that have been the utilitarian background everywhere else have been turned to gospel in this white-stone town. While other metropolises barter in cold cash, Washington has always been a city of rhetoric. Any trip around the monuments that form the core of this cathedral of words indicates that power in this town is the ability to spin beliefs and sympathies. The visitor may be overwhelmed by the broad avenues and carefully placed stone homages to what seems like every event in the nation's history, while political leaders across centuries have counted on the authority these sites command over whomever views them.

Placed carefully between the North and South of the United States along the Potomac River, so as to be unbiased of regional interest, the early government soon realized the difficulty of running a city whose only existence was to administer a distant and decentralized land. Even into the 20th century the city remained small and provincial, staffed mostly with bureaucrats and a persistent problem was that there was no regional interest—in the city itself! Even as Washington became more cosmopolitan during the 20th century, due to expanding government under Roosevelt and the advance of industry and technology into the South, John F. Kennedy could still see the flip side—he described it as 'a city of Northern charm and Southern efficiency'.

Though still a fairly transient town, the city that once changed populations with every new presidential administration has in recent times become a highly desirable place to live. This is particularly evident in Georgetown, where quaint brick houses—some of which were quarters for slaves, poor labourers and free blacks—now command million-dollar sums. Georgetown's Wisconsin and M Streets buzz with cosmopolitan restaurants, art galleries and expensive boutiques. Its quiet townhouse-lined streets are best explored on foot and its waterfront is the perfect spot for a stroll on warm evenings.

While Georgetown caters increasingly to well-heeled tourists and suburbanites, the Adams-Morgan neighbourhood attracts a more diverse, local crowd. 'Flavour' is the password to this vibrant international community just a few minutes' walk from Dupont Circle. From Cajun to Caribbean, Ethiopian to Hispanic, you name it and you're likely to find it (at bargain prices) along 18th St at Columbia Rd. Primarily a night-time neighbourhood, things change every September on Adams-Morgan Day when the streets explode with music, dance and ethnic food, as thousands of Washingtonians exchange their pinstripes for T-shirts and let it all hang out.

As downtown revitalizes, U-Street has become a trendy neighborhood.

Indeed, despite its bureaucratic image, DC is surprisingly youthful, due in part to a large student population—Georgetown, George Washington, American, Catholic, and Howard Universities are all located here. The city is home to an equally large international community that includes embassies, the International Monetary Fund, Inter-American Development Bank, World Bank and sizeable immigrant groups.

Fortunately for the traveller, crime is concentrated in residential areas that most tourists don't visit. The majority of attractions, accommodation and restaurants are located in safe areas. Even so, it is always advisable to travel with caution, especially at night.

Washington is a pleasant city to visit. There is a tremendous amount to see (mostly free) and it's cleaner and greener than most US cities, with a subway system that's graffiti-free, efficient and safe. The MCI Arena has breathed new life into the city's once moribund eastern downtown area. During the summer there is a constant stream of interesting events on the huge village green known as the Mall, especially the Smithsonian's Folklife Festival, but beware of the great heat, humidity and crackling thunderstorms. The most agreeable times to visit are spring, when daffodils, cherry trees, tulips, azaleas and magnolias bloom and autumn, when the air is crisp and clear and the museums are not overflowing with tourists. DC is divided into four quadrants—NW, NE, SW and SE—branching out from the Capitol Building. It's possible for the same street address to exist in all four quadrants, so be sure to pay attention to which section of the city an address is in. _www.washington.org_, _www.washingtonian.com_.

The telephone area code for Washington is 202.

Accommodation

Housing is more expensive than in other US cities and less abundant for the budget traveller. For longer, summer stays, be prepared to search long and hard as you will be competing with the hoards of interns who descend on the capital from May to September. The classified section of the free *City Paper*, out every Thursday and available from convenience stores and street vending machines, is packed with temporary/shared housing and summer sublets, _www.washingtoncitypaper.com_. Just be sure to move fast to get the one you want. It's also worth checking the Friday and weekend classifieds in the Washington Post, _www.washingtonpost.com_.

Allen Lee Hotel, 2224 F St NW, 331-1224/(800) 462-0186. Close to the Lincoln Memorial, State Department and Kennedy Center. S-$45-$58, D-$62-$74, $3 discount w/ISIC. Metro: Foggy Bottom. _www.allenleehotel.com_.

Braxton Hotel, 1440 Rhode Island Ave NW, 232-7800/(800) 350-5759. S-$70-80, D-$80. TV, bfast, tour pickup, 15 min walk to White House. Check-in 2pm, out 11am. 'Good value for money.' Metro: McPherson Sq/Dupont Circle. _www.braxton-hotel.com_.

Woodley Park Guest Home, 2647 Woodley Rd NW, 667-0218/(866) 667-0218. From $92, bfast included. Metro: Woodley Park-Zoo/Adams Morgan. _www.woodley-parkguesthouse.com_.

George Washington University Off-Campus Housing Office, Marvin Center, 800 21st St NW, 994-0334. Advertises apartments and shared houses available for the summer period. _gwired.gwu.edu/offcampus_.

Georgetown University publishes a good weekly listing of off-campus summer accommodation for rent. Contact the office of off-campus housing, M31 Darnall Hall, 3800 Reservoir Rd NW, 687-7764. You can either go in person to get a copy of the list or visit their website: *och.georgetown.edu*. Also, try the notice boards at local cafes (**Chesapeake Bagel Bakery** on Connecticut Ave and **Food for Thought** on 14th St have boards brimming with ads) and at Union Station.

Hotel Harrington, 436 11th St NW, 628-8140/(800) 424-8532, located downtown between Capitol and White House. From $89. 'Crowded.' 'Clean, safe & central location, near all tourist attractions, self-service cafeteria.' 'Brilliant.' Metro: Metro Center. *www.hotel-harrington.com*.

International Guest House, 1441 Kennedy St NW, 726-5808, 4 miles from downtown. From $20, includes bfast, tea and cookies at 9pm. Rsvs recommended. Check-in from 8am, out 10am. Closed Sun 10am-3pm, curfew 11pm. Metro: Columbia Heights (10mins bus ride) 'Very kind people; you can meet travellers from all over the world here.' *www.bedandbreakfast.com*.

Kalorama Guest House, 1854 Mintwood Pl NW, 667-6369. A Victorian-style home in Adams Morgan, From $55, 10% discount w/student ID. Rsvs preferred, check-in 1pm-8pm, out 11am. 'We were very well looked after.' Metro: Woodley Park-Zoo/Adams Morgan. *www.washingtonpost.com/yp/kgh*.

Washington International AYH Hostel, 1009 11th St NW, 737-2333. $29 AYH, $32 non-AYH. Linens free, towels provided, laundry facility, paid internet-access. Open all day, check-out 11am. Organises tours and outings. Rsvs strongly recommended. 'All the facilities you could need—the red jelly baby of the hostel world.' 'Excellent.' Metro: Metro Center. *www.hiwashingtondc.org*.

Washington International Student Center, 2451 18th St NW, 667-7681/(800) 567-4150. Dorms $28, free pickup from Amtrak and Greyhound (rsvs in advance), bfast, internet access. Metro: Dupont Circle/Woodley Park. 'Mixed reviews.' *www.hostel.com*.

Camping: Cherry Hill Park, 9800 Cherry Hill Rd, College Park, MD, (301) 937-7116/(800) 801-6449. $36, XP-$4. Pool, hot tub, sauna. Metro: College Park, then take #83 bus to Cherry Hill. *www.cherryhillpark.com*.

B&B: Bed and Breakfast Accommodations, Ltd., PO Box 12011, Washington DC, 328-3510: A great reservation service for dozens of B&Bs around the area, with rooms ranging from $50 (S) and $60 (D). *www.bedandbreakfastdc.com*.

Food

Near the Mall: Restaurants are scarce around the Mall and the distance between them can be daunting to a hungry stomach-on-legs. Most museums have a (crowded and noisy) cafeteria. A few government cafeterias are open to the public during working hours: '**Dept of Commerce** building cafeteria—good food at reasonable prices.' Just be aware that in the summer all the other visitors to the nation's capital are going to head for them too.

Au Bon Pain, at locations all over DC. Choose from a variety of different breads, pastries and salads, or design your own sandwich at little cost. 'Good places for BUNACers.' *www.aubonpain.com*.

The Cascades Cafe, in the basement of the **National Gallery of Art** between the old and new wings, 216-5966. Mon-Sat 11am-3pm, Sun 11am-4pm. Espresso and Gelato Bar: Mon-Sat 10am-4.30pm, Sun 11am-5.30pm. 'Tourist food, tourist prices, but it's beside a fabulous waterfall—it's like being a part of a sculpture. Worth a cup of coffee.' (The gallery also contains two other decent cafeterias.) *www.nga.gov/ginfo/cafes.htm*.

International Square, 19th & K Sts NW, 223-1850, French, Italian, Chinese, US, etc. Watch Washington lobbyists eat lunch. Mon-Fri 8am-6pm, Sat 10am-5pm.

Library of Congress Cafeteria, top floor of the Madison Building of the L of C, 1st St and Independence Ave SE. Open for bfast and lunch, standard cafeteria food at reasonable prices. Offers one of the best views of the city. Mon-Fri 9am-10:30am (bfast), 12:30pm-2pm (lunch), open 'til 3pm for snacks. *www.loc.gov/loc/visit/food.html*.

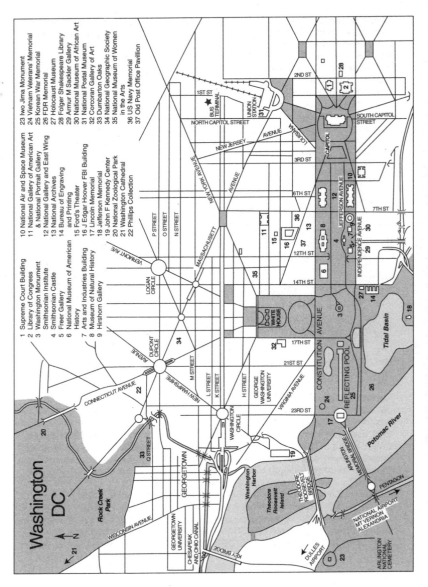

Washington DC

1 Supreme Court Building
2 Library of Congress
3 Washington Monument
4 Smithsonian Institute
5 Freer Gallery
6 National Museum of American History
7 Arts and Industries Building
8 Museum of Natural History
9 Hirshorn Gallery
10 National Air and Space Museum
11 National Gallery of American Art & National Portrait Gallery
12 National Gallery and East Wing
13 National Archives
14 Bureau of Engraving and Printing
15 Ford's Theater
16 J Edgar Hoover FBI Building
17 Lincoln Memorial
18 Jefferson Memorial
19 John F Kennedy Center
20 National Zoological Park
21 Washington Cathedral
22 Phillips Collection
23 Iwo Jima Monument
24 Vietnam Veterans' Memorial
25 Korean War Memorial
26 FDR Memorial
27 Holocaust Museum
28 Folger Shakespeare Library
29 Armur M Sackler Gallery
30 National Museum of African Art
31 National Postal Museum
32 Corcoran Gallery of Art
33 Dumbarton Oaks
34 National Geographic Society
35 National Museum of Women in the Arts
36 US Navy Memorial
37 Old Post Office Pavillion

Old Post Office Pavilion Food Court, 1100 Pennsylvania Ave NW, 289-4224. 'Large selection of reasonably priced places to eat—American, Greek, Indian, Chinese, etc,' plus entertainment. Summer hours: Mon-Sat 10am-8pm, Sun noon-7pm. _www.oldpostofficedc.com_.

Reeve's Bakery, 1306 G St NW, 628-6350. Excellent bakery with simple restaurant in the basement, burgers and sandwiches for reasonable prices (around $6). Open Mon-Sat 7am-6pm. _www.reevesbakery.com_.

Shops at National Place, 1331 Pennsylvania Ave NW, 662-1250. Plenty of inexpensive eateries. Mon-Sat 10am-7pm, Sun noon-5pm.

Soho Café & Market, at 6 locations throughout DC including 1101 Connecticut Ave NW, 466-2767 and 1901 Pennsylvania Ave, 223-3030. Open for buffet bfast, lunch and dinner, Mon-Fri 6:30am-5pm. Superb selection of hot and cold foods, sandwiches, salads, fruits and ice-creams. Priced by weight. Well worth a visit.

Union Station Food Court, 50 Massachusetts Ave NE, 289-1908/(800) LASA-LL4, houses a wide variety of eating places, everything from bagels to rice bowls to gourmet frozen yoghurt. Easy access by metro. _www.unionstationdc.com_.

US Senate Cafeteria, in the basement of the Dirkson Bldg, Capitol Hill, 224-4249. Famous for its Bean Soup. 'Try it—you'll know where they get their wind.' Open to public 7.30am-3pm for breakfast and lunch.

Ethnic food:

DC excels at cheap, authentic, ethnic restaurants. Generally speaking, look for Vietnamese food in the Vietnamese enclave in Arlington, VA (take the blue/orange metro line to the Clarendon stop); good Ethiopian and various types of Hispanic eateries in the Adams-Morgan 18th St & Columbia Ave NW area; and seafood at Market Lunch (in Eastern Market, 225 7th St SE) at the Eastern Market metro stop on the blue/orange line - try the excellent crab cakes; and on Maine Ave along the Potomac River in SW, Metro: Waterfront. If you're feeling spontaneous, go to Adams-Morgan and look around - it would be hard to go wrong, no matter which restaurant you stumble into. Some recommendations:

Bangkok Bistro, 3251 Prospect St, Georgetown, 337-2424. Fantastic contemporary Thai cuisine at reasonable prices, great selection of noodle and rice dishes, salads, seafood and soups. Entrees around $10. Mon-Thur 11:30am-10:45pm, Fri 'til 11:45pm, Sat noon-11:45pm, Sun 'til 10:45pm.

Burrito Brothers, 1718 Connecticut Ave NW, 332-2308. Carry out your quesadillas, tacos, etc, a few southward steps to Dupont Circle for a Mexican picnic amid an ever-changing crowd of bike messengers, chess players, musicians and protesters. Delicious and filling for a good price ($5-$7). Mon-Thu 11am-10.30pm, Fri-Sat 'til 11pm, Sun noon-9pm. Metro: Dupont Circle.

Cactus Cantina, 3300 Wisconsin Ave NW, 686-7222. Good value Mexican food, look for the big plastic cacti outside. Daily 11am-11pm, 'til midnight on Fridays and Saturdays. _www.cactuscantina.com_.

City Lights of China, 1731 Connecticut Ave NW, 265-6688. Absolutely the best Chinese food in Washington, even the fortune cookies are delicious! Try pan-fried dumplings and vegetable curl. $10-$16, 'moderately expensive but worth it'. Open Mon-Fri 11:30am-10.30pm, Sat noon-11pm, Sun 'til 10:30pm, _www.citylightsofchina.com_. Metro: Dupont Circle.

El Tamarindo, 1785 Florida Ave NW, 328-3660. Salvadoran and Mexican dinners, from $11, 15% discount w/student ID. By all accounts the cheapest and best in Adams-Morgan. Most potent margaritas in DC. Free tortillas and salsa; wash it all down with a Mexican beer. Open Sun-Thur 11am-3am, Fri-Sat 'til 5am.

Meskerem, 2434 18th St NW, 462-4100. Ethiopian restaurant renowned for quality cuisine and affordable prices. Eat upstairs sitting on floor cushions and soak in the ambience. Be warned though: you'll struggle to your feet after filling up on a plate of _injera_ and _wats_! Friendly staff and bright decor. Appetizers $4-$7, dinner $9-$13. Worth it: 'You won't have to eat for a week!' Noon-12am Mon-Thu, till 3am Fri-Sun. _www.meskeremonline.com_.

Mixtec, 1792 Columbia Rd at 18th, Adams Morgan, 332 1011. Tacos, tamales, tortas, etc, best value true Mexican food in DC! 'Highly recommended.' $3.95+

Nam-Viet Pho 79, 3419 Connecticut Ave NW, 237-1015. Across from the Uptown Theatre, some of the most delicious and cheapest food in the city! 'Pho' designates a special type of noodle soup, which must be tried, but a great variety of other foods await. Mon-Thur and Sun 11am-10pm, Fri-Sat 'til 11pm, _www.namviet1.com_.

Thai Room, 5037 Connecticut Ave NW, 244-5933. Sample real Thai food, dinner around $8. Don't get this mixed up with the more expensive and not-as-good Thai restaurant down the street. Open daily 11.30am-10pm.

White Tiger, 301 Massachusetts Ave NE, 546-5900. Lunch buffet $9 Mon-Fri, $10 w/ends. Indian dishes varying from eggplant to chick-pea to lamb. Open daily 11am-2:30pm (lunch), 5:30pm-10pm (dinner). Metro: Union Station.

Plain old American:

2 Amy's Pizza, 3715 Macomb St NW, 885-5700. Fantastic pizzas, eat-in or take-out, for around $10. Open Tue-Sat 11am-11pm, Sun 12pm-10pm.

Ben's Chili Bowl, 1213 U St, 667-0909. A Washington institution for forty years— every chili product under the sun, dirt-cheap. Open Mon-Fri 6am-2am, Sat 'til 4am, Sun 11am-8pm. _www.benschilibowl.com_.

Booeymonger's, 3265 Prospect St NW, 333-4810 and 5252 Wisconsin Ave NW, 686-5805. Great sandwiches, burgers and bagels $3-$7. Popular with students. Open 7:30am-midnight.

The Brickskeller, 1523 22nd St NW, 293-1885. Over 850 different beers from all over the world. Good, cheap food includes buffalo, 'Tastes like beef.' Beers from US microbreweries more potent than US domestic beers—you have been warned! Mon-Thu 11.30am-2am, Fri 'til 3am, Sat 6pm-3am, Sun 'til 2am, _www.the-brickskeller.com_. Metro: Dupont Circle.

Chesapeake Bagel Bakery, 818 18th St NW, 775-4690. Great coffee and bran muffins, as well as cheap bagels (also open for lunch and supper). Mon-Fri 6:30am-4pm, Sat 8am-3pm. Metro: Farragut North.

The Diner, 2453 18th St, Adams Morgan, 232-8800. You name it – they do it: breakfasts, burgers, sandwiches and homemade dinners, all very reasonably priced between $4-$13. Dine outdoors or indoors, 'great atmosphere'. Open 24hrs.

Lindy's, 2040 I St NW, near Tower Records, 452-0055. Perfect for lunch. Choose from 24 different varieties of burgers, each with vegetarian equivalent and lots of sandwiches, $4-$7. Tempting ice-cream store in the arcade next door. Open Sun-Thu 8am-2am, till 3am Fri-Sat. Metro: Foggy Bottom.

Luna Grill and Diner, 1301 Connecticut Ave, 835-2280. 'Fantastic atmosphere, great selection of food including lots of vegetarian dishes.' $5-$8 for a good meal. Open Mon-Thur 8am-11pm, Fri-Sat 'til 1am, Sun 'til 10pm. Metro: Dupont Circle.

Old Ebbitt Grille, 675 15th St NW, 347-4800. Near White House. Famous for their excellent bowls of chilli ($4-$5) served with sourdough, sour cream and chopped onions. Open Mon-Fri 7:30am-1:30am, Sat-Sun 8:30am-1:30am, _www.ebbitt.com_.

Atmosphere:

Barnes & Noble, 3040 M St NW, 965-9880. Georgetown. Three storeys, with café on top floor, which sometimes hosts concerts. Highly social coffee shop.

Food for Thought, 1811 14th St NW, 797-1095. Vegetarian and vegan food, whole-earth music nightly. Near to Black Cat nightclub. Bargain prices for substantial meals. Sun-Thur 8pm-1am, Fri-Sat 7pm-2am.

Kramerbooks and Afterwords Cafe, 1517 Connecticut Ave NW, 387-3825. Bookshop and cafe with jazz, folk and bluegrass music. The place to book-browse or people-watch. Order margaritas and split the atomic nachos, or chill out with a smoothie (blended ice-cream, fruit and liquor—delicious!), 7.30am-1am during the week, 24 hrs at w/ends. _www.kramers.com_.

La Madeleine, 3000 M St, Georgetown, 337-6975. This French bakery and café serves up tasty and inexpensive breakfasts, sandwiches, salads and crêpes. Open Sun-Thur 6:30am-11pm, Fri-Sat 'til midnight, _www.lamadeleine.com_.

La Ruche, 1039 31st St NW, 965-2684. Exquisite crab bisque and baked sandwiches, $4-$8, lovely outdoor patio. _www.cafelaruche.com_.

Politics and Prose Bookstore, 5015 Connecticut Ave NW, 354-1919. Mon-Thu 9am-10pm, Fri & Sat 'til 11pm, Sun 10am-8pm. _www.politics-prose.com_

Sweet tooth: The best ice cream in DC is **Max's Best Ice Cream**, 2416 Wisconsin Ave NW, 333-3111, where you can sample the best-selling Orange Chocolate Chip or one of their 149 other flavours. Open Mon-Thur noon-11pm, Fri-Sat 'til midnight, Sun 'til 10pm. Pop into **Thomas Sweets**, 3214 P St, Georgetown, 337-0616, try the cinnamon ice cream if you like 'Cheerios'.Daily 8am-11pm.

Of interest
Government buildings:
Botanic Garden, 1st St & Independence Ave SW, btwn Air and Space Museum and Capitol, 225-8333. Tired feet will enjoy a respite as you lounge on benches amid 500 varieties of orchids and other tropical flora. It features an indoor conservatory (open daily 10am-5pm) and the Bartholdi Park landscaped gardens (open daily dusk-dawn), free. Metro: Federal Center SW. _www.usbg.gov._

Bureau of Engraving and Printing, 14th & C Sts SW, 874-3019. Manufactures paper money, government bonds and stamps. Free guided tours Mon-Fri 9am-2pm. Get tkts for the tour at the ticket booth on Raoul Wallenberg Pl, which opens at 8am. 'No free samples.' Metro: Smithsonian. _www.bep.treas.gov._

The Capitol, 225-6827, on Capitol Hill, the central point of Washington from which the city is divided into quadrants. The city's most familiar landmark, it holds the chambers of the Senate and the House of Representatives. Of particular note are the works of Brumidi in the Great Rotunda and corridors. Free, guided tours cover the Rotunda, the National Statuary Hall and the Crypt. 'Very interesting tour, certainly worthwhile.' Tours leave every half hour, Mon-Sat 9am-4:30pm, from the temporary visitor receiving facility at the south end of the Capitol. The Senate and House galleries are open only when each body is in session. 'Most interesting part is the Senate Chamber-much smaller than you'd expect.' Get tkts for the tour from the Capitol Guide Service Kiosk from 9am, distributed on first-come, first-served basis, 1 per person, passport or photo ID required. Metro: Capitol South. 'Expect tough security checks.' _www.aoc.gov/cc/visit/index.cfm_ .

Folger Shakespeare Library, 2nd & East Capitol Sts SE, behind the Library of Congress's Jefferson Building, 544-4600. Here you'll find America's finest Shakespeare collection, including 79 copies of the _First Folio_ (the first published edition of Shakespeare's collected works)-more copies than anywhere else. At least one is always on display. Mon-Sat 10am-4pm, free. Metro: Capitol South. _www.folger.edu._

J Edgar Hoover FBI Building, Pennsylvania Ave btwn 9th & 10th Sts NW, 324-3447. Named after the man they couldn't get rid of because he had the goods on them all, even though, as it turns out, the Mafia had the goods on _him_. Guided tours postponed indefinitely as of 2005 – call or check website for updated info. 'Ugliest building in DC.' 'Disappointing.' Metro: Metro Center. _www.fbi.gov/aboutus/tour/tour.htm._

Library of Congress, 1st St and Independence Ave SE, opposite Capitol, 707-8000. The largest library in the world is made up of three buildings, but the one you'll want to see is the astounding **Jefferson Building:** walls, ceilings and floors are covered with inspiring, allegorical scenes representing such popular subjects as 'Truth, Beauty'. The cumulative effect is overwhelming (west entrance on 1st St is open for viewings of the Great Hall, Mon-Sat 10am-5.30pm. Tours available). Among the library's holdings are a perfect copy of the Gutenberg Bible (1450-the first book to be printed from moveable type), Jefferson's rough draft of the _Declaration of Independence_, Lincoln's drafts of the _Gettysburg Address_, a vast folk music collection you can listen to (by appt.) and a major portion of the books published in the US since the Civil War. Metro: Capitol South. _www.loc.gov._

National Archives, 8th St and Constitution Ave NW, 501-5000. Preserves and displays government records of enduring value such as the *Declaration of Independence*, *Bill of Rights*, *Constitution* and *Watergate Tapes*. Open daily Memorial Day weekend through Labour Day 10am-9pm, free. Metro: Archives/Navy Memorial. *www.archives.gov*.

Supreme Court Building, 1st St, btwn Maryland Ave & E Capitol St NE, facing the Capitol, 479-3211. The country's highest judicial body holds its sessions here. You can see the court in session by waiting in line, but the court is usually adjourned from the end of June until October. Mon-Fri 9am-4:30pm, tours hourly 9.30am-3.30pm, free. Metro: Capitol South. *www.supremecourtus.gov*.

White House, 1600 Pennsylvania Ave NW, 456-7041. Although he chose the site, George Washington is the only president never to have slept here. The White House has been rebuilt or redesigned inside and out many times, most memorably in 1814, courtesy of the British Army who burnt it down. The structural integrity may have been most severely tested in 1829 during Andrew Jackson's inaugural carouse - the new president's backwoods buddies nearly destroyed the place! Currently no tours are available to the public. Metro: McPherson Sq. The White House Visitor Center, 15th and E Sts, has great exhibits on various aspects of the mansion, open daily 7:30am-4pm. Metro: Federal Triangle or Metro Center. *www.nps.gov/whho*.

MONUMENTS: The National Park Service, which runs all of DC's monuments and major parks, has an amazing web site: *www.nps.gov*, or call 426-6841 for all monuments. Open daily 10am-10pm. Entrance to all the monuments is free.

The **Franklin D Roosevelt Memorial**, 376-6704, is situated near the cherry tree walk on the Tidal Basin, W Potomac Park. Each of FDR's four terms in office are represented by a stunning landscape of four outdoor rooms with inscribed walls and sculpted figures of pink Carnelian granite, surrounded by a profusion of waterfalls, trees and plants. Metro: Smithsonian. *www.nps.gov/fdrm/home.htm*.

Jefferson Memorial, on Tidal Basin south of Mall. A 19ft bronze Thomas Jefferson stands in the domed rotunda, designed to resemble Jefferson's own home at Monticello. Smaller crowds and the quiet serenity of the ionic columns create an intimate monument. See it at night, floodlit, for best effect. *www.nps.gov/thje/home.htm*.

Korean War Memorial, adjacent to the **Lincoln Memorial Reflecting Pool**. A sculptured row of 19 7ft stainless steel soldiers ready for combat and a 164 ft mural etched with over 2000 photographic images of service men and women, depicts in detail the hardship and tragedy of a war in which 54,000 Americans lost their lives. 24 hrs. Metro: Foggy Bottom. *www.nps.gov/kwvm/home.htm*.

Lincoln Memorial, at the foot of the Mall, 24 hrs. The large 19ft brooding figure flanked by two Lincoln addresses etched into the walls, is an impressive sight that no visitor to the city should miss. Rather than becoming an overgrown tombstone, this memorial has evolved into a living symbol of freedom and human dignity. *www.nps.gov/linc/home.htm*.

The **Vietnam Veterans Memorial** is just next door, a sombre granite slab that lists the names of all 58,000 American dead in the war and has a starkly direct power. The faces of the visitors tell more than the memorial does. The **Vietnam Women's Memorial**, across from the Wall, depicts three service women with a wounded soldier. Metro: Foggy Bottom. *www.nps.gov/vive/home.htm*.

Washington Monument, on the Mall at 15th St. This 555 ft obelisk, by law the tallest structure in DC, was built to honour the first president of the US. The view from the top of the recently re-vamped observation room is splendid. Get free tkts from the booth on 15th St—it's a good idea to go early, or book in advance and get tkts for $2 at (800) 967-2283. Don't believe anyone who tells you that the line about 3/4 of the way up the side of the monument is the 'high water mark' from spring floods (it's actually the point at which construction was halted during the Civil War and later resumed with a different colour of stone). 'Closes during thunderstorms!' Daily 9am-4:45pm. Ranger-led walk down tours of the inside at 10am and 2:30pm. Metro: Smithsonian. *www.nps.gov/wamo/home.htm*.

World War II Memorial, on the Mall, 17th St between Constitution Ave and Independence Ave. Opened 2004. 24 hrs. *www.wwiimemorial.com*.

SMITHSONIAN INSTITUTION. The world's largest museum and research complex, begun by British scientist James Smithson, who left his entire fortune (105 bags of gold) to finance it. The Smithsonian comprises the National Zoo and 15 museums and galleries, most of which are on the Mall between the Capitol and the Washington Monument. There are millions of catalogued items ranging from Lindbergh's plane to Glenn's capsule, from fossils to the Hope Diamond, from moon rocks to the First Ladies' gowns. All museums are free (nominal charge for films). General hours 10am-5.30pm (some museums extend their hours in summer). 357-2020 for 24 hr info on new displays and events; for general info call 357-2700. *www.si.edu*. Check *Washington Post Weekend Section* for exhibits.

The **Arthur M. Sackler Gallery** and the **National Museum of African Art**, both 10th St and Independence Ave SW. Underground museums behind the **Smithsonian Castle**. The former houses a collection of Asian art and artefacts, while the latter is the only museum dedicated to African art in the US. *www.nmafa.si.edu*. **The Freer Gallery**, 12th St & Jefferson Dr SW, has a wonderful collection of Asian and Asian-inspired art, with an underground link to the Sackler. *www.asia.si.edu*.

The **Smithsonian Castle**, the museum's original building, houses a Visitor's Center with info on all there is to see and do. Go and see one of the various and ever-changing exhibitions at **The Arts and Industries Building**, 900 Jefferson Dr. It is also worth making a stop at the **Anacostia Museum** and **Center for African American History and Culture**, 1901 Fort Pl SE. Metro: Smithsonian.

Hirshhorn Museum and Sculpture Garden on the Mall at Independence Ave, has a modern art collection not to be missed. The upper floors of the controversial, donut-shaped Hirshhorn display a fine permanent collection of 20th century art (1930-1970ish); the lounge has a nice view of the Mall. But the changing exhibits in the basement are where the avant-garde action is. The theatre in the basement occasionally screens free cutting-edge films. Metro: L'Enfant Plaza. *www.hirsh-horn.si.edu*.

Museum of Natural History, 10th St & Constitution Ave, is truly 'the nation's attic'— some 124 million artefacts—it even *smells* like mothballs and formalde-hyde! Scattered throughout seemingly endless hallways are wildlife dioramas, dinosaur bones, the Hope Diamond, a functioning coral reef, live insects, Indian skulls with partially-healed holes, a perfect crystal ball and the world's largest stuffed elephant. The museum has a 3D IMAX movie theatre. Metro: Smithsonian. *www.mnh.si.edu*.

National Air and Space Museum, next door to the Hirshhorn. This popular museum has everything from space capsules to U2 photographs of Soviet missile sites, to the earliest planes. 'Best thing we did in Washington, take a tape-recorded tour for most benefit.' 'A must.' See the 'mind-blowing' films such as *Infinity Express* on a 5-storey IMAX screen that gives you the impression you are voyaging through the solar system, past the Milky Way, to the very edge of the known universe and back. 'Highly recommended.' $8. Call 633-4629 for listings, or go to *www.smithsonian.org/imax* to buy tickets online. 'Good cafe.' Metro: L'Enfant Plaza. *www.nasm.si.edu*.

National Museum of American History, Behring Center, across the Mall at 12th St & Constitution Ave, has all sorts of Americana including Dorothy's ruby slippers, Fonzie's leather jacket, Archie Bunker's chair, and huge locomotives. 'A delve into the realms of American culture!' Don't miss the Information Technology exhibit.

Voted #2 among all DC area museums in the Washington Post's 2005 Best Bets Awards. Metro: Smithsonian. *www.americanhistory.si.edu*.

National Postal Museum, City Post Office Building, Massachusetts Ave & North Capitol St NE, a fascinating paean to not only the lowly stamp, but also the way the postal system has helped to define the country. Recently acquired John Lennon's childhood stamp album. Metro: Union Station. *www.si.edu\postal*.

National Zoological Park, 3001 Connecticut Ave NW, 673-4800. The zoo has over 2,700 animals belonging to 435 different species, best known of which are the giant pandas. Check out the *Amazonia* exhibit, an indoor tropical rainforest, watch an Asian elephant training demonstration, or visit the *Think Tank*, a mind-stretcher that delves into the realm of animal intelligence.   Summer 6am-8pm (animal houses 10am-6pm), winter 6am-6pm (animal houses 10am-4.30pm).   Free. Metro: Woodley Park Zoo *www.nationalzoo.si.edu*.

National Museum of the American Indian, 4th St and Independence Ave, 633-1000. 10am-5.30pm daily. The newest of the Smithsonian museums. One of three NMAIs in the US. Features exhibits on contemporary American Indian lives, 'Our Universes' and 'Our Peoples'. *www.nmai.si.edu*

National Portrait Gallery, due to re-open July 4, 2006. 275-1738. *www.npg.si.edu* and **Smithsonian American Art Museum**, **also** due to re-open July 4, 2006. A temporary site is the Renwick Gallery, 17th St and Pennsylvania Ave, 633-2850. 10am-5.30pm. *www.americanart.si.edu*.

More of interest

Dumbarton Oaks, 31st St btwn R & S Sts, 339-6401. Hidden away above Georgetown sits this discreet wonder. The gardens are simply heavenly, the design making every corner private, romantic and relaxing. The one real must see in DC.' Tue-Sun 2pm-5pm, gardens open daily 2pm-6pm, $7 admission to the garden. The museum is closed until 2007 for renovations, but gardens remain open. *www.doaks.org*.

Corcoran Gallery of Art, 500 17th St NW, 639-1700/(888) CORCORAN. Washington's oldest art museum. Open daily except Mon and Tue, 10am-5pm, Thur till 9pm, $8, $4 w/student ID. *www.corcoran.org*.

Ford's Theatre, 517 10th St NW, 426-6924 (box office 347-4833). Where Lincoln was shot by John Wilkes Booth in 1865. Beautifully restored; call first to avoid rehearsals and performances if just looking. Daily 9am-5pm, free. Interesting talks given in the theatre throughout the day. Excellent museum in basement. Opposite is the house where Lincoln died the next day, open daily 9am-5pm, free. Metro: Metro Center. *www.fordstheatre.org*.

Holocaust Memorial Museum, 100 Raoul Wallenberg Place SW, 488-0400. Intense, moving, thought-provoking record of the Holocaust and its victims between 1933 and 1945. Daily 10am-5.30pm, free (passes required—available from 10am at the 14th St entrance. Get there early!). 'Highly recommended.' 'Very moving, it will stay with you for the rest of your life.' Metro: Smithsonian. *www.ushmm.org*.

International Spy Museum, 800 F St NW, (866) SPY-MUSEUM. A museum with a mission to educate the public about espionage… hands-on fun! 10am-8pm daily, $14-18. *www.spymuseum.org*.

National Gallery of Art, 737-4215, sprawls magnificently along Constitution Ave at the upper end of the Mall. Though not part of the Smithsonian, the National Gallery takes a place of honour on the Mall and should be a priority on any trip. The west wing houses one of the world's greatest collections of Western European painting and sculpture, from the 13th century to the present and American art from Colonial times. Rembrandt, French Impressionists and Flemish, Spanish, German and British artists are all represented, plus one proudly displayed da Vinci, the sole work by that artist on the North American continent. Connected via an underground walkway, I.M Pei's **East Wing** is a work of art in itself. This modern structure, formed by unexpected juxtapositions of triangles, displays the gallery's modern art. Picasso, Mondrian, Rothko, Motherwell and O'Keeffe line the walls and magnificent changing exhibitions keep things lively. Mon-Sat 10am-5pm, Sun 11pm-6pm, free. Excellent underground café. Metro: Archives/ Judiciary Sq. *www.nga.gov*.

National Geographic's Explorers Hall, 17th & M Sts NW, 857-7588. The world famous magazine displays some of its work with interesting exhibits featuring some breathtaking photography. Mon-Sat 9am-5pm, Sun 10am-5pm, free. 'Quality museum.' Metro: Farragut North. *www.nationalgeographic.com*.

National Museum of Women in the Arts, 1250 New York Ave NW, 783-5000. One of the few museums devoted entirely to art created by women including Mary Cassat, Georgia O'Keeffe. Mon-Sat 10am-5pm, Sun noon-5pm, $6 w/student ID. 'Worth seeing.' Metro: Metro Center. *www.nmwa.org*.

U.S Navy Memorial and Heritage Center, 701 Pennsylvania Ave, NW, 737-2300. The outdoor memorial features an enormous, granite map of the world and its oceans, overlooked by the Lone Sailor. Free Navy band concerts on Tuesday evenings in summer. The Heritage Center includes interactive exhibits and the dramatic film, *At Sea*, shown Mon-Sat at noon. Mon-Sat 9.30am-5pm, free. Metro: Archives-Navy Memorial. *www.lonesailor.org*.

Old Post Office Pavilion, 1100 Pennsylvania Ave NW, 289-4224, has a short tour with a free ride in an interior glass elevator to a tower overlooking the city. Not as high as the Washington Monument, but the lines are not as long and the breezy arches afford an equally good—if not better—view of the city. Elevator runs Tue-Sat 9am-7:45pm, Sun 10am-5:45pm throughout the summer. There's entertainment in the food court daily. Open daily 7am-8pm. Metro: Federal Triangle. *www.old-postofficedc.com*.

Phillips Collection, 1600 21st NW at Q St, 387-2151. In a modest gallery and recent extensions sits a treasure house of art. While its centrepiece, Renoir's *Luncheon of the Boating Party*, attracts all the tourists, the Cézannes, Picassos, Delacroix', Goyas and a room of Rothko are equally worth a look. Excellent exhibitions. Tue-Sat 10am-5pm, Sun noon-5pm. $8, $6 w/student ID. 'Beautifully designed; superb collection.' 'A wonderful surprise.' Metro: Dupont Circle. *www.phillipscollection.org*.

Washington National Cathedral (Cathedral Church of St Peter and St Paul), Wisconsin and Massachusetts Aves NW, 364-6616. This beautiful cathedral dominates the skyline from wherever you are in DC, perched as it is on one of the city's highest points. Teddy Roosevelt laid the cornerstone in 1907 and it was finally completed in 1990. It has gargoyles of Washington lawyers and Darth Vader and a moon rock embedded in one of its stained glass windows. Woodrow Wilson is interred here and it was from this pulpit that Rev. Martin Luther King Jr. preached his last Sunday sermon. Mon-Fri 10-5.30pm, Sat till 4.30pm, Sun 8am-6.30pm. Metro: Tenleytown. *www.cathedral.org*.

Out of doors

The Harbour Front in Georgetown: a collection of expensive restaurants and bars along the Potomac River, interesting for its architecture and for people watching. Especially lovely at night, when the orchestrated fountain gushes in a colourful symphonetta. Water taxis stop here. While in the Georgetown area, go and climb the infamous, long, narrow **staircase from the Exorcist**, which leads from a gas station on M St up to Prospect St.

Kenilworth Aquatic Gardens, 1551 Anacostia Ave NE, 426-6905. Amazing collection of water lilies, lotuses and bamboo, grown in ponds along the Anacostia River. Hard to get to without a car and located in one of the grittier areas of the city, but still definitely worth the trip. Open daily 8am-4pm, free. Metro: Deanwood. *www.nps.gov/nace/keaq*.

National Arboretum, 3501 New York Ave NE, 245-2726. This park is in the middle of a somewhat run-down area of the city. With more than 400 acres of plants, picnic grounds, Bonsai and azalea collections, and trees from every state in the union, most visitors forget they're in the city. But, as arboretums go, not the world's greatest. Daily 8am-5pm, free. It's best to drive here, but you can also catch a free shuttle from Union Station every 40 minutes. *www.usna.usda.gov*.

Rock Creek Park, 895-6000. Almost 1,800 acres of rustic woods surrounding Rock Creek. There's a network of trails, riding stables, tennis courts, picnic areas and a nature centre. Daily 8am-dusk, free. The park occupies a large part of Washington's NW section and can be entered at several points. By Metro, the Woodley Park-Zoo/Adams Morgan, Cleveland Park, Foggy Bottom and Silver Spring stations are all within walking distance. *www.nps.gov/rocr*.

Theodore Roosevelt Island, Potomac Park NW, (703) 289-2530. This peaceful isle is accessed by footbridge from the car park off the northbound lane of the George Washington Pkwy. The 17ft bronze statue of Roosevelt, champion of nature and wildlife conservation, can be seen in the Statutory Garden. The island is also home to a wildlife refuge with over 2 miles of trails. Daily dawn-dusk. Metro: Rosslyn. *www.nps.gov/this*.

The **Tidal Basin** is surrounded by a ring of cherry trees, a gift from Japan in the early 1900s, best experienced during the **Cherry Blossom Festival**, late March to early April. The Tidal Basin Boathouse, 479-2426, rents peddle boats throughout the spring and summer months, daily10am-6pm; $8 for two-seater, $16 for four-seater. Metro: Smithsonian. *www.guestservices.com*.

The Mall. Evenings on the Mall are a treat for sports enthusiasts. 'Pick-up games of softball, hockey, football, volleyball and ultimate frisbee,' are always on the go. On w/ends you can also watch cricket and polo.

Sport

American Football: Redskins Stadium, in Landover, MD, (301) 276-6000, is the home of the **Washington Redskins** who play Aug (pre-season)-Jan. If you want to pay at minimum $125 to see this most American of spectacles, call Top Center Ticket Service: 452-9040, or Ticket City: 544-0919 about a week in advance. 'Fans are fiercely proud.' Metro: shuttle bus service from Addison Rd, Landover and Cheverly stations. *www.redskins.com*.

Baseball: RFK Stadium, E Capitol St, (866) 800-1275. Home of the new **Washington Nationals**, bought from the Montreal Expos in 2004. $7-45 per seat. *http://washington.nationals.mlb.com*. Metro: Stadium-Armory.

Basketball/Hockey: MCI Center, 601 F St NW, 661-5000. **The Washington Wizards** (men's basketball) play here Nov-Apr, tkts from $15, *www.washingtonwizards.com*. The women's basketball league is only a few years old, but the **Washington Mystics'** fans are intensely loyal and tickets are cheaper (from $8), Jun-Aug, *www.washingtonmystics.com*. **The Capitals** (hockey) play here Oct-Apr, tkts $10-$39, *www.washingtoncaps.com*. Call TicketMaster, 432-SEAT. Metro: Gallery Place/Chinatown.

Biking: DC and the surrounding area is home to hundreds of miles of trails for walking and biking. The Mall, Rock Creek Park and the C&O Canal are great spots for bike rides. Another scenic route is the **Mt. Vernon Trail** along the Potomac River, from Memorial Bridge through Alexandria to Mt. Vernon. **Bike the Sites**, 842-2453, runs 3 hr, 8-mile bicycle tours of Washington starting at 10am. The $40 price includes bicycle, helmet, water and snack. Call ahead for rsvs. *www.bikethesites.com*. Rent bikes from **Fletcher's Boat House**, Reservoir and Canal Rds NW, 244-0461, for $4/hr or $12/day, *www.fletchersboathouse.com*.

Canoeing - Thompson's Boat Center, 2900 Virginia Ave NW, 333-9543, rents bikes for $4-$8/hr or $15-$25/day, or take a canoe on to the Potomac for a nice aquatic view of the sights: $8/hr, $22/day. *www.thompsonboatcenter.com*. Both boat houses are located along the C&O Canal.

Ice Skating: the small **Sculpture Garden Ice Rink** on the Mall at Constitution Ave & 7th St NW, 289-3360, offers skating Nov-Mar, Mon-Thu 10am-10pm, Fri-Sat 'til 11pm, Sun 11am-10pm, $5 w/student ID, skate rental $2.50. Metro: Archives/Navy Memorial. *www.nga.gov/ginfo/skating.shtm*. **Pershing Park Ice Rink**, Pennsylvania Ave & 14th St NW, 737-6938. Intimate rink in the foreground of the ornate Willard Hotel, Nov-Mar, $6.50, skate rental $2.50. Metro: Federal Triangle. *www.pershingparkicerink.com*/.

Soccer: RFK Stadium, 547-9077. Home of **DC Freedom** (women's league), *www.washingtonfreedom.com* and **DC United**, a relatively new soccer team and winners of the '96, '97 and '99 MLS Championship, *www.dcunited.com*. Tkts from $16-$36, available at the RFK ticket booth or from TicketMaster, 432-SEAT.

Shopping

Department Stores and Malls: Hecht's at 1201 G St NW, 628-6661, (Metro: Metro Center) and **Lord and Taylor** at 5255 Western Ave NW, 362-9600, (Metro: Friendship Heights), are two of the biggest stores—watch out for constant sales with huge savings, *www.maycompany.com*. **The Fashion Centre at Pentagon City**, 1100 S Hayes St, Arlington VA, (703) 415-2400, is a state of the art, multi-level mall easily accessible on the Metro. 'Worth it just to see the building—amazing', *www.fashioncentrepentagon.com*. The region's best shopping mall is **Potomac Mills**, 20 miles south of DC on I-95, near Woodbridge, (800) VA-MILLS, one of the best-known discount outlet malls on the east coast. There are over 220 stores that have up to 70% discounts off suggested retail prices for all the major chains. Mon-Sat 10am-9.30pm, Sun 11am-7pm. Omni Bus (703) 730-6664/(888) 730-6664, departs for the mall from Franconia-Springfield Metro Station daily starting 12.50 pm, through 9.25 pm. **Shuttle bus** departs from several locations in DC, including Dupont Circle, Mon, Thur and Fri at 10:15am, Sat at 8.45am and 11:15am, Sun at 11:15am, $15 r/t, call (703) 551-1050 for more info. *www.potomacmills.com*.

Shops and Markets: Georgetown is the place to be seen shopping. Levis, Timberland, Gap, H&M, Banana Republic and assorted more interesting stores (try Commander Salamander at 1420 Wisconsin Ave NW and Second Hand Rose at 1516 Wisconsin) are here on Wisconsin Ave, but the real bargains will be elsewhere. **The Georgetown flea market** on Wisconsin Ave, Sun 8:30am-5pm, if you can stand the blistering heat, is like walking into an unexplored old attic full of bargain Levis, antique clothing, ethnic jewellery, Pentax cameras and even electric guitars. *www.georgetownfleamarket.com*. **Eastern Market**, 7th St SE on Capitol Hill, is an open-air farmers' market on Saturdays and flea market on Sundays. On both days you'll find handicrafts, artwork and used clothing on sale. The indoor section of the market is DC's last old-timey food market, open every day but Monday. Metro: Eastern Market. There's also a **farmer's market** every weekend at 18th & Columbia in the heart of Adams Morgan.

Tours

Capitol River Cruises, (301) 460-7447/(800) 405-5511. Cruises along the historic DC waterfront start on the sweeping curve of the Potomac River at Washington Harbour Pier in Georgetown. Apr 1st-Oct 28th: daily, noon-9pm on the hr, from the pier at 31st & K Sts, 45 mins, $10. *www.capitolrivercruises.com*. Also contact **Spirit Cruises**, 554-8000/ (866) 211-3811, who provide an alternative way to view the city. Pleasant cruise to Mount Vernon, $35, departs at 9am (be there at 8.30am) from Pier 4, 6th at Water St., Washington DC. There are also lunch and dinner cruises, $39 and $72. *www.spiritcruises.com*.

DC Ducks, 966-3825. A land and water tour in a WW2 amphibious landing craft. Vessels depart regularly from Union Station, 10am-4pm every hr on the hr. 11/2 hr

tour $26, 10% discount when tkts purchased online at _www.oldtowntrolleytours.com_.
Old Town Trolley Tour, 832-9800. A loop of DC taking in all the sites, you can hop
off and on again later. $28, 10% discount when tkts purchased online at _www.old-
towntrolleytours.com_. Non-stop tour lasts 2 hrs between 9am and 5pm.
Tourmobile, 554-5100, offers Washington and Arlington Cemetery tours for $20.
Passes are good for a day (9:30am-4:30pm) of unlimited re-boarding and you can
begin at any sight, a 2-day pass costs $30. Look for Tourmobile Sightseeing Shuttle
Bus Stop signs (main ones at Washington Monument, Lincoln Memorial); buses
run every 20 mins. 'Convenient and easy to use'. _www.tourmobile.com_.
Washington Walks, 484-1565, offers informative and entertaining walking tours
throughout the nation's capital city including the _I've Got a Secret_ tour, _Capital
Hauntings_ and the _Best Addresses_ tour. All $10, some tours require advance book-
ings. Go to _www.washingtonwalks.com_ for detailed info about times and dates.

Entertainment
For the best, most comprehensive listings and reviews of what's going on in the
area, pick up a free copy of the _City Paper_ on Thursday (in shops and from street-
corner boxes), the _Weekend_ section of Friday's _Washington Post_ and the NW neighbourhood paper, the _InTowner_, a free monthly paper available around Dupont
Circle and Adams-Morgan.
Festivals: The amazing **Smithsonian Folklife Festival**, held on the Mall for two
weeks around July 4th; **Adams-Morgan Day** (mid-Sept) on 18th St: ethnic music,
dance and food plus local blues and gospel sounds. **Taste of DC**, early Oct on
Pennsylvania Ave, food dished up from area restaurants, free concerts and entertainment. The **Smithsonian Kite Festival**, late March/early April, on the grounds
of the Washington Monument. Kite flying competitions and demonstrations fill the
sky with some of the most elaborate kites in the world. **Cherry Blossom Festival**,
late March to early April, throughout downtown DC. Several events, including a
race, sports tournaments, an arts and crafts show and a parade.
The Mall is the grassy stage for all manner of summer entertainment. On July 4,
fireworks and concerts are held there (for best viewing of fireworks get there early
and take a blanket). Monday nights in July are host to the 'Screen on the Green' festival—classic American movies start at dusk in front of the Washington Monument
absolutely free, but show up an hour ahead if you want to sit close enough to see
and hear the show. The Mall also plays host to sporting events every weekend,
including polo.
Theme Parks: Six Flags America, in Largo, MD, (301) 249-1500, a theme park and
expanded water park, features _Superman—the Ride of Steel_ with a terrifying plunge
and feats of superhuman speed, along with several other roller coasters and twelve
water rides. Admission is $40, but there are usually promotional discounts avail-
able (look out for coupons from CVS, Burger King, Wendy's and on Coke cans).
Open Sun-Thur 10:30am-9pm, Fri-Sat 'til 10pm, _www.sixflags.com_.
Nightlife: Much of it centres on and around bars. Many establishments in the
Dupont and Logan Circle areas cater to the gay crowd.
Childe Harold, 1610 20th St NW, 483-6702, this restaurant/bar is a centre of activ-
ity in Dupont Circle, open 11:30am-2am, _www.childeharold.com_; **Sign of the Whale**,
1825 M St NW, 785-1110, drink specials every night, Sun-Thur 11.30am-1.30am, Fri-
Sat 'til 3am and **The Big Hunt**, 1345 Connecticut Ave NW, 785-2333, pizza, beer and
pool, Mon-Thur 4pm-2am, Fri-Sat 'til 3am, Sun 5pm-2am.
Rhino Bar and Pumphouse, 3295 M St, Georgetown, 333-3150. A favourite with
students and young professionals, you are guaranteed a good time here. Big screen
TV, fantastic drink specials, pool tables and live DJ and dancing every night. Open
Mon-Thur   7pm-2am,   Fri   5pm-3am,   Sat   noon-3am,   Sun   'til   2am.
www.rhinobardc.com.

Eclectic music/spectacle: Birchmere, 3701 Mt. Vernon Ave, Alexandria, VA, (703) 549-7500. A highly renowned showplace for American folk/country/jazz/bluegrass that has hosted Dan Hicks and his Hot Licks, Diane Krall, Doc Watson and Bill Wyman. Times and prices vary, check out _www.birchmere.com_ for details.

Blues Alley, 1073 Wisconsin Ave, Georgetown, 337-4141, showcases best jazz artists in the country. Expensive and reservations necessary, but worth the entrance charge of $16-$40, 1/2 price tkts for 10pm show Sun-Thur w/student ID. Shows daily at 8pm and 10pm. Also serves Creole cuisine. _www.bluesalley.com_.

The Front Page, 1333 New Hampshire Ave NW, 296-6500. 'Popular bar for Happy Hour' (Mon-Fri 4pm-7pm). Cheap beer and free food. 'Good atmosphere, especially on Fridays.' 'Full of interns and would-be politicians.' Open Sun-Thur 11.30am-2am, Fri-Sat 'til 3am.

The Improv Comedy Club and Restaurant, 1140 Connecticut Ave NW, 296-7008. Tue-Thu at 8:30pm, Fri-Sat at 8pm and 10.30pm, Sun at 8pm, dinner served only at early show times. Tkts range from $15-$25. Metro: Farragut North. _www.dcimprov.com_.

Kelly's Irish Times, 14 F St NW, 543-5433. The place to go for those feeling homesick—full of Brits and Irish! A fair number of Americans too: fraternity boys ('sigma chi 'til I die!'), marines, fire-fighters . . . the world is here. Live music-place your requests and sing along. Has downstairs dance club. Open daily 11.30am-2.30am. Also worth a visit—**The Dubliner**, 737-3773, just down the road at 4 F St (can enter through the Phoenix Park hotel). Metro: Union Station. _www.dublinerdc.com/_.

Mr. Smith's of Georgetown, 3104 M St NW, 333-3104. College crowd, heated garden that's quiet enough to have a conversation in. Come for the 'super happy hour,' (4pm-7pm Mon-Fri) with $1-$1.50 off beers and half-price appetisers. Live music daily, piano bar Sun-Thur 9pm-1am, Fri-Sat 10pm-2am. Open daily Sun-Thur 11.30am-1.30am, Fri-Sat 'til 2:30am, _www.mrsmiths.com_.

Madam's Organ, 2461 18th St, in Adams Morgan, 667-5370. Where the beautiful people go to get ugly! Fun atmosphere, nightly blues, bluegrass and soul food to your heart's content. Cover charge varies. Open Sun-Thur 5pm-2am, Fri-Sat 'til 3am. _www.madamsorgan.com_.

The Tombs, 1226 36th St NW, at Prospect in Georgetown, 337-6668. College bar—rowing blades on the wall—food $8-25. Open Mon-Fri 11.30 am-1.15am, Sat 'til 2:15am, Sun 9:30am-1:15am. _www.clydes.com_.

For dancing:Dragonfly, 1215 Connecticut Ave NW, 331-1775. Ice-white interior, pod-like chairs, techno music and video projections. DJs every night. Happy hr Mon-Fri 5:30pm-8pm, open Mon-Fri 5:30pm-1.30am, Sat 7pm-2.30am. _www.dragonflysushibari.com_.

Lulu's, 2119 M St NW, 861-5858. Street lamps, rubber trees, and giant fireplaces add to the New Orleans decor. House downstairs, 70s and 80s music upstairs. Open daily 5pm-3am. Metro: Foggy Bottom or Dupont Circle. _www.lulusclub.com_.

9.30 Club, 815 V St NW, 3-930-930 (concert-line). It smells, it's dark, dingy and small but if indie's your thing, then this is it. Great live music: SuperGrass, Blur and The Charlatans have all played here, tkts $10-$30 (also available at _www.tickets.com_). Metro: U St/Cardozo. _www.930.com_.

For theatre and dance: Theatre in Washington gets better and better. The smart drama enthusiast visits **Ticketplace** at the **Old Post Office Pavilion**, 1100 Pennsylvania Ave NW, 842-5387, for half-price tickets on the day of a show, or on Sat for a Sun or Mon show (10% service charge). Open Tue-Sat 11am-6pm. Metro: Federal Triangle. _www.cultural-alliance.org/tickets_.

The Arena Stage, 1101 6th St SW, 554-9066, has one of the finest repertory companies in the nation. Metro: Waterfront. _www.arena-stage.org_.

Dance Place, 3225 8th St NE (3 blocks from Brookland stop on the metro's red line),

269-1600. Innovative modern dance performances, shows usually from 8pm, *www.danceplace.org*.

Folger, 201 E Capitol Street, SE 544-7077. Version of the Globe offering plays by Shakespeare and others, early music concerts and readings. Excellent company. Exhibitions based on extensive historical archives. *www.folger.edu*.

Ford's Theater, 511 10th Street, NW, 638-2367. Working theatre est 1863, Lincoln was shot here two years later. American musicals and plays. *www.fordstheatre.org*.

John F. Kennedy Center for the Performing Arts, 2700 F St NW, 467-4600/(800) 444-1324, has several theatres: the Opera House (ballet, plays, opera); the Eisenhower Theater (plays); the Terrace Theater; the Concert Hall, home of the world-class National Symphony; the Terrace Gallery (jazz) and the Film Theater. Students half-price for some performances. Daily evening performances at Millennium Stage in the Grand Foyer, 6pm, free. Terrace views of the Mall, Georgetown and Rosslyn across the Potomac are gorgeous, especially at night. Metro: Foggy Bottom. *www.kennedy-center.org*.

National Theatre, 1321 E St NW, 628-6161, also has some of the best performances in the city, direct from—or heading for—Broadway. 1/2 price student tkts sold in advance for Tue and Wed 8pm performances and Sun matinees at 2pm (need to go to box office w/student ID). Metro: Metro Center. *www.nationaltheatre.org*.

The Shakespeare Theatre, 450 7th St NW, 547-1122. Nationally acclaimed as one of the best Shakespeare companies, better than any other on the east coast. They also put on a free play at Carter Barron Amphitheatre, 619-7222, in Rock Creek Park, for two weeks in June. *www.shakespearetheatre.org*.

Source Theatre Company, 1835 14th St NW, 462-1073: some powerful productions on small stages. Prices are reasonable, but be careful in this area at night, *www.sourcetheatre.com*. In addition, the **DC Arts Center**, 2438 18th St NW, 462-7833, *www.dcartscenter.org*, **Stanislavsky Theatre Studio**, 1714 Church St NW, 946-4963, *www.sts-online.org*, the **Studio Theatre**, 1333 P St NW, 332-3300, *www.studiotheatre.org* and the **Woolly Mammoth Theatre Company**, in the Kennedy Center, 393-3939, *www.woollymammoth.net*, all deal in the off-beat and avant-garde, but put on stimulating traditional works as well. Look out for the **Washington Theater Festival**, Jul-Aug, 462-1073. In any event, check the *City Paper* and *Washington Post* for all listings.

Wolf Trap Park, 1551 Trap Rd, Vienna, VA, (703) 255-1900, the only US national park devoted to the arts. You can sit on the lawn or in the open-air theatre for top-notch ballet, symphonies, opera or popular music. Garrison Keillor's *Prairie Home Companion* broadcasts from here, when it's in the DC area. Lawn tickets are cheaper and you can picnic during the performance, but come early and bring a blanket. Metro: Orange line to West Falls Church and pick up a shuttle to Wolf Trap for $4, *www.wolftrap.org*.

US Marine Band, 433-4011, a nationally-renowned company, gives free concerts in summer throughout the city. Wednesday at 8pm on the west steps of the Capitol. Go to *www.marineband.usmc.mil* for more performance info.

Information

DC Chamber of Commerce Visitor Information Center, 1300 Pennsylvania Ave NW, (866) 324-7386, Mon-Fri 8:30am-5:30pm, Sat 9am-4pm. *www.dcvisit.com*.

Dial-a-Museum, 357-2020, info on current exhibits at the Smithsonian.

Dial-a-Park, 619-PARK, info on activities at memorials and park areas. *www.nps.gov*.

Washington Convention and Tourism Corporation, 1212 New York Ave NW, 789-7000, Mon-Fri 9am-5pm. *www.washington.org*.

Internet access

Martin Luther King Library, 901 G St NW, 727-1126. Free Internet use, 15 min or 1

hr slots, open daily 9.30am-9pm. Metro: Gallery Place. _www.dclibrary.org/mlk/_.
cyberSTOPcafe, 1513 17th Street NW, 234-2470. $8/hr, $6/half-hr. Metro: Dupont Circle. Open 7am-midnight. _www.cyberstopcafe.com/_.
Kramerbooks & Afterwords Cafe, 1517 Connecticut Ave NW, 387-1400. One computer available for free internet use, 15 min limit. Open daily 8am-1am, Fri-Sat 24hrs. Metro: Dupont Circle. _www.kramers.com_.

Travel

Confusion over the street layout here is forgivable. The same address may have four different locations, one in each quadrant. Just remember that NS streets are numbered, EW streets are lettered and the Parisian-style diagonal avenues are named after US states, one of the focal points being the Capitol, another is the White House.
Metro, 637-7000, Washington's space-age subway system is an experience in itself. Never-ending escalators descend below ground to reveal cavernous, museum-like vaults. This efficient, clean and safe system whisks you in minutes to museums, sights and shopping. Most places are within easy reach of a station, which are identified by brown posts marked with a white 'M.' Lines are denoted by colour and end-of-line destination. Downtown fare-cards cost $1.35 (more during rush hour and for longer journeys) obtained from machines before you reach the platform. One-day passes are $6.50, good after 9.30 am Mon-Fri and all day w/ends. Transfers to buses are $.35 (paid on the bus). Trains run Mon-Fri 5.30am-midnight, Sat-Sun 7am-3am. _www.metroopensdoors.com_.
Metrobus, 637-1328, is a complex but extensive system integrated with the Metro— practically every block in the city is reachable by bus. All buses stop every couple of blocks on their route. #30, 32, 34, 36 and 38 are very useful for Penn Ave, Georgetown and Wisconsin Ave. Exact fares are required—'carry a wad of $1 bills.' Flat fare is $1.25, an all-day pass is available for $3, bus-to-bus transfers are free. Find out more about the entire Metro system at _www.wmata.com_.
Circulator Crosstown bus service for $1. Daily 7am-9pm, every 5-10 mins. E-W between Union Station and Georgetown along K Street; N-S route from SW Waterfront to Convention Center via Mall and 7th Street, NW. Tickets on bus or from machines; free transfers from other Metro services. _www.dccirculator.com_.
Georgetown Metro Connection, 625-7433, is a fast, frequent and convenient shuttle-bus service that serves all metrobus stops in Georgetown and operates an express service between Georgetown and Foggy Bottom-GWU, Rosslyn and Dupont Circle metro stations. Buses are daily, every 10mins, Mon-Thur 7am-midnight, Fri 'til 2am, Sat 8am-2am, Sun 8am-midnight; $1 o/w. _www.georgetowndc.com/shuttle.php_.
Washington Flyer, (888) 927-4359, run airport shuttles from West Falls Church Metro to Dulles Airport. Buses run every half hr on weekdays 6:15am-10:45pm, w/ends 8:15am-10:45pm, $8. _www.washfly.com_. Also provide cabs to Dulles - call.
Airports: Reagan National Airport, (703) 417-8000, is close to the city, easy to get to on the Metro's blue and yellow lines. A taxi from DC would be from $15. Domestic flights only. _www.mwaa.com_.
Washington Dulles International Airport, (703) 572-2700, _www.mwaa.com_, is located about 26 miles from downtown Washington. Flights are generally cheaper here. A taxi from DC would be about $50, but the cheapest way to get here is by taking the #5A Metrobus from L'Enfant Plaza, which leaves hrly on the half hr 5:30am-10:30pm and takes you straight to the airport for just $2. Call 637-7000 for more info.
Baltimore Washington International Airport (BWI), (800) 435-9294, _www.bwiairport.com_, one hour north of Washington, is served by Amtrak, (800) 872-7245, _www.amtrak.com_, $14-$24 o/w and MARC commuter trains, (410) 539-5000, _www.mtamaryland.com_, $6 o/w.

Long-distance buses - Greyhound, 1005 1st St NE, (800) 231-2222. Terminal behind Union Station. 24 hrs. Not an area to be alone in at night. *www.greyhound.com*.

Washington Deluxe, (718) 387-7523/(866) BUS-NY-DC, a fantastic service with buses that go from Chinatown in DC to Chinatown in NYC for just $20 o/w and $35r/t. *www.washingtondeluxe.com*.

Rail - Union Station, 50 Massachusetts Ave NE, 289-1908, serves Amtrak, Maryland Rail Commuter (MARC), Virginia Railway Express (VRE) and Metro, just 8 mins from downtown. Day trips and overnights from here to Baltimore, Harpers Ferry, Fredericksburg. 24 hrs. Beautifully renovated, lots of eateries, shops and a multiplex cinema. *www.unionstationdc.com*.

Taxicabs are cheaper here than in most major cities, but the 'zone system' is often confusing for tourists. Instead of meters, the fare is based on your starting and ending zone. Almost the entire Mall and downtown area are covered by one zone (single non-rush hour fare $5.50; 2 zones is $7.60, 3 is $9.50). Visitors are vulnerable to the small minority of cabbies who may try to overcharge, but the lack of meters eliminates the incentive to take you out of your way. Before you get in the cab, ask the driver to tell you how much a ride will be. Fares shouldn't vary between cabs, so if you fear a quote may be too high, find another cab. There's a $1 sur-charge during rush-hours (7am-9.30am and 4pm-6.30pm), $1.50 for each extra passenger, $2 for each large bag and a $2 charge for radio calls. If you take a taxi from DC to Maryland or Virginia the driver will use the odometer to determine the mileage and the fare. Cabs are plentiful in the downtown area, but if you're in a quiet residential area you may want to call one. The biggest companies are **DC Flyer Radio Taxi**, 863-1136 and **Diamond Cab**, 387-6200. *http://dctaxi.dc.gov/dctaxi/ frames.asp?doc=/dctaxi/lib/dctaxi/Taxicab_Zone_Map.pdf*.

Car-pooling: Look in the *Washington Post* for shared expense rides, especially late Aug/early Sept when students are returning to college, *www.washingtonpost.com*.

NEARBY

Arlington National Cemetery, across the Potomac from DC, (703) 607-8000, is where more than 260,000 people are buried including JFK, Jacqueline Kennedy Onassis and JFK's brother, Robert, amidst engravings of the President's most stir-ring words. Changing of the Guard Ceremony at the **Tomb of the Unknown Soldier** takes place every half hour Apr-Oct, otherwise once on the hour. 'Impressive!' 'Beautifully serene—hard to believe Washington could be this peace-ful.' Apr-Sep 8am-7pm, Oct-May 'til 5pm. Metro: Arlington Cemetery. *www.arlingtoncemetery.org*. Close by is the **Iwo Jima Memorial**, a sculpture of 5 marines and a sailor hoisting an American flag on to Mt Surabachi on the island of Iwo Jima, mod-elled after a famous World War II photograph by Joe Rosenthal. 'Stunning, as is the view from here to Washington.'. *www.stayarlington.com*.   Right next door is the **Netherlands Carillon**, the perfect place for a picnic. Free concerts are given here May-Aug. Come on Saturdays at 6pm to hear the bells chime and take in one of the best views of Washington. Metro: Rosslyn. **The Pentagon**, (703) 697-1776, nearby, is no longer open for tours after the September 11th attack.

Alexandria,VA across from DC, a few miles down the George Washington (GW) Memorial Parkway, is a delightful mini-Georgetown, fifty years older than Washington, with over 100 18th century buildings, including the church attended by George Washington and Winston Churchill. Metro: King Street. Follow King Street east toward the river to get to the heart of Old Town. There's a pleasant walkway and bike path along the waterfront as far south as Mount Vernon, and north to DC via Oronoco Park, where you can see the start of the Alexandria Canal, which once crossed the Potomac in an aqueduct between Georgetown and Rosslyn. It opened in 1843 and connected with the C & O Canal (see below). Via the canals, coal from western Maryland, wheat, corn, whiskey, and flour were shipped to wharves in Alexandria until the canal was abandoned in 1886. *http://oha.ci.alexan-*

dria.va.us/oha-main/oha-alexandria-canal.html. **Ft Ward**, 4301 W Braddock Rd, (703) 838-4848, is the best preserved of 192 Union forts built to protect Washington during the American Civil War, well worth a visit. Includes a Museum. _http://oha.ci.alexandria.va.us/fortward_. Downtown Alexandria, don't miss the unique **Torpedo Factory**, 105 N Union St, (703) 838-4565, whose original purpose as a munitions plant has been subverted by artists in search of studio space. Daily 10am-5pm, free. _www.torpedofactory.org_. Metro: Alexandria/King St. You can also take a **water taxi** from Georgetown to Old Town Alexandria, which departs every 2 hrs on the 1/2hr Tue-Sat 12:30pm-10:30pm and Sun 12:30pm-8:30pm, $12 o/w. Call (703) 548-9000 or visit _www.potomacriverboatco.com_ for info. The place to eat in Alexandria is the **Hard Times Café**, 1404 King Street, where the Texas chili is addictive. _www.hardtimes.com/alexandria.htm_.

Chesapeake & Ohio (C & O) Canal. Until the advent of the railways, America made use of a considerable system of canals throughout the Northeast and Midwest. One of these is the Chesapeake & Ohio, running along the Maryland border from Washington DC to Cumberland. The canal is now a national historical park extending 185 miles, one of the longest of all national preserves. Mostly disused but leafy and beautiful, the banks of the canal are well worth a hike. The Canal passes through Georgetown, and the towpath makes for good cycling, walking or jogging. Summer horse-drawn barge trips from Thomas Jefferson St in Georgetown, 653-5190, $8, leave at 11am, 1.30pm, 3pm, Wed-Sun. _www.nps.gov/choh_ Upriver, the **Great Falls of the Potomac**, (703) 285-2965, are worth a look from either the MD or VA side. _www.nps.gov/gwmp/grfa_. Call the **Great Falls Tavern Visitors Center** on (301) 767-3714/(301) 739-4200, Mon-Fri 9am-4:45pm, _www.nps.gov/choh_.

Mount Vernon, 8 miles south of Alexandria via the GW Parkway and bike path, (703) 780-2000. Home of George Washington and a fine example of a Colonial plantation house, built in 1740. Original furnishings, plus key to the Bastille. George and Martha are buried here. Daily 8am-5pm o'wise Mar 1-Oct 31, 9am-4pm; $11. 'The restaurant has delicious, old-style peanut soup', _www.mountvernon.org_.

MARYLAND - Free State, Old Line State

Locals boast that Maryland is 'America in miniature'. The Mason-Dixon Line, surveyed by English astronomers Charles Mason and Jeremiah Dixon in 1767, marks the border between Maryland and Pennsylvania, but it has also come to represent the unofficial border between North and South. Maryland shows northern influences in its western mountainous area settled heavily by British and Germans and southern character along the eastern shoreline, famous for old antebellum mansions and delicious Chesapeake Bay crabs and oysters. Maryland's identity has become more complex in recent years, as the state has become increasingly urban in the areas surrounding DC and Baltimore and northern business and political interests have become more explicit.

The Chesapeake Bay dominates Maryland's cuisine and exerts a major influence on the state's economy, culture and politics. Don't leave without sampling Maryland's famous crabs and experiencing the Bay culture. If you're here in September be sure to visit the small town of Crisfield for its annual **Labor Day Hard Crab Derby and Fair**. This three-day event includes a crab race, parades, a beauty pageant, boat races, crab-picking contests and a carnival. If you have time, visit the tobacco auctions in Hughesville, La Plata, Upper Marlboro, Waldorf or Waysons Corner; the auctioneer's patter is riveting. _www.mdwelcome.org_.

BALTIMORE One of the nation's major seaports and not long ago considered Washington DC's ugly step-sister, today Baltimore enjoys one of the most successful urban renewal programs in America. The city's **Inner Harbor**, the centrepiece of its rebirth, was designed by the same prolific company that re-galvanised Faneuil Hall in Boston and designed the entire city of Columbia, a pleasant stopover near Baltimore.

On the sea-front **Fells Point** offers an unpretentious step back into the city's Colonial and sea-faring past. The country's oldest waterfront has, for the most part, avoided both development and tourism, resulting in a setting strikingly unchanged for some 200 years. But don't think this is just an historic area; 'real' people live and work here and, in addition to history, the Point has a great food market, bars, restaurants and summer festivals.

The city is fiercely proud of its baseball team, the Orioles, and of its heroes, which include baseball stars Babe Ruth and Cal Ripkin Jr, journalistic curmudgeon H. L. Mencken and writer Edgar Allen Poe. While you're here, don't miss out on tasting fresh crab and use correct pronunciation when referring to the city or state: it's 'Balmer, Merlin'! _www.baltimore.org_.

The area code is 410.

Accommodation
Travellers on a tight budget may find the *Baltimore Quick Guide* helpful, available from tourist offices in the Inner Harbor.

Best Western, 5625 O'Donnell St, 633-9500/(800) 633-9511, 4 miles from downtown. D-$109 for 2 people (2 double beds, XP-$10), continental bfast inc. Check-in after 3pm, out noon.

Days Inn Baltimore, 100 Hopkins Place, 576-1000. Great location in Inner Harbour. From $150, hospitality basket inc. Check-in 3pm, out 11am. _www.daysinnerharbor.com_/.

Food
Crab, Baltimore's speciality, is available practically anywhere. The scrumptious crustaceans are served by the dozen hot from the pot, peppered with volcanic Old Bay seasoning. Your only implements will be a mallet and a newspaper. Soft shell crabs are delicious too. Try **Phillip's Seafood Restaurant**, Light St Pavilion, 1st Level, 685-6600 and sample their famous crab cakes (small $7.99, large $10.99), _www.phillipsfamousseafood.com_. This is located at **Harbor Place**, (800) HARBOR-1, a giant Inner Harbor pavilion with countless fast food stalls and a few restaurants. 'Beautiful view of the harbour.' Subway: Shot Tower. _www.harborplace.com_.

Bertha's Dining Room, 734 S Broadway, Fell's Point, 327-5795. The restaurant's catch-phrase is 'EAT BERTHA'S MUSSELS!' and you can for about $9. Open Sun-Thur 11:30am-11pm, Fri-Sat 'til midnight. _www.berthas.com_.

Jimmy's, 801 S Broadway, Fell's Point, 327-3273. Good, filling bfasts and lunch at low prices: Specials from $5, entrees go from $7. 'Usually crowded, especially Sun mornings.' Open daily 5am-9pm.

Lexington Market, 400 W Lexington St, 685-6169. Historic public market established in 1782. Endless displays of food of almost every type and description. It's worth it just to come and watch the vendors in action. Mon-Sat 8.30am-6pm. Light rail/Subway: Lexington Market. _www.lexingtonmarket.com_.

Pete's Grille, 3130 Greenmount Avenue, 467-7698. 'A real diner with good, cheap food and a great atmosphere.' Winner of the local 'Best Breakfast' award 1993-2003, entrees $5-$7. Mon-Sat 6am-2pm, Sun 7am-1pm.

Of interest
Babe Ruth Birthplace and Museum, 216 Emory St, 727-1539. Memorabilia of

America's favourite slugger and other Maryland heroes. Daily in summer 10am-6pm (7pm when Orioles are playing). $6, $4 w/student ID. Light rail: Camden Yards. *www.baberuthmuseum.com*.

Baltimore Museum of Art, 10 Art Museum Dr, 396-7100. Owes its wonderful Matisse collection to the shrewd purchases of the Cone sisters from the artist himself. Also has a good Modernism section. Wed-Fri 11am-5pm, Sat-Sun 'til 6pm. $7, $5 w/student ID. *www.artbma.org*.

Baltimore Streetcar Museum, 1901 Falls Rd, 547-0264. Streetcar rides, tours and exhibits featuring a permanent collection of Baltimore streetcars from 1859-1944. Open year round on Sun noon-5pm (Jun-Oct: Sat also, noon-5pm), $6. *www.baltimoremd.com/streetcar*.

Edgar Allen Poe House and Museum, 203 N Amity St, 396-7932. Winding staircase leads to the tiny garret where Poe wrote 1832-1835. Sporadic hrs: Jul-Sept Fri-Sat noon-3:45pm, $3. Phone to check other hrs. NB: Poe was never wealthy and his former home is in a rundown area. Use caution. *www.eapoe.org/balt/poehse.htm*.

Eubie Blake National Museum and Cultural Center, 847 N Howard St, 225-3130. Features permanent exhibits on Baltimore jazz greats Billie Holiday and Cab Calloway, among others. Open Mon-Fri 10am-5:30pm, $2, $1 w/student ID. Light rail: Monument St. *www.eubieblake.org*.

Flag House & Star-Spangled Banner Museum, 844 E Pratt St, 837-1793. The house where Mary Pickersgill sewed the flag that inspired Francis Scott Key to write the *Star Spangled Banner*. Be sure to see the Great Flag Window, a glass wall the same size, colour and design as the original Star-Spangled Banner. Tue-Sat 10am-4pm. $6, $4 w/student ID. Subway: Shot Tower. *www.flaghouse.org*.

Maryland Historical Society, 201 W Monument St, 685-3750, has the original manuscript of *that* poem, which was later adopted in 1931 as the national anthem, as well as the art collection of the former Peale Museum. Open Wed-Sun 10am-5pm. $8, $6 w/student ID. Light rail: Centre Street. *www.mdhs.org*.

Federal Hill, 727-4500, a federal historic district of primarily brick late-19th century homes. To the north is Federal Hill Park, a Baltimore landmark with spectacular views of the Inner Harbor and downtown skyline. The Cross Street Market and the surrounding business district on S Charles and Light Sts have a wide range of moderately priced restaurants and taverns, as well as an eclectic mix of shops. *www.historicfederalhill.org*.

Fell's Point, 675-6750, a revamped harbour area around Aliceanna, Lancaster, Ann and Thames Streets. Shops and good places to eat. Can be reached by the water taxi that ferries people around the harbour. *www.fellspoint.us/*.

Fort McHenry National Monument and Historic Shrine, end of Fort Ave, 962-4290. Successful defence of the fort in the War of 1812 was the inspiration for Francis Scott Key to write the *Star Spangled Banner*. When Key saw that the garrison flag had been raised the morning after the British attack, he knew that the fort had not fallen. Today ancient cannons still cover the harbour. Daily in the summer, 8am-7:45pm, $5. Catch the water taxi across to the fort, leaves roughly every 1/2 hour from Inner Harbor. This $5 all-day pass allows you to get on and off at various points en route. 'Very worthwhile.' *www.nps.gov/fomc/index.htm*.

Jewish Museum of Maryland, 15 Lloyd St, 732-6400. America's leading museum of regional Jewish history, culture and community, with two synagogues. Tue-Thur and Sun noon-4pm. Tours at 1pm and 2:30pm, $8, $4 w/student ID. *www.jewishmuseummd.org*.

Maryland Science Center and Davis Planetarium, 601 Light St on the harbour, 685-2370. Hands-on exhibits, computer games, Chesapeake Bay and Baltimore City displays. $18.50 admission includes entrance to the planetarium and 5-storey IMAX theatre, $14.50 without IMAX. Sun-Wed 10am-6pm, Thu-Sat till 8pm. 'Not worth it.' *www.mdsci.org*.

National Aquarium, Pier 3, 501 E Pratt St, 576-3800. Take the elevator to the 4th floor, then the escalator to the rain forest where piranhas glower, sloths dangle and free-flying birds practically land on your head. 'Expensive, but worth it. Modern and interesting design; the shark tank is amazing.' Summer: daily 9am-5pm, Fri 'til 8pm, $17.95. Subway: Shot Tower. _www.aqua.org_.

Poe's Grave at Westminster Hall, 515 W Fayette St, 706-2072. The tombstone marking his grave is near the front gate. Cemetery open daylight hrs only, free. On Halloween the local Historical Society hosts a weirdly funny party in the grave-yard, during which 'Frank the Body-Snatcher' lectures on the perils of his profession. On Poe's birthday in Jan, Poe House organizes a special celebration in Poe's memory (call 396-7932 for more details). _www.westminsterhall.org_.

Top of the World at the top of the **World Trade Center**, 401 E Pratt St, Inner Harbor, 837-8439. The world's tallest pentagonal building, designed by I M Pei. Offers panoramic views of the harbour and city and exhibits on Baltimore's history. $4. Open daily 10am-6pm, Sat 'til 9pm. _www.promotionandarts.com_.

U.S.S. Constellation Museum, Pier 1, Inner Harbor, 301 E Pratt St, 539-1797. The only surviving Civil War era naval vessel and last tall-sail war ship built by the US Navy. Open daily 10am-5.30pm, $7.50. _www.constellation.org_.

Walters Art Museum, 600 N Charles St at Centre, 547-9000. One of the largest private collections in the world with something of everything from across the ages, including a floor housing Oriental decorative arts. Wed-Sun 10am-5pm. Newly reopened in a modern structure in 2001. $10, $6 w/student ID, free to all Sat 11am-1pm and the first Thur of every month. Light rail: Centre Street. _www.thewalters.org_.

Washington Monument, Charles St and Mt Vernon Pl. 178 ft high, the monument was built between 1815 and 1842, long before the one in DC.

Entertainment

Harbor Place is one hot spot and venue for various concerts and street performances. Also head for **Fell's Point**, east of Harbor Place, where the real fun is. Around 9pm or 10pm serious drinking and dancing gets underway in the numerous little bars filled with local rowdies, yuppies, bohemians, unrepentant pirates and assorted lowlifes, all in good fun. Just take the trolley from Inner Harbor, or follow Broadway toward the harbour until you run out of street.

Power Plant Live is a new entertainment district, located one block from the Inner Harbor at 34 Market Place, 727-5483, where you will find restaurants, bars, clubs and live entertainment. Visit _www.powerplantlive.com_ for more info.

Center Stage Theater, 700 N Calvert St, 332-0033. A nationally acclaimed professional theatre. Tickets from $10, student discounts with valid ID (up to 50% off some performances). _www.centerstage.org_.

Lyric Opera House, 140 W Mt. Royal Ave, 727-6000. Home of the Baltimore Opera Company and haunt of German director Werner Herzog, who does a suitably dramatic production from time to time. It also hosts musicals and other shows. Tkts from $37, 50% student discount 1 hr before a show. _www.baltimoreopera.com_.

Sport

Baltimore Orioles, Oriole Park, Camden Yards, 333 W Camden St, 685-9800. 'Great baseball in an electric atmosphere. Highly recommend.' _The_ place to go for a good time. 'Tasty roast beef sandwiches made on outdoor grills.' Tkts $8-$45. MARC runs trains from DC's Union Station to Camden Yards, $7r/t, (539-5000). Return bus service is provided when the game ends after the last train leaves. 'Great value and a real Oriole atmosphere even before you reach the ground.' _www.theorioles.com_.

Information

Baltimore Area Convention and Visitors Association, 100 Light St, 12th Floor, (800) 343-3468/(877) BALTIMORE. Open Mon-Fri 9am-6pm. _www.baltimore.org_.

Internet access
Enoch Pratt Free Library, 400 Cathedral St, 396-5430. Free Internet access, 30 min limit. Light rail: Centre St, Subway: Charles Center or Lexington Market. Call or check _www.epfl.net_ for more details.

Travel
Amtrak, Penn Station, 1500 N Charles St, 291-4263/(800) 872-7245, _www.amtrak.com_.
Baltimore/Washington International Airport (BWI), 859-7111, 10 miles south of Baltimore. Take the #17 Mass Transit bus, or light rail, from downtown, $1.60 o/w. _www.bwiairport.com_.
Greyhound, 210 W Fayette St, 752-7682/(800) 231-2222, _www.greyhound.com_.
Mass Transit, 539-5000, for bus, subway and light rail schedules for downtown and suburbs; $1.60 base fare, $3.50 all-day pass. _www.mtamaryland.com_.
Water Taxi service, Constellation Dock, Pratt St, (410) 563-3901. Calls at all major attractions around the harbour. $8 all-day unlimited use. Mon-Thur 10am-11pm, Fri-Sat 'til midnight, Sun 'til 9pm. _www.thewatertaxi.com/_.

ANNAPOLIS   Situated on Chesapeake Bay, the city of Queen Anne is the capital of Maryland and was the capital of the US for a while in 1783-1784. At the State House, George Washington resigned his command of the Revolutionary Army after his victory over British forces. It was here, in January 1784, that the US Congress ratified the Treaty of Paris, ending the Revolutionary War. Clustered behind the 18th century waterfront is one of the most beautiful of America's colonial towns.

Annapolis is synonymous with sailing and the United States Naval Academy. Now co-ed, the academy is still 'where the boys are' and acts as a magnet for young women, especially on weekends! The bars on the wharf are good for a beer and overhearing fishermen's stories of the Chesapeake Bay. Treat yourself to local oysters and a basket of hot crab, delicious and cheap and catch the Crab Festival in August. A trip around the harbour is a must. The movie _Patriot Games_ was shot here. _www.visitannapolis.org_.
The area code is 410.

Accommodation
Accommodation tends to be expensive in this trendy little town.
Annapolis Accommodations, 41 Maryland Ave, 263-3262/(800) 715-1000. Houses for short-term rent. _www.stayannapolis.com_.
Capital KOA Campground, 11 miles from Annapolis on Rte 3 north in Millersville, 923-2771/(800) 562-0248. Open Apr-Nov. Sites $32-42, cabins $55-79. _www.capitolkoa.com_.

Food
Chick and Ruth's, 165 Main St, 269-6737. Down the street from the state capitol, this deli has politically-named specials from around $5-$8. A homey and memorabilia-crammed atmosphere. Open Sun-Thur 6:30am-10pm, Fri-Sat 'til 11:30pm. _www.chickandruths.com_.
Historic Inns (Maryland Inn), Church Circle, 263-2641. Well-known early 18th century Inn. **The Treaty of Paris Tavern** is where the signatories of the treaty that ended the Revolutionary War came to celebrate. Beautiful, and a slice of history.
Market House, Market Space, City Dock. Restoration of an 1858 building with tons of fresh seafood and various other foods. 'Best value, tastiest seafood in town!' 'Best oysters in the east!' _www.ci.annapolis.md.us_.

Of interest

A **boat trip** around the harbour is the most pleasant way to experience the many facets of Annapolis; **Watermark Cruises**, Slip 20, City Dock, 268-7600, do 40 min harbour cruises, $8, which leave on the hour Mon-Fri 11am-4pm, Sat-Sun 11am-7pm. There is also the 90 min Scenic Severn River Cruise, $16, which departs at 12:30pm Thur-Sun. _www.watermarkcruises.com._

Maryland State House, State Circle, 974-3400. Oldest US State House in continuous legislative use. 9am-5pm daily, free tours at 11am and 3pm.

US Naval Academy, bordered by King George St & Severn River, 263-6933. Large, beautiful chapel has sarcophagus of John Paul Jones. Guided walking tours $7.50, depart from the Visitors Center, 52 King George St. Mon-Sat 9:30am-3pm. 'Excellent, interesting tour.' _www.navyonline.com._

Walking Tours: The Museum Store, 77 Main St, 268-5576, rents audio self-guided tours for $5. Open Sun-Thur 10am-8pm, Fri-Sat 'til 10pm. **Three Centuries Tours**, 263-5401, offers two walking tours daily. The 10:30am tour meets at the Visitors Center (26 West St) and the 1:30pm tour meets at the information booth on the city dock, $11, $6 w/student ID. _www.annapolis-tours.com._

Entertainment

Pick up copies of _Bay Weekly, Capital Entertainment_ and _Spin Sheet_, all free, for listings, news and reviews.

Information/Travel

The Annapolis and Anne County Conference and Visitors Bureau, 26 W Street, (888) 302-2852. _www.visitannapolis.org/._

Greyhound, 308 Chinquapin Rd, 263-7964, _www.greyhound.com._

ASSATEAGUE ISLAND   This narrow, 37 mile long barrier island on the Atlantic coast of Maryland and Virginia, is home to the threatened peregrine falcon and piping plover, as well as 275 other bird species. The Assateague horses, herds of wild horses of uncertain origin, have been roaming the island since the 17th century. **Assateague State Park**, (410) 641-2120, is a 2-mile stretch of beach and dunes directly across the bridge from the Maryland mainland. _www.dnr.state.md.us/publiclands/eastern/assateague.html._

   Chincoteague National Wildlife Refuge, (757) 336-6122, occupies most of the Virginia end of the island, _www.fws.gov/northeast/chinco/._ The rest of the island is managed by **Assateague Island National Seashore**, (410) 641-3030, _www.nps.gov/asis._ Camping is available in the State Park and the National Seashore: $16-$35, rsvs recommended. Lots of opportunities for hiking, as well as for canoeing and kayaking in the back bays. 'Delightful area,' be sure to bring plenty of insect repellent!

OCEAN CITY   Maryland's only major oceanside resort. The town has a lively boardwalk and a wide beach, but gets crowded in the summer. This is the place to go if you want a wild time and a summer job. 'Packed with British, Irish and other international students.' _www.ococean.com._

   The area code is 410.

Accommodation

Accommodation can be reasonable here during the off-season, but in the summer months even the tackiest dives can get away with outrageous rates. A rule of thumb is the further away from the boardwalk, the better. Accommodation is available—you just have to walk around to find it. 'Beware of those selling "cheap" accommodation at the bus terminal and realtors who are out to make money from summer employees.'

Bay Sails Inn, 102 60th St, 524-5634. $29-195, depending on season. Walk-in rates may vary. Closed for Winter. Pool. _www.baysailsinn.com_.

Cayman Suites Hotel, 12500 Coastal Hwy, 250-7600. $49+, depending on season. Glass-enclosed heated pool, fitness room. _www.caymansuites.com_.

Food/Entertainment

Ocean City has a league of bars, clubs and eateries.

The Angler, 312 Talbot St, 289-7424. Lively bar and restaurant. Happy hour 3pm-6pm daily, 75¢ drafts on Sun. 'Excellent!' Open 6am-2am. Cover $5 on Sun after 10pm.

La Hacienda, 8001 Coastal Hwy, 524-8080. 'Great Mexican food.' Most dishes under $10. Open daily from 5pm. _www.beach-net.com/laha_.

Information

Ocean City Convention and Visitors Bureau, 4001 Coastal Highway, 289-8181/(800) OC-OCEAN. _www.ococean.com_.

OC International Student Services has accommodation listings and offers help to overseas students. They are at: 304 S Baltimore Ave, (410) 289-0350 and can be contacted daily between 9am-3am. _www.ociss.com_.

SMITH and TANGIER ISLANDS   Tiny **Smith Island** (population 330) is Maryland's only inhabited island accessible exclusively by boat. The residents here are said to be direct descendants of the original inhabitants who came over from Cornwall, England, in 1657. The story goes that Capt. John Smith gave the island his name when he discovered it in 1608, and was so taken by the beauty of the place that he wrote in his log: 'Heaven and earth seemed never to have agreed better for man's commodious and delightful habitation.' Most of the 650 residents of nearby **Tangier Island, VA**, also trace their linage to single ancestor, John Crockett, who arrived in 1686. The islanders' extreme isolation has preserved a dialect of English that has been compared to that spoken in the Elizabethan Age. Tangier has 3 delicious seafood restaurants all within a walk of each other: **Chesapeake House** (757-891-2331), **Fisherman's Corner** (757-891-2900) and the **Waterfront Restaurant** (757-891-2248).

Summer cruises to the islands, with narration, run daily at 12:30pm (May-Oct) from **Crisfield, MD**. Call (410) 425-2771 for Smith Island, $24 r/t, _www.smithislandcruises.com_, or (410) 968-2338 for Tangier Island, $24 r/t, _www.tangiercruises.com_.

Accommodation is scarce. **The Inn of Silent Music**, (410) 425-3541, on Smith Island, has double rooms from $105 inc bfast and it's the site of the best and only seafood restaurant in town, _www.innofsilentmusic.com_. On Tangier Island, **Shirley's Bay View Inn**, (757) 891-2396, has eight cozy cottages, very friendly owners and some of the most beautiful sunrises and sunsets you will ever see. Call for rates. _www.tangierisland.net/. www.smithis-land.net_ and _www.tangierisland-va.com_.

ANTIETAM BATTLEFIELD   An interesting side-trip from Baltimore heading west on Rte 70—the site of the Civil War's bloodiest single-day battle, fought in 1862 and resulting in 23,000 casualties. The scene of the battle is now a national park with an excellent museum and diorama at its Visitors Center, (301) 432-5124, near **Sharpsburg**, off Rte 65 (Hagerstown Pike). Open daily 8:30am-6pm, $4, _www.nps.gov\anti_.

VIRGINIA - The Old Dominion, Mother of Presidents
Virginia is famed for its Colonial heritage, its historic homes and estates and its great battlefields on which the fate of the nation was decided in both the 18th and 19th centuries. Seven of the 15 pre-Civil War Presidents were born here. Virginia is the least southern of the old Confederate states in both geographical and cultural terms. Northern Virginia is a mainly urban collection of Washington suburbs, where a growing technology industry is fast converting the area into the Silicon Valley of the east.

Away from the DC suburbs, Virginia retains its mostly rural southern character and Virginians everywhere are fiercely proud of the state's long role in American history. West of DC, Virginia is old-money horse and wine country: Route 66 W to Rte 245 brings you through rolling green meadows and woods to **The Plains** (eat at the **Rail Stop**, once part-owned by Robert Duvall, _www.railstoprestaurant.com_), and thence to **Middleburgh**, full of pleasant coffee shops and quaint stores, at the heart of Virginia hunt country, where horse fences and jodhpurs blend in with the scenery.

Virginia has a great deal to offer from both a scenic and a historic perspective. In the east are sandy beaches and the amazing 171/2 mile **Chesapeake Bay Bridge Tunnel**, which links Virginia to Maryland; in the west, Skyline Drive and the Shenandoah National Park. Everywhere there are countless well-preserved links with the past. _www.virginia.org_.

RICHMOND   A provincial capital during the War of Independence, the capital of Virginia and of the old Confederacy, Richmond was partly destroyed by the Confederate Government. Today old and new gel, forming an attractive, bustling city with plenty of history and entertainment. Richmond also makes a good base for visiting nearby landmarks. _www.visit.richmond.com_.
The telephone area code is 804.

Accommodation
Days Inn, 2100 Dickens Rd, 282-3300. Newly renovated 2004. D-$59, bfast included, pool. Check-in 2pm, out 12pm. _www.daysinn.com_.
Massad House Hotel, 11 N 4th St, 648-2893. From $80. 'Good accommodation.' 24 hr restaurant nearby. Check-in anytime, out 11am. _www.massadhousehotel.com_.
Motel 6, 5704 Williamsburg Rd, 222-7600, six miles east of Richmond on Hwy 60, near the airport. From $36, free coffee in mornings. 'Good value for money.' Check-in anytime, out noon. _www.motel6.com_.
Radisson Hotel, 301 W Franklin St, 644-9871/(800) 333-3333. D-$109 (two double beds, up to 4 people), includes pool and gym. Check-in 3pm, out noon. _www.radisson.com_.
Pocahontas State Park, 10301 State Park Rd, 796-4255. 19 miles south of Richmond, (exit 61 off I-95 to Rte 10, take country road 655). Sites $23, showers, boating, biking and pool. 'Nice place.'

Food
Aunt Sarah's Pancake House, 7927 Broad St, 747-8284 and other Virginia locations. Regular pancakes under $5. Open Sun-Thur 6am-9pm, Fri-Sat 'til 3am.

Farmer's Market, on 17th St in Richmond's old town Shockoe Bottom near Shockoe Slip, 646-0477. Oldest continuously operating farmer's market in the country. Thur, Sat, Sun 8:30am-2pm. *www.17thstreetfarmersmarket.com*.

Mamma Zu, 501 S Pine St, 788-4205. Huge pasta dishes, large pizza will feed three for approx $10. Open Mon-Sat 11am-11pm.

3rd Street Diner, 218 E Main St, 788-4750. Popular with locals, 'fantastic sandwiches', $4-$6, bfast specials $5. Daily 24 hrs, bfast anytime.

Of interest

Take an historic walk through Richmond, starting from the Court end. Many attractions—national landmarks, museums and other notable buildings—are located within 8 blocks.

Hollywood Cemetery, 412 S Cherry St, 648-8501. US Presidents James Monroe and John Tyler and Confederate President Jefferson Davis are buried here, along with some 18,000 Confederate soldiers. *www.hollywoodcemetery.org*.

James River & Kanawha Canal, along the right bank of the James River, 649-2800/648-6549. Another 19th century attempt to connect the Ohio River to the Atlantic Ocean, but doomed by small budgets and the railroad. Today it is a beautiful landscaped public area starting in downtown Richmond and extending to the historic Tredegar Iron Works site. The most popular spot is between 5th and 17th Sts. *www.richmondriverfront.com*.

Monument Avenue, a beautiful tree-lined blvd with statues commemorating, among others, Arthur Ashe, JEB Stuart, and scientist and oceanographer Matthew Fontaine Maury.

Science Museum of Virginia, 2500 W Broad St, 864-1400/(800) 659-1727. 'Hands-on' exhibits and the excellent Universe Space Theater, where films are shown on a large planetarium dome providing sight and sound from every direction. Mon-Sat 9.30am-5pm, Sun 11:30am-5pm. Admission to museum $8, IMAX films $8.50, combo ticket $15.50. *www.smv.org*.

St John's Church, 2401 E Broad St, 648-5015. Built in 1741, this is where Patrick Henry made his famous 'Give me liberty or give me death' speech. A reenactment of this speech and other events of the Second Virginia Convention of 1775 are conducted at 2pm on Sun from Jun-Sept. Tours Mon-Sat every 1/2 hr 10am-4pm, Sun 1pm-4pm, $5. *www.historicstjohnschurch.org*. Nearby is the **'Poe Museum'**, 1914-16 E Main St, the oldest stone building in town, in which Poe never lived, but which houses lots of Poe memorabilia. Call 648-5523 for more details or visit *www.poemuseum.org*.

The State Capitol, Capitol Square, 698-1788, neo-classical domed building designed in 1788 by Thomas Jefferson, the first of its kind in America, with a life-size marble statue of George Washington by French sculptor Houdon directly under the dome. Upon observing it's life-like quality, General Lafayette stated, "I can almost realize he is going to move." Undergoing renovations. Tours available of the outside only. *legis.state.va.us*.

Steeplechase races, a Virginia tradition. In spring, private country estates throughout Virginia's Piedmont region open their doors to the public for steeplechase horse racing. Watching the ritual tailgate parties can be just as entertaining as the race. Steeplechase races are held at Colonial Downs in New Kent County (20 miles east of Richmond), 569-3200, in April. One car load $95-115 or take the shuttle-bus service from Richmond Raceway (600 E Laburnum Ave), $30-45 r/t and admission. *www.strawberryhillraces.com*.

Valentine Richmond History Center, 1015 E Clay St, 649-0711, has exhibits on the life and history of Richmond. Tue-Sat 10am-5pm, Sun noon-5pm. $7, $6 w/student ID. *www.richmondhistorycenter.com*.

Virginia Aviation Museum, 5701 Huntsman Rd, near the International Airport, 236-3622, houses an extensive collection of vintage flying machines. Mon-Sat 9:30am-5pm, Sun noon-5pm. $6. *www.vam.smv.org*.

Virginia Museum of Fine Arts, 2800 **Grove** St, 340-1400. A panorama of world art from ancient times to the present. Suggested donation $5. Wed-Sun 11am-5pm. *www.vmfa.state.va.us*.

White House and Museum of the Confederacy, 1201 E Clay St, 649-1861. Mon-Sat 10am-5pm, Sun noon-5pm. Museum $7, guided tour of White House $7, combo ticket $10. *www.moc.org*.

Biking and Hiking: There are over 200 miles of trails to explore in the Richmond-Petersburg area, many of which cut through surrounding battlefields. **Whitewater Rafting**: One of only a few 'urban' whitewater runs in the country rages right through the heart of historic Richmond. Contact the **Richmond Raft Company**, 4400 E Main St, 222-7238/(800) 540-7238, who do trips from $48-$60, *www.richmondraft.com*, or **James River Runners**, (434) 286-2338, tubing excursions from $16, rafting excursions for $26. *www.jamesriver.com*.

Entertainment

Cary Town, an entertainment district comprised of 9 blocks from Blvd to Thompson, with an eclectic mix of shops and restaurants unique to Richmond. This is also a fantastic people-watching spot.

King's Dominion, 20 miles north of Richmond on the I-95, 876-5000. 'Great rides—don't miss the Anaconda—a looping roller-coaster featuring an underwater tunnel.' Also try out Tomb Raider Firefall, new in 2005! Admission $46 or book online at *www.kingsdominion.com* and get $14 off.

Richmond Highland Games & Celtic Festival, Richmond Raceway Complex, 600 E Laburnum Ave, 569-3200. Held every year on the 4th w/end in Oct, this festival involves lots of music, lots of food and large men throwing stuff – Scottish athletics at its best! *www.richmondceltic.com*.

Shockoe Slip, Carey St btwn 12th & 14th Sts, old warehouses now store galleries and eclectic craft shops, hip restaurants, bars and nightclubs.

Information

Richmond Visitors Information Center, in the brand new Convention Center on Clay St (btwn 3rd and 5th Sts), 783-7450. *www.visit.richmond.com*.

Internet access

West End Public Library, 5420 Patterson Ave, 646-1877. Free Internet use, 45min limit. Mon & Wed 10am-8pm, Tue, Thur & Fri 'til 6pm, Sat 'til 5pm. *www.richmondpubliclibrary.org*.

Travel

Amtrak, 7519 Staples Mill Rd, 553-2904/(800) 872-7245. About 5 miles from downtown, but no buses available. Taxi fare $20. *www.amtrak.com*.

Greyhound, 2910 N Blvd, 254-5910/(800) 231-2222. (Charlottesville $17.50o/w, $29r/t: 1 1/4 hrs; Williamsburg $10 o/w, $18.50r/t: 1 hr). *www.greyhound.com*.

Richmond International Airport, 1 Richard E Byrd Terminal Dr, 236-3260. Buses to and from the airport are few and far between; call **Groome Transportation**, 222-7222, for pick-up service to downtown Richmond. Prices depend on which zone in Richmond you are travelling to. *www.groometransportation.com*.

FREDERICKSBURG One hour north of Richmond off the I-95, four great Civil War battles were fought here. You can tour the **Fredericksburg Battlefield** where Lee's army fought off wave after wave of charging Federals from Marye's Heights.

The town itself has several interesting old houses, among them the home of George Washington's mother, Mary Washington; **Kenmore**, the home of George's sister Betty Washington Lewis and the **Rising Sun Tavern**, owned by George's brother Charles. Antique shops selling overpriced Americana line the quaint streets, but there are some good and inexpensive places to eat. Try **Goolrick's Pharmacy**, 901 Caroline St, 373-9878, open Mon-Fri 9am-7pm, Sat 'til 5pm. Original soda fountain, milkshakes, soup and sandwiches will satisfy for under $5. *www.goolricks.com*. There is also **Sammy T's**, 801 Caroline St, 371-2008, where delicious vegetarian fare costs $5-$10, open daily 11am-8pm. *www.sammyts.com/*. *www.fredericksburgvirginia.net*.

The telephone area code is 540.

Information

Fredericksburg Battlefield Visitors Center, Lafayette Blvd, 373-6122. Museum exhibits, guided walking tours (in summer) and video that describe the four battles of Fredericksburg. Summer: daily 8:30am-6:30pm, otherwise 9am-5pm, $4. *www.nps.gov/frsp/vc.htm*.

WILLIAMSBURG

As state capital between 1699 and 1780, Williamsburg played a significant role in the heady days leading up to the American Revolution. Nowadays there's **Colonial Williamsburg**, with hundreds of houses painstakingly restored to create the look of earlier times and actors dressed up to give an air of reality. They even address the subject of slavery with actors 'living' a slave's life. Even so, this is, as one reader put it, 'a sort of Colonial Disneyland'. Major tourist area. *www.visitwilliamsburg.com*.

The telephone area code is 757.

Accommodation

Williamsburg is loaded with hotels, but even the modest ones can charge high rates. See *www.mywilliamsburgvacation.com* for great listings of B&Bs, motels and hotels.

Comfort Inn, 2007 Richmond Rd, 220-3888, 2 mi from Colonial Williamsburg. $89, $7 XP. Check in 3pm, check out 11am.

Bassett Motel, 800 York St, 229-5175. $58, $5 XP. Less than 1 mi from Colonial Williamsburg. Check in at 2pm, check out at 11am.

Camping: Williamsburg Pottery Campground, 901 Lightfoot Rd (exit 234 off I-64), 565-2101. $16. Showers. 5 miles from Colonial Williamsburg, 10 miles from Busch Gardens.

Food

Authentically decorated taverns in Colonial Williamsburg offer 18th and 21st century fare at 21st century prices.

College Deli, 336 Richmond Rd (opposite William and Mary College), 229-6627. Subs, pizzas and the 'best sandwiches in North America.' Entrees $6-$13. Open 10:30am-2am daily.

Paul's Deli Restaurant and Pizza, 761 Scotland St, 229-8976. Popular student hangout. Huge subs, pasta and seafood specials, $6. Open daily 10:30am-2am. *www.paulsdelirestaurant.com*.

Sal's Pizza, 1242 Richmond Rd (in the commercial part of town), 220-2641. 'Best pizza in town.' Pizzas $7-16. Open 11am-11pm daily.

Of interest

Busch Gardens, 3 miles east of Williamsburg on Hwy 60, (800) 343-7946. A fanciful re-creation of old-world Europe and action-packed theme park operated by the Anheuser Busch Brewing Co. Authentically-detailed European hamlets alongside wet, dry and mind-erasing rides with such fear-inducing names as 'Alpengeist' and 'Apollo's Chariot', one of the fiercest roller-coasters in the world! Summer:

open daily 10am-10pm, $49.99. A 3-day pass for admission to both Busch Gardens and Water Country USA is available for $74.95. *www.buschgardens.com*.

College of William and Mary. Founded in 1693, the second oldest in the nation. The **Sir Christopher Wren Building** at the west end of Duke of Gloucester St is purported to be the oldest academic building in continuous use in the US. Also part of the college is the **Muscarelle Museum of Art**, 221-2700, where permanent collections feature old master paintings, contemporary works and Colonial Virginia portraits. Wed, Sat and Sun noon-4pm, Tue and Thur 10am-4:30pm. $5 admission fee. *www.wm.edu/muscarelle*.

Colonial Williamsburg. Perhaps the best buildings are the Capitol, jail, Raleigh Tavern, Governor's palace and various colonial craft shops. Basic admission $39, or a 'Freedom Pass' provides yearly admission to all exhibits for $49. Buildings open daily 9am-5pm.You can also just wander for free without going into the houses at all. Start at Merchants Sq and continue in a rough counter-clockwise direction. Go first to the Visitors Center where you can see a documentary film that may make the visit more meaningful. Call (800) HISTORY for more info or visit *www.colonial-williamsburg.com*.

James River Plantations, take Rte 5 along the river to visit several plantation homes of early American leaders. *www.jamesriverplantations.org*.

Historic Jamestowne, the first permanent English settlement in America. Not that much has been restored, the visitor must often be content with looking at foundations. Plagues, Indians, starvation and fires hindered its development and when the peninsula finally became an island, Williamsburg and Yorktown prospered in its stead. The original settlement is about a mile from the more recent **Jamestown Settlement**, 5 min from Williamsburg on Hwy 31 south. In the park are replicas of three ships, a re-creation of the first fort, an Indian village and a museum. Daily 9am-5pm, $11.75. Under the same administration is **Yorktown**, where the battlefield and 67 18th century structures remain in good condition. The surrender of the British at Yorktown, in October 1781, ended the War of Independence, although the final peace treaty wasn't signed until two years later in Paris. The **Yorktown Victory Center**, in Yorktown on Rte 238, sits on the Colonial Parkway overlooking the York River. Built for the Bicentennial, it is a permanent museum dramatising the military events of the Revolution. Daily 9am-5pm, $8.25. A combo ticket to both parks is $17. For general information, call (888) 593-4682 or visit *www.historyisfun.com*.

Water Country USA, west of Williamsburg on the I-64, (800) 343-7946. This water park is the sister park to **Busch Gardens**. Open May-Sept. $35.99, 2-day pass for both Busch Gardens and Water Country USA is $64.95. *www.watercountryusa.com*.

Information

Colonial Williamsburg Visitors Center, on State Hwy 132-Y, (800) HISTORY. Daily 9am-5pm. Runs shuttle bus (9am-10pm) to historic section, free with admission ticket. *www.colonialwilliamsburg.com*.

Williamsburg Area Convention & Visitors Bureau, 421 N Boundary St, 253-0192/(800) 368-6511. *www.visitwilliamsburg.com*.

Travel

Amtrak, 468 N Boundary St, 229-8750/(800) 872-7245, *www.amtrak.com*.
Greyhound, 468 N Boundary St, 229-1460/(800) 231-2222, *www.greyhound.com*.

VIRGINIA BEACH   Continuing south east from Williamsburg and past Norfolk, you come to this fast-growing resort with a 28-mile beach, running from the landing dunes of America's first permanent colonists on Cape Henry to Virginia's Outer Banks. From here you can access the amazing **Chesapeake Bay Bridge Tunnel** for the northern drive up the Atlantic coastline. It's well worth stopping off to visit **Assateague National Seashore** (see Maryland) and the beautiful **Chincoteague Island**, Virginia's only resort island, famous for its oyster beds, clam shoals and the Chincoteague ponies (visit _www.chincoteaguechamber.com_ for more info) or _www.vbfun.com_.

The telephone area code for Virginia Beach is 757.

Accommodation
Angie's Guest Cottage, 302 24th St, 428-4690. $17.10 HI, $20.50 non-HI (10% ISIC discount for non-members), linens $2, cheaper rates off season. B&B: From $64. 'Friendly, clean and great atmosphere'. If they don't have space, they'll recommend others that might, although no one's prices come close to matching Angie's. _www.angiescottage.com_.
Sundial Motel, 308 21st St, 428-2922/(800) 626-7373. $39-129, 11/2 blks from the beach. _www.sundialvirginiabeach.com_.
Camping: Virginia Beach KOA Campground, 1240 General Booth Blvd (2 miles from beach), 428-1444/(800) KOA-4150.Tent $18-38. Showers, laundry, pool, mini-golf, volleyball and shuttle-bus to beach. _www.koa.com_.

Food
Junk food heaven! Fast food joints crowd the boardwalk, which at night becomes loud and luminous!
The Beach Pub, 1001 Laskin Rd, 422-8817. Seafood and American cuisine. Bfast $5, lunch specials $6. 'Great food, great value'. Open 6:30am-10pm daily.
Giovanni's Pizza Pasta Place, 2006 Atlantic Ave, 425-1575. Inexpensive Italian food. Lunch and dinner $6-$10. Daily noon-10:30pm. _www.vabeach.com/-giovannis/tour.htm_.
The Jewish Mother, 3108 Pacific Ave, 422-5430. Burgers, sandwiches, etc. Entrees $8.95-$16.95. 'Friendly place'. At night a popular bar with live music. Open Mon-Fri 10am-midnight, Sat-Sun 8am-midnight, bar open 'til 1:30am daily.

Of interest
Poe wasn't the only Edgar around these parts with a finger on the pulse of the paranormal: the work of Edgar Cayce, the 'best documented psychic of modern times' is explained in exhibits, lectures, movies and tours at the **Edgar Cayce Visitors Center**, 6700 Atlantic Ave, 428-3588/(800) 333-4499. You can learn about life after death and have your ESP (extra-sensory perception) tested too. Mon-Sat 9am-8pm, Sun Noon-8pm. Free. _www.edgarcayce.org_.
The Viva Elvis Festival, 491-7866, in late May/early June, has Elvis impersonators, Elvis films, Elvis food (fried peanut-butter-and-banana sandwiches) and a 'Flock of Elvi' skydiving to the beach, not to mention four days of Elvis karaoke contests! So if you've ever fancied yourself as a bit of a hound dog, here's your chance. _www.beacheventsfun.com_.
Virginia Beach is amusement park paradise. If you're looking for thrills try **Ocean Breeze Water Park**, 422-4444. Open Mon-Sat 10am-7pm, hours may vary. All-day pass $18.95, $9.95 after 4pm. _www.oceanbreezewaterpark.com_. There's also **Atlantic Fun House**, 422-1742, open noon-midnight. $5, _www.atlanticbeachclub.com_.

Sport
Virginia Beach is host to a leg of the annual **Bud Surf Tour**, attracting pros from around the world. If you fancy your chances, **Wave Riding Vehicles**, 422-8823, provide local surf reports and info on main surf areas. You can also rent surfboards from their store at 1900 Cypress Ave for $27/day. Open Mon-Sat 9am-9:30pm, Sun 10am-8pm. _www.waveridingvehicles.com_. Cycling, jogging and skating are popular

along the boardwalk and there are also a couple of fishing piers for those wishing to take things easy.

Information
The Virginia Beach Visitor Information Center, 2100 Parks Ave, (800) VA-BEACH. Free publications full of useful info and accommodation directories. *www.vbfun.com*.

CHARLOTTESVILLE Located in central Virginia and surrounded by beautiful dogwood-laden countryside and old estates, Charlottesville is one of the most interesting and charming places in the state. Several celebrities have moved here to enjoy the gentleman-farmer lifestyle including John Grisham, Sam Shepherd and Jessica Lange. A pleasant sample of Virginian craftsmanship can be found along the **pedestrian mall**, a bonanza of old shops and cafes that stretch between 1st and 6th Sts in the downtown area. Much of the architecture was either designed by Jefferson or influenced by his example. The elegant **University of Virginia** is testimony to his humanism and architectural genius. *www.soveryvirginia.com*.

The telephone area code is 434.

Accommodation
Budget Inn, 140 Emmet St (near the University), 293-5141. $48-78, free coffee in morning. Check-in 1pm, out 11am. *www.budgetinn-charlottesville.com/*.
Econo Lodge, 400 Emmett Dr, 296-2104, $47-58, free coffee and doughnuts in morning. Outdoor pool. Check-in 3pm, out 11am. *www.econolodgeuniversity.com*.

Food
Baja Bean Co, 1327 W Main St, 293-4507. California-style Mexican food, which you can wash down with a choice of 12 Mexican beers and 20 different Tequilas. 'Cheap and delicious.' Entrees $5-9. Open daily 11am-2am. *www.bajabean.com*.
Big Jim's Barbeque, 2104 Angus Rd, 296-8283. Huge burgers that you can't finish, Cajun-style, from $4. Open 11am-10pm daily.
White Spot Restaurant, 1407 University Ave, 295-9899. Small, basic diner food. Try the 'Gus,' an egg-cheese-cholesterol burger, with fries and a soda for less than $6. 'Friendly, helpful staff.' Open daily 8am-11pm.

Of interest
Ash Lawn, 21/2 miles beyond Monticello on Rte 53, 293-9539, the 535-acre estate of the 5th US president, James Monroe. The site was chosen by his close friend Thomas Jefferson. Daily 9am-6pm (Apr-Oct), 11am-5pm (Nov-Mar), $9. *www.ash-lawnhighland.org*.
Historic Court Square, E Jefferson St. Self-guided tour info available free at Albemarle County Historical Society at 200 2nd St NE (see Info section below).
Michie Tavern, 1/2 mile from Monticello on Rte 53, 977-1234. Re-creates 18th century tavern life. Story has it that Jefferson, Monroe, Madison and Lafayette met here. Converted log-house next door serves all-you-can-eat 18th century southern-style colonial buffet lunch (daily 11:15am-3:30pm, $13.50). Original Tavern Museum open daily 9am-5pm, $8, tours run every 1/2 hr 'til 4:30pm. With lunch the museum ticket is $2 off. *www.michietavern.com*.
Monticello, 3 miles south-east of the town on Rte 53, 984-9822. The architectural masterpiece where Thomas Jefferson and Sally Hemmings (his slave and mistress) lived. Built from his own design, this Palladian villa has many ingenious extras, such as the clock that sits over the front door. Daily 8am-5pm (Mar-Oct). $14, frequent tours every 5-10mins, 'Magnificent with fine views of the surrounding countryside.' *www.monticello.org*.

Entertainment

Durty Nelly's, 2200 Jefferson Park Ave, 295-1278. Bar/deli where you can choose from over 50 beers. Happy Hour specials (4:30pm-6:30pm Mon-Fri), live music on Tue, Thur and w/ends, cover $3-$4. Daily 11am-2am.

Friday After Five, on the mall during the summer: live entertainment and a festive atmosphere. *www.fridaysafterfive.com*.

Millers, 109 W Main St (near the mall), 971-8511. Bar with live music daily, free or low cover. 'Cheap American food'. Open daily 11:30am-2am.

Information

Albemarle Charlottesville Historical Society, 200 2nd St NE, 296-1492, for brochures on historic sites, museum features, law in Virginia and local history. Walking tours leave from here on Saturdays at 10am, $3. Open Mon-Fri 9am-5pm, Sat 10am-1pm. *www.albemarlehistory.org*.

Charlottesville Convention & Visitors Bureau, intersection of Rte 20 and I-64 (on the way to Monticello), 293-6789. Info on places to eat and stay and things to do; also has special Thomas Jefferson exhibits. *www.soveryvirginia.com*.

Travel

Amtrak, 810 W Main St, 296-4559/(800) 872-7245, *www.amtrak.com*.

Greyhound, 310 W Main St, 295-5131/(800) 231-2222. (Richmond $14o/w, $23 r/t: 1 hr 15 mins), *www.greyhound.com*.

NORFOLK   Named the 'Best Big City' in the South by *Money Magazine*, Norfolk has been reborn and revitalized. Within 10 blocks of the downtown area is a trendy restaurant and theatre district, shopping and harbour cruises (call Tall Ship Harbor Cruises on (757) 627-SAIL *www.american-rover.com/*). Don't miss the nationally acclaimed **Chrysler Museum of Art**, 245 W Olney Rd, (757) 664-6200, *www.chrysler.org*; **Nauticus – The National Maritime Center**, 1 Waterside Dr, (757) 664-1000/(800) 664 1080, *www.nauticus.org* and the **Battleship *Wisconsin.***

The best nightlife can be found around the **Waterside Festival Market-place**, 333 Waterside Dr, (757) 627-3300, *www.watersidemarketplace.com*. Weekend waterfront festivals at Town Point Park include **HarborFest** (the tall ships and maritime festival in June), the **Bayou Boogaloo and Cajun Festival** (June) and the **Town Point Virginia Wine Festival** (Oct); call (757) 441-2345 or visit *www.festeventsva.org* for more info. History buffs can follow the self-guided **Cannonball Trail** walking tour, tracing over 400 years of Norfolk and American history, or tour the **Norfolk Naval Base**, the world's largest naval base and home of the Atlantic Fleet, (757) 444-7955, *www.navy.mil*.

Information

Norfolk Convention and Visitors Bureau, 232 E Main St, (800) 368-3097. *www.norfolkcvb.com*.

NEWPORT NEWS   Just 30 minutes from Norfolk and known as one of the world's major shipbuilding centres, **Northrop Grumman (The Newport News Shipbuilding)**, with over 115 years of experience, has become the premiere shipyard for aircraft carriers, submarines and fleet services to the military and the private sector of maritime shipbuilding. It comes as no surprise, therefore, that the city boasts America's premier maritime museum, **The Mariners' Museum**, 100 Museum Dr, (757) 596-2222, where you can see the ongoing preservation and display of relics from the USS *Monitor*, the internationally famous Crabtree Collection of Miniature Ships, figureheads, antique navigation instruments and steam engines. *www.mariner.org*. For more info contact the **Newport News Visitor Center**, (757) 886-7777/(888) 493-7386, *www.newport-news.org*.

SHENANDOAH NATIONAL PARK Only 80 miles from Washington DC, the park is a lovely wilderness area. The 105-mile **Skyline Drive** runs along the crest of the Blue Ridge Mountains following the old **Appalachian Trail**, with an average elevation of over 3000 ft. The southern end of the drive meets the **Blue Ridge Parkway**, which takes the traveller clear down to the Smokies.

The route affords a continuous series of magnificent views over steeply wooded ravines to the Piedmont Plateau on the east and across the fertile farmlands of the Shenandoah Valley to the west. Check the weather before doing the Skyline Drive. If it's bad, you'll just drive through clouds.

There are over 500 miles of foot trails for every type of hiker. Campgrounds, lodges and shelters can be found throughout the park (see below). Look out for pioneer dwellings and homesteads. **Skyline Drive Entrances**: (North to south) Front Royal off Hwy 340, Thornton Gap near Luray off Hwy 211, Swift Run Gap near Elkton off Hwy 33, Rockfish Gap near Waynesboro off Hwy 250 or I-64. $10/vehicle. *nps.gov/shen*.

· *The area code is 540.*

Accommodation
Bear's Den Hostel, just off Rte 7, 601 S (near Bluemont), 554-8708. A stone lodge that sits on the Appalachian Trail overlooking the Shenandoah Valley. Office hrs daily 5pm-10pm, front gate locked at 10pm. Dorms $18 (linen inc), private room from $50 for two, cottage from $65 for two, camping $6 pp. Rsvs recommended. *www.bearsdencenter.org*.

Lodges: Skyland Lodge at milepost 41.7. Lodge units: Sun-Thur $85-$110, Fri-Sat $99-122; cabin rooms: Sun-Thur $62-$107, Fri-Sat $67-$114. **Big Meadows Lodge** at milepost 51, easy access to hiking trails and restaurants. Lodge units: Sun-Thur $85-$96, Fri-Sat $99-$106; cabin rooms: Sun-Thur $85-90, Fri-Sat $93-97. All rates based on double occupancy, XP-$10. Rsvs required (months in advance for fall): call 743-5108/(800) 999-4717. All campgrounds and lodges have rangers-in-residence who provide info on trails, natural history, etc. *www.visitshenandoah.com*.

Campgrounds: Mathews Arm at Skyline Drive milepost 22.1 (no showers), Big Meadows at milepost 51.3, **Lewis Mountain** at milepost 57.5 and **Loft Mountain** at milepost 79.5. Tent sites $16. All on first-come, first-served basis, except **Big Meadows** that requires reservations and charges $19. Call (800) 365-CAMP.

Of interest
Luray Caverns, 970 US Hwy 211 W, 743-6551. Eastern America's largest and most popular caverns, full of stalactites and stalagmites and the haunting sounds of the great stalacpipe organ, the world's largest musical instrument. Daily 9am-7pm (summer hrs). $19, 1hr tours leave every 20mins. 'Excessive.' 'Worth every cent.' *www.luraycaverns.com*.

Information
Shenandoah National Park Visitors Centers: Byrd Center at Big Meadows (milepost 51), 999-3283 (has info on camping within the park) and Dickie Ridge Center (milepost 4.6), 635-3566. *nps.gov/shen*.

LEXINGTON   At the southern end of the Shenandoah Valley. A quaint picturesque town where both Stonewall Jackson and Robert E. Lee lived. Visit the **Stonewall Jackson House**, 8 E Washington St, 463-2552, for a guided tour and information on Jackson's younger years, $6. Open Mon-Sat 9am-5pm, Sun 1pm-5pm. _www.stonewalljackson.org_. The **Lee Chapel and Museum** at Washington and Lee University, 463-8768, is where Lee and his beloved horse, Traveller, are buried. Free, Mon-Sat 9am-5pm, Sun 1pm-5pm. _leechapel.wlu.edu_. Nearby **Rockbridge Vineyard**, 30 Hill View Lane in Raphine, (888) 511-9463, offers tours and tastings of its award-winning wines. Free, Wed-Sat 11am-5pm, Sun noon-5pm, _www.rockbridge-vineyard.com_.

North of town on Rte 39 is the **Goshen Pass**, a breathtaking mountain gorge with miles of whitewater rapids, the perfect spot for swimming, tubing, fishing or hiking. The **Natural Bridge**, spanning 90 ft, lies just 16 miles from Lexington off the I-81, _www.naturalbridgeva.com_. The **Natural Bridge Caverns**, 291-2121/(800) 533-1410, have stalagmites and stalactites along with hanging gardens and flowstone cascades: $12 for the bridge, $18 for both the bridge and caverns. Stay in their lodge, starting from $69.95 for a double in summer. Camping is also available at the **Campground at Natural Bridge**, 291-2727, tent sites $25-$27, cabins $55 for two, _www.campnbr.com_.

WEST VIRGINIA - The Mountain State

A common image people have of West Virginia is of a poor but proud popu-lation struggling to make a living from coal mining and enduring a hard life between business cycles as rocky as the Appalachian mountains that cover the state. Though this image is partly accurate, fifty years of federal pro-grammes, a growing tourist economy and industries flourishing in other, less mountainous parts of the state have combined to alter the economic picture of West Virginia.

The most striking (and most lucrative) aspect of the Mountain State, however, remains its natural beauty. Tree-covered mountains, raging rivers, caves, waterfalls and gorges offer the visitor a variety of scenic vistas and wilderness adventures.

West Virginia is the only state born out of the conflict of the Civil War. The state seceded from the Confederacy and her mother state, Virginia, protest-ing inequality in taxation, unequal representation in the legislature and unequal distribution of funds for public works that favoured the eastern part of the state. Local bluegrass musicians can be heard in small towns and big cities alike. _www.callwva.com_.

The telephone area code for the entire state is 304.

CHARLESTON   Not to be confused with Charleston, South Carolina. This is the state capital and an industrial town. The new **Clay Center for the Arts and Sciences**, one of the most ambitious cultural and educational undertak-ings in West Virginia, has breathed new life into this previously rather dull city. Charleston is also a good base for a more interesting visit to the countryside. _www.charlestonwv.com_.

Accommodation

Budget Host Inn, 3313 Kanawha Blvd, 925-2592/(800) 283-4678. $31-70, free coffee am. Check-in up to 12pm, out 11am. *www.budgethost.com*.

Microtel Inn, 600 2nd Ave, 744-4900/(800) 248-8879. S-$41, D-$46, continental bfast included. Check-in from 12pm, out before 12pm.

Motel 6, 6311 MacCorkle Ave, 925-0471. From $46, free coffee am. Check-in anytime, out 12pm. *www.motel6.com*.

Parsley Motor Inn, 1607 Bigley Ave, 345-3500. From $36. Check-in anytime, out 11am. *www.parsleymotorinn.com/*.

Food

Capitol Roasters Café, 160 Summers St, 720-7375. Serves soups and sandwiches (around $6) in a warm and inviting atmosphere. Open Mon-Thur 7am-8pm, Fri-Sat 'til 11pm, Sun 8am-6pm.

Charleston Town Center Picnic Place and Restaurants, Clendin, Court, Lee and Quarrier Sts, 345-9525. 160 stores and restaurants, one of the largest downtown enclosed malls in the US. Mon-Sat 10am-9pm, Sun 12.30pm-6pm. *www.charleston-towncenter.com*.

Main Kwong, 1407 Washington St, 342-8899. The best Chinese in Charleston. Entrees: $4-$12, open Mon-Thur 11am-10pm, Fri-Sat 'til 11pm, Sun noon-10pm.

Soho's, 800 Smith St, 720-7646. Traditional Italian cuisine, lunch $6-$10, dinner $10-$20. Open Mon-Sun 11am-3pm (lunch), 5pm-9pm (dinner), Fri-Sat 'til 10pm.

Of interest

The Clay Center, 1 Clay Sq, 561-3500/(888) 241-6376. New in 2003, the Clay Center for Arts and Sciences is a 240,000 sq-ft complex of performance and exhibition spaces, an interactive science museum, planetarium and large-format theatre. Open Wed-Sat 10am-5pm, Sun noon-5pm, Thu 'til 7pm. General admission: $12.50. *www.theclaycenter.org*.

Coonskin Park, 2000 Coonskin Dr, 341-8000. Swimming pool, golf course, paddle-boat lake, skate park, soccer field and tennis courts. Open 8am-dusk. *www.kanawha-countyparks.com*.

East End Historic District, residential district bordered by Bradford, Quarrier, and Michigan Sts and Kanawha Blvd. Many fine examples of Colonial, Greek Revival, Late Victorian and Georgian homes.

State Capitol, Main rotunda, Building 1, Kanawha Blvd, 558-4839. Free tours Mon-Fri 9am-3.30pm, Sat 1pm-5pm. *www.wvculture.org*.

If your feet are sore and you are heading for an address on the 1500 block, be warned... The **1500 block of Virginia St** is considered the longest city block in the world!

Internet access

Kanawha Public Library, 123 Capitol St, 343-4646. Free Internet use on a first-come, first-served basis, must have valid ID to sign up. Open Mon-Thur 9am-9pm, Fri-Sat 9am-5pm.

Information/Travel

Convention and Visitors Bureau, 200 Civic Center Dr, 344-5075/(800) 733-5469. *www.charlestoncvb.com*.

Amtrak, 350 MacCorkle Ave SE, 342-6766/(800) 872-7245. *www.amtrak.com*.

Greyhound, 300 Reynolds St, 357-0056/(800) 231-2222. *www.greyhound.com*.

NEW RIVER GORGE In the southernmost part of the state, the New and Gauley Rivers churn some of the most exciting rapids anywhere and, logically, the greatest tourist attraction is to brave them in all forms of craft. The Gauley, in fact, is billed as one of the top ten whitewater rivers in the

WHITEWATER

North America's wildly beautiful and spectacular rivers make it ideal for whitewater rafting, a mind-blowing experience you'll never forget. These are some of the best whitewater rivers:

EAST: **Chattooga, Long Creek, SC**. 50 ft/mile drops through the most inaccessible canyons in the Southeast and passes the site of a scene from *Deliverance*. Best tackled in spring or early summer. Day trips $50-$109: call **Wildwater Limited**, (800) 451-9972. *www.wildwaterrafting.com*.
Cheat, Albright, WV. Try 'Big Nasty' and 'Coliseum' rapids, part of the largest natural watershed in the East. Only rafted Mar-Jun. Day trips $56-$76. For more info call **Mountain Streams**, (800) 723-8669, *www.mtstreams.com*.
Gauley, Summerville, WV. Don't try the upper section unless you've got rafting experience (or a death wish!). Day trips $75-$145 at **The Rivers Company**; for more info call (800) 879-7483. *www.riversresort.com*.
James, Richmond, VA. Raft past commuters in metropolitan Richmond. Call the **Richmond Raft Co**, (800) 540-7238, who do trips from $48-$60, *www.richmondraft.com*.
New, Lansing, WV. The world's second oldest river after the Nile. Lower section is known as the 'Grand Canyon of the East,' with a spectacular view of the longest, highest single-span bridge on earth. Day trips $85-$105; for more info call **Class VI River Runners** (800) 252-7784. *www.800classvi.com*.
Penobscot, Maine, through the steep-walled granite Ripogenus Gorge, one of the most scenic whitewater stretches in eastern USA. But no time for the view if you ride the 'Exterminator' Class V rapid—'intense'. Call **Northern Outdoors**, (207) 663-4466/(800) 765-7238. Prices depend on day and season, but day trips run from $69-$122. *www.northernoutdoors.com*.
Youghiogheny (The 'Yough' is pronounced Yock'), **Ohiopyle State Park, PA**. Splendid, challenging rapids. Prices depend on season and difficulty and range from $25-$120 for day trips. Contact the **Wilderness Voyageurs Inc**, (800) 272-4141, *www.wilderness-voyageurs.com*. The **Upper Yough, Friendsville, MD** ranks among the most challenging in the world, with rapid names including 'Meat Cleaver' and 'Double Pencil Sharpener'! An experienced rafter's dream, a beginner's nightmare!
USA Raft, (800) 872-7238, is the reservation company for several outfitters. They can help you choose from among 30 different outings, to suit all skill levels, on ten of the best whitewater rivers in the east. *www.usaraft.com*. For more info check out the American Whitewater Affiliation homepage, *www.americanwhitewater.org*.

WEST: **Colorado, Grand Canyon, AZ**. Over 150 world-class rapids between Badger Creek and Lava Falls, surrounded by canyon walls a mile high. Call the **Arizona Office of Tourism**, (888) 520-3434. *www.arizonaguide.com*.
Middle Fork of Salmon, Stanley, ID. Whitewater of unforgettable intensity and beauty, natural hot springs and waterfalls. **Snake, Lewiston, ID**. Rafting from Hells Canyon, the *deepest gorge in the US*, on 'reorganizer' rapids and warm water. For both rivers contact the **Idaho Outfitters and Guides Association**, (800) 494-3246. *www.ioga.org*.
For extended trips on Western rivers, contact **Gorp Travel**, Boulder, CO, (800) 444-0099, *www.gorptravel.com*. Also check out *www.westernriver.com* and *www.travelsource.com/rafting*.

CANADA: **Kootenay, Radium Hot Springs, BC**. The Kootenay tumbles through some of the most scenic passes of the Rocky Mtns. Contact **Kootenay River Runners**, (800) 599-4399. Day-long excursions cost around C$83. *www.raftingtherockies.com*. **Jasper National Park** also provides amazing scenery and exhilarating runs. Contact **Whitewater Rafting Ltd** for day trips, C$45-60, (800) 557-7238. *www.whitewaterraftingjasper.com*.

A beginner should check out *The Complete Whitewater Rafter* by Jeff Bennett, McGraw-Hill, NY, NY, for historical background on the sport and tips for handling the wildest of rivers. For more information on whitewater routes, consult *Whitewater Rafting in North America* (2nd Edition) by Lloyd D Armstead, Pequot Press, Chester, CT.

TIPS: Wherever you decide to go, bear in mind the following: look for an established outfitter that has been in business for a number of years and has a current license. Decide what you want and know the level of ability required (up to Class III for first-timers, IV-VI more advanced, difficult rapids). Plan ahead—deposits may be required; w/ends are more expensive than weekdays; find out what the price includes (meals, equipment, etc). Finally, if you fall out of the raft, fold your arms across your chest and point your feet DOWNstream.

world. The major town serving the region is **Beckley**, where accommodation and hiking equipment can be found. Get here by following I-77, the West Virginia Turnpike (toll).

Accommodation
Laurel Creek Cabins & Campground, Rt 19, Laurel Creek Rd, Fayetteville. Cabins with private bath $65 for 1-2 people, linens and towels provided. Campground-$7/person. Open Mon-Sat 11am-5pm, check-out 11am. *www.wvweb.com/www/ml*.
Midland Trail Motel, Rt 60, Ansted, 658-5065. S-$34.50, D-$39.50. Check-in after 4pm, out 10am. *www.newrivercvb.com/midlandtrailmotel*.

Food
Cathedral Café, 134 S Court St, Fayetteville, 574-0202. 'Phenomenal breakfasts' (around $4) and great lunches (around $6). Open Mon-Fri 7:30am-4pm, Sat-Sun 7am-4pm, Fri-Sat 5pm-9pm for dinner during the summer, *www.cathedralcafe.biz*.

Of interest
Cliffside Amphitheatre, in the New River Gorge National River area, near Beckley, 256-6800. Classic and modern drama by local repertory companies. June-Sept, Tue-Sun, 8.15pm. Tkts $14.
Exhibition Coal Mine, New River Park in Beckley, 256-1747. Learn about coal mining by going down into a real coal pit. April-Nov, daily 10am-5.30pm, $15. 'Take a sweater.' *www.beckleymine.com/*.
New River Gorge Bridge, on US-19 past Fayetteville. The world's second longest single-arch steel bridge spans the gorge at one of its most stunning points.
Whitewater Rafting. The New River CVB has brochures of many organisations that run whitewater rafting tours along the New and Gauley Rivers at various prices. $95 could buy you the thrill of a lifetime, but prices start as low as $49.
New River Gorge is surrounded by numerous State Parks, including **Babock, Bluestone, Carnifex Ferry, Hawk's Nest**, and **Pipestem**. All offer exceptional recreational facilities and camping, *www.wvstateparks.com*.

Information
New River Convention and Visitors Bureau, 310 Oyler Ave, Oak Hill, 465-5617/(800) 927-0263, *www.newrivercvb.com*.

MONONGAHELA NATIONAL FOREST Sounding like the name of a monster from a Japanese sci-fi flick, the Monongahela is actually a charming and beautiful forest covering much of eastern West Virginia. Unusual geological formations beneath the mountains have resulted in the creation of some of the largest caverns in the world, as well as warm mineral springs that bubble up in several valleys. There's coal under the mountains too and many of the back roads are made bumpy by the giant coal trucks that roll in convoy all day and all night.

Accommodation
Graham's Motel, Rte 219, **Buckeye**, 799-4291/(888) 887-8226. From $40, free coffee and pastries in the morning. 'Very laid-back and hospitable atmosphere.'
Camping: There are no camping restrictions in the forest, so if you have some of that pioneer spirit, just find a spot and camp down. State parks with campgrounds: **Greenbrier**, ex 175 off I-64, near **White Sulphur Springs**, 536-1944, has cabins suitable for groups; from $79 inc tax for four people, $83 inc tax on w/ends. Tent sites are $15, $19 w/hook-up, *www.greenbriersf.com*. **Watoga**, near Hillsboro, Rte 28, 799-4087. Tent sites $15, $19 w/hook-up, cabin for four $77, *www.watoga.com*.

Food
The Brazen Head Inn, Rte 219, Mingo Village, (866) 339-6917. A great Irish pub with West Virginia traditions. Home-made, country cooking – traditional Irish cuisine and there is always fish and chips on the go! Open Tue-Fri 4pm-9:30pm, Sat 8am-9:30pm, Sun 'til 8pm, _www.brazenheadinn.com_.

Harpers Front Porch, Seneca Rocks, 567-2555. Great home-made Italian-American cuisine. Pizzas, pastas and specialty sandwiches around $5-$7. Open daily 11am-9pm Apr-Oct. 'Great view of the Seneca Rocks.'

Of interest
Within a few miles of the town of **White Sulphur Springs** are the **Lost World Caverns** in Lewisburg, 645-6677/(866) 228-3778, filled with amazing rock formations and bats. Daily 9am-7pm. Wild tour $60, an expedition beyond the commercial caverns. Not for the faint-hearted! _www.lostworldcaverns.com_. Also along Hwy 219 is the **Droop Mountain State Park**, site of a Civil War battle. 11/2 hours northeast of White Sulphur Springs on Rt. 92 North is the **Cass Scenic Railroad**, 456-4300, where a coal-fired locomotive hauls visitors along old logging railways through the remote corners of the National Forest, late May through early Oct. 11/2 hr rides at 10.50am, 1pm and 3pm; $13; 5hr trip at noon (except Mon), $17. All w/end trips are $2 extra. _www.cassrailroad.com_.

Green Bank National Radio Astronomy Observatory, on Rte 28, 456-2011, is 10 miles away from the Cass Railroad. This is a major radio telescope that American scientists are using to map the universe and study its chemical composition. Free daily tours from mid-June to Sept between 9am-6pm. _www.nrao.edu_.

Information
Pocahontas County Convention and Visitors Bureau, Marlinton, (800) 336-7009, _www.pocahontascountywv.com_.

NORTHERN PANHANDLE The section of the state that sticks up between Ohio and Pennsylvania has two things worth visiting: **Grave Creek Mounds** at Moundsville, 843-4128, the largest pre-historic, conical Indian burial site in the US. Mon-Sat 10am-4.30pm, Sun 1pm-5pm, $3. **Prabhupada's Palace of Gold** in Moundsville, south of Wheeling on Hwy 250, 843-1812. This glittering gold complex is a Hare Krishna tribute to their departed leader and includes a temple and a spectacular rose garden. Open daily 10am-8pm Apr-Aug, 10am-5pm Sept-Mar, $6 donation, _www.palaceof-gold.com_. Also, if you happen to be in **Weirton**, be aware that this is the only place in the country where a state is only one city wide. It is bordered on the west by Ohio and on the east by Pennsylvania.

Information
Wheeling Convention and Visitors Bureau, 1401 Main St, Wheeling, (800) 828-3097, _www.wheelingcvb.com_.

HARPERS FERRY The National Park Service preserves this small, historic town where in 1859 John Brown raided the government arsenal and hoped to spark a general slave uprising. He was captured the following evening by Col Robert E. Lee and two months later was tried and publicly hanged in neighbouring Charles Town.

Highly recommended for Civil War buffs—Harpers Ferry changed hands 8 major times during the war—the area also appeals to nature lovers for the view from **Jefferson Rock**, so named because Thomas Jefferson stood here after returning from Europe and said, 'This scene is worth a voyage across the Atlantic'. Park Service tours throughout the day, 10am-3pm in summer; in winter talks are few and far between, but exhibits and orientation films are open 8am-5pm. Call 535-6298 for more info, *www.nps.gov/hafe*. Pedestrian bridge connects into C & O Canal Towpath over the river.

Nearby **Shepherdstown**, the oldest town in West Virginia and home of Shepherd College, offers shops, higher priced accommodation and restaurants. Worth a visit is the **Shepherdstown Opera House**, a movie theatre in a restored early 1900s building.

Charles Town is well known for the **Charles Town Races and Slots**, Flowing Springs Rd, (304) 725-7001/(800) 795-7001, where you can bet on the thoroughbreds and rid yourself of spare change on one of the 3,500 slots, *www.ctownraces.com*. Nearby there are plenty of motels and cheap eats, as well as country fairs, carriage rides and charming old houses. The first rural postal delivery service in the US began here.

Accommodation
Harpers Ferry AYH Hostel, 19123 Sandy Hook Rd in Knoxville, MD, 2 miles from Harpers Ferry, (301) 834-7652. $17 AYH, $20 non-AYH; $9 AYH camping, $12 non-AYH, includes access to showers and kitchen. Small store on site for general supplies and groceries. Check-in 6pm-10pm, out 7am-9am. Overlooking the Potomac and Shenandoah Rivers, this is a great location for hiking, biking, rafting and fishing. Shuttle bus from the train station, small charge. *www.harpersferryhostel.org*.

Food
The Anvil Restaurant, 1270 Washington St, Harpers Ferry, 535-2582. Open for lunch and dinner Wed-Sun 11am-9pm, specializing in seafood. Light fare available in pub, all entrees under $11.75. *www.anvilrestaurant.com*.
The Turf Rib Room, 608 E Washington St, Charles Town, 725-2081/(800) 422-TURF. Open for bfast, lunch and dinner. Great prime rib, fresh seafood, homemade biscuits and gravy. Open Mon, Wed and Thur 10am-9pm, Fri-Sat'til 10pm, Sun from 7am. *www.turfmotel.com*.

Of interest
Ghost tours, 725-8019. An exploration of Harpers Ferry's ghost-ridden past, Fri-Sat at 8pm (March-Oct), $4. Meet in front of Hot Dog Haven on Potomac St.
Whitewater Rafting on the Shenandoah, a tamer ride than the New River Gorge. Blue Ridge Outfitters, Hwy 340, 2 miles from the Harpers Ferry National Park, (304) 725-3444. Raft and canoe trips, Mar-Oct, from $50 raft, from $55 canoe. Rsvs recommended. *www.broraft.com*.

Information/Travel
Jefferson County Convention & Visitors Bureau, Harpers Ferry, (866) HELLO-WV, *www.hello-wv.com*.
Amtrak, Potomac St and Railroad Bridge, (800) 872-7245. *www.amtrak.com*.
MARC Line Trains, (800) 325-7245, also run from DC, Mon-Fri only, $9 o/w. You might also want to pass through here if you're on your way to the Skyline drive through Virginia's Shenandoah National Park. *www.mtamaryland.com*.

AMERICA'S UNDERGROUND RAILROAD
The once secret paths of liberation come to light

No single institution has had as serious and widespread an effect on the development of American society throughout history and in the present day, as the enslavement and forced transportation of as many as three million Africans to America, that persisted for 300 years. Prevailing economic conditions eventually polarized the attitudes of the industrialized North, which had outlawed slavery by the end of the 18th century and the South, where the invention of the cotton gin had secured the paramount importance of slavery, resulting in a civil war that was the bloodiest conflict in the nation's history.

By the 19th century, when the numbers of sympathizers in the movement to abolish slavery had grown in northern states, the north became the definite path to freedom. Escaping slaves were instructed to follow the "drinking gourd," or North Star, while they traveled under cover of night. A system of quilt symbols, kept top secret among blacks and sympathetic whites, allowed a draped design in broad daylight to be a quite secure direction or precaution for passing fugitives. Due to the continued passing of severe fugitive slave acts in which southern slave owners could employ bounty hunters to reclaim their 'property', even in northern states, Canada, where the British Parliament had outlawed slavery since 1833, became the ultimate destination. Perhaps 100,000 fugitives were eventually spirited north after 1830, a third of them ending up in Canada

The most heroic in these perilous ventures were former slaves themselves. The brave, such as Harriet Tubman who escaped—only to return into the midst of her predators, helped almost 300 others escape to freedom. The dangers of the journey north were epitomized in *Uncle Tom's Cabin* by Harriet Beecher Stowe. Some essential sites in the history of the Underground Railroad include:

Frederick Douglass National Historic Site, 1411 W St SE, **Washington, DC**, (202) 426-5961/(800) 967-2283. The 1877-1895 home of the famous escaped slave and prolific writer, orator, and advisor to the Great Emancipator himself, President Lincoln, in support of abolition and then equality. The house contains information and artifacts of his important role. Free 1hr guided tours are offered for groups of less than 5, over that rsvs required. There are 6 tours/day: 9am, 10am, 11am, 2pm, 3pm and 4pm. Daily, Apr-Oct 9am-5pm. *www.nps.gov/frdo*.

Levi Coffin House, 113 Route 27 N, **Fountain City, Indiana**, (765) 847-2432. Levi Coffin has been called the 'President' of the Underground Railroad, and for good cause. He wrote extensively in support of abolition, hid over 2,000 escaping slaves in clever passageways in his house and let them drink from an unconventional indoor well. $2, Open June-Aug, Tues-Sat 1pm-4pm and Sept-Oct, open Sat only. *www.waynet.org*.

The Johnson House, 6306 Germantown Ave, **Philadelphia, Pennsylvania**, (215) 438-1768. The Johnson family of the 1850s was highly active in the abolition movement, and their house was an important stop between north and south. Tours $5, $3 w/student ID. Mid-Sept to mid-Aug, Thu-Fri 10am-4pm (by appointment only), Sat 1pm-4pm.

Plymouth Church of the Pilgrims, 75 Hicks St, in Brooklyn Heights, **Brooklyn, NY**, (718) 624-4743. Henry Ward Beecher, a famous and fiery preacher for emancipation, hid blacks in the cellar of the church. Open to the public by appointment. *www.plymouthchurch.org*.

Rokeby Museum, 4334 Rt 7, **Ferrisburgh, VT**, N of Middlebury, (802) 877-3406. The location of this home and farm created a unique atypical opportunity for fugitives from American slavery, who worked openly on a Quaker farm for wages. Open mid-May to mid-October, tours Thu-Sun at 11am, 12.30pm and 2pm, $6, $4 w/student ID.

National Underground Railroad Freedom Center, 50 Freedom Way, **Cincinnati, Ohio**, (513) 333-7500. Focuses on the cooperation and courage of both fugitives and allies along the railroad network, and looks at later freedom movements, including women's suffrage. *www.freedomcenter.org*

The official **National Park Service** website has information about slavery and the Underground Railroad that goes into greater depth than can be achieved here and also has a list of related historical sites to visit across the Midwest and Northeast. *www.cr.nps.gov/nr/travel/underground/ugrrhome.htm*. **Traveling America,** (877) 782-2045, suggest trails of smaller and less-travelled sites stretching between Washington DC, upstate New York, West Virginia, Ohio and Kansas. *www.travelingamerica.com*.

THE MIDWEST

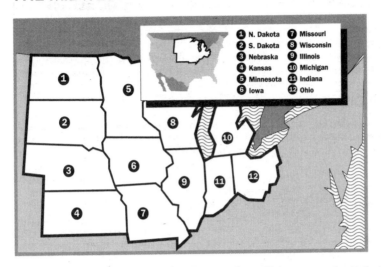

The Midwest (defined here as the 12 states from Ohio west to the Dakotas) is the rich, flat underbelly of the US whose glacier-scoured fertile lands yield massive quantities of corn, soybeans, hay, wheat and livestock. It's also the manufacturing, transportation and industrial heart of America. The region boasts the world's largest vehicle producer, General Motors Corporation of Detroit, Michigan, the first electrically lit city in the world (Wabash, Indiana) and the largest manufacturer of farm equipment, Deere & Company, (in Moline, Illinois).

But the recession of the early 1980's hit the Midwest hard. From some it earned the nickname 'the rust belt' for its deteriorating and closed-down factories. Falling prices and excessive debts trapped many farmers in a downward spiral toward bankruptcy, causing unprecedented suicides that tore at the fabric of a settled life. However, industry has revived somewhat and the Midwest is kicking back.

The essential quality of Midwestern life is its small-town character. Take time to meet its friendly and generous inhabitants, to get to know the prairie villages and the slow drawl of fields between them. Listen to the charming Scandinavian brogue of the northern states and on National Public Radio's weekly *Prairie Home Companion*. Try to find time to read the novels of Nobel Prize winner Sinclair Lewis (*Babbitt, Main Street, Elmer Gantry*), each of which was carefully mapped out by Lewis in quintessential Midwestern cities.

Mother Nature provides much of the drama here, from tornadoes in spring and summer to the fantastic electrical storm displays that illuminate summer evenings. The area is also seismically active: in 1811-1812 the biggest quakes in recorded history rolled through one million square miles, causing the Mississippi and Ohio Rivers to flow backwards.

The region's mighty rivers and Great Lakes serve as liquid highways for its produce, but also create liquid disasters such the great flood of 1993 that caused over $10 billion of damage and left millions of people homeless and (ironically) without water. Itself once 'the West', the Midwest in turn became the staging area for pioneer trails like the Santa Fe, Oregon and Mormon. With the advent of the railroad, the region became the distribution link between cattle ranch and consumer—a role it continues to play today.

ILLINOIS - The Land of Lincoln

Home to the nation's third largest city, Chicago, the tallest building in North America, the Sears Tower at 1,450 ft, and the tallest man in the world, who came from Alton and stood at a whopping 8ft 11inches, the state of Illinois is not one that does things by halves. Its very name originates from a Native American word meaning 'tribe of superior men', which is very fitting considering that Metropolis, the home of Superman, really exists in Southern Illinois. The story of this state, however, features more of Meriwether Lewis and William Clark than it does Clark Kent and Lois Lane. It was these two adventurers who, back in 1803, used Illinois as their launching pad for the historic expedition that would see them pave the way for westward expansion.

The birthplace of Ronald Reagan and Hillary Clinton, Illinois is also the final resting place of the state's favourite son, Abraham Lincoln. In the north of the state lies Chicago, a Midwestern metropolis which boasts stunning American architecture, and still vibrates with the sound of earthy Chicago blues. South of Chicago, endless fields of corn and soybean stretch for miles and it is here, in the countryside, that you'll taste Midwestern hospitality at its best, as sweet and honest as an ear of young corn. You'll also find, near Carthage in NW Illinois close to the banks of the Mississippi, the restored Nauvoo Temple, _www.nauvootemple.com,_ whence the Great Mormon Migration began in 1846, after the founder of the Mormons, John Smith, died at the hands of a mob in Carthage. About 70,000 Mormons made the arduous 1,300 mile trek from here to Salt Lake City, led by Brigham Young. _www.illinois.gov/visiting_.

CHICAGO   In the aftermath of the Great Fire of 1871, a Chicago realtor put up a sign that read: 'All gone but wife, children and energy!' That unquenchable spunk is still Chicago's trademark. The place hurls superlatives at you: tallest buildings, largest grain market, greatest distribution point, second busiest airport, biggest Polish populace outside Warsaw, highest concentration of practising psychics—the list is endless.

Chicago has two popular nicknames, The Second City and The Windy City. For decades it was the nation's second most populous area (after New York), but that title has since passed to Los Angeles. It's the politics, not the breeze sweeping in off Lake Michigan that explains Chicago's other nickname. Windy was the word for Chicago's politics. Then, for six terms until 1976, the ruthless Mayor Richard J. Daley—the 'Big Boss'—ran one of the last great political machines in America for a generation after World War II and made Chicago 'the city that works'.

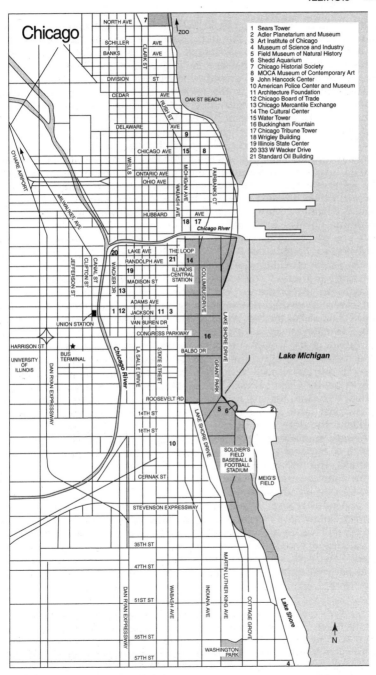

Chicago

1 Sears Tower
2 Adler Planetarium and Museum
3 Art Institute of Chicago
4 Museum of Science and Industry
5 Field Museum of Natural History
6 Shedd Aquarium
7 Chicago Historical Society
8 MOCA Museum of Contemporary Art
9 John Hancock Center
10 American Police Center and Museum
11 Architecture Foundation
12 Chicago Board of Trade
13 Chicago Mercantile Exchange
14 The Cultural Center
15 Water Tower
16 Buckingham Fountain
17 Chicago Tribune Tower
18 Wrigley Building
19 Illinois State Center
20 333 W Wacker Drive
21 Standard Oil Building

It still does, with clean streets filled with brightly-blooming summer flowers, miles of bicycle paths and an excellent, efficient transit system that includes six free trolleys downtown. Under Mayor Richard M. Daley, elected in 1989, Chicago has become 'a prosperous, well-governed model for the rest of the country', according to *The New York Times*.

The Millennium Park is the newest, dazzling addition to Chicago's waterfront. Among its outstanding features is the Jay Pritzker Pavilion, considered 'the most sophisticated outdoor concert venue of its kind in the US', designed by the renowned Frank Gehry. *www.millenniumpark.org.*

Although it was built on a swamp (the Indians called it the 'place of the stinking wild onions'), Chicago is also the fount of architectural innovation in the US. Downtown is a mind-boggling kaleidoscope of high-rise bravado, red, white, blue and green, with every new skyscraper more original and colourful than the next, designed by such towering talents and firms as Daniel Burnham, Mies van de Rohe, Louis Sullivan, Harry Weese and Skidmore, Owings, & Merrill.

If you have limited time, be sure to take the 90 minute **Chicago Architecture Foundation River Cruise** (312) 922-3432 (Michigan Ave and River), which provides expert commentary on over 50 historic and modern buildings and leaves you breathless and your neck slightly cricked! The cruise also covers the newest buildings, housing Chicago's escalating numbers of in-towners now revitalizing downtown, each recent structure as full of character as the last. Window washing takes on new meaning in these urban Himalayas! *www.architecture.org*.

Chicago is also a vital communications and trading centre and hub for both industry and agriculture in the Midwest, not only where east meets west via rail, but also where northern commerce meets the south via a canal dug to join the Great Lakes to the vast Mississippi River system. Pushed by Daniel Burnham, the city had the good sense to preserve its lakeshore as recreational land, giving it an extraordinary skyline along 27 miles of parkland and clean beaches.

Always pugnacious, Chicago in its gangland heyday (1920's-1940's) was a hive of criminal activity where there were hundreds of unsolved mob murders. The 1988 movie *The Untouchables* reveals the morbid underworld of the infamous criminal Al Capone and his gang. To stem the flow of guns into the city, in 1998, Chicago and Cook County, led by Mayor Daley, sued the gun industry for $433 million, accusing it of creating a public nuisance in the city. But, while Chicago's crime rate has dropped every year since 1992, the city still has the highest per capita murder rate in the nation. With this in mind, visitors should remember that the Loop and lakeshore areas are the safest. After dark, stay clear of parks and poorly-lit streets. These cautions hold particularly true for women. The South Side is very risky at night. *www.chicago.il.org. The telephone area code is 312 or 773.*

Accommodation

Chicago is a city of neighborhoods, such as Chinatown, the Loop, Streeterville, Gold Coast, Old Town and Lincoln Park: check which section you're staying in to get your bearings.

Arlington House Hostel, 616 W Arlington Pl, Lincoln Park, (773) 929-5380/(800) HOSTEL-5. Dorms $24.00, linen rental. Private room w/shared bath $54, w/private bath $68. Close to Chicago nightlife, internet access. Newly renovated. _www.arlingtonhouse.com._

Chicago International Hostel, 6318 N Winthrop Ave, Edgewater, (773) 262-1011. Dorms $21-23, linens incl. Private rooms w/bath $40, semi-private w/bath $27, semi-private w/out bath $24. All rates are per person, per night. Free coffee and bagel in the mornings. Closed 11am-2pm. Close to Loyola University and good, safe location. 'Recently renovated and near to El.' Must have photo ID. On-line reservations may be made at _www.hostels.com._

HI-Chicago, 24 E Congress Parkway, Downtown (South Loop), (312) 360-0300. Check-in 2pm, out 11am. Dorms $30 AYH, $33 non-AYH, incls linen. New 500 bed hostel located in restored loft building with easy access to attractions. Kitchen, a/c, student centre, library, on site cafes, internet access. Open 24 hrs. _www.hichicago.org_.

Fat Johnnies Last Resort Home Hostel, 2822 W 38th Place, Brighton Park, (773) 254-0836. Dorms $12, incls linens. Kitchen area, storage, 30 mins from downtown by bus.

Hotel Wacker, (Named after Charles H. Wacker, a great local brewer and preserver of the lakefront – so be respectful!), 111 W Huron St, Downtown, (312) 787-1386. Check-in 7am onwards, out 12pm. S-$60, D-$65, all w/baths, TV, a/c, phones. Close to entertainment district.

Also try **A1 Discount Hotels**, a hotel booking service that offers savings of up to 65% off regular rates, no fee required. Call (888) 511-5743 (U.S and Canada); (00) 5066-5066 (Europe), or book at _www.a1-discount-chicago-hotels.com._

Food

Local specialities: Chicago-style deep-dish pizza, stuffed pizza, kosher all-beef hot dogs and el-cheapo hamburgers called sliders. Pick up _Chicago Magazine, Where – Chicago_ and _This Week in Chicago_ from most hotels or tourist offices for comprehensive guides to eating out. Go online to _www.timeout.com/chicago_ or _www.Rocket99.com_ for bar and restaurant listings and reviews.

Ann Sather's, 929 W Belmont, (773) 348-2378. Bfast served all day, $6-$12, delicious Swedish Pancakes (similar to crepes) served with lingonberry jam, homemade cinnamon rolls. In ex-funeral home, murals and stain-glass windows. Daily 7am-10.30pm. Red Line to Belmont, few minutes from downtown. Three other locations in Lincoln Park. _www.annsather.com._

Berghoff's, 17 W Adams, (312) 427-3170. Over 100 years old and holds the city's first ever liquor license. German-American cuisine, a Chicago tradition. Big helpings. Mon-Thu 11am-9pm, Fri 11am-9:30pm, Sat 11:30am-10pm. Entrees–$10.95-$21.95. _www.berghoff.com._

Billy Goat Tavern, 430 N Michigan, (312) 222-1525. Cheap rib-eye steaks and cheeseburgers. Combos $7. 'Run by Greeks who holler your order across the Midwest: 'Cheezebooga, Cheezebooga, Pepsi, Pepsi! No fries, Cheeps!' Mon-Fri 6am-2am, Sat 10am-3am, Sun 11am-2am.

Bistro Pacific, 680 N Lake Shore Drive, (312) 397-1800. Korean, Japanese and Chinese cuisine. Great for romance on a budget, with dark, secluded, candlelit booths. Entrees $9-$11. Open Mon-Thu 11:30am-10pm, Fri until 11, Sat 4:30pm-11pm.

Cafe Ba-Ba-Reeba, 2024 N Halsted, (773) 935-5000. _The_ place to go for tapas and paella. Open Mon-Thu and Sun noon-10pm, Fri-Sat 'til midnight. Entrees-$11.95-$14.95. _www.cafebabareeba.com._

Ed Debevic's, 640 N Wells at Ontario, (312) 664-1707. 50s-style diner where the staff's deliberate rudeness gives you a break from Midwestern hospitality. 'Great American food. The most fun you can have eating out. You have to go in there just to read the outrageously rude messages posted around the restaurant'. Open Sun-Thu 11am-9pm, Fri-Sat 11am-11pm. Entrees $8. _www.eddebevics.com._

Edwardo's, 9 locations including 1212 N Dearborn, (312) 337-4490, on the near

North Side; 521 S Dearborn, (312) 939-3366, downtown; and 1321 E 57th St, (773) 241-7960, in Hyde Park. Pizza, pasta & salads. Entrees $10-$20. 10% student discount with ISIC card. Sun-Thu 11am-10pm, Fri-Sat 11am-11pm.

Fox & Obel, 401 E Illinois, near Navy Pier, (312) 410-7301. 40 seat café (with interesting breakfast selection) and food market catering to Chicago's new in-towners. Has, among other things, 75 prepared foods, over 400 types of cheese, some of best chocolate in Chicago, etc 'Definitely worth a sniff.' _www.fox-obel.com._ Open 7am-9pm daily.

Frontera Grill, 445 N Clark St, (312) 661-1434. Excellent Mexican food. Open Tue-Fri 11.30am-2.30pm, (lunch: $12.95-$16). Tue-Thu 5pm-10pm, Fri-Sat 'til 11pm (dinner: $15-$25), Sat brunch 10:30am-2.30pm. _www.fronterakitchens.com._

Gino's East, 633 N Wells, (312) 943-1124. 'Most well-known pizza house in Chicago.' Thin crust $11-$15, deep dish $11-$18. Mon-Thu 11am-9pm, Fri-Sat 'til 11pm, Sun 12noon-9pm.

Giordano's, 730 N Rush St, (312) 951-0747, and about thirty other locations. Voted best pizza by _Chicago Magazine._ 'The best pizza ever.' Open Sun-Thu, 11am- 11pm, w/ends 'til midnight. Pizzas $9-$24. _www.giordanos.com._

John Barleycorn Memorial Pub, 658 W Belden Ave at Lincoln Ave, (773) 348-8899. An English-style pub with artsy intellectuals. American cuisine. Entrees $7. Open Mon-Fri 4pm-2am, Sat 9am-3am, Sun 9am-2am. _www.johnbarleycorn.com._

Lou Malnati's Pizzeria, 439 N Wells St, (312) 828-9800. The pizza is _buonissima!_ Open daily 11am-11pm, Fri-Sat 'til 11.30pm, Sun 'til 10pm. Pizzas $14-$20. _www.loumalnatis.com._

Lou Mitchell's, 565 W Jackson, (312) 939-3111. A family operation since 1923, this venerable eatery gives free Milk Duds to the 'ladies', donut holes, prunes and oranges to all! Eggs served in skillets. Fresh-ground bottomless cups of coffee, Greek/French toast, malted waffles, and the 19 fluffiest omelettes in town. $4.25 - $8.45. 'Great atmosphere.' Open daily 5:30am-3pm, Sun from 7am. London _Times_ described it as 'Downfall of British Breakfast.' No credit cards.

Mitchell's Original, 101 W North Ave, (312) 642-5246. Good filling bfasts for $8-$10. Open Mon-Thu 6am-1am, Fri-Sat 24 hrs.

Miller's Pub, 134 S Wabash Ave, (312)263-4988, 'Good for breakfast, with friendly service, moderate prices and a good atmosphere.' Autographed celebrity photos adorn the walls. Ribs, steaks and Italian dishes. Entrees $8-$15. Open daily 11am-4am. _www.millerspub.com._

Nookies Tree, 3334 N Halsted, (773) 248-9888. Great value 3 course meals with refill coffee for $8-$10. 'Very wide selection from quality burgers to gourmet.' Sun-Thu 7am- midnight, Fri-Sat 24 hrs.

Oodles of Noodles, 2540 N Clark, (773) 975-1090. Great choice of different types of noodles, $6-$8. 'Friendly.' Sun-Thu 11:30am-9:30pm, Fri-Sat 11:30am-10pm.

Pegasus Restaurant and Taverna, 130 S Halsted St, (312) 226-4666. Exquisite Greek cuisine, à la carte menu. Entrees $9-$35. Enjoy appetizers and cocktails in the rooftop garden. Open Mon-Thu 11am-midnight, Fri until 1am, Sat-Sun noon-1am.

Scoozi, 410 W Huron, (312) 943-5900. Open for dinner Mon-Thu 5:30pm-9pm, Fri-Sat 'til 10pm, Sun 'til 9pm. Entrees $11-$22. As Italian as it sounds.

Shaw's Crab House, 21 E Hubbard, (312) 527-2722. Two restaurants in one: the Blue Crab Lounge (oyster bar) and the Main Dining Room which serves more than 40 fresh seafood entrees, chicken, prime steaks and pasta dishes. A fun place to go for seafood. Oyster bar, and main room: Entrees $16.95-$24.95. Live music on Tue, Thu and Sun 7pm-10pm. Entrees $10.95-26.95. Bar menu available. _www.shawscrabhouse.com._

Star of Siam, 11 E Illinois St, (312) 670-0100. A popular, funky and affordable Thai restaurant, with spices to suit all palates. Main courses $8 or less. Open Mon-Thu, Sun 11am-9:30pm, Fri-Sat 'til 10:30pm.

Of interest

If you are staying in Chicago for more than a few days, it is worth buying a **City Pass** for $49.50. It will save you around 50% off the regular admission price for the following attractions: *The Hancock Observatory, The Art Institute of Chicago, The Field Museum, Shedd Aquarium, Adler Planetarium and Astronomy Museum*, and the *Museum of Science and Industry*. It is valid for nine days from first use and is available from the aforementioned attractions, or you can buy online at: *www.citypass.com.*

Adler Planetarium and Astronomy Museum, 1300 S Lake Shore Dr, (312) 922-7827. Admission: Galaxy Package (+1 sky show) $16, Universe Package (+2 shows) $20, additional sky shows $5 each. 'Good show, interesting photos.' Daily 9:30am-4:30pm, in summer until 6pm. *www.adlerplanetarium.org.*

Architecture Foundation, 224 S Michigan, (312) 922-3432. Offers tours of outstanding Chicago architecture. 2 hr walk around the Loop costs $12, students $9. Times vary, check website. 'Good way to see a variety of Chicago architecture. Wear comfortable shoes.' Bus tour departs Sat at 9.30am in spring, summer and fall, for a 30 mile 3 hr tour including Frank Lloyd Wright's **Robie House**, $35, students $32. (Rsvs essential). Highly recommended: $1^1/2$ hr **Chicago River Architectural Tour**, daily from Michigan and River during summer (call for times), $23 on weekdays, $25 w/ends and hols. 'We had commentary by a docent with an amazing knowledge of every skyscraper in sight.' (312) 902-1500. *www.architecture.org.*

For a panoramic view of the city you can ascend the **Sears Tower,** (312) 875-9447, the second tallest (and one of the ugliest buildings) in the world, at Wacker Drive and Jackson. On a clear day from the Skydeck you can see four states-Illinois, Indiana, Wisconsin and Michigan. Go at night for a truly spectacular view of the city but forget the audio-visual show beforehand, it's a waste of time. Open daily May-Sept: 10am-10pm, Oct-Apr: 10am-8pm, $11.95. *www.theskydeck.com.*

Art Institute, 111 S Michigan Ave, (312) 443-3600. A magnificent collection of Impressionism, post-Impressionism—great Cézanne and Gauguin, modern American art and the Thorne Rooms: a series of minutely detailed period rooms—in miniature. Mon, Tue, Wed, Fri 10.30am-4.30pm, Thu 'til 8pm, Sat-Sun 10am-5pm. $12, $7 w/student ID, Tue free. Good basement cafe. 'Wonderful, well worth seven bucks.' 'Fantastic art collection. Give yourself a whole day if you want to see everything.' *www.artic.edu.*

Chicago Historical Society, 1601 N Clark St, (312) 642-4600. An impressive collection of exhibits about Chicago and Illinois. Outstanding on Lincoln with notebooks, letters, fashions, photos, manuscripts, furnishings. Mon,Tue,Wed noon-8pm; Thu, Fri, Sat 9.30am-4.30pm, Sun noon-5pm; $5, $3 w/student ID. Free on Mon. Research center being renovated, call for open hours. *www.chicagohistory.org.*

Chicago Mercantile Exchange, 30 S Wacker Dr, (312) 930-1000. The largest financial futures exchange in the world handles over 700,000 contracts each day (in June 2005), including those of pork bellies and other livestock. Gallery closed to public until further notice. However, lobby visitor center is open. Free. *www.cme.com.*

Field Museum of Natural History, 1400 S Lake Shore Dr, (312) 922-9410. Anthropology, botany, zoology, geology. Visit *Sue*, the largest T-Rex skeleton in the world, about 67 million years old. Daily 9am-5pm (last admission 4pm); $19, $13 w/student ID. 'There are interesting exhibits on American Indians and Eskimos.' *www.fmnh.org.*

Frank Lloyd Wright houses. There are many in the Chicago area; the Art Institute bookshop has good guidebooks. You need a car to see many of them, but FLW's own house and studio at 951 W Chicago Ave, Oak Park, is reachable by taking the CTA Green Line to Oak Park. From here, some of the houses are within walking distance. **Visitors Centre**, 158 N Forest Ave, (888) OAK-PARK, open daily 10am-5pm. Self-guided walking tour $9. Call for times. *www.visitoakpark.com*.

International Museum of Surgical Science, 1524 N. Lake Shore Dr, (312)642-6502. A sculpture of a surgeon holding his wounded patient marks the entrance to this museum, which takes you on a journey through the history of surgery. Open May-Sep 10am-4pm, Oct-Apr Tue-Sat only, $3 w/student ID. *www.imss.org*.

John Hancock Center, 875 N Michigan, (888) 875-8439. Tallest residential building in the world. Incredible views of the city from the observatory, where you can feel 'the windy city' on the Skywalk, the world's highest open air viewing area, complete with 'soundscopes', talking telescopes which tell you what you are looking at. Open 9am-11pm, $9.75, *www.hancock-observatory.com*. Reach dizzying heights in the **Signature Lounge** on the 96th floor, for a night of sophisticated live jazz with hors d'oeuvres and cocktails. No dress code. Sun-Thu 11am-12:30am, Fri-Sat 'til 1:30am.

The Loop. This 5-by-7-block city core is defined by the steel tracks of the elevated subway ('El'), a strangely loveable transit system with a voice like a giant trash compactor. Besides being fast and cheap, this gives free rein to voyeurism, letting you virtuously peep at a thousand fleeting tableaux as you flash past. Within the Loop are theatres, smart hotels and shopping districts, including the once pre-eminent **Marshall Fields** department store (still has the best Christmas windows anywhere). For chic stores such as **Neiman Marcus**, travel up the **Magnificent Mile** of upper Michigan Ave (take the Red Line to Grand).

The industrial Chicago suburb of **Des Plaines** is the birthplace of that most American of eateries, McDonald's. The original is now the **McDonald's # 1 Store Museum**, 400 N Lee St, (847) 297-5022. Free, call for days/hrs. Lots of 50's McDonald's memorabilia—but you can't eat here! Go to the *operating* McDonald's across the street for your Big Mac instead. In Oak Brook, the nation's only **Hamburger University** trains McDonald's managers, *www.mcdonalds.com.*

Michigan Ave, 20s and 30s facades, mortared with money, opulent restraint, shops for ogling only.

Museum of Contemporary Art, 220 E Chicago Ave, (312) 280-2660. The MCA's new building, located near the historic **Water Tower**, holds exhibits of fine art dating from 1945, as well as permanent collections featuring the works of Kline, Magritte and Warhol. It also houses a 300-seat theatre, along with a sculpture garden from which you can relax and enjoy the awe-inspiring view of Lake Michigan. 'Good Café.' Tue 10am-8pm (free 5pm-8pm), Wed-Sun 10am-5pm. $10, $6 w/ student ID, *www.mcachicago.org*.

Museum of Science and Industry, 57th St and Lake Shore Dr, (773) 684-1414. Visit the Apollo 8 Spacecraft, go for a simulated space shuttle ride, or see the latest Omnimax presentation. Mon-Sat 9.30am-4pm, Sun 11am-4pm. Admission $9, plus $6 extra for Omnimax Theatre. 'Best I've ever been to—easily spend a whole day here.' 'Magnificent place.' *www.msichicago.org*.

Shedd Aquarium, 1200 S Lake Shore Dr, (312) 939-2438. The world's largest indoor aquarium. Over 8000 aquatic species and an oceanarium with Beluga whales, dolphins, penguins, etc. Open daily 9am-6pm (last entry 4.30pm). Combined admission to Oceanarium and Aquarium $23. 'Very disappointing—save your money for the coastal aquariums in Boston and Baltimore.' *www.sheddaquarium.org*.

Six Flags Great America, 542 N Rt 21, Gurnee, (847) 249-4636. 12 roller coasters and over 40 rides and attractions, including the new Hurricane Harbor water park. Take I-94 or I-294 west, exit Grand Ave (Rt 132); 45 mins from Chicago. Late June-early Aug 10am-10pm, call for other times. Tickets $44.99; look out for discount coupons in Yellow Pages and local food outlets, or online deals at *www.sixflags.com/greatamerica*.

University of Chicago, 5801 S Ellis Ave, (773) 702-1234. 7 miles south of the Loop on the Midway. Dominating the Hyde Park neighbourhood is the beautiful campus of one of America's best universities. 'Wonderful examples of Gothic architecture' and the 'Nuclear Energy' sculpture, marking the site of the first sustained nuclear chain reaction. Although patrolled by Uni police, surrounding areas are dangerous, especially at night. *www.uchicago.edu*.

There is also a lot to see without having to spend a dime:

Millennium Park, downtown Chicago between Randolph and Monroe Streets, 24.5 acre park is a centre of art, music, architecture and landscape design. Free classical music presentations by the Grant Park Orchestra and Chorus. Features the Jay Pritzker Pavilion, designed by Frank Gehry. Beautiful gardens, ice rink and Millennium monument. *www.chicagotraveler.com/chicago millennium park.htm*.

Beaches: 18 sandy miles of 'em, free! The best is **North Avenue Beach** for a quick swim in the lake (change in the new restrooms), pick-up volleyball, or a lazy loll and try smaller **Oak St Beach** further south, in Lincoln Park down from **Lincoln Park Zoo**. 'The best beach we found in America. Clean, safe and a nice place to relax after seeing the city.' Cool off at the **Oak Street Beachstro** (312) 915-4100, overlooking the park, the beach and the lake, with strawberry daiquiris, mimosas and pina coladas. Also buffet brunch weekends 8 – 11.30 am. The area is pleasant and relatively safe. 'Makes Chicago seem like the seaside.' 'Quite pleasant walking along waterfront'. Free Trolley to Park from Water Tower. CTA Bus #72.

Buckingham Fountain Set in Grant Park along Chicago's lake front, the fountain is outlined against the skyscrapers of the Loop. At night a light show transforms the fountain into a dazzling, multi-coloured sculpture, May-Nov, 9pm. Especially inviting on a hot summer's day since it holds a million-and-a-half gallons of water.

Lincoln Park Zoo, 2200 N Cannon Dr, (312) 742-2000. One of the oldest zoos in America (1868). More than 2,000 exotic and endangered species, including special exhibits on big cats, primates and others. Nice cafes. Also features *At Home in the Woods*, interactive exhibit of N. American mammals. Mon-Fri 9am-6pm, Sat-Sun 'til 7pm, free. 365 days. *www.lpzoo.org*. CTA Bus #72 or #77.

Tomb-hopping America's most notorious gangster, Al Capone, has two graves in the city. One is at Mt Olivet, 111th St, (inscribed with 'qui riposa'), another at Mt Carmel ('My Jesus mercy'), Mt Carmel Catholic Cemetery, Harrison and Hillside Aves. *www.graveyards.com.*

Outdoor Art

Skyscrapers in Chicago are always amazing, continuing to rise like mushrooms in spring rain. There are at least 100 modern and historical skyscrapers of note - get a free list, including their architects, from the **Archicenter** at 224 S Michigan (312) 922-3432. Look up **The Standard Oil Building,** 200 E Randolph St, the world's fourth tallest; the **Hancock Tower;** the **Chicago Tribune Tower,** 435 N Michigan Ave, with its ornate faux-Gothic design and pieces of the Great Wall of China, Edinburgh Castle, etc., set in the building; the bifurcated **Wrigley Building;** and **333 W Wacker Dr,** famed for its elliptical, green mirrored offices that look out onto the river. Also, don't miss the wedge-shaped **Illinois State Center,** 100 W Randolph St, with its light, airy atrium and, of course, the black 'nine-tubed' monolith that is **Sears Tower.**

Sculpture fills the city. Outside the State Center sits Alexander Calder's *Flamingo*, a huge set of pink interconnecting girders; *The Picasso*, Daley Center Plaza at Washington and Dearborn, is a 63 ft steel woman with typical abstraction; *Untitled Sounding Sculpture* by Bertoia outside Standard Oil; *Batcolumn*, Claes Oldenburg's huge baseball bat in full erection at 600 W Madison; Miro's *Chicago*, a smaller homage to the city than most, Brunswick Plaza, 69 W Washington; and finally Marc Chagall's *Four Season's* 70ft mosaic wall that looks like graffiti, First National Bank Plaza.

Entertainment

Chicago was once home of the famous **Chess Records**, 2120 S. Michigan Ave, where Poland met Memphis and St. Louis. Here Muddy Waters, Willie Dixon, Bo Diddley, Howlin' Wolf, Sonny Boy Williamson and Chuck Berry got their mojos working. Among the many Chuck Berry numbers taped here was *Johnny B. Goode*, named after Chuck Berry's pianist Johnny Johnson, was taped here. The Rolling Stones came here to meet Muddy Waters and recorded (*I Can't Get No*) *Satisfaction* here in the mid 1960s. Mike Bloomfield and Paul Butterfield continued the Muddy Waters blues tradition here with feeling at Big John's. The studio is now a museum run by the **Blues Heaven Foundation**, (312) 808-1286, set up by Willie Dixon to preserve the blues legacy. *www.bluesheaven.com.*

Today Chicago is the Blues capital of the world and has one of the strongest folk scenes in America, not to mention all that jazz! Pick up a free copy of *The Reader* to find out where it's happening, published Fri and available at over 1,000 locations, or visit *www.chireader.com*. Also check the listings in *Chicago Magazine*. NB: Stick to Old Town, the Rush Street area and the North Side at night, even if you are in an armoured car.

B.L.U.E.S., 2519 N Halsted, (773) 528-1012. 'The people—exhilarating. The blues—totally overpowering.' 'Crowded, small, hot.' Sun-Fri 8pm-2am, Sat 'til 3am. Music starts at 9:30 pm. Cover $7-$10, *www.chicagobluesbar.com.*

Experience 'slam' poetry at the **Green Mill Lounge,** 4802 N Broadway, (773) 878-5552. Every Sun at 7pm local poets recite their work, one-on-one, in a bid to scoop $10 in winnings at this 95-year-old mobster hangout. Live music every night, $6-$15 cover. Sun-Fri noon-4am, Sat 'til 5am. Minimum age 21. *www.greenmilljazz.com.*

Hot Tix, 163 E Pearson St. and also at 72 E Randolph. 'Half-price tickets for same day performances—theatre, dance, the arts.' Tue-Sat, 10am-6pm, Sun noon-5pm. Must buy tkts personally. Show up 15-20 min before booth opens for your pick. *www.hottix.org*.

Andy's Jazz Club, 11 E Hubbard, (312) 642-6805. A great place to hear jazz, blues and Rock 'n' Roll. Mon-Thu 10:30am-1:30am, Fri-Sat 10:30-2am, Sun 4pm-12:30am. Cover $5, $10 w/ends, *www.andysjazzclub.com.*

North Pier Chicago, a restored warehouse on the Chicago River with shops, restaurants and **Dick's Last Resort**, 435 E Illinois St, (312) 836-7870, a large jazz bar. Close by is **Navy Pier**, 600 E Grand Ave, (312) 595-PIER, stretching into Lake Michigan. It offers a host of attractions, including an IMAX theatre, live entertainment, a ferris wheel and an amazing fireworks display every Wed (9:30pm) and Sat (10:15pm) throughout the summer, *www.navypier.com.*

Second City Comedy Revue, 1616 N Wells, (312) 337-3992. 'The place to see great comedians with a twisted sense of humour.' John Belushi, Chris Farley, Bill Murray and Mike Myers are among the egregious graduates of this establishment. Two sets of revues Fri & Sat ($19.50), one show Tue, Wed, Thu & Sun ($18). *www.secondcity.com.*

Sluggers World Class Sports Bar, Inc., 3540 N Clark, (773) 248-0055. Has acres of screens showing all sports and a games room with an indoor baseball-batting cage! Cheap beer and food. 'A right laugh.' Mon-Thu 3pm-2am, Fri-Sun 11am-2am. *www.sluggerschicago.com.*

Check out *www.barsonline.com/chicago.htm* for other suggestions.

Festivals For free festivals throughout the year incl. the **Tall Ships Festival** (end-July–early August) near the Navy Pier, (312) 744-3370, and annual **Chicago Jazz Festival** (late Aug in Millennium Park's new Pritzker Pavilion designed by Frank Gehry), check out *www.cityofchicago.org/specialevents*.

Theatres Chicago abounds in theatre – find out what's on at the dozens of equity and non-equity playhouses in *Performink*, Chicago's entertainment trade paper (free) and in the Chicago *Reader,* which gives thumbnail reviews of all major shows, with times and ticket prices. Newest is the **Lookingglass Theater** at the Water Tower Water Works founded by David Schwimmer of *Friends,* which opened in 2003 with a play adapted from a Studs Terkel work. Two Chicago theatres are especially well-known and have prices to match their fame. **The Steppenwolf Theater**, 1650 N Halsted St, (312) 335-1650, where Malkovich and Mamet grew up. Box office open daily 11am-5pm, tkts $10-$50, student discounts $10-15 w/student ID on day of performance. *www.steppenwolf.org.* **The Goodman Theater**, 170 N Dearborn St, (312) 443-3800. Box office open Mon-Sat 10am-5pm, Sun noon-5pm, later on days with evening performances; $12 w/student ID at 6pm on day of performance, *www.goodman-theater.org.* Both provide consistently good original work.

Sports

Chicagoans are sports mad. The **Chicago Bulls** basketball team was the NBA powerhouse of the 1990s, winning 6 championships in 8 years and drawing a huge following around the world. Although the Bulls have faltered since the departure of Michael Jordan, fans still flock to see their team play at the **United Center**, 1901 W Madison, (312) 455-4000. Call (800) 4NBA-TIX for tickets, *www.nba.com/bulls.* The **Blackhawks** play ice-hockey there in the winter, (312) 455-7000. NFL action and the **Bears** can be viewed at **Soldier Field**, McFetridge Dr and S Lake Shore Dr, (847) 615-2327, *www.chicagobears.com.*

Wrigley Field, 1060 W Addison, (773) 404-CUBS, is the home of the **Chicago Cubs** and one of the most beautiful baseball parks in the country, famed for its ivy-covered outfield wall. Intimate and packed to the rafters with people and atmosphere, it was the last park in the leagues to introduce floodlights: night games didn't arrive until 1988. An ideal way to taste the most American thing this side of apple pie; tkts $6-$36, *www.cubs.com.* The 2005 World Champions, **Chicago White Sox** play at the **U.S Cellular Field**, 333 W 35th St, (312) 674-1000, and have equally fervent supporters. Tkts range from $14-$40, *www.whitesox.com.* You can also get tickets from Ticketmaster: go to *www.ticketmaster.com.*

Internet and Wifi

Check out *www.internet-cafe-guide.com/chicago-internet-cafe.html* for a comprehensive list of Internet cafes.

Digital Café Chicago, 1331 N Ashland Ave, (773) 384-4881. $6/hr, open daily 9am-midnight.

Harold Washington Library Center, 400 S State St, (312) 747-4540, the computer connection is on the 3rd floor. Free access, time limit 1 hr; first-come-first-served basis. Mon-Thu 9am -6.30pm, Fri -Sat 9am-4.30pm, Sun 1pm-4:30pm.

The Map Room, 1949 N Hoyne Ave, (773) 252-9345. Free wifi access. Mon-Fri 6:30am-2am, Sat 7:30am-3am, Sun 11am-2am. *www.maproom.com.*

Information

Chicago Convention and Tourism Bureau, 2301 S Lake Shore Drive, (312) 567-6500. *www.choosechicago.com.*

Chicago Office of Tourism, 77 E Randolph St, (312) 744-2400/(877)-CHICAGO. Mon-Fri 10am-6pm, Sat 'til 5pm, Sun 11am-5pm. *www.ci.chi.il.us/tourism.*

Visitor Information Centers at Chicago Water Works (163 E Pearson at Michigan Ave), Chicago Cultural Center (77 E Randolph) and inside Sears on State (2 N State). (877) 244-2246. *www.877chicago.com.*

Travel

Transit: You can get almost everywhere in Chicago on the **CTA/RTA system**, which runs the famous 'El' rapid transit trains and 204 connecting bus lines throughout the metro area, for $1.75 a ride, long or short, plus $0.25 transfers. Buying Transitcards at El stations is recommended to speed your entrances. Call (312) 836-

7000 for fare and schedule info. Visit _www.rtachicago.com_ or check _www.transitchicago.com/maps/visitorinfor.html_. **Metra** runs 12 suburban commuter lines. _www.metrarail.com._

Boat Trips: Chicago is at its best from the lake. 'Best thing I did in Chicago.' **Mercury,** (312) 332-1353 and **Wendella,** (312) 337-1446. Boats leave from opposite sides of the Chicago River at Michigan and Wacker Dr: The longer the better as you sail further and proportionately less of your time is taken up with passing through the locks into Lake Michigan. Best of all is the 2 hr Sunset Ride for the dazzling lights. 'Boat stops in front of Buckingham Fountain—spectacular lights and colour show.' Daily 7:45pm, $18. Good deals are **Lake and River Taxis**, 474 N Lake Shore Drive, (312) 222-9328, to Navy Pier and Museum Campus (Field Museum, Aquarium) along the Lake and along Chicago River. Daily 10am – 6 pm, $6 O/W; All-day Pass $12.

Cabs: Cabs cost $2.25 to start, plus 50¢ for additional passengers, and run up fast. Be prepared to pay at least $5 for your ride in the downtown area – and check that the driver knows your destination.

Cycling: Bike Chicago, (312) 595-9600 and (800) 915-2453, locations at Navy Pier, North Ave Beach and 63rd Street. **Lakefront Trail** is 18 miles long, up and down from Navy Pier. 'Great way to tour the city.' Service includes free bike route maps and free guided tours, including to Hyde Park (19 miles r/t) and Lincoln Park (5 miles r/t) from Navy Pier, daily at 1.30pm. Bikes and in-line skates $8.75/hr, $35 daily. 4 day minimum rental $9.99, a day, 10% discount w/student ID. Rsvs recommended. _www.bikechicago.com_. Bikes also for hire at North Ave Beach. CTA has **Bike & Ride** facilities on trains (except rush hours) and buses, so you can literally go almost anywhere by bike—ask for brochures. Bikes go free.

Trolleys: The Free Trolley System (312) 836-7000, runs during the summer to Michigan Avenue (shopping), Navy Pier, the Museum Campus, State Street, Chinatown, Pilsen, the Prairie Avenue Museums and Lincoln Park. Brochures from hotels and Visitor Information Centers. **Chicago Trolley Co.**, 615 W 41st St, (773) 648-5000, covers a 13 mile route through the downtown area using trolleys and double-decker buses; you can hop on and off when you like, $25, or get a 2 day tkt for $35. _www.chicagotrolley.com._

Amtrak, Union Station, 225 S Canal St, (312) 655-2354/(800) 872-7245. Hub of the Amtrak intercity system. Think _The Untouchables_. _www.amtrak.com._

Auto Driveaway, 310 S Michigan, (312) 341-1900. 'Friendly.' 'Very helpful.'

Greyhound, 630 W Harrison St, (312) 408-5800/(800) 231-2222, _www.greyhound.com._

O'Hare International Airport, (773) 686-2200. The second busiest airport in the world, located 17 miles northwest of downtown Chicago. The CTA Blue Line provides 24 hr access between downtown and the airport and runs every 10 mins directly to and from the airport for just $1.75 (about 40 minutes from downtown). There are buses and cabs, but congestion is horrific and it'll take forever - a taxi is $35-$40. Alternatively, save money by using the shuttle service, (312) 454-7800/(800) 654-7871, which runs daily 6am-11.30pm, $17.50, from O'Hare to downtown and the northern suburbs. Visit _www.ohare.com_, for more information.

SPRINGFIELD The pleasant state capital has one main attraction: Abraham Lincoln. At the age of 28, 'The Great Emancipator' arrived in the city to practice law and ended up staying for twenty years until he became the 16th President of the US in 1861. From that moment on, the city's history and future have been inexorably tied to this beloved American citizen. Indeed, Lincoln himself declared 'to this place, and the kindness of these people, I owe everything'.

New in 2006 is the exciting **Abraham Lincoln Presidential Library and Museum**, the nation's largest presidential museum. Visitors are carried on a journey from Lincoln's bare log cabin in Indiana to Ford's Theatre, stopping along the way to view multimedia presentations, holographic theatre, and a Treasures Gallery (including the Gettysburg Address). The Museum is located at 212 N. Sixth (558-8844) Open Mon-Sun 9am-5pm, Wed. 'til 8:30. Admission is $7:50. Go to _www.alplm.org/home/html_ for in-depth information. Visit the **Lincoln Home National Historic Site,** 426 S 7th St, 789-2357, to see the only house he ever owned (daily 8:30am-5pm). Beautifully restored, it has a very useful visitor's bureau. _www.nps.gov/liho_. You can also visit the **Lincoln-Herndon Law Offices,** 6th & Adams, 785-7289, where Lincoln practiced law from 1843-1853, (Tue-Sat 9am-5pm). The **Lincoln Depot,** Monroe & 9th, 544-8695, is where he boarded the train to go to DC for his inauguration (daily 10am-4pm). Also of interest is the Lincoln **family tomb**, Oak Ridge Cemetery, 782-2717 (daily 9am-5pm) and the **Old State Capitol,** Capitol Plaza, 785-7961, where he was a member of the Illinois House of Representatives (Tue-Sat 9am-5pm). _www.illinoishistory.gov._

Northeast of the city on Rte 97 is **New Salem**, 632-4000, a reconstruction of the 1830's village where Lincoln lived as a young man (Wed-Sun 9am-5pm). All this is free. The state's other adopted golden boy, **Frank Lloyd Wright**, is also on show in Springfield. The **Dana-Thomas House,** 301 E Lawrence, 782-6776, _www.dana-thomas.org_ was built in 1903 for a local socialite. This prime example of the 'Prairie Style' that Wright pioneered also has furnishings by the man himself (Wed-Sun 9am-4pm). _www.visit-springfieldillinois.com. The telephone area code is 217._

Accommodation
Best Rest Inn, 700 N Dirksen Pkwy, 522-7961. TV, telephone, fridge available. Rooms $35-45.
Capitol City Motel, 1620 N 9th, 528-0462. Near the fairgrounds and with kitchenettes. S-$35, D-$40.
Mr. Lincoln's Campground, 3045 Stanton Ave, 529-8206/(800) 657-1414. 4 miles E of downtown, take #10 bus. Free showers, tent space $20 pp. Cabins $35 (4 or 6 people), $50 deposit.

Food
Try a **'cozy dog'** ($1.59) from the very diner that created the _corn dog_, a staple snack throughout the nation, at the **Cozy Drive In,** 2935 S 6th St, 525-1992, open Mon-Sat 8am-8pm. Closed major holidays. Also houses a selection of Route 66 memorabilia. _www.cozydogdrivein.com._
Feed Store, 516 E Adams St, 528-3355. Great for homemade soups and salads, daily special $5.85, Mon-Sat 11am-3pm.
Jungle Jim's Café, 1923 Peoria Rd, 789-6173. A cheap and cheerful spot for breakfast or lunch, dishes $4.50-$5.50. Open daily 6am-2pm.
Norb Andy's, 518 E Capitol, 523-7777. 2 blks from the Capitol Building and popular with the politicians, here you'll find a wide variety of steaks, burgers, pastas, seafood and sandwiches. Live music on Fri and Sat nights. Lunch $6.95, dinner $13.95. Mon-Fri 11am-11pm, Sat noon-11pm. (May be closed due to nearby construction)

Of interest
Executive Mansion, 410 E Jackson, 782-6450. Home of the Illinois governor and the

third oldest governor's home in the United States. Seven US presidents have been received here, including Lincoln. Three levels are open to the public; you are able to sneak a peek at Lincoln's bedroom. Tue, Thu, Sat 9.30am-11am, Tue & Thu 2pm-3.30pm, free. _www.illinois.gov/mansiontour.cfm._

Illinois State Capitol, 2nd & Capitol Ave, 782-2099. The centre for state government; watch the politicians in action from the balcony. Mon-Fri 8am-4pm, Sat-Sun 9am-3pm, free. _www.springfield-il.com/attract/ilstate.html._

Illinois State Museum, 502 S Spring St, 782-7387. Features the State's natural and cultural treasures. A new interactive exhibit, _Changes_, explores changes in climate, land, and life. Open daily, free. _www.museum.state.il.us._

Thomas Rees Memorial Carillon, Washington Park, 753-6219/544-1751. The third largest bell tower in the world. Go to the top for amazing views of the city. June-Aug: Wed-Sun noon-8pm, $1.50, includes tour through the tower's three floors. _www.carillon-rees.org._

The infamous 2,000-mile **Route 66** passes through the heart of Springfield. Labelled by John Steinbeck as 'The Mother Road' and immortalized in the song written by Bobby Troup in 1946 (sung by everyone from Nat King Cole to the Rolling Stones) ,it provided an escape route for the likes of Al Capone, and is now dotted with remnants of nostalgia. Capture the essence of this historic route by visiting **Shea's Gas Station Museum,** 2075 Peoria Rd, 522-0475, which features a collection of gas station memorabilia from the last 50 years. Tue-Fri 7am-4pm, Sat 7am-noon, free. Also check out _www.route66fest.com._

Information/Travel

Springfield Illinois Convention and Visitors Bureau, 109 N 7th, 789-2360/(800) 545-7300. Mon-Fri 8am-5pm. www.visit-springfielddillinois.com.

Greyhound, 2351 S Dirksen Pkwy, 544-8466/(800) 454-2487. $38.50 to Chicago (4 hrs 45 mins), 15% discount with Greyhound Student Advantage Card. Ticket Office open daily.

METROPOLIS It's a bird, it's a plane, it's Clark Kent's 'home town' in southern Illinois on the Ohio River. There's a giant mural of Superman in the park, a 15ft bronze Superman statue outside the Massac County Courthouse, free kryptonite from the Chamber of Commerce and for entertainment and the comics—the _Daily Planet_. If you're not suffering from Superman overload, go to the **Superman Museum,** 517 Market St, (618) 524-5518 and see the original costume worn by the first 'Superman' in the 1950s, along with movie props and rare toys; daily 9am-6pm, $3, _www.SuperMuseum.com._

No, this isn't where Superman was invented, or even where he was supposed to have lived. 'Metropolis' in the comic book was a big city; this Metropolis is a small town of a few thousand friendly souls. Nonetheless, locals hold a 'Superman Celebration' each year on the 2nd weekend in June. Call (800) 949-5740, or visit _www.SupermanCollectors.com./town.html_ for more information.

INDIANA - The Hoosier State

Indiana has a wholesome, almost cornball ingenuousness about it, so it's not surprising to learn that it's the home of Notre Dame, Orville Wright (Wilbur was born in neighbouring Ohio), Cole Porter, Amish villages of _Friendly Persuasion_ fame and David Letterman of late-night TV show notoriety. The state is called the Crossroads of America because it is centrally located in the United States and a great deal of the country's commercial activity passes through Indiana. The rural portions have the most to offer: rustic landscapes of country roads, covered bridges, notably in Parke County west of Indianapolis, and the Round Barns in Fulton County. In **Vevey** 'Steamboat' Gothic mansions that thrived during an era of brisk river trade are dotted along the Ohio River and many of the fine buildings are preserved. They now house restaurants and shops that include in their inventory antiques and crafts. Vevey Tourist Bureau: _www.1-800-hellovv.com._

Indiana has a huge steel industry that is mostly located in the northwest corner of the State. Do not come to the false conclusions that this state is limited in its exports. The main industrial cities such as Gary have their own attractions also. **Gary** lays on an impressive air show each July to celebrate the pioneering work of Octave Chanute. He was an engineer who in 1896 staged a series of glider experiments that proved instrumental in the development of powered flight by the Wright Brothers. _www.garychamber.com_ and _www.alllake.org_.

A note to travellers: Indiana doesn't use Daylight Savings Time – different counties use different time zones! Check the local time before you set your watch. In 2005, the state decided that in April 2, 2006, Indiana would no longer be counted as one of three states that do not _Spring ahead_ from 'standard' to 'daylight saving' time, but the issue still remains! Visit _www.enjoyindiana.com_ for more details.

INDIANAPOLIS Foursquare in the centre of the state, Indianapolis is: state capital; national headquarters for the American Legion; home of the Indy 500 auto race and cross-roads of America, so-called because a dozen or so major routes meet here.

The city is as exciting as mashed potatoes except during the month of May, when the '500' Festival, the Indy time trials and other pre-race madness stir things up. It's almost impossible to get seats for the race itself on Memorial Day Sunday (you must write for them a year in advance), but standing room and scalpers' tickets are available closer to race day. Time trials and qualifying runs begin 2-3 weeks before the main event and provide nearly the same thrills and mayhem as the big race. Bring beer, lunch and make a day of it. At night, party with the racing fans along Georgetown Ave. Call Speedway on 481-8500 for an application form, or write to: Tkts, Indianapolis Motor Speedway, PO Box 24152, Speedway, IN 46224. Check out _www.imstix.com_ for more information. The main festival parade, which leads up to the race and attracts global coverage, offers tkts up to a week before the race. Call 927-FEST or visit _www.500festival.com._

During spring, summer and fall, folk festivals take place by and around the Monument Circle area downtown. _The telephone area code is 317._

Accommodation
Basic Inn, 5117 E 38th St, 547-1100. D-$45, with $5 refundable deposit.
Indianapolis Motor 8, 3731 Shadeland, 545-6051. D-$44.85; cable TV.
Motel 6, 5241 W Bradbury St at Lyndhurst, 248-1231. D-$43.99.
Skyline Motel, 6617 E Washington St, 359-8201. D-$54, $5 key deposit.

Indianapolis Hotels. For budget and luxury accommodations call 1-800-839-6210 for listings or book online for even greater discounts at *www.indianapolis.com*.

Camping: For the more adventurous (i.e. with strong legs and country hearts) there are numerous campgrounds throughout the state. Few rent tents/trailers so bring your own.

The Indianapolis State Fair Recreational Vehicle Campground, 1202 E 38th St, 927-7510. 6 miles from downtown. Can be reached by bus. Tent space $16-$19; year round. All amenities.

Indianapolis KOA, 5896 W 200 North, Greenfield, 894-1397. 12 miles from downtown. Tent space-$19-35; full hook-up, $25.95, cabins $39-95 for 2 people.

Food

The Aristocrat, 5212 N College Ave, 283-7388. American and pub-style food. Prices start at $8.95. Open Mon-Thu 11am-10pm, Fri 11am 'til 12midnight, Sat 10am 'til midnight, Sun 10am 'til 9pm.

Bravo Italian Kitchen, 2658 Lake Circle Dr, 879-1444. Open Sun-Thu 11am-10pm, Fri-Sat 'til 11pm.

Broad Ripple Village, north of city centre at 62nd St, is a mall full of ethnic restaurants and quaint shops. *www.broadripplevillage.org*.

La Jolla, 921 Broad Ripple Ave, 253-5252. Home of the famous margarita; serves Mexican food. Prices start at $5.95. Sun-Thu 11am-10pm, Fri-Sat 11am-11pm.

Shapiro's Deli, 808 S Meridian, 631-4041. Cheap and good cafeteria style food. Daily 6:45am-8pm. Prices start at $5 for sandwiches.

Some Guy's Pizza, 6235 Allisonville Rd, 257-1364. Pizzas range from $4.25-$25 for supreme pizzas! Tue-Fri 11am-2pm, 4pm-10pm, Sat 'til 11pm, Sun 'til 9pm.

White Castle, opposite the Amtrak station and at several locations throughout the city. Fast-food burger joint. Open 24 hrs. 'Ideal for when your train from DC arrives at 4 am!'

Yorkshire Rose Pub and Deli, 1168 Keystone Way, 844-4766. Large selection of imported beers, soup, sandwiches, salads and entrees. Prices start from $6.50 for lunches and $10 dinners. Mon-Sat 11 am-midnight.

Of interest

Benjamin Harrison House, 1230 N Delaware Street, 631-1898. Home of the 23rd President of the US. Mon-Sat 10am-3:30pm, Sun (open only during July, August and December) 12:30-3:30pm. $6 adults and $3 for under 18's. *www.presidentbenjaminharrison.org*.

Conner Prairie Pioneer Settlement, 6 miles N of Indianapolis, Allisonville Rd, exit off I-465, (800) 966-1836. Restoration of a 30-building pioneer village *circa* 1836. Visit typical homes and work places of the era, eat frontier cooking, celebrate various festivals and meet inhabitants. Hosts events and summer concerts. Tue-Sat 9.30am-5pm, Sun 11am-5pm, $11. *www.connerprairie.org*.

Harrison Eiteljorg Museum, 500 W Washington, 636-9378. Located in the White River State Park it accommodates a private collection of American Indian and Western art. It is one of only two such museums east of the Mississippi. New wing includes education center, galleries and café. 'Lovely atmosphere.' Mon-Sat 10am-5pm, Sun noon-5pm; $7, $4 w/student ID. *www.eiteljorg.org*.

Indiana State Fair, 1202 E 38th Street, Rte 37, 927-1482. Two weeks of Hoosier hoopla in mid-August, with an audience of almost a million. 'Huge, mad, big name groups.' Purchase tkts at discount from local stores, $5 or on the day, $6. *www.state.in.us/statefair*.

Indianapolis Motor Speedway, 4790 W 16th St, 481-8500. The Speedway hosts three main races: Indianapolis 500, Brickyard 400 and the US Grand Prix. Tkts can be purchased online. Visit *www.brickyard.com* with many additional links.

Indianapolis Motor Speedway Hall of Fame Museum. Devoted to automobiles and racing, it houses a wide collection of memorabilia. Located on the infield of the Speedway, 481-8500. Open 9-5pm, 364 days a year, $3. A bus ride around the circuit is also $3; call for details. _www.indianapolismotorspeedway.com/museum_

Indianapolis Zoo, 1200 W Washington St, 630-2001. Houses 350 species of animals, a botanical garden with over 20,000 plants, and new 'Dolphin Adventure'including an underwater dolphin dome. Summer hrs: daily 9am-5pm, 'til 6pm Sat and Sun; $11.50. _www.indianapoliszoo.com._

Museum of Art, 4000 Michigan Road, 920-2660. Collections include European, American, Asian, Contemporary and African Art; this last lot largely donated by H. Eiteljorg contains African masks, figures and jewellery. Also has largest collection of paintings, drawings and prints by Turner outside of the UK: The collection has almost 4,000 items and spans more than 60 years of his life. Tue-Sat 10am-5pm, Thu 'til 9pm, free. _www.ima-art.org_.

Union Station, 200 S Illinois St. Built in 1888, one of the finest examples of Romanesque Revival architecture in the US. Galleries, restaurants, boutiques and passenger trains.

Entertainment
Chatterbox Tavern, 435 Massachusetts Ave, 636-0584. Fantastic jazz and good for a late drink. Cover $4. Open 'til 3am, closed Sun. Check-out reviews at _http://indianapolis.citysearch.com._

Crackers Comedy Club, 2 locations: 6281 N. College Avenue (Broad Ripple Village), 255-4211 & 247 S. Meridian St, 631-3536. Tue-Thu, shows at 8.30pm, extra show Fri-Sun at 8pm. Entry to over 18's. Tkts: $8-$14. _www.crackerscomedy.com._

Ike's and Jonesy's, 17 W Jackson, 632-4553. '50s and '60s music. Serve a selection of food all under $11, special drink prices also on selected nights e.g. Budweiser $1.75. $5 cover Thu-Sat. Open 11am-3am, closed Sun. _www.ikeandjonesys.com._

The Slippery Noodle, 372 S Meridian, 631-6974. Live blues 7 nights a week. Free Sun-Wed, $5 cover Thu-Sat, open 'til 3am. _www.slipperynoodle.com._

The Vogue, 6259 N College Ave, 259-7029. Music for the masses, '70s and '80s retro, pop, hip hop and techno. $3-$5 cover. Wed 9pm-3am, Fri & Sat 10pm-3am. Free entry for females: Fri and Sat before 11.30pm. _www.thevogue.ws_.

Information/Travel
Indianapolis Convention and Visitors Association, One RCA Dome, 639-4282/(800) 958-INDY. _www.indy.org_.

Metro Bus, 209 N Delaware, 635-3344. Runs the city buses, $1. _www.indygo.net._

Amtrak, 350 S Illinois St, 263-0550/(800) 872-7245.

Greyhound, Union Station, 1 block S of Pan Am Plaza, (800) 231-2222. Open 24 hrs.

Indianapolis International Airport, 7 miles W of downtown. Hop on the #8 'Washington' bus to get there, basic fares apply. From the airport to downtown, get a bus from Courtesy Vehicle Island. $1. Info: 635-3344. _www.indianapolisairport.com._

Internet access: Indianapolis Central Library, 202 N Alabama, 269-1700. Free access, 1hr time limit. Mon-Tue 9am-9pm, Wed-Fri 9am-6pm Sat 9am-5pm; computer labs close 30mins before the library. New state of the art facility will open in early 2006 at 40 E. St. Clair. _www.imcpl.org_.

AMISH COUNTRY
An hour north and east from Peru lands you in the counties of **LaGrange** and **Elkhart** — the heart of Amish country. _www.amishcountry.org_. _The telephone area code is 260._

Accommodation/Food
Country Inn and Suites, 3440 N. S.R. 5, Shipshewana 768-7780. 2 adults $99.
Amish Log Cabin Lodging & Campground, 5970 N S.R.5, Shipshewana, 768-7770.

www.amish.org. Log cabin, sleeps 4, $49; deluxe with 2 double beds $109-$129; camping facilities, $26 w/water and electric, $30 full hook-up.

5 & 20 Country Kitchen Restaurant, SR 5 & US 20, Shipshewana, (260) 768-4958. Daily specials with home-style cooking and great desserts! Conveniently located near the flea market.

Of Interest

The Town of **Shipshewana**, SR 5 off US 20, is a centre of Amish culture. Holds an auction and flea market every Tuesday 7am-5pm and Wednesday 7am-3pm, in the summertime, 768-4129 for info, or visit _www.tradingplaceamerica.com_. **Yoder's Department store**, (260) 768-4887, also carries Amish crafts and goods for those who miss the market days; open Mon-Sat 8am-5.30pm, check out _www.yoderdepartmentstore.com_ for details. To discover more about the Mennonite and Amish history and way of life, visit **Menno-Hof** across from the flea market on SR 5, 768-4117. Open Mon-Sat, 10am-5pm and Tue 'till 7, last tour starts $1/2$ hour before closing, $5, _www.mennohof.org_. In **Nappanee** on US 6, **Amish Acres**, (800) 800-4942, conducts tours of an Amish farm, complete with wagon rides. $11.95. Check out the **Pletcher Art Festival** from the 2nd Sat of August and the **Apple Festival** in late September. Amish Acres is home to the **Round Barn Theater**, 1600 West Market, US 6 West, where you can see live Broadway classic musicals in a 400-seat restored round barn theatre. Days and times vary but shows usually start at 2pm or 8pm and cost $25. _www.amishacres.com._

Information

Amish Country/ Elkhart County Convention and Visitors Bureau, (800) 250-4827. _www.amishcountry.org_.

LaGrange County Convention & Visitors Bureau, listings of good value dining, lodgings and attractions. 440 1/2 S. Van Buren St., Shipshewana, (800) 254-8090 or _www.backroads.org_.

BLOOMINGTON is a pleasant college town, home of Indiana University, an hour's drive south-west from Indianapolis on Rte 37. The movie _Breaking Away_ was filmed here and featured a bike race called the Little 500. The race is an annual event in mid-April and numerous abandoned stone quarries, also featured in the movie, now serve as swimming holes on hot summer days so you can feel like a movie star! _www.bloomington.in.us_.

An hour south-west from Bloomington takes you to the Wabash River town of **Vincennes**, site of **Grouseland**, 882-2096; the mansion was built in 1803 for the first Governor of Indiana and was the home of the shortest-lived US president—William Henry Harrison. At his inauguration, doubtless ignoring his mother's advice, Harrison gave a 2 hr speech in freezing rain, contracted pneumonia and died 31 days later, never having made a major decision as president. His 32-day term lasted from 4 March-4 April, 1841. The mansion is open Mon-Sat 9am-5pm, (last tour 4.30pm). $5, $3 w/ student ID. _www.grouselandfoundation.org._

Seventy-five miles downstream from Vincennes lies **New Harmony**, where two Utopian communities were set up in the early 19th century. In 1814 a grumpy Lutheran named George Rapp quit Germany to found New Harmony, where he awaited the coming of the Lord for 10 years. Being delayed for some reason, the Lord never appeared and Rapp departed, leaving New Harmony to Welsh expatriate Robert Owen, who founded a community of equality based on education. Kindergarten, co-ed public education and other new ideas in education were first tried here, and what remains is a historic district of 20 buildings, including a dramatic 'roofless church' designed by Philip Johnson. *www.newharmony.org*.

The telephone area code for the region is 812.

Accommodation/Food

Motel 6, Bloomington University, 1800 N Walnut St, 1 mile north of downtown, 332-0820, clean, spacious rooms and pool. S: Sun-Thurs $30-35, Fri-Sat $39.99-42.99 D: Sun-Thu $38.99, Fri-Sat $45.99.

Lake Monroe Village Campground, 8107 S Fairfax Rd, 824-2267. 8 miles S of Bloomington. Free showers, pool, hot tub. $25, $35 w/hook-up, cabins available, $85 for two, XP-$10. *www.lakemonroevillage.com.*

Nick's, 423 E Kirkwood Ave, 332-4040. Cheap hamburgers and beer. Mon-Sat 11am-2:30am, Sun noon-12midnight.

The Downtown Sq, features an abundance of restaurants within 2 blocks. Most found on Kirkwood City Ave, near College and W Walnut St.

Travel/Information

Greyhound, 219 W 6th St, 332-1522/(800) 231-2222.

IOWA - The Hawkeye State

In the movie *Field of Dreams*, Kevin Costner stood face to face in a spectacular baseball field with the ghost of his father. 'Is this heaven?' asked the ghost, his freshly-oiled leather baseball glove in hand. 'No, it's Iowa,' answered the son. Given the verdant beauty of the land, it's easy to see how he could have been confused. It is a land situated between the Mississippi River to the East and the Missouri River to the West in the heart of North America and there's an ethereal quality to this state, whose recent history reads like pages from the Bible. An agricultural mecca, Iowa is a veritable Eden that produces unfathomable quantities of corn, soybeans and cattle and quarter of the nation's porkers and generates over $10 billion annually from its agriculture. This bounty was destroyed in 1993 when Iowa was hit by the worst flood in history—a flood that turned the whole state into a National Disaster Area and left hundreds of thousands of people homeless and without water.

The weather has always been famous here. A freak Iowa blizzard resulted in the serendipitous development of the Golden Delicious apple, and the powerful electrical storms are amazing celestial displays. A strong Quaker community resides here whose most famous member was the 31st President, Herbert Hoover. Visit the **National Historical Site**, with the cottage where Hoover was born in 1874, his schoolhouse and Presidential library-museum. It is located in West Branch, Iowa, 10 miles east of Iowa City. Take I-80 to exit 254. It's open daily 9am-5pm, $5 (319) 643-2541. The Quakers here played an integral role in the success of the Underground Railroad— the pathway to freedom for thousands of slaves. It was to Iowa that black scientist and inventor George Washington Carver fled to escape persecution. Every four years the rest of the country remembers Iowans as they have first shot in the choice of the next President in the mid-winter political caucuses. *www.traveliowa.com* provides useful information.

DES MOINES Trisected by rivers, Iowa's capital (population approaching 200,000, excluding hogs) is a green and friendly place to catch your breath and take advantage of good food and lodging. Like Minneapolis, the city has a carpeted skywalk connecting major downtown buildings. 'A really beautiful city.' Worth a visit in June for 'Summer in the City', a volunteer effort to present musicians, artists, and food vendors every Saturday. www.des-moinesia.com. *The telephone area code is 515.*

Accommodation

Usually not difficult but watch availability in August during the State Fair.

A-1 Motel, 5404 SE 14th St, 287-5160. S or D-$35, TV.

Motel 6, 4817 Fleur Dr, 287-6364. Close to airport. S-$37 and D-$43.

Village Inn, 1348 Euclid at 14th St E, 265-1674. 'Large, clean, comfortable rooms.' $45-$54. www.villageinnmotel.com.

The Carter House Inn, 640 20th St, 288-7850. D $99. Student discount 15%. Huge breakfast is included in the price.

Acorn Valley Campground, 5600 NW 78th Ave, Johnston, 276-0429. Camping site located close to the picturesque Saylorville Lake. Take exit 131 off 1-80 on Merle Hay/NW Beaver Dr. Boating, fishing, swimming, along with hike and bike trails. Rsv 3 days prior to arrival, 14 day limited stay. Open May-Sept, sites $12-$22. www.reserveusa.com.

Food

Drake Diner, 1111 25th St, 277-1111. Frequented by local students. Daily 7am-11pm. $4-$14.

Famous Dave's Bar-B-Que, 2 venues, 1720 22nd Street, 267-0800 and 4351 Merle Hay Road, 331-3300. Wide choice of ribs, sandwiches and burgers. Lunch $6-$10, Dinner $8-$15. www.famousdaves.com.

Iowa Beef Steakhouse, 1201 E Euclid Ave, 262-1138. Quality steaks at reasonable prices. Open Sun-Thu 5pm-10pm, Fri-Sat 'til 11pm.

Java Joes, 214 4th St, 288-5282. Live music from Irish Jams to Jazz to an Open Mike night in a coffee house atmosphere. Internet access available. Great value, $2-$7. Mon-Thu 7am-11pm, Fri-Sat 'til midnight, Sun 9am-10pm. www.javajoecoffeehouse.com.

Manhattan Deli, 3705 Ingersoll Ave, 274-1208. Fabulous subs! From $3.50. Open Mon-Sat, 10am-3.30pm.

Stella's Blue Sky Diner, 3281 100th St, Urbandale, 727-4408. '50s vintage rock n' roll diner. Order a milkshake— the servers put on a show. Open Sun-Thu 10.45am-9pm, Fri and Sat 10.45am-10pm.

The Tavern, 205 5th St, 255-9827. 'The best pizza in town', with some of the most obscure toppings, $7.25-$18. Mon-Thu 11am-10pm, Fri-Sat 'til midnight, Sun noon-10pm.

Of interest

Adventureland, NE of city, 142A exit off I-80, 266-2121/(800) 532-1286. Over 100 rides, shows and attractions including the Tornado, the Sidewinder giant pendulum, and the Spaceshot. 'Lame'. Daily, Memorial Day-Labor Day, Fri-Sat 10am-10pm, Sun-Thu 10am-8pm; $27. www.adventureland-usa.com.

Iowa State Fair, 11 days in mid Aug. One of the oldest and largest in the country attracting thousands of visitors. $5, Top-notch. Camping at fairgrounds at Dean Ave, 262-3111, ex 265. Huge, good amenities, wooded area; $15 site. For more info call (800) 545-3247 or visit www.iowastatefair.org.

Jordan House, 2001 Fuller Rd, 225-1286. Built in 1852 by James C. Jordan, the first white settler in West Des Moines, it was a stopping point on the Underground Railroad. It features 16 period rooms, along with a railroad museum and a museum dedicated to the Underground Railroad. May through Sept: Wed & Sat 1pm-4pm, Sun 2pm-5pm, $3. www.thejordanhouse.org.

Living History Farms, I-35 and I-80 at Hickman Rd exit 125, 278-5286. Three operating farms: 1700's Indian, 1850's pioneer, 1900's farm; also 1870 town of Walnut Hill. Lots of special events and exhibits. Takes 3-4 hrs to see everything. May-Oct, daily 9am-5pm; $10. _www.livinghistoryfarms.org_.

Science Center of Iowa, 4500 Grand Ave, 274-4138. Home of the Digistar Planetarium, 'fabulous laser shows', and simulated shuttle flights. Mon-Wed 9am-6pm, Thu-Fri 9am-8pm, Sat 9-6, $7.50. _www.sciowa.org_.

White Water University Water Park, 5401 E University Ave, 265-4904. Enjoy the wave pool, tubing rides, water slides, miniature golf course, The Lazy River and twin-engine go-carts on an over/under track. May-Aug, daily 11am-6pm, also open Labor Day weekend. $15, $6.00 after 4.30pm. Extra $4.50 for carts and golf. _www.whitewateruniversity.com_.

Information/Travel
Des Moines Convention and Visitors Bureau, 405 6th Ave, suite 201, (800) 451-2625, Mon-Fri 8.30 am-5pm. _www.desmoinesia.com_.

Iowa Tourism Board and Visitors Bureau, 200 E Grand Ave, 242-4705, open Mon-Fri 8am-4.30pm, _www.traveliowa.com_, and at Des Moines International Airport, 256-5050, information desk, open 24 hours. _www.dsmairport.com_.

MTA city bus, 283-8111. Serves downtown, the fairgrounds $1. There is a bus service to the airport, but it is rather erratic and takes a tortuous route; take a cab to be sure, $12-$13, call the **Capitol Cab Company**, 282-8111.

Internet access
Des Moines Public Library, 100 Locust St, 283-4152, free access, 1/2 hr time limit. Call ahead to schedule time. Rsvs recommended. Mon-Thu 9am-7pm, Fri 'til 6pm, Sat 'til 5pm. _www.desmoineslibrary.com_.

Java Joes Coffeehouse, 214 4th St, 288-JAVA. $1/10 mins plus free wifi for your laptop. Smoke-free environment. _www.javajoescoffeehouse.com_.

EFFIGY MOUNDS NATIONAL MONUMENT In north-east Iowa, the 1500 acre monument stretches alongside the Mississippi River. The American Indian burial and ceremonial mounds date between 500 BC and 1300 AD and are dotted across the bluffs shaped like birds or bears. In the north unit, 'Great Bear' stretches 120 ft from head to tail. A visitor center sits 3 miles N of Marquette, 151 Hwy 76. It has an auditorium, museum, bookstore and displays as well as 11 miles of hiking trails. Opens daily 8am-6pm (summer); $3 per person ($5 per car maximum) includes entrance to the park, museum and trails, 873-3491. 'The March of Bears' lies in the south unit, where ten bear mounds and three bird mounds are strung together in one line. It's most impressive when outlined by snow. Greyhound goes no closer than Dubuque, IA or LaCrosse, WI, so car rental a must. For more details, go to _www.nps.gov/efmo_. If you are struggling and have no place to stay, SW of Dubuque is the **New Melleray Abbey** which may be able to accommodate you. $40 per day donation requested. Visit _www.newmelleray.org_ for more information and reservations.
The telephone area code is 563.

MADISON COUNTY This rural county boasts an ironic Hollywood legacy. It became a household name when Robert James Waller's book _The Bridges of Madison County_ hit the silver screen. The movie tradition, however, goes back even further. **Winterset**, the largest city in the county, was the childhood home of John Wayne. You can visit John Wayne's birthplace, 216

S. Second St, (515) 462-1044, $3, open 10am-4.30pm daily. See *www.johnwaynebirthplace.org*. Also check out the splendid covered bridges— of the original 19 bridges that dotted this county, five are still intact. For more information, contact the Madison County Chamber of Commerce at (800) 298-6119 or visit *www.madisoncounty.com.*

AMANA Settled by German mystics in 1854, the Amana Colonies (seven villages located one hour apart by oxen) became the longest-lived commune in the US. Reorganized along corporate lines in 1932, Amana residents no longer practice communal living but instead produce microwave ovens and other appliances along with woollens, wine and other hand-crafted goods. You can walk past the houses, factories and workshops (built along traditional German lines) and visit museums, but the main attraction is the food (heavy on pork and carbohydrates). *www.amanacolonies.com.*

The telephone area code for Amana, Brooklyn, Dyersville, Iowa City and Williamsburg is 319.

DYERSVILLE 'If you build it, he will come.' That's what a mysterious voice told Kevin Costner in the 1989 hit movie, *Field of Dreams*. Universal Studios built the famous baseball park in Dyersville and people do come…to the **Field of Dreams Movie Site**, (888) 875-8404. *www.fieldofdreamsmoviesite.com*. The 97 year old Lansing family farm, 200 miles west of Chicago, draws movie lovers and baseball fans by the carload each summer and you can pitch and bat all day. Dyersville sits on US-20, 175 miles from Des Moines. The farm and field are open April-Nov, 9am-6pm, free.

Accommodation/Food

Colony Inn, 741 47th Ave, Amana, 622-6270. 'Great breakfast—$8 all-you-can-eat: fruit salad, pancakes, eggs, sausage, bacon, fried potatoes and more!' Open Mon-Sat 7am-2.30pm, 4pm-8pm, Sun 7am-7.30pm. Prices average $14.

Comfort Inn, Exit 225 of I-80, 668-2700. Breakfast included in price. Two queen bed room is $68, at weekend it rises to $89.

Super 8 Inn, Exit 225 off I-80, Williamsburg, 668-2800. Rooms from $62-$69.

Of interest

Heritage Museum of Johnson County, 310 Fifth St, Coralville, 351-5738. 1876 school illustrates the culture and heritage of eastern Iowa and Johnson County through active teaching tours. Wed, Sat & Sun 1pm-5pm, Sun 'til 4, free. *www.iowacity.com/museums.htm#heritage*.

Kalona Historical Village, Hwy 22, D Ave, 656-3232. 17 miles south of Iowa City. Largest Amish community west of the Mississippi. Visit several historical buildings and 3 museums, including the Quilt and Textile Museum. 'Fascinating, especially to see the Amish form of transport (horse-driven 'buggies'). Advisable to have a car to travel around and, really, need a car to get there in the first place!' Summer: Mon-Sat 9.30am-4.00pm, $10 guided tour, lasts 1hr. *www.kalonachamber.org*.

Museum of Natural History, 10 Macbride Hall, 335-0480. Exhibits include a wide variety of displays interpreting Iowa's geology, early Native American cultures and ecology. Tue-Fri 10am-3pm, Sat 'til 5, Sun 1pm-5pm. Free. *www.uiowa.edu/~nathist*.

Tanger Factory Outlet Center, Exit 220 on I-80, 668-2811/(800) 406-2887. 90 miles east of Des Moines. More than 60 brand-name manufacturers and designer outlet stores. Save 40%-70% off regular retail prices. Mon-Sat 9am-9pm, Sun 11-6pm. *www.tangeroutlet.com* Visit website to claim a special savings card!

Information
The Amana Colonies Convention and Visitors Bureau, 39-38th Ave, Suite 100, 622-7625/ (800) 245-5465. Office hrs: Mon-Fri 8am-4.30pm. _www.amanacolonies.com._
Eastern Iowa Tourism, PO Box 189, **Dyersville**, (800) 891-3482. Mon-Fri 8am-5pm. _www.easterniowatourism.org_.
Iowa City Area Convention and Visitors Bureau, 408 1st Ave, **Coralville**, 337-6592/(800) 283-6592. Open daily. _www.iowacitycoralville.org._

Internet access
Iowa City Public Library, 123 S Linn St, 356-5200. Free internet access for 30 minutes. Mon-Thu 10am-9pm, Fri-Sat 'til 6pm, Sun 1pm-5pm. _www.icpl.org_.
Kalona Public Library, 511 C Ave, 656-3501. Free access, 60 minutes time limit; bring ID. Mon 10am-8pm, Tue-Wed 'til 6pm, Thu 1pm-8pm, Fri 1pm-5pm, Sat 10am-3pm. _www.kctc.net/kaloplib_.

KANSAS - The Sunflower State

Kansas is America's heartland—and the flag perhaps provides the best insight to the state's history. It consists of a dark blue field with the state seal in the centre. A sunflower lies above the seal, and the seal contains a landscape including a rising sun, representing the east; and a river and steamboat, representing commerce; and a settler's cabin with a man ploughing a field, representing the state's agriculture. A wagon train heads west and buffalo are seen fleeing from two Indians (the original inhabitants of Kansas). The quintessential prairie state has all the home-sweet-homeyness you could want. But there's still a wildness in the air here: namely, the wind.

This same unceasing wind has played a hand in the state's history—kicking up deadly dust storms and twisters (one of which sucked up poor Dorothy in _The Wizard of Oz_), driving lonely pioneer women insane with its howling. The survivors, however, must have been of good stock, for Kansas boasts the first female US senator, Nancy Landon Kassebaum; the most famous aviatrix, Amelia Earhart; and has produced both a US president and Vice-President. Dwight D. Eisenhower, raised in Abilene, was commander and chief of the Allied Armies in Europe during W.W.II. and president from 1953-61.

Kansas' bid for statehood was the fuse for the outbreak of the Civil War, 1867-1865, and ferocious anti-and pro-slavery factions earned it the epithet 'Bleeding Kansas'. In the rip-roaring cattle and railroad era of mid/late 1800's, cowhands drove one million cattle a year to Abilene, and 'blew' their $1-a-day wages on cards, rotgut and fancy 'wimmin'. The cow capital eventually moved west from Abilene to Wichita and Dodge City. In the early 20th century Kansas turned modern and began what is now the greatest airplane producing centre in the world. 'A remarkable state, well worth making an effort to discover.' 'At night, a magnificent and fulfilling stillness falls over the plains.' _www.accesskansas.org._

ABILENE Considering its associations with the Chisholm Trail and Wild Bill Hickok, Abilene's lack of westernness disappoints. Abilene is really Ike's Kansas—grain elevators, porch swings and funky little cafes and is the unlikely subject of the affectionate chorus, 'prettiest town I've ever seen'. The Eisenhower buildings are pompous but do stop for a look at Ike's simple boyhood home.

Visit _www.abileneks.com_ or _www.abelinecityhall.com_.

The telephone area code is 785.

Accommodation
Days Inn, 1709 N Buckeye, 3 blocks South off I-70, (800) 701-1000. Year-round. S-$47, D-$51. Free continental bfast.

Diamond Motel, 1407 NW 3rd St, Abilene, 263-2360. Year-round. S-$27, D-$33-38. Sml refrigerator and TV in room.

Super 8, 2207 N Buckeye, Take exit 275 off I-70, 263-4545. $52.

Food
Mr. K's Farmhouse Restaurant, 407 S. Van Buren St, 263-7995, Open Tue-Sat 11am-2pm and 5pm-9pm, Sun 11am-2pm only. Original American Fare. Lunch $3-$6.49, dinner $7-$18. _www.mrksfarmhouse.com._

Breadeaux Pizza, 306 NW 3rd Street, 263-7757. Hand tossed fresh baked pizza. Daily 11am-10pm.

Of interest
Great Plains Theatre Festival, 3rd & Mulberry St, 263-4574/(888) 222-4574. Kansas' premier professional regional theatre. May-Dec: performances Tue-Sun, tkts $16. _www.gptfdirect.org_.

Old Abilene Town and Museum, SE 6th at Buckeye. Recreation of historic Texas Street during the cowtown days. Take a tram or stagecoach ride. On the weekend, can-can girls perform and gunfights liven things up. Open daily. _www.abilenekansas.org._

Seelye Mansion and Museum, 1104 N Buckeye, 263-1084. Tours of 1905 Georgian mansion and gardens, along with _The Patent Medicine Museum_ which contains medical artifacts from the nineteenth and early twentieth centuries. Mon-Sat 10am-6pm, Sun 1pm-4pm (last tour 4pm), $10. _www.seelyemansion.com._

The Garden of Eden – yes, you read it here first – is in **Lucas**, 305 E 2nd St, 525-6395, 22 miles E of Paradise, west of Abilene on I-70, off Hwy 232. An eccentric Civil War Veteran by the name of SP Dinsmoor built this statue garden in the 1920s in his front yard, using 113 tons of concrete, among other things. Even more bizarrely, you can catch a glimpse of the late man himself; his corpse is on display in a glass-lid coffin. May-Oct: daily 10am-5pm, $4.50. _www.garden-of-eden-lucas-Kansas.com_. 12 miles from the geodetic centre of the US.

Information
Abilene Convention & Visitors Bureau, Located in Abilene Civic Center, 201 NW 2nd, (800) 569-5915. _www.abilene.com/visitors_.

ATCHISON The birthplace of Amelia Earhart and the Topeka, Atchison, and Santa Fe Railroad, Atchison sits alongside the Missouri River, a short trip north-west of Kansas City. Most of the town's attractions centre on its famous aviatrix daughter. _www.atchisonkansas.net_.

The telephone area code is 913.

Of interest
Amelia Earhart Birthplace Museum, 223 N Terrace St, 367-4217. Earhart amassed a long list of breakthroughs for women: first to fly Atlantic as a passenger, first to fly solo across Atlantic and first to fly solo across US. She was out to become the first

woman to fly around the world when she disappeared somewhere in the Pacific on July 2, 1937. Celebrate her birthday around July 24th at the festival held every year. Summer: Mon-Fri 9am-4pm, Sat 10am-4pm, Sun 1pm-4pm, $2 donation. *www.ameliaearhartmuseum.org*.

Nearby Warnock Lake is home to the **International Forest of Friendship**, an expansive woodland area dedicated to aviation and aerospace endeavours. Within the forest is a memorial to the 10 astronauts who have lost their lives in space exploration, as well as a life-size bronze statue of Earhart. A more recent addition to the forest is the Earhart Earthwork, a living portrait, created in 1997 from stones and plantings to celebrate her 100th birthday. Check *www.ninety-nines.org./fof.html* for more details.

Food/Lodging
Comfort Inn, 504 S 9th St, 367-7666. S-$48, D-$60, XP-$8.

Paolucci's Restaurant and Lounge, 113 South Third St, 367-1241. 'A casual, cosy restaurant and bar with panelled walls, where a hamburger, $3.25, and glass of Merlot, $2.50, hit the spot.' Serves Italian and American food. Mon-Sat 7am-9pm, Sun 8am-1pm.

WICHITA Wichita has Kansas' most worthwhile cowboy mock-up in its **Cow Town** ('authentic, much better than Dodge City'), with five original and 32 replica buildings. Boeing, Cessna and Beech—three major aircraft producers—make Wichita the 'Air Capital of the World'. 'Great place to hitch-hike by air.' *www.visitwichita.com.*

The telephone area code is 316.

Accomodation
Comfort Inn, 990 Connolly Court, 744-7711, 15 miles north of the airport on I-135. D and S-$70. Bfast included. TV, indoor pool and free internet.

Inn at Willowbend, 3939 Comotara, 636-4032. King room-$89. Bfast and 2 complimentary cocktails included. *www.theinnatwillowbend.net*.

Red Barn, 6427 N Greenwich Road, 744-9800. D-$75. Rsvs req. Privately owned house located on an ostrich farm. Features the *Kansas-Sunflower Room*, *Americana Room*, and the *Heritage Room*. Own bathroom. Shared hot tub. Bfast incl. TV on request.

Super 8, 6075 Aircap Drive, 744-2071. S/D-$49, incl bfast. TV.

Town Manor Motel, 1112 N Broadway at 10th, 267-2878. S-$28, D-$35, $5 key deposit.

Food
La Galette Bakery, 1017 W Douglas Ave, 267-8541. Mon-Sat 11am-3pm.

Miller's Bar-B-Que, 4601 E 13th St, 684-8080. Wed-Thu 11am-3pm, Fri 'til 6.45pm, Sat 12pm-6.45pm. Prices start at $4.50.

Hometown Buffet, 6820 W Central Ave, 942-4334. American food. Lunch $6.49, dinner $8.79. Mon-Fri 11am-8.30pm, Sat 8am-9pm, Sun 8am-8.30pm. *www.hometownbuffet.com.*

Of interest
Kansas African-American Museum, 601 North Water, 262-7651. This museum and cultural centre was established to give recognition to black participation in early Wichita. Their contributions in the fields of sports, government, entertainment, medicine, education and the military are depicted in the museum. Also exhibited are African artefacts, wood carvings, jewellery and dress. Tue-Fri 9am-5pm, Sun 2pm-6pm, free. Guided tours $2. *www.thekansasafricanamericanmuseum.org.*

Kansas Bike Trails: Shawnee Mission Park, Dornwood Park, The Levee, The

Bowls and Clinton Park. From Kansas City, take K-10 which switches to 23rd St. Go west until you arrive at park. One of the largest trails around. Lots of hills, rocks, and hikers to watch out for! _www.naturalkansas.org/shawnee.htm._

Old Cowtown Museum, 1871 Sim Park Dr, 264-6398. A 'living' historic village. Open April-Oct. Mon-Sat 10am-5pm, Sun noon-5pm. $7. _www.old-cowtown.org._

There are several good (free!) art museums, including the **Ulrich Museum at the Univ of Wichita,** 978-3664, which has on its outside wall an exquisite Miro mosaic with over one million pieces of glass. It also features an outdoor sculpture collection, with work by Henry Moore amongst others. Tues-Fri 11am-5pm, Sat-Sun 1pm-5pm. _www.ulrich.wichita.edu._

Kansas' skyscrapers hold wheat, not people, and you'll find the tallest grain elevators in the world in **Hutchinson,** 45 miles NW on SR 96. They hold 20 million bushels of grain. The annual **Wichita Beerfest** is held in early-Oct at the Century ll Convention Center, 1-5pm. Features over 350 beers and a selection of foods. Live bands, exhibits and bagpipes! Cooking demos and beer seminars! Must be 21yrs+ and present ID. Tickets go on sale end of Aug. Call 204-7364 or _www.midwestbeerfest.com._ Similar Winefest takes place in late April. Check out _www.midwestwinefest.com_ or call 204-7364.

Information

Kansas State Tourist Bureau, 1000 SW Jackson St, Suite 100, **Topeka,** (785) 296-5403/(800) 2-KANSAS. Mon-Fri 8am-5pm. _www.travelks.com._

Chamber of Commerce, 350 W Douglas, 265-7771. Mon-Fri 8am-5pm. _www.wichitakansas.org._

Kansas B&B Assoc., PO Box 2147, Stafford, TX 77497, 1-888-8-KS-INNS.

Wichita Visitors Bureau, 100 S Main, Suite 100, 265-2800. Stop here first for map and information. Open Mon-Fri, 8am-5.15pm. _www.visitwichita.com._

For more info try **Kansas Community Networks:** _www.ku.edu/heritage/towns._

Internet access

Wichita Public Library, 223 S Main St, 261-8500. Free, 1hr limit. Mon-Thu 10am-9pm, Fri-Sat 10am-5.30pm, Sun 1pm-5pm. _www.wichita.lib.ks.us._

THE SANTA FE AND OTHER TRAILS Because of its geographic position, Kansas was crosshatched with trails: the Santa Fe, Chisholm, Oregon and Smoky Hill, among others. Whether travelling through Kansas or settling it, pioneers needed grit and resilience. South of Colby (60 miles from Colorado), near I-70, you can examine an authentic sod house at the **Prairie Museum** _www.prairiemuseum.org._ **Fort Larned** (6 miles from Larned off Hwy 154) and graffiti-covered **Pawnee Rock** (NE of Larned on 156) still stand as trail markers. Along US 50, 9 miles W of Dodge City, wagon ruts of the Santa Fe Trail can be seen.

MICHIGAN - The Wolverine State

When you look at a map of Michigan, you'll be struck by its unique shape. It looks something like a hand— natives will eagerly indicate the part of the state they're from by pointing to it on their palm. The extended hand is indicative of a friendly people and a surprisingly friendly climate.

You cannot travel more than six miles in any direction before finding a body of water in Michigan. It features 150 waterfalls and like its neighbouring state, Minnesota, it has more than 10,000 lakes, two of which are the second and third largest in the world. Although it touches no ocean, it has 3200 miles of shoreline and more lighthouses than any other state.

A campers' and hikers' dream, Michigan has youth hostels, thousands of campsites (including the unspoiled northern pleasures of Isle Royale National Park) and a rich network of farm trails and roadside produce markets on its two peninsulas. The state produces a bounty of cherries, blueberries and other fruits that beg to be sampled as you're passing through. *www.michigan.org*.

DETROIT Detroit is famous for car manufacturing, Motown and race riots. Auto assembly lines and good soul music are both disappearing, while crime is ever present. A bustling inland port, the city is working to revive a decaying downtown with flashy complexes like the **Renaissance Center** snaring lucrative convention gigs, but parts of downtown still look like bomb sites. Homesick visitors may consider Detroit a desperately sad place to be, but natives are quick to defend Motown. Of course, they live out in the suburbs, primarily and that's probably where you should stay too!

The Motor City came by its name and fame quite by accident, largely because Henry Ford, Ransom Olds and other auto innovators happened to live and work in the area. The auto industry brought thousands of blacks to Detroit. One of them was Berry Gordy, founder in 1959 of the Motown sound (Smokey Robinson, the Supremes, the Temptations, etc.), who used to make up songs on the Ford assembly line to relieve the monotony. The movie *8 Mile* starring Eminem is possibly the most recent, recognisable export of Detroit. The film is littered with insider Detroit references, and effectively makes the city an active character, concentrating more on the American dream of a good job and family values rather than the murder-capital hellhole of some movies. *www.visitdetroit.com.*

The telephone area code is 313.

Accommodation
Check out *www.tripadvisor.com* for good deals in the Detroit area.
Cabana Motel, 12291 Harper Ave, 371-1220. D-$45. Located near Connor off I-94.
Falcon Inn Motel, 25125 Michigan Ave in Dearborn, between Telegraph and Beach Deli, on US 12, 278-6540. S or D-$40. Convenient for Greenfield Village.
Village Inn, 217 Michigan Ave at Oakwood Blvd in Dearborn. 565-8511. S-$50, D-$60. Near the Henry Ford Museum and Greenfield Village. *www.villageinnofdearborn.com.*
Park Avenue Hostel, 2305 Park Avenue, 961-8310. $15 a night.

Food
Strong ethnic communities here, so head for Greektown, Chinatown and the Polish community (called Hamtramck—actually an independent city within Detroit).
Jacoby's, 624 Brush St, 962-7067. 4 blocks N of RenCen. German and American food from $6. Open Mon-Thu 11am-10pm, Fri-Sat 11 'til 11pm, Sun until 3pm.
Mexicantown is home to many authentic Mexican restaurants and mercados.
Los Galanes, 3366 Bagley St, 554-4444. Lunches $5+, Dinners $7-$14. It often has dancing on weekends and live music, $5 cover. Mon-Thu 9am-11pm, Fri-Sun until 2am.
Markets: Hart Plaza btwn the RenCen & Civic Center holds w/end ethnic festivals all summer long. **Eastern Market** on Russell St has produce bargains.
Lafayette Coney Island, 118 W Lafayette Blvd, 964-8198. Open 9am-4am, serves

wieners smothered in chili and raw onions with a cup of bean soup on the side. Bargain prices, cash only.

Pizza Papalis Tavern, 553 Monroe in Greektown, 961-8020. Open daily 11am-1am. Deep-dish Chicago pizza, fresh pasta and large sandwiches. Around $6 pp.

Traffic Jam, 511 W Canfield, 831-9470, nr Wayne State campus. The extensive menu, in-house brewery, fresh-baked bread, and decadent desserts make this restaurant a Detroit favourite. Mon-Thurs 11am-10.30pm, Fri 'til midnight, Sat noon-midnight, Sun noon-8pm. _www.traffic-jam.com._

Of interest

Belle Isle, 852-4075. Series of islands connected by bridges, on the Detroit River. It has 4 sections: an aquarium, conservatory, both $2, a 'beach' with a waterslide $3, and the **Dossins Great Lakes Museum,** $2. Plenty of cafes around; however, it's a lovely area to take a picnic. _www.pps.org//gps_.

Detroit Grand Prix. Indy Cars World Championship race takes place in mid-June. The course follows the city streets by the RenCen. (800)489-7223.

Detroit Institute of Arts (DIA), 5200 Woodward Ave (off I-75, Warren Ave), 833-7900. From fine primitives to Picasso, plus Diego Rivera's famous and scathing mural on factory life. Also: has one of the best African art collections in the country. Cafe in Renaissance decor. Wed-Thu 10am-4pm. Fri 'til 9pm and Sat-Sun 'til 5pm. $4 donation. _www.dia.org_.

Ford Detroit International Jazz festival, 963-7622. This is the US half of the Swiss Montreux International Jazz Festival, North America's largest free jazz event and one of the most prestigious and widely recognised festivals. During the first weekend of Sept. _www.detroitjazzfest.com._

Gospel Music Hall of Fame and Museum, 18301 W McNichols, 592-0017. A far cry from Motown, this museum chronicles the history and development of gospel music. Record your voice in a live studio session and take home a CD. By appointment only, $4 donation. _www.gmhf.org_.

Greenfield Village and adjacent **Henry Ford Museum** in Dearborn, W of Detroit, 982-6150. Greenfield Village has 240 acres containing over 100 genuine historic buildings amassed by Henry Ford and set up in sometimes curious juxtaposition: Abe Lincoln's courthouse, Wright Brothers' cycle shop, Edison's lab (complete with vial said to contain Edison's dying breath). Almost everything runs or ticks or does something—a stunning microcosm of the roots of technological Americana. There is also an IMAX theatre, tkts $10. Horse carriages, steam trains, Model-T Fords, steamboats, horse-drawn sleighs. The fantastic 12-acre Ford Museum has a huge transportation collection and antique aircraft. Daily 9am-5pm, Sun from noon (closed Jan-Mar); $14 museum tkt, $20 village tkt. Day pass to both for $26 or 2-day tkt $48. Departing from the Ford Museum are tours of the **Ford Rouge Factory** where you can go behind the scenes inside one of the world's largest automotive complexes. Virtual reality theatre adventure, walking tour of assembly plant. April-Jan daily 9.30am-5pm, $14. Book in advance online at _www.thehenryford.org_.

Graystone International Jazz Museum and Hall of Fame, 1249 Washington Blvd, 963-3813. The oldest jazz museum in the world; specialising in jazz memorabilia from 1920 to the present. The collection includes musical instruments from the Graystone Ballroom, as well as artefacts of such great jazz artists as Count Basie, Duke Ellington, and others. The museum also organises travelling exhibits. Open Tue-Fri 11am-4pm, Sat by appointment only; $3.

Joe Louis Arena at Cobo Hall, 600 Civic Centre Dr, 983-6606, home of the **Detroit Redwings** and where sporting events, ice capades, concerts and the circus come to town. _www.olympiaentertainment.com./JLA_.

Motown Museum, 2648 W Grand Blvd, 875-2264. It all began here, Hitsville USA, as Berry Gordy Jr. called it. Motown sound was introduced to the world in the 1960s from this small home. Offices and recording studios remained here until the company moved to LA, California in 1972. Museum filled with gold discs, rare photos, vintage clothing, memorabilia and artefacts recapturing the history of this seminal era in American music. Exhibits feature musicians, songwriters and black singing groups such as Diana Ross and the Supremes and The Temptations. Tue-Sat 10am-5pm, $8. _www.motownmuseum.org._

Renaissance Center, the 'RenCen' on the river, 568-8000, is the world headquarters for General Motors. A mirrored fortress of four 39-story towers, protecting a newly renovated 73-story hotel. Houses shops, restaurants, along with a five-story glass-enclosed atrium overlooking the river.

Across the street is **Mariner's Church,** 170 E Jefferson Ave, open to the public. Detroit's earliest Gothic stone church whose bells still toll once each year for the sailors who perished on the freighter Edmund Fitzgerald in 1975 on Lake Superior.

Sport

Sporting venues in Detroit have undergone a renaissance themselves, with new, state-of-the-art playing fields for two of the city's teams. The **Detroit Tigers'** ballpark, **Comerica Park,** 2100 Woodward Ave, features a carousel, ferris wheel and a giant water feature in its complex. For tkts, call (248) 25-TIGER. _www.detroittigers.com._ Since August 2002 the **Detroit Lions** have resided at the lavish **Ford Field.** For tkt info 262-2003 or _www.detroitlions.com._ Detroit's other professional sporting teams include the **Pistons,** the city basketball team and the **Redwings** (ice hockey).

Winter sports: For info on events, sports and activities, call **Michigan Travel Bureau,** (800) 5432-YES or visit _www.skimichigan.net_ for a list of resorts.

Michigan Ski resorts include: Big Powderhorn Mountain, Bessemer (906) 932-4838/(800) 222-3131, D-$79 XP-$28. _www.bigpowderhorn.net_ and **Blackjack,** Bessemer (906) 229-5115, Near Lake Superior. Single condo, can sleep four: $59/night, $225/week or $385/month. _www.skiblackjack.com._ Check out Boyne USA for more resorts: **Boyne Highlands; Harbor Springs; Boyne Mountain; Boyne Falls.** Call (800) GO-BOYNE or visit _www.boyne.net._ Also check: **Crystal Mountain,** Thompsonville (800) 968-7686, _www.crystalmountain.com;_ **Indianhead Mountain Resort,** Wakefield (800) 3-INDIAN, _www.indianheadmtn.com;_ **Shanty Creek,** Bellaire (800) 678-4111 _www.shantycreek.com._

Windsor, Canada: this city that receives mixed reviews is _south_ of Detroit. It is reached via bridge or tunnel and recommended, but with a few warnings: 'I was given a difficult time because I was backpacking and had only $100 plus ticket home. Plenty of trucks outside immigration to ask for a ride though.' Once you get inside Canada, though, you'll find a bounty of good clubs and cheap eats, as well as beautiful parks. And unlike Detroit and the rest of the states, the drinking age in Windsor is only 19. NB: If returning to the USA, make sure you have passport and US visa documents with you.

Information

Michigan Travel Bureau, (800) 543-2937, _www.michigan.org._
Detroit Metro Convention & Visitors Bureau, 211 W Fort St, Suite 1000, 202-1800 or (800) 338 7648. Mon-Fri 9am-5pm, _www.visitdetroit.com._
Visitor Hotline, 1-800-DETROIT.

Travel

Detroit Department of Transportation, 933-1300/(888) DDOT-BUS. Runs buses in the downtown area; $1.50. _www.ci.detroit.mi.us/ddot._
Southeastern Michigan Area Regional Transit (SMART), 962-5515. Buses to Suburban areas. Basic fare $1.50. _www.smartbus.org._
Amtrak, Michigan Ave, between Southfield & Greenfield, 336-5407/(800) 872-7245. Not the best station or area to be stuck in at night. Open daily 7am-midnight, tkts sold until 11pm.

Greyhound, 1001 Howard St, between 6th and John C Lodge. 961-8011/(800) 231-2222.
Detroit Metro Airport (DTW), (734) 942-3550. Detroit's main airport is about 21 miles from downtown. Take a SMART bus #125 (will read airport) from Fort and Cass St. Direct bus takes about 1hr 20mins, $1.50. Alternatively, **Commuter Express,** 292-2000, runs private cars from major downtown hotels; rsvs req. takes approx. 45 mins, $42. Taxi: try **Detroit Cabs** 841-6000. Takes approx. 30 mins, $40-$45. *www.metroairport.com.*

ANN ARBOR An hour's bus ride west of Detroit, Ann Arbor is thoroughly dominated by the University of Michigan and loves it. As a consequence there are lots of good hangouts; live music including excellent bluegrass; cheap eats; support services; and events like the July Art Fair (begins annually on the third Wed of July). For info on the **Ann Arbor Film Festival,** held at the Michigan Theater annually every March, go to *www.aafilmfest.org* or call 995-5356. More info at *www.annarbor.org. The telephone area code is 734.*

Accommodation
Lamp Post Motel, 2424 E Stadium Blvd, 971-8000. Rooms $50, bfast included. Friendly management.
The Library Bed and Breakfast, 808 Mary Street, 668-6815. Room both S and D-$75, bfast included and vast library!
U of M, Conference & Catering Services, 603 Madison, 764-5297, 8am-5pm. Campus overnight guest rooms and short-stay apts. Rsvs required. Call for availability.

Food/Entertainment
Afternoon Delight, 251 E Liberty St, 665-7513. This place has all-natural muffins and pita sandwiches. Try the yoghurt shakes. Serves breakfast all day Sat & Sun. Daily 8am-3pm.
Rick's, 611 Church St, 996-2741/ 996-2748. Live music and discounted drinks, plus 'ladies nights' with free admission on selected evenings. Mon-Sat 7pm-2am.
Zingerman's Deli, 422 Detroit St, 663-5282. Serves every kind of sandwich; the menu is a good hour's read. Also stocks a tremendous inventory of cheese, smoked fish, meats, breads, coffees, etc. Daily 7am-10pm. $7-$12. *www.zingermans.com.*

Of interest
Many attractions are affiliated with the University, including the **Museum of Art,** 525 State St, 764-0395, which has a first-rate collection of Asian and Western art. Tue-Sat 10am-5pm, Thu 'til 9pm, Sun noon-5pm, $5 suggested donation. *www.umma.umish.edu.*
Ann Arbor Summer Festival, 647-2278, in June/July runs for $3^{1}/_{2}$ weeks. Offers a variety of performances and exhibits every day. Free-$25. *www.mlive.com/aass.*
Gerald R. Ford Presidential Library, 1000 Beal Ave, 741-2218. Here you can look through the original files of President Ford and other records of the post-WWII era. Not a museum. Free. Mon-Fri 8.45am-4.45pm. *www.ford.utexas.edu.*
Nichols Arboretum, 1610 Washington Hts, 998-9540,
 www.sitemaker.umich.edu/mbgna and **Gallup Park,** 994-2780, are next to the Huron River on the city's north-eastern edge. You can canoe, kayak, fish and take a ride in a paddle boat. The park and arboretum are open sunrise-sunset, *www.ci.ann-arbor.mi.us/PARKS/index.html.*

Information/Travel
Ann Arbor Convention and Visitors Bureau, 120 W Huron St, 995-7281. Mon-Fri 8.30am-5pm. *www.annarbor.org.*
Amtrak, 325 Depot St, 994-4906/(800) 872-7245.

Greyhound, 116 W Huron St, 662-5511/(800) 231-2222, at Ashley St, 1 block off Main St. Advisable to buy at the terminal and avoid fees.

Internet
Ann Arbor District Library, 343 S fifth Ave, 327-4200. Free access, unlimited, first-come-first served basis. Free wifi also. Mon 10am-9pm, Tue-Fri 9am-9pm, Sat 9am-5pm, Sun noon-6pm. *www.aadl.org*.

NATIONAL LAKESHORE/UPPER PENINSULA Michigan has two wilderness areas, the **Upper Peninsula** and the **Sleeping Bear Dunes National Lake Shore**. The Upper Peninsula is located just above Wisconsin. This multi-million acre forest is bordered by three of the Great Lakes. It provides a rare retreat into untouched wilderness; hiking, cross-country skiing, fishing and canoeing are available. For more information, contact Upper Peninsula Travel and Recreational Association, PO Box 400, Iron Mountain, MI 49801, call 774-5480/(800) 562-7134 or visit *www.uptravel.com*. Also the US Forestry Service, Hiawatha National Forest, 2727 North Lincoln Rd, Escanaba, MI 49829, 786-4062, can supply you with guides and maps. *www.fs.fed.us/r9/hiawatha*.

   Sleeping Bear Dunes, 45 mins from **Traverse City,** is known for its magnificent sand dunes and polar-bear swimming (Lake Michigan never seems to warm up). 'Traverse City has excellent sugar-sand beaches on its two Lake Michigan bays—it feels like the sea-side!' In Traverse City, catch the **National Cherry Festival** in mid-July, an excellent festival. **Interlochen Center for the Arts,** SW of Traverse City, showcases some of the most well-known musical acts in their summer concert series, superbly staged in Kresge Auditorium, (231) 276-6230. 'Musical nirvana on a warm summer evening!'

   The area code for the Upper Peninsula is 906; for Sleeping Bear Dunes, 231.

Accommodation/Food
Northwestern Michigan Community College, East Hall, 1701 E Front St, Traverse City, (800) 748-0566. S-$35, D-$40. About 1 mile from the bus station. Accommodation provided for one night only.
Dale's Donut Factory, 3687 South Lake Shore Dr, St Joseph, (269) 429-1033. 'The donut factory of donut fans' dreams!' Mon-Fri, 3am-6pm, Sat 'til 2pm.

MACKINAC ISLAND When you set sail for Mackinac Island, leave your cares, worries and rental cars behind. No motor vehicles are permitted here—your transportation choices are horseback, bicycle, surrey or shank's mare. Tranquil, beautiful and Victorian in design, Mackinac (pronounced 'Mackinaw') is especially nice during the June Lilac Festival. Chocoholics note: island specialty is homemade fudge. Boat runs hourly in summer.

   Take a peek at the elegant 1880s Grand Hotel, featured in the movies *This Time for Keeps* and *Somewhere in Time*. It has a porch that never ends, the longest in the world. Check out the Mackinac Island pages, created on the island by the islanders themselves. Rich in pictures, info, news and stories, the website is *www.mackinac.com. The area code is 906.*

Accommodation
Unfortunately, accommodation is rather expensive here and no camping is allowed on the island. Also, there are few lockers to be found here, or on the mainland at St Ignace and Mackinaw City, so you will be carrying your rucksack with you—'an

exhausting bind if you go over to the island intent on walking'. The moral of this? If you plan to go, plan ahead! Check the accommodation section of the Mackinac Island website. There are also the usual motel chains along I-75; they are probably your best bet. **The Tourism Board** is helpful, 847-3783.

Bogan Lane Inn, PO 482, Mackinac Island, 3/4 mile E of the boat docks, 847-3439. S/D-$75, XP-$20. All include bfast. Rsvs req. Open year round. _www.boganlaneinn.com._

Since camping isn't allowed on the island, try nearby **Mackinaw City**, (888) 455-8100, or **St Ignace** (800) 338-6660. **Tee Pee Campground**, PO Box 10, Mackinaw City, MI 49701, (231) 436-5391, is $1/2$ mile south of the city on US 23 and Lake Huron. Site $28 w/electricity and water, for up to 4 people. Open May-Oct. Visit _www.teepeecampground.com_ for details.

Information/Travel

Enjoy travel by water but watch you don't end up having to swim! Usually boats stop sailing around 8.30pm-9.30pm.

Mackinac Island Tourism Board, 847-3783. Daily 9am-5.45pm. _www.mackinacisland.org._

Arnold Mackinac Island Ferry, Box 220, 847-3351/(800) 542-8528. Depart from Mackinaw City, every $1/2$ hour, and St. Ignace, every 45 mins, $18 r/t. _www.arnoldline.com._

Shepler's Mackinac Island Ferry, Box 250, Mackinaw City, MI 49701, (231) 436-5023/(800) 828-6157. Serves Mackinaw City 9.30pm and St Ignace, $17 r/t. _www.sheplersferry.com._

Star Line Mackinac Island Ferry, 587 N State St, St Ignace, 643-7635/(800) 638-9892. Also serves Mackinaw City and St Ignace, $18 r/t. _www.mackinacferry.com._

ISLE ROYALE NATIONAL PARK This is the roadless, wild and beautiful 'eye' in Lake Superior's wolfish head. Natives shun the pretentious name, calling it 'Isle Royale' instead. Free camping by permit only, including use of screened shelters around the island. 'Boil surface water at least 5 mins.' Carry salt—inland lakes on the island have leeches. Island closed in winter. Visit the virtual visitors centre at _www.nps.gov/isro_ or call (906) 482-0984.

MINNESOTA - Land of 10,000 Lakes

Driving through Minnesota, you may well wonder if you took a wrong turn somewhere and wound up in Scandinavia. The Minnesota countryside almost duplicates the Nordic landscape, with fertile farmland in the south, dense pine forests in the north and 12,000 glacier-scoured lakes all around. Doubtless this is why so many immigrant Swedes and Norwegians moved here earlier this century; to them, the state looked like home.

Vikings may have learned of Minnesota's Nordic delights early on, if a Viking runestone dated from 1000 AD proves authentic. Much of the population still appears Nordic, and the countryside and cities are among the cleanest and most well-preserved in the US.

The land also seems to attract giants, both literal and figurative. It's the birthplace of J Paul Getty, Bob Dylan, Charles Lindbergh, F Scott Fitzgerald, Sinclair Lewis and the Mississippi River, as well as the home of Paul Bunyan the woodsman and the Jolly Green Giant of canned pea fame. Minnesota also holds the dubious distinction of being the only state governed by a former professional wrestler; pop culture fanatics cheered and political purists jeered when Jesse 'the Body' Ventura was elected in 1998.

The state is especially lovely during Indian summer; highway markers often point out the most vivid colour displays. Free maps of the fall colour routes are obtainable from the **Minnesota Tourism Bureau**, 100 Metro Sq, 121 7th Place E, St Paul. Call (800) 657-3700. Any time of year, **North Shore Drive** (US 61) along Lake Superior north to Canada is a top contender for the most beautiful camping and gawking route in America. Miles of well-kept biking paths criss-cross the state. **The Heartland Trail**, a 48 mile paved bike trail in north-central Minnesota, is one of the loveliest. While here be sure to go canoeing—a peculiarly Minnesotan tradition passed down from Chippewa Indians and French-Canadian trappers to present day. You can disappear into the north country wilderness and not see another person for days on end. Given the number of lakes, it's not surprising that fishing is hugely popular here. Beware the land of 10,000 lakes in the summertime—Minnesotans joke that the official state bird is the mosquito. For info visit _www.exploreminnesota.com_ and for lists of Minnesota's historic sites visit _www.mnhs.org/places/sites/index.html_.

MINNEAPOLIS/ST PAUL   Minneapolis and St Paul are 'Twin Cities' only in geographic terms, laced together by the Mississippi River. It's said that Minneapolis was born of water, St Paul of whiskey.

Minneapolis is young, Scandinavian, modern and relaxed, a working-class city freckled with lakes and home base of a number of Fortune 500 companies, headed by the biggest names in engineering. As in San Diego and Seattle, residents here sensibly take advantage of their versatile setting; many spend their lunch hour sailing in summer. Minneapolis was and is Mary Tyler Moore territory, as bouncy and clean as the Pillsbury doughboy, another local product.

St Paul began as an outpost with the uncouth name of Pig's Eye, described in 1843 as 'populated by mosquitoes, snakes, Indians and about 12 white people'. Perhaps to compensate for these rough beginnings, St Paul has become a conservative capital city of Irish and German Catholics, doting on history and Eastern refinement. F Scott Fitzgerald is a St Paul native, as is Charles Shultz of 'Peanuts' fame, whose cartoons were rejected by his high school yearbook. Today St Paul is home to the mythical 'Lake Wobegon' and Garrison Keillor's lively and laconically drole National Public Radio variety show, _Prairie Home Companion_. Between the two cities, they boast having more theatres, dance and concert venues than any other US destination, outside New York.

To the south is the younger sibling, **Bloomington**, where lurks the gigantic **Mall of America.** Reach it by shuttle, from both St Paul and Minneapolis. Out of the three metropolitan areas, Minneapolis offers most for the visitor: friendly, outgoing locals, a handsome downtown with mall, skyways, parks, a meandering waterfront and swimmable lakes. Stick to downtown, however: 'I am astonished—could other US downtowns be like this, given a chance? The rest of Minneapolis that I've seen is as ordinary and soulless as anywhere else in America.'

Check out the following websites: *www.minneapolis.org*, *www.stpaulcvb.org* and *www.bloomingtonmn.org*. *The telephone area code for Minneapolis is 612, for Bloomington, 952 and St. Paul, 651.*

Accommodation

Minneapolis International House, 2400 Stevens Ave, Mpls, 522-5000/(888)250-3315. Student rates: Private room $29, dorm $20. Linens incl. Bike hire $5 daily. Located in historic mansion district. Living room with piano and fireplace, outdoor patio. Recreational room with foosball and TV. Clean and relaxed. Close to major attractions, downtown, bus lines and lakes. New kitchen area. 'Friendly, helpful staff!' Book and confirm on-line at *www.minneapolishostel.com.*

Fraternities in the 16-1700 block of University Ave can sometimes offer room to travellers. 'Very cheap and plenty of lovely half-naked men wandering around—just what you need after two months in camp.'

Hillview Motel, 12826 Johnson Memorial Dr, Hwys 169 & 41, Blgton. 445-7111. Rates: $35-89. TV and linen incl.

Kaz's Home Hostel, 5100 Dupont Ave South, South Mpls, 822-8286. $10 pp; one bedroom with two beds. 5 miles from downtown. Curfew: leave by 9am, return after 5pm. Use of kitchen facilities.

Students Co-op, 1721 University Ave SE, (612) 331-1078. $10/night, and monthly rates available-only in summer. Kitchen, laundry, TV. 'Smashing place to live —full of friendly lunatics. Great social life.' Located on 'frat' row, near Dinkytown, an area dense with student cafes and cheap places to eat. *www.umich.edu/~nasco/gtcc/minnesota.html*.

LivInn, 285 Century Ave N, Maplewood, St Paul. 738-1600. S-$49, XP-8, D-$54. Close to airport, shops, and zoo.

Lebanon Hills Regional Park Campground, 12100 Johnny Cake Ridge Rd, Apple Valley, (952) 454-9211. Tent site $17, $22 w/electric, $27 w/full hook-up. 10 miles from d/town Minneapolis. *www.co.dakota.mn.us/parks/hillscamp.htm.*

Food

Be sure to try Minnesota specialities: wild rice, walleyed pike, sweet corn and Fairbault blue cheese. St Paul's soul dish is *boya*, a Hungarian stew served on the slightest pretext. For cheap munchies try some of the downtown and college bars during happy hour.

Al's Breakfast, 413 14th Ave, SE, Mpls, 331-9991. 'Best morning meal in town! Good things happen here; people's lives change. If you want a car, or an apartment, or a sweetheart, come in, have coffee and chat a while.' Mon-Sat 6am-1pm, Sun 9am-1pm. B/fast $3-$8.

Brit's Pub, 1110 Nicollet Mall, Mpls, 332-3908. Very popular with locals. Serves Brit fare. Open daily 11am-2am. *www.britspub.com.*

Cafe Latte, 850 Grand Ave, St Paul, 224-5687. Bakery and wine bar. Located in Victoria Crossing. Energetic urban cafeteria. 'Seductive sprawling triple-layer turtle cake.' Choice of four interesting soups every day. Bring a friend so you can try more than one. Open daily at 9am, Sun and Tue 'til 10pm, Wed-Thu 'til 11pm, Fri-Sat 'til midnight.

Cossetta, 211 West Seventh St, St Paul, 222-3476. An Italian market and deli. Fresh meats, cheeses and salads are served cafeteria style. Lunch or dinner for two with wine is about $20. Open Sun 11am-8pm, Mon-Thu 'til 9pm, Fri-Sat 'til 10pm.

Emily's Lebanese Delicatessen, 641 University Ave NE, Mpls, 379-4069. Great lunch spot! $3-$12.50. Closed Tue. Open 9am for take out, 11am for eating in. wk/days 'til 9pm, wk/end 'til 10pm.

Famous Dave's BBQ, 4262 Upton Ave S, Mpls, 929-1200. Delicious barbecue. Open daily 11am-9pm, Fri-Sat 'til 10pm. Average price $8.

Gasthof Zur Gemütlichkeit, 2300 University Ave NE, Mpls, 781-3860. German restaurant and bar that draws customers of all ages. Polka and live German music Fri & Sat. Order the 'boot'— a mammoth-sized glass boot filled with beer, shared with a large group. Restaurant open Tue-Thu 5pm-10pm, Fri-Sat 4pm-11pm, Sun 3pm-10pm. Bar stays open 'til 2am, Fri and Sat. Closed Mon. *www.gasthofzg.com.*

Green Mill, 2626 Hennepin Ave, Mpls, 374-2131. Excellent burgers, good pizza. Sun-Thu 11am-10pm, Fri-Sat 'til 11pm. Bar open 'til 2am.

Key's Cafe, 1007 Nicollet Mall, Mpls, 339-6399. 'Small and friendly café which serves good food at reasonable prices. All day bfast and daily specials are a good deal.' Bfast $3-$10, big portions. Mon-Wed 6.30am-8.30pm, Thu 7.30am-8.30pm, Fri-Sat 'til 9pm, Sun 8am-3pm.

Lotus. Two separate restaurants with one idea: Vietnamese food in a stylish setting! 313 SE Oak St, Mpls, 331-1781. Open Mon-Sat 11am-9pm, *www.lotusuofm.com*; and 3037 Hennepin Ave, near Calhoun Square, 825-2263. Open Sun-Thu 11am-10pm, Fri-Sat 'til 11pm.

North Country Co-op, 1929 S 5th St, 338-3110. Full grocery with fresh produce and bread. Daily 8am-9pm. *www.northcountrycoop.com.*

Origami, 30 N First St, Mpls, Warehouse District, 333-8430. The best sushi in Minneapolis. Open Mon-Sat 11am-9pm, Fri-Sat 'til 10.30, Sun 5pm-9pm.

Sawatdee, Has 5 locations in which to sample some of the best Thai food. 607 Washington Ave, S Mpls, 338-6451, open Sun-Thu 11am-9.30pm, Fri-Sat 'til 10.30pm; and 289 E 5th, St Paul, 222-5859, open Mon-Thu 11am-10pm, Fri-Sat 'til 11pm, are just two. The one in St Paul is older and better.

Seward Community Cafe, 2129 E Franklin Ave, Mpls, 332-1011. 'The Sunday bfast is very cheap and filling.' Bfast $4-$6. Mon-Fri 6.30am-2pm, Sat-Sun 8am-4pm.

Of interest: Minneapolis

Besides being the longest pedestrian walkway in the US, the outdoor **Nicollet Mall** is one of the most agreeable and attractive. It's full of flowers, fountains, friendly conversation, strollers, sandwich-eaters, bus stop shelters, wafting classical music and tempting boutiques. Overhead an enclosed Skyway system (designed for Minnesota winters) lets pedestrians cross in comfort from building to building connecting 70 downtown blocks.

The focal point of the Mall and Skyway complex is the 57-storey **IDS Center** at Nicollet and 8th St; Minneapolis' tallest skyscraper by 1ft! The **Crystal Court**, a 3-level arcade within the IDS complex, has a 'ceiling' of crystal pyramids and shapes which nicely diffuse the sunlight, creating a dappled effect as though one were strolling beneath trees. A 105ft waterfall is also reachable by walking North on the Mall to the Mississippi. Both the lighting and the vibrant cafe/meeting-place ambience are best absorbed at noon. **Basil's** has reasonably-priced lunch specials, and there's an info centre in the Crystal Court. Suggestions of scenic walks around the Twin Cities can be found in free leaflets from the info centre in the IDS Complex and **Minneapolis Convention and Visitor Assoc.**, 33 S 6th Street, Suite 4000, Mpls, MN 55402, (888) 676-6757. *www.minneapolis.org*.

Recommended: cross the Hennepin Ave bridge reachable by walking North on Nicollet Mall to the far side of the Mississippi and then return to downtown via the 3rd Ave/Central Ave bridge and view the only natural waterfall on the Mississippi. The area immediately across the river is called **Riverplace & St Anthony Main**, restored warehouses on the original cobblestone Main Street of Minneapolis. The 3rd Ave Bridge takes you across to St Anthony Falls; the Minneapolis side is lined with fine old warehouses and flour mills and the new **Mill City Museum**, 704 S. Second St, open Tue-Sat 10am-5pm, Thu 'til 9pm, and Sun noon-5pm. Multimedia, hands-on exhibits show the history of how Minnesota became the flour milling capital of the world. Students with ID, $6. *www.millcitymuseum.org*. Between the museum and S Washington Ave is the **Milwaukee Road Depot**, a restored wrought-iron train shed that now has a year-round indoor figure skating rink, indoor water park, four hotels and a restaurant/bar. A favourite **walk or bike ride** is along the Mississippi on either side. Others are around Lake of the Isles, Cedar Lake, Lake Harriet or Lake Calhoun, all in south Minneapolis. This is a city with 153 parks and 45 continuous miles of bike paths.

American-Swedish Institute, 2600 Park Ave, 871-4907. Shops, fine art, 33-room mansion with exhibits on Minnesota's Swedish heritage. Tue, Thu, Fri, Sat noon-4pm, Wed 'til 8pm, Sun 1pm-5pm; $5. _www.americanswedishinst.org._

Historic Orpheum Theater, 910 Hennepin Ave South, Mpls, 339-7007. Pop, jazz and rock events. 2,200-seat facility. Located in the LaSalle Plaza. Call (651)989-5151 for tkts. _www.hennepintheatredistrict.com._

Minneapolis Institute of Arts, 2400 3rd Ave S, 870-3046. Contains over 100,000 objects ranging from ancient art to art deco. Tue, Wed, Fri & Sat 10am-5pm, Thu 'til 9pm, Sun 11am-5pm; free, special shows have fees. Donations requested. _www.artsmia.org._

Minnehaha Falls and Park, south of city. 144-acre woodland with 53-foot cataract popularised (though never seen) by Longfellow in his _Song of Hiawatha._

University Theater, 110 Rarig Center, 330 21st Ave South, 625-4001. Musicals, comedies and dramas (Shakespeare /Classics/ Contemporary), featuring student and professional actors, designers and directors. _cla.umn.edu/theatre._

Walker Art Center, 725 Vineland Pl, 375-7622. A modern collection with over 8,000 works. Tue, Wed, Sat 10am-5pm, Thu-Fri 'til 9pm, Sun 11am-5pm; $8, $5 w/student ID. Free on Thu eve and on the first Sat of each month. On the grounds is the **Sculpture Garden,** including the enormous Spoonbridge and Cherry. Open 6am-midnight; free. More details at _www.walkerart.org._

Of interest: St Paul

Request a St Paul **Fun Pass** to take advantage of discounts on lodgings, dining and attractions. Visit _www.stpaulcvb.org_ or call (800) 627-6101.

Alexander Ramsey House, Irvine Park, 296-8760. Victorian home of early Minnesota governor, run by the Minnesota Historical Society. 1 hr tours Fri-Sat 10am-3pm, $7. _www.mnhs.org._

Historic Fort Snelling, junction of Hwys 5 and 55 near airport, 726-1171. Reconstruction and preservation of 1827-era fort. Film, exhibits and fort tours. June-Labor day: Mon-Sat 10am-5pm, Sun noon-5pm; $8. _www.mnhs.org./places/sites/hfs._

Indian Mounds State Park, Dayton's Bluff, east of downtown off Hwy 94. Burial site of at least two American Indian cultures. Pleasant picnic spot overlooking the Mississippi. Contact St Paul Parks & Recreation 266-6400. _www.nps.gov/miss/maps/model/mounds.html._

James J Hill House, 240 Summit Ave, 297-2555. 45-room Romanesque mansion and private art gallery that once belonged to the builder of the Great Northern Railway. $1^{1}/_{4}$ hr tour begins every 30 min, Wed-Sat 10am-3.30pm, Sun 1pm-3.30pm rsvs recommended; $8. _www.mnhs.org./places/sites/jjhh._

Padelford Packet Boat Co, 227-1100, Harriet Island, downtown St Paul. Paddlewheel boat tours of Mississippi River. Depart from Harriet Island in St Paul and Boom Island, Minneapolis. 2 daily $1^{1}/_{2}$ hr cruises June-Aug (noon and 2pm), Sat-Sun 2pm in May & Sept, $18. _www.riverrides.com._

Landmark Center, 75 W 5th St, 292-3225. The old Federal court building, now a focus for cultural events and houses the **Minneapolis Museum of American Art.** Worth going for the architecture alone. Mon-Fri 8am-5pm, Thu 'til 8pm, Sat 10am-5pm, Sun noon-5pm; free. _www.landmarkcenter.org._

Science Museum, 120 W Kellogg Blvd, 221-9488. Houses an omnitheatre, a huge, domed screen, 221-9444, as well as a 3D laser theatre. June-Labor day: Mon-Sat 9.30am-9pm, Sun 10.30am-6pm. Tkts: Exhibit $8.50, omnitheatre $7.50, combo tkt $16, incls laser show. _www.smm.org._

State Capitol, near the Science Museum, 296-2881. 45 min tour of building, governor's quarters, golden horses on top and base of dome for panoramic view. Open Mon-Fri 9am-4pm, Sat 10am-3pm, Sun 1pm-4pm; tours end 1 hr before closing times. Free. Go to info desk. *www.mnhs.org./places/sites/msc.*

Summit Avenue District. Summit Ave has the longest, uninterrupted row of Victorian houses in the US. Anchored by the **Cathedral of St Paul** and the **James J Hill House**, No 240, it was built up by wealthy business leaders and tycoons. Summit Avenue is also the address of other notable men, **F. Scott Fitzgerald** and **Hubert Humphrey** (former vice president of the U.S.) The **Governor's Mansion** is No. 1006, while Fitzgerald ended up living at No. 599, where he penned his first novel in 1919. Grand and Selby Avenues, near Summit Ave, are the heart of St. Paul's nightlife and shopping scene. The University of Minnesota campus has the **Goldstein Gallery**, 241 MacNeal Hall; displays on fashion, housing, and interior design. *www.ohwy.com./mn/g/gdstgall.htm.*

Nearby: Lake Pepin, 1 hr S of the Twin Cities, Hwy 61. Good swimming beaches.

Mall of America, 60 E Broadway, Bloomington, 883-8800, about 15 min from St Paul; take MTC bus #54. Mall attracts more visitors annually than Disney World, Graceland and the Grand Canyon combined. A feast for shopping gastronomes and also for added piquancy: a seven-acre indoor theme park with roller coaster and 28 rides. Also worth checking out is **Underwater Adventures**, with more than 1.2 million gallons of water and over 3000 sea creatures! Retail hrs: Mon-Fri 10am-9.30pm, Sat 9.30am-9.30pm, Sun 11am-7pm; times vary for other attractions. Visit *www.mallofamerica.com* for more details.

Minnesota Zoo, in Apple Valley 20 miles south of St Paul, Zoo (952) 431-9200 , IMAX 997-9720 . Buses from Twin Cities' downtowns via the Mall of America, Mon-Fri. 5 zones, from tropics to oceanic, with Siberian tigers, wolves and caribou; along with an IMAX Theatre. Memorial day- Labour day daily 9am-6pm. Other months, daily 9am-4pm. Zoo $12, Zoo and IMAX combo tkt $19, Parking $5. *www.mnzoo.com.*

Sauk Center. Sinclair Lewis' hometown and the setting for his book, *Main Street.* Located 2 hrs NW of St Paul on 94 West, (320) 352-5201. Interpretative Center and museum; Mon-Fri 8.30am-5pm, Sat-Sun 9am-5pm, free. Lewis' boyhood home open May-Sept only: weekdays, 8.30am-5pm, Sat-Sun 9am-5pm, $3. *www.saukherald.com./ftp/lewis/default.html.*

Taylor's Falls, located on the St Croix River near Wisconsin border. Spectacular falls and great rock climbing. *www.taylorsfalls.com*. On your drive up, stop in **Stillwater**. *www.ilovestillwater.com.*

Entertainment: Minneapolis

Pick up a free copy of the *City Pages* (comes out on Wed) at newstands and coffee shops for the latest word on what's going on or go to *www.citypages.com.*

First Avenue and 7th St Entry, 701 1st Ave N, 338-8388/332-1775. First Avenue was made famous by Prince in the movie *Purple Rain.* You probably won't see Prince, but you can see good rock groups in the Main Room. Also features dance nights Thu-Sat, 9pm-3am. 7th St. The **Entry** is around the corner: cheaper, lesser-known groups. Check out *www.first-avenue.com* for more details.

Festivals: summertime noon concerts throughout downtown Mpls, especially Nicollet Mall. **Peavea Plaza** has 'Tunes at noon' through June 11.30am-1.30pm and 'Hot Summer Jazz' in late June. Call 343-5943. For more info/listings go to *www.downtownmpls.com*. Activities on the lakes are featured in the **Aquatennial** in July, call (612) 376-7669 or visit *www.aquatennial.org* for detail; and the **Minnesota State Fair** is held late Aug-early Sept at 1265 Snelling Ave N, St Paul, (651) 642-2200/603-6806, admission $9; *www.mnstatefair.org.*

Guthrie Theater, 725 Vineland Pl, 377-2224/(1-877) 44-STAGE, was founded in the 1960s by Sir Tyrone Guthrie and has one of the finest repertory companies in the

US. Student discount, $5 off all performances. Low cost previews; enquire. Box office open Mon-Fri 11am-8pm, Sat 10am-8pm, Sun 2pm-7pm (10am-7pm for Sunday matinees) www.guthrietheater.org.

Orchestra Hall, 1111 Nicollet Mall, 371-5656/(800) 292-4141. Home of the Minnesota Orchestra. Cabaret in summer; jazz, pop and other concerts. Box office open Mon-Fri 9am-6pm, Sat 10am-3pm. www.minnesotaorchestra.org.

The Quest Club, 110 N 5th St, 338-6169. Club and concert venue. Cover ranges from $7-$23. 'Great night-club'. Admission 18+ and 21+, depending on event; need ID. $10 entry. www.thequestclub.com.

U of Minnesota Film Society, 17th and University Ave SE, 627-4430. On campus: 'the Film Society often has free or cheap screenings of recent flicks. See notice board in Student Union'. Movies are shown at **Bell Museum Auditorium**, 10 Church St, SE, and **Galtier Plaza Cinema**, 5th St & Jackson, St Paul; and at Oak St Cinema, 309 Oak St SE, Mnpls. www.ufilm.org.

The **Dinkytown** area near campus on the east side of the river is liveliest at night. Good country rock groups perform at many bars in the metropolitan area.

Entertainment: St Paul

Make sure you get a copy of the free *City Pages* available all around St Paul in coffee shops, etc. for up-to-date events. www.citypages.com.

Fitzgerald Theater, 10 E Exchange St, 290-1200. Home of Garrison Keillor's entertaining weekly public radio comedy and music show, *A Prairie Home Companion*. www.prairiehome.org. It also has a variety of concerts, lectures, and productions and hosts a Saturday night radio show featuring some of the finest in American folk music. Box Office: Tue-Fri, noon-6pm, Sat 10am-2pm. www.fitzgeraldtheater.org.

Minnesota History Center, 345 West Kellogg Blvd, (800) 657-3773. Museum hours: Tue-Fri 10am-5pm, Tue 'til 8pm, Sat 9am-5pm, Sun noon-5pm, open Mon in summer, $6. For latest events, check the website at www.mnhs.org.

The Ordway Center For The Performing Arts, 345 Washington St, near Landmark Center, 224-4222. The St Paul Chamber Orchestra and Minnesota Opera perform here. Check out www.ordway.org.

Winter Carnival, Rice Park, btwn 4th & 5th Sts and Market & Washington. Jan-Feb 10 days of parades, parties, sporting events and fireworks; $3.50 button, available throughout Twin Cities, entitles holder to participate in most activities. Check out Grande Day Parade, torchlight parade and ice-carving competitions. Call (800) 488-4023 or go to www.winter-carnival.com for info.

Information

Look for free newspapers (from street boxes and stores downtown), *Skyway News*, *Twin Cities Reader* and *City Pages* for events, accommodation and job tips.

Minnesota Tourism Bureau, 121 7th Place E, Suite 100, Metro Square, St Paul, (800) 657-3700. Mon-Fri 8am-4.30pm. www.exploreminnesota.com.

Greater Minneapolis Convention & Visitors Association, (800) 445-7412, Mon-Fri 8am-5pm. www.minneapolis.org.

St Paul Convention & Visitors Bureau, 175 West Kellogg Boulevard, Suite 502, St Paul, (800) 627-6101, Mon-Fri 8am-4.30pm. www.ci.stpaul.mn.us.

St Paul Parks and Recreation, (651) 266-6400 or www.ci.stpaul.mn.us/depts/parks.

Internet access

Cahoots Coffee Bar, 1562 Selby Ave, St Paul, (651) 644-6778. $1.25/15mins, $5/hr. Mon-Thu 7am-9.30pm, Fri-Sat 'til 11pm, 7.30am-9.30pm.

Minneapolis Public Library, 250 Marquette Ave, (612) 630-6000. Free access, 1hr limit. ID required. Mon, Wed, Fri 10am-5pm; Tue, Thu 11am-6pm; Sat noon-5pm, www.mplib.org.

South St Paul Public Library, 106 3rd Ave N, (651) 554-3240. Free access, 1 hr limit. Mon &Thu 9am-8pm, Tue,Wed & Fri'til 6pm, Sat 10am-3pm. *www.southstpaul.org/departments/library*.

Travel

Metropolitan Transit Commission (MTC), (612) 373-3333, runs the two cities integrated bus systems. Basic fare $1.50, $2.00-$2.75 during rush hour. *www.metrotransit.org*.

Amtrak, 730 Transfer Rd, St Paul, 644-6012/(800) 872-7245. On the *Empire Builder* route that connects Chicago and Seattle/Portland. 'Located on an industrial estate, no accommodation nearby.'

Greyhound, 950 Hawthorne Ave, Mpls, Nr corner of 10th St. 371-3325/(800) 231-2222.

Minneapolis/St Paul International Airport. Take the Route 7 CDEFG (sign must read '7C' etc.) bus from 4th St, Mpls, every 20 min. From St Paul take 54A/54M from 6th St, every 30 mins. About 45 min travel time. **Express Shuttle/Coach USA**, (612) 827-7777, runs a limousine service to downtown hotels, $11 St Paul; $13 Mpls. $2 discount on r/t. *www.supershuttle.com.*

DULUTH Situated on a steep hillside overlooking Lake Superior, Duluth has the world's largest fresh-water lake and is known for its unbelievably cold winters. The mines that used to provide the city with much of its income have all but disappeared. Now it's you, the happy tourist, who helps keep the place moving. It's access to the lake that attracts most visitors; there is a beautiful 4.6 mile walkway that traces the shore of the lake and along the harbour. Accommodation can be a problem in the busy summer when motels can bump up their prices, but try **Best Western Downtown Motel**, 131 W 2nd St, 727-6851/(800) 528-1234, S-$71, D-$59 (wk/days), breakfast included, free internet access. *www.bestwestern.com*. Visit the **Convention and Visitors Bureau**, 100 Lake Place Dr, 722-4011/(800) 4-DULUTH, for information on the best current deals. For a long list of activities, events, lodgings, attractions and dining check out *www.visitduluth.com*.

The telephone area code is 218.

HIBBING Famous for its Mesabi Range iron ore, Hibbing is also home of the original Greyhound buses and the birthplace of Bob Dylan. For those interested in digging up more knowledge about mining, the Minnesota Museum of Mining in Chisholm and the Iron Range Interpretative Center may be worth visiting. Hwy 73 takes you through a multicoloured mini-Grand Canyon, the mined-out maw of the Pillsbury open pit. Along the way are several vista points for viewing other gaping holes, some as much as four miles long and two miles wide. Visit *www.hibbing.mn.us*.

GRAND RAPIDS There's no place like Grand Rapids; it was home to Judy Garland, born there in 1922. Today it's the site of the **Judy Garland Birthplace Historic House and Museum**, (800) 664-JUDY. The annual Judy Garland festival is held at the end of June, featuring cameo appearances by some of the surviving Munchkins from her most famous movie, *The Wizard of Oz*. Opened in 1995, the house attracts some 10,000 Judy Garland fans a year. Before Garland's death in 1969 she told an interviewer: 'If we had stayed in Minnesota, my life might have been much happier.' Open daily 10am-5pm. $6. *www.judygarlandmuseum.com.*

NORTHERN MINNESOTA is known for the beauty of its wild areas. Among the best: **Chippewa National Forest**, a 1.6 million acre wilderness that contains over 1300 lakes and rivers with broad vistas of beautiful large and small lakes. Hiking trails have been developed and maintained for visitors. Bald eagles are the star attractions. For information write to 200 Ash Ave NW, Cass Lake MN 56633; call (218) 335-8600 or visit *www.fs.fed.us/r9/chippewa/index.htm*.

Try *www.paulbunyan.net/users/blawler/chipp.htm* for recreation opportunities and a complete list of campgrounds.

North Shore, Lake Superior. Superior National Forest, (218) 626-4300. *www.superiornationalforest.org*. If you have about a week, you can drive all the way around Lake Superior into Canada and Wisconsin. Otherwise, go to Duluth to see this beautiful shoreline. *www.visitnorthshore.com*.

There is a plethora of campgrounds scattered throughout the area. The best include **Grand Marais Municipal Campground**, 387-1712. Camp sites $19.50, $23.50-$26.50 w/hook up, located on Lake Superior. *www.boreal.org/cityhall/recharbor.html* and **Lamb's Campground**, Hwy 61, Lamb's Way, Schroeder, 663-7292. 60 wooded acres and $1^1/2$ miles of beach. Fishing, hiking, boat facilities. Call for current rates. *www.boreal.org/lambsresort*.

Superior National Forest stretches across Minnesota's north-eastern area from the Canadian border to the north shore of Lake Superior. It is especially known for the **Boundary Waters Canoe Area**, a million-acre protected wilderness area honey-combed with rivers. There are bugs, bears and a lot of portaging, but, if you come prepared, this adventure is well worthwhile. For information write to the Forest Supervisor, 8901 Grand Ave Place, Duluth, MN 55808, or go to *www.boundarywaters.com*; call the **Minnesota Tourism Bureau** in St Paul, 296-5029.

VOYAGEURS NATIONAL PARK On the Minnesota-Canadian border, this 218,054 acre expanse of forested lake country is well equipped for public use. The park takes its name from the intrepid Canadians who plied this network of lakes and streams in canoes, transporting explorers (some seeking the Northwest Passage), missionaries and soldiers to the West. They later returned by way of Montreal, carting vast quantities of furs with them. You can reach the park by car, but inside there are only waterways—you'll need to rent a boat. Free primitive camping in designated areas.

Other lodgings at nearby private resorts. No park entrance fee. There are various visitor and information centers; call **Ash River Visitor Center** (218) 374-3221 or **Crane Lake rangers station** (218) 993-2481. **Houseboats** can be rented on **Rainy Lake**, **Crane Lake** or the **Ash River**. For more information write to **Voyageurs National Park**, 3131 Hwy 53, International Falls, MN 56649-8904 or call (218) 283-9821. **Voyagaire Lodge and Houseboats**, Crane Lake, (800) 88-BOATS. Privately run by Jim and Gretchen Janssen who can direct you to the places where decades ago Native Americans etched their stones into the granite walls along the park's bluffs, *www.voyagaire.com*. For more details: *www.voyageurs.national-park.com*.

MISSOURI - The Show-Me State

Mix equal parts of the Old South, the Wild West and the modern Midwest and you've got the flavour of the Missourian: shrewd, salt of the earth, slightly cantankerous—nobody here believes anything unless they see it with their own eyes. The flat landscape is dominated and divided by the Big Muddy, the Missouri River, a wilful, sediment-laden powerhouse. Missouri has the second largest number of farms in the country and is the leading purebred livestock producer. It is also 12th in ice cream production and has also produced Harry S Truman, Mark Twain, TS Eliot, Jesse James and Generals Pershing and Bradley, as well as entertainers Chuck Berry, Brad Pitt, Don Johnson, Scott Joplin and Kathleen Turner.

In the south-west begins the Ozark Plateau, wooded, full of springs, unspoilt rivers and caverns. A portion of the Cherokee **Trail of Tears** runs through SE Missouri and has been made into a scenic camping and recreational area. _www.missouritourism.com._

ST LOUIS is associated with several great American traditions. It's here where St Louis Browns baseball fans first gobbled up hot dogs in 1893 and where 1904 World's Fair goers first contended with drippy ice cream cones and sampled hamburgers on buns. St Louis is where WC Handy wrote and sang the blues, where slave Dred Scott sued for freedom, where one-time resident Tennessee Williams set his _Glass Menagerie_ and where Charles Lindbergh got the bucks for his trans-Atlantic venture. It's here that Chuck Berry learned to sing at his father's church, and still plays from time to time at **Blueberry Hill**. 'If you tried to give rock and roll another name,' said John Lennon, 'you might call it Chuck Berry.' In 1998, St Louis captured the attention of baseball fans everywhere as Cardinals' slugger Mark McGwire shattered Roger Maris' record for a single season's home runs.

Huge, humid, full of unsavoury slums and heavy industry from meat-packing to beer-brewing, the city nevertheless has a vital cultural life, lots of free attractions and the elegant Gateway to the West arch. **St Louis Convention & Visitors Commission's** website, _www.explorestlouis.com_ has links to a calendar of events, attractions and nightlife. (800) 325-7962.

The telephone area code is 314.

Accommodation
Check out **A1 Discount Hotels,** (888) 511-5743, a reservation service which offers savings of up to 65% off regular rates. _www.a1-discount-st-louis-hotels.com._
Econo Lodge, 1100 N Third St, 421-6556, D-$60.

Food
Berkshire Grill, 12455 St Charles Rock Rd, Bridgeton, 298-1260. Excellent American classics, Italian and Mexican dishes. Open Mon-Thu 11am-11pm, Fri-Sat 'til midnight, Sun 'til 10pm.
Blueberry Hill, 6504 Delmar Blvd, 727-0880. Creative menu, live bands, outdoor seating in trendy University City Loop. In 2005, Chuck Berry was still doing gigs here. Open Mon-Sat 11am-1.30am, Sun 11am-midnight. _www.blueberryhill.com._
Brandt's, 6525 Delmar Blvd, 727-3663. Also in The Loop. Great décor and burgers. _www.brandtscafe.com._
Coffee Cartel, 2 Maryland Plaza, 454-0000, 24 hour coffee shop located in lively

Central West End. Good value sandwiches, desserts, ice cream, smoothies and coffee. Internet access available, $5/hr.

Crown Candy Kitchen, 14th St & St Louis Ave, 621-9650. A 1913 ice cream parlor with a blend of shakes and sundaes. Serves sandwiches, soups and chilis. Drink 5 malts in 30 min and pay nothing! Open Mon-Sat, 10.30am-10pm, Sun noon-9pm.

Culpeppers, 300 N Euclid Ave, 361-2828. Serves American fare, great food with outside seating in Central West End. Mon-Sat 11am-1am, Sun 11.30 am-midnight.

John D McGurks Irish Pub, 1200 Russell Blvd, 776-8309, Open Mon-Fri 11am-1.30am, Sat from 11.30am, Sun 3pm-midnight. Live music every night. *www.mcgurks.com.*

King Louie's, 3800 Chouteau Ave, 865-3662. American classics.

Morgan St Brewery, 721 N 2nd St, 231-9970. Not only a restaurant and micro-brewery, but also a separate dance club in historic Laclede's Landing. Open Tue-Sun 11am-2.30am. *www.morganstreetbrewery.com.*

Old Spaghetti Factory, 727 N 1st St, 621-0276. 'Massive helpings, good atmosphere, spaghetti dinners with dessert, coffee from $7.50-$10.' Open Sun-Thu 11.30am-10pm, Fri-Sat 'til 11pm. *www.osf.com.*

Remy's Kitchen, 222 S Bemiston Ave, 726-5757. One of St Louis' most popular restaurants. Make a reservation or you'll wait for hours. Also a wine bar. Open for lunch Mon-Fri 11.30am-2.30pm, for dinner Mon-Thu 5.30pm-10pm, Fri-Sat 5.30pm-midnight.

Rigazzi's, 4945 Daggett Ave, 772-4900. Another good choice for Italian. Open Mon-Thu 8am-11pm, Fri-Sat 'til midnight. *www.rigazzis.com.*

St Louis Bread Company, 10 S Central, 725-9666, and several other locations. Phenomenal sandwiches, bagels, soups and salads! Hours vary by location. *www.panerabread.com.*

Ted Drewes, 6726 Chippewa St, 481-2652, and 4224 S Grand, 352-7376. 'Naughty-but-nice frozen custard desserts. Take-away. 'Always draws a crowd—be prepared for large queues esp in eves and w/ends'. Open daily 11am-11pm. *www.teddrewes.com.*

There are also many inexpensive ethnic restaurants around **Laclede's Landing** and on the 4th flr of the **St Louis Center**, Locust & 6th St.

Of interest

Gateway Arch, St Louis Riverfront, (877) 982-1410. A unique 40-person tram ('don't go if you get seasick') mounts the core of each leg of this 630-ft stainless steel arch designed by Eero Saarinen, in response to a competition in which the architect would best represent St Louis as 'The Gateway to the West'. Once there, you overlook the city and the Mississippi. 'Getting up to the top is amazing. Each compartment holds five people; it's really small and bright white, like something out of Star Trek!' Get there before 11am to avoid queues. Daily 8.20am-10.10pm during summer; 9.20am-5.10pm, winter. $10 for tram ride; free to enter the grounds of the arch and the **Museum of Westward Expansion** complex beneath the arch. 'The museum is very atmospheric, giving vivid impressions of frontier life.' $7 for film depicting the construction of the arch.

The Old Court House, west of Arch at 11 N 4th St, 655-1600, was scene of slavery auctions and the unsuccessful attempt by slave Dred Scott to win his freedom in court; the ramifications of his case helped ignite the Civil War. Open daily 8am-4.30pm, free, audio tour $3. Trial room no longer exists, but you may see **Dred Scott's** grave in Section 1, **Calvary Cemetery,** 5239 Florissant Ave, 381-1313, gates open 8am-5pm daily. *www.stlouisarch.com.*

Forest Park, midtown, 5 miles W of Gateway Arch. *www.slfp.com./ForestPark.html.* A large and well laid-out park with numerous attractions; in 1904 the site of the centennial Louisiana Purchase Exposition and World's Fair. An electric signal from the White House simultaneously unfurled 10,000 flags, while fountains flowed, bands played, 62 foreign nations exhibited and 19 million people visited there to sample iced tea and ice cream cones for the first time. Of the 1576 buildings erected for the fair, only one was permanent; it's now the **St Louis Art Museum**, 1 Fine Arts Drive, 721-0072; one of the most impressive in the US. 'Interesting exhibitions in a peaceful setting.' Open Tue-Sun 10am-5pm, Fri 'til 9pm, free for permanent collection. _www.slam.org_. **The Jewel Box** is a conservatory located within Forest Park—a lovely place for a stroll. Also located here, **St Louis Zoo**, 781-0900; 'great sea lion show. You could spend a whole day here'. Daily 8am-7pm, Tue 'til 8pm. Free admission but fees for some attractions. _www.stlzoo.org_.

Nearby: Grant's Farm, Gravois Rd at Grant Rd (outskirts), 843-1700. Ancestral home of the Busch family, formerly owned by Ulysses S. Grant. Look at one of the largest breeding facilities of lovably huge Clydesdale horses anywhere. Also deer, buffalo, birds, and even elephants, thrown in. May-Oct Tue-Fri 9am-3.30pm, Sat 'til 4pm, Sun 9.30am-4pm. Free but $5 parking. _www.grantsfarm.com._

Missouri Botanical Gardens, Tower Grove & Shaw Ave, 577-51.00/(800) 642-8842. See the Climatron, first geodesic-domed greenhouse with computer-controlled climates maintained within. Also home of the largest Japanese garden in North America. Take the Metrolink to Central West End and then the Garden Express shuttle bus. Open daily 9am-5pm, Wed 'til 8pm in summer, opens Wed and Sat 7am for walkers, $7, _www.mobot.org_.

Outdoor Municipal Opera, located in Forest Park . Also known as 'The Muny', it is the largest, and oldest, outdoor musical theatre in the country with 1450 free seats at the back of a 10,800-seat amphitheatre. It holds West End, Broadway style musicals most nights in summer. 'Great for a summer's evening. Make a night of it and take a picnic—there are picnic tables outside the theatre.' Call 361-1900 for schedule. Box office open daily 9am-9pm. Visit _www.muny.com_ for more details.

Six Flags Theme Park, St Louis, PO Box 60, Eureka, (636) 938-4800. 30 miles NW of downtown St Louis on I-44. 'The inverted looping thrill ride Batman is totally awesome!' Tip: go in evening; less humid and possibility of discount. Also, ride The Boss, one of the biggest wooden roller coasters in the world, 'terrifying'. Ride the Tornado at Hurricane Harbor, a huge waterpark. Admission free with Six Flags admission, but there is a fee for locker and tube rentals; closes three hours before main park. Daily May-August, 10am-9pm, Sat 'til 10pm. $41.99 includes all rides and attractions. Get a discount at _www.sixflags.com._

St Louis Science Center, 5050 Oakland Ave, 289-4444/(800) 456-7572. Mon-Thu 9.30am-5.30pm, Fri-Sat 'til 9.30pm, Sun 11.30am-5.30pm. Free, but fees for special exhibitions. Check out _www.slsc.org_.

Union Station, Market St, btwn 18th and 20th, recently completed restoration of 19th century Gothic train station (it was once the world's largest train station!). Now full of shops, restaurants and old railroad cars. A cinema and carousel are located outside, within walking distance. _www.slfp.com./UnionStation.html_.

Just across the river from St. Louis lies the historic town of **St Charles** (visitor info. (800) 366-2427). Founded in 1769, St Charles whisks visitors back to the days when riverboats ruled the Midwest and 'prairie schooners' cruised the newly-settled western lands. Today the red-brick streets of Missouri's largest historic district are flanked with shops and restaurants. Visit the new **Lewis and Clark Boat House and Nature Center**, Bishop's Landing, 1050 Riverside Dr, (636) 947-3199, for historical background and hands-on activities about their incredible journey; open daily 10am-5pm, Sun from noon. $2, _www.lewisandclark.net_. St Charles is also home to the **First Missouri State Capitol**, 200 S Main, (636) 940-3322, the seat of state government from 1821-1826; open Mon-Sat 9am-4pm, Sun 11am-5pm, $2.50. While in St Charles, eat at the **Trailhead Brewing Co**, 921 S Main, (636) 946-2739. Open Mon-Fri 11am-10pm, Sat-Sun 'til 11pm. In the nearby town of **Defiance** is the **Daniel Boone Home**, (636) 798-2005, built by the famous pioneer and his son. The elder Boone lived there until his death in 1820. Collection of houses dated 1830-1860 also make up **Boonesfield Village**. Open daily 9am-6pm, (last tour 4.30pm); 1 hr tour $7, 2 hr tour $12.

Entertainment

Gateway Riverboat Cruises, below Gateway Arch, 621-4040. The oldest excursion company on the Mississippi offers sightseeing trips of varying duration and price on one of its two boats, *Tom Sawyer* and *Becky Thatcher*. 'Apart from a great view of the arch, there is very little else to see.' 1 hr sight-seeing tour $10; $37 for the cruise, including prime-rib dinner and band.

Paddlewheel steamboat trips are easy to find in St Louis, most of the boats dock in front of the arch.

UMB Bank Pavilion, 14141 Riverport Drive, Maryland Heights, 298-9944. Outdoor concert venue. Seats nearly 20,000 per show. For cheaper tkts sit on the lawn. 'Wonderful venue, really relaxed and you can get a good view from the lawn.' For information, visit *www.umbbankpavilion.com*; for tkts, call Ticketmaster, 241-1888.

St Louis nightlife unfolds on three different stages: **University City Loop,** the **Central West End,** and **Laclede's Landing.** U-City Loop draws a lot of college students, as does the Landing. The twenty-something's head to the Central West End while the older crowd is drawn to Washington Street in the Landing. The Soulard area has also grown to be a favourite college hangout. Also held in the Landing are the massive **Rocking on the Landing,** held annually July 4th and 5th and the **Big Muddy Blues Festival** held early September. Call **Laclede's Landing Merchant's Association,** 241-5875. *www.lacledeslanding.org*.

Information

Visitors Center: Gateway Arch, 655-1700, 7th and Washington and Kiener Plaza.
Missouri Travel Center, (800) 877-1234. Line open 24 hrs. *www.visitmo.com.*
St Louis Convention and Visitors Commission, 211 N Broadway, Suite 1100, 421-1023/(800) 325-7962. Mon-Fri 8.30am-5pm. *www.explorestlouis.com.*

Internet access

The Grind, 56 Maryland Plaza, 454-0202. Free access for customers at cybercafe in hip Central West End. No time limit, works on a 'common courtesy' basis.
St Louis Central Library, 1301 Olive St, 241-2288. Free access to library card holders. One 1 hr session, max 2 hrs per day. Mon 10am-9pm, Tue-Fri 10am-6pm, Sat 9am-5pm. Visit *www.slpl.lib.mo.us* for info. on other branches in the area.

Travel

Bi-State Transit, 231-2345, runs the city buses, one-day pass $4. *www.metro-stlouis.org*.
Metrolink, also run by Bi-State, is the light railway that can take you to most of the major sights. 'Very easy to use.' $1.50 basic fare, 25¢ transfer; day pass valid for both bus and Metro, $4.
Amtrak, 550 S 16th St, (800) 872-7245. Service to Chicago, New Orleans, Dallas and Kansas City; station closes at 11.45pm.
Greyhound, 1450 N 13th St, 231-4485/(800) 231-2222. Open 24 hrs.
Lambert/St Louis International Airport. About 10 miles from downtown and serviced by Bi-State buses and Metrolink: the easiest way is to take the bus to the airport from 6th and Washington, journey time of 36 min, $1.50 each way. Greyhound also runs buses from their terminal, $8, approx 30 min. Taxi to downtown approx $30, try **ABC Cabs,** 725-2111. *www.lambert-stlouis.com.*

HANNIBAL Mark Twain (*née* Samuel Clemens) spent his boyhood in Hannibal and his adopted hometown flogs Twain mania for all it's worth. Though brazenly commercial, it's good-natured hucksterism for the most part. The old rogue would no doubt approve, being no stranger to exaggeration himself: 'Recently someone sent me a picture of the house I was born in. Heretofore I have always stated that it was a palace but I shall be more guarded now.'

Twain's mother was a descendant of the Earl of Durham, who occupied Lambton Castle; his father's ancestors included one of the judges who delivered Charles I to the hands of executioners. Nevertheless, the Clemens family settled in modest Hannibal, where 'everybody was poor but didn't know it, and everyone was comfortable and did know it'.

Hannibal teems with classic Americana; as Twain writes, 'it's 'a little democracy which was full of liberty, equality and the Fourth of July'. Tom, Huck and Becky's old stomping grounds recall pleasant memories of whitewashed fences and frog races. Visit the **Becky Thatcher House** and **Judge Clemens' law office**. Eschew **Tom Sawyer's cave** (2 miles out of town and decidedly unspooky) and take a 1hr **Mark Twain Riverboat** trip on the Mississippi, 221-3222: departures at 11am, 1.30pm and 4pm (boards ½ hr before), $10; 2 hr dinner tour is also available from 6.30pm-8.30pm, $29.95 (inc. band). Bar extra. _www.marktwainriverboat.com._

Mark Twain's Boyhood Home and Museum, 206 Hill Street, 221-9010, is worth a look. The $8 ticket includes admission to the boyhood home and museum, plus Judge Clemens' law office, Grant's Drug Store and the new Mark Twain Museum Gallery, featuring 15 original Norman Rockwell paintings. Admission to Thatcher House is included in the price of admission. Daily 8am-6pm (summer). _www.marktwainmuseum.org._

Mysterious fact: Twain's birth coincided with the appearance of Halley's Comet and throughout his life, he predicted he would go out as he had come in. In 1910, right on cue, the comet reappeared and Twain snuffed it! For more information call the **Hannibal Convention and Visitors Bureau**, 505 N 3rd St, 221-2477 or go online, _www.visithannibal.com._

The telephone area code is 573.

KANSAS CITY Centrally located at the junction of the Missouri and Kansas Rivers, KC truly is the 'Heart of America'. It is within 250 miles of both the geographic and population centres of the US and is less than 1900 miles (half the distance from the east coast to the west coast) from every US city. The spirit of America plays heavily on the Missouri side of the dividing river—suburbs have names like Liberty and Independence.

Kansas City has been home to some notable Greats, such as Walter H. Beech (founder of Beech Aircraft), actress Kirstie Alley and Walt Disney (and therefore Mickey Mouse, as he was first penned here), and also has created the likes of the Eskimo Pie, the melt in-your-mouth-not-in-your-hands M&M candy coating and a legendary jazz scene. It is also home base of the Kansas City Royals and an important cattle market. No trip to the Midwest is complete without a pilgrimage to **Arthur Bryant's**, the Holy Grail of barbecuedom and a sufficient reason for visiting the city. In fact, _www.arthurbryantsbbq.com._ takes you to Bryant's personal homepage, with an amusing read of the history behind the restaurant and even photos of the renowned Arthur Bryant's barbecue sauce!

Once part of a great blues and jazz triangle with New Orleans and

Chicago, KC nurtured the careers of Count Basie, Duke Ellington and Charlie 'Bird' Parker; a new memorial dedicated to Parker, a 17ft bronze statue, is located outside the **American Jazz Museum,** 17th & Vine. KC's sister city is Seville, Spain, which explains the preponderance of Moorish arches, Spanish tiles and ornamental fountains around the Country Club Plaza. Try as they might, the Spanish architectural additions are unable to stifle the all-American spirit of the city. _www.visitkc.com._

The telephone area code is 816.

Accommodation

Try calling the **Convention and Visitors Bureau,** 221-5242/(800) 767-7700 or visiting _www.visitkc.com_ for hotel reservations and information.

Motel 6, 6400 E 87th St, 333-4468. Rooms $46.

Super 8 Motel, 4032 S Lynn Court Drive, Independence, 833-1888. S-$50, D-$55, B/fast incl., 10 min from KC.

Food

Arthur Bryant Barbecue, 1727 Brooklyn Ave at 17th, 231-1123. A sensational place to eat barbecue. Hot, grainy, opaque sauce (which you'll see ageing in the window). Get lots of sauce and take time to look at the memorabilia on the walls. A cartoon depicts Arthur entering heaven, with St. Peter asking him if he brought any sauce with him. 'World class BBQ ribs, swooning beef brisket sandwiches. Go on, stuff yourself!' Open daily from 10am. _www.arthurbryantsbbq.com._

Dixon's Chili, 9105 E 40 Hwy, 861-7308. Many locales in KC. Harry Truman loved KC chili—cheap and savoury. Open Mon-Sat 10am-10pm. Average $4.50.

Fric and Frac, 1700 W 39th St, 753-6102. Special deals each night like, 'Taco Saturday' and 'Shrimp Night', also 2-for-1 burger meals. 'Ideal place for mixing with the locals.' Open Sun-Thu 11am-midnight, Fri-Sat 'til 1.30am.

LC's Barbecue, 5800 Blue Pkwy, 923-4484. When all the tourists hit Arthur Bryant's, true barbecue aficionados head to LC's. A hole in the wall, but exquisite barbecue! Open Mon-Thu 11.30am-9.30pm, Fri-Sat 'til 11pm.

KC Masterpiece, 4747 Wyandotte on the Country Club Plaza, 531-3332. Another great choice for BBQ, its sauce is mass-marketed throughout the US. Open Sun-Thu 11am-10pm, Fri-Sat 'til 11pm. _www.kcmrestaurants.com._

Kansas Machine Shed, 12080 S Strang Line Rd in Olathe, (913) 780-2697. Authentic farm favourites served in a farm-like setting. Try their award winning pork entrees. Open Mon-Sat 6am-10pm, Sun 7am-9pm.

River Market Brewing Company, 500 Walnut, 471-6300. Kitchen open Mon-Thu 11am-10pm, Fri-Sat 'til 11pm, Sun 'til 8pm. _www.rivermarketbrews.com._

Of interest

Country Club Plaza, btwn Main St & SW Expressway. Oldest shopping mall in the US. Huge Spanish-style plaza with fountains, genuine Iberian art, beautiful night lighting, interesting food and shops (200 of 'em). At **47th & Nicholas,** a copy of the Giralda Tower in Seville. **47th & Central:** Spanish murals, exquisite Sevillano tilework depicting the bullfight. Splendid display of lights at Christmas. _www.countryclubplaza.com._

Crown Center, 2450 Grand Blvd, Main and Pershing Rd. 'City within a city,' built by Hallmark Cards. Features: shops; hotel; 5-storey waterfall; indoor gardens; restaurants; free events for kids and adults. In December, it houses the nation's tallest Christmas tree. 'Go Sat mornings when woodcarvers, artists, etc. are at work.' Attached to it is the **Hallmark Visitors Center,** 274-5672. Mon-Fri 9am-5pm, Sat 9.30am-4.30pm. Free exhibits showing how the company grew and the manufacturing process along with peddling sentiment and gushing rhymes. _www.hallmarkvisitorscenter.com._

Independence, a few miles east of KC and one-time home of the well-known haberdasher, former President Harry Truman. **Harry S Truman Home** is located at 223 N Main, 254-2720. Daily tours 9am-4.45pm; $3. Also visit the **Jackson County Courthouse** nearby where he was a judge and view a 30 min DVD presentation, *The Man From Independence*, 795-8200, $2, open 10am-3.30pm. Round out your Truman experience by visiting the **Truman Presidential Museum and Library**, 24 Hwy and Delaware St, 833-1400. Contains presidential papers, shows film presentations daily and his grave site in the courtyard. Mon-Sat 9am-5pm, Thu 'til 9pm, Sun noon-5pm; $7. *www.trumanlibrary.org.*

Kansas City Museum, 3218 Gladstone Blvd, 483-8300. Housed in the 50-room mansion of lumber king RA Long, are exhibits on natural, regional history, as well as a planetarium. Tue-Sat 9.30am-4.30pm, Sun noon-4.30pm; suggested donation $2.50. *www.kcmuseum.com.*

Nelson Atkins Museum of Fine Art, 4525 Oak St, 561-4000. Huge variety, especially of oriental art and crafts; one of the best collections of Chinese paintings outside Asia. Outdoor sculpture garden is great with its fine Henry Moore collection. Tue-Thu 10am-4pm, Fri 10am-9pm, Sat 10am-5pm, Sun noon-5pm, free. *www.nelson-atkins.org.*

The Livestock Exchange Building in the former Stockyard District is the last remnant of the Stockyard days, 12th & Genessee. **The Golden Ox** next door has good if somewhat pricey steaks.

Entertainment

KC's location on the Missouri river makes it a prime spot for riverboat casino-hopping. Try **Harrah's North**, 472-7777.

Westport, original city heart btwn 39th & 45th Sts, is famous for good taverns and nightlife. Try **Grand Emporium**, 3832 Main St, 531-1504, for live music and good bands, *www.grandemporium.com.* With luck, you may catch the **Jazz Pub Crawl** in May or Sept, a night of hopping in and out of 20 clubs with hot live jazz. Shuttle buses transport you safely from one to the next at your leisure. *www.jazzkc.org./jazzlovers.html.*

Kelly's Westport Inn, 500 Westport Rd, 561-0635. Cheap drink and a friendly atmosphere. Daily 8.15am-3am, Sun opens 11am.

Stanford and Sons, 504 Westport Rd, 756-1450. Comedy Club. Showtimes Wed-Thu at 8pm, Fri and Sat at 7.45 and 9.45pm. *www.stanfordscomedyclub.com.*

Information/Travel/Internet access

Convention and Visitors Bureau, 221-5242/(800) 767-7700. *www.visitkc.com.*

Kansas City Area Transportation Authority (Metro), 221-0660. Basic fare $1. *www.kcata.org.*

Amtrak, 2200 Main St, 421-3622/(800) 872-7245. For trains to St Louis, Chicago, and even LA.

Greyhound, 1101 Troost St, 221-2835/(800) 231-2222.

Kansas City International Airport, 243-5237, about 18 miles from the city. Take the #129 Metro bus, $1 from downtown 10th and Main, about 45 min. The **KCI Shuttle**, 243-5000, picks up from major hotels and costs $14 o/w; a taxi will cost $35-$40; try **Yellow Cabs** 471-5000.

Kansas City Public Library, 311 E 12th St, 701-3400. Free access, Courtesy limit. First-come-first-served basis. Mon-Thu 9am-8pm, Fri 9am-6pm, Sat 10am-5pm, Sun 1pm-5pm. *www.kclibrary.org.*

ST JOSEPH Over 100 young masochists applied to a less-than-appealing ad that read: 'Wanted: young skinny wiry fellows, not over 18. Must be expert riders willing to risk death daily. Orphans preferred. Wages $25/week. Apply Central Overland Express.' Thus, on 3 April 1860, the **Pony Express**

was born. Composed of 80 riders, 400 horses, 190 stations and 400 station hands, the Pony Express decreased the average delivery time of a letter from the east to California from 8 weeks to 10 days and played a crucial role in aligning California with the Union during the Civil War. Although the 2000 mile Missouri to California mail delivery system was only in operation for 18 months, it left a lasting impression on the world. The **Pony Express Museum** at 914 Penn Street, 279-5059/(800) 530-5930, preserves the original stables and other interesting memorabilia, well worth a visit; Mon-Sat 9am-5pm, Sun 1pm-5pm, $4. _www.ponyexpress.org._

Same day, but 22 years later, Bob Ford shot Jesse James for a $10,000 reward. The house where the shot was fired is now the **Jesse James Home and Museum**, 12th & Penn, 232-8206, which is full of original Jamesabilia and even has the hole left by the bullet in the wall. It as also the site of Pony Express headquarters 1860-1861; Mon-Sat 10am-5pm, Sun 1pm-5pm; museum $4, home $2, 232-8206. _www.stjoseph.net/ponyexpress._

The telephone area code is 816.

BRANSON   A postcard from Branson jokingly quips, 'Would the last one leaving Nashville for Branson please turn off the light?' Much of Branson (like this postcard) is a little bit corny, but it's spot-on. Branson proclaims itself the live entertainment capital of America. With nearly 50 theatres hosting over 100 shows, Branson has more theatre seats than Broadway – and has more on the way. While Branson was originally touted as a country music mecca, the entertainers also dazzle you with comedy, dance and magic. Branson is proud of its image as a source of wholesome family entertainment; its location in the heart of the beautiful Ozark Mountain region supports this claim with camping and outdoors activities for all ages. The shows are many and varied, but perennial favourites include the **Andy Williams Moon River Theatre**, 2500 W 76 Hwy, 334-4500, _www.andywilliams.com_, the **Jim Stafford Theatre**, 3440 W 76 Hwy, 335-8080, _www.jimstafford.com_, and the **Shoji Tabuchi Theatre**, 3260 Shepherd of the Hills Expy, 334-7469, _www.shoji.com_. Stop at Shoji's to use the bathrooms! They're like nothing you've ever seen. Also check the new **Branson Landing**, with its mile+ long boardwalk and nightly water shows. Show tickets can be pricey—look for discounts at tourist info centres and ticket outlets scattered around town.

In addition to live entertainment, Branson has great shopping. Leading names such as Ralph Lauren, the Gap, and J Crew have set up shop in 3 outlet malls, two located conveniently off Hwy 76 and the third off Gretna Rd, Branson Meadows. (Beware the main drag during the summer months, though, when traffic clogs the strip, making it impossible to get anywhere).

Branson has capitalised on the natural splendour of the Ozarks and the lively history of its pioneer past. **Silver Dollar City**, Hwy 76 at Indian Point Rd, (800) 952-6626, is a theme park staged in pioneer days. Daily 9.30am-7pm, $41 (look for discount coupons and promotions at ticket outlets). Also included in the admission price to Silver Dollar City is an hour-long tour of **Marvel Cave**, a geological wonder upon which the theme park was built. The cave is so large, hot air balloons have been used to ascend it; ordinary visitors use a cable car (326m) to rise to the top. Journeying down into the cave is not for the weak—you'll have to climb down about 600 steps! *www.bransonsilverdollarcity.com*.

Celebration City is a $40m theme park centered around the '90s, with 20 rides, fireworks and laser displays each night. It is affiliated with SDC and about 5miles away. A great nightspot as it opens 3pm-10pm daily. $27. Combo tkt available for $62, incl. 2 day pass for both parks.

One of the Ozarks' most popular attractions is **Lambert's**, 1800 W Hwy J, Ozark, 581-7655, a fun restaurant located north of Branson on Hwy 65, about 10 miles south of Springfield. Lambert's is the home of the 'throwed rolls'; as you're munching on mammoth-sized portions of country favourites, waiters toss soft, piping hot rolls to hungry diners. *www.throwedrolls.com*. Also check out *www.explorebranson.com.*

The telephone area code is 417.

CAVES Missouri has more known caves than any other state, many with guided tours to keep you from getting lost and driving up the owners' insurance premiums. For more information, write **Missouri Division of Tourism**, PO Box 1055, Jefferson City, MO 65101, or call (573) 751-4133, *www.missouritourism.org*. Some examples: **Bluff Dwellers' Cave**, two miles S of Noel, (417) 475-3666. A 45 minute tour includes stalactite curtains, corals, 10-ton balanced rock, as well as a 54-foot limestone dam. Open daily 8am-6pm; $10, includes museum. Check out *www.4noel.com/bluffd/bluffd1.htm* **Fantastic Caverns**, 4872 N Farm Rd, 4 miles N of Springfield, (417) 833-2010. They are as good as their name implies, and you don't even have to walk! Jeep-drawn trams transport visitors through the caves in modern comfort. Open daily (May-Aug) 8am-8pm; $17.50, *www.fantastic-caverns.com*

Meramec Caverns, Stanton, I-44 exit 230, Hwy W, (573) 468-3166, is one of the largest caves in the state. Rich in history: a hideout for Jesse James and once a station on the Underground Railroad. '1¹/₂ hr tour, lots of stunning formations in calcite and onyx including a very large botryoidal formation and 70 ft high stalactite; $14, well worth it!' Open daily 8.30am-7.30pm. *www.americascave.com* For in-depth details about each state park, check the official state parks listing at *www.mostateparks.com.*

NEBRASKA - The Cornhusker State

A huge, tilting plate of a state, it rises from 840 ft at its Missouri River eastern border to nearly 5000 ft as it approaches the Rockies. Through it runs the feeble Platte River, 'a mile wide, a foot deep, too thick to swim and too thin to plow', along which countless buffalo roamed until they were sought after by kill-crazy Buffalo Bills. As shallow as six inches in places, the Platte nonetheless made an excellent 'highway' and water supply for the 2.5 million folks who crossed Nebraska in Conestoga wagons, 1840-66. Even today, the most worthwhile things to see in the state are those connected with the pioneer trails west.

There's poetry in these plains, though. Willa Cather, one of the most skillful wordsmiths of the pioneer days used south central Nebraska as the backdrop for many of her works. Six of her twelve novels and many of her short stories are staged in Red Cloud and Webster County, where she spent her formative years. Cather recognised the beauty in the land around her: 'as I looked about me I felt that the grass was the country, as the water is the sea. The red grass made all the great prairie the colour of wine stains. And there was so much motion in it; the whole country seemed, somehow, to be running.'

Like the other plains states, Nebraska has perfectly miserable weather in the summer and winter. Its speciality is hailstones, which occasionally reach the size of golf balls. A leading producer of beef cattle, TV dinners and popcorn, Nebraska specialises in silos of both the grain and ICBM missile variety. _www.visitnebraska.org_.

OMAHA Once a jumping-off place for pioneers, Omaha is the Union Pacific train headquarters and has taken over the noisome title of 'meat packer for the world' from Chicago, although the once booming stockyards have long since moved to rural areas. Friendly, yes, but about as lively at night as a hog carcass, except around Old Market.

Hometown of Fred Astaire, Marlon Brando, Warren Buffett (the second-richest man in the US, behind Bill Gates), Montgomery Clift, Nick Nolte and Malcolm X, Omaha is the place where Father Flanagan started **Boys Town**, a home for troubled youth later immortalised by a Spencer Tracy movie of the same name. On a not-so-philanthropic note, it's also the underground **Strategic Air Command** (SAC) headquarters. A collection of aerial photos of Omaha, Omaha links and a photo map can be accessed through _www.novia.net/~sadams/Omaha_Pages/OMA_Pics.html_. Well worth it! Also, for more details: _www.visitomaha.com_, or call (866) YES-OMAHA.

The telephone area code is 402.

Accommodation
Ak-sar-ben Super 8, 7111 Spring St, 390-0700. Queen bed for 1 or 2 persons, $68. Astute readers will notice the name spells 'Nebraska' backwards.
The Bellevue Campground, Haworth Park, 291-3379, on the Missouri River 10 miles S of downtown at Rt 370. Use the infrequent 'Bellevue' bus from 17th and Dodge to Mission and Franklin, and walk down Mission. Camp sites-$7 tent, $15 RV w/hook-up.
Motel 6, 10708 M St, 331-3161. D-$46.
Satellite Motel, 6006 L St, 733-7373. D-$50. Rooms have microwave, fridge, TV and video.

Food/Entertainment
Try the cobbled streets of the **Old Market**, on Howard St, btwn 10th & 13th Sts. Has over 100 shops, and 30 restaurants and bars maintaining the ambience of 19th century Omaha.
Bohemian Cafe, 1406 S 13th St, 342-9838. 'Czech food and atmosphere—the duck is superb.' Also serves American food; imported Czech beer. Lunches start $5.75, dinners $8.50-$10. Daily 11am-9pm.
Delice European Bakery, 1206 Howard, 342-2276, a great place for dessert! Open Mon-Thu 7.30am-9pm, Fri-Sat 'til 11pm, Sun 'til 6pm.
The Diner, 409 S 12th St, 341-9870. True diner experience, lunch specials for under $6. Open Mon-Sat 6am-4pm, noon-3pm Sun.
The Dubliner, 1205 Harney St, 342-5887. Shoot electronic darts. 150 imported beers. Food available. Live Irish music at weekends, cover $2-$5. Open daily 11am-1am (lunch served 11am-2pm).

Johnny's Cafe, 4702 S 27th St, 731-4774. Omaha stockyard's steak house for three-quarters of a century. Every cut of steak available. Open Mon-Sat for lunch, 11am-2pm, for dinner Mon-Thu 5pm-10pm, 'til 10.30pm Fri-Sat.

Of interest
Boys Town, 137th St and W Dodge Rd, 498-1140. Founded in 1917 by Father Flanagan, this home for troubled youth is now a historic landmark. Includes Hall of History, featuring Spencer Tracy's Oscar from 1938 portrayal of Flanagan, as well as stamp and coin museum. 'Very interesting.' May-Aug: tours daily 8am-5pm; $1 guided tour, $2 audio tour. www.girlsandboystown.org.

General Crook House, 30th & Fort, 455-9990, the Italianate mansion of a Civil War and National Indian Wars hero. Also has beautiful Victorian gardens on the site of Fort Omaha; built in 1879 by the outpost's first commander. Mon-Fri 10am-4pm, w/end 1pm-4pm, $5, students $4. omahahistory.org./museum.htm.

Henry Doorly Zoo, 10th and Dear Park Blvd, 733-8400. Contains rare white Bengal tigers and a $4^1/_2$ acre aviary, the world's second largest; 'Lied Jungle', a simulated tropical rain forest with the accompanying wildlife; and an IMAX Theatre. Mon-Sat 9.30am-5pm. Visitors can remain in the park until dusk; $10.25 entrance, $8.25 IMAX tkts. www.omahazoo.com.

Joslyn Art Museum, 2200 Dodge St, 342-3300. Housed in Art Deco building, Indian and other art; pictures painted during the Maximillian Expedition up the Missouri River in 1833-4 are worth seeing. Free '**Jazz on the Green**' Thu eves in July & August. Open Tue-Sat 10am-4pm, Sun noon-4pm; $6, $4 w/ student ID. Free on Sat 10am-noon. www.joslyn.org.

Old Market, 10th & Howard. Cobbled streets, warehouses recycled into smart shops, galleries, restaurants. 'Most interesting place in Omaha.' See where oft eulogised and misrepresented black leader **Malcolm X**—*née* Malcolm Little—was born, 3448 Pinkey St. Then see the wider picture, **Great Plains Black Museum,** 24th & Lake St, has extensive exhibits on the black experience, including profiles of black cowboys, athletes and soldiers; as well as exhibits featuring the underground railroad. Summer: Mon-Fri 9am-5pm. Free. 320-5105.

Orpheum Theater, 409 S 16th St, 444-4750. 1927 vintage theatre featuring concerts, ballet, plays. Box office open Mon-Fri 10am-5.30pm.

Strategic Air & Space Museum, Exit 426 off of I-80, Ashland (between Omaha and Lincoln), 944-3100. Bombers, missiles, a *red phone* (hear the end of the world!) and the SR-71 Blackbird, the world's fastest plane. 'Nuclear nightmare at its *finest*! A must-see!' Also shows films in the 250 seat theatre. Daily 9am-5pm, $7. www.strategicairandspace.com.

Western Heritage Museum, 801 S 10th St, 444-5071. Housed in the wonderful Art Deco old Union Station, worth a look in itself, this museum has displays on Omaha and Nebraska history. Tue-Sat 10am-5pm, Sun 1pm-5pm; $6. www.dwhm.org.

Information/Travel
Nebraska Tourist Information, (800) 228-4307.

Student Center, U of Nebraska, 60th and Dodge St, Milo Bail Building 2nd fl, 554-2383. Helpful with accommodation, general info. Mon-Fri 7.30am-4.30pm.

Greater Omaha Convention and Visitors Bureau, 1001 Farnam St, #200, (800) 332-1819. Mon-Fri 8am-4.30pm.

Amtrak, 1003 S 9th St, (800) 872-7245.

Greyhound, 16th & Jackson, 341-1906/(800) 231-2222.

Internet access
Omaha Public Library, 215 S 15th St, 444-4800. Free access, 30 min limit. Mon-Wed, 9am-8pm, Fri-Sat 'til 6pm, Sun 1pm-6pm. www.omaha.lib.ne.us.

LINCOLN The **Nebraska State Capitol Building** dominates this cow town and its many miles of surrounding plains. This is home of the Unicameral, Nebraska's unique one-house, non-partisan legislative body—an improvisation made during the Depression to save money.

The capitol, 'Tower on the Plains', was not blown in by tornado, despite what its incongruent appearance may suggest, but architect Bertram Goodhue did come all the way from New York City in 1920 to design this early 'skyscraper'. The broad base of the building represents the plains; the tower, the aspirations of the pioneers.

Lincoln was home to **William Jennings Bryan**, a turn-of-the-century populist who three times was the Democratic Party's presidential candidate and finally made a monkey of himself at the notorious Scopes Trial in Tennessee. His house stands at 4900 Summer Street. For a virtual tour of downtown Lincoln, visit _http://db.4w.com./lincolntour_.

The telephone area code is 402.

Accommodation
Visit the **Nebraska Association of B&Bs** at _www.bbonline.com/ne/nabb_.
HI-USA, 640 N 16th St, on U of Nebraska campus, 476-0926. Dorm-$10 AYH, $13 non AYH. Check in by 11pm. Kitchen facs, linens incl. _www.hiusa.org/usa-hostels_
The Great Plains Budget Host Inn, 2732 O St, 476-3253. Rooms $37-42, mention student status and BUNAC guide for discount. Large rooms w/small fridge, TV.
The Town House Motel, 1744 M St at 18th, 475-3000. S-$50, D-$55. Super-suites with full kitchen, living room, TV, b/fast incl. _www.townhouseminisuites.com._
Camping: Nebraska State Fair Park Campground, Exit 399, 2400 N 14th St, 473-4287. Apr-Oct. Sites $18 for two w/hook-up. _www.statefair.org_. **Camp-A-Way,** 1st & W Superior, Exits 401 & 401-A, 200 Ogden Rd, 476-2282. Open year round. Tent sites $15, RVs $23.50-$29.50 full hook/up. All with cable TV. _www.campaway.com._
Cheap motels abound on **Cornhusker Hwy,** around the 5600 block (E of downtown).

Food
The Coffee House, 1324 P St, 477-6611, is a favourite hangout for locals. Muffins and bagels from $1.25. One of the few cafes in the area with a smoking section. Internet access $3/hr – if you make a purchase of $3 or more you receive 1 hr free! Mon-Sat 6.30am-midnight, Sun 8am-midnight.
P.O. Pears, 322 S 9th St, 476-8551. A college hangout with cheap beer, good burgers, and live music at the w/end. Open daily11am-1am. _www.popears.com._
Valentino's. Local pizza place, 2710 S 70th St, 437-9177. Buffet dinner available $8.50 pp. Daily 11am-9pm, Fri-Sat 'til 9.30pm. _www.valentinos.com._

Of interest
Sheldon Memorial Art Gallery, 12th and R St, 472-2461. Houses a fine collection of 20th century American art and sculpture garden. Tue-Sat 10am-5pm, Fri 'til 8pm, Sun noon-5pm, free. _www.sheldonartgallery.org_.
State Capitol, located at 15th & K St, 471-0448. Art Deco style with a little of everything inside. Mon-Fri 9am-4pm, Sat 10am-4pm, Sun 1pm-4pm; guided tours on the hour (every hr w/days in summer). Free. _www.capitol.org_.

Entertainment
Stroll around the restored 19th century commercial buildings in historic **Haymarket Square District,** between 7th and P St, to 9th and Q St, 435-7496. Today they're home to galleries, restaurants, unique shops, and antiques. _www.historichaymarket.com._
There are several nightspots in Lincoln, among them the notorious **Barry's Bar and**

Grill, Corner of 9th and Q St, 476-6511. Mon-Sat 11am-1am, food service 'til 10pm.
Panic Bar, 2005 18th St, 435-8764, is a great gay dance/video/patio bar. Daily 4pm-1am, Sat from 1pm.
Chocolate Lover's Fantasy, Holiday Inn, 9th & P St. This festive event features Lincoln celebrities, chefs, and fabulous chocolate in every form with a live and silent auction every February. 434-6900.
Jazz in June, Sheldon Sculpture Garden, 12th and R St. Free outdoor concerts with well known jazz musicians each Tue in June, 7pm-9pm. For good seats go early and take a blanket! *www.jazzinjune.com.*

Information/Travel
Lincoln Convention and Visitors Bureau, 1135 M St, 3rd fl, 434-5335. Open daily. *www.lincoln.org.*
Tourist Information Centre, 301 Centennial Mall S, 4th fl, 471-3796. Mon-Fri 8am-5pm. *www.visitnebraska.org.*
Amtrak, 201 N 7th, 476-1295/(800) 872-7245.
Greyhound, 940 P St, 474-1071/(800) 231-2222.

Internet access
Bennett Martin Library, 136 S 14th St, 441-8500. Free access, 45 min limit. Lab open: Mon-Thu 10am-8.45pm, Fri-Sat 10am-5.45pm, Sun 1.30pm-5.15pm. *www.ci.lincoln.ne.us/city/library/index.htm.*

ALONG THE PIONEER AND PONY EXPRESS TRAILS
The Oregon, Mormon and other pioneer trails plus the Pony Express routes followed the Platte River, which today is paralleled in large part by I-80 and by Hwys 30 E and 26 W.

The land outside of Omaha lies flat and is covered with farms. If you like corn, you'll be in heaven here. Two and a half hours west from Omaha, in the town of **Grand Island** on Hwy 34, is the **Stuhr Museum of the Prairie Pioneer,** (308) 385-5316, a 200 acre 1890s frontier village often used in Hollywood western sets. Daily 9am-5pm, Sun from noon. $8. *www.stuhrmuseum.org.*

Sixty miles south of Grand Island and 6 miles north of the Kansas border is the town of **Red Cloud.** *www.redcloudnebraska.com.* Home of Pulitzer prize-winning author Willa Cather, who deftly chronicled frontier life in her books, *O Pioneers!* and *My Antonia,* among others. The small town of 1200 people boasts 26 sites in the historic district. The Nebraska State Legislature dubbed the western half of Webster County, 14 miles north of Red Cloud, 'Catherland' in 1965. It's one of the largest historical districts dedicated to an author in the United States. An inscription at the **Willa Cather Pioneer Memorial** quotes the author: 'The history of every country begins in the heart of a man or a woman.' Guided tours explore 7 restored buildings, including Cather's childhood home. Mon-Sat 9.30am, 11am, 1.30pm, 3pm, tours last 1 hr 15 min; prices vary. Also self-guided walking and driving tours. Call (402) 746-2653 or visit *www.willacather.org.*

Going east to west: at **Gothenburg,** midstate, you can see two original **Pony Express** stations: one in Ehman Park (308) 537-2143 and the other is located at lower 96 Ranch on the Oregon Trail, 4 miles south of Gothenburg, and an old stagecoach stop with bullet holes still in the walls. An interesting website to check is *www.trailsandgrasslands.org* for info on planning prairie expeditions. At **Lafayette Park,** 314 27th St, (308) 537-2299, tent sites are $10, campers $15. **North Platte**, long-time home of scout and show biz personality, **Buffalo Bill Cody**, offers a free look at his ranch house—a pretty but prissy-looking Victorian affair, $2.50 per vehicle entrance fee, (308) 535-8035. Open daily, 9am-5pm. B Bill got his nickname for killing 4280 buffalo in 8 months while employed by the railroad to supply meat for its crews. _www.northplatte-tourism.com._

Travelling west to **Bayard**, the **Oregon Trail Wagon Train Company** offers one- and four-day treks that circle **Chimney Rock**. Meals (including pioneer items like vinegar pie and hoecakes), wagon driving or riding, and other activities from an Indian 'attack' to prairie square-dancing for about $200 a day. They also do three hour covered wagon tours to Chimney Rock and back, for $15 pp (min 5 people); leaving at 8.30am, returning 11am. Evening cookouts are also available, $19. Book through Oregon Trail Wagon Train, Rt 2 Box 502, Bayard, NE 69334 or call (308) 586-1850. _www.oregontrailwagontrain.com._

Scottsbluff and **Chimney Rock**, off Hwy 92 and 21 miles apart, in western Nebraska, are two rock formations that served as landmarks for the frontier families. Only **Scottsbluff** with pioneer graves and defined wagon ruts is climbable. The park rangers at Scottsbluff give daily lectures in summer and the pioneer campsite can be visited. Spectacular views. $5 vehicle fee, summer hours 8am-7pm. _www.nps.gov/scbl_. The visitor centre at the **Chimney Rock National Historic Site**, (308) 586-2581, houses museum exhibits, including the original maps from Captain Fremont's 1842-43 exploration of the Oregon Trail. Daily 9am-5pm, $3. _www.nps.gov/chro_. For accommodation, try **Lamplighter America Inn**, 606 E 7th St, (308) 632-7108. 2 miles from Scottsbluff Monument. Rooms $32-38, indoor pool and breakfast is included.

Box Butte County, Alliance, in the Nebraska panhandle offers one of the most unique sights you'll see on your trek across America. It's home to **Carhenge**, NE Hwy 87, (308) 762-1520 _www.carhenge.com_, in which stones are replaced by 1950s and 60s automobiles, planted in the ground trunk down. The result: a circle of cars with almost the same dimensions as the 4000 year old British model. J Reinders, the genius behind this attraction that draws 40,000 visitors annually, used cars because there aren't any stones in the area. Open daily, free. If you journey out to Box Butte County for a taste of synthetic Britain, take time for a taste of real America. The **Knight Museum**, 908 Yellowstone Ave, (308) 762-2384, contains Native American, Pioneer and area history. It also features an authentic one-room schoolhouse. May-Sept: Mon-Sat 10am-6pm, Sun 1pm-5pm. Free.

For more information on historic sites, visit _www.nebraskahistory.org_.

NORTH DAKOTA - Peace Garden State

Virtually border to border farmland, interspersed with missile sites, North Dakota grows lots of spring wheat, sugar beets and cattle. There are no notable national monuments to make you rush here although it does have the world's largest concrete buffalo (in Jamestown), concrete Holstein (in New Salem) and steel turtle with movable head (40,000 lbs in Dunseith). Not to mention the longest road without a curve—110 miles of tedium on

Rte 46. The fertile east is more densely populated than the west, first settled by the land-hungry Europeans who capitalised on the Homestead Act, 1862. It's also the east that bore the brunt of the damage of the horrific 1997 flood: 1.7 million acres of farmland were devastated, and the whole state was declared a disaster area.

The Badlands of North Dakota aren't as well known as their counterparts in South Dakota, but they are strikingly beautiful, with hills and valleys interspersed amongst the dusty rocks. Teddy Roosevelt owned a ranch out here before he entered political life, sparking his lifelong interest and commitment to environmental issues. 'I never would have been president,' he said, 'if it had not been for my experiences in North Dakota.' Roosevelt is remembered with a national park that bears his name and honours his memory. *www.ndtourism.com.The telephone area code for the state is 701.*

BISMARCK The Missouri river separates Bismarck from its sister city, Mandan, named after the Mantani Indians, meaning 'people of the bank'. The capital city's name was originally Edwinton, later changed to Bismarck by the secretary of the Northern Pacific Railroad who had a plan to secure Deutschmarks from Otto von B to finance railroad construction and attract Teutonic settlers. The first part was successful, the latter was not, and the name stuck. Bismarck overcame an early period of lawlessness and a major fire to become the state capital. *www.bismarck-mandancvb.org.*

Accommodation
AmericInn, 3235 State St, 250-1000. S-$60, D-$70, bfast included.
Expressway Inn, 200 E. Bismarck Expy, 222-3311, average room $50.

Of interest
State Capitol Building, 600 E Boulevard Ave, 328-2480, also known as the 'skyscraper on the prairie'. Famous sons and daughters in the Rough Rider gallery: Eric Sevareid, Peggy Lee, Lawrence Welk, Roger Maris. Take the elevator to the 19th floor to the observation deck and see for miles and miles over the prairies. 1 hr tours begin on the hour: Mon-Fri 8am-11am, 1pm-4pm; Sat 9am-11am, 1-4pm; Sun 1-4pm; free.
North Dakota Heritage Center (on Capitol grounds), 328-2666, has an Indian collection called one of the finest in the world. Many personal effects of Sitting Bull. Not to be missed: the Indian crafts store—outstanding and authentic artefacts for sale. Mon-Fri 8am-5pm, Sat 9am-5pm, Sun 11am-5pm, free. *www.state.nd.us/hist.*
United Tribes International Pow Wow, 3315 University Drive, 255-3285 ext. 293. Held at the United Tribes Technical College in early Sept. Premier cultural event of North Dakota. Represents over 70 tribes and features over 1500 dancers, drummers, and 20,000 spectators! A must see event. $15 Thu-Sun or $8 per day. *www.unitedtribespowwow.com.* Other events take place sporadically at Indian reservations; check with tribal offices at Ft Totten, Turtle Mountain and others.

Information/Travel
Bismarck Convention & Visitors Bureau, 1600 Burnt Boat Drive, 222-4308; Open Mon-Fri 7.30am-7pm, Sat 8am-6pm, Sun 9am-5pm.
North Dakota Tourism Dept, Century Center, 1600 E Century Ave, Suite 2, Bismarck, (800) 435-5663. Open Mon-Fri 8am-5pm. *www.ndtourism.com.*
Amtrak, 400 1st Ave SW, Minot, 852-0358/(800) 872-7245. Nearest station to Bismarck is on the *Empire Builder* Chicago-Seattle route.
Greyhound, 3750 E Rosser Ave, 223-6576/(800) 231-2222.

Internet access
Bismarck Public Library, 515 N 5th St, 222-6410. Free access, 1 hr limit, first-come, first-served. Mon-Thu 9am-9pm, Fri-Sat 'til 6pm, Sun 1pm-6pm. *www.bismarcklibrary.org*.

LEWIS AND CLARK TRAIL By auto or on foot, you can retrace the explorers' route of 1804-05 south along the Missouri River from Wood River, Illinois. Points of interest include: **Ft Yates** (Sioux national headquarters), **Ft Lincoln** (from which Custer and the 7th Cavalry rode to their destiny at Little Bighorn), **Ft Mandan** (where the French Canadian trader Charbonneau and his 15-year old Shoshone wife Sacagawea were hired as guides by Lewis and Clark in the winter of 1804-05), **Knife River Indian Village**, and **Sitting Bull Historic Site**, where the leader was originally buried on the Western edge of Ft Yates, 1890.

Well-located and affordable accommodation can be found at **Missouri River Lodge**, approx 6.8 miles N of Knife River Indian Village, between Forts Clark and Mandan, (877) 480-3498. *www.moriverlodge.com.* Check out *www.lewisandclarktrail.com* which takes you through the landmarks in their journey, with suggestions on what to see along the way. Before taking the trail, be sure to read *Undaunted Courage* by Stephen E Ambrose, for a breathtaking account of the momentous expedition.

BADLANDS AND ROOSEVELT NATIONAL PARK Called 'mako sica' (land bad) by the Sioux and 'les mauvais terres a traverser' by French settlers, the Badlands have been forming for over 600,000 years, largely due to erosion by the Little Missouri River. Described as 'grand, dismal and majestic', the Badlands formations are best seen in early morning and late afternoon. The south unit near **Medora** has a 36-mile loop with scenic overlooks. You can catch a glimpse of wild ponies, descendants of those who galloped about the rough terrain in the days of Sitting Bull. You'll also see herds of buffalo and families of prairie dogs, oblivious to the tourist's gaze.

The **Theodore Roosevelt National Park** honours the president's commitment to wildlife preservation. Concerned by the effects of development on the environment, he started the US Forest Service to monitor the destruction of grasslands and big game species. Compared to the other western National Parks, it's refreshingly low in tourists. Teddy's **Elkhorn Ranch** is very remote; the ranch ultimately showed a net loss of $21,000 but he loved the area, saying: 'I owe more than I can ever express to the men and women of the cow country'. No buildings remain, but the ranch site is located 20 miles up a dirt road, north of the south unit. Call for directions. Spend the night in the campground at **Cottonwood,** five miles from the park entrance; first-come first-served basis, no hook up or showers, sites $10. For park and campground information call 623-4466/842-2333, or visit *www.nps.gov/thro/home.htm*. You could also try **Sully Creek Campground,** three miles S of Medora: 'Primitive, can get cold but very convenient to Roosevelt if one has a car.'

INTERNATIONAL PEACE GARDENS On the US/Canadian border—the world's longest non-fortified border. The formal gardens commemorate years of peace between the countries. Enter via **Dunseith**. Front gate open 24 hours; $10 per vehicle. Call (701) 263-4390/(800) 432-6733 *www.peacegarden.org*.

OHIO - The Buckeye State

Ohio makes everything and more of it than anybody else: comic books, coffins, Liederkranz cheese, bank vaults, vacuums, false teeth, playing cards, rubber, jet turbine engines, soap, glassware—you name it. Small wonder that Ohio also produced America's first billionaire: John D Rockefeller. They're always tinkering in Ohio, the birthplace of the cash register, the fly swatter, the menthol cigarette and the beer can, not to mention one of the Wright brothers, Thomas Edison, John Glenn (the first astronaut to orbit the earth) and Neil Armstrong.

Get out of its highly industrialised cities and you'll discover a surprising amount of green and gentle countryside, full of lakes, wineries (85 of them, *www.ohiowines.org*), farms with roadside produce and local colour from Amish villages. Ohio also houses a fair share of oddities like Hinckley, the buzzard capital of the world (where you can satisfy that craving for a buzzard cookie). Sinclair Lewis used Ohio as his model setting for small-town America in *Babbitt*, a novel written in 1922 about a businessman whose individuality is eliminated by Republican pressures to conform.

The state also has some of America's best roller coasters and amusement parks, one of the largest state fairs in the US, over 1000 festivals (including Twinsday at Twinsburg) and is the birthplace of eight presidents. *www.discoverohio.com.*

CINCINNATI Unique in being a village that grew to cityhood on steamboat traffic, the Queen City of the West is also unique in having formerly elected Jerry Springer mayor (true to form, Springer thought the town was too polite)! The dual nature of Cincinnati—one of utility and burlesque—is part of its history as a port town. As many as 8000 boats a year docked at Cincinnati to take on passengers, lightning rods and lacy 'French' ironwork destined for New Orleans bordellos.

Valued for their transportation capacity, steamboats also provided a few less practical thrills... They were raced incessantly, causing huge sums of money to change hands and equally astonishing losses of life; in one five-year period, 2268 people died in steamboat explosions. Settled by Germans, the 'City of Seven Hills' became a leading producer of machine tools, Ivory soap, beer, gin and a variety of ham favoured by Queen Victoria, all without losing its liveable, likeable essence. Check out Cincinnati events such as the **Oktoberfest Zinzinnati** (Sept) and the **Queen City Blues Festival** (July) at *www.cincyusa.com.*

The telephone area code is 513.

Accommodation
Ramada Inn, 800 West St, 241-8660, $69-S/D.
Howard Johnson Inn, 5410 Ridge Ave, 631-8500, D-$47.
Camping: Cedarbrook, 760 Franklin Rd, btwn Cincinnati and Dayton in Lebanon, 932-7717, sites $22-$28. Visit *www.cedarbrookcampground.com.* for more details. Also, **Cincinnati South** KOA, I-75 exit 166, (859) 428-2000, 30 miles N of Cincinnati. Tent

sites $20 (primitive), $25 for two w/hook-up, cabins $35 w/hook-up (4 people max), www.koa.com.

Food

Cincinnati's Germanic tradition means it has a number of beer gardens. It's also noted for chili, served '3-, 4- or 5-way'; e.g. with spaghetti, beans, meat, onions, Cheddar cheese. Chili parlours abound, each with a secret recipe, although it's accepted that they all contain cinnamon. Cincinnatians eat more than 2 million pounds of chili each year, topped by 850,000 pounds of shredded cheddar cheese! During the last w/end in July you can sample a variety of chili, while enjoying a host of entertainment and music, at the **Annual Gold Star Chili Fest**, Yeatman's Cove along the Ohio River, free.

Camp Washington Chili, 3005 Colerain Ave, 541-8804. 'Prime source of 5-way Cincinnati-style chili: thick, spicy meat sauce atop a bed of plump spaghetti, garnished with beans, shredded cheese and chopped onions.' Small bowls $2.70, medium $4.20, large $8.05. Open 11am-11pm Mon-Thu, 11 am-midnight Fri-Sat, 4pm-1-pm Sun.

Gold Star Chili, 8467 Beachmont Ave, 474-4916/(800) 643-0465 and several other locations. Open Mon-Sat 10am-11pm, Sun 11am-10pm. www.goldstarchili.com.

Graeter's, 332 Ludlow Ave, 281-4749 and several other locations, is the locals' ice cream of choice. www.graeters.com.

Izzy's, 800 Elm St, 721-4241. A Cincinnati tradition, known for its corned beef sandwiches ($5.95) and potato pancakes ($1.75). Open Mon-Fri 8 am-8pm, Sat 10am-5pm. www.izzys.com.

For ribs, chicken, Saratoga chips, or anything covered in Montgomery Inn BBQ sauce, take a trip to the **Montgomery Inn,** 9440 Montgomery Rd, 791-3482. Open for lunch Mon-Fri 11am-3pm, dinner Sun 3pm-9:30pm, Mon-Thu 3pm-11pm, Fri and Sat 3pm-midnight. www.montgomeryinn.com.

Findlay Market, 1801 Race St, 665-4839. Produce and picnic items. Wed-Fri 8am-6pm, Sat 6am-6 pm, Sun 11am-4pm.

Of interest

The Beach, 2590 Water Park Dr in Mason, 20 miles N of Cincinnati (on I-71), 398-7946/(800) 886-7946. One of the ten largest water parks in the US with 40,000 sq ft area of white sand and over 40 rides, a 25,000 sq ft wave pool, as well as speed, giant inner-tube and body slides. May-June daily 10am-7pm, June-Aug 'til 9pm, Aug-Sept 'til 7pm; $26.99. www.thebeachwaterpark.com.

Carew Tower, 241-3888, 5th and Vine Sts. 48 story Art Deco building is Cincinnati's tallest building. Built in only 15 months during the Great Depression. From the 48th floor, take a gander at Cincinnati, the Ohio River and Kentucky opposite. Open Mon-Thu 9:30am-5:30pm, Fri-Sat 9:30am-9pm, Sun 11am-5pm, $2 admission to the 48th floor.

Cincinnati Art Museum, 953 Eden Park Dr, 721-5204. Open Tue-Sun 11am-5pm, Wed 'til 9pm, free. www.cincinnatiartmuseum.org.

Cincinnati Zoo & Botanical Garden, 3400 Vine St, 281-4700/(800) 94-HIPPO. Called 'the sexiest zoo in the US' for its successful breeding programme: lots of gorillas, elephants and an insectarium. 'Opened in 1875 and features over 700 different animal species and 3000 types of plants.' Now open: 'Wolf Woods', featuring a pair of Mexican gray wolves, the most endangered subspecies in N. America. Daily 9am-6pm, grounds close 7pm, $12.95. www.cincyzoo.org.

Contemporary Arts Center, 44 E 6th St, 721-0390, Mon 10am- 9pm, Wed-Fri 'til 6, Sat-Sun 11am-6pm. $7.50, $5.50 w/student ID. Exhibitions of 'cutting edge' contemporary art. www.contemporaryartscenter.org.

Krohn Conservatory, 1501 Eden Park Dr, 421-4080. One of the largest public greenhouses in the world, with over 1000 plant species. Seasonal floral displays. Daily 10am-5pm, donations encouraged. _www.cincinnati-oh.gov_.

Meier's Winecellars, 6955 Plainfield Pike, 891-2900/(800) 346-2941. Ohio's oldest and largest winery. Free video presentations about wine making and wine ageing, wine tasting $1. Tue-Sat 9am-5pm.

Newport Aquarium, just over the bridge in Newport, KY, (859) 491-346/(800) 406-3474. View 11,000 exotic creatures from around the world; underwater tunnels take you closer to sharks and other marine life; first showing of shark ray in the western hemisphere. Open daily 10am-7pm (last tkts sold at 5.30pm), $17.95. _www.newportaquarium.com._

Paramount's Kings Island, in Mason, off I-71 (exit 24), 754-5700/(800) 288-0808. The Midwest's largest and often busiest theme park contains the world's longest wooden coaster, 'The Beast'. Its successor, 'Son of Beast', stands as the tallest, fastest and only looping wooden roller coaster in the world. Over 100 rides and live shows, including 13 roller coasters, and the new 'Italian Job' stunt track. Admission to **WaterWorks**, the adjoining waterpark, is included with regular park admission ticket. Fireworks nightly (10pm or 11pm on Sat). 'The park is accessible via the Metro 71 and 72 bus from downtown Cincinnati. Two schedules in the morning, one in the afternoon.' Open Sun-Fri, 9am-10pm, Sat 'til 11pm (Memorial Day-Labor Day); $34.99. WaterWorks open daily Mon-Thu and Sun 11am-7pm, Fri-Sat 'til 8pm. _www.pki.com._

Taft Museum of Art, 316 Pike St, 241-0343. This Federal 1820 mansion houses collection of paintings (including Rembrandt and Whistler), Chinese porcelains, French enamel and portraits. 'Exquisite.' Open Tue, Wed and Fri 11am-5pm, Thu 'til 8pm, Sat 10am-5pm and Sun noon-5pm. $7, $5 w/student ID. _www.taftmuseum.org_.

The National Underground Railroad Freedom Center, 50 E Freedom Way, along the Cincinnati riverfront (513) 333-7500. $12, $10 w student ID. Tue-Sun 11am-5pm. Shows the plight of thousands of slaves through a range of exhibits, interactive media and live performances. For information, visit _www.freedomcenter.org_.

Tyler Davidson Fountain Square. The centre of downtown activity is around here. Free lunch-time concerts, pre and post-ballgame celebrations, shops and businesses.

Union Terminal, 1301 Western Ave, 287-7000/(800) 733-2077. An Art Deco gem with the world's highest unsupported dome that now houses the 'Museum Center', comprised of the **Museum of Natural History** where a cavern full of bats and the Ice Age (simulated) awaits; the **Cincinnati Historical Society** has a mock-up of a 1860s street to wander in; finally, pop over to the Omnimax to see those films on the big screen; $6.75. Museums open Mon-Sat 10am-5pm, Sun 11am-6pm; to one museum $7.25, to two $10.25 and for everything $13.25 (inc. Omnimax). Call to check Omnimax show times. _www.cincymuseum.org_.

Riverboats breeze past the public landing at the foot of Broadway. The revitalised riverfront area invites you to watch the boats from the Serpentine Wall. Cruises are generally heavily booked and rather pricey, but you can take in arrivals, departures and attendant hoopla and steam calliope-playing for free.

Cincinnati is home base of the _Delta Queen_, a genuine relic on the National Register of Historic Landmarks. This is an authentic paddlewheeler, not merely one of the ignoble beasties that ply the waters in hundreds of US cities and towns. _Showboat Majestic_, 241-6550, also docks here, with live theatre nightly (Wed-Sat 8pm, Sun 2pm and 7pm); $15, $14 w/student ID, _www.cincinnatilandmarkproductions.com/sbm_. On the Covington, KY, side is the _Mike Fink_, Greenup St, (859) 261-4212, a riverboat restaurant with a delectable New Orleans-style seafood bar. Not cheap but you may feel like splurging on catfish, crab legs and chocolate chip pecan pie. Open Mon-Fri 11am-9.30pm, Sat 'til

10.30pm, Sun 10am-8.30pm, _www.mikefink.com_. For information about year-round cruising, sightseeing, lunches and dinners aboard boats, contact **BB Riverboats**, at the foot of Madison Ave, (800) 261-8586. 1 hr sight-seeing cruises at $13.95; check out _www.bbriverboats.com_ for details. Located at Covington Landing.

Entertainment

Mt Adams, Cincinnati's answer to Greenwich Village, is where the yuppies are. For information visit _www.mtadamstoday.com_ The students hang out in the **Clifton area** of the University of Cincinnati. The place to go in this college town is **Calhoun St** or **Short Vine** (1 block off Vine St). Many bars and clubs, ranging in musical style, dress code and price in the U district. Many of the most popular places to eat and hang out are on the Kentucky side of the riverfront at Newport on the Levee, _www.newportonthelevee.com._

Cincy's always up for a festival— try to time your visit accordingly. Live music and top bands take the stage during **Pepsi Jamming** on Main St in Apr-May, **Oktoberfest** in mid-Sept, _www.oktoberfest-zinzinnati.com_ and the **Tall Stacks** riverboat expo in Sept-Oct (takes place every 4 years, last one was in 2003), provide lots of opportunities for dancing, eating and beer drinking in the downtown area. Check out _www.gccc.com_ for a calendar of events.

Arnold's, 210 E 8th St, 421-6234, btwn Main & Sycamore Sts downtown. Has jazz and bluegrass music along with sandwiches and dinners (entrees $7.50-$21.95). Cincinnati's oldest bar. Open Mon-Fri 11am 'til 1am, Sat 4pm-1am, Sun 4pm-1am.

Blind Lemon, 936 Hatch St, Mt Adams, 241-3885. Old-fashioned decor. Pop, acoustic guitar music, no cover. Open Mon-Tue 5.30pm-1.00am, Wed-Fri 5pm-2 am, Sat-Sun 3pm-2.30am.

Music Hall, 1243 Elm St by Lincoln Park Dr, 744-3344/721-8222. Classical music, discount w/student ID 45 mins before performances, $10. Box open Mon-Fri 10am-5.30pm, Sat 10am-1pm. _www.cincinnatiarts.org._

Playhouse in the Park, 962 Mt Adams Circle, 421-3888. Two theatres with plays Oct-June and sometimes cabaret in the summer. Student rush tkts on sale 15 mins before performances, $15 discounts. _www.cincyplay.com._

Sports

Cincinnati Reds games, 765-7000, at **Great American Ball Park** (new in 2003 and seats 42,256 people), America's first professional baseball team, originally called the 'Cincinnati Red Stockings'. Tkts are $5-$28, _www.cincinnatireds.com._ The **Bengals** football team play at the **Paul Brown Stadium**, downtown Cincinnati, 621-3550. Tkts $35-$54, _www.bengals.com._

Information

Greater Cincinnati Convention and Visitors Bureau, 511 Walnut St, (513) 621-2142/(800) CINCY-USA. Mon-Sat 10am-5pm, Sun noon-5pm. _www.cincyusa.com._ **State Information**, (800)-BUCKEYE.

Internet access

The Public Library of Cincinnati & Hamilton County, 800 Vine St, 369-6900. Free access, 90 min time limit. Mon-Wed 9am-9pm, Thu-Sat 'til 6pm, Sun 1pm-5pm. Check out _www.cincinnatilibrary.org_ for other branches and more info.

Travel

Southwest Ohio Regional Transit Authority, 1014 Vine St, 632-7575 for info and schedules. Basic fare: $1.00 within city limits. _www.sorta.com._

Amtrak, 1301 Western Ave, 651-3337/(800) 872-7245, _www.amtrak.com._

Cincinnati/Northern Kentucky International Airport, _www.cvgairport.com,_ is in Kentucky, about 13 miles away. Executive, (859) 261-8601/(800) 990-8841, runs shuttle buses to the airport from downtown hotels for $15 o/w, $25 r/t, _www.executivetranscincy.com._

Greyhound, 1005 Gilbert St, 352-6012/(800) 231-2222. A long walk from the city centre, *www.greyhound.com.*

COLUMBUS The capital city of Ohio, Columbus sits in the middle of the state, a centre of growth that preserves the state's historical heritage. The home of Ohio State University, Columbus has played host to several notable names. The writer O Henry produced some of his best stories while confined in a Columbus cell for embezzlement. Local humorist James Thurber attended Ohio State University briefly and set his play, *The Male Animal*, there.

Columbus is in a region of the Buckeye state intriguingly called 'Leatherlips', named after a Wyandot Indian chief who was executed by his people for siding with palefaces. *www.experiencecolumbus.com.*

The telephone area code is 614.

Accommodation
Motel 6, 5910 Scarborough Blvd (20 mins from downtown, off the I-70 at exit 110A), 755-2250. S-$31.99 inc. tax, D-$37.99. *www.motel6.com.*
German Village Inn Motel, 920 South High St, 443-6506. D-$79 1 mile from downtown.

Food/Entertainment
Try the Short North area, between downtown and the Ohio State Campus, for real bohemian atmosphere. The hippest shops, galleries, restaurants and night clubs are to be found here.
Blue Danube, 2439 N High St, 261-9308. Good, cheap restaurant with generous portions. Pub-style food, along with American, Greek and Mexican dishes. Holds one of the largest stocked bars in Ohio. Open daily 11am-2am.
Brenen's Café, 1860 N High St, 291-7751. This student-favourite hangout serves up huge sandwich baskets ($4.50) and baked goods like triple chocolate muffins. Open Mon-Thu 7am-11pm, Fri 'til 10pm, Sat 8am-10pm, Sun 'til 11pm.
There are good eating places in the **German Village** (bus from High St) and the Arena District, 375 N Front St, 857-2336. Also at **North Market**, 29 Spruce St, a century-old centre for produce. For nightlife, try **North High St**, 2 miles N of downtown. This is where the Ohio State University students go. Some of the better restaurants are to be found in the **Brewery District/German Village** and in rather off-beat places like **Grand View Ave** (NW of downtown). Bar bands are Columbus' speciality. Almost all have live music on w/ends. Grand View Ave is a hidden treasure with its 'Drexel' cinema, open air coffee houses and bookstores.

Of interest
Center of Science and Industry (COSI), 333 W Broad St, 228-2674/(888) 819-2674. Contains science, health, industry and history exhibits. Wed-Sat 10am-5pm, Sun noon-6pm. $12 general admission, $17 value pass (includes all exhibits plus any or all Extreme Screen movies). 'Worth it.' *www.cosi.org.*
Columbus Zoo & Aquarium, 9990 Riverside Dr, 645-3550/(800) MONKEYS. Exit 20, Sawmill Rd (off I-270 outer belt). 100-acre zoo. Impressive collection of great apes, including the first gorilla ever born in captivity. The only zoo in the world housing four generations of gorillas. Also features 'Manatee Coast,' one of only four manatee exhibits outside of Florida. Daily 9am-6pm, $9. Some activities involve additional charges. *www.colszoo.org.*
Dodge Skatepark, 667 Sullivant Ave, 645-8151. Concrete snake run, three bowls, pyramid and other obstacles suitable for skateboarding, in-lining and BMX. Open daily dawn-dusk, free. *www.columbusrecparks.com.*
Easton Town Center, Easton Way, off I-270, 337-2200. Mega shopping and

entertainment complex in northeast Columbus. Features shopping, dancing, dining, pottery-making, comedy clubs and GameWorks, a virtual reality video arcade. Free wifi access. Mon-Thu 10am-9pm, Fri-Sat 'til 10pm, Sun noon-6pm. *www.eastontowncenter.com.*

German Village, 588 S Third St, 221-8888. Open Mon-Sat. Restored 19th century community containing private homes, shops and restaurants. *www.germanvillage.org.*

Ohio Theatre, 39 E State St, 469-0939. A 1930s theatre/cinema with wonderful Titian red, gold-spangled baroque interior. Shows plays and classic movies (summer months only, $3.50). 'Amazing decor; organist rises through the floor.' *www.capa.com.*

Topiary Garden, 408 E Town St at Washington Ave, 645-3300. Topiary depiction of Georges Seurat 'A Sunday Afternoon ..' complete with 52 topiary people, 8 boats, 3 dogs and a monkey! Open dawn-dusk, free. *www.topiarygarden.org.*

Wyandot Lake Adventure Park, 10101 Riverside Dr (adjacent to the zoo), 889-9283, has over 45 rides. Daily10am-8pm, $25.90, *www.sixflags.com./parks/wyandotlake/index.asp.*

Information

Experience Columbus, 90 N High St, 221-6623/(866) EXP-COLS, open Mon-Fri 8am-5pm; **Visitors Center,** 3rd floor of the City Mall, (800) 345-4386. *www.experiencecolumbus.com.*

Travel

Central Ohio Transit Authority (COTA), 60 E Broad St, 228-1776, runs the local buses; $1.75 express routes, $1.25 basic fare, *www.cota.com.*

Greyhound, 111 E Town St, 221-0577/(800) 231-2222. Open 24 hrs, *www.greyhound.com.*

Port Columbus International Airport, E of downtown, *www.port-columbus.com.* Take the COTA #92 bus to Broad St ($1.35) and then the #10 bus to downtown. Call 228-1776 for more details. Taxis to downtown approx $18.

CLEVELAND Superman was born in Cleveland in 1933, the brainchild of two teenagers who in 1938 sold all rights for $130 and commenced upon a lifetime of generally fruitless litigation. This earthly urban version of Krypton is an entirely suitable birthplace for the 'Man of Steel'. Once an industrial powerhouse, it features an incredible array of bridges, yet still looks something like Dresden after the war. But iron and steel weren't the only things that brought money to Cleveland; its prime location on Lake Erie made it a natural centre for shipbuilding. John D Rockefeller watched his oil business here grow into one of the largest personal fortunes the world has ever known. Downtown Cleveland is thick with corporate headquarters, but industry isn't the only thing that flourishes here. The symphony orchestra, municipal art museum and other cultural endeavours rank amongst the finest in the US—a testament to the second renaissance the city has undergone.

Cleveland is also known for the **Rock 'n Roll Hall of Fame**, which opened in 1995 and was designed by I.M Pei. The choice of Cleveland was appropriate, considering the city's musical credentials: one of its ancestral disc jockeys coined the phrase 'rock & roll,' the city hosted the very first rock concert in 1952, and this is where Elvis Presley and Scotty Moore played their first concert outside the south, in 1955. The Hall graphically catalogues the decline of Rock 'n Roll from its passionate roots to its later

greedy mediocrity. _www.travelcleveland.com_ and _www.cleveland.com._
The telephone area code is 216.

Accommodation

There is not much downtown hotel accommodation for less than $80 (although look out for internet deals). It may be a better option to stay at one of the many motels near the airport.

Days Inn—Lakewood Manor Motel, 12019 Lake Ave, 226-4800. 5 miles W of downtown in Lakewood. S-$59 Mon-Thu, $69 Fri-Sun, D-$69 Mon-Thu, $79 Fri-Sun. Bfast included, cable TV, AC. _www.daysinn.com._

HI-Stanford House, 6093 Stanford Rd, Peninsula, 22 miles south of Cleveland, (330) 467-8711. Dorm-$15. Historic Greek revival farmhouse dating from 1847. Kitchen, laundry, dining room; adjacent to bike and hiking trails. _www.hiusa.org._

Knights Inn, 22115 Brookpark Rd, (440) 734-4500. S-D-$52-55, Bfast included. _www.knightsinn.com._

Red Roof Inn, I-90 & Crocker Rd, exit 156, Westlake, (440) 892-7920/(800) 733-7663. Rooms from $63 (Sun-Thu), $80 (Fri-Sat). Coffee in mornings. _www.redroof.com._

Camping: Woodside Lake Park, 2486 Frost Rd, (330) 626-4251. 35 miles E of downtown, off I-480 in Streetsboro. Sites $30 for two w/hook-up, _www.woodsidelake.com._

Food

Balaton, 13133 Shaker Square, 921-9691. Cleveland prides itself on delicious Hungarian food. Balaton is the best. Open Tue-Fri 11.30am-9pm, Fri 'til 10pm, Sat 12.30pm-10pm, Sun 'til 8pm.

Captain Tony's Pizza and Pasta Emporium, 13202 Shaker Square, 561-8669. Some of the best gourmet pizza in Cleveland. Open daily 10.30am-10pm. Pizzas $5 (small), $10 (large).

Geppetto's, 3314 Warren Rd, 941-1120. Six-time winner of the 'National Rib Burn-off', held in Cleveland on Memorial Day w/end, Geppetto's defeated some of the best ribs from all over the world. In spite of the prestige, the prices are reasonable. Open Mon-Thu 11.30am-11pm, Fri-Sat 'til midnight, Sun 'til 10pm. _www.geppettos.com._

Mama Santa, 12305 Mayfield Rd (in Little Italy), 231-9567. There are several wonderful Italian restaurants in Little Italy. This one is quite reasonably priced, with entrees between $5 and $11. Daily 11am-11.30pm.

Rock Bottom Brewery, 2000 Sycamore St, 623-1555. Great beer and sandwiches, steaks, seafood and pastas. Entrees $8.95-$19.95. Daily 11.30am-11pm (food), 'til midnight (bar). _www.rockbottom.com._

Watermark, 1250 Old River Rd (on the east bank), 241-1600. If you're going to splurge in Cleveland, this is the place to do it. Lovely riverside location. Fri night seafood buffet $18.95 (6pm-8.30pm). Sun brunch $17.95 (10am-2.30pm). Open Mon-Sat 11.30am-10pm, Sun 10am-2.30pm and 5pm-10pm. _www.watermark-flats.com._

West Side Market, W 25th and Lorain Ave, 664-3387. Head to this gastronomic cross-section for mouth-watering old world selections at low prices. Open Mon & Wed 7am-4pm, Fri-Sat 7am-6pm. _www.westsidemarket.com._ Across the street is **Market 25,** a new food court with some great cafes and restaurants.

Of interest

Great Lakes Science Center, 601 Erieside Ave, 694-2000. Hands-on science museum with an Omnimax theatre. Open daily 9.30am-5.30pm; $8.95 for the museum or the Omnimax, $12.95 for combo tkt. _www.greatscience.com._

Museum of Art, 11150 East Blvd at University Circle, 421-7340/(888) 269-7829. Free and first-rate, second only to the NY Metropolitan, with over 40,000 works. Tue, Thu, Sat, Sun 10am-5pm; Wed & Fri 10am-9pm. Free. _www.clevelandart.org._

Museum of Natural History, Wade Oval University Circle, 231-4600/(800) 317-9155. Its hi-tech planetarium features a projector that can show the positions of over 5000 stars – the only one of its kind in the world. Mon-Sat 10am-5pm, Wed 'til 10pm, Sun noon-5pm; $7, $5 w/student ID. *www.cmnh.org.*

Rock and Roll Hall of Fame and Museum, 1 Key Plaza, North Coast Harbor, 781-7625. The world's greatest repository of R'n'R memorabilia, incl Lennon's Sgt Pepper outfit, Madonna costumes, Michael Jackson's glove, a comprehensive tribute to Elvis, a myriad selection of lyric sheets and guitars and other entertaining historical artefacts/exhibitions. Daily 10am-5.30pm, Wed 'til 9pm; $20. Takes 3-4 hrs to tour. Check out *www.rockhall.com.*

Shaker Historical Museum, 16740 S Park Blvd, Shaker Heights, 921-1201. Tue-Fri & Sun 2pm-5pm, Free. *www.ohiohistory.org/places/shaker* Once the site of a rural commune begun by the Shakers, a religious sect who turned their backs on industrialisation for 10 mins—and along came Cleveland! Today's Shaker Heights is a ritzy suburb with good (and not always expensive) restaurants. It's also home of the nation's second-oldest shopping centre. Visit *www.shaker-hts.oh.us* for more information.

Geauga Lake and Wildwater Kingdom, 1060 N Aurora Rd, Rt 43, (330) 562-8303. This theme park includes 50 rides and attractions including Texas Twister and X-Flight, and a water park. Open 10am-10pm daily. Admission $24.95 (look out for special discounts on Coke bottles and cans). *www.geaugalake.com.*

Entertainment

Pick up a free copy of the *Cleveland Free Times, www.freetimes.com* or the *Cleveland Scene www.clevescene.com* for the latest in entertainment news.

Cleveland Orchestra, Severance Hall, 11001 Euclid Ave, 231-7300/(800) 686-1141. World-famous symphony orchestra established in 1918, presenting a variety of concerts. Tkts $18-$38. *www.clevelandorchestra.com.*

Playhouse Square Center, 1501 Euclid Ave, 771-4444. The second largest performing arts centre in the country, with 5 theatres. Call 241-6000/(800) 766-6048 for tickets. Visit *www.playhousesquare.com* for more details.

The Flats, NW of Public Square, where the Cuyahoga River meets Lake Erie, is the centre of Cleveland's nightlife. Many rock bars and good eating establishments, as there are in the **Warehouse District,** 2 blocks from downtown Cleveland, 334-3937, *www.warehousedistrict.org* The **Nautica Stage** at the Flats plays host to a number of outdoor summer concerts (rock, jazz, classical etc). Call 861-4080 for details, or check out *www.nauticaflats.com* Take a lunch or sunset dinner cruise on the *Nautica Queen,* 696-8888, for a breathtaking view of downtown Cleveland, from $24-$45. Lunch cruises: Mon-Fri noon-2pm, Sat 11am-1pm. Dinner: Mon-Thu 7pm-10pm, Fri-Sat 7.30pm-10.30pm, Sun brunch 11am-1pm. *www.nauticaqueen.com.*

Sport

The **Cleveland Browns** are one of the most storied American football franchises and boast a rich history. They play their home games at the **Cleveland Browns Stadium,** which sits on the shores of Lake Erie next to the Rock 'N' Roll Hall of Fame. Be sure to sit in 'The Dawg Pound', a low-priced section of seats in the stadium known for its costumes, partying and general rowdiness. Call (440) 891-5050 for tkts, *www.clevelandbrowns.com* Despite not winning a World Series title since 1948, the **Cleveland Indians** baseball team hosted sell-outs for a record 482 straight games in the late 1990s and early 2000s. Tickets are easier to come by now and Jacobs Field, 2401 Ontario St, 420-4200, remains one of the premier baseball stadiums in America. Tkts $5-$40. *www.clevelandindians.com.*

The **Cleveland Cavaliers'** home is Gund Arena, located right next door to Jacobs Field, 420-CAVS. American basketball phenom Lebron James, predicted to be the next Michael Jordan and rewarded with more than $100 million in endorsements before his first professional game, will play for the Cavaliers through 2007 and possibly beyond, _www.clevelandcavaliers.com_ Fans of ice hockey can catch the **Cleveland Barons**, a minor league team, at **Gund Arena** during the winter, _www.clevelandbarons.com_ and if a surge of homesickness arises, the **Cleveland Force** compete in America's Major Indoor Soccer League, _www.clevelandforce.com._

Information
Cleveland Convention and Visitors Bureau, 3100 Terminal Tower, 50 Public Sq, 621-4110/(800) 321-1001. Mon-Fri 8.30am-5pm. _www.travelcleveland.com._

Internet access
Cleveland Public Library, 325 Superior Ave, 623-2800. Free access. Mon-Sat 9am-6pm. Check out _www.cpl.org_ for other locations.

Travel
Amtrak, Lakefront Station, 200 Cleveland Memorial Shoreway, 696-5115/(800) 872-7245. Like the Greyhound Station, this is not a safe part of town. Most trains arrive in the early hours, so use caution when leaving the station. Either take a taxi or wait until daylight before venturing out. Open daily 5pm-8.30am. _www.amtrak.com._
Cleveland Hopkins International Airport, 265-6000. About 11 miles from downtown. The easiest, cheapest and quickest way to get there is to take the Rapid Transit train service (every 15 mins from and to Tower City Shopping Center), $1.50 o/w. _www.clevelandairport.com._
Greyhound, 1465 Chester Ave, 781-0520/(800) 231-2222. 'High crime area—take extreme care, especially at night, even in the restrooms.' _www.greyhound.com._
Regional Transit Authority, 566-5124, runs buses and the rapid rail system. Basic fare on buses $1.25, express buses/rail $1.50, $3 all day pass. _www.riderta.com._

TOLEDO AND NORTHWEST OHIO
A must-see in Ohio is the **Toledo Museum of Art**, 2445 Monroe Street at Scottwood Ave, Toledo, (419) 255-8000/(800) 644-6862. Houses the finest collection of glass in the US, founded by Edward Libbey, who brought the glass industry to Toledo in 1888. Tue-Thu & Sat 10am-4pm, Fri 'til 10pm, Sun 11am-5pm, free, _www.toledomuseum.org_. A good day trip from Cleveland or Detroit. Toledo's past, preserved through time in magnificent photographs, drawings and documents dating back to the 1860s, comes alive at the **Toledo Public Library,** 325 North Michigan, 259-5207 in their Local History and Genealogy Department's collection of over 150,000 images. Open 9am-9pm Mon-Thu, Fri and Sat 9am-5.30pm, Sun 1:pm-5.30pm. Also worth a visit is the **Toledo Zoo,** 2700 Broadway, (419) 385-5721, home to over 4,000 animals. You can view hippos underwater at the Hippoquarium, walk through an African Savanna and check out the Arctic Encounter that features underwater polar bear and seal viewing. Open 10am-5pm (May 1st–Labor Day), 10am-4pm (Labor Day–April 30th), $9, _www.toledozoo.org._

Further east lies the town of **Port Clinton**. From there, sail over to **South Bass Island**, an historical island-turned-raging-bar-scene. The island's principal city, **Put-in-Bay**, is home to the world's longest bar. Its famous watering hole, the **Beer Barrel Saloon**, 1618 Delaware Ave, (419) 285-7281, boasts a 405 ft counter, 160 bar stools, 56 beer taps and holds up to 3,200 people! Open daily 11am-midnight, _www.beerbarrelpib.com._

In **Sandusky**, perhaps spend a day or two at **Cedar Point**, 1 Cedar Point Drive, (419) 627-2350. The nation's second oldest amusement park and largest in the world: Known as 'America's Rollercoast', the park features 68 rides and 16 roller coasters, more than any other amusement park on the planet. Open daily during the summer 10am-11pm. $44.95, $27 after 5pm, _www.cedarpoint.com_. **Toft Dairy**, 3717 Venice Rd, (419) 625-4376, is famous for serving up phenomenal ice cream. Open daily 8am-11pm, _www.toftdairy.com_. After a hot, gruelling day at Cedar Point, head just southwest of Sandusky to **Bellevue**, where you can dig into a thick, juicy steak at **McClain's**, 137 E Main St, (419) 483-2727. Open Mon-Thu 11am-9pm, Fri 'til 9.30pm, Sat noon-9.30pm. Lunch entrees $3.50-$6.95, dinner $12.95.

Information
Greater Toledo Convention & Visitors Bureau, 401 Jefferson Ave, (800) 243-4667. Open Mon-Fri 8am-5pm, _www.doToledo.org_.

SERPENT MOUND STATE MEMORIAL and HOPEWELL CULTURE NATIONAL HISTORICAL PARK Serpent Mound, located near **Peebles**, (937) 587-2796/(800) 752-2757, is the largest Indian effigy mound in the US, built by the Fort Ancient peoples circa 1000 BC. 'Unforgettable, majestic and truly amazing that it's still around at all.' In the summer, green grass covers the enormous coils that the mound builders formed out of stone and clay. Park and museum open Tue-Sun in the summer 10am-5pm. Museum open weekends only in fall and spring. $7/vehicle, _www.ohiohistory.org_.

Hopewell Culture National Historical Park, located just north of **Chillicothe** at 16062 State Rte 104, (740) 774-1125, dates back 2000 years. The 23 mounds located at Mound City were used for various ceremonial activities including burials, cremations, weddings and public gatherings. Four additional Hopewell Culture sites are located nearby. The park is open from dawn-dusk and the visitor centre and museum are open 8.30am-5pm daily, 'til 6pm in summer. A recreation entrance fee is charged $3/person or $5/car load. _www.nps.gov/hocu_.

SOUTH DAKOTA - The Mount Rushmore State

South Dakota is living proof that bad weather (from 40 below zero to a blazing 116 degrees) can't be all bad. To look at its tourist brochures, you'd think the place was full of nothing but jolly Anglo hunters, ranchers and fishermen. It has, however, a large (mostly Sioux) Indian population on nine reservations, regarded as 'uppity Injuns' (and worse) for their determination to win back more of their traditional lands. It was the discovery of gold in the Black Hills (verified by that catalytic figure, General Custer, in 1874) that further exacerbated relations with the Sioux. The land in question had been granted to the Sioux by an 1868 treaty, and they were not willing to concede it. Settlers came by the wagonload anyway to extract the mineral. In spite of their fervent mining, gold continues to be South Dakota's most abundant mineral today.

Concentrate on the scenic western section: Mt Rushmore, the Black Hills, the Badlands. Because of distances and lack of public transit, it's difficult to sight-see without a car. Wyoming's Devil's Tower is only 35 miles from the South Dakota border, but you'll need a car to reach it as well.

One of the state's most popular tourist attractions is what Kevin Costner left behind— the sets from his highly acclaimed epic, _Dances With Wolves_. A visit to **Ft Hays,** (888) 343-3113, four miles south of Rapid City on Hwy 16, enables you to walk (free of charge) through some of the buildings used in the film production and pick up souvenirs at a number of gift shops; the Sioux winter camp setting that ends the film is in Little Spearfish Canyon in the Black Hills National Forest. The official state home page is _www.state.sd.us_. _The telephone area code is 605._

RAPID CITY A strategic spot for exploring the Black Hills and Badlands, the city itself is a hodgepodge of tourist 'claptrapery'. Visit the city guide compiled by the Rapid City Convention and Visitors Bureau at _www.rapidcitycvb.com._

Accommodation/Food
Big Sky Motel, 4080 Tower Rd, 348-3200/(800) 318 3208. Average price $47. Credit card number needed for rsvs. 30 mins to Mt Rushmore.
College Inn Motel, 321 Kansas City St (part of National American University), 394-4870/(800) 529-010. Popular with conference groups. Open June-Aug. 6 blocks from bus depot. Pool, laundry, cafeteria. 'Clean, well furnished.'
Lamplighter Inn, 27 St. Joseph, 342-3385. Room D-$65. Heated pool, free coffee. Book early.
Tally's, 530 6th St, 342-7621. Downtown; good food for not much money. 'Nice food and good locale.' Homemade American fare, $3-$7. Open Mon-Sat 7am-2.30pm.

Of interest
The Journey Museum, 222 New York St, 394-6923. 2.5 million years of history shown through interactive exhibits that explore the region and the Sioux Nation. The museum has 5 collections: the Museum of Geology, Sioux Indian Museum, Archaeological Research Center, Minnilusa Pioneer Museum and the Dumahel Plains Indians Artifacts Collection. Open daily 9am-5pm; $7. _www.journeymuseum.org_.
Caves in the Rapid City region: Sitting Bull Crystal Caverns, 342-2777, 9 miles S on Hwy 16 (heading toward Mt. Rushmore), has calcite dog-spar crystals. June-Aug daily 7am-7pm; $7.50. 45 min tours leave every 20 min. _www.sittingbullcrystalcave.com_. **Crystal Cave,** 342-8008, 2 miles W on Hwy 44, is closest and offers complete tours, 35-40 min, that aren't very strenuous: 'Quite long but very pleasant walk.' Open May-Oct, 8am-8pm, $8.

Information
Chamber of Commerce, Rushmore Plaza Civic Center, 343-1744. Useful maps. Ask for the _Rapid City Vacation Guide_, with a dandy section on panning for gold and rock hounding. 'Very helpful people.' Mon-Fri 8am-5pm, _www.rapidcitycvb.com._
South Dakota Tourism, 444 Mt Rushmore Rd, (800) 487-3223. _www.travelsd.com_. Provides in-depth travel info, including calendar of events.

Travel
Gray Line Tours, 1600 E St Patrick Street, (800) 456-4461. Different itineraries to the Black Hills and Mt. Rushmore. Pickup from various hotels. $35-$79 for the day. The fully narrated 9 hr Black Hills tour at $42 is 'quite extensive; well worth the money'. _www.blackhillsgrayline.com._
Stagecoach West, 343-3113. Visits to the Black Hills and Mount Rushmore, with treks to the _Dances With Wolves_ film set and the Crazy Horse Memorial. Enjoy $0.99 Cowboy Bkfst. Variety of packages priced at $39 or $54, some including supper. _www.rushmoretours.com._

Internet access
Rapid City Public Library, 610 Quincy St, 394-6139. Free access, 1 hr limit; once a

day. First-come, first-served. Mon-Thu 9am-8pm, Fri-Sat 'til 5.30pm. _www.rapidcitylibrary.org_.

DEADWOOD   Twenty-eight miles NW of Rapid City via I-90, Deadwood calls itself 'where the West is fun'! Once the lively stomping ground for Calamity Jane, Wild Bill Hickok and Deadwood Dick, it may be having a revival thanks to the popularity of the TV series, 'Deadwood' featuring the nefarious town characters. For links to Deadwood and other Old West sites, click on _www.deadwood.net_.

Accommodation/Food
Penny Motel, 818 Upper Main St, 578-1842. Trolley transportation to and from nearby historic sites. D-$59-69. _www.pennymotel.com._
Super 8 Motel, 196 Cliff St, 578-2535. D-$70. 12 miles S of main street, 50¢ bus available every ¹/₂ hr to downtown. 'Pool, hot tub and 24 hr casino; friendly, very clean.'
The many competing casinos in the downtown area often offer cheap deals for meals. Breakfast for 50¢ is not unheard of.

Of interest
Adams Museum and House, 54 Sherman St, 578-1714. The oldest history museum in the Black Hills; featuring Wild Bill Hickok and Calamity Jane memorabilia. Open summer Mon-Sat 9am-7pm, Sun noon-5pm, free. 'Interesting.' _www.adamsmuseumandhouse.org_.
Mt Moriah 'Boot Hill' Cemetery. Good place to do gravestone rubbings: Calamity and Wild Bill are here. Open year round.
Old Style Saloon #10, 657 Main St (800) 952-9398. Offers gaming tables, Italian steak restaurant and bar. See the chair where Wild Bill Hickok was gunned down while holding a poker hand of 2 aces and a pair of eights—still called 'a dead man's hand'. Hickok was never punished for any of his killings, several of which were clearly murders; his killer, however, was hanged. _www.saloon10.com._
Nearby: Spearfish, (800) 457-0160, home of the _Black Hills Passion Play_ since 1939. Performances take place on the largest outdoor stage in the country. June-Aug, at 8pm on Tue, Thu & Sun; $20-25. Visit _www.blackhills.com/bhpp_ for information.

THE BLACK HILLS   are neither black nor hills; they are actually ancient mountains cloaked with spectacular pine forests. The impressive result— a green citadel above the expansive tawny plains— was considered sacred ground by the Sioux. For links to everything in the Black Hills and South Dakota, search _www.blackhills.com._

Of interest
Custer State Park, 255-4515/(800) 658-3530. Free if you drive through on Hwy 16A, otherwise $5 pp, $12 for a 7-day vehicle permit, $15 per campsite. Rsvs recommended. The **State Game Lodge**, 255-4541, will take you on a Buffalo Jeep Safari, where you can see some of the park's 1500 buffalo during a 2 hr jeep ride for $30, include a cookout for $60. If you prefer horseback riding, call the **Blue Bell Lodge**, 255-4571. They'll arrange it for you for $26/hr or $38/2 hrs. _www.custerresorts.com._
Any tour through the Black Hills should include **Needles Hwy,** past spectacular volcanic pinnacles. Someone once wanted to carve these pillars into Wild West heroes, the genesis of the Rushmore idea. Hike to the top of **Harney Peak**; at 7,242 ft, it's the highest point in the US east of the Rockies.
Crazy Horse Monument, 4 miles N of Custer on Rte 16/385, 673-4681. The Oglala

Sioux leader, Crazy Horse, resisted white encroachment on Indian lands and was 33 when stabbed in the back by an American soldier under a flag of truce. After completion the 3-dimensional monument will dwarf Rushmore, ultimately standing 563 ft high and 641 ft long— the world's largest mountain carving. Korczak Ziolkowski started work in 1948 at the request of Native Americans and blasted away some 7 million tons of rock before his death in 1982. His family carried on and you can see work in progress daily 7am-9pm. Check with the many tour companies for scheduled trips or drive through; $10 pp, $24 per car. *www.crazyhorse.org*.

Jewel Cave National Monument, 673-2288. Dogtooth crystals of calcite sparkle from its walls in the 3rd longest cave system in the world. Bring a jacket—it gets quite chilly, even in the summer. Take the Introductory tour for $4, the Lantern tour for $8, or the Historic tour for $8 which is more strenuous but fun. Go early to avoid a long wait. Open daily 8am-7.30pm ('til 6pm from mid-Aug), tours 8.30am-6pm. *www.nps.gov/jeca*.

Mt Rushmore, 574-2523. Includes a 14 min film, evening amphitheatre programmes at 9pm. It took 14 yrs to create the 60-ft-high granite faces of Washington, Jefferson, Teddy Roosevelt and Lincoln, carved by Gutzon Borglum and partly paid for with South Dakota school kids' pennies and it's still not finished. Most beautiful in morning light and when floodlit, summer eves. Visitors Center, daily 8am-10pm. Sculptor Studio, where models and tools are displayed, 8am-5pm, summer only; free. $8 parking fee. *www.nps.gov/moru*.

HOT SPRINGS Long before white settlers discovered these waters, they were a point of contention between Sioux and Cheyenne Indian tribes. The warm, mineral-laden waters were also a popular watering hole for mammoths 26,000 years ago. The sides of the sinkhole were quite slippery, however, and some 100 mammoths are believed to have drowned. Today you can follow in the footsteps of the Indians and mammoths alike by bathing in the 87 degree, spring-fed indoor swimming pools at **Evans Plunge**, 1145 N River St, 745-5165, with water slides, hot tubs, tubes and floats. Open Mon-Fri 5.30am-10pm, Sat-Sun 8am-10pm; $9. *www.evansplunge.com*.

The first of the star-crossed mammoths was uncovered in 1974; the **Mammoth Site of Hot Springs**, 1800 Hwy 18, 745-6017, is the world's largest mammoth research facility, where you tour an active paleontological dig and view ice age fossils in-situ (bones left as found). Open daily 8am-8pm, (last tour 7pm); $6.48. *www.mammothsite.com*.

Black Hills Wild Horse Sanctuary, (800) 252-6652, is located 14 miles west of Hot Springs. See hundreds of wild mustangs, displaced from other ranges in the west, running free. Guided 2 hr bus tours available daily at 9-11am, 1-3pm; $20. *www.wildmustangs.com*.

If you haven't had your fill of caves yet, take time to visit **Wind Cave National Park**, 11 miles north of Hot Springs, 745-4600. Discovered in 1881, the 10 mile deep cave is named for the winds (caused by changes in barometric pressure) that whistle in and out of it. Open daily 8am-7pm, 60min-90min scenic tours; $7-$9. The two hour candlelight tour ($9) is recommended, as is the four hour caving tour ($23). 'The candlelight tour is great.' Dress warmly. Above ground, take advantage of superb animal watching and photographing deer, buffalo, antelope and prairie dog towns. Dawn and dusk are the best times. *www.nps.gov/wica*.

BADLANDS NATIONAL PARK Locals used to say that it looks like hell with the fires put out, but there's something quite heavenly about the 207 square miles of weird and beautiful buttes, canyons and brilliantly coloured rock formations. At sunset, the sandstone slopes blush with shades of pink and purple. Bones of sabre-toothed tigers, three-toed horses and Tyrannosaurus Rex have been found in this dried-up swampland. 'Absolutely amazing—the surprise package of our tour. Come into it at dawn with the sun at your back—it'll blow your mind, it's that good.' 'Well worth the 10 mile hike along rough track to watch the sunset' and spend the night at **Sage Creek** primitive campground, 433-5361, 35 miles from park entrance; free, 14 day maximum stay. No water on site. _www.badlands.national-park.com._

Of interest
Kadoka, an authentic Western backwater town east of the Badlands on I-90, is the best place to stay overnight to make the favoured dawn drive through the Badlands, emerging at **Wall**. Excellent visitor centre at the **Cedar Pass Badlands** entrance, includes video. To stay, try the **Best Western Plains Motel,** 712 Glenn St, in Wall, 279-2145; D-$62.

Wall is notorious for **Wall Drug,** 510 Main St, 279-2175, a drug store that mutated into a kitschy tourist trap. Roads leading to and from Wall are peppered with some 3000 billboards hawking the place; other signs can be found at the North and South Poles, a Kenyan rail station and in the Paris Metro, informing potential customers of the number of miles it is to Wall Drug. Sip free iced water and nickel coffee, buy a rattlesnake ashtray and puzzle over a jackalope, a cross between a jackrabbit and an antelope. Open daily, 6am-10pm. _www.walldrug.com._

MITCHELL If passing through, take time to see the **Corn Palace**, 601 N Main St, (866) 273-2676, a vaguely Russian fantasy of onion domes and dazzling pointillist murals, formed from 3000 bushels of coloured corn cobs. Watch artists construct new murals each summer on the outer wall of the civic auditorium. Summer: daily 8am-9pm; free. _www.cornpalace.com_. Also in Mitchell, the **Oscar Howe Art Center**, 119 W 3rd St, 996-4111. Combined history gallery and art center based on the history of the middle border region; paintings by legendary Sioux artist. Tue-Sat 10am-5pm, free. Area lodging: **Best Western Motor Inn,** 1001 S Burr, 996-5536. D $45. For more info contact the Chamber of Commerce, (866) 273-CORN.

WOUNDED KNEE 'I did not know then how much was ended. When I look back from this high hill of my old age, I can still see the butchered women and children lying heaped and scattered all along the crooked gulch as plain as when I saw them with eyes still young. And I can see that something else died there in the bloody mud, and was buried in the blizzard. A people's dream died there. It was a beautiful dream. The nation's hoop is broken and scattered. There is no centre any longer, and the sacred tree is dead.' —Black Elk.

The symbolic end of Indian freedom came at Christmas-time, 1890, at the so-called Battle of Wounded Knee when the US Cavalry opened fire with rifles and field guns on 120 Indian men and 230 Indian women and children. Most were murdered instantly; some wounded crawled away through a terrible blizzard. Torn and bleeding, many did not crawl far: a returning army burial party found numerous bodies frozen into grotesque shapes against the snow.

A shabby monument marks the spot 100 miles southeast of Rapid City, a few miles off Rte 18 near Pine Ridge. Movements for a larger memorial have met resistance from the Lakota, who bristle at the thought of surrendering more of their land to the US government for any reason.

Their unquiet mass grave nearby continues to serve as a rallying point for Native Americans. In 1973, at the second battle of Wounded Knee, two Indians died in the 71-day siege of the American Indian Movement, and the story is far from over.

NB: although the reservation has a motel, museum and other tourist facilities, don't expect uniformly friendly attitudes toward white faces. The Wounded Knee homepage is located at _www.dickshovel.com./WKmasscre.html_ with excellent links to related Native American sites and images.

MOBRIDGE On a high hill across the Missouri from Mobridge in north-central South Dakota is **Sitting Bull's grave**. One of the events preceding the massacre at Wounded Knee was the murder of Sitting Bull, the great Sioux leader, organiser and victor at Little Bighorn. It was carried out by Indian policemen under the eye of the US Cavalry.

The authorities always felt uncomfortable with Sitting Bull alive, regarding him as a subversive figure. In death, however, he became something of a commodity. Originally buried in North Dakota, Sitting Bull's body was snatched by South Dakotans, who planted him in Mobridge. A large stone bust was placed over the grave, just to be sure Sitting Bull stays put. Mobridge has a sculpture of Sitting Bull by Korczak Ziolkowski and ten fine murals by Sioux artist Oscar Howe in the municipal auditorium. Mobridge Chamber of Commerce has a fantastic city guide at _www.mobridge.org_.

WISCONSIN - The Badger State

Wisconsin is known for its liquids: beer, milk and water of all sorts. Like its neighbour, Minnesota, Wisconsin has more inland lakes than it knows what to do with. Wisconsinites gave names to 14,949 of their inland lakes before giving up in despair. On Lakes Michigan and Superior, the state sports no less than 14 ocean-going ports. In addition to the surplus of fresh water, the world's largest water park is also located within the state boundaries. Wisconsin is also rich in mineral deposits; while other places had gold rush, Wisconsin had a 'lead rush'.

The cities here are clean, amiable and altogether charming. Of course, so is the countryside, but watch out for mosquitoes the size of aircraft carriers (it's the price you pay for all those lakes). Many of the old railroads that used to cross the state have been converted into trails for bicycling, running, hiking and skiing. More info. available at _www.travelwisconsin.com._

MILWAUKEE There's a comfortable, old-shoe feeling about Milwaukee, enhanced by its reputation for good beer, 'brats', (a particularly succulent variety of German bratwurst, boiled in beer and served with a tangy sauce) and baseball. Remarkably short on grime and slums while big on restaurants and festivals, the city is a good-natured mix of ethnic groups, especially Germans, Poles and Serbs. In quantity of beer produced, Milwaukee has now been aced out by Los Angeles. For quality, however, this is still Der Platz. *www.officialmilwaukee.com*. *The telephone area code is 414.*

Accommodation

The Wisconsin B&B Assoc, 108 South Cleveland St, Merrill, 54452, (715) 539-9222, will assist with info on motels, B&Bs and country inns; check out *www.wbba.org.* The **Wisconsin Innkeepers Assoc** also has an interactive website at *www.lodging-wi.com.*

Eagle Home Hostel, S91 W39381 State Road 59, Eagle WI, (262) 594-2473. Re-opened in May 2005 under new non-HI management, this hostel is in surroundings laden with adventure activities 35 miles from Milwaukee. Try the 10,000 year old, 1000 mile long, Ice Age Scenic Hike Trail just a block from the hostel's door. $17 per bed, plus $10 daily park vehicle sticker, rsvs required. *www.hostellingwisconsin.org.*

Exel Inn, 115 North Mayfair Rd, Wauwatosa, 257-0140. Room $75, incl. continental b/fast. *www.exelinns.com.*

Red Roof Inn, 6360 S 13th St, Oak Creek, 764-3500. Average rate $65.

Camping: WACO Campground Directory/info on campgrounds across the state, *www.wisconsincampgrounds.com.*

Food

Besides Wisconsin's famous cheeses, Milwaukee is noted for 'beer and brats'. If you don't go to a Brewers baseball game and gorge in the sun on beer'n'brats, you've blown it. Also try local frozen custard at places like **Kopp's Frozen Custard,** 5373 N Port Washington Rd, Glendale, 961-3288. Other locations include 18880 W Bluemound Rd, Brookfield, (262) 789-9490; and 7631 W Layton Ave, Greenfield 282-4312. All open daily 10.30am-11.30pm. 'No matter when you come, it's always mobbed. Sundaes are the speciality of the house—each comes with its own blueprint detailing the exact ingredients and their placement!' *www.kopps.com.*

German and Serb restaurants are your best ethnic bets, but also check to see if Milwaukee is celebrating one of its famous summer festivals at the lakefront.

Crocus, 3577 S 13th St, 643-6383. This neighbourhood Polish restaurant offers the strange brew Czarnia—'a sweet brown syrup, thick with little dumplings, beans, shreds of duck, and plump raisins'. One full meal under $12. Mon-Fri 11:30am-2pm, Thu, Fri & Sat 4.30pm-9pm.

Karl Ratzsch's, 320 E Mason St, 276-2720. An early dining menu, Mon-Fri 4.30pm-6pm, is under $16pp. Famous for its German food, there are five German beers on tap, but also a whole array of liquors and a non-German food menu, too. Mon-Sat 4.30pm-closing, Wed-Sat lunch 11.30am-2pm. *www.karlratzsch.com.*

Real Chili, 419 E Wells, Milwaukee, 271-4042. Open since 1931. Serve Green Bay-style chili for under $5. Lunch and dinner served Mon-Sat 11am-midnight.

Of interest

America's Black Holocaust Museum, 2233 N 4th St, 264-2500. A sombre memorial to slavery in America. Open Thu-Tue 9am-5pm. $3 students.

Discovery World Museum, 815 N James Lovell St, 765-9966. Science, economics and over 150 interactive technology exhibits. Mon-Sat 9am-5pm, Sun noon-5pm; $7 incls live theatre shows and science demonstrations. *www.discoveryworld.org.*

Harley-Davidson, 11700 W Capitol Dr, Wauwatosa, 535-3666. Free 45 min tours let you see how a motorcycle is born and guides you along factory floor. Mon-Fri 9.30am-1pm, arrive early to avoid queues. *www.harley-davidson.com.*

Miller Brewery Tour, 4251 W State St, 931-2337. Free 1 hr indoor/outdoor tours, ending with your chance to sample the local brew all courtesy of Miller! Mon-Sat 10.30am-3.30pm. *www.millerbrewing.com.*

Milwaukee Art Museum, 700 N Art Museum Dr, 224-3200. Galleries with some of the finest late 20th century American art, German expressionism and Haitian art in the country. The *Quadracci Pavillion* features a 90ft high, glass-walled reception hall with a sunscreen that can be raised and lowered to create unique moving sculptures. Daily 10am-5pm, Thu 'til 8pm. $8, $4 w/student ID. *www.mam.org*.

Milwaukee County Zoo, 10001 W Bluemound Rd, 771-3040. With $25 million spent on renovations and over 2500 animals, this zoo is one of the finest. May-Oct: Mon-Sat 9am-5pm, Sun 'til 6pm; $9.75, parking $8. *www.milwaukeezoo.org*.

Mitchell Park Conservatory, 524 S Layton Blvd, 649-9800. Three 7-storey glass domes with different luxuriant botanical gardens: desert oasis, tropical jungle and a seasonal display. Daily 9am-5pm; $5. *www.county.milwaukee.gov*.

Pettit National Ice Center, 500 S 84th St, 266-0100. The nation's largest ice centre, open daily for public skating. Also an Olympic training complex. Mon 7pm-9pm, Tue-Fri 11am-1pm and 7pm-9pm, Fri 'til 10pm, Sat 12 noon-4pm and 7pm-10pm, Sun 7pm-9pm; $6, $2.50 skate rental. *www.thepettit.com*.

Public Museum, 800 W Wells St., 278-2702. Natural history and cultural museum featuring three floors of exhibits. Walk amidst live butterflies and see live exotic insects up close. Study a Costa Rican rain forest from roots to leaves and see dinosaur bones millions of years old. Stroll the *Streets of Old Milwaukee*, experience an American Indian powwow and explore cultures from Europe, Asia and the Americas. Mon - Sat 9am-5pm, Sun noon-5pm; $8. *www.mpm.edu*.

The County Parks around Milwaukee all hold varied events throughout the summer. Try **Johnsons Park**, *Jazz and Blues in the Park*, open air concerts every Fri and Sat eve in July & Aug; free. Call 881-9268 or visit *www.wjzi.com* for details. Look at *www.countymilwaukee.gov* for more listings.

Nearby: Germantown is the essence of old world Milwaukee. The town features restored German buildings, shops and restaurants in the **Dheinsville Historical Park**. Check out *www.germantouwnchamber.org* for more details. Just outside of Germantown is **Holy Hill**, atop of which is perched the **National Shrine of Mary**.

Old World Wisconsin, Hwy 67, Eagle, (262) 594-6300, is a 576-acre living history museum with 10 historic areas depicting 1800s rural America. Costumed guides lead you through authentic farmhouses and barns and a 1870s Crossroad village from the pioneer days. May-Oct: open Mon-Fri 10am-5pm, weekends 10am-5pm; $14, incls all-day tram pass and audio guide. *www.wisconsinhistory.org*.

Entertainment

African World Festival: Held in early August, this ethnic event showcases the best in African garb, jewellery, authentic foods, heritage, gospel, blues, R&B. Held at **Henry Maier Festival Park**, 200 N Harbor Dr, noon-midnight. Call 372-4567 for more info.

Downtown Milwaukee is well-known for its line-up of many colourful, varied summer festivals. Access the guide at *festivals.onmilwaukee.com*. Festivals include: **Summerfest**, (800) 273-FEST, huge music festival is held over 11 days, on 13 stages, in June & July, overlooking Lake Michigan. 'Groups, beer, funfair, massive.' $12. *www.summerfest.com*. **Festa Italiana** celebrates Italian heritage in mid-July with a combo of music, gondola rides and authentic food: 'delicious', *www.festaitaliana.com*. The Polish (June), German (July) and Irish (Aug) festivals are also cause for celebration.

Marcus Center for the Performing Arts, 929 N Water St, 273-7121. Home of the Milwaukee Symphony. Hosts opera, ballet and Broadway shows. Tckts range from $15-$60, student discount available depending on show. *www.marcuscenter.org*.

Milwaukee Repertory Theater, 108 E Wells St, 224-9490. 50 year old professional, non-profit theatre, hosts first-class plays. Sept-May. $2 off tkt price w/student ID. *www.milwaukeerep.com*.

Information/ Internet access

Visitors Bureau, 400 W Wisconsin Ave, 273-7222/908-6205 *www.milwaukee.org*.

Milwaukee Public Library, 8th and Wisconsin Ave, 286-3000. Visitors should see librarian for access. Limit of 2 hrs per day. Mon-Wed 9am-8.30pm, Thu-Sat 9am-5.30pm. *www.mpl.org.*

Travel

Milwaukee County Transit System, 344-6711. Run metro buses, $1.75 basic fare, 10 ride pass $13 or unlimited weekly pass $13. Available from grocery stores and cheque cash centers. *www.ridemcts.com.*

Amtrak, 433 W St Paul Ave, 271-0840/(800) 872-7245.

Greyhound, 606 N James Lovell, 272-2156/(800) 231-2222.

General Mitchell International Airport, 5300 S Howell Ave, 747-5300. *www.mitchellairport.com.* Take the #80 bus, which must read 'Airport', from 6th & Wisconsin, $1.75; 30 min, or the **Airport Connect** shuttle bus which provides a door-to-door service. Call (800) 236-5450 for info. Takes 25 mins, $10. *www.mkelimo.com.*

MADISON Madison, wrapped picturesquely around two lakes, is the bastion of enlightened civilisation. More famous for being a college town than a state capital, its history of radical activism mirrors that of Ann Arbor and Berkeley. It probably has the highest under-employment anywhere; your taxi driver no doubt has a PhD in Medieval Philosophy and your waiter a degree in Set Theory Topology. The east side houses the alternative community, while the liberal west side is overrun with card-carrying members of the ACLU and the Women's Political Caucus. There's a lot packed into this pretty town, and cheap eats abound. Try both of the open-air farmers' markets for picnic fare. Rent a bike to get around. The **Madison City Guide** can be found at *www.ci.madison.wi.us/recTourism.html. The telephone area code is 608.*

Accommodation

Exel Inn, 4202 E Towne Blvd, 241-3861. Average rate D-$57.

HI-Madison Hostel, 141 S Butler St, 441-0144. Dorm-$18 AYH, $21 non-AYH; Private-$41 AYH, $44 non-AYH. Linens/towels included. Kitchen, laundry, library, tv and videos. *www.madisonhostel.com.*

The Lowell Center, 610 Langdon, 256-2621. $62-72, bfast incl. Indoor pool and sauna. On fraternity row. Great frat parties in the vicinity.

University Inn, 441 N Frances St, 257-4881/(800) 279-4881. D-$99 with continental bkfst. Heart of downtown. *www.visitmadison.com.*

Food

Best eateries are on or near campus, try **State Street.**

Amy's Cafe, 414 W Gilman St, 255-8172. Greek and American style salads and sandwiches. Open daily 11am-10pm. *www.amyscafe.com.*

Babcock Hall Dairy Store, 1605 Lynden, in Babcock Hall, 262-3045. Delicious ice cream and lunch specials. Mon-Fri 9.30am-5.30pm, Sat 10am-1.30pm. *www.wisc.edu/foodsci/store.*

Ella's Kosher Deli, 2902 E Washington, 241-5291. A real deli, standby of natives; sit and shmooze for hours. There's even a carousel to play on. Open Sun-Thu 10am-10pm, Fri-Sat 'til midnight.

Gino's, 540 State St, 257-9022. Known for stuffed pizza. Daily 11am-midnight.

Dane County Farmers Market, Capitol Sq, 424-6714. There's no shortage of fresh fruit and veg at this market, the largest of its kind in America. Summer outdoor and winter indoor markets. 'Beautiful local produce with a festival atmosphere.' April-Nov, Wed 8.30am-2pm, Sat 6am-2pm. *www.dcfm.org.*

Library Mall, UW campus, State St. A good choice for a pleasant day—food vendors gather en masse, offering a variety of choices. Call the university info line 263-2400 to hear about scheduled events on the Mall.

Monty's Blue Plate Diner, 2089 Atwood, 244-8505. All-American food and fabulous desserts. Mon-Thu 7am-9pm, Fri 'til 10pm, Sat 7.30am-10pm, Sun 7.30am-9pm. _www.foodfightinc.com._

Sunprint Café, 1 S Pickney, on the Square, 268-0114. Specialities are coffee, soups, sandwiches and pastries. An especially good place to have breakfast omelettes. Open Mon-Fri 7am-2pm.

Willy St Co-op, 1221 Williamson St, 251-6776/(888) 762-6776. A well-run co-op on Madison's east side. You'll be at the heart of Madison's alternative culture while you buy veggies. Daily 8am-9pm. _www.willystreet.coop/index.html._

Of interest

It all revolves around the campus—a must for briefing yourself on social action, people, and activities throughout the town. Pick up a copy of _Isthmus_ or check out _www.thedailypage.com._

American Players Theater, nr Spring Green, 40 miles W of Madison, 588-7401 (Box office open 10am-5pm, Mon-Sat, 2.30-6.30 Sun). In its 24th season this outdoor classical theatre is set in 110 wooded acres. It has quality Shakespearean and classical drama performed in the open air. Bring a picnic and enjoy the beautiful venue. Performances on Tue-Sun evenings June-Oct; from $29. _www.playinthewoods.org._

Henry Vilas Zoo, 702 S Randall, 266-4732. This zoo has improved in recent years. Vilas Park also has lovely beaches and is a nice place to take a walk. June-Sept: daily 9.30am-5pm; free. _www.vilaszoo.org._

Lake Shore path, start behind the Union terrace and walk out to **Picnic Point.** You'll meet many joggers and Madisonians talking over their problems.

Monona Terrace Community Center, 1 John Nolan Dr, 261-4000. Designed by Frank Lloyd Wright, the Center opens out to a beautiful view of the lake. Guided tours focusing on Wright's organic architecture are given daily at 1pm, $2 students. _www.mononaterrace.visitmadison.com._

Olbrich Botanical Gardens, 3330 Atwood Ave, 246-4551. Especially beautiful in summer, when the roses are in bloom. The outdoor gardens are open daily 8am-8pm; free. The **Bolz Conservatory's** daily hours are 10am-4pm, $1. Free Wed and Sat, 10am-noon. _www.olbrich.org._

State Capitol, 2 E Main St, 266-0382. The story goes that it is just a foot shorter than the one in Washington DC. Free tours: Mon-Fri 9-11am, 1-4pm, Sat 'til 3pm, Sun 1pm-3pm.

Nearby: Wisconsin Dells, 53 miles N of Madison, I-90/94. 'Magnificent rock and river scenery but terribly commercialised. Only visible by boat.' _www.wisdells.com._ Cure those hunger pangs and try the daily All-you-can-eat meals at **Paul Bunyan Northwoods Cook Shanty,** 254-8717; breakfast (7am-noon), lunch and dinner (noon-8.30pm). Also home of **Noah's Ark,** 1410 Wisconsin Dells Pkwy, 254-6351. America's largest water park, with over 60 water rides and attractions. Open Memorial Day-Labor Day, 9am-8pm; $28 for all-day pass. _www.noahsarkwaterpark.com._

Baraboo, about 40 miles NW of Madison. In May 1884, the five Ringling Brothers began their world-renowned circus in a modest way, behind the Baraboo jail. Their former winter quarters is now the site of the excellent **Circus World Museum,** 550 Water St, 356-8341. Big Top Circus performances 11.30am and 3.30pm. Open daily 9am-6pm; $15, _www.circusworldmuseum.com._ While in Baraboo, visit the **International Crane Foundation,** 356-9462. It's the only facility in the world that raises cranes for breeding and release into the wild. Open 9am-5pm, April-Oct., tours at 10am, 1 and 3pm. _www.savingcranes.org._

Taliesin, near Spring Green, 45 mins W of Madison. A walk through Frank Lloyd Wright's Wisconsin estate is a journey through his evolution as an architect. Tours go through Hillside Studio (designed as a school in 1902) and theater, the grounds or through the house. From $15-$75. Reserve tkts online at *www.taliesinpreservation.org*.

FLW may have been more famous, but the prize for sheer originality has to go to Alex Jordan for his spectacular **House on the Rock** in **Dodgeville**, south of Taliesin on Rt. 23, 935-3639. Described by *Roadside America* as 'the Palace of Versailles converted into a Tussaud wax museum by a Kuwaiti sheikh', House on the Rock is a mind-boggling conglomeration of mermaids, angels, antiques, enormous things (fireplace, steam locomotive, carousel, theatre, organs), catwalks and bisque dolls. Then there is the heart-stopping 'Infinity Room', a horizontal glass-enclosed needle stretching 218 ft out into the clear Wisconsin air with no visible means of support. See it! Takes approx 4 hrs to see everything. Daily 9am-7pm (tkt office closes at 6pm); $19.50. *www.houseontherock.com.*

Entertainment

The liveliest Madison nightlife is, obviously, near campus. Head to **State St**— it connects the campus and the Capitol; no cars are allowed. Bars to try near campus: **State St Brats**, 603 State St, 255-5544 and **Brothers Bar,** 704 University Ave, 251-9550. Both are crowded on w/ends.

Concerts on the Square: Capitol Square, every Wed eve, July.

Madison also hosts some fun summer festivals. **The Art Fair on the Square,** mid-July, colours the area around Capitol Square with some 500 artists present, and the worlds largest **Brat Fest** is becoming a Madison Tradition. Held Memorial Day w/end, it is an opportunity to sample a Johnsonville Brat and Pepsi for only $1. Proceeds go to charity, *www.bratfest.com* or call 345-2220. **Taste of Madison,** early September, is another opportunity to sample local dishes, this time from the best local restaurants. *www.madfest.org/taste.*

Information/ Internet access

Greater Madison Convention & Visitors Bureau, 615 E Washington Ave, 255-2537. Mon-Fri 8am-5pm. *www.visitmadison.com.*

Madison Public Library, 201 W Mifflin St, 266-6300. Free access, 1 hr time limit. Mon-Wed 8.30am-9pm, Thu-Fri 'til-6pm, Sat 9am-5pm. *www.madisonpubliclibrary.org.*

LAKE SUPERIOR REGION In NW Wisconsin, there are two areas to explore; **Indian Head Country,** (800) 826-6966, extending from the shore of Lake Superior to the Mississippi River. Tourist information is also available online at *www.wisconsinindianhead.org.* The **Apostle Islands,** (715) 779-3397, offer another chance to relax and unwind with a national lake shore known for its peaceful beauty. Also look online at *www.nps.gov/apis.* The **Turtle Flambeau Flowage** alone offers 19,000 acres of angling and wildlife watching opportunity. *www.turtleflambeauflowage.com.*

In these parts, fishing is almost a religion. See a testimonial to Wisconsin fish-worship at the **National Fresh Water Fishing Hall of Fame,** on Hwy 27 in **Hayward,** (715) 634-4440. Daily 15 Apr-1 Nov, 10am-4.30pm; $5. *www.freshwater-fishing.org/museum.html.*

AMERICA'S AMAZING AMUSEMENT PARKS

America's incredible amusement parks have evolved from trolley company-sponsored carnivals, a ploy to attract passengers, to today's megaparks that entertain over 130 million visitors annually in hundreds of inductions of heights, sights and stomach-gripping accelerations of all sorts. The thrill rides you'll find here have an all-American spirit, though the concept of coasters themselves has its roots in Eastern Europe.

The first "coasters" were, in fact, ice-covered slides built for winter amusement in 15th century Russia. The rides evolved, and eventually the idea arrived in the US. By March 2005, according to *American Coaster Enthusiasts (ACE)*, there were 260 parks with 712 coasters in North America, almost a third of the 1,800 or so operating worldwide. (Internationally Japan comes second in coaster numbers to the US – 232, followed by Britain – 152.) Of the 634 coasters in the US, 73 are in California, 49 in Pennsylvania, and 48 in Ohio. The past few years have been a building blitz for the major competing theme parks, so expect roller coasters that plunge more than 25 storeys, reaching 100 mph and more! *www.aceonline.org*.

In May 2005, **Six Flags Great Adventure** in New Jersey launched the tallest and fastest roller coaster yet, the *Kingda Ka*, which zooms at 128 mph. According to ACE, first riders reported 'a more intense, yet smoother launch than any coaster before it, a breathless dive and delay before the twist, and incredible views from both the summit at 456 feet and the 129-foot-high float hill.' The second fastest coaster in the world is the *Top Thrill Dragster* at **Cedar Point**, Ohio, which reaches 120 mph. *www.rcdb.com/rhr.htm*.

THEME PARKS. Disney's California Adventure Park, Anaheim, (714) 781-4565, celebrates (in a Disneyfied sense) the bounty of the Golden State, whether it be wildlife, aviation or wine. Includes Hollywood backlot, seaside boardwalk, $56. *www.disneyland.com*. **Coney Island - Astroland**, Brooklyn, New York, (718) 372-0275/265-2100. At the site of America's first roller coasters in the long-gone Luna Park, indulge in nostalgia of the sort featured in Woody Allen's *Radio Days* and countless other films. Ride the *Cyclone* - one of the most revered coasters of all time, first operated 1927, wooden track with 27 elevation changes, six 180 degree turns; designated National Historic Site in 1991. $5, $4 for second ride. *www.astroland.com*. **Disneyland**, Anaheim, CA, (714) 781-7290. The original Disney park and 2nd most visited, includes *Space Mountain* roller coaster, and *Star Tours* ('a ride to the Moon of Endor'). $56. *www.disneyland.com*. **DisneyWorld**, Orlando, FL, (407) 824-4321. The largest and most visited park in America features Epcot Center, MGM, Magic Kingdom, Animal Kingdom, Typhoon Lagoon and Blizzard Beach water parks and Downtown Disney/Pleasure Island (night-club extravaganza). *www.disneyworld.com*. **Hershey Park**, Hershey, PA (717) 534-3900. Besides more than 60 rides, this park features a tour of Hershey's Chocolate World, along with free samples. *www.hersheypa.com*. **MGM Studios,** CA, (407) 824-4321, currently featuring the *Indiana Jones Epic Stunt Spectacular*, *Fantasmic!*, *Aerosmith's Rock 'n' Roll roller-coaster, and the Twilight Zone Tower of Terror*; *www.disneyworld.com*. **Universal Studios Florida,** Orlando, FL, (407) 363-8000. The Orlando branch has 110 acres of rides, shows and attractions *www.universalorlando.com*. **Universal Studios Hollywood**, (800) 864-8377, a westcoast version of Universal Studios Florida, featuring *Mummy Returns-Chamber of Doom, Terminator2 3-D, and Shrek 4-D*. *www.universalstudios.com*.

ROLLER COASTER PARKS. The fastest, highest and biggest US roller coasters are in the flat Midwest. These parks don't mess around with themes or excessive corporate promotion-their selling point is pure speed and thrill. Among the most well known: a 'terrifying' place to start, according to the *New York Times*, is **Cedar**

Point, Sandusky OH, (419) 627-2350, the largest amusement park in the world, with 16 roller coasters. This park is home to the *Millennium Force*. It was the fastest and tallest roller coaster in the world, now second to Cedar Point's *Top Thrill Dragster*, 420 ft tall with a speed of 120 mph! If you are anywhere *near* Ohio, this is not one to pass up. Cedar Point's most recent aquatic addition is *Snake River Falls*. With 80ft drops at 50-degree angles, this is the world's tallest, steepest and fastest water-ride. *www.cedarpoint.com*. **Worlds of Fun** (and **Oceans of Fun** water park next-door), Kansas City, MO, (816) 454-4545, have the *Mamba*-a shocker with an initial plunge of 205 ft! Also notable are the speedy *Timber Wolf* and coiled *Orient Express*. *www.worldsoffun.com*.

Paramount's Kings Island, Mason, OH, (513) 754-5800/(800) 288-0808. Eight banked turns and 70 mph speeds make the wooden roller coaster *The Beast* the world's longest with 7400 ft of tracks (lasting a death-defying 3 mins 40 secs), while the newer *Son of Beast* topped the world in height for a wooden coaster. *www.pki.com*. **Paramount's King's Dominion**, Doswell, VA (804) 876-5561, home of the *Hypersonic-XLC*. Riders are launched horizontally by compressed air from 0 to 80 mph in 1.8 seconds! Enough to blast a politician's toupee clear off, eh? It then ascends 17 storeys at 90 degrees. Also has its own water park area, incl. in price. *www.kingsdominion.com*.

Six Flags America, Largo, MD (301) 249-1500, a theme park and water park, features the *Superman-Ride of Steel*, a hyper-coaster that ends up leaping a 197 ft building and flying faster than a speeding bullet. *www.sixflags.com*. **Six Flags Great America**, Gurnee, IL (847) 249-4636, offers the double-track triple helix wooden *American Eagle* which reaches speeds of over 66 mph; *Batman*, a two minute suspended outside looping thrill-of-a-lifetime; and *Superman-Ultimate Flight*. **Six Flags St. Louis**, MO, (636) 938-4800, features the *Excalibur* and *Ninja*, which has spirals, drops, a sidewinder and 360 degree loop. In the south, **Six Flags over Texas** in Arlington, (817) 530-6000, features the *Texas Giant*, which used to get our recommendation – that is until the *Titan* came along, with an 85mph drop into a 120ft tunnel.

At **Six Flags Astroworld,** Houston, TX, (713) 799-1234, try the *Texas Cyclone*, a long-time favourite, and the *Ultra Twister*, once compared to 'riding inside a giant slinky, with a nine-storey free-fall to start'. **Six Flags Over Georgia,** nr Atlanta, (770) 739-3400, opened spring of 2001, with the *Déjà Vu*, in which you fly through a 110 ft inverted boomerang twist – and then do it all again – backwards! **Six Flags Magic Mountain**, Valencia, CA, (661) 255-4111, where the world's largest looping roller coaster at 188 ft, the *Viper*, reaches 70 mph and achieves seven inversions. 'The initial drop is truly heart-stopping!'

Check out *www.themeparks.about.com*, *www.ultimaterollercoaster.com*, *www.aceonline.org*, and *www.ridezone.com* for info on just about every roller coaster and theme park in the country.

WATER PARKS. Of growing popularity and ingenuity, especially in the warmer states, are America's 136 water parks. In Florida, **Typhoon Lagoon,** Orlando, FL (407) 560-4141 has one of the world's largest wave pools *www.disneyworld.com* but **Waterworld's** *Thunder Bay*, Denver, CO, (303) 427-7873, also releases mammoth waves. *www.waterworldcolorado.com*. **Adventure Island**, Tampa, FL (813) 987-5600, is home of the *Tampa Typhoon*, a slide that shoots down from a height of seven storeys. *www.adventureisland.com*. **Water Country USA**, Williamsburg VA, (800) 343-7946, boasts the *Rampage*, a nearly-vertical water slide of 75 ft. Get more into at *www.4adventure.com*. **Wet 'n Wild** parks, located in Orlando FL, (407) 351-3200 and Las Vegas, NV, (702) 734-0088, as well as **Six Flags Hurricane Harbor** in Dallas, TX, (817) 265-3356, all feature fast, helical rides on water mats and sensational free falls. Explore *Wild Rivers Mountain* with 25 water rides, at **Wild Rivers**, Irvine, CA, (949) 768-9453.

THE MOUNTAIN STATES

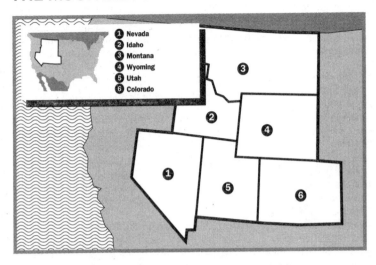

Nevada
Idaho
Montana
Wyoming
Utah
Colorado

After the endless horizontality of the Midwest, with its carefully manicured patterns of fences, townships and agriculture, the landscape of the Mountain States bursts upon you, young, rangy and wild as a colt. The Rockies, the San Juans and the Grand Tetons are intimidating, yet seductive. Crossing them is a pilgrimage; just imagine how their sharp white beauty must have made pioneers' hearts sink into their boots.

Like the first western immigrants, modern day visitors will immediately be astounded by the great magnitude and diversity of the land. From Montana's Big Sky country to the extreme verticality of southern Utah, everything in the west is, in a word, Big. Great distances separate cities, attractions and often, people. The extreme weather of the west strikes a precarious balance between the calm sunshine that fills most days and the violent and unpredictable storms that descend upon the unsuspecting throughout the year. For these reasons and others, the western wanderer may find exploration impossible without a car. Check the introduction for tips on buying and renting.

The topography doesn't limit itself to mountains, either. In this six-state cluster, you are treated to geysers, glaciers, buttes, vast river chasms, vivid canyons in paintbrush colours. The greater portion of this beauty is protected in National Parks and Monuments, among them: Rocky Mountain, Yellowstone, Craters of the Moon, Glacier, Devil's Tower, Zion and Bryce Canyon. In stark contrast to all this natural grandeur is the flagrant plasticity of Las Vegas, Reno and Hoover Dam/Lake Mead, without a doubt the most wondrously artificial trio of spots on earth.

Weather throughout the region tends to be dry and hot in summer and, with the exception of Las Vegas, cold and snowy in winter. Even summer evenings can be cold, and violent thunderstorms are common.

COLORADO - The Centennial State

Horace Greeley, the newspaper editor famous for his advice: 'Go West, young man', actually found the west a bit raw for his tastes. In 1860, he described what he saw on the frontier: 'They had a careless way of firing revolvers, sometimes at each other, at other times quite miscellaneous—so I left.'

Like other mountain states, Colorado has a lusty, shoot-'em-up past filled with gold seekers, gold diggers, cattlemen and con men. Many former mining towns remain, some recycled into ski resorts, others spruced up for tourism but still in settings of unparalleled grandeur. Modern day Colorado gold has been discovered by the technologically inclined and politically aware. Components for the Hubble telescope were manufactured here, and the state is the second-largest employer of federal government workers. Given its natural beauty, colorful history and highly acclaimed skiing, Colorado is a prime tourist destination. Known as the nation's backbone, the state has 54 peaks over 14,000 feet. Over 75 percent of US land over 10,000 feet is concentrated in Colorado.

The eastern section, a monotony of rangeland cluttered with dun-coloured tumbleweeds and fenced 'hog-tight, horse-high and bull-strong', has little to offer. Concentrate instead on the western half, where you find four **national parks**: **Rocky Mountains** *www.nps.gov/romo/*; **Mesa Verde** *www.nps.gov/meve/*; **Black Canyon of the Gunnison** *http://blackcanyonofthegunnison.areaparks.com/* and **Great Sand Dunes** *www.nps.gov/grsa*, awesome scenery and an extraordinary display of summer wildflowers (some 5000 species).

Colorado's many youth hostels, among the best in the US, include ranches, historic hotels and ski lodges. For the best deals, head to the Rockies from late August to early October after the summer mountaineers have retreated but before the snows descend. For camping facilities in Colorado you can reserve a place at *www.reserveamerica.com/client/client_co.jsp*. Also check *www.coloradodirectory.com*.

The four telephone area codes for Colorado are 303, 720, 719 and 970.

DENVER Impressively situated against a backdrop of snowy peaks, Denver is a welcome end to a gruelling, 'are we there yet?' journey across the Great Plains. In spite of its picturesque setting, much of the unpleasant urban sprawl, crime and pollution that plague other American cities has arrived in Denver. After a painfully awkward decade of rapid development, Denver now sports a modern, well-finished look, befitting its role as banking, government, and industrial capital for the Rocky Mountains.

Perched at the confluence of Cherry Creek and the South Platte River, Denver began as a mining outpost. Its convenient foothills location nicely met the needs of Rocky Mountain miners, who rushed westward in the 1860s to find gold. The city didn't ascend to real prominence, however, until it linked up to the transcontinental railroad in 1869. A silver rush further catalysed the city's growth a decade later. Denver—complete with Colorado's first saloon—became the state's capital. Today, people pour into Denver by the million, many at Denver International Airport, *www.flydenver.com*. It looks like a tented Bedouin city but is the most modern, technically advanced airport in the US; in 2004, it was the world's 10th and the nation's 5th busiest airport, handling over 40 million passengers.

With a median age of 30, over 200 parks and more days of sunshine (300) than San Diego or Miami Beach, the 'Mile High' city is a welcome place for sports and outdoors enthusiasts. Its undying love of professional sports teams has moved beyond the Broncos as local teams take turns bringing home championship trophies. Catch one of the many team games while in town. The Broncos football team, *www.denverbroncos.com*, 649-9354, play from September–January and have a stadium capacity exceeding 76,000. In the LoDo district (Lower downtown) is **Coors Field,** *www.mlb.com,* home to baseball's Colorado Rockies from April–September, with a crowd capacity of 50,000 and the **Pepsi Center,** *www.pepsicenter.com* hosts both the Nuggets basketball team from November–April and the Avalanche ice-hockey team from September–April. Denver also boasts possibly the world's largest sporting goods store, **Gart Sports**, *www.gartsports.com*, 10th St and Broadway, since 1928, where you can if needs be, shop from a golf cart!

The nation's No 1. sports town conjures a city full of beefed-up sports jocks, but more people attend cultural events annually than all four pro sports teams combined. Denver is today the most educated city in the US with more high school grads per capita than any other city. As such, a lively cultural life throbs in Denver when the sun goes down. The city also brews more beer than any other and the largest brewpubs are located in LoDo with a choice of over 80 varieties. Wynkoop Brewing Company, *www.wynkoop.com*. In June, the LoDo Beer Festival closes down the streets offering music and beer samples from all 70 Colorado breweries.

Downtown Denver revolves around 16th St Mall, a mile-long promenade lined with shops and eating places. *www.downtowndenver.com/bid/16thstmall.htm* and *www.denver.org*.

The telephone area code is 303.

Accommodation
Innkeepers of the Rockies, 1717 Downing St, 861-7777. Dorm $17. Private rooms $35 in Guest Haus (5 blocks away). Friendly, busy neighbourhood with many restaurants, Internet available, and cable TV. 'Clean, comfortable and well equipped.' 'Owners very knowledgeable about sights and attractions.' New owner in 2005. *www.innkeeperrockies.com.*

Motel 6, 3050 W 49th Ave, 455-8888. S-$45-$54, D-$51-$60. AC, indoor pool, TV. Bus stop 1 blk away. 'Friendly staff, good service.' Also on Wadsworth Blvd, 232-4924. *www.motel6.com.*

Melbourne Hotel and Hostel, 607 22nd St, 292-6386. $13 AYH, $16 non-AYH, private rms D-$32, AYH, $35 non-AYH. 6 blocks from Greyhound stn. If arriving at airport call for directions. 'Brilliant.' 'Good, clean rooms. Staff very helpful.' 'Reservations strongly recommended.' *www.denverhostel.com*.

New House Hotel, 1470 Grant St, nr State Capitol, 861-2415. 70 rooms, first come first served basis. S-$29.50-$35, shared bath. S-$41, private bath and colour TV. Both w/additional refundable $5 key deposit. No rsvs.

Camping: Delux R.V. Park, 5520 N Federal Blvd., I-70 exit 272. 433-0452. 4.5m from downtown. Tent site $20, RV full hook-up $31. *www.deluxrvpark.com*.

Food
Try Rocky Mountain trout and rattlesnake, the local specialties. This is also the

home of 'Rocky Mt oysters' or 'swinging steaks', an indelicate dish made of French-fried bull testicles. The *Official Visitor's Guide* (avail. at Visitors Bureau) lists dozens of places to eat in Denver, and includes an extensive ethnic restaurant guide. 'Larimer & 17th Sts, variety of quite cheap places to eat—Turkish, Greek, Chinese, French, pizza.'

Casa Bonita, 6715 W Colfax, 232-5115. The all-you-can-eat Mexican platter is not the half of it: This isn't a restaurant, it's a Mexican carnival—with gun fights, cliff divers, mariachi bands. 'Disappointing.' Open Sun-Thur 11am-9:30pm, Fri & Sat 'til 10pm. *www.casabonitadenver.com*.

Cherry Cricket, 2641 E Second Ave, 322-7666. Bar and restaurant, famous for hamburgers. Also serves Mexican fare. Open daily 11am-12am, happy hour 4:30-6:30pm. *www.cherrycricket.com*.

Duffy's Shamrock, 1635 Court Pl, 534-4935. 'Good service, excellent value.' 'A godsend for the traditional boozer. Longest bar west of Mississippi—78ft. $6 specials, home-made red and green chili.' 'All-American food.' Open Mon-Fri 7:00am-2am, Sat 8:00am-2:00am and Sun 11:00am-2:00am.

The Market, 1445 Larimer St, 534-5140. 'A trendy place to sit and drink coffee, buy health foods, watch people.' $5.50-$6, self-service deli. Open Mon-Thur,   6.30am-11pm,   Fri   6.30am-12:00am   Sat-Sun   7:30am-12am. *www.larimersquare.com/restaurants.html*.

The Old Spaghetti Factory, 1215 18th St, 295-1864, dinners with drink and dessert, $5-$8 with antique surroundings incl. tables made out of beds. Mon-Thur 5:00pm-9:30pm, Fri 5:00pm-10:30pm Sat 12.00pm-10.30pm, Sun 'til 9.30pm. *www.osf.com*.

20th St Cafe, just behind Greyhound bus station at 1123 20th St, 295-9041. $2-$6; chicken/fried steak special. 'Good cheap breakfast and lunch in clean and friendly surroundings.' Open Mon-Fri 6am-6:45pm, Sat 7am-1.30pm.

Of Interest

Art Museum, 100 W 14th Ave Pkwy, (720) 865-5000. Striking, fortress-like building covered with a million sparkling tiles. Seven floors of well-displayed art from totem poles to Picasso, incl. Native American and European collections. 'Exhibits on Indians more interesting and paintings better than in many small US galleries.' The expansion project which includes The Hamilton Building will be opening in Fall 2006. Tue-Sat 10am-5pm, Wed 'til 9pm, Sun noon-5pm. $8, $6 w/student ID. *www.denverartmuseum.org*.

Black American West Museum, 3091 California St, 292-2566. Black pioneer history. Founded by Paul Stewart, who was inspired to discover the forgotten history of the West's African Americans as a child when he was told that he could only play the role of the Indian –since 'there are no black cowboys'. The museum also pays homage   to   western   black   women.   Summer   daily   10am-5pm, $6. *www.coax.net/people/lwf/bawmus.htm*. *www.blackamericanwest.org.*

Colorado History Museum, 13th and Broadway, 866-3681/2. The 112-ft time line spans 150 years of Colorado history, with documents, maps, photos, and artifacts. Library and Native American exhibits. Open Mon-Sat 10am-5.00pm, Sun noon-5.00pm; $5. $4.50 w/student ID. *www.coloradohistory.org*.

Governor's Residence Tours, 400 E 8th Avenue, 866-3682. Tour the current governor's residence, donated to the State in 1960. Free, 1pm-3pm, every Tues in the summer. *www.coloradohistory.org/join%5Fus/volunteers/ResidenceTour.htm*.

Larimer Square, 14th to 15th Sts. Denver's restored Victorian and highly commercial   'heart',   with   gas   lit   lamps   and   horse-drawn   carriages. *www.larimersquare.com* Larimer Square runs into **16th Street Mall**, the heart of Denver's business, convention and theatre district with more shops and eateries. Free shuttle buses are the limited traffic allowed in this strip and travel the length of the Mall in about 7 minutes. Nearby is the glittering **Tabor Center**, a completely glass-enclosed shopping complex, named after a 1890s gold rush bonanza king. *www.taborcenter.com.*

Denver Zoo City Park, 2300 Steele St, Denver's City Park, 376-4800. Home to nearly 4000 animals representing 750 species. See the Komodo Dragons Tropical Discovery, featuring waterfalls, mountain cave, tropical streams, temple ruins and a jungle river. The painting rhino is also a must-see! Open daily 9am-6pm, admission gate closes at 5pm, $11. *www.denverzoo.org.*

Denver Museum Nature and Science, 2001 Colorado Blvd in City Park, 322-7009/(800) 925-2250. Dinosaur displays, mummy exhibits and the world's most advanced Space Odyssey planetarium (fully interactive exhibition about life beyond earth). $15, $6 w/student ID. Combo tkts w/IMAX giant screen cinema, $20, $10 w/student ID. 'Exhilarating experience.' Daily 9am-5pm. *www.dmns.org/main/en/.*

The Molly Brown House Museum, 1340 Pennsylvania St, 832-4092. Learn the true details of the ill-fated Titanic. Ms Brown was one of few survivors and earned herself fame & the name 'the unsinkable Molly Brown'. Tours operate daily with the last one at 3.30pm, arrive early. 'Interesting story, uninteresting museum.' June-Aug Mon-Sat 10am-3.30pm, Sun from noon; winter, closed Mon. $6.50 *www.mollybrown.org.*

Six Flags Elitch Gardens, 2000 Elitch Circle, 595-4386. Over 50 rides and attractions – including a tropical water park. Experience the newest extreme water ride with Edge to the edge of the other side. Memorial Day to Labor Day, 10am-10pm. $37.99, online tickets for $25.99. 'Not for the faint-hearted.' *www.sixflags.com.*

State Capitol, 200 E. Colfax 866-2604. This dome has been gold-leafed 3 times since 1907, but of true value is the Colorado onyx (the world's entire supply) used in the interior of the Capitol. Ascend to the top deck; a brass marker identifies nearby peaks. Free 45-min tours Mon-Fri 9am-3.30pm. *www.state.co.us/gov_dir/leg_dir/lcsstaff/tourwelcome.htm.*

Nearby: Golden - Coors Brewery, 13th and Ford, 277-2337. Free 45 min tours and sampling every 30 min, Mon-Sat 10am-4pm. Bring ID. 'Very nice people.' *www.coors.com.* Overlooking Coors, high above on Lookout Mt, is **Buffalo Bill Grave and Museum,** 526-0747. Wild West shows and Pony Express artifacts dedicated to this flamboyant figure who symbolised the West. Learn how Cody earned his fame and also understand his true relationship with the Native Americans. On the 1st Sunday in June, take part in a recreation of his burial in 1917. Daily 9am-5pm. $3. *www.buffalobill.org.*

Glenwood Springs: Greyhound, (800) 123-2222 run buses. 'Day trip from Denver; take 8.15am bus service to Glenwood Springs. Glorious Rocky Mt scenery along the way. If the bus is not late, you arrive at lunchtime. Swim, eat strawberry waffles at Rosie's Bavarian Restaurant across the street from the bus station. It's a 3 hr and 40 min trip both ways - a long day, but worth it.' *www.ci.glenwood-springs.co.us.*

Rosie's, 141 W 6th St, (970) 928-9186. German and American fare. Open for b/fast daily 7am-noon, $6 and for dinner Wed-Sat 5pm-9pm, $15. 'Best breakfast restaurant in town.'

Entertainment

Pick up a copy of *Westword,* a free weekly, for info about the arts in Denver. *www.westword.com.*

Buckhorn Exchange, 1000 Osage St, 534-9505. Pricey downstairs restaurant ($30-$40) with buffalo and elk entrees. Stick to upstairs, Denver's oldest western saloon. Outdoor covered patio with food cooked on a chuck wagon. Thu-Sat live music in cocktail lounge (cowboy music and 'old ballads'). Open Mon-Fri 11am-2pm and 5.30pm-9pm, Fri-Sat 5.00pm-10pm, Sun 5pm-9pm. *www.buckhorn.com.*

Denver Performing Arts Complex (PLEX), 950 13th st, 640-2862. Covers 4sq blocks and is the largest arts center in the US. Eight theatres, over 10,000 seats and the center of Denver's art community. *www.artscomplex.com*.

El Chapultepec, 20th and Market, 295-9126. Jazz bar since 1924; daily live performances, no cover charge. Food $3-$10. 'A real dive, but good jazz.' Open 9:00am-2am daily.

Glendale is Denver's 'singles scene' with over a dozen discos, saloons and restaurants crammed into a small area. Bars with discos, outdoor volleyball courts, saddles for bar stools ... you name it.

Mercury Cafe, 2199 California, 294-9281/58. Charismatic and bohemian entertainment; swing dance, salsa and belly dancing are all on offer. Dance classes for all levels. Diner open Tues-Sun 5.30pm-11pm, nightclub open 'til 2am. Coffee, drink and dessert served 'til 1.30am. Low prices. 'Laid back and popular with locals.' Call or visit website for times, prices and schedules. *www.mercurycafe.com*.

Pepsi Center, 1000 Chopper Circle, nr 16th St Mall, 405-1111. 20,000 seat arena, home of the NBA Denver Nuggets and NHL Colorado Avalanche. Also holds concerts and other events. *www.pepsicenter.com*.

Red Rocks Amphitheater, located in 816-acre Red Rocks Park, 17 mins W of Denver, nr Morrison, 640-2637. Summer rock, country & western, pop and classical concerts surrounded by 440-ft red sandstone bluffs. 'Any concert here is a must—the most beautiful setting in the world with spectacular views over the prairies and Denver.' Park admission is free; shows range from $8-$80. A visitor's center is also here so it's an interesting venue to visit at any time. Daily 5am-11pm. *www.redrocksonline.com*.

The Snake Pit, 608 E. 13th Ave. 831-1234. Funky club. Guest DJ's from the UK! Cover ranges from free to $5. Open daily 5pm-2am. Food available inc pizza…

Wazee Supper Club, 15th and Wazee, LoDo, 623-9518. Pizza place and downtown bar w/jukebox. 17 beers on tap, $2-$3.75 per glass. Open 11am-2am Mon-Sat, Sun noon-midnight, Happy Hour 4pm-6pm. *www.wazeesupperclub.com*.

Wynkoop Brewing Company, 1634 18th St, 297-2700. Colorado's oldest brewery. Minimum ten beers on tap at all times, all brewed on premises. Stout, porter, light and medium ales, bitter beers. Tours of brewery Sat 1pm-4pm. Open 11am-2am, Happy Hour 3pm-6pm. *www.wynkoop.com*.

Shopping

Cherry Creek Shopping District, 3000 East 1st Ave, 388-3900. It's huge - 400 stores, 75 restaurants and 25 art galleries – and has everything, including Tiffany & Co, that a shopper could ever desire. Mon-Fri 10am-9pm, Sat 10am-8pm, Sun 11am-6pm. *www.shopcherrycreek.com*.

Tattered Cover; 2 locations in central Denver: 2955 East 1st Ave, nr C.C. Mall, and 1628 16th st, LoDo, (800) 833-9327. One of the nation's most outstanding bookshops (so said the *NY Times*). Four storeys with reading lamps and comfy chairs to aid browsers. *www.tatteredcover.com*.

Information

Visitors Bureau, 918 16th St, 623-0655/892-1505 and 1555 California Street, 892-1112/(800) 645-3446. *www.denver.org*.

Colorado Tourism Office, 1625 Broadway, (800) 433-2656. *www.colorado.com*.

Internet access

Cafe @ Netherworld, 1278 Pennsylvania, 861-8638. Bar, restaurant, pool hall and cyber café. $5/hr however, connect your own laptop for $2/hr, spend $5 between 11am-2pm and receive free access. Daily, 11am-2am. *www.netherworld.com*.

Denver Public Library, 10 W 14th Ave, (720) 865-1111. Free access, common courtesy basis. Mon-Tue 10am-9pm, Thur-Sat 10am-5.30pm, Sun 1pm-5pm. For other branches visit *www.denver.lib.co.us*.

Travel

Greyhound, 293-6555/(800) 231-2222, 1055 19th St & Curtis. Bus service to Salt Lake City is one of the most scenic routes in America. 'The best part is the first 3 hours out of Denver.' 'Do not do it at night, fantastic scenery, too great to sleep through.' _www.greyhound.com._

City Bus, RTD, 299-6000, $1.25 basic fare. $3.50 to Boulder. _www.rtd-denver.com._

Amtrak, Union Station, 17th and Wynkoop Sts, 534-2812/(800)872-7245. The _California Zephyr_, Chicago-Oakland, CA route runs through Denver and the stretch to Salt Lake City is one of the best in the US, with the train running slowly up into the mountains, through one of the longest tunnels in the US, into beautiful gorges otherwise inaccessible to humanity. 'Get off at Glenwood Springs to see natural steam rising behind the station.'

Car rental: Best way to see the state is to drive, try: **Cut Rate Rent a Car,** 8000 E. Colfax, 393-0028. Min 2 day rental; lowest price $14.95/day or $100/week. _www.cheaprentacar.com._ Also try **Auto Driveaway,** 5777 E Evans, 757-1211. Ships cars across the country. $350 refundable deposit (if returned in one piece), all you pay for is the gas. _www.autodriveaway.com._

Hiking

The 500-mile **Colorado Trail** begins at **Waterton Canyon** nr **Chatfield Reservoir,** 10 miles S of Denver. As the trail winds across the state to Durango, it crosses 8 mountain ranges, 7 national forests, 6 wilderness areas, and 5 river systems. For a more feasible day's hike, try **Devil's Head Lookout in Rampart Range,** 30 miles SW of Denver. The Devil's Head lookout tower has been in service since 1919. This national historic treasure is accessible via a 1.4 mile long foot trail. The rise of 940 vertical feet takes most people 45-90 minutes, but the reward is a 360 degree panorama of the Spanish Peaks to the south, Mt Evans to the north, South Park to the west and the plains to the east. Bring lots of water. More details call the Range Manager 275-5610 or visit _www.fs.fed.us/r2/psicc/spl._ For more hiking ideas, visit **Mike's Hikes** online at _www.mtnds.com/hikes._

HEADING NORTH TO THE ROCKIES Leaving Denver on I-70 W, one of the most scenic routes north—the **Peak-to-Peak Highway**—begins near **Central City**, a well-preserved Victorian town with honky-tonk saloons. The discovery of gold in Central City in 1859 turned fledgling Denver into little more than a revolving door. Everyone cleared out overnight to strike it rich. You can still pan for gold in what was 'the richest square mile on earth'.

The final leg of this road, Highway 7, leads to the east entrance of the Rocky Mountain National Park. An alternate route to this entrance at Estes Park, Highway 36, passes through Boulder.

BOULDER Although it's become too popular for its own good, Boulder still makes a scenic and lively alternative to Denver for explorations in northern Colorado. It is just an hour's drive northwest from Denver and offers a wealth of cultural, culinary and outdoor activities. It's largely a laid-back student town with 25,000 university students in residence here. Boulder's current trendy center is along the Pearl Street Mall: 'fun on Sundays, clowns, magic shows, good eats, lots of young people'. 'Quite a magical place and altogether more interesting than Denver.' 'One of my favourite places in the whole USA. A medium-sized university town, full of life and young people.' _The telephone area code is 303._ _www.bouldercoloradousa.com_ , _http://www.ci.boulder.co.us/_

Accommodation
Boulder International Youth Hostel, 1107 12th St, 442-0522. Dorm $20 with $10 refundable deposit. S-$42, D-$49, $10 ref. deposit, both shared bath. Kitchen, laundry; deposit for fans, phones, refrigerators. 20 mins to mountains; city or charter buses available. 'Friendly, relaxed.' 'Ill-equipped kitchen.' 'Rather cramped.' *www.boulderhostel.com.*
New West Inns, 970 28th St, 443-7800/(800) 525-2149. S-$75, D-$80. Bfast incl. Outdoor pool.

Food
Boulder is the only city in the US to own a glacier. This once served as a delicious water supply and the UMC food service, on campus, will be happy to serve you ice cold H_2O but also has an extensive choice of catering facilities to fill you up. Try **Alfred Packer Memorial Grill,** U of Colorado, Memorial Bldg, Broadway and Euclid, 492-6578. Mon-Fri 7am-2.30pm, Sat-Sun closed during summer. Named after the only man ever convicted of cannibalism in the US. Alf's culinary treat took place in 1874, when he and 5 others were trapped by blizzards. Only he survived. The presiding judge, who convicted him said: 'There were only 6 Democrats in Hinsdale County and you, you son-of-a-bitch, ate 5 of them!' *umc.colorado.edu/food*.
Boulder Dushanbe Teahouse, 1770 13th St, 442-4993. Like nothing you've ever seen. The teahouse was a gift from Boulder's sister city of Dushanbe, Tajikistan, handcrafted and reassembled over the course of 8 years. Sun-Thurs 8am-9pm, Fri-Sat 'till 10pm. International menu. *www.boulderteahouse.com*.
Buchanan's Coffee Pub, 1301 Pennsylvania (On the Hill), 440-0222. Pastries, sandwiches and flavoured coffees from $1.10. Summer, Mon-Fri 7am-11pm, Sat-Sun 8am-11pm. *www.buchananscoffee.com.*
The Mediterranean, 1002 Walnut St, 444-5335. Widely considered the best restaurant in town, the 'Med' offers a cornucopia of delicious and inexpensive food. The paella is not to be missed. *www.themedboulder.com*.
Old Chicago Pizza Parlour, 1102 Pearl, 443-5031. Huge selection (110+) of beers. Beer monsters can try the 'World Tour of Beers Special' in the bar: win prizes while you get sloshed! But don't forget the food: 'Best pizza I've ever tasted.' $2.50 Guinness pints on Thu. 11am-2am daily, Happy Hour Mon-Fri 3pm-6pm. *www.oldchicago.com*.
Traling's Oriental Cafe, 1305 Broadway, 449-0400. Popular cheap and cheerful Chinese dishes. Hip with students. Sun-Wed 11am-9.30pm, Thu-Sat 'till 2:30am. *www.traling.com.*
TridentBooksellers & Cafe, 940 Pearl, 443-3133. Consistently voted 'Best Coffeehouse' by Boulderites. Browse in the adjoining bookstore, and then sit outside and sip bottomless cups of gourmet coffee.

Of Interest
Arapaho Glacier, 28 miles W of Boulder, the glacier (more a snow-field now) is about $1/2$ mile long and 50-100ft thick. Can't get too close, but a trail does run along the south edge and makes for an interesting hike. *www.fs.fed.us/r2/arnf/recreation/trails/brd/arapaho-glacier.shtml*.
Celestial Seasonings Tea Co, 4600 Sleepytime Dr, 581-1202. Free 45-min tasting tours of the Boulder factory include; a stroll through their herb garden and a stopover in the refreshing 'mint room'. Mon-Sat 10am-3pm, Sun 11am-3pm. Tours leave on the hour, arrive early. *www.celestialseasonings.com*.
Colorado Chautauqua, 900 Baseline, 440-7666. Dining, lodgings and events hosted in the dining hall est. 1898 and auditorium. Events list at *www.chautauqua.com*. A variety of hiking trails also start near here, including one to the beautiful **Flatirons Glacier.** 'Great views over Boulder—but take plenty of water!' Ranger cottage, 441-3440 or *www.ci.boulder.co.us/openspace*.

Eldorado Springs, located off I-93, 499-1316. Swim in fresh artesian spring water. The pool has a slide and is surrounded by towering mountains. $6 fee. 'Scenic place to cool off or rock-climb but you need transport.' 10am-6pm daily. _www.eldoradosprings.com_.

Fiske Planetarium, 492-5001/2, Regent Drive, on campus: 'Worth a visit, especially the laser show'. Opening times and shows vary, esp during summer. Laser show $5. _www.colorado.edu/fiske_.

Glider rides, 5534 Independence Rd, 527-1122. $60-$170; rides from 15 mins. Daily 9am-5pm. _www.milehighgliding.com_.

U of Colorado, 429-6161. 600 acre campus is the big party place in town, with a mass of summer events; schedule at _www.colorado.edu_.

Entertainment

Catacombs Bar, 2115 13th St, 443-0486, cool basement bar with live music, Mon, Wed, Fri and Sat. Daily 4.30pm-1.30am, Sun from 7.30pm. Happy Hour 'till 8pm daily, Sun 'til midnight. _www.catacombsbar.com_.

Colorado Shakespeare Festival, 277 U of Colorado. Outdoor and indoor theatre; Jul-Aug. One of the best in the US. Tkts 492-0554, $10-$52. _www.coloradoshakes.org_.

Rockies Brewing Company, 2880 Wilderness Pl, 444-8448. Open Mon-Fri 11am, 'til 8pm Mon-Tue, 'til 9pm Wed-Fri. Closed Sat-Sun. Free tasting tours Mon-Fri 2pm. _www.boulderbeer.com_.

Sundown Saloon, 1136 Pearl, 449-4987 has a wide selection of microbrews. 'Plenty of pool tables downstairs.' Open daily noon-2am. _www.thesundownsaloon.com._

The Mall, 449-3774, downtown pedestrian Mall along **Pearl St**. Variety of lunch and evening performances. 'Superb spectacles any summer evening—all free.' _www.boulderdowntown.com_ for events calendar.

The Walrus, 1911 11th St, 443-9902. Located near the mall. Good mix of students and locals. 'Cozy, friendly atmosphere.'

Information

Boulder Convention and Visitors Bureau, 2440 Pearl St, 442-2911/(800) 444-0447. _http://www.bouldercoloradousa.com._

Boulder Ranger District, Arapaho and Roosevelt National Forests Hiking. 2140 Yarmouth Ave, 541-2500. _www.fs.fed.us/r2/arnf/about/organization/brd/index.shtml._

ESTES PARK A hairbreadth away from the entrance to Rocky Mountain National Park, Estes may be the most convenient place to lodge if you're without wheels. Commercial campgrounds here have showers and are close to everything. The Estes Park Welcome Center website, _www.estes-park.com_, is a comprehensive guide with helpful links for lodging and recreation information in the area. Also try _www.estesparkresort.com_ or call (800) 44-ESTES. _The area code is 970._

Accommodation

YMCA Estes Park Center, 2515 Tunnel Rd. 586-3341. Adjacent to park and great value if travelling with friends. Private cabin w/double bed and bunk beds for $91 or main lodge with three Queen beds - sleeps 6 people and private shower for $110. Recreational activities abound. Rsvs advisable in July. _www.ymcarockies.org_.

Food/Entertainment

Estes Park Brewery, 470 Prospect Village Drive, 586-5421. Open daily 11am-10pm. 'Pool tables, pinball, basic food and free tasting bar anytime.' _www.epbrewery.net_.

Poppy's Pizza and Grill, 342 E Elkhorn, 586-8282. Pizzas from $3.50. 'Nice cheap restaurant with big patio, frequented by locals.' Open daily, 11am-9pm. _www.poppyspizzaandgrill.com._

The Stanley Hotel, 333 Wonder View Ave, (800) 976-1377. A must-see if you're in

Estes; this striking 1909 white building was King's inspiration for the *The Shining* and it is also part location for the movie *Dumb and Dumber*. *www.stanleyhotel.com*.
The Wheel Bar, 132 E Elkhorn, 586-9381. Cheap liquor, entrees around $15.50. Open daily 10am-2am.

ROCKY MOUNTAIN NATIONAL PARK To the Indians and early trappers, these were the Shining Mountains, gleaming with silvery lakes, golden sunrises, blue-white glaciers and snowpacks. Later settlers prosaically dubbed them 'Rocky', but there is nothing prosaic about this wildlife-rich range of mountains and valleys crowned by a cross-section of the Continental Divide. Over 60 peaks in the park are 12,000 feet or more. Even the untrained eye can see the clear traces of glacial action in the five visible active glaciers that remain. **Longs Peak** is the highest, at 14,259 ft.

Be sure to take the **Trail Ridge Road** (Hwy 34), the highest fully paved road in the US, which follows a 50 mile old Ute and Arapaho trail along the very crest of a ridge. Along 11 miles of trail, you actually overlook 10,000 ft peaks! View alpine lakes, spruce forests and wildflower-spangled meadows and reach the highest point at 12,183ft above sea level if you don't suffer health problems. The trail is particularly delightful when the flowers are at their peak, in June and July; indeed, snow keeps this and other park roads impassable until the end of May and from late October on. Look out for elk, moose, hawks, coyote, bighorn sheep and mountain lions.

Other routes lead hikers to a variety of long and short trails. One excellent trail is the 5.6 mile hike from **Glacier Gorge Junction** to **Bear Lake** and **Lake Haiyaha.** At the end of the hike, catch the free park bus back to Glacier Gorge (runs mid-June to Labor Day). For more hiking suggestions and photos, visit one of the many websites available; try Mike's Hikes, at *www.mtnds.com/hikes*. Horseback riding is also popular; horses can be rented at Estes Park and Grand Lake. (Also at Glacier Creek and Moraine stables in the National Park.) The park has 355 miles of trails; for good maps visit the Beaver Meadows Visitor Center (Park HQ), open all year (in summer 8am-9pm), 2 miles west of Estes Park on Hwy 36 and check the NPS website. Park entrance fees are $10 per person and $20 per car for seven days: open 24 hrs. 586-1206. Other centres are scattered throughout the park. *www.nps.gov/romo*, *www.rocky.mountain.national-park.com* and unofficially *http://estes.on-line.com/rmnp*.

The telephone area code is 970.

Accommodation/Food

Campgrounds near east entrance cost $20 per night: Moraine Park, Glacier Basin require booking. Call National Park reservations (800) 365-2267, *http://reservations.nps.gov/index.cfm*. **Aspen Glen, Longs Peak** and **Timber Creek** (latter nr West entrance) are first-come, first-serve and also cost $20. A $20 fee applies to all backpackers and permits are available at Back Country Office, Rocky Mtn National Park, Estes Park, CO 80517, 586-1242. 'Glacier Basin has a free bus to the main hiking area. Campsites have no shops or showers so it is difficult without a car.' Shuttle runs along Bear Lake Rd. *www.nps.gov/romo/pphtml/camping.html*.

Near southwest entrance. Travelling N from Denver stop for pastries, homemade bread and more, at **Carvers Bakery,** 93 Cooper Creek Way, off Hwy 40, 726-8202. Open 7am-1pm daily, Sat-Sun 'til 4pm, closed Fri. **Base Camp**, behind Conoco gas station in Winter Park (U.S. 40), 726-5530, breakfast and lunch for very little money,

7am-2pm daily. Find good lodging at **Shadowcliff AYH, Grand Lake**, off Rt 34, 627-9220. $15 AYH, $18 non-members. Private S/D: $45 plus XP $11, up to six per room with shared bath. 'Brilliant Scandinavian-style hostel on cliff overlooking lake.' Reserve ahead. _www.shadowcliff.org_.

Travel/Info
The best way to get to the park is by car; see car rentals under Denver. **Gray Line** offers Sun, Tues, Thurs, Fri 10-hr tour of the park, leaving from Denver, (303) 289-2841/(800)348-6877.$80 Rsvs req _www.grayline.com/franchise.cfm/action/details/id/117_
Grand Lake Chamber Commerce, 14700 US hwy 34, 627-3372/3402 or (800)531-1019. _www.grandlakechamber.com_.
Rocky Mountain National Park Office, 1000 Hwy 36, Estes Park, 586-1206. _www.nps.gov/romo/index.htm_.

COLORADO SPRINGS
Two hours south of Denver sits a town at the foot of 14,110ft high **Pikes Peak**, an exhilarating sight to behold. Founded by bonanza kings, as a resort and retirement center, the Springs has grown though to become the second largest city in Colorado and home to the US Air Force Academy and US Olympic Training Centre. The city makes a good base to explore **Garden of the Gods, Cripple Creek** and **Royal Gorge.**

The telephone area code is 719.

Accommodation
Buffalo Lodge, 2 El Paso Blvd., 634-2851. S-$62, D-$72 (could sleep up to 4). AC, outdoor pool, TV, laundry facilities, b/fast, bus stop 2 blks, 15 mins to downtown. _www.buffalolodge.com_.
Motel 6, 3228 N Chestnut St, 520-5400. Sun-Thu S-$44, D-$58, Fri-Sat S-$50, D-$64, XP-$3, AC, outdoor heated pool. View of Pike's Peak from rooms.
Garden of the Gods Campground (AYH), 3704 W Colorado Ave, 475-9450/(800) 248-9451. Cabins $40 for 2. Tent site $28-$38 for 2, XP-$3. RV, full hook-up $35. Pool avail. during summers only. _www.coloradocampground.com_.
Golden Eagle Ranch Campground and May Museum Center, 710 Rock Creek Canyon Road, 576-0450. 5 mls S of Colorado Springs, Hwy 115. Tent and RV sites: $20 basic; $22 full hook-up. Museum houses 8000 insect displays, space exploration wing, and NASA movies, $4.50. _www.maymuseum-camp-rvpark.com_.

Entertainment/Food
Barney's Diner, 129 W Las Animas St, 632-1756. Open Mon-Fri 6.30am-3pm, Sat 7.30am-2:30pm; special roast dinners and hearty breakfasts for under $5.
Poor Richard's Feed & Read, 324 N Tejon St, 632-7721. Part of an entertainment complex with restaurant, toy and bookstore as neighbours. Poor Richard's has local art on display and excellent vegetarian dishes for under $8. Open daily 11am-10pm.

Of Interest
Cave of the Winds, I-25 exit 141, go W on Hwy 24, 685-5444. Offer tours of the caves. Discovery tour of history and geology is run daily, $16. The lantern tour recreates the early 1800s cave treks using lanterns, daily $20. Nightly laser shows during the summer, $10, bring a blanket. _www.caveofthewinds.com_.
Garden of the Gods, NW of Colorado Springs off Hwy 24; Visitors Center, with free interactive exhibits is located at 1805 N 30th St, 634-6666. 940 acres of stunning red sandstone formations with views of Pikes Peak, especially striking at sunrise or sunset. Free. 'Outstanding scenic beauty—next best thing to Grand Canyon.' 'Well worth a visit.' Follow links from _www.springsgov.com_.
Ghost Town Wild West Museum, 2 miles from downtown, Hwy 24, 634-0696. Step

back in time to an 1800s ghost town, pan for gold and try your skill at the shooting gallery. Daily 9am-6pm, Sun from 11am, $6.50. *www.ghosttownmuseum.com*.

Pike's Peak. Panoramic views extend over 100 miles, *www.pikes-peak.com*. Hike the **Barr National Recreation Trail**, 8 hr hike suitable for beginners or take the 19-mile auto highway that climbs to the summit, $10/adult or $35/car; difficult mountain road. This is the course of one of the most harrowing and oldest car races in the world, held in July, *www.ppihc.com*. At the top is the view that inspired Katherine Lee Bates to write *America the Beautiful* in 1893. **Pike's Peak Cog Railway**, open April-Dec is $29 to the summit. Rsvs advised, call 685-5401. *www.cograilway.com*. Follow one of the trails for as long as you like and then walk down. 'The view is breathtaking.' 'Take a sweater.'

Rock Ledge Ranch Historic Site, across from G. of the G. Visitors Center, 578-6777. This living history programme chronicles 4 historic time periods: 1775-1835 American Indians; 1860s Galloway Homestead; the 1880's restored farm; 1907 Orchard House. Historically dressed interpreters. Wed-Sun, 10am-5pm; $5. *www.springsgov.com*.

Seven Falls, 10 mins from downtown C. Springs on Cheyenne Blvd, 632-0765. Called 'the grandest mile of scenery in Colorado', seven separate falls splash off a sheer granite cliff from a height of 181 ft. Stunning! Audio tours and illuminated at night. Daily 8.30am-10.30pm, $8.25, $9.75 after 5pm. *www.sevenfalls.com*.

US Olympic Complex, 1750 E Boulder St, 866-4618. Potential Olympians train here every year. The complex is also centre for sports medicine and scientific research. An Olympic highlights free tour is available every $1/2$ hr Mon-Sat, 9am-4pm. *www.usolympicteam.com*. If you're seeking still more Olympic experience, visit the **World Figure Skating Museum and Hall of Fame**, 20 First St, 635-5200. Mon-Sat, 10am-4pm; $3. *www.worldskatingmuseum.org*.

Nearby: Bishop's Castle, 11 mi S of Canon City in Beulah. Every man wants his own castle; Jim Bishop took that dream a little further. He has been building a castle since 1969 on a mountainside in central Colorado, by himself. Some are amazed by his feat, others think he's crazy. Decide for yourself. Eventually he hopes to add a moat and drawbridge, as well as a roller coaster on the castle's outer wall. Free. *www.roadsideamerica.com/attract/COBEUcastle.html*.

Canon City, the town from which Tom Mix launched his cowboy career. It may also look familiar to movie-goers as the shooting site of *Cat Ballou* and *True Grit*. If you're bored by the natural beauty of the area, visit **Buckskin Joe's Frontier Town and Railway**, 275-5149, where you can relive the wild west, complete with live hangings! Daily, 9am-6.00pm, $16. *www.buckskinjoe.com*. Staying with the rampant theme of lawlessness, there's also the **Prison Museum**, 201 N First St, 269-3015. Get inside an actual gas chamber or pose for souvenir photo behind bars in black and white-striped overalls. Daily 8.30am-6pm, $7. *www.prisonmuseum.org*. Little else of interest except **Royal Gorge Bridge and Park**, 275-7507. Has the highest suspension bridge at 1,053 ft, in the world - an acrophobe's nightmare! 'Tourist claptrap of all sorts predominates (including the sickening aerial tram), but the view is stupendous.' $20 includes tram ride across gorge; a train ride to bottom and trip on a mule-drawn wagon. Daily 10am-7pm. Elevation of 6,688 ft. *www.royalgorgebridge.com*.

Cripple Creek, opposite side of Pike's Peak, (877) 858-GOLD. The picturesque, but difficult route is via Gold Camp Road (follow Old Stage Road then join up with Gold Camp to avoid the tunnel cave-in)—$2^1/2$ hrs of gravel and curves (Teddy Roosevelt called it 'the trip that bankrupts the English language'). Far easier is the route by Hwy 24 that turns on to Hwy 67 S, about $1^1/2$ hrs. In its heyday, Cripple Creek yielded more than $25 million in gold in one year and had the honour of being called a 'foul cesspool' by Carry Nation for its brothels and 5 opera houses. Today the gold continues to arrive through tourism and the many casinos. Despite both being in overabundance, the place has considerable charm. Don't miss the **Mt Pisgah cemetery** (wry epitaphs, wooden headstones, etc.) *www.cripple-creek.co.us*, or **Mollie Kathleen Gold Mine**, 689-2466. $15—'very worthwhile, free gold ore'—and takes you 1000ft down. Daily 8am-6pm. *www.goldminetours.com*. For accommodation try: Victorian relic, **Imperial Casino Hotel**, 689-2922, S/D-$65 w/day, $75 w/end, XP-$10. With a casino and restaurant. *www.imperialcasinohotel.com.*

Information
Colorado Springs Convention and Visitors Bureau, (800) 888-4748. *www.coloradosprings-travel.com*.
Cripple Creek Visitors Welcome Center, 689-2169. *www.cripple-creek.co.us*.
Greyhound, 120 S Weber St, Colorado Springs, 635-1505. $14 o/w or $24 return trip to Denver. Leaves daily between 5.00am and 9pm.

WESTERN COLORADO In the north west is **Steamboat Springs,** a reasonably priced ski resort ('fun and friendly—great skiing'), with many state parks, trails and even a balloon rodeo in July for entertainment, (877) 754-2269 or *www.steamboatsummer.com*. Three hours farther west is **Dinosaur National Monument,** which overlaps into Utah. The monument presents striking and lonely canyon vistas (used by Butch Cassidy and his gangs as hideouts) and the fossil remains of stegosaurus, brontosaurus and other big guys, exposed in bas relief on the quarry face. You may still be lucky and catch more bones being exposed before your eyes. 'Not at all gimmicky; fascinating to anyone even vaguely interested in paleontology or geology.' NB: quarry and visitor centre are in Utah; see that section.

The major route west from Denver is the I-70, which passes through some of the best skiing in the world, and some of the most reasonable in Colorado, the mountain towns near **Breckenridge** (west side of the Eisenhower Tunnel); **Vail** and **Glenwood Springs.** Glenwood Springs makes for an invigorating place to pause for a dip in the world's largest open-air natural pool and an excellent base camp for exploring the surrounding mountains. Wyatt Earp's sidekick, Doc Holliday, lies buried here; his headstone reads: 'He died in bed.'

The scenic interstate follows the Colorado River all the way to **Grand Junction,** the last town of any size in Colorado and the nexus of any trip in Western Colorado. While a stay in Grand Junction could probably be avoided, the city does serve as an important gateway to the towering spires and canyon wilderness of **Colorado National Monument,** which is on the eastern edge of the Colorado Plateau. Call 858-3617, $5/car/week and $3 on foot. Tent site $10/night for up to 7 people. *www.nps.gov/colm*.

Further south is **Black Canyon** of the **Gunnison National Park** ('a very special place—deer wander regularly through campsites') near **Montrose,** *www.nps.gov/blca* and take Hwy 550 journeying further south through **Ouray,** near **Telluride** to **Silverton** and then **Durango.** Ouray, the 'Switzerland of America', strikingly beautiful and tiny (population of 800) is noted for its natural hot springs and **Camp Bird Mine**, which produced $24 million for the Walsh family. With some of the loot, papa Walsh bought his daughter the Hope Diamond.

Between Ouray and Telluride the views are spectacular, the road, hair-raising. Dizzy Gillespie once said, 'if Telluride ain't paradise, then heaven can wait'. Wait it did for Butch Cassidy, who pulled his first bank job here. Interesting buildings from the mining era have earned **Telluride** national historic landmark status. Telluride is also well known as a ski resort and festival centre, featuring summer music events from bluegrass to jazz, and the remarkable **Film Festival**, second only to Cannes, on Labor Day weekend _www.telluridefilmfestival.org_. 'For me, there is only Telluride...' said Louis Malle.

The telephone area code is 970.

Accommodation
First check _www.visitgrandjunction.com/visitors/lodging/hotels.cfm_.
Grand Junction: Hotel Melrose, 337 Colorado Ave, 242-9636. Private S-$33+ w/shared bath, Dorm beds $20. Refurbished. Centenary in 2008. VCR, cable, free local calls. Walking distance to bus and rail stns. Has info on hiking tours in the area. _www.hotelmelrose.com._

Travel/Information
Amtrak: (800) 872-7245. **Glenwood Springs,** 413 7th St; **Grand Junction,** 339 S 1st St. Both stops on the beautiful _California Zephyr_ route.
Greyhound: (800) 231-2222. **Glenwood Springs,** 118 W 6th St, 945-8501; **Grand Junction,** 230 S 5th St, 242-6012.
Visitors Bureau's and Chambers of Commerce for each of the ski resorts in Western Colorado can be found via _www.colorado.com_, or call (800)-COLORADO. Breckenridge, 453-6018; Durango, (800) 463-8726; Glenwood Springs, 945-6589; Grand Junction, (800) 962-2547; Montrose, 240-1414; Vail, 476-1000.

DINOSAUR NATIONAL MONUMENT Camping at Dinosaur National Monument is plentiful with 6 different sites. $10 per car entrance fee to the park but campsite fees vary, depending on how intimate you want to get with mother nature, from free-$12; motels at nearby Dinosaur, CO and Vernal, UT. The monument has no direct transit, but take the bus to Vernal, Utah, where you can rent a car. See also Utah. Call the Visitors Center, (435) 781-7700 or visit: _www.nps.gov/dino_.

BRECKENRIDGE Home of several major resorts, the small towns in this area offer unparalleled deals and striking beauty to distract the less fortunate of Denver's pocketbooks. _www.gobreck.com_.

Accommodation
Alpen Hutte Lodge, 471 Rainbow Dr, Silverthorne, Off the I-70, 468-6336. $18-$29 dorm beds, linens $2. Shuttle service throughout town and to neighbouring ski areas. Strict midnight curfew, laundry, TV lounge, kitchen, no hard liquor. 'Really nice, clean kitchen.' Call ahead for rsvs. _www.alpenhutte.com_.
Fireside Inn, 114 N French St. 453-6456. Summer dorms: $26; winter dorms $30-$38. Hot tub, cable TV and kind British proprietors will cook a full breakfast for $8 or provide a continental brekkie for $4. Internet access $4 per $1/2$ hour. _www.firesideinn.com_.

Food
Old Dillon Inn, 321 Blue River Pkwy, **Silverthorne**. 468-2791. Open 4.30pm 'till 10pm. An old wooden barn transported from the neighbouring town of Dillon. The 'Inn' serves killer Mexican food for under $10 and has great drink specials. Live music Fri & Sat.

ASPEN 158 miles south west of Denver on Hwy 82, Aspen is a tasteful, beautiful ski resort and classical music festival site (mid-June to mid-Aug), set amid National Forests and more recently the multi-million dollar spreads of Jack Nicholson, Don Johnson, Melanie Griffith and Cher, among others. Most things cost the earth in Aspen but reasonable accommodation can be found with a short one-hour ($6) bus ride down the hill to **Glenwood Springs**. _www.aspenchamber.org_.

Accommodation
Call the **Aspen Chamber Resort Assoc.** (800) 670-0792/925-1940, as they do work with many hotels in the area and can offer surprisingly good prices. NB: rates are highest in winter, lowest in spring and autumn. _www.aspenchamber.org_.
St Moritz Lodge, 334 W Hyman, 925-3220/(800) 817-2069. Hostel beds $30-44, XP-$15 throughout year. Shared bath, incls linen and bfast. Pool/whirlpool and steam room. _www.stmoritzlodge.com_.
Camping: Free wilderness camping w/running water in **White River National Forest**, 2-4 hrs W of Denver on I-70. Covers nearly all of Pitkin County. Closest: E Maroon, 1 mile NW of Aspen on Hwy 32. _www.fs.fed.us/r2/whiteriver_.
In **Glenwood Springs**:
Glenwood Springs Hostel, 1021 Grand Ave, 945-8545. Centrally located and with lots of activities available. Dorm style, $14, $44/ 4 nights, Private room S-$21, D-$29. Linens $2. Large record collection and internet access avail. $1/15mins.. Will pick up from bus or train with advance notice, although is easily walkable. Kitchen, laundry. 'Comfortable'. Organises half-day white-water rafting trips $34; caving and gondola trip $18; disc. for ski areas and Vapour Caves; mountain bike rentals $15 and free transport for hiking. $7 bus to and from Aspen. _www.hostelcolorado.com_.

Food
The Big Wrap, 520 E. Durant Ave, 544-1700. Great wrapped sandwiches and smoothies are offered all day long. Tacos from $5. Mon-Sat 10am-6pm.
Rusty's Hickory House, 730 W Main, 925-2313. 'Good breakfast, lunch, reasonably priced.' $7 and $8 lunch specials. Open daily 8am-2:30pm, 5pm-10pm. _www.hickoryhouseribs.com._

Of Interest
Aspen Music Festival, 925-9042 box-office. 9 weeks, late June-Aug. Rivals Tanglewood's Berkshire Festival in prestige. 'The combination of setting, fresh air and music blew my mind.' Many open rehearsals and other free events. _www.aspenmusicfestival.com_.
Gondola ascent of Mt Ajax to 11,212 ft, 925-1220; $18/wkdays and $20/wkends. _www.aspensnowmass.com_.
Hot Pool, Glenwood Springs, 945-6571/(800) 537-SWIM. Natural water outdoor pool. 'Exhilarating.' 'Especially superb at night.' $14.25 daily/ $9 at night, towel rental $2.50. Daily 7.30am-10pm. _www.hotspringspool.com_.

Information
Stay Aspen Snowmass Visitor Center, 425 Rio Grande Place, (800) 262-7736. The airport lies 5 miles from town. _www.stayaspensnowmass.com_. A free county bus runs from the highway outside the airport. This free efficient service by Roaring Fork TA is also available throughout Aspen Valley. _www.rfta.com_.
Glenwood Springs Chamber Resort Association, 1102 Grand Ave, 945-6589. Open Mon-Fri 9am-6pm, w/ends 10am-3pm. _www.glenwoodchamber.com_.

SOUTHWESTERN COLORADO Perhaps nowhere in Colorado are the land and the people so diverse as in the southwestern corner of the state. Jagged, snow capped mountains seem to tear the clouds apart while millennium-old dwellings hide from the elements and all but the most intrepid explorers. Durango, the de facto capital of this former gold country is an excellent base for a trip into one of the least visited, but most rewarding regions of the west. *The telephone area code is 970.*

Accommodation
At Silverton: French Baker Teller House, 1250 Greene St, 387-5423. D-$64/ shared bath, $89/private bath, incls bfast. 'Town worth visiting.' *www.tellerhousehotel.com.*

Of Interest
South to Durango:
Ouray: bus route from Grand Junction, Hwy 50 then 550 to Durango passes through Montrose, Ouray and Silverton. 'Unparalleled scenery; exceeds the Denver-Salt Lake City run. Canyons through 11,000 ft red rock mountains. Best from mid-Sept when aspens have changed to gold.' 'Wrecked cars 500 ft below, left as warning to other motorists.'
Million-dollar highway, between Ouray and Silverton. A 6-mile stretch, numbered among the most spectacular roads in the US.
Telluride: jeep trail to Ouray over 13,000-ft Imogen Pass. 'Astounding' in a jeep, a truly remarkable accomplishment when covered on foot—as many people do each Sept in a 17-mile race. Visitors Bureau (888) 605-2578. *www.visitelluride.com.*

DURANGO Located in the southwestern corner of the state, Durango is as authentically western as a Stetson hat. Billy the Kid and other outlaw types used to make Durango their headquarters. Before that, the Spaniards came looking for gold, found it and lost it again when local Ute Indians got fed up with them. Durango's location 40 miles east of Mesa Verde makes it a natural base for sightseeing.

Accommodation
Spanish Trails Inn, 3141 Main Ave, 247-4173. Summer S-$59-$69, queen bed suitable for sharing, D-$79-$89. Free coffee, outdoor pool. *www.spanishtrails.com.*

Of Interest
The main local attraction is the circa **1882 narrow-gauge railway to Silverton,** 479 Main Ave, 247-2733. Coal-fired train runs 45 miles one way and climbs 3000 ft through the saw-toothed San Juan Mts. Round trip takes 9 hours, costs $62 ($109 if you reserve seat in the elegant parlour car). Runs 3 times daily, May through Oct. It is recommended that you book 'at least 6 weeks in advance'. Although you may get lucky arriving 6.30am the day before, the odds are against you. Alternatively, take the am bus to Silverton and then catch the train back to Durango. The bus takes only $1^1/_2$ hrs and costs $69 'Plenty of seats on south-bound journey.' 'Beautiful scenery, worth every dollar.' *www.durangotrain.com.*
Toh-Atin Galleries, 145 W 9th and Main Ave, 247-8277/(800) 525-0384. Native American and Southwestern art gallery with fine Navajo weavings, jewellery, sculptures and original paintings. Free. Mon-Sat 9am-6pm, Sun 10am-5pm. *www.toh-atin.com.*

Food/Entertainment
'If you're feeling flush, try fresh trout at the **Palace Restaurant**,' 505 Main Ave., 247-2018. Open daily 11am-9pm. Average entrée, $17/lunch, $22/dinner. *www.palacerestaurants.com.*
Diamond Belle Saloon, in the **Strater Hotel**, 699 Main Ave, 247-4431. 'Authentic saloon atmosphere with ragtime piano.' Live music daily. Open 11am-midnight.

www.strater.com/belle.php. Also in hotel: **Diamond Circle Theater** has melodrama and one other show every summer night but Sun, 7.30pm, $20. *www.diamondcirclemelodrama.com.*
Mama's Boy, 2659 Main St. 247-0060. For less than $10, one finds inexpensive and authentic Italian food in the heart of Durango. Open nightly, 4.30pm to 10 pm.

Information
Durango Chamber of Tourism Office, 247-3500. *www.durango.org.*

MESA VERDE NATIONAL PARK 'Far above me, set in a great cavern in the face of the cliff, I saw a little city of stone, asleep.' —Willa Cather.

No matter how limited your tourist plans for the West might be, a visit to Mesa Verde, the finest of the prehistoric Indian culture preserves, reflecting more than 700 years of history, is a must. The 80-square-mile area sits at an altitude of 6,200ft and rises another 2000 ft above the surrounding plain, gashed by many deep canyons. The tableland you see today bears little to no resemblance to the land of the past. Junipers and pine trees grow where these ancestral Native Americans once tilled their squash, beans and corn. From the depths of the canyon they drew their drinking water from springs. Originally they built their pueblos on the flat surface, but later for security, dug their homes into the sheer canyon walls.

There are two loops to the park: one leads to **Cliff Palace.** Built by the Anasazi tribe in 1100-1275 AD, the palace is a large medieval-looking town, containing 200 living rooms, 23 kivas and eight floor levels, all within a single cave. You can climb on parts of it. The other loop, to **Mesa Wetherill,** provides good vantage points for viewing the ruins scattered thoughout the canyons. The dwellings were occupied for about a century beginning in the 1200s and were vacated for unknown reasons (probably due to drought).

To really enjoy the park, give yourself at least a day and read the park service pamphlet on the history of human habitation here. A visit to the museum, with its extensive exhibits of tools, clothing, pottery and dioramas depicting the Anasazi way of life is also a must for understanding the culture. Open daily 8am-5pm. Admission to park, $10; ranger-guided tour of Cliff Palace and a balcony house $2.50. *www.nps.gov/meve.*

Accommodation
In **Cortez: El Capri Motel,** 2110 S Broadway, 565-3764. S-$43, D$46. Cheaper in winter. AC, TV.
In **Mesa Verde Park: Morefield Campgrounds,** 529-4465/(800) 449-2288. Tents/RV sites, $20 or $25 w/hook-up. Showers, store, snack bar, laundry and lots of amenities close by. 'Gets very cold at night in fall and spring; need warm sleeping bag as well as tent.' *www.visitmesaverde.com, www.nps.gov/meve/pphtml/camping.html.*

Of Interest
Four Corners, Southwest Colorado. The meeting of Colorado, Utah, Arizona and New Mexico is commemorated with a slab of inscribed concrete. You can sprawl to have your picture taken as you perform the amazing feat of being in 4 states at once! In summer, Indians from Navajo and other tribes come in their pickups and sell their handcrafted wares, often at much better prices than you'll find in the tourist centres or trading posts.

Travel
ARAMARK Tours, (800) 449-2288. From **Morefield** and **Far View Lodge** in the

park for a half-day tour of the Mesa-top dwellings, 9am, returning noon and 1pm returning 4pm, $39.

IDAHO - The Gem State

With over 80 recognised ranges, Idaho is the most mountainous of all Rocky Mountain States. The land with 50 peaks over 10,000 feet, wild rivers and deep chasms, such as **Hell's Canyon** on the **Snake River** (the deepest in North America) is dappled with fishing lakes and hot springs. Idaho is like Colorado without the people or the public transit. _www.visitid.org_.

Appropriately called the Gem State, Idaho produces 72 different precious and semi-precious stones, some of which are unique to the area. The state was settled by French trappers and followed by a mix of Basques, Mormons and WASPS who came to raise livestock; mine silver, log timber and grow lots of delicious Idaho spuds. Idahoans are a taciturn lot; interesting, then, that the most famous figures associated with the state were noted for eloquence. One was Chief Joseph of the Nez Perce Indians, who surrendered to the US Army by saying: 'From where the sun now stands, I will fight no more forever'. The other, writer Ernest Hemingway, was an adoptive Idahoan who chose to live, write (parts of _For Whom the Bell Tolls_), commit suicide and be buried in Idaho.

The most scenic section is the northwest panhandle region, crowned by the shattering beauty of **Lake Coeur d'Alene**. Follow the Lewis and Clark expedition trail, journeyed 200 years ago in the area, or more practically take Greyhounds northern route from Boise to Coeur d'Alene. There is no Greyhound service that takes you south toward the **Craters of the Moon** national monument and near **Sun Valley** (commercial ski area), but Sun Valley Express runs a luxurious service from Boise, which means you can take in the stunning vistas of this area in style. _www.sunvalleyexpress.com_. Car rental may be a good option, try Thrifty Car, (888)432-8687 from $30/day. _www.thrifty.com_.

National Park: Yellowstone (though this is mostly in Wyoming). For main entrances to park, see Montana. State parks visit _www.idahoparks.org_ or go to links from _www.visitid.org_. _The telephone area code for Idaho is 208._

BOISE If travelling past an endless trail of small farmhouses has left you comatose, you'll probably be delighted to arrive in Boise, the largest metropolitan area for 300 miles around, settled between mountains and desert. The capital of Idaho, Boise is a very pleasant and liveable town. It makes an excellent base for the start of any trip through Idaho and is the only bastion of cosmopolitan life in this otherwise provincial state.

Accommodation
Budget Inn, 2600 Fairview, 344-8617. S-$35, D-$46.

Cabana Inn, 1600 Main St, 343-6000. S-$42, D-$50. Spacious rooms with cable TV and free local calls.

Hostel Boise, 17322 Can-Ada Rd, Nampa, few miles W of Boise, 467-6858. Great hostel in center of attractions. Dorm, $15.50 AYH, $18.50 non-member; private $31, $35 for two. Internet access $1/20mins. No curfew, patio, kitchen, free local calls. Will pick you up from airport, $10 w/rsvs. Check out their 3-day auto rental special-$10/day! _www.hostelboise.com_.

Food

Boise has many places to eat. Check _http://boise.areaconnect.com/restaurants_ and _www.boiseweekly.com._

Downtown, centered around **8th and Main Street** has a wide choice of delis, coffee shops and restaurants to suit all palates and price range. Grab a great breakfast at **Moons Kitchen,** 815 W Bannock St, 385-0472. $4.50-9. A must to try is the shakes, from $3.40, which have been blended here since '55. Mon-Fri, 7am-7.30pm, Sat 8am-7.30pm, Sun 9am-2pm. _www.moonskitchen.com._

Noodles, 1802 Franklin, 466-4400, a 15 min drive from downtown in Nampa and serves a lunch special for $8.25 and diner special for $11.25. Daily 11am-9pm, w/end 'til 10pm.

At **8th Street Marketplace** are several small cafes and shops, such as **Cafe Ole,** 404 S 8th St, 344-3222, with $5.95 Mexican lunch specials. Mon-Thu, 11am-10pm, Fri-Sat 'til 11pm, Sun 3pm-9pm. _www.cafeole.com._

Pengilly's Saloon, 513 W Main St. 345-6344. Introduce yourself to the local cowboy culture at Boise's 'favourite old time tavern'. 3pm-2am, closed Sun.

Of Interest

It's likely that some event will be going on throughout the summer at **The Bank of America Center, The Morrison Center,** or **The Boise State University Pavilion,** each of which hosts the big performances within Boise. Free events are also hosted in the downtown public plaza, **The Grove,** on most summer evenings. _Alive after 5_ is held here every Wed evening, May-Sept. _www.downtownboise.org._ For the latest goings-on, get Friday's _Idaho Statesman, www.idahostatesman.com,_ and read the events calendar in _Scene._

Julia Davis Park, along Boise River is home to several museums and also the zoo: **Boise Art Museum,** 670 Julia Davis Dr, 345-8330. Idaho's only public art museum with 2000 pieces of art focused on 20th century American works. Summer: Tue-Sat 10am-5pm, Thu 'til 8pm, Sun noon-5pm. $8, $6 w/student ID. _www.boiseartmuseum.org._

Idaho Black History Museum, 508 Julia Davis Dr, 433-0017. Features historical photos, crafts and other articles reflecting black culture. Summer: Tue-Sat 10am-4pm. Donation accepted. _www.ibhm.org._

Idaho Historical Museum, 610 North Julia Davis Dr, 334-2120. Relates the Idaho history from prehistoric times through pioneer settlement, including Indian, Basque and Chinese influences. Summer: Tues-Sat 9am-5pm, Sun 1pm-5pm; $2. _www.idahohistory.net/museum.html._

Zoo Boise, 355 Julia Davis Dr, 384-4260. See exotic animals as well as Idaho's native wildlife. Daily 10am-5pm; $6, Thu $3.75. _www.cityofboise.org/parks/zoo._

Basque Museum and Cultural Center, 611 Grove St, 343-2671. The museum explores the rich history of the Basques in Idaho and their old-world origins. Tue-Fri, 10am-4pm, Sat 11am-3pm. Donation appreciated. _www.basquemuseum.com._

Idaho State Capitol Building, Capitol Blvd and Jefferson, 334-2470. Smaller version of the nation's capitol. Self-guided tours begin at the Visitors Center in the lower level. Mon-Fri 8am-5pm, Sat 9am-5pm; free. _www.state.id.us._

The Big Easy, 8th Street Marketplace, 367-1212. Concert house, Cajun-style restaurant and nightclub which has live music Wed, Fri and Sat nights. Hosts national acts and local bands. Dinner: Mon-Sat (burgers $6.95), 4pm-10pm. _www.bigeasyconcerts.com._

World Center Birds of Prey, 5668 W Flying Hawk Lane, 362-3716. You can see the Harpy Eagle (the world's largest eagle), plus observe a pair of California Condors. Everything you ever wanted to know about birds of prey. 90 min tour available. Daily 9am-5pm; $3. _www.peregrinefund.org._

Nearby: Elmore County. Bruneau Dunes State Park, 18 mi SW of **Mountain Home** off Hwy 51, 366-7919. The Bruneau Dunes are unique in the Western hemisphere in their formation and rise to over 470 ft making them the tallest in North America; $4/vehicle. **Camping** is also available on a first-come, first-serve basis; $12 per tent site, $16 w/ hook-up. Also houses one of the largest public observatories in the US; provides breathtaking views of space. _www.idahoparks.org_. Accommodation is also readily available in **Mountain Home**, try the cheapest at **Highlander Motel**, 587-3311, S-$39, D-$42. **Chamber of Commerce**, 587-4334, has helpful staff.

Idaho City, 38 mi NE of Boise on Hwy 21, a mining town that captures the all-too-wild spirit of the West. Once the largest town in the Pacific Northwest, only 28 of the men, women and children buried here are believed to have died of natural causes. Idaho City has been rebuilt since its gold mining days, with some of the original buildings still in use. Duck into the local museum and arts and crafts to explore the gold rush history. If you find yourself unwilling to leave, you can stay at the **Idaho City Hotel**, S-$39 D-$44 a night, (392-4290).

Travel/Information

Amtrak, (800) 872-7245 and Greyhound, 343-3681/(800) 231-2222 are both at 1212 W Bannock. Amtrak no longer operate trains out of Boise but contracts Greyhound buses to get passengers to Portland train station (9 hrs), $51 o/w.
Idaho Travel Council, 700 W State St, (800) 635-7820. _www.visitidaho.org_, _www.visitid.com_.
Boise Convention and Visitors Bureau, 2676 S. Vista, (800) 635-5240; Mon-Fri 8.30-5pm. _www.boise.org_.

Internet access

Boise Public Library, 715 S. Capitol Blvd, 384-4114. Free access, 1 hr limit. _www.boisepubliclibrary.org_.

NORTH CENTRAL IDAHO hosts a trove of geological treasures. It's no wonder that Lewis and Clark called this region 'paradise'. Among the most famous is **Hells Canyon**, on the **Snake River**. Everything about the river is big. Big river, big waves, big views, big cliffs. The canyon is the deepest gorge in North America, at 7,828 ft it's several thousand feet deeper than the Grand Canyon. To see it by car, travel along US-95 towards Riggins, where you can access Heavens Gate and the Seven Devils area. The Oregon end of the river also boasts spectacular views. White water tours are available, but are generally expensive. **Granite Creek Tours**, (800) 262-8874, offer a 200 mile trip for $120. _www.snakeriveradventures.com_.

Near Hells Canyon are the **Seven Devils Peaks**, (509) 758-0616, one of Idaho's highest and most spectacular mountain ranges. The peaks tower a mile and a half above the Snake River below. From **Heaven's Gate Lookout** on the peaks, you can see into the three surrounding states!

North Central Idaho is also home of the **Nez Perce National Historic Park and Museum**, 843-2261. 38 sites of the Park are scattered across the states of Idaho, Oregon, Washington and Montana and have been designated to commemorate the stories and history of the Nimiipuu and their interaction with explorers, fur traders, missionaries, soldiers, settlers, gold miners, and farmers who moved through or into the area. Staff answer questions on the area, Nez Perce People, their historic trail and the war and surrender of 1877. Summer daily 8am-5.00pm ('til 4:30pm in winter). _www.nps.gov/nepe_. Contact **Outfitters and Guides Association**, PO Box 95, Boise ID 83701, 342-1919, for more info. Mon-Fri, 8am-4pm. _www.ioga.org_.

COEUR D'ALENE The depth and fire of this utterly beautiful lake remind one of sapphires. The resort city of Coeur d'Alene and its floating boardwalk (the world's largest) is similarly not to be missed.

Accommodation
Down **motel row** (Sherman Ave) are several similarly priced rooms, such as the infamously-named **Bates Motel,** 2018 E Sherman Ave, 667-1411, S- $43-$48, D-$48-$53. Watch out for the night manager, "Norman"! No reservations and just kidding!.

Food
Crickets Steakhouse and Oyster Bar, 424 Sherman Avenue, 765-1990. Offers lunch, dinner and late dinner! 'Specializing in the best beef in the area'. Open daily 11am-2am.

Rustlers Roost, 9627 N US-95 in Hayden, 772-6613. 10 mins by car. Serves the city's only barbeque at dinner. Sandwiches w/fries from $4.25. Open daily 6am-2pm. _www.rustlersroost.com_.

Of Interest
Be sure to take the $1^1/_2$hr **lake excursion,** $16.75, leaving from **Independence Point** near the clock tower, starting at 12:30pm. Last tour leaves at 4:30pm. Call **Lake Cruisers,** (800) 688-5253, for departure schedules and other cruise packages. Fishing permits are $10.50 per day, available at any marina or tackle shops.

Digging for rare star garnets at **Emerald Creek** south of St Maries ranks somewhere between gardening and an Indiana Jones adventure. (Take Hwy 3 south 25 miles to Rd 447; SE 8 miles to Parking Area, then hike a $^1/_2$ mi to 81 Gulch.) All-day digging permits are issued at the A-Frame (Gulch) for $10; call 245-2531. They have very limited equipment that you can rent for $1 or bring your own container and shovel. Guides will show you what to do. These black and blue garnets are found only in Idaho and India. Wear old shoes and clothes—it's wet and muddy. _www.fs.fed.us/ipnf/rec/activities/garnets_.

Silverwood Theme Park, 15 mins north, on Hwy 95, Athol, 683-3400. Attractions, rides and shows at Idaho's largest theme park, including the **Boulder Beach Water Park**. $29.99, Sun-Thu 11am-9pm, Fri-Sat 11am-10pm, Boulder Beach 'til 7pm. _www.silverwoodthemepark.com_.

Travel/Information
Coeur d'Alene Convention and Visitor Bureau, 202 Sherman Ave, (800) 292-2553. _www.coeurdalene.org_.

Chamber of Commerce, PO Box 850, Coeur D'Alene, ID 83816, 664-3194/(877) 782-9232. Office is located at 1621 N 3rd St. Mon-Fri 8am-5pm. _www.coeurdaleneidaho.org_.

Greyhound, 137 E. Spruce Ave, 664-3343.

TWIN FALLS is home to the breathtaking **Shoshone Falls,** 40 ft higher than Niagara and set on a pretty stretch of the Snake River. Evel Knievel's famous and beautiful jump site, 5 miles northeast of town, can be viewed from the **Perrine Bridge,** Hwy 93, that spans the Snake River. Twin Falls is a good starting point for a journey into **Sun Valley** and **Sawtooth National Forest.** West off US 30, the 40 ft-tall **Balanced Rock** rests on a base only a few feet in diameter. No sneezing! If you haven't had your fill of falls yet, venture to Idaho's **Thousand Springs** and **City of Rocks.** Natural springs pour forth from canyon walls. Legend has it that the Lost River in central Idaho drops into the ground at the base of the **Lost River Mountains** and comes out here. As you head north to Sun Valley on Hwy 75, cool off at **Shoshone Ice**

Caves, a 1000 ft lava tube, with naturally frigid temperatures and fascinating ice formations. Daily 8am-8pm from May-end Sept; $6.50, 886-2058. Guided tours 45-60mins. 'Bring your coat.'

Accommodation
Gooding Hotel, 112 Main St, Gooding, 934-4374/(888) 260-6656. Head 30 miles W from Twin Falls, 10 mi from I-84, exit 141 or 157 on Hwy 46. S/D-$65-$90, XP-$20, full breakfast incl. Kitchen and lounge.

Of Interest
City of Rocks National Reserve, 55 miles S of Burley on Hwy 77, 824-5519. Granite columns climb 60 storeys in this eerie, dreamlike landscape. Campsites are $7 a night. _www.nps.gov/ciro_. On the way to City of Rocks stop at **Oakley,** a town with Idaho's greatest concentration of old buildings, recognized by National Register of Historic Places.

Hagerman Fossil Beds National Monument, 837-4793. 35 miles N of Twin Falls on Hwy 84. Experience history as far back as 3.5 million years. Fossil beds have remains of mastodons, saber-toothed tigers and ancient zebras. Take a day to enjoy the natural hot springs and beautiful trout fishing. _www.nps.gov/hafo_.

Malad Gorge, East of Bliss, I-84, exit 47, 30 mi NW of Twin Falls. 837-4505. This spectacular gorge dips down 250 ft, where the river tumbles over a 60 ft waterfall, emptying into Devil's Washbowl below. A footbridge spans the canyon, offering spectacular views. _www.idahoparks.org/parks_.

Info/Travel
Greyhound, 1390 Blue Lakes Blvd N, 733-3002.
Twin Falls Travel Bureau, 858 Blue Lakes Blvd N, 733-3974/(800) 255-TWIN. _www.twinfallschamber.com_.

Internet access
Twin Falls Public Library, 201 4th Ave E, 1 block from Court House, 733-2964. Free, 30 min limit. _www.twinfallspubliclibrary.org_.

CRATERS OF THE MOON NATIONAL MONUMENT Located at the northern end of the Great Rift system, this grotesque grey landscape of extinct cones, gaping fissures and cave-like lava tubes is the largest basaltic lava field in the contiguous US. The area erupted 2000 years ago and the next eruption is anticipated at the end of the next millennium, but that fact shouldn't trouble visitors for a few generations!

The most extravagant formations can be seen from one 7-mile loop road (Nordic Ski track in winter) in the 83-square-mile preserve; $5 per car, good for seven days. US moon astronauts spent a day in training here, rockhounding; free guided walks explore the extensive caves here about three times/day, call for schedule. Camping: $10/night; no reservations, no hook-ups available. Loose rock, so bring sturdy ground cloth. No public transport to park and it's 18 miles to the nearest town-**Arco.** Call (208) 527-3257 for visitor and camping info or visit _www.nps.gov/crmo_. **Mt Borah,** the highest peak in Idaho at 12,662 ft, towers over the wasteland. At the base of the peak lies a fault, created by a 1983 earthquake that rocked central Idaho. As a result of this quake, the mountain grew 2 feet, while the surrounding valley fell 5 feet.

This chilling, stark landscape, which looks like the day after an atomic attack, was the home for much nuclear testing and tinkering. 30 miles east is the Idaho National Engineering Laboratory. Nearby **Arco** was the first town lit by atomic power. The area has more nuclear reactors per citizen than anywhere else in the world, and **Atomic City** needs no explanation: 52 nuclear reactors were built in this area, now it's home to only about 25 daring residents. Keep within park limits!

SUN VALLEY/KETCHUM In the 1930s, railroad mogul Averell Harriman asked Count Felix Schaffgotsch of Austria to search America for a site 'of the same character as the Swiss and Austrian Alps'. The Count selected Sun Valley, and thus, the first ski resort destination was born. World-class skiing on ol' Baldy has attracted world-class spenders, with their thirst for ultra-resort fare in tow. Go to nearby Ketchum; it's more congenial and much less ostentatious—but still expensive.

Accommodation
Try **Ketchum Property Managers,** Sun Valley for some great deals, 200 W River St, (800) 521-2515. *www.resortquest.com/sunvalley.*
Lift Tower Lodge, 703 S Main St, Ketchum, PO Box 185. 726-5163/(800) 462-8646. 14 unit motel, showers, TV. S/D-$75 D-$85, continental breakfast and outside jacuzzi.
Camping: Pitch a tent for around $11 in designated areas in Sawtooth National Recreation Area, 8 miles N on Hwy 75. *www.fs.fed.us/r4/sawtooth.* One of the most beautiful valleys in the States, $3 user fee (for hiking etc.). Although the sites at the North end of the valley are unbeatable, camping outside designated areas costs $13 and up. Call (877) 444-6777. *www.reserveusa.com.*

Food/Entertainment
Desperado's, 4th & Washington, 726-3068. Tacos for $3.50 and a selection of 15 Mexican beers. Open Mon-Sat 11.30am-10pm.
Pioneer Saloon, 308 N Main St, 726-3139. Prime ribs & fresh fish, prices from $8. One of only a handful of traditional Western bars left, with a handcrafted back bar. Nightly 4pm-2am, restaurant opens at 5pm. *www.pioneersaloon.com.*
Whiskey Jacques, 251 Main St., 726-5297. Grab a stiff cheap drink at this former Hemingway watering hole. Cheap deals and live music combine in this popular Sun Valley bar. Open 4pm-2am. *www.whiskeyjacques.com.*

Of Interest
You're in one of the best kept secrets of the west. Spend some time hiking in **Sawtooth,** then relax in one of the many hot springs in the area. The closest is **Warm Springs** near the Sun Valley Ski Resort, but go three miles further to **Frenchman's** for a free dip. The ski lift is open in summer and for $20 you can spend the day racing down the steep mountain slopes on a mountain bike and ride up the hill on a chairlift. $15 gets you up the hill one time. Sun Valley also rents bikes for a steep $38-$40 so check around town for deals. Ice shows at the **Outdoor Resort Ice Rink,** off Sun Valley Road, 622-2194, feature Olympic athletes on Sat evenings, mid-June to mid-Sept. The rink is open to the public all year ($9.50 plus $3.50 for skates). *www.sunvalley.com.* July 4th and Labor Day are big days here; catch the arts and crafts shows, Sun Valley Symphony, motorised parades, rodeos and bull riding. Twenty-four jazz bands from the US, Canada and Europe arrive in mid-October for the **Sun Valley Jazz Jamboree** festival; (877) 478-5277; tickets $20 w/student ID for the whole festival. *www.sunvalleyjazz.com.*
If you have time, take a day trip up to **Salmon** on the Montana/Idaho border. It's a lovely turn of the century western town and a good place to spend a day. The lodging costs are, however, as much as those in Sun Valley so it may be a good idea to make this a day trip out of the Sawtooth area. *www.salmonidaho.com.*

Tourist and Visitor's Bureau, 411 N Main St, Ketchum, 726-3423/(800) 634-3347. *www.visitsunvalley.com*.

The Salmon Valley Chamber of Commerce, 200 Main St, (800) 727-2540. *www.salmonbyway.com*.

EASTERN IDAHO Though not as scenic as the west, as a neighbour to Yellowstone and Teton National Parks it shares their beauty and a few other reasons to visit. The **Grand Tetons,** the youngest mountains in the Rockies, flank the eastern portion of the state. The town, **Blackfoot** is the site of the **Idaho Potato Exposition,** Hwy 91, 130 NW Main. The exposition has the world's largest concrete potato and had the world's largest potato chip— a 23-in Pringle donated by Proctor and Gamble in 1990.

On offer is the chance to sample potato cookies, potato fudge and potato ice cream! Open daily, 10am-5pm; $3. *www.ida.net/users/potatoexpo*. **St Anthony Sand Dunes,** off Hwy 20 are another rather unusual site. The dunes mass to 600 feet tall and contain 10,000 acres, providing endless opportunities for Off Highway Vehicle recreation; ATV's dune buggies and horses ride the open mounds. *www.id.blm.gov,, www.duneguide.com/sand_dune_guide_st_anthony.htm*

MONTANA - Big Sky Country

Touted as the 'Big Sky' country, Montana is an immense, Western-feeling state, rich in coal, sapphires and chrome, a grower of wheat and cattle and a major centre for tourism. A regular record-breaker when it comes to the hottest, coldest, windiest and snowiest weather in the lower 48 states, Montana achieved a mind-numbing 76°F below in the early 1980s. However, don't let the wild temperatures detract you from the wild beauty of the state. John Steinbeck wrote, 'I am in love with Montana; for other states I have admiration, respect, recognition, even some affection, but with Montana it is love'.

While in Montana one can choose from a wealth of outdoor activities and events—catch fish in **Glacier National Park** or take in a Saturday night rodeo in one of Montana's cities. Don't overlook the work of the local artists such as the late Charles M. Russell whose cowboy days are brilliantly depicted in oils and bronze in the museum in **Great Falls** and in **Helena's Capitol Building**. Helena is also the starting point for the **Gates to the Mountains** boat trip, 458-5241, which retraces Lewis and Clark's 1804-05 eventful expedition along the wild and scenic Missouri River; $10. *www.gatesofthemountains.com*.

One of America's great train journeys is the *Empire Builder* route across northern Montana— especially the portion that loops around Glacier National Park. Both east and westbound trips are in daylight or at dusk.

Montana's only sizeable minority are the American Indian and Alaskan Natives. About 56,000 Crows, Northern Cheyennes, Blackfeet, Flatheads, Grox Ventres, Chippewas and Rocky Boys make up the seven main reservations, representative of eleven tribes. Montana's the place where the Indians put paid to the whites, not only at Little Bighorn but at the Battles of

Big Hole and Rosebud. The tribes offer numerous events and facilities to visitors and are generally very friendly. _www.discoveringmontana.com_.

National Parks: Glacier and **Yellowstone** (mostly in Wyoming). For a recreation guide and accommodation listings, contact **Montana Travel**, (800) 541-1447. _www.visitmt.com_. Important note: while most of Yellowstone lies in Wyoming, three of the main entrances and the gateway towns of West Yellowstone and Gardiner are in Montana and are best reached via Greyhound from Montana cities or from Idaho Falls, Idaho. Read both Montana and Wyoming sections when trip planning for the park.

Telephone area code for the whole state is 406.

BILLINGS Montana's largest and most sophisticated city, Billings is on the Yellowstone River – an ideal stopover point for travellers from North or South Dakota en route to Yellowstone. This is a good route to the park, via the scenic Cook City, Hwy 212. 'A spectacular mountain view— pass 10,000 feet up and lots of elk and buffalo along the way! Don't go before mid-June, though, otherwise you may find yourself snowed in.' _www.ci.billings.mt.us_.

Accommodation/Food
Billings Inn, 880 N 29th St, 252-6800. S/D-$63-$67.50, XP-$5, incls bfast and free popcorn.

Stella's, 110 N 29th St. 248-3060. 'Stop in to get one of the best breakfasts of your life. They make everything here from scratch.' Big portions, under $7. Mon-Sat 5.30am-4pm, Sun 7am-1pm.

Of Interest
Foucault Pendulum, in First Citizen's Bank Building, 1st Ave S, 247-4100. Two storeys tall, this **California Academy of Sciences'** pendulum is modeled on the same principles that account for the earth's rotation. One of 16 in the US. Free.

Western Heritage Center, 2822 Montana Ave, 256-6809. Exhibits change twice a year, but the theme in general is an 'Interpretive program reflecting on the history of the Yellowstone Valley River region' and the city's frontier past. Open Tue-Sat 10am-5pm; Sun 1pm-4pm in summer, donations suggested. _www.ywhc.org_.

Yellowstone Art Center, 401 N 27th, 256-6804. Museum of modern and Western art housed in 1916-vintage jail. Tue-Sat 10am-5pm, Thurs 'til 8pm, Sun noon-5pm in summer; $7, $5 w/student ID. _yellowstone.artmuseum.org_.

Chief Black Otter Trail. N of the city: spectacular views, Native American scout grave, and a monument to settlers. Distraught braves who lost their families to smallpox are said to have ridden their ponies and themselves over Sacrifice Cliff, which lies along the trail.

Pictograph Cave State Park, 2300 Lake Elmo Drive, 247-2940. See 4,500-year old Indian drawings whose origins are still a mystery. $5 per vehicle or $1 pp. May-Sep daily 8am-8pm. _www.pictographcave.org_.

Pompey's Pillar, 28 miles east of Billings, 875-2233. A National Landmark along the Lewis and Clark trail. 150 ft tall sandstone butte 'signed' by Capt William Clark in 1806 and named by him in honour of the faithful Sacagawea's son, Pompey. $3 per vehicle. 8am-8pm in summer. 9am-5pm till Labor Day. _www.pompeyspillar.org_.

Travel/Information
Greyhound, 2502 1st Ave N, 245-5116, (800) 231-2222.

Chamber of Commerce, 815 S 27th St, 252-4016/(800) 735-2635. Summer open daily. _www.billingscvb.visitmt.com_ or _www.billingschamber.com_.

Internet access: Your Place or Mine Cyber Cafe, 344 Grand Ave, 254-9874. Open Mon-Sat 9am-9pm; $7/ hr. _www.yourplaceormine.com_.

CUSTER BATTLEFIELD NATIONAL MONUMENT Here on the Little Big Horn River, just under 60 miles east of Billings, General George Custer imprudently attacked the main camp of the Sioux, Hunkpapas and others. The date was 25 June 1876. 'I did not think it possible that any white man would attack us, so strong as we were,' said one Oglala chief. A Cheyenne recalled that after he had taken a swim in the river he looked toward Little Big Horn in the direction of Sitting Bull's camp. 'I saw a great dust rising. It looked like a whirlwind. Soon a Sioux horseman came rushing into camp shouting: 'Soldiers come! Plenty white soldiers!'

Before they could be moved to safety downstream, several women and children were killed, including the family of warrior Gall. 'It made my heart bad. After that I killed all my enemies with the hatchet.' Brilliantly led by Sitting Bull and Crazy Horse, the tribes routed the soldiers and surrounded Custer's column, killing all 263 of them. Who killed Custer is not known. Sitting Bull described his last moments: His hair 'was the colour of the grass when the frost comes. Where the last stand was made, the Long Hair stood like a sheaf of corn with all the ears fallen around him.' The visitors center, 638-2621/3204, is open daily during the summer, 8am-9pm; spring and fall 'til 6pm and in the winter 'til 4.30pm; $10 vehicle or $5 pp. _www.nps.gov/libi_.

THE GOLD COUNTRY Once the rough and tumble region of the state where miners, trappers and traders converged in an orgy of violence and lawlessness, the southwest corner of the state is now the host to a motley group of ghost towns, scenic rivers and tourists. Yet while the fortune seekers of old have long since gone, the region is still alive with the spirit of the Wild West.

BUTTE In the early 1900s Butte was a booming mining center dominated by copper, and was described as the 'Richest Hill on Earth' for over 100 years, due to the vast wealth of ores beneath its surface. Today, Butte is a city in transition to a more diverse economy, including tourism, education and energy research. America's largest Madonna figure, 'Our Lady of the Rockies', stretches 90 feet upward and peacefully observes the city from atop the Continental Divide. Butte's location, a mile above sea level in South-western Montana, and its inexpensive lodging market make it a good base for exploring Helena, the ghost towns and Indian battlefields roundabout. 'Road from Butte to Helena is great—lots of cliffs, narrow canyons, etc.' Butte offers little in the way of scenic beauty, however; unless one has an insatiable interest in mining history, it is possible to get one's fill of the city in a single day.

Accommodation
Capri Motel, 220 N Wyoming St, 723-4391. S/D-$44, D-$55, incls coffee and muffins.

Finlen Motor Inn, 100 E. Broadway 723-5461/ (800)729-5461, within walking distance of major sites uptown. S/D-$44-$48. _www.finlen.com_.

King's Motel, 307 S Main, **Twin Bridges**, (50 mi S on Hwy 41 from Butte), 684-5639/ (800) 222-5510. Offers clean, inexpensive cabins and fly fishing lessons; close to Virginia City. S-$55, D-$59, $69 w/kitchenette. _www.kingsflatline.com_.

Of Interest
Visit the **Mineral Museum at Montana Tech** or the **World Museum of Mining,**
723-7211, on a shaft-mining site with a new Underground exhibit, W of Montana
Tech on Museum Way. Plenty of antique mining equipment. At the same location,
Hell's Roaring Gulch is a replica of a pioneer village including a sauerkraut
factory, Chinese laundry and general store and more; both museum and village,
Daily 9am-5.30pm, 'til 9pm in the summer, $7. *www.miningmuseum.org*.
Copper King Mansion, 219 W Granite, 782-7580. 34-room mansion of copper
baron W. A. Clark. Daily 9am-4pm; $7 Also a B&B, prices range from $60-$95.
www.goldwest.visitmt.com/listings/931.htm.
Our Lady of the Rockies, (800) 800-LADY, visitors centre: 4304 Main. 90 ft statue
on East Ridge overlooking Butte, only 20 ft shorter than the Statue of Liberty.
Finished in 1985, it was built by volunteers from many religious sects with donated
materials. To get to the statue, take a tour bus from Butte Plaza Mall, round-trip
takes $2^1/2$ hours, rsvs required; $12. *www.ourladyoftherockies.org*.

Travel/Information
Greyhound, 101 E Front, 723-3287, Mon-Fri 1am-9am and 2pm-8pm, Sat-Sun 1am-
7am and 2pm-8pm. (800) 231-2222, 24hrs.
Chamber of Commerce, 1000 George St, 723-3177/(800) 735-6814. Summer, daily
8am-8pm. *www.butteinfo.org*.

HELENA Montana's pretty little capital city was crowned "Queen City of
the Rockies" following an 1864 gold strike and was listed as one of the top
100 artistic and cultural small towns in America. Situated along the Lewis
and Clark Trail, it's also a good place from which to launch your own Corps
of Discovery. Stroll down **Last Chance Gulch** (today's Main Street) to see
historic buildings and mansions dating back to the 1870s. The **Montana
State Capitol,** 6th St and Montana St, 444-4789, is decorated with interior
murals featuring themes of Montana's history (Free, Mon-Sat 9-3, Sun 12-4).
www.montanacapitol.com.

  St Helena Cathedral, 530 N Ewing, 442-5825, nicely complements its
lovely mountain setting. It's a replica of another well-known alpine church,
the Votive Church in Vienna. The **Kleffner Ranch,** located just east of town,
495-9090, is one of the most unique ranch properties in the state. The
octagonal stone house and enormous 3-storey barn were both built in the
1800s. Tours available by appointment, *www.kleffnerranch.com*. When you
get hungry, stop in at the **Staggering Ox,** 400 Euclid, 443-1729 and grab the
'world's best sandwich', the Clubfoot, from $4.75 to $6.95. Mon-Thu 9am-
8pm, Fri-Sat 11am-9pm, Sun 11am-7pm. *www.staggeringox.com*.
  Chamber   of   Commerce,   225   Cruse   Ave,   (800)   743-5362.
www.helenachamber.com.

GHOST TOWNS About 60 miles south east of Butte are **Nevada** and **Virginia
Cities;** Nevada City is restored village of 100 buildings and a museum.
'Don't miss the deafening collection of organs, pianos, and old RR
carriages.' To pan for gold and garnets in nearby streams, visit the **River of
Gold** in Nevada City, 843-5526; share a $13 bucket of 'dirt' to pan for gold
with. 'Takes lots of patience to pan for gold outside RR station to end up
with a few tiny specks of the yellow stuff.' Daily, 10.30am-6pm. (NB come
early to avoid the heat.) Restored in '97, the **Alder Gulch Short Line Train**

covers a two-mile stretch to **Virginia City.** Described as a 'working ghost town', the city has been heavily restored and offers numerous shops, restaurants and, of course, daily Western shootouts. _www.virginiacitymt.com_. When you get thirsty, kick back with a libation from Montana's first Brewery, The **H.S. Gilbert Brewery** and enjoy a performance of the Brewery Follies. _www.experiencegoldwest.com_.

Between Virginia City and **Bannack** (Montana's first boom town and territorial capital) was the 'Vigilante Trail'. In six months, 190 murders were committed here and gang activity got so notorious that miners secretly formed a vigilante committee. When they caught up with the gang leader, it turned out to be their sheriff, who was duly hanged on his very own gallows. 'Bannack: the best old Western town I've seen. Still has gallows, jail. View from top of Boot Hill unbelievable.' **Castle** (Calamity Jane's home town) and **Elkhorn** (300 old buildings still standing) are other interesting local destinations. **Anaconda,** 27 miles west off I-90, is home to the country's tallest smokestack. At 585 ft, it's tall enough for the Washington Monument to fit inside. _www.anacondamt.org_.

Big Hole National Battlefield is the site of the Nez Perce victory over US troops in 1877. Chief Joseph and his band were in flight to Canada, having refused to accept reservation life. Pursued by troops, they fought courageously and intelligently under Joseph's masterful military leadership. Despite their win, they were pursued and ultimately beaten at Bear Paw, less than 30 miles from the Canadian border. Visitors Centre, 9am-6pm in the summer and 'till 5pm in the winter. $5 per car or $3 per person. For info, call National Parks Service, Wisdom, 689-3155. _www.nps.gov/biho_.

MISSOULA AND THE FLATHEAD LAKE REGION The region continuously fights for the tourists' attentions with intriguing and, occasionally, disturbing festivals and non-stop beauty that will shake the knees of even the most jaded traveller. Only in western Montana could you find yourself sampling 'balls' for lunch at the Annual Testicle Festival and then spend the evening watching Shakespeare's classics performed by a roving group of thespians. **Flathead Lake** is the largest freshwater lake west of the Mississippi, State Parks and resorts line the 28 mile waterway, which varies in width from five to 15 miles. South of the lake is the **Flathead Indian Reservation.** This is modern Montana, and in many ways it is the most untamed, fascinating, and fun region of the state. _www.fcvb.org_.

MISSOULA A town of contradictions and culture, don't be surprised if you find yourself listening to cutting edge indie music in a century old cowboy bar or catch a long-haired bohemian wax poetic about the oft-overlooked merits of the WTO. The town is the self-proclaimed culinary capitol of the state; but don't take their word for it, let your palate be the judge. Lodging in this region can be expensive, although Missoula is reasonable. The camping, however, is excellent and inexpensive. For info on town happenings pick up a free copy of the _Independent_.

Accommodation
Sleepy Inn, 1427 W. Broadway, 549-6484. S/D-$48-$51 includes HBO, local calls and laundry facilities.

Royal Motel, 338 Washington, 542-2184/(888) 541-2006. S-$44-$52, D-$48-$52; all rooms have microwave and fridge. 3/4 of a mile from university. Rsvs advised.
City Center Motel, 338 E. Broadway, 543-3193. S/D-$45, D-$55. AC, cable and coffee. Rsvs preferred.

Food/Entertainment
Bagels on Broadway, 225 W Broadway, 728-8900. Best bagels in town, with a choice of fillings and sandwiches on offer. NB. Try the cheesecake! Mon-Fri 6.30am-5.30pm, Sat-Sun 7.30am-3.30pm.
The Depot, 201 W Railroad, downtown, 728-7007. Open-air deck restaurant has a large selection of reasonably priced pizzas, sandwiches and salads. 'Great quesadilla.' Daily 4pm-10.00pm, Sat-Sun 5.30-10.30pm. Bar is open 'till 2am.
Stockmans Bar and Lunch, 125 Front St. 549-9668. Bring your poker face to this Missoula classic. Serves classic American fare. Stockman's offers, 'liquor up front, and poker in the back', everyday, 1pm-2am.
The Rhinoceros, 151 Ryman, 721-6061. Come here on a full moon and all of the 52 draft beers that the Rhino offers are $1.74. Don't worry, for the other 27 days this popular bar hosts a great happy hour from 4-6pm. Mon-Sat 11am-2am, Sun opens at noon.

Of Interest
The Smokejumper Center, 5765 W. Broadway, 329-4934. Learn about those brave souls who jump into the centre of uncontrollable forest fires. Daily 8.30am-5 pm but show up at 10,11,2,3 or 4 for the tour. Donation. *www.visitmt.com*.
Lolo Hot Springs, 38500 W. Highway 12, (800) 273-2290. Head 30 mi. S of Missoula and relax in the hot pools of Lolo. Daily 10am-10pm, $6. *www.lolohotsprings.com.*
Western Montana Fair and Rodeo, First week in August, 721-3247. Fair $6/day, rodeo $10/night. *www.westernmontanafair.com*.
Testicle Festival, Rock Creek Lodge, Clinton, I-90 to exit 126. 825-4868. Yuppies, cowboys and the strange converge 22 miles E of Missoula each mid-September for a weekend of debauchery and deep-fried bulls testicles, $10. 4-day entrance and camping $20. *www.testyfesty.com*.
Miracle of America Museum, 58176 Hwy 93, 883-6804. Halfway between Missoula and Glacier. See America pay tribute to itself. With 6 acres of exhibition, it's been dubbed the 'Smithsonian of the West'. Summer daily 8am-8pm, $4. *www.cyberport.net/museum*.

Travel/Information
Greyhound, 1660 W. Broadway, 549-2339. Open when buses are in town, usually four times a day. Call ahead.
Missoula Convention and Visitors Bureau, 1121 E Broadway, Suite 103, 721-4750/(800) 526-3465. Open Mon-Fri 8am-6pm. *www.missoulacvb.org*.
Internet access: Cyber Quest, 821 S Higgens, 542-2985. $3/hr, 30 mins minimum. Snacks, munchies, drinks and an espresso bar!

GLACIER/WATERTON NATIONAL PARK 'Nothing that I can write can possibly exaggerate the grandeur and beauty of their work.' So wrote naturalist John Muir about glaciers. Nowhere are his words truer than here, surely one of the top contenders for the title of 'most beautiful place on earth'. The joining of **Glacier** in Montana and **Waterton** in Alberta created this 'International Peace Park', the first park in the world to cross national boundaries. *www.nps.gov/glac/*.

The Glacier section is traversed east to west by the **Going-to-the-Sun Highway**. Open mid-June to mid-Oct (snowed in the rest of the year), these 50 miles of remarkable beauty are most impressive coming from the west:

hugging the side of a cliff for dear life, the road grinds its way up a dizzy precipice along a fantastic hanging valley backed by angry peaks to **Logan Pass.** (Centre of the hwy) From Logan Pass visitors centre, there are some great day hikes—the 7.6 mile **Highline Trail** to the north, or 1.5 mile **Hidden Lake hike** have stunning scenery and aren't too strenuous. Also stop at **Mt Oberlin Overlook**; meet the friendly mountain goats that populate the area and get a spectacular eagle-eye view of the park.

Around 750 miles of trails wind among rugged mountains and cirque glaciers, leading to wildflower-scattered alpine meadows, trout-splashed lakes and quizzical mountain goats. Glacier's dangerous and unpredictable grizzlies are not one of the tourist attractions! Park naturalists lead parties along different trails; specifics can be found on the web or call one of the many visitor centers. A must see is the **Triple Divide,** a unique point from which water trickling through tiny streams must choose its ultimate destination: west to the Pacific; southeast to the Gulf of Mexico; or northeast to Hudson Bay.

When it comes to scenery, the Canadian side is no slouch, either. To reach **Waterton,** you must leave Glacier Park at the **St Mary** east entrance, and re-enter just at the US-Canada border. The Canadian park, much smaller than its sister to the south, centres on Waterton Lake. The **Shoreline Cruise Co.,** (403) 859-2362 has a $27 r/trip that lasts two hours from the north shore to the south, that is wonderful. _www.watertoninfo.ab.ca_. The hike around the lake's east side has been called Canada's best.

It's generally warm in summer, with occasional storms and invariably cold nights; by October, some of the park is liable to be snowed in. Excellent trout fishing but if you don't fancy catching your own; **Eddy's,** in **Apgar Village,** on the west side of park, 888-5361, (at the foot of Lake McDonald), is famous locally for good $12 trout dinners; 7am-9.30pm (summer). The park costs $20 per vehicle or $10 pp.

Accommodation

Glacier Park makes reservations at the 4 hotels and 3 motels within the park. They recommend rsvs 6 months in advance, (406) 756-2444. Last minute cancellations may make space available. Rooms start at $43 for a basic wood cabin, $96 w/bath. _www.glacier.national-park.com_.

Backpackers Inn, 29 Dawson Ave, East Glacier, 226-9392. Hostel accommodation in cabins $10; bring a sleeping bag—it gets cold at night! Private rooms available, $20 for 1 & $30 for 2. Linens/sleeping bag provided for $1. Outdoor BBQ grill. 'Good bulletin board.' Internet access across the street.

Brownie's Grocery and AYH Hostel, 1020 Montana Hwy 49, 226-4426. 6 blks from Amtrak station—will pick up. $13 AYH, $16 non-AYH, rooms $18-$26 AYH, $26-$29 non-AYH. Check-in 7.30am-9pm. Kitchen, linens provided. Park is 8 miles away. 48 hr cancellation policy.

Many lodges at **East and West Glacier,** just outside park. Best prices for doubles, triples or quads, so it pays to bunch up.

Super 8 Motel, 1341 1st Ave E, Kalispell Glacier, 755-1888/(800) 800-8000. S/D-$74-$88, D-$95/$116.

Parks 13 Campsites, (800) 365-CAMP, cost $12-$17. Back country camping free with permit from park office. $10 entrance fee to park. Watch out for bears. Information: Call the park office, 888-7800. _www.nps.gov/glac_.

Travel

In summer **Amtrak,** (800) 872-7245, stops at **East Glacier** and **Belton** on the west side of the park. There is no public transport between this station and the park although the **Red Jammer,** 892-2525, old-fashioned tour bus, takes you on a fantastic trip through the park with an informative commentary on all the sights. *www.glacierparkinc.com.* **Greyhound** only goes as far as Great Falls.

In summer horses can be rented in the east at **Mini Glacier** and in west Glacier at **Lake McDonald,** 888-5121. The **Great Northern Llama Company** offers 4-day llama pack trips. Cost is $222 pp per day, incls meals. Call 755-9044 or write 600 Blackmer Lane, Columbia Falls, MT 59912. *www.gnllama.com.*

River rafting trips by Glacier Raft Co. and others, 888-5454/(800) 235-6781, all equipment provided; $42 half-day, $73 whole day—incls BBQ steak lunch. *www.glacierraftco.com.* **Blackfoot Indians** will take you on a cultural tour of the park, incl short hikes (but not the entry fee), for $35-$65 depending on where you get the tour from; call Sun Tours, 226-9220/(800) 786-9220. *www.glacierinfo.com.*

GREAT FALLS If Glacier has left you tired of striking mountain peaks and vistas, head southwest to the Montana Plateau and the state's second largest city. This was the home base for American artist Charles M. Russell and houses an outstanding collection of his work; it's also home base for a fearsome array of Minuteman missiles at Malmstrom AFB. The home of the state fair in August, Great Falls is a likeable town. Lewis and Clark spent a month foraging around these parts in June 1805. While certainly not a destination, it is a useful and rewarding stopover between Glacier and Canada and Yellowstone and the Southern parts of the state.

Accommodation

Super 8 Motel, 1214 13th S, 727-7600. S-$60-$70, D-$66-$73. Centrally located.

Of Interest/Internet/Travel

C. M. Russell Museum, 400 13th St N, 727-8787. Outstanding collection of his Western paintings, bronzes and wax models. Over 30 other artists are also on show, including J Sharp and O.C. Seltzer. Open 9am-6pm daily in the summer, Tue-Sun 10am-5pm in the winter, $8, $3 w/student ID. **Russell's house and studio** are at 1300 4th Ave N, free with museum ticket. *www.cmrussell.org.*

Giant Springs Heritage State Park, NE of town, 454-5840. Site of the world's shortest river, the Roe, which is also one of the largest natural cold water springs in the world. Park open dusk 'til dawn; $2. The park is also home to the newest **Lewis and Clark interpretive site,** $5, open 9am to 5pm daily, 727-8733. *www.lewisandclark.state.mt.us.*

Malmstrom Air Force Base Museum, 228 75th St, 731-2705. Impressive collection of aircraft and missiles. Mon-Fri, 10am-4pm, call for weekend and holiday schedules; free. *www.malmstrom.af.mil.*

Internet access: Great Falls Public Library, 301 2nd Ave N, 453-0349. 1 hr limit. Free. *www.greatfallslibrary.org.*

Travel

Greyhound, Rim Rock Railway, 326 1st Ave S. 453-1541/(800) 823-1982; open 12pm-6.30pm and Sat-Sun opens at 2pm.

GATEWAY CITIES TO YELLOWSTONE, the oldest National Park in the world, **BOZEMAN, GARDINER** and **WEST YELLOWSTONE.** Of *Zen and the Art of Motorcycle Maintenance* fame, **Bozeman** is a college town and agricultural centre. It lies on the Butte to Billings Greyhound route; south from

Bozeman, Hwy 191 dips in and out of Yellowstone Park, coming at length (90 miles) to West Yellowstone. It's also here that you'll find the **Museum of the Rockies,** 600 W Kagy Blvd, 994-DINO. It became famous worldwide through the work of its chief palaeontologist, dinosaur hunter Jack Horner. Dr. Grant, of Michael Crichton's *Jurassic Park*, was fashioned after Horner. Planetarium and laser shows are also a daily feature on site. Daily, 8am-8pm. Museum $9.50, call for Planetarium and Laser Shows. *www.museumoftherockies.org.*

Gardiner, a small village on Yellowstone's central north border, has the only entrance open year-round. **West Yellowstone**, a few blocks from the west entrance to Yellowstone has numerous lodgings, bike/car rentals and other amenities for exploring the park. $20/vehicle and $10/person entrance fee for 7 days applies. The park has a published paper, *Yellowstone Today*, available on the web, *www.nps.gov/yell* with information, fees and more on all the entrances and the park itself.

Accommodation

In **Bozeman: Royal 7 Motel,** 310 N 7th Ave, 587-3103/(800) 587-3103, S-$52, D-$60, incl b/fast.

Bozeman International Backpackers Hostel, 405 W Olive St, 586-4659. $16, private room $35. Kitchen, laundry, nr downtown.

In **West Yellowstone: Madison Motel,** 139 Yellowstone Ave, 646-7745/(800) 838-7745. $22 AYH, non-AYH, $24, private rooms from S-$29, D-$39, S/D-$39-$49 with private bath, linens incl. Hotel part circa 1912, reflects early, pre-auto days of Yellowstone. 'Romantic old log house.' 'Very friendly.' Internet $5/hr, $2 minimum. Blk from W gate.

Wagon Wheel and Rustic Wagon Campgrounds and Cabins, Both off Gibbon Ave, 3 blks apart. Very nr. Greyhound. Wagon Wheels is a little cheaper, 646-7872. Tent site $26. 'Very generous host. Shower block is palatial.' 5-min walk to **Running Bear Pancake House.** *www.rusticwagonrv.com* and *www.wagonwheelrv.com.*

Travel/Information

Buffalo Bus Tour Company, 646-9564/(800) 426-7669. Leave from West Yellowstone daily; Upper/Lower Loop tours cost $45. Combo tkt $84. 10 hrs, on average. Packages, incl accommodation can be arranged. *www.yellowstonevacations.com.*

Car rental: 'If travelling from Bozeman and returning, try hiring a car for a round trip in 24 hours. Four of us did and it worked out cheaper than busing.' Hertz: (877) 388-6939.

Greyhound, 1205 E Main, 587-3110.

Park Information, (307) 344-7381. *www.nps.gov/yell*. An additional website, great for accommodation and activity lists with hundreds of links is *www.yellowstoneparknet.com.*

NEVADA — The Silver State

'Stark' describes the Silver State. It's a flat and monochrome universe of sagebrush, raked with north-south mountain ranges that rise like angry cat scratches from the dry desert floor. Five territories exist in the state and the two smallest seem to have the most to offer: **Las Vegas Territory** in the South with bright lights and bold attractions and **Reno-Tahoe Territory**, bordering California in the west with a more scenic, historic colouring.

About two million people rattle around in this state that measures 110,000 sq miles. Las Vegas and the surrounding area has been logged as the fastest growing city in the country for a number of years and has 70% of the state's population. Nevada had humble beginnings, admitted to the Union in 1864 on the strength of gold and silver from the Comstock Lode that helped finance the Union side of the Civil War.

The half-century that followed the war brought boom-and-bust cycles but a few factors positively intervened: In 1931 construction on the **Hoover Dam** commenced, drawing workers whose pay cheques were welcomed that same year by recently re-legalised gambling. Gaming, which would grow to become one of the state's largest sources of revenue, generating $10.6 billion in 2004 in Las Vegas alone, fulfilled the insatiable desires of government employees who were provided with good jobs and also a generous amount of radiation when the U.S. tested nukes north of Las Vegas. Today Nevada produces 76% of the gold mined in the US and 13% of the world's supply.

Nevada's trademarks may be glitter, fallout, prostitution and quickie marriages; but it's also a land of ranches, Native American pow-wows, Basque and Mormon communities and natural wonders like the **Valley of Fire,** weirdly beautiful **Pyramid Lake,** and the world's oldest tree, in Nevada's only National Park, **Great Basin.** The past and the future also meet here. There are ghost towns such as **Virginia City,** built overnight in 1869 upon the spilt champagne of lucky speculators—and new towns such as **Primm** and **Mesquite** built almost as quickly upon the loose change and gas money of the escaping, and the evicted, Strip visitors. Bring your sunglasses and no more than you are willing to lose. _www.travelnevada.com_.

LAS VEGAS There is a point at which overwhelming vulgarity achieves a certain grandeur and Las Vegas is living proof. In the blue velvet hours, it's an opulent oasis of neon jewels, endless breakfasts and raucous jackpots, a snug, clock-less world that throbs with unwarranted promise and phony glamour. As daylight approaches, the mirage wavers and melts away and the oasis becomes a banal forest of tacky, overweight signs whose oppressiveness is only challenged by an unforgiving summer heat. The town began when the San Pedro, Los Angeles and Salt Lake Railroad Co. created a town site called Las Vegas along its way in 1905.

The splashiest hotel-casinos are along **The Strip,** where it didn't all start with gangster Bugsy Siegel and **The Pink Flamingo** as Hollywood said in the movie _Bugsy_. The seminal Las Vegas joint opened its doors in 1941, the **El Rancho Vegas.** _www.vegas.com/map.html_. Like the movies, the scenery is ever-changing. Some of the latest mega-resorts are kitschy reflections of Europe, including a 55-storey replica of the Eiffel Tower at the **Paris,** an upscale Tuscan-village-meets-shopping mall at the **Bellagio,** and canal-lined shopping and serenading gondoliers of the **Venetian.** In 2000, the **Desert Inn** made famous by Noel Coward, closed to make way for a new, 42-story hotel called **Wynn Las Vegas**, which opened last year, the newest addition to what has become an increasingly entertainment-oriented town. Today, the amazing Cirque du Soleil, magician David Copperfield, comedian Jay Leno, and Celine Dion are among the standard headliners in Vegas. On _www.vegas.com_ you can get shows by type and price range.

Three miles from The Strip lies the **'Glitter Gulch'**, the downtown area and high-wattage cluster of 15 hotel casinos that share the covered, and county-funded, **Fremont Street Experience**—a free nightly light and music show. The Gulch tries harder with looser slots, cheaper eats and a more tolerant and friendly attitude towards newcomers and low-rollers in a, somewhat unsuccessful, attempt to distract visitors from the homelessness and Strip competition that plagues downtown. _www.vegasexperience.com._

There are lots of cheap lodging and food deals both on and off the Strip, so keep your eyes peeled. A word of warning for those under the magic stateside age of 21—Nevada doesn't like you. If you're under 18, you're not even allowed on the strip past 9pm and those under 21 are prohibited from gambling. And although confidence may allow those who look over 21 to avoid being 'carded' when they start playing, it certainly won't if you start winning. Finally, a little advice from _Fear and Loathing in Las Vegas_ and the Doctor, Hunter S. Thompson: '... this is not a good town for psychedelic drugs. Reality itself is too twisted'. Check out _www.lvol.com_ and _www.vegas.com_.

The area code is 702.

Accommodation

Since the casino owners want to encourage visits by unwary tourists, cheap lodging is possible in Las Vegas. Lodgings are cheapest in the summer when the temperatures hover around 115°F, and are cheaper midweek than on weekends. Avoid public holidays and big conventions (November and January) if you can. Sometimes there are astonishing bargains even at big flashy Strip hotels. 'Don't be afraid of bargaining.' If you find it difficult to get a room on a summer weekend, try one of the big places—more likely to have vacancies and it can still work out cheaply for 2 or more people. Beware of booking agents, 'they tell you the city is fully booked, just one free room. They then charge you $20 to book it. Don't be fooled by the free fun books they offer—you can get them anywhere'.

Also, compare freebies (eg coupons for gambling, shows, meals) between hotels—they can make a big difference to your overall expenses. Many of the big hotels also have free airport shuttles so remember and ask! Local radio and giveaway papers advertise the latest bargains, as do the _LA Times'_ classified ads. Hotels in Vegas offer big rewards for examining their websites. Often, technologically inclined gamblers will find rates that are half those offered by reservation agents. Speaking of the web, check out the wit of _www.cheapovegas.com_ to get the low-down on deals.

Downtown - close to bus station, and generally cheaper than the strip, but often dangerous—especially at night:

Budget Inn, 301 S Main St, 385-5560/(800) 959-9062. Across the street from Greyhound. 'Spotless.' S & D $50-$81. Greyhound special can apply! Call ahead. _www.budgetinnhotel.com._

Las Vegas International Hostel, 1322 Fremont St, 385-1150/(800) 550-8958. $17-$25 dorm, less $1 for members and BUNACers. Private rooms start at $41. $10 key deposit, Internet $1/10mins, TV, games, 24-hr pool, free pancake b/fast. Daily excursions to canyons, casinos and clubs. 'Real friendly.' 'Ants a problem in summer.' Check the web for latest prices, various room packages and internet specials. _www.usahostels.com/vegas._

On or near The Strip - NB-Casinos will not rent rooms to those under 21. Also, these rates will fluctuate dramatically depending on occupancy—always call ahead:

The Aztec Inn Casino, 2200 Las Vegas Blvd S, 385-4566. Rooms start at S/D-$35. A refundable $55 deposit is required if you use cash so have a credit card handy! 'In easy reach of all casinos with brilliant rooms.' Stick to the strip in this neighbourhood, next door to Stratosphere (see 'of interest').

Casino Royal, 3411 Las Vegas Blvd. S, (800) 854-7666. You can't beat its location (across from Mirage.) S/D-$99-$119. Pool and casino. *www.casinoroyalehotel.com*.

Circus Circus, 2880 Las Vegas Blvd S, 734-0410/(800) 634-3450. Thousands of rooms, TV, pool, amazing themed amenities and even acrobats! S/D-$40, XP-$13. max 5 persons. $90 plus on w/ends. Payment of first night req in advance; 48 hrs cancellation policy. 'Excellent.' The pyramid-shaped **Luxor** (888) 777-0188 and **Excalibur** (877) 750-5464 are similarly priced sister resorts of Circus Circus and at certain times may offer better rates. *www.circuscircus.com*; *www.luxor.com*; *www.excalibur.com*.

Howard Johnson Airport Inn, 5100 Paradise Rd, 798-2777/(800) 297-0144. S/D from $35, ($60-$80 w/ends). 2 pools, lounge, 24-hr shuttle service to airport and the Strip.

Sahara Hotel, 2535 Las Vegas Blvd S, 737-2111/(888) 696-2121. S/D from $40. Moroccan themed resort. 'First class. Amazing pool.' *www.saharavegas.com*.

Stardust Hotel, 3000 Las Vegas Blvd, 732-6111/(866) 642-3120. Possibly the most garish on the Strip, with 1,552 AC rooms. Prices from S/D$49 w/days, starting from $90 w/ends, with frequent specials advertised in newspapers and elsewhere. 2 pools, 5 restaurants. 'Sparkling room.' *www.stardustlv.com*.

Food

As a ploy to keep you gambling, many casinos dish up cheap and/or free meals to keep your strength up. You don't have to gamble to take advantage, either. Do read the fine print, though; some of the largesse has strings attached. Free or cheap breakfasts are commonplace. Every casino has an all-you-can-eat buffet, some, like the **Bellagio's,** 693-7111, are exquisite with fresh lobster and grilled to order steaks. Try their international cuisine daily 8am-10pm. Others, like **Circus Circus',** are 'terrible' but amazingly cheap. The local daily paper, *Review Journal*, prints a list of the all-you-can-eat buffets and other cheap deals at all hotels and casinos. Check Food and Dining on *www.reviewjournal.com*. It is possible to eat remarkably well (Las Vegas is host to some of the nation's finest restaurants) and it is possible to eat for next to nothing—it is rarely possible to do both though.

Capriotti's, 322 W Sahara, 474-0229. Perhaps the best sandwich on this side of the Mississippi, try a homemade turkey, a cheesesteak or the 'bobbie'. Mon-Fri 10am-5pm, Sat opens at 11am. $6-$12. Several locations but this is closest to the Strip.

Carnival World Buffet, at the Rio, 3700 W Flamingo, 252-7777. Good value buffet, bring your appetite. $13 for bfst, $15 for lunch and $23 for dinner. Mon-Fri 7am-10pm, opens at 7.30am on the weekends. *www.harrahs.com*.

Kilroys, 1021 S Buffalo, 363-4933. Las Vegas locals love Kilroy's burgers. And for $7 you'll soon see why. Open Mon-Sat 11am-11pm (bar is 24 hrs).

P.F. Chang's, 3 locations, (Strip—In the **Aladdin's**). 836-0955. Trendy atmosphere and good Chinese; $9-$14. *www.pfchangs.com*.

Roberto's Taco Shop, Multiple locations, (Strip—6711 LV Blvd. S Bldg S) Great, greasy, cheap Mexican food served 24 hours. Makes for a great late-night meal.

The Plaza Buffet, 1 Main St. 386-2110, Under $10 deals! 24 hrs.

Luv-It Frozen Custard, 505 E Oakley Blvd (one block east Strip), 384-6452. On hot Vegas days, this is the spot to be—best in Vegas. Tue-Thurs 1pm-10pm, Fri-Sat 'till 11pm, closed on Sun-Mon. *www.luvitfrozencustard.com.*

Of Interest

The Strip is the prime sightseeing attraction. Stroll through New York, Paris, medieval Europe, ancient Rome, you name it. Along the way check out the active volcano outside the **Mirage,** a pirate battle next door at the **Treasure Island,** statues that come alive inside the Forum Shops of **Caesars Palace,** a choreographed water show at the **Bellagio,** and a reenactment of Mardi Gras at the **Rio**—all for free.

If you've had enough of the bright lights, head inside the **Bellagio,** (877) 957-9777, to find a small, respectable gallery. It has housed pieces by Andy Warhol, Picasso and Monet. Exhibits change habitually: The last one (2005-2006) was *The Impressionist Landscape from Corot to van Gogh,* including 34 masterworks. Daily 9am-10pm, $15 ($12 w/student ID). *www.bgfa.biz.*

To gain a different impression of Las Vegas head 90 mi NE to **Crystal** and check out the **World Famous Brothel Art Museum,** (775) 375-5251. This annex to the local house of vice has a small collection of uninteresting exhibits, random pictures and quirky articles detailing Nevada's history of legalized prostitution. Free. *www.brothelmuseum.com.*

Stratosphere Hotel and Casino, 200 LV Blvd, (800) 998-6937 is more like a theme park. An observation deck (the tallest free standing structure in the US) gives spectacular views of Glitter Gulch, The Strip, the desert and mountains beyond, $9.95. You can try the High Roller for extra $4. Also encounter 4G's as you become the tallest object in Vegas for a split second on the **Big Shot,** $8. Combination rides $16-$30. The hotel rates can be reasonable, specials start at $32. *www.stratospherehotel.com.*

If the world's highest doesn't excite you, head out to **Primm,** (800) 386-7867 and ride what was until recently the world's tallest and fastest. The 'Desperado' drops 225ft. and is well worth $7. Finally, if you just can't bear that 40 mile drive you can walk to **Circus Circus** (734-0410) for the largest indoor roller-coaster, the Rim Runner, a ride that takes you through a water fall and other abundant attractions. $22.95 regular pass. *www.adventuredome.com.*

Liberace Museum, 1775 E Tropicana Ave at Spencer, 798-5595. A memorial to the entertainer who personified the Las Vegas life style. Free shuttle available from The Strip, 474-6507. Mon-Sat 10am-5pm, Sun 12pm-4pm, $12.50, $8.50 w/student ID. The world's largest rhinestone is also here. *www.liberace.com.*

Fashion Outlet at Las Vegas, a 35 mile shuttle ride from Aladdin or the MGM, call to rsv, (888) 424-6898. If you win big, don't save your money on the pricey boutiques of the strip, come here instead. The shuttle costs $15 r/t, the earliest leaves 9.15am and the latest returns 6pm. *www.fashionoutletlasvegas.com.*

The Luxor Hotel, 3900 LV Blvd. (800-557-7428) and **Caesars Palace,** 3570 LV Blvd. (877-427-7243) are both home to IMAX theatres. The Luxor hosts films for $9.99.

Flyaway Indoor Skydiving, 200 Convention Centre Dr. (877) 545-8093. If you've always wanted to skydive but couldn't bring yourself to jump out of a plane, $60 will buy you time in a 140 mi/hr wind tunnel. Daily 10am-7pm. *www.flyawayindoorskydiving.com.*

Red Rock Canyon, 20 miles west of Vegas. **Casino Travel and Tours,** 798-3020/(888) 444-9928, operates various daily tours from downtown. The Luxor tour bus leaves at 8.25am and returns approx 6 hrs later; $55—look out for discount coupons. 'Very beautiful.' *www.casinotravel.com.*

Cowboy Trail Rides, 948-7061 at Red Rock Canyon Stables offers horse back riding, mustang viewing and cowboy poetry. Daily 8am-10pm; starting at $89 for 2hrs. Pick-up at Excalibur Hotel at 7am. *www.cowboytrailrides.com.*

For a simple, free way to relax in Las Vegas, hop into any of the fancy Strip **hotel pools**. Several readers have written to say that no one asked if they were guests at the hotel. The key is to look like you belong there. But be careful, as a Las Vegas Cabana Host warned, 'That trick may slide at any other pool but when it comes to my pool…you're going to need a key!'

Entertainment

Las Vegas is famous for big-name superstar shows. Any given weekend may find Jerry Seinfeld entertaining in the **Caesars Palace** showroom and the Rolling Stones kicking off another 'final tour' at the **MGM Grand.** Championship boxing matches, golf tournaments and other sporting events also take place here. Paris-style revues, soft-core sex shows and lounge singers are all Las Vegas standards. Few shows are free, but like the restaurants and lodgings, they are less expensive here than most places, and the drinks are usually cheap or free.

If you are gambling, waitresses are glad to serve all manner of free, inhibition-releasing, beverages. 'To get free drinks, go to casinos where they are playing 'Keno'. Sit down and pretend to play by marking sheets provided. The waitresses then come and take your drink order for free!' Also, play nickel slots.

Las Vegas is home to so many good bars and nightclubs that it would be hard to go wrong anywhere. Favourite bars include **O'Shay's** across the street from Caesars Palace where what they lack in décor they make up for with $1 Guinness. **Fat Tuesday's** serves up $1 jell-o shots, mixed tropical drinks and $1 shots in their counter in the back of the MGM Grand. They can help ease the pain that the bars in the **Bellagio** charge for the best drink in town—A Cable Car ($10). To see the beautiful people get down, dress to the nines and around midnight head out to **Ra** in the **Luxor** or **Rum Jungle** at the **Mandalay Bay**. If you are particularly attractive give Baby's a shot, it's behind an unmarked door in the back of **The Hard Rock Hotel and Casino**. If you want to get down with the locals, try **The Beach**, 365 Convention Center Dr. Just don't forget your wallet.

Information/Internet
Las Vegas Convention and Visitors Bureau, 3150 Paradise Rd, across from the convention centre, 892-0711/(800) 332-5333. _www.vegasfreedom.com_.
Nevada Tourism, 401 N Carson St, Carson City. (800) NEVADA-8. _www.travelnevada.com_.
What's On guide, fortnightly magazine entertainment guide: (800) 494-2876. _www.ilovevegas.com_.
Internet access: Las Vegas Library, 833 Las Vegas Blvd N, 507-3500. Free, 2 hr limit. Wireless available. Open daily. _www.lvccld.org_.

Travel
Greyhound, 200 S Main St, downtown, 384-9561 (800) 231-2222.
No **Amtrak** station, bus service only, 200 S Main St, (800) 872-7245.
Auto Driveaway, 4343 N Rancho Dr, 658-8500. Mon-Fri 8am-4pm. Transport a car and catch Las Vegas en route. _www.autodriveaway.com_.
McCarran International Airport, 5 miles south of downtown. Lavish, carpeted. 'Large couches, ideal for dozing.' Don't play slots here. Take the CATRIDE #108 or #109 _Maryland Pkwy_ bus from 300 N Casino Center, $1.25, takes about 45 minute (CAT-RIDE: 228-7433), 24 hr regular service. _www.catride.com_. A few hotels also have free airport shuttles.
Scenic Airlines, 638-3300/(800) 634-6801, does 15 different trips from Las Vegas to the Grand Canyon. Best value probably the 8-hr air-ground tour over Hoover Dam and all along the Canyon in a small plane. Expensive at $279, but well worth it for a unique experience. Shorter flight-only tours cost $159. Book in advance. Special fares and offers can be found at _www.scenic.com_.

HOOVER DAM and LAKE MEAD NATIONAL RECREATION AREA One hour's
drive from Las Vegas is proof that engineering can be elegant as well as massive. Hoover's 726 foot vaguely Art Deco wall holds back Lake Mead, irrigates over one million acres, and keeps the lights on in LA and elsewhere. 'You can see the best of it by just driving past.' 'Fantastic value. Don't just drive past!' Self-guided tours 9am-4pm, $10; (702) 294-3523. There is a museum, visitors center and exhibit hall; takes approx 2 hours to see everything. 'Tour goes right inside the workings of the dam.' 'Probably

absorbing for the student engineer but not for the artistically inclined.'

An oasis of trees and shade by the shore of Lake Mead is the **Boulder Beach Campground,** (702) 293-8906, tent site $10/night. NB: do not stay here in summer, when the temperature is 100°F at 4am and the air is wall-to-wall insects! 'You'd have to camp in the lake to get a decent night's sleep.' www.usbr.gov/lc/hooverdam and www.nps.gov/lame.

RENO Although it tries hard to peddle greed, instant gratification (eg. quickie marriages/divorces) and fantasy like its Big Brother, Las Vegas, Reno doesn't quite make it. Despite the worst of intentions, little glimpses of culture, humanity and scenic beauty keep peaking through: its tree lined parkway along the **Truckee River;** its friendly university; its jazz festivals; its good Basque restaurants. Close to enchanting **Lake Tahoe** and only a day's drive from San Francisco, 'the Biggest Little City' makes a pleasant base to explore **Virginia** and **Carson Cities** and the emerald blue waters of Lake Tahoe's east shore. For an outstanding view take the **Mt Rose Hwy,** south of Reno on Rte 431; it climbs 8,911 feet up the highest pass in the state before descending into the **Tahoe Basin.** www.cityofreno.com.
The area code is 775.

Accommodation/Food
Reno takes the same attitude towards sleeping and eating that Vegas does, only Reno does it cheaper. Deeply discounted rooms can commonly be found at the downtown casinos and cheap buffets are the foundation of any Northern Nevada culinary escapade. Try **Circus Circus** (800-648-5010) for good deals.
El Cortez Hotel, 239 W 2nd St, 322-9161. S-$26, $29 w/ends, $5 deposit.
Motel 6, 866 N Wells Ave, 786-9852/(800) 466-8356, S/D $40/$45, w/end $49/$56.
Top Deck Restaurant, 2nd and Virginia St., (877) 777-7303, In the Club Cal-Neva. Super cheap coffee shop. Serves a variety of foods 24 hours Fri-Sun, weekdays 7.30am-10pm. www.clubcalneva.com.

Of Interest
National Automobile Museum, 10 S Lake St, Downtown, 333-9300. Mind-boggling collection of over 220 classic autos: Bugattis, a 1938 Phantom Corsair Coupe, entertainers' custom vehicles. Mon-Sat 9.30am-5.30pm, Sun 10am-4pm, $8. www.automuseum.org.
Nevada Historical Museum, 1650 N Virginia St, nr campus, 688-1190. Washoe Indian Dat-So-La-Lee was one of the finest weavers of Native American baskets in the country. Her work, as well as mining history and the development of casino industry, is on display here—the state's oldest museum. Mon-Sat 10am-5pm, $2. dmla.clan.lib.nv.us.
Nearby: Virginia City, A $25/week reporter for the local *Territorial Enterprise,* Mark Twain, wrote of this semi-ghost town in its boisterous prime: 'It was no place for a Presbyterian, and I did not remain one for very long'. The **Mark Twain Bookstore,** 111 So C St, 847-0454, displays some Mark Twain memorabilia. www.marktwainbooks.com. **The Sundance Saloon,** now a T-shirt shop, still houses the city's oldest bar. The city also has a melting pot of **cemeteries,** from Masonic and Catholic to Chinese and Mexican. Explore also the museums on C St—one of the best being **The Way It Was,** 847-0766, full of mining and local history. Daily 10am-6pm, $2.50. Don't miss the annual camel, ostrich and water-buffalo races, held on the weekend following Labor Day, fees apply; from $10. The Chamber of Commerce can tell you more, 847-0311. www.virginiacity-nv.org.
Carson City. Loaded with Victorian gingerbread homes and refreshingly situated

in the green Sierra foothills, this is the smallest capital city in the lower 48. Mark Twain lived at 502 N Division St with his brother, who was the first territorial secretary of state. Take the free self-guided **Blue Line** tour, 687-7410/(800) 638-2321, to explore the city and local history. _www.visitcarsoncity.com_. Sights include a rare collection of natural gold formation at the Carson Nugget; displayed at the **Carson Nugget Casino**, 507 N Carson St. _www.ccnugget.com._ The former US mint, now the State Museum, 600 N Carson is located just across the street, $5. The **Nevada State RR Museum**, 2180 S Carson St, 687-4810, is one of the finest railroad museums in the US. Operates historic equipment daily, 8.30am-4.30pm, $4. _www.nsrm-friends.org_. Call the **Carson City Chamber of Commerce** for local events, 882-1565. _www.carsoncitychamber.com_.

LAKE TAHOE One of the deepest and most beautiful lakes in the world. A voyage over **Spooner Summit** (Hwy 50) or **Mt. Rose** will be rewarded with awe-inspiring views of its crystal blue waters. Lake Tahoe is a haven for outdoor enthusiasts, offering every imaginable activity from parasailing to snowboarding. The Casinos on the south shore provide 24-hour excitement while the tranquil community of **Incline Village**, on the north shore, is home to solace seeking celebrities and quiet family cottages. Visit the local Chamber of Commerce at _www.laketahoechamber.com_ (N shore), and _www.tahoechamber.com_ (S shore). NB: also see California.

Travel/Information
Amtrak, E. Commercial Row & Lake St, 329-8638, (800) 872-7245.
Greyhound, 155 Stevenson St, 322-2970/(800) 231-2222.
Reno Convention and Visitors Authority, E 1st St, (888) HIT-RENO. Mon-Fri 8am-5pm. _www.renolaketahoe.com_.

GREAT BASIN NATIONAL PARK Opened in 1986, Great Basin was the first new national park in the lower 48 in 15 years. 400 miles to the west of Carson City on Hwy 50, it is the centrepiece of the 'loneliest road in America', a highway that follows the route of the historic **Pony Express Trail.** Great Basin's role as a National Park probably has more to do with federal politics than with one-of-a-kind beauty or environmental precaution: The federal government owns most of Nevada but until 1986, Nevada was the only western state without any of the prized, federally designated park lands. The park nonetheless makes for a nice place to stretch one's legs. The nearest town to the 77,100-acre Great Basin is the miniscule **Baker** whose population of 50 boasts half a dozen houses, a gas station, a two-room school, post office, a motel, restaurant/bar and a small convenience store.

Scenery within the park varies from spectacular mountains, topped by the 13,063ft **Wheeler Peak,** to sagebrush-studded desert, alpine lakes, deep limestone caves, lush meadows and groves of gnarled bristlecone pines—the oldest living trees. The vistas are 'unbelievable, absolutely outstanding'. Park headquarters and visitor centre is at **Lehman Caves;** 30, 60 and 90 min ranger-guided tours of the caves run from 8am-4.30pm, and cost $4, $8 and $10 respectively. If you really, really love the desert, campsites are $12. For park information phone (775) 234-7331. _www.nps.gov/grba_.

EXTRATERRESTRIAL HIGHWAY The remote desert area that the E.T. Hwy snakes through probably wouldn't be visited by tourists if it wasn't believed to be frequented by aliens. After the success of the film, *Independence Day*, 100 miles of Hwy 375 were dubbed the Extraterrestrial Highway, attracting thousands of UFO-hungry tourists to an otherwise desolate area. The government's infamous research centre, **Area 51**, is located just outside of **Rachel**. Don't expect to sneak inside— security is tight and fines for sneaking in are stiff. Every Wednesday night, people flock to the highway for a weekly UFO watch. No extraterrestrial activity has been verified, though. The only aliens you're likely to see are those depicted in the combination restaurant/bar/museum/gift shop/motel in **Alamo**, the **Little A'Le'Inn**, (775) 729-2515. *www.littlealeinn.com*, *www.angelfire.com/nv/dreamland51*.

UTAH - The Beehive State

Although the US government owns 70 percent of Utah's land, the Beehive state is, for all intents and purposes, under Mormon control—a unique situation indeed considering the American insistence on separation of church and state.

The Church of Jesus Christ of the Latter-Day Saints (LDS, *www.lds.org*) began in 1827 when New Yorker Joseph Smith was led by an angel named Moroni to some gold tablets. Translated (with the help of Moroni and two seer stones called Urim and Tummim) into English, the writings became the scriptures of the *Book of Mormon*. The fledgling sect was pushed westward from New York but didn't encounter any significant antagonism until Smith introduced polygamy at Nauvoo, Illinois. A hostile mob promptly killed Smith and his brother. The mantle fell to Brigham Young, who ably led his band west to the bleak wilds of northern Utah in 1847, in which no one, not even the local Ute Indians, seemed terribly interested.

The industrious Mormons established their new state of Deseret and applied repeatedly to the US government for admission to the Union but were turned down over the issue of polygamy, which was still going strong. (Brigham himself ultimately had 27 wives and 56 children.) After years of wrangling, in 1890 the Mormons gave in and banned polygamy among themselves. A number of dissenters left and their descendents can be found living quietly and polygamously in Mexico, Arizona and elsewhere.

The importance of Mormonism makes Utah—especially **Salt Lake City** and environs—sharply different and in many ways better than other states. Hardworking Mormons have built clean, prosperous, humanistic cities and settlements. From early settlement days, Utah has supported the arts; it is home not only to the world-famous Tabernacle Choir but galleries, museums, opera, theatre and the **Sundance Film Festival**. On the negative side, it's hard to find a drinkable cup of coffee anywhere. Mormons discourage the use of coffee and stimulants and apparently feel the same way about seasonings. Liquor laws, once extremely stringent, have eased somewhat but getting a drink in a restaurant can still be a baroque procedure.

All of Utah's five National Parks are in the south, an area studded with magnificent monuments of the greatest historical, geological and scenic importance. Take a tour or rent a car, allow ample time for exploration and reflection. Explore the natural attractions on the **Utah/Arizona border** and further south, such as **Monument Valley,** the **Navajo reservation** and the north rim of the **Grand Canyon** (via Kanab). A boat trip through the flooded canyons of the **Glen Canyon** National Recreation Area is also an unforgettable (albeit pricey) experience. *www.utah.com*.

National Parks: Zion, Bryce Canyon, Canyonlands, Capitol, Reef Arches.
The telephone area code is 801. Also 435 where indicated.

SALT LAKE CITY Host to the 2002 Winter Olympics and not just a state capital but the Mecca/Vatican/Jerusalem for Mormons worldwide. Salt Lake City has a joyful, almost noble air about it. Founder Brigham Young knew how to design a city; Salt Lake City is cradled by the snowy **Wasatch Mountains** in a setting of remarkable grace. Add to that streets broad enough for a four-oxen cart to turn in, a tree for every citizen, clean air and ecclesiastical architecture that succeeds in being impressive without being dull, and you have quite a place.

'The beauty of this city is that nearly everything worth seeing is within ten minutes walk of the Greyhound terminal. I managed to see a great deal in the four hours' break I had between buses. I found Mormonism really interesting but it's easier to stomach if taken with a pinch of salt.'

Not hard to do, since **the Great Salt Lake** lies just 18 miles west of the city. The lake is a mere remnant of Lake Bonneville, a vast prehistoric sea that covered much of Utah and parts of Nevada and Idaho. The outline of the ancient sea is still visible from the air.

Accommodation
Avenues Hostel, 107 F St, 359-3855. $15.50 dorm; S-$28, D-$31.50. Internet access $3/30mins.Rsvs should be made a week in advance for busy dates, need a credit card or money order. 'Spacious, well-equipped, kitchen, launderette.' *www.hostels.com*.
Carlton Hotel, 140 East South Temple St, 355-3418/(800) 699-1500. S-$74, D-$79. Nr bus depot. 'Super place with lovely bathrooms, restaurant.' Call for student discounts $180/week.
Crystal Inn Downtown, 230 W 500 S, 328-4466/(800) 366-4466. S/D or 2 queen beds-$100-$149. Microwave, fridge, hot buffet b/fast, free airport shuttle, sauna,
Ute Hostel, 21 E Kelsey Ave, (801) 595-1645. Opened 1994, friendly hostel; dorm S-$15, D-$35, shared bath and kitchen facilities. *www.infobytes.com/utehostel*.

Food
Toasters Deli, 151 W 200 S, 328-2928. Great toasted sandwiches, soups, salads, bagels and coffee. Mon-Fri 8am-8pm, Sat 10am-4pm. Sun closed. All under $10.
Old Salt City Jail, 460 S 1000 E, 359-6090. Steak, chops and seafood served in a jail, with a singing sheriff for authenticity! Daily 11am-9pm, Sat-Sun opens at 5pm. $10-$20 entrees.

Of Interest
Temple Square Visitors Center, in the north and south parts of the square, (801) 240-2534. Run by the Mormon Church, a number of free tours are offered; start 9am. Excellent walking tour maps are also available. 'Guided tour conducted by Mormons who must have been trained to sell insurance. Intimidating.' Daily, 9am-9pm. *www.mormon.org*.
LDS Church Office Building, 50 East North Temple, (801) 240-2190. Free tours

Mon-Fri 9am-5pm. 'Fantastic view from 26th floor.' Check 'Other Resources – Places to Visit' at _www.lds.org_

Genealogical Library, 35 NW Temple, 240-2854/(800) 346-6044. Because Mormon doctrine recommends the baptism of adherents' long-dead ancestors, the church has been accumulating and organizing genealogical records from all ages and all corners of the earth since 1894. With more than 2 billion on record, the library has become a major world centre for genealogical research. If you know the birth date and birthplace of an ancestor before 1900, the library can probably help you trace your family tree back for generations (they have a separate section for British ancestry). The collection includes over 2.4 million rolls of microfilmed records; 742,000 microfiche; 310,000 books, serials, and other formats; 4,500 periodicals; and 700 electronic resources. Mon 8am-5pm, Tue-Sat till 9pm. Free tour and help. _www.familysearch.org_.

Mormon Temple, Temple Square. This monumental structure in Mormon Gothic took 40 years to build and was finally completed in 1893. It cost $3.5 million. Notice the golden statue of the angel Moroni on one of the towers; according to LDS doctrine, this was the being that appeared to church founder Joseph Smith. 'Even if you're only passing through, go to see the temple. Fantastic the way it's lit up.' Not open to non-church members. Check 'Temples' at _www.lds.org_

Mormon Tabernacle, home of the Mormon Tabernacle Choir. To witness the weekly radio and TV broadcasts, be in your seat by 8.30am Sun morning to be sure of a place. 'An acoustic wonder.' This is one place where if you stand in the back you can still hear a pin drop in the centre. Call Visitor's Centre, 240-2190, for more information. _www.mormontabernaclechoir.org_.

Additional Mormonabilia: 'This is the Place' monument at **Pioneer Trail State Park,** Emigration Canyon, east edge of city, 582-1847. Also a living history museum; walk through the 50 homes with pioneers explaining the history. 'Mormons are obsessed with the pioneers but they don't try to convert you—in fact, I found Mormonism quite fascinating.' $6. _www.thisistheplace.org_.

Brigham Young's Grave, cemetery on 1st Ave between State and A St.

Beehive House, 67 E South Temple, 240-2671. BY's first residence. Free 30 min tours every 12 minutes, Mon-Sat 9.30am-6.30pm, Sun 10am-1pm. The tiny dorm rooms in the upper hall and main floor of the adjoining Lion's House was home for 19 of BY's wives. Legend has it that after supper the great man would climb the stairs and chalk an X on the door of his lady for the night. Sometimes a rival would erase the X and chalk another on her door before the absent-minded stud came back upstairs. In this fashion, BY brought 56 new Mormons into the world.

Abravanel Hall, 123 W South Temple, 533-5626. A glorious glass wedge of a place that houses the Symphony Opera and Orchestra. _www.utahsymphonyopera.org_. Close by are the **Salt Palace**, the **Capitol Theater** and the **Delta Centre**. At the latter center NBA's **Utah Jazz** team play, Oct-May. _www.nba.com/jazz_. For those into sports, the **Grizzlies** play ice hockey near by in **West Valley City** at the **E Center**, Oct-April. _www.utahgrizzlies.com_.

Utah Museum of Fine Arts, 410 S Campus Center Dr. 581-7332. Tue-Fri 10am-5pm, Wed 'till 8pm, Sat-Sun 11am-5pm, $4. _www.utah.edu/umfa_.

Across the 'U's' campus is the **Utah Museum of Natural History,** 1390 E Presidents Circle 581-6927. Mon-Sat 9.30am-5.30pm, Sun noon-5pm, $6. _www.umnh.utah.edu_.

Shopping: Brigham Young established the first department store in the US, the **Zion Cooperative Mercantile Institution** (ZCMI Center Mall), 36 S Main. At one time it was the biggest covered mall in the country. Is being re-developed with in conjunction with Crossroads Plaza, also owned by the LDS. Good browsing too at Trolley Square. _www.thedowntownmalls.com_.

Great Salt Lake, 18 miles west. 2500 sq miles and with salinity levels between 10 and 20 percent, second only to the Dead Sea. The Mormons used to put joints of beef in the water overnight, retrieving them tolerably well pickled. Then the lake was saltier; more fresh water is added each year when the snow melts off the mountains.

Sundance, 328-3456. Established by Robert Redford in 1981, the Sundance Institute sponsors the annual **Sundance Film Festival** in **Park City** each January. Over 10,000 people attend the film festival to catch rising stars, emerging screenwriters and directors. _www.sundance.org_.

Entertainment

Days of '47 Festival, 3rd week in July. Rodeo, parades, free concerts, dances, and a sunrise service by the Mormon Tabernacle Choir. 'Fun.' _www.daysof47.com_.

Raging Waters, 1200 W 1700 S, 972-3300. Utah's largest water theme park. Open summer: Mon-Sat 10.30am-7.30pm, Sun from noon. $19.13. Nightwater 4pm-7.30pm, $11.14. _www.ragingwatersutah.com_.

Utah Winter Games, 1760 Fremont Dr, 973-8824; try a bobsled run with the professionals or watch luge and ski-jumping events. 'Hairy but exhilarating!' _www.utahwintergames.org_.

Information/Internet access

Salt Lake Convention and Visitors Bureau, 90 South West Temple, (801) 521-2822/(800) 541-4955. _www.visitsaltlake.com_.

Salt Lake City Public Library, 210 E 400 S, (801) 524-8200. Free, limit of 1hr. _www.slcpl.lib.ut.us_.

Utah Official Travel Council, (800) 200 1160. _www.utah.com_.

Travel

Amtrak, 340 S 600 W, 322-3510/(800) 872-7245. Catch the _California Zephyr_ between Oakland, CA and Chicago from Emeryville (5885 Alndregan St, (510) 450-1081) just outside Salt Lake City.

Greyhound, 300 S 600 W, 355-9579/(800) 231-2222.

Gray Line Tours, trip to Bingham Canyon and the Great Salt Lake, $42. Leave daily 2.30pm and last $4^1/_2$ hrs. Departs from Shilo Hotel, 200 SW Temple, or call 531-1001. 'Bus to San Francisco drives along the lake anyway.' _http://www.saltlakecityutah.org/sightseeingtours.htm_.

Utah Transport Authority (UTA), 743-3882. Buses: $1.40 basic fare with free transfers available, good for 2hrs. _www.rideuta.com_.

Salt Lake City International Airport, 776 N Terminal Dr, about 4 miles/10 mins west of downtown. Catch the #50 bus from N Temple and 300 W, $1.40; goes straight there.

PROMONTORY About 80 miles north of Salt Lake City is the **Golden Spike National Historic Site,** that marks the spot where North America's first transcontinental railroad was 'supposedly' completed on May 10th 1869. After a symbolic gold-spike ceremony, Leland Stanford and Thomas Durant, the heads of the railroads thus joined, were scheduled to pound in the final iron stake. Stanford missed and Durant was too woozy from the previous night's revelry to even try; a professional spike-pounder standing nearby was called in to do the job. Or so the story goes—it's more historical myth than fact.

The actual Golden Spike (which was only 73% gold) is found in the **Art and History Museum** at **Stanford University in Palo Alto,** California. Stanford, the Governor of California, purchased the spike and brought it back home with him. An alternate account insists that the junction of the two railroad lines did not, in fact, take place at Promontory Point, but rather

15 months later near **Strasburg, Colorado.** Nevertheless, the gold-spike ceremony is re-enacted each May 10th, the 2nd Saturday of August and on weekends at 1pm and 3pm during the summer.

The **Visitors Centre,** (435) 471-2209—ext.18, is open in the summer, daily 9am-5pm, $7/vehicle. _www.nps.gov/gosp_.

DINOSAUR NATIONAL MONUMENT This park overlaps two states (see also Colorado) but the major attractions lie mostly in Utah. **Vernal** has a superb **Field House of Natural History,** corner of 500 E and Main, (435) 789-3799. It offers natural science, geology, rocks, minerals and a Native American hall with educational explanations of ancient fossils and 18 life-sized dinosaurs including a Utah Raptor. Summer months 8am-9pm, winter 9am-5pm; $5. _www.stateparks.utah.gov/park_pages/field.htm_. Twenty one miles from Vernal is **Dinosaur Quarry,** where you are on eye level with half-exposed brontosaurus and other remains. See Indian petroglyphs as you look down into the gorge beside the quarry.

The road from Vernal to Daggett is called 'the Drive through the Ages' for the billion years of earth's history that lies exposed on either side. There are numerous campgrounds in and around the Dinosaur National Monument (emphasis on RVs, though).

The **Visitors Center,** (435) 789-7894, at Field House is full of free maps and info and even Dinosaur Hunting Licenses-get your own permit to hunt a live dinosaur. See 'Colorado' for more information about the Eastern half of the park. _www.nps.gov/dino_.

ZION NATIONAL PARK Though not as famous as Yosemite or the Grand Canyon, tiny Zion's outstanding landscapes rank up there with the best. Zion has a huge, painted gorge of magnificent and constantly changing colours; its floor is an oasis of green. Cottonwoods grow on the lush canyon floor, where you can camp at two sites: Watchman or South Campgrounds. So delightful was the sight that the first Mormons called it Zion. They were later corrected by Brigham Young who proclaimed, 'It is not Zion'. (It remained 'Not Zion' for some years.)

The 6-mile drive into the canyon (only accessible by shuttle bus from April-October) passes the **Great White Throne, Weeping Rock** and the trail to the **Emerald Pools,** but for a better look you are advised to walk. There are numerous trails, with fantastic geological features; info about all of them is available from the **Zion Canyon Visitors Center** at the park's south entrance, bordering Springdale. You can walk alone, or take a guided tour with a park ranger. These tours leave daily at 9am from the visitor's center, as do the free shuttle buses. The free tour shuttle service tickets go quickly and its advisable to get yours the day before the trip from the visitors center. Before setting off on any trail, long or short, check with rangers for advice on availability of drinking water in certain areas, sudden summer cloudbursts with flash flooding and falling rock. Remember also to take a bottle of energized water, to avoid dehydration.

'We liked the Emerald Pools Footpath, a gentle stroll for a hot day— beautiful waterfall.' 'Try walking up to **Angels' Landing,** 5-mile round trip rising 1488 ft. Incredible views.' 'Angels' Landing walk—strenuous but very rewarding.' (NB: sheer drops along path—not for acrophobes.) The best view of the **Great White Throne,** a colossal multicoloured butte, is from the **Temple of Sinawava.** Also worth seeing is the **Kolob Arch.** With a 310 ft span, one of the world's largest. The park entry fee ($10 for individuals, $20 for vehicles) is good for 7 days; backcountry passes are required prior to overnight hikes and for the more adventurous trails. ($10 for 1-2 people). For further info call the **Parks Office HQ,** 772-3256, 8am-7pm. _www.nps.gov/zion_ and _www.utah.com/nationalparks/zion.httm_.

The area code is 435.

Accommodation
For Park lodgings, check _www.zionlodge.com/galleries/lodging.htm_
Best Value Inn, 323 S Main, **Cedar City,** 586-6557. S/D-$55-$60. AC, TV, b/fast, spa, pool. _www.bestvalueinn.com_.
At Kanab: Canyonlands International Hostel. 143 E 100 South, 644-5554. NB. _Just closed at time of going to press._
Camping: (800) 365-CAMP, _www.nps.gov/zion_. 286 sites, all unreserved apart from Watchman Campground; arrive by noon to snag one. $16 basic site, $18 full hook-up, $20 for sites adjacent to the Virgin River. Toilets but no showers. Motels, groceries, and gas station in **Springdale,** bordering the south entrance. **Cedar City,** 40 miles north of Zion, 16 miles from **Cedar Breaks National Monument** (called 'Little Bryce' for its spires, perhaps more intensely coloured than anywhere else— good camping) makes a good base.

Travel
Greyhound, 2569 N Main St, (800) 231-2222. Stop only so can't buy tickets here. Goes to Salt Lake City and Las Vegas.
Within Zion: The free **Zion Canyon Loop Shuttle** operates daily 5.45am-11pm from Visitor Center to Temple of Sinawava; and the free **Springdale Loop Shuttle,** which operates daily 5.30am-11.15pm from Zion Canyon Theater to Majestic View. _www.nps.gov/zion_ and _www.zionpark.com/Shuttle.htm_.
Car Rental, 2281 Kittyhawk at Cedar City Airport, 586-4004. Must be over 21. _www.nationalcar.com_.

BRYCE CANYON NATIONAL PARK Bryce's landscape belongs to God's Gothic period—delicately chiselled spires, colonnades and crenulated ridges in vivid to pastel pinks, madders, oranges, violets. Most stunning when seen against the sun: west rim in morning, east rim in afternoon. Named for Ebenezer Bryce, an unpoetic soul who described the canyon as 'a hell of a place to lose a cow'. From the pine-covered cliff tops (site of the visitors centre and other facilities), the horseshoe-shaped amphitheatres reveal surreal formations that have been likened to houses, sunburned people and petrified sunsets. For hiking, descend the canyon to the **Peek-a-boo Trail** or take a short trip along the **Navajo and Queen's Garden trails,** which link at the bottom (about $1^1/_2$ hrs for a quick trot).

There is a 16-mile auto road but the views are less spectacular. On full-moon nights, take the free 'moon walks' down Navajo Trail or try a star walk on w/ends of dark-moon nights at 8.30pm. 'Wall Street is more spectacular than Queen's Garden.' In order to alleviate the traffic snarls that have plagued Bryce Canyon (one parking space available for every four cars that enter the park during high season!), the park has instituted a shuttle service to transport people to the major sites. Visitors who wish to bring their cars into park will be subject to a $20 fee, while those who ride the free shuttle only pay $20/day/group for up to 5 persons. **Park HQ:** 834-5322. Pedestrian fee is $10 and is good for 7 days. Camping costs $10/night for up to 6 people per site. 'Arrive by noon to be sure of a place.' _www.nps.gov/brca_. *Area code is 435.*

Accommodation
Most accommodation is in **Panguitch**, 24 miles SW of Bryce. _www.panguitch.org_.
Bryce Canyon Pines Motel, Only 6 miles from Bryce entrance, on Hwy 12, Mile Post 10, 834-5441/(800) 892-7923. S/D-$55-$75 summer, $30-$55 in winter. AC, pool, and homey dining room with good home cooking. Horseback riding: $10 for half-hour; $90 full day. _www.brycecanyonmotel.com_.
Paria Outpost and Outfitters, located between Mile Posts 21 and 22, Hwy 89, (928) 691-1047. One-of-a-kind B&B and restaurant. $50/night with discount for multiple night's stay. Offer a Trail Head shuttle and guided tours, start at $60. _www.paria.com_. Next door is the **Paria Guest Ranch,** (928) 660-2674, with campsites, $7.50 and bunkhouse, $12. Horseriding is also available here, $45/2hrs and you can rent kayaks $40/day/2 people. Makes a good day's activity at Lake Powell. _www.pariacampground.com_.

MOAB A former uranium mining town on US 163 in east-central Utah, Moab makes a convenient centre from which to visit **Canyonlands, Arches** and **Capitol Reef National Parks.**
It's also a place to book a tour to one of these parks. Try **Navtec Tours,** 321 N Main, 259-7983/(800) 833-1278. The most popular trip is the land/river combo, $89-$95. _www.navtec.com_. Other operators in town offer bike rentals and tours, horseback riding and white-water rafting. The **Visitors Center** at Center and Main can help you sort out options. Daily summer hrs: 8am-9pm, (800) 635-6622 _www.discovermoab.com_. For rafting ($36/half day, $48/day) contact **Tag-A-Long Tours,** 452 N Main St, Moab, 259-8946/(800) 453-3292. _www.tagalong.com_.

Accommodation
Check Moab's website _www.moab-utah.com_ for info, maps, lodging and activities.
Inca Inn Motel, 570 N Main, 259-7261. S/D-$50 bath, XP-$6. Continental Breakfast included. Cable TV, AC, pool. _www.moab-utah.com/inca/inn.html_.
Lazy Lizard Hostel, 1213 S Hwy 191, 259-6057. Dorm-$9, Private S/D $22/$24. Separate bath/shower room and hot tub; shared kitchen and laundry facs. Cabins for 1-6 people range from $27-$47. _www.lazylizardhostel.com_.
Virginian Motel, 70 E 200 St S, 259-5951. S/D-$59-$89 in summer, $25-$30 in winter, XP-$10. Fridges, cable TV, AC, rsvs recommended. _www.moabutah.com/virginian/motel.html_.

ARCHES, CANYONLANDS, CAPITOL REEF The 76,500 acres of **Arches National Park** contain water worn natural bridges and over 2000 arches of smoky red sandstone carved by the tireless wind. 'Our most memorable national park.' Entrance $5/individual, $10/vehicle for 7 days. NB: If you plan on visiting more than one of these parks, the $25 local annual passport may be a good bet—good for 4 parks in southeast Utah. **Camping** in Arches is $10 Mar-Oct. No rsvs. But campers must register at visitors centre starting at 7.30am in summer, (winter, first come first serve). For more information, call (435) 259-8161. _www.nps.gov/arch_.

Natural Bridges is noted for three rock bridges, the foremost a 268-ft span—the 2nd largest in the world. Less well-known features are the hundreds of Anasazi cliff ruins and the world's largest photovoltaic solar generating plant, which runs the park's electrical system. Entrance $3/individual, $6/vehicle. Call (435) 692-1234 for info: _www.nps.gov/nabr_.

Canyonlands is invitingly rich in colour and landforms: towering spires, bold mesas, sky-scraping needles, precarious arches, roaring rapids, peaceful sandbars and intricate canyons. Entrance to this park is $10/vehicle and $5/person. For info call (435) 719-2313. _www.nps.gov/cany_. The park is also full of petroglyphs, pictographs and ruins: the **Maze District** with its Harvest Scene and the **Needles District** south of Squaw Springs campground are particularly good. Needles campsite is $10/night, (435) 259-4711. If you enter Canyonland Park at the **Maze District Visitors Center,** (435) 259-2652, there is no entrance charge but you will need a backcountry camping pass, $15, good for 14 days. A campsite is $30/car or individual. The district with a 'superb view from **Dead Horse Pt,** just outside park' is **Island in the Sky.** $5/night at Willow Flat campsite, (435) 259-4712.

Capitol Reef, rising 1000 feet above the Fremont River and extending for 20 miles, is the most spectacular monocline (tilted cliff) in the US. The bands of rock exposed along its length are luminous, rich and varied in their colour, and often cut with petroglyphs of unusual size and style. Its formations were named 'sleeping rainbows' by the Navajos. The entrance fee is $5, overnight backcountry permit is free. _www.nps.gov/care_.

GLEN CANYON, MONUMENT VALLEY The soaring pink sandstone arch of Rainbow Bridge and the beauties of boating in Glen Canyon can be undertaken from Moab, but closer bases would be Page, AZ. and Kanab UT. $5/person, $10/vehicle in Glen Canyon. _www.nps.gov/glca_.

On **Navajo land,** Monument Valley's landscape of richly-coloured outcroppings was the scene of many a John Ford western. _www.navajonationparks.org_. Two campsites: 'the best is in the **Tribal Park** among the mesas—quiet, hot showers'. $10/night for up to 6 persons, plus $5 entrance fee, (435) 727-5872. Near Monument Valley, **San Juan State Park,** (435) 678-2238, (no entrance fee) boasts its famous land formations, the Goosenecks. The San Juan River snakes back and forth, covering a distance of five miles while progressing only one linear mile towards the Colorado River and Lake Powell. _www.desertusa.com_.

GRAND STAIRCASE ESCALANTE AND VERMILLION CLIFFS NATIONAL MONUMENTS The two newest national monuments in the country. The **Grand Staircase Escalante** covers 1.9 million acres of rugged, primitive land in South Utah and includes a unique combination of archaeological, historical, paleontological, geological, and biological resources. It stretches east of Bryce on Hwy 12 down to Lake Powell, then to Bull Frog and up to Escalante. **Vermillion Cliffs National Monument** is located along Hwy 89, between Kanab, UT. and Page, AZ. and supplies a great hiking trail along the **Paria River.** A good base from which to reach both these National Monuments is the **Paria Outpost and Outfitters and Guest**

Ranch. (See Bryce Canyon NP Accommodation). *www.zionnational-park.com/gsgeology.htm*.

WYOMING – The Equality State

When Buffalo Bill first saw this land in 1870, he called it 'the foothills of heaven'. The name 'Wyoming' itself has much more mundane origins— it's an Algonquin Indian word that means 'wide prairie place'. The name first belonged to a valley in Pennsylvania—easy to swallow, since the Algonquin-speaking tribes lived thousands of miles away from modern-day Wyoming, on the East Coast. In semantics terms, however, the name is a perfect fit.

Cowboy machismo and women's rights might seem an odd mixture, but Wyoming is nicknamed the Equality State for good reason: it had the first women's suffrage act, the first female governor, juror, justice of the peace and director of the US Mint. Buffalo Bill was among the early feminists of Wyoming, declaring: 'if a woman can do the same work that a man can do and do it just as well, she should have the same pay'.

A horsy, folksy, gun-totin' state, home of the notorious Hole-in-the-Wall Gang in the 1890s, Wyoming has ranches so huge they're measured in sections instead of acres. Everyone knows about the twin treasures of **Yellowstone** and **Grand Teton** National Parks, but Wyoming also keeps a few tourism secrets. **Devils Tower** is now imprinted on the world's retina as an extra-terrestrial landing pad and **Salt Creek**, the world's largest light oil field, was the site of the infamous Teapot Dome scandal in 1927. *www.wyomingvisitor.com*.

National Parks: Grand Teton, Yellowstone (largely in Wyoming but slivers of the park are in Montana and Idaho; see Montana section for additional information).

The telephone area code is 307.

YELLOWSTONE NATIONAL PARK Established in 1872, the park is the oldest and perhaps the most well-loved of national parks. It comprises 2.2 million acres and as such is larger than Delaware and Rhode Island combined. The land covers the entire northwest corner of Wyoming before dribbling over into Idaho and Montana. Three of the five entrances are in Montana; they and the gateway cities of Gardiner, Bozeman and West Yellowstone are discussed in the Montana section. Wyoming park entrances are from the east via **Cody** and from the south via **Jackson/Grand Teton National Park.**

Drought and 40 to 70-mile-per-hour winds set the stage for the uncontrollable forest fires of 1988. The fires burned a mosaic pattern throughout nearly 800,000 acres. Fortunately, only half of this acreage was blackened and much of this quickly rejuvenated. None of the major attractions was disturbed.

Yellowstone is one of the world's most impressive thermal regions. There are more geysers and hot springs here than in the rest of the world combined. Besides **Old Faithful** (which blows up to 184-ft, dispelling 3,700-8,400 gallons of water every 76 minutes or so), there are some 10,000 thermal features including geysers, hot springs, colourful paint pots and gooey mud pools—an uncanny array of colours, temperatures, smells, disquieting sounds and eruptions. Old Faithful is the most famous geyser, but there are many others nearby that erupt more frequently. Also worth visiting is the **Norris Geyser Basin**, where you can see hundreds of geysers and pools on a walk of $2^1/4$ miles.

Another priority should be the **Grand Canyon of the Yellowstone River**. This 20 mile long gorge is 'one wild welter of colour', as Rudyard Kipling put it. 'Breath-taking—even better than the Arizona one.' The river tumbles into the canyon through the **Lower Falls**, twice the height of Niagara Falls. **Artist Point** gives possibly the most scenic view of Yellowstone—look over the sheer drop of 700 feet to the canyon below. Don't miss the 110 miles of shoreline and sublime scenery along **Yellowstone Lake**, also famous for its trout. Leave yourself enough time to also visit **Sapphire Pool**, a deep sapphire blue pool in the **Biscuit Basin** area, 3 miles north of Old Faithful. Upstream towards Old Faithful, park along the side of the road and bring your swimsuit down to the river. The river runs warm with the hot water of the geysers if you find the right spot.

A wildlife sanctuary, the park is home to around 318 species of birds (including the trumpeter swan, the largest of all North American wildfowl) and 50 species of mammals including deer, moose, bison, and bear. Because so many people fed the bears (often being hurt in the process by these naturally wild, 3ft tall, 300-400 pound animals), the park has removed many of them to remote areas. Human meddling has turned a number of these bears into serious menaces, and over 100 of them have had to be shot. If you do sight bears, do not feed them, do not get close to them (less than 100 yards is prohibited) and do not come between an adult and cubs. The bears are wild and meant to stay that way.

Cars were not admitted to the park until 1915; today, about 800,000 of them enter, with attendant traffic jams, accidents, pollution and parking problems. But as in other parks, visitors tend to congregate in the same places, leaving the rest of the park refreshingly empty.

Challenging hikes include the $3^1/2$ mile walk to the summit of **Mt Washburn** (stay on trails, don't take shortcuts). If you have more time, rent a canoe at West Yellowstone and canoe/camp the **Lewis River** to the **Shoshone Lakes**—a pristine, wildlife-filled journey. Many campsites (free permit required) along the route and at the lake. 'Don't forget Canyon and Upper Falls—on a par with Grand Canyon!'

The park is open year-round; $20/vehicle and $10/person entrance fee for 7 days applies. The official season runs May to September. During the fall and winter, bus service and other facilities cease and you run the risk of getting caught in a heavy snowstorm. In the off-season (Nov-May), the only roads and entrance open are via Gardiner. You can, however, take a (very expensive) snow coach from West Yellowstone (Dec-March). Yellowstone in winter is enchanting: the animals move in close to the warmth of the geysers and thermal springs—awesome to see them in the swirling mists. You can actually ski or snowshoe close to bison and elk. *www.nps.gov/yell*.

Park Information: 344-7381. The published paper, *Yellowstone Today*, available on the web has info, fees and more on all the entrances and the park itself. *www.nps.gov/yell/publications/pdfs/YellToday*.

Accommodation

Lodging outside the park is discussed under West Yellowstone and Gardiner, Montana. See also Cody. _www.travelyellowstone.com_.

Within the Park: Call 344-7311. Nine different lodges and cabin clusters are available for individuals and small groups. Prices range from $48 for 2/night in a cabin, up to $130 for fully equipped lodges. **Roosevelt Lodge** is one of the cheapest, from $56, 'only place worth the money'. Other bargains are **Lake Lodge**, from $65 and **Old Faithful Lodge and Cabins**, from $92. 'Beds are very comfy'. Lodges open and close at different times in spring and fall. You must make rsvs. _www.nps.gov/yell_.

Camping: 12 campgrounds with more than 2300 sites are available for $18/night. The few campgrounds that may be reserved are **Canyon**, **Madison**, **Grant Village**, **Bridge Bay** and **Fishing Bridge** (for RVs only, $34). The rest are usually filled by noon in summer on a first-come first-served basis. Campsites, Canyon and Grant are the only two that have shower facilities, $3.25, so 'arrive before 8pm if you want a shower—or use hotel as we did.'

Camping can be very cold, even in July, so check the elevations of the campgrounds first (Madison gets the chilliest) and bring a warm sleeping bag. To camp outside the developed sites and away from all the RVs, obtain a free permit at one of the park's visitor centres, where you can also buy a necessary hiking map. Do not sleep with food near you: At night some bears can't distinguish between bags of crisps and bags of people! You will need a bear box or secure car at the campgrounds to secure food. **Mammoth** Campground is the only one open all year.

Food

Six concessions in the park, none of which is particularly cheap. If you can, bring in groceries from West Yellowstone. All lodging facilities do have dining rooms though, and fast-food outlets.

Travel

Most travelers have their own cars; there is no public transport in the park.

Xanterra Parks and Resorts, the NPS-authorized concessionaire in Yellowstone, 344-7901, has full, grand loop available June-Sept, dep Mammoth Hot Springs Hotel 8:30am, returns 5:45pm. $50. _http://travelyellowstone.com/static/162.htm_. 'Clerks at West Yellowstone very helpful with advice.' 'You can make your own combinations.' You get to see a lot during the day.' _www.nps.gov/yell_.

Greyhound: see W. Yellowstone, MT. _www.travelyellowstone.com_.

GRAND TETON NATIONAL PARK In **Moose**, 20 miles due south of Yellowstone and 15 minutes north from Jackson, lies the totally different world of the Grand Teton Mountains. As awe-inspiring as Yellowstone, this park comprises nearly 310,000 acres and reminds one of alpine Europe rather than the American West. The Tetons rise without preliminaries from a level valley to sharp pinnacles above 12,000 ft, separated by deep glaciated clefts. On their crags and flanks, you see remnants of the last great glaciation that once covered North America, some 10,000 years ago. Although these are the youngest mountains in the Rockies, you'll see some of the oldest rock formations in North America. Besides peaks, valleys like Jackson Hole, the lakes and the winding Snake River all complement the stunning environment. **Jackson Hole**, **Jenny Spring** and **Solitude Lakes** make for good if icy swimming.

Warm clothes and sturdy shoes are essential here for tackling the many excellent hiking trails. This is mountaineering country; several schools have their headquarters in the area. Free backcountry permits for climbing must be obtained from **Jenny Lake** visitor's center, where rangers go over safety conditions. Be careful—it's not for novices.

One of the best ways to absorb the Tetons is to float down the **Snake River** on a large raft steered by boatmen. In the forests at river's edge, look for some of the wapiti (elk). The largest migrating herd in North America is found here in the Grand Tetons. Commercial river rafting tours abound, but depending on your karma you may meet up with a group of locals who are already going. Join in—but remember that the 1056 mile long Snake River's rapids require skillful handling.

Admission to the park is combined with Yellowstone: a $20 vehicle pass ($10 if you're on foot) is good for 7 days in both areas. **Visitor centres** are located in **Moose** (open all year), **Colter Bay, Jenny Lake** and **Flagg Ranch,** 739-3300. _www.nps.gov/grte_.

Accommodation
Lodging both in the park and in nearby Jackson can be more costly than at Yellowstone and vicinity. Call (800) 628-9988 or visit _www.gtlc.com_ for details of **Colter Bay Village Cabins** (May-Sept) in the park, and **Jackson Lake Lodge**. Both reasonable. At Colter Bay, one room (6 people) in a tent cabin w/shared bath is $38 for 2 people. A two person log cabin costs $75-$112. The tent cabins are cheaper and more 'adventurous', constructed of canvas and logs, with outdoor grill and wood burning stoves. Bring own bedding for bunks. Rooms at Jackson Lodge start at $173 for two. Try also **Signal Mountain** cabins in **Moran**, 543-2831/(800) 672-6012. D-$99. _www.signalmountainlodge.com_. Make rsvs. They also have a range of activities available from rental of kayaks ($11/hr) to guided Snake River raft trips.

JACKSON John Colter first stumbled upon this area in 1807. A former member of the Lewis and Clark Expedition, Colter arrived here by himself to lure other settlers to the lovely area he'd found. Modern Jackson, pretty and gentrified, is a cross between Aspen and Boulder, drawing crowds of boisterous tourists in summer. In winter, on the other hand, the tiny village entices gentler, nobler visitors when over 7,000 elk come to graze at the edge of town.

Capture some of this magic on a one hour sleigh ride through the elk refuge, 733-9212, $15, leave (Dec-March) daily 10am-4pm from the **National Museum of Wildlife Art**, Hwy 26/191, 2.5 miles north of Jackson. _http://nationalelkrefuge.fws.gov_. In the spring, local scouts collect and sell antlers, some of which end up as aphrodisiacs in the Far East. Visit Jackson's annual antler auction on the 3rd Saturday in May. NB. Jackson is a playground for the rich, so can be expensive.

Accommodation
Bunkhouse Hostel, 1 blk N of town square, 215 N Cache D, 733-3668/(800) 234-4507. Dorm $25, Private rooms from $54. Lounge with TV and kitchen. _www.anvilmotel.com_.
Hostel 'X', McCollister Dr, Teton Village, 12 miles N of Jackson, 733-3415. S/D-$55 or up to 4 people-$68. Free internet access, games room, lounge with fireplace. _www.hostelx.com_.
Cottages at Snow King, 470 S King St. 733-3480. Will put a microwave and a fridge in your room at no extra charge. S/D-$72, 2 queen beds-$80. B/fast: fruit and beverages.

Food
Bubba's, 515 W Broadway, 733-2288. Good home cooking; breakfast and sandwiches for around $4-$7. Daily, summer 7am-10pm.

Mountain High Pizza Pie, 120 W Broadway, 733-3646. Reasonable, traditional, deep-dish and wholewheat crusts. Outdoor seating. Daily, 11am-10pm.

Entertainment

Grab a copy of Jackson Hole *News and Guide*, a combination of two papers, both previously awarded 'best weekly in the nation', a good read and useful calendar of events. *www.jacksonholenews.com*. Try **Cowboy Bar**, 25 N Cache, 733-2207. Pull a saddle up to the bar and pound 'tall boys' in this authentic western bar. *www.milliondollarcowboybar.com*. **JJ's Silver-Dollar Bar**, 733-2190, with 2,000 silver coins embedded in the counter (11.30am-midnight). **The Rancher**, 733-3886, facing the town square. Large pool hall, with live DJ 3 nights/week and bar food. Mon-Fri, 1pm-2am, Sat-Sun from noon. **The Snake River Brew Pub**, 265 S Millward, 739-2337 has 12 beers incl stout, porter and lagers; take a free self guided tour. *www.snakeriverbrewing.com*. For good music, try **Stagecoach, Wilson**, east on Hwy 22, 733-4407; disco on Thurs nights, bluegrass Mon and Stagecoach band, Sun. **The Mangy Moose**, in Teton Village, 733-4913 has live bands, $5-$40 cover (Open 9am-10pm). *www.mangymoose.net*.

Jackson Hole Llamas, 739-9582/(800) 830-7316. Expensive but an experience! Day trek, $95, includes lunch. 3-5 day treks, include food and accommodation, from $570-$895, by group request only, 8-10 people. Also available: longer guided trips to west slope of Teton's and Yellowstone. *www.jhllamas.com*.

Town Square Shootout. Features a lively re-enactment of frontier justice in the Jackson Town Square six nights a week during the summer at 6.15 pm. Free.

Teton Village, 12 miles NW of Jackson is Jackson Hole Mountain Resort, 733-2292/(888) DEEP-SNO. Ski resort with accommodation (from $40 at Hostel X), and many restaurants. Home to the longest continuous vertical drop in the USA—4139 ft to Rendezvous Peak. Try dogsledding, heli-skiing or take the 63-passenger aerial tram, summer: 9am-6pm, $17. A day's ski-pass is $66, after 3-days, discounts apply. *www.jacksonhole.com*.

Grand Targhee Resort, 45 min drive from Jackson Hole, (800) 827-4433. Various events. Attend the annual Bluegrass Music Festival; August. *www.grandtarghee.com*.

Travel/Information

Start Buses, 733-4521, runs a service between Jackson and Teton Village several times a day, $3. Also run a free shuttle service throughout Jackson. *www.startbus.com*.

Jackson Hole Airport, 733-7682, about 8 miles from town. **Alltrans**, (800) 443-6133, runs a shuttle service from the town's hotels to the airport, $15 o/w or $26 r/t. Phone ahead to request service. *www.jacksonholealltrans.com*. For a taxi, try **Buckboard Transportation**, (877) 791-0211, is min. $26 for 1-2 people.

Jackson Hole Chamber of Commerce, 990 W Broadway, Jackson Hole, 733-3316/. For all local information and help. *www.jacksonholechamber.com*.

Internet access

Jackson Hole Public Library, 125 Virginian Lane, 733-2164. Free, 15 min limit. Call to rsv a computer for 1 hr. *www.tclib.org*.

CODY It may look like an endless stretch of motels, but be not dismayed. Cody possesses a superlative, five-in-one museum complex and an Old Trail Town that are well worth your attention. 53 miles east of Yellowstone, Cody is the namesake of William F, also known as **Buffalo Bill**—a bison hunter/army scout/Pony Express rider-turned-showman. His Wild West show players earned a living by touring the US, Canada and Europe with a mawkish morality play of brave cowboys and savage redskins—very popular at the time. Royalty loved it; Queen Victoria gave Cody a diamond brooch, saying his show was so exciting she found it 'almost impossible to sit'. Annie Oakley and Sitting Bull were among Buffalo Bill's prize 'exhibits'; the mythology created thereby was later recycled by Hollywood.

East of Cody, the vividly coloured strata of **Shell Canyon** along the winding stretch of Highway 14 between Shell and Sheridan is highly scenic; to reach **Custer's Last Stand** in Montana, turn north at Sheridan.

Accommodation
Irma Hotel, 1192 Sheridan Ave, 587-4221/(800) 745-IRMA. $100-122 (annex rooms-$73-$95), Grand historic place built by Buffalo Bill and named after his daughter. If you don't stay, have a drink at the incredible cherrywood bar, a gift from Queen Victoria after BB's command performance in England. Lunches ($4.25-$11.50) and even dinners ($6.95-$20) are good value at the **Irma Grill.** *www.irmahotel.com*.
Pawnee Hotel, 1032 12th St, 587-2239. $32-42.
www.cjswalkerswyoming.com/PawneeHotel.
Rainbow Park Motel, 1136 17th St, 587-6251/(800) 710-6930. $54-80 in Summer. *www.rainbowparkmotel.com*.
Ponderosa Cabins and Campground, 1815 8th St, 587-9203. Basic cabins S/D $36. TV. Showers/bathrooms not in the cabins but nearby. Very central.

Of Interest
Buffalo Bill Historical Center, 720 Sheridan Ave, 587-4771. Home to 5 museums devoted to Western cultural and natural history: The **Buffalo Bill Museum** holds memorabilia of the showman and entrepreneur, W. F. Cody. The **Plains Indian Museum** has one of the country's largest and finest collections of Indian art and artifacts. The **Whitney Gallery of Western Art** presents a collection of masterworks including stirring bluechip artists such as Remington, Catlin, Russell and Bierstadt. The **Cody Firearms Museum** traces the role of the firearm in shaping the US and has the largest collection of American firearms in the world. The **Draper Museum of Natural History** leads visitors down an interactive trail of the Yellowstone ecosystem. Hours vary by season. June-Sept 15, daily 7am-8pm. $15, $10 w/student ID. *www.bbhc.org*.
Buffalo Bill Dam Visitors Centre, 5 miles W of Cody, Hwy 14, 527-6076. Exhibits, natural history; interactive displays show how this beautiful dam was built and wildlife. Daily 8am-8pm, free. *www.bbdvc.org*.
Old Town Trail, 587-5302, 2 miles W in Shoshone Canyon, Yellowstone Hwy. A collection of historic pioneer buildings and relics from all over Wyoming from Cassidy and Sundance's hideout to Jeremiah Johnson's grave. 'Non-gimmicky.' Open mid-May to mid-Sept, Daily 8am-8pm, $6. *www.nezperce.com/trltown.html*.
Rodeos, (800) 207-0744, early June-Aug. Held nightly on the west side of town at Stampede Park. 8.30pm, $17. *www.codystampederodeo.com*.

Information
Cody Chamber of Commerce, 836 Sheridan Ave, 587-2777/(800) 393-2639. *www.codychamber.org*.

DEVILS TOWER NATIONAL MONUMENT Accorded inter-galactic notoriety in *Close Encounters of the Third Kind*, Devils Tower was declared the nation's first national monument by Theodore Roosevelt in 1906 in recognition of the special part it played in Indian legend. A landmark also for early terrestrial explorers and travellers, the monolith is a fluted pillar of sombre igneous rock rising 865 ft above its wooded base and 1,267 ft above the **Belle Fourche River.** Open year-round, $8/vehicle, $3/person entrance fee. NB: 'Tower can be climbed safely only by experienced rock-climbers and takes about 4 hours. Descent 1 hour.' In one year, about 4,000 people make the climb. The scene is 'creepily impressive, much more so than the movie'. In the park are prairie-dog villages, an outdoor amphitheatre and free ranger programmes in summer. **Park Visitors' Center**: 467-5283; open 8am-8pm summer, shorter hours in winter. _www.nps.gov/deto_.

Accommodation
Campsites at the monument, approx. April-Oct; $12/night-all basic sites.
Hulett (10 miles) and **Sundance** (28 miles) are towns closest to the park and have good accommodation available. **Spearfish**, S Dakota, 1¹/₂ hrs away, is a larger college town.
Arrowhead Motel, 214 Cleveland St, Sundance, 283-3307. $55-70. 'Most clean and attractive. Friendly, helpful and bright.' _www.arrowheadmotel.com_.

CHEYENNE Formed in 1867 when Union Pacific Railroad tracks were laid and named after the Indian people who inhabited the area, Cheyenne was once fondly called 'hell on wheels' for its volatile mix of cowpokes, cattle rustlers and con-men. Wyoming's Capital, Cheyenne now contents itself with having the purest air and the most frequent hailstorms in the US. A little of the old buckaroo flavour returns each July during the week-long **Frontier Days Rodeo,** the largest outdoor rodeo in the US.

Accommodation
Home Ranch Motel, 2414 E Lincolnway, 634-3575. Summer: $35-45.
Motel 6, 1735 Westland Rd, 635-6806/(800) 466-8356. $44. Free coffee.
Rodeo Inn, 3839 E Lincolnway, 634-2171. Ave. $50.

Food
For full list, check _www.cheyennenetwork.com/entertainment/dining_.
Albany Cafe and Restaurant, 1506 Capitol Ave, 638-3507. Restaurant and bar, good for meeting people. 'Not a pickup bar, not gay, not expensive, good music. Can this be true?' Mon-Sat 11am-9pm, dinner from 4.30pm. Happy hour daily 3-6pm.

Of Interest
Frontier Days, 778-7200. 'Daddy of 'em all' rodeo, last full week in July (in 2006, it will be July 21-30) from 1pm. 4 parades, chuckwagon races, free pancake breakfasts, and perhaps the best rodeo in the US. For tkts and prices, check _www.cfdrodeo.com_. 'During rodeo, the whole town goes wild on Saturday night but forget it at other times'; 'Cheyenne is dead as a doorpost on Saturday night.' However, there are planned entertainments every evening, eg. country music, Indian dancing at an Indian village. **Laramie County Fair,** first week in August, _www.laramiecountyfair.com_ follows the Frontier Days events.
Holiday Park is home to the world's largest steam locomotive, Old Number 4004. The "Big Boy" was retired by the Union Pacific Railroad in 1956.
State Museum, 2301 Central Ave, 777-7022. Worthwhile cowboy, Indian and pioneer museum. Free tours available on request (48 hrs notice req). Open Tues-Sat 9am-4.30pm, free. _http://wyomuseum.state.wy.us_.

Travel/Information
Greyhound, 222 Deming Dr, 635-1327/(800) 231-2222. NB. No **Amtrak** service.
Cheyenne Area Convention and Visitors Bureau, 309 W Lincoln Way, 778-3133/(800) 426-5009. _www.cheyenne.org_.

Internet access
Laramie County Library, 2800 Central Ave, 634-3561. Free, first come first served basis. _www.lclsonline.org_.

SKIING AND SNOWBOARDING IN THE USA

In 1935 there were no ski resorts in the USA. When Sun Valley, Idaho, introduced the world's first chairlift in 1936, Hollywood stars such as Clark Gable thronged to the slopes and the glamour tag has stuck ever since. Winter sports still have a reputation for being expensive but it's quite possible to ski or snowboard thousands of vertical feet at over 300 resorts and countless miles of backcountry terrain on a budget - and sometimes for free.

And don't forget **Canada** which has great resorts such as **Whistler-Blackcomb,** the continent's largest ski area with a ski-able area of 7,071 acres, near Vancouver, the 2010 host of the Winter Olympics, and at **Banff, Alberta**, where **Ski Banff, Lake Louise** and **Sunshine** total over 7,700 ski acres, surrounded by breathtaking scenery.

TRIP TIPS

Lift tickets eat into any budget so avoid peak times such as holidays and weekends; lowest prices are usually from Oct to mid-Dec and in April, with some great deals between Thanksgiving and Christmas. Look out for multiple-area discount cards and reduced-rate mid-week or evening lift passes w/student ID. If you have time, volunteering for community programs such as working with handicapped skiers or helping out at ski competitions will often earn you a valuable free season pass. Some resorts allow you to 'try before you buy'— just return your lift pass within 1 hr of purchase for a full refund or credit voucher for another day.

Cross-country skiing is less expensive than downhill skiing and is free in areas such as **Sunlight Mountain Resort, Glenwood Springs, Colorado,** (970) 945-7491, _www.sunlightmtn.com_. **Mammoth Mountain Resort, Mammoth Lakes, California,** (760) 934-2571, _www.mammothmountain.com_ and **Silver Run Mountain, Red Lodge, Montana**, (406) 446-1770, _www.silvermt.com_. If you don't have your own equipment, check out unlimited all-season rentals, for as low as $80. The smaller rental shops often have the best deals. Try **Sunlight Ski and Bike Shop,** Glenwood Springs, (970) 945-9425, _www.sunlightmtn.com_.

If you're planning on skiing for a short time, daily equipment rentals (around $15-$30) are your best bet. Look out for pre-season sales in late Oct and 'swaps' in major cities for discounted and nearly new gear. Clip coupons in local papers for discount meals and drinks; local supermarkets will often run deals with major resorts. Weekly resort entertainment nights are also great for free beer and snacks. For a rundown on all things related to or about skiing, visit _www.skicentral.com_.

**EAST COAST:** **Sugarloaf USA, Maine**, (207) 237-2000, _www.sugarloaf.com_. Close to the Canadian border with 2,800ft of skiable vertical, snowboarding, cross-country and ice-skating; popular with advanced skiers, discounts w/student ID. **VERMONT: Killington,** (800) 621-MTNS, _www.killington.com_ boasts the highest vertical in the east at 3,150 ft and the longest ski season, but known to be crowded with long lift lines. Three hrs from Boston, it's a pricey resort with buzzing après-ski. Call about the **Collegiate Snowfest** held in Dec and Jan; discounts on ski passes, accommodation with student ID.

Nearby **Okemo,** (802) 228-4041/(800) 78-OKEMO, _www.okemo.com_ is smaller but not as crowded as Killington, discounts on lift tickets with student ID. **Suicide Six,** (800) 448-7900, _www.onthesnow.com/VT/437,_ is a cheap place to learn during the mid-week. It holds a special place in American skiing history;

it's here where, in 1934, a Model T Ford was rigged up to power America's first ski tow. **Jay Peak,** (802) 988-2611, *www.jaypeakresort.com*, 8 miles from the Canadian border, offers spectacular scenery and excellent snowboarding – and is cheaper than **Mount Snow/Haystack.** (800) 245-7669, *www.mountsnow.com*. The closest major Vermont resort to New York and Boston. Also have student discounts available with ID. Lots of little ski areas in the **'NE Kingdom'** area of Vermont/New Hampshire.

NEW HAMPSHIRE: Mt. Washington Valley, Chamber of Commerce, (800) 367-3364, *www.mtwashingtonvalley.org*, comprises several downhill and cross-country resorts including **Shawnee Peak, Black Mountain, King Pine, Bretton woods, Attitash Bear Peak, Cranmore Mountain,** with good weekend prices and **Wildcat,** good for strong skiers and snowboarders. **Waterville Valley,** New Hampshire, (800) 468-2553, *www.waterville.com*, has an exclusive snowboard park called the 'Wicked Ditch of the East' and some of the best cross-country trails in the nation. Various student passes and reduced rental fees.

NEW YORK: Windham Mountain, Catskill Mtns, (800) 754-9463, *www.skiwindham.com* and **Hunter Mountain,** (518) 263-4223, *www.huntermtn.com*, twenty minutes away, just 2 hrs N of New York City, offer strong intermediate slopes but they are packed at weekends.

Best areas for après-ski: **Mt Washington Valley, NH** and **Killington, VT.** Best areas for vertical: **Killington** and **Cannon, Franconia Notch, NH,** (603) 823-8800. *www.cannonmt.com*.

MOUNTAIN STATES: **COLORADO** offers extensive skiing for all levels with 300 days of sunshine per year. **Aspen,** (800) 308-6935, *www.aspensnowmass.com* and **Vail,** (303) 504-5870/(888) 222-9324, *www.vail.snow.com*, are noted for celebrities and astronomical prices. (Vail is the second largest ski area in North America, after Whistler in Canada.) Head instead for **Sol Vista** (970) 887-3384/(800) 754-7458, *www.solvista.com* and **Arapahoe Basin,** (888) ARA-PAHOE, *www.arapahoebasin.com*, which are also cheaper than nearby **Winter Park** and **Keystone. Purgatory at Durango Mountain Resort,** (970) 247-9000/(800) 693-0175, *www.durangomountainresort.com* is an active student haunt with roller coaster runs and a snowboard park. They have various student discounts. A shuttle bus runs between Purgatory and **Durango,** which is about 25 miles away, $2.50 o/w. **Durango** is the place for cheap lodging and wild night-life during Spring Break.

IDAHO: Ski 'Baldy' at **Sun Valley Resort,** (800) 786-8259, *www.sunvalley.com*; 3,400 ft of vertical and 50 km of back country trails through impressive wilderness. For budget skiing try **Silver Mountain Resort**, (800) 204-6428, *www.silvermt.com*. Purchase the season pass in the springtime for great discounts the following winter.

UTAH: Host to the 2002 Winter Olympics, **Salt Lake City,** *www.visitsaltlake.com*, has 7 ski areas less than 1 hr from the city centre. Call the Visitors Centre, (801) 521-2822, for discount coupons. **Alta,** (801) 359-1078, *www.alta.com*, has low-price student passes, check out the pre-season pass, available 'til early Sept. Skiing here is great for powder-hounds but no snowboarding. **Solitude,** (800) 748-4SKI, *www.skisolitude.com* and **Brighton,** (1¹/₂ miles apart) (801) 532-4731, *www.skibrighton.com*, are great values with intermediate and beginner slopes and challenging canyon walls for experts.

The **Canyons,** (435) 649-5400/(888) CAN-YONS, *www.thecanyons.com*, has ski-jumping and extreme chutes plus free bus service from **Park City,** 30 miles east of Salt Lake City.

MONTANA: Long on powder, short on sun. **Big Mountain,** (406) 862-1900/(800) 858-4152. _www.bigmtn.com_. With student ID ski all day for around $40. Ski rentals are also very low, just 'talk to Tom for good deals'.

NEW MEXICO: 18 miles from the city of Taos and 2,000 ft higher, at the fringe of Carson National Forest, **Taos Ski Valley,** (505) 776-2291/(800) 347-7414, _www.skitaos.org_, will challenge experts. (No snowboarding.) Multi day discounts and selected dates are reduced.

WYOMING: **Jackson Hole,** (307) 733-2292/(888) DEEP-SNO, _www.jacksonhole.com_, is laid back with cheap lodging. For deep powder go to **Grand Targhee,** (307) 353-2300/(800)-TARGHEE, _www.grandtarghee.com_. Call before Sept for discounts.

Best apres-ski: **Aspen** (pricey) and **Durango**. Highest verticals: **Big Sky, Montana** (4,180 ft), **Jackson Hole, WY,** (4,139 ft). Best night skiing: **Mt Hood Skibowl, Oregon.** _www.skibowl.com_.

WEST COAST: CALIFORNIA: the **Lake Tahoe** area, 200 miles east of San Francisco has world-class ski areas and casino-based nightlife. If you're willing to forgo difficult terrain, then avoid the larger, pricier resorts and head out to **Diamond Peak**, Nevada, (775) 832-1177, _www.diamondpeak.com_, with 655 skiable acres. Also try **Ski Homewood,** (530) 525-2992/(877) 525-SNOW, _www.skihomewood.com_, for outstanding lake views and great slopes. **Kirkwood,** (209) 258-6000/(877)-KIRKWOOD, _www.kirkwood.com_, has the best terrain for all abilities, the best prices and the best snow but a quiet après-ski. Don't miss **Badger Pass**, Yosemite National Park, (209) 372-1000, _www.yosemitepark.com_, noted for its stunning location and cross-country tracks.

OREGON Mount Hood Ski Bowl, (503) 272-3206/(800) SKI-BOWL, _www.skibowl.com_, has cheap passes, challenging runs, a snowboard obstacle course, a halfpipe and bungee jumps.

ALASKA: Catch the northern lights at **Alyeska,** (907) 754-2285/(800) 880-3880, _www.alyeskaresort.com_. Other various activities here include: helicopter skiing, dog sledding, whale watching and cruises. Forty miles southeast of Anchorage. _www.alyeskaresort.com_.

For detailed info on the best spots to ski and snowboard, check out _www.goski.com_, an excellent on-line resource that includes maps, prices, accommodation, events, weather and the latest gear. Also useful: _Skiing on a Budget_, Claire Walter, Better Way Books, $15.99 and _The Rites of Winter: A Skier's Budget Guide to Making It on the Slopes,_ by Bruce Jacobsen and Roland Riggs, $15.99.

SKI JOBS There are thousands of seasonal jobs in ski resorts—from casual bartending to certified instruction. Job fairs are held throughout the country in the autumn but check _www.coolworks.com_ for a head start; it's a huge directory of current opportunities, addresses and details of benefits such as free lift passes and accommodation. Some ski resorts will organize work permits for overseas applicants. Otherwise you will have to find a way to get the correct working papers yourself before you enter America. "I worked at Sun Valley and got in over 100 days of skiing on the mountain as 'bowl patrol'—cleaning bathrooms. Best ski-bum job in the universe! Assuming it snows. . . ."

THE PACIFIC STATES

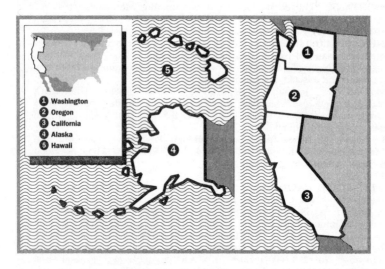

1 Washington
2 Oregon
3 California
4 Alaska
5 Hawaii

The Pacific states have everything and more. From ancient redwoods to modern cities, from lumbermen to film stars, from Polynesian huts to Arctic igloos, plus every one of these states is home to some of the most exciting scenery in America. The Chinese may have discovered this part of America as early as 1421 AD (later to look for gold) and the Russians, British, French, Spanish and Mexicans have all had claims here. Although Americans swept west under the conquering banner of Manifest Destiny, some of the old influences survive.

But the Pacific is also where the rainbow ends, where expectations must finally prove themselves. Enthusiasm reigns everywhere, and that is probably the region's most enjoyable quality.

ALASKA - The Last Frontier

Aleut for 'great land', Alaska has a penchant for superlatives: biggest, coldest, costliest, highest peak, longest coastline, richest animal life, longest (21+ hours) and shortest days (6 hrs 20 mins on December 21).

Although the state was jeered at as 'Seward's Folly' when President Lincoln's Secretary of State bought it from the Russians for 2¢ an acre in 1867, no one laughed for very long. In 1897-1898, the discovery of gold in the Yukon inspired a deluge of opportunists, virtually created towns such as Skagway, and inspired the Lancashire-born, Glasgow-bred Robert Service to wryly portray the lives of gold miners in spell-binding ballads such as *The Cremation of Sam McGee*, *The Shooting of Dan McGrew*, and *The Prospector*: 'For once you've panned the speckled sand / and seen the bonny dust, / Its peerless brightness blinds you like a spell; / It's little else you care about; / you go because you must, / And you feel that you could follow it to Hell.'

Alaska proved fruitful again when, in 1968, one of the world's richest caches of petroleum was discovered in Prudhoe Bay. But those oil resources are now dwindling – they've fallen by 75 percent since 1987 and only natural gas may soon be pumped from here, provided a pipeline is built to transport it through Canada. Otherwise fisheries and canneries (employing 25,000+ Latinos) are the state's main economic staple. Alaska is breathtakingly beautiful and well worth visiting, particularly in summer when daytime temperatures are surprisingly warm. There's plenty of daylight and the Northern Lights appear after 10pm 243 nights of the year.

The land route of the **Alaska Highway** from British Columbia to Fairbanks and Anchorage is an adventure, but the finest approach is by boat from Seattle or Prince Rupert. State-run, inexpensive ferries ply the Inside Passage year-round, allowing close-up looks at glaciers, islands, fjords, whales and stopover privileges at the various ports of call, all the way west to Dutch Harbor. For unlimited travel on participating ferries, trains and buses, consider the Alaska Pass during the summer (May 15-Sept 15), from $599 for 8 travel days out of 12 to $749 for 12 out of 21 days of travel, plus booking fee of $75. _www.alaskapass.com_. Call (800) 248-7598 / (206) 463-6550. Travel info at _www.travelalaska.com_. For hostel info, check _www.hostelalaska.com/alaskahostels.htm._

National Parks: Denali, Gates of the Arctic, Glacier Bay, Katmai, Kenai Fjords, Klondike Gold Rush, Lake Clark, Wrangell-St. Elias.

The telephone area code for the state is 907.

THE INSIDE PASSAGE and THE PANHANDLE Warmed by the Japanese Current and protected from the open sea by a necklace of islands, this southeastern waterway enjoys the state's mildest weather. The state operates an extensive ferry system called the **Alaska Marine Highway**, an appropriate name since five of the seven ports in the Panhandle have no overland highway access to the outside world. 'Just the sight of a humpback whale breaching is enough to make the journey a memorable one.' 'Good vessels, interesting places to stop over, many opportunities to meet people.' 'In summer, Tongass Forest interpreters give free talks, film shows, on board. An imaginative and interesting service.' **National Forest and National Park Services**, 8465 Old Dairy Rd, Juneau. (907) 586-8751. Mon-Fri 8am-5pm. Provides info and permits for Forest Service cabins in **Tongass National Forest,** which stretches from south of Ketchikan to north of Juneau. _www.fs.fed.us/r10/tongass_.

KETCHIKAN First port of call going north is Ketchikan, a salmon centre that is increasingly dependent upon cruise ship traffic. Weather beaten houses on stilts and the harbour give it a New England flavour, but it never rained like this in Massachusetts. The record here is 223.8" a year.

Accommodation/Food

For Lodging, Food visit _www.ketchikanalaska.com_ **Ketchikan Reservation Service**, 800-987-5337, provides info on B&Bs (from $60). _www.ketchikan-lodging.com_. **HI-Ketchikan Hostel**, First United Methodist Church, Grant and Main Sts, Ketchikan, 225-3319. June-Aug. $12 AYH. 4-night limit. Open for late-arriving ferries if call beforehand. _www.akohwy.com/k/kayhostl.htm_. **Signal Creek Campground**, 6 miles N of Ketchikan ferry terminal on Tongass Hwy, features attractive views and pleasant nature trails. Call (877) 444-6777 or go to *www.reserveusa.com* for resv. Most camping at state parks costs $10. In **Ketchikan**, the US Forest Service manages Ward Lake area campgrounds, 225-2148, $10; 2-week limit June-Aug.

For places to eat, visit *www.ketchikanchamber.com/dining.html* **The Narrows Inn & Restaurant**, 4871 N Tongass Hwy, 247-5900. Try Alaskan King Crab and local oysters. Rooms $125 inc bfst. *www.narrowsinn.com.* **Tatsuda's**, 633 Stedman at Deermount St, 225-4125. The most convenient supermarket to downtown. Daily.

Of Interest

Totem Heritage Center, 601 Deermount St, 225-5900. The largest collection of authentic, pre-commercial 19th C totem poles in the US. Daily 8am-5pm, $5. Go and see Totems 160 yrs old as well as more contemporary ones. *www.city.ketchikan.ak.us/departments/museums/totem.html*. Next door, the **Deer Mountain Tribal Hatchery**, 1158 Salmon Road, 225-5158, offers a guided tour on the nuances of salmon sex. Open daily 8am-4.30pm. $9 (incl. Heritage center). To learn about the nuances of human sex check out historic **Creek Street**, the old redlight district. The colourful neighborhood of renovated stores and galleries, is home to **Dolly's House**, 24 Creek St, 225-2279/209-0801, a brothel turned museum. The **Tongass Ketchikan Museum**, 629 Dock St, 225-5600, displays local history, art, the native heritage and fishing exhibits. Mon-Sun 8am-5pm; $2. **Saxman Village** totem park S of Ketchikan features the Abraham Lincoln pole.

Ketchikan Visitors Center, 131 Front Street, 225-6166, (800) 770-3300, on waterfront. *www.visit-ketchikan.com*, and *www.ketchikanalaska.com* .

SITKA Once capital of Russian America on the west coast of Sitka Island, and beautifully situated at the foot of Fuji-like Mt Edgecumbe, Sitka has a reconstructed Russian cathedral full of icons, plus interesting gravestones from this period. James Michener spent much time here researching his book, *Alaska*.

HI-Sitka Hostel, United Methodist Church, 303 Kimsham St, Sitka, 747-8661. PO Box 2645, Sitka, AK 99835. Open June-Aug, $10 AYH. Bring sleeping bag.

Of Interest

Sitka National Historical Park, is home to most of the major attractions that this town has to offer (*www.nps.gov/sitk*). Among them is **Castle Hill** the actual spot where the sale of Alaska took place. The **Russian Bishops' House**, 501 Lincoln St, 747-4927, is the largest and last remaining Russian-built home in Alaska. Daily guided tours in summer 9am-5pm, ($3). **St. Michael's Cathedral**, 747-8120, is a stunning Russian Orthodox church, open 11am-3pm Mon-Sat. See Tlingit Indian craftsmen and artists at work from 8am-5pm daily in summer at the **Southeastern Alaska Indian Cultural Center**, (747-8061). **Sheldon Jackson State Museum**, 104 College Dr, 747-8981, an impressive collection of artifacts, representing all four native groups of Alaska. Open daily in summer, 9am-5pm; ($4 summer, $3 winter). **Sitka Visitor's Bureau**, 303 Lincoln, 747-5940. 8am-5pm. *www.sitka.org*.

JUNEAU Alaska's capital, climbs steep wooded hillsides with wooden stairways and a kaleidoscope of architectural styles. It's a great irony (and a bone of contention) among many Alaskans that the capital city is reachable only by air or water. The water, the **Inside Passage**, is home to some 600 humpback whales during the summer months. **Mendenhall Glacier**, 6 miles long and 1.5 miles wide, is 15 minutes from Juneau by car, and has camping. **Admiralty Island**, a few miles from Juneau, has the largest concentration of brown bears in North America, about 1600. From **Haines**, the **Old Dalton Trail** leads off to the **Klondike**. First come first served camping near Juneau is available at **Mendenhall Lake Campground**.

Of Interest
Alaska State Museum, 465-2901, 395 Whittier St for good artifacts; $5 ($3 in winter). Open daily. *www.museums.state.ak.us/asmhome.html*.
Glacier Bay National Park, 50 miles NW of Juneau, 697-2225. Beautiful and untouched wilderness of seals, whales, bears and 20 glaciers. Access by boat or plane only, expensive. 'Awesome.' *www.nps.gov/glba*.
Juneau Visitor's Centre, One Sealaska Plaza, (800) 587-2201. Open Mon-Fri 8.30am-5pm, Weekends 9am-5pm. *www.traveljuneau.com*.

HAINES At the northern end of America's longest fjord, Haines is surrounded by 20 million acres of protected wilderness. **Glacier Bay National Park** is less than 25 miles by air, and Canada's **Kluane National Park** and **Tatshenshini-Alsek Provincial Park** are accessible by road from here. **Skagway** is 14 miles to the north by ferry. Near Haines is the world's largest concentration of bald eagles at **Chilkat Preserve**; best months are November thru March, when eagles number 4000. *www.haines.ak.us* **Bear Creek Camp & Hostel**, Small Track Road, Haines, 766-2259. 1½ miles from Haines. $3 pickup/drop off from ferry. Summer: $18pp, wood-heated cabins. Private cabins, $48 for two. Hot showers, kitchen, laundry and camping from $10 for first person, $4 XP. *bearcreekcabinsalaska.com/.*

SKAGWAY was big-city size. Now down to a population of 825, it's reaping a new gold rush of tourists to photograph its well-preserved wooden sidewalks, false-front buildings and memorials to Soapy Smith, the local con-man and thief. 'On his birthday, locals urinate on his grave.' Best during the old-time fervor of the **Sourdough Days** of September.

Of Interest
Skagway: Klondike Gold Rush National Park, Broadway and 2nd Ave, 983-2921. The 7-block historic Broadway Street contains many restored structures, leftovers from the Gold Rush days. The **National Park** at Skagway includes the ruins of the short-lived **Dyea** and the 33-mile **Chilkoot Trail** that served as the route for over 20,000 stampeders to the interior gold fields up the Yukon. An 8-hour stay in Skagway permits a spectacular $3^1/_2$ hr train ride over **White Pass**, where in the winter of 1897 some 3000 horses died, as Jack London wrote: 'like mosquitoes in the first frost'.
Before you go, read *The Klondike Stampede* by Tappan Adney, and the verses of Robert Service, *The Spell of the Yukon* and *Ballads of a Cheechako*: '…it isn't the gold that I'm wanting /So much as just finding the gold. /It's the great big broad land 'way up yonder; /It's the forests where silence has lease; /It's the beauty that fills me with wonder, /It's the stillness that fills me with peace.' Daily 8am-8pm. *www.nps.gov/klgo*. Also check out the **Trail of '98 Museum**, 983-2420, in the Arctic Brotherhood Hall, 700 Spring St.
Skagway Visitors Center, In Arctic Brotherhood Hall, 983-2854. Daily 8am-6pm, Oct-Apr Mon-Fri 8am-5pm. *www.skagway.org*.

Travel
Alaska Marine Highway, (800) 642-0066. Contact for rsvs, schedules and other info. Alternatively, place a reservation by filling out an online form via *www.dot.state.ak.us/amhs/index.html*. Meals, staterooms cost extra but run at or below hotel prices. 'Board early.' 'Boat deck is heated, has camping beds, showers and lockers provided free.' 'Cafeteria good value, but taking your own food

definitely advisable.' From Ketchikan the longest non-stop ferry ride in the US goes to Bellingham, Washington, 39 hours, o/w $193 exc meals or berth.

Gray Line, (800) 544-2206. Buses run across Alaska throughout the summer but are very expensive.

THE ALASKA HIGHWAY For years nearly all gravel or dirt-surfaced, the highway nowadays is paved from top to bottom. Beginning at Dawson Creek, British Columbia, it's 915 miles to Whitehorse in the Yukon and a total of 1,420 to its official end in Delta Junction. The **HI-TOK Hostel,** Mile 1322 1/2 Alaska Highway, 883-3745. Hours away from any large city, offers clean air, solitude and starry skies for $10. Drop in during summer only.

'Make sure your car is in good running order and carry a few of the more essential spare parts. Garages charge what they like for spares.' Gas stations are every 20-50 miles, occasionally as far apart as 100 miles. Before you set out on your journey, pick up a copy of the free pamphlet *Help Along the Way* at a visitors bureau, or contact the **Department of Health and Social Services**, 465-3030, *www.hss.state.ak.us*. Includes exhaustive listing of emergency medical services and emergency phone numbers throughout Alaska and western Canada, plus tips on preparation and driving.

ANCHORAGE The largest city (260,000) in Alaska, makes a good excursion base for exploring the southern part of the state. Besides its transportation links and a fairly rambunctious nightlife, Anchorage also dabbles in the business of love: its *Alaskamen*, published every two months, provides profiles and photos of eligibles for women in the lower 48, and boasts 3-5 matches per month. The first Saturday every March, 70 mushers and a thousand or more dogs set off on the 1049 mile **Iditerod Trail Sled Dog Race** to Nome, trying to break the record of 8 days, 22 hours set in 2002 by Marin Buser.

Accommodation
Alaska Private Lodgings / Stay With A Friend, in **Wasilla,** 235-2148, can refer you to B&Bs from $55 p/n. *www.alaskabandb.com*.

Spenard Hostel International, 248-5036, 2845 W 42nd Ave. Rsvs rec. $18 cash price. Chores traditional. *www.alaskahostel.org*.

South of Anchorage on the New Seward Hwy, in **Girdwood,** the place for mountain biking in the summer, skiing in the winter: **Alyeska Camping: Chugach State Park;** 694-798, two of the best areas are **Eagle River,** $15, and **Eklutna,** $10, respectively 12½ miles and 26½ miles NE of Anchgorage along Glenn Hwy.

Food/Entertainment
Blondie's Café, at corner of 4th and D St, 279-0698. All-day bfast for $5.25. After 5pm, dinners for about $12. Sun-Thu 5am-10pm, Fri-Sat 'til 11pm.

Chilkoot Charlies, 2435 Spenard Rd, 272-1010, huge sawdust-on-the-floor venue, live music, bar food. Sun-Thu 10.30am-2.30am, Fri-Sat 'til 2.45am. Cover around $4.

Moose's Tooth Pub & Pizzeria – Brew Pub, 3300 Old Seward Hwy, 258-2537, live music Thurs. Mon-Thu 11am – 12pm, Fri-Sat 11-1 am *www.moosestooth.net*. Related **Bear Tooth Theatre Pub,** 1230 West 27th. Off Spenard, 276-4200.

Of interest
Alaska Experience Theater, 705 W 6th Ave, 276-3730. 40 mins of Alaskan adventures on the inner surface of a hemispherical dome. Every hr, 10am-9pm; $8.

Earthquake Park, close to town off Northern Lights Blvd. Recalls the 1964 Good

Friday earthquake. The quake was the strongest ever recorded in North America; 9.2 on the Richter scale. Walk, bike or skate along the **Tony Knowles Coastal Trail**, an 11 mile paved track that skirts **Cook Inlet**. The second largest tide in the world, 38.9 ft, occurs in Cook Inlet.

The **Museum of History and Art**, 121 W 7th Ave, 343-4326, has historic and ethnographic art from all over Alaska, as well as national and international art exhibits. Tue-Thu 9am-9pm, every other day, 9am-6pm, $6.50. *www.anchoragemuseum.org*.

Nearby: Eklutna Burial Grounds, 26 miles N on Glenn Hwy. Indian cemetery with spirit houses that look like doll houses, interesting gravesites. Get info from visitors bureau. 'Fascinating.'

Portage Glacier, 53 miles S of Anchorage, is Alaska's most visited tourist attraction. Award winning film *Voices from the Ice* shown at Portage Glacier Visitors Information Center (end of Portage Hwy), 783-2326, 9am-6pm daily, $1. 'Superb.' 'A must.' **Gray Line**, 277-5581, and other tours available from Anchorage call at **Alyeska Ski Resort**, 754-2108, 40 miles S, on the way.

Information/Internet access

Anchorage Convention & Visitor's Center, 524 W Fourth Ave, 276 4118 Free Visitors Guide from (800) 478-1255. *www.anchorage.net*.

Log Cabin Visitor Information Center, 546 W 4th Ave, 274-3531. Dispenses lots of maps, including bike trails guide.

Alaska Public Lands Information Center, 605 W 4th Ave, 271-2737. 'Helpful; friendly people.' *www.nps.gov/aplic*.

Alaska Public Library, 3600 Denali St, 343-2975.

Travel

Anchorage International Airport, 266-2525. Nearly every airport in Alaska can be reached from Anchorage. *www.dot.state.ak.us/anc/index.shtml*.

The 80-yr-old **Alaska Railroad**, (800) 544-0552 runs daily May-Sept btwn Anchorage and Fairbanks via Denali National Park ($143-179 o/w), to Seward ($59) and to Whittier ($52). *www.alaskarailroad.com*. Daily bus service by **Gray Line of Alaska**, (800) 544-2206. All major car rentals, plus **Affordable Car Rental**, 4707 Spenard Rd, 265-2491. *www.thecityofanchorage.com/autorental*.

DENALI NATIONAL PARK Mount McKinley has twin peaks, the south being higher at 20,320 ft. Although native Indians originally named the mountain (and the park) Denali, meaning 'the tall one', it was renamed for US president William McKinley while he was campaigning. President Jimmy Carter had the mountain officially renamed Denali in 1979.

This giant, tallest in North America, surveys a vast kingdom of tundra, mountain wilderness and unusual wildlife (caribou, Dall sheep, moose, grizzlies). The highway over **Polychrome Pass** into the **Valley of Denali** is astonishing: a huge bowl, rimmed with frozen Niagaras of clouds tumbling over the encircling cliffs, spreads out before you.

Eighty-six miles of gravel road allow you to see much of the park by bus (you can go into the park only 12 miles by car, unless you have a campsite reserved), but hiking one of the trails radiating from McKinley Park Hotel is the best way to enter into the spirit of the place. Best views of the mountaintop at **Wonder Lake**—'have to go at least 8 miles into the park to see the mountain'. Visitors Center half a mile up Park Rd, 683-1266/1267, daily 7am-8pm 'til late September. Pick up info on shuttle buses to Wonder Lake here. 'Fantastically situated; caribou come right up to the centre.' No food or gas in the park except at Park entrance. Don't overlook a trip to Yentana, the 'Galloping Glacier'—most beautifully coloured on earth. $10 entrance fee good for 7 days. Denali's National Park's website is at *www.nps.gov/dena*.

Accommodation

Denali Mountain Morning Hostel, Mile 224 of Parks Hwy. (907) 683-7503. $25 hostel beds, $1 one time fee for extra blankets. $65 private rooms. Morning /afternoon shuttles in/out park $3. *www.hostelalaska.com*.

Seven **campgrounds** within the park line Denali Park Rd. Sites $16 ($4 resv. charge). Must have permit to camp inside park. For resv, call (800) 622-7275 or 272-7272; arrive early! Hikers waiting for a backcountry permit or a campsite can find space in **Morino Campground**, $6, next to hotel.

Grizzly Bear Cabins, 6 miles S of main entrance, 683-2696. Tent Sites $17.50, tent cabins, D-$26,T-$30, bath with showers with hot water nearby. Other cabins $52-$188. Rsvs rec (by VISA only), closed by Sep 10th. *www.denaligrizzlybear.com*.

Travel

Frequent shuttle bus service to all 7 campgrounds in park until Labor Day. Booked up quickly but stand-bys available from 5.30 am. From $17.50. Shuttle buses leave Denali Visitor Center, daily, 7.30am-1pm. Reservations- (800) 622-PARK.

Camper buses, $18.50, move faster, transporting only people with campground permits/backcountry permits. Leave visitors centre 5 times daily. Good strategy for dayhiking/convenient for park explorers.

FAIRBANKS Warmest place in Alaska in summer and one of the coldest in the winter, Fairbanks was once a frontier town with 93 saloons in one three-block stretch. Today the second largest city, a direct result of the pipeline and oil boom, it is 150 miles south of the Arctic Circle. Try to time your visit for one of its many festivals: the Eskimo/Indian Olympics (dancing, blanket toss, etc.) each July and the **Midnight Sun Festival and Run**, in June (call the Downtown Association of Fairbanks at 452-8671) are among the wildest. Play or watch midnight baseball, played without lights for 97 years, at the latter. 'Definitely the rough frontier town.' 'Surprisingly nice—lots of trees.' *http://www.downtownfairbanks.com*.

Accommodation

Ah! Rose Marie, 302 Cowles St, 456-6193: 'Loves students.' Centrally located. $60+ singles, $75+ doubles *www.akpub.com/akbbrv/ahrose.html*.

Alaska Heritage Inn Youth Hostel, 1018 22nd Ave, 451-6587. Outfitted canoe and raft trips, wildlife viewing, horseback riding. $15 dorm; $40 private room, XP $20. *www.koontzalaska.com/Inn/heritage-inn.html*.

Billie's Backpackers Hostel, 2895 Mack Rd, 479-2034, $25 a night. Shuttle from train station/airport. Free 24-hr high-speed internet. *www.alaskahostel.com.*

Grandma Shirley's Hostel, 510 Dunbar St, 451-9816. 'Beats all other hostels!' Showers, free towels, common room, free bike use; co-ed room with 9 beds; $16.25.

Food/Entertainment

Howling Dog Saloon, junction of Elliot and Steese Highways, 456-HOWL (4695). Out of town, but good fun and great Cajun food on the cheap. Live bands and midnight volleyball. Opens at 4pm. *www.howlingdogsaloon.com*.

Pikes Landing, 4438 Airport Way 479-6500. Bar/restaurant serving good food on a deck overlooking the Chena River.

Of interest
Pioneer Park (formerly **Alaskaland**), 2300 Airport Way, 459-1087. Open 11am-9pm. The 44-acre site, developed to commemorate the Alaska Centennial in 1967, portrays state history with gold rush cabins, a sternwheeler, Indian and Eskimo villages and a mining valley. Free, closes Labor Day. Food pricey, but gets praise: 'Alaska Salmon Bake—all you can eat; salmon, halibut, ribs, etc.—lovely!' **The Fairbanks Summer Folk Fest** is held here in July. **Univ. of Alaska Museum of the North**, 907 Yukon Drive, $4^1/2$ miles NW of city, 474-7505. Features exhibits ranging from displays on the aurora borealis to a 36,000 yr old bison recovered from the permafrost; Eskimo arts and crafts. Daily 9am-7pm. $5. 'Superb, don't miss it.' 'Definitely one of Alaska's highlights.' *www.uaf.edu/museum*.
Eagle Summit, 108 miles along the Steese Hwy, from where you can watch the sun fail to set on 21 and 22 June.

Information
Alaska Public Lands Information Center (APLIC), 250 Cushman St #1A, Fairbanks 99707, 456-0527. Has info on parks and protected areas of Alaska. Open daily. *www.nps.gov/aplic/center*.
Convention and Visitors Bureau Log Cabin, 550 1st Ave, 456-5774/(800) 327-5774. Check comprehensive website for dozens of B&Bs, inc daily vacancy info etc. Daily 8am-7pm (summer), M-F 10am-5pm (winter). *www.explorefairbanks.com*.
Univ. of Alaska Student Union: info board for digs, rides, etc.

Travel
Alaska Railroad, 1745 Johansen Expressway, 458-6025/ (800) 544-0552. *www.alaskarailroad.com*.
Municipal Commuter Area Service, 501 Cushman, 459-1011. Runs 5 rtes. Fare $1.50. 'Fairbanks very difficult without a car.' *www.co.fairbanks.ak.us/Transportation.*
Parks Hwy Express, 479-3065 or (800) 770-7275, runs daily to Denali ($46 o/w) and Anchorage ($91 o/w, free stop off at Denali). *www.alaskashuttle.com*.

CALIFORNIA - The Golden State

California. The word beckons, like an incantation: the Far West inspires images of sun, sand, surfing, Hollywood, adventure, healthy foods, healthy people, new age mysticism and an easy life. But California is much more complex than its popular image implies. Time does not offer enough here. It has the natural beauty of several states combined: rich redwood groves containing the tallest trees on earth; the stark superlatives of Death Valley; and the dizzying glacier-carved heights of Yosemite Valley. Like Shangri-La, California is cut off from the rest of the world by uninviting terrain: the volatile Trinity Alps in the north and the Sierras in the east; the Mojave Desert in the south; and to the west, over 1200 kms of coastline and rocky precipices on the Pacific Ocean coast.

When pioneers crossed the prairie to California, they found a land with potential for riches beyond mere gold, a promise that has since been fulfilled. There's more of everything in California: more people (over 36 million), more money (it's the world's 5th largest economy, trailing only Japan, Germany, the UK, and France – the state produces nearly $1.5 trillion worth of goods and services annually) and more science activity (a disproportionate share of the US's pure science research and more Nobel laureates than the former Soviet Union). A key partner in the Pacific Basin economy, California leads the nation in agricultural and industrial output, from avocadoes to animation, from Silicon Valley to the Sunset Strip. For more information go to: *www.state.ca.us.*

Over the last decade, however, the state's golden image has become a little tarnished. The tech slowdown has decimated Silicon Valley while the southland continues to struggle with an increasingly diverse population. Neither this nor Mother Nature's omnipresent danger can slow California's growing population. As an illustration of nature's uncertainties, go no further than the horrendous wild fires which in 2003 raged for days across southern California costing many their homes and businesses. So while the state gets more and more crowded, traffic more and more congested and electricity more and more scarce, the area moves closer and closer to another round of rapid change.

If you are planning a trip to California, plan to rent a car. Crossing the Golden State on public transportation is almost as difficult as staking out the state in a covered wagon. Unless you have plenty of time and plenty of patience to navigate the state's discordant network of transit options, save yourself the grief. *www.visitcalifornia.com.*

National Parks: Channel Islands, Death Valley, Joshua Tree, Lassen Volcanic, Redwood, Yosemite, Sequoia and Kings Canyon.

Accommodation overview

Perhaps in response to its popularity, California offers a great variety of lodging options, many of them dead cheap.

Hostels: number about 100+, with new ones opening all the time. Always enquire locally—you might find a better deal. *www.totalescape.com/lodge/hostels/calif.html.*

Motel 6: The chain began here, in the state that invented the motel. This mega-chain offers basic rooms at very reasonable rates. Call (800) 4-MOTEL-6 or go to *www.motel6.com* to reserve a room anywhere in California. No pampering: their 6pm 'show up or lose your rsvs' policy is extremely firm; be sure you'll be able to arrive on time. **B&B Inns:** A comprehensive directory of Golden State B&B Inns is available on the net or in printed form, produced by the **California Association of B&B Inns (CABBI)**. From San Diego to the Oregon border, the directory showcases over 250 California B&Bs. Contact (831) 462-9191, or *www.cabbi.com.*

University lodgings: Many universities offer dorms for travelling students in the summer; also, most have housing offices that may list information on temporary housing.

Camping: National Park and monument fees are from $6-$20 (often in addition to the park's entrance fees). Some of the best campsites in California are state operated, of which those located along the Pacific Coast Hwy are the most stunning, with many sites located directly on the beach. While the fees may be steep, a reservation is usually the only way to secure one of these sites in the summer. **To reserve campsites:** for rsvs and campsite availability in CA state parks: call (800) 444-7275. Cost varies btwn sites plus $7.50 service charge, sites can accommodate up to 8 people. For national forests throughout the West Coast, call (877) 444-6777, $10-$30 per site plus another $9 service charge, depending on whether the campsite is **National Forest** or **Corps of Engineers**. Check *www.reserveusa.com* to be certain. Most campsites at national parks are first come, first served; however, sites at Yosemite and Sequoia can be reserved five months in advance by calling (800) 436-7275/(800) 365-2267. *http://reservations.nps.gov.*

NORTHERN COAST The Northern Coast region is a land of rugged shoreline and pounding surf, of towering redwood forests and rushing rivers, of verdant hills and bountiful vineyards. Time spent here is time spent in Paradise.

During the age of the dinosaurs, Redwoods existed here in great quantity, though they severely diminished in number during the Ice Age. A narrow strip, stretching more than 400 miles north of San Francisco to the Oregon border, was all that survived of the coastal species of *sequoia sempervirens*, this remnant was further depleted by logging early in this century.

You can see these majestic survivors in the very northwesternmost corner of the state along two stretches of Hwy 101, considered one of the most picturesque drives in the world: **Humboldt Redwoods State Park**, (take a detour off the hwy north of **Garberville** to see the **Avenue of the Giants**); and **Redwood National Park**, which stretches from **Orick** to **Crescent City** and encompasses three state parks. This 'UNESCO World Heritage Site' features the world's tallest trees, one over 367 ft tall! *The North Coast Redwoods* brochure gives an idea of what each park has to offer; available from Humboldt Redwoods State Park and other hostels.

The telephone area code is 707.

Accommodation
This area is saturated with pricey bed and bfast inns. However, inexpensive local motels and interesting hostels makes affordable accommodation possible.

HI-Redwood Hostel, 14480 US 101, Klamath at **Wilson Creek**, 482-8265. The northernmost link in the California coastal chain of hostels, this one is located in mist-shrouded Redwood National Park and International Biosphere Reserve. Dorm $16-19. Private rooms $45. Linen free. Dining room, laundry, kitchen, and sundecks overlooking ocean. *www.norcalhostels.org/redwoods.*

Camping: Emerald Forest, 753 Patrick's Pt., 677-3554, **Trinidad**, offers secluded tent sites in the midst of a redwood grove for $24 (summer)/$21 (autumn) a night for 2 (incl laundry, video aracade and hot showers), XP-$3 and cabins for $79-$189. Rsvs ahead. *www.rvintheredwoods.com.*

Redwood National Park, 464-6101/(800) 444-7275, encompasses 3 state parks that offer campsites with showers, $15 p/night, rsvs req in summer. *www.nps.gov/redw.*

Humboldt Redwoods State Park, 946-2409/(800) 444-7275. 6 campgrounds, $15 spring/$20 summer for up to 8 people, extra vehicle $6. *www.humboldtredwoods.org.*

Food
Moosse Café (at the **Blue Heron Inn**), Albion and Kasten, 937-4323, in **Mendocino**, serves organic eclectic Californian cuisine in casual environment. Daily 11.30am-3.15pm for lunch and 5.30pm-9pm for dinner.

Orick Market, 488-3225, daily 8am-7:30pm to stock up on supplies.

Palm Café, Rte 101 in **Orick**, 488-3381. A locals' joint with delicious homemade fruit pies. Daily 5am-8pm.

Prairie Creek: Rolf's Park Cafe, 2 miles N of **Orick** on Hwy 101, 488-3841. Chow down on elk, buffalo and boar as well as traditional American food; $15-$22 dinners. Open daily, eve only. Close Nov-Mar.

Of interest
The Northern Coast offers dozens of parks and beaches strung like pearls along the way; here you can experience nature at its most diverse and best. Take a leisurely cycle through vineyard country, hike in primeval forests, or ramble along clifftops for spectacular views of the ocean. Raft down racing rivers, soak in hot mineral springs or luxuriate in the ultimate mud-bath! **In Eureka:** Many examples of Victorian architecture can be found both here and in nearby **Arcata,** such as **Carson House Mansion**, 2nd & M St, a quintessential Victorian Gothic-style mansion.

www.eurekaheritage.org/the_carson_mansion.htm. The town's old bank is home to the **Clarke Historical Museum**, 240 E St, 443-1947. Tue-Sat 11am-4pm. *www.clarkemuseum.org*. Heading south: **The Pacific Lumber Company**, 125 Main St, **Scotia**, 764-2222. A historic logging museum; tour passes issued Mon-Fri 8am-2pm, free. 'Fascinating.' *www.palco.com*.

Rockefeller Forest in Humboldt Redwoods State Park, 946-2263, contains the largest grove of old-growth trees in the world, some over 2200 yrs old; nearby in **Founder's Grove**, find towering redwoods over 360 ft tall, allow a half hour for the loop, extended via the **Mayhem Plaque Trail**. *www.humboldtredwoods.org*.

Not to be missed is the **Avenue of the Giants**, just north of **Garberville** off US 101. A 33 mile scenic hwy winds its way through majestic redwoods. 16 miles S of Garberville, in Leggett, is the **Drive-Thru-Tree**, 925-6363, where for a $3 park entrance fee, you can do just that (as many times as you wish!) *www.drivethrutree.com*.

Skunk Train, Laurel St, Ft Bragg, (800) 777-5865. Founded in 1885; steam and diesel engines take you for a 40 minute ride past giant redwoods on a picturesque old logging run to Willits. You could 'smell it before you could see it coming'. $35 two trains daily, 9am, 2pm. June–Aug. *www.skunktrain.com*.

Pygmy Forest, btwn Navarro and Big Rivers on Hwy 1; particularly visible around Jug Handle Creek, south of Ft Bragg. Two paths from entrance of **Van Damme State Park**, 937-5804: the **Fern Canyon Trail** is 4^1/$_2$ miles, and the **Little River Airport Rd** is 3^1/$_2$ miles. A 3 hr hike will take you back five hundred thousand years in time to see how the ocean has shaped this countryside. The 5 mile (r/t) trail dubbed the **Ecological Staircase** meanders through terraces carved by the Pacific. The fifth terrace is the **Pygmy Forest**, a land of stunted cypress and Bolander pine unique to this area. A 50 yr old tree may grow to no more than an inch in diameter and two to five feet in height.

The town of **Mendocino** on Hwy 1, an artists' colony by the sea, is a wonderful place to stop, stretch and stroll. Artisans show and sell at Gallery Faire (crafts) and Studio 2 (jewellery), among others. The town appeared as Cabot Cove in the TV series *Murder, She Wrote*. Be sure to visit **Mendocino Headlands State Park** while you're there. When they shot the movie, *The Russians are Coming*, along the Mendocino coast, they were wrong: the Russians have been here and gone. See the well-restored proof at **Ft Ross**, 847-3286, a 19th century seal-hunting outpost, and the only genuine Russian military installation in the lower 48 states.

Information/Travel

Crescent City Area Visitors Center, at 1111 Crescent St, 464-6101 x 5064. Daily 9am-5pm. *www.nps.gov/redw/pphtml/facilities.html*.

Garberville Chamber of Commerce, 773 Redwood Dr, 923-2613. Daily 9am-5pm. *www.garberville.org* .

Prairie Creek Redwood Visitors Center, 464-6101 ext 5301. *www.parks.ca.gov/default.asp?page_id=415*

Greyhound, 500 East Harding Dr, 464-2807/(800) 231-2222, in Crescent City.

MOUNT SHASTA and LASSEN VOLCANIC NATIONAL PARK A hideaway for city-dwelling Californians to recharge their batteries, 160 miles northwest of Sacramento lies the Shasta Cascade. Towering mountains, stunning waterfalls, dense forests and glistening lakes create a dramatic landscape dominated by the 14,162-ft **Mt Shasta**, the white-haired patriarch of Northern California.

Younger, shorter, hotter-headed sister to Mount Shasta is the live 10,457-ft **Lassen Peak**, which last erupted in 1917 – a wink of the geologic eye, a member of the Pacific 'Ring of Fire'. Brilliantly bizarre moonscape, nasty mudpots, pools of turquoise and gold and sulphurous steam vents reveal the region's volcanic history, especially in the **Bumpass Hell** area. You are free to climb the two and a half miles to the three craters of Lassen: main road takes you near, trail is easy, fine views of Shasta and the devastation to the northeast. Excellent summer programmes: Ishi, the last Stone Age man in America, was found near Lassen and the Manzanita Lake info centre has photo displays of him. Passes are valid for 7 days, $10 per car, $5 on foot. 'Yosemite is tame by comparison.' Park Info, 595-4444, daily 9am-6pm. *www.shastahome.com/lassen-volcanic/park.htm*.

Take the time to explore the seven national forests and 10 national and state parks in the area. **Cool Mountain Nights** in Mount Shasta at the end of August, features an outdoor concert, street fair, classic car show, blackberry bluegrass festival, Tin Man Triathlon and community bfast. *www.shastacascade.org*.

The telephone area code is 530.

Accommodation
Alpenrose Cottage, 204 E Hinkley Street, Mount Shasta, 926-6724, $30 ($175/wk) semi-private room, linen incl, kitchen, laundry, etc. Rsvs nec. *www.snowcrest.net/alpenrose*.
Swiss Holiday Lodge, 2400 S Mt Shasta Blvd, Mount Shasta, 926-3446. Pretty chalet, Tremendous view of Mt Shasta. S/D-$50-$60. Inc continental bkft. Pool, jacuzzi, communal kitchen. *http://users.snowcrest.net/swissholidaylge.*
Camping: Lake Siskiyou, 4239 W.A. Barr Rd, Mt Shasta, 926-2618, a popular recreational lake featuring boating, swimming, fishing, sailing, campground, RV park, grocery/deli, $18 per tent for 2 ppl, w/full hook-up $25. *www.lakesis.com*.
Lassen Volcanic National Park, Mineral, 595-4444. Volcanic lava flows, hot springs, mud pots and old emigrant trails. Season is June thru October. Admission $10, includes ranger-guided programmes. *www.nps.gov/lavo*.
Trinity Lake, US Forest Service, Weaverville, 623-2121. Formally known as Clair Engle Lake, includes secluded bays and coves ideal for camping, fishing, houseboating, swimming and other water sports. *www.fs.fed.us/r5/shastatrinity.*

Travel
Amtrak, serves Redding and Dunsmuir, (800) 872-7245.
Greyhound, 1321 Butte St, Redding, and at 4th and Mt. Shasta in Mt. Shasta, 241-2070/(800) 231-2222.

SACRAMENTO Known as Gold Country for a reason; in 1839 Swiss immigrant John Augustus Sutter landed on the banks of the American River intending to create a trading post and haven for European immigrants; within a decade a sawmill was built in the nearby foothills. A foreman inspecting Sutter's Mill one morning in 1848 made a discovery that was to change history—a gold nugget glinting in the sun.

A month later, three Chinese disembarked in San Francisco on the first sailing ship to the US from China, the first of thousands that would follow to gold mining camps near Sacramento. Perhaps they were not the first Chinese to sail to the US: Buried deep under a sandbank in the Sacramento River, there has been a recent discovery of a medieval Chinese junk of Zhou Man's fleet, which Gavin Menzies, in his absorbing book *1421 – the Year China Discovered America*, thinks is almost certain proof that the Chinese discovered America before Columbus.

Today, the state's capital, at the confluence of the Sacramento and American Rivers, has a pleasant, mid-western feel, that offers to transport visitors back to the height of the gold stampede in the 1850s-1870s. *www.sacramentocvb.org*.

The telephone area code is 916 except Nevada County where it is 530.

Accommodation
Check *www.discovergold.org/visitor/accommodations.cfm* for places to stay.
Good Nite Inn, 25 Howe Ave, 386-8408. From $40. 2 miles from downtown.
HI-Sacramento Hostel, 925 H St, 443-1691. From $20. Private rooms available. 'Fabulous hostel.' *www.norcalhostels.org/sac/index.html*.
Motel 6, 1415 30th St, 457-0777. Close to Sutter's Ft, accessible by bus. From $46. Pool, AC, coffee, noisy (freeway nearby). *www.motel6.com*.

Food
Delta King Pilothouse Restaurant, Hotel and Saloon. 1000 Front St, Old Sacramento, 441-4440. The riverboat is located on the river, providing food and entertainment. Lunch Mon-Sat 11.30am-2pm, Dinner Sun-Thu 5pm-9pm, w/end 5pm-10pm. *www.deltaking.com*.
Fanny Ann's Saloon, 1023 2nd St, 441-0505. Philly, turkey sandwiches, salads. 'A pleasant change from burgers.'
Fox and Goose, 1001 R St, 443-8825. Real British pub fare, meals under $10. *www.foxandgoose.com*.

Of interest
While in this area, be sure to read up on the amazing Lola Montez, sample the wonderful gold rush tales of Bret Hart, and read Mark Twain's story, *The Celebrated Jumping Frog of Calaveras County*. For information on local museums, check *www.sacmuseums.org*.
California State Railroad Museum, 111 I St, Old Sacramento, 445-6645. $4 includes a 'step-a-board' section onto the steam locomotive. Steam train excursions are also available along the scenic Sacramento river and depart from the **Central Pacific Freight Depot** on Front & K Sts, summer w/ends, 11am-5pm, on the hr; 6 mile trip taking 40 mins, $6. *www.csrmf.org*.
Crocker Art Museum, 216 O St, 264-5423. A restored Victorian mansion with staid old paintings; catch the sometimes-wild modern art exhibits upstairs. $6, $3 w/student ID. *www.crockerartmuseum.org*.
Old Governor's Mansion, 16th & H Sts, 323-3047. Charming wedding-cake Victorian building, now a state museum with furnishings donated by 13 former state governors, including Ronald Reagan. Tours daily 10am-4pm. 'Best sight in city,' 'good tour and stories'. *www.parks.ca.gov/default.asp?page_id=498*.
Old Sacramento, 28-acre historic district on Sacramento River. The riverfront encompasses 26 acres of shops and restaurants in 1849 to 1870-vintage buildings. Especially evocative at night. Includes **Sacramento History Center, Old Eagle Theatre, Pony Express Monument** and **California State Railroad Museum**. *www.oldsacramento.com*.
Old Sacramento Riverboat Cruises, 110 L St Landing, (800) 433-0263. Brunch tour, 2 hrs, cruise only $20, w/brunch $37.50. Luncheon, 2 hrs $20, w/lunch $35. Sightseeing, 1 hr, $12.50. Sunset Cruise, 2 hrs, $20, w/dinner $37.50. *www.spiritofsacramento.com*.
Self guided **walking tours** of Old Sacramento, free maps available from Visitors Centre.
State Capitol Museum, 10th and L St, 324-0333. Superbly restored to its 19th century grandeur; wander through, under the magnificent dome and crystal chandeliers, and on the marble mosaic floors. Eat lunch in the reasonably-priced

basement cafeteria or picnic on the lawn under massive deodar cedars (the species originated in the Himalayas). Mon-Fri 9am-4pm; hourly tours. Stroll the surrounding **Capitol Park** filled with thousands of varieties of plants. *www.capitolmuseum.ca.gov*.

Sutter's Ft, 2701 L St, 445-4422, should fascinate anyone interested in history; self-guided tours through exhibit rooms which include a blacksmith's shop, a bakery and prison. **State Indian Museum**, on the same park-like grounds, displays examples of an Indian sweathouse and a barkhouse. Fort open daily 10am-5pm, Museum Tue-Fri by request; $4 for Fort, $2 for the Indian Museum. **Living History Days** are held on various Saturdays during the summer. Performed in **Sutter's Fort State Historic Park**, 2701 L St. $4. For other special events, call 445-4422. *www.parks.ca.gov/default.asp?page_id=485* .

Nearby: You can trace the path of the '49er miners on their way through **Gold Country** by following Hwy 49 which links many of the 19th century mining communities in the Mother Lode. The flavour of the Gold Rush still lingers in rustic ghost towns, especially **Coloma**, where James Marshall found the nugget that set off the Rush.

Nevada County is dotted with historic landmarks. *www.aboutnevadacounty.com* and *mynevadacounty.com*. **Nevada City** claims to be the most complete gold town left in California. Victorian houses and flat-topped 'false front' buildings, popular in western frontier towns, line the streets, lending the town a feeling of a living museum. Head north on Hwy 49 to **Empire Mine State Historic Park**, in **Grass Valley**, this was the largest, deepest and richest of California's mines; restored buildings, exhibits and an illuminated mine shaft are included on park tours. W/end tours also incl living history and cottage tours, with interpreters in 1905-period costume, call 273-8522. *www.empiremine.org*. Head south on 49 to **Coloma** and the **Gold Discovery Site State Park**, 622-3470, 8am-sunset. Nearby is **Placerville**, where Studebaker began making wheel-barrows for miners in 1848 and home to a typical Mother Lode mine, in **Gold Bug Park**, 642-5207, which remains untouched by the cave-ins and flooding that destroyed others. Open daily 8:30am-5pm, $4 admission, audio tour tape $1. Also take in the Stamp Mill, where the gold was separated from the ore. *www.goldbugpark.org*.

Information
Nevada County Chamber of Commerce, 248 Mill St, Grass Valley, 273-4667, *www.gvncchamber.org*.
Sacramento Convention & Visitors Bureau, 1608 I St, 808-7777, *www.sacramentocvb.org*.
Old Sacramento Visitors Bureau, 1004 2nd Street, Sacramento, 442-7644.

Travel
Amtrak, 4th & I St, (800) 872-7245.
Greyhound, 715 L St, 444-7270/(800) 231-2222. 'Gambler's buses to Tahoe, Reno—if you can afford to lay out the fare. On arrival several casinos give you money in chips and food vouchers. Details in local papers—a great day out.' To main terminal in Reno $23 o/w.
Regional transit: buses and a light rail system, 321-2877. $1.50 basic fare, valid for 90 mins from purchase, $3.50 day pass. You can walk from 6th and K to Old Sacramento (5 blocks). *www.sacrt.com*.
Sacramento Airport, NW of town, is served by numerous shuttle bus companies who pick up from downtown areas. *www.sacairports.org/int*. The journey takes 15 mins, approx $13 o/w. Good service to use is **Super Shuttle**, (800) BLUE-VAN.

LAKE TAHOE
For two adjacent states, California and Nevada seem worlds apart: one is verdant, varied and mellow; the other, desiccated, monotonous

and frantically on the make. Nowhere is the contrast greater than on the shores of the lake these two states share, Lake Tahoe, a sapphire in a mountain setting two hours east of Sacramento. On the California side, South Lake Tahoe is a ski-bum village in winter, a granola filling station for hikers in summer. Across the border in Stateline, Nevada, casino-dwellers pump the one-armed bandits year-round, rarely venturing out into the light of day. Make sure you find a way to take the amazing drive round the lake, even if by public transport (see below).

Greater Lake Tahoe's web pages can be found at _www.virtualtahoe.com_. _The telephone area code is 530 in California and 775 in Nevada._

Accommodation
Check _www.laketahoe.com_ . All the following are located in South Lake Tahoe.
Alpenrose Motel, 4074 Pine Blvd, 544-2985. Summer rates: D-$70-$100, XP-$10. TV, free coffee, access to private beach. 7 mins walk from Nevada casinos. _alpenroseinntahoe.com_.
Econolodge, 3536 S Lake Tahoe Blvd, 544-2036. D-$39-$89, much more expensive during the ski-season. _www.visitlaketahoe.com/econo._
Camping: for up-to-date info on camping in state parks and forests around Lake Tahoe, contact the **Forest Service** or the California State Reservation system at (877) 444-6777. _www.reserveusa.com_.

Food
Izzy's Burger Spa, Hway 50, 544-5030, Sun-Thu 11am-9pm, w/end 'til 10pm. Izzy's serves up the best burgers in the basin, under $5.
Sprouts, 3123 Harrison Ave (at corner of Hwy 50), 541-6969, open 8am-9pm, not to be missed vegetarian, even if you're not a vegetarian.
Chris' Café, 3140 Hwy 50, **Meyers**, 577-5132 Open daily 6am-2pm, a locals' favourite for breakfast, worth every minute of the 20 min drive west on Hwy 50.
New York Pizza, 1034 Al Tahoe Blvd, 541-0401., ask anyone, this is the best pizza on this side of the Hudson, Open daily 11:30am-10pm. Less than $10.
Beacon Bar and Grill, on the lake in **Camp Richardson**, 541-0630. The attention that their rumrunners (special concoction of diff rums and juices) attract makes the lake jealous, $3 Wed and happy hours, daily, 4-7 pm. _www.camprichardson.com._

Of interest
There are way more activities to get involved in, at and around the lake than can possibly be listed here. Clearly, though, the outdoors is the main attraction. For information about permits, fees and helpful tips stop by the **National Forest Visitors Center** at **Taylor Creek**, 3 mi North of S. Lake Tahoe on Hwy 89, where you can also catch several good hikes. Call 543-2674 or check out _www.r5.fs.fed.us/ltbmu._
Take a sunset cruise on Lake Tahoe any night during summer on the **MS Dixie 2** paddle wheeler by calling (775) 588-3508. The $46 cruise includes dinner and wine, other cruises $29-57. _www.laketahoecruises.com._
Truckee near **Donner Pass** on Hwy 80 is a quaint town with wooden buildings and a frontier atmosphere. 2 miles W of Truckee is **Donner State Park** where, in the winter of 1846-47, the 89-member Donner party was trapped by 22-ft snows, (memorial statue there is as tall as the snow was deep that year). Only 47 survived the ordeal by resorting to cannibalism.

Information
South Lake Tahoe Visitors Center, 3066 Lake Tahoe Blvd, 541-5255, open Mon-Sat, 9am-5pm. For lodging info call (800) 288-2463, _www.tahoeinfo.com_.

Travel
Anderson's Bike Rental, 645 Emerald Bay Rd, South Lake Tahoe, 541-0500. Deposit (ID) req. Daily 9am-6pm. Less than $10 for half a day. Very good value. 10% disc avail in trail map at rental shop.
www.tahoevacationguide.com/Activities/bikerentals.html.
Greyhound: Caesars, Nevada, (800) 231-2222.
Public Transportation: The STAGE is an extensive service of buses and trolleys across the south shore of the lake, 542-6077, $1.25, $2 all day. It meets up with the Tahoe Area Regional Transport (TART), public buses, at **Emerald Bay**. The TART service, (800) 736-6365, connects the west and north shores from Tahoma to Incline Village, $1, $2.50 all day. Buses run daily 6am-6.30pm (some on south shore run much later) and schedules and maps are avail on the bus. *www.placer.ca.gov/works/tart.htm*.

WINE COUNTRY Both **Napa Valley** and its neighbour **Sonoma Valley** are noted for superlative viticulture; these areas produce everything from world-class cabernets to sassy jug wines. Just two hours by car from San Francisco, the scenery alone is worth the trip. Bus service to both valleys is good, but renting a car is the best way to tour. That way, you can alternate wine-tasting with farm stops, roadside stands, cheese factories, delis and other tasty locales.

Besides wine, you can taste the sparkling mineral water that bubbles out of the ground at **Calistoga**, home to California's **Old Faithful Geyser**; watch gliders and hot air balloons over the vineyards; visit **Jack London's Beauty Ranch** near old-worldly **Glen Ellen** and maybe even pause a moment at the **Tucolay Cemetery** near Napa, where Mary Ellen Pleasant, aka Mammy Pleasant, is buried. A 19th century black civil rights advocate and entrepreneur who owned a string of San Francisco boardy houses and restaurants, Mammy Pleasant gave $30,000 to finance John Brown's raid on Harper's Ferry, and aided the smuggling of hundreds of slaves to freedom via the Underground Railroad. In 1868, she successfully sued at the Californian Supreme Court for the right of blacks to ride San Francisco streetcars, more than 80 years before Rosa Parks refused to give her seat on a bus to a white person in Alabama.

Visit Napa Valley's wineries, food, lodging, etc., virtually at *www.napavalley.com*.
The area code here is 707.

Accommodation
Budget accommodation in the wine country is hard to find. B&B prices hover around $60-$225, tending towards the high end of the scale! It is best to stay in Santa Rosa, Sonoma or Petaluma for budget accommodation, otherwise you are advised to camp.
Triple-S Ranch, 4600 Mountain Home Ranch Rd, **Calistoga**, 942-6730. These all-wood cabins are a good deal: from 2 pp-$90, inc. cont. bfast. Rsvs rec on w/ends.
Camping: Bothe-Napa Valley State Park, 3801 St Helena Hwy, 942-4575. For rsvs call Destinet at (800) 444-7275. Sites $16, hot showers. Check-in 2pm-12am. *www.napanet.net/~bothe*. NB Summer temps may reach 105 F, but nights are usually cool. **Napa County Fairgrounds**, 1435 Oak St, **Calistoga**, 942-5111, dry grass in a parking lot with showers and electricity, tent site w/full hook-up, $25. Closed late June-early July.

Food

Restaurant fare tends to be dauntingly expensive in most instances, but there are numerous delis and supermarkets with picnic makings and many wineries have pleasant picnic areas. Get suggestions for good grocery stores and bakeries from the locals. Some good ones are the **Sonoma** and **Vella Cheese Factories**, 2 W Staine St, 996-1931/315 2nd St, 938-3232; the **Twin Hill Ranch** near Sebastopol (applesauce bread), 1689 Pleasant Rd, 823-2815; and the **Oakville Grocery** in Oakville, 7856 St Helena Hwy, 944-8802. Calistoga has at least 7 all-different bfast places.

Nicola's Delicatessen & Pizzeria, 1359 Lincoln Ave., **Calistoga**, (707) 942-6272, Big breakfasts, great sandwiches and handmade pizzas are served from 7am-9pm daily. Bfast from $4.

Of interest

Wineries: There are over 300 in Napa Valley alone. The tiny ones tucked away on side roads are informal and fun, but you need a car to get to them. NB You must be over 21 to sample wines and access sites. The big five wineries, from north to south, are: **Robert Mondavi**, $1/2$ mile N of Oakville, 226-1246, Cliff May building, 'technical tour', picnics on the lawn *www.robertmondaviwinery.com*; **Sterling & Beaulieu**, 1111 Dunaweal Ln/1960 St Helena Hwy, 942-3344/967-5200. Open daily 10am-5pm, tastings $5. Their aerial-tram (Sterling) offers 'spectacular views', *www.aboutwines.com*; **Beringer**, 2000 Maine St, 963-7115, whose Gothic Rhine House is a landmark, *www.beringer.com*; and **Charles Krug**, 2800 Maine St, 967-2200 the oldest in the valley, founded 1821 *www.charleskrug.com*. Other good wineries: **Stag's Leap**, 5766 Silverado Tr., Napa, has superb wine that measures up to the Continent's best; call 944-2020 to arrange a tour and tasting between 10am-4:30pm, $10. *www.stagsleapwinecellars.com*. For champagne, hit **Korbel Brothers**, 824-7000, in Sonoma Valley since 1822, daily 10am-3.45pm, *www.korbel.com*. Around Sonoma are 4 more standouts, from **Sebastiani**, *www.sebastiani.com/home.asp*, to **Buena Vista**, which is the oldest winery in California. The latter is the original winery of Agoston Haraszthy, the Hungarian 'count' who brought European vinestock to the US. Green Hungarian is good; Mozart Festival here in summer: *http://buenavistawinery.com/history.* Most wineries have tasting at the end of tours, 10am-5pm or so. 'Christian Brothers last tour of the day is more like party-night than wine tasting—you get half glasses to taste!' In August, the **Napa Valley Fairgrounds** hosts a summer fair that includes wine-tasting, rock music, juggling, a rodeo and rides. 253-4900, *www.napavalleyexpo.com*.

Jack London State Historic Park, off Hwy 12 on Arnold Dr. in **Glen Ellen**, 938-5216, contains ruins of the author's **Wolf House**. Museum hours, 10am-5pm, park open daily 9.30am-5pm, $6 p/vehicle. *www.jacklondonpark.com*.

Robert Louis Stevenson Park, in **St Helena**, 11 miles N of Calistoga on Hwy 29, 942-4575, for great trails (trail leading to former site of RLS house).

Sonoma is still centred around its lush plaza, where in 1846 Yankee rebels raised a grizzly-bear flag and established the short-lived Republic of California. The republic gave way 40 days later to US control, but the flag, and its symbol, stuck. Remnants of Spanish control still exist here, including the **Mission** and **Lachryma Montis**, home of General Vallejo, who once governed much of California. If you have the chance, take the hwy from Sonoma to Hwy 80; it's a beautiful drive any time of year.

Information

The local **Napa Visitor Center**, 101 Antonia Drive, American Canyon, 642-0686 is helpful. Be sure to pick up their farm trails brochures, including *Inside Napa Valley* for maps, winery listings and weekly events. *www.napavalley.com/napavalley/nsvc.* Also, **Chambers of Commerce** in: **St Helena**, 1010A Main St., 963-4456. *www.sthelena.com*. **Calistoga**, 1458 Lincoln Ave, 942-6333. *www.calistogachamber.com*.

Travel
It's best to rent a car, but there are buses and bike tours.
Public Transportation: a hodgepodge of counties and municipalities offer bus service throughout the valley that is patchy at best. **Golden Gate Transit,** 455-2000, operates out of Santa Rosa (#72, 73, 80) to San Francisco, *www.goldengate.org*.
Sonoma County Transit, 576-RIDE, and Napa Valley Transit's VINE service, (800) 696-6443, operates throughout the valley including the Napa Downtown Trolley, *www.nctpa.net/vine*.
Greyhound, (800) 231-2222, frequent service to Sonoma and twice daily service to Napa and Calistoga that requires an overnight stay.
Gray Line, (888) 428-6937/ (415) 558 9400, offers $140 7-hour Napa tour from San Francisco. Pier 43$^{1}/_{2}$.
Napa Valley Bike Tours, 6488 Washington St, Yountville, (800) 707-2453, rents bikes and operates numerous bike tours throughout Napa and Sonoma Valleys. From $115. Open daily 8.30am-5pm, *www.napavalleybiketours.com*.
Napa Valley Balloons, 253 2224, in Yountville offer the ultimate view for around $205 and incl. small breakfast and gourmet lunch. *www.napavalleyballoons.com*.

MARIN COUNTY Linked to San Francisco by the slender scarlet bracelet of the Golden Gate Bridge is Marin County, whose predominant hues are two shades of Green—green hills and green money. The western edge, facing the Pacific, is wild, windblown, solitary and beautiful. Among its treasures is the 70,000-acre **Pt Reyes National Seashore**, which falls precariously along the **San Andreas Fault**. At the very point of Pt Reyes is a lighthouse and from December to February, migrating gray whales can sometimes be seen from here. Further up the peninsula is **Tomales Bay State Park**. **Drake's Beach** is another gem, where Sir Francis may have landed when he claimed all of Nova Albion for Elizabeth I.

Near Pt Reyes are other public wilderness sanctuaries, among them popular **Stinson Beach** (closest swimming beach to San Francisco, enquire locally about the sea serpent) and **Muir Woods**, 6 miles of cool trails through a hushed and fragrant cathedral of *sequoia sempervivens*, some as tall as 240 ft. **Mt Tamalpais**, favourite of hikers and bicyclers, commands fantastic views; its trails link up with Stinson's, Muir Wood's and others.

Inner Marin is stuffed with plush communities that line the northwest shore of San Francisco Bay. From **Tiburon** you can take a ferry to nearby **Angel Island**, *www.angelisland.org*, which has seen several incarnations as a duelling field, military staging ground for three wars, quarantine station for Asian immigrants and a missile site. The island is now a state park with campsites, friendly deer, bicycling trails and the ghostly ruins of Civil War officers' houses to explore. A former whalers' harbour, **Sausalito**, is home to the best views of San Francisco. 'A fantastic way to get a feel for the area is to take a ferry to Sausalito and walk back across the Golden Gate Bridge. Once across, you can catch a bus back to downtown.' Marin County Visitors Bureau, *www.visitmarin.org*. *The telephone area code for Marin County is 415.*

Accommodation
Angel Island camping, $20 per site (8 people max). To stay in one of the island's 9 camps, call 435-3522 or (800) 444-7275 for rsvs. Rsvs are accepted up to 7 months in adv., which is just about how far ahead you'll have to make them if you plan to stay on a Sat night or for a holiday. *www.angelisland.org/*.
HI-Marin Headlands Hostel, 941 Fort Barry, **Sausalito**, 331-2777, sits on a hillside

in the serene Marin headlands, just across the Golden Gate Bridge. 'Very spacious hostel. You'll need a car to get into the city 12 miles away, no public transport. 'Popular but far from centre of town, or anywhere else.' 'Friendly, courteous staff'. Sumptuous location. Open year-round, $18, private room $54, but difficult to reach on public transit. Rsvs recommended in summer. *headlandshostel.homestead.com*.

HI-Point Reyes Hostel, Box 247, Point Reyes Station, CA 94956, 663-8811. Hostel is spread btwn 2 cabins on a spectacular site. Hiking, wildlife and Limantour beach all within walking distance. From $16. Write to reserve beds. *www.norcalhostels.org/reyes*.

Food/Entertainment

This area has many organic groceries where you should buy supplies then picnic in one of Marin's countless parks. For one of the best people-watching places, try **The Depot Bookstore and Café**, 87 Throckmorton Ave, **Mill Valley**, 383-2665. Food and drink at reasonable prices. Open daily 7am-7pm. *www.depotbookstore.com*.

Priscilla's, 12781 Sir Francis Drake Blvd., off Hwy 1 in **Inverness**, 669-1244. 'Huge, excellent pizzas.'

Treviso, 39 Caledonia, **Sausalito**, 332-4500. Come see Marin mellow out in this restaurant/bar.

Mayflower Inn, 1533 4th, near Shaver, **San Rafael**, 456-1011. A genuine British pub with darts, raucous singing, bangers, pasties, fish & chips and pints of Guinness in front of a blazing fire. Guaranteed to cure any case of homesickness. Open for lunch Sun-Fri, dinner daily.

No Name Bar, 757 Bridgeway, **Sausalito**, 332-1392, genuine beat hangout, great atmosphere.

Marin County Fair, San Rafael, first weekend in July, includes pig races, pie competitions, fireworks, high-tech exhibits, music and carnival rides! Call 499-6400 for info. *www.marinfair.org*.

Of interest/Information

Ferries from Tiburon to Angel Island, 21 Main St, Tiburon, 435-2131, leave four times daily on weekdays, more frequently on summer weekends. $10, $1 for transporting bikes. Sunset cruises $12, 6.30pm-8pm on Fri/Sat. Call **Angel Island State Park** direct on 435-1915 for more info on Angel Island, *www.angelislandferry.com*.

Marin County Civic Center, 3501 Civic Center Dr, 499-6646, **San Rafael**, *www.co.marin.ca.us/depts/CU/Main/mc*. Reminiscent of a Roman aqueduct, the civic center is a riot of pink and turquoise against emerald hills and azure California sky. Some people love this Frank Lloyd Wright structure; some call it the Bay Area's biggest sore thumb. Whatever your opinion, you shouldn't miss seeing it—and if you travel through Marin County on Hwy 101, you won't. Tours given Wed at 10:30am, free, meet in gift shop on second floor. **Rainbow Tunnel**, Hwy 1 northbound from Golden Gate Bridge to Marin County. A monument to a Cal Trans engineer's whimsy. You'll know it when you see it.

San Francisco Bay Model, 2100 Bridgeway, 332-3871. Constructed by the Army Corps of Engineers, the hydraulic model simulates tides, oil spills, etc. Tue-Fri 9am-4pm, Sat/Sun 10am-5pm. *www.co.marin.ca.us/depts/CU/Main/mc*.

SAN FRANCISCO The city-by-the-bay, San Francisco flows like a magic carpet of images: hills, bridges, cable cars, fog, ferryboats, gays, painted Victorians, earthquakes, movie car chases. Known to all simply as 'the City' ('Frisco' warrants the death sentence), San Francisco occupies a peerless setting on the tip of a green and hilly thumb separating ocean from bay. A narrow strait, fraught with dangerous undertows, is spanned by the silent, shimmering drama of the Golden Gate Bridge.

Seen from afar, the city is by turns a citadel shining in the sun, a bank of diamonds glittering in the night, a coquette peeking over a ruff of fog, heartbreakingly lovely. Closer examination reveals imperfections: slums, cold corporate canyons, porno districts and boxy tract homes and the ever-present fear of the 'big one'. But even with its flaws, San Francisco is still way ahead of whoever is in second place.

History and geography have conspired to make San Francisco a city of neighbourhoods in the European manner. Ethnic differences are not assimilated but, instead, encouraged, imparting a cosmopolitan flavour that comes as a welcome relief to the monotony of much of urban America. This westernmost of Western cities, paradoxically, is America's door to the East—to China, Japan, and the rest of Asia—with which California does more business than with Europe.

San Francisco's heritage was truly born in 1848 when gold was found across the bay and thousands poured into the city to seek their fortunes. Here in 1853 Bavarian immigrant Levi Strauss opened his dry goods store (later co-patenting copper rivets to make denim jeans), butter sold for six dollars a pound, fortunes were spent at over 600 liquor stores and taverns, and ladies of the evening charged up to a hundred dollars a night, a year's wages of the day in the US. In the 1850s, there were 12 women for every man in the city, every second person was a foreigner, and many newspapers spawned the stimulating intellectual tradition that survives in the city today.

It's hard to have a bad time in San Francisco. The wealth of things to see and do, the diverse and delicious foods and, most of all, the San Franciscans themselves, make visiting a delight. People migrate here not to be successful but to be (or learn to be) happy and human. Their efforts make San Francisco a city of good manners, full of little kindnesses and occasional gallant acts, whether saving whales or cable cars.

Temperatures are mild year-round. Spring and autumn offer the most sunshine, but come prepared for brisk winds and chilly weather at any time. Unexpectedly, summer is when the city's famous fog crosses the line into infamy. Mark Twain, it is said, once complained that the 'coldest winter I ever spent was a summer in San Francisco'.

San Francisco's central location is perfect for day trips to nearby attractions. Berkeley, Santa Cruz, Marin County and the Napa and Sonoma wine country can be reached within two hours by public transport. It's more than likely that, when it comes time to leave, you'll have to tear yourself away. When in San Francisco, remember three things: wear strong shoes, watch for seagulls and keep an eye on your heart at all times; otherwise as the song says, you'll probably leave it here. _www.sfvisitor.org_.

The telephone area code is 415.

Survival

San Francisco's **Greyhound** depot is located in a scruffy-to-rotten district, bearable during the day but predictably worse at night. When seeking accommodation, bear in mind that the large triangle formed by Market, Divisadero and Geary is a high crime area, which tends to spill over to the other side of Market, where the Greyhound depot is. The worst section, though, is the Western Addition, bounded by Geary, Hayes, Steiner and Gough. Stay out, day or night (no reason to visit, anyway). Other dicey streets at night are the first four blocks of Turk, Eddy and Ellis. That doesn't mean you shouldn't stay here—just be aware and exercise caution, particularly after dark.

Accommodation

NB: The best accommodation goes quickly, especially in youth hostels, so check in early. If arriving late, phone ahead. Accommodation info also available at Greyhound. For all in-town and nearby hostels, check www.norcalhostels.org/ourHostels.html. See also hostel listings for Marin County.

Adelaide Hostel, 5 Isadora Duncan, (877) 359-1915. Dorms from $20, S/D from $55, XP-$10. Continental bfast included, free internet. www.adelaidehostel.com.

Central YMCA, 220 Golden Gate Ave, 345-6700, dorms-$28, S-$39, D-$60. Private rooms req. Credit card reservations. www.ymcasf.org/accomodations.html.

Golden Gate Hotel, 775 Bush, btwn Powell and Mason, 392-3702. S/D-$85/95, shared bath, $115 w/private bath. Excellent location, within walking distance to just about everything. This safe and clean hotel has a 'very friendly and helpful staff' who serve continental bfast and afternoon tea for free, as well as internet access. www.goldengatehotel.com.

Grand Central Hostel, 1412 Market St, 703-9988, S/D-from $20, 4-bed dorm $12, free kitchen, laundry, TV room. This place and its poor location gets mixed reports.

Grant Hotel, 753 Bush St, btwn Powell and Mason, 421-7540, (800) 522-0979, about $75, coffee and TV, excellent and safe location. 'Our double rm was $65 p/night; we asked for an extra bed and fridge and got them. Large common room, very comfortable hotel!'

Green Tortoise Guest House, 494 Broadway, (off Kearny), 834-1000, $22 dorm, $56 private, (plus $20 key deposit). 'Very friendly, clean hostel on edge of Chinatown,' which can be 'a bit cramped'. But there is 'free tea and bfast if you get up early enough', plus the internet'! Laundry, common room, sauna. www.greentortoise.com/san-francisco-hostel/index.php.

HI-San Francisco Downtown Hostel at Union Square, 312 Mason St, 788-5604. $24-member, $28-non-member. 276 beds. A block from the excitement of Union Sq, in the theatre district, this hostel provides double and triple rooms. Union Sq is a great place to people watch or enjoy a picnic under the palm trees. Outside the hostel is a variety of restaurants, shops and art galleries. 'Excellent on-site information desk, central location.' Kitchen, library, free linen and vending machines but 'not enough showers!' as well as internet and laundry. Open 24 hrs, 21 nights max stay. www.sfhostels.com/locations/downtown.php.

HI-San Francisco Fisherman's Wharf Hostel, Bldg 240, Ft Mason, on Bay & Franklin, 771-7277. Take #42, #47 or #49 bus from Van Ness. Located in the Golden Gate National Recreation Area, an urban national park on the bay. Dorm overlooking the bay. 'Arrive early—fills very quickly.' Fort Mason is also home to museums, galleries and theatres. Fisherman's Wharf, Chinatown and Ghirardelli Sq all nearby. 'The abundance of British students makes it a good place to head for if you're alone and want to share costs.' Dorm $22-29, private $68-78, facilities inc kitchen, laundry and bfast. www.sfhostels.com/locations/fishermans_wharf.php.

Interclub Globe Hostel, 10 Hallam Pl, 431-0540, on Folsom btwn 7th & 8th. From Greyhound take bus #14 or a 15 min walk. Dorm $12, $40 private rooms. In nightclub district, no curfew, internet $1/10 mins. $10 key deposit. Although located in a 'druggy area' the 'good cafeteria' and 'brilliant atmosphere' draw an 'alternative crowd' and rave reviews —'best hostel I stayed in'.

Olympic Hotel, 140 Mason St, 982-5010. '1 block from AYH — rec. for hostel overspill.' This hotel has 'friendly and helpful' staff and shared doubles from $65, includes complimentary continental bfast and 24-hr internet. www.olympichotelsf.com/Olympic-Hotel-Boutique-San-Francisco-Hotel-site-map.html.

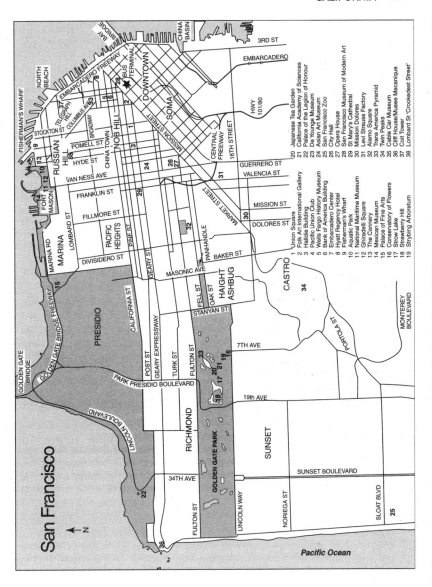

San Francisco

1 Union Square
2 Folk Art International Gallery
3 Haldie Building
4 Pacific Union Club
5 Wells Fargo History Museum
6 Bank of America Building
7 Embarcadero Center
8 Hyatt Regency Hotel
9 Fisherman's Wharf
10 Aquatic Park
11 National Maritime Museum
12 Ghiradelli Square
13 The Cannery
14 Mexican Museum
15 Palace of Fine Arts
16 Conservatory of Flowers
17 Strow Lake
18 Strawberry Hill
19 Strybing Arboretum
20 Japanese Tea Garden
21 California Academy of Sciences
22 Palace of the Legion of Honour
23 De Younge Museum
24 Asian Art Museum
25 San Francisco Zoo
26 City Hall
27 Opera House
28 San Francisco Museum of Modern Art
29 St Mary's Cathedral
30 Mission Dolores
31 Levi Strauss Factory
32 Alamo Square
33 Trans America Pyramid
34 Twin Peaks
35 Cable Car Museum
36 Cliff House/Musee Mecanique
37 Coit Tower
38 Lombard St 'Crookedest Street'

Pacific Tradewinds Hostel, 680 Sacramento St, 433-7970. Converted by two former backpackers. $17-$24 per night ($5 key deposit may be req), free internet, coffee/tea, linen and security box. Centrally and conveniently located in Chinatown, close to Market St and public transport. For $6 they will wash your laundry! No curfews. Rsvs recommended in summer. While this 'very friendly and homely atmosphere' was enough for some—'Best accommodation I stayed in.'

Others have complained that it was 'not very clean'. _www.sanfranciscohostel.org_.
Super 8, corner of O'Farrell/Taylor, (800) 843-8709. Own shower, cable TV, bfast.
Easy access to Chinatown/Market St. 'Friendly staff, clean rooms.' S-$79, D-$109,
XP-$10. _www.sanfrancisco.com/super8_.

Food

Food is one of the things San Francisco does best; sampling the amazing variety of
local cuisines is a top priority. The city grew as a seaport, so eat like a sailor:
Dungeness crab and sourdough bread, Irish coffee and Anchor Steam, the local
beer. Move on to other cultures in one of the many excellent and cheap ethnic
restaurants—Persian and Basque, Salvadorean and Greek, Sichuan and Russian,
Italian and Vietnamese. To really understand SF dining you'll have to do the grunt
work yourself and eat your own way through the city. For menu listings, check
www.themenupage.com/sf.html   and   _http://www.themenupage.com/sf.html_
www.sfstation.com. For places open late, visit _www.posthoc.com/24hours.htm._
Atmosphere: Buena Vista Cafe, 2765 Hyde St, 474-5044. Go on a foggy night and
listen to foghorns moan and cable cars clang while you nurse an Irish coffee
(introduced to the US in 1953 by SF newspaperman Stanton Delaplane). 'Extremely
crowded.'
Tommy's Joynt, 1101 Geary, 775-4216, 'Great decor, huge buffalo stew ($6.50).'
Daily 11am-2am. _www.tommysjoynt.com_.
Breakfast: Pinecrest Restaurant, 401 Geary (at Mason St) 885-6407. Dinner and
bfast served, all day. 24 hrs.
Sears Fine Foods, 439 Powell, 986-1160. Try French toast made from sourdough
bread. 'Excellent bfast, go extra early.' Open daily 6.30am-2.30pm.
www.themenupage.com/sears.html.
Burritos: Taqueria La Cumbre, 515 Valencia, near 16th, 863-8205. Daily 11am-9pm.
'Mouth-watering.'
Hamburgers: Hayes Street Grill, 320 Hayes St, 863-5545. Intimate, small-
restaurant cooking up the finest modern California cuisine. **Original Joe's**, 144
Taylor, btwn Turk & Eddy, 775-4877, serves 12-ounce burgers—regular or
charbroiled (after 5pm)—for around $8-10. The single best burger in the country.
'Only Brits can finish them,' so they've invented a 'junior' for wimps. European
soccer teams eat here. Open daily, 10am-midnight.
Italian: Tomasso 1042 Kearny, 398-9696, for pizza. Tue-Thu 5pm-10.30pm, Fri/Sat
'til 10.45pm, Sun 4pm-9.45pm. _tommasosnorthbeach.com/OurNews.asp_.
Asian: Best tempura at **Sanppo**, 1702 Post, 346-3486, Mon-Sat 11.30am-12am, Sun
'til 10pm; best Sichuan at **Tsing Tao**, 3107 Clement, btwn 32nd & 33rd, 387-2344,
open 10am-10pm. **House of Nanking**, 919 Kearny St, 421-1429, Mon-Fri 11.30am-
10pm, w/end from noon, a seemingly typical tourist spot serving a typically great
Chinese at prices you'd find in China.
French: Numerous French restaurants line the street of Belden Pl, (between Pine
and Bush). Two of the best are **Plouf**, 40 Belden Place, 986-6491 and **Café Bastille**,
22 Belden Pl , 986-5673, both have very reasonable prices and excellent food.
Sourdough bread: Boudin Bakery, several locations (Pier 39, Fisherman's Wharf,
Ghiradelli Square), 988-1849, hey, sometimes the biggest _is_ the best. Began in 1849
when Isidore Boudin created the Original San Francisco Sourdough French Bread;
they've kept the culture alive for over 150 years! _www.boudinbakery.com_. Now has 3
bakeries and 20 cafes throughout California.
Steaks: Tad's Steak House, 120 Powell, 982-1718. Steak, salad and bread for $11.
'Excellent food.' Daily 7am-11.30pm. _www.tads-steakhouse.com._
Sweet tooth: Gelato Classico, 576 Union, 391-6667. The standard of excellence in
Italian ices. **Just Desserts**, locations on Buchanan, Church St and Embarcadero.
'Best cheesecake, chocolate cake in the city.'

Of interest

Don't go looking for 'sights' and miss the best one: San Francisco itself. The best way to take it all in is to alternate walking with cable car or bus riding. Spend a half day (at most), in the tourist' ghettos of Fisherman's Wharf, The Cannery, Pier 39, Ghiradelli Square, etc., all of which are aimed squarely at your wallet. You've missed an essential part of the city's heart if you don't do one or more of the following: take a ferry to Sausalito past **Alcatraz**, the infamous prison; inch up and down the near-cliffs locally known as 'hills' while dangling from the down slope end of a cable car; hop on a MUNI tram for a tour of the peninsula; or stand on the Marin headlands north of the Golden Gate Bridge in the evening, watching the lights of the city come on. Unlike LA, San Francisco is fairly compact, easy to comprehend and well equipped with public transport to give your legs a much-needed break on its 43-plus hills.

Alcatraz, Pier 41, 705-5555. 3-hour ($16) trip to 'the Rock', where the likes of Al Capone, Machine Gun Kelley and the 'Birdman' were incarcerated from Civil War times to 1963. 'Dress warmly.' Tours year-round, 9:30am-4:15pm, every $1/2$ hr. Evening tour ($23.50) captures what it's really like to be stuck on the island. 'Must pre-book tkts but well worth it.' 'Long queues—get there early.' 'Best tour I went on in whole of US.' _www.telesails.com_.

Alamo Square, Take a walk to this green square for the best view of the **Painted Ladies**, the coloured Victorian houses that epitomise SF living.

Bank of America Building, this building, the second tallest in the city, is pretty obvious, but for the record it's at 555 California St. The Carnelian Room, 433-7500, a posh restaurant on the 52nd floor, offers an excellent view along with prices you can't afford. Cocktails are served between 3pm-11pm if you don't want to splash out on dinner, but jackets are required after 5pm. Restricted viewing is also possible from the 27th floor of the **Transamerica Pyramid**, at Montgomery St, a $34 million corporate symbol that has, amazingly, given the Golden Gate Bridge a run for its money as the City's symbol as well. The view of the Bay and hills beyond is nice, but it's more fun to go right up to the edge of the plate glass window—a plate glass wall, really—and just look down. For a good panoramic view of the city, have a drink at the Carnelian Room, _www.carnelianroom.com_.

Chinatown: more Chinese live here than in any other Chinatown in the states. Inhabiting Grant and Stockton btwn Bush and Broadway, SF's Chinatown can be a crowded confusion of sights, smells and sounds. 'Do yourself a favour and spend a couple of hours just wandering around taking it all in, especially the seafood shops.' All the tourists go to Grant; you should explore Stockton, Washington and little side streets to see: herbal shops at 837 and 857 Washington; fortune cookies being made at **Mee Mee**, 1328 Stockton _www.meemeebakery.com_ ; and T'ai-Chi practiced in the morning at Portsmouth Sq, RL Stevenson's old hang-out btwn Clay and Washington, where the city began.

Civic Center: between Franklin, Larkin, McAllister and Hayes. Its centre is **City Hall**, unhappy scene of the 1978 dual murder of the mayor and one of the city's gay supervisors by a former supervisor; both the crime and minimal punishment provoked rioting, outrage, and jolted SF's image as a tolerant mecca for gays.

Cow Hollow also known as Union Street—upwardly mobile locals shop and drink coffee away from the downtown bustle.

Cruises around the Bay: from Piers $43^1/2$ and 41, the **Red and White Fleets**, 447-0597, and the **Blue and Gold Fleet**, 705-5555, make frequent departures. Dress warmly and wait for clear weather. Blue and Gold specializes in tours to Alcatraz while both offer Bay cruises. Blue & Gold has a $2.25 per ticket phone reservation fee, but it's worth it especially for Alcatraz; **Golden Gate Ferries**, 923-2000 to Sausalito and Larkspur ($6.15 o/w), departing from the Ferry Building on Embarcadero, at the foot of Market Street. _www.goldengateferry.org_.

Embarcadero: Vaillancourt walk-through fountain, a 710-ton assemblage of 101 concrete boxes, unveiled in 1971 to cries of 'loathsome monstrosity', 'idiotic rubble', etc. A must-see.

Financial District: Montgomery St. is the 'Wall Street of the West'. **Wells Fargo History Museum**, 420 Montgomery, 396-2619. The bank whose symbol is a stagecoach pays homage to its worst enemy, Black Bart, who robbed Wells Fargo 28 times in 7 years (successfully all but once). Also includes other mementoes of the Old West. Free, Mon-Fri 10am-3pm. *www.wellsfargohistory.com*.

Fisherman's Wharf/Pier 39: Minuscule amount of wharf, surrounded by a frightening quantity of souvenir rubbish, overpriced seafood, dreary wax museums and bad restaurants. The working wharf is a series of 3 finger piers, just past Johnson and Joseph Chandlery. **Pier 39** is a carefully hokey construct of carnival and commerce, but **do not fail to see the sealions!** Dive among the sharks under San Francisco Bay at **Aquarium of the Bay**, 623-5300/(888) 732-3483, America's first 'diver's-eye view' aquarium. Inches away, witness a spectacular array of 10,000 rays, salmon, crabs, jellyfish, and other underwater wildlife via the two 150ft acrylic tunnels. Open weekdays 10am-6pm, weekends 10am-7pm, summer 9am-8pm, $13.95. *www.aquariumofthebay.com*.

Aquatic Park, 3 blocks left of Fisherman's Wharf. The 6 vessels moored here as well as the nearby **National Maritime Museum** (Free, daily 10am-5pm), 561-6662, are charming, 'especially the restored ferry'. $5 to enter **Hyde Street Pier**, where you can board 3 of the ships, including the 1886 *Balclutha*, 9.30am-5pm. Elsewhere is docked the liberty ship *Jeremiah O'Brien* and the WWII sub *Pompanito*, all with boarding fees. Also at the Aquatic: free swimming beach, cold but fairly clean, with free showers. Nearby is open-air seating where wonderful conga and jam sessions take place on fine Sat-Sun afternoons. Btwn Aquatic and the Wharf are **Ghiradelli Square** and **The Cannery**, both mazes of specialty shops, restaurants and contrived street colour covered by a thin veneer of history. *www.maritime.org*.

Asian Art Museum, 200 Larkin St, 581-3500, houses regularly changing special exhibits. $10, $6 w/student ID, Tue-Sun 10am-5pm, Thu 'til 9pm ($5 on Thursdays after 5). *www.asianart.org*.

Golden Gate Bridge: it's painted orange-red but glows gold in the afternoon sun. Perhaps the most famous suspension bridge in the world, the $1^1/_2$ mile Golden Gate links SF with the green Marin headlands (honeycombed with war fortifications). You can walk or bike across for free (dress warmly); pedestrian walk closes at sunset. At midpoint, you'll be 260 ft above the water, a drop that has drawn over 1000 suicides. By car, the bridge is free northbound, $4 southbound. 'Take Golden Gate Transit buses #28 or #29 from Civic Center to bridge then stroll along beach all the way back to Fisherman's Wharf. Lovely way to spend a day.' Other ways to do the bridge: walk from SF to Marin on the Bay side, and once across, keep going down Alexander Dr to Sausalito (about a mile, downhill all the way) and catch the ferry back to SF—the best of both worlds.

Golden Gate Park and West SF: An exceptional park of 1017 acres, larger than New York's Central Park, is filled with a vast array of plantings, foot and bridle paths. *www.nps.gov/goga* and *www.nps.gov/goga/home.htm.* Lots of free events and admissions, especially on first Wed of every month. On Sundays cars are prohibited. Sunday concerts on the **Band Shell**; lovely **Conservatory of Flowers**; **Stow Lake** (rent a rowboat) and **Strawberry Hill**; **Strybing Arboretum and Botanical Gardens** (661-1316), with 55 acres of global specimens. *www.strybing.org*. Get to the enchanting **Japanese Tea Garden** early or late to miss tour bus hordes. The 1894 garden is home to exquisitely manicured greenery matched with impressive pagodas and expertly brewed tea. Also to 'Lindy in the Park' swing dancers on Sundays mid-day. The gardens are open weekdays 8am-4:30pm, wkends and hols, 10am-5pm. 752-4227. There is also a Beach Chalet at Ocean

Beach, dating to 1925, with WPA murals, that serves breakfast, lunch and dinner (386-8439) For info on places and events within the park, call the Visitor's Center at 751-2766 or San Francisco Recreation and Parks Department, 831-2700.

Within the park: The California Academy of Sciences, 875 Howard Street, info line 750-7415, $7, $4.50 w/student ID, includes admission to the **Steinhart Aquarium**, which has huge, open tanks, and the **Natural History Museum**, with the Earthquake Exhibit. Also part of the Academy is the **Morrison Planetarium**, an additional $2.50, Free 1st Wed of every month except Planetarium, 9am-8:45pm. Daily opening 10am-5pm. _www.calacademy.org_. The **De Young Museum** and the **Palace of the Legion of Honor** are part of the **Fine Arts Museums of San Francisco**. (750-3636). The De Young Museum is located in the Golden Gate Park and is free, open Tue-Sat 10am-4.45pm. The Palace is in Lincoln Park, at 34th St and Clement, and includes Rodin sculptures and impressionist works. Open Tue-Sun 9.30am-5pm, $8, free every Tue. Keep in mind a warning though that was received by the local police, 'Don't walk to the park from the bus station unless you want to find out what it is like to be mugged or raped.' _www.thinker.org_. Under 10,800 panes of glass, the **Victorian Conservatory of Flowers in the Park** (666-7001) beckons to budding horticulturists with aquatic gardens, highland tropics, carnivorous Nepenthe pitcher plants, and 8-ft-wide lilies from the Amazon. Tue-Sun 9am-4.30pm, $5/$ with stud ID. _www.conservatoryofflowers.org_.

Haight-Ashbury, south of the Golden Gate panhandle, was famous in flower-power days, now spiffed up in what is sometimes called the 'creeping gentrification' of the city, typified by the Gap store at the intersection of Haight/Ashbury. Take a stroll down Hashbury Lane: **Janis Joplin's pad** at 112 Lyon, now home of a charitable organization, and **Jefferson Airplane's hangar** at 2400 Fulton. SE of Haight is **Noe Valley**, a sunny version of Greenwich Village, whose main drag, **Castro St**, gave birth to the modern gay pride movement. **Twin Peak** provides (on clear days) a fine view of San Francisco. To see it, take bus #37 from Market Street.

Hyatt Regency Hotel, 5 Embarcadero Center, 788-1234. Glittering seven-sided pyramid, its lobby filled with trees, birds, flowers and fountains. Ride the twinkly elevators to the 18th floor for costly drinks in **Equinox**, a restaurant that revolves, with a magnificent view of the Bay Bridge. 'Romantic, delightful—$10 cocktails.' 'Required to buy drink.' _www.sanfranciscohyattregency.com._

Japantown covers approx. 12 sq blocks with Japancenter Mall at the core. Between Fillmore and Octavia, Geary and Bush. Plenty of authentic Japanese restaurants, and a street fair 1st wknd in Aug.

Mexican Museum, Bldg D, Ft Mason, 202-9700. Don't pass up this rich panorama of folk, colonial and Mexican-American works, from masks to pottery to Siquieros lithos. Outstanding special exhibits. Wed-Sat 11am-5pm. 2005 was their 30th anniversary. _www.mexicanmuseum.org_.

The Mission District: Fri and Sat nights come alive on Mission between 16th and 24th as the local Chicano youth strut their mechanical stuff with their highly customised vehicles. Witness for yourself their low riding antics and the street carnival that ensues in this area rich with murals, culture and pride. See for yourself at the mini-park btwn York and Bryan on 24th; in Balmy Alley btwn 24th and 25th; and on Folsom at 26th. **Mission Dolores** at 16th and Dolores (621-8203) is a simple, restored structure with an ornate basilica peering over its shoulder. Daily 8am-12pm, 1pm-4pm, $3 donation. Interesting cemetery; drop in any time for free. _www.missiondolores.citysearch.com_.

Nob Hill: Cable car lines criss-cross here; transfer point. **Cable Car Museum**, Washington & Mason, 474-1887: 'the cable cars are powered from here, see how they work, very interesting'. Daily 10am-6pm Apr-Sep, 'til 5 the rest of the year; free. _www.cablecarmuseum.com_. North of Union Square is the grande dame of SF hills; prior to the quake it was crowded with mansions, of which only the **Pacific Union Club** was left standing. If you're dressed for it, take the elevators to the view bars atop the **Fairmont** and Mark **Hopkins Hotels**.

North Beach. This, the birthplace of the beat movement, fends off Greenwich Village's claim to the same by maintaining even now a certain junkyard style. Once the centre of the rip-roaring Barbary Coast, the area now hosts topless, bottomless, seemingly endless clubs along Broadway's 'mammary lane'. Clashing crazily with this gaudy neon fleshpot are clubs, coffeehouses and bookstores that reek of intellectual prestige or pretention, depending on your point of view. Among the greatest (if not the latest), is **City Lights Bookstore**, 261 Columbus, 362-8193. Open daily 10am-12am. Still owned by Lawrence Ferlinghetti, still stocked with Alan Ginsberg. Original mecca for the Beat writers. _www.citylights.com_. The alley next to the store is named in honour of Jack Kerouac. Look for **29 Russell St**, where he wrote _On the Road_. Get _triste_ at **Cafe Trieste**, 609 Vallejo, at Grant, 982-2605, to the tune of an aria from a tragic Italian opera performed by the owner (Sat 2pm), and drown your sorrows in a cafe latte; 'the highlight of my trip'! Pay your respects at **Vesuvio Bar**, 255 Columbus, 362-3370. When the beat movement bit the dust, the detritus gravitated here. Once, Kerouac and Dylan Thomas bent elbows at Vesuvio; the drinks are still cheap. 6am-2am every day. _www.vesuvio.com_.

Pacific Heights, with its unsurpassed collection of Victorian mansions, many of them colourfully painted. Webster, Pine and the 1900 to 3300 blocks of Sacramento contain many charming examples.

Palace of Fine Arts, 3301 Lyon St, (415) EXPLORE. Built for the 1916 Panama-Pacific Exposition out of plaster of Paris, the palace was not expected to hold up, as it did, for fifty years. It was restored with cement in 1967 and now houses the **Exploratorium**, a carnival of science and art that explains principles of physics and human perception through hands-on exhibits. Tue-Sun, 10am-5pm, $13, $10 w/student ID.To see the super-popular Tactile Dome: rsvs are req. $16 will get you into both the dome and the museum. 'Don't miss it!' _www.exploratorium.edu_.

San Francisco Museum of Modern Art, 151 3rd St btwn Mission and Howard, 357-4000. All the bluechips: Miro, Klee, Jasper, Pollock, etc. Free 1st Tue of every month, otherwise $11, $6 w/student ID. Open Thu-Tues 11am-6pm and Thu 'til 9pm (half price from 6pm), closed Wed. The building is worth a visit in itself. _www.sfmoma.org_.

San Francisco Zoo, Sloat and 45th, 753-7080. It is the largest zoological park in N California. $11, 1st Wed of every month is free, 10am-5pm daily. _www.sfzoo.org_.

Seal Rocks: Cliff House, a spooky, Gothic-style reconstruction of a seaside resort on a cliff above the crashing sea. It offers a panorama from a walk-in _camera obscura_.

SoMA (South of Market): Anchor Brewing Company, 1705 Mariposa, 863-8350. See how SF's own Anchor Steam Beer is created. Tasting follows $1^1/2$ hr-2 hr tour, Mon-Fri 1pm. Resv in advance, up to 2 months, free. _www.anchorbrewing.com_.

St Mary's Cathedral, Geary & Gough. Almost extra-terrestrial in feeling, with a free-hanging meteor shower over the altar. 'Well worth seeing.' Free.

Telegraph Hill/Russian Hill: Romantic Telegraph Hill is topped by the Coit Tower, _www.coittower.org_. Does it look like the nozzle of a firehose to you? $3 for the elevator to the top. 10am-5pm daily. Russian Hill was the gathering place for bohemian writers, artists and poets, from Ambrose Bierce to George ('cool grey city of love') Sterling. It boasts not 1 but 3 steep streets that make it the most vertical district in SF. The most famous is, of course, **Lombard**, with its 8 switchbacks and 90-degree angles (almost impossible to photograph but featured in movies such as _What's Up Doc?_ and _Foul Play_). Telegraph Hill is also the home of a flock of wild red-and-green parrots, still there, which featured in _The Wild Parrots of Telegraph Hill_, a wonderful documentary that is as much about Mark Bittner, a dharma bum and customer at Cafe Trieste, who fell in with the endearing birds.

www.wildparrotsfilm.com. **Filbert** btwn Hyde and Leavenworth and **Union** btwn Polk and Hyde are also of notable verticality, although not as interesting (unless you have a manual transmission).

Union Square: City centre, named on the eve of the Civil War. In 1906, the square served as emergency camp for earthquake refugees. Nearby is **Maiden Lane**, once a red-hot red-light district, now a charming cul-de-sac with the only Frank Lloyd Wright building in the city and home to the **Xanadu Gallery**. A striking tunnel entrance and interior ramp leads to the entrance, the prototype for the Guggenheim Museum of New York City. The Gallery is at 140 Maiden Lane, 392-9999, free. *www.xanadugallery.us*. North at 130 Sutter is the progenitor of the modern glass skyscraper, the 1917 **Hallidie Building**. Superb stores abound; even Woolworth's is nice, although Gump's is the local landmark among them.

Entertainment

Whatever your sexual proclivities, it takes quite a bit of cash (and often a smart appearance) to explore the singles bars, meat-rack taverns and gay watering holes of SF. Some tips: go at happy hour, when drinks are cheaper and hors d'oeuvres available; Union St is hetero, Castro-Polk is gay. A better tip: SF has a high VD and herpes rate, and the action has calmed down considerably since the advent of AIDS. Emphasis is now on 'safe sex', but sex that's totally safe hasn't been invented. In unfamiliar environs, your best tip is to relax, enjoy the atmosphere and music, and save your hunting for your home turf.

The City's 'happening' nightlife scene is constantly changing due to fashion and nightclubs changing names or going bust (as in any city). The area south of Market is usually quite lively. The best sources of info for events, clubs, music are the *BAM* monthly, the free *Bay Guardian* (on Weds, *http://sfbayguardian.com*, which includes guide to nude beaches in Northern Cal*)* and the *Pink Datebook* in the Sunday *Chronicle* – see *SFGate. www.sfgate.com/chronicle.*

330 Ritch Street, between 3rd and 4th, 541-9574, in the heart of fashionable Mission district. Alternative, dance, and hiphop, cover around $5-$15.

Club Fugazi, 678 Green Street, 421-4222, Beach Blanket Babylon venue; the longest running production is SF—book in adv, tkts $25-$70. They serve liquor, so you must be 21 to enter! *www.beachblanketbabylon.com*.

DNA Lounge, 375 11th St, 626-1409. Subterranean disco-club open for all-night dancing. $10-$20 cover at weekends. *www.dnalounge.com*.

Edinburgh Castle, 950 Geary Street, 885-4074, a little bit of Scotland in SF; not the nicest part of town though. *www.posthoc.com/edinburghcastle.htm*.

Pier 23 Cafe, The Embarcadero, 362-5125. Cafe/nightclub, has bay view, funky atmosphere. Open Mon-Thu 11.30am-10pm, Sat 10am-10pm, Sun brunch 10am-3pm, music menu 3-9pm. *www.pier23cafe.com*.

Rasselas Jazz Club and Ethiopian Restaurant, 1534 Filmore St, 346-8696. Jazz, blues and cabaret-style evenings. Restaurant opens at 6pm, (bkfast and lunch 7am-2pm weekdays, 9am-3pm wkends), live music wk days 8pm, w/end 9pm, close at 2am. *www.rasselasjazzclub.com*.

Slim's, 333 11th St, 255-0333. No age limit, over 21's get a stamp entitling them to a drink. 'Good for local bands.' Cover and opening times depend on band. *www.slims-sf.com*.

Sigmund Stern Grove Concert Series, 19th Ave and Sloat Blvd, 252-6252. Bring a picnic and listen to opera/jazz/classical in a bower of eucalyptus and redwood trees. Free, Sun 2pm, mid-June-mid-Aug. *www.sterngrove.org*. Music, dance and theatre offerings are abundant; see the *Datebook*. **The San Francisco Symphony**, Davies Symphony Hall, Grove St, 864-6000, has inexpensive (around $19) open rehearsal seats; call for details, otherwise normal prices start at $20. Last minute tickets for centre terrace avail 2 hours before show time, *www.sfsymphony.org*.

Also: 'You can usually get a standing ticket for $10 cash at the **San Francisco Opera**

House, 301 Van Ness, 864-3330, on the day of performance. Otherwise student rush tickets are sometimes available, 2 hrs before for $15, call ahead. _www.sfopera.com_.
Festivals: San Francisco is home to so many festivals for so many varied interests that even a quick summation of the big ones would be impossible. Check with the _Guardian_ to see what's happening while you're in town.

Sport
For professional baseball lovers, the **Giants** play in the beautiful **PacBell Park**.The **49ers** professional football team play down on Gilman Ave at **3-Com Park**. Tickets for both teams can be very hard to come by so plan well in advance and check the web for specials: _www.sf49ers.com_ and _www.giants.mlb.com_.

Information
Redwood Empire Association, Pier 39 (upper level), within the **Californian Welcome Center**, 956-3493. This helpful and friendly organisation offers a free guidebook and info about all the 'Redwood' counties—SF and north. Open daily 10am-9pm. _www.redwoodempire.com_.
San Francisco Convention and Visitors Bureau Information Center, 900 Market at Powell in Hallidie Plaza and on Pier 39, 391-2000. Multilingual, helpful, open daily, _www.sfvisitor.org_.

Internet access
Main Library, Larkin & Grove Sts, across from the Civic Center, 557-4400, free (15 min limit).If you have your own laptop, the library is a Hotspot. _www.sfpl.org_.

Travel
San Francisco has a public transportation system that cities around the world envy, but its size and comprehensiveness can create confusion even for the locals. Feel free to ask for help or advice and avoid driving as much as possible. Parking in the city can cost as much as sleeping in the city and spots are harder to find than beds. Be sure to pick up BART, Golden Gate Transit and MUNI Maps, (all are free). The comprehensive _www.transitinfo.org_ is a godsend when it comes time to navigate the system.
A/C Transit services East Bay from Transbay Terminal, 817-1717. Often faster than BART in rush hours. _www.actransit.org_.
Amtrak, (800) USA-RAIL. Free shuttle from Ferry Building to Emeryville and from Transbay to Oakland depot where you get daily service on the _Coast Starlight_, _Capitol Corridor_, _California Zephyr_ and _San Joaquins_ trains.
BART, (510) 465-BART in East Bay. Sleek, carpeted, comfortable 'Bullet-Beneath-the-Bay,' connecting SF with Oakland, Berkeley, etc. Fares $1.25-6.05. BART ticket machines accept nickels, dimes, quarters, $1, $5, $10, and $20 bills; some accept credit and debit cards. Long waits during rush hours and on Sun. Service ends at midnight. _www.bart.gov_.
Caltrain and San Mateo Transit, (650) 817-1717 and (800) 660-4287 (locally), Frequent trains between SF and Gilroy (S of San Jose), but call for info; $2-9.50, depending on distance. NB: Some San Mateo bus routes do not accept luggage. _www.caltrain.com_.
Golden Gate Transit, 455-2000, operates the Golden Gate Bridge along with numerous ferries and buses; fares run between $2 and $5 each way, depending on distance and means. _www.goldengate.org_.
Green Tortoise Bus, 956-7500 or from outside CA, toll-free (800) TORTOISE. Counterculture service to East Coast, Baja, Alaska, Seattle, New Orleans, the Grand Canyon, Yosemite and just about anywhere, in converted old diesels with sleeping platforms. To everything there is a season—and the Tortoises migrate accordingly: Mexico in winter, Alaska in summer, California anytime. _www.greentortoise.com_.
Greyhound, 425 Mission St, 495-1569 or (800) 231-2222, open 24 hrs.

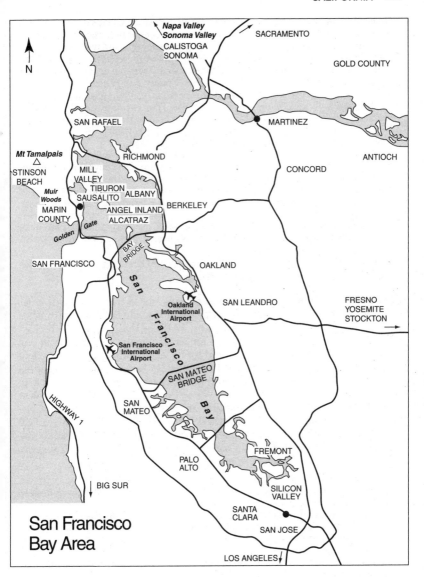

San Francisco
Bay Area

MUNI Local Transit, 673-MUNI. Began in 1912, now a 1000+ mile integrated network of buses, Metro streetcars, and cable cars with frequent service, friendly drivers and good transfer system. Basic fare is $1.50, inc free transfer. The fabled cable cars are $5 o/w. MUNI "Passports" allow unlimited rides on cable cars, buses, and streetcars for $11 all day, $18 for 3 days or $24 for 7 days plus discounts at participating museums and attractions. The MUNI "Weekly Pass" is $15 and allows for unlimited bus travel, (cable cars are an extra $1). Both are available at

Visitors Information Centres and cable car tix booths. Don't forget to pick up a MUNI map for $3 and 'make sure you get the front seat on the cable car for the best experience'. _www.sfmuni.com_. Also see _www.transitinfo.org_ for SF Bay area transit

San Francisco International Airport, (SFO) 12 miles S, (650) 761-0800, 744-7742. BART has rapid rail directly into the International Terminal at the airport ($4.95 from downtown), serving northern San Mateo County, San Francisco, and the East Bay, with a connection to Caltrain at Millbrae Station. Caltrain operates rail service to the Peninsula and South Bay between San Francisco and Gilroy. Weekday express trains operate between Millbrae and San Francisco during commute hours. For shuttle buses, of which there is bewildering array, see _www.toandfrom.org/airport/sanfrancisco.html_, _www.flysfo.com_.

Car Rental: Renting a car in San Francisco is probably the worst possible thing a traveller can do in this city. If you are forced to, be prepared to pay more to park the car than to rent it. **Thrifty Car Rental**, 229 7th St, (415) 621-8989, seems to offer the best value. There are massive daily surcharges for insurance, and those under 25 must pay an extra $25 per day, rsvs at least 1 week in advance during summer. _www.thrifty.com_.

For tours: Gray Line, Pier 43 Embarcadero 434-8687 or (888) 428-6937, Offers city tours, Muir Woods, Sausalito and Bay cruises from 1 hr to all day from $28-89. _www.graylinesanfrancisco.com_.

San Francisco Helicopter Tours, (800) 400-2404, 60-90 km flights over city and bay $130-170 per person. _www.sfhelicoptertours.com_.

BERKELEY and **OAKLAND** Like Siamese twins, these two neighbour cities blend imperceptibly into one another physically, while each demonstrates a personality of its own. Easily reached by BART or bus, this area—the East Bay—offers good day trips; Berkeley for its university and accompanying cultural and social dividends, Oakland for its Jack London Square, excellent lakeside museum, blues clubs and baseball team known as the 'Athletics'. Both cities are short on cheap lodgings and long on streets that are unsafe to walk at night.

In Berkeley concentrate on the area in and around the university, the closest you'll come to the fabled Berzerkley of free speech, anti-war, radical fame. 'Rather bohemian atmosphere, good for buying secondhand rare books, homemade trinkets or discussing Marxist ideology with a stranger in a coffeehouse.' *The telephone area code is 510.*

Accommodation
Easily the greatest challenge to visitors is trying to find somewhere cheap to sleep in the East Bay. One source is the advertised housing of the *Daily Californian*, the newspaper of the University of California, Berkeley. _www.dailycal.org._ Also, try the 35 UC Berkeley fraternities—easy access to city and inexpensive. _www.calgreeks.com/chapters_, 'but for that price, who cares?' Each fraternity determines for itself whether or not to accept guests, and policies are subject to change. If the frats turn you down (or vice versa), here are some more possibilities:
Motel 6, 8480 Edes, at Oakland airport, 638-1180, S-$49.
YMCA, 2001 Allston Way, Berkeley, 848-6800. S$39-46, D$50-60 includes use of facilities. _www.baymca.org/index.php/d_hotel.html._

Food
Berkeley For all East Bay places to eat and to check out menus, visit _www.themenu-page.com/eastbay.html_.
Blondie's Pizza, 2340 Telegraph, 548-1129. Delicious slices for $3.50.
Cafe Milano, 2522 Bancroft, 644-3100. Nicknamed 'Cafe Pretentious'. 'This is a

must if you're going to sample the atmosphere of Berkeley properly.' **Cheeseboard**, 1504 Shattuck Ave., 549-3191, this bakery and accompanying pizza parlor three doors down has both the crowds and the critics raving. Apple-apricot muffins from $1.50. http://cheeseboardcollective.coop.

Crèpes a Go Go, 2125 University Ave., 841-7722, and 2334 Telegraph, 486-2310. Ooh la la, these 'fantastically delicious crepes' will have you coming back for more. Daily 8:30am-9/10 pm.

Pasand, 2286 Shattuck, 549-2559. Indian food, excellent and cheap. www.pasand.com.

Spenger's, 1919 4th, 845-7771. Forget Fisherman's Wharf, this is the Bay Area institution for seafood. Happy hour Mon-Fri 4pm-6pm & 9:30pm-11pm. www.themenupage.com/spengers.html.

With the exception of the multi-lingual and multi-ethnic **International House** at the top of Bancroft, avoid the expensive and drab univ. cafeterias.

Of interest

On campus: Black Oak Books, 1491 Shattuck, 486-0698. Open 10am-10pm daily, with new and used books on all subjects. Readings most evenings at 7.30pm, often given by some very well-known authors and poets. 'A gem, Go!' www.blackoakbooks.com. **Lawrence Hall of Science**, Centennial Dr, 642-5132, sits above campus in the Berkeley hills, take bus #65 from downtown. Open daily 10am-5pm, $9.50, $7.50 w/student ID. www.lawrencehallofscience.org. 'Top of the mountain, excellent view, amazing museum, spent whole afternoon playing computer games.' Both the **Campanile (Sather Tower)** in the centre of campus and the Lawrence Hall of Science on the hill above, have excellent views of Berkeley and the bay. Spot the football stadium that rests directly atop the Hayward fault, a branch of the San Andreas; a large vertical crack may be seen through the upper tier. The Main Library (where Mario Savio and Joan Baez addressed the first major student demonstration against the Vietnam War in 1964) has the world's largest collection of Mark Twain materials. 'Try the browsing room (Morrison Room)— British newspapers, headphones to listen to records.' The **Phoebe Hearst Museum of Anthropology**, adjacent to Kroeber Hall, 642-3682, has excellent Indian costumes and crafts, $4, students $1. Wed-Sat 10am-4.30pm, Sun from noon, free on Thu. hearstmuseum.berkeley.edu. The **University Art Museum**, 2626 Bancroft Way, 642-0808, is home to video, performance art and modern works, $8, $5 w/student ID. Wed-Sun, 11am-5pm; Thur 11am-7pm, closed Mon/Tues. 'Not worth it.' Also located in the museum building is the **Pacific Film Archives**, 2675 Bancroft, 642-0808. Nightly showing, more at term time. $8 for the first show, $5 w/student IDs. www.bampfa.berkeley.edu.

Off campus: Telegraph Ave is the figurative, if not the literal, heart of Berkeley. This was the street that gave birth to both 1960's revolutionaries and 1980's punks. Throughout the decades the drag has stayed true to its roots and is now home to countless coffee shops, record stores, tattoo parlours, restaurants, street people and various student politics. **Tilden Park**, in the Berkeley Hills, rests high above the anarchy below and allows visitors a stunning bay vista.

Amoeba Music, 2455 Telegraph Ave, 549-1125, this legendary establishment hosts the best and largest collection of obscure and underground music on the west coast. www.amoebamusic.com.

Moe's Bookstore, 2476 Telegraph, 849-2087. Huge and politically hip—4 floors of books. Daily 10am-11pm. www.moesbooks.com.

Takara Sake USA Inc., 708 Addison at 4th, 540-8250. Museum, video and free tastings of wine and sake, noon-6pm daily. www.takarasake.com.

Oakland: Jack London Sq, 10 mins from BART City Center station. Visit Jack London's cabin from his Klondike days, have a drink at the First and Last Chance Saloon, where London and RL Stevenson used to tipple. 'Village is excellent reconstruction of the wharf area.' In the square you'll find **Yoshi's Jazz House**, 510 Embarcadero West, 238-9200, here Jazz and Sushi meet in harmony at the bay's best jazz spot. Resv req, *www.yoshis.com*.

Lake Merritt, downtown Oakland, is the largest saltwater lake within a US city; overlooking it is the **Oakland Museum** at 1000 Oak St (Lake Merritt BART Stn), 238-2200. Art, history and natural science of California—interesting. $8, $5 w/student ID. Wed-Sat 10am-5pm, Sun noon-5pm, first Fri of the month open 'til 9pm. *www.museumca.org*.

Entertainment/Sport
Berkeley: Ashkenaz, 1317 San Pablo, 525-5054. Multi-ethnic folk dancing. 'Cheap fun.' *www.ashkenaz.com*.

Freight and Salvage Coffeehouse, 1111 Addison St, 548-1761. Mixed bag of traditional country, bluegrass, ethnic groups and comedy. No alcohol or smoking! Daily 7.30pm-midnight. *www.freightandsalvage.org*.

Blakes on Telegraph, 2367 Telegraph, 848-0886. Big-name hiphop, funk and rock bands. 'Lively restaurant/bar with good local bands.' 'Lively part is downstairs.' Daily food served 11:30 am - midnight, 7 days a week; $5-$9 a dish. Cover $10. *www.blakesontelegraph.com*.

Triple Rock, 1920 Shattuck, 843-2739, a great bar with beer brewed on premises, enjoy one on their redwood deck. *www.triplerock.com*.

See the **Oakland A's** baseball team at the **Coliseum**, 568-5600. Tickets $9-36. *www.oaklandathletics.com*.

Survival
Berkeley Free Clinic, 2339 Durant, 548-2570. Mon-Fri they offer medical service from 7pm to 10pm. Call during the afternoon for a same-day appointment. On Sat, offers a women's clinic; on Sun, an STD clinic. *www.berkeleyfreeclinic.org*.

Information/Travel
A/C Transit, 839-2931, extensively serves the East Bay, *www.actransit.org*.

Oakland International Airport, 563-3300. *www.flyoakland.com.* Take bus or BART to Colosseum station, AirBART bus from there ($2), every 10-20 mins, Mon-Sat from 5am, Sun from 8.30am. 465-BART, *www.bart.gov/guide/airport/oak.asp.* NB: this is the airport to fly into if you are visiting the Bay. It is considerably cheaper than SF and more accessible.

UC/Berkeley Shuttle, 643-5708. From Berkeley BART stations to campus, Botanical Gardens, Hall of Science, etc. Fare $0.50-1.00, 7am-9pm w/days only, limited service during summer. *http://pt.berkeley.edu/beartransit.*

SANTA CRUZ-MONTEREY This stretch of coast rivals the section north of San Francisco in its scenic beauty. Not nearly so unpopulated, though—tiny hamlets and larger towns line Hwy 1 (also known in this area as the Cabrillo Hwy). The first major city, **Santa Cruz**, is 90 miles S of SF and similarly suffered considerable damage in the October '89 earthquake. Jumping nightlife, lots of movies and bookstores, surfers aplenty and a rowdy beach and boardwalk scene earn the town its name, as pronounced by natives: 'Sanna Cruize.' The **University of California** campus, home of the 'Battling Banana Slugs', is a special jewel. Eight colleges, independent of one another are hidden in the redwoods on a hill above the town; can you find them all?

Nearby is **Capitola-by-the-Sea**, a doll's village of Victorian houses and beach bungalows; its name comes from the days when this sleepy seaside resort was California's capital *www.capitola.com*. Catch the Begonia Festival if you're here in September. Further south are the towns of **Soquel/Aptos**.

Around the curve of the **Monterey Bay**, the towns of **Pacific Grove, Monterey, Pebble Beach** and **Carmel-by-the-Sea** cluster on a knob of land jutting out into the Pacific. Here, the cheap glitz of the Santa Cruz boardwalk gives way to much more expensive glitz, and the soft warm beauty of the coast turns angular, dramatic and cold. You don't need to shell out $8.50 for the **17-Mile Drive** to see it, though—bike it for free, or just north of the drive is an even more beautiful stretch, beginning at Ocean View Blvd and 3rd St in Pacific Grove: **Sunset Drive**, which also happens to be the best time to see it. And it's also free. *www.santacruzca.org* has links to restaurants, clubs and more and *www.carmel-california.com* about all the goings on in the area. *The telephone area code is 831, except San Jose, 408.*

Survival
This is a resort area, which means the necessities of life—food and shelter—tend to be treated as luxuries here: you can spend exorbitant amounts on either. Fortunately, Santa Cruz has a culture that generally welcomes students, transients or people who combine both qualities at once; the Monterey and Carmel area can be hostile to the same.

Accommodation
HI-Monterey Hostel, 778 Hawthorne St, Monterey, (831) 649-0375;. $20-23 dorm incl linen, private rm $54 up. *www.montereyhostel.com.*

HI-Pigeon Point Lighthouse Hostel, 210 Pigeon Point Rd, **Pescadero**, (Hwy 1, 50 miles S of San Francisco), (650) 879-0633, perched on a cliff on the central California coast, the 115 ft Pigeon Point Lighthouse is one of America's tallest. It has been guiding mariners since 1872. Today the boardwalk behind the fog signal building guides whale watchers eyes during the whales' annual migration. Walk through the tidepool area or through the amazing 1,000 yr old redwoods nearby. Dorms are $18 (members), $25 (non-members); private rooms from $46; outdoor hot tub and kitchen. Rsvs essential. *www.norcalhostels.org.*

HI-Point Montara Lighthouse Hostel, 16th St at Hwy 1, 25 miles S of San Francisco, (650) 728-7177. Restored lighthouse in an exceptionally beautiful place. Explore the coastline and watch the annual migration of gray whales btwn Nov and April. Several great beaches for swimming, surfing, jogging, horseback riding and windsurfing. $18-$21, private room $54. *www.norcalhostels.org.*

HI-San Jose Sanborn Park Hostel, 15808 Sanborn Rd, **Saratoga**, (408) 741-0166. This beautiful log house hostel is surrounded by a forest of redwoods and madrones in Sanborn County Park. It's also close to the Winchester Mystery House, the Rosicrucian Egyptian Museum and the Technology Center Museum. $14 HI, $16 non-HI. *www.sanbornparkhostel.org.*

HI-Santa Cruz Hostel, 321 Main St, **Santa Cruz**, 423-8304. 15 min walk from Greyhound. Hostel is located at the Carmelita Cottages (restored 1870's cottages), on Beach Hill. Only 2 blocks from beach, boardwalk, amusement park, and wharf; 5 blocks from downtown. Extensive bus system makes this a great starting point to state parks in the nearby mountains. Outside lockers store bags of early arrivals, garden, fireplace, barbecue, free evening snack. $18, $21 (non-members). 3 night maximum,11pm curfew. Rsvs essential in summer *www.hi-santacruz.org.*

Discover Inn, 1106 Fremont Blvd, **Seaside**, 394-3113. 1 block from Monterey, close to beach, $59-79 during summer, (less in winter). 'Good accommodation.'

Camping: Big Sur Campground and Cabins, 667-2322. Rsvs essential in summer. 2 miles N of Pfeiffer-Big Sur State Park on Hwy 1, 26 miles S of Carmel. This and other campgrounds at *www.bigsurcalifornia.org/camping.html*.

Food
Generally, be wary of any restaurant that caters too obviously to the tourist trade.

Plenty of places, particularly in Santa Cruz, have a reputation with the locals for serving overpriced, mediocre food; the restaurants in Monterey and Carmel are merely overpriced. Here are some eateries that are more in line with a hungry budget traveller's needs:

Charlie Hong Kong, several locations, orig. at 1141 Soquel Ave, 426-5664, **Santa Cruz**, this fast and filling noodle joint gets rave reviews for both its creativity and its prices. Check it out—daily 11am-11pm. _www.charliehongkong.com_.

Mr Toots, 221A Esplanade, **Capitola**, 475-3679. Grab a bran muffin and watch the seagulls from the outside deck. 'A bargain!' Daily 7am-10.30/11.30pm.

Village Corner, Dolores & 6th, **Carmel**, 624-3588. Mediterranean food from $8 at lunchtime, good bfasts around $8, 'try the eggs Benedict', informal setting. Daily 7am-10pm. _www.carmelsbest.com/villagecorner_.

Zachary's, 819 Pacific, **Santa Cruz**, 427-0646. Huge, good bfasts for cheap. Go early unless you're keen on queues!

Of interest

Coming down Hwy 1 from SF, you get to **Pt Ano Nuevo State Beach** before Santa Cruz. If it's winter, you may be able to see breeding elephant seals lazing in the rookery there. Critters of another sort romp on the area's nude beaches. Coming into town, glimpse **UC Santa Cruz** on the swelling green hills to your left; from roads leading to its colleges nestled in the trees, you can get spectacular views of Monterey Bay. The vista from **Cowell College** is particularly good.

If you get weary of squishing discarded hot dogs btwn your toes, wander over to the **Pacific Garden Mall**, which has organic restaurants, organic clothing stores and organic people roaming the streets. Just north of the boardwalk is West Cliff Drive, which leads to **Natural Bridges State Beach**, 423-4609, though only one of the sandstone bridges still stands. _www.parks.ca.gov/default.asp?page_id=541_.

Roaring Camp & Big Trees Narrow Gauge Railroad, 335-4484. Its $20 round trip from Santa Cruz to Felton, or Felton to Bear Mountain through redwoods, $18, takes place on original 19th century steam trains. Call for times, _www.roaringcamp.com_.

Also, stick around for a number of festivals around the beginning of July, such as the annual **Tahiti Fete** in Santa Cruz Wharf, a Polynesian dance competition with arts & crafts, music and dancing. _www.santacruzwharf.com_. **Cannery Row**, **Monterey**, once immortalized by John Steinbeck, the defunct sardine canneries now make wonderful homes for little shops. Open daily 8am-7pm. _www.canneryrow.com_. There's a Steinbeck Festival here every August.

Kalisa's La Ida Café, 851 Cannery Row, **Monterey**, 644-9316, was once a brothel, now they serve great cups of coffee and have belly-dancing at night. Across the street, the more cerebral **Monterey Bay Aquarium**, 886 Cannery Row, 648-4888, displays species native to the Monterey Bay in huge tank settings so natural that visitors get the impression that they are the ones behind glass. Daily, 10am-6pm in summer; $19.95, $17.95 w/student ID. 'Great value for money. Fantastic for biologists and non-biologists alike.' _www.mbayaq.org_.

Carmel is an acquired taste. The town draws hordes of curiosity seekers, all of whom want to catch a glimpse of actor and one-time mayor Clint Eastwood at his Hog's Breath Inn, at San Carlos and 5th. You won't, but stop by anyway for a look, maybe a drink—in a setting that would make Bilbo Baggins feel right at home.

The Mission, Rio Rd off Hwy 1, **Carmel**, 624-1271, $1/2$ mile from downtown, has a star-shaped window framed by vines, fountains and flowers, $4. The white sand beach nearby is great for running barefoot on but don't attempt to swim in the cold and treacherous surf, open Mon-Fri 9:30am-4:30pm, wkends 10.30am-4:30pm _www.carmelmission.org_.

Point Lobos State Reserve, 624-4909, 2 miles S of Carmel. Monterey-Salinas Transit stops here several times a day, on its way to Big Sur. $8 p/car, walkers get in free.

(You can park your car on the hwy and walk in to avoid the fee!) 450 acres of natural beauty: coves, islands, fearless animals and birds. Best of all are China Cove and the beach beyond (take lunch). Daily 9am-7pm. *www.pointlobos.org.*

Pfeiffer-Big Sur State Park, 667-2315, is only one tiny part of the 90 mile stretch of scissored coastline btwn Carmel and San Simeon known as 'Big Sur'. The stretch is almost pristine and wholly soul satisfying. Pay for entrance to one park in California and get into any other state park free, otherwise it's $5. Do stop on Hwy 1 for the obligatory open-air quaff and sea gaze at **Nepenthe**, 667-2345, an ambrosia burger perhaps? This was originally the home of Rita Hayworth and Orson Welles; **Cafe Amphora** on the lower deck actually has the better view. Big Sur was home to the beats and Henry Miller and today continues to be inhabited (sparsely) by rugged individualists. *www.nepenthebigsur.com.*

Information
Carmel Tourist Information Center, on San Carlos between 5th and 6th Sts, 624-2522, open Mon-Fri 9am-5pm. *www.carmelcalifornia.org.*

Monterey Visitors Center, Daily 9am-6pm, Lake El Estero at Franklin & Camino 649-1770, and **Monterey Convention and Visitors Bureau**, 150 Oliver St, 657-6400. Mon-Fri 9am-5pm. *www.montereyinfo.org.*

Santa Cruz County Visitors Council, 1211 Ocean St., 425-1234. *www.santacruzca.org.*

Travel
Greyhound, 425 Front St (downtown Santa Cruz), 423-1800, has service from SF to Monterey. Daily 7am-6.45pm.

Monterey-Salinas Transit, 899-2551 (from Monterey), 424-7695 (from Salinas). $2 per zone, free transfers. Or get an all day pass for $4.50-9. All downtown routes stop at Munras/Tyler/Pearl St triangle. Serves Monterey, Pacific Grove and Carmel; spring and summer service to Big and Little Sur as far as Nepenthe. *www.mst.org.*

Santa Cruz Metro, 425-8600. Lots of routes, $1.50 each way or $4.50 for the day. *www.scmtd.com.*

SAN LUIS OBISPO and SANTA BARBARA COUNTIES

Called the central coast, this region stretches from Big Sur south to Santa Barbara. Among its highlights are **San Simeon**, site of **Hearst Castle**, built by William Randolph Hearst, newspaper magnate and the *Citizen Kane* of Orson Welles' film. This Spanish-style castle houses Hearst's $75 million art collection, which includes now-priceless tapestries, rugs, jade, statuary, even entire antique ceilings and fireplaces and assorted loot from all over Europe, including Cardinal de Richelieu's bed. 'A two-hour trip into paradise.' *www.hearstcastle.com.*

Further down the coast, **Morro Rock** makes a monolithic landmark at water's edge, the first in a series of volcanic peaks that march picturesquely through San Luis Obispo County. You can follow them along Hwy 1 (also the bus route). Beaches and camping opportunities abound; the amiable character of the inland town of **San Luis Obispo** adds to the area's appeal.

South of Morro Bay on Hwy 101 is **Solvang**, a charming coastal replica of a Danish town: 'worth a visit with its reasonably priced accommodation and restaurants'. *www.solvangca.com.* Further south, **Santa Barbara** beckons. Far and away it is the loveliest of coastal cities, from its setting against the Santa Ynez Mountains to its beautiful Spanish adobe architecture. Despite its wealth, Santa Barbara is a non-stuffy, youthful city, with a big UC campus, sophisticated nightlife and the best sidewalk cafe idling anywhere in the US. Readers constantly comment on this 'elegant little town with a lot happening', and the area's 'beautiful unspoilt beaches'. It's also the home and location (Santa Teresa) used by Ross Macdonald in his detective stories, and current resident Sue Grafton's *A to Q*, etc., gumshoe Kinsey Millhone. *www.suegrafton.com*.

The telephone area code is 805.

Accommodation

Farm Hostel, PO Box 723, **Ojai**, CA 93024, 646-0311. An independent backpackers lodge located in the beautiful Ojai Valley, gateway to the Southern California outback. It's a central location, (50 miles N of LA, a 40 min drive from Santa Barbara and 20 min from Ventura Beach), close to hot springs. Their 12 beds require phone resv and a passport but they will pick up from the Ventura Greyhound, $15. *www.hostelhandbook.com/farmhostel*.

HI-San Luis Obispo SLO Hostel, 1617 Santa Rosa St, 544-4678, a gateway to Big Sur, the hostel is within walking distance of downtown shops, restaurants and theatres. Don't miss the downtown Farmer's Market every Thur night! With its ideal year-round climate, San Luis Obispo is a mecca for outdoor enthusiasts. Members are $18, non-members-$20 for dorm beds. Private rooms-D-$45-55. All hostellers enjoy homemade sourdough pancakes each morning and those who stay longer than 3 days get a bike for a day (otherwise $10), fac inc laundry, patio, barbecue, sports equipment and a beautiful garden. Resv private rooms way in advance, *www.hostelobispo.com*.

Hotel State St, 121 State St, **Santa Barbara**, 966-6586. 'Excellent; staff very nice and helpful.' *www.hotelstatestreet.com*.

Santa Barbara Tourist Hostel, 134 Chapala St, 963-0154, near excellent bars and shopping, dorms-$21, private rooms-$65 (shared bath). *www.sbhostel.com*.

Camping: Morro Bay State Park info line: 772-7434/(800) 444-7275 for all parks in the area. $11-25 tent sites hold up to 8 people. Camping available at **San Simeon** and **Atascadero Beach**. *www.parks.ca.gov/default.asp?page_id=594.*

Of Interest

UC Santa Barbara and **Cal Poly** (San Luis Obispo) are two of the biggest party schools in the country and a visit to either of these cities would not be complete without finding out why. Cal Poly throws the biggest Mardi Gras party outside of New Orleans while UC Santa Barbara revels in its status as the stereotypical S. CA party school. **Isla Vista** is the capital of said revelry. This small densely populated student ghetto sees near nightly hysteria break out on its main drag, Del Playa, as students blow off the stresses that beautiful weather, surfing, drinking, copulating, and the occasional book inherently bring. Don't drive if you've been drinking and, when the streets start clearing off at midnight, follow the crowds indoors (the police strongly enforce a midnight curfew).

Farmers Market on Higuera Street, San Luis Obispo, every Thurs evening, 6pm-9pm—stalls, music, food.

Giant Chessboard, Embarcadero at Front, Morro Bay. The local chess club plays each Sat noon-5pm, on a 16'16' board with redwood pieces that weigh as much as a small child! Possible to rent during the week. $38 all day.

Hearst Castle, State Hwy 1, 927-2020. Incredible palatial over-indulgence of 1930s. The influence for Xanadu in *Citizen Kane*, and where William Randolph Hearst entertained presidents, kings and Hollywood stars. 'Absolutely fascinating.' Book at least a day in adv, (800) 444-4445. $24 for one of four tours covering different aspects of the castle; $30 for evening tour. 'Take Tour 2 or 3—smaller groups, more personal and informative.' Each tour lasts about 2 hrs. Take in the 'companion film' also, which documents the history of the castle and is shown on a 5-storey screen, daily 8am-3pm. *www.hearstcastle.org*.

Old Mission Santa Barbara, upper end of Laguna St, Santa Barbara, 682-4713. Noble facade with columns and towers, many unusual touches, from Moorish fountain to Mexican skulls in the 1786 'Queen of the Missions.' *www.sbmission.org*. More beautiful still is the **County Courthouse**, Osos & Palm Sts: a 1929 Hispano-Moorish treasure, inside and out.

Festivals: Robert Burns Night in San Luis Obispo, January 24th. Celebration features Scottish foods, music and dancing! First w/end May is the **Annual Garden Festival**, San Luis Obispo. Call the local Chamber of Commerce at 781-2777 for more info. In Santa Barbara, the **International Film Festival** is held at diff dates in the Spring and is host to premieres and screenings of international and American films. Call 963-0023 for more info. *www.sbfilmfestival.org*. **The Ojai Music Festival**, first weekend in June, is an outdoor classical music festival featuring world-renowned musicians and an arts and crafts show. Call 646-2094. *www.ojaifestival.org*. In July, the **Santa Barbara County Fair** in Santa Maria is a 4-day celebration including nightly performances by nationally known musicians, arts & crafts, carnival and food. Contact (800) 549-0036. *www.santamariafairpark.com*. Don't miss the **Santa Barbara Chumash Pow Wow** in mid-Sept, where more than 300 dancers represent 40 tribes in a Native American dance competition and features traditional arts and crafts.

Food
In Santa Barbara: **Joe's Cafe**, 536 State St, 966-4638: 'bustling atmosphere, lashings of food at low prices; a favourite student meeting place'.
The Natural Café, 508 State St, 962-9494. Healthy sandwiches and delicious smoothies. Under $6. *www.thenaturalcafe.com.*
Freebird's Burritos, 879 Embarcadero Del Mar, **Isle Vista**, (803) 968-0123, some Santa Barbara students eat nothing else during their 4+ here.
In SLO: Your best bet for food is to head for Higuera St. Try **Big Sky Café**, 1121 Broad St, 545-5401; *www.bigskycafe.com* and **Woodstock's Pizza Parlor**, 1000 Higuera St, 541-4420, for good chow. *www.woodstocksslo.com/pg/AboutUs.htm#*.

YOSEMITE An Oxford don once said, 'Think in centuries.' In Yosemite, it's inescapable. Cut in jewel facets by a glacial knife, the park encompasses nearly 1,200 square miles of incredible beauty—luminous lakes and dashing streams; groves of redwood elder statesmen and aged incense cedar; salt-and pepper boulders comically abandoned in boggy alpine meadows by the retreating glaciers of past millennia.

People bemoan the popularity of Yosemite, but not even four million visitors per year can ruin it. One-third of them choose to jam the park between July and August, and most of those content themselves with a stay in Yosemite Valley (just call it 'nature's parking lot'), leaving vast areas untrampled. Despite its congestion, you shouldn't miss the Valley's supreme vistas of **Bridalveil Falls** and **Glacier Point**, as well as the steel-blue shoulders of Half Dome and El Capitan. A mountaineers' heaven, **Half Dome** is the sheerest cliff in America, just 7% off vertical, and a full day's hike (summer only) for those who choose not to suffer from vertigo. **El Capitan** is the biggest block of exposed granite in the world and so vast that you need binoculars to see the climbers who take up to a week to scale it.

A fine way to see the park is to travel up Hwy 41 from Fresno to the south entrance near **Mariposa Grove**, the home of the Giant Sequoias, *www.redwoodsinyosemite.com/sequoias.htm*. The exit from **Wawona Tunnel** into the valley is absolutely spine-tingling. If you have the time, don't leave the park right after seeing the valley. Instead, take the high road, Hwy 120, over **Tioga Pass** towards shimmering and endangered **Mono Lake**. Continue south on Hwy 395 through **Owens Valley**, a neglected gem in a dusty corner of the state where **Mt Whitney** is visible from the highway.

Open year-round, Yosemite Valley is at its best in spring and early autumn; in summer visitors pay for the beautiful weather by watching the once spectacular waterfalls fade to a trickle. Winter is the time hardy souls and true Yosemite afficionados love best. With the season's first dusting of snow, the valley becomes a stark, eerie, white-on-black tableau—a living Ansel Adams photograph. A 7-day pass to the park is $20 per vehicle or $10 each for hikers. 'Keep your ticket—checked on exit.' More info at _www.nps.gov/yose_.

The telephone area code is 209.

Accommodation
Within the park: More than any other spot in California, you must book cabin, lodge or camping accommodation well in advance to avoid disappointment. _www.nps.gov/yose/trip/camping.htm._ 'Urbanised' campsites can be reserved through MISTIX, (800) 365-2267. Book on the internet at _reservations.nps.gov/index.cfm_.

Outside Park: Motel 6, 1410 V St, Merced, 384-2181. From $44. _www.motel6.com_.

HI-Midpines—Yosemite Bug Hostel, 6979 Hwy 140, **Midpines**, 966-6666. So-called because its 'infectious' nature!, this hostel is 20 miles E from Yosemite in several forested acres. The area is great for cycling and mountain biking, skiing, rafting and, of course, hiking. 'Clean, comfortable and set in a beautiful location.' 'Fantastic! Can't recommend this place enough!' Tent cabins are $30-$50, private room with shared baths-$40-$70 while dorms are $15-18 and campsites are available for $17. Free wireless internet. _www.yosemitebug.com_.

Campsites: Sunnyside, Tioga Pass and Bridalveil: $12 for a walk-in, and your only hope if you haven't booked way in advance. If you have a wilderness permit it is possible to take the shuttle to **Backpacker's Camp**, a quiet retreat behind North Pine's campground. _www.nps.gov/yose/wilderness/specialuse.htm._

Other cabins: For reservations at **Curry Village, Yosemite Lodge, White Wolf Lodge and Housekeeping Camp**, call (559) 252-4848. Curry Village offers tent or wooden cabins for $108. Some have commented that you can 'pay for 2, fit 6 in'! but that it 'was too cold to get undressed when I was there in Sept'. Showers 'often overtaxed.' _www.yosemitepark.com/content2hdr.cfm?SectionID=26&PageID=54_   At **Housekeeping Camp**, 1 mile S of Yosemite Village, $67, mattress beds (sans bedding) are provided in three-wall concrete shelters. Summer only. _www.yosemitepark.com/content2col.cfm?SectionID=27&PageID=59._

Food
Food is costly and often poor in the park. Readers recommend Yosemite Valley's burger shop and pizza house. The **Recovery Café** at The Yosemite Bug Hostel offers bfast, pack lunches, dinners, espresso drinks, beer and wine on tap, pool table and games in the rustic Main Lodge with view decks. Grocery stores, restaurants and cafeterias are located at Yosemite Valley, Curry Village, Wawona, Tioga Lake, White Wolf, Fish Camp, El Portal and Tuolumne Meadows.

Of interest
Everything! If you're adventurous, climb **Half Dome** by hiking around to the back via a 17-mile round-trip trail and hauling yourself up a stiff cable-and-slats 'stairway' to the top. The payoff is the view: the panorama of Yosemite Valley and beyond, and the dizzying drop-off from the cliff. Beware, though, the cost of the

view could be your life if you're not prepared. Half Dome is a serious hike and requires a full day, sturdy shoes, gloves (have you ever tried to pull yourself up 1,000 vertical feet of steel cable with your bare hands) and more water than you'd expect. Try hiking **Nevada Falls** first; climb up to **Vernal Falls**, through the **Mist Trail** (a serious understatement), then follow the river up to the face of the Nevada Falls; on your way back down swing along the ridges of the Panorama trail and pant into the drinking fountain at the base of Vernal. 'Met a bear—terrifying.' If all this sounds a bit much, hike (or drive) to Glacier Point for an unbeatable view of the whole valley.

Information
Park Information, (559) 253-5635 has info on lodging in the park. *www.yosemitepark.com.*
Visitors Center, 372-0200 at village mall in Yosemite Valley. Shuttle bus stop #6 & #9. Open daily 8am-8pm.

Travel
Service to Yosemite from Merced: **VIA Adventures Bus Line,** from the Greyhound Depot in Merced, 384-1315 . *www.via-adventures.com.*
Tours: Yosemite Tours, (888) 307-6194. Various 1-3 day tours from San Francisco. Rsvs nec. $121+, *www.yosemitetours.us.*
Incredible Adventures, 350 Townsend St, San Francisco, (800) 777-8464. Run 1-3 day tours to Yosemite from San Francisco. $129+. *www.incadventures.com.*
Green Tortoise also runs 2 and 4-day adventure tours for $114/$154+food from San Francisco, 1-800-TORTOISE. *www.greentortoise.com.*
Driving: Park open year-round except Hwy 120 at Tioga Pass. Fill up on gas before you enter the Park!

SEQUOIA-KINGS CANYON NATIONAL PARKS These two parks, established around 1890 and administered jointly since WWII, straddle a magnificent cross-section of the high Sierras, including 14,495-ft **Mt Whitney**, the highest peak in the lower 48 states. Here you'll find the beautiful and impetuous **Kings River**, remnants of Indian camps, and wildlife that may venture into view in early morning or at dusk. Here, too, stand giant sequoia; like their redwood cousins along the coast, these trees are survivors of Ice Ages and lumber companies. One of their number, the 2500-year-old **General Sherman**, is the world's most massive living thing, in all its 275-foot-high, 2145-ton glory. **Congress Trail** leads away from the general's shadow and delves 2 miles into the depths of the Giant Forest.

Access to the parks is by road from the west and southwest or by foot from the east. Bus service is available from Visalia to trailheads on both sides of the Sierras. 'Road to Owens Valley gives very pretty views and climbs to about 4000 ft above sea level.' *www.nps.gov/seki* has its own virtual visitor centre.

The telephone area code is 559.

Accommodation
Outside parks: The remote location keeps the crowds out of both your view and park lodgings, leaving little reason to stay in the small, boring and, quite frankly, ugly towns that surround the park. If a random summer weekend, however, finds the crowds out in force and you in a pinch, check the parks' web page. It has a valuable database with links to extra-park lodging opportunities.
In parks: Camping: $20, no rsvs required as getting a site 'shouldn't be a problem,' according to rangers, or call (800) 365-2267. Free backcountry camping with permit

(resv for $10 fee) or pick up at Visitor's Centre. Also, free camping is avail on Sequoia National Forest lands near park.

Information/Travel
Sequoia and Kings Canyon National Park Information, 565-3341, gives general information for both parks. For **backpacking** info call 565-3708. 'Helpful and informative.' Parks open year-round, 24 hours. $10 p/vehicle for 7-day access. Access via hwys 198 and 180.

DEATH VALLEY NATIONAL PARK Covering 3.3 million acres, most of them about a million miles from nowhere, Death Valley has cornered the market on hottest, driest and lowest (282 ft below sea level) place in the US (interestingly, less than 100 miles from Mt Whitney, the highest point in the lower 48). High peaks ringing the valley prohibit moisture, and white sand and hills reflect light in a blinding glare. But the definition of Death Valley is heat: one July day in 1972, Furnace Creek lived up to its name with a ground reading of 201 degrees (that's not a typo), while the air maintained a balmy 128 degrees.

Late October to early May is the sanest time to gaze at the tortured landscapes of **Zabriskie Point** and **Dante's View**, climb the **Ubehebe Crater**, explore **Scotty's Castle**, and slide on the sensuous sand dunes at **Stovepipe Wells**. Scotty's Castle is no prospector's shack. Located 60 mi. north of Furnace Creek this $2 million, 18-room Spanish fortress with an 1100-pipe organ, a large waterfall in the living room and other astonishing features was built by a wealthy midwestern businessman. Scotty, however, was a local and colourful con man who convinced newspapers, neighbours and the IRS that it was his. Tours daily 9am-5pm last 1 hr and cost $11; call 786-2392. Always dramatic, the desert can bring forth storms of wildflowers in March and April as suddenly as it does storms of water or sand. _www.nps.gov/deva/Scottys/Scottys_main.htm._

Visitor Information at Park headquarters, **Furnace Creek**, 786-2331, has a museum of geological interest; also info at Scotty's Castle. _www.nps.gov/deva_. _The telephone area code is 760._

Accommodation
Death Valley lies 300 miles NE of Los Angeles and 135 miles NW of Las Vegas; the only bus is from Las Vegas. Park lodging boils down to **camping** for $10-$16 per site, the costly **Furnace Creek Ranch**, 786-2345, _www.furnacecreekresort.com_, and the **Stove Pipe Wells Motel**, 786-2387, _www.stovepipewells.com_. 'During summer, arrive by 6pm. Otherwise no key.' Both located on Highway 190. A cheaper option is the gas station/motel at **Panamint Springs**, 10 miles W of the park. 'A welcome relief in the middle of nowhere.'
HI-Desertaire Death Valley Hostel, 2000 Old Spanish Trail Hwy, 852-4580. Only 1 hr drive from Death Valley National Monument, the hostel is an excellent base to explore desert peaks and canyons. Don't miss the free **Tecopa Hot Springs Baths**— 107 F natural mineral water located just 3 miles from hostel. Also, hiking, biking, patio, watchtower deck, laundry, volleyball. Camping $15; rooms $45-$55. _www.tecopahotsprings.org/baths.html_.

JOSHUA TREE NATIONAL PARK In the high desert 54 miles east of Palm Springs is this 870-square-mile sanctuary of startling rock formations, mountain lions and kangaroo rats, colourful cacti and giant 50-foot agave trees with manlike arms and twisted bodies. These odd plants were named in the 1850s by Mormon pioneers, who recalled a line from the *Book of Joshua*: 'Thou shalt follow the way pointed for Thee by the trees'.

Entrance to the park is $10 per vehicle for a 7-day pass. Campsites charges $10—call (800) 365-2267. No shower and you need to bring food, water and firewood. Good exhibits, museum and ranger-guided tours (in autumn/winter only) from park headquarters at **Twentynine Palms**, and the **Cottonwood Springs Visitor Centre**, 8am-5pm daily. From 5185-foot **Salton View**, you get a splendid panorama of the Coachella Valley, the Salton Sea and Palm Springs. On a clear day you can see Signal Mountain in Mexico. Also, don't miss the annual **Village Street Fair**, held in the Park during the first weeks of May and September, featuring food, beer, games and entertainment. Call the Chamber of Commerce on 366-3723 for details, *www.nps.gov/jotr*.

PALM SPRINGS A flat desert town hugging snow-capped mountains, Palm Springs is a class act—from artfully weathered New Mexican adobes to its view of 10,831-foot Mt San Jacinto. Even the Indians are millionaires here, but don't let that put you off. During the hot, dry summer, prices melt like ice cubes and swimming pools can be reached within microseconds from air conditioned rooms. *www.palmsprings.com*.

The telephone area code is 760.

Accommodation
Each hotel seems to set its own dates for low season, approximately June through Sept. Rates always lowest Sun-Thu. To find the best deal, check newspaper specials, ask the Visitors Bureau, call around and don't be afraid to haggle. Except for Motel 6, winter rates are generally shocking.
Motel 6, 595 E Palm Canyon Dr, 325-6129 and 660 S Palm Canyon Dr, 327-4200. Lush setting, pools, book ages ahead. Rates from $42. *www.motel6.com*.

Food
In summer, they practically give the food away; check local paper, giveaway tabloids for 'early bird' brunch and other specials.
Las Casuelas, 222 S Palm Canyon, 325-2794. 'Great Mexican food.' Mon-Fri from 11, w/end from 10am 'til whenever they feel like it! *www.lascasuelas.com*.
Louise's Pantry, 44491 Hwy 111, 346-9320, queues form out the door as those in the know bombard this local landmark for its sumptuous American favourites.

Of interest
Aerial Tramway, off Hwy 111, 325-1391. 10 mins, 8516 ft, and 5 climatic zones later, you're on Mt San Jacinto and it's 30-40 degrees cooler (in summer); you may even need a jacket. At the top: restaurant, mule rides, backpacking, events and free camping. 'Can see part of San Andreas fault from top.' Mon-Fri 10am-8pm, w/end 8am-8pm, $21.50. *www.pstramway.com*.
Cabot's Indian Pueblo Museum, 67-616 E Desert View Ave, in Desert Hot Springs (E of I-10 on Palm Drive), 329-7610. Eccentric 3-storey pueblo, built of found objects by Cabot Yerxa, inc mementos of Battle of Little Bighorn and Eskimo and Indian relics. Fri-Sat 10am-3pm, Oct-July. *www.cabotsmuseum.org*.
Palm Springs Desert Museum, 101 Museum Dr, 325-7186. Displays arts, performing arts and natural sciences. Tues-Sat 10am-5pm, Thu 12pm-8pm (free 4pm-8pm) Sun 12am-5pm. $12.50, $5 with student ID. *www.psmuseum.org*.
Living Desert Zoo & Gardens, 47900 Portola Ave, Palm Desert (E of Palm Springs

off Hwy 111), 346-5694, 1200 acres of native plants, gazelles, Bighorn sheep and other desert denizens. 'After sundown' room displays with nocturnal beasties. Summer 8am-1pm, winter 9am-5pm, $11.95 in season, $7.95 summer. *www.livingdesert.org*.

Palm Springs International Film Festival, Mid-Jan, more than 150 films are screened and an awards gala honours filmmakers' careers. Call 322-2930 for more info. *www.psfilmfest.org*.

Information/Travel

Chamber of Commerce, 190 W Amado Rd, 325-1577. *www.pschamber.org*.
Palm Springs Visitors Bureau, off Hwy 111 in the Atrium Design Center, #201, 770-9000. Mon-Fri 8.30am-5pm. *www.palm-springs.org*.
Greyhound, 311 N Indian Ave, (800) 231-2222. On Phoenix-LA route.
Sun Bus Transit, 343-3451, operate local buses. *www.palmsprings.com/bus.html.*

LOS ANGELES Everything you have ever heard about LA is true. The place is so large and diverse that it will become whatever you wish to make it. There is urban angst and alienation downtown, and sun-seeking hedonism at Zuma beach. There is Greek sculpture in Malibu and a Cadillac stuck into a Beverly Hills roof. There is the film director sipping Perrier in Venice and the Vietnamese fisherman angling for dinner off the Santa Monica Pier. Remember that this city specialises in creating fantasy. The only way to find your own LA is to jump in with both feet.

Whatever you find, you'll be in good company. Ten million Angelenos speak 100 languages, and it's true—most do say 'have a nice day'; some even mean it. It's part climate, and part culture—LA has always drawn more from the Far East and Latin America than from New York and the grimy East Coast. The pace is a bit slower here, and the attitudes more tolerant. Easterners may deride LA as shallow and vain, but there is little doubt among Angelenos that theirs is a city struggling with social, economic and artistic questions difficult for outsiders to appreciate.

Most difficult to grasp is the great fear that one day the California Dream may be over. The place where people came to live a dream is slowly becoming less than that. The freeways are clogged, the air is smoggy and there is a constant worry about water. When in May 1992 four white police officers were acquitted of beating black motorist Rodney King, the riot that ensued did not just leave more than 50 people dead but left the city with a profound sense of identity crisis. Then came the massive earthquake on the 17th January, 1994. More than 50 died and many people were left homeless and stranded. The dream had become a nightmare.

Despite the growing congestion, the youthful LA sense of unlimited possibilities is easily restored with a trip along Mulholland Drive. Named for the engineer of LA's first aqueduct, Mulholland twists along the spine of mountains separating LA from the San Fernando Valley. A drive here offers sweeping vistas out over the enormous possibilities of the LA basin. At night the city lights stretch down to the sea, covering a seemingly limitless expanse. Clearly this was a city meant to dream dreams.

If you haven't acquired a car, it is surely now or never. You will no doubt get lost, spend countless hours looking for parking, but there's a sly exhilaration to driving LA freeways. It's like urban surfing. Once you've experienced the silken pull of seamless traffic, conquered a complex exchange as cars confidently curl on and off into new trajectories, and got a taste of life in the fast lane, you'll probably agree.

Check out LA Yahoo! Metro at *la.yahoo.com*; the *LA Times* has a great entertainment guide at *www.calendarlive.com*; an up-to-date and stylish site thrives at *www.losangeles.com*; similarly the Visitors Bureau makes pleasant viewing of all the city's areas at *www.lacvb.com*.

The area code for downtown LA is 213, for Hollywood is 323, for Santa Monica and the West Side is 310, the San Fernando Valley is 818, Long Beach is 562, Orange County is 714 and Pasadena is 626; beware, though, LA area codes change about as often as hot fashions do.

Geography

LA is immense and the first thing you need to do is get a sense of how to find your way round. For convenience sake, we'll assume that you have landed at the airport, and you're looking at a map. The airport is close to the coast, in the middle of the **Santa Monica Bay**. Moving south along the coast you come to **Long Beach** (the *Queen Mary* is moored here, and Disneyland is about 10 miles inland from here in Anaheim) and then the resort areas of **Huntington Beach, Newport Beach, Laguna Beach** and, eventually, **San Diego**, 125 miles south of LA.

Moving north along the coast from the airport, you first come to **Marina Del Rey**, the largest man-made marina in the world, and then to the beach community of **Venice**, a bohemian beach hang out. When LA people let it all hang out, this is where it hangs. Moving along, you come to **Santa Monica**, once called Soviet Monica for its liberal leanings, this area is a pleasant beach community with a large British population.

Malibu Beach is about a 45 min drive north from here along the Pacific Coast Hwy. Moving inland from Santa Monica along **Sunset Blvd** you come to Westwood, home of UCLA. Further along Sunset, in **Beverly Hills**, the feeling is decidedly posh, and anything but collegiate.

Sunset passes through **Beverly Hills** and **Hollywood** and into **Downtown**. Below Hollywood is the **Melrose/West Hollywood** area, the cutting edge of LA chic. Hopping over the Hollywood Hills to the north, you enter **North Hollywood** and the **San Fernando Valley**. The TV and movie studios are located in Burbank and the North Hollywood area.

If you arrive by train or bus you will come into downtown. By bus it is possible to arrive at Santa Monica, Hollywood, Pasadena, Glendale and North Hollywood stations, but by train you have no other choice. Of course, LA is a tough city in places, particularly Downtown and East LA—'Never go near, especially at night'. Sticking to the West Side—Beverly Hills, Westwood and parts of Hollywood—is generally safe.

Accommodation

Getting around LA can be a battle, so you should choose lodging near where you will want to spend the most time. Beverly Hills, Westwood and the West Side are centrally located to many sights. Do not stay downtown just because it sounds as though all the sites are there. They're not.

Downtown: (close to Union Train Station/bus station):
Motel de Ville, 1123 W 7th St, (213) 624-8474. Located on a busy street, the motel's basic facilities have been called 'good value'. 'Don't hesitate to bargain,' though, in this 'terrible area'.

Beverly Hills/Hollywood/West Side: (close to entertainment, shopping, movie sites):
Banana Bungalow, 7950 Melrose Ave, W Hollywood, (323) 655-1510 or 800-4-HOSTEL. 'Fantastic' resort-style facility: cable, private bath, café, free linen. Diff

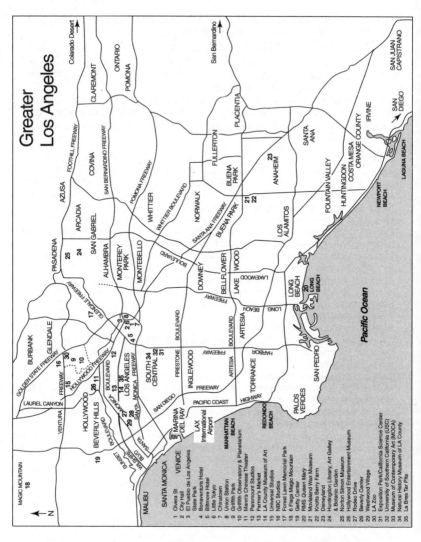

Greater Los Angeles

1 Olvera St.
2 City Hall
3 El Pueblo de los Angeles State Park
4 Bonaventure Hotel
5 Biltmore Hotel
6 Little Tokyo
7 Chinatown
8 Union Station
9 Griffith Park
10 Griffith Observatory & Planetarium
11 Mann's Chinese Theater
12 Paramount Studios
13 Farmer's Market
14 LA County Museum of Art
15 Universal Studios
16 NBC Studios
17 Forest Lawn Memorial Park
18 6 Flags Magic Mountain
19 Getty Center
20 RMS Queen Mary
21 Movieland Wax Museum
22 Knotts Berry Farm
23 Disneyland
24 Huntingdon Library, Art Galley & Botanical Garden
25 Norton Simon Museum
26 Hollywood Entertainment Museum
27 Rodeo Drive
28 Beverly Center
29 Westwood Village
30 LA Zoo
31 Exposition Park/California Science Center
32 University of Southern California (USC)
33 Museum of Contemporary Art (MOCA)
34 Natural History Museum of LA County
35 La Brea Tar Pits

types of tours avail. Free shuttle from LAX at certain times, $12 the rest of the week. $18-20 mixed dorm.

Student Inn International Hostel, 7038½ Hollywood Blvd, (323) 469-6781 or (800) 557-7038. Call for rsvs. Dorms $17, shared Queen size bed in dorm $28, private $20/person, XP $15. Kitchen and free 'light bfast'. Close to the Hollywood Greyhound. Mixed reports. _www.studentinn.com_.

Airport and South Coast: Hostel California, 2221 Lincoln Blvd, (310) 305-0250. $12.75-$16; private rooms $40; passport req. _www.hostelcalifornia.net_.

Backpackers Paradise at Adventurers Hotel, 4200 West Century Blvd, Inglewood, (800) 852-0012. Dorms $15, D-$22 pp, (special discount for BUNAC members).

Rooms D-$60.Includes free morning bfast java and muffin. Shuttle to and from airport, Greyhound and Amtrak. *www.backpackersparadise.com.*

Colonial Inn Hostel, 421 8th St, Huntington Beach, about 20 miles S of airport, (714) 536-3315. Run by a self-described 'funky old lady having a good time'. TV, nice garden and porch, kitchen etc. $21 ($130/wk) dorm, D-$06; 'were disappointed on arrival'. 'Full of Aussie surfers and hard to get to on public transport.' *www.huntingtonbeachhostel.com.*

Hacienda Hotel, 525 N Sepulveda Blvd, El Segundo, (800) 421-5900. 'Expensive but safe, excellent facilities, TV, swimming pool. Most important factor is the free shuttle to LA Airport.' S/D-under $100. *www.haciendahotel.com.*

HI-Hostel LA South Bay, 3601 S Gaffey St, # 613, San Pedro, (310) 831-8109. Has a panoramic view of the Pacific Ocean and Catalina Island, and features spectacular sunsets. Prime location for whale watching cruises to observe gray whales on their annual Alaska-Baja journey (Christmas to April). It's 'clean and friendly', $20+, private room $22.80. *www.hiusa.org/usa-hostels/ca/ca-state.shtml.*

Santa Monica: HI-Hostel Santa Monica, 1436 2nd St, Santa Monica, (310) 393-9913. Library, kitchen, TV room, open courtyard, laundry, travel store. 2 blocks from beach, dorms $25, D-$62 (non-members add $3). 'Fantastic facilities, but too many rules.' *www.hilosangeles.org.*

Venice Beach: Cadillac Hotel, 8 Dudley Ave., (310) 399-8876. S/D-$89-$99, w/private bath. This 'really friendly' hotel has a gym, sauna, laundry, sun deck; will pick you up from the airport. *www.thecadillachotel.com.*

Venice Beach Hostel, 701 Washington Blvd, (310) 306-5180. Free airport pick-up Dorms $13+, D-$34+, incl breakfast, a relaxed atmosphere, kitchen, lounge and sundeck. 'Very sociable hostel but not for those who need privacy.' 'Staff have lots of info on what to do in LA, just ask.' 'Sharing bathroom with at least 14 people!' *www.venicebeachhostel.com.*

Near Disneyland: Anaheim Inn (Best Western), 1630 S Harbour Blvd (1 block S of Hwy 5), (714) 774-1050. 'Good location, just across from Disneyland theme park.' $79-$169, up to 5 people.

HI-Hostel Fullerton, 1700 N Harbour Blvd, (714) 738-3721. Closest hostel to Disneyland (4 miles S; 10 min drive). Hostel is situated in Brea Dam Park with a picnic area and golf driving range. Quiet, restful place to relax while in LA area with a kitchen, linen rental $2 and tours avail. Dorms $25 for members (+$3 for non-members). Take the 'Airway' super-shuttles from airport to the door, $21. *lahostels.org/fullerton.htm.*

Food

The greater LA area has over 25,000 eating establishments. Does this city love to eat out, or what? In fact, during recessions, people in Los Angeles eat out more often than they did before the downturn. One reason for this obsession may be the mobile lifestyle, and the rich mix of ethnic cultures. Don't be surprised to find kosher burritos, Thai Tacos and more. Check out *www.latimes.com/features/food/ www.calendarlive.com/dining*, or *www.at-la.com/dining* to taste what's here, and *http://cuisinenet.com/city/city-13842/?v=237* for menus.

Downtown: Cassell's, 3266 W 6th St, (213) 480-8668. Beautiful hamburgers but too crowded any time after noon, cafeteria-style dining. Mon-Sat 10.30am-4pm.

Cole's PE Buffet, 118 E 6th St, (213) 622-4090. Oldest restaurant and saloon in LA since 1908. 'Atmosphere hole-in-the-wall cafeteria.' Try the house speciality, French dip, a west coast sandwich. Mon-Sat 9am-7.30pm. *www.colespebuffet.com.*

Clifton's Cafeteria, 648 S Broadway, (213) 627-1673, offers a vast array of cheap dishes ($2.75-$7.99), soothing decor from a redwood forest with real waterfall to the Art Deco touches at 7th St. Daily 6.30am-7.30pm. *www.cliftonscafeteria.com.*

Dupar's, 6333 W 3rd St at the Farmer's Market (also at 12036 Ventura Blvd), (323) 933-8446. Old-style coffee shop specialising in savory pot pies and desert pies, legend bfast pancakes, with the option of buying batter ready to take home! Daily 6am-10pm. *www.dupars.com*.

Café El Tepayac, 812 N Evergreen, (323) 267-8688, is home to the Manuel Special, an enormous burrito requiring two people to finish. This Salvadorian barrio hang out draws an unusual mix of police, locals and Mexico food junkies. Daily 7am-10pm. $6-$12.

Mandarin Deli, 727 N Broadway in Chinatown, (213) 623-6054, authentic multi-lingual establishment (sans English). Try the jiao tzi, $5 for eight. Daily exc Thur 11am-7.30pm.

Original Pantry Cafe, 877 S Figueroa, (213) 972-9279. Huge helpings of basic meat and potatoes fare for less than $15. The Pantry is famous both for its food and its unassuming presence, an anomaly in trendy LA. Open 24 hrs.

Pho Hoa, 640 N Broadway, (213) 626-5530. 'Good Vietnamese restaurant with large portions and reasonable prices.' Open daily 8am-6pm.

West Side: Apple Pan, 10801 W Pico Blvd, (310) 475-3585. Unassuming steak or hickory burger $5.45 and apple pie, $4. Great food with locals lining up behind the counter stools (no tables) waiting for a spot at the trough! Closed Mondays.

Barney's Beanery, 8447 Santa Monica Blvd, (323) 654-2287. Things haven't changed too much since Janis Joplin used to hang out here. The pool tables still need new felt, the vinyl in the booths is still bright, and the action at the bar is still pretty fierce. Excellent chili. Breakfast served all day. Great place to meet locals, Open daily. *www.qsbilliards.com/barneysbeanery*.

Canter's Deli, 419 N Fairfax, (323) 651-2030, in LA's old Jewish section close to CBS Television City. There is no better deli or bakery in town, especially at 3am; awarded 'Best Pastrami in Town' by *LA Times*. Open 24 hours. Full bar, 'Tibbits Room' with entertainment such as open mike nights. *www.seeing-stars.com/Dine2/Canters.shtml*.

Dolores' West Restaurant, 11407 Santa Monica Blvd at Purdue, (310) 477-1061. 24 hr old-fashioned burger joint. Bottomless coke and the renowned JJ Burger. **Musso And Franks**, 6667 Hollywood Blvd, (323) 467-5123. This old bar and grill dates from 1919, the oldest restaurant in Hollywood. Once a haunt of Chandler, Fitzgerald, Hemingway and Faulkner, etc it's now a regular for film industry types (and the Rolling Stones). It offers a touch of the golden era of Hollywood elegance at prices that match. Breakfast all day. Open Tue-Sat 11am-11pm.

Nate 'n' Al's, 414 N Beverly Dr, (310) 274-0101. The Beverly Hills power schmooze takes place here early in the am. Plates tend to hover around $15. Daily 7am-9pm. *www.seeing-stars.com/Dine2/Nate&Als.shtml*.

Tail O' the Pup, 329 N San Vicente at Beverly, (310) 652-4517. A hot-dog shaped stand complete with bright yellow mustard oozing out of the sides! Hot dogs, burgers. Daily 6am-5pm. *www.seeing-stars.com/Landmarks/TailOfThePup.shtml.*

The Valley: Arturo's Puffy Taco, 15693 Leffingwell Rd., **Whittier**, (562) 947-2250, while it may be well off the beaten path, this seminal taco shop is already a local favourite. Don't be surprised if you run into Westside celebs grubbing down on these unique tacos. Open Mon-Sat 10am-10pm.

Dupar's, 12036 Ventura Blvd, Studio City (also at 6333 W 3rd St, Farmers Market, and Thousand Oaks), (818) 766-4437, great pies, burgers, and one of the best coffee shops in town. Coffee $1.65, pies $4. Open 6am-2am. 'This is a real hang-out late on a Friday or Saturday,' when they stay open 'till 4am. *www.dupars.com.*

Patrick's Roadhouse, 106 Entrada just off Corner of Pac Coast Hwy and Entrada Dr (across the street from Will Rogers State Beach), (310) 459-4544, open Mon-Tue 8am-3pm, Wed-Sun 8am-9pm. Make rsvs for w/ends. Where Arnie had his bachelor party, and where everybody who's anybody comes to feed. 'Good homemade fish and chips.' *www.patricksroadhouse.com* (Palm Springs version).

Venice: Rose Cafe and Deli, 220 Rose Ave in Venice, (310) 399-0711. Pretty place serving healthy food to beautiful people. Visitors are greeted by a mural of a bright red rose. Open daily 8am-3pm. Reasonable prices.

Santa Monica: Many good places to eat along the 3rd Street Promenade, outdoor tables etc. One of the best is **Broadway Deli**, 1457 3rd Street Promenade, (310) 451-0616; **Ye Olde King's Head Pub**, 116 Santa Monica Blvd, (310) 451-1402, a real ghetto for expatriate Brits, complete with darts, chips, everything! _www.yeoldekingshead.com_.

Of interest

For convenience, sites have been grouped geographically. It would be wise to plan day trips around one important site. The MTA has an excellent self-guided tour booklet for people using the bus. *LA Weekly*, the weekly events calendar, is the online source to check for cafes, clubs and comedy, _www.laweekly.com_.

Downtown: Despite rumours to the contrary, downtown LA does exist. In fact, film producers use it as a double for Manhattan. Old and graceful structures survive, especially around the beautiful **Pershing Square Park**, but the area is dominated by soaring skyscrapers. To get oriented take DASH, (800) COMMUTE or (213) 626-4455, a bus system that covers all of downtown, 25c each ride, _www.ladottransit.com_.

City Hall, Spring St, (213) 485-212, was, at one point, the tallest building in LA. It features an eclectic style of Babylonian and Byzantine architecture, and has an observation deck on the 27th floor. The *Los Angeles Times* **Building** (213) 237-5757 is across the street and offers free tours on w/days, both 45 mins. You can either do the editorial tour, which takes you through history and production, or the Printing tour, which takes you to the ultra-modern 4-storey high press. You'll also get a free replica of the first edition in 1881; resv a week in adv.

Just a few blocks from City Hall around First and San Pedro Sts, is **Little Tokyo**, a bustling area which has grown like mad in the last few years. LA has had an important Japanese community since the 1880s, although they were rounded up during WWII and herded into camps. The community has rebuilt since that shattering experience. This is a good place to walk around. Be sure to visit the **Japanese American Cultural and Community Center Gardens**, 244 S San Pedro, _www.jaccc.org_, the koi pool at the **New Otani Hotel** and the many Japanese speciality shops.

Walking along Broadway away from Little Tokyo towards Pershing Square, you would think you were in Mexico. This bustling Hispanic area becomes the garment and diamond districts near 7th St. If you turn west on 5th St off Broadway you come to Pershing Square—a graceful park in the middle of downtown. On the site of an Indian (later Spanish) trail, the **Biltmore Hotel**, 506 S Grand, 612-1567, is the square's most charming and sumptuous hotel complete with a fountain and wood-beamed ceiling in the Spanish-style entrance. JFK stayed in the $2400-a-day suite when he won the Democratic presidential nomination in 1960. A graceful architectural counterbalance to the skyscrapers is the Byzantine style **Los Angeles Central Library**, 630 W 5th St btwn Flores and Grand Ave, (213) 228-7000. Free wi-fi (also at several other branches). Open Mon-Thu 10am-8pm, Fri/Sat 10am-6pm and Sun 1pm-5pm. _www.lapl.org_.

Each of the enormous skyscrapers surrounding the Library—the **Arco Towers**, the **Citicorp Center**, and the **Bonaventure Hotel**—are small cities in themselves. They house underground shopping, parking and restaurants and are connected to one another by skywalks and underground passages. The Bonaventure in particular offers a stunning atrium and impressive glass elevators that whisk you along the outside of the building to a restaurant at the top. On clear days the view is remarkable. _www.at-la.com/westinbv_

Hop on the DASH bus, or walk north along Broadway to get to **Chinatown** and **Olvera St.** Just off Main St, in the preserved Olvera St area, is the original Spanish settlement led by the succinct Felipe de Neve, who christened the outpost as **El**

Pueblo de Nuestra Senora la Reina de los Angeles del Rio Porciuncula, (which was later shortened to LA by hip studio execs). **El Pueblo de Los Angeles Historic Monument**, (213) 485-6855, founded in 1781, is the oldest section of LA, *www.ci.la.ca.us/elp*, but Olvera St, and the **Iglesia de Nuestra Senora** across the street are colourful reminders of LA's Spanish roots.

This is a good area to have a Mexican lunch (try **La Luz Del Dia,** 1 Olvera Street) and to shop amongst the colourful Mexican and Central American stalls. Since the Spanish-style **Union Train Station** is nearby on Alameda St, you may want to save Olvera St 'til your last day in LA. Walk up Main St to Ord and head left to Broadway, and Mexico gives way to China, and **Chinatown**. While not as classy as Little Tokyo, it is chock full of good places to eat. The street life is a bit more old-fashioned here. Between crates of live chickens stacked helter skelter on the sidewalk, merchants still hold live birds upside down while old Chinese women poke the breast bones to check for tenderness.

Your best orientation to the rest of LA is to take **Sunset Blvd** west, away from Downtown (MTA #2). Beginning in El Pueblo Park, Sunset shoots out towards **Hollywood**, and morphs into the **Sunset Strip** before winding through the posh areas of **Beverly Hills** and **Bel Air**, and finally dips down to the Ocean. Sunset Blvd cuts a grand path through LA's many attractions. It is central to the city, and indeed, people measure their success in life by whether or not they have managed to acquire a home on the fashionable 'North Side' of 'The Boulevard'.

Hollywood: At Sunset and Los Feliz Blvd, head north to **Griffith Park**. The largest city park in America, Griffith offers trails, bridle paths, a zoo, the **Greek Theater**, three golf courses, and an observatory and planetarium. Performances in the Greek Theater take place from June through September; for info call *Ticketmaster* (213) 480-3232. The park observatory is free, and the 65' long, 12' wide refractor telescope is open to the public, from sundown 'til 9.50pm. The ocean breeze generally blows the smog away, and visibility is good. There is also a free **Hall of Science**, the **Griffith Observatory** (planetarium), (323) 664-1191, closed for renovation 'til 2005. For astronomical info dial **Sky Report**, (323) 663-8171. *www.griffithobs.org/skyreport.html*.

From the Planetarium you will not need a telescope to see the famous **Hollywood Sign**. The 50 foot letters were built by a real estate developer, and originally spelled out **Hollywoodland**, the name of his development (but that too was also shortened). Not far from the observatory you'll find the stars are on the street along Hollywood Blvd. Over 2500 names of stars are laid into the terrazzo sidewalk above bronze symbols of microphones, cameras, television sets or records denoting the craft that brought them fame. For the list of names, visit *www.hollywoodchamber.net.* Do not expect Hollywood to glitter as brightly as her sidewalks. The area has been a somewhat shabby, red-light district since the 50's. Children who run away from home for the glamour of Hollywood are often suckered into prostitution and worse. The Art Deco **Pantages Theater**, recalls the glamour of by-gone days. Built in 1929, the Pantages for many years housed the Academy Awards, and today draws many Broadway musicals. **Fredericks of Hollywood**, 6608 Hollywood Blvd, (323) 466-8506, is LA's original, and uninhibited, sexual image-maker. Mon-Sat 10am-9pm, Sun 11.30am-6.30pm. Free museum. *www.fredericks.com*.

The most popular Hollywood attraction is **Grauman's Chinese Theater**, 6925 Hollywood Blvd, (323) 464-8111. *www.manntheatres.com/chinese*. The theatre opened in 1927 with the premiere of DeMille's *King of Kings* and was christened by Norma Talmadge who accidentally stepped in wet cement that night, the birth of a Hollywood tradition. Some of the world's most famous anatomy is imprinted here, including Michael Jackson, Donald Duck, R2-D2, Trigger and Marilyn Monroe. The building itself is a strange blend of Polynesian and Chinese Imperial architecture.

Grauman's offers one of the best sound systems, and largest screens in LA. Just steps away is the **Hollywood Entertainment Museum**, 7021 Hollywood Blvd, (323)465-7900, daily 10am-6pm, $12, $5 w/student ID, is a state-of-the-art museum featuring original sets of *Star Trek: Next Generation*, *Cheers* and Agent Mulder's office in *X Files*. There is also a display called *Hollywood in Miniature*. www.hollywoodmuseum.com.

Hollywood offers several other architectural styles: Frank Lloyd Wright designed two homes near here—**Hollyhock House** and **Sowden House**. Neither is open to the public. The **Hollywood Bowl**, 2301 N Highland Ave, a large ampitheatre with near-perfect acoustics. The bowl hosts major jazz, classical and rock concerts. www.hollywoodbowl.com Call *Ticketmaster* on (213) 480-3232 for tkts or log on to www.ticketmaster.com.

Off Hollywood, on Vine St is the **Capitol Records** office, designed to look like a stack of 45s with a huge 92' needle on top. The red beacon on the needle spells out Hollywood in morse code. After leaving Hollywood, but just before Beverly Hills, Sunset Blvd banks into the famous **Sunset Strip**—an exciting night spot lined with inventive, hand-painted billboards, and the best rock clubs in LA. At the other end of the frenzied Strip, Beverly Hills is as calm as a bank vault on Sunday. Everyone who has seen *Beverly Hills Cop* knows how rich and bizarre the residents are here. **Rodeo Drive** (pronounced Row-DAY-o) near Wilshire Blvd is the most expensive retail strip in the world. The Gucci side is the most fashionable. If you want to see the nearby homes of the stars—Gene Kelly lived at 725 Rodeo, Carl Reiner at 714—you'll need to rent a car, take the bus or a mainstream coach tour. Don't bother buying a 'Map of the Star's Homes' from the street vendors—many are inaccurate and out of date, and you rarely can get close to the properties anyway.

For a more affordable shopping experience head to the massive **Beverly Center**, corner 3rd and La Cienega. Next to the center, the Cadillac sticking out of the roof marks the spot of the **Hard Rock Cafe**. Be sure and stop in at the **Beverly Hills Hotel**. The bright pink decor is hard to miss. The film industry does its business at the Hotel bar called the **Polo Lounge**. Bring your wallet and don't forget to have yourself paged. Sunset continues on along the northern edge of **Westwood Village** and **UCLA**. Tucked in with the campus, Westwood Village is one of LA's few walkable districts, and chockful of cinemas, shops, street buskers and socialising places. 'Fri and Sat nights are like a circus here.' Celebs also frequent Westwood. The campus area is a live party spot. 'Frat parties along Gayley from 21 Sept on. Free beer, spirits, food, entertainment and the best-looking women in the world.' On a quieter note, **Westwood Village Cemetery**, 1218 Glendon, has the most visited grave in LA, that of Marilyn Monroe; Natalie Wood is also buried here. Continuing past Westwood, Sunset winds through miles of exclusive **Pacific Palisades** real estate (Ronald Reagan lived here) finally reaching the Pacific Coast Hwy and **Malibu**.

The Valley: Made famous by the song *Valley Girl* (sung by Frank and Moon Zappa) the **San Fernando Valley** is really like a totally coooool bedroom community for like kids who drive really bitchin Camaros. The shopping is, like, totally excellent at the **Sherman Oaks Galleria**. The most totally kickin' part of the valley fer shur is near the studios in the **North Hollywood** area. Other than like, those, the major sites are, like, the **LA Zoo** in **Glendale**, and the famous **Forest Lawn Memorial Park**, 1712 S Glendale Ave, (800) 204-3131. This is the American way of death as depicted in Evelyn Waugh's *The Loved One*: odourless, spotless, artistically uplifting, almost fun, at least for the survivors. It's hard to keep from giggling at the crass wonder of it all, from repros of the Greatest Hits of Michelangelo and Leonardo da Vinci to the comic-book approach on the 'Life of Jesus' mosaics. Take a copy of Ken Schessler's, *This is Hollywood* along (but keep it out of sight—park officials won't allow the book on the grounds) to find where the notables are planted. Free, daily 8am-5pm. _www.forestlawn.com_ (The cemetery also has five franchises in the region, each with its own artwork, patriotic themes and style.) Outside of the sheltered preteens and dead people, the Valley plays host to a thriving porn industry.

Museums and art galleries:

Downtown: Exposition Park, corner of Exposition & Figueroa Blvds. Built in the early 1900s and houses LA's oldest museums and a beautiful rose garden.

California Science Center, 700 State Drive, Exposition Park (323) SCIENCE, contains Creative World, World of Life, and Science Plaza exhibitions, many hands-on exhibits. Daily 10am-5pm. Admission is free but some exhibits require a nominal fee, such as the IMAX theatre, $8, $5.75 w/student ID (call or check website for show times-last film 5.30pm). _www.casciencectr.org_.

Natural History Museum of LA County, 900 Exposition Blvd, (213) 763-DINO, exhibits include 'battling dinosaurs,' habitat halls with mounted animals placed in natural settings, and the American History Halls covering the Revolutionary War to 1914. Also impressive are the California and Southwest History Halls and the Pre-Columbian—Meso American Hall covering Maya, Inca, and other civilizations, including the world's largest collection of Latin American artifacts. The Hall of Gems and Minerals is the West's largest display of such stones and includes the 102-karat Ashberg Diamond, thought to have been a part of the Russian crown jewels. Open Mon-Fri 9.30am-5pm, w/end 10am-5pm, $9, $6.50 w/student ID. _www.nhm.org_.

Nearby is the **Coliseum**, site of the 1932 and 1984 Olympics, and **USC**. Best known for its, once great, football team and revered alumni, such as OJ Simpson, USC is affectionately called the University of Spoiled Children, although the spoiled children claim that the school's real name is the University of Southern California. _www.lacoliseum.com_.

MOCA, Museum of Contemporary Art, 250 S Grand Ave btwn 2nd and 4th, (213) 62-MOCA-2. Famous Japanese architect Arata Isozaki designed this newest museum on the LA scene. The building itself is a work of art, integrating primary shapes into abstract patterns. Most impressive is the large polished onyx gable window above the ticket booth. The collection includes many modern artists from the 1940s to the present—Louise Nevelson, Robert Rauschenberg, David Hockney and others. Mon & Fri 11am-5pm, closed Tue & Wed, w/e 11am-6pm, $8, $5 w/student ID, all day. Free Thur 5-8pm. MOCA's other buildings are the **Geffen Contemporary**, 152 N Central Ave and the **Pacific Design Center**, 8687 Melrose. Tkts are good at all the locations. Both downtown locations can be visited on the same day and a valid ticket is good for 30 days at the Pac Design Ctr. _www.moca.org_.

LACE, Los Angeles Contemporary Exhibitions, 6522 Hollywood Blvd, (323) 957-1777, is devoted to artists who are still alive. LACE offers everything from performance art to video art, suggested donation $3, students $2. Open Wed-Sun 12pm-6pm, Fri 'til 9pm. If there is an avant-garde in LA, it stays one step ahead by coming here, _www.artleak.org_.

West Side: Los Angeles County Museum of Art, mercifully abbreviated to LACMA, 5905 Wilshire Blvd, (323) 857-6000. LACMA has grown impressively in the last few years. The Anderson building houses the collection of 20th century works by Picasso, Braque and Matisse. The older Armand Hammer Building houses an impressive collection of Far Eastern works. LA art often looks west for inspiration. An ode to this phenomenon is found at the **Pavilion for Japanese Art**, which houses the Shin'enkan collection of Edo period screens and scrolls. Widely regarded as the most outstanding collection of its kind, the 32,100-square-foot pavilion is a world-class centre for Japanese art, Open Mon, Tue & Thu 12pm-8pm, closed Wed, Fri 'til 9pm, Sat/Sun 11am-8pm, $9, $5 w/student ID, free after 5pm and the 2nd Tue of the month. _www.lacma.org_.

La Brea Tar Pits are nearby. Ancient sources of natural tar, the pits were often covered with a light layer of dust and water. Ice Age animals seeking water became ensnared in the tar and their bones were preserved for history, making the Tar Pits the single richest fossil find in the world. **The George C. Page Museum of La Brea Discoveries**, 5801 Wilshire Blvd, (323) 934-PAGE, exhibits of fossils in atrium. Open pit to watch excavating in summer months. Still millions of fossils. Mon-Fri 9.30am-5pm, 10-5 w/ends, $7, $4.50 w/student ID, free first Tues of month. *www.tarpits.org*.

The Museum of Tolerance, 9786 W. Pico, (310) 553-8403, museum examines the Holocaust and race and prejudice in America. Interactive exhibits such as the Tolerancenter test your own prejudices. Open Mon-Thu 10am-6.30pm, Fri 10am-5pm, Sun11am-7.30pm. Closed Sat; $10, $7 w/ stud ID. *www.museumoftolerance.com.*

The Getty Center, 1200 Getty Center Drive, (310) 440-7300. The museum is free, but if you're driving there is a $7 parking fee. Metro bus #761 stops at the entrance. Tue-Thu 10am-6pm, Fri/Sat 10am-9pm, Sun 10am-6pm. Collection of high quality art, from Greek and Roman sculpture, impressionists and photography, housed in a fantastic building and with spectacular views of the city. In 2005, had Rembrandt exhibition. *www.getty.edu*.

UCLA Hammer Museum, 10899 Wilshire Blvd., (310) 443-7078, Another Oil Baron whose incredible art collection outlived him, the Hammer Musuem hosts frequent exhibitions of contemporary works and a diverse collection whose centrepiece is Van Gogh's *Hospital at Saint Rémy*. Admission is $5. Opens everyday at 11am, closes at 7pm Tue, Wed, Fri and Sat, Thu at 9pm (free day) and Sun at 5pm. *www.hammer.ucla.edu*.

Pasadena: Huntington Library, Art Collections and Botanical Gardens, 1151 Oxford Rd. in San Marino, an impressive and well-housed collection of Gainsborough and 18th Century British art. Summer—Tues-Sun 10:30am-4:30pm, $15, $12 w/student ID. Free 1st Thu of the month. English tea is offered Tues-Fri 12pm-4pm, w/end 10.45am-4pm in the Rose Garden, rsvs rec. $13 for limitless buffet, call (626) 683-8131 for. 'The gardens are mind-blowing.' *www.huntington.org*.

The Norton Simon Museum of Art, 411 W Colorado Blvd, (626) 449 6840. The worst day in the history of the LACMA was the day that Norton Simon got mad and decided to take his ball and go start his own game. So, Simon, who had been on the museum's board, opened his own museum in Pasadena. Simon's extensive collection includes Degas and Rodin (the *Burgers of Calais*) and a garden graced by Henry Moore's sculptures arranged along a fountain. $8, free w/student ID. Open daily noon-6pm, Fri 'til 9pm. *www.nortonsimon.org*.

Amusement parks:

Best to go in **off-season** (as it is cheaper and less crowded), on a **school day**, or when everyone is somewhere else, (e.g. watching the Superbowl). **Arrive early**, before the gates open and check for discounts.

Disneyland Resort: Disneyland has a young sibling in its quest to take over the imaginations of the world's children: **Disney's California Adventure** theme park, now over 50 years old, is Disney's ode to the Golden State. But first things first: **Disneyland**, 1313 S Harbor Blvd, Anaheim, (714) 781-4400. 9am-Midnight. This is the original **Magic Kingdom** and the culmination of Walt Disney's dream. Disney designed the 51 attractions to provide wholesome entertainment for adults and children in this flawlessly clean park. Attractions are grouped into 7 theme parks: you enter the park through Main Street, a re-creation of Walt Disney's home town, Marceline, Missouri. **New Orleans Square** houses the infamous *Pirates of the Caribbean*. **Adventureland** is devoted to the explorer spirit of African safaris. **Fantasyland** recreates the magic of the animation classics; the entrance is through Sleeping Beauty's castle, right next to the *Matterhorn Bobsleigh* roller coaster. In

Frontierland, you can journey through the old west on an incredible mining train roller coaster, the *Big Center Mountain Railroad*. A visionary himself, Disney took special interest in the future. You can do this at **Tomorrowland**, which includes the legendary *Space Mountain* roller coaster, *Honey 3-D*; and *Star Tours*, the original motion simulator set to a *Star Wars* theme. Finally, **Critter Country** features the popular *Splash Mountain*, a water flume attraction themed around *Song of the South* adventures. There is year-round entertainment (e.g. Big bands, the Videopolis Dance Club) but the *Parade of the Stars* is only during the summer, 4.45pm/8pm. Since all this is available for the $56 admission fee, you really have to ask yourself why you should see any of the other parks in town. 'Get there as early as possible. Lines for good rides become enormous by noon.' 'Take a full day.' 'Avoid Saturday!' 'Don't miss the parade of Disney Characters.' 'Don't leave luggage at Greyhound—station closes at 9pm, Disneyland at midnight.' 'Tomorrowland is best—see it first.' *www.disneyland.com.*

Disney's California Adventure is located next door to Disneyland and boasts 28 attractions, as well as Hollywood studios, cable cars, Napa Valley wineries, fish filled wharfs, sandy boardwalks and high flying roller coasters: If you don't have time to see the entire state of California, Disney built its own version just for you. The *Electric Light Parade* (9pm) with hundreds of light-bedecked floats and fireworks, is available summer evenings. The hours are similar to Disneyland's and admission prices are the same ($56). Special combination tickets are available ($105 for a 2-day "hopper" pass to both or $139 for a 3-day pass). *http://disneyland.disney.go.com/disneyland/home/home?name=HomePage.* To get to the parks, try MTA, (213) 626-4455, from downtown (1½ hrs): take #460 W on 5th—$3.35 (runs as late as 11.50pm in summer). Or take Greyhound to Anaheim and then the local **Orange County Transit Authority (OCTA)**, (714) 636-7433 from the Greyhound terminal to the park, #43. Bus runs every 15 min. (714) 999-1256 / (800) 231-2222. *www.octa.net.*

Knott's Berry Farm, 8039 Beach Blvd, Buena Park, (714) 220-5200. Call for opening hrs. The gift shops outnumber the rides and attractions 10 to 1 but its *Montezooma's Revenge* (with 360-degree upside-down loops) is nauseatingly effective, allowing you to meet yourself (and possibly your lunch) coming back. 'Hurts, but must be tried.' Rides include *The Boomerang*, a 54 second reverse looping roller coaster; the *Wilderness Scrambler*, an outdoor ride that spins you round and round; the *Ghostrider*, and the *Bigfoot Rapids*. Lots of special celebrations, rock concerts and discount promotions, so check the papers. Admission is $35. *www.knotts.com.*

Movieland Wax Museum, 7711 Beach Blvd, Buena Park, 1 block N of Knott's, (714) 522-1155. Go see 200-plus movies and TV stars captured (not always successfully) in wax. The big event is the Chamber of Horrors, based on 13 scary movies, including *American Werewolf in London, Dracula, The Exorcist* and *Psycho*. Here you can also be fooled by moviestar look-alikes of Clint Eastwood, Michael Jackson, Marilyn Monroe and Bette Davis, and newcomers Britney Spears and Keanu Reeves. Daily 10am-6pm, $12.95, *www.movielandwaxmuseum.com.*

RMS Queen Mary, (562) 435-3511, located on Pier J at 1126 Queens Hwy in **Long Beach**. Open daily 10am-6pm; $29.95. *www.queenmary.com.*

Six Flags Magic Mountain, **Valencia**, N of LA, (661) 255-4100. $47.99, open 10am-10pm. Home of the most roller coasters on earth, Alton Towers has nothing on this place. Experience some of the biggest rollercoaster rides in the world: *The Viper, Collossus, The Revolution* and the *Ninja* are all here. Also, extreme adventure is in store for those who experience the *Dive Devil*, a 60mph 50ft skydive/bungee jump freefall! 'Arrive early, by the afternoon 2 hr queues are not uncommon.' No outside food or drink allowed. *www.sixflags.com.*

Universal Studios, 100 Universal City Plaza, (818) 508-9600. $53 includes a 45 min tram tour through the 420-acre lot, plus all the usual rides and attractions. Shows include *Spiderman* and *Shrek*. Tours leave throughout the day and the park is open from 9am-10pm during the summer. Hours vary in the off-season. Get there early to avoid crowds. 'Get right-hand seat on tram—most scenes, Jaws, etc., to the right.' Catch a tidal wave of action and an ocean of thrills in the more recent attraction: *Waterworld*. Or journey deep into the Jurassic Jungle on a turbulent water ride to face a towering T-Rex in *Jurassic Park—The Ride*. While 'not on a par with Disneyland,' a free shuttle is avail. from Anaheim—call to make resv. Alternatively, the Red Line Subway runs to the park from downtown. While you are there, check out the *Universal Citywalk*, a virtual city centre with restaurants, shops, bars and clubs. *www.universalstudios.com*.

North Hollywood
The Industry:
What the cognoscente call the movie business. To get a feel for it, read the trade magazines *Hollywood Reporter* and *Variety*. More hands-on experience can be gained by hanging out at the Polo Lounge, or Ma Maison Restaurant, but for those without the necessary wallets, TV shows are free, and you can watch them being taped at any of the major studios. Tkts avail from the Visitors Center, from the TV reps in front of tourist attractions like Grauman's Chinese Theater in Hollywood; or by calling Audiences Unlimited, (818) 506-0043, beware, though, it can take up to 4 hrs to get *one* 22 min episode wrapped up. To find location filming, call the LA Film and Video Permit Office on (323) 957-1000 or go online to *www.eidc.com*.
NBC Studio Tour, 3000 W Alameda, (818) 840-3537. To see a show taped, arrive early at the ticket office on the west side of the NBC complex off California St. Tickets are dispersed to waiting crowds at 8am. If this sounds like too much work, you can catch studio and grounds tours from the same location, 70-min tour is on a 'first come first served basis'. Mon-Fri 9am-3pm; July, Aug also on Sats 10am-2pm. $7. *www.nbc.com*.
Eddie Brandt's Saturday Matinee, 5006 Vineland Avenue, (818) 506-4242, is home to hardcore movie fans and 4 million rare videos, movie stills and posters, movies renting from $6. Tue-Fri 1pm-6pm, Sat 8.30am-5pm. *www.ebsmvideo.com.*

Other Attractions
Beverly Hot Springs, 308 North Oxford Ave (north of Beverly Blvd), (323) 734-7000. Separate spas for males and females, each featuring a giant tiled pool filled with piping hot water, a cool pool to calm down in, a steam room perfumed with fresh-cut eucalyptus branches and a dry sauna. The main spa treatment is a 55 min shiatsu massage ($80), the quintessential Japanese acupressure technique; there's a good deal of stretching, tweaking, twisting and even pounding! Open daily 9.30am-9pm, $60 on Fri-Sun and $50 during the rest of the week. *www.beverlyhotsprings.com*.

Entertainment
The **Sunset Strip**, with new clubs and restaurants opening in the past few years, is once again becoming LA's cultural epicenter and a destination of choice for both visitors and the truly hip residents. The Strip is divided into three loosely defined zones. **Laurel Canyon West** to **La Cienega Blvd** is a largely pedestrian-free stretch that includes some of the Strip's newer clubs such as the **Bar Marmont, Roxbury, The House of Blues** and **Dublin's Irish Whisky Pub**, a sports bar. West of La Cienega is one of the few enclaves tailored for pedestrian traffic, **Sunset Plaza**: two blocks of upscale open-air cafes. From here, the Strip winds toward Doheny where there is an abundance of commercial take-away eateries. The six blocks here are also home to the last of the area's clubs, the **Viper Room, Roxy, Whiskey** and **Billboard Live**. *BAM*, a free monthly paper, lists gigs up and down the West Coast. Also pick up *The Reader* and *LA Weekly*, free, full of entertainment listings. All available at record/bookstores and newsstands, all are published on Thursdays.

Anti-Club, 4658 Melrose, (323) 661-3913. Everything from cow-punk, video poetry and South African cheap beer. *www.rockandrollroadmap.com/anti.html.*

The World Famous Baked Potato, 3787 Cahuenga Blvd (near Universal), (818) 980-1615. Oldest major contemporary jazz watering hole. Tiny, but Lee Ritenour, Larry Carlton, among others established themselves here. Get there early for enormous spuds stuffed with whatever you want (7pm 'til 2am). Showtimes 9.30pm & 11.30pm, *www.thebakedpotato.com*.

Avalon Hollywood (formerly The Palace), 1735 N Vine St, Hollywood (323) 467-4571. Rock out in a restored old theatre.

The Troubadour, 9081 Santa Monica Blvd, (310) 276-1158, ageing but legendary launching pad for top rock acts; small and smoky. Cover plus 1 drink min, cheaper on Mon hoot nights. Open nightly.

Whisky a Go Go, 8901 Sunset Blvd, (310) 652-4202. Cream of rock triumvirate and hang-out of the stars. Cover, naturally. Legendary Sunset Strip club where Jim Morrison and Van Halen have played. *www.whiskyagogo.com*.

Theatre/Comedy: LA comedy clubs not only feature some of the hottest up-and-coming comedians, they also enjoy routine surprise visits from comedy legends and almost always have entertainment industry types in the audience seeking the next superstar. Cover charges tend to range from $10-$20, with a two-drink minimum. Besides **The Comedy Store**, 8433 Sunset, (323) 656-6225, *www.thecomedystore.com* , here are some of the other hot spots:

The Laugh Factory, 8001 Sunset, (323) 656-1336. Hosts industry showcases and special benefits. Comedy legends pop up from time to time. *www.laughfactory.com*.

The Ice House, 24 N Mentor Ave, Pasadena, (626) 577-1894. This place books star-powered headliners who do full, hour-long shows in comparison to the Hollywood-based clubs' 10 min specials. *www.icehousecomedy.com*.

Theatres: LA has an enormous number of larger theatres, including the **Mark Taper Forum**, the **Shubert** and **Ahmanson**. The best theatre is often at the small equity-waiver houses where struggling actors hone their skills while waiting for the big break. Check the *Reader* and *Weekly* for listings. Best bets are usually the **Group Repertory** or **Odyssey**.

Cinema: As you would expect from the world's film capital, there are a lot of movies around town. Westwood is the place where most films premiere. Dial 777-FILM to get location and schedule information for current films and purchase tkts in adv. You may wish to check *http://cinematreasures.org* for locations.

Mann Village Theater (was The Fox), 961 Broxton Ave., (310) 248-6266, built in 1931, has been, and continues to be, the home of Hollywood's biggest premiers. This Westwood legend is the one theatre you should see a movie in, if you only see one movie while in LA.

The Nuart, 11272 Santa Monica Blvd, (310) 281-8223. Revival/art house par excellence. *www.landmarktheaters.com/Market/LosAngeles/NuartTheatre.htm.*

Arclite Hollywood, 6360 Sunset Blvd, (323) 464-4226, this large-screen cinerama geodesic dome-shaped theatre housed the premiere of *Apocalypse Now*, and others. Open Daily 10.30am. Now it may host 14 other theatres, but the historical dome still stands. *www.arclightcinemas.com.*

Out of doors

Catalina Island, 26 miles off Long Beach, a romantic green hideaway, 85% of which is still in its natural state. Well worth a trip to see the perfect harbour of Avalon and its delightful vernacular architecture, plus the natural beauties of the place. Snorkelling is best at **Lovers Cove**, but look out for sharks. 'Beautiful.' The ride is $44 r/t and departs (daily at 9 am, return 4.30 pm) from Balboa Pavilion. Call Catalina Passenger Service, (949) 673-5245 (Newport). Rsvs req. *www.catalinainfo.com*.

Malibu Canyon, just north of Malibu offers one of the most stunning day trips in

Los Angeles. Take this canyon road to the Malibu State Creek Park for trails into the rugged Santa Monica Mountains.

Sport
Southern California is paradise for sports lovers. You can catch every major professional sport (with the exception of pro football). The Dodgers baseball team plays downtown at **Dodger Stadium**, 1000 Elysian Park Ave (323) 224-1448. *www.dodgers.mlb.com*. The World Champion **Lakers** (basketball) play down at the **Staples Centre** downtown. Tickets for Lakers games are hard to come by and extremely expensive ($100 for 'cheap' seats), *www.nba.com/lakers*. Instead, catch the Not-So-World Champion **Clippers** (LA's other pro basketball team) play in the exact same arena for less than $20. Call (213) 742-7555, *www.nba.com/clippers*.

Information
Bus and train info, (800) COMMUTE. 24 hrs.
Human Services Hotline, 24 hr, (323) 686-0950, locates doctors, emergency medical help.
LA Visitors Information Center, 685 Figueroa St, by the Hilton Hotel, (take DASH Bus A), (213) 689-8822. Mon-Fri 9am-5pm. Hollywood Visitor Information Center, 6801 Hollywood Blvd. at Highland. (323) 467-6412. Mon-Sat 10am-10pm; Sun 10am-7pm. Very helpful multilingual staff. Offer free maps, bus and rail info, TV taping tkts, and run-downs of special events. *www.lacvb.com*.

Internet access
Free Internet access and wi-fi is available at the **LA Public Library**, 630 W 5th St downtown, (213) 228-7000, and about 20 branches of the library. *www.lapl.org*.

Travel
Amtrak, 800 N Alameda, (800) USA-RAIL. Also stations in Fullerton, Santa Ana, San Juan Capistrano, San Clemente and San Diego. *The Coast Starlight* to Seattle is highly recommended for socialising and scenery.
Auto Driveaway, 3407 W 6th St, #525, (323) 666-6100. Open Mon-Fri. *www.autodriveawayla.com*.
Ride board, Floor B, Ackerman Union, UCLA, postings of ridesharing opportunities.
Car Rentals: Costless Car Rental (800) 770-0606, 4831 W. Century Blvd, a limited selection of cars and limited levels of employee competence are the prices you pay for these cheap rentals, from $30 a day. Fox (310) 641-3838, *www.foxarentacar.com*. **Thrifty**, (800) 367-2277, call for rates, Rsvs required 1 week in adv; and **Midway**, 2629 Wilshire Blvd., (213) 487-4700, all charge similar prices. Apparently it is possible to 'bargain with [Midway] over rates and mileage.' *www.midwaycarrental.com*.
Greyhound-Trailways Information Center, 1716 E 7th St (downtown), (800) 231-2222. Call for fares, schedules and local ticket info. Inside, a huge, clean but cheerless terminal; outside, the meanest streets anywhere—a zoo. Don't plan any overnights here. 'Friends twice approached by vicious druggies and tramps outside station—be careful.' 'Stay on the upper level.' If you want to avoid the dodgy downtown terminal, Santa Monica is accessed by Greyhound—picks up and drops off at the back of the Santa Monica Plaza—no signposts though!
Guideline Tours (800) 604-8433. Mainstream tours, only really worth doing if you are strapped for time—City tour $47, Universal Studios $68/69, Disneyland (including entrance) $79 etc. *www.guidelinetours.com*.
Hollywood Fantasy Tours, 6231 Hollywood Blvd, (323) 469-8184, 2 hr Beverly Hills Movie Star tour, 1 hr Hollywood tour, or combo by trolley. Runs daily 10am-5pm. *www.hollywoodfantasytours.com*.
Los Angeles International Airport (LAX), is on the west side of town, just south of

Venice, served by 90 passenger and cargo airlines. Information (310) 646-5252. *www.lawa.org/lax/welcomeLAX.cfm.* Transportation to and from downtown is fastest and least complicated using one of the numerous shuttle companies. Many accommodations offer free airport pick-ups so check beforehand. In general, shuttle companies will pick-up/drop-off from any major hotel, 24 hrs, req 1-day notice. **Super Shuttle**, (310) 782-6600, *www.supershuttle.com/htm/cities/lax.htm.* Venice Beach is a $15 cab ride from LAX. LA Taxi *www.la-taxi.com* and Yellow Cab *www.layellowcab.com* have $38 flat fare between LAX and downtown. Free shuttle bus service is provided to the LA MTA Metro Rail Green Line Aviation Station. Wait under the LAX Shuttle Connections sign on the Arrival Level islands in front of each terminal, and board the "G" Shuttle. You also can take the "C" Shuttle from the same pick-up point to get to the LA MTA Bus Center to board city buses serving the LA area. For transit info call (800) 266-6883. Other bus lines serving LAX are Culver City Bus Lines, Santa Monica Big Blue Bus, and Torrance Transit. Santa Monica Big Blue Bus #3 goes from Broadway Santa Monica to Parking lot C at LAX, then free shuttle to your terminal. Metrorail (213) 626-4455 goes closest to LAX on the Green Line Then get the free shuttle to your terminal, 24 hrs.

LA City Tours, (888) 800-7878, (323) 960-0300; *www.lacitytours.com.* Local LA tours—night club tour, city tour, Disney etc., plus further afield to Mexico, Las Vegas, Grand Canyon, etc. Specialise in small groups and gives discounts to BUNAC members.

MTA Buses and Metrorail: (213) 626-4455 or (800) COMMUTE, or check them out on the Net before you go: *www.mta.net.* $1.25 base fare, 25c transfers. Can be purchased at over 850 retail locations around the city. Buses: Bottom level of Greyhound terminal. 'Excellent value.' 'From the airport, change buses at Broadway.' **Metrorail:** This multi-billion dollar system 'doesn't seem to go anywhere useful': 20 miles of Blue Line light rail south from 7th & Figueroa downtown to Long Beach hits 22 stations; the 16-station Red Line E-W subway from Union Station/Civic Center downtown to the Wilshire Center, Hollywood and on to San Fernando Valley. The Green Line runs from Norwalk to Redondo Beach.

Orange County Transit District, (714) 636-7433, *www.octa.net.*

Santa Monica City 'Big Blue' Bus, (310) 451-5444, operates a good service throughout the Westside, with 13 routes and more than 1,000 stops from beaches, parks and shopping areas to businesses, colleges, inc downtown LA and LA International Airport. Basic fare 75¢, free transfers, #10 Express bus downtown $1.75. *www.bigbluebus.com.*

Taxis: Checker, (213) 482-3456, **Independent**, (213) 385-8294. *www.taxi4u.com*, and **LA Taxi** (323) 428 6896 *www.la-taxi.com*. Bear in mind that LA covers huge distances—cabs get expensive.

THE COAST TO SAN DIEGO First stop **Huntington Beach**, famed party beach and surfer capital. 'The local surfers love to take a complete novice in hand so don't hesitate to ask how it's done.' Also, check out **Huntington Beach Skatepark #2**. Located next to Huntington Beach High School on Main St near Yorktown and absolutely free.

Laguna Beach, 30 miles south of LA, buffered against urban sprawl by the San Joaquin Hills, has a **decided** Mediterranean look, from its indented coves to its trees and greenery right down to the waterline. The long white sand beach has superb snorkelling, surfing (for experts) and safe swimming at **Aliso Beach Park**. In winter, the whale watching and tidepooling are excellent. Long a haven for artists, Laguna is famous for its 7-wk Pageant of the Masters each July-Aug, but the accompanying **Sawdust Festival** (crafts, live music, jugglers, food) is both more accessible and more fun. While here, plan to eat at **The Cottage**, 308 N Coast Hwy (949) 494-3023, or **The Stand** at 238 Thalia St, (949) 494-8101 recommended by a Lagunian for its 'great Mexican food, smoothies and tofu cheeseless cake'. 'Laguna has excellent atmosphere, very picturesque.' Both open daily.

Newport Beach: Terribly yachty and formal except on **Balboa Island**, a mecca for boy/girl-watching. 'Try the Balboa bars and the frozen bananas at the ice cream kiosks.' Also, **T-K Burgers** at 2119 W Balboa Blvd (949) 673-3438 is the most popular hangout for the non-deckshoe set.

Orange County/Anaheim: San Juan Capistrano, 12 miles inland from Laguna and 22 miles south of Santa Ana. This mission town is well served by Greyhound, Orange County buses and Amtrak, so you have little excuse for passing up its mission, easily the best in California. The chapel, oldest building still standing in the state, is almost Minoan in proportions, feeling and colour. Also on the grounds are the romantic ruins of the great church tumbled by an 1812 earthquake and now a favoured nesting place for the famous swallows. The Indian graveyard, jail and various interesting buildings are well worth your dollar. Take lunch.

SAN DIEGO One glimpse of San Diego, and it's hard to believe that when Juan Cabrillo first landed here in 1542, he found not a single tree or blade of grass. Today, this desert-defying city is green, green, green by a blue, blue sea. Developed as a naval port, San Diego is strategically (for the tourist) located 100 miles south of Los Angeles and as close to Tijuana as any sane person may want to get.

The town is breezy and casual, famous for top-notch Mexican and seafood restaurants, monstrous 'happy hour' spreads, a historic old town, and great beaches accessible by bus from downtown. Lavish sunshine and its citizens' personal wealth haven't entirely eliminated the small-town flavour of San Diego and it is one of America's nicest and fastest growing cities. Check up on _www.sandiego-online.com_ for updates.

The telephone area code is 619.

Accommodation
Golden West Hotel, 720 4th Ave, 233-7596 (near Horton Plaza). $30, all shared bath. Also have some suites.

International House, 4502 Cass St (Above Tokyo House Restaurant), (858) 274-4325, and 3204 Mission Blvd, 539-0043. $23, wk rate $110. Incl bfast. Free internet. 'Super-friendly staff. Hostel has homely, personal atmosphere. People take the time to know your name. Arty décor.' _www.ih-sandiego.com._

Ocean Beach International Backpacker Hostel, 4961 Newport Ave, (800) 339-7263. Free pick-ups from bus/train/airport. Free bfast at 8am. Free BBQ Tue & Fri. Laundry, TV & videos, lockers, free use of surfboards, no curfew, alcohol allowed. From $16 (winter), rates higher in Summer. 'Clean and well-kept.' 'Brilliant! Friendly, laidback, hostel located right on beach—easy bus route to downtown.' 'Well recommended!' Seaworld a 15 min walk, San Diego Zoo a 30 min bus ride. _www.californiahostel.com/._

HI-Point Loma Hostel, 3790 Udall St, 223-4778. 6¹/₂ miles from downtown; take #35 bus to Ocean Beach. San Diego Zoo, Mission Bay Park, Sea World, Balboa Park and Old Town are close by. 'Well equipped, nr cheap markets, 20 min walk from beach.' Staff plans activities such as barbecues and beach bonfires. Member dorms-

$19, private rooms avail. _www.sandiegohostels.org/pointloma.htm._

HI-San Diego Downtown Hostel, 521 Market, 525-1531. Second gateway hostel to Mexico, it is located in the soul of the city's historic Gaslamp Quarter. Close by trolley, city bus. Few miles from Balboa Park, the Zoo, Sea World and beaches. Laundry, kitchen, $10 bike rentals are nearby. $19-$22 dorms and private rooms available, $47-55.50. _www.sandiegohostels.org/downtown.htm._

USA Hostels—San Diego, 726 5th Ave, 232-3100. In the heart of San Diego's Gaslamp District, this gateway-to-Mexico hostel is close to pubs, clubs and shops. Staff are experienced backpackers. Tons of info on travel, cheap fares and Mexico. 'If we don't have the info, we'll get it for you!' Day tours to Tijuana, pub crawl, free bfast, dinner available usually around $4, no curfew. Dorms (summer) $23 ($21 if booked via internet), private rooms $59 ($55); weekly rates available. _www.usahostels.com/sandiego/s-index.html._

Food

See _http://entertainment.signonsandiego.com/section/restaurants_ for complete listings by type and neighbourhood; another source for food in the city area is _www.sandiegomag.com/diningguide05/dining0805._ For 24-hour diners, visit _www.hoboes.com/html/Diner/AM/24.shtml._ In San Diego, you're likely to find some of the best Mexican food in the city, and plenty of places to choose from.

Chuey's Cafe, 1894 Main St, 234-6937. String beef tacos, other outstanding Mexican dishes under $12. Nearby murals at Chicano Park on the Coronado Bay Bridge make a fitting post-comida stroll.

El Indio Tortilla Shop, 3695 India St, 299-0333. Situated in an artists' district. 'Heavenly chicken burritos ($4.45), 50 takeout items so park across the way and pop in!' Dishes under $8, Sun-Wed 8am-9pm, Thu-Sat 7am-9pm.

Roberto's, many locations in and around the city, a wonderful greasy-spoon dive, popular with the locals and among the best for Mexican food. 'Great place, try the rolled tacos.'

Non-Mexican: Boll Weevil Restaurants, 15 locations around San Diego. Excellent, inexpensive burgers. $3.39-$6.65. 'More flavour than any other burger I had in three months.' _www.bollweevilinc.com._

Big Kitchen, 3003 Grape St, 234-5789. A bfast-and-lunch place with characters. Bfast/lunch $5-$10. Look for comedienne Whoopi Goldberg's graffiti on the kitchen wall, she once bussed tables here. Mon-Fri 7.30am-2pm, Sat-Sun 'til 3pm.

Chicken Pie Shop, 2633 El Cajon Blvd, 295-0156. North Park area. Scrumptious chicken & turkey pies for $1.70 to go, $3.95 to sit down with side dish, $5.25 pie-dinner. Daily 10am-8pm.

Filipe's Pizza, 4 locations in San Diego. 'Best Italian food in San Diego, try the lasagne; really superb.'

Of interest

Old Town, a snippet of the city's original heart, along San Diego Ave. Free walking tours from the Plaza at 2pm make the few historical remnants come to life. The **Visitor Center** is at 4002 Wallace Street, 220-5422. Up the hill is **Presidio Park**; its Serra Museum, 2727 Presidio, 297-3258, houses exhibits on history of San Diego, $5, $4 w/student ID. _www.sandiegohistory.org._

Balboa Park: Take the #7 bus or bike to this superlative 1074-acre park, whose pink-icing Mexican Churriguera-esque buildings were designed by Bertram Goodhue for the 1915-16 Panama-California International Exposition. 'Beautiful. Worth going to just for the architecture.' The park has over 20 museums and galleries. The best way to see it all is to purchase a Balbao Park Passport, which allows admission to 13 museums over 7 days and costs $30. Pick it up at the Visitors Centre or one of the museums. Rotating 'free Tuesdays' system ensures that several museums are free each Tues—check with the Visitor Centre. Balboa

Park is also home to the world-class San Diego zoo, a brass ring style carousel, pipe organ concerts, free sidewalk entertainment, free facilities for everything from volleyball to frisbee golf and occasional free festivals and performances. **Visitor Center: House of Hospitality**, 1549 El Prado, 239-0512, 9:30am-4:30pm daily, *www.balboapark.org/visitors.html* .

Inside the park: Museum of Art, 1450 El Prado, 232-7931. Tue-Sun 10am-6pm, Thu 'til 9pm. $10, $7 w/student ID; *www.sdmart.org*. **Natural History Museum**, 1788 El Prado 232-3821. Daily 10am-5pm, $9, $6 w/student ID; *www.sdnhm.org*. **Aerospace Museum**, 2001 Pan American Plaza, 234-8291. Daily 10am-5pm, $9; *www.aerospacemuseum.org*. **Museum of Man**, 1350 El Prado, 239-2001. Daily 10am-4.30pm, $6; *www.museumofman.org*. **Museum of Photographic Art**, 1649 El Prado, 238-7559, $6, $4 w/student ID, *www.mopa.org*. **Reuben H Fleet Science Center**, 1875 El Prado, 238-1233, IMAX films, laser shows, simulator ride (*Deep Sea*) and galleries, $6.75-$15. Daily 9.30am-4/8pm, Fri 'til 9pm. 'Science portion is small, while no great shakes await, the 360-degree films are exhilarating.' *www.rhfleet.org*.

Also at Balboa: summer light opera at the **Starlight Bowl Theatre**, box office 544-STAR, free concerts at organ pavilion. Check for student discounts. *www.starlighttheatre.org*.

Cabrillo National Monument, Pt Loma, 557-5450, take a #26 bus from downtown San Diego. A splendiferous view of the site where Juan Cabrillo first touched land at San Miguel Bay. Excellent tidepools, nature walks, films on whales, exhibit hall. Open summer 9am-5.15pm. Fee: $5 per car or $3 a person, *www.nps.gov/cabr*.

Coronado / Hotel Del Coronado, 1500 Orange Avenue. The hotel is where Edward VIII first met Mrs Simpson, then a Coronado housewife, and where *Some Like it Hot* was filmed. It's a wonderful old building situated right on one of America's best beaches. Take the **Trolley Tour** (see below). *www.hoteldel.com.*

Gaslamp District south of Broadway. Sixteen blocks of restored frontier San Diego, filled with smart shops and cafes. *www.gaslamp.org*.

La Jolla, (pronounced 'La Hoya') the jewel of San Diego, from sculptured rocks at Windansea to the St Tropez-like La Jolla Shores and limpid La Jolla Cove. On La Jolla Bvld, rent snorkels and roam in this fabulous underwater park and wildlife preserve. The beach is trying to lose its stuffy image and redraw the tourists and locals who, in recent years, have flocked to **Mission Beach**. The community is home to the **Museum of Contemporary Art**, 1001 Kettner Blvd, 234-1001. The free museum is open 11am-5pm everyday except Wed (closed). *www.mcasandiego.org*.

Mission Bay Park, 2581 Quivira Ct, 221-8900. 4600-acre marine park, the largest facility of its kind in the world with sailing, fishing, water skiing, wind surfing on 27 miles of beaches. Mission Beach has a reputation for hedonism, fun, sun and beautiful bodies to rival 'Baywatch'. *www.aboutmissionbay.com.*

San Diego Zoo, off Park Blvd in Balboa Park, 234-3153, is one of the world's best—a luxurious setting for the 3200 animals. General admission is $21—$32 includes bus tour, the aerial tram ride, and zoo. Open daily 9am-9pm ('til 4pm after Labor Day); gates close at 4pm. Don't miss the walk-through hummingbird aviary, the koalas and the primates. Plan to spend an entire day here, *www.sandiegozoo.org*.

The San Diego Wild Animal Park, is located 32 miles N of the San Diego Zoo off Hwy I-15 near **Escondido**, (760) 747-8702. 1800 acres of animals freely roaming in their natural habitats; view from a 60 min ride on the **Wgasa Bush Line** monorail. Spanish architecture. 'Lots to see—don't miss bird shows. Best monorail run is 4.30pm for most animal activity.' 'Amazing.' Also, Mombasa Lagoon is an interactive attraction where you can climb inside a giant stork eggshell, hop across the water on extra large lily pads, or explore an oversized spider's web. $28.50 includes entrance, monorail, hidden jungle and all live shows. Two-park ticket with Zoo—$54.45. Daily 9am-4pm. *www.sandiegozoo.org/wap/index.html.*

Sea World, 1720 South Shores Rd, 222-6363, on Mission Bay north of downtown.

Expensive at $56.95, so you'd better like performing whales, dolphins and seals! 'Don't miss the seal and otter shows.' **Shamu Backstage**, a 1.7 million gallon killer whale habitat allows visitors to touch, train and feed the killer whales, even wading with them in their 55-degree water. 'An all-day affair.' Open daily—hours vary; _www.seaworld.com_.

San Diego County Fair, Del Mar Fairgrounds, north of San Diego, (858) 755-1161. Some of everything: outdoor flower and garden show, arts, gems, minerals, hobbies, crafts, jams, jellies, hundreds of animals and a three week carnival mid-June to early July. Horseracing takes place in summer months. _www.sdfair.com/index.php?fuseaction=fair.general info._

Entertainment
In Cahoots, 5373 Mission Center Rd, Mission Valley, 291-1184. Popular Country and Western bar, 'Always a party! Something cookin' every day of the week.' $1.75 drinks 'til midnight. 5pm-2 am daily. _www.incahoots.com._

Humphrey's, 2241 Shelter Island Dr, 224-3577. Great happy hours Mon-Fri 4.30pm-6.30pm and live entertainment every day. _www.humphreysbythebay.com_.

Princess Pub and Grille, 1665 India St, downtown, 702-3021. '_Real_ beers on tap. Biggest surprise is when you walk out of the door and back into California.' Daily 11am-midnight. Happy hours Mon-Fri 4-7pm _www.princesspub.com_.

Croce's Top Hat Bar and Grill, 818 5th Ave, 233-4355. Live rhythm & blues nightly music nightly at this local hot spot. Dinner entrees $6-$30. Mon-Fri 5:30-12pm. Also open for bfast Sat-Sun 8:30am-12:30pm, _www.croces.com/tophat.shtml._

Festivals: There are many: **National Whale-Watching Weekend**, mid-Jan/Feb, sees special speakers and presentations at the Cabrillo whale-watching station at Point Loma. Take **San Diego Transit's #26.** 557-5450. _www.nps.gov/cabr/whales.html._ Also, **Street Scene** is an annual food and music festival held late July, featuring more than 100 blues, Cajun, zydeco, rock, jazz, and reggae bands. (888) **487-4347.** _www.street-scene.com._

Sport
The San Diego's **Padres** baseball team play at **Petco Park,** accessible by trolley and San Diego Transit, routes 4, 11, and 25. 795-5012. _www.padres.com._ The NFL **Chargers** also play here, 874-4500. _www.chargers.com._

Shopping
Bazaar del Mundo International Marketplace in Old Town, open 10am-10pm. Horton Plaza; **San Diego Factory Outlet Center**, 4498 Camino de la Plaza; **Seaport Village**, 14-acre complex at West Harbor Dr and Kettner Blvd.

Information/Internet access
International Visitor Information Centers, 1040 1/3 West Broadway (at Harbor Drive), 236-1212, (800) 4SANDIEGO, multilingual staff. Daily 9am-5pm. _www.sandiego.org/visitorcenter.asp._ Also at 7966 Herschel Ave in Village of La Jolla.

Balboa Park Info Center, 1549 El Prado, Balboa Park, 239-0512. Other centres in Old Town, at airport. Daily 9.30am-5pm. _www.balboapark.org/visitors.html._

Public Library, 820 E St, 236-5800 has Free access.

Travel
Amtrak, 1050 Kettner Blvd at Broadway, (800) 872-7245. Romantic 1915 depot with twin Moorish towers. _Pacific Surfliner_ has 12 daily roundtrips to LA, about 2 hrs 45 mins ($26 o/w), and Paso Robles. _www.dot.ca.gov/hq/rail/depots/stops/san.htm._

Greyhound, 120 W Broadway, (800) 231-2222. 24 hrs.

San Diego International Airport (Lindbergh Field) lies at northwestern edge of downtown. _www.san.org._ Shuttle (Flyer #992) connects airport with waterfront, Amtrak, light rail, and downtown, every 10 minutes. $2.25.

Auto Driveaway, 7590 El Cajon Blvd, 671-7800. _www.autodriveaway.com._

Bargain Auto Rentals, 3860 Rosecrans St, 299-0009. One of the only places to rent to 18 year olds, cash deps req, credit card essential. Open daily. Cars allowed to Mexico. _www.bargainautorentals.com_.

San Diego Regional Transit, 233-3004. Runs a 'very efficient and easy-to-understand' bus system. Basic fare $1.75-$4. Shuttle routes $1. 'Daytripper' one-day pass, $5. _www.sdcommute.com._

San Diego Trolley, 233-3004, which makes frequent breaks for the US border near San Ysidro; $6 r/t. 'Buy a r/t ticket to Tijuana, you won't want to stay long.' 'Quick, comfortable' and cheaper than Mexicoach and Greyhound. _www.sdcommute.com/Rider_Information/trolley/index.asp_.

Trolley Tour, 298-8687. Get on/off where you like; city tours and Coronado (across the amazing Coronado Bridge) are worthwhile. $27. _www.trolleytours.com._

ANZA-BORREGO DESERT and **EASTERN SAN DIEGO COUNTY** The 600,000-acre state park is in San Diego's back yard, at the end of a scenic 90-mile climb through forests, mountains and the charming gold mining village of **Julian**, ultimately spiralling down 3000 ft to the **Sonoran Desert** floor. _www.anzaborrego.statepark.org, www.parks.ca.gov/pages/638/files/ABDSPmap.pdf._ The route can be traversed by bicycle (tough) or car, but there's also a cheap bus service via the **San Diego Rural Bus,** (800) 858-0291, four trips going and coming (#s891 and 892) on both Thu and Sat from El Cajon, east of San Diego, to Julian, Borrego Springs and other points, that charges $3 a person. The park, the largest desert state park in the continental US, is open daily 24hrs, free vehicles.

At once desolate and grand, the **Anza-Borrego Desert** (NB. _Borrego_ is Spanish for bighorn sheep.) embraces sandstone canyons, rare elephant trees, pine-rimmed canyons, oases and wadis. Springtime brings wildflowers, which you can see year-round at the excellent sound and light presentation at the **Visitors Center**, 767-5311, daily 9am-5pm. For rsvs: (800) 444-7275. Best months are Nov-May; it's terribly hot thereafter. If you don't want to camp, stay in Julian at one of the B&Bs or cottages rather than in expensive Borrego Springs. Either way, don't miss out on the spectacular apple pies ($3) made at the **Julian Pie Company,** (760) 765-2400, and sold in restaurants all around the area. For places to eat and stay in historic Julian, check _www.julianbnbguild.com/thingstodo.html_ and _www.julianfun.com._

The telephone area code is 760.

HAWAII - Aloha State

When your plane touches down, congratulate yourself—you've made it to paradise. Hawaii has its poor and its homeless, but paradise still exists in this tourist-trampled state and it's not hard to find.

Hawaii was first inhabited sixteen hundred years ago by Polynesians who had set out in their canoes from the Marquesas Islands, in what is now French Polynesia. For centuries they grew their taro, hunted pigs, and occasionally had each other over for dinner (one-way tickets only), undisturbed by 'civilisation'. Captain Cook, when he arrived at Kona in 1778, inadvertently brought an end to that, but the Hawaiians brought an end to him, which was irony, if not justice. Not for nothing did he name Hawaii the 'Sandwich Islands'; he had inside knowledge!

Polynesian-blooded Hawaiians now number about 250,000, and are well outnumbered by the descendants of the immigrants brought in to expand the sugar industry in the late 19th century: Europeans/Americans, Chinese, Japanese, Koreans, and, lately, Filipinos, Samoans and Vietnamese. The pure Hawaiian is almost, as Mark Twain put it, 'a curiosity in his own land'. The 'missionaries' banned the teaching of the Hawaiian language (as well as removing some letters from the alphabet!), so that by 1987 fewer than 2,000 people spoke the native tongue. Now, though, children can be taught in Hawaiian if they wish.

Hawaii's island chain has been formed (and is still being formed) by volcanic activity. The islands are actually the tips of the tallest volcanic mountains on earth—Mauna Kea on the Big Island is 13,796' above sea level, and over 19,000' below! The oldest sizeable island (Kauai) is to the west, but the newest island (Hawaii itself, the Big Island) is still growing in the east as tectonic plate movement pushes the islands off the volcanic hot spot below. The most popular islands (from left to right: Kauai, Oahu, Maui and Hawaii) are readily accessible by air and are all worth visiting for their differing flavours, scenery and beaches. All of Hawaii's beaches are public and most are excellent.

From **Oahu**, with its cosmopolitan capital, Honolulu, you can island-hop via the reasonably priced local airlines. Don't be discouraged by the astronomical prices of the big resort hotels. Good, cheap motels and bed and breakfasts abound. (**B&B Honolulu**, 3242 Kaohinani Dr, Honolulu, 96813 (800) 288-4666, _www.hawaiibnb.com_, operates throughout the state, rooms also from $55, often including bfast.)

National Parks: Haleakala and Hawaii Volcanoes. _www.nps.gov/hale_ and _www.nps.gov/havo_, _www.gohawaii.com_.

The telephone area code is 808.

OAHU Most urbanized and brutalised of the islands, Oahu is also the most resilient. While Honolulu absorbs the brunt of Hawaii's approx 4.5 million visitors each year, much of the rest of the island is ignored by the masses. Within a 30 minute drive, outside of Honolulu you'll discover an island that remains relatively unblemished by the tourism factories on the southern coast. Oahu is also the cheapest island to get to and to stay on.

Honolulu is the state's capital and home to one of the nation's busiest ports and tourism industries. Don't come here looking for miles of untouched beaches, Hawaiian villages, charm or quiet. You'll find in Waikiki a postage-stamp sized beach covered with bodies in various shades of red. Crowded with traffic and people, Waikiki is a place to act the tourist: shop at the **International Market** for muu-muu's (traditional Hawaiian costume); sip mai tais at the **Hard Rock Café**; eat puupuus (Hawaii's hors d'oeuvres) and have a good time when the sun goes down.

Don't miss sampling poi, a Hawaiian staple made of taro root. Packaged in plastic bags and sold in local stores, the squishy grey stuff looks remarkably like wallpaper paste, (some say it tastes like it too), but be open-minded and decide for yourself. Although they are somewhat buried in the barrage of tourist ballyhoo.

Honolulu's historical sites, particularly, **Pearl Harbor** and the **Punchbowl**

Crater, are tasteful and moving. Get a fantastic view from the old military fortifications atop **Diamond Head**, a volcanic crater overshadowing the city.

Following Hwy 72 E, you come to **Koko Head State Park**. Home to **Hanauma Bay**, _www.hawaiiweb.com/html/hanauma_bay_beach.html_. This is a snorkeler's heaven. Coral reefs form large tunnels and deep pools, through which you can chase elusive sea turtles and colourful fish. To the northeast of Honolulu lies the steep, grooved ridges of the **Koolau Range**, which, like most Hawaiian ranges, drips with lush foliage. Cutting through the mountains, **Nuuanu Pali Pass** offers splendid views of the ocean. It was here that **King Kamehameha the Great** defeated the Oahuans in 1795, literally forcing them over the cliffs; the victorious king became the first ruler of the united Hawaiian Islands.

Near **Hauula** on the northeast coast, a tough one-mile climb along a rough mountain ravine brings you to the **Sacred Falls**, one of the loveliest sights on the island: 2500-foot cliffs form a splendid backdrop to the falls, which drop 87 feet into the gorge. Oahu's northern side boasts the incredible beaches of Sunset and Waimea Bay. In the winter, these beaches see some of the world's most incredible surf. In the summer, the waters are like glass. Further on is the **Puu O Mahuka Heiau**, where humans were once sacrificed to the gods (the practice has since been discontinued). Check _www.visit-oahu.com_ or call (877) 525-6248 for a _Travel Planner_.

Accommodation
Waikiki, a couple of miles east of downtown, is crowded with low-cost digs, many with kitchens, most a couple of blocks from the beach. Rsvs advised year-round. NB: city buses take backpacks 'at the discretion of the driver'.

Big Surf Hotel, 1690 Ala Moana Blvd (near boat harbour), 946-6525. Ave $60.

Central YMCA, 401 Atkinson Dr, across from Ala Moana Shopping Center, 941-3344. First come, first served; pool, weight room, 4 racquet ball courts, $33 male, $41-48 women (private bath), 18+only, $10 key deposit. 'Convenient for all buses.' _www.centralymcahonolulu.org_.

HI-Honolulu Hostel, 2323A Sea View Ave, 946-0591. Across the street from **Univ of Hawaii**; from the airport, take #19 or #20; transfer to bus #6, #4, or #18 to the university. Small and peaceful. Kitchen, TV room, patio under coconut trees, laundry, clean single-sex facilities. 3 night max for non-members, $19. Members can stay up to a week, $16. Check-out 11 am, lights out 11 pm. 'Very busy.' Rsvs essential. _www.hostelsaloha.com_.

HI-Waikiki Hostel, 2417 Prince Edward St (2 blocks off beach), 926-8313. 3 night max for non-members, $23. Members can stay up to a week, $20, private doubles - $48 & $54. Kitchen and free use of snorkelling gear! No lockout or curfew. Rsvs advised. _www.hostelsaloha.com_.

NB: Camping is not recommended on Oahu; locals gather at campsites and may feel you are encroaching on their turf.

Food
In the local parlance, Hawaiians don't eat, they 'grind.' Grinding episodes start with puupuus which reflect the state's ethnic diversity, such as egg rolls and falafel. This is the home of the _mai tai_, a nobly proportioned ration of rum, pineapple juice, chunks of fruit and a baby orchid. Another local poison is the blue Hawaii, a toxic-looking concoction made from Blue Curacao, vodka and pineapple juice.

There's good ethnic eating at the Japanese delis, Chinese noodle shops and especially along **Hotel Street**. If you're still not stuffed, tap into Honolulu's lavish happy hour spreads, or better still, a luau. Read the free _Waikiki Beach Press_ and other local papers for Church luaus that are, generally, friendlier, cheaper, tastier and more fun than those at the big hotels. Be sure to sample shaved ice, Hawaii's deeply improved version of the snowcone. Try the variety of ethnic restaurants located btwn the 500 and 1000 blocks of **Kapahulu Ave** and the region's many seafood specialties. **Kaimuki, Moili'ili** and the downtown districts thrive with good food and nightlife. *http://the.honoluluadvertiser.com/section/dining* may be helpful.

Eggs and Things, 1911-B Kalakaua Ave., 949-0820, opens at 11pm and closes at 2pm, this night owl's haven serves breakfast—really, really good breakfasts, for less than $10. *www.eggsnthings.com*.

Queen Kapiolani Hotel, 150 Kapahulu Ave, Honolulu, 922-1941, open for all three meals and offer a buffet lunch Fri-Sun from 11am-2pm. *www.queenkapiolani.com.*

Rainbow Drive-In, 3308 Kanaina Ave, 737-0177, tasty cuisine at rock-bottom prices (c $5). Open daily 7:30am 'til 9pm.

Of interest

In Honolulu: Academy of Arts, 900 S Beretania, (take #2 #13 bus from Waikiki), 532-8701, Tue-Sat 10am-4.30pm, Sun 1pm-5pm; closed Mon. $7, $4 w/student ID. 30 galleries housing everything from Polynesian to avant-garde, including one of the finest collections of Asian Art in America and James Michener's renowned collection of Ukiyo-e woodblock prints surrounds six garden courts. Call 532-8768 for listings and show times. *www.honoluluacademy.org*.

Bishop Museum and Planetarium, 1525 Bernice St, 847-3511, $14.95 includes gallery tours, dance performances, craft demonstrations of incredible feather cloaks (treasured as booty by the ancient kings) and other Hawaiian and Polynesian artefacts. *www.bishopmuseum.org*.

Capitol District Walking Tour gives extensive coverage of Honolulu's historic district and may be picked up from the **Hawaii Visitor Bureau**. *www.visit-oahu.com*.

Foster Botanical Garden, 50 N Vineyard Blvd, 522-7066, a cool oasis of rare trees, orchids and flowers. Wear insect repellent! Guided tours weekdays 1pm. Take #4 bus from Waikiki to corner of Vineyard Blvd. Daily 9am-4pm, $5.

Hilo Hatties, 700 N Nimitz Hwy, (888) 526-0299, the definitive tourist trap offers a free shuttle from Waikiki with complimentary refreshments. Huge selection of 'Hawaiian' clothes and gifts, open daily, 8am-6pm, and have many stores throughout the islands. *www.hilohattie.com*.

Honolulu Zoo, 151 Kapahulu Ave, 971-7171, Daily 9am-4.30pm, $6, is home of the world's finest group of tropical birds. *www.honoluluzoo.org*.

Iolani Palace, King and Richards St, 522-0832, Tue-Sat 8am-3.30pm. Closed Sun/Mon, $20. Only royal palace on American soil, used just 11 yrs by the Hawaiian monarchs. 90 min tours begin every 30 min. Queen Liliuokalani wrote *Aloha Oe*, easily the most famous Hawaiian song, while imprisoned here. Very popular; rsvs necessary, call 522-0832. *www.iolanipalace.org*.

Hawaii's post-modern **State Capitol** stands at the corner of Beretania and Richard Sts. Mon-Fri 9am-4pm; free.

Outside Honolulu: USS Arizona National Memorial at Pearl Harbor, 422-0561, a 23 min film on the Japanese attack on Pearl Harbor in the Visitors Center is followed by free Naval boat tours of the harbour and memorial. The ghostly outline of the USS Arizona is still visible through the limpid water, wherein lie hundreds of sailors who died on 7 Dec 1941. Take #20, #42 or City Express A bus from Waikiki, (1-1/4 hr), or catch a shuttle bus (see TRAVEL). Daily tours 8am-3pm. Free, but arrive early and dress respectably, (queue forms at 7am for same-day tkts). The Visitors Center is open daily 7.30am-5pm. *www.nps.gov/usar*.

USS Bowfin, next to the Arizona Memorial, 423-1341. Self-guided tours (w/hand-held receiver) of this WW2 submarine are available daily from 8am-5pm (last tour 4.30pm), $10. *www.bowfin.org.*

Sea Life Park, Makapuu Point (16 miles E of Waikiki on Hwy 72), 259-7933. The huge reef tank offers a unique view of brilliant fish, coral and sharks. Open daily 9am-5pm; $25, 'cheaper and better than the mainland aquatic parks.' *www.sealifeparkhawaii.com*.

Beaches: Queen's Surf Beach is close to downtown and attracts swimmers, skateboarders and in-line skaters. Also, try the **Sans Souci Beach**. If you seek more secluded beaches, head east on Diamond Head Rd until you reach Kahala Ave. **Hanauma Bay** is home to the islands best shore based snorkelling, #22 Bus from Waikiki. Closed Tue, $3. Equipment can be rented for $6, 'they take your passport as deposit'. Tour parties were banned in 1991 to cut down on damage to the fragile ecology. Other snorkelling beaches include **Magic Island, Kahe Point State Park** and **Waimea Bay** (in summer). Tremendous waves pound the island's north shore in winter but are no more than ripples in the summer; instead summer months see swells along the eastern coast. In the beaches by Hanauma Bay, such as Sandy Beach, you'll find world-class bodysurfers. *Aloha!* is a guide to Oahu's popular beaches, *www.aloha.com/~lifeguards*.

Entertainment

The **Hilton Hawaiian Village** has free shows, with a torch lighting ceremony at 6pm on Sat & Sun, and a more impressive Polynesian show with fireworks on Fri nights at sunset, 949-4321.

The Wave, 1877 Kalakaua, 941-0424, live music every night, 9pm-4am; $5 'til 10pm, then $7 cover, must be 21-yrs+. *www.wavewaikiki.com.*

World Café, 1130 N. Nimitz Hwy, 599-4450, has good tunes, drink specials and is cool with the under 21 set.

Festivals: May 1st is **Lei Day** and culminates in the crowning of the Lei Queen, a celebration that is accompanied by huge festivities and various concerts. Remember that a lei is always accompanied by a kiss! One of the best parades is held on June 12 in Honolulu, to honor **Kamehameha the Great**, the warrior king who unified the island chain in the early 19th century.

Information/Internet access

Oahu Visitors Bureau, 2250 Kalakaua, Royal Hawaiian Shopping Centre, 5th flr, 924-0266. Mon-Fri 8am-4.30pm. *www.visit-oahu.com.*

The **Waikiki-Kapahula Public Library** offers free internet access. One catch: you need a library card, $10 (for 3 months), good for all the libraries in Hawaii. Access at **Waikiki-Kapahulu** branch 400 Kapahulu Ave, 733-8488, requires res.

Travel

Honolulu Intl. Airport, 300 Rodgers Blvd, 836-6413. Airport Waikiki Express from airport to any hotel in Waikiki, every 25 mins, $8. *www.honoluluairport.com* and *www.hawaii.gov/dot/airports/oahu.*

The Bus, 848-5555, offers good bus service around the island; $2 gets you anywhere, inc the airport. *www.thebus.org.*

Waikiki Trolley, 591-2561 or (800) 824-8804, four lines link Waikiki and downtown Honolulu. *www.waikikitrolley.com*.

MAUI Twenty-five flying minutes southeast of Honolulu is Maui, the trendiest of the islands and famous for its beaches, parties, sweet onions, potato chips, humpback whales and Maui Wowie, a potent variety of the local marijuana. Formed by two volcanic masses linked by a wasp-waisted isthmus, Maui is marked by an extraordinary variety of terrain and climate, from the cold dryness of 10,023-foot **Haleakala** volcanic crater to the lush wetness of **Hana** (to describe it adequately would require a new vocabulary for hues of green). The former whaling port of **Lahaina** is touristy and social; the upcountry eucalyptus land around **Makawao** is rural and mellow.

Once you get past the endless condos of **Kihei** and **Wailea**, there are superb beaches and camping opportunities at **Makena** and further south at Haleakala National Park, 572-4400, $10 per car. The 'House of the Sun' has the largest dormant (for the last 200 years, anyway) volcano in the world, 21 miles in circumference. If you go there, you will be told repeatedly that the crater is big enough to swallow all of Manhattan (you might as well hear it here first).

Often huge cumulus clouds will pour over the crater lip and pile up like whipped cream. At dawn and dusk you may find a gigantic shadow of yourself projected against the clouds and encircled by rainbow light—the **Spectre of Brocken** effect. Sunrise at Haleakala is like a slow-motion fireworks display that is best seen near the Puu Ulaula Observation Centre. NB: Dress warmly! _www.nps.gov/hale_.

Hookipa Beach Park, on Maui's north shore, is the Mecca of the windsurfing world.

Accommodation/Food

Flown-in food is costly on Maui, so stick to local products: seafood, pineapples, lettuce, tomatoes, world renowned sweet onions, 'Maui Kitch'n Cook'd Potato Chips', 'Maui blanc' (pineapple wine) and, of course, Maui ribs (ask any local).

Banana Bungalow, 310 N Market St, Wailuku, (800) 8-HOSTEL, uncrowded rooms and numerous facilities, including free hi-speed and wireless internet connection. Dorm (incl taxes) $22.50, S-$44.40, D-$55.50, T-$66.60. Cheap meals, island tours, beach shuttles and a free dropoff at the airport are all included. _www.mauihostel.com_.

YMCA Camp Keanae, 13375 Hana Hwy on the east side (36 miles E of airport), 248-8355, this isolated and beautiful setting requires a couple of compromises. One, bring your food with you and two, be in by 9pm. $17 pp, (no linens), kitchen, usual facilities with check-in from 4pm-6pm. Cabins of 4 to 60 bunks. Call before you go. _www.mauiymca.org/campk.htm._

Of interest/Travel

Blue Hawaiian Helicopter Tours, 871-8844, start from $165 p/p and although expensive, may be worth the one-of-a-kind views you'll be able to catch of the Haleakala Crater, rainforests and rugged shores of Maui. From the mainland call (800) 745-BLUE. _www.bluehawaiian.com_.

In **Hana**: 54 miles of bad but beautiful road kept Hana private. If you are willing to let someone else do the driving, try a tour, $80-105 for full day trips, **Ekahi Tours** (888) 292-2422 / 877-9775, _www.ekahi.com_; Charles Lindbergh loved Hana enough to live and be buried here. 'Don't miss the crystal clear **Oheo Gulch**—just like paradise.' A free shuttle runs btwn Lahaina and Kaanapali every 25 min and stops at the Royal Lahaina, Sheraton, Marriott, Kaanapali Beach and Hyatt.

View the humpback whales which mate and calve in the **Lahaina Channel** every winter; lots of whale-watching tours leave from the harbour. Also, see the **Whalers Museum** in Kaanapali, 3rd floor of the beachside **Whalers Village**, 661-5992. This 'small but stunning and poignant' museum houses whaling artefacts, photographs, and antiques from 19th C. Open Daily 9.30am-10pm, free. _www.whalersvillage.com/museum/museum.htm._

Information/Travel

Word of Mouth Rent-a-Car, 150-A Hana Hwy, Kahului, 877-2436 / (800) 533-5929, _www.mauirentacar.com_.

Maui Visitors Bureau, 1727 Wili Pa Loop, Wailuku, 244-3530. Mon-Fri 8am-4.30pm. _www.visitmaui.com._
Visitor Information Kiosk, 872-3893, at Kahului Airport baggage claim areas, daily 7.45am-9.45pm. _www.hawaii.gov/dot/airports/maui/ogg/._

HAWAII The Big Island is the youngest, fireiest and, some believe, prettiest of the islands. It's known locally as the Orchid Island because of the 22,000 varieties that grow wild on the mountainous slopes. Unlike its sister isles, which draw crowds to their beaches, Hawaii's main attraction is inland— **Hawaii Volcanoes National Park**, a cracked and crumpled moonscape created by the living volcano **Mauna Loa**. Each day the volcano adds to the island's real estate, annually dumping 650,000 cubic yards of red-hot lava into the ocean, enough to pave a thin sidewalk to New York. Nearby **Mauna Kea** has earned new fame: From its peak scientists discovered a galaxy 12 billion light years away. This and **Kilauea** are two of the world's most active volcanoes.

The island's black sand, pink sand, and red sand beaches are incredible—but stick to the white sand when it comes time to lie down. The island is home to more climates than some continents. Make sure to take the time to explore the jungly mystery of the east side; the desert bleakness of the south; the commercialised carnival of the Kona Coast to the west with its coffee-laden breezes; and the rolling hills of the north, the Hawaiian cowboy country.

Mark Twain, one of the many writers inspired by the island's beauty (such as Jack London, Somerset Maugham and Robert Louis Stevenson), wasn't alone in his sentiments that Hawaii is 'the only supremely delightful place on earth'. Here the Aloha Spirit has yet to fade and people still get together to 'talk story' and watch the sun set. _www.bigisland.com._

Accommodation
The Kona Coast on the western side is where the high-priced hotels are; Hilo on the east retains an unspoiled, if dilapidated charm.
Arnott's Lodge, 98 Apapane Rd, Hilo, 969-7097. $20 bunk, S-$42, D- $52, ensuite $130, tents $10, all inc tax. Right on the beach, daily tours & eco-expeditions, free shuttle to / from airport, bikes, snorkels to rent, internet access, laundry, kitchen & TV lounge. Check in before 8pm. _www.arnottslodge.com._
Dolphin Bay Hotel, 333 Iliahi St, Hilo, 935-1466, prices start from D-$79, T-$99 all rms have kitchens. Free bfst pastries and all-you-can-eat Papaya in their wonderful garden. _www.dolphinbayhotel.com._
Hotel Honokaa, Mammane St, Honokaa, (800) 808-0678, dorms start from $15. Private D from $50, 'luxury' D-$75, Rsvs required. This 'very simple', hotel/hostel has been going over 80 years. _www.hotelhonokaa.com._
Kona Tiki Hotel, 75-5968 Alii Dr, Kailua-Kona, 329-1425, all rooms inc fridges, ocean views and bfst., freshwater pool. D-$60-85. _www.konatiki.com._
My Island B&B Inn, 19-3896 Old Volcano Rd, Volcano Village, 967-7216. Beautiful rooms in a historic mission-style home. From S-$55, D-$70, XP $20, incl full bfst. _www.myislandinnhawaii.com._
Camping: The County runs beach parks where you can camp for $5 pp; permits required, from one of the four County Parks offices on the island. Call 961-8311 or go online for info _www.hawaii-county.com/parks/parks.htm_. In **Volcanoes National Park**, find the only free campsites in the state at **Namakani Paio** (inc. running water) and Kulanaokuaiki. _www.nps.gov/havo_

Food/Of interest

Kona coffee and macadamia nuts are the indigenous items on the menu; restaurants seem to put the nuts in everything. Be sure always to ask for 100% Kona coffee. Taste it at **Royal Kona Coffee Mill and Museum**, 83-5427, on Mamalahoa Highway towards **Captain Cook**, 328-2511, open daily. *www.koacoffee.com/coffeehistory.html*.

Only in America—drive-in-volcanoes at Hawaii **Volcanoes National Park**, 985-6000, *www.nps.gov/havo* $10 per car, good for 7 days, via Hwy 11 from Hilo, **Crater Rim Drive** takes you through the **Kilauea Caldera**, almost into the gaping maw of the **Halemaumau Firepit**. Here lives Pele, the notoriously bad-tempered Hawaiian fire goddess. Going south on Hwy 11, the magnificent vista of the island's desert south comes into view.

You can visit the legendary black sand beaches at **Kaimu** and **Punaluu**, but be warned, the 'sand' is really volcanic rubble. Walking on it is a little like walking on broken glass, so bring shoes. The sand is green at **Ka Lae**—that is, if you can find any sand among the huge boulders that cover most of the shore. This is the most southerly point in the US, and the Hawaiian version of Plymouth Rock; here, Polynesian explorers first beached their canoes and established Hawaii's oldest known settlement, circa AD 750. Ka Lae is not developed for tourists and most car rental agencies prohibit customers from travelling this road.

Further north on the island's western side is **Captain Cook's Monument**, accessible only by sea. Here the European discoverer of the Islands, once regarded by natives as a god, suffered a massive drop in popularity in 1779. The marker showing where he was killed (while intervening in a dispute) is under water.

Kahaluu Park Beach, south of **Disappearing Sands Beach** on Alii Drive is home to amazing snorkeling amongst flashy fish. It's like swimming through an aquarium. If you've forgotten your mask and fins, rent them from the park or at **Jack's Diving Locker**, just down the road from the Kona Inn Shopping Village in **Kailua-Kona**, at 75-5813 Alii Drive, (800) 345-4807, daily 8am-9pm. *www.jacksdivinglocker.com* Watch for **Manta Rays** at the **Kona Surf Hotel** nightly. The hotel spotlights the ocean where huge rays come to feed, free and thrilling. Taking Hwy 19 from Kailua-Kona, you pass through the verdant hills of northern Hawaii.

Turn onto Hwy 24 at **Honokaa** to see the dreamlike **Waipi'o Valley**, a little green world captured by steep cliffs. The road goes all the way down to the valley, but the last part is too steep for cars. Jeep transport is available for a fee. Spare yourself the expense and the gear-grinding heart-attack ride down by hoofing it; if you're in reasonably good shape, you'll make it back up, too. Your reward: playing in the surf at the wonderful beach below.

The **Waipi'o Lookout**, offers one of the most striking panoramas in the islands. NB: A road to avoid is Hwy 200, the 50-mile, high fatality, **Saddle Road** that cuts btwn the twin behemoths of Mauna Kea and Mauna Loa. Once you're on it, there's no turning back: attempting a U-turn on the narrow road lined with lava rock guarantees a flat tire or worse.

Information/Travel

Big Island Visitors Bureau, 250 Keawe St, Hilo, 961-5797, open Mon-Fri 8am-4.30pm. *www.bigisland.org* and *www.hawaii-county.com/parks/parks_geninfo.htm.*

Hilo Airport *www.hawaii.gov/dot/airports/hawaii/ito/.* Has eight rent-a-car agencies, including **Dollar** 961-6059/ (800) 342-7398, and **Avis** 935-1290/ (800) 331-1212. A cab ride from the airport to Hilo is $12.

Hilo Mass Transit, 961-8744, from Mooheau Bus Terminal on Kamehameha Ave. Operates one service each day from Hilo to Volcano NP, Mon-Fri, (return next day). Has numerous other routes on the island - find out more at *www.co.hawaii.hi.us/mass_transit/transit_main.htm.*

Tour companies There are many land tour companies – for a list check _www.alternative-hawaii.com/activity/bitourlf.htm._

KAUAI Once the 'Garden Island' was known as the 'undiscovered isle', but no more. Now Kauai has its share of supermarkets, condos, huge resorts, canned tours and streams of rental cars. Mother nature, however, continues to make much of the island impassable and undiscovered. The highway that almost-girdles the island may flow with tourists, but the speed by which everything moves is considerably slower than on Kauai's sister islands. The landscape that lent the backdrop for the filming of _South Pacific_ in the 1950s still endures: **Lumahai** and **Haena** beaches on postcard-perfect Hanalei Bay.

The best patches of paradise are not gone; they just have to be discovered, and while the heavenly waterfall where France Nuygen cavorted with her GI beau has been closed due to tourist overload, hundreds of others still remain. The only thing this island is missing is nightlife. Learn how you can experience Kauai on an exciting helicopter tour or an exhilarating boat trip and by driving past some of the most scenic spots imaginable. _www.kauaidiscovery.com_ and _www.jans-journeys.com/kauai_.

Accommodation
Garden Island Inn, 3445 Wilcox Rd, Nawiliwili (2 miles from Lihue), (800) 648-0154. Ocean views from D-$90. _www.gardenislandinn.com._
Hotel Coral Reef, 1516 Kuhio Hwy, Kapaa, 822-4481, some rooms with ocean view (pay extra), rsvs advised. Coffee, homemade bread and fruit each morning, car rentals available. Rooms from S/D-$99. _www.hotelcoralreef.com._
Kauai International Hostel, 4532 Lehua St, Kapaa, (808) 823-6142, Located opposite beach and restaurants, great base for exploring; friendly backpacker crowd and staff with full kitchen, TV, pool table and laundry. Dorms $20, private rooms from $50. _www.kauaihostel.net._
Camping: Kauai County Parks Office, 4444 Rice St, Lihu'e, 241-4463, has $3 permits for camping in county parks. _www.kauai.gov/Default.aspx?tabid=176._

Food
Visit _www.alternative-hawaii.com/rest/khaw.htm_ for a local food guide.
Kauai is the proud birthplace of **Lappert's Ice Cream & Coffee**, 1-3555 Kaumualii Highway, Hanapepe, 335-6121, including such Aloha flavours as Guava and Macadamia Nuts, Pineapple, Mango, Kona Coffee, and Coconut. _www.lapperts.com._
Green Garden, 1-3749 Kaumualii, Hanapepe, 335-5422, home to incredible pies, specializing in delectable lemon chiffon and lilikoi cream (passion fruit) versions.
Korean BBQ 4-356 Kuhio Hwy, **Wailua**, 823-6744, 'Best bet for a bargain meal.'

Of interest
National Tropical Botanical Gardens have four locations on Kauai— the **McBryde Garden** in the Lawai Valley, 252 acres of garden and preserve, and HQ of the NTBG (3530 Papalina Road, Kalaheo); neighboring **Allerton Garden** at Lawai Kai; **Limahuli Gardens**, a thousand acres on Kauai's wet north shore in Haena in a valley covering three distinct ecological zones; and on the Hana coast of Maui, **Kahanu Garden** amid lava flows full of plants from other Pacific Islands). Tours $10-30; details at 332-7324. _www.ntbg.org._
North from Lihue on Hwy 56: Rent kayaks in Wailua (plenty of rental places are down by the river, upstream from the highway) and paddle up the **Wailua River** towards the Fern Grotto, a sea of green that nearly blocks out the sun. Don't stop here, though, continue up the river towards the **Wailua Falls**. After a short hike

you'll come across the Falls, where you can cool off in the stunningly beautiful pool below.

Past Wailua, turn off the road for a panoramic ocean view from **Kilauea Lighthouse**. Further north is the aforementioned Hanalei Bay; don't let its beauty distract you from the oriental splendour of **Hanalei Valley**, inland from the hwy. Wet and dry caves are right on the road; pull off and explore! Hwy 56 ends at **Ke'e Beach**, where the cliffhanging trail along the gorgeous Na Pali Coast begins.

A mellow but challenging hike takes you through some of the best scenery in the Hawaiian Islands: as you round one crucial corner, you get your first breathtaking view of a series of precipices plunging into the sea. The beach at the end of the hike is a beautiful stretch of sand. It's best to avoid the temptation to swim; incredibly strong undertows suck back with vacuum force.

South from Lihue on Hwy 50: two historic sites of European interest—the **Old Russian Fort (Ft Elizabeth)**, now a brush-covered rocky ruin; and **Captain Cook's Landing** (Jan. 1778) at **Waimea Bay**. Take a side trip to see the Menehune Ditch, an ancient aqueduct built, some say, in a single night by the Menehunes—Hawaiian leprechauns! All archaeologists know is that someone built the aqueduct years before the first Polynesian explorers arrived in Kauai. Inland on Hwy 550, **Kokee State Park** has the breathtaking 'Grand Canyon of the Pacific', **Waimea Canyon**.

Information
Kauai Visitors Bureau, 4334 Rice Street, **Lihue**, 245-3971. Has free travel planner, maps, guides. _www.kauaidiscovery.com/about.html_.

OREGON - Beaver State

In 1805-1806, Lewis and Clark explored this region, following the mighty Columbia River to its mouth—'the Columbian valley, wide and butiful...' wrote Meriwether Lewis. Their favourable reports brought pioneers along the 2000-mile trail—at first a trickle, swelling by the 1840s into a flood. A remarkably homogeneous bunch they were, too: farmers from the Midwest and South running from the economic depression of 1837-1840, looking for good soil, rainfall and an environment with neither malaria nor snow. Later, Astoria was founded near the mouth of the Columbia River to promote trade with China.

Oregon became a US territory the year of the California gold rush and promptly lost two-thirds of its males to the gold fever. A few struck it rich; more returned home and started selling wheat and lumber to the miners. At one point, Oregon wheat was actually made legal tender at $1 a bushel.

The heavily forested Beaver State has suffered in recent years from a decline in the demand for lumber but is still the largest producer of plywood in the US, the process having been invented here a hundred years ago, in 1905. Wineries (_www.oregonwine.org_) and fruit and flower growing are increasingly important. You can see 2500 varieties of English roses in the Willamette Valley, and peonies, lilacs—daffodils, hyacinths, and tulips there, too, plus the odd windmill.

Tourism is now the fourth-largest industry. Fortunately, Oregonians work hard to preserve the state's natural beauty and like Vermonters, they have banned the construction of new billboards and kept crass tourist traps to a minimum (with noticeable exceptions along the coast). In 1991, Oregon was judged 'Greenest state in the US' by environmentalists.

The biggest magnet for visitors is the 400-mile coastline, protected as an almost-continuous series of state beaches. At times cold, foggy and windy, this region offers a kaleidoscope of magnificent sights: offshore rocks, driftwood-piled sands, cliffs, caves, twisted pines and acres of rhododendrons. Coastal villages seem to specialise in weather-beaten charm with picturesque barns, covered bridges and historic villages that make the area from the coast to the East Willamette Valley a fun area to explore. Unless you're bent on speed, avoid the dull ribbon of interstate freeway that un-seams the valley north to south.

Both the youth hostel and the bed and breakfast networks are alive and well in Oregon. Biking is extremely popular here; just remember that it, like other outdoor activities can be rained out at any moment. Most of the time, it's a slow mournful drizzle, the kind that drove Lewis and Clark nearly crazy during their winter sojourn at Fort Clatsop.

Though many east coasters have drifted west to this state and find it much more beautiful than its more-popular neighbour to the south, Oregon has not drawn nearly the number of converts as California has. This makes Oregonians happy: while there you may spot one of the bumper stickers that define the 'Oregon attitude': 'Don't Californicate Oregon.' Furthering the wry underselling of the state, another slogan warns: 'In Oregon, you don't tan; you rust'. Travellers are welcome, however, as long as they're passing through. The most popular bumper sticker reads, 'Welcome to Oregon. Now go home'. _www.traveloregon.com_. **National Park:** Crater Lake.

PORTLAND In 1843, a couple of canoeists en route to Oregon City liked what they saw here and staked a 'tomahawk claim' by slashing trees in a 320-acre rectangle. The naming of the town was similarly impromptu: settlers flipped a coin and the losing name was Boston.

Portland, the City of Roses, modestly revels in its sparkling mountain and riverside setting, its luxuriant rose gardens with its month-long **Festival of Roses** in May/June, _www.rosefestival.org_, and its low-key neighbourliness. Opportunities abound for good eating and social action in this city of booklovers, art lovers and ardent joggers. '...No place on earth, with the exception of Paris, has done as much to influence my professional life,' wrote renowned Portland-native chef James Beard in his memoirs _Delights and Prejudices_.

Portland makes an ideal base to explore the Columbia River Gorge: take Hwy 84 east along the river to Troutdale and turn off onto the Columbia River Scenic Hwy. For an excellent free guide to the Gorge, including windsurfing, contact _www.hoodriver.org_. The old highway stops south of Bonneville Dam (its fish hatcheries are nice), but the scenic beauty doesn't. Further east on Hwy 84, the surrounding land dries up. Towns and farms line the river like oases, in stark contrast to the surrounding high desert cliffs. This is a drive that shows the state at its best. The Portland _Low-Budget Guide_ is an alternative offering to what the local Chamber of Commerce may typically offer. _www.pova.com._ For a fun and very informative read, go to _www.alt.Portland.or.us/index.shtml_.

The telephone area code for the city is primarily 503.

Accommodation
McMenamins Edgefield Hostel, 2126 SW Halsey St, Troutdale. (800) 669-8610.

Converted farm, this lodge shares estate with a winery, brewery, movie theatre and two restaurants. Two single-sex dorms, showers, tubs, $30, but no outside food or laundry. *www.mcmenamins.com*.

HI-Portland Northwest, 1818 NW Glisan St, 241-2783. New hostel close to cafes, shops, brew-pubs and nightlife. Van tours available to Oregon Coast, Mt. Hood etc.; Kitchen, laundry, bike storage, espresso bar. Resv recommended, $16-$19; private room $49-59. *www.2oregonhostels.com/nw_home.htm.*

HI-Portland Hawthorne Hostel, 3130 SE Hawthorne Blvd, 236-3380. Catch #14 bus from bus / rail terminals. Homey hostel with yard, BBQ, garden and covered porch. All-day van tours run year-round to Mt St. Helen's Volcano, Oregon Coast and Mt. Hood. Women's rooms fill up quickly in summer; rsvs or walk-in very early. Coffee-houses, live music clubs and a $1 cinema-pub are within walking distance. No curfew. All-you-can-eat pancakes, $1. Baggage storage available if arriving before 10 am. Free internet access. Dorms from $16, nonmembers $19. *www.portlandhostel.org*.

Camping: Ainsworth State Park, 37 miles E of Portland at Exit 35 off I-84. Close to noisy expressway but the drive through gorge is well worth it. Hot showers, flush toilets, hiking trails. $14 / $16 w/hook-up. *www.oregonstateparks.org/park_146.php*

Champoeg State Park, 7679 NE Champoeg Rd, off Hwy 219S. $16 / $20 w/hook-up. Call State Park Reservations: (800) 452-5687. Check for many state park facilities: *www.oregonstateparks.org*.

Food

The tastiest thing in Oregon is free—the drinking water. Grocery prices are high in town, even for local produce. You'll do better at the roadside produce stands, particularly along the Columbia River, where the peaches are huge and drip all over your shirt when you bite into them. Don't miss local specialities: blackberry and boysenberry pie, razor clams (hideously expensive, but with a licence you can dig your own), scallops, smelt and Dungeness crab. There are farmers markets in every town and city, listed on *www.aglink.org*. For an extensive list of breweries, eateries and wineries, visit *www.pova.com/visitors/visguide/dining.html.*

Bijou Cafe, 132 SW 3rd, 222-3187. 'A must for visitors. Great value for money with a friendly and relaxed atmosphere.' Daily for bfast and lunch, $4-$9.

Bread & Ink, 3610 SE Hawthorne, 239-4756. Local favourite for lunch. 'Best burgers.' Also pasta, fish specials, Vietnamese, Italian, Mexican and Jewish! Open daily. 'Nicest restaurant in town.'

Dan and Louis Oyster Bar, 208 SW Ankeny, 227-5906. Outstanding oysters, stew, marine atmosphere. Open daily.

Fuller's Coffee Shop, 136 NW 9th Ave, 222-5608. Old-fashioned luncheonette with freshly made cinnamon rolls, four-star French toast, and omelettes accompanied by classic hash browns. Try fried razor clams for lunch. Open daily.

Jake's Famous Crawfish, 401 SW 12th Ave, 226-1419. A daily blackboard of sea creatures, hauled in fresh, choice includes salmon, crab and sole. (11:30am to 10pm wkds, Sat-Sun only dinner from 4pm.). $1.95 happy hour!

Old Wives' Tales, 1300 E Burnside, 238-0470. Multi-ethnic vegetarian, vegan, chicken and seafood; also soup and salad bar. 'New Age, classical and jazz music round out the eclectic atmosphere.' Daily for bfast, lunch and dinner.

Papa Haydn's at two locations, 5829 SE Milwaukee, 232-9440, and 701 NW 23rd Ave, 228-7317. A Viennese coffee-house with dynamite pastries. 'Milwaukee location hard to find.' Open daily.

Of interest

The **Oregon Museum of Science and Industry (OMSI)**, 1945 SE Water Ave (at the corner of Clay St), (800) 955-6674, is open daily Tue-Sun 9.30am-5.30pm, summer, (call for winter) $9, extra charges for OMNIMAX Theatre ($8.50), planetarium etc.

Cheap planetarium shows ($5.50). Don't miss 'state of the heart,' a preserved human heart; software that checks your cardio-vascular health; and a biofeedback train that goes faster as you get warmer. All three attractions cost $19. *www.omsi.edu.*

Pioneer Courthouse Square, SW Broadway and Yamhill, is an open-air city centre square paid for by the sale of 65,000 bricks used to build it, with benefactors' names inscribed on each one. Over 300 free performances and year-round events. See the 'weather ball,' a meteorological glockenspiel. 'Silly noon-time fanfare.' In summer, the "Noon Tunes" attract huge numbers of jazz and folk music lovers, Tues & Thurs noon-1pm. *www.pioneercourthousesquare.org.*

Portland Art Museum, 1219 SW Park Ave, at the South Park Blocks, 226-2811. European, 19th and 20th century American, pre-Columbian, West African, Asian and Pacific Northwest Indian art. $10, $9 w/student ID. Tue-Wed 10am-5pm, Thu-Fri 'til 8pm, Sun 12pm-5pm. *www.pam.org.*

Portland Building, btwn Main and Madison, 4th and 5th. Architect Michael Graves, knowingly or not, has taken a page from Frank Lloyd Wright's notebook by designing a controversial pink and blue public building for a mid-sized American city (cf. 'Marin County' in California section). Outside is the Portlandia sculpture.

Skidmore Old Town Historic District, New Market Block, SW 1st and Ankeny. Interconnected townhouses with open plaza, colonnade, outdoor stands. Old Town also marks the end of Waterfront Park, an excellent place to picnic, fish, stroll and enjoy community events.

National Sanctuary of Our Sorrowful Mother, known simply as **The Grotto**, 8840 NE Skidmore, 254-7371. Natural grotto in huge cliff, resembling grotto at Lourdes. It's worth seeing the monastery above (take elevator) for rose gardens, Marian art and one of the best views you can get of Portland, the Columbia River and Washington State beyond. Open daily. *www.thegrotto.org.*

Some of Portland's most pleasant features are its **fountains**: the **Lovejoy**, SW 3rd & Harrison; the **Rose Fountain**, at O'Bryant Sq, 408 SW Park; **Ira Kellar Fountain**, SW 4th Ave btwn Market & Clay Sts, and the **Skidmore Fountain**, 1888 SW 1st & Ankeny.

Washington Park, west of town, has **Japanese Gardens**, 611 SW Kingston Ave, 223-1321, with 5 traditional styles, especially lovely with the white cone of Mt Hood framed by maple leaves and pagodas. $6.75, $5 w/student ID. Tue-Sun 10am-7pm, Mon 12pm-7pm. Daily tours. *www.japanesegarden.com*. Also in the park is the **Rose Test Garden**, 400 SW Kingston Ave, free, with over 8000 rosebushes. *www.parks.ci.portland.or.us/Gardens/IntRoseTestGarden.htm.* From here you can take 'the world's smallest railroad', $3, through the forest to the **Zoo-OMSI** complex (the Washington Park and Zoo Railway). The **Zoo**, 4001 SW Canyon Rd, 226-1561, daily 9am-7pm (last admission 6pm), $9.50, has a huge chimp collection and large elephant herd. *www.oregonzoo.org/index.htm.*

Outside Portland: the **Columbia River Gorge**, stretches east from Portland to The Dalles and offers truly magnificent scenery. Sailboard enthusiasts flock from around the world to catch the intense winds that are funnelled down the canyon. Take a car up and along the Historic River Hwy which parts with I-84 at Troutdale to enjoy spectacular views of the Gorge and see some of the numerous waterfalls en route (**Multnomah** is the biggest and most impressive). For real escapism, go up to the tranquil setting of **Lost Lake** and a close-up of **Mt Hood**, the state's tallest mountain. 'Spectacular, picture-book scenery.' Greyhound and Amtrak both serve the area; 'Amtrak is best for views'. **Bonneville Dam**, with its salmon farms and fish ladders is also worth a look.

Hwy 30 West. A beautiful 100-mile drive to **Astoria** that romps up hill, down dale, beside the Columbia and its wooded islands, past roadside stands, houseboats, picturesque backwaters, juicy blackberries—there's even a pull off to see **Mt St Helens. Westport**, with its Wahkiakum ferry across the river, is good for lunch.

Shopping
Oregon has **no sales tax** so make the most of your dollars!
Lloyd Center, 282-2511, has 200 shops around an indoor ice-rink. Open daily. *www.lloydcentermall.com.*
Niketown Store, 930 SW 6th, 221-6453. TVs in the floor, sculptures of famous sports stars and various artefacts such as jerseys and shoes. Open daily. *http://niketown.nike.com.*
Powells City of Books, 1005 W Burnside, 228-0540. Allegedly the world's biggest bookstore—takes up one whole block and visitors are given a map on entry! Open 9am-11pm daily. *www.powells.com.*
Saturday Market, under west end of Burnside Bridge in Skidmore, SW 1st and Ankeny, 222-6072. 'Original buyers market.' Stalls with homemade everything. 'Wonderful.' Sat 10am-5pm, Sun 11am-4.30pm. *www.saturdaymarket.org.*

Entertainment
The best entertainment listings are in Friday's *Oregonian* and various free handouts. Check the *Willamette Weekly* (put out each evening on street corners and in restaurants) for listings of good local blues and rock bands. There are 16 **microbreweries** in the state, many in Portland. A favourite, **Bridgeport Brew Pub**, 1313 NW Marshal, 241-7179, offers several cask-conditioned ales 'till 11pm wkds and midnight on weekends. Or watch inexpensive movies at **Bagdad** (sic) **Theater and Pub**, 3702 SW Hawthorne, 236-9234, as you sample seasonal brews. Great pizza and beer. **Festivals**: Portland hosts excellent festivals: the **Blues Fest** in July, 973-FEST, *www.waterfrontbluesfest.org*, **The Bite** in mid-August, 248-0600, *www.biteoforegon.com* and others.

Information/Internet access
Portland Oregon Information Center in **Pioneer Courthouse Square** 701 SW Sixth Ave, 275-8355. Mon–Fri 8.30am–5.30pm; Sat 10am–4pm. 'Maps and a bounty of info.' Pick up the *Portland Book. www.travelportland.com.*
Free internet access at **Portland Central Library**, 801 SW 10th St, 988-5123. The Multnomah County Library system (17 branches) has more than 500 computers.

Travel
Amtrak, 800 NW 6th Ave, 248-1146/(800) 872-7245.
Gray Line, 4320 N Suttle Rd, 694-1022. Lots of day tours: Mt Hood, Mt St Helens, the Columbia River Gorge, coast, around town. $34-$75+. Pickup at local hotels. *www.grayline.com/franchise.cfm/action/details/id/127.*
Greyhound, 550 NW 6th Ave, next to Union Station, (800) 231-2222.
Tri-Met city bus, Streetcar, and MAX rail, 238-7488 for rates and info. Free downtown zone in the "Fareless Square," $1.50-$1.80 to other areas, $3.75 all-day pass. *www.trimet.org*. Streetcar runs 3 miles, every 15 mins, from Legacy Good Samaritan Hospital at NW 23rd Avenue and SW River Parkway and Moody at RiverPlace. Fares same as Tri-Met. *www.portlandstreetcar.org*. MAX is the light rail system part of Tri-Met with three lines joining downtown Portland with Beaverton, Gresham, Hillandale, the Expo Center and the airport. Fares same as Tri-Met.
Portland International Airport (PDX) is located about 13 miles E of the city. MAX Red Line tram takes about 30 mins to/from airport. Alternatively take the Gray Line Express bus, 285-2895, $12 o/w. *www.flypdx.com.*
Broadway Cab, 448-8888, and **Radio Cab**, 227-1212. Cabs won't stop on streets.

THE OREGON COAST Hwy 101 runs along the Pacific coast from the southernmost tip of California to the Canadian border, but the Oregon

stretch, especially the pristine 225-mile section from the California boundary to **Newport**, is surely the loveliest. It's also the driest part of the Oregon coast (it gets about half the amount of rain as the stretch north of Newport), a definite attraction for those camping out. 'Best way to see this is by camping; buy a tube tent; light, compact, about $12.' The coast offers driftwood hunting, whale watching, clam digging and rock hounding, from agates to jasper.

While you're on the beach, nose-to-sand, look for glass floats, the ultimate beachcombing prize. The powerful combo of the Japanese Current and a westerly wind wash these green, amber and turquoise buoyancy balls from Japanese fishing nets all the way across the Pacific. December through March is the best time to search; look for non-rocky beaches with moderate slope and go early to beat other float-hunters. Swimming is dangerous in many areas and cold everywhere; enquire locally.

Going north to south, the Oregon coast starts at **Astoria**, a miniature San Francisco at the mouth of the Columbia River. Founded in 1811 by John Jacob Astor as a base for the Pacific Fur Company, the town survived as the first permanent US settlement on the Pacific Coast due to successful trading with China. While there, check out the rococo Flavel House and Shallon Winery; try scallops at Pier 11 and Finnish limpa bread at local bakeries. Also of interest is **Ft Clatsop**, a few miles SW of town (8am-6pm, $5 in summer) where Lewis and Clark spent the stormy winter of 1805. If you're in a car, cross the Megler Bridge to Washington, spanning 4.6 miles and barely skimming the surface of the water. Back on Hwy 101, turn west to **Ft Stevens**, a historic park with a picturesque shipwreck.

Seaside, with its boardwalk, arcades and popular swimming beach, is a candyfloss sort of town, noted for cheap seafood at Norma's and the official end of the Lewis & Clark Trail. **Cannon Beach** merits a pause: monolithic **Haystack Rock**, a charming art-village with 40+ studios and galleries, and great windy walking at **Ecola** (Chinook for whale) **State Park** are some of its pluses.

Near **Tillamook**, take the **Three Capes Rd**, a 39-mile loop through a succession of scenic vistas, villages and lighthouses to **Three Arch Rocks National Wildlife Refuge**, with its herd of Steller sea lions. Tillamook, with more cows than people, provides tasting of its namesake cheese and others, along with wine, at the Blue Heron and Tillamook Cheese Factories. The lively little fishing and beach town **Newport**, on a sheltered and beautiful bay, is a good place to eat Dungeness crab and browse with other holidaymakers. 'A friendly young community on NW cliff, where there are quaint wooden summer cottages facing the ocean.'

Of interest here is the **Oregon Coast Aquarium**, 2820 SE Ferry Slip Rd, (541) 867-FISH, next to the Science Center. The aquarium offers various exhibit galleries of 15,000 Oregon marine creatures, including a walk among sharks in an underground viewing pool 'passages of the Deep.' Open daily summer 9am-6pm (10am-5pm in winter), $11.25. _www.aquarium.org_. Neighbouring **Depoe Bay** is noted as an excellent whale-watching spot, Nov-March; along its seawall, geyser-like sprays of ocean water often arch over the highway.

Beverly Beach to the south is the nearest campground and has hiker/biker spots. South of Newport is a likeable tourist trap called **Sea Gulch**, a village of carved life-size figures. The carving is done freehand— with a chainsaw! —and you can watch. **Yachats** (that's Yah-hots) is worth a stop; especially in smelt season May-Sept, or better yet, during the annual Smelt Fry in early July. It's nothing to eat a dozen of the silvery mini-fish and fun to watch the catch, too. Good non-fish offerings at the Adobe Hotel and others. Between rhododendron-happy **Florence** and Yachats are the **Sea Lion Caves**, 547-3111, _www.sealioncaves.com_, the world's largest sea caves, reached via elevator and reeking of perennial, fishy sea lion halitosis. Open daily 9 am 'til dusk, $8; you can also see the huge creatures more distantly from various points near the caves.

Oregon Dunes, some as high as 600ft, stretch for 40 miles to Florence; duneside camping is possible but crowded at **Honeyman State Park**; the **Umpqua Lighthouse State Park** (hiker/biker section), 6 miles south of Reedsport, is better. Biggest town in SW Oregon, **Coos Bay** is a fishing and lumber port good for a night's stopover, with a grimy bar, good meals at the **Blue Heron Bistro**, and myrtlewood factories.

Hwy 101 turns inland at Coos Bay, but you can follow secondary roads nearer the coast to spectacular scenery at **Sunset Bay** (camping) and **Shore Acres State Park**. At cranberry-growing **Bandon** you have a cheese factory, the makings of an art colony, a youth hostel, and natural beauty all around. Further along, the panorama of **Humbug Mountain** and the rock-strewn coast are a worthwhile stop; 3-mile hike to the top. An excellent campground with a low-cost hiker/biker section is found at **Gold Beach** on the banks of the Rogue. The river is an officially designated wild river and a prime spot for rafting and fishing. Good smoked salmon here. Explore the Oregon coast from Astoria to Brookings Harbor through links on _www.oregoncoast.com/orcoast.htm_.

The telephone code for the area is primarily 541.

Accommodation
For lists and websites of lodgings on the coast, check _www.oregoncitylink.com/newport/stay.htm_, _www.oregoncoastlodging.com_ and _www.stateoforegon.com/directory_oregonlodging.php_

Adobe Motel Resort, 1555 Hwy 101 N, **Yachats**, 547-3141. Fireplace, sauna, excellent bfasts and dinners. B&B D-$105-$120 with ocean view, $75 without, inc tax, lower the longer your stay, lower after Sept. _www.adoberesort.com_.

City Center Motel, 538 SW Coast Hwy, **Newport**, 265-7381, (800) 687-9099.

Sea Star Guesthouse, 370 1st St, **Bandon**, 347-9632. Located in the historic 'Old Town Waterfront District', halfway btwn San Francisco and Seattle on the Oregon Coast Bicycle Route. See some of Oregon's most scenic coastlines: dunes, cliffs, rock formations and white sandy beaches. Café, fireplaces, sleeper sofas, mini-kitchens, and courtyard overlooking harbour, day use, equipment storage area, information desk, kitchen, laundry facilities, linen. Dorms $19, private and semi-private rooms available for $35, internet access. _www.seastarbandon.com_.

HI-Seaside Hostel, 930 N Holladay Dr, **Seaside**, (503) 738-7911. European style hostel on river, 4 blocks from beach. Canoes and kayaks available; outdoor decks with river view; on-site espresso and pastry bar; movies shown every evening; internet access; nature programs. Dorms $16 exc tax, nonmembers $19, private rooms D-$38-$59. Greyhound stops at hostel. _www.2oregonhostels.com/ss_home.htm._

Camping: There are over 50 campgrounds in Oregon's state park system; $14-18 for tent site; yurts (yes, yurts!, sleep 5, 16´ in diam, "filled with comfy furniture") available in many parks at $27-30. Some sites have hiker/biker sections, set away from vehicles, from $4. Call (800) 452-5687 for rsvs, (800) 551-6949 for info. Check state park website: _www.oregon.gov/OPRD/PARKS/camping.shtml_. **William M. Tugman State Park,** near **Lakeside**, 759-3604, open mid-April-Labor Day, comes highly praised: 'best campsites in the US'. Oregon Dunes Recreation area is less than a mile away. Greyhound will drop you where you like. Warm sleeping bag advised, also food as parks usually far from shops. Tent sites $16. Has 13 yurts.

CRATER LAKE NATIONAL PARK
Mt St Helens was a minor firecracker compared with **Mt Mazama**, which exploded some 6,800 years ago to form Crater Lake. This inky blue well, in a densely forested part of southern Oregon's Cascade Range, cannot be bettered for dramatic settings: approached through a moonlike landscape and rimmed by 500 to 2000-ft cliffs (all that is left of 12,000-ft Mazama), Crater Lake descends to depths of 1932 ft, making it one of the deepest lakes in the world. Poking through the surface are **Phantom Ship Island** and **Wizard Island**, itself an extinct volcanic cone. Boat excursions visit Wizard, where you can hike to its 760-ft summit and down into its 90-ft-deep crater. The 33 mile **Rim Drive** is open mid-July to October; also recommended are the 1 mile hike down to the lake from Cleetwood Cove and the $1^1/_2$ miles **Discovery Pt Trail**.

From high points in the park, you can see **Mt Shasta**, 100 miles to the south. Wonderful bird-watching, wildflowers and nature programmes. Crater Lake is even more beautiful in winter, when snow-capped conifers are reflected in the deep blue iris of the lake. _www.nps.gov/crla_.

The telephone code for the park is 541.

Accommodation
Motel 6, 5136 S 6th St, 884-2110 in **Klamath Falls** and 779-0550 in **Medford. Camping:** In the park, **Mazama Campground**, on the South Entrance Road: 200 sites, no reservations, Open mid-June to Oct, depending on snow conditions, and **Lost Creek Campground**, (800) 551-6949, at the East rim of the crater, 16 sites. Nature Trail begins here. Grocery store at Mazama Village and excellent fishing in early summer. Backcountry sites free. _www.nps.gov/crla/pphtml/camping.html._

Food
Best to buy food at the **Klamath Fort General Store**, 52608 Hwy 62, **Ft Klamath**, (541) 381-2265. Open in summer daily, 7am-9pm. There is a **Safeway** supermarket in Klamath Falls at Pine & 8th St. _www.klamathcounty.net._

Information/Travel
For information on lodgings, food, and other sights in the Klamath basin area, visit _www.greatbasinvisitor.info_.
Amtrak, 1600 Oak St., (800) 872-7245.
Greyhound, 3817 Hwy 97, Klamath Falls, 882-4616/(800) 231-2222.
National Park: Steel Visitor **Center**, next to park HQs, **594-3100.** Provides free backcountry camping permits. Open all year, daily, summer 9am-5pm. **Rim Village** Visitor Center open June-Sept 9:30am-5pm, 594-3090. Park entry fee $10 p/car. Enter the park via Hwy 62 South or West. _www.nps.gov/crla/._

SOUTHERN OREGON
South and west of Crater Lake are a cluster of worthwhile destinations, made more appealing by well-placed hostels and other good lodging. **Ashland**, (_www.el.com/to/ashland_, _www.thebestofashland.com_)

America's answer to Britain's Old Vic, has three theatres (including a pleasant one outdoors) and an 8-month play schedule that includes the nation's best Shakespeare Festival. _www.osfashland.org._ Not far away is **Jacksonville**, an intelligently restored gold mining town. Stagecoach rides are offered to the cemetery and 80-odd homes there.

Nearby are the **Rogue River** and **Oregon Caves National Monument**, (541) 592-2100 x 232, open 9am-5pm daily, $8 for tours, _www.nps.gov/orca_ ; the latter are set deep in the marble heart of **Mt Elijah** and full of stalagmites & stalactites, flowstone formations and strenuous hikes that challenge even the greatest spelunkers. Near **Cave Junction** is **Takilma**, a former hippy mecca, which still has a hippy hospital. Nowadays the area is populated with 'survivalists'; apparently the natural convection of the land would eliminate the danger of radiation in the event of nuclear attack. To visit the wine growing areas here, including extensive lists of places to stay by area and town, check _www.winesnw.com_. For info on southern Oregon, check _www.sova.org_.

Telephone code for the area is 541.

Accommodation
Check for hostels, hotels and other lodgings at _www.all-oregon.com/hotels/southern_oregon.htm._

Ashland Hostel, 150 N Main St, Ashland, 482-9217. 3 blocks to Shakespeare Festival. Large kitchen, laundry; located in historic home. Open year round. Dorm $21, rooms $50. Resv. recommended. _www.ashlandhostel.com_.

Manor Motel, 476 N Main St, **Ashland**, 482-2246. Downtown. TV, AC. Rooms with kitchen also available. Advance rsvs and deposit required.

CENTRAL AND EASTERN OREGON The much less visited interior of the State does not have the scenic drama of the coastal region, however there are a number of sights and pleasant towns in which one can while away a few hours. Central Oregon Visitors Association (800) 800-8334, _www.visitcentraloregon.com_.

Eugene is the state's second city, situated between the Cascade Mountains and Coastal ranges, and as home to the University of Oregon, has a youthful feel to it. Sports enthusiasts will not be disappointed with many trails for running and cycling—this was the place where the Nike running shoe was tried and tested. The area has numerous covered bridges to be explored and photographed. Contact the visitor's centre at 754 Olive between 7th and 8th, (800) 547-5445 / (451) 484-5307, also known as the Convention & Visitors Association of Lane County Oregon (CVALCO). _www.visitlanecounty.org_.

On the eastern side of the Cascades, **Bend** is a good base for visiting central Oregon. Greyhound run daily from Eugene and Portland. The town centre, set on the Deschutes river, has a laid-back feel, with several lovely cafés with a Californian ambiance. The climate here also, is less extreme than on the coast; Bend is said to receive 250 days of sunshine a year. The **Bend Visitor's Center** is located at 917 NW Harriman, 382-8048/ (800)949-6086. _www.visitbend.org_ lists cafés, delis etc.

Further inland still, **Baker City**, (800) 523-1235, is an old gold-rush town and commemorates the **Oregon Trail** at the **National Historic Trail**

Interpretative Center, Flagstaff Hill, 523-1843, 5 miles from town. _www.nps.gov/oreg/oreg/site10.htm_ Over 150 years ago, thousands of Americans made the 2000-mile trail west to the 'Promised Land', over treacherous rivers and rugged mountains. Ten percent of them didn't make it. The Centre also has exhibits on the Native Americans who first settled the land. Open daily, 9am-6pm (summer), 9am-4pm (winter). Far in the Northeastern corner of the state, the Snake River has gouged **Hell's Canyon**, a National Recreation Area, and the **deepest canyon on the continent**. Unlike the Grand Canyon, you can't just go to the edge and peer in. There are numerous other lookout points, though, and one may take a boat tour along the river. Contact the Hells Canyon National Recreation Area Headquarters/Wallowa Mountains Visitor Center 88401 Hwy 82, Enterprise, (541) 426-5546; for general HCNRA Information, call (509) 758-0616; for float info and res: (509) 758-1957 and powerboat info/res: (509) 758-0270. The website has links and listing of outfitters and local communities: _www.fs.fed.us/hellscanyon._

WASHINGTON - The Evergreen State

Unofficially known as _The State of Nirvana_, there is a persistent legend that the original name proposed for Washington was 'Columbia'; the idea was dropped to avoid confusion with the nation's capital, the District of Columbia, and settled on the no-less confusing Washington. True or not, Washington has always been haunted by its name, to the extent that the state once advertised itself to tourists as 'The _Other_ Washington,' thereby selling itself short.

Like neighbouring Oregon, Washington is mountainous, rainy and green in the west, and flat, dry and tawny in the east. Likewise, it has but one pre-eminent city, Seattle, which enjoys a pugnacious rivalry with Portland. Once a stronghold of the radical labour movement (the Wobblies were here in the 1930s), Washington now builds more Boeings, raises more apples, tulips, and daffodils, processes more seafood, and stores more nuclear waste than just about anyone else and is the home of the world's most successful software company, Microsoft.

Washington isn't all work and no play—the **Yakima Valley** has produced 75% of the hops grown in the US since 1868 and nearly fifty microbreweries participate in the state's various brewfests every June, September and October, complete with coaster championships and keg tosses. _www.washingtonbrewfest.com_. The **American Hop Museum** is in **Toppenish** (509) 865-4677, _www.hopsdirect.com/spotlight/9805_. Wine grapes were first planted in the state by the enterprising Hudson Bay Company in 1825; now there are over 240 wineries in five appellations of the state, making it the 2nd largest US wine producer, aided, believe it or not, by two hours more average summer sunlight per day than in California's top wine areas. Production of wines in the state has more than doubled over the past decade. See _www.washingtonwine.org_ or _www.winesnw.com_ for the lowdown on Washington wines by region.

Way to the east of the state, there's another American capital, of lentils, in the **Palouse** region, _www.tourism.wa.gov/RegionPage_pid-106600_R5.html_.

And north of Seattle, there's tulip frenzy in the **Skagit Valley** in April each year, where as the *NY Times* notes: 'the neat lines of color look like rainbow rows on a giant chenille bedspread'. *www.tulipfestival.org*.

A large share of the state's scenic beauty is within reach of Seattle: **Puget Sound** and its hundreds of islands; the still, dark **Olympic Rain Forest**; omnipresent **Mt Rainier,** *www.mount.rainier.national-park.com*, and the obtrusive upstart, **Mt St Helens**, 75 miles south, *www.fs.fed.us/gpnf/mshnvm*. Other sights are further flung. **North Cascades National Park**, an expanse of alpine loveliness, with canyons, glaciers, peaks and grizzlies along the British Columbia border. *www.nps.gov/noca*. In the eastern part of Washington one will find the 550 ft **Grand Coulee Dam**, *www.recreation.gov/detail.cfm?ID=1889*, the largest single power producer in the world, the **Palouse River Canyon,** the deepest gorge in North America, deeper even than the Grand Canyon and the '**Scablands'**, a weird, scarred landscape left thousands of years ago by a glacial flood that inundated much of the Columbia Plateau. The Long Beach peninsula, though part of SW Washington is more conveniently reached from Astoria, Oregon.

Rain is endemic to the Northwest, but Seattle gets most of its 34 inches per year between October and May; the Olympic rain forest gets up to 150 inches annually. **National Parks:** Olympic, Mount Rainier, North Cascades. *www.travelwashington.com*.

The five telephone area codes for the state are 206, 253, 360, 425 and 509.

SEATTLE   Long before the advent of 'grunge,' before Nirvana, Soundgarden *et al*, the 'Emerald City' was a place to be. With becoming flower-bedecked arrangements of hills, houses, water and mountains, Seattle has long been a mecca for those who like life with a more laid-back attitude, including *Frasier* whose apartment has a magical location within sight of downtown. *www.seeseattle.org*.

To the southwest, the skyline is dominated by snowy 14,410ft Mt Rainier. To the west, the city's great deepwater harbour opens on to island-studded Puget Sound and the Olympic Mountains. Urbanisation is further subdivided by lakes and parks, from tiny to massive, girding the downtown district into a compact and pleasing shape, much of it laid out in the early 1900's by the firm of Frederick Law Olmsted. The look is an idiosyncratic mix of sleek and traditional, of contemporary ranch houses and bohemian houseboats and over 23,000 public steps with a collective altitude higher than that of Mt Everest.

All this adds up to a rose and poppy-filled city that feels similar to another great Pacific metropolis whose initials are 'SF'. Don't tell Seattlites that; they defend their city's individuality. And rightly so. Seattle, named after a local Indian chief, does have a certain flair. It's not every city that would make a Wagnerian opera cycle (sung in German and English) its major cultural event, or outfit its waterfront with vintage 1927 Australian, Tasmanian mahogany streetcars and its airport with a meditation room.

Considering that it's a major gateway to, and trade partner with the Orient, Seattle shows few Asian influences of the non-gustatory kind. At its core the city is boisterous, adventurous and optimistic, no doubt a legacy of its logging and Klondike goldrush past. Jimi Hendrix and Bruce Lee were born, raised, and buried here and the world's richest man, Bill Gates, lives in nearby Bellevue where his company, Microsoft, is based.

If coffee is your amour then Seattle is the place to get in some serious drinking. The city seems to run on caffeine, supplied by some of the strongest espressos you will ever taste. There are over 660 coffee bars and cafes everywhere all serving 'damn fine cups of joe', as Agent Cooper would say. You'll be wired for weeks. Needless to say, Starbucks started here in Pike Place more than 35 years ago, naming itself after the mate in Herman Melville's *Moby Dick*. Check out *www.seattleweekly.com* for arts, current entertainment, shared housing ads, etc; hardcopies are free.

The telephone area code for Seattle is 206.

Accommodation

B&B's: lots of options including **B&B International** and **Northwest B&B**; details in *Accommodation Background*. Also: **Pacific B&B**, *www.seattlebedandbreakfast.com* or call 439-7677 or (800) 684-2932; **Traveller's Reservations Service**, 364-5900, specialises in B&B's. Covers Seattle and most of the Northwest, including Puget Sound, Tacoma, Olympia, Spokane, Victoria and Vancouver Island, BC.

College Inn Guest House, 4000 University Way NE, 633-4441. Continental bfast plus all-day coffee, tea. Antique; registered as a historical landmark. From aver $70, all shared bath.

Green Tortoise Backpacker's Hostel, 1525 2nd Ave, 340-1222 or 888-4AHOSTEL. All rooms have own wash basin. Kitchen, free bfast, laundry and discount cards. Internet access. 'Staff really nice.' Call hostel for pick-up. $23 dorm, private rooms avail. *www.greentortoise.net*.

Moore Hotel, 1926 2nd Ave, 448-4851. 'Clean, modern, spacious—offered us the best deal.' 'Excellent hotel, warm and friendly.' Rates range from $45 - $79. *www.moorehotel.com*.

HI-Seattle Hostel, 84 Union St (next to the Pike Place Market), 622-5443/ (888) 622-5443, is a former US immigration station with a modern interior. Take bus #174 from bus station to Union & 4th Sts. $19-35. Rsvs essential. *www.hiseattle.org*.

HI-Vashon Island Ranch Hostel, 12119 SW Cove Rd, Vashon Island, WA 98070, 463-2592. A ferry ride from downtown, this hostel offers a getaway from the city in a unique setting. Nine Sioux Indian tepees offer couple and family rooms, or sleep in covered wagons surrounding a campfire. Free, self-made breakfast, then enjoy beautiful, rural Vashon Island on bikes provided free at hostel. Rsvs req. 'Check ferry timings carefully—few and far between at weekend. Will pick up from Thriftway Grocery Store on island; on return, take bus from Vashon to ferry.' $13 (AYH), $16 (non-member), Private rooms avail. *www.vashonhostel.com*.

Food

Washington is famous for superb fruit (especially peaches, apples, and berries), Dungeness crab, Olympia oysters, razor and littleneck clams, and the indigenous candy, 'Aplets' and 'Cotlets,' a sort of jellied fruit bar covered with powdered sugar and guaranteed to be addictive. Seattle is a prime place to sample them all. Excellent Chinese, Thai, Japanese and Vietnamese restaurants, too. For a comprehensive directory by neighbourhood or type, see *www.seattledining.com* and *www.seattleweekly.com/food*.

Bakeman's, 122 Cherry St, 622-3375. Turkey or meatloaf; white or wheat; mayo or mustard — make your mind up and move down the line! Open Mon-Fri only, 10am-3pm. Prices 'insanely low'.

Caffé D'arte, 1625 2nd Ave, 728-4468 (2 blocks from Commodore Hotel). The best coffee shop in Seattle! T-shirts, mugs etc., good to buy as souvenirs. Mon-Fri 6am-6pm, Sat 9am-6pm. Coffee is roasted in Seattle at S Myrtle St *www.caffedarte.com*.

Elliott Bay Book Company, 101 S. Main, 624-6600. Cafe and literary gathering place, with over 100,000 titles. Cafe Mon-Sat 9:30am-10:00pm, Sun 11am-7pm. _www.elliottbaybook.com_.

Emmet Watson's Oyster Bar, 1916 Pike Place, 448-7721. Best oysters anywhere, three dozen kinds of bottled and draft beer, good ceviche (marinated fish), exquisite Puget Sound salmon soup, and cioppino. Savour hangtown fry (oyster omelette) for bfast. 'Nice back garden.' Inexpensive, under $15.

Gravity Bar, 415 Broadway E, 325-7186. A trendy, stainless steel decked juice bar serving things like 'Milano', a double shot of wheat-grass with fresh garlic.

Hi-Spot Café, 1410 34th Ave, 325-7905. Bfast is a must-eat Seattle meal here! Open daily 8am-2:30pm. _www.hispotcafe.com_.

Bimbo's Bitchin' Burrito Kitchen, 506 Pine, 329-9978, cheap and hearty burrito's in this one-of-a-kind spot. $5-$7.

Ivar's Acres of Clams Restaurant, Pier 54, 624-6852. Seattle seafood tradition since 1938. Great old photos and waterfront view. Sun-Thu 11am-10pm, Fri-Sat 'til 11pm.

Lowells, Pike Place, 3 stories overlooking Puget Sound. Main courses $7.50-15. 7am-8pm.

Old Spaghetti Factory, Elliot and Broad, near Pier 70, 441-7724. A chain serving so-so pasta. Daily specials. Open daily.

Pike Place Bar & Grill, 90 Pike St, 624-1365, b'fast till 2 pm with huge market breakfasts. Sun-Thu 9am-10pm, Fri-Sat 'til 11pm.

Pike Place Market is the place to purchase fresh produce, meat, fish and takeaway items; it's a bustling warren of entertainers and ethnic treats from Filipino lumpia to Spanish tapas to Estonian piloshkys and coffee & coffee & coffee, plus its own micro-brewery.

Rock Bottom Brewery, 1333 5th Ave, 623-3070 has delicious dishes in $7-8 range, inc wild mushroom swiss burger, chipotle chicken pizza, and patty melts, plus handcrafted beers such as Peashooter Pale Ale, Rain City Red and Faller Wheat. _www.rockbottom.com_.

Trattoria Mitchelli, 84 Yesler Way (Pioneer Sq area), 623-3883. 'Try the Skid Row scramble—and other scrambles. Pleasant, laid-back ambience.' Sun-Thu 11:30am-11pm, Fri-Sat 'til 4am.

Streamliner Diner, 397 Winslow Way NE, Bainbridge Island, 842-8595.Daily; bfast and lunch; local institution for more than twenty years; American, mainly breakfasts all day $6-10; reach the island via ferry from Seattle, Pier 51.

Of interest

Mt St Helens. The Indians called it 'Loowelit-klah,' or 'smoking mountain,' and they knew what they were talking about. On 18 May, 1980, the mountain erupted, blowing away a cubic mile of earth, killing 57 people and 2 million mammals, birds and fish, and exhaling smoke and ash to 72,000 ft to circle the globe. Since then, Mt St Helens has erupted sporadically but on a smaller scale; quakes and ominous rumblings are commonplace. Plan on spending all day on your trip, whether from Seattle or Portland. 'A beautiful place.' To experience the mountain, options include: **air flyovers** from nearby **Toledo**, **Cougar** or **Randle**, which give the best views of flattened trees, debris-choked rivers and devastated landscape slowly regenerating itself; **bus tours** run from Seattle through a loop road leading to the mountain, also accessible by car. Check in with the Forest Service info centre (turn W off I-5 on exit 49) to enter the volcano zone.

Hikers can make a difficult but worthwhile trek from **Meta Lake** to **Independence Pass**, which overlooks ruined **Spirit Lake**, chilling views of desolation and crumpled human artefacts. The **Norway Pass** trail is also excellent.

Seattle Aquarium at Pier 59, 386-4320, offers a fishbowl—where you are in the bowl, and the fish swim overhead. 'Marvellous.' June-Aug 9.30am-7pm, Sept-May reduced hrs, $12. Watch out for the 'Coconut Crab' exhibit. _www.seattleaquarium.org_.

The Underground Tour. For 'Dirt! Corruption! Sewers! and Scandal!' take an amazing and 'extremely entertaining' but discombobulated underground tour of Seattle's Pompeii, 608 1st Ave (near Pioneer Sq), 682-4646. When Seattle burned down in 1889, the city simply built the new on top of the old. What's left below is an odd warren of storefronts, brothels, speakeasies, opium dens, and tunnels where drunken miners swayed and sailors are popularly supposed to have been shanghaied. Tour passes through bank vault rebuilt to accommodate the gold from Alaska and ends (naturally) at a gift shop. Has underground café that features (what else) espressos and local microbrews. 'Touchy feely vision of life as it really was.' 'Highly amusing account of Seattle's early sewage system. Never thought crap could be so funny.' ('Tides in, poop's out.') Tours last $1^1/_2$ hrs; $11, $9 w/student ID. *www.undergroundtour.com*.

Experience Music Project, 325 5th Ave near the Space Needle, (206) EMP-LIVE, designed by the architect of the Guggenheim in Bilbao, Frank Gehry, this bizarrely-undulating interactive 'museum-cum-music-college', through which Seattle's monorail passes, allows you to listen, learn, and be a play-it-yourself rock-star on a virtual stage for the day. Designed to celebrate and explore creativity through popular music 'exemplified by Rock 'n' Roll', EMP features a fascinating story of how the guitar became electric with a related movie *Quest for Volume* featuring selected giants as Merle Travis, Les Paul and Bonny Raitt. Via computerized hand-held remotes, EMP traces an irritatingly-quick history of rock and roll and features Seattle-native Jimi Hendrix and NW bands in special galleries. Included are a Sky Church with the world's largest indoor video screen, and interactive sound, demo, digital, and learning labs. Funded by one of the Microsoft co-founders, EMP still charges a hefty $19.95 entrance fee. 'Interesting, but somehow not involving. Need lots of time.' Open Mon-Thu 10am-5pm, Fri-Sun 'til 6pm. *www.emplive.com*.

Government Locks, connecting Puget Sound, Lake Union and Lake Washington, were built in 1916 and at that time second only to the Panama locks in size. 'Best free sight in Seattle. Boats and leaping salmon passing through all day.' 'Some salmon nearly jump onto the footpath!' 'Interesting historical/ecological display in building.' A National Historic Place; Visitor Center is at (206) 783-7059. *www.nws.usace.army.mil/PublicMenu/Menu.cfm?sitename=lwsc&pagename=mainpage.*

International District, btwn Main & Lane, 4th & 8th. Culturally-neutral official name for Seattle's Chinatown, bright with Buddhist temples, restaurants, herbal shops and the Bon Odori Festival in Aug.

Klondike Gold Rush National Historical Park, 117 S Main (Pioneer Sq), 553-7220. Beginning July 1897, when two ships carrying more than three tons of gold berthed in Seattle harbour, the Klondike stampede was outfitted in Seattle and the city's Assay office processed over $200 million in gold from the northern fields. Exhibits, free films and gold panning demos. 'Watch Chaplin's *The Gold Rush* free on 1st Sun every month.' Daily 9am-5pm; free; *www.nps.gov/klse*. (*Also see* Skagway.)

Lake View Cemetery, next to **Volunteer Park**, at 14th Ave & E Prospect. Divided by nationality—Chinese, Japanese, Polish, etc. Also **Bruce Lee's grave**, covered with letters to him, martial arts trophies, mementoes, flowers, etc., left by devotees. NB: For those with a gruesome frame of mind, Kurt Cobain's residence has been torn down, and he isn't even buried in Seattle—sorry.

Museum of Flight, 9404 E Marginal Way S, 764-5720. Over 40 aircraft from the beginnings of aviation to an Apollo command module. Newest exhibits include a full-scale F-18 mock-up where you can sit in the cockpit and—yes—Concorde! Daily 10am-5pm. $14. *www.museumofflight.org*.

Pacific Science Center, 200 Second Ave. North, 443-2001, includes 6 buildings: spacerium, planetarium, computer rooms, seismograph, Indian longhouse, lots of science toys. Tue-Fri 10am-5pm, Sat-Sun 10am-6pm. $9.50 entrance fee; $15 includes IMAX or laser shows. IMAX info line: 443-IMAX. 'Laserium Rock is an exciting presentation.' The Center also has many shops, eateries and entertainment from opera to rock to folk festivals. *www.pacsci.org*.

Pike Place Market, Pike & 1st, 682-7453. Begun in 1907, this multi-level maze of regional colour boasts over 250 permanent businesses, includes dozens of restaurants, stand-up bars and takeaway places, plus local produce and seafood. The Market was featured in *Sleepless in Seattle*, and is where the first Starbucks opened. There are oils at Tenzing Momo apothecary, indigenous art at Northwest Tribal Art, carvings from Mt St Helen volcanic ash, berries, flowers, hand-made soaps, broaches, scents, etc, Also bookshops, coffeehouses, bars, second-hand shops, crafts and 'excellent free entertainment by buskers and street musicians.' Check the tongue-in-cheek, free *Pike Place Market News* (subhead: *Attack of the Organic Vegetables*) for map, listings, and events. *www.pikeplacemarket.org*.

Pioneer Square, around 1st & Yesler, heart of old downtown. The original 'skid road', so-named because logs were 'skidded' down a 49 degree road greased with dog-fish oil in lumberjack days which gave rise to 'Skid Row', a term widely imitated in several cities from LA to NYC. Nicely restored, but little life on the streets; good walking tour map available. Music places open at night. 'People talk and smile all the time here—very laid back.' *www.cityofseattle.net/tour/pioneer.htm.*

REI store, 222 Yale Ave N, 223-1944. The biggest and best outdoors shop in the west; has a mountain bike test trail, gear-testing stations, and a 65-foot climbing wall, among other things. REI is a coop, Recreational Equipment, Inc., begun in 1938 by a group of local climbers: It's the largest consumer cooperative in the US with over two million members. *www.rei.com/stores/seattle*.

Seattle Art Museum, 100 University St, 654-3100. Newly-designed museum designed by Robert Venturi, who designed the National Gallery extension in London and it is his usual post-modern joke of differing styles from Egyptian to neo-classical. Be sure to visit the Northwest Art Gallery on the 3rd floor to see stunning Native American art including Haida argillite carvings, an octopus bag, vivid red button robes, xoots kudas (bear shirts), and masks that will scare the living daylights out of you. Tue-Sun 10am-5pm, Thu till 9pm; Suggested admission prices $7, $5 w/student ID. First Thu of every month, free. *www.seattleartmuseum.org*.

Seattle Asian Art Museum, 1400 E. Prospect, is the Seattle Art's sister institution, $3. *www.seattleartmuseum.org*.

The Space Needle, 400 Broaed St., 905-2200, a 605-ft relic of the 1962 Seattle World's Fair that was designed by Edward Carlson on a coffee house placemat, has stunning views, best at night when the city is lit up. $13 for fast glass elevator ride to the top and info-tour. Find out where *Frasier's* apartment would have to be for *that* view! 'Kitschiest souvenir shop in Seattle on top.' Revolving restaurant at 500 ft. On the grounds of **Seattle Center**, where various fairs take place over the summer; Fun Forest amusement park is there, too. *www.spaceneedle.com*.

University of Washington, 15th Ave NE. 'Beautiful, like Berkeley.' On campus, an arboretum and Japanese tea garden, gift of Seattle's sister city, Kobe. Info centre on NE 40th. Visitors Info Center 022 Odegaard, 543-9198 (temporarily in 2006). *http://depts.washington.edu/visitors/*

The waterfront is the soul of any port town, and Seattle is no exception. The working piers for the Alaska halibut and salmon fleet and the large freighters are remote, but the tourist's waterfront is front and centre. Piers 48 through 70 have steamships to Victoria and also the Victoria Clipper Catamaran, a **waterfront park** and a **fire-fighting museum**.

Nearby: Boeing Aircraft Factory, 3303 Casino Rd S, **Everett**, 30 miles north of Seattle, exit 189 W off I-5. Call (800) 464-1476 for tour info. See jumbo jets in the making in the building where the world's largest jetliners are manufactured. Very heavily booked in summer; 90 min tours $5. Mon-Fri 9am-4pm. Tkts available from 8:30am for the day but beware—can be sold out by 9am. *www.boeing.com/companyoffices/aboutus/tours/background.html*.

Entertainment

The 5th Ave Theatre, 1308 5th Ave, circa 1926 vaudeville house patterned after Imperial Chinese architecture of the Forbidden City, renovated in 1980 for $2.6 million, now hosts Broadway shows. Free tours daily 9:30am-5pm by appt, 625-1418. 'Absolutely smashing place.' *www.5thavenuetheatre.org*.

Gasworks Park, *www.cityofseattle.net/parks/parkspaces/GASWORKS.htm*.   See beautiful kites being flown high up in the sky, or go get your own from **Gasworks Kite Shop**, 3420 Stone Way, 633-4780. On the other hand, if you feel inspired to go sailing on Lake Union, **Urban Surf**, 2100 N Northlake Way, 545-WIND, rents windsurfing boards for $45 daily, and in-line skates, $5 p/h or $16 p/day. *www.urbansurf.com/index.html*. During lunch hours in the summer, the free **Out to Lunch** series brings music and dancing to all parks, squares and offices downtown Seattle. Call 623-0340 for more info.

Pioneer Square, Volunteer Park and the campuses of **University of Washington** and **Seattle University** (downtown at E Cherry & Broadway) are all nuclei for daylight and after-dark activities. Plenty of good beer, live music and psyched crowds! For a joint cover, you may wander from bar to bar and club to club within the Pioneer Square area; **Color Box** is recommended for typical Seattle bands and good old grunge. Read the *Post-Intelligencer* and the *Seattle Times' Tempo* mag for listings and the *Hot Tix* column with discount and free stuff.

Seattle Opera, 1020 John St, 389-7676/(800) 426-1619, at the Seattle Center. Get there with stud ID two hours before curtain-up for half-price 'student rush' tickets; on day of performance, standing room tickets avail at $12. Box office opens 5.30pm. *www.seattleopera.com*.

The Seattle Symphony, 215-4747/ (866) 833-4747, performs in the new **Benaroya Hall** at 200 University St. *www.seattlesymphony.com*.

Paramount Theater, 911 Pine St, 467-5510. Rock and pop acts, as well as legitimate theatre. Not cheap but good acoustics. *www.theparamount.com.*

Festivals: Northwest Folklife Festival, annually at the Seattle Center, late May, 684 7300, has amazing array of NW performers, 'One of Seattle's most significant cultural events—for over 30 years.' Will be 35 in 2006. Free. *www.nwfolklife.org*.

The Seattle Arts Festival, Bumbershoot, also annually at the Seattle Center, over Labor Day w/end. Bands, food, art, etc. 'Amazing, very popular.' Hotline 281-7788. *www.bumbershoot.com*.

Information

Pick up free copies of *Seattle Weekly*, *www.seattleweekly.com*, for details of all local events, places to eat and stay etc. The *Seattle Post-Intelligencer, Best of the North West http://seattlepi.nwsource.com* , lists top attractions of the city and Puget Sound, free sights, art, architecture, summer concerts, etc.

Citywide Concierge Center, 461-5840, at the Washington State Convention and Trade Center, downtown on Pike Street between 7th and 8th Avenues, on Galleria level, 9am-5pm, daily. Visitors' info of all kinds, inc res. *www.seeseattle.org*.

National Park Service, Pacific Northwest Outdoor Recreation Information Center, (ORCI), 222 Yale Avenue North, in REI Center, 470 4060. Daily 10am-6pm. *www.nps.gov/ccso/oric.htm*.

Internet access

The home of good coffee has discovered that web-browsing is a complementary activity, and there are many cyber-cafes:

Seattle Public Library, 29 branches. At Central Library at 100 4th Ave: free wi-fi; 400 PCs, usually pretty busy, 1 hr limit, must have library card (free), 386-4636. Mon-Sat 10am-6pm, Sun 1pm-5pm *www.spl.org*.

Online Coffee Co, 1111 1st (Spring & Seneca), 381-1911, and 1720 E Olive Way (Olive & Harvard), 328-3731, open 7 days. 1 min/12c, First 30 min free with beverage purchase.
Capitol Hill Internet Cafe, 216 Broadway Ave E, 860-6858, has free wi-fi.
FedEx Kinko's, 735 Pike St (Convention Center), 467-1767. Most of the 12 Seattle locations have wi-fi and open daily. _www.fedex.com/us/officeprint/main/index.html._

Travel
Land: Metro Transit local public buses, 201 S Jackson, 553-3000 / (800) 542-7876. Within the 'Magic Carpet' downtown area, all buses are free 6am-7pm; otherwise $1.25-$2, depending on zone. _http://transit.metrokc.gov/tops/bus/bus.html._ All-day visitor's unlimited passes $5. _http://transit.metrokc.gov/tops/bus/fare/vp-home.html._ Waterfront Streetcar Line, with Australian trolley cars, every 20 mins from International District, via Pioneer Square, the waterfront along Elliott Bay, to Myrtle Edwards Park; follows metro rates. Transfers good for 90 minutes.
Amtrak, King St Station, 303 S. Jackson, (800) 872-7245. The _Coast Starlight_ to Oakland/SF and LA offers a beautiful ride down the coast; the _Empire Builder_ travels a mammoth 42 hr trip to Chicago via Minneapolis.
Gray Line, 624-5077/(800) 426-7532, various tours and to airport from the Westin Hotel, Space Needle and other points. _www.graylineofseattle.com._
Greyhound, 811 Stewart, (800) 231-2222. Serves Bellingham for ferry services north, daily to Sea-Tac Airport, Spokane, Portland, Tacoma and Vancouver, BC.
Sea: Ferries-Washington State Ferries, Pier 52, (206) 464-6400. To islands, Olympic Peninsula, Bainbridge, Bremerton, Vashon Island and other points. 'Excellent way to see the Sound and the islands around Seattle.' 'Always breezy—bring a jacket.' Local ferries for the San Juan Islands and Sidney, British Columbia depart from Anacortes (north of Seattle). See 'San Juan' section. _www.wsdot.wa.gov/ferries._
Victoria Clipper, 448-5000 / (800) 888-2535, offers passenger-only ferry service to Victoria, British Columbia, from Pier 69, twice a day in summer: $72 o/w, from $120 r/t. Once-daily two hour high speed catamaran trips—Clipper IV is the fastest passenger ferry in North America, $81/$133. To Friday Harbor, San Juan Islands (3 hrs), once daily $42.50/$68. Many tours in Seattle/Victoria/Vancouver area. _www.victoriaclipper.com/victoria_clipper_ferry_service._
Alaska Marine Highway System: to Alaska and the Inside Passage. Departs approx 6pm Tue & Fri from port in **Bellingham**, 89 miles N of Seattle. Call (360) 676-8445 for info; rates vary (cheapest: approx $200, 39 hours to Ketchikan). _www.akferry.org_ and _www.dot.state.ak.us/amhs_
Bainbridge Island Harbour Ferries, Pier 52, 464-6400, $6.10 r/t without car. _www.wsdot.wa.gov/ferries/schedules/current/index.cfm?route=sea-bi,_ 35 mins, smooth as a pond, see Mt Rainer, Seattle Skyline. The island is brimming with strawberries, flowers. Walk to the block-long village, sample BBQ pork at **Café Nola**, 101 Winslow Way E, 842-3822, (Mon-Fri 11am-3pm). Pubs and art galleries on the island, even a winery: **Bainbridge Island Winery**, 8989 Day Road East, 842-WINE. A free informal tour of the winery, the only estate grown winery on Puget Sound is offered every Sun at 2pm. Otherwise open Fri-Sun 11am-5pm. _www.bainbridgevineyards.com._ In July experience the bee-kissed aroma of lavender at nearby **Sequim Celebrate Lavender Festival** (877) 681-3035 _www.lavenderfestival.com._
Air: Seattle-Tacoma International Airport (Sea-Tac), about 12 miles S of the city. Beware: although signs are in English, Japanese, Chinese and Korean, Sea-Tac is poorly signposted. Gray Line's Airport Express to 7 downtown locations every 30 mins, 626-6088 or (800) 426-7505, $10.25. Water taxi from Pier 55 at the foot of Spring Street, 12 mins. $3. Taxi is $28-32. Bus from downtown take #194 or 174, Mon-Sat, $1.25-2. 30 mins. _www.portseattle.org/seatac._

OLYMPIC NATIONAL PARK Sparkling mountains and lush forests occupying 1400 sq miles in the centre and along the coastline of the Olympic peninsula, making this a crown jewel of US national parks. Hwy 101 circles the park, but only a few roads penetrate inward; its wilderness is further fortified by vast tracts of national forest around it. A hikers' park indeed.

Massive glacier-cut peaks are the park's signature. The highest at 7965 ft, was named **Mt Olympus** by an English sea captain in 1788. Use the **Port Angeles** entrance to get here. 'Don't miss the 18 mile drive from sea level to one mile high at **Hurricane Ridge**—what views of Mount Olympus and its glaciers!'

The park proves that rain forests are not solely a tropical phenomenon. West of Olympus in the **Bogachiel, Hoh, Quinault and Queets River Valleys** is the great Olympic Rain Forest, the world's only coniferous rain forests with the world's largest specimens of cedar and Sitka spruce. Jewelled with moisture, tree limbs cloaked in clubmoss, this cool Amazon suffused by primordial light gets 150 inches of rain in an average year. Best access is via the 20 mile drive up the **Hoh River**. Don't overlook the intelligent displays at the visitor centre and the views along **Quilcene River**. Follow the **Hoh Rainforest Trail** which begins at the **Hoh Rainforest Visitor Center**.

Dense forest runs almost into the sea along the pristine, rocky coastal strip. The best view is at the southern end where Hwy 101 passes close to shore, but the best part is **Lake Ozette**, reached only by trails. Here the undergrowth is extravagant and the ground is boggy; much of the trail is bolstered by boards. Bears sometimes lumber down to the water in search of a meal. About 4 miles from the lake is beautiful **Cape Alava**, especially when silhouetted at sunset. 'Make every effort to see this park—fantastic.'

Admission to the park is $10 per vehicle (at the more built-up entrances), good for 7 days, and $5 per hiker/biker. **Campgrounds** in the park offer tent sites from $8-$16. No food stores in the park, so purchase beforehand in Port Angeles. NB: This is bear country—food should be stored appropriately.*www.nps.gov/olym*.
The area code is 360.

Information/Travel
Clallam County Transit, (800) 858-3747, 452-4511, $.75, throughout county, *www.clallamtransit.com*.
Olympic Bus Lines, 417-0700 operates a shuttle from Port Angeles and downtown Seattle, airport, Amtrak and Greyhound. *www.olympicbuslines.com.*
Olympic National Park Visitors Center, 3002 Mt Angeles Rd, 565-3130. Information on self-guided trails, camping, backcountry hiking, fishing and generally fields questions about whole park. Displays a map of locations of other park ranger stations. Daily 9am-4.30pm. *www.nps.gov/olym/pphtml/facilities.html*.

PORT TOWNSEND and **THE SAN JUAN ISLANDS** Port Townsend shows you that western Washington isn't uniformly soggy; it lies in the 'rain shadow' of the great Olympic Mountains, and gets a mere 18 inches a year. Sunny weather, a vital cultural life, ebullient Victorian architecture and two nearby hostels make Port Townsend an excellent place to base for exploration.

In 1859 the US gained the 192-island chain of the **San Juans** in the great

'Pig War,' precipitated when a British pig recklessly invaded an American garden and was shot. The resulting squeal of outrage had US and British troops snout to snout on island soil, but diplomacy won out. With Kaiser Wilhelm the unlikely mediator, the US got the San Juans and the British got bangers, one supposes.

Connected by bridges to the mainland and each other are the islands of **Whidbey, Fidalgo** and **Camano**. The city of **Anacortes** on **Fidalgo** is a major ferry connection, and site of the San Juan jazz festival _www.anacortes.org_. Despite their accessibility, these islands are quite rural. Further north and well served by ferry are **Orcas, Lopez** and **San Juan**. All have excellent camping, unsurpassable shorelines and scenery with good clamming and some fine beaches. Lopez is best for bicycling and has a good swimming beach at **Spencer Spit**, though water temperatures average a chilly 55 degrees. More eagles nest in the San Juans than in any other region of the US mainland. Visit the excellent website _www.ptguide.com_ for events, history, visitors, travel, lodging, food, transportation, and other useful information on Pt Townsend; and _www.sanjuansites.com_ on San Juan and Orcas.

Accommodation

Nordland: HI-Marrowstone Island, 10621 Flagler Rd. (360) 385-1288 located in **Fort Flagler State Park**, (360) 385-3701, twenty miles from Port Townsend. _www.parks.wa.gov/parkpage.asp?selectedpark=Fort+Flagler&pageno=1._ With 784 acres of forest and seven miles of pristine beaches, the Park is a wonderful place to enjoy hiking, biking, clamming, sea kayaking, fishing and deer grazing. Olympic National Park is only an hour's drive. _www.nps.gov/olym_ and _www.northolympic.com/onp._ Hostel has large common room with wood stove, crab pots, info desk. Bikes to borrow. Not very well insulated, rural, and only 14 beds. 'The place to ebb out for a while.' June-Sept, rsvs recommended, call 8am-10pm or 5pm-10pm. $14 members, otherwise $17. Private room $34.

Port Townsend: HI-Olympic Hostel, 272 Battery Way, (360) 385-0655, in **Ft Worden State Park**, _www.fortworden.org/park.html_ . The hostel has outstanding views of the Cascade and Olympic ranges and the Strait of Juan de Fuca. The 433-acre park is host to music festivals (country, jazz, blues), kite flying and kayak gatherings, the Marine Science Center, and has miles of trails and beaches to explore. _www.parks.wa.gov/parkpage.asp?selectedpark=Fort%20Worden&pageno=1._ The hostel is near the town and a sandy beach, where Richard Gere, Debra Winger, and Lou Gossett filmed _An Officer and a Gentleman_. Call 7.30am-noon or 5-10pm. $17 members, nonmembers $20, private rooms $42. _www.olympus.net/personal/olyhost_.

Manresa Castle, 7th and Sheraton, 385-0755. From D-$99. TV, brass beds, antique decor. Bus stops 1 block up street. _www.manresacastle.com_.

On the San Juans: Doe Bay Resort and Retreat, 107 Doe Bay Rd, Olga, **Orcas Island,** (360) 376-2291. Offers yoga and ayurvedic retreats, all organic produce, and cafe over the water. New owners in 2005. Showers, fully equipped kitchen, beach, hot tubs, $10 pass, (clothing optional), 'Wonderful view over Otter coast.' Hostel beds $25, cabins $65+, yurts D-$75, camp sites $35. _www.doebay.com_.

Palmer's Chart House, 102 Upper Road, **Orcas Island**, 376-4231.(Island website: _www.orcasisland.org_ has long lodging list.) Open year-round, warm place with private baths and entrances, decks, lots of amenities. Overlooks Deer Harbor. 1 hr ferry ride to Orcas from Anacortes; from Orcas 1 hr to Sidney. Highly rec for an unusual American experience. S-$60, D-$80.

San Juan Island Camping: Snug Harbor Resort, 1997 Mitchell Bay Rd. **Friday Harbor**, (360) 378-4762. Cabins for 4+ $209, May-Sep. _www.snugresort.com_ ; **Lakedale Campground**, 4313 Roche Harbor Rd, **Friday Harbor**, $26 per site, call

378-2350. **NB:** a reader warns that San Juan island camping is crowded and the other islands are booked up in August. Rsvs early. *www.lakedale.com*.
State Park Camping: Call (800) 452-5687 for resv. at **Moran** on Orcas, 151 sites $14+$7 res fee. First-come, first-serve is normally avail. during the week. *www.sanjuansites.com/thingstodo/parks/moran/orcasislemoran.htm.*

Of interest

Two excellent guides to the area are *The San Juan Islands Afoot and Afloat* and *Emily's Guide*, with detailed descriptions of each island, both available at bookstores/outfitting stores on the islands and in Seattle.
Anacortes Jazz Festival, *www.anacortes.org/jazz_festival_2005.cfm* gives details on the annual jazz and music festival held on Fidalgo Island in mid-September.
Whale Museum, 62 First St N, **Friday Harbor,** (360) 378-4710. Exhibits of whale skeletons, brains; reading materials. Includes videos on Orcas and other whaling subjects. $6, $3 w/student ID. 'Small but very good.' Daily. 9am-6pm in summer. *www.whale-museum.org*.
Whale watching at **Lime Kiln Point,** no entrance fee. From the cliff above the water you can see both Orcas and Minke whales come close to the rocks to feed on salmon. Peak whale-watching is June and July. 'Usually arrive in afternoon.' *www.parks.wa.gov/parkpage.asp?selectedpark=Lime%20Kiln%20Point.*
Orcas Island: Moran State Park in Eastsound, (360) 376-2326, has 33 miles of hiking trails ranging from a light 1 hr stroll to a full day's adventure climbing Mt Constitution (2,027 feet in 4.3 miles). Trail guides available from the registration station. *www.orcasisle.com/~elc/trailmap.htm.*

Information/Travel

Orcas Island Chamber of Commerce, 376-2273, *www.orcasisland.org*.
Port Townsend Visitor Information, (888) 365-6978 / 385-2722, 2437 E Sims Way. *www.ptguide.com*.
Public transport is available, and often free, in every Puget Sound county, with the exception of San Juan County. Travels are often difficult to coordinate but rewarded with big savings. Check out *www.jeffersontransit.com/public.html#1* and its accompanying links for more help: **Jefferson County Transit** (360) 385-4777/ (800) 371-0497. Fares $1.25, inc day pass. About $4 to Sea-Tac Airport.
Ferries travel daily from Anacortes to Shaw, Lopez, Orcas, San Juan and Sidney, BC. *www.wsdot.wa.gov/ferries.* Westward journey to any island: $12.20 per passenger (peak), $10.10 non-peak. Intra-island hops are free. Numerous ferry and land combinations are possible; study the free ferry schedules and maps: call (206) 464-6400 or (800) 542-7052 (in Washington) for more info. **Victoria Clipper,** 448-5000 or (800) 888-2535, has daily ferries to **Friday Harbor** from Seattle, Victoria, some including whale searches. *www.victoriaclipper.com.*
Bike rentals also make for an interesting, fun, and relatively inexpensive way to explore the islands, (ferries don't charge extra for bikes). **Island Bicycles,** 380 Argyle Ave, **Friday Harbor,** 3 blocks up from ferry landing, 378-4941, is one of many rental options: $7 an hour, $35 a day. Open daily. *www.islandbicycles.com.*

MOUNT RAINIER NATIONAL PARK It was the enterprising 18th century British Admiral Rainier who got this 14,410-foot active volcaano named after himself. Today Mt Rainier, 80 miles south of Seattle and clearly visible from there, is surrounded by a national park that should interest the most jaded peak peeker. With 575 inches of snow piling up in an average year, little of the mountain shows beneath the glittering whiteness. More than 40 glaciers crown Mt Rainier – it has the largest single-peak glacial system in the US, and lush conifer forests line its lower slopes, interrupted by meadows bright with wildflowers in July and August. _www.nps.gov/mora_.

The Wonderland Trail wanders for 90 miles around the mountain, passing through snowfields, meadows and forests, with shelter cabins at convenient intervals. The full walk can take 10 days, but there are lesser trails for those with lesser ambitions. Near the park's southeast corner is the **Trail of the Patriarchs**, leading through groves of massive red cedar and Douglas fir. The best place for seeing wildflowers is to march up from **Paradise Valley**. In the northeast, excellent hiking trails branch out from **Sunrise**, the highest point in the park that can be reached by road.

July through Sept are often warm and clear, sunsets and sunrises over the mountain are unforgettable. It rains even in summer, and cloudy, rainy or foggy weather is the rule the rest of the year. Always bring raingear! Entrance is $10 per car, $5 for hikers/bikers or bus riders.

The **Cascade foothills**, north of Rainier, are a closer alternative. Drive 30 miles east to North Bend, then follow south fork of the **Snoqualmie River** for 15 miles. Take dirt track marked **Lake Talapus** to car park. From there, a 2 mile hike to the lake. Gorge yourself on blueberries, swim and dive off rocks, kill bugs—on a sunny day, this beats any city tour. 'This is the real America.' _www.nps.gov/mora_.

Telephone code 360.

Accommodation

Backcountry camping is free but hikers need a permit to use the trailside camps scattered in the park's backcountry. First come, first serve permits are free but can be resv. for $30, for 12 mos. Sites have access to toilets and (untreated) water.

Campgrounds: Ranging in price from $8 to $15 nightly the park has a plethora of camping facilities, two take resv. but the others are first-come, first-serve. Arrive early. Open summers only, except for Sunshine Point, but come equipped for cold— higher altitudes have snow on the ground, and often in the sky, even in the dead of summer. _www.nps.gov/mora/recreation/camping.htm._

Mt Haven Campground & Cabins at Cedar Park, 569-2594. Tent site $25; cabins $124 for 4 w/kitchen, bath, shower, fireplace and laundry. _www.mounthaven.com_.

Paradise Inn, 569-2413, at 5400 ft. Open mid-May to early Oct. From S/D-$92; $137 w/ private bath. Rsvs 569-2275. _www.guestservices.com/rainier_.

Information/Travel

Greyhound, 1319 Pacific Ave, Tacoma, (800) 231-2222.

Mount Rainier National Park Headquarters, call 569-2211 for info on weather and road conditions, food, lodging, camping, hiking, visitors centres and more. _www.nps.gov/mora/pphtml/facilities.html._

Jackson Visitors Center, largest in park, nr Paradise Inn, 5400' up, 569-6036. Daily in summer 10am-6pm, closed week-days rest of year. A/V programs including the 25-minute _Rainier: THE Mountain_, walks and talks on a variety of natural and cultural resource topics. Has exhibits on the natural and cultural history of the park. Jackson Grill (food service)and gift shop.

Climbing Information Center at the Paradise Guide House, at Paradise. 569-6009. Open daily in summer. Issues climbing permits for routes from Paradise.

Longmire Museum, 569-2211 x. 3314. One of the oldest museums in the National Park Service, est 1928. Exhibits on natural and cultural history. Open daily.

Longmire Wilderness Information Center, in SW corner of the Park, six miles E of Nisqually Entrance. Elevation 2700'. 569-4453. Open daily in summer, closed rest of year. Has large relief map of Park. Issues wilderness camping reservations and permits for the entire park, climbing permits for routes off Westside Road.

Ohanapecosh Visitors Center, in SE corner of Park, off Hwy. 123. 569-6046 . Info and wildlife displays. Open daily in summer.
Sunrise Visitors Center, at Sunrise, in NE of the park. Elevation 6400'. Has exhibits, snacks and a gift shop. Walks and talks on a variety of natural and cultural resource topics are offered. Open daily in summer.

NORTH CASCADES NATIONAL PARK Spectacular scenery in the Cascade Mountains: razor-backed peaks, plunging waterfalls, high snowfields and deep lakes. From Seattle, take Hwy 5 N to Hwy 20 E. No entrance fee to park; most areas are wilderness, inaccessible by road. You can, however, drive to three **campgrounds** in the park: **Colonial Creek, Goodell Creek** and **Newhalem**, $10-12. Park info 856-5700 ext. 515. The HQ Visitors Center is in Sedro-Woolley, along the North Cascades Highway (Route 20), about an hour and a half north of Seattle. _www.nps.gov/noca_.

LONG BEACH PENINSULA On its long sandy finger of land in extreme southwest Washington, the Long Beach peninsula harbours an immense clam and driftwood-filled beach, covered with huge dunes (great for escaping the wind) and backed by pines hiding hundreds of old-fashioned beach cottages. The peninsula is a great place to whale watch and hosts summer festivals for kite flyers, garlic and cranberry lovers and seafood connoisseurs.
Besides the windswept beauty of the area, visit the **Lewis and Clark Interpretative Center**, 642-3029, 10am-5pm daily, $3 adults, $1 children, near **Cape Disappointment Lighthouse**, a superb audio-visual evocation of the extraordinary hardships and wonders of the explorers' epic journey. The display ramps lead you to the same magnificent ocean overlook that climaxed Lewis and Clark's trip in 1805. Read Stephen E Ambrose's account of their journey in _Undaunted Courage_. The website, _www.funbeach.com_, includes directions by car, lodging options and a link to the visitors' bureau for the peninsula. For information on all of Washington's lighthouses, see _www.lighthousefriends.com/pull-state.asp?state=WA_.

Accommodation
The Whale's Tale Motel, 620 S. Pacific, **Long Beach**, (800) 55-WHALE or (360) 642-3455, is conveniently located in the heart of downtown Long Beach. Large multi-room accommodations with full kitchens and separate bedrooms are $60-$70 in summer but as low as $35 in winter, (XP-$5); free use of fishing gear, small boat, sauna and rec. room. _www.thewhalestale.com_.

AMERICAN BEACHES

From the rugged and lonely north Pacific shoreline to the crowded, hedonistic playgrounds of Florida's coasts, America's beaches have something for everyone. Even to the landlocked, the scent of coconut oil strikes a deeper chord than that of traditional apple pie. For a truly American experience, try these beaches:

WEST COAST and **HAWAII** The best: **Redondo Beach**, south of Los Angeles. Hawaiian George Freeth introduced the Polynesian art of surfing to the mainland here. **Most beautiful**: the 17 miles of seals, sea lions and multicoloured ice plants that lie amongst the jagged cliffs and sheltered bays between **Pacific Grove** and **Carmel. Princeville**, Kauai, is home to a view of Hanalei Bay and the Na Pali coastline that will make your heart stop at sundown. **Most fashionable: Malibu**, with its bleached sandy beaches and celebrity homes that dot the hills above. A close second is **La Jolla**, near San Diego, CA, a ritzy, cove-lined beach frequented by upscale beachcombers, divers and surfers. **Strangest: Venice Beach**, near LA, has rollerskating grannies, graffiti, and a lot of muscle. **Snorkelling: Hanauma Bay**, Oahu, Hawaii—The best. **Surfing: Sunset** and the other beaches of **Oahu's North Shore**, Hawaii: there is no better place in the world for waves in the winter. A close second is **Maverick's**, California, south of San Francisco, where man and Mother Nature duke it out amongst this deadly stretch of treacherous surf. Here surfers need to be pulled by Jet Skis to even ride these waves. Forget going in the water here, instead, find a calmer plot of sea and try 'Boogie-boarding', so-called because participants 'boogie' down waves upon shorter rectangular boards. If you can't swim give 'Skim- boarding' a shot: using the thin, waxed wooden skimboard try to 'skate' atop the shallow edge of the wave. It's not as easy as it sounds or appears to the casual beach goer. **Windsurfing: Hookipa Beach Park**, Maui— unrivalled as the world's No. 1 location due to constant trade winds and exceptional wave conditions. 'Fun just to watch.' **Most forgotten: Santa Catalina Island**, 26 miles off of Long Beach (CA) is accessible by ferry, home to great scuba diving and swimming. **Most peaceful: Long Beach**, on Vancouver Island's west coast, BC, 12 miles of sea, sand and solitude.

THE EAST COAST Hampton Beach, New Hampshire, has boardwalk, arcades, and waterslides. **Virginia Beach**, Virginia, is a fast growing resort with 28 mi of beach. **Brunswick**, Maine, hosts excellent Beach Bluegrass Festival over Labor Day weekend. **Ocean City**, Maryland, crowded with Washingtonians, IS wild. **Myrtle Beach**, South Carolina, is the third most-visited spot on the East Coast behind Disneyworld and Atlantic City. Nearby **North Myrtle** becomes a student mecca in early mid-May. **Atlantic City**, New Jersey, birthplace of salt water taffy and showplace of Miss America. It's also the East Coast's answer to Las Vegas, with plenty of casinos, hotels and celebrity shows. **Asbury Park**, decaying but still can lay claim to Bruce Springsteen. **Brighton Beach**, Brooklyn, New York, the only American beach where Russian is the native language!
Sanibel Island, Florida, for the best seashells, starfish. **Cocoa Beach**, Florida, has cosmic surfing and the added attraction of being near the blast-off site for the Space Shuttle flights. **Fort Lauderdale**, Florida, midway between Palm Beach and Miami is a glut of beer, raw lust and sports cars. NB: while the vast majority of America's beaches are public, rules governing beach access differ from state to state, always inquire locally.

For a full rundown, go to _www.petrix.com/beaches_ which lists best beaches in the US ranked by Dr Stephen Leatherman (50 factors considered), including 2005's ranking of Best Beaches (with photos); best walking beaches (hard-packed sand, gently sloping); best wild beaches (sparsely populated, limited access, nature abounds); best romantic beaches (natural beauty, privacy, good sand and water quality); and best nightlife beaches. Dr Leatherman, also known as Dr Beach, is author of _America's Best Beaches._

THE SOUTHWEST

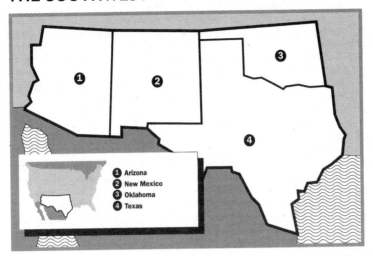

1. Arizona
2. New Mexico
3. Oklahoma
4. Texas

Much of this area is exactly as you would expect from seeing Westerns—whether shot in Spain or elsewhere. Purple mountains, searing deserts, cactus, cowboys and Indians all inhabit Arizona, New Mexico and west Texas. Contrasting with this region are the lush farmlands of east Texas and Oklahoma and the parks and ski resorts of northern Arizona and New Mexico on the tailbone of the Rocky Mountains.

Hardly passing through an intervening industrial stage, the Southwest since World War II has leapt from a simple economy into the nuclear-industrial-aerospace age and is now the bright buckle of the Sun Belt. But the past has not been lost—old Indian and Spanish influences remain.

For several decades after it was blazed in 1822, the Sante Fe Trail served emigrants and traders between Missouri and the Southwest. Now the major thoroughfares are the I-40 (the legendary 'Route 66') to the north and the cross-country I-10 to the south. To enjoy the natural splendour of the region and get a sample of day-to-day life here, stay off I-40 as much as possible.

ARIZONA - Grand Canyon State

Once called the 'Baby State' (the words of one of the state's first senators) because it is the youngest of the lower 48, Arizona has slid comfortably into its mature role as a mecca for retirees and families on vacation. The low cost of living and unique quality of life are now also drawing younger residents in large numbers. A land of vast silences and arid beauty, the Grand Canyon State (its new moniker) also contains sharp and sometimes troubling contrasts. One-quarter of Arizona is Indian land, containing the incredibly ancient and artistically advanced cultures of the Hopis, Navajos and others, and one in twenty inhabitants is a Native American. Yet Native Americans in the state were not allowed to vote until 1948.

Arizona's works of nature are among the grandest in the US, if not the world, beginning with the Grand Canyon and continuing through 21 other highly varied national parks, monuments and recreation areas. But the works of man range from banal to short-sightedly destructive: water-greedy cities, a borrowed London Bridge, and dam-drowned canyons. Even the upper portion of the Grand Canyon—the Marble Canyon—was threatened with a dam at one time!

The southern section from Tucson east is the richest historically. It was once the stomping ground of Wyatt Earp, Billy the Kid (_www.aboutbil-lythekid.com_), Apache chiefs Geronimo (_www.indians.org/welker/geronimo.htm_) and Cochise and assorted prospectors, padres and gunslingers. Northern Arizona, with its stark mesas and richly coloured canyons, offers the great-est scenic drama. In the north, Glen Canyon and Monument Valley, both spilling over into Utah, and Canyon de Chelly should all be high on the visitor's list, after the mandatory pilgrimage to the Grand Canyon.

The vast distances between cities and parks—not to mention the sprawl within Phoenix and Tucson themselves—make a car a smart acquisition. Car rentals at Phoenix airport have a 30 % tax added. Take a bus to the city and rent downtown.

National Parks: Grand Canyon, Petrified Forest, Saguaro. For more info see _www.arizonaguide.com_, _www.stepintoplaces.com_, _www.arizonavacationvalues.com_.

The telephone area codes for the state are 480, 602, 623, 928 and 520.

PHOENIX Huge, hot and horizontal, Phoenix is quite possibly the worst city for pedestrians, who faint on the sizzling sidewalks during the city's three months of 110?F plus temperatures. The city isn't a convenient gateway to anywhere-although at the rate it's sprawling, Phoenix may one day ooze right up to the lip of the Grand Canyon.

Actually the suburbs can be more interesting than the metropolis itself. **Tempe** is home to Arizona State University, with the largest student body in the west. **Scottsdale**, the destination for the moneyed traveller, boasts some upscale resorts. _www.phoenixcvb.com_.

Accommodation
NB: In general, expect much higher rates Oct-May in large Arizona cities like Phoenix and Tucson. In summer, check rates at the posh resorts - opulence can be had for less than $50 nightly. Check out the ranch-style motels on **Van Buren St** and **Main St** (aka **Apache Trail**).

Mi Casa-Su Casa, (800) 456-0682/(480) 990-0682. Lists rooms in 250 B&B's statewide and across Southwest. From D-$49 inc. bfast. Loves foreign travellers. _www.azres.com_.

In Phoenix: Budget Lodge Motel, 402 W Van Buren St, (602) 254-7247, $35-$85. Pool, AC, TV.

AYH-Metcalf House, 1026 N 9th St btwn Roosevelt & Portland, 2 blocks E of 7th St, (602) 254-9803. $15. 'Good for help and info. Common room (day use), no curfew, scheduled activities, kitchen, laundry. Glad to provide free sound advice when purchasing a car esp. if planning to resell. 'Very family style atmosphere promoted - liked everyone to have dinner together, etc.' 'Clean and quiet, the cheapest place to stay in Phoenix.' First come, first serve, members and those who show up at 5pm

are guaranteed a bed. Dinner at 6pm. Closed in Aug. *www.hiayh.org*.
YMCA, 350 N 1st Ave, (602) 257-5150. Co-ed, 1 floor for women. S-$20; $2 for access to pool and athletic facilities. 'Clean.' *www.valleyymca.org*.
In Mesa: Motel 6, 1511 S Country Club, (480) 834-0066, From $33. *www.motel6.com*.
Near Airport: Days Inn, 3333 East Van Buren, (602) 224-8244, Summer specials:-D-$40. Excellent location and facilities. Free 24-hr airport transportation. *daysinnphoenix.com.*
Tempe Travelodge, 1005 E Apache Blvd, (480) 968-7871. From $65, continental bfast incl. *www.tempetravelodge.com*.

Food
Essentially an expensive gringo resort area, with fast food and a 24 hr convenience store seemingly on every corner. In Tempe, near the university, along Mill Ave at University Ave, are low-cost bars and nosheries where students congregate.
Club Rio, 430 N Scottsdale Rd, Tempe, (480) 894-0533. 'Huge burgers.' (Mon & Thu burgers $4). For a splurge, try steaks cooked Indian-style, over mesquite, a technique that originated here. The restaurant is open during the day Mon-Fri 11am-3pm, club nights Fri/Sat. *www.clubrio.com*.
La Tolteca, 1205 E. Van Buren St, (602) 253-1511. Incredible deals await at this authentic Mexican stand. Open every day 6:30am-9pm.
Pinnacle Peak Patio, 10426 E Jomax Rd in Scottsdale, (480) 585-1599, is where locals go for cheap and excellent mesquite-broiled fare. Mon-Thu 4pm-10pm, Fri-Sat 'til 11pm, Sun 12pm-10pm. *www.pppatio.com*.
Los Dos Molinos, 8646 S Central Ave, (602) 243-9113. Features live music at lunch and dinner. Huge menu offering enchiladas and burritos. Tue-Sat 11am-3pm then 5pm-9pm, Sat 11am-9pm.

Of interest
Always phone first or check with the visitors' bureau; sights are far apart and the summer heat is intense - lows in July are around 90°F.
In Phoenix: Camelback Mountain, take Echo Canyon Park Rd. Tallest peak in the Phoenix Mountains, 2,704 ft. Phoenix's most visible landmark offers scenic views, picnicking, good trails, including Summit Trail, just over 1 mile. Call the Parks and Rec. dept. for more info on local parks, (602) 256-3220. *www.ci.phoenix.az.us*.
Desert Botanical Gardens, 1201 N Galvin Pkwy, (480) 941-1225. On the border of Phoenix, Scottsdale and Tempe in Papago Park, by the zoo. Carefully maintained colourful collection of cacti, some twice as high as a human being and 20,000 desert plants to show how the desert ecosystem works. Summer, 7am-8pm. $9, $5 w/student ID, *www.dbg.org*.   Half a mile west is the **Phoenix Zoo,** 455 N Galvin Parkway, (602) 273-1341. Specialising in Arizona wildlife; recently refurbished **Arizona Trail** inc. indigenous species from the state. Walk around or take a guided tour via tram. Summer weekdays 7am-1pm, weekends 7am-4pm, after Labor Day 9am-5pm; $14. $9 during summer, *www.phoenixzoo.org*. The zoo is located within **Papago Park** on Galvin Parkway past Van Buren St, (602) 256-3220; 1200 acres of desert hills and volcanic rock. Museums, picnic areas and the **Hole in the Rock**.
Heard Museum, 2301 North Central Ave, (602) 252-8848. Recently rebuilt and reopened in May, 2005. Outstanding collections of native American handicrafts, silverwork, weavings, basketry, plus most of former Sen. Barry Goldwater's collection of Hopi Kachina dolls. Museum also promotes the work of contemporary Native American artists, and sponsors occasional lectures and Native American dances. Take guided tour of the core exhibits of SouthWestern Indian collections. Daily 9.30am-5pm. $10, $5 w/student ID. "Shop has wonderful selection of authentic Native American jewellery though one may prefer to buy more directly from vendors or makers. Beware of SouthEast Asian copies." **Heard Museum North,** 34505 N Scottsdale Rd, (480) 488-9817. A single gallery and shop, $3. *www.heard.org*.

Mystery Castle, 800 E Mineral Rd, (602) 268-1581. Bizarre pueblo mansion operating tours of the 18-rooms (none on the same level or in the same shape) and 13 fire places, $5. Thu-Sun 11am-4pm Oct-June, closed July-Sept.

Paolo Soleri's Gallery and Studio, 6433 Doubletree Ranch Rd, Scottsdale, (480) 948-6145/(800) 752-3187. Now houses the Cosanti Foundation. Open to walk around 9am-5pm. *www.cosanti.com*. **Arcosanti,** (928) 632-7135, Soleri's futuristic vertical city in the making, is N of Phoenix, exit 262 off I-17. Free. Visitors Centre open daily 9am-5pm, tours 10am-4pm, $8 donation. Must have a car. *www.arcosanti.org*.

Phoenix Art Museum, 1625 N Central, (602) 257-1222. Western and Latin American exhibits. Tue-Sun 10am-5pm, Thu free and open `till 9pm. $9, $7 w/student ID. *www.phxart.org*.

Pueblo Grande Museum and Archaeological Park, 4619 E Washington St, (602) 495-0901. Explore a trail through the ruin and full-size replicas of Hohokam houses. While in the museum there are exhibits featuring the ancient Hohokam and archaeology and a changing gallery. Mon-Sat 9am-4.45pm, Sun 1pm-4.45pm. $2. Free Sun. *www.pueblogrande.com* .

South Mountain Park, 10919 S Central Ave, (602) 495-0222. Largest municipal park in the world; dramatic rock formations and cacti; hiking trails, spectacular lookouts, *www.phoenix.gov/parks*.

Rawhide's 1880s Western Town, Wild Horse Pass, (480) 502-5600. Includes Old West shoot-outs, saloon, a steakhouse (with deep-fried rattlesnake on the menu), rodeo country music and stage coach rides. Daily 5pm-10pm; free. Must purchase tickets to the attractions. *www.rawhide.com*.

Taliesin West: 114th St and Frank Lloyd Wright Blvd, Cactus Rd intersection, **Scottsdale,** (480) 860-2700. Frank Lloyd Wright's winter home and workshop. Guided tours avail. lasting 1-3hrs. 1 hr tours, $14, $12 w/student ID, 3 hr $25 tour inc. refreshments. Fri night tour, $22.50, also inc. refreshments and the chance to see the fire-breathing dragon! Call for exact timings. *www.franklloydwright.org*.

In Tempe: the ASU Art Museum, 10th St and Mill Ave, 1 block S of Uni, (480) 965-2787, built in 1989, is an avant-garde showcase housing 5 galleries of changing exhibits, Tue-Sat 10am-5pm. Winter Tue till 9pm. Free. *asuartmuseum.asu.edu*. On the same block is the **Ceramics Research Center,** which houses a collection of 3,500 ceramics, 'probably the largest and strongest contemporary collection of British and American ceramics in the USA'. Free. The **Gammage Center for Performing Arts,** corner of Mill and Apache Sts, (480) 965-3434, a building designed by Frank Lloyd Wright. Free $1/2$ hr tours can be reserved Mon-Fri, Sep-May. Student rush discount tickets are available before some performances at the box office Mon-Fri 10am-6pm. Elsewhere on the ASU campus, most offices are not open in summer.

Nearby: Casa Grande Ruins National Monument, 1100 Ruins Drive, Coolidge, (520) 723-3172, $3 pp. A 4-storey structure built by the Pueblo Indians in 1300 and protected from further erosion by a hilarious 'umbrella', courtesy of the US government. Daily 8am-5pm; *www.nps.gov/cagr*. Far more spectacular are the ruins at **Tonto National Monument,** nr Roosevelt, (928) 467-2241. 700 yr old cliff dwellings of the Salado people. 'The Apache Trail follows Rte 88 to Tortilla Flats and Roosevelt Lake through superb desert scenery with views of Superstition Mountains and Weavers Needle. Make a day trip of it.' $3 pp, open 8am-5pm daily, trail closes at 4pm *www.nps.gov/tont*.

Entertainment

Mesa Golf-land & Sun Splash, 155 W Hampton Ave, Mesa, (480) 834-8319. The surf reaches 5ft on this $2^1/2$ acre, 2 million gallon wave pool; no surfing any more but swimming still permitted. Giant water slides and waving palms complete the oasis illusion. Open Mon-Thu 10am-8pm, Fri-Sat 10am-9pm, Sun Noon-10pm May-Aug, $21 ($17 after 4pm) plus $5 for tube rental. Lockers available, $8. See website for discount coupons. 'Most indulgent moment of my holiday.' For the after-hours scene, grab the free *New Times Weekly* and the *Cultural Calendar of Events* guide. *mesa.golfland.com*.

Check out **Char's Has The Blues,** 4631 N 7th Ave, (602) 230-0205. Sports dozens of junior John Lee Hookers! 'Arizona's best blues bar' Doors Sun-Thu 7:30 pm, Fri-Sat 7pm; cover w/ends. *www.charshastheblues.com*.

Sport

Arizona Diamond Backs play at Bank One Ballpark on E Jefferson St, (602) 514-8400/462-6799. *www.arizonadiamondbacks.com*.

Phoenix Suns, major league basketball team play at America West Arena, (602) 514-8321. Season starts in Oct.

Information/Internet/Wi-Fi

Arizona Office of Tourism, 1110 W Washington, Suite #155, (602) 364-3700; Open Mon-Fri 8am-5pm, *www.arizonaguide.com*.

Casa Grande Chamber of Commerce, 575 N Marshall St, (520) 836-2125. *www.casagrandechamber.org*.

Greater Phoenix Convention & Visitors Bureau, 400 E Van Buren St, (602) 254-6500. *www.phoenixcvb.com*.

Scottsdale Chamber of Commerce, 4343 N Scottsdale Rd Suite #170, (480) 421-1004. Mon-Fri 8am-5pm. *www.scottsdalecvb.com*.

Tempe Convention & Visitors Bureau, 51 W 3rd St, Suite #105, (800) 283-6734. *www.tempecvb.com*.

Internet access

Burton Barr Central Library, 1221 N Central Ave, (602) 262-4636, open daily. All Phoenix public libraries provide internet access. Free, from 15 mins-1 hr. The Central Library, Desert Broom and Cholla branches provide free Wi-Fi. *www.phoenixpubliclibrary.org/libcomp.jsp*.

Travel

Valley Metro Public Transport, (602) 262-7433. $3.60 all day pass, basic fare $1.25, free transfer. Most routes operate Mon-Fri 5am-10pm. DASH is free between State Capital/downtown/Arizona Center till 6pm. *www.valleymetro.org*.

Discount Cab, (602) 266-0240.

Greyhound, 2115 E Buckeye Rd, 1 mile W of airport, (800) 231-2222/(602) 389-4200, 24 hrs. Also picks up from Terminal 4 at airport. In **Mesa:** 1423 S. Country Club Rd. (480) 834-3360.

Sky Harbor International Airport, SE of downtown, (602) 273–3300. Allow time in the terminal to see the abundance of contemporary art exhibits depicting Arizona's cultural life. Showers and lockers available. From downtown, Mon-Sat take the 'Red Line' bus from Central Station at Central & Van Buren, $1.25. *phoenix.gov/AVIATION/index.html*.

TUCSON Once capital of the Arizona Territory, Tucson (pronounced Too-sawn) is now part university town, part giant retirement home. The city is also capitalising on its new age background and is a burgeoning arts and crafts center. Folksiness notwithstanding, Tucson is, like Phoenix, a big, tough town with its share of crime, poverty and drugs. Watch your step in downtown, particularly at night and especially if you are female.

Most worthwhile sights are well away from downtown: the Desert Museum, Mission San Xavier del Bac, Saguaro National Park, Old Tucson and the interesting Yaqui Indian tribe. The Yaquis have been immortalised in the books of Carlos Castaneda, a renegade anthropologist who claims that members of this tribe possess ancient knowledge of true sorcery. Whether or not you buy this view, the Yaquis are a highly spiritual and musical people whose rites combine native and Catholic traditions. Their public performances (around Pascua, a village south of Tucson) are especially magnificent during Holy Week and at Christmas.

Both Tucson and Phoenix are in the Sonora Desert, surrounded by giant saguaro forests, cacti and mountains, all within driving but not walking distance. Tucson is 65 miles north of Nogales, an agreeable town on the Arizona/Mexico border. For more info see: _www.ci.tucson.az.us_ or _www.dotucson.com_.

The area code for much of Southern Arizona is 520.

Accommodation
Motel strip row runs along South Freeway, the frontage road along I-10.
Hotel Congress & Tucson International Hostel, 311 E Congress St, 622-8848. Historic railroad hotel built in 1919, conveniently located across from the Greyhound and Amtrak stations. Dorm $20-29. Private room (hotel) $59-89. 'Best value in USA.' 'Wild progressive nightclub in lobby. Great fun.' The hotel also hosts live music or DJs throughout the week. 'Only 40 miles to Mexico!' *www.hotel-congress.com*.
Camping: Travel via the Catalina Hwy. **Mount Lemmon Recreation Area** in the Coronado National Forest, 300 W Congress St, 670-4552, offers beautiful campgrounds, $10-15, free off-site camping in certain areas. *www.fs.fed.us/r3/coronado*.

Food
Tucson is the place to get great Mexican food, especially *chimichangas*, reportedly invented here. *Chimichangas* are essentially fried pastry stuffed with beef, chillies, onion, cheese and salsa. Follow your nose, or pick up a free *Tucson Weekly*.
Caruso's, 434 N 4th Ave, 624-5765. Entrees $6-10. 'Great lasagna.' Tues-Thu 4.30pm-10pm, Fri & Sat till 11pm, Sun from 4pm.
El Charro, 311 N Court, 622-1922, original of four in Tucson. Open Mon-Thu 11am-9pm, Sat till 10pm, Sun noon-8pm. A fortress of Mexican-American food since 1922. Tasty *carne seca* (air-dried beef), $6-15, a speciality of Mexican cattle country. Noisy and sociable, packed with tourists, Tucsonians, healthnuts and burrito hounds spooning it all up! *www.elcharro.com*.
Jacks Original BBQ, 5250 E 22nd St, 750-1280. BBQ and grill. Open Mon-Sat 11am-9pm, Sun noon-9pm. *www.jacks-bbq.com*.
Saguaro Corners Restaurant, 3750 South Old Spanish Trail, 886-5424. Unique experience-view wild animals while you dine. Tue-Sat noon-2.30pm 5-9.30pm, Sun noon-9.30pm. Entrees from $3. *www.saguarocorners.com*.

Of interest
Arizona-Sonora Desert Museum, 2021 N Kinney Rd, 14 miles W of the city, 883-2702. A museum, zoo and nature preserve rolled into one. Detailed look at Sonoran desert from tunnels that let you peer into snake and prairie-dog households to outdoor habitats of Gila monsters and mountain lions. Plants and rocks of the desert are also represented, in a museum that has been called 'the most distinctive in the US'. 'Don't miss this place.' Visit early am or late pm to see max. animal activity; Summer 7.30am-10pm daily. $9. Entrance fee includes admission to the **Earth Sciences Center** with a manmade limestone cave showing subterranean rock and life forms, and explanations of volcanic activity. *www.desertmuseum.org*.
North of the museum, **Saguaro National Park,** 733-5153; 2 sections, one east and one west of Tucson, both open 7.30am-sunset. The Saguaro cacti, the protection of which the park was created for, are found naturally only in the Sonora desert (although pirated plants may be seen as far away as LA). These cacti can grow upto

59 ft and live for as long as 200 yrs. In late May, waxy white flowers sprout from the tips of cacti arms—a charming and improbable sight. **East Park (Rincon mountain)**, 3693 S Old Spanish Trail, has the oldest stands. $10 to drive the loop; $5 p/pedestrian or cycle. Miles of trails and a scenic drive lead through the cactus forest. Get a free permit from the visitors center for backcountry camping (before noon) if you are prepared to brave the summer temperatures of upto 115F. **West Park (Tucson mountain)** 2700 N Kinney Rd, 883-6366. Hiking trails, auto loop, and paved nature walk near visitors centre. **Gates Pass** is an excellent spot for watching the sun as it rises and sets. *www.nps.gov/sagu.*

Kitt Peak National Observatory, 56 miles SW of Tucson, on Rte 86, 318-8200. Centre for astronomical research. Daily 9am-3.45pm. Tours at 10am, 11.30am and 1.30pm. Tours 1hr. $2. 'Fascinating.' Rsvs nec. For night-time viewing $36, $31 w/student ID. *www.noao.edu/kpno.*

Old Tucson Studios, 201 S Kinney Rd, 883-0100. Sun-Fri 10am-3pm, Sat 10am-4pm. Tours every 45 mins $12.95. Setting for some of Hollywood's finest western movies, inc. *Rio Bravo, Eldorado, and Young Guns II.* Daily shoot-outs, saloon entertainment and rides. Also check out **Mescal**, it's sister city, where *Tombstone, The Quick and The Dead, and Young Riders* were shot. *www.oldtucson.com.*

Sabino Canyon, 5700 N Sabino Park Rd, 749-2861 and **Seven Falls,** two of the area's most popular and breathtaking hiking, picnicking and biking areas (bikes before 9am/after 5pm only, except Wed/Sat). Either take a tram up the canyon, $7.50, or walk. The falls can be reached only by a $4^1/_2$-mile hike. No overnight camping. Call for best directions. **Visitors Centre** Mon-Fri 8am-4.30pm, Sat/Sun 8.30am-4.30pm. *www.sabinocanyon.com.*

Pima Air and Space Museum, 6000 E Valencia Rd, 574-0462. Huge aeroplane cemetery. Tour the plane used by Presidents Kennedy and Johnson. Daily 9am-5pm, $9.75. *www.pimaair.org.*

Titan Missile Museum, exit 69 on I-19 nr Green Valley, 625-7736. Don a hardhat and see the only Titan 2 ICBM (cruise missiles to the uninitiated!) silo in the world open to the public. Open daily Nov-April 9am-5pm; Closed Mon-Tue. May-Oct $8.50. 'A chilling, frightening and all-powerful must see.' *www.pimaair.org/tmm/index.html.*

Tucson Museum of Art, 140 N Main Ave, 624-2333. Outstanding collection of Pre-Columbian, Spanish Colonial and Latin American folk art. Mon-Sat 10am-4pm, Sun noon-4pm. Closed Mon during summer. $5, $2 w/student ID, free Sun. *www.tucsonarts.com.*

Worthwhile **museums on UA campus: Center for Creative Photography,** 1030 N Olive Rd, 621-7968. Magnificent museum that houses 50,000 fine art photos, including the Ansel Adams and Richard Avedon archives. Mon-Fri 9am-5pm, Sat & Sun from noon; make appointment to view prints & archives. Free. *www.creativephotography.org.* **Arizona State Museum,** Uni Blvd & Park Ave at Uni gates, 621-6302. Archaeology and photography artifacts as well as a pottery collection ranging from middle archaic to contemporary. Mon-Sat 10am-5pm, Sun noon-5pm. Free, donations rec, *www.statemuseum.arizona.edu.* **Flandrau Science Center Planetarium,** 1601 E Uni Blvd, 621-STAR; exhibits on space and astronomy. Mon-Sat 9am-5pm, Thu-Sat 7-9pm, Sun 1-5pm. Admission to the Science Centre is $5.50, $4.50 matinees (summer only). *www.flandrau.org.* The campus is also home to the **Mineral Museum,** Uni Blvd & Cherry Ave, Mon-Sat, 9am-5pm, Sun 1-5pm, entry is incl. with Planetarium. *www.geo.arizona.edu/minmus.*

Nogales: An hour's drive south from Tucson brings you to this border town, the largest crossing between Arizona and Mexico. It is actually two towns, either side of the border, and it is worth crossing just to see the contrast between the tumbling white-washed Mexican houses clinging to the slopes, and the ordered streets on the American side. *www.nogalesmainstreet.com.*

Entertainment

UA students are renowned for rocking and rolling on **Speedway Blvd**. Pick up a copy of the free *Tucson Weekly* or the w/end sections of *The Star* or *The Citizen* for current entertainment listings. Head up 4th Ave to **O'Malley's,** 623-8600, which has food, pool tables. During **Downtown at Dusk,** 547-3338, Congress St is blockaded for a celebration of the arts with outdoor singers, crafts, and galleries, and twice monthly on Thursdays Oct-May, the **Artwalk,** (480) 990-3939, takes place. *www.downtowntucson.org.*

The Bum Steer, 1910 N Stone, 884-7377. Good lunch specials for under $6 on Thu & Sun. 'A must. Good luck lads and don't forget Happy Hour.' 'Try the house special-'Jiffy Burger' (Peanut butter, bacon and jack cheese). Open daily 11am-1am, at w/ends it hosts a nightclub with DJs playing hip hop and r'n'b.

The Maverick; King of Clubs, 6622 E Tanque Verde Rd, 298-0430; honky-tonk cowboy hoe-down.

Near UA Campus: The Shanty Cafe, 401 E 9th, 623-2664. 'Good friendly pub and student watering hole.' Good selection of beers. Open daily till 1am.

Gentle Ben's Brewing Company, 865 E University Blvd, 624-4177. Open 11am-1am, closed Sun during summer. *www.gentlebens.com.*

Information/ Internet access

Metropolitan Tucson Convention and Visitors Bureau, 110 S Church Ave, (800) 638-8350. Ask for a bus map, the *Tucson Official Visitor's Guide,* and an Arizona campground directory. *www.visittucson.org.*

Main Library, 101 N Stone Ave, 791-4393. Open daily. First-come first-served, use ltd to 1 hr. All 22 public libraries in the Tucson-Pima area provide internet access, each with different res policies.Check *www.lib.ci.tucson.az.us/publicpcs.htm#software.*

Travel

Sun-Tran public buses, 792-9222, basic fare $1 exact change. Ltd. service hrs.

Amtrak, 400 N Toole Ave, 1 block N of Greyhound, (800) 872-7245/623-4442. On the Sunset Ltd LA-Miami route. Opening hours limited.

Greyhound, 2 S 4th Ave, (800) 231-2222/792-3475. 'Girls near depot should stay on the move. This is the local prostitutes' pitch—clients are very persistent and extremely unpleasant.'

Tucson International Airport, 573-8000, from downtown take #6 S to airport. *www.tucsonairport.org.* After bus hours, call **Arizona Stagecoach,** 889-1000, pick-up/drop-off at downtown hotels, $17-30. Rsvs rec. for departure (24 hrs). *www.azstagecoach.com.*

Yellow Cab taxis, 624-6611. Open 24 hrs.

Budget Car Rental, 3085 E Valencia Rd, 889-8800.

TOMBSTONE, BISBEE and **APACHE COUNTRY** This rugged terrain, once subject to the raids of Mexican revolutionary Pancho Villa, was originally Apache territory. *www.ojinaga.com/villa.* Cochise, who fought the US Cavalry until 1886, was never captured and lies buried somewhere in the **Coronado National Forest,** about 60 miles east of Tucson. *www.fs.fed.us/r3/coronado.*

Tombstone was named as a bit of death-defying bravado by the prospector who founded the town. Told that in this wild Apache country, he would find 'only his own tombstone', he struck silver instead. The silver was short-lived (1877-90), but the tombstones survive in this city that lives off the tourists it traps. **Boot Hill Cemetery** (closes at dusk) is the resting place for both Christian and Jewish wild west pioneers and is one of the few sights in town that is free. It also displays the epitaph of the Clanton Gang,

'Murdered on the Street of Tombstone'—by Marshal Wyatt Earp, Earp's brothers and Doc Holliday at the shootout at **OK Corral**, 308 E Allen St, 457-3456. Open daily, 9am-5pm, $5.50, $7.50 includes shoot-out daily at 2pm, orientation and museum. _www.ok-corral.com_.

There are various other shoot-outs, entrance fees apply. Check out the **Helldorado Amphitheatre**, 457-9153 and **Six Gun City**, 457-3827, both on Toughnut St. 'Whole place is a little false but great fun.' **Legends of the West Saloon**, 457-3055, offers cool drinks and you may even catch a public mock hanging! **The Bird Cage Theatre**, 457-3421, where the legendary Lola Montez danced (the Madonna of the Gold Rush era) is still standing and houses a museum. $5, _www.tombstoneaz.net_.

Visitors Center, 4th & Allen Sts, Tombstone, 457-3929. _www.tombstone.org_.

South of Tombstone by 25 miles, **Bisbee** clings to the sides of steep hills and is a mining town of great character and considerable charm. Over $2 billion in silver, gold and copper came from these hills, but today Bisbee is famous for a special variety of turquoise, on display at **Bisbee Blue Jewelry**. Don't miss the delightful Art Deco courthouse or the nearby 'Lavender Pit Queen Mine'. _www.bisbeearizona.com_.

If you're here in the summer, take heart: Bisbee is 5500 ft above sea level, making it much cooler than Tombstone. Worth a visit is the **Copper Queen Mine**, 478 Dart Rd, 432-2071. Daily tours, $12 at 9am, 10.30am, noon, 2pm and 3.30pm, last 1 hr—'cold, so dress warmly'. 'Extensive, informative, good value.' For local information pick up a copy of the _Tombstone Epitaph_, the town local newspaper. It was saved from bankruptcy by U of Arizona and is now published by students. _www.tombstone-epitaph.com_.

Accommodation
In Cochise, on Route 191: **Cochise Hotel,** exit 331 off I-10 Cochise, 384-3156. S-$37, D-$53, suites $69—sleeps 3. Booking mandatory for this authentic relic of the Old West. Brass beds, costumed guests, quilts, and chamberpots bring 1882 to the modern traveller but with modern plumbing.
In Tombstone; Larian Motel, 457-2272, 410 Fremont St. Clean and close to downtown. S-$49 D-$69. _www.tombstonemotels.com_.
In Bisbee: Bisbee Grand Hotel, 61 Main St, (800) 421-1909/432-5900. From $75 inc. full bfast. _www.bisbeegrandhotel.com_. Also **Jonquil Motel**, 317 Tombstone Canyon, 432-7371. Call ahead especially in winter. $50-75. _www.thejonquil.com_.
Copper Queen Hotel, 11 Howell Ave, 432-2216. From D-$93. Beautiful, regal, once the headquarters for everyone from Teddy Roosevelt to 'Black Jack' Pershing, hot on Pancho Villa's trail. Good dining room, sidewalk cafe, pool, saloon. 'Many rooms with antique furniture—a trip back in time when this was a bustling mining town.' _www.copperqueen.com_.
Camping: can be found for free but sites are $10 pn in Coronado National Forest, 826-3593. _www.fs.fed.us_.

FLAGSTAFF Gateway to the Grand Canyon, a college town with character, Flagstaff is home of 'NAU' (Northern Arizona University). Other scenic splendours nearby are Oak Creek Canyon and Montezuma Castle to the south; Meteor Crater, Petrified Forest and Canyon de Chelly to the east; and Sunset Crater and Wupatki to the north. Santa Fe Ave, the main drag, used to be part of the infamous Route 66, with the Santa Fe railroad right alongside. Somewhat closer to the Grand Canyon is **Williams**, which has some

lodgings and good camping. _www.flagstaffarizona.org_ provides current info on events in the city. City elevation is about 7000 feet making summer weather quite pleasant (relative to areas of lower elevation).
Throughout northern and western Arizona the area code is 928.

Accommodation

'Worth getting into a casual conversation with a Northern Arizona University student. Tell them of your exploits and ask for a bed for the night. It worked for me and some others.' Alternatively, cruise historic Rte 66 to find cheap motels. But, while accommodation is cheaper along Rte 66, the volume of freight train traffic, ie every 15 minutes, and the trains whistling, can be annoying.   The _Flagstaff Accommodations Guide_ available at the Visitors Centre, prices all area hotels, motels, hostels and B&Bs. Tip: if seeing the Grand Canyon, check the noticeboard in your hotel/hostel; some travellers leave their still—valid passes behind. Rates begin falling after Labor Day and are cheapest Nov-May.

Best Value Inn & Suites, 1990 E Santa Fe Ave, 774-2779. Approx. $60.

Grand Canyon International Hostel, 19 S San Francisco St, (888) 442-2696. 1 block from Amtrak. Dorm-$18, private rooms D-$36, all include bfast. Free pickup/drop-off from Greyhound station. No curfew. 'Day trips to Sedona, Grand Canyon and the best staff anywhere in America!' 'Helpful staff.' 'Nice clean rooms; kept bags for us while we saw Canyon.' _www.grandcanyonhostel.com_.

Hotel du Beau Hostel, 19 W Phoenix, (800) 398-7112, directly behind Amtrak. Dorm $18, D-$38, inc. private bathroom. A once famous motel, this friendly and fun hostel has free coffee, fruit and doughnuts for bfast. Runs tours to the Canyon, $50 inc. lunch and entrance, and Sedona $25. Free Greyhound pickup. Rsvs nec. June-Sept. 'Cheap, clean, friendly, but not the place for a good night's sleep—don't go if you're a light sleeper!' 'The best hostel I stayed in.' 'Looked after our rucksacks as we visited the Canyon.' 'Best night in America.' 'A real travellers' haven.' _www.dubeauhostel.com_.

Weatherford Hotel, 23 N Leroux, 774-2731. Spacious rooms, bunk beds and funky furniture. $50-$55 nr Amtrak & buses. 'Lively area at night.' 'Excellent bar with good entertainment, English beer on draught.' Rsvs rec.

Camping: KOA Campground, 5803 N US 89, 526-9926, 6 miles NE of Flagstaff. Local buses stop nearby. Showers, Fr + Sat nightly movies. Tent sites $21-23, cabins $38-42 (must bring linens). _www.koa.com_. For info on campgrounds in the surrounding **Coconino National Forest,** From $14; call the Coconino Forest Service to check restrictions, 527-3600. 'You'll need a car to reach the designated camping areas. Pick up a forest map, $6-7, at the **Visitors' Center**. _www.fs.fed.us/r3/coconino_.

Food/Entertainment

Alpine Pizza, 7 N Leroux, 779-4109, praised for its Italian food. A popular spot for beer, pool and pizza. Daily 11am-10pm, later at w/ends.

Beaver St Brewery, 11 S Beaver St, 779-0079. Fantastic menu; great beer, dips, fondues and huge sandwiches. Daily 11.30am-1am.

Downtown Diner, 7 E Aspen, 774-3492. 'Excellent,' 'best value.' Mon-Wed 5.15am-9pm, Thu till midnight, Fri & Sat till 2.30am, Sun 7.30am-3pm.

Macy's, 14 S Beaver St, 774-2243 (behind Hotel Du Beau). Hippy student hangout serves fresh pasta, veggie food, sandwiches, pastries and coffee. Daily 6am-9pm, Fri & Sat till midnight. _www.macyscoffee.net_.

Mary's Cafe, 7136 N Hwy 89, 526-0008. Open daily 5am-1am. 'Huge homemade cinnamon rolls.'

The Museum Club, 3404 E Rte 66, 526-9434; log cabin roadhouse which began life housing a collection of stuffed animals, now hosts country music entertainment Thu-Sat. Open 11am-2am, Fri & Sat till 3am. _www.museumclub.com/profile_.

Of interest
Museum of North Arizona, 3101 N Fort Valley Rd, 774-5213; 3 miles N of Flagstaff. Focuses on the fine arts, native culture, and natural sciences of the Colorado Plateau. Houses excellent exhibits on native American life; Indian Craft Shows in summer with original items for sale; also find out as much as is known about how the Grand Canyon and Colorado Plateau were created. Daily 9am-5pm, $5, $3 w/student ID. *www.musnaz.org*.

Near Flagstaff: Lowell Observatory, 1400 W Mars Hill Rd, 774-3358. Founded in 1894, the Observatory includes telescope through which Percivall Lowell 'discovered' canals on Mars and where Pluto was first sighted in 1930 by Clyde Tombaugh. Hands-on astronomy exhibits. 'Worth it if only for view over Flagstaff.' Open daily Apr-Oct 9am-5pm, other hrs vary according to season. $5, $4 w/ student ID. *www.lowell.edu*.

Nearby: Mt Agassiz has the area's best skiing. **The Arizona Snow Bowl & Ski Lift Lodge,** 779-1951, daily 8am-4pm. Also offers Scenic Skyride and horseback riding. *www.arizonasnowbowl.com*.

Walnut Canyon, 10 miles E of Flagstaff lays a lush canyon filled with cliff-hanging ruins. The day-use trail is strenuous in places (involving 240 steps over 185ft). Ranger led hikes avail. in summer, rsvs nec. **Visitors Centre** 526-3367. 'Wildlife and Indian relics, very worthwhile and not crowded.' Trail closes at 4.45pm, admission $5 for park. *www.nps.gov/waca*.

Internet access
Cyber Cafe, 1520 S Riordan Ranch Rd, 774-0005. Open Mon-Sat 9am-10pm, Sun 10am-9pm. Fee charged.
Coconino County Public Library, 300 W Aspen, 779-7670. Open Mon-Thu 10am-9pm, Fri till 7pm, Sat till 6pm. $5/hr. *www.flagstaffpubliclibrary.org*.

Travel
Mountain Line Transit, buses, 779-6624. Routes cover most of town, $.75, $2 for day pass, buses run once every hour.
Amtrak, 1 E Rte 66 (Santa Fe Ave), (800) 872-7245. *Southwest Chief* between LA and Chicago stops here. USA Rail Pass holders can use shuttle bus to Canyon for a fee.
Greyhound, 399 S Malpais Lane, across from NAU campus, (800) 231-2222/774-4573. Open 24 hrs.
To get to Grand Canyon: 638-7888, NB: Entry fee $20 p/vehicle, $10 p/pedestrian.
Gray Line/Nava-Hopi Tours, 114 W Rte 66 (800) 892-8687. Shuttles buses to Grand Canyon and Phoenix. Call for times and prices.
Seven Wonders Scenic Tours, 526-2501. Full-day tours with very knowledgeable driver offering flexible day-trips with plenty of freedom at destinations! Tours to various points in Arizona: Grand Canyon $70 inc. entry fee. Also Lake Powell, Petrified Forest, Indian Reservation and Sunset Crater. *www.tourthesouthwest.com*.
Budget Car Rentals, 4800 N US Highway 89, 527-1996, daily 7am-7pm, w/ends till 6pm. 'Push for a student discount.' 'Probably the best way to see the Canyon, if you can round up three other people to split the cost.'
Peace Surplus, 14 W Rte 66, 779-4521. Camping equipment rental; tent, pack and stove rental, plus a good stock of cheap outdoor gear. Mon-Fri 8am-9pm, Sat 8am-8pm, Sun 8am-6pm. Reasonable but 3-day rental min. *www.peacesurplus.com*.

OAK CREEK CANYON and **SEDONA** Going down Hwy 89A from Flagstaff, the road descends into this brilliantly tinted canyon carved by Oak Creek. As you drive down 89A, be prepared to be stunned by the shapes and colours of the cliffs and mesas. From the **Oak Creek Natural Area**, a footpath takes you along the floor, through a dense growth of pines, cypresses and junipers, repeatedly crossing the swift-running brook.

After the descent you come to **Sedona**, a pretty artists' colony and setting for many of Zane Grey's Western novels. The town of Sedona itself is rather touristy and expensive. Take Hwy 179, south of Sedona, and the landscape opens up into striking vistas punctuated by mesas and serrated sandstone cliffs of red, pink, ochre and buff. You can visit the Frank Lloyd Wright **Church of the Holy Cross**, 4 miles off of Hwy 179 at 780 Chapel Rd, 282-4069, a amazing concrete shadowbox set against rust-coloured cliffs with amazing views.

Accommodation
The Sedona Chamber of Commerce, corner of Forest Rd at Rte 89A, 282-7722. Distributes listings for accommodation and private campgrounds in the area. _www.sedonachamber.com; www.visitsedona.com._
Star Motel, 295 Jordan Rd, 282-3641, From $60.
La Vista Motel, 500 N Rte 89A, 282-7301, comfy rooms with TV, fridge from $55.
Camping: There are a number of campgrounds within Coconino National Forest, 527-3600, along **Oak Creek Canyon** on US 89A (sites $16 p/vehicle). **Cave Springs** (877) 444-6777, 10 miles N of Sedona is a busy campground. $18. Free backcountry camping is allowed in the forest, anywhere outside of Oak Creek and more than 1 mile from any official campground. _www.reserveusa.com._

Of interest
Sedona Arts Center, 15 Art Barn Rd, 282-3809. Touring exhibitions which change every 5 weeks; very diverse media and subject matter. Daily 10am-5pm. Free. NB: Sedona is itself a centre for contemporary and traditional arts. _www.sedonaartscenter.com._
Slide Rock Park, 282-3034. 7 miles N of Sedona on US 89A. Takes its name from a natural stone slide into the waters of Oak Creek. Daily in summer 8am-7pm; spring&fall till 6pm, winter till 5pm. $8 p/car for up to 4 people. $2 p/individ. _www.pr.state.az.us._
Red Rock State Park, 282-6907, SW of town on US 89A. Rangers lead day-hikers into the nearby red rocks, including nature and bird walks. Daily 8am-6pm. $6 p/vehicle for up to 4 people. The land was part of a ranch owned by Jack and Helen Frye. Jack was partner with Howard Hughes in the founding of Trans World Airlines as seen in the movie _The Aviator_. Their house, _House of Apache Fires_ is on top of the small mesa within the park.

MONTEZUMA CASTLE NATIONAL MONUMENT   Further south on I-17 is **Tuzigoot National Monument**, exit 287 on Hwy 260, 634-5564, $3 pp, a pueblo ruin atop a mesa overlooking the Verde River. But for a better example, cut across to exit 289, I-17 to **Montezuma Castle**, 567-3322, built in 1000-1400AD the castle is far more picturesque and intact. Neither a castle nor connected with Montezuma, this was a cliff dwelling inhabited by Sinagua. Visitors view the 'castle' from a paved path below. Daily 8am-6pm summer, 8am-5pm winter; $3pp. _www.nps.gov/moca._ **Fort Verde State Park**, south on I-17 is Camp Verde, an historic fort from the period of the American Indian Wars. 3 restored houses and a museum document period of US Army base there. Gen. George Crook who convinced Geronimo, the last warring Indian chief, to surrender, was here. Must for anyone interested in tragedy of white-Indian interactions of the late 19th century. Better to visit museum before the restored houses.

PETRIFIED FOREST NATIONAL PARK   This 94,000-acre park actually contains the varicoloured buttes and badlands of the Painted Desert as well as

Indian petroglyphs at **Newspaper Rock**, pueblo ruins, two museums and a large 'forest' of felled and petrified logs. This part of the US was actually at the Equator during the Triassic period. The trees date back to the Triassic period and were probably brought here by a flood, covered with mud and volcanic ash, preserved by silica quartz and laid bare once again by erosion. Most of the fossilised remains are jasper, agate, a few of clear quartz and amethyst. Like the red, yellow, blue and umber tones of the Painted Desert, these vivid colours are caused by mineral impurities. A road bisects the park north to south. The park is open daily 8am-5pm, longer during the summer 7-7pm; $10 p/vehicle. **The Painted Desert Inn** contains murals by noted Hopi artists, open 8am-5pm, while the **Visitors Centre**, at the north entrance, I-40, shows an info-film about the park. Open daily 7am-7pm, off-season 8am-5pm. At the South Entrance, US Hwy 180, **Rainbow Forest Museum and Visitors Center** has further information. _www.nps.gov/pefo_.

Accommodation
No lodging in the park. However, lodging is available in **Holbrook**, 27 miles away, or **Gallup, New Mexico**, but prices are not always cheap. Budget travellers should return to Flagstaff.
Camping: There are no established campgrounds in the park, but free backcountry camping is allowed in several areas (hikers only) with a permit from the museum.

Travel
There is no public transportation to either part of the park. **Nava-Hopi Bus Lines**, and **Gray Line Tours** offer services from Flagstaff.

NAVAJO and **HOPI RESERVATIONS** The **Navajo** nation occupies the nort east corner of Arizona (plus parts of Utah and New Mexico), an area the size of West Virginia. On it dwell a shy, dignified, beauty-loving people, the largest and most cohesive of all Native American groups. Nearly all Navajos are fluent in their native tongue, a language of such complexity that Japanese cryptographers were unable to decipher it during the Second World War, when the US military used Navajos to send secret information.

Originally a nomadic culture, the flexible Navajos adopted sheepherding and horses from the Spanish, weaving and sand-painting from the Pueblo Indians, and more recently such things as pickup trucks from the whites. The reservation, while poor, is a fascinating mix of traditional hogans and wooden frame houses, uranium mines and trading posts, all in a setting of agriculturally marginal but scenically rich terrain, anchored by the four sacred peaks of Mounts Blanca, Taylor, Humphrey and Hesperus.

Amidst the 150,000 Navajos is an arrowhead-shaped nugget of land upon which sit the three mesas of the **Hopis**, a strenuously peaceful and traditional tribe of farmers and villagers. The 6,500 Hopis have planted corn and ignored Spaniards, Navajos and Anglos alike for nearly a thousand years, their religion and culture still poetically and distinctly non-Western.

Rte 264 crosses both reservations, allowing you access to the Hopi mesa villages and the Navajo settlements and capital at **Window Rock** on the Arizona-New Mexico border. Neither group is particularly forthcoming with non-Natives, but you can bridge their suspicion by respecting their strong feelings about photographs, alcohol, tape recorders and local customs. Always ask permission to take pictures; if you are allowed, expect to pay and live up to your bargain. If you are lucky enough to witness dancing or healing ceremonies, behave as the Indians do to avoid giving offence.

Oraibi on the Third Mesa vies with the Pueblo Indians' Acoma as the oldest continuously inhabited settlement in the US. To enter the village, you must ask permission of the chief and pay a fee—absolutely no cameras, however. One of the most intriguing Hopi villages is **Walpi**, high atop the narrow tip of the Second Mesa. Dating from the 17th century, this classic adobe village of kivas and sculptured houses remains startlingly alien. 'Hire a four-wheel drive to get up very steep roads, dirt tracks.'

Besides looking at the masterful rugs, pottery, jewellery and other crafts, be sure to sample Indian food. Navajo specialties include fried bread, mutton stew and roast prairie dog. Interesting Hopi dishes are nakquivi or hominy stew and the beautiful blue cornmeal bread served with canteloupe for breakfast. **The Hopi Cultural Center** has accommodation, Sun-Thu S-$90, XP-$5, Fri & Sat $95, XP $5 (rsvs rec.), and also a restaurant serving traditional Hopi food, 734-2401, on Rte 264 at the 2nd Mesa; Open at 6am daily. _www.hopiculturalcenter.com_. More info from the **Navajo Tourism Dept**, 871-6436/810-8501; _www.discovernavajo.com_.

Navajo National Monument in the north of the reservation, off State Hwy 564, has impressive Anasazi ruins. No entrance fee, Visitors Centre open daily 8am-7pm, has information and a gift shop. One of the highlights includes **Betatakin**, a 135-room structure nestling half way up a 700 ft sandstone cliff. There are ranger led hikes daily in summer to the ruins, takes around 6 hrs. Phone Park Information 672-2700 for details. _www.nps.gov/nava_.

MONUMENT VALLEY The scene of countless John Ford films and full of Navajo sacred places, this sprawls across Arizona-Utah state lines and can be reached via Hwys 160 and 163 from the south. The views here epitomise just about everyone's perception of the wild west; towering rock pinnacles and sandy mesas; a day's visit should be almost obligatory. It is possible to get a hint of the landscape from Hwy 163, but it is well worth paying the $5 admission to the **Monument Valley Tribal Park** to get a close-up. The most distinctive formations are **The Mittens**—you will know them when you see them. If you're lucky, you'll be able to spend the night at the **Mitten View Campground**, around $10 pn (up to 6 people), close by the Visitors Centre, (435) 727-5874. It won't be the most comfortable night you've ever spent-only a thin layer of sand covers the rocky mesa—but you will be well rewarded by the unforgettable sunrise and sunset, as the mighty rocks and wide sky directly ahead of you change colour by the minute.

Venture onto the valley floor with either a **jeep tour** or on **horseback**—both led by Navajo Indians who will tell you some of the legends and the history of the sites as you travel around. You may even get to hear some of their traditional songs, complete with tom-toms. 'A truly spiritual experience.' Other highlights include the **Eagle's Eye Rock** and the **Trading Post Totem Pole**, a giant needle jutting out of the desert floor. Various stalls outside the Visitors Centre operate tours. There is also the chance to experience life in an Indian Hogan, the traditional six-sided desert home, where crafts are still practised and on sale. An early ride/tour is recommended to beat the glare of the midday sun.

A car is almost a necessity, both here and elsewhere on the reservations. There is some bus service via Nava-Hopi from Window Rock to Tuba City, which stops at **Kearns Canyon** in **Hopiland**. For more info see _www.monumentvalleyonline.com_.

Accommodation
Discover Navajoland, and _The Visitors' Guide to the Navajo Nation_ are available from the **Navajoland Tourism Department**, 871-6434/810-8501. Handy and detailed maps are available for a nominal fee. Mon-Fri 8am-5pm. Plan to camp at the national monuments or the Navajo campgrounds. Alternatively, you can make your visit a hard-driving day trip from Flagstaff or Gallup. _www.discovernavajo.com_. **Greyhills Inn**, Warrior Dr, Tuba City, 283-4450. On a Navajo reservation. 'Easy access' to Grand Canyon. From $22. Check-in 3pm. Rsvs rec.

CANYON DE CHELLY NATIONAL MONUMENT
Surrounded by Navajo land, Canyon de Chelly (about 30 miles north of Hwy 264 and pronounced 'Canyon de Shay') has the powerful beauty of a bygone Garden of Eden. Canyon de Chelly is inhabited by Navajos, who live among 800-year-old pueblo buildings. Both are upstaged by the fantastic walls of the canyon itself, 1000 ft of sheer vertical orange rock.

A road runs along the rim with several lookouts to view **White House Ruin** and **Spider Rock**. The only descent you're allowed to navigate solo is the White House Trail; all others require a Navajo guide. The 1¼ mile (o/w) trail to White House Ruin winds down a 600-ft face through an orchard and across a stream. Take an organised jeep tour or, if you happen to have your own 4 wheel drive vehicle, get a free permit from the Visitors Centre, 674-5500, daily 8am-6pm, and pay a Navajo guide ($15/hr) to show you around.

Although a National Monument, Canyon de Chelly is on Navajo land and is therefore subject to certain restrictions designed to limit intrusion into Navajo privacy. It is also quite isolated, and you would need to consider staying nearby overnight. _www.nps.gov/cach_.

Accommodation
There is no budget accommodation anywhere in Navajo territory. **Farmington, NM**, and **Gallup, NM**, are the closest major cities with cheap lodging. **Free camping**: in the park's **Cottonwood Campground**, 1½ miles from Visitors Center, 674-5500. With over 90 sites which are allocated on a first-come first-served basis, facilities incl. restrooms, picnic tables, water and dump station.

Travel
No public transport to either the Monument or Chinle. Inside the Monument, jeeps tour (six or more passengers) the canyon floor for a good look at ruins and pictographs, $39.50 pp half day, $64.50 pp full day (inc. lunch), through **Thunderbird Lodge**, (800) 679-2473 (rsvs rec. in summer). S-$59-97 D-$65-106 _www.tbirdlodge.com_.

SUNSET CRATER and WUPATKI NATIONAL MONUMENTS
Less than an hour's drive from Flagstaff on US 89A is the entrance to a long volcanic region, **Sunset Crater**. It erupted most recently about AD 1064/5, leaving a colourful cone on a jet black lava field. From the rim, over 8 volcanic peaks,

including those of the **San Francisco Range**, can be seen. The self-guided **Lava Flow Nature Trail** wanders 1 mile through the surreal landscape surrounding the cone, $1^1/2$ miles E of the Visitors Center. The volcanic ash from Sunset made good fertiliser, and a number of Indian groups built pueblos nearby at **Wupatki**. There are over 800 ruins on mesa tops, 5 are open to the public, and a museum to interpret the finds at this long since abandoned settlement. $5 pp, inc. entry to both Sunset Crater and Wupatki. At **Wupatki Visitor Center** is the most complete ruin surrounded by vibrant red limestone outcrop. The ruin is thought to have had 100 rooms. _www.nps.gov/wupa_. _www.nps.gov/sucr_.

Sunset Crater Volcano National Monument's Visitors Center, 10 miles N of Flagstaff on Hwy 89, 526-0502. Open daily during the summer 8am-6pm (seasonal hrs apply).

Wuptaki National Monument Visitors Centre, 679-2365.

Camping: Bonito Campground, 526-0866, in the **Coconino National Forest** at the entrance to Sunset Crater, provides the nearest camping, 44 sites, $15, first-come first-served.

FOUR CORNERS The only point on the United States map where four states meet can be reached from the northeast of Arizona. Here you can have one leg in Arizona, one in New Mexico; an arm in Colorado and another one in Utah. A quadrangle housing the flags of each state marks the spot. Reached by I-160.

THE GRAND CANYON According to legend a Texas cowboy riding across the Arizona desert came to the edge of the Grand Canyon unprepared for what he would see, 'Good God,' he exclaimed, 'something happened here'. This astonishment is probably repeated daily. Approached from a flat, sloping plain on all sides, the Grand Canyon is a startlingly abrupt gash. The Colorado River traverses a magnificent, 277-mile-long canyon through a landscape filled with 270 animal species and containing five of the seven known life zones. To the visitor on the rim, the colourful buttes amid early-morning mist appear as a dreamlike valley of palaces. The proportions of the canyon are deceptive and can best be viewed from **Grandview Point**.

No-one is quite sure how the canyon was created. The spectacular sandstone and limestone formations were not carved out by the river, but are a result of erosion by the wind and extreme cycles of heat and cold. An analogy commonly used by park rangers compares the Colorado River cutting the Grand Canyon to cutting a cake by holding the knife still and having someone lift the cake. The rock on the canyon floor is some of the oldest exposed land on earth.

The Grand Canyon has 3 parts: the **South Rim**, open year-round, access from Williams is via Hwy 64 and from Flagstaff via Hwy 180/64; the **North Rim**, open mid-May to mid-Oct, access via Hwy 67 from Jacob Lake; and the **Inner Canyon**, open year-round, access from the rim by foot, mule or boat (Apr-Oct) only. To get from the North to the South Rim or vice-versa is 215 miles/5 hours by car or an arduous 26-mile hike down and up. If you're not able to take your time in the park, you should choose early on which rim you want to visit.

The South Rim is easy to reach and has the best views as well as the lion's share of the lodgings and amenities. The North Rim boasts special autumn colours, an abundance of animal life and uncrowded serenity. A quarter-million tourists per year visit here versus three million on the south side. The North Rim is best taken in on a loop through Zion and Bryce National Parks.

If you're at all fit, you'll want to hike to the **canyon floor**, or at least part of the way. If you make it to the bottom, don't forget to touch an outcropping of black vishnu schist; this metamorphic rock, the lowest layer in the canyon, was formed when the earth was half the age it is now. 'Hard work, but an awesome and breath-taking spectacle.' 'Do read the hiking tips under *Of Interest* before setting out; the heat, the stiff 4,500 foot climb, the high altitude of the entire area and the need to carry large amounts of water are all factors you must prepare for.' 'No 2-D picture could ever do justice to this scene of nature at her most imposing form. Even if you have to go to great lengths to get here, that first sight of the canyon ... you'll have no regrets.' The scenery is often enhanced or spoiled, depending on your point of view, by the haze coming over from Los Angeles and Las Vegas, which can give the whole place an even more magical aura.

Park entrance fee is $20 per car. It's $10 for someone on foot or on a bus. You will come across a wealth of info through any browser, but *www.kaibab.org* is a worthwhile site to explore for its virtual photo footage. Also see *www.nps.gov/grca*. It's quite feasible to return to Flagstaff on USI-80-180 at night but take elk signs seriously as the animals cross the road without warning and are quite large.

Accommodation

Most accommodation on the South Rim is very expensive. It is recommended that you make reservations for lodging, campsites or mules well in advance - prepare to battle the crowds! Some accommodation, like **Phantom Ranch**, the only lodge on the canyon floor, gets booked up by hikers a year in advance. Brisk weather and fewer tourists in winter, but some hotels and facilities close. **The North Rim** campgrounds are only open May to October.

Check exact dates if you plan to travel at this time. Some campgrounds can be booked up to 5 months in advance over the internet at *reservations.nps.gov*. A comprehensive summary of the accommodation options can also be found at *www.nps.gov/grca/grandcanyon*. **TIP**: check at the visitors' centre and the Bright Angel transportation desk after 4pm for vacancies.

South Rim:

Inside park; Grand Canyon Lodges. Xanterra Parks & Resorts handles accommodation for all 6 lodges and hotels within the park. Call (888) 297-2757. Book 6-9 months in advance. Prices start at $28 dorm room, $67 private bath. *www.grand-canyonlodges.com*. **Bright Angel Lodge and Cabins** are usually the least expensive. **Maswik** and **New Yavapai** are also reasonable. 'Book well ahead, even after Labor Day.' **Outside park**: There are numerous hotels and motels in **Tusayan**, 7 miles south of the South Rim: **Quality Inn**, Hwy 64, (800) 221-2222, 638-2673; S/D-$118 approx. Or try further out in **Williams: Quality Inn Mountain Ranch Resort**, 6701 E Mountain Ranch Rd, 6 m E of Williams on I-40, (800) 228-5151/635-2693. $79-109, pool and spa. *www.mountainranchresort.com*.

Camping: inside the Park there are 2 established campgrounds: **Mather Campground, National Park Reservations** (800) 365-2267/(301) 722-1257, $15 pn for up to 6 people. Rsvs usually 5 months and at least 1 day, in advance. Later in summer, thunderstorms deluge the area. Campsites fill quickly June through Sept, so get there very early (allocated from 10am). **Desert View Campground,** 26 m E of Grand Canyon Village, first-come first served, May-Oct only. $10, no hook-ups.

Outside park: Camper Village, (928) 638-2887, 7m S of Grand Canyon Village on Hwy 64, opposite IMAX theatre. Tent site $18, XP-$2. Massive campground, 'always have a site'. **Kaibab National Forest;** campground overflow generally winds up in the National Forest, along the south border of the Park, where you can pull off a dirt road and camp for free, but not within $1/4$ m of a Hwy. 'OK as long as you remain within $1/2$ mile of public telephone.' For more info, contact the **Tusayan Ranger District, Kaibab National Forest,** 635-8200/638-2443. They also operate the Ten-X Campground, 2 m S of Tusayan, April-Sep, $10 no hook-up. *www.fs.fed.us.*

Backcountry camping: Any overnight hiking (or camping away from designated campgrounds) within the park requires a Backcountry Use Permit, $10, plus an impact fee of $5 per night pp. This applies if you are within the canyon, not on the rim. Demand again exceeds supply. Applications in writing only, up to 4 mths in advance, to **Backcountry Office,** PO Box 129, Grand Canyon, AZ 86023, fax 638-2125; check the parks' website for more info and to download an application: *www.nps.gov/grca.* There are a very limited number of permits available 24 hrs beforehand; put your name on the waiting list at the Backcountry Office, 638-7875, $1/2$ mile S of the **Visitors Centre.** Daily 8am-noon, 1pm-5pm. Phone queries in the afternoon only. 'As soon as you arrive, go to the Backcountry Office by 7am for a chance at unclaimed permits.' Keep in mind that there's a heavy fine for those caught camping without a permit.

Inner Canyon: Phantom Ranch, (888) 297-2757, dorms $28, cabins $72, XP $10.50, based on double occupancy. Booked up long in advance, rsvs rec. 12 mths ahead. 'Air conditioned, very comfortable.' NB: Anything you buy down here is bound to be expensive, and that includes food. Leave excess luggage on the rim for a fee. Must book any meals in advance.

North Rim: Inside park: Grand Canyon Lodge, Call Xanterra or, for last minute (48 hrs) reservations, call 638-2611. Late May to mid-Oct only. $93-124. Campsite rsvs and trail info at Lodge, but no place to check luggage.

Outside park: Jacob Lake Inn, 44 miles N Hwy 89A & 67, 643-7232. Open year-round: cabins up to 2 people $72; 2 rm cabin $86-91 (dependent upon number of people). *www.jacoblake.com.*

Camping: North Rim Campground is the only National Park operated camp ground inside the park; $15 per site. Rsvs (800) 365-2267, outside North America call (301) 722-1257, can be made up to 5 months in advance. *www.reservation.nps.gov.*

Outside park: Kaibab Camper Village, $1/4$ m S of Lake Jacob on Hwy 67, 643-7804 (summer), 526-0924 (winter). Tent site $13 for 2, XP $2. *www.kaibabcampervillage.com.*

Part of the Kaibab National Forest is also located north of the canyon, and it is possible to camp here. Call the North Kaibab Ranger District, 643-7395. 'Often necessary to camp outside park on National Forest land the night before, arriving in park early am to nab site.'

Food

Expensive and generally poor everywhere in the park, even at cafeterias, although it is possible to find meals for fast food prices. Best bets: **South Rim: Canyon Village Market Place,** 638-2262, across from Visitors Center, also at Desert View, East Rim, and Tusyon. Stock up at this store which also has a deli counter and reasonably priced supermarket. Summer 7am-9pm.

North Rim: The Grand Canyon Lodge, 638-2611. The restaurant serves bfast $3-7 and dinners from $8 (rsvs only). Sandwiches at cafeteria. There is also a bar. Cafeteria open daily 5:30am-10:30pm. Dining room daily 6.30am-9.45pm.

Of interest

Hiking Tips: Whether you descend into the canyon or not, guard against heat exhaustion and dehydration by drinking the park-recommended juice mixture. Water alone will not satisfy your body's requirements, as the rangers will tell you. Other hiking tips: wear a hat, don't wear sandals, always check beforehand to make sure your trail is open. For hiking into the canyon, plan to carry 4 litres of water per person per day. Also carry permit, pocket knife, signal mirror, torch, maps, matches, first-aid kit and importantly, food. Buy energy food at the Visitors' Centre. Rangers say people make the mistake of drinking too much water without any food which can be just as dangerous as no water. Calculate 2 hrs up for every hr going down. If you do get lost or injured, stay on the trail so they can find you. Rangers threaten the cost of an air rescue, which runs in to the $1000s.

The park service warns against hiking to the Colorado River and back in one day. BUNACers add: 'Do take notice of time estimates.' BUT, 'be aware of what you personally can do. Rangers will try and dissuade you from hiking to the bottom and back in one day precisely because so many idiots try and do it without proper planning. Those who are fit, and used to the heat and above all act sensibly should not have problems, and the times estimates can be wildly pessimistic.' 'If you plan to camp at the bottom, you need a minimum of equipment, it reaches 100 degrees in summer.' 'Hardly worth the effort to carry tent.' A final recommendation: 'when camping at the bottom, start the ascent at 3am, escaping the midday heat, seeing sunrise over the Canyon, and catching the 9am bus back to Flagstaff.' 'Start at 5am to go down and up in one day. No shade all day.'

Along the **South Rim:** The most remarkable views are from Hopi, Yaki, Grand View and Desert View points. Yaki Point is especially recommended for viewing the changing colour of the rocks at sunset. A 9 mile trail from Yavapai Museum to Hermit's Rest follows the very edge of the Canyon. Pick up relevant leaflets from the visitors centres before setting out. The South Rim is also the starting point for the South Kaibab and Bright Angel Trails to descend into the canyon.

Bright Angel Trail, trailhead at the Bright Angel Campground, usually has water (May-Sept only) and is 8 m to the river, 9 m to Phantom Ranch. 'A good one-day hike is Bright Angel to Plateau Point via Indian Gardens and back, 12 miles. Great scenery.' 'Gives you time to sit and take in the scenery.'

South Kaibab Trail, trailhead at Yaki Point, is 6 m down, no campgrounds and little shade; don't attempt it in summer. A nice couple of hours walk is just down to Cedar Ridge and back, at least gives you the experience of being in the Canyon, 3 m round-trip. 'Colorado River is nice to paddle in—too strong for anything else.'

From the North Rim: The North Kaibab Trail is 10 m with seasonal water supply. 'NOT recommended for a day hike—this is from an experienced hiker, and not a Ranger whose job it is to be over-cautious.' It is a 27.6 mile round-trip to Phantom Ranch. A good day hike would be to Roaring Springs and back, 9 m. The entire Kaibab Trail is 29 m and connects North and South Rims. Views from the North Rim include **Cape Royal** (nature talks in summer), Angel's Window, overlooking the Colorado River, and the much-photographed Shiva's Temple, a ruddy promontory of great beauty.

Air tours depart from LA, Las Vegas, Phoenix, Flagstaff, Williams and the Grand Canyon National Park airfield. Dozens of small companies offer tours; by day the sky above the canyon is filled with buzzing planes (much to the disgust of environmental groups and visitors who value serenity). For a lot of visitors, this is the most memorable aspect to their trip. Not quite everybody is impressed though: 'not worth the $94 helicopter ride—just as good views from the viewpoints'. Check Chambers of Commerce and Yellow Pages in those cities under Airline Tours. **Grand Canyon Airlines,** 638-2407, operate a 45 min tour for $99 pp. _www.grand-canyonairlines.com_. **Papillion Helicopter Tours,** (800) 528-2418/638-2419, costs $115 for 30mins, $175 for 45-50mins, _www.papillon.com_. Copters and planes once flew below canyon rim, but this practice was banned after a 1986 crash in the canyon.

Grand Canyon Caverns, 22 m W of Seligman on Rte 66, 422-3223. Descend 21 storeys into the welcome 56-degree caves of coloured minerals, by elevator. 45 min tours, daily 8am-6pm, $12.95. Flashlight tour $14.95. _www.gccaverns.com_.

Grand Canyon Railway, Williams depot; 233 N Grand Canyon Blvd. (800) 843-8724. Train leaves from Williams to Grand Canyon for the 21/4 hr journey, by steam Memorial w/end- end Sept. Vintage 50's diesel locomotive runs through the rest of the year, from $60, there is also a layover avail. for those travelers who wish to stay longer at the Canyon, when prearranged. William's depot includes museum and Old West shoot-out. _www.thetrain.com_.

For a special experience that few park visitors get to enjoy, hike in to **Havasupai Falls** from the **Havasupai Indian Reservation** adjacent to the park on the southwest side. The heavy calcium content of **Havasu Creek** has resulted in coral-like circular deposits that form a stairstep sequence of turquoise pools. Bathers can catch impromptu rides where the water bubbles over the top (watch out-the 'coral' is sharp!). A trail follows the creek downstream to the **Colorado River**. Ask around for directions, or call the **Havasupai Tourist Enterprise** (whose land the creek is on) at 448-2121.

IMAX Theater, just before the South entrance to the Park, Hwy 64, 638-2203. For $10 you can almost experience what it must have been like to be one of the first to come across the canyon, before its existence was generally known. _www.grand-canyonimaxtheater.com_.

Mule Rides into the canyon: from South and North Rims (summer only). While outrageously popular and often booked up 23 months in advance, you may be able to secure a last minute booking if there is a no-show. On the South Rim they are operated by **Xanterra Parks & Resorts,** (720) 842-5271. 7 hr trips, $136 pp, incl. lunch, overnight trips, $367, incl. 3 meals and accommodation. The following restrictions apply: you can't be pregnant or handicapped or weigh more than 200 pounds and you must be at least 4'7" tall, speak fluent English (the mules don't like people who talk funny) and not be afraid of heights. Guaranteed rsvs require pre-payment. For the North Rim call **Canyon Trailways** (435) 679-8665, $55 half day, $105 full day. _www.canyonrides.com_.

Ranger programmes are highly recommended; they conduct guided hikes, do evening slide shows, etc. In winter, programmes are inside the Shrine of Ages building. Also check the sunrise and sunset photo walks by the Kodak rep. Check at visitor centre for current topic or look in _The Guide_.

Whitewater boat trips down the Colorado: the park office has list of companies. If you're in two minds about it, see the IMAX presentation which shows the rapids ranging from mild III's to the toughest of all, level VI's. The duration for most rafting adventures is 3 days to 2 weeks, of camping, hiking and braving the rapids. Try **Grand Canyon Expeditions,** (800) 544-2691/(435) 644-2691, 8/14 night packages; operating for 40 years. _www.gcex.com_. **Tour West** (800)453-9107/(801) 225-0755. 3,6, 8 or 12 night packages. _www.twriver.com_.

Information

The Guide is the park's weekly free newspaper; check for ranger programmes, bus timings, and any other park info.

South Rim:Visitor's Center, (928) 638-7771, 4 miles N of South entrance station.

Info Line 638-7888. Ask for the free and informative _Trip Planner_ to be sent to you. Details of weather/river conditions, lodging, shuttle buses, etc.

Equipment Rental from **Canyon Village Market Place,** 638-2262. Rents hiking boots (socks included), sleeping bags, tents, etc. Deposits required on all items. Daily in summer 8am-8pm.

North Rim: Visitor's Centre, 638-7864, 100 yards from Grand Canyon Lodge. Info on North Rim viewpoints, facilities and some trails.

Travel
Transportation Information Desk, Bright Angel Lodge, 638-3283. Last minute rsvs. Open 6am-8pm.
Gray Line in Phoenix, (800) 732-0327/(602) 495-9100. From $115 full day-$375, 3-day trip. Office in Las Vegas and other large cities. 'Surprisingly reasonable tours'. _www.graylinearizona.com_.
Nava-Hopi Bus Lines, (800) 892-8687, times vary by season, so call ahead.
Within the Canyon: Shuttle Bus service rides the West Rim Loop, daily 7.30am-sunset and the Village Loop, daily 6.30am-10.30pm, every 10-15 mins; from Grand Canyon Village; various stops. 'Very crowded in summer.' **The Hiker Express** (928) 774-1697 runs every 15 mins btwn Grand Canyon Village and South Kaibab Trailhead at Yaki Point.
Trans-Canyon Shuttle, 638-2820, run buses between North and South Rim, specifically with hikers in mind. Leaves from Bright Angel Lodge in the South and North Rim Lodge. Rsvs nec. From $70. Open late May-Oct. 'A waste of money.'

LAKE POWELL and **GLEN CANYON** North of the Grand Canyon, on the border with Utah, Glen Canyon is another natural wonder, combined with the monumentally ambitious Glen Canyon Dam, begun in 1957-1967 to provide hydro-electricity and water storage. The flooding of the vast canyon, when the dam was completed, took 17 years to fill. The whole of the Glen Canyon is now a National Recreation Area, covering hundreds of square miles, and with plenty of opportunities for lakeside relaxation. Beaches and rocky outcrops abound, perfect for swimming and diving, and five marinas supply all your watersports needs. **The Carl Hayden Visitors Centre** in **Page**, 608-6404, provides an orientation film, 3D model of the area and information on the dam and lake, the dam itself is open for free tours.

The canyon, named for its glens, was 'mapped' by John Wesley Powell in 1869. It is ironic that so much of the canyon he named should now be submerged by a lake named after him. Some of the highlights include the fantastic **Antelope Canyon**, sometimes known as 'Corkscrew Canyon' for the twists and turns the rocks take.

Much of the steep-sided canyon is almost cavern-like with rock above, as well as on all sides; shafts of light filtering through add to the effect. Situated on Navajo land, only authorised tours are allowed into the canyon. Try **Eki's Antelope Canyon Tours**, 645-9102, _www.antelopecanyon.com_. They organise a number of trips, including a specialist photographers tour which takes best advantage of the changing light. Just as spectacular is **Rainbow Bridge**, the world's largest natural rock bridge, rising 290 ft. It can be reached by a rather arduous hike, or the much more pleasant leisurely boat tour from one of the marinas. **Aramark**, (800) 528-6154/645-2433, offer a number of options, including a full day tour from **Wahweap**, 6 miles from the town of **Page**; $114, or half day $49, (resv. rec). _www.lakepowell.com_. The admission charge to the Recreation Area is $10 p/car, $5 for pedestrians. _www.nps.gov/glca_.

Accommodation:
There are numerous hotels/motels in **Page**, and camping is allowed inside the Park. A National Parks Service - run campground at **Lee's Ferry**, 355-2234, charges $10 per site. There are a couple of lodges at **Wahweap** and **Bullfrog**. Call (800) 528-6154 for reservations in the recreation area.

Information
The site *www.desertusa.com* gives a good overview of the area with some excellent photos to give you a taster.
The Carl Hayden Visitors Centre general info line is 608-6404.
Page-Lake Powell Chamber of Commerce and Visitors Centre, 644 N. Navajo Dr. Page, Suite B, 645-2741. *www.pagelakepowellchamber.org*.

LAKE HAVASU CITY If you wanted to hide London Bridge where no one would ever think of looking for it, where would you put it? That's right—in the middle of a big fat desert at Lake Havasu City spanning the Colorado River! Built in 1831, the old London Bridge couldn't handle the traffic across the Thames and by 1962 was falling down. It was sold to Robert McCulloch, founder of Lake Havasu City, and McCulloch Oil Corp, for $2,460,000. They apparently thought that it was Tower Bridge they were buying!

London Bridge together with a Tudor Village and double-decker bus makes this a must for the discerning British visitor. Hwy 95 south to Parker traverses a beautiful stretch of scenery; if you continue all the way to Quartzsite, view the Hi Jolly (Hadji Ali) Grave, adorned with a pyramid; a tribute to the Syrian who tried to introduce camels to this desert.

Lake Havasu Tourism Bureau, 314 London Bridge Rd, (800) 2HAVASU/453-3444 can direct you. There's also a **Visitor's Center** located in the English Village open daily. **Outback Off-Road Adventures** offer 4-wheel drives out into the desert for the day or half a day; 680-6151. Recreationally, the city's lake is described as 'a lake to rent', since all types of water sports are available here from paddle boats to jet-skiing. *www.golakehavasu.com*.

NEW MEXICO - Land of Enchantment

Travel industry hyperbole aside, New Mexico *does* enchant. It possesses a dramatic landscape heightened by the scalpel-sharp clarity of the desert air; natural wonders like the Navajo's and the Carlsbad Caverns; and the finest array of Indian cultures, past and present, in the country. In human terms, New Mexico is incredibly ancient, having been inhabited for over 25,000 years. More significantly, it is the only state that has succeeded in fusing its venerable Spanish, Indian and Anglo influences into a harmonious and singular pattern. You will notice the benign borrowings everywhere, from sensuous adobes tastefully outfitted with solar heating to the distinctive New Mexican cuisine, currently very chic.

New Mexico inspires awe for more than its beauty. On 16 July 1945, at the appropriately named Jornada del Muerto (Journey of the Dead) Desert, the world's first atomic bomb belched its radioactive mushroom into the air. (Physicist Enrico Fermi reportedly took bets on the chances that the test would blow up the state.) Today, the state is a leader in atomic research, testing, uranium mining and related fields. Blithe as locals may be about nuclear materials (the Alamogordo Chamber of Commerce still sponsors a twice-annual outing to Ground Zero the 1st Saturdays in April and October), think twice before visiting the Alamogordo-White Sands region. Your genes may thank you some day.

Instead, concentrate on the fascinating and diverse Indian populations: the 19 pueblo villages, each with its own pottery, dance, arts and style include the Navajos, whose capital is at Window Rock and the Jicarilla and Mescalero Apaches, noted for dancing and coming of age ceremonies. Celebrations open to the public are so numerous that you could plan an itinerary around them. The state has a comprehensive, well-designed site for visitors, *www.newmexico.org*, that includes brochures, maps, and food and lodging in each city. *Viva New Mexico!* at *www.vivanewmexico.com* provides interesting information about New Mexico's writers and artists and how to buy Indian jewelry and pottery, etc.

National Park: *Carlsbad Caverns.*

The telephone area code for most of the state is 505. Greater Albuquerque is 575.

ALBUQUERQUE Named for a ducal viceroy of Mexico, Albuquerque is the state's largest city, containing over a third of its 1.9 million residents. Although it has most of the state's tacky motels and urban sprawl, the University of New Mexico allows it to hold onto a youthful feeling.

The city's setting and scenery are spectacular and Albuquerque does make a good base for day trips to the Indian pueblos and to the Sandia Mountains. The best times to visit are during the June Arts and Crafts Fair, the September State Fair, the amazing October Hot Air Balloon Fiesta and at Christmas, when city dwellings are outlined with thousands of luminarias—candles imbedded in sand, their light diffused by paper. For hints on what to see and do, go to *www.albuquerque.com; www.abqcvb.org* or *www.nmstatefair.com*.

Accommodation

Central Ave, formerly Route 66, is the north-south divider; railroad tracks divide east-west. 'Cheap hotels on Central SE. Walk to the other side of railroad, right side of Greyhound terminal to Central SE, then straight ahead.' 'Use caution; many are dangerous.'

Econo-Lodge, 817 Central NE, 243-1321. S-$39, D-$45-52. *www.econolodge.com*.

Route 66 Hostel, 1012 Central Ave SW, 247-1813. Beautiful, newly renovated private rooms. Dorm $15, private rooms from $20; $5 key deposit, $1 linen for dorms. 'Friendly, no curfew.' Full communal kitchen. Free coffee, tea, snacks and cereal. Must help out with chores!

Silver Moon Lodge, 918 Central SW, downtown, 243-1773. $50-89, prices differ during the year. 'Very friendly and clean, but not in good side of town.' *www.silver-moon-lodge.com*.

University Lodge, 3711 Central Ave NE, 266-7663. Has basic motel rooms and a pool. $33-51. *www.university-lodge.com*.

Camping: Albuquerque North KOA (off I-25), 867-5227. Tent sites $18-34. Rsvs rec. *www.koa.com*.

Food

Check out the inexpensive eateries around the University of New Mexico.

M & J Sanitary Tortilla Factory, 403 2nd SW, 242-4890. Neighbourhood chilli parlour; excellent Mexican food, written up in the *New Yorker*; interesting art by locals on walls. Mon-Fri 9am-4pm.

Flying Star, 3416 Central SE, 255-6633, is a bakery, coffee shop and ice cream store. Salads and sandwiches under $9, specials from $8. Open Sun-Thu 6am-11.30pm, Fri & Sat till midnight. *flyingstarcafe.com/locations.htm*.

Of interest
Old Town, 1 block N of Central NW, bounded by Rio Grande Blvd and Mountain Rd. Shops, restaurants and occasional live entertainment. The only nugget of Spanishness left in the city. 'Well worth a visit.' On the plaza is the **Church of San Felipe de Neri** founded in 1706 and museum open Mon-Sat 10am-4pm, 243-1242. *www.sanfelipedeneri.org*.
Indian Pueblos all over the state are particularly accessible from Alberquerque. Dances, fiestas and ceremonials are sacred and held throughout the year (recording may not be permissible at these events). *www.itsatrip.org/visitors/americanindian*.
Albuquerque Museum, 2000 Mountain Rd NW, 243-7255. Permanent and changing exhibits on history of Albuquerque and southwest US. Tue-Sun 9am-5pm; $4. Tours of sculpture garden, Tue-Sat 10am. Entrance includes Walking Tour of Historic Old Town. Tue-Sun 11am. *www.cabq.gov/museum/index.html*.
Hot Air Balloon Fiesta, Balloon Fiesta Park, off I-25, 821-1000. About 750 balloons from around the world assemble for 9 days in early Oct. The first launch is at 5.45am, get there 5am-7am. $6, + $5 per vehicle. *www.aibf.org*.
Indian Pueblo Cultural Center, 2401 12th St. nr I-40, 1 mile E of Old Town, 843-7270. Excellent exhibit and sales rooms by the 19 Pueblo Indian groups allow comparison of techniques and styles. High quality, prices to match. 'Only thing of interest in this town.' Open daily 9am-4.30pm, $4, $1 w/student ID. Also Indian Pueblo Dance performances, schedule varies; cameras allowed with permission. Restaurant serves traditional pueblo food. 8am-3pm. *www.indianpueblo.org*.
National Atomic Museum, 1905 Mountain Rd, 245 2137. $5, daily 9am-5pm. Disquieting look at selection of nuclear weapons casings, plus 'oops' items like the A-Bomb the US accidentally dropped on Palomares, Spain, in 1966. Regular screenings of *Ten Seconds that Shook the World*. *www.atomicmuseum.com*.
New Mexico Museum of Natural History and Science, 1801 Mountain Rd NW, 841-2800. Evolutionary history of New Mexico presented through new hi-tec Dynamax Theatre, and an 'Evolator time machine,' unique to the museum, taking you millions of years back through time. Planetarium ($6).'Fantastic. Don't miss your chance to stand inside an "active" volcano.' Open daily 9am-5pm, exp. Mon during Sept & Jan. Combo for three $16. *www.nmnaturalhistory.org*.
Petroglyph National Monument, 6001 Unser Blvd NW, 899-0205. Open daily, Los Imagines Visitors Centre 8am-5pm. Free entry but parking $1, ($2 on w/ends) at Boca Negra Canyon. Rsvs needed to take part in Ranger-led hikes. *www.nps.gov/petr*.
Sandia Peak Aerial Tramway, NE of town, take Tramway Rd, exit 234 off I-25, 856-7325. At 2.7 miles, the world's longest aerial tramway, climbing to 10,378ft. Fantastic panorama which sometimes includes hot air balloons and hang gliders in the area. Open daily 9am-9pm. 15 min ride, $15. *www.sandiapeak.com*. Mountain biking is also available. Take the ski lift to the top and bike down 24 miles of trails. $38 bike hire per day inc. lift & helmet, plus deposit.
Maxwell Museum of Anthropology, 1 University of New Mexico, Albuquerque. West end of campus btwn Martin Luther King & Las Lomas, 277-3700/4405. Tue-Fri 9am-4pm, Sat 10am-4pm. Free. *www.unm.edu/~maxwell*. Fine Arts Museum 277-4001, inc. sculptures, photography and paintings. Tue-Fri 9am-4pm (Tue 5pm-8pm), Sun 1pm-4pm. Free. *http://unmartmuseum.unm.edu*.

Information/ Internet access/Wi-Fi
Visitor's Information Centers: Albuquerque Convention and Visitors Bureau, 20 First Plaza NW, Suite 601, (800) 284-2282/842-9918. Three other locations throughout the city. *www.itsatrip.org*.
Main Public Library, 501 Copper Ave NW, 768-5141, Mon-Sat 10am-6pm. One off

fee of $3 for access card. Internet use ltd. to 3hrs per day. Wi-Fi available free at nine city libraries, including the Main. *www.cabq.gov/library*.

Travel
Sun-Tran Transit, 100 First St SW, 243-7433. The local city buses, basic fare $1, $4 for a 3-day pass. *www.cabq.gov/transit/tran.html*
Amtrak, 214 1st St SW, (800) 872-7245. Open daily 10am-5pm. *www.amtrak.com*.
Greyhound, 300 2nd SW, 243-4435. Clean, safe depot with all-night cafe. *www.greyhound.com*.
Sandia Shuttle Express, (888) 775-5696. Shuttle vans daily to Santa Fe, $23, o/w. Rsvs needed. *www.sandiashuttle.com*.
Albuquerque Cab Co, 883-4888. Provides airport service. *www.albuquerquecab.com*.
Albuquerque International Airport, S of downtown, next to the airforce base. Take Route #50 bus from downtown, $1, 6am-5.30pm w/days, less frequent w/ends. *www.cabq.gov/airport*.

CARLSBAD CAVERNS One of the world's largest and very possibly the most beautiful caves in the world. The Carlsbad Caverns began their stalactite-forming activities about 250 million years ago. In contrast, the famous Mexican freetail bat colony has been in residence a mere 17,000 years. Once numbering seven million, give or take a bat, the colony's population has recovered from the effects of insecticides, which had brought the population down to only 250,000, and is now home to over 1 million of the little buggers. It was the eerie sight of bats pouring like smoke from the cave openings that led to Carlsbad's discovery in 1901.

The caves became a National Park in 1930, but the big bucks locally came from the sale of 100,000 tons of prime bat shit ('guano' to the genteel) to California citrus growers. No, the bats don't drink blood-and few harbour rabies, but the superstitious should keep the throat and other parts covered while the blind zoom overhead! For more info see *www.nps.gov/cave*, *http://carlsbadcaverns.areaparks.com*. *www.carlsbad.caverns.national-park.com* or *www.chamber.cavern.com*.

Accommodation
Advised to drive to Carlsbad for cheaper accommodation.
White's City Resort & Best Western Inns, 17 Carlsbad Cavern Hwy, White's City, (800) CAVERNS. Pool. 7 miles from the caverns. Mixed reports. Sometimes cheap deals are avail. But often as much as $100 a night. Campground is cheapest option. Call for rates. *www.carlsbadcaverns.com*.
Oscuro Hostel, 648-4007, located on the ranch past the railroad tracks on Rt 54, 15 miles S of Carizozo. $14 dorm, D-$27.
Carlsbad RV & Campground, 4301 National Parks Hwy, Carlsbad, 885-6333, indoor pool, shop, games room, laundry, $16.50 primitive camping for up to 4 people, $19.50 w/hookup. *www.carlsbadrvpark.com*.

Of interest
Carlsbad Caverns National Park, 785-2232, is open all year. **Self-Guided Cave tours: Natural Entrance Tour**, open winter, 8.30am-2pm, summer till 3.30pm. **Big Room Tour**, 1 mile, about 1 hr. Open winter, 8.30am-3.30pm, summer till 5pm. Both tours have plaques to guide you along. $6 gets you a 3 day pass to these self-guided tours, $9 w/audio. **Slaughter Canyon Cave** is more rugged and only for those in good shape. Rsvs and a torch are required for this twice daily tour, summer 10am & 1pm, winter Sat & Sun at 10am, $15. Temperature inside the cave is 56°F, refreshing in summer but bring a jacket. 'Rangers will not let you descend into the caverns

unless you are wearing sensible shoes: i.e. not flip-flops, sandals, or anything with heels.' 'Free nature walks around cavern entrance at 5pm, something to do while waiting for the bats.' (Try to plan your visit to the caves for the late afternoon in order to see the nightly bat flight at dusk.) Rsvs for all guided tours available through (800) 967-2283.

Bat facts: bats are in residence Spring through mid-Oct only and are at their busiest May-Sept, just before sunset. They leave the cave at dusk to fly up to 120 miles, consume an aggregate five tons of insects, return at dawn to spend the day sleeping in cosy bat-fashion, 300 per sq. ft. Call **Visitor's Center**, 785-2232 for more bat-data. 'No one should miss the incredible sight of a million bats flying a few feet over one's head. Just like Dracula, in fact.' No flash photography allowed. *www.nps.gov/cave*.

Lake Carlsbad & Beach, a three-mile spring-fed water playground with free swimming, boat ramp and docks, water skiing, picnic area, tables, fireplaces and fishing, 887-1191.

Travel

Texas, New Mexico and Oklahoma Coaches (TNM&O), 887-1108, runs buses via White's City from El Paso. Talk to driver for drop off at White's City. *www.tnmo.com*.

ROSWELL A mecca for UFO freaks, this is the spot where an alien spacecraft was said to have landed on the night of July 4th 1947. The rapid cover-up and denials exacerbated the rumours, and as is to be imagined, many theories abound as to the real nature of the 'incident'. For sci-fi drama (or tacky tat to the non-nerd population) head to the **International UFO Museum**, 114 N Main St, 625-9495, open daily 9am-5pm, $2, *www.iufomrc.org*. For UFO links and town information including that on its annual **UFO Festival** in July see *www.roswell-online.com/ http://roswellcvb.com*.

SANTA FE This state capital is a city for walkers, full of narrow, adobe-lined streets that meander round its Spanish heart, the old plaza where the Santa Fe trail ends. A crossroads for trade routes and the oldest seat of government in the US, Santa Fe has witnessed a remarkable amount of history. But the age of the place doesn't prepare you for its beauty, the friendliness of its locals and the vitality of its artistic and cultural life. The town has a strict architecture policy that requires that all the buildings must be in 17th century pueblo style and painted in one of 23 varying shades of brown, all of which gives the place a pleasing unity.

On the other hand, some have commented that much of the city cultural charm has been lost in the boutiques that cater too much to wealthy Americans. If you find yourself overwhelmed by the excesses of **Santa Fe** make a pilgrimage to **Los Alamos**, where the first A-Bomb was built and the ghost town of **Madrid**. For more info see *www.santafe.org*, *www.visitsantafe.com*.

Accommodation

For the lowdown on budget accommodations, call the **Santa Fe Detours Accommodations Hotline**, 983-6565, *www.sfdetours.com*.

Motel 6 North, 3007 Cerrillos Rd, 473-1380. From S-$46, D-from $52, more w/ends. 'Motel row' is along Cerrillos. *www.motel6.com*.

Santa Fe International Hostel, 1412 Cerrillos Rd, 988-1153. $14 AYH; $15 non-AYH; S-$25 for private room, XP-$10. 'Excellent hostel; no curfew; friendly people, full of information.' 'More than adequate facilities: cooking, showers, library.' Rsvs in writing with a money order for the full payment.

Camping: Santa Fe KOA, 466-1419. RV w/full hook-up $31 for 2 people. Tent site $24-30 Mar-Oct. _www.koa.com_. **Santa Fe National Forest,** 438-7840, has campsites from $8 and free backcountry camping in the beautiful Sangre de Cristo Mountains and Pecos region. _www.publiclands.org_ and _www.fs.fed.us/r3/sfe_.

Food

Santa Fe is the home of Southwestern cooking, a cuisine based on humble indigenous ingredients—beans, corn and chilli, in imaginative combinations with other foods. Sample a bowl of _posole_, the hominy-based stew served with spicy pork that New Mexicans love. If you have a strong stomach and Teflon tastebuds, try the green chilli stew. Prepare your mouth for a rerun of the Mt. St. Helens eruption. For complete places to eat, visit the excellent _www.santaferestaurants.net_ or _www.santafenow.com/rest/rest.htm_. The site _www.newmexico.org/food/index.php_ also has info on all the wineries in New Mexico, several of which are in the Santa Fe area. The Santa Fe Wine and Chile Festival is held in late September. _www.santafewineandchile.org_.

Burrito Company, 111 Washington Ave, 982-4453. 'Tasty Mexican food at cheap prices, varied clientele-many artists.' Open Mon-Fri 7am-5pm, Sat 7.30am-5.30pm, Sun 8am-5pm.

The Shed, 113 1/2 E Palace, 982-9030, in circa 1692 adobe. Good New Mexican lunches, crowded. Lunch Mon-Sat 11am-2.30pm; dinner Mon-Sat 5.30pm-9pm + rsvs rec. Lunch $6.50-9, dinner $8-12.

Tia Sophia's, 210 W San Francisco St, 983-9880. A locals' hangout, the food is exceptional. Try the Atrisco ($7)-chilli stew, cheese enchilada, burritos, beans, _posole_ and a _sopapilla_! Mon-Sat for bfast 7am-11am, $5; lunch 11am-2pm, $6.

Of interest

NB: Despite its compact size, Santa Fe can wear you out - its altitude is 7000ft. Pace yourself.

The Plaza de Santa Fe: city heart, popular gathering place since 1610, and terminus of both the Santa Fe and El Camino Real trails, the Plaza has seen bullfights, military manoeuvres and fiestas. Billy the Kid was exhibited here in chains after causing much trouble in the area. When the Kid vowed to kill territorial governor Lew Wallace, the intended victim hid out in the Palace of the Governors, fronting the north side of the Plaza. While cloistered, Wallace began writing _Ben-Hur_. _www.ben-hur.com_.

The oldest public building in America (1610) and seat of 6 regimes, **The Palace of the Governors,** 105 W Palace Ave, 476-5100, _www.palaceofthegovernors.org_ is one of five museums of **The Museum of New Mexico.** Both the Palace of the Governors and the Museum of Fine Arts are free Fri 5pm-8pm, otherwise each museum can be visited separately for $7, or $15 gets a 4-day ticket allowing entry to all. Tue-Sun 10am-5pm. The museum houses historical exhibits and has Indian craft and jewellery for sale under its portal (better quality than elsewhere in town) _www.museumofnewmexico.org_. Nearby is the **Museum of Fine Arts,** 107 W Palace Ave, 476-5072. Includes an amazing collection of 20th century Native American art and temporary exhibitions of more recent works. Further out is the **Museum of International Folk Art,** 706 Camino Lejo, 476-1200. 'Well worth the walk.' Call for special performing arts events. A gallery handout will help you appreciate the fascinating, though jumbled, exhibit. _www.moifa.org_. Finally, the **Museum of American Indian Arts and Culture,** 710 Camino Lejo, 827-6463, is the first state museum devoted to Pueblo, Navajo, and Apache Indians, with exhibits on history and ethnology from the Laboratory of Anthropology as well as contemporary native arts. _www.miaclab.org_.

Georgia O'Keeffe Museum, 217 Johnson St, 946-1000, houses the largest collection of work by this famous adopted local, open daily 10am-5pm, Fri 10am-8pm. $8, free Fri 5-8pm, free daily for students w/ID. _www.okeeffemuseum.org_.

Churches: Santa Fe is home to several notable ones, among them: **El Cristo Rey**, 983-8528, noted for its size and stone reredos; the **San Miguel Chapel**, 401 Old Santa Fe Trail, 983-3974, the oldest mission in the US; the French Romanesque **St Francis Cathedral**, 131 Cathedral Place, 982-5619, built by Archbishop Lamy (subject of Willa Cather's *Death Comes for the Archbishop*) to house La Conquistadora, a 17th century shrine to the Virgin Mary; the **Loretto Chapel**, 207 Old Santa Fe Trail, 982-0092, is a Gothic structure whose so-called 'miraculous' spiral staircase is of mild interest, *www.lorettochapel.com*; the charming **Santuario de Guadalupe**, 100 Guadalupe St, 988-2027, is the spot where 18th century travellers stopped to give thanks after their hazardous journeys from Mexico City.

Bandelier National Monument, 35 miles NW of Santa Fe, 672-0343, contains ruins of an Indian settlement and 75 miles of backcountry trails. Visitors Center open daily, 9am-6pm. Park open from dawn till dusk. $10 per vehicle. Camping on a first-come first served basis, $10pn. 'Need a car to get to it, but well worth seeing.' Ask for directions in Santa Fe. *www.nps.gov/band*.

Fiesta de Santa Fe, 988-7575, early to mid-Sept, first held in 1692, the oldest non-Indian celebration in the US; great community spirit. 'Zozobra or Old Man Gloom, a 40 ft dummy, is burned amidst dancing and fireworks. Most spectacular!' 'Fantastic.' *www.santafefiesta.org*.

Indian Market, Downtown Plaza, 983-5220, held annually in August. The largest market of Indian arts and crafts in the world, with 1200 Indian artisans selling handmade jewellery, sculpture, pottery, baskets, beadwork, sand-painting, feather-work, etc. Avoid the initial 8-deep crush in front of the stands by going after 11am. Besides artists' wares there are practical demonstrations, Pueblo dance showcases and a fashion show of traditional and modern Indian dress. NB: Beware of the non-authentic tourist-trap vendors who set up stalls in hotels, parking lots and side streets. The market is free but admission is needed to see the dances. Hotels get very booked up at this time-rsvs rec. For a schedule of events see *www.swaia.org*.

Nearby: Los Alamos, 30 miles N of Santa Fe is the sight where the first atom bomb was built, Bradbury Science Center, 15th & Central, 667-4444, has replica of 'Fat Man' bomb. Tue-Sat 10am-5pm, Sun-Mon 1pm-5pm; free. 'Helpful, friendly staff. Fantastic scenery.' *www.losalamos.com*. *www.lanl.gov/museum*.

Santa Fe Opera, (800) 280-4654/986-5955, one of America's truly great opera companies. Tkts for performances (July & Aug) $24-142; standing room for less. You can also take a 1 hr tour of the open-air opera house, set amid hills and white petunias 7 miles N of Santa Fe. Call the box office. NB: Unless you have a tkt for a performance or are part of a tour, you won't be allowed in. *www.santafeopera.org*.

Wheelwright Museum of the American Indian, 704 Camino Lejo, 982-4636. 'This is the best museum in the area.' Designed to resemble a traditional Navajo hogan, the Wheelwright contains the artistry of many Indian cultures. Rotating displays. The gift shop is designed as a replica of a turn-of-the-century Navajo Trading Post. Mon-Sat 10am-5pm, Sun 1pm-5pm. Free, donations rec. *www.wheelwright.org*.

Interesting neighbourhood: Canyon Road is home to adobe art galleries, studios and shops.

Information/ Internet access

Chamber of Commerce, 8380 Cerrillos, 988-3279. Very helpful with details of Pueblo Indian dances, ceremonials, etc. Good maps, booklets. *www.santafechamber.com*.

Santa Fe Convention and Visitors Bureau, 201 W Marcy St, (800) 777-2489. Pick up the useful *Santa Fe Visitors Guide*. Also, an information booth, located at Lincoln & Grant.

Santa Fe Public Library, 145 Washington St, 955-6780, Mon-Thu 10am-9pm, Fri & Sat at 10am-6pm, Sun 1pm-5pm. Free, printed pages ltd. to 10. Free internet use ltd. to 1 hr.

Travel
Amtrak goes to nearby Lamy and provides a shuttle bus into Santa Fe, $16. (800) 872-7245.
Capital City Taxi, 438-0000.
Greyhound, 858 St Michael's, (800) 231-2222/471-0008, open Mon-Fri 7am-5.30pm, 7:30pm-9:45pm; sporadic hours at w/end. Bus station is 3 miles outside town.

TAOS Set against the rich palette of the crisp, white **Sangre de Cristo Mountains**, the earth tones of soaring Indian pueblos and the turquoise sky of northern New Mexico, Taos (pronounced to rhyme with 'mouse') has long been a haven for artists and writers like Georgia O'Keefe, John Fowles and D H Lawrence, as well as housing the **Kit Carson Home,** $1/2$ block E of Taos Plaza on Kit Carson Rd. Period rooms (1850s), Indian, gun and Mountain Man (how the fur-trappers lived) exhibits, daily 9am-5pm; $5. Next to which is **The Stables** showing the best of local artists.
   The town also has excellent skiing opportunities: **Taos Ski Valley**, 15 miles N of Taos, offers powder conditions in bowl sections and short, steep downhill runs. The ski lift works in summer too, and the area has excellent hiking opportunities. Although Taos has become expensive, get to know its traditional Indian and Hispanic communities for a glimpse of the real Taos.
   Other places of interest are the **Blumenschein Home**, 222 Ledoux, 758-0505, _www.taosmuseums.org_; **Millicent Rogers Museum**, 1504 Millicent Rogers Road, 758-2462, _www.millicentrogers.org_; while **San Geronimo's Feast Days** are not to be missed at the end of September. _www.taoswebb.com_ and _www.taosvacationguide.com_.

Accommodation
HI-Taos, The Abominable Snowmansion, Arroyo Seco, 10 miles N of Taos, Rte 150, 776-8298. Kitchen, pool table, games in main bldg. Check-in 8am-12am, 4pm-10pm. Dorms, cabins, and Indian tepees, camping $9, non-AYH $12, dorm beds-$15 AYH, $18 non-AYH, S-$34, D-$42 in summer, more expensive in ski-season. _www.snowmansion.com_.
The Budget Host Inn and Taos RV Park (800) 323-6009/758-2524, rooms $39-69, inc. private baths, free cable, cont. bfast and local calls. Tents $16.50, 758-1667. _www.taosbudgethost.com_.
Camping: easy for those with a car. Check out the **Carson National Forest,** 758-6200, which operates more than 30 campgrounds, approx $15. Backcountry camping requires no permit; call for more info. _www.fs.fed.us_.

Information
Chamber of Commerce, 1139 Paseo del Pueblo Sur (Rte 68), (800) 732-8267. Distributes maps and tourist literature. Make sure you ask for a guide to Northern New Mexican Indian pueblos. _www.taoschamber.org_.

SILVER CITY Located in the southwest mining country, Silver City is an attractive town, whose history is steeped in the black and white cowboy films of the last century and is now a haven for artists. **The San Vincente Artists of Silver City** sponsors free self-guided artwalks, 534-0269. For more information pick up a brochure from Yankee Creek Gallery, 302 N Bullards St. _www.silvercityartists.org/index.html_. A couple of free museums show the history of the pioneers and the native Americans before them;

Silver City Museum, 312 W Broadway, 538-5921, 9am-4.30pm Tue-Fri, Sat & Sun 10am-4pm. Free. *www.silvercitymuseum.org*.

The **Western New Mexico University Museum,** 1000 W College Ave, 538-6386 Mon-Fri 9am-4.30pm, Wed 1pm-4.30-m, Sat & Sun 10am-4pm. Free, donations rec. *www.wnmu.edu/univ/museum.htm*. The town is also close to the **Gila National Forest**, a wild and lovely terrain of blood-red gorges, ghost towns and Indian ruins. **Visitors Center** at the **Gila Cliff Dwellings National Monument**, 536-9461, open daily 8am-6pm. $3 pp entry to cliff dwellings. In this region, Geronimo eluded US Cavalry troops for years. *www.nps.gov/gicl*. Amtrak and Greyhound go to Deming; from there take the **Silver Stage Lines** shuttle bus to city centre, runs once a day (rsvs nec. a day in advance: (800) 522-0162), they also go to El Paso airport.

Accommodation
Palace Hotel, 106 W Broadway, 388-1811, an 1882 historic hotel, rooms $41-68. *www.zianet.com/palacehotel*.
Camping; Gila National Forest, 388-8201. Most sites free although some are approx. $15 pn. Allocated on a first come first served basis.

CHACO CULTURE NATIONAL HISTORIC PARK Situated in the northwest of the state, this is a massive 11th-century ruin, its largest pueblo containing 800 rooms and 39 kivas (sacred chambers) contemporary with Mesa Verde, but much less visited, 786-7014. $8 per vehicle, open year-round, but roads can be impassable in inclement weather so check forecast before travelling. **Visitor's Centre**, 8am-5pm. No food or drink avail. Campsites at $10 pn.

Stay at **Circle A Ranch Hostel**, 510 Los Pinos County Rd, 289-3350. 2.5 hours drive northwest from Santa Fe. Adobe hacienda in Sante Fe National Forest, remote area but near hiking trails and swimming hole. Rsvs strongly advised. Open May-Oct. Bunks: $20, D-$45-50. 'Lovely adobe ranch, friendly people—felt part of the family.' *www.nps.gov/chcu; www.circlearanch.info*.

INDIAN GROUPS ELSEWHERE IN NEW MEXICO There are 19 Tewa-speaking Native American groups in all, called collectively the **19 Pueblos**. The website *www.indianpueblo.org* has links to each of the pueblos, or contact the **Indian Pueblo Cultural Center** in Albuquerque, (800) 766-4405/843-7270. Among the most interesting of the Pueblos' cities is **Acoma**, (800) 747-0181; the 'Sky City', 60 miles west of Albuquerque, and occupying a huge and spectacular mesa. The ground is so stoney that the Indians had to haul soil 430 ft for their graveyard. Inhabited since AD 1075, the Pueblo vies with the Oraibi in Hopiland as the oldest settlement in the US. Noted for high quality pottery with intricate linear designs. Pueblo admission $10, if you wish to take photos it's an extra $10 per camera. The dollar is embraced readily enough at the Pueblo **Casino**, 552-6017/747-0059, open 8am-4pm Sun-Wed, 24 hr on Friday and Saturday. Buses leave from the bottom of the mesa daily, $10. Call the pueblo for further information. *www.skycitycasino.com*.

Santa Clara, 753-7330, between Santa Fe and Taos, is famous for its black polished pottery. More outgoing and open to visitors than other Pueblos, the Santa Clarans have fewer restrictions on photography (fee may still be charged). This is an excellent place to take in the dancing at the late August festival.

The Jicarilla Apaches, 759-3242/759-4218, in the northwest and the **Mescalero Apaches**, 671-4494, in the southeast have numerous tourist facilities and both offer camping on their lands. Their ceremonies are very striking, especially the female puberty rites which take place during summer months. Visitors may respectfully watch the principal activities. As with Pueblo Indians, call ahead to ensure the reservations will be open when you plan to travel and for more information generally.

OKLAHOMA - The Sooner State

Originally set aside as an Indian Territory, between 1889 and 1895 "Okla humma" (translation- "red people") was thrown open to settlers in one of the most fantastic land grabs ever (think *'Home & Away'* film fame). Thousands of homesteaders impatiently lined up on its borders, and at the crack of a gun raced across the prairie in buckboards, buggies, wagons and carts, on bicycles, horseback and afoot to lay claim to the two million acres drawn up by the federal government. Some crossed the line ahead of time, giving Oklahoma its nickname, the Sooner State, admitted to the Union in 1907. Oklahoma has suffered, from broken promises over Indian lands in the nineteenth century, to the flight of the 'Okies' in the 1940's, immortalized in John Steinbeck's book, *The Grapes of Wrath*.

Experience Oklahoma's prairies, generous forests and rolling mountains by the 400 miles of historic Route 66, *www.oklahomaroute66.com*. Alternatively, if you want to take life at a slower pace, check out the world's first parking meters, which date from 1935, in Oklahoma City. For more info see *www.travelok.com; tourism.state.ok.us; www.oktourism.com*.

The area code for Oklahoma City is 405; western Oklahoma is 580; for eastern Oklahoma and Tulsa it is 918.

OKLAHOMA CITY Oklahoma City was established in a single day when 10,000 land grabbers showed up at the only well for miles around in what had till then been scorched prairie-land. In 1911 the state capital was moved from nearby Guthrie to Oklahoma City where oil was discovered in 1928. Now six oil wells slurp away in the grounds of the Capitol Building.

Until September 11th, 2001, the city was also the scene of the biggest domestic terrorist action to take place on American soil; the Oklahoma City Federal Building was bombed on April 19th 1995, taking 168 lives. For more info see *www.okconline.com; www.visitokc.com* and *www.allaroundoklahomacity.com*.

All of the following listings use the local area code (405) unless otherwise stated.

Accommodation
Accommodation in downtown OKC is scarce, although main hotel/motel chains are located along S. Meridian Ave.

Motel 6 Airport, 820 S Meridian Ave, 946-6662. From $37. *www.motel6.com*.

Super 8, 311 S. Meridian, 947-7801. Close to state fairgrounds with remote cable TV, free local calls and coffee. From $48. *www.super8.com*.

Camping: RCA, A state-run campground is located on **Lake Thunderbird,** 30 miles S of OKC at **Little River State Park,** 360-3572. Swim or fish in the lake or hike the cliffs for a view. Tent sites $7-22, showers avail.

Food

Most places downtown close early in the afternoon. The best and cheapest steaks can be had near the stockyards at **Cattlemen's Cafe,** 1309 S Agnew, 236-0416, Sun-Thu 6am-10pm; Fri & Sat 'til midnight. Steaks from $10. _www.cattlemensrestaurant.com_.

Flip's, 5801 N Western, 843-1527. An Italian restaurant and wine bar, food is served in an artsy atmosphere. Lunch dishes $7-10, dinner $10-20. Open daily 11am-2am. Sun brunch served 11am-3pm.

The Spaghetti Warehouse, 101 E. Sheridan Ave, 235-0402. Good-value Bricktown place that proves that there's more to Oklahoma City dining than steaks. Lunch dishes $5-9. Sun-Thu 11am-10pm, Fri & Sat 11am-11pm.

Of interest

Myriad Botanical Gardens, 301 W Reno, 297-3995. The gardens are a 17-acre oasis in downtown Oklahoma, but the highlight is undoubtedly the **Crystal Bridge,** a glass-enclosed cylinder 70 ft in diameter containing both a desert and a rainforest. Open Mon-Sat 9am-6pm, Sun noon-6pm. $6. _www.myriadgardens.com_.

National Cowboy Western Heritage Center, 1700 NE 63rd, 6 miles N of downtown along I-44, 478-2250. $8.50, 9am-5pm daily. $8. The museum has tripled in size since 1995 and is 'America's premier western heritage museum'. Features art by famous western painters. But beware, some have found it: 'boring, and not worth it'. _www.nationalcowboymuseum.org_.

Oklahoma City Zoo, 2101 NE 50th St, 424-3344. Open 7:30am-6pm in summer, 'til 5pm in winter, but visitors can stay till dusk, ($7). Rated one of the top zoos in the nation with over 110 acres housing over 2,100 animals. _www.okczoo.com_.

Omniplex, 2100 NE 52nd St, 602-OMNI/(800) 522-7652, _www.omniplex.org_, houses 8 museums and galleries: **Air Space Museum** has exhibits on the state's contribution to aviation and space; the **International Photography Hall of Fame** holds examples of work by leading photographers around the world. There is also the **Red Earth Indian Center, the Hands-on Science Museum, Planetarium, Kirkpatrick Galleries, Kirkpatrick Gardens and Greenhouse,** and finally the Omnidome, Oklahoma's first large format movie screen. Admission is $7.50, ($13.50 incl. Omnidome, $3 for Planetarium). Mon-Fri 9am-5pm, Sat till 6pm, Sun 11am-6pm.

State Capitol, 2300 N Lincoln Blvd, 521-3356. Six derricks make politics pay; one of them is 'whipstocked' (drilled at an angle) to get at the oil beneath the Capitol, itself an unimpressive structure, one of the few state capitols without a dome. Open daily, 7am-7pm; guided tours 9am-3pm on the hour, free. Rsvs rec.

State Museum of History, 2100 N Lincoln Blvd, 522-5244. 'Interesting Indian relics.' Mon-Sat 9am-4.30pm. Free.

Six Flags, Frontier City I35 south of 122nd St. 478-2412. $28. + parking fee. Buy online for $14. Also Six Flags, Whitewater Bay 943-9687, off I-40 & Meridian. $23. Opening hours vary. _www.sixflags.com_.

Nearby: Indian City USA, near Anadarko, 65 miles SW of Oklahoma City on Hwy 8, 247-5661/ (800) 433-5661. Authentic re-creation of Plains Indian villages, done with help of Univ. of Oklahoma's Anthropology Dept. Dancing, demonstrations, ceremonies, camping, swimming. Open daily 9am-5pm. Camping also avail. Call for rate and info. _www.indiancityusa.com_. Also see the **Hall of Fame for Famous American Indians,** 247-5555. Free, open Mon-Fri, 9am-5pm, Sun 1-5pm, on the same site.

Norman (_www.visitnorman.com_), home of University of Oklahoma (over 22,000 students), 30 mins from Oklahoma City. Student life dominates the town, so there's usually plenty to do.

Bartlesville (_www.visitbartlesville.com_) 50 miles from Tulsa. Houses the only Frank Lloyd Wright tower. **Price Tower,** 510 Dewey Ave, 336-4949. $8. Open Tues-Sat 10am-5pm, Sun from noon. _www.pricetower.org_.

Festivals: Festival of the Arts, 270-4848, held annually every April at Myriad Gardens & Festival Plaza. Highlights visual, culinary and performing arts. *www.artscouncilokc.com.* **The Red Earth Festival,** 427-5228, held annually every June, is the country's 3rd largest celebration of Native America. Includes intense dance competitions in which dancers from different tribes perform for prize money. *www.redearth.org.*

Entertainment
For nightlife ideas, pick up a copy of the *Oklahoma Gazette* or try the Bricktown district on Sheridan Ave, especially the **Bricktown Brewery,** 1 N Oklahoma Ave, 232-2739. Dine (main meal more than $7) and watch the beer brew. The second floor houses live music. Cover charge, 21yrs+ *www.bricktownbrewery.com.* Or try **In Cahoots,** 2301 S. Meridian Ave. 686-1191. Popular dance hall and saloon with nightly live music ranging from country to indie.
Oklahoma State Fair, August/Sept (405) 948-6704, *www.oklahomastatefair.com; www.okstatefairpark.com.*

Information
Oklahoma City Convention and Visitors Bureau, 189 W Sheridan, 297-8912 / (800) 255-5652. *www.okccvb.org.*
Norman Chamber of Commerce, 115 E Grey St, 321-7260. *www.normanok.org.*

Travel
Greyhound, Union Bus Stn, 427 W Sheridan & Walker St, (800) 231-2222/235-6425. 24 hrs; crummy area, but station has security guards (until midnight).
Oklahoma Metro Area Transit, 300 SW 7th St, 235-7433. Bus service Mon-Sat approx. 5.30am-7.30pm. No service Sunday. $1.25 basic fare. *www.gometro.org.*
Yellow Cabs, 232-6161 in OKC; 329-3333 in Norman.
Will Rogers International Airport, 7100 Terminal Dr, 680-3322. No buses run directly there. Take the #38 from 10th & Harvey to Meridian, then take the #29 to the airport. *www.flyokc.com.*

TULSA What began as 'Tulsee Town' in 1836 under a sturdy oak tree, which still stands at 18th and Cheyenne Streets, is today the second largest city in Oklahoma. In its art-deco heyday, Tulsa was once known as the 'oil capital of the world'; now Tulsa has slid technologically sideways to 'aerospace capital of ... Oklahoma'. Its setting among rolling green hills on the Arkansas River and located on Route 66, is prettier than OKC but it's just as windy. (The whole state is notorious for wild weather).
For more info *www.urbantulsa.com; www.visittulsa.com.*
All of the following listings use the local area code (918) unless otherwise stated.

Accommodation
Try the budget motels on I-44 and I-244.
The Baymont, 4530 E Skelly Dr off I-44 (exit 229, Yale), 488-8777. Free continental bfast, USA Today, local calls and pool. D-$59-74.
Motel 6 Tulsa West, 5828 Skelly Dr, 445-0223. From $33. *www.motel6.com.*
Camping: Tulsa KOA Kampground, 19605 E Skelly Dr. (off I-44), 266-4227. Pool, laundry, showers, game room. $27 (full hook-up).

Food
McDonalds, Will Rogers Turnpike Vinita, 40 m NE of Tulsa on I-44, (918) 256-5571. The Notre Dame of McD's rests on old Route 66 – this is the largest franchise in the World.
Metro Diner, 3001 E 11th St, 592-2616. Salads, sandwiches, burgers, and pasta. Dishes from $6. W/day 7am-10pm. W/end 7am-midnight.

Of interest

Creek Council Oak Tree, 18th St. and Cheyenne Ave. known as 'Tulsa's First City Hall', the tree was a meeting place for the first group of Creeks to come from Alabama to Oklahoma in 1828.

Oklahoma in general and Tulsa in particular are in Bible-Belt country; here you'll find **Oral Roberts University,** 7777 S Lewis, (800) 678-8876. Founded by the evangelist after a vision from God so specific that he was told what style to build the place in, ORU looks like a fifties version of the future, as seen in those classic B movies. *www.oru.edu.*

Thomas Gilcrease Institute of American History and Art, 1400 N Gilcrease Museum Rd, (888) 655-2278/596-2700. The treasure house of Western American art, plus 250,000 Native American-Indian artefacts, interesting maps and documents like the original instructions for Paul Revere's ride, the first letter written from the North American continent by Christopher Columbus' son, etc. Free/donations rec. Daily 10am-5pm. *www.gilcrease.org.*

Tulsa Zoo, E 36th St N, 669-6600. Open daily 9am-5pm. $6. *www.tulsazoo.org.*

Nearby: Cherokee Heritage Center, Willis Rd, **Tahlequah**, 70 m from Tulsa, 456-6007. *www.cherokeeheritage.org.* Summer performance of the *Trail of Tears* performed June through August, Thu–Sat at 8pm in a lovely amphitheatre, telling the story of the tragic march 1838-39 from eastern Tennessee, in which 4,000 of 16,000 Cherokees died of hunger, disease and cold, and were forced to begin life anew in the territory that would become the state of Oklahoma. Haunting music and dance. To understand the full gravity of the march, read John Ehle's *Trail of Tears.* Also houses the **Cherokee National Museum,** $8.50, Mon-Sat 10am-5pm, Sun 1pm-5pm, and the **Tsa-La-Gi** Village, a replica of a 17th century Cherokee village staffed by Cherokee who portray the life of their ancestors, including braves, kids and villagers; 45 min tour.

When you are leaving Oklahoma, go by way of **Quapaw,** 542-1853, in the north-east corner of the state where Oklahoma cuts a corner with Kansas and Missouri. In this area you may be lucky enough to see the Tri-State Spook light, described as a 'weird, bobbing light' along State Line Road. Scientific explanations (light refraction from an unknown source, underground quartz crystals) have been given for this phenomenon. But everyone knows the spook light is really caused by UFOs on their way to North Dakota.

There is also a **Pow Wow,** off I37, Beaver Spring, 542-1853, where 4th July celebrations are held, *www.quapawtribe.com.*

Entertainment

Pick up a free copy of *Urban Tulsa* at local restaurants. Bars on Cherry St (15th St, E of Peoria) and S Peoria. The intersection of 18th and Boston caters to the young adult crowd.

Bostons, 18th & Boston, 583-9520 is a popular blues venue, with the best performances at w/ends. 12pm-2am.

Events: Tulsa State Fair, 744-1113, Sept/Oct. *www.tulsastatefair.com.*

Jazz on Greenwood, Aug, 587-3193, outdoor jazz festival in the historic Greenwood district of the city, *www.jazzongreenwood.com.*

Information/ Travel

Chamber of Commerce/Convention and Visitors Division, 2nd St Williams Centre Tower Two, 2 W 2nd St, 585-1201. *www.tulsachamber.com.*

Greyhound, 317 S Detroit, (800) 231-2222/584-4428.

Metropolitan Tulsa Transit Authority, 582-2100. Basic fare $1.25, express $1.50, transfer free, more limited service at w/ends. *www.tulsatransit.org.*

River Trail Bicycles, 6861 S Peoria, 481-1818, $7-10/hr. or a fixed fee. Credit Card

needed for overnight rentals, otherwise photo ID accepted. _www.tomsbicycles.com_.
Tulsa International Airport, 838-5000, just off Hwy 11, about 6 miles NE of down-
town _www.tulsaairports.com_.
Yellow Checker and City Cabs, 582-6161.

TEXAS - Lone Star State

Texans may have had to tip the stetson of 'biggest state' to Alaska but they
haven't lost their talent for beer drinking, braggadocio, rodeos, BBQ, Texas-
sized steaks and making Dallas-sized mountains of money. This state has
the size, colour and raw energy of a Texas longhorn steer, and it'll wear you
out if you try to cover it. Consider just one or two of its seven regions and its
cities of charm, San Antonio, Austin, and perhaps the gulf coast: driving
cross state, which takes about sixteen hours from one end to the other, often
consists of languishing looks at tumbleweed and endless horizons—
although initially charming, it quickly loses its appeal.

The Texan scenery may vary from desert to mountains to vast rolling
plains but everywhere in the summer months there is one constant—-the
heat. Temperatures of 90-100 degrees are the norm and in Houston, especially, there is also high humidity—'Gulf weather' it's called.

Always intensely political, Texas has seen six regimes come and five go,
from Spanish, French and Mexican, to a brief whirl as the Republic of Texas
and finally Confederate. Through it all, Texas remains good ole' boy
country, a terrain of hard-bitten little towns and hard-edged cities whose
icons are Willie Nelson, the Dallas Cowboys, LBJ, and the two George
Bushes. These towns wouldn't be complete without 'Guns and Gold for
sale' shops, the epitome of which must be 'Gun Barrel City'. _www.tour-
texas.com_ and _www.traveltex.com_, _www.txlodging.com_. For the self-proclaimed
best food in Texas, visit _www.texas-best.com/foods.html_ .

National Parks: Big Bend, Guadalupe Mountains.

_Multiple area codes exist throughout Texas; ten-digit dialing is necessary in the
larger cities._

SAN ANTONIO Situated about 75 miles south of Austin with over a million
people, initially began in 1691 as an Indian village with the wacky name of
'drunken old man going home at night', which the Spaniards bowdlerised
to San Antonio.

Despite the early Spanish (and later Mexican) presence in Texas, by the
1830s, most inhabitants were Anglo and the resultant friction caused skirmishes and ultimately the 'Battle of the Alamo'. During the Alamo's 13-day
siege in March 1836, 200 Americans gallantly fought to the last man against
the 5000-man Mexican army of Santa Ana. Afterwards, the rallying cry of
'Remember the Alamo' aided Sam Houston and his troops to defeat the
Mexicans and establish the Republic of Texas, 1836-1845. Now the downtown action centres round the San Antonio River and its pleasant green
Riverwalk, which hosts a myriad of things to do, see and eat year-round.
www.sanantoniocvb.com.

All of the following listings use the local area code (210) unless otherwise stated.

Accommodation

For cheap motels, try Roosevelt Ave (an extension of St Mary's), Fredericksburg Rd and Broadway (between downtown and Brackenridge).

El Tejas Motel, 2727 Roosevelt Ave, 533-7123. Close to missions, 3 miles from downtown. Bus #42 to door. Approx. $45. AC, TV.

HI-San Antonio International Hostel, 621 Pierce St, 223-9426. Private rooms with AYH discount, S/D start at $39. Dorm rooms $18 AYH, $21 non-AYH. $10 key deposit. Linen $2, bfast $5. Pool, kitchen. Fills quickly in summer. From bus station take #11 to Grayson St at Pierce. 'A friendly, ranch-style hostel in a quiet neighbourhood.'

Motel 6, 5522 N Pan-Am Expressway, I-35 and Rittiman Rd, 661-8791. From $38; TV, AC, pool. Also, Motel 6, downtown at 211 N Pecos St, 225-1111. From $60 weekends, weekdays from $46, TV, AC, pool. Other Motel 6 locations avail at _www.motel6.com_.

Travelers Hotel, 220 Broadway, 226-4381. Downtown, 1 block from the Alamo. From $26. Extra people are just $20 each!

Villager Lodge, 1126 E Elmira St, (800) 584-0800. Large, well-furnished rooms. TV/AC. 'Very caring management.' From $34.

Food

San Antonio has a Spanish/Mexican flavour that's tangible, with its majority Latin population; it has far better Mexican food than most Mexican border towns. Most of the town's reasonably priced restaurants can be found on Broadway.

Cadillac Bar & Restaurant, 212 S Flores St, 223-5533. Open Mon-Fri 11am-2am, Sat 5pm-2am. With a choice of Tex-Mex food and a patio out back, it's off the tourist track and a hit with the locals. _www.cadillacbar.com_.

Earl Abel's, 4210 Broadway, 822-3358. Open 6.30am-1am. Try fried catfish or chicken.

Henry's Puffy Taco, 815 Bandera St, 432-7341. Open 11am-9pm, till 10pm w/ends.

Mexican Manhattan, 110 Soledad St, 223-3913. Open Mon-Sat 11am-10pm. Free happy hour weeknight buffet. Otherwise dishes start at $6. _www.mexicanmanhattan.com_.

Mi Tierra, in El Mercado (Market Sq) 225-1262. Open 24 hrs, dishes $7.50-$21.95. Dynamite Mexican food. Order the Chalupa Compuesta and the super cheap Caldo (soup), _pan dulce_ also rec. _www.mitierracafe.com_.

Pig Stands, 1508 Broadway, 222-2794 and 807 S Presa (off S Alamo), 227-1691. Open 24 hrs offering cheap country-style food. The Broadway location parking lot fills with classic cars every Fri night.

Rio Rio, 421 E Commerce St, 226-8462, 11am-11pm w/days, till 12pm w/ends. Great location on Riverwalk, large portions, most lunch specials under $5, good vegetarian choice. _www.rioriocantina.com_.

Of interest

The Alamo, Alamo Plaza near Houston and Alamo St, 225-1391. Texas' most visited tourist attraction, the restored 1718 presidio-mission is free and open daily 9am-5.30pm, Sun from 10am. Free, donations rec. Mural inside of heroes Bowie, Crockett and Travis. Pass up the slide show across the way-ear splitting and redundant. 'Boring-don't bother.' _www.thealamo.org_.

Also in Old San Antonio: **San Fernando Cathedral,** main Plaza, where Alamo heroes are buried. _www.sfcathedral.org/history.htm_. Behind city hall is the beautiful Spanish Governor's Palace, 105 Plaza de Armas, 224-0601. Mon-Sat 9am-5pm, Sun 10am-5pm, $1.50.

Brackenridge Park, 3900 N St Mary's St (3 miles NE of downtown on Hwy 281). Take bus #8. Free Japanese sunken gardens, a skyride, riding stables, and the **San Antonio Zoo,** 3903 St Mary's St, 734-7184. Open daily 9am-8pm, Last admission at

6pm. $8. _www.sazoo-aq.org_. **El Mercado**, at junction of Santa Rosa and Commerce Sts. Typical Mexican market with stalls of fresh fruits and meats, cheap clothes and crafts from Mexico.

HemisFair Park: The **Institute of Texan Cultures**, 801 S Bowie at Durango (behind the Federal building), 458-2300, has displays on 26 ethnic groups; Tue-Sat 10am-6pm, Sun noon-5pm. $7 adults, _www.texancultures.utsa.edu_. The view from the 750 ft **Tower of the Americas**, 600 HemisFair Park, 207-8615, Sun-Thu 9am-10pm, Fri & Sat till 11pm, is worth the $3 fee.

San Antonio has 5 missions, counting the Alamo. Unless you're mission-mad, skip the other three and see **Mission San Jose**, 6701 San Hose Dr, 932-1001, known as the 'Queen of the Missions'. (Take the hourly S Flores bus marked 'San Jose Mission'). Designated a National Historic Site it has an interesting granary, Indian building, and barracks. Try to time your visit for Sun mass when the mariachis play, usually noon-1pm. Free but donations requested.

La Villita, btwn Nueva & S Alamo Sts, downtown restoration of the city's early nucleus, with cool patios, banana trees, crafts demos and sales. Daily 10am-6pm. _lavillita.com_.

Natural Bridge Caverns, 26495 Natural Bridge Caverns Rd, 651-6101. The caverns' 140-million-year-old phallic rock formations are guaranteed to knock your socks off! 75 min. tours every 30 min. Open daily 9am-7pm in summer, $15. _www.natural-bridgecaverns.com_.

Paseo del Rio. The jade green river is echoed by greenery on both sides, cobblestone walks, intimate bridges at intervals, and lined with restaurants and bars with Happy Hours. A civic as well as tourist focal point. 'Free lunch, evening concerts in summer.' 'Free dancing along the Riverwalk.' 'The hub of San Antonio's nightlife.' 'Very pretty but outrageously hyped and a bit fake and plastic—the Mexican Village is a lot more authentic.'

Rio San Antonio Cruises, operate narrated boat tours of the Paseo del Rio (800) 417-4139. Tkts $6.50, available from the River Center Mall, under the Commerce St Bridge or across from the Hilton. Open 9am-10.30pm.

San Antonio Museum of Art, 200 W Jones Ave, off Broadway, 978-8100. Housed in a restored turn-of-the-century brewery, the museum now exhibits Greek and Roman antiquities, Mexican folk art, 18th-20th century US art and Asian art. $8, $5 w/student ID. Wed-Sat 10am-5pm, Tue 10am-8pm, Sun noon-6pm. _www.sa-museum.org_.

Sea World of Texas, 16 miles NW of downtown, at Ellison Dr and Westover Hills Blvd, (800) 700-7786. $170 million park - aquariums, flamingoes, waterfowl, a 12.5-acre lake for water skiers, two water rides (log flume and river raft), two roller coasters and a 3-D theatre. Open daily in high summer, otherwise w/ends only-call for times. $45. _www.seaworld.com_.

Entertainment
For evening fun, any season, stroll along the **River Walk**. The _Friday Express_ or weekly _Current_ is a good entertainment resource.

Arneson Theater, Alamo & Nuevo, 207-8610. Showcases everything from flamenco to jazz to country; river separates you from stage. Fiesta Noche del Rio, 226 4651, variety show is $15, June-August, Fri and Sat at 8.30pm.

Floore Country Store, 14492 Old Bandera Rd, btwn Old & New Hwy 16 in Helotes, 695-8827. One of the oldest Honky-Tonk hangouts and a favourite of Willie Nelson. Open w/days till 8pm. Misc. entertainment Fri-Sun evenings; cover from $7 on Sat nights. _www.liveatfloores.com_.

For authentic _Tejano_ music (Mexican-country!) head to **Cadillac Bar,** (see listing in Food section). Dancing frenzy heaven. _www.cadillacbar.com_.

Diez y Seis (translated: 16th) on or around 16th Sept, Market Sq, (800) 447-3372, marks Mexico's independence from Spain with street parades, floats and events citywide. **Fiesta San Antonio**, 227-5191, April. Plenty of Tex-Mex action with 10 days of concerts and parades citywide, to commemorate the victory at San Jacinto and honor the heroes at the Alamo, *www.fiesta-sa.org*. Also, numerous fiestas, music events and blowouts (**most** free) throughout the year; during St Patrick's week, San Antonians dye both their beer and their river green!

Information/ Internet Access
Convention and Visitors Bureau, 203 S. St. Mary's St, 2nd floor, (800) 447-3372/207-6700. *www.sanantoniocvb.com*.
Internet free at the San Antonio Public Library, 600 Soledad, 207-2500, Mon-Thu 9am-9pm, Fri/Sat 9am-5pm, Sun 11am-5pm. Access ltd to 1 hr if others waiting.

Travel
VIA, runs local buses, 362-2020. Basic fare 80¢, transfer 15¢, express $1.60 (half price for students) day-tripper pass $3. Operates daily till 10pm, but many routes stop at 5pm. Also runs the El Centro old-fashioned trolleys that circle downtown, 80¢, students 40¢. *www.viainfo.net*.
Amtrak, 350 Hoefgen St, (800) 872-7245.
Greyhound, 500 N St Mary's St, (800) 231-2222/270-5824. 24 hrs.
San Antonio International Airport, About 5 miles N of downtown; take #2 'Blanco-Airport' bus from Soledad & Travis Sts, 80¢.
Yellow Checker Cab, taxis, 226-4242.

AUSTIN   Capital City, originally known as 'Waterloo', Richard Linklater made his film, *Slacker*, here for a reason. With its laid-back attitude it doesn't seem like 'real' Texas but it does seem like the most enjoyable city in the state. Truly an oasis, socially and culturally, in the middle of a desert, it has a huge student population that adds a vigour to the place. Austin is *the* place to go to see bands, hang out, drink too much and party hard. It's also, strangely enough, a centre for approx. 1.5 million Mexican free-tail bats, the largest urban bat colony in North America. In summer, the little critters roost under the Congress Ave Bridge. Every evening, at around 8pm, a crowd gathers to see them all leave to feed. Bat Hotline: 416-5700 (*Category 3636*). *Austin 360* is an online newspaper with info on the Austin music scene, sports and news. *www.Austin360.com* and *www.austintexas.org*.
   All of the following listings use the local area code (512) unless otherwise stated.

Accommodation
Congress St is cheap hotel/motel row. The **University of Texas** operates Co-op's that offer room and board (3 meals a day) at great rates, $20-25. June-Aug. For more info: **ICC Student Co-ops** on 476-1957.
HI-Austin International Hostel, 2200 S Lakeshore Blvd (nr Barton Springs), (800) 725-2331/444-2294. Dorm rooms $16.75 AYH, $19.75 non-AYH, inc linen. Lock out 11am-5pm. Extremely clean, well-kept, kitchen, lockers, internet, laundry facilities, AC, free parking and live music. It's in a good location with friendly staff and a cavernous 24 hr common room that overlooks Town Lake, *www.hiaustin.org*.
Motel 6, 8010 N I-35 at Rundberg Ln Exit #241/240-A, 837-9890, offers a pool, laundry, AC, TV. From $34. Rsvs required at w/ends. *www.motel6.com*.
Red Roof Inn, 8210 N. Interregional Hwy 35, (800) 733-7663/(512) 835-2200. Located 6 miles N of downtown. From $36, includes pool, coffee, newspaper, TV, no AC. *www.redroof.com*.
Camping: The Austin Lone Star RV Resort, (800) 284-0206 (rsvs line)/444-6322, 7009 S. I-35, offers a pool, hot tub, clean private bathrooms, laundry and a grocery store. $25-$68. *www.austinlonestar.com*.

Food

Great pickings, but you'd better like Texas BBQ, Mexican food and Texas chili. Lots of student hangouts along Guadalupe.

The Filling Station, 801 Barton Springs Rd, 477-1022. Get 12oz ethyl-burgers or a gasket platter. 'Try the high-octane speciality drink, the Tune-up, guaranteed to clean out your spark plugs!' Dishes under $10. Mon-Thurs 11am-10pm, Fri & Sat night till 12, Sun noon-10pm.

Furr's Cafeteria, 4015 S Lamar, 441-7825. Two other branches in Austin. All-U-Can-Eat, $5.79 (lunch) $6.29 dinner, 11am-8.30pm.

Sandy's Hamburgers, 603 Barton Springs Rd, 478-6322. Open 10.30am-10.30pm. Try the frozen custard.

Texas Chili Parlor, 1409 Lavaca St, 472-2828. World-class chili joint and saloon, also serves cocktails. Open daily 11am-2am. *www.cactushill.com/TCP/home.htm*.

Texas Showdown Saloon, 2610 Guadalupe, 472-2010. Small menu. Beer garden sometimes has live music; 'Texas-style' atmosphere, average drinks $3. Open 11am-2am. Happy hour daily 2pm-7pm.

Threadgill's, 6416 N Lamar, 451-5440. A stronghold of Texas food, and run by Eddie Wilson, a founding father of Austin's music scene, this soul-food joint has free seconds (veggies) and was an early stomping ground of the original screamer, Janis Joplin. Eddie plays the place down. 'I've got easily the best restaurant in the history of the globe!' Kitchen's motto is 'we don't serve all you can eat, we serve more than you can eat'. Mon-Sat 11am-10pm, Sun till 9pm. *www.threadgills.com*.

Of interest

Barton Springs, Zilker Park, 2201 Barton Springs Rd, 867-3080/476-9044. Open-air swimming hole (not chlorinated) fed by underground springs. 'Reached by lovely 40 min riverside walk, beautiful setting.' Pool's temperature rarely rises above 60F though! Alternatively, walk upstream and swim at any nice-looking spot! Open daily 5am-10pm, $2.50 w/days, $2.75 w/end. Also **Hamilton Pool** Hamilton Pool Road on Texas 71 West, 264-2740, a favourite with Texan students. 60ft waterfall cascades into a jade green pool. Monitored—closed if bacteria levels are too high. $8 parking fee, $3 walk-ins, 9am-6pm daily.

Capitol Building, Congress Ave & 11th St, 463-0063. 7ft higher than the one in Washington D.C. Free tours every 15 mins; entry to public areas, including galleries from which you can observe debates during session. Call for opening hours.

Museums: Austin Museum of Art, Laguna Gloria, 3809 W 35th St, 458-8191. 8 miles from the State Capitol. Blends art, architecture, and nature, overlooking Lake Austin. Free, donations rec. Now has a new location downtown, 823 Congress Ave, 495-9224, quadrupling the museum space. $5, $4 w/student ID, Tue $1. Open Tue-Sat 10am-6pm, Thu till 8pm, Sun noon-5pm. *www.amoa.org*.

O. Henry Museum, 409 E 5th St (cross Naches), 472-1903, free. Personal effects of the popular short-story writer who lived in Austin from 1885-1895. Wed-Sun noon-5pm. *www.ci.austin.tx.us/parks/ohenry.htm*. Also, **Republic of Texas Museum,** 510 E Anderson Lane, 339-1997. Indispensable museum for anyone interested in Texas or Civil War history. $2. Mon-Fri 10am-4pm. *www.drt-inc.org/Museum.html*.

University of Texas, Guadalupe and 24th St, north of Capitol. Huge, rich, highly social school. *www.utexas.edu*. Has several museums and the **LBJ Library** at 2313 Red River St, 721 0200. Free, daily 9am-5pm. A/V displays, replica of the Oval Office and tapes of LBJ's twang. LBJ's birthplace, home, ranch and grave are west of Austin, in and around **Johnson City.** Also: **Harry Ransom Center,** 21st & Guadalupe on UT campus, 471-8944. Housing one of the world's four copies of the Gutenburg Bible, lots of Evelyn Waugh and manuscript collections of James Joyce, T.S. Eliot, and D.H. Lawrence. Gallery Tue-Fri 10am-5pm, Thu till 7pm, Sat & Sun noon-5pm. Free. *www.hrc.utexas.edu*.

Entertainment

Austin is a major music centre; check *The Daily Texan* and the free *Austin Chronicle* to see who's playing where. Guadalupe Ave, called The Drag, is a hot spot for student and non-student activity. For nightclubs and fancy bars it has to be 6th St, wall-to-wall music and a great Halloween street party. Lately, much nightlife has headed to the **Warehouse Area** around 4th St, west of Congress. Also, check out:

Austin City Limits, an excellent nationwide TV country show broadcast weekly for over 30 years on public television in the US. *www.pbs.org/klru/austin*.

Antone's, 213 W 5th St, (512) 263-4146. Has drawn the likes of BB King, John Lee Hooker, Muddy Waters, Fats Domino. Daily 8pm-2am. *www.antones.net*.

Broken Spoke, 3201 S Lamar, 442-6189. Authentic C&W dive with live music that dates back to Bob Wills and the Texas Playboys, Texas two-step dancing, chicken-fried steaks. Cover varies $5-20. *www.brokenspokeaustintx.com*.

Information/ Internet access

Convention and Visitors Bureau, 201 E 2nd St, (800) 926-2282/478-0098. Daily 9am-6pm through the summer. Free literature available, *www.austintexas.org*.

Austin Public Library, 800 Guadalupe, 974 7400. Mon-Thu 10am-9pm, Fri/Sat 10am-6pm, Sun noon-6pm. Free.

Travel

Capital Metro, 474-1200. Local bus company; basic fare 50¢, free transfers. *www.capmetro.org*. The Dillo Bus, serves downtown area to uni campus; green trolleys run daily (free).

Greyhound, 916 E Koenig Lane, (800) 231-2222/458-4463. 24 hrs.

Amtrak, 250 N Lamar Blvd, (800) 872-7245.

Austin Bergstrom International Airport, 3600 Presidential Blvd, S of city, opened in 1999. #100 buses travel from the uni/ downtown, every 40 mins. 50¢. *www.ci.austin.tx.us/austinairport*.

Yellow Checker Cab Co, 452-9999.

DALLAS/FORT WORTH Big D pushes culture but its finest achievements are Neiman-Marcus, the glittering emporium of the conspicuous consumer, and Tolbert's Chili Parlor, where serious chili-heads used to go to eat a bowl of red before they die. 'Dallas is a hard-nosed business environment with entertainment geared to the relaxing businessman.' One of the world's largest permanent trade fairs is located here. The city seems to go on forever and attractions are not centralized. If you are not travelling by car, you may want to visit a city more accommodating to the pedestrian.

An airport larger than Manhattan is the umbilical cord linking Dallas with **Fort Worth**, its cattle-and agriculture-based sister city. Fort Worth, surprisingly, has a lot more of interest to see and do, with a number of top-notch museums and art collections, most free and conveniently clumped in Amon Carter Square. As befits an overgrown cowtown, the honky-tonk country and western scene is alive and well, more cowboy than urban. Forty miles and a heap of freeways separate these two behemoths, so don't plan to lodge in one and visit the other; *www.fortworth.com*; *www.dallascvb.com*.

The Dallas/Ft. Worth area has five area codes – 817, 682, 972, 469 and 214 – ten-digit dialing is required for all local calls.

Accommodation

NB: Budget accommodation in either city does not exist in the downtown areas. We suggest you rent a car and schlep out to one of the Motel 6s ringing the area, or make your visit a brief one.

B&B Texas Style, (800) 899-4538, Mon-Fri 8.30am-4.30pm. Rooms in private homes and B&B's around town, starting from $55. *www.bnbtexasstyle.com*.

Hotel Lawrence, 302 S. Houston St., (877) 396-0334, while expensive this nicely appointed hotel features a free continental bfast, from $80. Check *www.hotellawrencedallas.com* for special deals.

Motel 6, 2660 Forest Lane, I-635 at Josey Lane/Denton Drive. (972) 484-9111. From $37. For more locations and their rates call (800) 466-8356 or visit *www.motel6.com*.

Food

In Dallas: For the lowdown on dining, pick up Friday's *Dallas Morning News*.

Celebration, 4503 W Lovers Lane, (214) 351-5681. 'A real discovery for both its ambience and good food. Magnificent home cooking.' *www.celebrationrestaurant.com*.

Gennie's Bishop Grill, 321 N Bishop Ave, (214) 946-1752. Cafeteria-style, lines are short and functional. 'Garlic chicken is a must.' Mon-Fri 11am-2pm.

Mecca, 10422 Harry Hines Blvd, (214) 352-0051. A happy-go-lucky roadhouse 'where a squadron of feisty waitresses rule the loose-jointed dining room/joint'. Chicken-fry and cinnamon rolls are specialties. Open Mon-Fri 5.30am-2.30pm, Sat 5am-2pm.

Sonny Bryan's, original location at 2202 Inwood Rd, (214) 357-7120. 'Best urban barbecue in Texas.' Their funky, run-down atmosphere is shared with 14 other Dallas locations. Mon-Fri 10am-4pm. *www.sonnybryans.com*.

In Fort Worth: **Kincade's,** 4901 Camp Bowie Blvd, (817) 732-2881. Feast your eyes (and mouth) on their world-renowned half-pound hamburger! Mon-Sat 11am-6pm.

Paris Coffee Shop, 700 W Magnolia, (817) 335-2041. Home-baking prepared daily, ave. $8. Mon-Fri 6am-2.30pm, Sat till 11am. 'The best breakfast and lunches in town.'

Cattlemen's Steak House, 2458 N Main St, (817) 624-3945. A Fort Worth institution thanks to its steaks and margaritas. Dishes $17-35. *www.cattlemenssteakhouse.com*.

Of interest

In Dallas: You have probably seen the Zapruder footage so often that there will be no problem in retracing the route that **John F Kennedy** took to his death on 22 Nov 1963. He was driven on Main to Houston and Elm where Lee Harvey Oswald is alleged to have fired the shot from the sixth floor of the **Texas School Book Depository,** 411 Elm St, (214) 747-6660. Now a museum to the Kennedy life and legacy, it is easily reachable from the Greyhound station during a rest stop. Open daily 9am-6pm (last entry 5pm), $10, $13 incl. audio tour, *www.jfk.org*. 'Very moving and sensitive.' Overlooking the scene is an **obelisk**. A Philip Johnson-designed cenotaph is on Main St at Market. JFK spent his last night in the **Fort Worth Hyatt Regency**.

Dallas Museum of Art, 1717 N Harwood at Ross, (214) 922-1200. Anchors the new Arts District with its excellent collections of Egyptian, Impressionist, modern and decorative art. Sculpture garden lies adjacent. Some pre-Colombian works. Tue-Sun 11am-5pm, Thu till 9pm, Closed Mon. $10, $5 w/student I.D. *www.dallasmuseumofart.org*.

Frontiers of Flight Museum, Dallas Love Field terminal, mezzanine, (214) 350-1651. Collection of aviation artefacts including the fur parka worn by Adm. Richard E Byrd in 1929 on his first flight to the North Pole. Mon-Sat 10am-5pm, Sun 1pm-5pm, $8. *www.flightmuseum.com*.

For a Dallas-sized shopping experience head for the **Galleria,** LBJ Fwy & Dallas Pkwy, (972) 702-7100 with 200 stores and an ice rink, open Mon-Sat 10am-9pm, Sun 12pm-6pm, *www.galleriadallas.com*.

West End Historic District, Market Street from Pacific to McKinney is the restored old town, including the not-so-authentic **West End Marketplace Mall** at the north end of Market St.

Architecture: both the **Hyatt Regency** and **Reunion Tower** at 300 Reunion Blvd, (214) 651-1234, get high marks: 'best things in Dallas', 'especially beautiful at sunset'. There is an observation deck 50 stories high, $2, a good way to see and get a feel for the whole city before you start walking. Open 10am-10pm. Call first since frequent parties close the deck to the public. Also, worth a look is the 1914 **Union Rail Station**, connected to the tower by underground walkway.

Parks: Fair Park, 3809 Grand Ave, (214) 670-8400. Open 9.30am-4.30pm. 277 acres, home to the annual (Sept-Oct) State Fair, The Cotton Bowl Football Stadium, Parry Ave (214) 692-2600, and the **African-American Museum**, 3536 Grand Ave, (214) 565-9026, a multimedia collection of folk art and sculpture, donation, daily 10am-7pm, free admission. _www.aamdallas.org_. Also, the Science Place, $7.50, **IMAX Theatre**, $7, and **Planetarium**, $3, all at Main Building, 1318 2nd Ave, Grand Ave Park entrance, (214) 428-5555. Mon-Sat 9.30am-5.30pm, Sun 11.30am-5.30pm. A $13.50 ticket for IMAX and Exhibit is available, _www.scienceplace.org_.

Nearby: White Rock Lake provides a haven for walkers, bikers, and inline skaters. _www.whiterocklake.org_. Ft Worth: the **Amon Carter Museum**, 3501 Camp Bowie Blvd (817) 738-1933, with its splendid Western art collection of Russells and Remingtons, Tue-Fri 10am-5pm, Thurs till 8pm, Sun 12pm-5pm, admission free. _www.cartermuseum.org_. **The Kimbell Art Museum**, 3333 Camp Bowie Blvd, (817) 332-8451, is Louis Kahn's architectural tour de force. Home to Asian, pre-Columbian and late Renaissance works, the museum is open Tue-Sat 10am-5pm, Fri noon-8pm, Sun noon-5pm, free, _www.kimbellart.org_. **The Museum of Science and History**, 1501 Montgomery St, (817) 255-9300, Mon-Thu 9am-5.30pm, Fri & Sat 9am-8pm and Sun 11.30am-5.30pm, $7. Their **Omni Theatre**, $7, screens science movies, and also offers **The Planetarium** $3.50. Combo ticket, $13. _www.fwmuseum.org_. A truly Texan experience is to be had at **Billy Bob's** 2520 Rodeo Plaza, the Yards (817) 624-7117, 'the worlds largest honky tonk', where rodeo, bull ring, BBQ restaurant, pool tables, souvenir shop, 42 bars, line dancing and honky tonk performances regularly collide, producing a hoard of loyal, uniformed Stetson, wrangler and cowboy boot wearers. Open daily 11am-2am, closed Fri 5pm-6pm. Offers an array of dance classes, free class 7pm-8pm, cover $1-9 + surcharge dependent on bands. _www.billybobstexas.com_.

Fort Worth Stockyard District, (817) 625-1025 for more info see Stockyards Gazette avail. at the **Visitors Information Center**, 130 Exchange Ave. (817) 624-4741, Open daily Mon-Fri 9am-7pm. The Stockyards host **Weekly Rodeos**, Coliseum at 121 E. Exchange Ave. (817) 625-1025, Fri and Sat nights at 8pm, $9.50. _www.fortworthstockyards.org_.

Sundance Square, between 1st & 6th Sts is the heart of downtown. Red-paved blocks filled with shops, cafes and bars.

Entertainment

The free weekly _Dallas Observer_, out every Wednesday, can help you assess your entertainment options. Check out **West End Market Place**, off Houston St, where there is a plethora of galleries, eateries, and dance clubs. _www.westendmarketplacedallas.com_.

Six Flags Hurricane Harbor, I-30 btwn Dallas & Fort Worth, in Arlington, exit Texas 360N, (817) 265-3356. $29.99 plus $7 parking. Open daily in summer, otherwise w/ends only - call for details.

Six Flags Over Texas, I-30 & Hwy 360 intersection, 20 min W. of Dallas in Arlington, (817) 640-8900. $41.99 plus $9 parking-check for deals online _www.sixflags.com_. Price includes all rides and shows. Open daily May-Aug w/ends thereafter. The original of this ever-expanding chain, the 'six flags' referring to the six regimes that Texas has seen. Especially nauseating are the Texas 'Chute-Out',

'Superman: Tower of Power', 'Gargantuan', and 'Titan' roller coaster that travels at 85 mph. Also 5 hrs of air-conditioned shows each day.

Sport: Football is a religion in Dallas. **Texas Stadium** on the E. Airport Freeway is home to the **Dallas Cowboys,** (info) (214) 253-6060 (NB: tkts are scarce). _www.dallascowboys.com_. The **Texas Rangers** play baseball in Arlington, off the I-30. Call (817) 273-5100, or tkts online at _www.texasrangers.com_.

Information

Dallas Convention and Visitors Bureau Information Center, 'Old Red' Courthouse, 100 S Houston St. (800) 232-5527/(214) 571-1300. _www.dallascvb.com_.
Fort Worth Convention and Visitors Bureau Information Center, 415 Throckmorton, (800) 433-5747 / (817) 336-8791. _www.fortworth.com_.

Internet access

In Dallas: free at the **J Erik Johnson Central Library,** 1515 Young St, (214) 670-1400. Use limited to 1 hr. 25¢ per printed page.
In Fort Worth: Houston Central Library, 500 W. 3rd St, (817) 871-7701. Use limited to 1 hr per person per day. 25¢ per printed page.

Travel

Dallas: Amtrak, Union Station, 400 S Houston St, (800) 872-7245. 'The bars upstairs in the terminal also worth a visit—cheap, and wonderful architecture.'
Dallas Area Rapid Transit (DART) (214) 979-1111, local buses and light rail, $1.25, premium routes $2.25, day pass $2.50 local, $4.50 premium. Routes radiate from downtown; serves most suburbs. _www.dart.org_.
Greyhound, 205 S Lamar St (3 blocks E of Union Station), (800) 231-2222/(214) 655-7082. 24 hrs.
Dallas-Fort Worth International Airport, between the two cities. To get there take train from Dallas Union or Fort Worth T&P station direct to Center Port, DFW Airport, from where you catch the free DFW shuttle to individual terminals (remember to take a free transfer slip). Or take a Super Shuttle, (817) 329-2000, from one of the main downtown hotels in either Dallas or Fort Worth $15-20 o/w. Rsvs only, 24 hrs in advance. _www.supershuttle.com_.
Dallas Love Field Airport, 8008 Cedar Spring Road, (817) 670-6080/6073, take #39 'Love Field' bus from one of the blue bus stops on Main and Griffin. _www.dallas-lovefield.com_.
Fort Worth: Amtrak, 1001 Jones St, (800) 872-7245.
Greyhound, 901 Commerce St, (800) 231-2222/(817) 429-3089, 24hrs.
Yellow Checker Cab Co, (817) 534-5555 Fort Worth and (214) 426-6262 Dallas.

HOUSTON The newer skyscrapers that crowd Houston's skyline have sleek skins of black sun-reflecting glass, the same material used for astronaut helmet visors. Seems appropriate, since this city shares its name with the first word spoken from the moon on 20th July 1969, and from which its inextricable links with NASA began. 'Space City' was originally founded by brothers John and Augustus Allen who paid $1.40 for 6642 acres in 1838. Later, in 1901, the discovery of oil perpetuated the swell of inhabitants, now more than 1.9 million, and made Houston the fourth largest city in the USA, swelled in 2005 by evacuees from Hurricane Katrina.

Houston is a sprawling city unconstrained by zoning and you really must have an air-conditioned car to combat the hot and humid summers: 'Houston is a huge, modern city but has hardly any attractions. It is probably the most boring city I've been to. The tremendous humidity makes it even worse.' BUNACers complain that 'downtown is dead'!
www.houston-guide.com, _www.houstonet.com_.

All of the following listings use the local area code (713). However, it is important to note that Houston also has (832) and (281).

Accommodation

HI- Houston International Hostel, 5302 Crawford at Oakdale St, 523-1009. $15. 'Friendly, clean and efficient with AC.' Laundry. Lock-out 10am-5pm. Within walking distance of museums. *www.houstonhostel.com*.

Houston Inn, 2200 S Wayside Dr, 928-2800, rooms from $40. AC, TV, pool, free continental bfast served 6-10am.

Motel 6, 5555 W 34th St (800) 466-8356. From $36. AC, TV, pool and unlimited local phone calls. There are a number of Motel 6s around the outskirts of town. See *www.motel6.com* for other locations.

Red Roof Inn, 15701 Park Ten Pl, (800) 733-7663/(281) 579-7200. From $42, AC, TV, free tea & coffee. *www.redroof.com*.

Food

The diverse Houston cuisine reflects the 90+ languages that are spoken here; no wonder then that Houstonians eat out more than residents of any other city. Reasonably priced restaurants along **Westheimer** and **Richmond Ave**, intersecting with **Fountainview**.

Backstreet Café, 1103 S Shepherd Dr, 521-2239. Food is 'new American' but with an international flavour. The shaded dining area provides a respite for the weary traveler. Entrees $10-20. Open Sun-Thu 11am-10pm, Fri & Sat till 11pm.

Bellaire Broiler Burger, 5216 Bellaine Blvd, 668-8171. 'Burgers are delicious, shakes are real!' Burgers approx. $5. Open Mon-Sat 11-8pm.

Berryhill Hot Tamales, 2639 Revere St, 526-8080. 'Check out the recommended fish tacos ($3.99) and the shrimp-and-avocado salad.' Open Mon-Fri 10am-10pm, Sat 9am-10pm, Sun 9am-9pm. *www.berryhilltamales.com/baja*.

Cabo Mix Mex Grill, 419 Travis St, 225-2060, 'reasonably priced Mexican fare'. Open Mon-Wed 11am-midnight, Thu-Sat till 2am, Sun till 10pm. *www.cabomixmex.com*.

Goode Company Barbeque, 5109 Kirby Dr, 522-2530/523-7154. Pig out on crunch-crusted pork ribs, melt-in-the-mouth brisket, chicken, ham, duck, or turkey with peppery pinto beans and luscious jalapeno cheese bread on the side. Dishes approx. $10. Busy at w/ends. Open daily 11am-10pm. *www.goodecompany.com*.

Otto's BBQ, 5502 Memorial Dr, 864-2573; best ribs in town since 1963. Open Mon-Sat 11am-9pm.

Of interest

Houston Livestock Show and Rodeo. The largest rodeo in the world attracts more than 1.8 million visitors each year in spring. Reliant Stadium, 840 Kirby Dr, (832) 667-1000, from $16, depending on the show. *www.hlsr.com*.

Menil Collection, 1515 Sul Ross Ave, 525-9400, Wed-Sun 11am-7pm. Free. Large private art collection including African, Byzantine, Indian and surrealist works. *www.menil.org*.

Museum District: home to 11 'museums' in the loosest sense of the word. Includes **Hermann Park** *www.hermannpark.org*, **Japanese Gardens**, as well as actual museums or galleries. The **Contemporary Arts Museum,** 5216 Montrose Blvd, 284-8250, has multimedia exhibits. Free; open Tue-Sat 10am-5pm, Thu till 9pm, Sun noon-5pm, *www.camh.org*. Across the street is the **Museum of Fine Arts**, 1001 Bissonet, 639-7300. Exhibition wing designed by Mies Van der Rohe. Renaissance art plus renowned Hogg collection of 65 paintings, watercolours by Frederick Remington. Tue & Wed 10am-5pm, Thu till 9pm, Fri & Sat till 7pm, Sun 12.15pm-7pm. $7, $3.50 w/student ID, free Thu. *www.mfah.org*.

Cullen Sculpture Garden, 'the most beautiful acre in Houston', 5101 Montrose Blvd, includes pieces by artists such as Matisse and Rodin. Daily 10am-10pm, free.

Museum of Natural Science, 1 Hermann Circle Drive, 639-4629, has moon-landing equipment. Open Mon-Sat 9am-6pm, Tue till 8pm, Sun 11am-6pm. $6, free Tues 2pm-8pm. The museum also houses a **Planetarium** ($5) and an **IMAX** Theatre ($7). Inside the museum's **Cockrell Butterfly Centre** in a tropical paradise of 80F, there are more than 2000 butterflies. **Rothko Chapel**, in Montrose area at 1409 Sul Ross, 524-9839. A multi-faith chapel, its walls bedecked with Rothko's exercises in controlled simplicity. Daily 9am-6pm. *www.hmns.org*.

Zoological Gardens, 1513 N. MacGregor, Gorillas, hippos, reptiles and rare species of other animals. Also hosts a macabre bat colony. You're allowed to see them quaff their daily blood—'fascinating, repellent'. Admission $8.50; 533-6500, open daily 10am-6pm. *www.houstonzoo.org*.

Hundreds of shops and restaurants line the 18 mile **Houston Tunnel**, which connects all the major buildings in downtown Houston, Civic Center to the Hyatt Regency, open w/days during business hours. Also, try the **Galleria**, 622-0663, 5085 Westhiemer St, an enormous shopping mall with over 300 shops. Open Mon-Sat 10am-9pm, Sun 11am-7pm.

NASA-LBJ Space Center, 1601 NASA Rd (20 miles S of downtown via I-45), (281) 244-2100. Open daily 10am-7pm (summer and w/ends), 10am-5pm (winter); $17.95. Admission includes a free, guided tour: see spacecraft, shuttle trainer, moon rocks, NASA films. 'No need to book Mission Control tours. First come, first served basis.' 'Very exciting seeing Mission Control in action. We watched a test run for the next shuttle mission.' 'Very informative.' The complex also houses models of Gemini, Apollo and Mercury as well as countless galleries and hands-on exhibits. You too can try to land the space shuttle—on a computer simulator! *www.spacecenter.org*.

Port of Houston, a deep channel that runs 50 miles S to the Gulf of Mexico and allows Houston to be the 3rd largest port in the US and the 6th in the world. From the observation platform at Wharf 9 you can watch huge ships in the Turning Basin. Free $1^1/2$ hr boat trips, Tue & Wed, Fri & Sat 10am & 2.30pm, Thu & Sun 2.30pm, closed for maintenance during Sept. Call Sam Houston, 670-2416 for rsvs. 'A free look at the bayou and a stunning perspective of the skyline'. 'Book well ahead in summer' *www.portofhouston.com*.

Sam Houston Park, downtown at 1100 Bagby St, 655-1912. Nice mélange of historic Greek revival, Victorian, log cabin and cottage against a canyon of office buildings. Daily, guided tours of the buildings and grounds, Tue-Sat 10am-4pm, Sun 1pm-4pm. $6, $4 w/student I.D. Not far away is **Tranquillity Park** at Bagby and Walker, named in honour of lunar landings. 'Truly an oasis in the desert.'

Entertainment

In the last couple of years there have been concerted efforts to improve downtown nightlife in Houston, especially in the Montrose district. For some chills and thrills, wander down the more established **Richmond Ave**, btwn Hillcroft and Chimney Rock.

Continental Club, 3700 Main St, (713) 529-9899, live music. *www.continentalclub.com*.
Danny's Sports Bar, 12126 Westheimer Rd, (281) 558-8693, 11am-12am. *www.dannysportsbar.com*.

Miller Outdoor Theatre, 100 Concert Dr, 284-8350, has free symphony, ballet, plays, drama and musicals in the summer. 'Get there 30 mins early for good position.' Tkts required for seats, box office 11am-1pm.

Six Flags Astroworld, opposite the infamous Astrodome at 9001 Kirby Dr, 799-8404. One in a chain of theme parks. $41.99, discount tickets available at Kroger or Fiesta grocery stores for. Hours vary. Splashtown $29.99. *www.sixflags.com*.

Minute Maid Park, 501 Crawford, adjacent to Union Station, (713) 259-8000, home ground of the Houston Astros baseball team. At least $10.

Information/ Internet access
Greater Houston Convention and Visitors Bureau Information Centre, 901 Bagby St, 713 437-5200. *www.houston-guide.com*.
Internet free at the **Houston Central Library**, 500 McKinney, (832) 393-1313, Mon-Thurs 9am-9pm, Fri-Sat till 6pm, Sun 2pm-6pm. Access limited to $1/2$ hr, additional $1/2$ hr possible. 15¢ per printed page. *www.hpl.lib.tx.us*.

Travel
Metro Transit Authority, 739-4000. Local METRO buses, basic fare $1. Reliable service within the 'loop' of I-610. Less frequent at w/ends. *www.ridemetro.org*.
Amtrak, 902 Washington Ave, (800) 872-7245. Unsafe neighbourhood.
Greyhound, 2121 S Main St, (800) 231-2222. Open 24 hrs - unsafe neighbourhood.
Houston Intercontinental Airport (HIA), 25 miles N of downtown. Take Metro bus #102 (Express) on Travis going north; last bus out 11.39pm, last into downtown 12.13pm; $1.50. No w/end service. There's also the Airport Express bus, 523-8888, leaves from next door to Hyatt Regency on Louisiana, every half hour from 7am-11.30pm, $28 o/w.

GALVESTON History rich, hurricane prone Galveston Island was named for Bernardo de Gálvez, governor of Louisiana and later viceroy of Mexico in the late 1700's. However, the modern city dates from 1817 when headquarters were established by pirate Jean LaFitte, who liked its 32 miles of sandy beaches (so handy for burying bullion). Galveston, a resplendent little city of scarlet oleanders, nodding palms and fine 19th century mansions, served briefly as capital of the Republic of Texas in 1836. Come here to getaway with the city slickers, gorge on bay shrimp, and imbibe the placid, slightly decayed Southern feeling of the place with its cute boardwalk and seafood restaurants.
  Unfortunately, the beach here isn't as fine as those further to the south. Camping is permitted in the state park and access to the Island is via causeway and by free ferry from Port Bolivar to the east. *www.galveston.com*.
All of the following listings use the local area code (409) unless otherwise stated.

Accommodation/Food
Galveston Island State Park, west on 61st St, 737-1222, has camp sites for $15, plus $3 pp park entry. Rsvs rec on w/ends. There are hotel rooms to be had, although these can be expensive during the summer - best to try one of the roadside motels.
Along **Seawall Blvd**, check out the bountiful seafood and traditional Texas barbecues. Try **The Original Mexican Café**, at 14th & Market, 762-6001, the oldest restaurant on the island. Tex-Mex meals with homemade flour tortillas. Daily lunch specials ($5-10). Open daily 8am-9pm.
Captain's Table, 11126 FM 3005, West End of town, 744-0881, claims to hold 'the best kept secret on the island within its swinging doors'. One thing is certain, though, a great meal can be had here for $10. Open 4–10pm daily.

Of interest
Texas Seaport Museum, Pier 21, # 8 at end of Kempner (22nd) St, 763-1877. Home to *Elissa*, a Scottish-built square-rigged sailing ship restored to its 1877 condition. Daily 10am-5pm, $6. *www.tsm-elissa.org*.
Some of the **architecture** worth seeing: **Ashton Villa**, 2328 Broadway, 762-3933, an elegantly restored 1859 Italianate mansion. $6, ($5-students), summer opening 10am-4pm daily except Sun (noon-4pm). **The Bishop's Palace**, 1402 Broadway, 762-2475, 1402 Broadway, extravagant 1886 home, $6, Open daily 10am-5pm. Tours every half hour.
The Strand contains a fine concentration of over 50 19th Century iron front build-

ings, which house cafes, restaurants, gift shops and clothing stores. Stop by Moody Gardens, (800) 582-4673. This l0-story glass pyramid encloses a tropical rainforest, 2000 exotic species of flora and fauna, a six-story 3D **IMAX Theater** and a **Bat Cave**. Open Daily 10am-9pm, last entry 8pm. Each attraction has a separate admission, but a comprehensive $35.95 ticket is available; _www.moodygardens.org_.

Information/Travel
Galveston Island Convention and Visitors Bureau Information Centres, (888) 425-4753; daily 8.30am-5pm, two locations, 2428 Seawall Blvd and 2215 Strand. _www.galvestoncvb.com_.
Kerrville Bus Lines, (affiliated to Greyhound), 714 25th St, 765-7731. Four buses daily btwn Houston and Galveston, approx $15.

CORPUS CHRISTI and **THE SOUTH TEXAS COAST** A large port city with a growing population, Corpus Christi (translated as 'body of Christ') makes a good gateway to **Padre Island**, a long lean strip of largely unspoilt National Seashore with white beaches that points toward the Texas toe. Once inhabited by cannibals, the shifting blond sands of Padre have seen five centuries of piracy and shipwrecks and no doubt conceal untold wealth. However, the natural wonders of the 110 mile long island are today quite sufficient for most people.

It's a prime area for vacationing American students during their summer break and although it can become a little overcrowded, it has a real 'youth' vibe with everyone geared to enjoy themselves. The island is linked to the mainland by a long causeway and so most accessible to those travelling by car. You can camp free at a number of idyllic and primitive spots at the South Padre end of the island, accessible via Hwy 100 only. Camp on the seaward side of the dunes; the grassy areas may have poisonous rattlesnakes. Besides Galveston and Padre, the South Texas coast has hundreds of miles of coastline and various other islands.

South Texas border towns are numerous but not particularly appealing. Avoid **Laredo**: 'A dump with rip-off hotels.' **Brownsville/Matamoros** is probably the best and certainly most convenient to South Padre. 'Got free tourist card from Mexican consulate at 10th and Washington Streets in 5 mins.' For links to attractions check out: _www.ccbayarea.com_; _www.sopadre.com_; _www.south-padre-island.com_; _www.ci.corpus-christi.tx.us_.

All of the following listings use the area code for the region (361) unless otherwise stated.

Accommodation
Cheap accommodation is scarce in downtown Corpus Christi. For the best motel bargains, drive several miles south on **Leopard St** (bus #27) or I-37 (take #27 express). Campers should head for the **Padre Island National Seashore** 949-8068, $8 pn on campground incl. water or **Mustang State Park**, 749-5246. The latter offers elec, water, showers and picnic tables for $15 incl. utils or $7 for primitive camping on the beach, both + $3 pp park admission. Must pick up a camping permit from the ranger station at the park entrance.
Best Western, 5701 Padre Blvd, (800) 528-1234, From $63. Free continental bfast. Rec off peak stay.

Food
Rockport is recommended for its seafood and gumbo, while Corpus Christi, South Padre and the entire area are rich in roadside stands that sell cheap, fresh boiled

shrimp and tamales—the local speciality. Best to check out the south side, around **Staples St**, and **S Padre Island Drive**.

La Bahia, 224 N. Mesquite, 888-6555, Serves up authentic Mexican dishes at authentic prices. Open daily 7.30am-2pm, w/end 5pm-9pm.

Howard's BBQ, 1002 Antelope St, 882-1200. Ample beef and sausage plate, salad bar buffet and drink ($5). Mon-Thu 11am-3pm.

202 Bayside Bar & Grill, 202 W Whiting St, (956) 761-8481. Platters from $11. Open daily 11am-12pm.

Tom & Jerry's, 3212 Padre Blvd, (956) 761-8999, offers original American food with burgers from $5 and steaks at $17. Open daily 11am-10pm.

Charlotte Plummer's, 202 N Fulton Beach Rd, 729-1185, open daily 11am-9.30/10pm. Seafood galore. *www.charlotteplummers.com*.

Of interest
North and east of Padre Island and Corpus Christi is the **Aransas Wildlife Refuge**, (361) 286-3559, $3 pp or $5 per vehicle, where you can go by boat from Rockport and see (in season and at a distance) the world's remaining 150 whooping cranes (bird), best time to see them is btwn Oct & Mar. Open daylight hours.

Information/Travel
South Padre Tourist Bureau, 600 Padre Blvd, (800) 767-2373. *www.sopadre.com*.
Corpus Christi Visitors Bureau, main office at 1823 N. Chaparrel, (800) 678-6232/766. *www.corpuschristi-tx-cvb.org*.
Greyhound, 702 N Chaparral, (800) 231-2222/882 2516.

EL PASO and **BIG BEND** The biggest Mexican border city, El Paso feels neither Hispanic nor Texan. Originally known as 'Franklin', the first Europeans came to the area in 1581.

Backed by mountains, El Paso's main focus is the Rio Grande River, where early Spanish expeditions used to cross. The river also serves as one of the country's most casual borders. Other than sampling the sleazy delights of Ciudad Juarez, there's little reason to tarry in El Paso.

It can serve as a base for Carlsbad Caverns in New Mexico or Texas' national parks. 'Unless your journey necessitates going via El Paso, take another route.' A one-stop information centre is located at *www.elpasoinfo.com*. See also *www.elpasocvb.com* and *www.desertusa.com*.

All of the following listings use the area code for the region (915) unless otherwise stated.

Accommodation
HI-El Paso International Hostel in the **Gardner Hotel,** 311 E Franklin Ave, 532-3661. Small dorms, beautiful, spacious kitchen, common room with pool table, TV and couches for lounging and socialising in basement. From $22. Rsvs.
Gateway Hotel, 104 S Stanton St, 532-2611. Close to San Jacinto Sq. Clean, spacious large beds and closets. Diner downstairs. Check out 4pm. S-$33, D-$38.

Food
Burritos are the undisputed local speciality!
Forti's Mexican Elder Restaurant, 321 Chelsea Dr, close to I-10, 772-0066. The fajitas and shrimps are 'superb'. Dishes from $9. Sun-Thu 9am-9pm, Fri-Sat 9am-11pm.
H&H Coffee Shop, 701 E Yandell, 533-1144. Adjoins H&H Car Wash; nip in for a quick cuppa! Renowned for its hangover cure (Sat only). Mon-Sat 7am-3pm.
Smitty's, 6219 Airport Rd, 772-5876. Tender brisket, lunch and dinner served. Mon-Sat 10am-9pm.

Of interest

Simply stroll through downtown to see the colourful remnants of **El Paso's Wild West history**. Hop aboard one of the **Border Trolleys,** 544-0062, that depart from El Paso Civic Center and the Convention Centre, for a whirlwind exploration of the streets. $13 round trip.

Ciudad Juarez, 4th largest city in Mexico, is poor by western standards, though wealthy by Mexican standards. The shopping for leather and rugs is excellent. Three bridges span the Rio Grande between El Paso and Ciudad Juarez. The main bridge is Cordova, which is free. Other bridges charge-usually under $5. 'Mexican immigration didn't even give us a glance.' 'You can also ride the bus over. If you do, hold on to your passport and don't surrender your DS-2019 to the US authorities.'

El Paso Museum of History, moving to Cleveland Square 2006. Tells the story of the Indian, Conquistador, Vaquero (Mexican cowboy), cowbo, and the US Cavalryman, all of whom fought and bled to win the Southwest. Tue 2-5pm, Wed & Thu till 12, free/donations. _www.elpasotexas.gov/history_.

Fort Bliss Replica Museum, in north El Paso, Pleasanton Rd & Pershing Drive, 568-4518, houses several museums on the base exploring the history of the Civil War, the 3rd Armored Cavalry, and air defence. Open daily 9am-4.30pm. Free, donations requested.

Missions: El Paso has three missions located along the Camino Real, (the Royal Highway, considered to be the oldest road in the US), 90 years older than the more famous ones in California. The jewel is **Nuestra Senora del Carmen (Yseleta Mission),** 100 block of Old Pueblo Rd, originally built in Mexico, only now in the US because of changes in the flow of the river—the border is said to lie at the deepest channel of the Rio Grande. Open daily.

San Jacinto Plaza, the historic city square plays host to street musicians. In Feb, El Paso hosts the Southwestern Livestock Show & Rodeo, 532-1401. _www.elpasostockshow.com_.

Information

El Paso Convention and Visitors Bureau, 1 Civic Center Plaza, (800) 351-6024/534-0600. Open 8am-5pm. _www.elpasocvb.com_.

Travel

Sun Metro, 533-1220. Local bus service, basic fare $1, departs from San Jacinto Plaza.

Amtrak, Union Station 700 San Francisco St, (800) 872-7245.

Greyhound, 200 W San Antonio, (915) 542-1355. 24 hrs.

El Paso International Airport, (915) 780-4749, about 5 miles NE of downtown. Take #31/35 to 5 points terminal and change onto the #33. _www.elpasointernationalairport.com_.

Yellow Cab, 533-3433.

BIG BEND NATIONAL PARK is a 329 mile drive southeast of El Paso and it is recommended that you take at least a couple of days to visit this preserved desert environment. The nearest transport links are at **Alpine,** 100 miles away, served by Greyhound and Amtrak. The park, situated on the bend of the Rio Grande, encompasses spectacular deserts, mountains and deep limestone canyons. The river serves as the border with Mexico for a thousand miles in Texas, so this is also where countries and cultures meet. The extreme climate, over 100 degrees in summer, but often freezing in winter, and the isolation of the park, mean that visits should be carefully planned. You will need to be almost totally self-sufficient for the time you are here.

Recommended sites include the **Ross Maxwell Scenic Drive**, which takes you down to the Rio Grande and is the trailhead for the short hike to **Santa Elena Canyon**. There are over 200 miles of hiking trails in the park. More information can be found at the **Visitors Centres** at **Panther Junction** and in **Chisos Basin**.

Accommodation/Food

Park Information is (915) 477-2251, and the entrance fee is $15 per vehicle, good for 7 days. Camping fac. WC, running water, grills, picnic tables, no hook-ups. RVs over 20 ft not rec. **Accommodation** is at the **Chisos Mountain Lodge**, (915) 477-2291, or at three developed **campgrounds**, $10; water but no hook-up; no rsvs, first-come, first served. Primitive camping is also available with a permit. _www.nps.gov/bibe_.

Terlingua, on the western edge of the park, is an old mining ghost town quietly emerging as an alternative tourist centre, and a base for adventurers rafting the Rio Grande. A couple of restaurants and cafes live up to the New Age/South Western traditions with the stunning scenery as a backdrop. Especially recommended is the **Starlight Theatre, Bar and Restaurant,** 371-2326. Stay in nearby Lajitas. A reconstructed Old West Resort town, **Lajitas** RV Park, Hwy 170, (915) 424-3467 has tent sites for $10. If you a visit this place then pay a visit to the local mayor—a beer-drinking goat who lives outside the **Lajitas Trading Post**. _www.terlinguatx.com_. _www.lajitas.com_.

GUADALUPE MOUNTAINS NATIONAL PARK located 110 miles east of El Paso, the rocky and rugged terrain includes **El Capitan**, a 8085 ft cliff, and 8749 ft **Guadalupe Peak**, highest in Texas. Also worth a stop is the **McKittrick Canyon**. For hikers, there are 80 miles of trails, some steep, mostly rugged, but there are also chances to view desert wildlife.

The park has two main campgrounds, **Pine Springs** and **Dog Canyon**, $8, no rsvs. The park's 10 **Background Camps** are primitive but free. All camping requires free permit, avail. from the **Visitors Centre** located at Pine Springs, open 8am-6pm, longer in summer. Park Information is (915) 828-3251, no entrance fee, _www.nps.gov/gumo_.

Nearest lodging is in **White's City**, New Mexico, 35 miles away.

LUBBOCK   The 'Chrysanthemum Capital of the World,' with over 80,000 plants throughout the city, is better known as home of the **Red Raiders** (Texas Tech Football Stadium) and **Walk of Fame**, 8th St and Ave A; a collection of plaques commemorating West Texas stars. **Buddy Holly's Memorial** was Buddy's birthplace and also where he is buried. **Mackenzie Park,** off E Broadway and Ave A is home to wild prairie dogs which once could be found all over the state, and also to the **Joyland Amusement Park**. _www.joylandpark.com_.

BUNACers recommend the **Midnight Rodeo**, 7301 S. University, 745-2813; closed Mon, a huge dance bar in the middle of town, for the traditional Texan two-step and lots of drinks specials. Open from 6pm. There are plenty of chain motels in the area offering reasonable **lodging**, and the **Convention and Visitors Bureau** is at 1301 Broadway, (800) 692-4035/747-5232. _www.lubbocklegends.org_; _www.lubbocklegends.com_.

NATIONAL PARKS—SOME TOP CHOICES

It can take a lifetime to visit all of North America's 522 National Parks. If you're planning to go to several in the United States, think about buying The National Parks Pass ($50, valid from first use for a year) from any one of the **parks** charging entrance fees. Call (888) GO-PARKS or visit _www.nationalparks.org_. Before you go, check the U.S. National Park Service homepage at _www.nps.gov_ and the Canadian Parks website at _www.pc.gc.ca_. If you only have time to see a few, here are some of the best:

Acadia/Maine, (207) 288-3338. America miniaturized with beaches, forests, lakes, and Mt Cadillac, the highest point on the Eastern seaboard. $5/person, $25/vehicle. _www.nps.gov/acad_.

Banff and Jasper/Alberta, (403) 762-1550. Banff, Canada's oldest park, offers mountain grandeur and hot mineral springs. Alongside is Jasper with more mountains, glaciers and lakes. Columbia ice fields, between the two, is the place to spot various big-horned sheep, moose, bears and wapiti (elk). Breathtaking. ($8/person, $16/2-7 persons a day or $55/person, $/2-4 persons for an annual pass to all of the Canadian Parks East of Manitoba). _www.pc.gc.ca/pn-np/ab/banff/index e.asp_

Everglades/Florida, (305) 242-7700. Covers 1.5 million acres and about one seventh of the entire Everglades. Wildlife is diverse with panthers, bobcats and alligators and bug sprays essential! The public seems to agree that it has a lot to offer, over a million visit the park every year. $5/person or $25/vehicle. _www.nps.gov/ever_.

Fundy/New Brunswick, (506) 887-6000. World famous high tides, inter tidal zones and great hiking in the backcountry of Acadian Forest. $6/person $15/vehicle. _www.pc.gc.ca/pn-np/nb/fundy_.

Waterton-Glacier International Peace Park, (406) 888-7800. 10,000 years ago glaciers carved peaks, valleys and ripples here. 50 glacier crumbs remain. Straddles the US/Canadian border but cooperative management protects the park's environment. $10/day or $25/year. _www.nps.gov/glac_.

Grand Canyon/Arizona, (928) 638-7888. Deeper, wider and more colourful than you could have thought possible; you cannot prepare yourself for this one. $10/person, $20/vehicle. If possible, see it in full context with Bryce and Zion National Parks. _www.nps.gov/grca_.

Great Smoky Mountains/Tennessee, (865) 436-1200. Highly accessible home to Clingman's Dome, the highest point in the Smokies. Try any of the 850 or so miles of hiking paths along the Appalachian Trail. No fees.

Olympic/Washington, (360) 565-3130. Boasts three ecosystems in one park. Glacier topped mountain ranges, with Mt Olympus, the tallest at 7,965 ft, grey whales along the Pacific coast and rainforests providing cover inland. Due to its isolation the park has several unique species of plant and animal. Look out for the endemic, Olympic Salamander and Yellow-Pine Chipmunk. The original plant species are also beautiful, especially Flet's violet. Free entry. _www.nps.gov/grsm_.

Yellowstone/Wyoming, (307) 344-7381. The world's first national park and largest in the Lower 48, its myriad attractions include Old Faithful and other geysers, wildlife, mud pots and much more. $10/person, $20/vehicle. _www.nps.gov/yell_.

Yosemite/California, (209) 372-0200. Home of the incredible El Capitan, Half Dome, Bridal Veil Falls, Glacier Point and redwoods. $10/person, $20/vehicle. _www.nps.gov/yose_.

To avoid the crowds and high prices that have plagued the National Parks in recent years, consider visiting in the off-season. Another option would be to visit one of the less touristy but perhaps equally beautiful parks, such as Washington's **North Cascades**, Alaska's **Glacier Bay**, Oregon's **Crater Lake**, North Dakota's **Theodore Roosevelt** or Minnesota's **Voyageurs.**

THE SOUTH

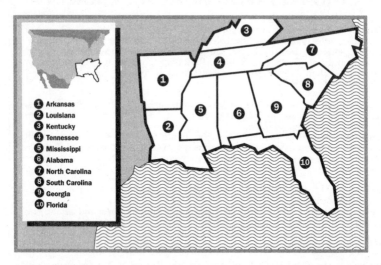

Arkansas
Louisiana
Kentucky
Tennessee
Mississippi
Alabama
North Carolina
South Carolina
Georgia
Florida

Although Northerners may hate to admit it, the South has given birth to much of the best American music, architecture and literature. The plaintive call of the blues rose up from the Mississippi Delta and from the hills of Appalachia came the early strains of country music. Exuberant jazz echoed from the alleys of New Orleans; from Memphis burst rock n' roll. In contrast to the pristine architecture of Puritan New England, Spanish and French sensibilities contributed to the refined antebellum architecture of the Deep South. Together, romantic notions of the plantation, the isolation of agricultural life, and rigid social and racial stratification have inspired the works of Southern writers such as Chopin, Faulkner, Welty, Williams and Wright.

The legacy of slavery has also been one of the defining characteristics (and burdens) governing the development of southern society. Today, remnants of the Underground Railroad, the active struggle to help free slaves to follow the 'drinking gourd' to the North and Canada, still exist in some southern states. Go to _www.freedomcenter.org_ to find the various locations of these sites.

From a Southern perspective, the Civil War was a Northern attack upon a different way of life—a planters' aristocracy dependent on slavery. The passions the war unleashed are difficult to appreciate. The fight was to the death, and most of the old South was in fact destroyed. Although the United States had one-sixth the population in 1860 that it had in 1960, six times as many men died in the Civil War as in Vietnam. In spite of their defeat, Virginian General Robert E. Lee and Confederate President Jefferson Davis are still honored with statues and parades in the central square of every Southern city. _www.jeffersondavis.net._ These celebrations have recently come under fire from civil rights activists as symbolic of the more ugly racial realities and motives behind the war. _www.civilwarhome.com._

Only recently has the South begun to come out from under these economic and racial clouds of the war. The dream of equal rights, deferred since the Civil War, was brought closer to realization by the hard-fought civil rights movement that forced legislative and social change in the 1960s. Today black mayors run many cities, economic success is open to all and schools and businesses are integrated, but signs of a 'white backlash' remain, revealing that tensions still run deep. Meanwhile high technology in Alabama, banking in Atlanta and research in North Carolina testify to the growing economic power of the 'New South'. In fact, the rapidly developing south has had to rein in urban sprawl that continues to threaten remaining rural and wilderness spaces.

The entire Gulf coast of this region was hit severely by a force-5 hurricane, Katrina, in September 2005. The most destructive storm ever to hit the US, caused the evacuation of many coastal communities including the entire population of New Orleans, the complete destruction of parts of the city and neighboring towns, and extensive damage to the local economy including the port, off-shore oil operations, and coastal casinos. Recovery and reconstruction of the area and its economy have been continuing since then, and, while dampened, the exuberant spirit of the delta region will undoubtedly live on.

While you explore its quirks, the South is bound to treat you well. Being polite counts down here. You won't be travelling long before you are introduced to simple, but gracious 'Southern Hospitality'. Perhaps the sultry weather contributes to a slower, more Mediterranean pace of life. If you travel in the summer, be prepared to sweat it out. It will be hot and humid as you never imagined possible. Do make sure to sample Southern cooking—hearty food, like pecan pie, chicken and catfish fried to crisp, juicy perfection. And don't pass up spicy Cajun cooking in New Orleans! See _www.dixiedining.com._

ALABAMA - The Yellowhammer State

Fifty years ago the ways of the Old South were dear to the 'Heart of Dixie', (so called because the old $10 notes issued here before the Civil War bore the word 'dix', French for ten). Segregation was still the law; Governors stood in the doorways of white schools barring blacks. The world's attention focused on Alabama's racism in 1955 when blacks, led by a young minister named Martin Luther King, Jr, began a peaceful revolt against the Jim Crow laws that walled them in. Today, the civil rights struggle has borne fruit in the form of integrated buses and schools and the first elected black officials since reconstruction. _www.thekingcenter.org._

Economic changes have been as far-reaching. Share-cropping and agrarian poverty still exist, but King Cotton no longer rules Alabama's economy. Medical research in Birmingham, aircraft engines in Mobile and rockets from Huntsville are major industries. Tourism follows close behind, thanks to the Gulf Coast, the Tennessee Valley lake country in the north, and graceful architectural touches of the Old South in Mobile and Montgomery. The humble peanut provides the base for another booming industry; there are acres of peanut fields in the southern Wiregrass area of the State, and each autumn the town of Dothan hosts the National Peanut Festival _www.nationalpeanutfestival.com._

'The State of Surprises' is home to many of America's most prominent African-Americans, including Joe Louis, the boxer, Hank Aaron, the baseball home run king, W C Handy, father of the blues, Jesse Owens, Olympic athlete, and the singer Nat King Cole. The state was the setting for the classic Oscar-winning comedy _My Cousin Vinny_ (1992) with Joe Pesci and Marisa Tomei, that starkly highlighted the cultural differences between America's north and south.

With the scenic Appalachian foothills in the north and beaches in the south, Alabama's diverse geography makes it a perfect destination for those who love the outdoors. 4 national forests (_www.nps.gov_), and 22 state parks (_www.alapark.com_) leave you with no shortage of places to camp, hike, walk, fish and hunt. _www.touralabama.org_.

The area code for Mobile is 251. Montgomery is 334. For Birmingham, use 205. If calling Huntsville, use 256.

MOBILE The flags of France, Spain, England and the Confederacy have all flown over this attractive port city on the Gulf of Mexico. The town's varied history is best reflected in the architecture of the old quarter, at its loveliest in March and April when the azaleas are in bloom. The people of Mobile have been celebrating Mardi Gras since 1703—longer than anywhere else in the US. Those who have seen it say it is second only to the one in New Orleans, 150 miles west.

The area is not as attractive as it once was. Hurricane Frederick struck in 1979, destroying many charming old buildings that have since been replaced by paper mills and typical highway eyesores.. Still, Mobile features some of the most beautiful streets in the South and _Time Magazine_ has ranked it one of the top fifteen 'hottest cities'. Hurricane Katrina struck in 2005, but most of the town's attractions appear to have escaped unscathed. _www.mobile.org_.

Accomdmodation
Olsson's Motel, 4137 Government Blvd, 661-5331. S-$40, D-$49.

Food
Rousso's, 166 S Royal St, 433-3322. Open Mon-Sat 11am-10pm. 'Good food, quite reasonably priced.' _www.roussosrestaurant.com._

Wintzell's Oyster House, 605 Dauphin St, 432-4605, and 6700 Airport Blvd, 341-1111. Lunch under $8, dinner from $11. 'Very popular place.' Sun-Thurs, 11am-10pm (Fri-Sat 11pm). _www.wintzellsoysterhouse.com._

Of interest
February is a good time to visit Mobile, when Mardi Gras is in full swing, or in March when the 27-mile **Azalea Trail** blooms. Enjoy parades, floats, costumes and the carnival atmosphere. It's nice to wander around the old squares and streets dating back to the 1700s when the French held sway in Mobile. **Bienville Sq, De Tonti Sq** and **Church Street** have been restored. Check with the **Mobile Visitor's Center** at **Fort Conde** for walking and driving maps of the neighbourhoods.

Among the houses open to the public are: **Condé Charlotte House,** 104 Theatre St, 432-4722. Tues-Sat 10am-4pm, $5 _www.alabamamuseums.org/c ccmh.htm_; and **Oakleigh**, 350 Oakleigh Place, 432-1281, 1833 antebellum mansion furnished by the

Historic Society, *www.azaleacity.com/oakleigh,* $5, $3 w/student ID. Admission includes tours of the mansion and the nearby Creole Cottage, Mon-Sat 10am-4pm.
Alabama Constitution Village, 109 Gates Avenue, Mobile, 564-8100. Open Tue-Sat 9am-5pm. Villagers dressed in period clothing guide visitors through the reconstructed federal style buildings. *www.earlyworks.com/village.html.*
The Museum of Mobile, 111 S. Royal St, 208-7569. Exhibits cover the history of Mobile from the 17th century to the present day. Mon-Sat 9am-5pm, Sun 1-5. $5, $3 w/ student ID. *www.museumofmobile.com.*
U.S.S. Alabama **Battleship Memorial Park,** Mobile Bay, Battleship Pkwy, 433-2703. Before Katrina, you could roam around the historic WW II battleship moored here on the river along with the submarine *U.S.S. Drum.* See also the B-52 bomber *Calamity Jane,* a SR-71 Blackbird spy plane and other military exhibits. The battleship is now a state shrine. 'Can be explored from bow to stern.' $10. As of late 2005, was closed indefinitely due to 'immense damage from Katrina'. The *Drum,* however, was apparently spared from the hurricane. *www.ussalabama.com.*
Cathedral of the Immaculate Conception, 4 S Clairbourne St, 434-1565. Designed by Claude Beroujon in 1835 and now named a minor basilica. Open 7am-3pm. 'Worth a look.' *www.stainedglass.org/main_pages/sgq/cathedral.html.*
Dauphin Island, 30 miles S of Mobile, is a quiet place where you can camp, swim and wander. *www.dauphinisland.org.* Off the hwy just before the island, blooms Bellingrath Gardens, 973-2217, designed by the founder of Coca-Cola. Open 8am-5pm. *www.bellingrath.org.*
Mobile's picturesque location on Mobile Bay makes it a good place from which to explore the Gulf Shores. Relax on the 32 miles of sugar-white sand at Gulf Coast or visit Adventure Island on Orange Beach for a round of miniature golf, 24559 Perdido Beach Blvd, 974-1500. To get there, take I-65 to the Gulf Shores Pkwy. *minigolf.golfdirectory.biz.*

Information
Mobile Visitor Center/Fort Condé Welcome Center, 150 S Royal St, (800) 252-3862. Inside reconstructed 1724 fort complete with cannons and costumed guides. Open Mon-Fri 8am-5pm and for conventions. *www.mobile.org.*
Alabama Visitor's Bureau, 1 South Water St. 968-7511. For general info call (800) 252-2262. *www.800alabama.com.*

Internet access
Kinkos, 3980 Airport Bvld, 344-1122, $12 per hr.

Travel
Amtrak, 11 Government St, 432-4052/(800) 872-7245. Daily 5.30am-midnight.
Greyhound, 2545 Government Blvd, (800) 231-2222 or 478-6649.
Mobile Transit Authority aka The Wave, 344-6600. Major depots, Bienville Sq, Royal St parking garage, and Adams Mark Hotel. $1, transfers 50c. NB: There is no service to the airport. For a taxi call **Mobile Cab and Baggage Company,** 476-7711.

BIRMINGHAM Once known as the steel town of the South, Birmingham is now a major centre for biomedical research, finance, manufacturing, engineering, and wholesale/retail industries, representing a quarter of Alabama's entire retail sales.

The great civil rights marches of 1963 began here—protests that threw Martin Luther King, Jr. into the city's jail. Sixteen years later, Birmingham elected its first black mayor. The booming steel industry lured immigrants to Birmingham; touches of their ethnic heritages still linger. Birmingham stretches for 15 miles along the Jones Valley—be sure to take in the views from the top of nearby Shades and Red Mountains. *www.birminghamal.org.*

Accommodation
Tourway Inn, 1101 6th Ave N, 252-3921. S-$40, D-$45. TV, pool. Downtown.
Oak Mountain State Park, 620-2520. 15 miles S of Birmingham, off I-65 in **Pelham** (exit 246). 10,000 acres of thick forest offer hiking, golf, horse-riding and an 85-acre lake. Entrance $2. Sites $10.55, w/hook-up $16.65. _www.alapark.com._

Food
See _www.bhamdining.com._
Bogues, 3028 Clairmont Ave, 254-9780. Cheap diner serving southern fare. Mon-Fri 6am-2pm, w/end 6am-11:30am.
Kobe, 3501 Grandview Pkwy, 298-0200. Japanese Steakhouse and Sushi bar. Mon-Thu 11am-10pm, Fri/Sat 11am-11pm.

Of interest
Arlington Antebellum Home and Gardens—the birthplace of Birmingham, is at 331 Cotton Ave SW, 780-5656. Home features an array of 19th century southern decorative arts. $5. Tue-Sat 10am-4pm, Sun 1pm-4pm. 'Something out of old Dixie.'
The Vulcan Statue sits high atop Red Mountain; it is the largest cast iron statue in the world and in the US, is second only to the Statue of Liberty in height. Erected to honour the steel industry, Vulcan is 55 ft tall and stands on a 124-foot pedestal; his massive head alone weighs 6 tonnes. _www.vulcanpark.org._
Birmingham Civil Rights Institute, 520 16th St N, in historic civil rights district, 328-9696. Documents the Civil Rights Movement since the 1920s. More than just a museum; it also promotes ongoing research and discourse on human rights issues. Drama performances often held here at night. Tues-Sat 10am-5pm, Sun 1pm-5pm. $9, $4 w/ student ID. _www.bcri.bham.al.us._
Alabama Sports Hall of Fame, 2150 Civic Center Blvd, 323-6665, pays tribute to all-time greats such as Jesse Owens and Birmingham's own prize hitter, Willie Mays. Mon-Sat 9am-5pm. $5, $3 w/student ID. 'Arrive early.' _www.ashof.org._
Botanical Gardens, 2612 Lane Park Road, 414-3950. Rose Garden, Japanese Garden with teahouse and the largest conservatory in the Southeast. 150 types of hybrid roses. Open daily. Free. _www.bbgardens.org/media/html/home/index.php._ Across the road is **Birmingham Zoo,** 879-0408, the largest zoo in the Southeast which houses nearly 800 mammals, birds and reptilea over 100 acres. 9am-5pm daily. $11. _www.birminghamzoo.com._
Alabama Jazz Hall of Fame, in the historic, art deco Carver theater, 1631 4th Ave near 17th St, 254-2731. Find out how a Birmingham native wrote jazz anthem 'Tuxedo Junction' and browse around this collection of memorabilia. Tues-Sat 10am-5pm. $2. _www.jazzhall.com._
Reynolds Historical Library, on the U of Alabama campus, one of the top historical science libraries in the nation, has original letters from George Washington and Florence Nightingale. Mon-Fri, 8am-5pm. _www.uab.edu/reynolds._
McWane Center, 200 19th St N, 714-8300. Birmingham's newest attraction is this hands-on science museum featuring interactive displays and IMAX theatre presentations. $9 admission, $9 for IMAX, $16 for both. Open 10am-6pm Mon-Sat, Sun Noon-6pm. _www.mcwane.org._
Close to Birmingham, two miles off Hwys 72 and 43 in Colbert County is **Tuscumbia**, home of **Ivy Green**—the **Helen Keller Birthplace, (**256) 383-4066, open Mon-Sat 8:30am-4pm, Sun 1pm-4pm. $6. _www.helenkellerbirthplace.org._

Internet access
Birmingham Public Library, 1803 11th Ave S, 933-7776, free.

Information/Travel
Visitors Bureau, 2200 9th Ave N, 252-9825, (800) 962-6453. Mon-Fri 8.30am-5pm. _www.bcvb.org._
Greyhound, 619 N 19th St, (800) 231-2222. 24 hrs.

MONTGOMERY The capital of Alabama, Montgomery was once capital of the Confederacy until the honour was transferred to Richmond. The proud confederate tradition lives on in modern Montgomery; the Senate Chamber is kept just as it was the day secession was voted and the tree-shaded streets lined with ante-bellum homes carry you back a hundred and more years.

It was not until 1955, almost 100 years after the Civil War, that Rosa Parks helped to usher in a time of great social change. She was arrested here after refusing to give up her bus seat to a white male passenger. _www.grandtimes.com/rosa.html_. Montgomery blacks voted to stage a bus boycott on Dec 2, 1955, launching a new era in the civil rights protest. A young preacher named King helped organize the boycott. _www.visitingmontgomery.com_. Rosa Parks, who became known as the 'Mother of the Civil Rights Movement', died in Detroit, October 2005 aged 92. After her death she became the first woman to lie in honour in The Capitol Rotunda in Washington DC. The memorial service in Washington Cathedral was attended by thousands including Oprah Winfrey who said: 'I would not be standing here today, nor standing where I stand every day, had she not chosen to sit down'.

Accommodation
The Inn South, 4243 Inn South Ave, 288-7999. Near I-65. S-$36, D-$38.
Town Plaza, 743 Madison Ave, 269-1561, S-$40, D-$45.
Fort Toulouse Jackson Park, 7 miles N of Montgomery on Rte 6 off US 231, 567-3002. 39 campsites in woodland w/hook-up. Tents $11, RV hookup $14.

Food
Chris's Dogs, 138 Dexter Ave, 265-6850. Famous for its chili sauce. Open daily 10am-7pm. Hot-dogs $1.60, fries $1.35.
Martha's Place, 548 Sayre St, 263-9135. 'Country lunch'—entree with drink, sides, and dessert, $6. 'The only place you'll find better lemonade is in heaven'. Mon-Fri, 11am-3pm.
Montgomery Curb Market, 1004 Madison Ave, 263-6445. Sells homemade pies, fresh produce. Tue, Thurs, Sat mornings. Also try **Montgomery State Farmers' Market**, 1655 Federal Dr, 242-5350, a 28-acre complex including cafe serving breakfast and lunch, garden centre and stalls selling farm produce, home baking, and crafts. Daily 7am-6pm.

Of interest
State Capitol, Bainbridge St at Dexter Ave, 242-3935. A gold star marks the spot where Jefferson Davis was inaugurated as president of the Confederacy in February 1861. Note also the impressive murals depicting state history and the graceful hanging spiral staircases. Mon-Fri, 9am-5pm, Sat, 9am-4pm.
First White House of the Confederacy, 644 Washington Ave, across the street from the Capitol, 242-1861, contains memorabilia of Confederate President Jefferson Davis and family. Mon-Fri 8am-4.30pm. Free. 'Worthwhile.' _www.land-we-love.com/confederacy_white_house.htm_.
Civil Rights Memorial was designed by the architect of the Vietnam War Memorial in Washington, DC. Visitors can view the memorial at the corner of Washington Ave and Hull St, 965-8200. _www.splcenter.org/crm/memorial.jsp_.
Dexter Ave King Memorial Baptist Church, 454 Dexter Ave. Where Martin Luther King, Jr. was pastor for 6 years. Tours given Mon-Thurs, 10am or 2pm, Fri 10am, Sat 10:30am-1:30pm, walk-thru Sat 1:30-2:00. 263-3970. Donation appreciated. _www.dexterkingmemorial.org._
Montgomery Museum of Fine Arts, 1 Museum Dr, in W M Blount Cultural Park

off Woodmere Blvd, 244-5700. Tues-Sat 10am-5pm, Thurs 10am-9pm, Sun 12-5pm. Free. *www.fineartsmuseum.com.*

W A Gayle Space Transit Planetarium, 1010 Forest Ave in Oak Park, 241-4799. Simulated space journeys. Mon-Thurs, show at 3pm, Sun show at 2pm. $3. *montgomery.troy.edu/planet/default.cfm.*

The Alabama Shakespeare Festival, 1 Festival Dr, 271-5300. The only American Shakespeare troupe to be invited to fly the flag of Britain's RSC. Performances running from Oct-Sep. Tkts from $25. *www.asf.net.*

Scott and Zelda Fitzgerald Museum, 919 Felder Ave, 264-4222. Home to novelist F Scott and wife Zelda from October 1931 to April 1932, during which time Scott worked on *Tender is the Night.* Works of both writers on display. Wed-Fri 10am-2pm; Sat/Sun 1pm-5pm. $1.

Hank Williams Museum, PO Box 310 at nearby **Georgiana,** at Exit #114 off I-65, (334) 376-2396 contains memorabilia of the famous country singer and has a yearly festival. *www.hankmuseum.com.*

About 40 miles northeast of Montgomery is the noted **Tuskegee University,** a co-ed university founded in 1881 by former slave Booker T Washington. *www.tuskegee.edu.* For museum and tours for **Booker T Washington's home** go to historical site's visitor centre, open daily 9am-5pm, 727-3200.

Information
Montgomery Visitor Information Center, 300 Water St, 262-0013. Mon-Sat 8am-5pm, Sun 12pm-4pm.

Internet access
Montgomery Public Library, 245 High St, 240-4999, free.

Travel
Greyhound, 950 W South Blvd, 286-0658 or (800) 231-2222. 24 hrs.
Montgomery Area Transit System, 240-4012. Buses run Mon-Fri, 6am-6pm. $1-$2.
Yellow Cab, 262-5225. $1.95 first mile, $1.50 each additional mile.

HUNTSVILLE Founded by John Hunt in 1805 as the first English settlement in Alabama, this one-time sleepy town has become rather more 'spaced out'. Since 1960, it has been host to one of the state's biggest attractions, the **US Space and Rocket Center**. The Centre is now the focal point for the research and development of the NASA Space Program due to the pioneering work on the Saturn V Moon Rocket of the late German scientist Wernher von Braun. Among its many attractions is the only full-size model of the space shuttle and a 67ft domed screen showing breathtaking films of space flight. Open 9am-6pm, $14 w/o Spacedome show, (256) 837-3400. *aero.com/museums/us_space_and_rocket/wmuusr01.htm.*

It is possible to experience the wonders of the wild at the **Harmony Safari Park**. This federally licensed nature preserve holds free-ranging exotic and endangered animals including ostriches and buffalos. Sat/Sun, Apr-Oct 10am-sunset. Hobbs Island Road, go 9 miles, then turn right, (877) 726-4625.

An hour's drive west of Huntsville is **Muscle Shoals**, a town known to few people outside the music business. *www.cityofmuscleshoals.com. Time's better there* according to Deep River Blues. Several recording studios are in and around the town and musicians ranging from WC Handy to Elton John to Doc Watson have come here to play. Studio tours available free. *mssound.com/index1.html.* Call Muscle Shoals Sound, 381-2060, in advance. *www.huntsville.org.*

ARKANSAS – The Land of Opportunity

Arkansas was named after the native Quapaw Indians, who were called 'Akansea' by other tribes. The name (meaning 'South Wind') was misspelled by early French explorers – hence its present form – which is pronounced 'Ark-an-saw'. The land of opportunity was admitted to the Union in 1836 as the 25th state.

Arkansas's widely varied landscapes are home to a history rich in intriguing subplots. A trip across the state can lead from Mississippi River bottomlands to mid-America's most prominent peaks; from a legacy of Deep South cotton culture to a town on a Wild West frontier.

Eastern Arkansas, with its long hot summers and rich alluvial soil well-suited for the cultivation of tobacco, corn and cotton, became prime plantation country. Arkansas has always drawn its income from agriculture; only in the last two decades has industrial production increased substantially. A predominantly Democratic domain, and home state of Bill Clinton, Arkansas has only elected 6 Republican governors in its history— against 38 Democrats and other political representatives, including the Whigs. _www.clintonfoundation.org._

With hills, forests and the colourful Ozarks Mountains to the north, western Arkansas maintains strong frontier undertones. Settler opinion caused the state to hesitate before seceding from the Union. The Ozark and Ouachitas areas retain a strong folksy flavour with a distinct mountain culture which has left its mark on national folk art, legend and music. Although Little Rock is the geographical, legislative and commercial centre of the state, look to Hot Springs National Park and the Ozarks for the truly rustic Arkansas. _www.arkansas.com_.

The area code for Little Rock and Hot Springs is 501, for the north it's 870.

LITTLE ROCK Considered the 'heart of Arkansas', it was named after a local landmark on the bank of the Arkansas River. This one-time hunter and trapper outpost is now the state capital. Known to its residents as the 'City of Roses,' Little Rock came to the world's attention back in 1957 with the attempt to ban nine black children from the segregated Central High School. It came to everyone's attention again in 1992 when former governor Bill Clinton moved to the White House and seemingly took half the town with him. Heady days in Little Rock! Don't neglect the surrounding countryside: west of the town is Hot Springs, and to the northwest lie the Ozarks. _www.littlerock.com_.

Accommodation
Motel 6, 7501 I-30, 7 miles outside town, 568-8888, S-$35, D-$50. Pool, AC.
KOA Campground, in North Little Rock on Crystal Hills Road, 758-4598, 7 miles from downtown btwn exit 12 on I-430 & exit 1-48 on I-48. Sites $26, w/hook-up $30, cabins $37. _www.koakampgrounds.com._

Food
River Market, btwn Commerce and Rock Sts on E Markham, 375-2552. Fresh crops, food stops and speciality shops by the Arkansas River. Sun 10am-5pm, Mon-Sat 7am-6pm. _www.rivermarket.info._

David Family Kitchen, 2301 Bdway, 371-0141. Serves Southern-style big-portion meals at low cost. Mon-Fri 6am-6pm, Sun 6-4.

Of interest

The only city to have three capitol buildings. The hand-hewn, oak-log territorial capitol is part of the **Historic Arkansas Museum**, a collection of 14 restored buildings dating to the 1820s, E 3rd and Scott Sts, 324-9351, hourly tours, 9am-5pm, $2.50. _www.arkansashistory.com_. The aristocratic **Old State House**, 300 West Markham St, 324-9685, regarded as one of the most beautiful antebellum structures in the South, was used from 1836 to 1912. Mon-Sat 9am-5pm, Sun 1pm-5pm. Free. _www.oldstatehouse.com._ The present **State Capitol,** Woodlawn and Capitol Ave, 682-5080, was based on the US Capitol in Washington. Don't miss the beautiful gardens and the brass doors made by Tiffany's of New York. Daily, self-guided tours with audio-headsets, 7am-5pm Mon-Fri, 10am-3pm, Sat/Sun. _www.sos.arkansas.gov/tours.html_.

The **Quapaw Quarter,** a 9 sq mile area, is the original Little Rock with many 19th century additions, both business and residential, including the Governor's Mansion _www.arkansasgovernorsmansion.com;_ the **Pike Fletcher-Terry Mansion**, home of three colourful and famous Arkansans, and now a part of the **Arkansas Arts Center**, 372-4000. Daily 10am-5pm, free. _www.arkarts.com._ Included in the quarter is the Old Arsenal in **MacArthur Park**, birthplace of Gen Douglas MacArthur. Also of interest is the **Arkansas Museum of Discovery**, 500 E. Markham St. 396-7050. _www.amod.org_. 9am-5pm daily, $6.35. Of the 49 state parks in Arkansas, **Burns Park**, 758-1424, in N Little Rock is one of the country's largest, over 1,500 acres, offering camping, golf, tennis, hiking, and more. _www.arkansasstateparks.com._

Riverfront Park btwn the Statehouse Plaza and the Arkansas River has lighted brick walkways, fountains, benches, and a pavilion with a pictorial display of the city's history. The park is also the site of **Riverfest** on Memorial Day Weekend, 371-4770. _www.riverfestarkansas.com._ The distinctive **Clinton Presidential Center** jutts out over the Arkansas River – 'building a bridge', in the former president's words. Open 9am-5pm, Sun 1-5pm. $7. _www.clintonfoundation.org/cpc-index.htm_.

Information/Travel

Little Rock Convention and Visitors Bureau, Markham and Broadway, 376-4781, has maps, info, and helpful staff. Mon-Fri, 8.30am-5pm. _www.littlerock.com._
Greyhound, 118 E Washington St in North Little Rock, 372-3007 or (800) 231-2222.
Amtrak, 1400 W Markham & Victory Sts, 372-6841/(800) 872-7245.
Local Transit Authority, 375-1163. Basic fare $1.10. To reach the airport, take the E6 bus from 4th and Louisiana. Taxis to the airport cost around $12. Call 374-0333.

Internet access

Little Rock Public Library, 823 N Buchanan St, 663-5457, free.

HOT SPRINGS NATIONAL PARK Pure and bubbling up from the ground at 143 degrees, the waters of the Hot Springs mix with cool water from natural reservoirs to create the ideal 100 degree bath. The hybrid town/national park is cradled between two peaks in the Ouachita Mountains, about an hour south of Little Rock on US 70. From February to April, lodging and bathing costs rise to match the demand of flocking tourists.

Although actual bathing is prohibited in the park, the Visitors Center does offer a free **Thermal Features Tour** during the summer, (mornings only in very hot weather) and information on private bathhouses during the rest of the year. Located at 369 Central, in the middle of Bathhouse Row, the center is open daily 9am-6pm in July, 9am-8pm Fri/Sat, 624-3383. Camping in the park is $10 per night, no showers or hook-ups though. Elsewhere on the Row, look for baths for about $18-$20 and massages as well as a string of moderately-priced motels. Rooms start at around $25 but the prices double from Feb-April. Cheaper lodging can be had at the motels clustered on Hwys 7 and 88 or at one of several campsites, including two nearby state parks. Contact the **Hot Springs Convention and Visitors Bureau**, 321-2835, (800) 772-2489. _www.hotsprings.org._

THE OZARKS The once-majestic Ozark Mountains have softened into attractive wooded hills and limestone bluffs, refreshed by gushing springs and rivers. It's a good area for white water canoeing, fishing, hiking, cycling and camping, or just getting away from it all. The **Ozark National Forest** is bound on the east by the **White River** and on the west by the **Buffalo National River**. Featured here are **Blanchard Springs Cavern**, **Cove Lake** and **Mount Magazine**, the highest point in the state. _www.fs.fed.us/oonf/ozark._ Stop at the **Ozark Folk Center** in **Mountain View**, 870-269-3871, for Ozark music and crafts. Open 10am-5pm daily. Music shows 7.30pm-9.30pm. _www.ozarkfolkcenter.com_.

Summers are very hot, and don't forget to arm yourself with mosquito repellent. Best months to visit are August and September when it's cooler, drier and bugless, or in October, when the trees don their spectacular autumn foliage.

When visiting the area, make the small university town of **Fayetteville** your home base. And don't forget to wear red—the town explodes with pride for its famed Arkansas Razorback athletic teams. _www.fayettevilletourism.com._ Also worth a stop is the Victorian spa town of **Eureka Springs**. _www.eurekasprings.com._ Fashioned like a village in the Bavarian Alps, **Eureka Springs** has its own version of the Oberammergau passion play, _The Great Passion Play_, every year from April to October—just look for the 7 storey tall Christ, weighing in at 2 million pounds. Tkts $23-$25, (800) 882-7529. _www.greatpassionplay.org._

If you want to leave the natural state with more than just pleasant memories, visit the **Crater of Diamonds State Park** in **Murfreesboro**, (870) 285-3113, open 8am-8pm. For $5, you can scour the park's 36 acres for diamonds and other precious and semi-precious stones—and you get to keep what you find. Over 70,000 diamonds have been found there, including the largest diamond ever uncovered in the US. _www.craterofdiamondsstatepark.com._

FLORIDA - The Sunshine State

Still beautiful although in some places a little damaged by the successive hurricanes of 2004 and 2005, definitely tacky, over-touristed and overflowing with Miami-sized vices, Florida draws sunseekers young and old from around the world. The climate is warm and gentle, the beaches broad and sandy, the citrus plentiful. Ponce de Leon arrived in 1513 and named this land after the Spanish for Easter—Pascua Florida, having come to the easy conclusion that the Fountain of Youth could be found here. Students from around the country flock here during Spring Break, while senior citizens reclaim their childhood in the sun. High-rise resorts, nightclubs and retirement communities dominate.

Due to its southerly location and plantation-rich panhandle, Florida was one of the hardcore Confederate states. But Florida wasn't entirely plantation country—the southern part of the state remained tropical wilderness. In some areas, such as the swampy Everglades, it's still that way today. During America's revolution, conservative Brits in the northern states fled the conflict by migrating here. Today the state bears few reminders of traditional Dixie culture, but shows its southern hospitality by welcoming tourists from all over the US and Canada. Florida has also become a popular destination for European travellers, competing with Spain for northern Europe's summer holidaymakers.

Overdevelopment has created its fair share of problems. Rapacious real estate developers have littered the beaches with bland highrise hotels. The buccaneers who plundered the coasts in the 1700s have given way to the drug lords of the 1980s and 90s. Although authorities have reacted strongly by implementing ultra-strict drug laws, the problem persists. Florida's Spanish heritage lives on in the ethnically rich population. Spanish is as common as English in Dade County where the hispanic population weighs in at over 55 percent, including a sizable group of Cubans. Most people who call Florida home did not grow up in the state. The tourism-based economy has prevented a developed sense of community.

If you try hard, you may be able to ignore all the bronzed beach babes, the klatches of complaining New York retirees and rowdy confederates. Once you catch a glimpse of Florida's stunning beauty—primeval Everglades, palms, mangroves, and tropical vegetation and miles of sandy beaches groomed by warm seas, plus Cape Kennedy Space Center and the vast empire of Walt Disney World ... well, you'll be hooked. Take full advantage of the underwater world available in Florida. Look at the main website for more information.

Note: All hotel prices are for the summer/autumn season. Winter/spring rates are generally double. Shop around for cheap car rental deals, particularly off season, and also good airfares to and from the northern states. _www.flausa.com_.

The Area Code for the Panhandle and the Northern Coast is 904, for Daytona Beach it's 386, Space Coast is 321; Central Florida it's 407 and 561; Ft Lauderdale 954; Miami and the Keys 305; for Tampa use 813; and for St. Petersburg it's 727.

THE NORTHEAST COAST The most popular Florida coast where history meets tourists head-on. It begins unimpressively near the Georgia border in the port city of **Jacksonville**. The only site worth seeing is the **Fort Caroline National Monument**, 12713 Fort Caroline Rd, which marks the 1564 demise of the Huguenot Colony. Open daily 9am-5pm, free, 641-7155. _www.jacksonvilleflorida.com/Parks/fortcaroline.asp_. Also take time to visit nearby Amelia Island's delightful white sand havens at **Fernandina Beach** and **Fort Clinch State Park**. _www.ameliaisland.org._

St. Augustine, 40 miles further south, started as a Spanish colony in 1565 and outlasted a jealous rivalry with the French settlers to the north. Pointedly proud of being the oldest city in the United States, the place works diligently to commercialise its heritage. It is, however, worth investigating the region's spooky side by utilising the **Ghosts Tours of St Augustine** (riding, sailing or walking) 461-1009, $10-35. _www.ghosttoursofstaugustine.com._ By Florida standards, this is a tranquil town, picturesquely set on a quiet bay. _www.see-staugustine.com._

Accommodation
Inexpensive hotels are difficult to find—especially in summer. Your best bet here may be camping.
International Haus, 32 Treasury St, 808-1999. Near Greyhound Station. Dorm rooms $18, private rooms Mon-Fri $55, Sat-Sun $65. Check-in after 12pm.
North Beach Campground, 824-1806, 4 miles N of town, on west side of A1-A. $38 for two, XP-$3. 'Best campsite in the USA—jungle-type setting.' Rsvs nec at w/ends. _www.northbeachcamp.com._

Food
St. George Street Eatery, 3 St. George St., 824-8914. Daily 10am-5pm. Burgers and subs from $4.

Of interest
Among the old Spanish buildings in St. Augustine are the **Castillo de San Marcos** _www.nps.gov/casa_, the **Cathedral of St Augustine, Mission of Nombre de Dios** _www.missionandshrine.org_, **Old Spanish Inn, Oldest House** _www.staugustinehistoricalsociety.org_, **Old Store Museum** and the **Old Slave Market.** A 208 ft stainless steel cross marks the spot where the pioneer Spaniards landed in 1565, although the present mission church dates only from earlier last century.
The Spanish Quarter, 825-6830, is the restored area of the old city. Blacksmiths' shops, crafts shops, and morning cooking demonstrations can be had for the $6.89 admission. 'A lot of it is disappointing, however, since a number of the lovely old buildings are now the home of junk and trash shops.' 9am-5.30pm daily. _www.historicstaugustine.com/csq/history.html._ If you haven't had enough of Spain yet, you'll want to catch the **Days in Spain Fiesta,** held in the heart of the city every September when St. Augustine celebrates its birthday. Tourist-trap museums—the wax museum, Ripley's Believe it or Not, etc., abound.
Nearby on Hwy A1-A to the south is **Alligator Farm,** 824-3337. Established 1893, the farm isn't just another man-vs-gator wrestling/souvenir stand but rather a place where people actually learn the difference between a crocodile and alligator and more. Open daily 9am-6pm, $17.95, 20% discount coupon available on website. _www.alligatorfarm.com._

Information/Travel accommodation
Convention and Visitors Bureau, 88 Riberia St, (800) 829-1711, 8am-5pm Mon-Fri. _www.visitoldcity.com._
Greyhound, 100 Malaga St, 829-6401/(800) 231-2222. St Petersburg, Mon-Thu $92 r/t, w/end $98 r/t.

Internet access
St John's County Public Library, 1960 N Ponce de Leon Blvd, 823-2650, free.

DAYTONA BEACH Daytona Beach stretches out along the old Buccaneers' Trail, fifty miles south of Saint Augustine. The fast ships of the buccaneers have been replaced by the fastest cars of the NASCAR circuit. The Daytona International Speedway draws the best racers in the world, and the warm Feb-Apr temperatures draw thousands of US students on Spring Break. _www.daytonabeach.com._

Accommodation

Rates are highest in summer and lowest after Labor Day. After Labor Day—
'haggle'. There are many hotels on the beach, among those recommended:

Candlelight Motel, 1305 S Ridgewood Ave, 252-1142. Rooms $47, XP-$5. 'Loves
having Brits.'

Lido Beach Motel, 1217 S Atlantic, 255-2553. S-$35 D-$45 w/bath, shower, TV.
'Basic, clean rooms. Short walk to main pier and few seconds from beach.'

Ocean Court Motel, 2315 S Atlantic, (800)-532-7440. From $58 (no extra to share for
BUNACers, or 10% discount), great rates on efficiencies, balconies, ocean view
rooms all the time, rates drop in mid-August. *www.oceancourt.com*.

Skyway Motel, 906 S Atlantic Ave, 252-7377. S-$25-30, D-$35-40, XP-$5, opposite
beach.

Surfview Motel, 401 S Atlantic, 253-1626. S-$38, D-$45. $10 key deposit.

Camping: Daytona Beach Campground, 4601 Clyde Morris Blvd, 761-2663. From
I-95, take exit 86A. Sites $24 for two, $30 w/hook-up, XP-$5. 7th night free. 5 miles
from beach. Also **Tomoka State Park,** 676-4050. Tent site $11, $14 w/hook-up. **Nova
Campground,** 1190 Herbert St in Port Orange, 767-0095. Tent site $16, $18-22
w/hook-up, XP-$3. Various other grounds at Flagler Beach.
www.floridastateparks.org.

Food/Entertainment

Aunt Catfish, west end Port Orange Causeway, 767-4768. Name says it all.
Seafood, burgers, BBQ, $8-$18. Sunday brunch $12. Mon-Sat 11.30am-9.30pm, Sun
9am-2pm. *www.auntcatfish.com.*

Ocean Deck, 127 S Ocean Ave, 253-5224. Reasonably priced menu served 11am-
2.30am, live music most nights, karaoke Sat/Sun at 4pm—plus 4 beach volleyball
courts! *www.oceandeck.com.*

Oyster Pub, 555 Seabreeze Blvd, 255-6348. Sandwiches ($5-$7), seafood ($8-$16)—
or try the raw oysters: $6.95 p/doz, $3.50 p/doz happy hr, 4pm-7pm. 11.30am-3am
daily. *www.oysterpub.com.*

Sweetwaters, 3633 Halifax Dr in Port Orange, 761-6724. Lunch from $6.50, dinner
from $8, daily 11.30am-10pm.

Of interest

With major automobile and motorcycle races scattered throughout the year,
Daytona International Speedway, 1801 Volusia Ave is always going at full throttle.
The Daytona 500, one of the premier races in the US, caps off Speed Week in mid-
February. Tkts to any of the races normally start at approx $70. Call 253-7223 for
race details. *www.daytonaintlspeedway.com*.

But it's probably the 23 miles of white sand, not the 500 miles of auto racing, that
brought you to the **'World's Most Famous Beach'. Downtown Daytona** is right in
the middle. The bulk of the crowds congregate near Main St and Seabreeze Blvd
though quieter spots can be found to the north and south. A variety of shops in the
commercial district rent surf boards while shops along the community's western
boundary, the Halifax River, rent sail boards and jet skis. Although overnight
camping on the beach is illegal, drivers can take cars onto the beach and roam its
length 8am-7pm; the fee is $5 per car. Be careful when sunbathing!
www.volusia.org/beach. **Ponce de Leon Inlet Lighthouse,** 4931 S Peninsula Dr, 10
miles south of Daytona Beach, offers self-guided tours of the second tallest
lighthouse on the eastern US at 175 ft. Call 761-1821 for info. Open 10am-8pm, close
at 9pm, $5. *www.ponceinlet.org.*

Sport

Daytona Beach offers a wide variety of sporting activities both on land and in the
water. Sailing, surfing, scuba diving, and jet skiing are popular off-shore, while
everything from skateboarding to karate can be found along the boardwalk and

beyond. Baseball fans should head to the **Jackie Robinson Ballpark**, 105 E Orange Ave, 257-3172, home of the **Daytona Cubs**, the Chicago Cubs Class-A affiliate in the Florida State League. Tkts $6 general. *www.daytonacubs.com.*

Information/Travel
Convention and Visitors Bureau, 126 E Orange Ave, 255-0415 or (800) 854-1234. Mon-Fri 9am-5pm. *www.daytonabeach.com.*
Amtrak, 100 North Atlantic Avenue, Fairfield Hilton, (800) 872-7245.
Greyhound, 138 S Ridgewood Ave, 255-7076 or (800) 231-2222. A long way from the beach.
Voltran Transit Company, 761-7700, bus service around county and trolley through city. Fare $1.

Internet access
Holly Hill Public Library, 1066 Ridgewood Ave, 239-6454. Free. Call ahead to reserve time. Open Tue-Sat 9am-5pm.

SPACE COAST Space is America's final frontier—the closest you can get to it for now is halfway down the Atlantic side of the Florida peninsula on the Space Coast, the home of the US space program. Because of its close proximity to Orlando and Daytona Beach, the area from Titusville to Melbourne has become a primary stop for anyone travelling through the state. And because it plays second to the other cities' better known attractions, the Space Coast is one of the better values in the state. But be aware of the shuttle launch schedule—lodging prices skyrocket.

Visit **Titusville**, home of the **John F. Kennedy Space Center** and **Cape Canaveral** if you want to catch a shuttle launch. But be prepared—crowds of people clog US 1; some camp out nearly a week in advance to watch lift-off. For an up-to-date launch schedule, call (800) 572-4636 (in state only). *www.kennedyspacecenter.com.*

Spaceport USA, 452-2121, is NASA's tourist centre. Admission is $30 and includes 2 IMAX movies, a museum, a rocket garden and a full-size shuttle. From I-95, take Rte 50 exit from the north, 407 exit from the south. The Spaceport is open daily from 9am-7pm. **Cocoa Beach** is the nearest Greyhound stop.

The rockets blast off over spectacular wild-life on **Canaveral National Seashore** and **Merritt Island Wildlife Refuge**. The reserve's visitor center, (386) 428-3384, is located on Rte 406 north of Titusville and is open 9am-5pm. *www.nps.gov/cana*. The seashore's southern entrance at **Playalinda Beach** is at the end of Rte 406. Primitive backcountry camping is allowed. On summer evenings, marvel at the flying fish.

Cheap **accommodation** abounds along US 1. Rooms are hard to find in the winter and spring. You'll have an easier go of it in the summer. In **Cocoa Beach**, you can stay at **Fawlty Towers**, 100 E Cocoa Beach Causeway, 784-3870. From D-$79-$99. *www.fawltytowersresort.com.* For camping, try **Jetty Park Campground**, 400 E Jetty Rd, 783-7111. Sites $18 for six w/o hook-up. 'Best location of the campgrounds.'

Down the coast from **Melbourne** at **Jensen Beach**, 700 pound sea turtles lumber ashore. The **Jensen Beach Turtle Watch** offers late night (Tue and Thurs) sea turtle egg-laying and hatching tours in June and July, suggested donation $5. Call **Hobe Sound Wildlife Refuge** to see if the turtles are up to it, (561) 546-6141, reservations necessary—tours book quickly. *hobesound.fws.gov.*

More information on the area is available through the **Cocoa Beach Area Chamber of Commerce** (*www.cocoabeachchamber.com*), 400 Fortenberry Road in Merritt Island, 459-2200 and the **Titusville Area Chamber of Commerce**, 2000 S Washington Ave, 267-3036. *www.titusville.org.*

FORT LAUDERDALE An area that has more than 300 miles of waterways has earned the title of 'Venice of America'. Don't be fooled by this nickname, however, this region is all Florida, replete with family attractions, swaying palms and wide, sandy beaches.

A once popular Spring Break destination, students from all over America would flock to Ft Lauderdale for their own 'carnevale'—where artsy masks and costume parades give way to skimpy bikinis and wet t-shirt contests. Local authorities have cracked down on the revellers in recent years, causing somewhat of an exodus to Daytona Beach and Clearwater. Still, March and April can be crazy months in this otherwise fairly sedate vacation place and yachting mecca.

To the north is the little town of **Palm Beach**, where it is illegal to own a kangaroo, or even hang a clothesline and it is impossible to find cheap lodging. Complete with its sunny palm-lined streets, elite shopping and oceanfront estates, Palm Beach is crowded with homes of Kennedys and lesser millionaires. You can look, but if you have to ask the price, you can't afford to shop in the posh stores of **Worth Ave**. For a real taste of the wealth that circulates here, walk through the **Breakers Hotel** (*www.thebreakers.com*) and stroll down **Millionaire's Row**. The home of the man who built Palm Beach is now the **Henry Flagler Museum**—an impressive demonstration of what money can buy. *www.flagler.org.*

Ft Lauderdale has undergone extensive urban redevelopment with a $1.5 billion investment—mostly in office space, but also in the **Las Olas Riverfront**, 300 SW 1st Ave, where new restaurants and shops have opened. *www.riverfrontfl.com.*

Accommodation
All rates here are for the off-season. Expect to pay more during winter and spring.
Floyd's Hostel, 462-0631. Call ahead for address and free pick-up. $35-40, $240 weekly. Laundry, central location, international students only. 'Excellent reports.' *www.floydshostel.com.*
Lafayette Motel, 2231 N Ocean Blvd, 563-5892, from $78 w/kitchenette, weekly rates available. 'Bright, simply furnished rooms with very friendly and helpful staff.'
Merrimac Hotel, 551 N Atlantic Blvd, 564-2345. From $59. Pool, right on the beach. Rsvs nec. 'Excellent.'
Seagate Apt Motel, 2909 Vistamar St, 566-2491. From $55. Pool, close to beach. 'Highly recommended.'
The Seville, 3020 Seville St, 463-7212. S-$39. 'Very clean, 5 mins from beach.' *www.sevillehotel.com.*

Food
Fast food joints and expensive restaurants live off the students who flock to Fort Lauderdale. Lots of bars and discos along Atlantic Blvd. Some have happy hours with free food.

Big Louies reputedly has the best pizza, 1990 Sunrise, 467-1166. Open daily 11am 'til 1am. Food $5-$20. _www.biglouies.com._

Southport Raw Bar, 1536 Cordova Road, (877) 646-9808. Cheap seafood and sandwiches. Open 11am-2am w/end 11-3am. Friendly staff: 'Come on down: it's great!' _www.southportrawbar.com._

Of interest
Tacky tours proliferate along the coast. Choose carefully.

Everglades Park, 21940 Griffin Road West, 434-8111. Free admission to park. 1 hr airboat tour for $16.50. Open 9am-5pm daily. _www.evergladesholidaypark.com_.

Hugh Taylor Birch State Recreation Area, 3109 E Sunrise, 564-4521. One of the few natural sights on the concrete beach, includes trails, fishing and canoeing. $4   per   car,   pedestrians $1.   Open   daily   8am-8.15pm. _www.floridastateparks.org/hughtaylorbirch/default.cfm._

Museum of Art, 1 East Las Olas Blvd, 525-5500. Features exhibitions on Auschwitz and King Tutankhamun. Daily 11am-7pm, $6, $3 w/student ID. _www.moafl.org._

Museum of Discovery and Science, 401 S W 2nd St, 467-6637. The state's most widely visited museum. Hands-on and interactive exhibits, virtual reality, and 5-storey IMAX theatre. Mon-Sat 10am-5pm, Sun noon-6pm. Museum, $9; IMAX, $9; Combination, $14. _www.mods.org_.

Information/Travel
Greater Fort Lauderdale Convention and Visitor's Bureau, 100 East Broward Boulevard, suite 200, 765-4466. _www.sunny.org._

Greyhound, 515 NE 3rd St, 764-6551/(800) 231-2222.

Amtrak, 200 SW 21st Terrace, 587-6692/(800) 872-7245.

Broward County Transit (BCT), 357-8400. $1 basic fare, all day pass $2.50. This stretch of coast is served by airports at Fort Lauderdale and West Palm Beach. The BCT runs regularly to and from Fort Lauderdale airport (#1) and connects with **Palm Beach County Transit** (233-1111) at the **Boca Mall**, and **Dade County Transit** at the **Aventura Mall**. From West Palm Beach airport, catch the #4 bus to downtown. Call (561) 272-6350 for times. _www.co.broward.fl.us/bct/welcome.htm_.

Internet access
Broward   County   Library,   100   S   Andrews   Ave,   357-7444,   free. _www.broward.org/library._

MIAMI Miami's mayor once called his city 'the Beirut of Latin America'. He meant it as a compliment—Beirut used to be the intellectual and economic trade centre for a region, as Miami is for Latin America. Unfortunately, most Americans believed the analogy to Beirut's violence was more appropriate for Miami's legendary crime problems.

Be cautious while visiting Miami, but don't believe everything you see on television. Boatloads of poor Haitians and Cuban criminals feed the legend. But while racial tension exists under the surface, it's not intrusive: for the most part the Anglos, Hispanics and blacks live peaceably alongside one another. Nicaraguan and Cuban transplants give the city a right wing political flavour. Symbolizing the bubbly spirit, cultural diversity and musicality of America's Latin diaspora is the Univision Escándalo TV program broadcast live every day from Miami, starring Charytín Gokco and her colleagues, Marisa y Felipe.

Take advantage of this diverse region. Join in the spontaneity that surrounds Southeast Florida, where historic homes give way to modern mansions, and the sidewalks of big cities lead to the sands of your own private island. The high-speed Metrorail, a people mover and an excellent bus system enable you to easily navigate the city without a car. *www.ci.miami.fl.us/pages/visitors.asp*.

Accommodation/Food

Not many motels within Miami are safe, clean and cheap. Smarter to stay at Miami Beach and commute to Miami attractions by bus or rail.

Airways Inn and Suites, 5001 NW 36th St, 883-4700, From $49, pool, movie channel, restaurant. Newly renovated. Pick up at airport. *www.miamiairway-sinnsuites.com.*

Canton Too, 2614 Ponce de Leon Blvd, Coral Gables, 448-3736. Reputedly the best Chinese food in Miami. Sun-Thu 11am-11pm, Fri/Sat 11am-12pm.

Charcuterie Restaurant, 3612 NE 2nd Ave, 576-7877. Interesting selection from a French/eclectic menu for lunch. Open daily 11:30am-3pm.

Café Sambal, 500 Brickell Key Drive, 913-8251. Panpacific cuisine. Price of plates $15-26. Open daily 6.30am-11pm.

Of interest

Seaquarium, Rickenbacher Causeway on Key Biscayne, 361-5705. Oldest and best: dolphins, sharks and killer whales; home of TV star Flipper, Lolita the 10,000 lb killer whale, Salty the Sea Lion. Open 9.30am-6pm, $26. Tkt office closes at 4pm. *www.miamiseaquarium.com/index.htm.*

Bayside, Biscayne Blvd and 4th St, 577-3344. $95 million complex of shops, restaurants and nightspots highlighting downtown. Mon-Thurs 10am-10pm, Fri and Sat 'til 11pm, Sun 11am-9pm. *www.baysidemarketplace.com.*

Little Havana, lies btwn SW 12th & SW 27th Ave with Calle Ocho (SW 8th St) housing most of the restaurants. Cigar and pinata manufacturers also. *miami.about.com/cs/maps/a/calle_ocho.htm.* **Bay of Pigs Memorial** commemorates the failed US-backed invasion of Cuba in 1961, at SW 13th Ave and SW 8th St.

Vizcaya Museum and Gardens, 3251 S Miami Ave, 250-9133. An Italian-style mansion created by millionaire James Deering in 1916, now the **Dade County Art Museum.** Open daily 9.30am-5pm, $12. Free tours of the home and formal Italian gardens. *www.vizcayamuseum.org.*

For wildlife visit **Monkey Jungle,** 14805 SW 216 St, 235-1611. Monkeys run wild, you view them from cages: look smart and they might give you a cream bun. $18, daily 9.30am-5pm. Tkt office closes at 4pm. $1 discount w/student ID. *www.monkeyjungle.com.* Also see **Parrot Jungle,** 11000 SW 57th Ave, near US 1, 666-7834. A huge cypress and oak jungle filled with exotic birds, some on roller skates. $25, student $23, daily 10am-6pm. Trained bird shows 10.30am-5pm. *www.parrotjungle.com/jsps.*

Museum of Science and Planetarium, 3280 S Miami Ave, 646-4200. Open daily 10am-6pm (last tkt 5pm); $10, $8 w/student ID. *www.miamisci.org.*

Coconut Grove, in the southern suburbs, for a look at a 'Florida-style subtropical Chelsea scene'. Galleries, boutiques, boat hiring. Get there via bus 14 going south to Main Hwy. The bulletin boards in Coconut Grove are said to be good for rides going north. *www.coconutgrovemiami.com.* South of Miami in Homestead is **Coral Castle,** US 1 at SW 286th St, 248-6345. Designed by a jilted lover who waited for his fiancée by creating a 1,100 ton estate out of coral, the castle stood originally in Florida City; in 1939, it was moved in its entirety to its present location. Open daily 7am-9pm $9.75, for self-guided tour. *www.coralcastle.com.*

Water Sports: surfing at **Haulover Beach Park** and **South Miami Beach,** but beware, the waves are small; good swimming at **Cape Florida State Park, Matheson Hammock, Tahiti Beach, Lummus Park,** etc. *www.floridastateparks.org.* Sailing, jet skiing and windsurfing on **Hobie Beach** off Rickenbacher Causeway.

Information/Internet access
Greater Miami Convention and Visitors Bureau, 701 Brickell Ave #2700, 539-3000, (800) 933-8448, Mon-Fri 8.30am-4.30pm.
Dade County Library, 1400 NW 37th Ave, 638-5255, free.

Travel
Greyhound, 4111 NW 27th St, 871-1810 or (800) 231-2222.
Amtrak, 8303 NW 37th Ave, 835-1221/(800) 872-7245.
Metro Dade Transportation, 770-3131. Extensive network of buses (Metrobus), subway (Metrorail) and downtown people mover (Metromover). Services airport. Bus and rail fare $1.50. Metromover free. 'Best tour of the city for a quarter.' _www.co.miami-dade.fl.us/transit._

MIAMI BEACH Situated on a long, narrow island, across Biscayne Bay from Miami, Miami Beach would like to think of itself as the ultimate in opulence. True to its reputation, for many it's the dream place for retirement. Eighty years ago this was a steamy mangrove swamp. Now, this area summons images of perfection, and, of course, the beach which attracts many European visitors. This makes it harder to get the good hotel rates that used to be available during the summer. It's still worth bargaining, however. The peak season is from late December to April. _www.gmcvb.com/Index.asp_.

Accommodation
Bayliss Guest Home, 504 14th Street, 538-5620. Double room $40 for BUNAC travellers.
Banana Bungalow, 2360 Collins Ave, 538-1951. $15 dorm room, $85 weekly. Pool, bar, breakfast. 'Rooms cramped but great atmosphere.' _www.bananabungalow.com_.
The Tropics Hotel, 1550 Collins Ave, 531-0361. Dorms start at $22. Art Deco building with pool and good kitchen facilities. _www.tropicshotel.com_.

Food
Nemo, 100 Collins Ave, 532-4550. American style with Malta influence. $10-$35. Open daily 12pm-12am. _www.nemorestaurant.com/direct.shtml_.
Nexxt Café, 700 Lincoln Road, 532-6643. All round American cuisine. Huge portions. $7-$20. Open daily 11am-11pm.
Puerto Sagua, 700 Collins, 673-1115. Specializes in seafood and Latin food. Try the paella. $5-$15. Open daily, 7:30am-2am.
San Loco, 235 14th Street, 538-3009. Tex-Mex take out, $3-$7. Open 11am-5am.

Of interest
Whimsical and gaudy, the **Art Deco District** is as close to high art as Miami Beach comes. The art is characterized by a distinct Miami Beach flavour known fondly as 'Tropical Deco'. While considered gaudy by some, it's notable enough to grant the area status as a National Historic District. The most impressive sights can be found along Collins Ave and Ocean Dr. The homes are part of a depression-era development and can be seen on a Preservation League tour, 672-1836. _www.mdpl.org_. Thurs at 6.30pm and Wed, Fri, Sat and Sun at 10.30am, $15 (student w/ID). Self-guided audio tours are available, $10 (student).
Different areas of **The Beach** cater to different groups: punks and surfers stick to the area below 5th St, volleyball players hang out at 14th St, gays gather on 21st St and the rich and famous flee to **Bal Harbor**, near 96th St. Airboat rides $7.
Miccosukee Indian Village, mile marker 20, Hwy 41, 223-8380. Guided tours show Miccosukee craftsmen at work. Museum has Indian artifacts. 9am-5pm daily, $5. _www.miccosukee.com/mivillage.html_.

Internet access
North Miami Beach Public Library, 1601 NE 164th St, 948-2970, free.

THE KEYS The only living coral reef in America is draped alongside the Florida Keys—the scimitar-shaped chain of islands curving southwest from Miami to Key West.

You pick up the toll-free Overseas Hwy at Key Largo for the 100-mile run down to Key West. En route, the road hops from island to island; at times you can travel up to seven miles with only the sea around you. It's worth a brief stop in **Key Largo**, as Arnold Schwarzenegger found in *True Lies*, to visit the **John Pennekamp Coral Reef State Park** and pay a brief tribute to Humphrey Bogart. *www.pennekamppark.com.* The *African Queen* is permanently docked outside the Holiday Inn. Locations along the highway are designated by milepost markers.

Key West itself is the southernmost point of the United States and embraces an eclectic mix of history, eccentricity and lush, island charm. Hemingway once lived here and it remains a favourite place for gays, writers and artists. Key West is not typical America; it's more like a Caribbean island. Even the food—turtle steak, conch (pronounced 'conk') chowder, Key lime pie—suggests this.

Don't miss sunset over the Gulf of Mexico—the whole town turns out on **Mallory Square** to watch the show, both in the sky and on the ground. Sundown here is usually accompanied by some kind of performance, such as a water-ski display, a magician or a folk singer. 'Key West was virtually deserted when we were there in September and October; very quiet and idyllic.' *www.fla-keys.com*.

Accommodation

Key Largo: John Pennekamp State Park Campsite, mile marker 102.5, (800) 326-3521, Sites $24, $26 w/hook-up. Rsvs rec. 'Take more mosquito spray than you ever believe you'll need. Nice campsite, good swimming, it's just a shame the bugs spoil it.'

Jules Undersea Lodge, world's first underwater hotel, 51 Shoreland Drive, milepost 103.5, 451-2353. A diver's dream; a pinch at $295 inc dinner, unlimited snacking and diving! Worth a peek, if you can scuba! *www.jul.com.*

Key West: Angelina Guest House, 302 Angela St, 294-4480. D/T-$59-$109. 'Clean and simple. Very friendly.' *angelinaguesthouse.com.*

Caribbean House, 226 Petronia St, 296-1600 or (800) 543-4518. D-$60, 4 people, w/bath. 'Excellent.' 'Very friendly and central.' TV & bfast. *www.caribbeanhousekeywest.com.*

El Rancho Motel, 830 Truman St, 294-8700, Rooms from $85. Prices change depending on day/month of arrival. Pool, within walking distance of downtown. 'Excellent, quiet.' *www.elranchokeywest.com.*

Key West B&B, 415 William St, 296-7274, S-$49, From $59 off-season, from $99 peak season. *www.keywestbandb.com.*

Food

In Key West, the more expensive restaurants line Duval St while the side streets offer a more eclectic selection. Don't forget to try authentic Key Lime pie.

Sloppy Joe's, 201 Duval, 294-5717. Hemingway was an enthusiastic regular. Live entertainment seven days a week, 9am-4am. Conch fritters $7.25. Open 365 days a year! 'Don't miss it.' *www.sloppyjoes.com.*

Nightlife is in abundance in Key West. Take a walk along Duval St for some alternative choices—try **Ziggie's Gumbo and Crab Shack**, 83000 Overseas Hwy, 664-3391. Wide range of crab dishes. Price range $10-$20, open 11am-10pm daily, and **Camille's**, 703½ Duval, 296-4811, a landmark diner with cheap food and friendly service, 8am-3pm, 6pm-10.30pm. _www.camilleskeywest.com._

Of interest
Hemingway Museum, 907 Whitehead St, 294-1136. Papa left Paris and moved to Key West in 1928. This became his home in 1931 until he left for Cuba in 1940. He wrote *A Farewell to Arms* and *For Whom the Bell Tolls* among others in this 1851 house. On discovering that the house was as Hemingway left it when he died, the present owners decided to turn it into a museum. 'Full of the overfed descendants of Hemingway's cats.' Open daily 9am-5pm, last tour 4.30pm, $11. _www.hemingwayhome.com._

Conch Tour Train, 294-5161. Takes you about 14 miles in $1^1/_2$ hrs and includes 65 points of interest such as Hemingway's house, **Truman's Little White House** _www.trumanlittlewhitehouse.com_, **Audubon House** _www.audubonhouse.com_, where the artist stayed while sketching birdlife over the Keys, **the turtle kraals, the shrimp fleet**, etc. Tkt office, 501 Front St or 3840 N Roosevelt, 9am-5.30pm, 294-5161, $20 for the whole island. _www.conchtourtrain.com._

Tours of the area are also available by **glass-bottomed boat**. **Fireball**, 296-6293, Glass Bottom Boat Tour, $30 for 2 hr trip at 12pm and 2pm, $35 at sunset, 6pm. **Key Largo Princess** leaves 10am, 1pm and 4pm daily, 451-4655, $22. And try snorkelling trips over the coral reefs. 'Well worth splashing out $20 or so—and maybe even buying an underwater camera.' 'Explore the island by foot if you have more than one day in Key West, or rent a bike.' **Tropicar Inc.**, 1300 Duval Street, 294-8136. Mopeds are the most popular mode of transport on the island, from $18. _bellsouthpwp.net/t/r/troprent._

Information/Travel
Florida Keys Chamber of Commerce, 402 Wall Street, 294-2587. _www.florida-keys.fl.us/chamber.htm._
Key West Visitors Bureau, (800) 352-5397, _www.fla-keys.com_.
Key West Welcome Center, 3840 N Roosevelt Blvd, 296-4444, (800) 284-4482. _www.keywestwelcomecenter.com._
Greyhound, 3535 S. Roosevelt Blvd. in Key West, 296-9072/(800) 231-2222. For a taxi to the airport, call 296-6666, Approx. $20.

EVERGLADES and BISCAYNE NATIONAL PARKS The Everglades lies further south than any other area of the US mainland and is the last remaining subtropical wilderness in the country.

A world-renowned sanctuary for rare and colourful birds, this unique aquatic park is characterised by broad expanses of sawgrass marsh, dense jungle growth, prairies interspersed with stands of cabbage palm and moss-draped cypresses, and mangroves. The level landscape gives the impression of unlimited space. _www.nps.gov/ever/index.htm._

The western entrance to the park lies near **Everglades City** on Rte 29, but the only auto road leading into the area is Rte 9336. Take it from **Florida City**, 11 miles to the east. The $5 (pedestrian/cyclist) admission will give you up to 7 days access. Camping is $14 per night. Get out and walk along the paths if you really want to understand the place. Try the **Anhinga Trail**, 2 miles past the entrance. The **Royal Palm Visitors Center** has great displays on the unique Everglades' ecology. At the northern end of the park off US 41, the **Shark Valley Visitors Center** provides access to the **Tamiami**

Trail. The 15-mile trail can be explored by foot, bike or two hour tram ride, $13.25, 221-8455. Shark Valley entrance is $10.

The weather in this southernmost part of Florida is quasi-tropical. Winter temperatures generally range between 60 and 85 degrees F. The rest of the year, the temperature soars past 90 degrees by mid-morning, and the high humidity makes it feel even hotter. Bring sunglasses, suntan oil and gallons of insect repellent. Accommodation, restaurants, sightseeing and charter boats and other services are found in **Flamingo**, at the end of the main park road, about 50 miles from the park entrance. From the Gulf Coast of Florida, you can enter the park at Everglades City.

Biscayne National Park is a jewel for snorkellers and scuba divers, with 95% of it lying underwater. Most of the marine park's treasures are underwater in living coral reefs. Above ground, exotic trees, colourful flowers and unique shrubbery form dense forests. The main entrance is at the western side of the park at the **Dante Fascell Visitor Center**, 230-7275, 9 miles east of **Homestead** on North Canal Drive, 9am-5pm daily. For snorkelling equipment and canoe rental or info on glass-bottomed boat tours, call the **Biscayne Aqua Center** in Homestead, 247-2400. _www.nps.gov/bisc/index.htm_.

Accommodation
Everglades International Hostel, 20 SW 2nd Ave, Florida City, 248-1122 or (800) 372-3874. 15 min to Everglades National Park and Biscayne National Park. One mile south of Homestead Greyhound Station. Canoe and kayak rentals, discounts to local attractions. $13 AYH, $16 non-AYH, $33-$38 private room. _www.evergladeshostel.com_.
Everglades Motel, 310 Collier Avenue, 695-4224, from $60 in the summer. AC, TV, fridge. _www.evergladescitymotel.com._
Flamingo Lodge, in Flamingo, 38 miles inside the park, (800) 600-3813. D-from $68. Higher rates at w/ends. _www.flamingolodge.com._
Camping, $14 a site in winter, at **Lone Pine Key** and **Flamingo.** The park office, 242-7700, doesn't charge for camping in summer because they feel sorry for anyone who would brave the clouds of mosquitoes to do it. For the truly adventurous, 19 backcountry sites are accessible by motorboat or canoe. Just don't try swimming or paddling in the lakes or ponds—'unless ya' wanna 'gator to getya'! You must have a backcountry permit, if you want to do your own canoe trip overnight. Note: in summer you'll need to bring food if you camp.

Tours
Gray Line Tours from Miami and Miami Beach, but for a group of people it would be better and cheaper to hire a car for a day. _www.grayline.com_.
Everglades National Park Boat Tours, (239) 695-2591 offers boat tours of the park every day, starting at 9am and leaving every half hour until 4:30pm. $21.

ORLANDO Located 35 miles from the east coast in the heart of the Florida lakes area, Orlando is perhaps the most visited place in the state. Tourism has boomed since the opening of Walt Disney World, and the area's easy access to nearby Kennedy Space Center ensures its ongoing popularity. A favourite EU tourist spot, you're likely to meet folks from home here. It has the chaotic atmosphere of a boom town, so choose carefully before you set out to see the sights—many of them are waste-of-time, money-grabbing parasitical spinoffs. Cheap car rentals may be the best bet to visit all these attractions. _www.orlandoinfo.com_.

Accommodation

A zillion hotels have opened here in the last decade to lure the folks visiting all the nearby worlds. Most are expensive, but a few inexpensive chains like Motel 6 and Days Inn have staked their claim to the action. It may prove cheaper to stay in a more expensive motel nearer to Disney, etc. and get free shuttles to the attractions.

Quality Inn Plaza, 9000 International Dr, 345-8585/(800) 999-8585. Rates vary but are based on room. Around $90 for two adults. _qualityinnplaza.orlandofloridareservations.com._

Rodeway Inn International, 6327 International Drive, 996-4444. Minutes from all Orlando attractions. Pool, guest service desk offers day trips and attraction tickets. Ave $69.

Travelodge, 409 Magnolia Ave, 423-1671. Pool, laundry room. Shuttles to Disney. $58. 'Very friendly and helpful.' Rsvs rec in June/July.

KOA Disneyworld, Bronson Memorial Hwy, off US 192 in Kissimmee, 396-2400. Sites $38 for two w/hook-up.

KOA Orlando, 12345 Narcoossee Road SE (Hwy 15, 4½ miles S of Hwy 528), 277-5075. $25.

Food

Fat Boys Bar-B-Q, 1605 W Vine St, Kissimmee, 847-7098. 'Good steak.' Juke box. Daily 11am-9pm daily.

Flea World, 4311 North Highway 17-92, 330-1792. America's largest flea market, 1700+ dealer booths and 14 food concessions. Provides entertainment every w/end. Fri/Sat/Sun 9am-6pm. _www.fleaworld.com._

Fox and Hound Pub, 3514 W Vine St, Kissimmee, 847-9927. English/Irish decor and beer. British staff. 'Worth a visit.'

Of interest

Prime your smile, open your wallet because a huge mouse with better name recognition than George Bush is waiting for you at **Walt Disney World**. The huge complex of 4 theme parks, 3 water parks, an entertainment complex and thousands of hotel rooms sits glistening at Lake Buena Vista, about 15 miles S of Orlando on I-4. All this Disney magic comes with a hefty price tag. A day ticket for one of the major theme parks is around $50; For the enthusiasts among you, you would be better off purchasing a multi-day pass that you can use to visit any combination of the parks on any given day (5-day $165, 7-day $167). Prices fluctuate greatly, call on the day you plan to visit. Arrive early to avoid the long, hot afternoon queues or wait until late afternoon and evening, when crowds thin and early park-goers retire. The 'Fastpass', which assigns appointment times for the most popular rides, has alleviated some of the worst queues. General info number 824-4321. _www.disney.go.com/Disneyworld/index2.html._

Magic Kingdom. The park that's the equivalent to Disneyland in Los Angeles and Tokyo. This is the place to sing _It's a Small World_, sail along with the _Pirates of the Caribbean_ or to watch all 41 US presidents come to life in one room. When the soft side of Disney gets to be too much, spook yourself with the ExtraTERRORestrial **Alien Encounter** or zip through **Space Mountain**. The Magic Kingdom exceeds its older sister, Disneyland, as a magnificent architectural, technological and entertainment achievement. 'You definitely need 2 days.' 'Great! I feel like a child again.' 'Better than it's hyped up to be.' 'Don't miss _Space Mountain_ (only if you like roller coasters), _Pirates of the Caribbean_, and the amazing 3-D movie at the Kodak pavilion.' 'Visit after Labor Day to avoid queuing 1 hr for everything.' 'Buy tickets beforehand to avoid queues.' 'Food expensive.'

Epcot Center (Experimental Prototype of Community of Tomorrow). Billed by some as an 'adult' amusement park and as 'dull' by others, the $1 billion Epcot is the second of the Disney theme parks. Epcot consists of two worlds: Futureworld and the World Showcase. The former has exhibits and rides based on science, nature and society. Don't miss the 3-D film, *Honey I Shrank the Audience*. In the **Wonders of Life** pavilion, Cranium Command explores the brain of a lovesick 12 year old boy in a simulator designed by George Lucas, the father of *Star Wars*. 'Hilarious.' **The World of Motion** is home to the General Motors *Test Track* that promotes itself as the longest and fastest attraction in the Disney complex. While some readers describe the pavilions as: 'mind-boggling boredom', some are applauded as 'wonderful', eg. the incredible dinosaur ride in the Energy Pavilion. The World Showcase comprises pavilions from 11 different countries. All the employees in the showcase come from their host countries. Epcot has built a reputation as having the best food of any of the parks; visitors should make lunch and dinner reservations as soon as they enter the park at Spaceship Earth. The best bargain is the all-you-can-eat Norwegian smorgasbord. Be sure to view the park's nightly spectacular laser display, *Illuminations*. 'Unique, contemporary—very good.' 'Not worth the price; very modern and technical, no place to have fun like in Disneyworld.'

Disney/MGM Studios Theme Park. Inspired by the success of Universal Studios Orlando, Disney opened their response to movie madness in 1989 to great reviews and huge crowds. The park, designed as a movie set, is inhabited by various Disney characters as well as 'directors' and 'stars'. In addition to the standard rides and attractions, there is a backstage Studio Tour which offers a behind-the-scenes look at film making. Production for some Disney and Touchstone (its adult subsidiary) releases takes place here, but the main goal of the park is to bring in tourists and their dollars. *The Great Movie Ride, Rock and Rollercoaster, Catastrophe Canyon, Star Tours,* the *Animation studio* and the *Indiana Jones Stunt Spectacular* are the main highlights. The action culminates at the **Twilight Zone Tower of Terror**, where you plunge 13 stories down a darkened elevator shaft—twice! Be sure also to catch the *Muppet-Vision* 3-D movie, and don't miss the chance to be a millionaire, only virtually unfortunately! Take part in surroundings mirroring that of the show, and though you won't win a million dollars if you get to the end, you can win some great prizes on the way!

Disney's Animal Kingdom Park is the latest addition to the Disney family. Land and water habitats radiate outward from the Tree of Life, the park's centerpiece. Animal Kingdom is more than just a glorified zoo—you can go on a Kilimanjaro Safari in Africa, take in one of DinoLand's thrill rides, and catch the live animal performances at the Pocahontas Colors of the Wind theatre. The park is home to countless animals—real, imaginary and extinct. Costume appearances by some of Disney's most famous animal characters remind you that you're still in the Magic Kingdom.

Other Disney Parks: the scorching Florida sun can be quickly remedied by a stopover at one of the 2 water parks, **Typhoon Lagoon** and **Blizzard Beach**. Typhoon Lagoon is a traditional waterpark, complete with twisting water slides and a wave machine. The newest water park, Blizzard Beach is the world's only combination ski resort and water adventure park. The artificial snow and -ice winter landscaping won't do much to beat the Florida heat. Instead, shoot down the Summit Plummet, a 120-ft tower from which you plunge straight down at 60 miles per hour! Admission around $30. For a taste of Disney nightlife, venture to **Pleasure Island**. Eight distinct nightclubs, as well as numerous shops and restaurants, inhabit the island. Open 7pm-2am, one admission charge of $21 allows you to visit all of the clubs.

SeaWorld, on I-4 btwn Orlando & Disneyworld, (800) 432-1178. $60. 9am-10pm. Features sharks, killer whales, walruses, multimedia fish and dolphins. 'One of the most spectacular aquatic animal displays I've ever seen.' *www.seaworld.com*.

Wet n' Wild Amusement Park, off I-4 10 miles NE of Disney, 351-3200. Water park with slides of all degrees of daring including two 7 storey spectacular slides. 'Brilliant day out.' $39, cheaper after 5pm. 9am-9pm daily.

Universal Studios Orlando, near I-4 and the Florida Tnpk, 10 miles SW of downtown, 363-8000. Open since May 1990, the largest movie studios outside Hollywood stretch for 444 acres and feature such attractions as *ET Adventure*, a *Back to the Future* ride with seven-storey high OMNIMAX screens, and the newest attraction, *Twister*—a unique chance to see a tornado from the inside. Even more recent is the *Shrek* addition, which picks up where the film ends and puts you in the action, and *Jimmy Neutron*, where you embark on a wild chase an evil scientist through your favourite Nicktoons. There is also a tour of famous film sets, which include *Jaws*, and the Bates Motel from *Psycho*. Watch scary creatures come to life at The Gory, Gruesome and Grotesque Horror Make-up Show. Don't miss the *Terminator 2, Battle Across Time* ride or the display of dinosaurs used in the filming of *Jurassic Park*. Open daily 9am-9pm. 1-day pass $60. You might also consider purchasing a Flex Ticket, entitling you to up to 14 days of unlimited admission to SeaWorld, Universal Studios, Wet 'n' Wild Water Park and the **Universal Studios Island of Adventure,** a newer addition with more traditional rides themed on Marvel superheroes (The Hulk and SpiderMan) and the ever-lucrative Jurassic Park franchise. $185. *www.universalstudios.com/index.php.*

Information
Orlando-Orange County Visitors and Convention Bureau, 363-5872, several miles SW of downtown in Mercado, 6700 Forum Dr. #100. Open daily 8am-7pm. Pick up *Orlando* for city info and ask for a **free Magic Card,** to receive discounts at various shops, restaurants, hotels and attractions. *www.orlandoinfo.com.*

Internet access
Orlando Public Library, 101 E Central Blvd, 835-7323. Must buy a 'technology card', $5, valid for week.

Travel
Orlando International Airport, 825-2001. 'Amazing airport, with fake monorail operated completely automatically. Taxis or shuttles recommended over public transport. *www.orlandoairports.net/goaa/main.htm.*

Amtrak, 1400 Sligh Blvd, 843-7611/(800) 872-7245. Take bus #34 to downtown.

Greyhound, 555 N John Young Parkway, 292-3440/(800) 231-2222. Take bus #25 to downtown.

Lynx, (407) 841-LYNX. Local bus system serving downtown, airport, International Drive and all the tourist areas. Fare $1.50. 'Good service.' *www.golynx.com.*

THE GULF COAST Broad, blindingly white and generally cleaner than those in the East Coast, the beaches of the West Coast are another reason why many people vacation in Florida. Although the area between Fort Myers and St Petersburg (St Pete), where the best beaches are found, is growing rapidly, areas of relative isolation are fairly easy to come by. The largest concentration of retiree transplants can also be found here.

FT MYERS 'There is only one Fort Myers, and 90 million people are going to find out' wrote Thomas Edison (*www.thomasedison.com*). Located on the south bank of the Caloosahatchee River, south of Tampa, Ft Myers, incorporated in 1886, has one major claim to fame – it was Edison's 14-acre winter home, built that same year. It adjoins that of Henry Ford (purchased 1916).

Today the **Edison and Ford Winter Estates** at 2350 McGregor Blvd, (239) 334-7419, are open to the public, $16 for a tour that is mesmerising for the breadth of the story it tells of Edison, holder of 1093 patents. He invented among many other things, the first stock-ticker (1871), electric vote counter, record player (1878), carbon filament incandescent light (1879), motion picture maker (1888), and alkali battery (1909). 'I shall make the electric light so cheap,' he wrote, 'that only the rich will be able to burn candles.' Besides the displays and early model Fords, the estate includes Edison's remarkable botanical garden 'where perfumed zephyrs forever kiss the gorgeous flora', which includes rubber varieties on which he experimented, and an amazing banyan tree given to Edison in 1925. It has a 390 foot circumference of aerial roots, the largest of its kind in the continental US. *www.edison-ford-estate.com*.

North of Ft Myers, a set of sandy keys hugs the coast towards Tampa, separated from the mainland by an intracoastal waterway. Best visited in the off-season, these beaches have a pleasant uncrowded atmosphere. On your way to Tampa, stop in at **Venice**, visit the **Soda Fountain**, 349 W Venice Ave, (941) 412-9860, which specialises in old fashioned fountain delights such as phosphates, egg creams, floats, malted milks, ice cream sodas, sundaes and brownie supremes ($2-$6), plus sandwhiches and hot dogs. *www.tasteofthepast.com/home.html*.

TAMPA/ST PETERSBURG Tampa, located 22 miles east of St Pete and best known for its cigars, is the area's business centre. **Clearwater** is the most popular beach destination among the under 25-set. But don't let appearances fool you. Tampa's only real draws are Ybor City, a unique Latin quarter, and **Busch Gardens**, an amusement park. Clearwater has not-so-pleasant crowds and tall nondescript hotels. The best finds on the Sun Coast, as the area is called, are tucked away and tough to get to. But once there, the beauty and relaxed atmosphere are sublime.

At the other side of the bay is sedate St Pete, the 'Sunshine City', whose retirement community reputation—*Cocoon* was filmed here—obscures several interesting attractions as well as miles of excellent beaches. See *www.gotampa.com* and *www.floridasbeach.com*.

Accommodation

Clearwater Beach International Hostel, (727) 443-1211 at the Sands Hotel, 606 Bay Esplanade Ave, Clearwater Beach. $14 AYH, $15 non-AYH, private rooms $39, linen $2. AC, bike rentals $5, pool. Rsvs rec. 'Excellent, friendly & fun.' *www.clearwaterbeachhostel.com.*

Days Inn, 2901 E Busch Blvd, on Rte 580, 13/4 miles E of jct I-75, exit 33, (813) 933-6471. Rooms $49-59, up to 4 people, depending on day of arrival. AC, TV, coin laundry, pool. 10 mins from **Busch Gardens**. *www.daysinn.com/DaysInn/control/home*.

Shirley Ann Hotel, 936 1st Ave N, (727) 894-2759. D-$65. 'Clean, comfortable. Owners are lovely people.' Near buses to Orlando.

Camping: St Petersburg KOA, 5400 95th St N, (727) 392-2233. $34 for two, $47 w/hook-up. Extra person charge. 'Great.'

Fort DeSoto Camp Grounds, (727) 582-2267, near St Pete Beach, follow signs on Pinellas Bayway. Wildlife sanctuary composed of five islands. Sites from $25. Call for availability but must make rsvs in person at camp grounds, or 150 5th St N, #146, in St Pete, or 631 Chestnut St in Clearwater. *www.fortdesoto.com.*

Food/Entertainment

Cha Cha Coconuts, The Pier complex in St Petersburg, (727) 822-6655. Mon-Thu 11am-11.30pm, Fri-Sun 11-1.30am. Sandwiches and ribs. 'Not your typical tropical bar', they claim.

Hurricane Seafood Restaurant, 807 Gulf Way in St Petersburg Beach, (727) 360-9558. Right on Pass-A-Grille beach, famous for its grouper sandwich and other seafood selections from $8. Open daily for bfast, lunch and dinner. Live music. _www.thehurricane.com._

Carmine's, 1802 7th Ave in Tampa's Ybor City, (813) 248-3834. Italian and Cuban fare, $7-17 for dinner. Mon/Tue 11am-11pm, Wed/Thurs 11-1am, Fri/Sat 11-3am, Sun 11-6pm.

Cafe Creole, 1330 9th Ave E in Tampa's Ybor City, (813) 247-6283. Delicious Cajun cuisine from $. Mon-Sat 11.30am-10pm, closed Sun. Live Cajun music and Dixieland jazz Wed-Sat.

Of interest

St Petersburg: Almost everything worth seeing in St Petersburg is located downtown but use caution after dark and stay in well-lit areas. The city's focal point and the centrepiece of the waterfront is **The Pier**, 2nd Ave NE, 821-6164. Mon-Sat 10am-9pm, Sun 11-9, a 5 storey-upside-down pyramid in the middle of Tampa Bay that houses a variety of shops, restaurants and the **University of South Florida Aquarium**, 895-7437, $2, free on Sundays, 10am-8pm. For miles in both directions of The Pier, you can walk through waterfront parks, beaches and marinas. _www.stpete-pier.com._

Salvador Dali Museum, 1000 3rd St S, 823-3767. Largest collection of surrealist works by the Spanish master. $14, $9 w/student ID, Mon-Sat 9.30am-5.30pm (Thurs 'til 8pm), Sun noon-5.30pm. _www.salvadordalimuseum.org._

Sunken Gardens, 1825 4th St N, 551-3100, is a 5-acre sinkhole filled with tropical flora and fauna, 'gator wrestling and trained macaws. Open Mon-Sat 10am-4.30pm, Sun noon-4.30; $8. _www.stpete.org/sunken.htm._ 30 miles N of St Petersburg off the hellish Hwy US 19 is **Tarpon Springs**, a small colony of Greek fisherman who have been harvesting sponges for generations. Stroll through the village and dine on Greek fare. _www.tarponsprings.com._

On the Beaches: Of the group, **Pass-A-Grille Beach** and **Caldesi/Honeymoon Islands** are 'supreme'. Pass-A-Grille, at the southern tip of St Petersburg Beach, nicely balances dunes and quaint shops with dolphins and casual sun worshippers. Take I-275 to the Bayway exit, the last exit before leaving the peninsula, then head west to the beach.

Caladesi Island State Park and Honeymoon Island State Recreation Area have preserved the pristine state of the gulf shore while providing miles of white sand for beach goers. Side-by-side, one admission price admits you to both islands, but the only way to get to Caladesi is by ferry, $8 r/t. Call 469-5918 for info. Ferry runs hrly 10am-4pm Mon-Fri, half-hourly 10am-4pm w/ends. If you're from Florida, it's cheaper (otherwise $5 per car). Located between Tarpon Springs and Clearwater, take US 19 to State Road 586 and head west to the end of the road. Max length of stay on Caladesi, 4 hrs.

Tampa: Watch the banana boats dock and unload at Kennedy Blvd and 13th St. A stroll along Bayshore Blvd brings you a string of southern mansions.

Adventure Island, 4500 Bougainvillea Ave, 1 mile northeast of Busch Gardens, 987-5660, is one of the better water parks in Florida complete with water slides, rapids, wave pool, etc. $33. Open daily in summer, Mon-Fri 9am-7pm, Sat/Sun 'til 8pm. _www.adventureisland.com._

Busch Gardens—The Dark Continent, just off Rte 580, 987-5171. $56, open daily in summer although opening hours change monthly, call for details. Take an African safari to view more than 1000 animals, as well as dolphins and belly dancers, rollercoaster rides, shows, etc. *www.buschgardens.com*.

Museum of Science and Industry, 4801 E Fowler Ave, 987-6000, Features a simulated hurricane. $16 admission includes ticket to IMAX theatre. Open daily Mon-Fri 9am-5pm, Sat/Sun 9-7. IMAX open until 12am Fri and Sat. *www.mosi.org*.

The Tampa Theater, 274-8982, a genuine old-time movie palace from the 1920s, designed in Rococco. Mediterranean styles dominate. The theatre shows old movies and art films at good prices, and when the show starts, watch the stars come out on the ceiling above. Franklin St in downtown Tampa. $8, $6 w/student ID. Before 6pm, $6 for everyone. *www.tampatheatre.org*.

Ybor City, was once the 'cigar manufacturing headquarters of the world' and is now in the process of being gentrified: Ybor retains a stylish Latin influence. Learn of its history and that of the cigar industry at the **Ybor City State Museum,** 1818 9th Ave, 247-6323. Open daily 9am-5pm, tours Sat at 10:30am, $3. *www.ybormuseum.org.* The **Cigar Festival,** held in November, features street shows, dancing and food, call 247-1434 for details. Although several restaurants with live music and dance bars are in the area, use caution when walking through Ybor at night.

Information
St Petersburg Chamber of Commerce, 100 2nd Ave N, 821-4069. *www.stpete.com.*
St Pete Beach Chamber of Commerce, 6990 Gulf Blvd, 360-6957. *tampabaybeaches.com.*
Tampa Bay Convention and Visitors Bureau, 400 N. Tampa St. 223-2752. *www.visittampabay.com.*

Internet access
St Pete: St Petersburg Public Library, 3745 9th Ave, 893-7724, free.

Travel
Tampa: Amtrak, 601 Nebraska Ave, 221-7600/(800) 872-7245.
Greyhound, 610 Polk St, 229-2174/(800) 231-2222.
Hillsboro Area Regional Transit, 254-4278, $1.30, $3 for unlimited daily travel. #30 btwn airport and downtown. *www.hartline.org.*
St Petersburg: Greyhound, 180 9th St N, (727) 898-1496 or (800) 231-2222.
Pinellas Suncoast Transit Authority, 530-9911. $1.25 basic fare, $3 for unlimited daily travel. *www.psta.net.*

THE PANHANDLE This strip of land jabbing into Alabama has more in common with the states of the Deep South than it does with sub-tropical South Florida. Winter is distinctly cooler here and the terrain is broken up by an occasional hill.

Hidden away in the hills and forests is **Tallahassee**, the state capital. *www.talchamber.com.* The town has resisted tour bus invasions much as it avoided capture by the Union forces during the Civil War. This is a city of real Floridians, not transplanted northerners. There's still much of its 19th century architecture to see and a slower way of life to appreciate.

Moving further west along the Panhandle, you come to **Panama City** and the commercialised resort of **Panama City Beach**. Panama City runs on Central Standard Time and so is one hour behind the rest of Florida. It used to be a peaceful fishing village but now developers are invading, thanks to their triumphs down the road at Panama City Beach. The beach really is lovely and the sea is clear and warm, but everything is over-priced and overpopulated. *www.cityofpanamacity.com*.

Further west still lies **Pensacola**, the last city in Florida. Since the first successful settlement here in 1698, Pensacola has flown the flags of five nations and has changed hands 13 times. The British used it as a trading post in the 18th century. Business must have been good, for here Scotsman James Panton became America's first recorded millionaire. It's also the place where Andrew Jackson signed the treaty that enabled the United States to purchase Florida from Spain in 1821. *www.visitpensacola.com*.

The 52 miles of white sandy beaches near Pensacola are among the best in Florida; after a dip you're on your way west to **Gulf Islands National Seashore** (see Biloxi, Mississippi) and to New Orleans. **Information Center** in Gulf Breeze, (850) 934-2600, (800) 635-4803.

GEORGIA - Peach State

Georgia has seen some rough times. Named after George II, the state began as an English debtor's colony. Many of the original settlers died before the swampy lands could be cleared for planting cotton. Although antebellum Georgia thrived, the Civil War brought destruction. When things were beginning to look up for the weakened Confederate forces, Union **General Sherman** broke through rebel defenses at **Chattanooga** and launched his 60 mile march to the sea. *ngeorgia.com/people/shermanwt.html*.

Whilst proud of its past, the Peach State chooses to look to the future, and since the Second World War has been rising on the crest of an industrial boom. Peanut farmer **Jimmy Carter** marched out of the anonymity of **Plains** to become president in 1976 and Savannah challenges Charleston's claim to be the most beautiful city in the South. It is worth checking out **Amicalola**, the greatest waterfall in Georgia, standing at an impressive 729 feet, (706) 265-4703, off highway 52.

The area code for Atlanta is 404, for Stone Mountain 770, for Savannah and Southern Georgia it's 912.

ATLANTA Host to the 1996 Olympic Games and home of CNN (*www.cnn.com*), Ted Turner (*www.tedturner.com*), Coca-Cola (*www.coca-cola.com/flashIndex1.html*) and UPS. Atlanta's story has been one of fast-growing success. In the past decade, Atlanta has been the fastest expanding urban area in the entire nation in terms of size of building and infrastructure development. Founded in 1837 as the southwestern terminal of the Western & Atlantic Railroad, Atlanta was the commercial and industrial centre of the Old South. In 1864, General Sherman 'drove old Dixie down' with his devastating march to the sea, during which Atlanta was bombarded and then burned to the ground, as immortalised in *Gone with the Wind*.

The city rose again to show that progress counts more than prejudice. Atlantans elected their first black mayor in 1973. It was here that **Martin Luther King** was raised and first preached and Atlanta is now host to many well-to-do black immigrants from the North. Segregation used to be the norm here, but nowadays each neighbourhood is indicative of the diversity that now exists. Its skyscraper skyline, crisscrossing expressway system, and ultra-modern airport, which is the busiest in the US, proclaim Atlanta's leadership of the 'New South', but tend to be boring and charmless.

However, Peachtree Street (be careful, there are 32 Peach Tree streets in

Atlanta), financial hub of the ante-bellum South, still retains its dignified presence and away from downtown, the city's hills—especially Stone Mountain, wooded streets and numerous colleges—Atlanta University, Clark College, Emory University and the Georgia Institute of Technology—create a pleasant atmosphere. The **Dogwood Festival** here in April is the highlight of the year. _www.dogwood.org._

As with most American cities, be advised to be on your guard when out at night. _www.atlanta.com_.

Accommodation
'Go to the Visitors Bureau. Lots of deals and discount vouchers.'

Atlanta International Hostel, 224 Ponce de Leon Ave, 875-9449. 4 blocks E of N Ave MARTA. From $19. Private rooms from $55. 'Clean, safe and friendly.' Free coffee and doughnuts until 9am. Internet access available. _www.hostel-atlanta.com._

La Quinta Inn Duluth, 2370 Stephens Center Drive, (800) 957-0500. D-$79. Includes fitness centre and complimentary breakfast.

Villa International, 1749 Clifton Rd NE, 633-6783. 'A ministry of the Christian community.' Situated near Emory U, pleasant, safe suburb, next door to the Center for Disease Control. 'Quiet with a very helpful staff, though a little shabby.' S-$36 w/shower, sm D-$24 pp, lrg D-$27.50 pp. No TV/tel. _www.villa-atl.org_.

For further listings, it is worth calling **lodging.com**, toll-free: (888) 563-4464. _www.lodging.com._ They specialise in cheap hotels in Atlanta. There are numerous budget motels, e.g. **Comfort Inn, Days Inn, Motel 6, Red Roof Inn,** in the Atlanta area, but you'll need a car and they usually cost more here than elsewhere, from $40-$100. Look around Myrtle, Piedmont, Peachtree and Ponce De Leon.

Stone Mountain Campground, (770) 498-5710. Tent sites from $23. 'Beautiful sites on the lake.'

Food
Atlanta's specialties are fried chicken, black-eyed peas, okra and sweet potato pie.

Barkers Red Hots: buy 'Atlanta's Best Hot Dog' from street vendors at various locations around town, from $3.

Harold's Barbecue, 171 McDonough Blvd SE, 627-9268. 'Home-down cooking' at its best, a temple to the cult of the pig, single meal around $10. Open daily 10:30am-7.45pm. Cash only.

Mary-Macs, 224 Ponce DeLeon Ave NE, 876-1800. Good, cheap food (try the green turnip soup and corn muffins). 11am-9pm. 'Where the natives eat!'

The Varsity, North Ave at I-75, 881-1706. World's largest drive-in, next to Georgia Tech campus. Serves 15,000 people with 8,300 colas, 18,000 hamburgers, 25,000 hot dogs each day. 'Clean, fast, cheap and good.' Sun-Thurs 10am-11:30pm, Fri-Sat 10am-12:30am. _www.thevarsity.com._

Of interest
Atlanta Botanical Garden, Piedmont Ave at The Prado, 876-5859. A tranquil oasis with tropical, desert and endangered plant species. Tues-Sun 9am-7pm, $12, $7 student. _www.atlantabotanicalgarden.org_.

Memorial & Grave of Martin Luther King Jr, in Ebenezer Baptist Churchyard at 413 Auburn Ave NW, 524-1956. The inscription on the tomb reads: 'Free at last, free at last, thank God Almighty, I'm free at last.' Includes inter-faith Peace Chapel. Mon-Fri 9am-6pm. 'Be careful in this area.' _www.nps.gov/malu_.

State Capitol, Washington at Mitchell, 656-2844. Modelled on the Washington DC capitol building and topped with gold from the Georgia gold field at Dahlonega, brought to Atlanta by special wagon caravan. Houses **State Museum of Science and Industry, Hall of Flags** and **Georgia Hall of Fame**. 8am-5.30pm Mon-Fri. Tours at 10am, 11am, 1pm, 2pm. Free. _www.sos.state.ga.us_.

Underground Atlanta, downtown around Upper Alabama St. 12-acre complex housing more than 130 restaurants, shops and nightclubs. Impressive 10-storey light tower at main entrance. Shops open Mon-Sat 10am-9.30pm, Sun 'til 5.30pm; restaurant/club hours vary. *www.underground-atlanta.com.*

World of Coca-Cola, 55 Martin Luther King Dr, 676-5151. Adjacent to Underground Atlanta; the pavilion includes historic memorabilia, radio and TV retrospective, a futuristic soda fountain and an 18 ft coke bottle! Cool off in the hospitality room with free Coke samples, all you can drink. 'Watch the film and hear how Coca-Cola helped win World War II! ... Brilliant museum, brilliant value.' Mon-Sat 9am-5pm, Sun 11am-5pm; $9. *www.woccatlanta.com.*

Science and Technology Museum of Atlanta (SCI Trek), 395 Piedmont Ave, 522-5500. Said to be one of the top ten physical science museums in America; over 100 hands-on science exhibits. Mon-Sat 10am-5pm, Sun noon-5pm, $7.50 for students. *www.scitrek.org.*

The Atlanta History Center, 130 West Paces Ferry Rd. NW, 814-4000. 34 acres of landscaped gardens and trails. Library, archives, exhibitions and films on Atlanta and its history. Mon-Sat 10am-5.30pm, Sun noon-5.30pm. $12, $10 w/student ID, includes admission and guided tour of historic houses and grounds. *www.atlhist.org.*

Atlanta Preservation Center, 327 St.Paul Ave, 688-3353. $1^1/_2$ hr guided walking tours of Atlanta's historic districts. 7 tours available. $10, $5 w/student ID. *www.preserveatlanta.com.*

Jimmy Carter Presidential Center, 1 Copenhill, 435 Freedom Parkway, 331-3942. Take bus #16 to Cleburne. *www.nps.gov/jica.* **Museum on the Carter Presidency** also features other US presidents. Mon-Sat 9am-4.45pm, Sun noon-4.45pm, $7, $5 w/student ID. 'Well worth it.'. *www.jimmycarterlibrary.org.*

Cyclorama, in Grant Park, 658-7625. 103-yr-old circular painting (one of the largest in the world) with 3-dimensional diorama complete with lighting and sound effects, depicting the 1864 Battle of Atlanta. Don't miss the *Texas,* of the Great Locomotive Chase of the Civil War (immortalised by Buster Keaton in *The General*). Open daily 9.20am-4.30pm: $7. Further **Civil War memorabilia** in the area include the breastworks erected for the defence of the town in Grant Park, Cherokee Ave and Boulevard SE—and Fort Walker, Confederate Battery, set up as during the siege. *www.atlantanation.com/cyclorama.html.*

Stone Mountain, Grant Park. In massive bas-relief the equestrian figures of Generals Robert E Lee, Stonewall Jackson and Confederate President Jefferson Davis have been cut from a 600-ft-high granite dome, the world's largest exposed mass of granite. Astride this mountain, looking down on Lee and Davis you can understand why King, in his 'I have a dream' speech said, 'Let freedom ring from Stone Mountain in Georgia.' A cable car runs to the top, or you can climb it. Also in the 3200-acre historical and recreational park are- an ante-bellum plantation, an antique auto and music museum, a game ranch, riverboat cruises, a 5-mile steam railroad and more. Park entrance $8 p/car, general admission, $20. Dazzling nightly laser show at 9.30pm at no extra cost (June-Aug only). 'Worth waiting 'til dark: brilliant effects.' 25 miles E of Atlanta off Hwy 78, (770) 498-5690. Gates open 6am-midnight, attractions, 10am-5pm, 8pm in summer. *www.stonemountainpark.com.*

Marriott Marquis, 265 Peachtree Center Ave, 521-0000. One of a genre of spectacular hotels featuring a breathtaking atrium. A must-see if you are in Atlanta. Most expensive construct and the largest hotel in the southeast.

CNN Center, Marietta St at Techwood Dr, 827-2400. Tour the studios of this 24 hr all news network. $10. Daily 9am-5pm, every 10 mins. *www.cnn.com/studiotour.* Next door is the **Omni Coliseum,** home of the **Atlanta Hawks** basketball team. Ticketmaster: 249-6400. *www.nba.com/hawks.* **Turner Field,** 755 Hank Aaron Blvd, the stadium built especially for the Olympics, is now the home of the **Atlanta Braves** baseball team. _www.atlantabraves.com_. Ticketmaster. American football is played by the **Falcons** at the **Georgia Dome**, which hosted the '94 Superbowl and was also host to some Olympic events in '96. _www.atlantafalcons.com_.

Centennial Olympic Park, International Blvd and Techwood Dr, 222-7275, commemorates the 1996 Olympic Games. The park was made famous when a bomb exploded here during the Games. Visit the **Fountain of Rings**—the largest fountain in the world featuring the Olympic symbol. _www.centennialpark.com._

Margaret Mitchell House, 990 Peachtree St, 249-7015. Tour the historic home where Mitchell wrote _Gone with the Wind_ and relive antebellum Atlanta, unless frankly, my dear, you don't give a damn. Open daily 9.30am-5pm, $12, $9 w/student ID. _www.gwtw.org_.

Entertainment

Read the free, weekly _Creative Loafing_, _Atlanta Gazette_ and _Where Magazine_ to find out what goes on. 'Atlanta, especially midtown, is known second only to San Francisco for a large gay community.'

Piedmont Park, free open-air jazz and classical concerts, Atlanta Philharmonic Orchestra, throughout the summer. First week in Sep, **Atlanta Jazz Festival**. 'Not to be missed. People dance, drink; on a good evening it can be like the last night of the proms. Also watch the fireflies do illuminated mating dances.' _www.atlantafestivals.com._ Park also has an open-air swimming pool, 892-0117. 'Beautiful; great for a rest and a free shower. Friendly pool attendants.' 1.30pm-7.30pm Mon-Fri; free btwn 1.30pm and 4pm, 12am-7.30pm w/ends, $2. Keep eyes open at night; not too friendly neighbourhood. _www.piedmontpark.org/index.html_.

Six Flags Over Georgia, 12 miles W on I-20, 948-9290. One of the nation's largest theme parks, home to the 'Georgia Cyclone' rollercoaster and such rides as 'Mind Bender' and 'Splashwater Falls.' Sun-Thurs 10am-9pm, Fri, Sat 10am-10pm. 1-day pass $44. Take MARTA to Hightower Station, then bus #201. 'Don't go on Saturdays as you will spend the whole day in queues.' _www.sixflags.com_.

The Fox, 660 Peachtree, 881-2100. Second largest movie theatre in America and now a national landmark. One of the last great movie palaces. Built in 1929; Moorish design. Now a venue for concerts, theatre and special film presentations. Call for listings. **Atlanta Preservation Society**, 876-2040, operate a history tour of the interior; Mon, Wed, Thurs, at 10am, Sat at 10am and 11am, $10, $5 w/student ID. _www.foxtheatre.org_.

Information

Convention and Visitors Bureau, Harris Tower, 233 Peachtree St NE, Suite 2000, 521-6600. Mon-Fri 8.30am-5.30pm. 'Far more helpful than Chamber of Commerce.' Satellite locations in Lenox Square Mall and Underground Atlanta. _www.atlanta.net._

Chamber of Commerce, 235 Andrew Young International Blvd, across from Omni Building, 880-9000. 'Very helpful.' _www.metroatlantachamber.com._

Travel

MARTA (Metropolitan Atlanta Rapid Transit Authority), 848-4711, combined bus and rail serves most area attractions and hotels. Basic fare $1.75, weekly pass $13, unlimited usage. Subway runs 5am-1am. _www.itsmarta.com._

Greyhound, 232 Forsyth St, (800) 231-2222. Use caution in this area. Savannah approx. $80, Orlando approx. $138.

Amtrak, Peachtree Station, 1688 Peachtree St NW, (800) 872-7245. The NY-New Orleans _Crescent_ stops here daily.

Hartsfield International Airport is situated 12 miles S of the city, an impressive, innovative piece of building; 530-7300, customer service. MARTA buses can take you downtown, 15 min rides run frequently. _www.atlanta-airport.com._ Shuttle service available. Taxis downtown (209-4193), $25.

Internet access
Fulton County Library, 514 state Rd 25, 857-3895, free. _www.fulco.lib.in.us._

SAVANNAH Like many cities in the South, Savannah is rich in history, Southern charm, and old-fashioned manners. When **Ray Charles** sings _Georgia on My Mind_, it's surely Savannah and not Atlanta he's mooning over. Laid out in 1733 by English General James Oglethorpe, Savannah was America's first planned city and Georgia's oldest. In one of the earliest evangelical movements, Charles and John Wesley accompanied Oglethorpe as missionaries, later establishing in the city the Wesleyan Methodist Church. After seeing what Sherman had done to Atlanta in 1864, Savannah wisely decided to surrender, protecting her charming gardens, public squares and old homes from certain destruction. What Sherman spared, however, seemed almost doomed by declining cotton prices.

The town was rundown until restoration efforts began on Trustees Garden in the 1950s. Today, the city (which has no less than 21 squares) resonates with reminders of its colonial past and has been restored to its former glory. Warehouses that once stored clouds of cotton now house shops and restaurants along the Savannah River. Monthly parades, concerts and other events take place here; St. Patrick's Day celebrations are said to rival those of New York. The first steamship (the _Savannah_, of course) crossed the Atlantic to Liverpool (in 1819) from here, the 10th largest port in the US. And an old seamen's pub referred to in **Robert Louis Stevenson's** _Treasure Island_ still survives as the Pirate's House. _www.savannah.com/index.cfm._

Accommodation
Bed and Breakfast Inn, 117 W Gordon at Chatham Sq, 233-9481. In the heart of the historic district, an 1853 townhouse. 'Clean and well maintained.' Average $119. _www.savannahbnb.com._
Savannah International Youth Hostel (HI-AYH), 304 E Hall St, 236-7744. Renovated Victorian mansion in historic district. $22. Check-in 7am-10am and 5pm-11pm. No curfew. Call ahead for late check-in. Maximum stay 3 nights. Internet access available.
Thunderbird Inn, 611 W Oglethorpe Ave, (866) 324-2661. Around $100. Nr bus sta. _www.thethunderbirdinn.com._
Skidway Island State Park, 6 miles SE of downtown on Waters Ave, 598-2300, inaccessible by public transport. $18 1st night, $16 thereafter. Bathrooms and heated showers.

Food
Spanky's Pizza Galley and Saloon, 317 East River St, 236-3009. 'River Street's favourite good-time saloon.' Dinner from $8. Mon-Thu 11am-12am, w/end 'til 2am.
Toucan Café, 531 Stevenson Ave, 352-2233, serving all kinds of international food, sandwiches and salads, $5-$20. Open daily for lunch 11.30am-2pm, Mon-Thurs 5pm-9pm, w/end 'til 10pm. _www.toucancafe.com._
Wally's Sixpence Pub, 245 Bull St, 233-3151. Mon-Thurs 11.30am-midnight, w/end 'til 2am. 'A haunt of unusual and interesting characters.' Featured in the Julia Roberts' film _Something to Talk About._

Of interest

Old Savannah offers cobbled streets, charming squares, formal gardens and several beautiful mansions. Among the stately houses of the town is the **Owens-Thomas House**, at 124 Abercorn St, 233-9743, at which Lafayette was a visitor in 1825. Tue-Sat 10am-5pm, Sun 2pm-5pm, Mon 12-5pm; $8, $4 w/student ID. *oldsavannahtours.com.*

Green-Meldrim House, Madison Sq, 233-3845, is where General Sherman enjoyed his victory, $5, $2 w/student ID. The Green-Meldrim serves as Parish house for the Gothic Revival style **St John's Episcopal Church,** built 1852. Tue, Thurs, Fri 10am-4pm, Sat 10am-1pm..

Savannah Waterfront. Pubs, shops, restaurants and night spots housed in old cotton warehouses along cobblestone streets. 'Beware: it's a tourist trap with masses of souvenir shops and over-priced beer.' In the same vein is City Market, at St Julian and Jefferson Sts. *www.savriverstreet.com.*

Christ Episcopal Church, 28 Bull St, 232-4131. First church in Georgia; the present building was erected in 1840. John Wesley preached here in 1736-37, arousing extraordinary emotions in the congregation. He also founded the first Sunday school here. *www.christchurchsavannah.org/index.htm*.

Temple Mickve Israel, 20 E Gordon, 233-1547. Seeking religious freedom, a group of Sephardic Jews from England were among the first to settle here in 1733. The oldest congregation practicing reform Judaism in the US. The synagogue looks like a church, complete with a steeple, choir loft, and gothic design. No one is sure why the Orthodox congregation built it this way. Two of the Torahs, the oldest in America, are from the original congregation. Tours of museum and archives, Mon-Fri 10am-noon, 2pm-4pm. $3. Services Fri 6.30pm at selected congregants' homes, Sat 11am, all welcome. *mickveisrael.org.*

Entertainment

Kevin Barry's, 117 W River St, 233-9626, Irish pub immortalised in a song, offering good, cheap Irish food, Guinness on draught (not so cheap!) and Irish folk music at 8.30pm. Mon-Fri 4pm-3am, Sat 11:30am-3am, Sun 12.30-2am.

Also check out **Wet Willies,** 101 E River St, 232-5650, for 'irresistible frozen daiquiris'. Mon-Thurs 11am-1am, Fri-Sat 'til 2am, Sun from 12:30pm. *www.wetwillies.com/happen_view.cfm?id=1*.

Information/Travel

Chamber of Commerce Convention and Visitors Bureau, 101 E. Bay St, 644-6401, Mon-Fri 8:30am-5pm. *www.savannahchamber.com. www.savcvb.com.*

Savannah Visitors Center, 301 Martin Luther King Blvd, 944-0460. Literature, maps, a self-guided walking tour leaflet, slide show. Many tours start here. Open daily 8.30am-5pm.

Amtrak, 2611 Seaboard Coastline Dr, 234-2611/(800) 872-7245.

Chatham Area Transit (CAT), 233-5767. Public transportation system serving Savannah and surrounding area. Buses run 6am-midnight, basic fare $1. *www.catchacat.org.*

Greyhound, 610 W Oglethorpe Ave, 232-2135/(800) 231-2222.

Gray Line Bus Tours, 215 West Boundry St, 236-9604. *www.grayline.com/index.cfm.*

OKEFENOKEE SWAMP This large swamp area lies in southeast Georgia. Eight miles S of **Waycross** on Hwys US 1 and US 23, is the **Okefenokee Swamp Park**, 283-0583. This private park offers a half-hour boat tour, $16, hour boat tour $20, two-hour boat tour $30 (includes admission), and the walkways enable you to take in the cypresses, flowers, aquatic birds, bears and alligators without getting your feet wet. There is also a museum telling the story of the 'Land of the Trembling Earth' (the old Indian name for the swamp). _www.okeswamp.com._

Entrance to the park is $12, 9am-5.30pm daily. For info on the **National Wildlife Refuge**, call 496-7836 7am-5.30pm daily. The park offers 2-5 days canoe trips (reserve in advance), from $20 (excluding canoe hire).

KENTUCKY - Bluegrass State

Legendary for the duels, feuds and stubborn spirit of its earlier inhabitants (such as the infamous **Daniel Boone:** _earlyamerica.com/lives/boone_), Kentucky's bluegrass hills invite travellers to sample its bourbon whiskey, fried chicken, fast horses and even faster bluegrass music. Since Boone cleared the Wilderness Trail in 1769 to settle the first lands west of the Allegheny Mountains, Kentuckians have quietly elevated country living into an art form. Bluegrass music involves complex guitar-picking, banjo-strumming and fiddle-playing. While sometimes tedious in its traditional forms, it can be exhilarating in its progressive modes. Kentucky is the home state of **Merle Travis**, whose famous parlour-guitar, Travis-style picking is a noted method of bluegrass playing today. _www.countrymusichalloffame.com/inductees/merle_travis.html_.

Kentucky produces 87% of the world's bourbon (from Bourbon county) and bottles almost half of the nation's whiskey. The abundance of fertile bluegrass (which is not actually blue—it's green and blossoms blue in spring) attracted livestock farmers and their horses. The Kentucky equine passion has developed into a refined, multi-million dollar international obsession indulged annually at Louisville's **Kentucky Derby**. _www.kentuckyderby.com/2006._

Hardy country living has bred many proud Kentucky natives, among them **Henry Clay, Jefferson Davis, Abraham Lincoln** and **Mohammed Ali.** Kentucky's fighting spirit, important reserves of coal and strategic location made it a decisive factor in the Civil War. The hostility of the Civil War would not condone a state's remaining neutral, but nevertheless, that's what Kentucky tried to be. A worried Lincoln was said to have remarked that he hoped to have God on his side, but he had to have Kentucky. _www.kentuckytourism.com_.

The area code for Louisville, Frankfurt and western KY is 502, for Lexington, it is 859, and for eastern KY, 606.

LOUISVILLE The most prestigious horse race in the country, the **Kentucky Derby**, is held here the first week in May amidst a festival atmosphere of parades, concerts and a steamboat race.

Founded by George Rogers Clark as a supply base on the Ohio for his Northwest explorations, Louisville is now a commercial, industrial and educational centre that specialises in things that are supposed to be bad for you. Fast food, bourbon, whiskey and cigarettes are made here in abundance. This is also the hometown of the **Louisville Lip**, though the boulevard named after him is called Mohammed Ali.

En route from here to Mammoth Caves are various folksy attractions, including Abraham Lincoln's birthplace at Hodgenville, Stephen Foster's original 'My Old Kentucky Home' and the Lincoln Homestead nearby. Note: Louisville is pronounced Loo-AH-ville. _www.gotolouisville.com_.

Accommodation

Emily Boone Guest House, 102 Pope Street, (502) 585-3430. $10 plus 20 mins of chores. No curfew but respectful behaviour required. Rsvs req.

KOA, 900 Marriot Dr, (812) 282-4474. I-65 N across bridge, exit Stansifer Ave. 'Very handy for downtown.' Free use of pool, mini-golf and fishing lake at motel next door. Sites $24 for two, $29 w/hook-up, XP-$4, cabins for two, $40.

Thrifty Dutchman Budget Hotel, 3357 Fern Valley Rd, 968-8124. Off I-65. S-$40, D-$50. XP-$6.

Food

Look along **Bardstown Rd** for budget cafes serving a wide variety of local and international cuisine. BBQ's, burgoo stew and cured ham are all Kentucky delicacies, unlike the famed fried chicken.

Check's Cafe, 1101 Burnett, 637-9515. Local favourite where hamburgers start at $2. Oyster specialty. Open Mon-Thurs 11am-9pm, Fri/Sat 'til 11am, Sun 1pm-8pm.

The Old Spaghetti Factory, 235 W Market St, 581-1070. Full dinner with pasta, salad, bread and dessert around $10. Sun-Thurs 11.30am-2pm and 5pm-10pm. Fri/Sat 'til 11pm. _www.osf.com._

Phoenix Hill Tavern, 644 Baxter Ave, 589-4957. 4 stages offering live blues and rock, with dance music out on the deckbar. Wed/Thu/Sat 8pm-3.30am, Fri from 5pm. Cover $2-$5. 'Cheap sandwiches.' _www.phoenixhill.com._

The Rudyard Kipling, 422 W Oak St, 636-1311, 7 blocks S of downtown in Old Louisville. 'Hearty food and drink from all around the world.' Try a bowl of Kentucky burgoo (a meat and veg stew). Often live music; theatre is performed on the in-house stage during Sept and Oct. 'If you eat one meal in Louisville, eat it here.' Mon-Sat 6.30pm-midnight, sometimes Sundays. _www.therudyardkipling.com._

Of interest

Churchill Downs, home of the **Kentucky Derby**, 700 Central Ave, (800) 283-3729. On the morning of Derby Day, the first Saturday in May, arrive around 8am to ensure entry. Those without tickets are permitted to seat in certain areas. The big race starts at 5pm, but the partying goes on all day. Potent mint juleps, the drink of the South, are available from vendors. Racing also takes place from late Apr-early Jul and late Oct-late Nov. At gate 1 stands the **Kentucky Derby Museum**, 637-1111, Mon-Sat 8am-5pm, Sun noon-5pm, $9. Shows run twice hourly. Includes exhibits on horse racing and breeding, and an exciting 360 degree movie theatre that puts you in the middle of the race (hourly). _www.derbymuseum.org_. Each August Louisville hosts the **Kentucky State Fair,** which features the World Championship Horse Show for American saddlebreds—Kentucky's native horse breed. _www.kystatefair.org_.

A pleasant way to spend an afternoon is to take a cruise on the Ohio River on the _Belle of Louisville_, 574-2992, an old sternwheeler. The boat runs from April until October and departs from the landing at 4th St and River Rd, Fri/Sat 12pm-2pm, Sun 1pm-3pm, $12. 'Sunset cruises,' Tue and Thurs 6pm, $12. Nighttime Dance Cruises, Fri 9pm-11pm, $15. **Spirit of Jefferson** cruises also available. _www.belleoflouisville.org_. The **Corn Island Storytelling Festival,** one w/end in September, 245-0643, uses the _Belle_ for a storytelling tour along the river. The most popular festival event is the long run Park ghost story event, which is held at the Louisville waterfront. Festival tkts for all the events are $50, $90 for two. Individual event tkts available, $10 pp. _www.cornislandstorytellingfestival.org._

Howard Steamboat Museum, 1101 E Market St, (812) 283-3728, Tue-Sat 10am-4pm, Sun 1pm-4pm, $5, $3 w/student ID. Billed as the 'only museum of its kind in the

US', models of steamboats, tools and pilot wheels are on display. Located across the Ohio River from Louisville in Jeffersonville, Indiana. *www.steamboatmuseum.org*.

Jim Beam's American Outpost, 543-9877. 10 min movie and self-guided tour that shows you the joys of bourbon-making. (Bourbon is made using at least 51% corn and must be aged at least 2 yrs, preferably in a charred white oak container. Anything less is 'just' whiskey.) The tour is free, Mon-Sat 9am-4.30pm, Sun 1pm-4pm. Follow I-65, 22 miles S from Louisville, then E on Rte 245 toward Clermont.

America hoards her gold at **Fort Knox,** 25 miles SW of Louisville on US 31 W-60. Don't expect to see the metal, but if you're in a military frame of mind, visit the Gen Patton, KB, OBE, **Museum of Cavalry and Armor,** Building 4554, Fayette Ave, in Fort Knox, 624-3812. 200 yrs of military history, from the old frontier fort to displays of weapons, equipment and uniforms dating back to the Revolutionary War. Also see the 'ivory-handled Patton pistols' and war booty that Old Blood and Guts gathered in WW II. Donation appreciated. Mon-Fri 9am-4.30pm, w/end 10am-4.30pm. *www.knox.army.mil/museum.*

Information/Internet access
Kentucky State Dept. Of Tourism, (502) 564-4930. *www.kentuckytourism.com.*
Visitors Information Center, 400 S 1st St, corner of Liberty, (502) 584-2121/ (800) 792-5595. Mon-Fri 8.30am-5pm, Sat 9am-4pm, Sun 11am-4pm. Later in summer.
Louisville Free Public Library, 301 York Street, 574-1611, free. *www.lfpl.org.*

Travel
TARC, 585-1234, local buses serving most of metro area. Daily 4.45am-1am. Fare $1. *www.ridetarc.org.*
Greyhound, 720 W Muhammad Ali Blvd, 561-2805/(800) 231-2222.

MAMMOTH CAVES NATIONAL PARK Halfway between Louisville, Kentucky, and Nashville, Tennessee, lies Mammoth Caves National Park. Above ground this is a preserve of forest, flowers and wildlife, while below ground it's several hundred miles of passages, pits, domes, gypsum and travertine formations, archaeological remains and a crystal lake. The caves rival in size the better-known Carlsbad Caverns and may be explored on foot, or afloat during conducted boat trips. The boat trip does not go through Mammoth Caves itself, just the caves at Bowling Green. Call the park office for more info: (502) 758-2180.

Keep to the caves within the park and do not stray into the trashy/commercial/privately-owned/exploited caves nearby. There are several campgrounds within the park. Various tours leave regularly from the Visitors Center. **Cave City** is the service centre for the Park. Lots of motels here. *www.nps.gov/maca.*

A short drive north from Cave City is **Hodgenville** where you can visit the modest **Lincoln Birthplace and National Historic Site**. Nearby Knob Creek Farm was Abe's boyhood home, 549-3741, 8.30am-4.30pm. *www.nps.gov/abli.*

LEXINGTON Named in honour of its New England counterpart, Lexington was described by one traveller as 'an interesting historical town with a rich economy, not such a 'hillbilly image as people say'. Sheik Mohammed bin Rashid al-Maktoum would certainly agree. He makes time for the annual horse sales at Keeneland Race Course. He has been known to snatch up prized thoroughbreds for $1 million plus.

Lexington horse-traders have a certain shrewdness born of their unique trade. Luckily, the local industry leaves little non-organic pollution to spoil the rolling bluegrass hills of the countryside. _www.visitlex.com_.

Accommodation
Knights Inn, 2250 Elkhorn Dr, Exit 110 off I-75, 299-8481. S-$35, D-$37. Rsvs recommended. _www.knightsinn.com/KnightsInn/control/home_.
Kentucky Horse Park Campground, 4089 Ironworks Pike, 233-4303. 9 miles N of downtown off Newton Pike. Showers, pool, ball courts, laundry, free shuttle to horse park. Sites from $15.

Food
Alfalfa Restaurant, 557 S Limestone St, 253-0014, across from University Memorial Hall. Wide variety of seafood, meat and vegetarian dishes from $6. Lunch and brunch $6-10, dinner $8-$16. Restaurant hrs Mon-Thu 11am-9pm, Fri 'til 10pm, Sat 10am-10pm, Sun 10am-9pm. No cover.
Perkin's Family Restaurant, 2401 Richmond Road, 269-1663. Traditional Southern cuisine. Bfast from $6, lunch from $7 and dinner from $11.

Of interest
Some of the most magnificent horses in the world have been raised on **Three Chimneys Farm**, 873-7053. Dynaformer and Wild Again are two of the most famous studs hard at work making future Derby winners. Tours by appointment only; with fillies going for up to $10.2 million, many of the farms have decided not to interrupt the horseplay with buses of gawking tourists. _www.threechimneys.com_.
Bluegrass Tours, 252-5744, provides a once-daily tour from 9am-12pm of the area, which takes you past the paddocks of the famous thoroughbred farms, $26, Rsvs required. Famous farms include **Donamire** and **Cobra Farm**. _www.bluegrasstours.com_. Also visit the **Kentucky Horse Park**, Iron Works Pike, 6 miles N on I-75, exit 120, 233-4303. 'Well worth a visit, especially for horse lovers.' Daily 9pm-5pm, $19.50. Self-guided tour, incl option to ride on horse trolley for 15 mins. _www.imh.org_.
Ashland, Richmond Rd at Sycamore Rd, 266-8581, was the home of politician Henry Clay, the engineer of the great Missouri Compromise on slavery. The compromise allowed slavery below, but not above the 36th parallel. Ultimately proving unworkable, the compromise pushed the war back for years, $7 includes guided tour. 10am-4pm daily. _www.henryclay.org_.
The Mary Todd Lincoln House, 578 W Main St, 233-9999, built 1803, is where Abraham Lincoln's wife lived as a girl. Lincoln himself stayed here several times. Mon-Sat 10am-4pm. $7. _www.mtlhouse.org_.
The first college west of the Alleghenies was **Transylvania University**. Folklore has it that the old administration building burnt down and 10 students suffered nasty deaths because of a curse placed upon the school. Inside the new administration building at Old Morrison Hall lies the crypt of a professor named Rafinesque, which was placed there to remove the curse. Students celebrate the tale each Halloween. _www.transy.edu_.
The University of Kentucky, 257-3595, gives free campus walking tours, Mon-Fri. Visitor Center open daily 8am-4.30pm. _www.uky.edu_. Also worth seeing is the **University Art Museum,** 257-5716, featuring over 3500 works including drawings, paintings and sculpture. Tue-Sat noon-5pm, Fri 'til 8pm, free. _www.uky.edu/artmuseum_.
Outside Lexington: Shaker Village, in **Harroldsburg**, 25 miles SW of Lexington on US 68. This community was established by the Shaker sect in 1805 and by the middle of that century numbered 500 inhabitants. The Shakers have departed, but their buildings, with the help of some restoration, still stand. The museum preserves Shaker furnishings, $12.50, $16 includes river boat ride. To relive the

Shaker life, you can stay in one of the buildings, furnished in the Shaker style, $78-$94. Call (800) 734-5611 for rsvs. 7 miles from the original Kentucky settlement at Fort Harrod. *www.shakervillageky.org*.

In the SE corner of the state, the **Cumberland Gap National Historical Park** and the **Daniel Boone National Forest** provide a beautiful retreat into untouched wilderness. The Park Headquarters and Visitors Center, on Hwy 58, (606) 784-6428, 8am-6pm, has info on tours, camping and hiking in the Gap area. No rsvs. For info on hiking and camping in the Daniel Boone National Forest call 745-3100. *www.nps.gov/cuga/index.htm*.

Information/Travel

Convention and Visitors Bureau, 301 E Vine St, 233-1221, (800) 845-3959. *www.visitlex.com.*

The Visitors Center is in the same building, Suite 363. Mon-Fri 8.30am-5pm.

Greyhound, 477 New Circle Rd NW, 299-8804/(800) 231-2222. There are no buses serving the airport. For a cab, call 231-8294, reasonable fare.

LexTran, 255-7756. Buses depart from the Transit Center, 220 W Vine St. Serves university, metro and surrounding area. Daily 6.20am-12.40am. Fare $1.

Internet access: Lexington Public Library, 140 E Main, 231-5500, call to reserve time. Free. *www.lexpublib.org.*

LOUISIANA - The Pelican State

Louisiana culture has a rhythm all its own—a suite of jazz riffs, zydeco swing, Cajun and gospel harmonies, making it a state unlike any other. The Creole State has given the United States some of its most exotic cooking, its best party—Mardi Gras—and most flamboyant politicians. Depression-era Huey Long vowed to 'Soak the Rich!', former Governor Edwin Edwards claims that losing $1 million in Vegas was part of his hobby.

Louisiana's cultural heritage is rich and colourful. The original French and Spanish settlers brought old world architecture to the state, while their African and Caribbean slaves laid the musical foundations for what would become jazz music. And, after the British expelled them from Nova Scotia in 1775, the French Acadians, now called Cajuns, brought fur-trapping, Cajun cooking, dialects and their special zydeco music to the bayou.

Caribbean pirates, Mississippi riverboat gamblers and plantation owners have given way to a more respectable economy based upon thousands of offshore oil wells, a huge trade in grain and coffee, and a growing number of offshore casinos, but Louisiana, whose state flower is the magnolia, still beguiles visitors with a carefree, genteel atmosphere unlike anywhere else in America.

In September 2005, Katrina, the worst hurricane ever to hit the US, burst ashore, devastating and flooding New Orleans, South Louisiana and the neighbouring coast of Mississippi. At the time of writing, the area is still recovering and beginning to be rebuilt. Nevertheless, the entries in this Guide should all be double checked for their current details.

It is even possible that some places listed here may no longer exist. *www.louisianatravel.com.*

The telephone area code for New Orleans is 504, for Baton Rouge, 225 and for Acadiana it's 337.

NEW ORLEANS Until Katrina in September 2005, this was a party that never ended. First hosted by the French in 1718, the Crescent City was secretly sold to the Spanish in 1762 and the citizens didn't find out until 1766. It was returned to France just before the Americans bought it from Napoleon for $15 million in the Louisiana Purchase of 1803. Centuries of cross-pollination have resulted in a magnificent mixture of different cultures: Spanish architecture, French joie de vivre and a Caribbean sense of pace. A limitless supply of alcohol and music have contributed to New Orleans' reputation as the 'city that care forgot' and helped to earn its nick-name, *The Big Easy, www.bigeasy.com.*

Visitors are drawn by the Vieux Carré above Canal Street, where gracious homes, walled gardens, narrow streets overhung by iron-lace balconies, and delicious Creole food struggle to retain a mellow atmosphere against encroaching plastic America. The French Quarter, which mercifully escaped huge damage from Katrina, is one of the most nearly European areas in the US, and is always full of life. *www.crescentcity.com.*

And of course there's jazz that began here, first played on the discarded instruments of civil war army bands by legends such as Louis Armstrong (*www.redhotjazz.com/louie.html*), Buddy Bolden, Bunk Johnson (*www.bunkjohnson.org*), Jelly Roll Morton (*www.redhotjazz.com/jellyroll.html*), King Oliver (*www.redhotjazz.com/kingo.html*) and Kid Ory (*www.redhotjazz.com/ory.html*). They've all stomped here in Storyville. More recently, Pulitzer-prize winning local, Wynton Marsalis has continued the tradition. One the newest local entertainers to keep New Orleans pinned on today's map is comedienne Eleanor DeGeneres.

Writers too have been seduced by the city: Truman Capote was born here, William Faulkner and Sherwood Anderson wrote novels here; F. Scott Fitzgerald wrote *This Side of Paradise* in New Orleans; Lafcadio Hearn's prescient *Chita* described a tidal wave that engulfed Louisiana in the 19th century; O. Henry, the famous American short-story writer, wrote four of them about New Orleans; Longfellow's poem had *Evangeline* waiting for her Gabriel in a nearby bayou; Mark Twain's *Life on the Mississippi* tells of the city where he began and ended his piloting career; Walt Whitman worked for the New Orleans *Crescent;* Tennessee Williams immortalized the city in *A Streetcar Named Desire;* and more recently, Anne Rice's vampire tales are set there.

Edgar Degas, the only impressionist to visit North America, captured the atmosphere of the city during his visit here in 1872-73 with some of his paintings, including *The Cotton Exchange of New Orleans. www.passion4art.com/articles/french_impress.htm.*

Rock and roll, born on the banks of the Mississippi, also tells some great stories of New Orleans, including *Jambalaya* by Jerry Lee Lewis, *King Creole* by Elvis, and the poignant *You Never Can Tell* by Chuck Berry about Pierre and his mademoiselle: "They bought a souped-up jitney, 'twas a cherry red '53, They drove it down to New Orleans to celebrate their anniversary, It was there that Pierre was married to the lovely mademoiselle, "C'est la vie", say the old folks, it goes to show you never can tell." *www.chuckberry.com.*

The New Orleans police have gained a reputation for brutality towards, and general ill-treatment of, young foreign visitors. Be careful. Following

Katrina's devastation in 2005, the entire half million population of New Orleans was evacuated and large areas flooded, so the entries in this section should all be checked for their current details - see *www.nawlins.com* for updates.

Accommodation

Many of these rates do not apply during Mardi Gras, the Jazz Festival and the Sugar Bowl. Check first. Off-season rates prevail Memorial Day to Labor Day.

India House, 124 S. Lopez St, 821-1904. $17 dorm, $35 private room. Mid-city area, mins from French quarter. Pool, table tennis, kitchen, laundry, TV room, Internet access. *www.indiahousehostel.com.*

Parisian Courtyard Inn, 1726 Prytania St, 581-4540. From $44. $1/2$ hr walk to French Quarter, 1 block off streetcar route.

Marquette House Youth Hostel, 2249 Carondelet St, 523-3014. $18 AYH, $21 non-AYH, private rooms from $50. More during Mardi Gras/Jazz Festival. Nr Garden District and St Charles streetcar. Rsvs recommended. AC, internet access. 'Clean and comfy.' Nr laundry and supermarket. 'Very friendly and helpful.' 'Excellent.'

Prytania Park Hotel, 1525 Prytania St, 524-0427. Average $100+. AC, TV, includes bfast. Near French Quarter. 'Luxury.' *www.prytaniaparkhotel.com.*

St Charles Guest House, 1748 Prytania St, 523-6556. B&B 10 mins from French Quarter by streetcar, nr Garden District. Backpacker rooms $45, D-$65. Pool and sun deck. 'Near small supermarket and laundry.' 'Free bfast and newspapers.' 'Owners are very friendly and as kind and generous as anyone could be.' *www.stcharlesguesthouse.com.*

Camping: New Orleans KOA West, 11129 Jefferson Hwy, River Ridge, 467-1792. Site $24-46, $31, pool, laundry. RTA bus and various tours pick up from grounds. *www.neworleansrvcamp.com.*

Bayou Segnette State Park, 7777 Westbank Expressway, 736-7140. Bus service runs to park, but is located 1 mile away. Site $12, cabin up to 6 people (Mon-Fri only), $65. Rsvs essential for cabins. *www.lastateparks.com/bayouseg/byusegne.htm*.

Food

Hot, spicy Cajun food abounds, as does old fashioned stick-to-your-ribs Southern cooking. Gumbo, jambalaya, and crawfish are specialties. Try chocolate pecan pie and beignets—a hot, square doughnut without the hole. *www.foodfest.neworleans.com.*

Bayona, 430 Dauphine St. (b/t Conti and St. Louis Sts.), 525-4455. New-world cuisine in a Mediterranean atmosphere. Cream of Garlic Soup is a perennial favorite. Mon-Fri 11.30am-1.30pm, 6.30pm-9.30pm, Sat 'til 10.30pm. Call for rsvs.

Café du Monde, 800 Decatur, (800) 772-2927, in the French Market. Open 24 hrs. This is the place to get your beignets! 'An experience not to be missed.' Begin and end every day here. *www.cafedumonde.com.*

Café Maspero, 601 Decatur, 523-6250. Sandwiches, fried seafood. Open daily 11am-11pm, later at w/end. 'Good food—substantial meal $6.' Steak and seafood platter at only $10. All meals under $15. 'Expect to queue for a seat.' 'Low prices, big portions.' Cash only.

Coops Place, 1109 Decatur, 525-9053. Cajun food, dinner $6-$14. 'The real thing, unpretentious local restaurant.' Daily, 11am-3am.

Emeril's, 800 Tchoupitoulas St. at Julia St, 528-9393. A bit more expensive, but worth it; named Restaurant of the Year by *Esquire* magazine. Lunch 11.30am-2pm, dinner 6pm-10pm, Fri/Sat 'til 11pm, call for reservations. *www.emerils.com/restaurants/neworleans_emerils.*

The Fudgery, 1 Poydras St., 522-8030. Delicious homemade fudge. 'Watch them make it right in front of you—yummy!' Open Mon-Sat 10am-9pm, Sun 'til 7pm.

K Paul's Louisiana Kitchen, 416 Chartres St, 524-7394, in the French Quarter, looks like a hole in the wall but is actually world famous. If you're there at dinnertime,

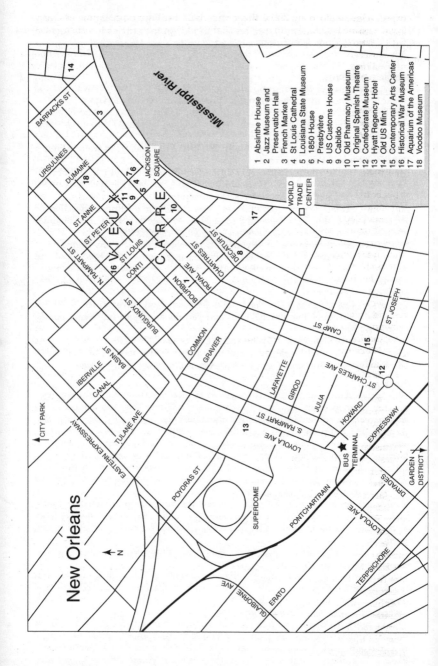

New Orleans

Mississippi River

VIEUX CARRE

1 Absinthe House
2 Jazz Museum and
   Preservation Hall
3 French Market
4 St Louis Cathedral
5 Louisiana State Museum
6 1850 House
7 Presbytère
8 US Customs House
9 Cabildo
10 Old Pharmacy Museum
11 Original Spanish Theatre
12 Confederate Museum
13 Hyatt Regency Hotel
14 Old US Mint
15 Contemporary Arts Center
16 Historical War Museum
17 Aquarium of the Americas
18 Voodoo Museum

WORLD
TRADE
CENTER

JACKSON
SQUARE

SUPERDOME

BUS
TERMINAL

CITY PARK

GARDEN
DISTRICT

BARRACKS ST
URSULINES
DUMAINE
ST ANNE
ST PETER
ST LOUIS
CONTI
N. RAMPART ST
BURGUNDY ST
BASIN ST
IBERVILLE
CANAL
TULANE AVE
EASTERN EXPRESSWAY
BOURBON
ROYAL AVE
CHARTRES ST
DECATUR ST
COMMON
GRAVIER
LAFAYETTE
GIROD
JULIA
S. RAMPART ST
LOYOLA AVE
POYDRAS ST
CAMP ST
ST CHARLES AVE
HOWARD
ST JOSEPH
EXPRESSWAY
PONTCHARTRAIN
GLAIBORNE AVE
ERATO
TERPSICHORE
DRYADES
LOYOLA AVE

expect to see a looooong line waiting to get in. Chef Paul Prudhomme has made Cajun cuisine famous worldwide. Excellent, but expensive, $26-$36. Lunch Thurs-Sat 11.30am-2.30pm, Dinner Mon-Sat 5:30pm-10pm. *www.kpauls.com.*

You can learn to cook Cajun food from Chef Joe Cahn at the **New Orleans School of Cooking,** 524 St. Louis, 525-2665 for info and rsvs. Demonstration classes available 10am-1pm $27, 2pm-4pm $22. Includes meal and recipes. Open daily. *www.neworleansschoolofcooking.com.*

Of interest

French Quarter or **Vieux Carré** (Old Square), the heart and soul of New Orleans, includes about 70 blocks of the old city between the river and Rampart St and Canal and Esplanade Sts. Apart from the pleasure of simply wandering around the streets, and through back alleys, you will find the city's most noteworthy buildings. Caution—do not wander down dark streets at night. As picturesque as they may be, the French Quarter's dark back alleys are good places for the foolish traveller to find trouble. *www.frenchquarter.com.*

The Quarter is a National Historic District, within the **Jean LaFitte National Historic Park and Preserve.** Lafitte was a famous New Orleans pirateer, who worked under the command of the French and the Columbians and helped, in small part, defeat the British at the Battle of New Orleans. Legend has it that his most audacious plan was to rescue Napoleon from his British captors, though this does not hold much credibility among New Orleaneans. *www.nps.gov/jela.* The park service **Folklife and Visitors Center,** 589-2636, 419 Decatur Street offers maps, informed rangers, and one tour of the French Quarter. It lasts for 60 mins and is free, departing at 9.30am. A good starting point in the Quarter is **Jackson Square.** The old Place d'Armes parade ground, Jackson Square has been the central gathering place in the city since it was first laid out in 1721. The square is named after Andrew Jackson, the hero of the battle of New Orleans. The statue honouring 'Old Hickory,' as the scrappy populist was called, was erected in 1856. *www.jackson-square.com.*

St Louis Cathedral, 525-9585, Jackson Sq's exquisite centrepiece was rebuilt in 1794 after a fire destroyed the original and remodelled in 1850. It is a minor basilica and the oldest active cathedral in the United States. Free guided tours Mon-Fri 10am-3pm. Sun mass 8am, 10am, noon, and 5pm. *www.cathedralstl.org.* Next to the Cathedral is the old Spanish governor's residence, **The Cabildo,** based in the State Museum, site of the US/French negotiations for the Louisiana Purchase. No 2 at the museum is The Presbytere, on Chartres St facing the Square. Dates to 1791 and houses New Orleans architecture exhibits and changing collections, specialising in Mardi Gras artifacts.

The Louisiana State Museum, 568-8214, includes several historical buildings in the Quarter which may be toured in combination. Individual museums $5, $4 w/student ID. Combination ticket $16.80, $12.60 students. All museum attractions open Tue-Sun 9am-5pm. **The 1850 House,** in a portion of the **Pontaba Apartments,** facing the Square, offers a glimpse of elegant Southern living. Said to be the oldest apts in the United States, the Pontabla Buildings were built for Baroness Pontabla and are furnished in the traditional antebellum style. Finally, the **Old US Mint,** 400 Esplanade, houses historical documents and jazz. A working mint from 1838-62 and 1879-1920, it's 'O' mintmark is a favourite among coin collectors worldwide.

Other historic buildings of the French Quarter include:

Absinthe House, 240 Bourbon St, 523-3181. The house where the LaFitte brothers, Pierre and Jean, 'plotted against honest shipping'; in others words, the Battle of New Orleans. Now a bar and literary landmark. Daily 9am-3am. *www.oldabsinthehouse.com.*

US Customs House, 423 Canal St, 589-6731. Dates from 1848; used as headquarters during Civil War Union occupation. Mon-Fri 8am-5pm. Free.

Contemporary Arts Center, 900 Camp St, 528-3805. 'Visual arts, music theater; stunning interior to building.' $5, $3 students, some exhibitions are free. Tues-Sun 11am-5pm. *www.cacno.org.*

Old Pharmacy Museum, 514 Chartres St, 565-8027. It was first used as a pharmacy in 1823, and was the first licenced pharmacy in the US. It is now an interesting museum of old apothecary items, voodoo potions, medical instruments and hand-blown pharmacy bottles and 'show globes'. Tue-Sun 10am-5pm, $5, $4 w/student ID. *www.pharmacymuseum.org.*

Historical Wax Museum, 917 Conti St, 581-1993, features a recreation of 'Congo Square,' the voodoo center of old New Orleans, as well as the popular Haunted Dungeon. Open 10am-5.30pm Mon-Sat, Sun from 12pm-5pm, $6.75, $5.75 w/student ID. *www.neworleanswaxmuseum.com/index.html*.

Le Petit Theatre du Vieux Carre, 616 St Peters St, 522-2081. They pride themselves on being one of the city's most beloved and historical theatres. It can also hold the title for the oldest continuously operating community theatre in the US. Built in 1789, Le Petit Theatre replicates the early 18th century abode of Joseph de Pontalba, Louisiana's last Spanish governor. About five performances are delivered each year. Thurs-Fri 8pm, Sun 2pm. Tkts approx. $16-21 for students. *www.lepetittheatre.com.*

Confederate Museum, 929 Camp St, 1 block off Lee Circle, 523-4522. Has memorabilia of the Civil War. 'Ten out of ten.' Mon-Sat 10am-4pm. $5, $4 w/student ID. *www.confederatemuseum.com*.

Take the **St Charles St Streetcar,** the oldest streetcar line in America still in operation and one of only 2 remaining in the city, through the fashionable Garden District ($1.25, 25¢ transfer). The line is an excellent way to get to know the city. *www.inetours.com/New_Orleans/St_Charles_Streetcar.html*. Once you reach the **Garden District,** get out and wander among the sumptuous houses built by rich antebellum whites to rival the Creole dwellings in the Vieux Carre. The District stretches from Jackson to Louisiana Aves between St Charles and Magazine Sts. *www.gardendistrict.neworleans.com.* Further down the streetcar line, you reach **Audubon Park** and the Audubon Zoo, 6500 Magazine, (866) 487-2966. One of the 'top 10 zoos in the US.' Natural habitats for 1800 animals. Open Mon-Fri 9.30am-5pm, w/end 'til 6pm, $12. Check website for special offers. *www.auduboninstitute.org.*

Another prime attraction outside the French Quarter is **City Park,** at Esplanade and Carrollton Sts, 482-4888, site of the famous **Duelling Oaks,** where New Orleans society settled their differences 'under the Oaks at dawn'. The fifth largest park in the USA, 1500 acres. Enjoy its magnificent oaks, statues and fountains, sports and recreational facilities. Botanical gardens, sports stadium, golf course, tennis courts, carousel and fairy-tale themed playground can be found here also. More like a lifestyle than a park. Free, but charges for activities. *www.neworleanscitypark.com.*

The New Orleans Museum of Art, 488-2631, is located in the park. The collection includes works by the Russian jeweller, Fabergé, an extensive decorate arts section and a large collection of French impressionist paintings. A floor of the museum is dedicated to Asian, African and Oceanic art. It suffered little damage by hurricane Katrina. Tues-Sun 10am-5pm, $8, $7 w/student ID. *www.noma.org*. More modern sites include the **Hyatt Regency Hotel,** Poydras and Loyola, with a free spectacular view. Not free and once spectacular is the **Louisiana Superdome,** 1500 Poydras St, 587-3663. Opened in 1975, it is the world's largest indoor stadium with the largest single room in the history of man. It was severely damaged by Katrina losing part of the roof and sheltering some 20,000 evacuees. The repair bill is put at about $125 million and it is expected to be the end of 2006 before the arena is open again. *www.superdome.com*.

Cruises on the Mississippi: The New Orleans Steamboat Co, 586-8777 offers three worthwhile tours: A dinner-jazz cruise, a harbour jazz cruise, and an aquarium zoo cruise. *www.neworleanssteamboat.com*. *The Cajun Queen*, 524-0814, offers a bayou, plantation, and battlefield cruise. *www.neworleanspaddlewheels.com*. Readership consensus is that the boat rides are generally 'boring' and 'not worth it,' but the Bayou trips by bus and boat are highly recommended if you want to see alligators 'au naturel'. These sights are found on the **Swamp Tour**; pick up from 223 N Peters, 592-0560/(800) 445-4109. Day tour $40, night tour plus airboat $65. *www.jeanlafitteswamptour.com*.

The **Aquarium of the Americas** on Canal St, (800)-774-7394, recreates the underwater environments of the American continent. Open 9.30am-7pm daily. $20 admission includes ticket to IMAX theatre. *www.auduboninstitute.org/aoa*.

Entertainment

New Orleans *is* entertainment. This is a city that knows how to have a good time and it's not only during Mardi Gras. Here you are likely to find a celebration of some kind at any time of the year. **Bourbon St**, though somewhat sleazy, is a perpetual party zone and a visit to this city would not be complete without at least one night's stroll down this crazy stretch of decadence, which survived Katrina in 2005. Although the jazz revival in New Orleans has brought back many good musicians, there are also, on Bourbon St, the typical tourist traps: over-priced nightclubs, flashy restaurants, endless clip joints, and plenty of bad music. Choose carefully (always check prices before you buy a drink, as you are sometimes paying for the band with them) and carry ID. Check *Gambit* and *Wavelength* newspapers for current listings.

New Orleans' temple of jazz is the **Preservation Hall**, 726 St Peter St, 522-2841 (days), 588-9192 (nights), where pioneers of jazz have always performed—and still do, hear jazz in its quintessential form. Doors 8pm, arrive early. 8.30pm-12am nightly, $8 standing. 'An absolute must." 'I'd pay $10 to go and see it again—a magical experience.' 'Whatever you read/hear will never do it justice—Go!' *www.preservationhall.com*. In **Jackson Square**, various jazz concerts are held throughout the year. Visit the website for more info. *www.jackson-square.com*.

Club 360, World Trade Center, 2 Canal St, 595-8900. America's largest revolving cocktail bar is 33 storeys high, and makes one revolution every $1^1/_2$ hrs (3ft per min). 'Visit in the evening and watch the sunset over the city.' Cover will vary. Open daily from 11am, closing times depend on number of customers, but usually around 2am.

Pat O'Brien's, 718 St Peter St, 525-4823. Reputed to be the 'busiest and the best' in the French Quarter. Popular with local students. 'Great atmosphere, no cover, closes 4am.' 'Home of the Hurricane Cocktail. Don't miss it.' $6 ($9 w/souvenir glass). Open Mon-Thurs 11am-3am, w/end 10am-4am. *www.patobriens.com*. Also try **Snug Harbor and Storyville** for sweet soulful music. *www.snugjazz.com*. Uptown New Orleans, around Maple, Oak and Willow Sts, down St Charles from Canal. 'Where the locals go. Good bars and clubs. Better music and cheaper.'

Information

New Orleans Welcome Center, 529 St Anne Street, 565-5661. In the French Quarter, free city and walking tour maps.

Metropolitan New Orleans Convention and Visitors Bureau, 2020 St. Charles Ave, 566-5011. *www.neworleanscvb.com*.

Internet access

New Orleans Public Library, Main Branch, 219 Loyola Ave, 529-7323. $3 an hour.

Milton H. Latter Memorial Library, 5120 St. Charles Avenue, 596-2625, free.

Situated in an historic mansion that is worth a look by virtue of the architecture alone! Visit it on a trip southwest on the St. Charles streetcar.

Travel
New Orleans Regional Transit Authority (RTA), 700 Plaza Dr, 242-2600. City bus and streetcar, the latter runs 24 hrs. $1.25, transfers 25¢. All-day pass $5, 3 days $12, obtainable from major hotels. *www.regionaltransit.org.*
Louisiana Transit Authority, 818-1077. Bus from airport to downtown, $1.60, exact change. Last bus leaves airport at 11.30pm.
Amtrak, 1001 Loyola Ave, 528-1610/(800) 872-7245. *Crescent* to NY, *City of New Orleans* to Chicago and *Sunset Limited* to LA originate here. Not safe after dark.
Greyhound, 1001 Loyola in train station, 524-7571 or (800) 231-2222. 'Bad neighbourhood.' Accommodation board here has been recommended. Try Tulane and Loyola for their ride boards.

BATON ROUGE During the first 150 years of its short history, Louisiana experienced considerable difficulty in deciding on a state capital. Opelousas, Alexandria, Shreveport and New Orleans all enjoyed such status. Finally, in 1849, Baton Rouge was chosen over New Orleans, largely due to concern over the state government being based in such a 'careless' city!

Situated in the heart of plantation country, 60 miles northwest of the 'Big Easy' on the Mississippi, Baton Rouge was named after the cypress tree used by the Indians to mark hunting boundaries between rival Native American tribes. Today it is the state's second largest city and one of the nation's largest ports, profiting mainly from petro-chemical and sugarcane production. The abundance of magnolia and cypress trees belies this industrial bias and the city still retains a small-town character. Of special interest are the 34 storey **New State Capitol Building**, 342-7317, 8am-4:30pm; the observation tower on the 27th floor closes at 4pm; the **Old State Capitol Building**, 342-0500 is open Tue-Sat 10am-4pm, Sun noon-4pm; the great white **Old Governor's Mansion,** 387-2464, Tue-Fri 10am-4pm and the two universities (Louisiana State and Southern). Call (225) 383-1825 for tourist info. *www.eatel.net/~meme/BR.html*.

CLOUTIERVILLE If it weren't for Kate Chopin, no one would probably visit Cloutierville. Chopin herself described the peaceful French settlement as 'two long rows of very old frame houses, facing each other closely across a dusty roadway'. The highly-celebrated author and her husband moved to his family's plantation after falling on hard times in New Orleans. Today the plantation is known as the **Kate Chopin Home**, (318) 379-2233, and is also home to the **Bayou Folk Museum**. The two-storey house is a monument to Bayou life and to the author who chronicled it so well. The museum features an old doctor's office, a blacksmith's shop. Cloutierville lies 20 miles south of Natitoches, off of I-49, about 260 from New Orleans. The house and museum are open Mon-Sat 10am-5pm, Sun 1pm-5pm, Admission charged. *www.natchitoches.net/melrose.*

ACADIANA True bayou country, complete with alligators and Spanish moss hanging from trees, begins in the Cajun area called Acadiana. The original French Acadians came to Louisiana after the British overran their native Nova Scotia. The British insisted that the Acadians swear allegiance to the

British crown and renounce Catholicism. During the war with France in 1775, the British deported shiploads of Acadians in *le grand derangement*, 'the Great Upheaval'. Other Acadians refused, moving instead to Louisiana where they became known as Cajuns. Using their knowledge of fur-trapping, the Cajuns quickly adapted to the ways of the swamp. (One ingenious adaptation was the use of moss for bedding.) In the 1920s, Louisiana passed laws forcing Acadian schools to teach in English, but this was not a state to be pressurized and the state is now officially bilingual.

Today's Cajuns still speak some Creole French and the bayous of Louisiana continue to account for much of the fur-trapping in the United States. Cajun cooking and music are currently in vogue, led by *Buckwheat Zydeco* and *Beau Soleil*, which sings mainly in French. *www.rosebudus.com/beausoleil.* Paul Simon's *Graceland* was heavily influenced by Cajun Zydeco music, a version of which makes for wonderful rock and roll. Modern Cajun life centers around **Lafayette**, **New Iberia** and **St Martinville**, about 120 miles northwest of New Orleans.

Accommodation/Food
Most lodging centered in **Lafayette**. Try the **Jameson Inn**, 2200 NE Evangeline Thruway, (337) 291-2916, c $75 (*www.jamesoninns.com/Hotel_Detail.asp?ID=57*), or **Lafayette Travel Lodge**, 1101 W Pinnhook Road, 234-4702 (Approx. $70-100) *www.travelodgelafayette.com.*

Mulate's Cajun Restaurant, is arguably the most famous Cajun restaurant in the world. 'Not to be overlooked. Not cheap but meals can be split—worth it.' Open daily 11am-10pm. Live Cajun music nightly, 7pm. *www.mulates.com.*

Of interest
In Lafayette: Lafayette Museum, 1122 Lafayette St, 234-2208. With Mardi Gras costumes and LA heirlooms. Tues-Sat 9am-4.30pm, Sun 1pm-4pm, $3, $1 w/student ID. *www.glmart.org.* Just outside Lafayette, the **Acadian Village**, 200 Greenleaf Drive, 981-2364, is a good place to learn about Cajun culture. Somewhat touristy, but with authentic Cajun houses, tools, and furnishings. Open daily 10am-4pm, $7. *www.acadianvillage.org.* The **Festival International de Louisiane**, 232-8086, is a 5-day fete celebrating music, art, theatre, dance, cinema, and southern cuisine and takes place in late Apr. Free. 'Don't miss it.' *www.festivalinternational.com.*

Just N of the city lies the **Academy of the Sacred Heart**, 662-5494, the only known exact spot of a miracle in the US. It was here that St John Berchmans, a Jesuit novice, appeared in response to the prayers of a dying woman. She recovered and Berchman returned to heaven. *www.ashrosary.org.*

In **Eunice**, about 30 miles N on US-190, every Sat night a live Cajun radio show is staged at the **Liberty Center for the Performing Arts** featuring Zydeco music, humourists and recipes, $5, 6pm-8pm. *www.eunice-la.com/libertyschedule.html.*

In New Iberia/St Martinville: Shadows on the Teche, 317 E Main St, New Iberia, 369-6446, a famous plantation on the banks of the Bayou Teche. D W Griffith stayed here as did Cecil B DeMille, and 4 generations of the family lived here until 1958. Open daily 9am-4.30pm, $7. *www.shadowsontheteche.org.*

Evangeline Oak on Port St at Bayou Teche marks the legendary first landing of the Acadians in bayou country.

cajunmoon.vastcity.com/louisiana/stmartinville/evangelineoak.html. Nearby is the statue of Evangeline beside **St Martin de Tours Catholic Church**, one of the oldest in Louisiana. Evangeline was one-half of the legendary pair of Acadian lovers immortalised by the Longfellow poem. The reputed home of Evangeline's beau, Gabrielle, is in the **Longfellow-Evangeline Commemorative Area**. A must-see quirk of history is the Roman-era **Statue of Hadrian** standing guard, appropriately, in front of a bank, on the corner of Weeks and Peters Sts.

Jungle Gardens, 369-6243, at end of Hwy 329 about 7 miles S of New Iberia, features a 1000 year old Buddha set in a swamp garden. Daily 9am-5.30pm, $6.25. If you doubt that Cajuns like hot food, you should know that Tabasco was invented nearby at the **Avery Islands Tabasco Pepper Sauce Factory**, 373-6129, free 20 min tours daily 9am-4pm, but you can't witness the filling of the bottles Fri-Sun. _www.tabasco.com/tabasco_history/visit_avery_island.cfm._

In the bayou: Louisiana swampland is unique, and tours into the swamps abound. Choose carefully, though, as rip-offs exist. Try **Cajun Jack's Swamp Tours** of the Atchafalaya, the largest swamp in N America, (985) 395-7420. See first hand how the Cajun people live as their ancestors did hundreds of years ago. Tour across 45 miles of scenery. Trips at 9am and 2.30pm, $25. _www.cajunjack.com._ If you are heading to Texas, try the drive along Hwys 82 and 27 through the **Creole Nature Trail**. _www.creolenaturetrail.org._

Information

Lafayette Convention and Visitors Commission, 1400 NW Evangeline Thruway, 232-3808/(800) 346-1958. _www.lafayettetravel.com._

Iberia ParishTourist Commission, 2513 Hwy 14, 365-1540.

MISSISSIPPI - The Magnolia State

The blues, King Cotton, southern hospitality, southern pride, civil rights, and riverboat rides are the images that spring to mind of this state—Mississippi is the Old South, a state that has had its fair share of strife. A dependence on slavery, and subsequent racial conflict and economic ruin are more visible here than anywhere else in the US.

Like any myth, parts of it are true—Mississippi folk *are* more polite than their Yankee neighbours. The graceful plantation homes that survived the Civil War do speak eloquently for the sensibilities of a lost time, before the last stand of the Southern gentleman on the battlefield of Vicksburg. And, in the hot, humid Delta backwoods, the rhythms that once consoled the slaves have been pressed gradually into the modern blues by such Mississippi giants as John Lee Hooker (_www.johnleehooker.com_), John Hurt Son House (_www.bigroadblues.com/features/sonhouse.shtml_), Elmore James and Muddy Waters (_www.muddywaters.com_). Tupelo was the home of Elvis Presley. Oprah Winfrey too is a Mississippi native.

The Old South begat other legends in the works of Tennessee Williams _www.tennesseewilliams.net_ and William Faulkner, Mississippi's most famous literary sons, and Pulitzer Prize-winner Eudora Welty whose house is in Jackson _www.eudorawelty.org_. From the lazy beat of Williams' long, hot summer to the radical civil rights battles that exposed the ugly, violent underbelly of Southern life in the 1960s, Mississippi has struggled to rid itself of its negative associations, epitomized in such films as the tense multiple-Oscar winning thriller *In the Heat of the Night* with Sidney Poitier and Rod Steiger (1967). Today, the Magnolia State concentrates on its contrasting wonders: from the antebellum mansions of the Natchez to the bustling excitement of metropolitan Jackson.

The Natchez Trace Parkway stretches diagonally across Mississippi along the historic highway of bandits, armies and adventurers. You can drive along it or explore the old trails on foot. Along Mississippi's Gulf coastline there runs another trail, the old Spanish Trail, that ran from St Augustine, Florida, to the missions in California. US 90 from Pascagoula to Bay St Louis follows the trail through the state. *www.visitmississippi.org*.

The telephone area code for Jackson, Vicksburg and Natchez is 601; Oxford is 662; for Biloxi and the Gulf it's 228.

JACKSON Set on the west bank of the Pearl River, the capital city of the state began as a trading post reputedly established by Canadian Louis LeFleur. General Sherman coined the phrase 'war is hell' here in Jackson and then went on to prove it by commanding his victorious Federal troops to burn the original Jackson to the ground in 1863. Locals renamed their devastated home 'Chimneyville'. It was not until early this century that Jackson recovered to become Mississippi's largest city. The discovery of natural gas in the area saved it from the economic ravages of the depression. Visit the website for details of tours. *www.visitjackson.com*.

Accommodation/Food
Motel 6, 6145 I-55 North, I-55 at County Line Road, exit 103, 956-8848. S-$37-39, D-$42-45, XP-$6. TV, pool. Free coffee in the morning.
Timberlake Campgrounds, 100 Timberlake Dr, 992-9100. Popular site with pool and tennis courts. Sites, $15, $20 w/hook-up.
Abner's, 681 S. Pear St, 889-9295. Dine-in/carry-out. Famous chicken tenders. From $5.

Of interest
Eudora Welty House, 1119 Pinehurst Street, (601) 353-7762. Where Eudora Welty lived for most of her life and wrote almost all of her fiction and essays, filled with books and intact as when she lived there. Welty was an avid gardener: the garden is open Wed 10am-2pm, Mar-Oct. Free, but res req. *www.eudorawelty.org*.
Mississippi Crafts Center, Natchez Trace Parkway at Ridgeland, 856-7546. Traditional and contemporary folk arts and crafts. Demos on different art techniques avail Sat & Sun. Call for further info. Open 9am-5pm daily. Free.
Mississippi Museum of Art, 201 E Pascagoula, 960-1515. Jackson's first art museum; opened in 1978. Presents as many as 40 exhibitions each year. Mon-Sat 10am-5pm, Sun 12pm-5pm. $5, $3 w/student ID. *www.msmuseumart.org*.
Russell C Davis Planetarium, 201 E Pascagoula St, 960-1550. The largest in the Southeast, and one of the best in the world. Exhibits are free, but special feature films are $2-3 for students. Times and programming vary. Call for further info. *www.city.jackson.ms.us/CityHall/planetarium.htm*.
The Oaks, 823 N Jefferson, 353-9339. Jackson's oldest house built around 1850, occupied by General Sherman during the Jackson siege in 1863. Period antiques on display including original furniture from Abraham Lincoln's Office. Open Tue-Sat 10am-3pm. $3, $2 w/student ID.
The Old State Capitol, at the intersection of Capitol and State Sts, 359-6920. Houses the **State Historical Museum**. The building has survived 3 torchings and is Mississippi's second state house. Displays artifacts from Native American settlements and documents Mississippi's volatile history both before and after the Civil Rights movement. Open 8am-5pm Mon-Fri, Sat 9:30am-4:30pm, Sun 12:30pm-4:30pm. *www.mdah.state.ms.us/museum.*
The 'magnificent' **New State Capitol,** at Mississippi and Congress, 359-3114, is where the state legislature currently gathers. 30 min guided tours 9am, 10am, 11am and 1.30pm, 2.30pm, 3.30pm. Mon-Fri 8am-5pm, free.

Information/Travel
Jackson Visitor Information Center, 921 N President St, 960-1891. Mon-Fri 8am-5pm.
Amtrak, 300 W Capitol St, 355-6350/(800) 872-7245.
Greyhound, 300 W Capitol St, 353-6342/(800) 231-2222. 'This area is best avoided at night.' No buses to/from the airport. For a taxi, call 355-8319.

Internet access
Jackson-Hinds Library, 300 N State St, 968-5825, free.

OXFORD When westward explorers first arrived at this quaint little town, they decided to name it Oxford in the hope of inspiring the state government to open a university here. Consequently, the University of Mississippi – *Ole Miss* – was established. The school gained notoriety in the early 1960s when a courageous student by the name of James Meredith shattered two centuries of white Southern tradition by becoming the first black graduate in 1963.

Literature has blossomed out of this small town, nestled in corn, cotton and cattle country in the north of Mississippi. Pulitzer and Nobel Prize winner William Faulkner based his fictitious Yoknapatowpha County on Oxford as he wrote about the anguish of a decaying South and the plight of the blacks.

Today, the mega-selling author of *The Client*, *The Chamber*, and *The Runaway Jury*, John Grisham, lives in Oxford, alongside some beautiful ante-bellum mansions. His 2001 work, *A Painted House*, is an introspective look at a childhood in the poor south in an area similar to this one. *www.oxfordms.com*.

Accommodation/Food
Comfort Inn, 1808 Jackson Ave, (877) 270-9434, from $70, free breakfast.
Food is best found in **Courthouse Sq,** at Jackson Ave and Lamar Blvd.
Ajax Diner, 118 Courthouse Sq, 232-8880, cooks excellent meat-and-vegetable platters, under $10, accompanied by jalapeno cornbread. Traditional po' boy sandwiches, $7. Mon-Sat 11.30am-10pm.

Of interest
Blues Archive 'N' Center for the Study of Southern Culture, 915-5993, Barnard Observatory, Sorority Row and Grove Loop, holds a huge amount of Southern music and literature, including B.B. Kings' personal collection of 10,000 recordings. Mon-Fri 8am-5pm. The centre also holds the Annual **Faulkner Conference** in late July, which draws scholars from around the world. If you go, first read *The Sound and the Fury*, *As I Lay Dying* or *The Reivers*. *www.olemiss.edu/depts/south*.
William Faulkner's Home, called Rowan Oak, Old Taylor Rd, 234-3284. Tucked back in the woods, unmarked from the street, Faulkner's home until 1962 can be reached by walking down S Lamar Street. Free.
Square Books, 160 Courthouse Sq, 236-2262, has impressive collection of Southern writers, and a cafe upstairs. Mon-Thu 9am-9pm, Fri/Sat 9am-10pm, Sun 10am-6pm. *www.squarebooks.com*.
On the way to Vicksburg is the **Delta Blues Museum,** 627-6820, 1 Blues Alley. Containing archives, books, records and instruments, the admission is $7, and the museum is open Mon-Sat 9am-5pm. The museum hosts the **Sunflower River Blues and Gospel Festival** on the first w/end in Aug, with the best contemporary blues and gospel around. Free. *www.deltabluesmuseum.org*.
University of Mississippi Museum, 915-7073. Self-guided tours of the 1848

campus, where a handful of the original buildings survive. Tues-Sat 9.30am-4.30pm, Sun 1-4pm.

Information
Tourist Information Center, 107 Courthouse Square, 234-4680, Mon-Fri 8am-5pm. _www.touroxfordms.com._

Internet access
Oxford Lafayette Library, 401 Bramlett Blvd, 234-5751, free.

VICKSBURG Lincoln had a simple, but brilliant two-part strategy for winning the Civil War: blockade Southern cotton from reaching European ports, then split the South in two by driving a wedge down the Mississippi river. The wedge fell upon Vicksburg, the stronghold of the South's Mississippi defense. The campaign lasted more than a year and climaxed with 47 days of siege led by Gen. Ulysses S Grant. 'The Gibraltar of the South' finally fell to Union troops on Independence Day, July 4, 1863, giving the Union control of the entire Mississippi River. The city did not revel in Independence Day celebrations until the late 1940s, however. Not surprisingly, the city has many Civil War sites and antebellum mansions. _www.vicksburgcvb.org._

Accommodation/Food
Ramada Hotel, 4216 Washington St, 638-5750. S/D-from $80.
Scottish Inn, 3955 Hwy 80 East, $1/4$ mile from battleground, 638-5511. S-$37 D-$39, XP-$5.
Walnut Hills Restaurant, 1214 Adams St, 638-4910. Southern cooking, sandwiches, soup, salads. From $5.75. Mon-Fri 11am-9pm, Sun 11am-2pm. _www.walnuthillsms.net._
Look along **Washington St,** for cafes, bars and local flavour.

Of interest
Old Courthouse Museum, 1008 Cherry St, 636-0741. Considered by many to be one of the finest Civil War museums in the South. Confederate troops operated from here during the siege of Vicksburg in 1863. Mon-Sat 8.30am-4.30pm, Sun 1.30pm-4.30pm, $5. _www.oldcourthouse.org._ Marble monuments, over 1,600 of them, recreate the fury of the battle at **Vicksburg National Military Park,** 636-0583. The Pantheon-like **Illinois monument** is the largest. Entrance and Visitors Centre on Clay St, about $1^1/2$ miles E of town on I-20, take exit 4B. $8 per vehicle, $4 bus-passenger. Open daily 8am-5pm. Upon entrance, an 18-minute movie recounts the campaign. A Civil War soldier's life is described by actors who dress in period costume and fire muskets and cannons, Jun-July. 'Need a whole day if you plan to walk the park. Bring water.' _www.nps.gov/vick._
The *U.S.S Cairo* **Museum,** 636-2199, also on park grounds, houses the Union gunboat of the same name, sunk by the Confederacy in 1862, and raised 100 years later. Open 8:30am-5pm, winter, 9:30am-6pm, summer. A climb up to the Vicksburg Bluffs by the overlook yields a great view of the Mississippi. _www.nps.gov/vick/cairo/cairo.htm._
Among several impressive ante-bellum mansions to see are: **McRaven House,** 1445 Harrison, 636-1663. Mon-Sat 9am-5pm, Sun 10pm-5pm $5; and **Martha Vick House,** 1300 Grove St, 638-7036. Mon-Sat 9am-5pm, Sun 1pm-5pm, $5.
Museum of Coca-Cola History and Memorabilia and the **Biedenharn Candy Co,** 1107 Washington, 638-6514. Where Coca-Cola was first bottled in 1894. Open Mon-Sat 9am-5pm, Sun 1:30pm-4:30pm, $2.95. In the summer you can get cokes in an 1800-old antique soda fountain. _biedenharncoca-colamuseum.com/bottle.htm._

S of Vicksburg, beautiful **Port Gibson** was considered by Union General Grant to be 'too beautiful to burn'. A good stop on the way to Natchez.

Information/Travel
Vicksburg Convention and Visitors Bureau, Clay St and Old Hwy 27 (exit 4B off I-20), (800) 221-3536. _www.vicksburgcvb.org._
Greyhound, 1295 S Frontage, 638-8389/(800) 231-2222. Daily 7am-9.30pm.

NATCHEZ   Natchez is the Old South. An important cotton trading centre, the port generated some of the great fortunes of the 1850s. Cotton planters, brokers, and bankers settled in the small town named after the Indian tribe that first settled the area. Non-commercialised, Natchez is one of the finest historical towns in the US.

The favoured architectural style of the Old South was Classical Greek and Roman, as promoted by Palladio, Inigo Jones and Thomas Jefferson. Natchez families have carefully preserved their ancestral treasures. For the visitor, a block's walk off Main Street is a retreat to the splendour of the antebellum South. _www.natchez.ms.us._

Accommodation/Food
Days Inn, 109 US Hwy 61 S, 445-8291. D-$59. Complimentary continental bfast, room with cable TV.
Natchez Historic Inn, 201 N.Pearl Street, 442-8848. Pricey, but atmospheric. $100. _www.natchezhistoricinn.com._
Fat Mama's Tamales, 500 S Canal St, 442-4548. Mild or spicy tamales and other regional specialities. $6.50/dozen. Mon-Thurs 11am-9pm, Fri/Sat 'til 10pm, Sun noon-7pm. _www.fatmamastamales.com._
Mammy's Cupboard, 555 Hwy 61 S, 445-8957. This unusual restaurant is shaped like a woman and the dining area lies under her skirt! Soup, sandwiches on homemade bread, and one hot Dixie lunch special every day. Everything under $10. Tue-Sat 11am-2pm.

Of interest
There are so many truly stunning homes here, that one can easily see how Natchez housed the most millionaires per capita of any city in the US in the 1830-60 period. **30 homes and gardens** are thrown open to visitors during the Pilgrimages each spring and fall while 8-12 residences are kept open year-round. The most impressive homes are **Dunleith** (Greek Revival style), **Rosalie** (Brick Federal) and **Longwood** (Moorish style—octagonal with a whimsical cupola). The **Pilgrimage Tours Headquarters**, 446-6631, at the Canal St Depot, on the corner of Canal and State St, has maps and literature on the area. _www.natchezpilgrimage.com_.
The once notorious **Natchez-Under-the-Hill,** (800) 467-6724, was the old cotton port and steamboat landing where gamblers, thieves and good-time girls scandalised the local residents. More respectable shops and a restored saloon fill the area now, against a spectacular backdrop of riverboats cruising along the Mississippi.
The Natchez Trace, 446-5790, _www.nps.gov/natr_. Natchez is named for the Indian tribe, which lived in the area before the white man came. The Trace was the centre of Indian activity from 1400-1729. An archeological site inside the city has uncovered the **Grand Village of the Natchez**, 446-6502, Daily 8am-5pm. The Indians forged the Natchez Trace, which winds its way north to Nashville. A beautiful drive, the trace is also full of history. **Emerald Mound**, 442-2658, one of the largest Indian Burial mounds is 1 mile off the pkwy, 11 miles NE of Natchez. Built in 1300, the mound covers 8 acres and is the third largest such site in the US.

Free. Davy Crockett travelled the trace, and the Bowie knife was forged at a campfire along the way. In 1812 Old Hickory (Andrew Jackson) led his troops against the British at New Orleans using the trace. The Visitor's Center at the trace, Pinehaven Drive, (601) 946-7484, is worth a visit.

Elvis Presley was born along the Trace in the little town of **Tupelo.** Elvis gave a benefit performance in '56 and in '57 for his hometown, which raised enough money to create a park out of the King's first 'shotgun' (read hovel) home. Tours through the home, 205 Elvis Presley Dr on Tupelo's east side, (662) 841-1245 Mon-Sat 9am-5pm, Sun 1pm-5pm. $2.50, museum, $6. Fans donated for the construction of a chapel in Presley's honour on the site. *www.elvispresleybirthplace.com.* (The **Tupelo McDonald's,** 372 S Gloster, is a temple to the King.)

Information/Travel
Mississippi State Welcome Center, 640 S. Canal St, 442-5849. Provides maps, lists of tours and homes.
Natchez Convention and Visitors Bureau, 640 Canal St, 446-6345. *www.natchez.ms.us.*
Tupelo Convention and Visitors Bureau, 399 E Main St, (662) 841-6521/(800) 533-0611. *www.tupelo.net.*
Greyhound, 103 Lower Woodville Rd, 445-5291. 7am-5.30pm daily.

BILOXI Although it's situated amongst the scenic white sand beaches of the Gulf Coast, Biloxi's economic backbone has not been tourism—it's been a shrimping community since the Civil War. In early June, the fleets are ritually blessed with bountiful shellfish harvests. At the harbour front down the end of Main Street and in the Back Bay area, you can watch the fishermen carry on with their lives, oblivious to the stares and snapshots of curious tourists.

The French landed here in 1699, but were not the only ones to have had control of this town: Biloxi has also been under the flags of Spain, Britain, the West Florida Republic, the Confederacy and the US. In 2005, the hurricane Katrina devastated the city – all entries should be checked: visit the town's website for the latest rebuilding news at *www.mississippi.gov/frameset.jsp?URL=http://www.biloxi.ms.us.*

Accommodation
Beach Manor Motel, 662 Beach Blvd, 436-4361. Nr Greyhound. D-from $65. Refrigerator, microwave.
Motel 6 Biloxi, 2476 Beach Boulevard, 388-5130. From $40.
Camping: Southern Comfort Camping Resort, US 90 at 1766 Beach Blvd, 432-1700, 3 miles from town. Sites $20 for two, $23-$25, XP-$2. Across from beach and pier.

Food
Mary Mahoney's French House Restaurant, 138 Rue Magnolia, 1 block N of US 90, 374-0163. In a 1737 home, not cheap, but excellent regional cuisine. Open Mon-Sat 11am-10pm. *www.marymahoneys.com.*
McElroy's Harbour House Restaurant, 695 Beach Blvd, 435-5001. Everything from local seafood to steaks and burgers, $8-$18. Bfast $6. Open daily 7am-10pm.

Of interest
Beauvoir, 2244 Beach Blvd, (800) 570-3818. The last home of Jefferson Davis, President of the Confederacy. See the Presidential Library built in his honour, the out building where he wrote the rise and fall of the Confederacy, and the Tomb of the Unknown Confederate Soldier. Open daily 9am-5pm, $7.50, $4.50 w/student ID. *www.beauvoir.org.* The famous cast iron 65-ft **Biloxi Lighthouse,** built in 1848

and one of the few remaining iron lighthouses is on US 90. $2, $1 students.

Other than Biloxi's **white-sand beaches**, the most enticing site along the coast is the **Gulf Islands National Seashore.** The seashore stretches into Florida, but there are 4 islands off the Mississippi coast that can be visited—West and East Ship, Petit Bois (pronounced Petty Boy), and Horn Island. _www.nps.gov/guis_. The islands have a unique ecosystem. They are anchored by sea oats, which keep the sand from washing away. The islands are also great places to bird-watch. **Ship Island ferry** runs from Gulf Port Harbour, (800) 338-3290, located at I-49 and I-90. This passenger boat runs 12 miles into the Gulf of Mexico. Runs Mon-Fri 9am, noon and 3.30pm, and in addition at 10.30am and 2.30pm w/ends, $20 r/t. _www.msshipisland.com_. The main site there is **Fort Massachusetts**, a linchpin of Lincoln's effort to blockade the south.

J L Scott Marine Education Center and Aquarium, 115 Beach Blvd (US Hwy 90), 374-5550. The 'Mississippi's Window to the Sea' public aquarium includes the 42,000 gallon 'Gulf of Mexico' tank which houses sharks, sea turtles, eels, and other large reef fish. Mon-Sat 9am-4pm. $5. _www.aquarium.usm.edu_.

Information/Travel
Biloxi Visitor Center, 710 Beach Blvd, 374-3105. Mon-Fri 8am-4.30pm, Sat 9am-4.30pm.
Greyhound, 166 Main St, 436-4335/(800) 231-2222.

Internet access:
Biloxi Library, 139 Lameuse St, 374-0330, free.

NORTH CAROLINA - The Tarheel State

American writer H L Mencken (_www.mencken.org_) once described North Carolina as 'a valley of humility between two mountains of conceit'. Wedged between Virginia and South Carolina, this photogenic 'land of beginnings' was the birthplace of English America and powered flight. A subtle population, tarheels are proud but humble about their rich heritage, unspoiled beaches, rugged mountains and stimulating cultural and intellectual life.

Few North Carolinians deigned to participate in the typical Southern racial discrimination. Only a small number held slaves and a formidable anti-slavery sentiment reigned until the 1830s, when organised agitation by Northerners provoked a defensive reaction. When shots were fired at Ft Sumter, Lincoln rallied troops against the Southern cause. Only then did North Carolina quietly step out of the Union.

The Tarheel State, first in the US in tobacco, textiles and furniture manufacturing, has attracted so many people that some native North Carolinians find themselves resisting the influx of 'Yankees'. Northern companies have flocked into the area around Raleigh-Durham, the so-called 'research triangle', helping to make it an internationally renowned centre for science and technology.

In just a few years, the triangle has grown to house more PhDs per capita than anywhere else in the country. Outside of the triangle, however, especially in the Asheville area, the economy has not benefited from high tech employment. Areas of the Appalachian Mountains are still some of the poorest in the country.

The approachable North Carolinians have welcomed filmmakers to their celluloid-friendly state, too. Parts of *Blue Velvet* were filmed here, as was the brutal tale of native Indians and colonists, *Last of the Mohicans*. From Cherokee history to modern folk-art, diversity is one of North Carolina's greatest attractions. *www.visitnc.com*.

The area code for Asheville is 828. For Charlotte it's 704, for Raleigh and Durham, it's 919. For the rest of the Coast, use 252.

THE COAST The 'Outer Banks' is the name given to the three curving island strips that shelter the North Carolina mainland from the Atlantic surf, **Ocracoke** (*www.ocracokeisland.com,* **Hatteras** (*www.hatteras-nc.com*) and **Bodie Island** (*www.nps.gov/caha/bodielh.htm*). The sandy beaches are relatively unspoiled and offer some of the best surfcasting in the country.

At the northern end of the Banks, fishing gives way to flying. The first power-driven flight was made near **Kitty Hawk** at **Kill Devil Hills** on 17 December 1903 by brothers Orville and Wilbur Wright. *www.kitty-hawk.com.* Now housed in the Smithsonian Institution in Washington D.C., their plane was aloft for 12 seconds, achieving a speed of 35 m.p.h, and covering 120 feet across the sands of the Outer Banks. Orville later explained that he and his brother had remained bachelors because they hadn't means to 'support a wife as well as an aeroplane'.

From the popular sands of Kitty Hawk, the Banks stretch south past the large dunes at **Jockey's Ridge** towards the primitive wildlife refuge of the country's first National Seashore, **Cape Hatteras**. The deadly currents and frequent hurricanes off the Cape earned this strip of land the nickname 'graveyard of the Atlantic'. Ships, ranging from tankers to U-Boats lie buried under its waters; over 600 have foundered on the Outer Banks' southern shores. Two hundred years ago, pirates used the currents to their advantage and, according to legend, led unsuspecting ships to their doom by tying a lantern to a horse's neck and walking it up the beach towards Diamond Shoals. Before a navigator realized that the lighthouse he was steering by was moving, he had run aground. Cape Hatteras lighthouse, the tallest in the US (196 ft), now warns ships away.

Ocracoke Island was home to America's most famous pirate, Edward Teach, better known as Blackbeard. Teach enjoyed the protection of several colonial governors until he was finally murdered by the Virginia Militia. *www.ocracoke-nc.com/blackbeard.* Today, the hurricanes and treacherous waters seem to have scared off developers and the Banks' abundant wildlife has largely been left in peace. **Pea Island National Wildlife Refuge**, 987-2394, shelters Great Snow geese among others. Open daily 9am-4pm.

Further south along the coast, the historic city of **Wilmington** is a good base for exploring the **Cape Fear River** and coastline. *www.navigator.com/wilmington.* Don't let the movie scare you off—the name supposedly originates from sailors' battles with the strong currents at the river mouth. *www.outerbanks.org*.

Accommodation
Camping: There are 4 National Park Service campgrounds along the 125-mile national seashore. The first three, at **Oregon Inlet** (south of Nags Head), **Cape Point** and **Frisco** (on Cape Hatteras) are filled up on a first-come, first-served basis for $18. The fourth camp is on **Ocracoke Island**, which can only be reached by

ferry. Sites on Ocracoke must be reserved in advance by calling 1-(800) 365-2267 or going to _www.reservations.nps.gov_ and entering the password CAPE. All campgrounds open until Labor Day. Private campgrounds are also scattered around the area, $20 w/shower; for more info contact Hatteras National Seashore, 995-4474.

Kitty Hawk: Outer Banks Youth Hostel (HI-AYH), 1004 Kitty Hawk Rd, 261-2294. $17 AYH, $20 non-AYH. Private rooms $32 AYH, $35 non-AYH, linen $2.50, towels $1.50.

Ocracoke: The following motels are located off Rte 12. **Blackbeard's Lodge**, 928-3421, from D-$85, _www.blackbeardslodge.com;_ **Sand Dollar Motel**, 928-5571, from S-$70, D-$75, XP-$10, _www.ocracokeisland.com/sand_dollar_motel.htm;_ and the **Pony Island Motel**, 928-4411, from D-$89 (10% discount for stays of a week or more), _www.ponyislandmotel.com._

Wilmington: Econo Lodge Intown, 2929 Market Street, (910) 763-3318. Ave-$72. Rooms include kitchenette, cable tv and modem lines. Free local calls. Complimentary bfast.

Food

Not far from the Wright Brothers Memorial is **Kelly's Outer Banks Restaurant and Tavern**, 2316 S. Croatan Hwy, 441-4116. Seafood, steak, chicken, pasta. Open daily; food served 5pm-10pm, live entertainment 'til 2am. _www.kellysrestaurant.com._ At Nags Head Causeway is **RV's**, 441-4963. Sandwiches, steak, seafood. 11:30am-9.30pm daily.

Of interest

Just on the mainland side of the Banks lies the mysterious small town of **Manteo**. 117 English men, women and infants led by Sir Walter Raleigh built a small fort and settled near here in 1587. When an expedition from Britain set out for the colony three years later they found that the entire community had disappeared without a trace. The only clues to their fate were the word 'Croatoan' scratched onto a palisade post and 'cro' on a tree trunk. **Fort Raleigh**, 473-5772, and **Elizabeth Gardens**, 473-3234, mark the likely site of the lost colony. Both are located at the N end of Roanoke Island on Rte 64. Fort open 9am-6pm; free. _www.nps.gov/fora._ Gardens open Mon-Sat 9am-8pm, Sun 'til 7pm, $6, $4 students. _www.elizabethangardens.org._ Lost Colony, 473-2127, is an outdoor drama which tells the story of the Roanoke Island Colony, held early Jun-late Aug, $16-20, Mon-Sat, 8:30pm, _www.thelostcolony.org_, and the _Elizabeth II_, a representation of the ship that brought the first English settlers to North America, is moored 4 miles S on Rte 400, Manteo St across from the waterfront. $8, self-guided tours aided by interpreters in costume. 10am-7pm, 473-1144. _www.outer-banks.com/eliz2.asp._

Nags Head Woods Preserve, 441-2525, 15 miles N of Manteo, is a nature preserve with five walking trails, open daily sunrise to sunset. _www.nags-head.com/nh-woods.htm._

Nearby in **Kitty Hawk,** the **Wright Bros Memorial and Museum** on Rte 158, 441-7430, pays homage to the great inventors. Open 9am-6pm daily, $3. What better way to celebrate a visit to the place where man first took flight than with an airplane tour from **Kitty Hawk Aerotours**, 441-4460, coastal tours, pricey-$150. Icarus fans may want to try the nearby hang-gliding operations: call **Kitty Hawk Kites**, 441-4124. $89 for a 3 hr lesson including training film, ground school, 5 flights and completion certificate. $129 for tandem flight (attached to instructor). _www.kittyhawk.com._

Lighthouses: at **Cape Hatteras, Ocracoke, Corolla** and **Bodie.** Visitors are not permitted to climb up the Bodie tower but are free to wander the grounds. The Chicamacomico Life Saving Station, on Hatteras Island near Rodanthe, records how private rescue companies of the 19th century operated.

Cape Fear Museum, 814 Market St btwn 8th & 9th St, Wilmington, (910) 341-4350. Established in 1898, it features nearly 40,000 artifacts from the Lower Cape. Learn how North Carolina earned its nickname, 'the Tarheel State', Mon-Sat 9am-5pm, Sun 1pm-5pm. $5, $4 w/student ID. *www.capefearmuseum.com.*

Information
Outer Banks Chamber of Commerce, 101 Town Hall Dr, Kill Devil Hills, off milepost 8½, 441-8144. *www.outerbankschamber.com.*
Aycock Brown Welcome Center off Rte 12 and US 58 (milepost 1-1½) in Kitty Hawk, 261-4644.
Cape Hatteras National Seashore Information Centers; Bodie Island, 441-5711 and **Hatteras Island,** 995-4474. **Ocracoke Island,** 928-4531, open daily 9am-5pm.
Cape Fear Coast Visitors Bureau, 24 N Third St, (877) 406-2356.

Travel
Car Ferry btwn Cedar Island and Ocracoke Island, daily, 8 crossings, 2 hrs, $15 car (book several days ahead on summer w/ends), $1 pp. For more info, call (800) 368-8949. Free ferries across Hatteras Inlet btwn Hatteras and Ocracoke daily, 5am-midnight, 40 mins.

TOBACCO ROAD North Carolina's backbone consists of a 150-mile-long arc of cities stretching between **Raleigh** and **Winston-Salem**. I-40 and I-85 pass through the rolling Piedmont hills, home of major tobacco-growing farms and factories. The state capital is in Raleigh and the **Raleigh/Durham Triangle** area is home to three major universities and has one of the nation's highest number of PhDs per head of population.

Accommodation
In Durham: Carolina-Duke Motor Inn, 2517 Guess Rd, off I-85, exit in Durham, 286-0771/(800) 483-1158. D-$55. Pool, AC, TV.
Budget Inn, 2101 Holloway St, Hwy 98, 682-5100. S-$38, D-$43. Pool, TV, laundry.
In Raleigh: Days Inn, 300 N Dawson, 828-9081. S-$59, D-$65. Cable TV, AC, complimentary continental bfast.
Microtel Inn, 104 Factory Shops Rd, 462-0061. S-$60, D-$70. Continental bfast.
In Winston-Salem: Days Inn North, 5218 Germanton Rd, (336) 744-5755. $54, complimentary contintental bfast.
Motel 6, 3810 Patterson Ave, (336) 661-1588. I-40 exit to US 52 N, exit Patterson Ave. $34, free coffee in the morning.

Food
In Durham: 9th Street Bakery, 136 East Chapel Hill, 286-0303. Cheap pastries and bakery items, sandwiches from $4.75. Mon-Fri 7am-5pm. *www.ninthstbakery.com.*
Satisfaction, 905 W. Main St, 682-7397. Big Duke hangout. Pizzas, sandwiches, burgers. Lunch, dinner, Mon-Wed 11am-1am, Thu-Sat til 2am.
In Raleigh: Applebee's Neighborhood Grill & Bar, 4004 Capitol Blvd, 878-4595. American fare (burgers, chicken, steaks) $10-20. Open Sun-Thu 11am-11pm, w/ends 'til midnight.

Of interest
Durham: Duke Homestead State Historic Site, 2828 Duke Homestead Rd, 477-5498, ancestral home of the Dukes, with early tobacco factories and outbuildings. Tue-Sat 10am-4pm, free. *www.ah.dcr.state.nc.us/sections/hs/duke/duke.htm.* **Duke University** is a gothic wonderland built with tobacco money. *www.duke.edu.* It's also the site of **Duke Chapel,** which boasts a 210 ft tower with 50-bell carillon and over 1 million stained glass pieces fitted in 77 windows. *www.chapel.duke.edu/home.*
Nasher Museum of Art, Duke University Rd and Anderson St, 684-5135, features

Medieval sculpture, American and European paintings, drawing and prints, and Greek and Roman antiques. _www.duke.edu/duma_. **Sarah P Duke Gardens,** 684-3698, contains 55 acres of landscaped and woodland gardens with a 5-mile trail among waterfalls, ponds, pavilions and lawns. 8am-dusk daily. _www.hr.duke.edu/dukegardens/dukegardens.html_.

Chapel Hill is a college town 15 miles SW of Durham on US 501. Home of the **University of North Carolina,** the first public university in America. _www.unc.edu._ Visit the **Morehead Planetarium** on Franklin St, near campus, 962-1236. $5, $4 w/student ID, opening hrs vary greatly so ring in adv. _www.moreheadplanetarium.org/index.cfm_. **Franklin St** is also the place to find cheap food and student bars and clubs. For those who have had enough of sight-seeing, **Cane Creek Reservoir,** 8201 Stanford Rd, 942-5790, offers boating, fishing, canoeing, and picnic and sunbathing areas. Thu-Sat 6:30am-6pm, Sun 1pm-6pm.

Raleigh: Mordecai Plantation House Historic Park, 1 Mimosa St, 857-4364. Birthplace of Andrew Johnson, features antebellum plantation house and other historic buildings. Tue-Sat 10am-4pm, Sun 1-5pm, $5. _www.itpi.dpi.state.nc.us/vvisits/mordecai.html._

North Carolina Museum of Art, 2110 Blue Ridge Rd, 839-6262. European paintings from 14th century, American 19th century paintings, as well as Egyptian, Greek and Roman art. Tue-Sat 9am-5pm, Fri 'til 9pm, Sun 10am-5pm. Free. _www.ncartmuseum.org_.

North Carolina State Capitol, 1 E. Edenton St, 733-4994. Greek revival style, built btwn 1833 and 1840. 'One of the best preserved examples of a Civic Building in this style of architecture.' Across the street is the **North Carolina Museum of History,** 807-7900. Explore the state's history through hands-on exhibits and 'innovative' programs. 'Check out the Sports Hall of Fame and Folklife galleries.' Changing exhibits provide detailed glimpses of the past. Tue-Sat 9am-5pm, Sun noon-5pm. Free. _www.ncmuseumofhistory.org_.

Winston-Salem: Reynolda House Museum and Gardens, Reynolda Rd, (336) 725-5325, houses 18th-20th century American paintings, sculpture, and prints associated with the founder of R J Reynolds Tobacco, including Church's The _Andes of Ecuador_. Tues-Sat 9.30am-4.30pm, Sun 1.30pm-4.30pm, $10, w/student ID free. _www.reynoldahouse.org._

Historic Bethabara, 2147 Bethabara Rd, 924-8191. Reconstruction of the first 18th century Moravian Village in NC, with 130 acre park, archaeological sites and other historic buildings. Settlers first came to this area in 1753. Tue-Fri 9:30am-4:30pm, open 1:30pm on w/ends, $2. _www.bethabarapark.org_.

Old Salem, 600 S Main St, 721-7350. Costumed interpreters re-create Moravian life. Daily demonstrations, bakery, restaurant and shops. Open Tue-Sat 8.30am-5.30pm, Sun 1pm-5pm, $21. _www.oldsalem.org._

The newer art is at the **Southeastern Center for Contemporary Art,** 750 Marguerite Dr, 725-1904. Wed-Sat 10am-5pm, Sun 2pm-5pm; $5, $3 w/student ID. _www.secca.org._

Greensboro, on I-40 btwn Winston-Salem and Raleigh, was the birthplace of the 1960s national student sit-in movement for civil rights. It was here where four local African-American students sat down in Woolworths and refused to move. The legacy of their courage is chronicled in the **Greensboro Historical Museum,** Lindsay St at Summit Ave, (336) 373 2043. Tues-Sat 10am-5pm, Sun 2pm-5pm. Free. _www.greensborohistory.org._

Emerald Pointe Waterpark, 3910 S Holden Rd, (336) 852-9721, one of the world's largest waterparks, offers giant wave pool, tube slides, drop slides, drifting river and more. All day tkts $27, $19 after 4pm. Open Sun-Fri 10am-8pm, Sat 9am-8pm. _www.emeraldpointe.com._

On I-85 at **Asheboro,** about 30 mins S of Greensboro, is the **North Carolina**

Zoological Park, (800) 488-0444. The world's largest natural walk-through habitat zoo. Open daily 9am-5pm, 'til 4pm in winter, $10, $8 w/ student ID. *www.nczoo.org*.

Information
Chapel Hill: Chamber of Commerce, 104 S Estes Dr, (919) 967-7075. *www.carolinachamber.org.*
Durham: Convention and Visitors Bureau, 101 E Morgan St, 687-0288. *www.durham-nc.com.*
Raleigh: Capital Area Visitor Center, 221 E Lane St., 733-3456, Mon-Fri 8am-5pm, Sat 9am-4pm, Sun 1pm-5pm.
Winston-Salem Visitors Center, Brookstown Ave, (336) 728-4200, *www.winstonsalem.com*.

Internet access
Raleigh: Cup@Joe, Mission Valley Shopping Center, 2109-142 Avent Ferry Rd, 828-9886, $1.50 for 15 min. *www.cspot.com.*
North Regional Library, 200 Horizon Dr, 870-4000, free.
Winston-Salem: Forsyth County Public Library, 660 W 5th St, 727-2264, free. *www.co.forsyth.nc.us/library.*

Travel
Durham: Greyhound, 820 W Morgan St, 687-4800/(800) 231-2222, open daily.
Durham Area Transit Authority, 683-DATA. Public bus service runs daily, schedules vary, fare $1.
Raleigh: Amtrak, 320 W Cabarrus St, 833-7594/(800) 872-7245.
Greyhound, 314 W Jones St, 834-8275/(800) 231-2222. Open 24 hrs.
Capital Area Transit, 833-5701, public bus service runs Mon-Sat, schedules vary, fare 75c.

ASHEVILLE AND AREA Travellers to this area find the simple, unhurried charm that is fading elsewhere in the busy 'New South'. The crafts and folklore of the Appalachian Mountains flourish in the shops and markets here, and the region's natural beauty is protected from overdevelopment. If you put your feet up anywhere in North Carolina, do it here, amidst this picturesque landscape. Great website: *www.ashevillechamber.org*.

Accommodation
Mountain Meadows Motel, 5793 Gerton Hwy, 625-1025. $55-75. Small fridge and microwave in rooms.
Log Cabin Motor Court, 330 Weaverville Hwy, 645-6546. Cabins from $45 for two. *www.cabinlodging.com.*
Super 8 Motel, 1329 Tunnel Rd, 298-7952. From $60.

Food
Boston Pizza, 501 Merriman, 252-9474. Popular student hangout, pizzas $5-$20. Try the 'Boston Supreme!' Sun-Thu 11am-10pm, w/ends 'til 11pm. *www.bostonpizza.com/home/index.cfm.*
The Hop, 507 Merriman, 252-8362. Homemade ice cream in 50's style joint. Open daily, 12pm-9pm.
Three Brothers Restaurant, 183 Haywood St, 253-4971, serves everything, about 20 different types of sandwiches. Open Mon-Thu 11am-9pm, Fri 'til 9.30pm, Sat 4pm-9.30pm.

Of interest
Biltmore House and Gardens, (800) 624-1575, America's largest privately-owned home and built by the Vanderbilt family is an opulent exception to the area's humble charms. Peter Sellers' last film *Being There* was filmed at this 250-room

European style chateau. Includes garden, conservatory, winery, and four restaurants. Take exit 50 or 50B on I-40 south of Asheville. Tkt office daily 8.30am-5pm, house open 9am-6pm, winery and gardens open 11am-7pm. $39 all inclusive. *www.biltmore.com*.

Chimney Rock Park, (800) 277-9611, lies 25 miles SE of Asheville near intersection of US 64 and 74. A 26-storey elevator runs inside the mountain and ascends to 1200 ft. $14. 'Spectacular views over the Appalachian Mountains.' *www.chimney-rockpark.com*. Also various nature trails through the nearby **Pisgah National Forest**, natural 100ft rock slides at **Sliding Rock** and a 404 ft waterfall, 877-3265. *www.westernncattractions.com/PNF.htm*.

For literary interest head to **Flat Rock**, once home to poet Carl Sandburg (*carl-sandburg.com*), and current site of the **Flat Rock Playhouse**, North Carolina's State theatre, 693-0731. *www.flatrockplayhouse.org*. Sandburg's home for 22 years, **Connemara**, 693-4178, has books and videos of the writer-poet's life. His wife's champion goats live on. Guided tours of the home daily 9am-5pm, every 30 mins, $5. *www.nps.gov/carl*. **The Thomas Wolfe Memorial**, 48 Spruce St (next to the Radisson Hotel), 253-8304, honours Asheville's most famous son. Wolfe's best-known novel, *Look Homeward Angel* (titled after Milton's poem of the same name), was inspired by childhood experiences; his father was the town stonecutter. *www.wolfememorial.com*.

Asheville is a prime spot to shop for local crafts. Traditions are lovingly preserved. The **Mountain Dance and Folk Festival**, 258-6111, on the first w/end in Aug has been going more than 60 yrs. **The World Gee Haw Whimmy Diddle Competition** is held annually in Sept at the Folk Arts Center, 298-7928, and includes demonstrations of this native Appalachian toy, made from laurel wood. About 70 miles NE of Asheville is **Grandfather Mountain**, (800) 468-7325, the highest peak in the Blue Ridge Mountains and the first private preserve set apart by the United Nations as a Biosphere Reserve. Known as the most biologically diverse mountain in the east, it's also the site of the annual **Highland Games**, (828) 733-1333, a celebration of Scottish dancing, piping, and Gaelic culture held each July. Tickets $10-$55. *www.gmhg.org*. Entrance to the mountain itself is off US 221, 2 miles north of Linville. $14. Open daily, 8am-7pm. *www.grandfather.com*.

Information/Travel

Asheville Convention and Tourism Bureau, 151 Haywood St, 258-6101. Open Mon-Fri, 8:30am-5:30pm, w/end 9am-5pm. 'A very helpful staff.' *www.exploreasheville.com*.

Asheville Transit, 253-5691. Serves city and outskirts. Fare 75¢, 10¢ transfer. *www.ci.asheville.nc.us/transit.htm*.

Greyhound, 2 Tunnel Rd, 253-8451/(800) 231-2222. 2 miles E of downtown, served by Asheville Transit buses #13 & #20. 8am-9pm.

Internet access:

East Asheville Library, 902 Tunnel Rd, 298-1889, free.

GREAT SMOKY MOUNTAINS NATIONAL PARK The name 'Great Smokies' is derived from the smoke-like haze that envelopes these forest-covered mountains. The Cherokee Indians, the area's original inhabitants, called it the 'Land of a Thousand Smokes'. World renowned for the diversity of its plant and animal resources, the beauty of its ancient mountains, and the remnants of Southern Appalachian mountain culture. The park is one of the largest protected areas in the east. Part of the Appalachian Mountains near the southern end of the Blue Ridge Parkway, it has been preserved as a wilderness that includes some of the highest peaks in the eastern US and 68 miles of the Appalachian Trail. Camping is possible in the three main parks: **Smokemont**, **Elkmont** and **Cade's Cove** at $17 per site (can sleep up to 6), call (865) 436-1200; _www.nps.gov/grsm_.

The **Great Smoky Mountain Railroad** runs $4^1/_2$ hr trips through Nantahala Gorge and Fontana Lake, from $28. 'Waste of time. What mountains? Telephone cables obscured view of scrap yards.' 7 hour raft and rail trips, from $71 (includes picnic lunch and guided raft ride). All departures from **Bryson City**. Call (800) 872-4681 for rsvs.

The area near **Cataloochee** affords an excellent impression of the obstacles facing the earliest pioneers on their push into the west. Cabins, cleared acreage and other pioneer remnants dot this section of the park. Perhaps the most fascinating visit is to the **Cherokee Reservation**, (800) 438-1601. There's a recreated Indian village ($13), and a production of _Unto These Hills_, an Indian drama about their land and the meaning it holds for them, a museum, and casinos—a controversial but common feature of the modern Indian reservation. Mid-June to late Aug, $16-18. _www.oconalufteevillage.com_.

The North Carolina entrance to the park is on US 441 at Cherokee with the visitor centre located at **Oconaluftee**.

SOUTH CAROLINA - Palmetto State

In its semi-tropical coastal climate, the Palmetto State, named after the tree that grows abundantly in coastal areas, was the first to secede from the Union and marks the beginning of the Deep South. South Carolina also typifies the New South. Since the Second World War, manufacturing has boomed, especially textiles and chemicals, but not at the expense of the state's traditional charm and lovely countryside. Factories, based in the Greenville area, replaced sleepy cotton fields and cotton itself has been replaced by tobacco as the major cash crop. Modernization has not come without a struggle, however, as enraged ancestors of confederate veterans saw their battle flag, a remembrance of the dead for some and recognised symbol of hatred for many others, removed from atop the state house in 2000.

South Carolina has, however, something of a split personality. Charleston beckons the visitor with its graceful streets and refined architecture. Myrtle Beach entices with all the subtlety of a tourist-howitzer. South Carolina has her slower country charms, but other than Charleston, few compare favourably with her neighbours. The beaches are less cluttered in North Carolina and the mountains are grander in Tennessee. _www.travelsc.com_.

The area code for Columbia is 803, for Charleston and Myrtle Beach it's 843.

CHARLESTON The curtain rose here on the Civil War to the cheers of society ladies and the blasts of harbour canon. Charleston's exuberance found a less violent expression in the 1920s when a dance dubbed the Charleston became a national obsession. Dance was better suited to the genteel Charleston nature that epitomises Southern graciousness. Settled by aristocracy, Charleston has always been concerned with architecture, art and the length of the family tree. It is also home of the oldest municipal college in the country, established in 1837, and is one of the busiest ports in the Southeastern US.

More recently in 1989, this lovely old town was severely battered when hurricane Hugo roared through. Many of the historic buildings suffered severe damage, so much so that the town will never look the same again. The redeveloped **Waterfront Park,** along the battery, is picturesque, a 'beautiful place to take an evening stroll by the river.' *www.charleston.com*.

Accommodation
Bed, No Breakfast, 16 Halsey St, 723-4450. Guest house in Harleston Village near College of Charleston, S/D-$78-$98. Coffee and tea service avail every morning. Rsvs nec. 'Comfortable.' 'Limited space.' 20 min drive to the beach. *www.virtualcities.com/ons/sc/z/scz6801.htm*.

Historic Hostel and Inn, 194 St Phillip St, 853-0846. $19, $45 private room. Free Internet, linen, laundry, all-you-can-eat pancake bfast, and free plane, bus, and train pick-up.

Rutledge Victorian Inn, 114 Rutledge Ave, 722-7551. B&B, From S-$69 w/shared bathroom. AC, TV. Favourite stop for BUNAC travellers and owners helpful in finding work in area. Rsvs rec. *www.bbonline.com/sc/rutledge.*

Food
The **Gourmetisserie** in the City Market is junk food centre—hamburger, pizza stands. 'Great meeting place.'

Andolini's Pizza, 82 Wentworth St, 722-7437. Voted Charleston's best pizza 11 years running by *The Upwith Herald*. 19" pies are hand-tossed, made to order while you watch, the calzones are the biggest in town, everything's freshly made, and prices start low. Sun-Thu 11am-10pm, w/ends 'til 11pm. *www.andolinis.com*.

A.W. Shuck's Seafood Restaurant, 70 State St, 723-1151. Local fav. Offers everything from famous Seafood casserole to crab-stuffed shrimp. Sun-Thurs 11.30am-10pm, w/ends 'til 11pm. *www.a-w-shucks.com.*

Of interest
A tremendous city pride exists in Charleston, and there are excellent documentaries on the city shown in the downtown area. *Forever Charleston*, a video on the city, is shown at the **Visitor Reception and Transportation Center**, 325 Meeting St, 720-5678, from 9am-4.30pm daily; $2.50. The **Preservation Society**, 147 King St at Queen, 722-4630, is a useful place to learn about Charleston history and volunteers welcome foreign visitors. Maps, pamphlets and walking books available. Mon-Sat 10am-5pm. *www.richassoc.com/charleston_airport.htm*.

Charleston is famous for its fine houses, squares and cobblestone streets. Start your walk along **Church Street**, the vision Heyward and Gershwin used to create Catfish Row in *Porgy and Bess*. The Battery, along the Cooper and Ashley rivers, has blocks of attractive old residences. The only **Huguenot church** in the US (*www.cr.nps.gov/nr/travel/charleston/fre.htm*) is at Church and Queen street while the **Dock Street Theater** is across the street (*www.loc.gov/bicentennial/propage/SC/sc_s_hollings1.html*). Topping the list of restorations is the **Nathaniel Russell House**, 51 Meeting St, 724-8481, probably the best house to visit. Dating from 1808, it has a famous 'free-flying' spiral staircase and lavish furnishings. Open Mon-Sat 10am-5pm, Sun 2pm-5pm. $8. *www.historiccharleston.org/russell.html*.

Basket-weaving traditions inherited from Africa and handed down by generations of slaves can still be seen at the **Market**, Meeting and Market Sts. Bazaar-orientated with masses of junk and some beautiful handicrafts. Watch the ladies making baskets—and then buy one. 'Lively and colourful.' 'Baskets are very expensive—at least $20 for even the tiniest basket.'

Daughters of the Confederacy Museum, 188 Meeting Street, 723-1541, offering artifacts and memorabilia from the war. Tue-Sat 11am-3.30pm, $5.

Gibbes Museum of Art, 135 Meeting St, 722-2706. Displays early art and portraiture of South Carolina and one of the finest collections of miniatures in the world. 'Worthwhile: some quite impressive early American paintings, and some even more impressive modern woodwork.' Tues-Sat 10am-5pm; Sun 1pm-5pm. $7, $6 w/student ID. *www.gibbesmuseum.org.*

Kahal Kadosh Beth Elohim, 723-1090, founded by Sephardic Jews in 1749. The current temple was built in Greek-Revival style in 1841 and is the oldest synagogue in continuous use in the US, also an early centre of reform Judaism. Tours Mon-Fri 10am-noon, Sun 12.30-3.45pm, free. *www.kkbe.org.*

The Charleston Museum, 360 Meeting St, 722-2996. Built in 1773, it is the oldest museum in the country. Exhibits include a full-scale replica of the Confederate submarine, *HL Hunley;* you can peer into the open side of the sub. 'Creepy.' Mon-Sat 9am-5pm, Sun 1pm-5pm, $10. *www.charlestonmuseum.com.*

The Old Exchange and Provost Dungeon, 122 E Bay at Broad St, 727-2165. Built btwn 1767 and 1771; delegates to the first Continental Congress were elected here in 1774. The dungeon was used as a prison by the British during the Revolution. Open daily 9am-5pm for self guided tours of the building and narrated tours of the dungeon, $7, $3.50 w/student ID. *www.oldexchange.com.*

Citadel Military College, 953-5000, is known as the West Point of the South. The male-only tradition at the citadel formally ended in 1999 when Nancy Mace became the first female graduate. The college, at Moultrie Street on banks of Ashley River, offers tours and a free museum, open Sun-Fri 2pm-5pm, Sat 12pm-5pm. Don't miss the dress parade every Friday when the cadets are in session, times vary. *www.citadel.edu.*

The Confederate bombardment of Federally-garrisoned **Fort Sumter,** just across the harbour, began the Civil War. Now Fort Sumter is a national monument, 883-3123, with its history depicted through exhibits and dioramas. *www.nps.gov/fosu.* Free to look around whatever time you dock. Fort Sumter is accessible only by boat. Be careful to take a boat that actually lands on the fort! **Ft Moultrie,** 883-3123, on Sullivan's Island but easily reached by car, has served as the bastion of security for Charleston harbour since the revolutionary war.

Also just outside Charleston is **Boone Hall Plantation**, 884-4371, 7 miles N near US 17. Beautiful house and gardens; the Avenue of Oaks leading to the mansion is stunning. The owner was the first to provide education to his slaves and built brick homes for them. Mon-Sat 8.30amam-6.30pm, Sun 1pm-5pm, $14.50. *www.boonehallplantation.com.*

Charles Towne Landing, 1500 Old Towne Rd, 852-4200, 6 miles outside Charleston, marks the site of the first permanent English speaking settlement in South Carolina. See *The Adventure,* a working reproduction of a 17th century sailing vessel. Also guided tram tours, animal forest, bike paths and walkways. Open 8.30am-5pm daily, $5.

Summers can be scorching, but you can cool off at **Folly Beach,** off Rte 171, with public parking and showers. 15 mins from downtown. 'Excellent beach, very long, deserted and clean.'

Information

Charleston Visitor Reception and Transportation Center, 375 Meeting St, 720-5678. Open daily 8.30am-5.30pm. Good maps available. 'Helpful.' *www.ci.charleston.sc.us/dept/content.aspx?nid=383.*

Even the **Chamber of Commerce** is historic—it is one of the nation's oldest civic commercial organisations; 81 Mary St, 577-2510/853-8000. *www.charlestonchamber.net/splash.asp.*

Internet access
Cooper River Memorial Library, 3503 Rivers Ave, 744-2489, free.

Travel
Charleston Area Rural Transportation Authority (CARTA), 747-0922. Daily 5.20am-1am. Fare $1.25. *www.ridecarta.com/splash/default.aspx.*
Amtrak, 4565 Gaynor Ave, 9 miles W of town on Hwy 52, 744-8263/(800) 872-7245. 6pm-2.50pm. The *Silver Meteor* calls here from NYC.
Greyhound, 3610 Dorchester Rd, 744-4247/(800) 231-2222.
Charleston Airport is located 13 miles N of downtown. Taxis $19-$22, 767-1100. Shuttle $10 available at airport. *www.chs-airport.com.*

MYRTLE BEACH AND THE GRAND STRAND The 60 mile stretch of South Carolina's northern coast known as the Grand Strand has seen almost frightening growth in the past two decades. It's loaded with countless amusements, fast food joints, and tacky boutiques with merchants selling the inevitable Myrtle Beach T-shirts and trinkets. In summer, the 23,000 population of Myrtle Beach swells to around 350,000.

Brookgreen Gardens, on US-17S, 20 minutes south of Myrtle Beach, 235-6000, seems out of place here. In a serene setting, the world's largest outdoor collection of American sculpture—over 900 works of art are on show, set against 2000 species of plants. The gardens also feature a wildlife park and aviary. 'Worth spending the whole day—the sculptures are amazing.' Open daily 9.30am-5pm, $12. *www.brookgreen.org.*

Further south is pretty and famous **Pawleys Island**. One of the oldest resorts on the Atlantic coast, this was originally a refuge for colonial rice planters' families who fled a malaria epidemic. Residents work hard to preserve its more elegant, less commercialised feeling. The well-known Pawleys Island Hammock is hand-woven and sold here—you can watch them being made by local craftsmen. *www.townofpawleysisland.com/index.html.*

Georgetown, on Hwy 17 at the southern end of the Grand Strand, was established in 1526 by the Spaniards and named 200 years later in honour of King George II. Concentrating on the export of rice, Georgetown became a thriving port in the 18th century. In the early 19th century, it became the biggest exporter of rice in the world. Although this trade has now gone, there are still many things worth seeing, such as the old docks along the waterfront that have been converted into **Harborwalk**, a promenade of restaurants and shops. Venture to Broadway at the Beach, 29th Ave N, and check out the **Ripley's Aquarium**, 916-0888. Awarded the Governor's Cup for being the best tourist destination in South Carolina, the Aquarium gives you the unique opportunity to walk through underwater tunnels while sharks and sting rays swim over your head. Open daily 9am-11pm, $17. *www.ripleysaquarium.com* and *www.mbchamber.com.*

Accommodation/Food/Entertainment
Although hotels are everywhere, they are generally expensive in season. There are a few bargains, though. **Rainbow Court Motel,** 405 Flagg St, 448-3857, has been recommended. D-$75. *www.rainbowcourt.com.* Fortunately Myrtle Beach claims 12,000 campsites and calls itself the 'Camping Capital of the World'. Try **Myrtle Beach State Park** on Rte 17 South, 238-5325, site $17-19. Some sites can be rsvd, others first-come, first-served basis. **The Myrtle Beach Chamber of Commerce,**

1200 N Oak St, 626-7444, has a complete guide to the area's campsites. *www.mbchamber.com.*

Peaches Corner, 900 Ocean Blvd, 448-7424.'Best burgers on the beach—try a famous 'Peaches Burger'. Mon-Fri 11am-midnight, w/ends 'til 1am or later.

The Filling Station, 1913 10th Avenue N, 626-9435. All-you-can-eat buffet for $8 lunch, $14 dinner. Salad, soup, sandwiches, pizza, desserts and more. Open daily 11am-10pm.

McAdoo's Oceanfront bar and grill, 3rd Ave. S, on the beach, 448-3863. Live bands on weekends. 'A bar with great atmosphere, outside tables with view of the ocean.' Open daily, 11am-2am.

2001, 920 Lake Arrowhead Rd, 449-9435. Three clubs in one building. Choose from **FunkyTown, Touch,** and **Razzles.** Open Tue-Sat 8pm-2am, cover $6-$10. Check local papers and hotels for coupons.

Information/Travel
Myrtle Beach Chamber of Commerce, 1200 N Oak St, 626-7444. Pick up copies of *Beachcomber* and *Kicks* for local events and entertainment listings. 'Also has useful accommodations directories.' *www.mbchamber.com.*

Greyhound, 511 7th Ave N, 448-2472/(800) 231-2222.

Coastal Rapid Public Transport Authority (CRPTA), 488-0865, bus service around Myrtle Beach area. Fare 75c-$1.25.

Internet access
The Living Room (a.k.a. coffee bar and used books), 1293 38th Ave, 626-8363. $1.50 per 10 mins. Mon-Fr 7am-midnight, Sat/Sun 9am-midnight. Free Wi-Fi.

COLUMBIA In the middle of South Carolina at the junction of three interstates sits Columbia, one of the first planned cities, the state's largest city, and capital since 1786 (farmers in The Piedmont lobbied for the seat of government to move from Charleston to the centre of the state). Although growing rapidly, the city is mild by Charleston or Myrtle Beach standards. Lake Murray, with 520 miles of scenic lakefront, is less than 20 miles away. Columbia's biggest claim to fame is the success of a local band, Hootie and the Blowfish. *www.columbiasc.net.*

Accommodation/Food
Along the interstates are the best places to find cheap and clean rooms.

Baymont Inn, 1538 Horseshoe Drive, 736-6400. D-$65, complimentary continental bfast.

Off-Campus Housing Office, Room 235, the Russell House, Green St, 877 895-1234, can direct visitors to people in the university community with rooms to rent. Open 9am-5pm. Check their website for information: *www.sa.sc.edu/ochs.*

For food and entertainment, head to **Five Points**—a business district at Blossom, Devine and Harden Sts—frequented by students. *www.fivepointscolumbia.com.*

Columbia State Farmer's Market, Bluff Road across from the USC stadium. Fresh produce daily. Mon-Sat 6am-9pm. Sun 1pm-6pm.

Groucho's, 611 Harden St, 799-5708, Columbia's renowned New York-style Jewish deli. Cheap, filling sandwiches for around $6. Open daily 11am-4pm.

Yesterday's Restaurant and Tavern, 2030 Devine St, 799-0196, is an institution. Open daily for lunch and dinner, lunch from $5-$13, dinner from $6-$15. Open daily 11.30am-midnight, bar 'til 2am. 'Friendly manager!' *www.yesterdaysec.com.*

Of interest
Many of the city's attractions are located in or around the **University of South**

Carolina. A mall-like area lined with stately buildings built in the early 19th century, with the **Horseshoe** marking the campus centre. _www.sc.edu_. On the Horseshoe facing Sumter St is the **McKissick Museum**, 777-7251. Large collection of Twentieth Century Fox film reels and science exhibits. Open Mon-Fri 8.30am-5pm, Sat 11am-3pm. Free. _www.cla.sc.edu/mcks/index.html_.

Columbia Museum of Art, within walking distance from the McKissick at Main and Hampton Sts, 799-2810. It houses Renaissance and baroque art as well as oriental and neoclassical Greek art displays. Open Wed-Sat 10am-5pm, Fri 'til 9pm, Sun 1pm-5pm. $5, $2 w/student ID, free on Sat. _www.colmusart.org_. Adjoining **Gibbes Planetarium**, has been closed for renovation but reopens in 2006. **South Carolina State Museum**, 301 Gervais St, 898-4921, housed in a renovated textile mill, focuses on art, history, natural history, and science and technology. Tue-Sat 10am-5pm, Sun 1pm-5pm, $5, $1 on the first Sunday of every month. _www.museum.state.sc.us_.

State Capitol, at Main and Gervais Sts, 734-2430. Built in 1855, the six bronze stars on the outer western wall mark cannon hits scored by the Union during the Civil War. Tours hourly on $^1/_2$ hr, Mon-Sat 9am-5pm, Sat 10am-4pm, Sun 1pm-5pm.

Information/Travel
Columbia Metropolitan Convention and Visitors Bureau, 1101 Lincoln St, 545-0000. Mon-Fri, 9am-5pm, Sat 10am-4pm. _www.columbiacvb.com_.
Amtrak, 850 Pulaski St, 252-8246/(800) 872-7245.
Greyhound, 2015 Gervais St, 256-6465/(800) 231-2222.

Internet access
Columbia Public Library, 931 Woodrow St, 799-5873, free.

TENNESSEE - The Volunteer State

Tennessee is music country. Memphis has been fertile ground for blues musicians and rock and rollers alike. Nashville brought country music down from the hills to mainstream America. The difference in music reflects deeper social differences within the state. The east is 'Hill Country'—backwoods and fiercely independent. The west is flat in texture and southern in demeanor, drawing life from the Mississippi River. The two cultures clashed violently during the Civil War, and several of the war's most costly battles were decided on Tennessee soil.

Tennessee's transition from its backwoods past into the 21st century has not been easy. After a famous trial in 1925, a Tennessee teacher named John Scopes was fined for teaching the theory of evolution. The eastern half of the state is less isolated today thanks to the Tennessee Valley Authority (TVA) built by the Franklin Roosevelt Administration. TVA was a massive effort to both tame a river and to civilise an entire region. People still argue over the proper role of government power in projects such as TVA. The state is so broad, it takes 10 hours to drive from one end to the other. _www.tnvacation.com_.

The area code for Nashville is 615. For the east it's 931 and 423. For Memphis and the west, dial 901.

NASHVILLE Capital of the state and the so-called Hollywood of the South, Nashville sparkles with the rhinestone successes and excesses of her country music stars. Bulging with moral character, Nashville is a centre of education and has more churches per capita than anywhere else in the country. *www.nashvillecvb.com.*

Accommodation
Most cheap motels are several miles outside town. 'Difficult to find cheap accommodation unless you have a car.'

Knights Inn, 99 Spring St, 259-9160. From $45. AC, TV, pool and bfast.

Motel 6, 311 W Trinity Lane, 227-9696. Junction of I-24 east and I-65 north. From $34. TV, AC, free coffee.

Camping: Many campgrounds are clustered around Opryland. Try **Nashville Travel Park,** 889-4225, site $24.45 for 2 ppl, XP-$4. Pool, mini-golf. *www.kiz.com/campnet/html/ZP/TN/0409/0409.HTM.*

Food
Bluebird Cafe, 4104 Hillsboro Pike, 383-1461. Mon-Sat 5.30pm-midnight, Sun 6pm-midnight. Live music and entertainment nightly, cover $8-$15. Sandwiches, french bread pizzas.

Elliston Place Soda Shop, 2111 Elliston Pl, 327-1090. Mon-Fri 7am-7pm, Sat 7am-5pm. 50s diner.

Of interest
The District. Broadway, 2nd Ave, Printer's Alley and Riverfront Park, make up the historic heart of Nashville. Renovated, turn-of-the-century buildings house shops, restaurants, art galleries, bars and nightclubs.

Country Music Hall of Fame and Historic RCA Studio B, 222 Fifth Avenue, 416-2001. Now in a brand-new building, still number one on any tourist list. Where Elvis Presley cut 100 records from 1963-71. See the King's solid gold cadillac, alongside exhibits, rare artifacts and personal treasures of other legendary performers. 9am-5pm daily, $17, $15 w/student ID. 'Watch out for bogus Hall of Fame on next street.' 'Not worth it.' *www.halloffame.org.*

Frist Center for the Visual Arts, 919 Broadway, 244-3340. Forum for rotating art collections, including an Ottoman exhibit. $6.50. w/student ID. *www.fristcenter.org.*

Music Row, btwn 16th and 19th Aves S. The recording studios for Columbia, RCA and many others are here. For a taste of historic Nashville you can tour the 'mother church of country music', the restored **Ryman Auditorium,** 116 Fifth Ave N, 254-1445/889-3060 for show info and tkt rsvs. The 100-yr old venue now offers daytime tours and live-performances every evening. *www.ryman.com.*

The *General Jackson* cruise, 458-3900, departs from the Gaylord Opryland Hotel, 2800 Opryland Dr. This 2 1/2 hr cruise incl lunch buffet and musical variety show, *Now That's Country,* $40. *www.gaylordhotels.com.*

The 20,000-seat **Gaylord Entertainment Center,** btwn 5th and 6th Aves, is home to the **Nashville Predators** hockey team and host to a variety of concerts and special events. Call for details, 255-9600/770-2000 *www.nationalpredators.com* and *www.gaylordentertainmentcenter.com.*

Nashvillians are hot on reproductions. Their pride and joy is the **Parthenon Pavilion,** the world's only full-sized replica of the original, located adjacent to Centennial Park on West End Ave, which has a 42ft statue of **Athena,** 862-8431, Tue-Sat 9am-4.30pm, Sun 12.30pm-4.30pm, $3.50.

Fort Nashborough, 1st Ave N btwn Broadway and Church Sts, is a replica of the original fort from which the city first grew. For some real history, leave town on I-40 (Old Hickory Blvd exit) and head 12 miles E to **The Hermitage,** 4580 Rachel's Lane, 889-2941, the home of Andrew Jackson, a backwards orphan who became US president (1829-1837). He is buried on the grounds. Open 9am-5pm daily, $12. *www.thehermitage.com.* **Belle Meade Mansion,** 5025 Harding Pike, 356-0501. Was the largest plantation and thoroughbred nursery in Tennessee. Mon-Sat 9am-5pm, Sun 11am-5pm, $11. *www.bellemeadeplantation.com.*

Entertainment

Topping the entertainment list is the show that made Nashville, **The Grand Ole Opry**, 2802 Opryland Dr, 871-OPRY. Radio WSU, and later television, broadcast this country music show out to a receptive nation. Tkts are tough to get during Fan Fair, the annual jamboree of country music held in June. The rest of the year you stand a decent chance. From $20 admission for the 2 shows each Friday and Saturday nights with cheaper matinees in summer. Option for waiting list. 'If you have up to number 15, you stand a chance.' 'Nothing quite like it.' **Opry Mills** is a mega-shopping and entertainment complex, (877) SHOP FUN. Walk through the garish **Opryland Hotel** where tropical vegetation, southern architecture, a Liberace impersonator and a waterfall co-exist under one enormous roof. For info on all Opry attractions call 871-6100 or _www.opry.com_.

Printer's Alley is Nashville's standard club strip.

Tootsie's Orchid Lounge, 422 Broadway, 726-0463. Top Country/Western bar, springboard for future Opry stars. Merle Haggard and other country greats may drop in to see how things are going. 2 bars, 2 bands, 2 floors. Open daily 10.30am-3am, no cover. _www.tootsies.net_.

Also try the **Station Inn**, 402 12th Ave S, 255-3307. Open from 7pm, shows start at 9pm. The area near Vanderbilt Campus has more student-oriented entertainment. _www.stationinn.com_.

Information

Convention and Visitors Division, Chamber of Commerce, 211 Commerce St, 743-3000.

Visitor Information Centre at the Nashville Arena, corner of 5th and Broadway, 259-4747. Open daily 9am-5pm.

Internet access

Bongo Java, 2007 Belmont Blvd, 777-2233. Mon-Fri 7am-11pm, Sat/Sun 8am-11pm. _www.bongojava.com._

Café Coco, 210 Louise Ave, 329-2871. _www.cafecoco.com._ 24 hrs.

Travel

Greyhound, 200 8th Ave and Demonbreun St, 2 blocks S of Broadway, 255-3556/(800) 231-2222. 'Use caution in this neighbourhood.'

Metropolitain Transit Authority (MATA), 862-5950. Running times vary. Murfreesboro Rd/Airport Bus, #18M. Fare approx. $1.50. _www.nashvillemta.org._

EASTERN TENNESSEE AND THE GREAT SMOKIES The **Great Smoky Mountains National Park** is one of the most heavily visited parks in the United States. Named by the Cherokee Indians for the haze which shrouds the mountain peaks, the 800 miles of trails offer an immense variety of wildlife and landscapes. _www.nps.gov/grsm._ One of the many routes you can take to the park entrance will bring you to **Gatlinburg**. 'Commercialism at its worst,' Gatlinburg specialises in wax museums, Elvis memorabilia, UFOs and Jesus knickknacks, all for sale to the gullible tourist. The only things worth doing, perhaps, are to ride the ski lift or to climb the space needle from where you get a good look at the mountains. _www.gatlinburg.com._

North of Gatlinburg on US Hwy 441 is **Pigeon Forge**, home of **Dollywood**, 1020 Dollywood Lane, (865) 428-9488, the only Tennessee attraction to rival Graceland. The theme park is devoted to the life and career of Tennessee's own Queen of Country, Dolly Parton, and includes music shows, restaurants, rides and 'jukebox junction', devoted to the 50s—

all with an 'old-time' atmosphere. 'You won't be disappointed!' Daily 9am-8pm, $44. _www.dollywood.com_. For accommodation look towards **Smoky Mtn Lodge**, 3661 Parkway, (865) 453-9732. From $40.

The park has three visitors centres, the main one being **Sugarlands**, two miles south of Gatlinburg, on Newfound Gap Rd, where you can get maps, and info on the park's unique history and wildlife. (865) 436-1200 is the park info line which links all three centres, the others being at **Cades Cove** and **Oconaluftee**. You must get a free permit at the centre in order to stay overnight at any of the 100 back-country campsites which dot the park. For three of the 10 developed campgrounds at **Smokemont**, **Elkmont** and **Cades Cove**, you have to make reservations. Call (800) 365-2267 enter code GREA, or go on-line to _reservations.nps.gov_, sites $14-20. The other campgrounds are first-come, first-served, $12-$17. If you decide to stay over in the park, you will need to bring your own food; there are no restaurants.

Getting around the park requires a car. The best way to see the mountain peaks is to drive along **Foothills Parkway** towards Walland, or along I-40 skirting the park's northeast flank. Take this for the more scenic route. Only one road, Hwy 441, which becomes New Found Gap Road, actually crosses the park, and can get quite crowded. Along the way there are numerous turnouts and trailheads. A ranger at the visitors centre can direct you to quiet walkways (trailheads with only one or two parking spaces) that offer more challenging and private trails, or you can stick to the more touristed, but impressive main turn-outs at the well-known vista points. **Cades Cove** in the western part of the park offers some of the best wildlife and a collection of historic buildings. Come early if you want to see the animals. Rangers offer guided tours on summer evenings from most campgrounds in the park.

CHATTANOOGA In the southeastern corner of the state, this was the site of an important Civil War battle. Union troops were pinned down under siege for two months before reinforcements allowed them to break free from the mountains and down into the plains of Georgia. Among Chattanooga's attractions: **Ruby Falls**, 1720 S Scenic Hwy, 821-2544, the world's highest underground waterfall, at 145ft. $13 for 1hr guided tour. Open daily 8am-8pm _rubyfalls.com/fun/plain/index.html;_ **Ross's Landing**, where the Cherokees began their Trail of Tears; **Chattanooga Choo Choo**, the restored 1909 railway station that once welcomed visitors to the South _www.choochoo.com;_ the **Tennessee River Park**, with 22 miles of trails; and the amazing **Walnut Street Pedestrian Bridge**, one of the world's longest. 'A lovely city. One of the nicest places I visited in the USA.' _www.chattanoogafun.com_.

Of interest
For both the view and the history, take the incline railway up **Lookout Mountain**, site of the famous Battle Above the Clouds. The mountain was an important signalling point for troops in the field. The gradient is 72.7% at its maximum; open daily 8.30am-9.30pm, $9 r/t. Often a long wait. There is a **Visitors Center**, 821-7786, at the top, which has displays on signalling in the Civil War. Also a 13ft x 30ft painting, _The Battle Above the Clouds_. 'Cheaper to pay for bus right to top and back. Bus leaves from near Greyhound.' 'While at the top, follow road to park and see the

cannons and memorials, and imagine the battle. The view is still better from up here.' _www.lookoutmtnattractions.com_. Just over the border with Georgia, on Hwy 27 is **Chickamauga** and **Chattanooga National Military Park**, (706) 866-9241. The Union forces were driven from here into Chattanooga after a fierce battle in which 48,000 men were wounded or killed. _www.nps.gov/chch_. The **Battles for Chattanooga Museum**, (423) 821-2812, has an excellent map show of the battle. Open daily 9am-6pm, last show 5.30pm, $7. _www.battlesforchattanooga.com_. If you are heading to Chattanooga from Nashville, you may want to stop at the **Jack Daniel's Distillery**, Hwy 55 in Lynchburg, (931) 759-4221. Free tours daily 9am-4.30pm but don't expect free samples, the distillery of the potent whiskey is in a dry county. 'Best tour in America; the smell of whiskey is all around!'

MEMPHIS Cradled in a bend of the Mississippi River, this city gave birth, via such legends as James Cotton (_www.jamescottonsuperharp.com_), WC Handy, Howlin' Wolf and Junior Wells, to the urban blues. And, as the birthplace of rock 'n' roll' in the 1950s, it is easy to see why Chuck Berry (_www.chuckberry.com_), Carl Perkins, Jerry Lee Lewis (_www.jerryleelewis.de_), Elvis Presley (_www.elvis.com_) and so many others have called Memphis home – thanks in the main to Sam Phillips at his **Sun Studios.**

After a long spell of urban decay, Memphis has reconstructed its downtown waterfront. Beale Street, famous for its blues clubs, is once again worth visiting. And Mud Island, in the Mississippi River, has several river-related attractions reachable by monorail. The river connects Memphis with the Deep South, giving the city the most southern feeling of Tennessee's large cities. There are excellent views of the Mississippi as she broadly sweeps away to the southwest just below the city.

Despite attempts to spruce up the city, vast sections remain depressed, reminding the visitor that this is a town where dreams have died. The number one attraction in Memphis is Graceland, where rock 'n' roll king Elvis Presley is buried. And in April, 1968, Martin Luther King, Jr was assassinated at the Lorraine Motel. _www.memphistravel.com_.

Accommodation
Admiral Benbow Inn, 4720 E. Summer Ave, 682-4601. D-$37, $5 key deposit. TV, AC, pool. 'Excellent.'

Super 8 Motel, 340 W Illinois Ave, 948-9005. From $48, free coffee and doughnuts. Close to Graceland. Next to Mississippi river.

Camping: T.O Fuller State Park, near Chucalissa Indian Village, 543-7581. $14.50 for two. 24 hrs. 'Very good.'

Food
Memphis is famous for pork BBQ, with over 100 BBQ restaurants.

Corky's, 5259 Poplar Ave, 685-9744, 30 mins from downtown. Renowned both nationally and locally, sit-in or drive-thru. BBQ platters with sides $7-$18. Open Sun-Thurs 10:45am-9.45pm. _www.corkysbbq.com._

The North End, 346 N Main St, 527-3663. Southern-style cooking; good, cheap vegetarian dishes. Live music, open daily 11am-3am.

Of interest
The best sights in Memphis are the many musical shrines, the most holy of which is Elvis Presley's home, **Graceland**, 3734 Elvis Presley Blvd, 10 miles S of town, 332-3322. Mon-Sat 9am-5pm, Sun 10am-4pm. The 'Platinum Tour', takes in the 23-room, 14-acre mansion, the _Lisa Marie_, a 96-seat airplane/penthouse in the sky, Elvis' tour bus, a stunning car museum, plus the Meditation Garden where Elvis

and family are buried. $27, $24.30 w/student ID. The 'Mansion Tour,' includes a 20 min video presentation and tour of the house only, $20, $18 w/student ID, but you will not want to miss the costumes, gold-wrapped grand piano, and 'jungle' playroom. Walking through the amazing 80 ft long 'Hall of Gold' lined with the King's gold records is almost breathtaking. Only by walking down this hallway can you begin to comprehend the enormity of Elvis's success. Catch the #43 bus to Graceland from just outside Greyhound station, $1.25. 'Free shuttle from Beale St.' 'I toured house hurriedly with 15 middle aged fans brought to tears in midst of disgusting bad taste. Plastic souvenirs are everywhere.' 'Worth it for the experience and insight into a great American icon.' _www.elvis-presley.com_.

Sun Studio, 706 Union Ave, 521-0664, now a National Historic Landmark, was the true birthplace of rock 'n' roll, launching the career of many legends including Elvis Presley and Jerry Lee Lewis. The gifted founder of Sun Studio, Sam Phillips, recorded Elvis' first of many hits with the seminal, symbiotic guitarist Scotty Moore, _That's All Right,_ here in July 1954. Two years later, Phillips recorded Jerry Lee Lewis's _Crazy Arms,_ followed by _Whole Lotta Shakin' Going On_ (which sold six million copies) and _Great Balls of Fire_ in 1957. John Lennon said: "That's the music that inspired me to play... There's nothing conceptually better than rock and roll. No group, be it Beatles, Dylan or Stones, has ever improved on _Whole Lotta Shakin' Goin' on_ for my money." _www.sunstudio.com_.

L&A City and Sightseeing Tours, 370-6666. Comprehensive bus tour of Graceland and Elvis 'sites'. Pick up from most downtown hotels. $38, city tour only $25.

Chucalissa Indian Village, Indian Village Drive, T.O Fuller State Park, 785-3160. Reconstructed 1000-year-old Indian village. Choctaw Indians live on the site and demonstrate Indian crafts. Tue-Sat 9am-5pm, Sun 1.30pm-4.30pm, $5. _cas.memphis.edu/chucalissa._

Dixon Gallery and Garden, 4339 Park Ave, 761-5250. Good collection of French and American Impressionist paintings. Tue-Fri 10am-4pm, Sat 10am-5pm, Sun 1pm-5pm, $5, free w/student ID. _www.dixon.org_.

The **Memphis Pink Palace and Planetarium,** 3050 Central Ave, 320-6320, is one of the largest museums in the Southeast, and specialises in science and history. Originally housed in the adjoining pink marble mansion. Tue-Sat 9am-5pm, Sun 12-5pm. $8 museum, IMAX theatre shows, $7.50 (call for show times), $4.25 planetarium. $16.75 all three. _www.memphismuseums.org._

Mud Island, 576-7241, situated offshore from main downtown area and accessible by a monorail. 52-acre park and entertainment complex devoted to life on the Mississippi River. Park entrance is free, but tkt for museum, monorail ride and riverwalk guided tour is $8. In the **River Museum**, tour 18 diff galleries, incl a towboat pilot house, see also a film about disasters on the river, and the dioramas that tell you about the river's history. The 5 block long Mississippi River scale model, complete with flowing water, follows the river's path to the Gulf of Mexico. Open 10am-6pm. Concerts in the summer. _www.mudisland.com_.

National Civil Rights Center, 450 Mulberry St, 521-9699. Houses exhibits and films on the individuals who led the civil rights movement and has two constantly changing galleries. The centre is housed in the **Lorraine Motel**, site of the 1968 assassination of Martin Luther King, Jr. Mon-Sat 9am-6pm, closed Tue, Sun 1pm-6pm, $11, $9 w/ student ID. _www.civilrightsmuseum.org/about/about.asp_.

The 32-storey, 6-acre **Pyramid,** is the 3rd largest pyramid in the world and has held concerts by the likes of The Rolling Stones, Billy Joel, and Elton John. Arena has seating for 21,000. _www.pyramidarena.com_.

Entertainment

Beale St, 4 blocks of nightclubs, galleries and restaurants. The place where WC Handy blew the notes to make him 'Father of the Blues'. His house is now a museum, 352 Beale St, 522-1556. Live music nightly and outdoor entertainment year-round. _www.bealestreet.com_.

Rum Boogie Cafe, 182 Beale St, 528-0150, Daily 11am-2am. Cover charge. _www.rumboogie.com/home.htm_.

During the day, **Abe Schwab's,** 163 Beale St, 523-9782, an eclectic and amusing drugstore, sells just about anything. 'Lively and bustling rapping, blues and loud records combine to create a unique atmosphere.' Open Mon-Sat 9am-5pm.

At the **Peabody Hotel** (800) 238-7273, 149 Union Ave, dating to 1869, the famous VIPs (Very Important Poultry) perform the March of the Peabody Ducks twice-daily. _www.peabodymemphis.com/defaultFlash.htm_.

Listen to **WDIA**, 1070 AM, the famous black radio station where B.B. King used to spin records and an important station for the early growth of the blues, and RnB scene. Try to plan your trip for Elvis Week in August, 'in the week he died, there are Elvises everywhere!'

Information
Memphis Convention and Visitors Bureau, Riverside and Jefferson, 543-5333. Daily 9am-6pm. _www.memphistravel.com._

Travel
Greyhound, 203 Union Ave, 523-9253/(800) 231-2222. Use caution in this area at night.

Amtrak, 545 S Main St, 526-0052/(800) 872-7245. 'Surrounding area very dangerous, even during the day, watch out!'

Memphis Transit Authority (MATA), Union Ave & Main St, 274-6282.

Buses to **Memphis International Airport** depart from downtown, catch the #50 to Popler and Hollywood, then change to #32, Mon-Fri 5.45am-5.45pm. Erratic service, total fare $1.25, students $1 plus 10c transfer. For a taxi call checker-cab company 577-7777. Approx $25.

GREAT AMERICAN BREAKFASTS

Breakfasts, and their weekend cousin, 'brunch', have a special place in American culture. Don't give in to the bagel-and-cream-cheese temptation (except in the world capital of bagels, New York) without first ordering a heaping tower of warm, syrupy pancakes. The south in particular knows how to sate a lumberjack-sized hunger for the whole day starting with a greasy-spoon breakfast—try extra hard to find an unassuming diner if visiting the region, as they surprisingly will often have the best food and prices.

For the great all-American breakfast, try:
The Bunnery, 130 N Cache Dr in **Jackson, WY**, (307) 733-5474, *www.bunnery.com*, which boasts wonderful buttermilk coffee cake and much more. For excellent coffee, try **Caffe Trieste**, 1465 25th St in SF, where Jack Kerouac probably began his day, (415) 982-2605, *www.caffetriste.com*. In **San Diego**, sample the homemade granola and delectable pumpkin waffles at **Cafe 222**, Island Ave at 2nd Ave., (619) 236-9902, *www.cafe222.com*. A spicier wake-up call awaits at **Cisco's Bakery**, 1511 E Sixth St, **Austin, TX**, (512) 478-2420. Its Tex-Mex-brex includes huevos rancheros powerful enough to open even the most stubborn lids. **Colony Inn**, at 471 47th St., **Amana, IA**, (319) 622-6270/ (800) 227-3471, offers a plentiful spread of all the traditionals.

Lou **Mitchell's**, 565 W Jackson St & Jefferson, at the start of Route 66 in downtown **Chicago, IL**, (312) 939-3111, is the quintessential old fashioned family-owned American breakfast place, great value and service, a must visit. Also in Chicago, **Ann Sathers**, 929 W Belmont, (773) 348-2378, *www.annsather.com*, has Swedish pancakes (similar to crepes) served with lingonberry jam, and delicious cinnamon rolls. Near Chicago in **Willmette, IL, Walker Brothers Original Pancake House**, 153 Greenbay Rd, (847) 251-6000, is noteworthy for pancakes of all kinds, with apple at the top of the list.

Visit **Lowell's**, 1519 Pike Place 'Market' in **Seattle, WA**, (206) 622-2036, for fine 'scrambles' and an inexpensive self-serve breakfast with a nice view of Puget Sound. **The Mad Batter**, 19 Jackson St. in **Cape May, NJ**, (609) 884-5970, *www.carrollvilla.com*, turns out monster sized stacks of pancakes, of course, but for the adventurous, the *Crabs Benedict* must be sampled as well. A notable breakfast by the sea can be netted at **Mangrove Mike's**, milepost 82 in the **Florida Keys**, (305) 664-8022, which turns out a solid southern breakfast (grits, home fries and rib-eye steak).

At **Original Pantry**, 877 S Figueroa St, **Los Angeles**, (213) 972-9279 (24 hrs), try hot cakes or French toast. **Uncle Bill's Pancake House** resides by the sea at 1305 Highland Ave, facing **Manhattan Beach** in LA, (310) 545-5177, in an historic orange and blue building with an ocean view from the porch.

Reeve's Restaurant and Bakery 1306 G St NW in **Washington, DC**, (202) 628-6350 also masters the key element of southern breakfast—fried foods galore. Sample their pastries—favourites are strawberry pie and shortcake. Also try **The Diner**, 2453 18th St in Adams Morgan, (202) 232-8800. Wide variety of plates, $4-$13. 24 hrs, dine indoors or out, feasting on delights ranging from the Spanish and Feta omelet to the Croque Monsieur/Madame (French loaf, béchamel sauce and melted gruyere).

In **New York City, Ellen's Stardust Diner** at 1650 Broadway at 51st (212) 956-5151, *www.ellenstardust.com*, features NY's only Sunday Jazz Brunch buffet, 11.30am to 3 pm in its Iridium jazz club. **Sara Beth's**, (212) 496-6280, makes its own preserves, home-baked muffins, sticky buns and offers a wide range of other breakfast foods. It has 4 locations on Amsterdam Ave north of 80th St, on Madison and 92nd, in the Whitney Museum, and the Chelsea Market (bakery only).

2. CANADA

INTRODUCTION

BACKGROUND

Before you go

Citizens and legal, permanent residents of the United States currently do not need passports to enter Canada as visitors although they will be asked for identification (proof of citizenship or Alien Registration card) at the border. All other visitors entering Canada must have valid passports. Since Immigration officials have enormous discretionary powers, it is wise to be well dressed, clean- cut, and the possessor of a return ticket if possible. The following persons do not need a visa if entering only as visitors:

1. British citizens and British Overseas Citizens who are re-admissible to the United Kingdom;
2. Citizens of Andorra, Antigua and Barbuda, Australia, Austria, Bahamas, Barbados, Belgium, Botswana, Brunei, Cyprus, Denmark, Finland, France, Germany, Greece, Iceland, Ireland, Israel (National Passport holders only), Italy, Japan, Liechtenstein, Luxembourg, Malta, Mexico, Monaco, Namibia, Netherlands, New Zealand, Norway, Papua New Guinea, Portugal, Republic of Korea, St. Kitts and Nevis, St. Lucia, St. Vincent, San Marino, Singapore, Solomon Islands, Spain, Swaziland, Sweden, Slovenia, Switzerland, United States, and Western Samoa;
3. Citizens of British dependent territories who derive their citizenship through birth, descent, registration or naturalization in one of the British dependent territories of Anguilla, Bermuda, British Virgin Islands, Cayman Islands, Falkland Islands, Gibraltar, Montserrat, Pitcairn, St. Helena or the Turks and Caicos Islands;
4. Persons with passport issued by the Government of the Hong Kong Special Administrative Region of the People's Republic of China;
5. Persons holding passports or travel documents issued by the Holy See.

Nationals of all other countries should check their visa requirements with their nearest Canadian consular office. If there is no official Canadian representative in the country, visas are issued by the British embassy or consulate. Those requiring visas must apply before leaving home. *www.cic.gc.ca/english/visit/visas.html.*

To **work in Canada**, a work visa must be obtained from the Canadian immigration authorities before departure. To qualify you must produce written evidence of a job offer. If you are in the UK, contact the **BUNAC** London office, (020) 7251-3472, for information about the *Work Canada* programme which gives eligible students and young people up to age 35 temporary work authorisation—for up to a year. Similar opportunities are open to students of a few other countries. Check with your nearest consulate. If you plan to **study in Canada** you will need a special student visa, obtainable from any Canadian consulate. You must produce a letter of acceptance from the Canadian college before the visa can be issued.

Visitors who plan to re-enter the United States after visiting Canada must be sure to keep their US visa documentation and passport to regain entry into the US. (*See Background USA chapter for information on the Visa Waiver programme.*)

Customs permit anyone over 18 to import, duty free, up to 50 cigars, 200 cigarettes and 200g of manufactured tobacco.

Along with personal possessions, any number of individually wrapped and addressed gifts up to the value of $60 each may be brought into the country. Each visitor who meets the minimum age requirements of the province or territory of entry may, in addition, bring in 1.14 litres of liquor or wine, or 24 x 355 ml bottles / cans of beer or ale, duty and tax-free. *www.cbsa-asfc.gc.ca.*

Further details on immigration, health or customs requirements may be obtained from the nearest High Commission, embassy or consulate.

Getting there from the USA

As a rough guide to fares from New York City to major eastern Canadian cities, the current fares to Toronto are: by train, 12-13 hrs, US$79 one way, US$178 r/t via Amtrak (*Maple Leaf*), *www.amtrak.com*, depending on when you travel, but also check out *www.viarail.ca*; by Greyhound bus, 10-13 hrs, US$80 o/w, US$150 r/t. *www.greyhound.com.* Airline prices from NYC have been known to start as low as US$130-140 o/w, US$285 r/t, but your best bet is to look up the cheapest deals on sites such as *www.expedia.com*, *www.travelocity.com*, *www.orbitz.com* or to check directly with the airlines flying to your destination at the time of travel. Flying time is about 90 minutes. On the west coast, Amtrak's *Cascades* goes to Vancouver from Eugene, Oregon, via Seattle and Portland. By train, Vancouver is about 4 hours from Seattle; 11 hours from Eugene; US$57 from Eugene.

Should you cross the border by car it's a good idea to have a yellow 'Non-resident, Interprovincial Motor Vehicle Liability Insurance Card' (phew!), which provides evidence of financial responsibility by a valid automobile liability insurance policy. This card is available in the US through some insurance agents. This evidence is required at all times by all provinces and territories. In addition, Québec's insurance act bars lawsuits for bodily injury resulting from an auto accident, so you may need some additional coverage should you be planning to drive in Québec. If you're driving a borrowed car, it's wise to carry a letter from the owner giving you permission to use the car.

Climate and what to pack

"It is only here in large portions of Canada that wondrous *second wind*, the Indian summer, attains its amplitude and heavenly perfection – the temperatures, the sunny haze; the mellow, rich, delicate, almost *flavoured* air: Enough to live – enough to merely be." Walt Whitman, 1904.

Summers in Canada are usually wonderfully warm and sunny. In all the major urban areas, afternoon temperatures in July are in the 20-27 C range (70-80s F); to the west, Vancouver has the warmest climate overall of any Canadian city, and Kelowna, in the heart of BC's wine area, has the nation's warmest summers. If you're looking to bathe in the sun, during the summer you'll find more of it up north in Yellowknife, Northwest Territories, where the sun shines 24-hours a day during the solstice. The sunniest year-round though, are the three Prairie Provinces – Alberta, Saskatchewan, and Manitoba.

Given Canada's huge mass, from the Arctic on south, not everywhere is so nice. In the Territories above the 60th parallel, as you go north, temperatures drop accordingly and even summer temperatures may be cool. Be warned that nights, even in high summer, can be chilly and it's advisable to bring lightweight sweaters or jackets. Yellowknife has an *average* August temperature of 58F (14.2C) for instance, and nights in the mountains can be pretty cold.

Snow can be expected in some places as early as September – generally in winter, Canada is very cold and snowy everywhere. Sir Edwin Arnold, an English traveler quoted by Mitchell Brown, wrote in 1891: "As for the climate of Canada, winter is not perpetual, but merely, in most parts, somewhat long." Parts of Quebec have the most snow. Along with it, Canada has every snow and ice-sport imaginable, starting with ice hockey. *www.members.tripod.com/~MitchellBrown/almanac.*

When you've decided which areas of Canada you'll be visiting, note the local climate at Environment Canada: *www.climate.weatheroffice.ec.gc.ca* and pack clothes accordingly. Plan for a variety of occasions, make a list, and then cut it by half! Take easy-to-care-for garments. Permanent press, non-iron things are best. Laundromats are cheap and readily available wherever you go. Remember too that you'll probably want to buy things while you're in North America! Canadians, as well as Americans, excel at producing casual, outdoorsy clothes, T-shirts, etc. The farther north you plan to go and the more time you intend to spend out of doors, the more weatherproof and/or waterproof the clothing will need to be. And don't forget insect repellent.

It's important too to consider the best way of carrying your clothes. Lugging a heavy suitcase is not fun. A lightweight bag or a backpack is possibly best. A good idea is to take a smaller flight-type bag in which to keep a change of clothes and all your most valuable possessions like passport, travellers cheques and air tickets as well, but always hand carry the bag containing your passport and money. For extra safety many travellers like to carry passport documents and travellers cheques in a special neck/waist pouch or wallet. It's worth making photocopies of key documents, in case they get lost, and keeping them separately. When travelling by bus, be sure to keep your baggage within your sights. Make sure it's properly labelled and on the same bus as yourself at every stop! And when going by plane, be sure off take off previous baggage tags, so that your bag isn't sent somewhere else!

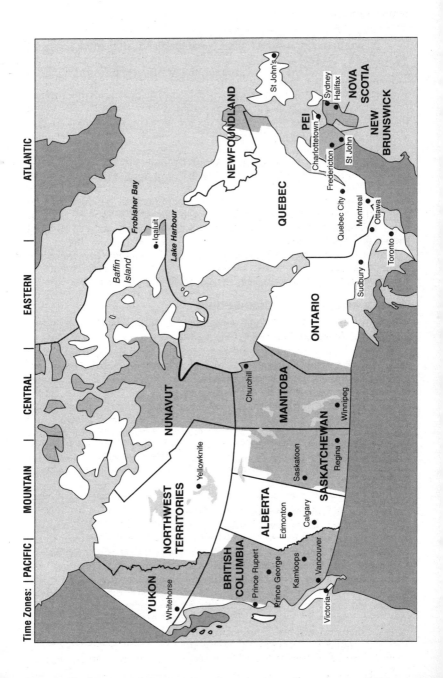

Time zones

Since 1884, Canada has had six time zones:

1. Newfoundland Standard Time: Newfoundland, and part of Labrador (GMT – 3½ hrs).
2. Atlantic Standard Time: Labrador, the Maritimes, far eastern part of Québec (GMT – 4 hrs).
3. Eastern Standard Time: Nunavut, most of Québec, and all of Ontario east of 90 degrees longitude (GMT – 5 hrs).
4. Central Standard Time: Ontario west of 90, Manitoba, Saskatchewan, most of Nunavut (GMT – 6 hrs).
5. Mountain Standard Time: Alberta, Northwest Territories, part of Nunavut, part of northeastern British Columbia (GMT – 7 hrs).
6. Pacific Standard Time: most of British Columbia and the Yukon (GMT – 8 hrs).

From the first Sunday in April through the last Sunday in October, Daylight Saving Time (DST) is observed everywhere except Fort St. John, Charlie Lake, Taylor and Dawson Creek in British Columbia, Creston in the East Kootenays, and most of Saskatchewan (except Denare Beach and Creighton). Time Zones and DST in Canada are regulated by provincial and territorial governments.

http://inms-ienm.nrc-cnrc.gc.ca/time_services/daylight_saving_e.html.

History and the Canadian People

Although Canada's First Nations have lived for thousands of years in the region north of the 49th parallel, it was the French who first gave Canada its name. In 1535, Jacques Cartier, seeking a passage to India via what is now called the St Lawrence River, was told of a *kanata* by native chiefs, and mistakenly thought this Iroquoian word for village was in fact a vast territory to the west, ruled by native peoples.

There was a vast territory to the west, to be sure, and indeed Cartier was the first European to trade for furs with its indigenous peoples, but Canada's character and quality of life today is more to do with the amazing formative imprint of a British fur-trading enterprise established by Royal Charter in 1670, the Hudson's Bay Company (HBC), that still exists today. www.hbc.com The domain of the HBC was immense, likened to a company town extending, at one point, over a quarter of the entire North American continent. But the social legacy established by the HBC and the North West Company, which it absorbed in 1821, is more significant.

Curiously, two hardy Frenchmen, Pierre-Esprit Radisson - once adopted by Mohawks - and Médard Chouart, Sieur Des Groseilles (known to the English court of the time, and to Canadian school children today, as "Messrs Radishes and Gooseberries") were the driving force behind the establishment of the London-based HBC; a German, Prince Rupert of the Rhine, cousin of Charles II, was its chief sponsor; and most of the HBC's leaders and many of its intrepid voyageurs were formidable Scots - many from the Orkneys - with a Calvinist zeal for hard work, loyalty, perseverance and survival. Their clan upbringing helped in their relations with local Indian bands across the continent.

HBC's mercantile empire was focussed almost entirely on fur trading with the native peoples, sustained by a web of 173 trading posts ("forts") that stretched as far south as Wyoming and north to the Arctic Circle, the furs transported by birch-bark canoes via the region's near total navigability. The Company had strict rules in dealing with Indians, whom it considered to be partners, that never produced a vigilante mentality, as noted by Peter Newman in his excellent *Empire of the Bay*, in contrast with the settlement of America's West that amounted to military conquest of Indian lands.

In pursuit of their business, the non-altruistic HBC and North West Company (NWC) also eschewed colonizing, which would upset the beavers and other animals on which the business depended, but would go to heroic lengths to expand their empire. It was the NWC's Alexander MacKenzie, for example, who both paddled (unknowingly) north up his name-sake river to the Arctic Ocean in search of another passage to India, and was the first European to reach the west coast of North America by land, in 17983 at Bella Coola in what is now British Columbia, a dozen years before Lewis and Clark crossed the US.

In HBC's entrepreneurial forts, presided over by company factors and strategically far apart, survival amid Canada's sometimes brutal climate and conditions necessitated allegiance, collective conscience over individual excellence, and respect for the proper order of things. Today's Canadian mentality, as Newman points out, is rooted in the HBC's principles of loyalty and organic growth of tradition rather than individual assertion of revolutionary will as in the US.

The English Canadian accent you hear today is decidedly North American, with a vague hint of a Scottish lilt. The French spoken in Québec differs from Parisian French by about three hundred years – Quebecois closely resembles the 17th century "central" French of the kings. In some ways the Québecois are more French than the French – they prefer 'stationnement' to 'parking' and 'fin de semaine' to 'weekend', words used freely in France – but the influence of North America is inevitable, as in getting caught in a traffic – 'jammer'. While the British eventually prevailed in colonizing Canada after 1759, culminating with the initial confederation of 1867 and belting it together with a transcontinental railroad, – the Canadian Pacific, in- 1885, it was the French quest to establish sovereignty in a "New France" that spearheaded Canada's original settlements.

Under royal charter, the French were the first to establish a European agricultural village on Canadian soil in 1605, at Port Royal on the west coast of Nova Scotia. The first permanent settlement in Canada was by the zealous Catholic Samuel Champlain at Québec in 1608. In 1610, a protégée of Champlain, Etienne Brulé, was probably the first European to explore the Great Lakes. And in the 1700s and 1800s nearly all the thousand or more extraordinary *voyageurs* who paddled furs in birchbark *canots de maître* for the NWC, to Lachine on the St Lawrence from Fort Chipewyan on Lake Athabasca and beyond, were French. These "magnificent river rats" were capable of prodigious physical feats, including portaging upto 180 lbs per man. (*Empire of the Bay*, Newman). The French, as well as the Scots they worked with, intermingled comfortably with the Indians, creating both a half-blood society – the Metis – and an enduring relationship with the Native community.

Today most of Canada's seven million French-speaking population live in Québec Province, the country's largest single religious group is Roman Catholic, and the charming walled old city of Québec calls itself, with pride, the "Cradle of French Civilization in North America". The distinctive French dialect of Québec is still found here, as in the delightful Canadian comedy, *La Grande Séduction - The Seduction of Dr. Lewis*. (Sainte-Marie-la-Mauderne in the film is actually Harrington Harbour, 300 km east of Anticosti Island in the Gulf of St. Lawrence, an isolated English-speaking village.)

The Scottish heritage remains vividly alive too, especially in the west: British Columbia even has a provincial tartan, and Canada's Scottish heritage is marked by dozens of highland games across the nation and at least 165 bagpipe bands. *http://web.ripnet.com/~nimmos/pipe_bands.html*.

Although Canada, like its neighbour to the south, is a comparatively young country, Canadians feel that they have finally emerged as a major world power in their own right - long gone are the days when Canada could only function in the shadow of Great Britain or the United States. The Queen, as Canada's head of state, appears on Canadian coins, is represented by a Governor General, visits Canada often and has an accepted role as sovereign, but otherwise Canadians are increasingly independent.

Of the last provinces to join, Saskatchewan and Alberta were formed in 1905 and Newfoundland entered the federation in 1949, all amazingly recent. Nunavut, meaning 'Our Land' in Inuit, was created in 1999: The element of self-rule allowed the Inuit is a milestone for the First Nations of the whole continent. For this reason, although undoubtedly proud of their country, Canadians are fiercely defendant of their home provinces and may well declare themselves an Albertan (or Québecois, whatever) first and Canadian second.

Despite a reputation for appearing to be puritanical, conformist, humourless and dull, you will more likely find Canadians to be charming, hospitable and anxious to share their land with you – from cricket to dragon boats, fringe festivals, wineries, bath-tub racing, bush pilots, sledding, real cowboy rodeos, fantastic Rocky Mountains, world-class skiing, marvelous Northern Lights and 24-hour golf at summer solstices. They will be most anxious to uphold Canada's uniqueness and show that Canada is not the same as America, despite apparent social similarities.

Try and see something of the *real* Canada. Get behind the stereotypical images and try to meet Canadians at the many local fairs and annual festivals. 'Man-made 21st century Canada will impress you, but it is the Canadian way of life and the natural beauty of the land that will really dazzle you.'

Economics and Politics

Rich in natural resources and with money in the bank, Canada's economy has had an enviable performance since the mid-1990s, including the fastest ongoing economic growth and strongest budget position of any industrial nation. Little wonder then that Canada has produced a quality of life in its major cities that is among the highest in the world, according to *Mercer Consulting*. Vancouver is rated by *Mercer* as having the third highest ranking of any city for overall quality of life; Toronto, Ottawa, Montreal, and Calgary all come in the top 25. For safety and security, according to *Mercer*, Canadian cities top all rankings in North America.

Among the rising stars of Canada's economy are a $2 billion a year movie industry in Vancouver, diamond mines extracting millions of carats in the Northwest Territories, and hundreds of vineyards and wineries in the Niagara area and Okanagan Valley of British Columbia (whose chief export market is…Australia!).One of Canada's star economic assets is its petroleum, with reserves second only to those of Saudi Arabia, expanding production, including over a million barrels a day from Alberta's fast developing oil sands, and the highest oil exports to the US of any country.

Second only in size to Russia, Canada has a population of roughly 32 million, with practically everyone living along its southern strip. The majority of its people are descendants of white Europeans, either Gallic or Celtic, with native peoples numbering about a million, most of whom live in Ontario and provinces to the West. As Canada continues to open its doors to the rest of the world, Canadian society has increased its cultural, racial, and political diversity. In January 2006 however, the Conservative Party headed by Stephen Harper was voted back into power after a 12-year absence from government.

Continuing to maintain its centre-stage prominence is the perennial issue of Québec. The primary objective of the Bloc Québecois, led by Gilles Duceppe, is the sovereignty of Québec, Canada's second most-populous province. *www.blocquebecois.org/fr.* You will notice the phrase *Je me souviens* on license plates in Québec: Québeckers, while acknowledging the english world since General Montcalm's forces were defeated on the Plains of Abraham by General Wolfe in 1759, naturally want to maintain their heritage and remain the distinct society that they are within Canada – a society that is as distinct from France today as New England is from England. Most of the rest of Canada not only respects the right of Québeckers to maintain their identity, but also loves the charms of this delightful and interesting province.

The values and traditions of individual provinces are strong and Canadian politics is renowned for its bitter inter-provincial and provincial-versus-federal rivalries, mostly based on so-called revenue sharing issues. This is particularly true of oil-rich Alberta, which has no debts and which pays Ottawa far more in taxes than it gets back. Constitutional proposals designed to keep Québec within the federation and everyone else happy as well, have not yet gained approval. Though bitter feelings still stem from the conflict, there is no doubt that this unsubtle blend of French and British influence adds an extra *quelque chose* to the Canadian cultural picture.

BACKGROUND INFORMATION

Languages. Canada's Constitution provides that English and French are its official languages and, under the Official Languages Act have 'equality of status and equal rights and privileges as to their use", overseen by a Commissioner of Official Languages. Consequently, government and most other institutions have signs and descriptive information side-by-side in both English and French. *www.canadianheritage.gc.ca/progs/lo-ol/index_e.cfm.*

Canada has an *Aboriginal Languages Initiative* that maintains and revitalizes Aboriginal languages, about a dozen of which are official in particular provinces and territories. *www.canadianheritage.gc.ca/progs/pa-app/progs/ila-ali/index_e.cfm.*

The Metric System. Everything in Canada is metric. Milk, wine and gasoline are sold by the litre; groceries come in grams and kilograms; clothing sizes are in centimetres, fabric lengths in metres; temperatures are Celsius; distances are in kilometres; and, most importantly, driving speeds are in kilometres per hour. All measurements in this section are given in metric terms. See the conversion tables in the Appendix. Electricity is on the US system: 110v, 60 cycles AC, except in remote areas where cycles vary.

Health. Canada operates a universal subsidised health service. The federal government sets national health-care standards while provincial ministries run the actual system locally, paid for through taxes. Three provinces (British Columbia, Alberta and Ontario) charge premiums. Most provinces cover most hospital and medical services of their inhabitants, although a minimum of three months' residency is required in Québec and British Columbia. The short-term visitor to Canada, therefore, must be adequately insured *before* arrival. For medical services, you'll need to show a provincial health card or pay directly.

In some provinces, temporary workers and students are eligible for the cards, in which case, apply for them as soon as possible after you arrive from the Ministry of Health where you live, (*www.chp-pcs.gc.ca/CHP/index_e.jsp?pageid=10042*) with an application form obtainable from the ministry, or in any doctor's office, hospital or pharmacy. *www.cic.gc.ca/english/newcomer/fact_health.html*.

Money, Banks and Tax. Canadian currency is dollars and cents and comes in the same units as US currency, i.e. cent, nickel, quarter and dollar, as well as $2 coins. The dollar coin has a great name, the 'loonie' (a loon [bird!] is featured on one side). Occasionally the $2 coin is subsequently referred to as a 'twonie'. One American dollar is worth about C$1.25 and you will find your dollars go a lot further here than in the US. This has not always been the case; for a long time Canadians would cross the border to make large purchases. To avoid exchange rate problems, it is a good idea to change all your money into Canadian currency or travellers cheques. (At the time of writing £1 = C$2.26.) Visit *www.bankofcanada.ca/en/exchange.htm* for updated exchange rates.

NB: There is generally no problem using US dollars in Canada, albeit with a loss on the exchange rate, but this is never possible vice-versa.

Unless otherwise stated, all prices in this section are in Canadian dollars.

Travellers' cheques are probably the safest form of currency and are accepted at most hotels, restaurants and shops. They may be used in the same way as cash at major stores or businesses in Canada.

Credit and debit cards. Barclaycard, Visa and MasterCard are all widely accepted and you can draw cash from these cards at banks and through

ATM's for a fee. You will be charged commission for every transaction you make. Switch and Delta debit cards can be used in the same way.

Bank hours are generally 10am-4pm, Monday to Friday and often with a later opening on Friday. If you are planning an extensive trip to Canada and the USA, you might consider opening a bank account offering a cash-card that works on both a Canadian and a US bank system.

All you need to open an account in Canada is cash. It is a simple matter of filling out one form. Since opening an account with a Canadian bank means corresponding with them through the mail, you will want to look into it well in advance of your trip. The Royal Bank of Canada offers a 'personal client card' that is valid in Canada and at all 'Plus' system machines in the US. *www.rbcroyalbank.com/cards/client_cards/personal*. ATMs are common in big cities and at most banks and normally accept cards with a Visa/MasterCard sign. Check with your bank for availability and charges and make sure you know your PIN!

Sales Tax and Rebates. Canada has a countrywide **Goods and Services Tax (GST)** of 7% and **Provincial Sales Taxes (PST).** Overseas visitors may be able to claim a rebate of **GST** paid on some items such as short-term accommodation and on consumer goods; it cannot be reclaimed for travel, car hire or meals. To complicate matters further, in Newfoundland, Nova Scotia and New Brunswick, the GST and PST have been combined into the **Harmonised Sales Tax (HST)** of 15%. The HST and GST can all be reclaimed and in Québec and Manitoba, so too can the PST. Keep your receipts! Each receipt must normally be for a minimum of $50 before taxes, expenses must total at least $200, and the goods must have been taken out of Canada within 60 days.

Details from: *www.cra-arc.gc.ca/tax/nonresidents/visitors* where you can download application forms for GST refunds. Visitors Rebate Program, Revenue Canada, Summerside Tax Centre, Summerside, PEI, C1N 6C6, (800) 668-4748. Outside Canada phone (902) 432-5608. You can also email enquiries to *visitors@ccra-adrc.gc.ca*. Application forms are also available in duty free shops and airports.

Provincial Sales Tax (PST) applies on the purchase of goods and services. This varies from province to province. In Ontario for instance, the rate is 8%, although there are exceptions such as on shoes under $30, books, groceries and restaurant meals costing less than $4. Liquor tax is 10%, in addition to the 7% GST. Alberta, the NW Territories, Nunavut and the Yukon do not have any PST. *www.taxtips.ca/provincial_sales_tax.htm.*

In Ontario there is a refund of the **Retail Sales Tax**, i.e. the PST levied on retail sales only, paid on goods permanently removed from Ontario within 30 days and totalling $50 (in tax) or more. More information from: Retail Sales Tax Branch, Refund Unit, 1600 Champlain Ave, Whitby, Ontario, L1N 9B2, (905) 432-3431 or (800) 615-2757.
www.trd.fin.gov.on.ca/userfiles/HTML/cma_3_29052_1.html.

Tipping, as in the USA, is expected in eating places, by taxi drivers, bellhops, baggage handlers and the like. 15% is standard.

COMMUNICATIONS

Mail. At present it costs 85¢ to send a letter to a US address and $1.45 to

Europe and other overseas destinations. Within Canada the rate is 50¢. Canada Post is *very* slow. Post offices are not generally open at weekends. The postcode is a must if sending mail to Canada. If you do not know where you will be staying, have your mail sent care of 'General Delivery' ('Post Restante' in Québec). You then have 15 days to collect. *www.canadapost.ca*. For rates go to *www.canadapost.ca/personal/rates/default-e.asp.*

Telephone. Local calls from coin telephones usually cost 25¢ and from private phones are usually free. Dial 0 for the operator. Check local directories for the cheapest times to place a long distance call—usually between 11pm and 8am. Telephone cards are available in Canada, buying you $5, $10 or $20 worth of time. 'Information' (Directory Enquiries in Britain) is the area code you want followed by 555-1212. **NB:** Toll-free numbers (those that begin with 800, 887 and 888) can only be dialed from within North America. Consumers in Canada have a choice of local telephone service providers, 15 of which are currently listed by the Canadian Radio-television and Telecommunications Commission (CRTC), the agency responsible for regulating Canada's broadcasting and telecommunications systems, including Allstream (formerly AT&T Canada), Bell West, Call-Net Communications, ExaTel, EastLink, and FCI Broadband. *www.crtc.gc.ca*.

Internet and Wi-Fi Access: Most libraries in all major Canadian towns and cities have both internet and wi-fi access. Wi-fi is available in establishments in nearly every Canadian community – for details, visit *www.wififreespot.com/can.html*. Please also refer to the *Background USA* section of this book.

PUBLIC HOLIDAYS

New Year's Day	1st January
Good Friday/Easter Monday	Variable
Victoria Day	3rd Monday in May
Canada Day	1st July
Civic Holiday	1st Monday in Aug in all provinces except Québec, Yukon and Newfoundland
Labor Day	1st Monday in September
Thanksgiving Day	2nd Monday in October
Remembrance Day	11th November
Christmas Day	25th December
Boxing Day	26th December

INFORMATION

Tourist Information. Tourist information centres abound and are indicated on highway maps. Especially recommended is the information published by the provincial tourist offices. If you plan to spend any length of time in one province, it is well worth emailing them and asking for their free maps, guides and accommodation information. To obtain provincial travel guides, consult provincial tourism authorities via the following links to their guide order forms:

Alberta: *http://www1.travelalberta.com/cfforms/freestuff*
British Columbia: *http://www.hellobc.com/bcescapes/request_start.asp*
Manitoba: *http://www.gov.mb.ca.travelmanitoba.com/freestuff/kitshtml.*
New Brunswick: *http://wwwwww.tourismnewbrunswick.ca ca /*
Cultures/en-CA/FreeStuff.htm?UserPref=culture%5Een-CA
Newfoundland & Labrador: *http://www.gov.nf.ca/tourism/*
mainmenu/buildaguide/order/default.htm.
Northwest Territories: *http://www.explorenwt.com/travel-guides/index.asp*
Nova Scotia: *http://www.novascotia.com/publicationsandmore/default.htm.*
Nunavut: *http://www.nunavuttourism.com /Master.ASP?ID=70*
Ontario: *http://www.ontariotravel.net*
t/TcisCtrl?language=EN&site=consumers&key1=travelGuides
Prince Edward Island: *http://www.gov.pe.ca/visitorsguide e*
/help/request.php3?PHPSESSID=85a667203b227e678db30ecf62fcecf0
Quebec: *http://www.bonjourquebec.com/anglais/utiles/brochures/index.php*
Saskatchewan: *http://www.sasktourism.com*
www.sasktourism.com/default.asp?page=111
Yukon: *http://www.datapathsystems.net/touryukon/freeguides.asp?*
CampaignSource=www.gov.yk.ca.
For more general tourist information, check *www.travelcanada.ca* , the site
of the Canadian Tourism Commission, which takes you in any direction you
choose to go.

CANADIAN CULTURE

FOOD

It is customary in Canada to eat the main meal of the day in the evening,
from about 5pm onwards. Canadian food is perhaps slightly more
Europeanised than American and in the larger cities you will find a great
variety of ethnic restaurants, anything from Chinese or Japanese to Swedish
and French.

Canada's original Indian recipes once included, according to Hrayr
Berberoglu, a specialist on Canadian food, such items as moose meat soup,
sweet pickled beaver, fried woodchuck, stuffed whale breast, boiled
porcupine, baked skunk, dried buffalo meat, baked salmon, roast or boiled
corn, and acorn bread.

Today's Canadian delicacies include a wealth of local specialities such
as Alberta beef, Arctic char, Atlantic lobster, Belon oysters and Bras d'or
from Nova Scotia, Prince Edward Island mussels and oysters, Brome
Lake Duckling, cod tongues, corn fed pork, domesticated buffalo, fiddleheads, farm-raised pheasants, Lake Erie sturgeon caviar, Matane shrimps,
Pacific oysters, quails, reindeer, five types of wild salmon, salmon caviar,
smoked Gaspe salmon, wild rice, and Winnipeg gold eye.
www.foodreference.com/html/artcanadianfoods.html.

Québec offers Brome Lake duck, apples from Rougemont, Matane
shrimps, cider vinegar, maple syrup, honey, salmon and cheeses. Advises
Berberoglu, the following cheeses are worth hunting down: Bluebry,
Cabriole, Cheddar (8 and 9 year old), Ermite, Le Bleu de la Montonniere, Le
Metis, Le Pied de vent, and Mamirolle.

Neighboring Ontario is famous for back bacon, superb maple syrup, strawberries and raspberries, with the Ottawa Valley known for wild blue-berries, and to the south, the Niagara Peninsula for fruit and vegetables.

These days, Canadian wines have really come into their own, especially in the two wine grape growing areas of British Columbia (Okanagan Valley) and Ontario in the Niagara Peninsula, both of which have established world-class wine quality standards. These wines includeing Cabernet Sauvignon, Chardonnay Merlot, Riesling, Sauvignon Blanc, and Syrah, among others, and have some delicious vintages at reasonable prices. You should not leave Canada without sampling their exquisite ice wines.

Cigarettes, Drinking, Drugs

Cigarettes. The cost is currently about $4-$6 for a packet of 25, depending on the brand. Foreign brands are widely available. Smoking is discouraged in many public places, with penalties and level of enforcement depending on the province, under Canada's Federal Tobacco Control Strategy.

In Québec, for example, it is against the law to buy tobacco by mail order, over the internet, on school grounds or in a health-care, social services or child-care facility. In some provinces you must be 19 or older to purchase tobacco products. In March 2005, Canada's Supreme Court ruled that provinces wanting to limit tobacco displays have the right to do so, following its ruling that allowed Saskatchewan to reinstate a law ordering storeowners to keep tobacco products behind curtains or doors. _www.hc-sc.gc.ca/hecs-sesc/tobacco/index.html._

Drinking. Liquor regulations come under provincial law and although it's generally easy to buy a drink by the glass in a lounge, tavern or beer parlour, it can be pretty tricky tracking down one of the special liquor outlets which can be few and far between. Beer, wine and spirits can only be bought from liquor stores which keep usual store hours and are generally closed on Sunday. The exception is Québec, where alcohol is available in supermarkets. The legal drinking age is 19, except in Alberta, Manitoba, and Québec where it is 18. Carry ID just in case. Restrictions on alcohol in Nunavut are determined by each community.

Drugs. Narcotics laws in Canada are federal rather than provincial and it is illegal under the _Controlled Drugs and Substances Act_ to possess or sell drugs such as cannabis, cocaine and heroin. The penalties for possession of cannabis range from a fine of up to $2000, to imprisonment for up to five years, or both. The penalty for trafficking (selling), or possession for the purpose of trafficking, of cannabis ranges from a term of imprisonment not exceeding five years less a day, to imprisonment for life.

The penalties for possession of cocaine or heroin range from a fine of up to $2000, to imprisonment for up to seven years, or both. The penalty for trafficking (selling), or possession for the purpose of trafficking, of cocaine or heroin is imprisonment for life. _http://laws.justice.gc.ca/en/C-38.8/_ and _www.hc-sc.gc.ca/hecs-sesc/ocs/index.htm_.

SHOPPING & ENTERTAINMENT

Shopping. Stores are generally open until 5:30 or 6 pm, with late opening on Thursday or Friday. Stores in the cities may well stay open later more fre-quently. Usually only shops located in tourist areas will be open on

Sundays. Canada is big on shopping malls (the inventor of which was a Canadian). In the large cities there are huge underground shopping malls concourses so that you don't need to go outside at all in the harsh Canadian winter, but can move underground from mall to mall, or mall to office, to subway or train station.

Entertainment. Until recently Canada was viewed as a cultural wasteland. Even now, for preference, Canadians watch US or British television programmes and read US or European magazines. Traditionally, talented Canadians moved from Canada to the USA in order to succeed. However, this been changing. This, in part, is because the government has legislated a minimum level of Canadian content in radio and television and implemented a strict 'hire Canadian' policy throughout the arts and entertainment industry. Radio stations must ensure that 35% of their popular musical selections are Canadian, and the CBC, private and ethnic TV stations must achieve a yearly Canadian content of 60%.

There are now thriving movie industries in Vancouver and Toronto. In 2004, almost a $1 billion worth of movie and TV productions were shot in Toronto *www.city.toronto.on.ca/tfto*, and $2 billion worth in Vancouver.

Canadian culture is also flourishing more as a reflection of new-found Canadian pride. Visitors will be impressed with the high standards in ballet, theatre and classical music.

Summer in Canada, everywhere, is extremely festive. Folk music and the visual arts thrive and Canada boasts a number of exceptional museums and restorations that are well worth visiting for a glimpse of Canada's past.

There are also huge annual spring and summer festival scenes in Canada. From major cities to small towns, from Shakespeare to summer solstices to jazz, you'll find a celebration of some kind wherever you go. At least 19 towns and cities across the country have Fringe Theatre Festivals modeled after the Edinburgh Fringe, usually in July, spread over a week or more. The biggest are those in Edmonton (2nd only to Edinburgh in size), Montreal, Toronto and Vancouver. The one in Montreal, for example, is a 'bilingual, bicultural, international festival of free artistic expression''with participation determined by Lottery with no restrictions on content. Over the 15 years through 2005, the Montreal Fringe had hosted over a thousand new performance companies. *www.montrealfringe.ca/lynx.htm.*

For details of more general festivals throughout Canada's provinces, check *www.culture.ca/canada/events-activites-e.jsp.*

SPORTS & THE GREAT OUTDOORS

Sports and Recreation. Canada has hosted almost every major sports competition: the summer and winter Olympics, Commonwealth Games, Pan-American Games and World University Games, including the 2001 World Athletic Championships (held in Edmonton). Vancouver/Whistler is set to host the 2010 Olympics. Surprisingly perhaps, the national game is lacrosse.

Canadians love to camp, hike, fish, ski and generally enjoy the outdoors. The list of outdoor sports in Canada is almost endless, from surfing in Tofino to para-skiing in Whistler, to long-distance kayaking and canoeing in the Yukon, to cricket in Victoria, to sailing off Newfoundland.

Winter sports (naturally) are very popular, from ice-skating to snowmobiling. Ice hockey is the biggie for watching. There is a Canadian version of American football. Baseball is also popular: the Toronto Blue Jays won the World Series in baseball in 1992 and 1993. In 2004, however, the Montreal Expos migrated to become the Nationals in Washington DC, so now there is only one Canadian baseball team playing in the American leagues. (See *Winter Sports* and *Baseball* boxes for more information)

The Great Outdoors. It's hardly surprising that, with all those wide-open spaces, Canadians are very outdoors-minded. Greenery is never far away and the best of it has been preserved in a system of wonderful national parks. Canada's national parks range in size from eight (St Lawrence Islands) to 44,000 sq kms (Wood Buffalo) and in type from the immense mountains and forests of the west to the steep cliffs and beaches of the Atlantic coastline, located in 39 designated natural regions, from the southern border to the furthest Arctic north. Thirteen of them are UNESCO World Heritage Sites including the birthplace, in 1885, of Canada's national park system at Banff. Eleven more Canadian parks are under consideration by UNESCO. There are also over 1,500 national historic parks and sites and many fine provincial parks.

Entrance to the national parks costs $5-7 for a one-day pass, more for season passes. All but the most primitive offer camping facilities, hiking trails and facilities for swimming, fishing, boating and other such diversions. Parks Canada offers a standardized campground reservation service in 18 national parks across, on-line, 24 hours a day, at *www.pccamping.ca*, or call (877) 737-3783 toll-free, 7am to 7pm.

Most of the national parks are included in this Guide. For more detailed information, email the individual parks or write: **Parks Canada**, 25 Eddy St, Hull, Québec, K1A 0M5. Call (888) 773-8888 for a copy of the free booklet *National Parks of Canada*, or visit their website, which includes details of all parks, entrance fees, and facilities: *www.parkscanada.pch.gc.ca* . These are Canada's major national parks:

Banff, Alberta	Mount Revelstoke, British Columbia
Cape Breton Highlands, Nova Scotia	Nahanni, Northwest Territories
Elk Island, Alberta	Pacific Rim, British Columbia
Forillon, Québec	Point Pelee, Ontario
Fundy, New Brunswick	Prince Albert, Saskatchewan
Georgian Bay Islands, Ontario	Prince Edward, Prince Edward Island
Glacier, British Columbia	Pukaskwa, Ontario
Grasslands, Saskatchewan	Riding Mountain, Manitoba
Gros Morne, Newfoundland	St Lawrence Islands, Ontario
Gwaii Haanas, British Columbia	Terra Nova, Newfoundland
Ivvavik, Yukon	Tuktut Nogait, Northwest Territories
Jasper, Alberta	Wapusk, Manitoba
Kejimkujik, Nova Scotia	Waterton Lakes, Alberta
Kluane, Yukon	Wood Buffalo, Alberta
Kootenay, British Columbia	Yoho, British Columbia.
La Mauricie, Québec	

ON THE ROAD
ACCOMMODATION
For general hints on finding the right accommodation for you, please read the 'Accommodation' section for the USA. The basic rules are the same. There are so many sources of lodging information that we advise you to check out several, if you can, to be sure you get the best deals.

All Canada's provincial tourist offices publish comprehensive accommodation lists, many of them on their websites, and some with rankings. These listings are obtainable in hard copy from Canadian government tourist offices or directly from provincial tourist boards and have details of all approved hotels, motels and tourist homes in each town. These guides are excellent and highly recommended.

City tourist guides may only list accommodation belonging to local Chamber of Commerce members, but many have comprehensive lists that include the complete range of what's available, from hotels to camping grounds.

CanadaSelect at *www.canadaselect.com*, provides national accommodations ratings for a range of bed and breakfasts, cottages, hotels, motels, inns, and resorts, with listings providing links to individual accommodation websites. The service does not provide comparative pricing info. Under the same site is CampingSelect, giving similar info on Canadian campgrounds.

Bed and Breakfasts. Several guides to bed and breakfast establishments are published in Canada and can be picked up in bookshops everywhere. In general, B&Bs can be pricier then tourist homes or hotels. In SW Ontario, for example, a B&B will cost $50 - $90 per double-occupied room per night, but most have higher rates. On Vancouver Island, there are some B&Bs with room rates as low as $60, but most are $95 per night or more. *BBCanada.com*, the first Canadian B&B site, now has over 9,000 members.

Another site provides another, more limited directory of B&Bs across Canada, including country inns, lodges, boutique hotels, and small resorts. *www.bandbinfo.com.* A further source is *Canada Bed and Breakfast*, which has more limited listings, but with greater individual details, at *www.1000inns.com/canada*.

Always check out local listings from regional and local tourists centres, which may be far more extensive than these websites and may provide better bargains.

Hotels and Motels The major difference between the hotel/motel picture here and in the US is that the budget chains like Super 8 and Motel 6 have not yet made it to Canada in force. Motel 6, for example, has just seven places in Canada, five of which are in Ontario. It shouldn't, however, be a problem to find independent, reasonably priced motels on highways between the major cities. In less populated areas distances between motels can be very great indeed – don't leave it too late to find a place to stay!

For the budget traveller it is likely that a tourist home or a hostel will nearly always be a less expensive alternative.

Besides regional and city tourist information listings, an excellent place to start looking is on *www.hotel—canada.com* which provides both comprehensive coverage of hotels and motels throughout Canada, by province and city, with room rates in both Canadian and US dollars, and availability by date. It also makes about two million reservations, at two million a year. A good site to compare price ranges of available hotels in a given town in Canada is *www.hotels-and-discounts.com/Canada/Canada-Hotels.html*. A website focusing on mid-level hotels is *www.choicehotels.com*, an international source covering Clarion, QualityInn, ComfortInn, SleepInn, MainStay Suites, Econo Lodge, and Rodeway Inn. This site gives you a range of available accommodation among the hotels in a given place.

Tourist Homes. A bit like bed and breakfast places in Britain and Europe, only without the breakfast. In other words, a room in a private home. Usually you share a bathroom and your room will be basic but perfectly adequate. Such establishments are scattered very liberally all over Canada, with prices starting from around $25-$30. Certainly if hostels are not for you and your budget doesn't quite stretch to a motel, then these are the places to look for. Again, the local tourist bureaus will be able to provide you with a list of possibilities.

Hostels. Hostelling International Canada has over 80 member hostels across the country with at least one hostel in each major city. In British Columbia, for example, there are 17 hostels, and another 17 in neighboring Alberta, with hostels clustered in some of the best parts – there are five in Jasper alone, for example ensuring that the National Parks in Alberta are well covered. You can save money with an International Youth Hostel Card from your own country, since non-members usually pay about $2-$5 more per night. There is no limit to a stay. For detailed information and lists of hostels write to: HI-Canada, 205 Catherine St, Suite 400, Ottawa, Ontario, K2P IC3, (613) 237-7884/(800) 663-5777, or check *www.hihostels.ca*. Two-year membership is $35 plus tax, or you can collect six welcome stickers at $4 each time you stay—this will also give you annual membership. If you're resident in the UK, it's currently cheaper to join the AYH in Britain.

There are also many independent hostels under the aegis of Backpackers Hostels Canada, with beds typically $20 a night, and $4 for breakfast. In British Columbia, for example, Backpackers lists 38 hostels all over the province. For information on its their hostels and their rates check *www.backpackers.ca* cor contact Backpackers Hostels Canada, Longhouse Village, RR 13, Thunder Bay, ON P7B 5E4, (888) 920-0044/(807) 983-2042. Email: *info@backpackers.ca*, *www.backpackers.ca*.

YM/YWCAs. Ys have weight lifting machines, pools and aerobics classes for those in need of an exercise fix, but standards vary; not all have overnight accommodation and in some cities the Y is predominantly a doss-house for the local homeless. For a complete list and information on Canadian Ys visit *www.ywca.ca* (36 YWCAs across Canada including 14 in Ontario), or *www.ymca.ca* (includes 61 YMCAs and YMCA-YWCAs) or contact: YMCA National Council, 42 Charles St E, 6th Floor, Toronto, Ontario M4Y 1T4, (416) 967-9622.

University Accommodation. There is much campus housing available during the summer. Look for student owned co-operatives in cities such as Toronto, which provide a cheapish service, often with cooking facilities. University housing services and fraternities will also often be able to help you. In general, college housing starts at about $20 single, but can be as high as $35 single. Staying on campus usually gives access to all the usual facilities including cafeterias, lounges, etc. and often a pool and gymnasium and athletic fields. The drawback about campus accommodation is that it is usually not available after mid-late August when Canadian students begin returning to college.

Camping. Canadians are very fond of camping and during the summer sites in popular places will always be full. Usually, however, campgrounds are not as spacious as those in the USA and less trouble is taken with the positioning of individual sites. Prices range from around $15-$40 per site. There are many provincial park campgrounds, as well as sites in the national parks and many privately operated grounds, usually to be found close to the highways. Campgrounds are marked on official highway maps.

Nearly all Canada's national parks include campgrounds. You can find out about them and their fees by province and park at Parks Canada: *www.pc.gc.ca*.

The *Camping-Canada* search engine is geared to RV camping but you can plug in tenting to their directory preferences. This found 219 tent campgrounds in Ontario, 114 in British Columbia, and 78 in Alberta, listed alphabetically by city, with number of sites available at each campground, utilities available and telephone numbers. *www.camping-canada.com.*

Another resource is *Campgrounds Campings Canada* (CCC), 2175 Sheppard Avenue East, Ste 310, Toronto, Ontario, M2J 1W8, (416) 971-7800, which provides extensive background information on camping locales and links.

The Rand McNally *Campground and Trailer Park Guide* covers Canada as well as the USA. Also, the Canadian Tourism Commission publishes guides on camping across Canada: Canadian Tourism Commission, Suite 600, 55 Metcalfe St, Ottawa, Ontario, K1P 6L5, (613) 946-1000.

The much recommended KOA now has about 50 campgrounds in Canada. Details from: KOA Inc, PO Box 30558, Billings, Montana 59114-0558, (406) 248-7444. They will send you a free directory of campsites (costs about $54 in postage). For more details, check out: *www.koa.com/where/-canada.htm*.

Both the provincial tourist guides and local tourist bureaus are other sources of excellent information on where to find a campgrounds. The government-run parks tend to have the more scenic tent sites. Most campsites are open summer months only, July- September.

For real outdoor camping in Canada you need a tent with a flyscreen. Black flies and mosquitoes are a serious problem in June and July and the further north you go the worse the little darlings are. It gets cold at night too as early as August, so be prepared for colder temperatures and wetter weather than in the US. Other hazards of camping in Canada include bears and 'beaver fever', a rare intestinal parasite (*giardia lamblia*).

TRAVEL.

There is a good set of Canada travel links by rail nation-wide and by rail and bus by province at: www.apta.com/links/international/canada.cfm.

Air. Canada has two main airlines and a host of local scheduled carriers that can transport you almost anywhere there is an airport, from Windsor,

Ontario, in the south, to north of the Arctic Circle. Details of these local carriers, some of which are puddle jumpers with float planes, are given in the province and territory sections.

Canada's major airline, **Air Canada** _www.aircanada.ca_, offers various discount fares, starting with "websavers" between Canadian cities that usually must be booked in advance by a certain date. 'Tango' fares are the best value. Always check on the website for special deals or call (888) 712-7786 (from Canada or the US) and ask for any special deals available on a given flight or for a given destination. **Air Canada Jazz,** a regional airline owned by Air Canada and based in Halifax, Nova Scotia, serves 72 destinations in Canada and the US, with hubs in Toronto and Vancouver, with reservations handled by Air Canada. _www.flyjazz.ca._

West Jet, based in Calgary, is Canada's expanding low-fare airline with flights operating from Victoria on Vancouver Island across the country to all major points between, as far east as St Johns, Newfoundland. Westjet have low fares all the time and some great specials. Best to fly Wednesdays for the cheapest fares: (403) 250-5839 or visit _www.westjet.com_.

CanJet, based in Halifax, Nova Scotia, has 'everyday low unrestricted o/w fares', Most of its flights are from places in eastern Canada, but it serves the west too (Calgary and Vancouver), with international services to Florida. It has a set of promotional fares (click on Promotions on its website _www.canjet.com_).

Students (with an ISIC card) may be able to get student discounts on flights through Travel CUTS, the Canadian Universities Travel Service Ltd, 187 College St, Toronto, ON, M5T 1P7, (866) 246-9762/(416) 979-2406, or at any of their other offices throughout Canada. _www.travelcuts.ca_.

Biking. Canada loves bikes. For information on the best routes for biking in all areas of Canada, check _www.canadatrails.ca/biking/index.html_ which has details of bike routes (and other trails) for each province. The site has details of the **Trans Canada Trail,** which Canada is in the process of constructing, as the world's longest recreation pathway. When completed, it will total more than 16,000 km (10,000 miles) from St. Johns, Newfoundland to Victoria, BC (the latter,with 7,000 bicycle commuters, was proclaimed bicycle capital of Canada by the Queen, in the year 2000).

There are also many provincial and regional trails, including in national parks. _www.canadatrails.ca/tct/index.html._ The Canadian Cycling Association at 702-2197 Riverside Dr, Ottawa, Ontario, K1H 7X3, (613) 248-1353 also may be helpful. _www.canadian-cycling.com_.

Bus. Bus travel is usually the cheapest way of getting around, fares generally being less than half that of the airfare. Every region in Canada has different bus companies: Acadian Lines, Greyhound Canada and Voyageur are the largest. Greyhound Canada has scheduled services from Montreal in the east to points on Vancouver Island in the west, and as far north as Whitehorse in the Yukon, serving 1,100 locations.

Nationwide, there's the **Greyhound Travel Pass**, available for 7, 10, 15, 21, 30, 40, 45, or 60 day lengths of unlimited travel on any of the Acadian Lines, Orleans Express, or Greyhound Canada lines throughout Canada, with discounts available for students. For seven days, the fare for students is $287, for 60 days it's $656, with grades in between.

North America-wide, there's the Greyhound **Canam Pass** for 15, 21, 30, 45 or 60 day lengths of unlimited travel on any of the Acadian Lines, Orleans Express, Greyhound Canada and Greyhound US routes. For 15 days, the student fare is $584, ranging to $899 for 60 days anywhere you want go on the continent.

Greyhound Canada _www.greyhound.ca_ has several special fare deals of which the _Go Anywhere Fares_ are the best; with this you buy tickets in advance one day, seven or 14 days ahead, valid for trips beginning on Greyhound Canada, Greyhound Lines, Grey Goose or Voyageur and all participating carriers; the fares include GST. Often, there is a substantial discount, if you book at least seven days ahead. For example, at the time of writing, for the three day trip from Toronto to Vancouver, the regular fare is $342.50 (ex GST); if you book one day ahead, the fare is $200; seven days ahead it's $159; and 14 days ahead it's $135.

On Greyhound Canada, students with a valid International Student Identity Card (ISIC) receive 25 per cent off adult tickets. You can also get a 10-percent discount off regular adult one-way or return tickets, if you present your valid Hostelling International (HI) membership card.

Greyhound Canada also has a _Companion Fare_ deal: _Travel in Twos, Travel for Less_ - your companion goes for 75 percent off when you buy one adult, senior or student ticket at the regular price at least three days in advance of travel, good for both o/w and r/t.

The **Greyhound (USA) Ameripasses** are only valid in Canada on specific routes, e.g. Buffalo or Detroit to Toronto. However, as detailed in the _USA Background_ chapter, Greyhound also offers the **CanAm pass**, valid for travel in _both_ countries. A 15-day, high season, All US/Canada Pass is currently US$377, US$419 for 21 days, US$459 for 30 days, US$539 for 45 days and US$599 for 60 days. Good student discounts are available.

All passes are non-refundable once any portion of the pass has been used and should be purchased before departing for Canada. In Canada, for more information call: (800) 661-8747 or visit . The International North American CanAm Pass can be purchased in Canada by non-US and non-Canadian residents at the gateway cities: Calgary, Edmonton, Ottawa, Toronto or Vancouver. Passes can be booked on line.

Always check for the cheapest 'point-to-point' fare or excursion fare when making a journey without a bus pass. Toronto to Vancouver, for instance, could cost $340 o/w, whereas a ticket booked 14 days in advance would cost just $134.

The Canadian bus companies will never check baggage through to a destination without its owner. So bags cannot be sent on ahead. If you are simply seeking a way to dump them for a day or so while you see the sights, lockers are usually available at bus stations.

In Ontario and Québec the **Rout-Pass** offers access to the routes of 35 intercity bus companies anywhere in the provinces between mid-May 1 and mid2th an-d Dec 11th. It offers coupons for travel within aconsecutive 7 or, 14 or 18 day periods. It can be purchased from intercity bus terminals in Toronto, Ottawa, Montréal, Québec City and other major terminals. The 14 day pass costs $199 GST for seven days, $249 GST for 14 days. Tel: (800) 661-8747 or call Montréal Bus Station on (514) 842-2281, or visit _www.routpass.com_.

The Moose Travel Network/BigFoot Adventure Tours operate hop-on/hop-off bus routes in the east (the Moose Run) and west (BigFoot Adventure) with a connecting service between the two. They go off the beaten track and allow you to meet other 'like-minded' travellers. Call (888) 244-6673 (west) or (888) 816-6673 (east), or go to *www.moosenetwork.com* and *www.bigfoottours.com* for more information.

Car. In general, Canadian roads are good, speed limits are higher than in the USA and there are fewer toll roads than south of the border. Canadian speed limits have gone metric and are posted everywhere in km/hr. The most common freeway limit is, 100 km/hr and is the most common freeway limit;, 80 km/hr is typical on two-lane rural highways and 50 km/hr operates most frequently in towns. Canadians, of course, drive on the right! Note that the wearing of **seat belts** by *all* persons in a vehicle is compulsory. Many parts of Canada are open spaces with huge distances between towns, especially in the Territories. Plan accordingly for your gasoline and supplies – see the checklist in the introduction to the Territories.

Car rental normally will cost from about $30-$45/day, $200/wk, with with free kms up to a point and a cost per km of about 5¢-20¢. Thereafter; the big companies often offer unlimited mileage. You may pay a surcharge for renting from the airport location; check with different branches of the same company. Most now have websites for information and online bookings—again these rates sometimes differ from those you pay booking in person. It's a lottery! As always, shop around for the best available rates. Try *www.budget.com* or *www.enterprise.com*. and finally, bear in mind there will be another surcharge for more than one driver and a hefty one if you are under 25; some companies will still refuse to rent to you at all. To hire an RV camper is a lot more expensive, but of course you wouldn't be paying as much for accommodation.

Third party **insurance** is compulsory in all Canadian provinces and territories and can be expensive; it's not unusual for it to double the total amount you pay. British, other European and US drivers licences are officially recognised by the Canadian authorities. Membership of the AA, RAC, other European motoring organisations, or the AAA in the US, entitles the member to all the services of the **Canadian AA** and its member clubs, free of charge. This includes travel info, itineraries, maps and tour books, as well as emergency road services, weather reports and accommodation reservations.

Gas is sold by the litre and costs upwards 88¢-99¢/litre. Gas stations can be few and far between in remoter areas and it is wise to check your gauge in the late afternoon before the pumps shut off for the night. Check on latest gas prices anywhere in Canada at *www.garnetknight.com/gas/locations.php*.

One **hazard** to be aware of when driving in Canada is the unmarked and even the marked railroad crossing. Many people are killed every year on railroad crossings. Trains come and go so infrequently in remote areas that it's simply never possible to know when one will arrive. Be particularly alert at night – which is long and longer in winter as one goes north. In the Territories, watch out for wandering caribou and keep your headlights on the whole time.

Hiking. Trail walking is one of Canada's best offers – there are trails everywhere, short ones, breath-taking ones, arduous ones, and really long ones – such as the Canol Heritage Trail in the North West Territories/Yukon *http://canoltrail.tripod.com* , the multi-purpose Trans-Canada Trail, or the purely footpath National Hiking Trail, now in preparation. There is so much wilderness space that it really would be a crying shame to spend any length of time in Canada without experiencing something of The Great Outdoors. *www.canadatrails.ca/hiking/index.html.*

Some of the best, of course, is in the national parks. A good guide to hiking trails in the national parks is: *The Canadian Rockies Trail Guide: A Hiker's Manual to the National Parks*, by Bart Robinson and Brian Patton.

Hitchhiking. Our advice is: don't do it.

Rail. Canada is strewn with railways that have had diverse fortunes. Some of them have seen better days but are just beginning a return to the limelight with economic changes such the expansion in trade with Asia. Many others are being revived locally as grand tourist excursions because of the spectacular scenery through which they were engineered, scenery that Canada has in abundance, especially in the Rockies and the west. Throughout the provincial and territory sections, be sure to check out the regional railways and the trips they offer.

One of the conditions for the entry of British Columbia into the Confederation was the building of the Canadian Pacific Railway to link east and west and with the completion of the track in 1885, Canada finally became a reality as a transcontinental nation. Later came Canadian Northern and the Grand Trunk Pacific, nationalised into Canadian National in 1923 after both companies had gone bankrupt.

Until 1978, Canada possessed two rail systems, the privately operated but viable Canadian Pacific, and the state-owned, often floundering, Canadian National. With the formation of **VIA Rail Canada** in 1978, the routes and fare structures of both became totally integrated. To cross Canada ,by train was quite an adventure, one of the world's great railway journeys.

Unfortunately, the Canadian government has now scrapped the famous transcontinental track through the Rockies via Banff as part of a mammoth, more than 50 per cent, cut in rail services nationwide. However, the more northerly route via Jasper. still operates but only three times a week. VIA Rail now has a 14,000-km network linking Canada from one end to the other with comfortable and civilised trains that have good eating and sleeping facilities. 'A much recommended way to travel.' (888) VIARAIL, *www.viarail.ca*.

The one way adult fare, Montréal to Vancouver, Comfort Class (Economy), coast-to-coast, is currently about $758, and the journey takes three days.

The service cuts initiated by the government in the formation of VIA Rail meant that many small, more remote communities can no longer be reached by train, but in the past ten years or so lots of local railways have been revived privately - always enquire about local passenger services.

In the East, VIA Rail Canada runs high speed *Rapido* trains along the so-called Ontario-Québec corridor, which connects Montréal with Windsor, Ontario. The Toronto to Montréal trip, takes less than 5 hours, has wi-fi on some trains and currently costs about $80 o/w Super Comfort Class including taxes, $68 o/w w/student ID. There is also the overnight *Enterprise* on this route, with sleek new *Renaissance* cars, that takes 8 hours+. The Toronto-Niagara Falls train goes via Oakville, Aldershot, Grimsby and St. Catharines in the Niagara wine country. The service leaving Toronto in the morning continues on to the US, travelling via Buffalo to New York City. On the way back, it leaves New York in the morning, arrives in Niagara Falls in late afternoon, and gets to Toronto in the early evening.

VIA Rail's **northernmost route** is in the Prairie region, from Winnipeg 1,600 kms to sub-Arctic Churchill on the Hudson's Bay, where you can look for beluga whales and polar bears, among other things. This service, the *Hudson's Bay*, allows you to get off the train anywhere you want, provided you tell them in advance. In the **West**, there are the scenic *Skeena* routes from Jasper to Prince Rupert and the Victoria-Courtenay trip up Vancouver Island – the *Malahat*.

Discounts. Advance discounts are offered, as available, on all VIA Rail trains in Comfort (Economy) classes called **Comfort Advantage** (allowing changes) or **Super Comfort** (lowest fare, changes allowed for $15 fee) - provided you buy tickets 5 days or more in advance, and provided there are seats still available. There are some black out dates. It is recommended you book Super Comfort fares well in advance; but differences between these and other Comfort prices may not be so steep. **Student fares** are available to those 18+ with an International Student Identity Card (ISIC), with photo ID with proof of age, or a valid ISIC card, required when you pick up the ticket. They must also be shown on the train upon request; and you must travel by 'comfort liberty fare.'

Various **system-wide various discount fares** are also available. These vary according to the time of year, day of the week, length of stay, age of traveller etc., so always enquire about the 'cheapest possible fare' when planning a trip. If you have an ISIC card, be sure to show it, discounts are often up to 35%.

Nationwide, VIA Rail offers the **CANRAIL Pass**, which gives 12-15 days of travel within a 30-day period on VIA trains and is good value for someone planning to do a lot of travelling since it can be used anywhere VIA goes, from the Atlantic to the Pacific, and up to Hudson's Bay. You can make as many stops as you like.

During peak travel times (June 1st-October 15th) for the entire system in comfort class a student (with ISIC) pass currently costs $687 excluding taxes; and for adults it's $763. Extra days (up to 3 in a 15 day period) are $59 (student) and $63 (adult). Low season rates are: student $425, adult $475. Extra days are also cheaper: student $37, adult $41. NB: Seats reserved for CANRAIL Pass holders may be limited, so it is recommended that you book tickets as soon as possible. In all cases tax must be added, which and this varies from place to place.

The **Corridorpass** gives you 10 days' travel in **southern Québec and southern Ontario**. For a single price, you can visit Québec City, Montréal, Ottawa, Toronto, Kingston, Niagara Falls, Kitchener, Stratford, London, Sarnia and Windsor, including all stations between these cities, within a 10 day period. The cost is $249 for adults, $224 for students, in comfort class.

In addition, there is a combined VIA Rail/Amtrak **North American Rail**

Pass, (800) USA-RAIL. This pass covers unlimited travel on both rail systems, covering 900 cities, for 30 days. Current high season rates: student, $904, adult $1004; and student $573, adult $637 in low season.

The trains are comfortable and civilised and have good eating and sleeping facilities. A much recommended way to travel. 1st Rail, Trafford House, Chester Road, Old Trafford, Manchester, M32 0RS, 0845-644 3553, are the main agents in the UK. Or call VIA at (888) VIARAIL.

Urban Travel. Town and city bus or subway fares are generally charged at a standard rate. Exact fares are often required and are around 90¢-$1.50 and upwards. Transfers, allowing passengers to change routes, or change from bus to subway routes, are generally available in cities and are usually free.

Taxis are usually pretty expensive unless shared by two or three people. In rural areas (much of Canada outside the major population centres) there is little in the way of public transport and failing ownership of a car, taxis may be the only way. Check under individual towns and cities for more detailed information on local travel.

FURTHER READING

History
The very readable books of Pierre Barton including: *My Country: The Remarkable Past, Klondike, The Promised Land, Arctic Grail* and *Welcome to the 21st Century: More Absurdities of Our Time*.
Empire of the Bay, Peter C. Newman. Highly recommended.
The Laughing Bridge, A Personal History of the Capilano Suspension Bridge, Eleanore Dempster.
A Short History of Canada (5th Edition), Desmond Morton. Highly recommended.
A Brief History of Canada, Roger Riendeau

General
Aurora Montrealis, Monique Proulx
Canadian French, Pierre Corbeil
Chicken Soup for the Canadian Soul, Jack Canfield, Mark Victor Hansen, Janet Matthews and Raymond Aaron
Culture Shock! Pang Guek Cheng and Robert Barlas
Literary Lapses & *Sunshine Sketches of a Little Town*, Stephen Leacock
O Canada: An American's Notes on Canadian Culture, Edmund Wilson
So, you want to be Canadian, Kerry Colburn & Rob Sorensen

Fiction
Anne of Green Gables, L. M. Montgomery
Klee Wyck, Emily Carr
Legends of Vancouver, E. Pauline Johnson
Maria Chapdelaine, Louis Hémon
The Call of the Wild & *White Fang,* Jack London
The Ice Master, John Houston
The Man from the Creeks, Robert Kroetsch
The Shipping News, Annie Proulx
The novels of Margaret Atwood, Margaret Laurence, Carol White and Robertson Davies and the poetry of Robert Service, eg. *The Spell of the Yukon* and *Ballads of a Cheechako*.

MARITIME PROVINCES AND NEWFOUNDLAND

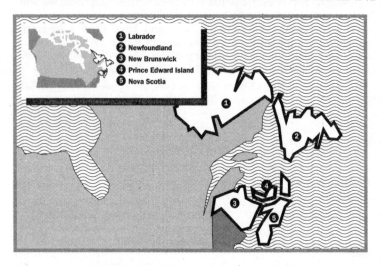

These lovely Atlantic-lapped provinces were the early stop-off points for eager explorers from Europe, many of them looking for a passage to China. Subsequently the Maritime provinces became one of the main battlegrounds for European colonial ambitions. From the start the chief combatants were France and Britain and, as a result, strong Gaelic, French and English threads are woven throughout the Maritimes culture and history that you will find thriving there today. It now seems certain that the Irish Saint Brendan reached Newfoundland in his ox-hide boat sometime after 500 AD. The first recorded visitor from Europe to North America was Prince Henry St Clair, who arrived there from Scotland in 1398 AD, almost a century before Columbus set foot on the continent.

Cape Bonavista on the coast of Newfoundland is thought to be the first land in the New World sighted by Giovanni Caboto, aka John Cabot, in 1497, where he claimed the territory for England by marking it with an English flag (and one from Venice too). But it was in **Chaleur Bay**, between today's New Brunswick and Québec, where Jacques Cartier, in 1535, made the first recorded exchange of furs between the Indians and Europeans, the first such trading exchange of any kind since the Norse voyages. (See *A Brief History of Canada*, Roger Riendeau). Little did Cartier know that his exchange would be the impetus for the vast empires of the French and English fur trading companies that would later span the continent.

Later, it was at **Port Royal** on the coast of Nova Scotia that the French were the first to establish a European agricultural village on North American soil in 1605, three years before Jamestown.

The story of the Maritimes is the story of a people who have fished, travelled and died at sea. The Grand Banks, the huge, shallow Continental

Shelf ranging from Massachusetts to Newfoundland, is the most fertile fishing ground in the world; thousands of fishermen from Europe are thought to have visited the Banks long before recorded history of the area. (So thick were the seas with cod that Cabot found his sailors could catch them merely by lowering baskets into the ocean!) Today, the economy of the Maritimes is based on forestry, tourism and the Grand Banks, with more fishery-related PhDs per capita here than almost anywhere in the world.

The region is beautiful in the summer, full of lake and sea swimming, excellent seafood, forest hikes and breathtaking scenery. Winters are long and hard with much snow, ice and general wintry chills to contend with! Spring comes late and autumn, as elsewhere in north eastern North America, is colourful and spectacular. Summer or autumn are recommended as the best times to visit the Maritimes.

NEW BRUNSWICK

New Brunswick is bounded mostly by water, with over 1,300 miles of coastline—a constant reminder of the importance of the sea in the culture of the province. To the west it is bordered by Maine, Québec and part of the Appalachian mountain range. Inland there is rugged wilderness, accounting for the popularity of huntin', fishin', campin' and hikin'.

The Vikings are said to have come here some thousand years ago, but when French explorer Jacques Cartier arrived in 1535, the area was occupied by Micmac and Maliseet Indians. Later the province became a battleground for French Acadian and British Loyalist forces. In 1713, by the Treaty of Utrecht, New Brunswick was ceded to the British along with the rest of Acadia (PEI and Nova Scotia). Many of the French fled south to the United States and settled in Louisiana. There, 'Acadian' was corrupted into 'Cajun', a word still used to describe the French in Louisiana. As a result of this early French influence, New Brunswick today remains 35% Acadian, most in the north and east of the province.

While in New Brunswick, be sure to sample the great variety of shellfish available, as well as the province's speciality—fiddleheads. Also, try a pint of the local Moosehead beer—although it is now available nationally, the sea air of New Brunswick itself is essential for a successful taste test! The coastline also has a number of whale-watching opportunities, especially in the summer and early autumn.

For a place so small, New Brunswick has more than its share of festivals that run from May to October. You may be interested in the Shediac Lobster Festival in early July, or Chocolate Fest in August! Visit _www.tourismnewbrunswick.ca_.

The telephone area code is 506.

FREDERICTON The City of Elms is the capital city of the province and its commercial and sporting centre. Clean and green, this is 'a good Canadian town', which got started in 1783 when a group of Loyalists from the victorious colonies to the south made their home here, naming the town after the second son of George III. They chose for their new town a spot where there had previously (until the Seven Years War) been a thriving

Acadian settlement. During hostilities the settlement was reduced by the British and the inhabitants expelled.

Fredericton's great benefactor was local boy and press baron, Lord Beaverbrook. His legacy includes an art gallery, a theatre and the university library. The latter is named Bonar Law-Bennett Library, after two other famous sons of New Brunswick, one of whom became Prime Minister of Great Britain, the other Prime Minister of Canada.

The town is situated inland on the broad St John River, the 'Rhine of America', once an Indian highway and a major commercial route to the sea. This area is one of scenic river valleys and lakes. *www.city.fredericton.nb.ca*.

Accommodation

Auberge Wandlyn Inn, 958 Prospect St, 462-4444. Outdoor & indoor pool. S-$75-150, D-$75-160. Convenient uptown location.

HI-Fredericton International Hostel, 621 Churchill Row, 450-4417. S-$20, $24 non-member, D-$16 pp, $20 non-member. Open year-round. 2 blocks from bus station; luggage storage, laundry facilities, free parking. *www.hihostels.ca*.

University of New Brunswick, Residents Admin. Bldg, Bailey Dr, (a red brick building with a clock) 453-4891. S-$27 inc tax, $22 exc tax w/student ID; D-$22 inc tax pp, $18 exc tax pp w/student ID; weekly: S-$100, D-$90 pp, monthly: S-$350, D-$310 pp, students only. 24 hrs. Close to downtown. 'Friendly and helpful.' University accommodation only available May-mid Aug. *www.unb.ca/housing*.

Camping: Mactaquac Provincial Park, 12 miles W on Hwy 2, 363-4747. 300 sites, laundry facilities, showers, recreation centre, kitchen shelters, and convenience store. Sites $21.50 inc. tax for four, $24 w/hook up. *www.tourismnewbrunswick.ca/en-CA/Products/Attraction/E672D27B-1E57-4889-8C3D-0D*.

Food

Boyce Farmers' Market, 655 George St, Regent St and Brunswick St, 451-1815. Have bfast or an early lunch in the market hall, then check out the fresh produce and local arts and crafts. Over 200 stalls. Sat only 6am-1pm. *www.boycefarmersmarket.com*.

Crispin's, King's Place Mall, King St, 459-1165. Deli/bakery with cafe. Great for cheap lunches ($5), soups, salads and sandwiches. Mon-Wed 7am-5:30pm, Thur & Fri 'til 9pm, Sat 9am-5pm.

Lunar Rogue, 625 King St, 450-2065. Good pub food and some interesting variations; sandwiches and snacks $5-$10, meals $10-$12. Huge order of Rogues Nachos for $9.50. Daily 11am-1am; bfast served Sat 10am-2pm, Sun 11am-2pm. Daily specials. Half-price appetizers Monday nights. *www.lunarrogue.com*.

Molly's Coffee House, 554 Queen Street (opposite Officers Square), 457-9305. Fine coffee and tasty snacks in this little café, which is also licensed – it has 50 imported beers and 40 malts! Variety of vegetarian food: entrées $7.95. Daily 9:30am-11pm.

Of interest

Beaverbrook Art Gallery, 703 Queen St, 458-8545. A gift to the province from the press baron, here you will find, besides extensive examples of Canadian art, such as that of Emily Carr, and an outstanding collection of British art from the Elizabethan to the modern era. Salvador Dalí's *Santiago el Grande* is on permanent display. There is good section on the history of English porcelain. Daily 9am-5.30pm, Thur 'til 9pm. $5, $2 w/student ID. *www.beaverbrookartgallery.org*.

Christ Church Cathedral, 168 Church St, 450-8500. A National Historic Site, opened in 1853, it's considered to be the first cathedral in North America to adhere to the exacting standards of mid-19th century Gothic Revival church architecture. It was modeled after the medieval St. Mary's, Snettisham, Norfolk. Worth a visit for its beautiful stained-glass windows. Free tours during the summer: *www.christchurchcathedral.com*.

Harvest Jazz and Blues Festival, Atlantic Canada's greatest celebration of jazz, blues and world music, five days every September, call 454-2583 or (888) 622-5837) for ticket and performance info. *www.harvestjazzblues.nb.ca*

Kilarney Lake, Route 8, North of Fredericton, 460-2230. Fresh-water lake, supervised, with change-house, washrooms and walking trails. Might be a bit nippy outside of the height of summer, though!

Kings Landing Historical Settlement, at Prince William, 23 miles W of Fredericton on Rte 2 (exit 253), 363-4999. Re-created pioneer village showing the life of rural New Brunswick as it was in the 1800s. Features homes, school, church, theatre and farm. Daily 10am-5pm; $14, $12 w/student ID. *www.kingslanding.nb.ca*.

Provincial Legislative Buildings, 706 Queen St, 453-2527. Includes, in the library, an Audubon bird painting and a copy of 1783 printing of the Domesday Book. Free tours include visit to legislative chamber. Mon-Fri 9am-4pm, July and August Mon-Fri 9am-5pm, Sat, Sun, Holidays 10am-4pm. *www.gov.ns.ca/legislature*.

University of New Brunswick, University Ave, 453-4666. Traces its beginnings back to 1785, making it one of the oldest English language provincial institutions of higher learning in North America. Buildings on campus include the **Brydone Jack Observatory,** 458-7855, Canada's first astronomical observatory. Tours available during the academic term, free. Call for opening times. *www.unb.ca*.

York-Sunbury Historical Museum, 571 Queen St, 455-6041. In Officers Square, this military museum depicts the history of Fredericton and New Brunswick. Summer: daily 10am-5pm, otherwise Tue-Sat 1pm-4pm. $3, $1 w/student ID. 'Kind of neat.'

Information/Internet/Travel

Fredericton Tourist Information, 11 Carleton St, City Hall, 460-2041/(888) 888-4768. 'Very helpful.' Also another info booth on the Trans Canada Hwy btwn Rtes 640 & 101, open 'til 9pm. *www.fredericton.ca*.

Tourism New Brunswick, (800) 561-0123 for general telephone information. Mon-Fri 8am-5pm. Also see *www.tourismnewbrunswick.ca*.

Fredericton Public Library, 12 Carleton St, 460-2800, has **internet** access. *www.gnb.ca/publiclibraries*.

Bus Terminal, 458-6007, 101 Regent St, **Acadien Bus**, to destinations throughout the Maritime provinces. *www.acadianbus.com*.

TRIUS Taxis, 454-4444. To the airport, costs around $18 o/w.

MONCTON This unofficial capital of Acadia is a major communications centre, but really has only two tourist sites of any importance: **Magnetic Hill** and the **Tidal Bore**. At Magnetic Hill, go to the bottom of the hill by car or bike, turn off the ignition and by some freak of nature you'll find yourself drifting up the hill!

The Tidal Bore is at its highest when it sweeps up the chocolate banks of Petitcodiac River from the Bay of Fundy, reaching heights of 15ft along the way. **Bore Park** is the spot to be when the waters rush in, all in 30 minutes. Check the schedule published in the daily paper, *The Moncton Times*, for the times when the tide is at its highest. Magnetic Hill is located at the corner of Mountain Road (Hwy 126) and the Trans Canada (Hwy 2). Bore Park is at the east end of Main St. An annual **Arts & Crafts Fair**—the biggest in the Maritimes—is held at Victoria Park in mid-August.

There is a nice beach with the warmest waters north of Virginia at **Shediac,** on the Northumberland Straight. This is also the place to catch the annual lobster festival in July. It's a short bus ride from Moncton and there is plenty of camping space nearby. Continuing the water theme, there is the **Magic Mountain Water Theme Park,** on Magic Mountain Rd. *www.gomoncton.com*.

Accommodation

Ask at the Tourist Bureau or call Tourism New Brunswick; 753-3876/(800) 561-0123, for a list of local B&Bs; prices range from D-$60-$85. Open Mon-Fri 8am-9pm, Sat-Sun 9am-5pm. *www.tourismnewbrunswick.ca*.

Université de Moncton, 858-4008/(800) 363-8336 x 1. Lafebra & La France residence halls have accommodation during summer only, May-late Aug. $20-$49 w/student ID, $41-$79 non-student. Go to corners of Crowley Farm Rd & Morton St for the best entrance. Check for current prices. *www.umoncton.ca/logement*.

Camping: Campers City, 138 Queensway Dr, Exit 454 on Hwy 2, 10 mins from downtown, 384-7867/(877) 512-7868. 180 sites. Sites $24, $26.50 w/hook up, showers. *www.campercity.ca*

Magnetic Hill Campground, 384-0191. 120 sites. Sites $22 inc. tax, $26-$28 w/hook up. Close to Magnetic Hill and open May 1 - Oct 31. Showers and laundry.

Information/Travel

Tourist Bureau, 10 Bendview Crt, 853-3590/(800) 363-4558. Summer: Mon-Fri 9am-8pm, otherwise 8:30am-4:30pm. *www.gomoncton.com*.

Codiac Transit, 857-2008. Public transport system serving Moncton, Riverview and Dieppe. Basic fare $1.75. *www.codiactransit-moncton.com*.

Bus Depot, 961 Main St, (800) 567-5151. Acadian Bus services to other Maritimes destinations. See under Saint John for other buses. *www.acadianbus.com*.

VIA Rail Train station, behind Highfield Square, Main St, 857-9830. Services to Halifax, Montreal. *www.viarail.ca*.

CARAQUET Situated on the scenic **Baie des Chaleurs** in the north of the province, Caraquet is the oldest French settlement in the area. Just west of town is a monument to the first Acadian settlers, who came here following their expulsion by Britain. On St Pierre Blvd E there is an interesting museum of Acadian history, the **Acadian Museum,** 726-2682, May 29-Sept 3 daily 10am-6pm, Sept 4 to Oct 8 daily 10am-5pm. $3, $1 w/student ID.

Off Hwy 11 to the west of town is the **Acadian Historical Village,** 726-2600, May 29-Sept 3 daily 10am-6pm, Sept 4 to Oct 8 daily 10am-5pm; $14, $11.50 w/student ID. The buildings here are all authentic (they were brought here and restored) and there are also crafts and demonstrations showing the Acadian lifestyle. *www.villagehistoriqueacadien.com*.

CAMPBELLTON This pretty waterfront town has the claim to fame of hosting the world's largest salmon and an 8.5 m sculpture dominates the aptly-named Salmon Plaza. A **Salmon Festival** takes place each July. Salmon aside, the town is an interesting base from which to explore. *www.campbellton.org*. **Mount Carleton,** $1^1/2$ hours west of Campbellton in St Quentin, is the highest point in the Appalachians and Sugarloaf Mountain has a chairlift for the less active. You can also stay in Canada's only **Lighthouse Youth Hostel (HI-Campbellton),** 1 Ritchie St, 759-7044. 20 beds. Dorm-$16, $20 non-member; June to mid-Aug only.

KOUCHIBOUGUAC NATIONAL PARK Pronounced 'Koo-she-boo-gwack', this park has some wonderful beaches as well as coastal forests and bog-lands. The main attraction is **Kelly's Beach,** with warm swimming water, nature trails, etc. Inland, the park is also home to vicious insects—wear repellent! The park has a number of campgrounds—reservations taken on 876-1277, or call the park direct: 876-2443. There is a $6 entrance charge per person. *www.parkscanada.gc.ca/kouchibouguac*.

SAINT JOHN Known as the Loyalist City and proudly boasting a royal charter, Saint John was founded by refugees—those intrepid American settlers who chose to remain loyal to Britain after the American Revolution. The landing place of the Loyalists is marked by a monument at the foot of King Street, the shortest, steepest main street in Canada. Before the Seven Years War, however, Saint John was occupied by the French. The first recorded European discovery was in 1604, when Samuel de Champlain entered the harbour on Saint John's Day—hence the name of the town and the river on which it stands. Saint John is Canada's oldest incorporated city.

Largely as a result of its strategic ice-free position on the Bay of Fundy, Saint John has become New Brunswick's largest city and its commercial and industrial centre. The waterfront is a pleasant place to visit and the bustling downtown streets are dotted with shops, cafes and historic properties. Good times to visit are during the **Festival-by-the-Sea** in August and **Loyalist Days,** the third week in July. (Incidentally, Saint John is never abbreviated, thereby making it easier to distinguish from St John's, Newfoundland.) *www.tourismsaintjohn.com* and *www.uptownsj.com.*

Accommodation
Admiral's Quay Motel, 1711 Manawagonish Rd, 672-1125/(888) 612-4244. Rooms from $65, all with private bath. Ten mins drive to downtown and the Nova Scotia ferry. *www.admiralsquay.com.*
Earle of Leinster B&B, 96 Leinster St, 652-3275. S-$56.52-$82.61, D-$65.21-$91.31, all with private bath. Historic house, walking distance to all attractions, bfast included. *http://earleofleinster.tripod.com.*
Camping: Rockwood Park, off Rte 1, in the heart of the city, 652-4050/657-1773. 2,200 acres. Sites $17, $23 w/hook-up. Two swimming lakes, horse riding in park.

Food
Market Square, renovated building with 19th century exterior and trendy, modern interior; on the waterfront. Lots of places to eat and shop.
Grannan's, 1 Market Square, 634-1555, is *the* place if you're a lover of raw oysters (half dozen $10.95), chowders from $5.95, other seafood from $7.95, fish & chips special $9.95. Daily 11am-Midnight. *www.grannanhospitalitygroup.com.*
Reggie's Restaurant, 26 Germain St, 637-2220, 657-6270. Imports smoked meat from Ben's, the famous Montréal deli. Inexpensive, filling meals for $5.50 or so. Daily 6am-5.30pm. *www.reggiesrestaurant.com.*
Saint John City Market, 47 Charlotte St, 658-2820. In the centre of town, the market opened in 1876, when it was presided over by the 'Pie Powder Court'. Fresh produce, crafts and antiques. Great for browsing and buying. Mon-Thur 7:30am-6pm, Fri 'til 7pm, Sat 'til 5pm. *www.sjcitymarket.ca.*

Of interest
There are three self-guided **walking tours** around Saint John: Prince William's Walk, the Loyalist Trail and a Victorian Stroll. Each takes around $1^1/_2$ hrs and shows you the highlights of the historic streets of Saint John. Among these are **Loyalist House,** 120 Union St, a Georgian house built in 1810; the **Old Loyalist Burial Ground** opposite King Sq; the spiral staircase in the **Old Courthouse,** off King Sq; **Barbour's General Store,** fully stocked as in the year 1867, with a barbershop; and **Old City Market,** Market St, Canada's first common law market, dating back to 1876. Pick up a map at **Tourist Information,** 1 Market Sq. Guided walking tours, operated by Gray Line New Brunswick, 633-1224, depart from **Barbour's General Store,** mid June-mid Sept, daily at 10am and 2pm; $15. *www.grayline.com.*

Carleton Martello Tower, 454 Whipple St, 636-4011. Fortification erected during and surviving the War of 1812. Spectacular view of the city. Summer: daily 10am-6pm, $4. *www.pc.gc.ca/lhn-nhs/nb/carleton/index_e.asp.*

Fort Howe Blockhouse, 658-2855. Magazine St. Replica of blockhouse built by the British during 1777 in Halifax, then disassembled and re-built to protect Saint John Harbour. A peace and friendship treaty between the British Crown and Native Indian tribes was signed here on September 24, 1778. Free.

New Brunswick Museum, 1 Market Sq, 643-2300. This museum, founded in 1842, was the first in Canada. It features a variety of historic exhibits, both national and international, a natural science gallery with a full-sized whale skeleton, artwork and Canadiana. Tue-Wed & Fri 9am-5pm, Thur 'til 9pm, Sat& Sun noon-5pm. $6, $3.25 w/student ID. *www.nbm-mnb.ca.*

Reversing Falls Rapids. The town's biggest tourist attraction. Twice a day, at high tide, waters rushing into the gorge where the Saint John River meets the sea, force the river to run backwards creating the Reversing Falls Rapids. There are two good lookouts for watching this phenomenon: the Tourist Bureau lounge/sun deck on Bridge Rd and Falls View Park.

Reversing Falls Jet Boat Rides, Fallsview Park, 634-8987. Choose a sightseeing boat ride, or a thrill ride, through the Reversing Falls and its whirlpools. $35. Or, try the more extreme sport of running the white water 'Bubble'-ride the rapids in a 10-foot inflatable bubble!!! $110. *www.jetboatrides.com.*

Rockwood Park. A beautiful park within the city limits. Fresh water lakes, sandy beaches, camping, golf, hiking trails and a zoo.

Sport

Canoeing/kayaking: Eastern Outdoors Inc., 39 King St, Brunswick Sq, 634-1530/(800) 565-2925. Also at 3 other locations. The place to go for rentals: canoe-$35/day, single kayak-$35/day, double-$45/day. Guided tours-$45/day. *www.easternoutdoors.com.*

Skiing: Poley Mountain Ski Area, in Sussex (51 miles E on Hwy 1), 433-POLEY. Lift ticket $24, $17 w/ student ID. *www.poleymountain.com.*

Information

Saint John Tourist Information, 1 Market Sq, (888) 364-4444/658-2855. Daily, summer 9am-8pm, winter 9.30am-6pm. **Reversing Falls Visitor Centre,** 100 Bridge Rd, 658-2937, May-Oct daily 8am-8pm; **Highway 1 West** (seasonal), on Hwy 1 west of harbour bridge, 658-2940, summer daily 9am-8pm, rest of year till 5 or 6pm. *www.tourismsaintjohn.com.*

Travel

Northumberland & Bay Ferries Ltd., (888) 249-7245, operate a car ferry service from Saint John to Digby, Nova Scotia—a 3 hr trip; mid May-Jan 1st. Nice scenery, but rather pricey: car $80 o/w in summer, $75 off-season, $35 for walk-on passengers ($25 w/student ID) /$20 off season ($18 w/student ID). Crowded in the summer. NB: Saint John bus stops at Woodville St – a 10 min walk to the ferry terminal. *www.nfl-bay.com.*

Saint John Transit, 658-4700. Local, city service. Basic fare $2.25. Check out *www.saintjohntransit.com.*

Acadian Bus Lines, 300 Union St, 648-3500. Bus to Moncton $24 o/w ($20 w/student ID), about 2 hrs *www.acadianbus.com.*

FUNDY ISLANDS Campobello Island: Going west on Hwy 1 from Saint John, you can catch a ferry from Back Bay that will take you, via Deer Island and Campobello, to Lubec, Maine: $14 for car and driver, $3 walk-on passengers. Call **East Coast Ferries,** 747-2159 or visit _www.eastcoastferries.nb.ca_. On Campobello is the 2,800-acre **Roosevelt Campobello International Park**, 752-2922. Visitors can see the 34-room 'cottage' maintained as it was when occupied by FDR from 1905-1921. Daily 10am-6pm, June-Oct, free. _www.fdr.net_. Also here is the **East Quoddy Head Lighthouse**, the last working lighthouse with the St George's Cross facing east. The cross symbolises safety and peace to those at sea. The lighthouse stands on its own island, accessible only at low tide. In July and August, it's a great spot for whale watching from the land. _www.campobello.com/lighthouse_. Campobello is also linked to Maine by the Franklin D Roosevelt Memorial Bridge.

Grand Manan Island: The largest island in the Bay of Fundy is a haven for bird and whale watchers. Try **Sea Watch Tours**, 662-8552, offering boat tours to sight puffins ($75), mid June-mid Aug, or combined whale (guaranteed sighting) and bird-watching trips, $55, from early July-late Sept. _www.seawatchtours.com_. Call from the mainland for weather info, as cancellations due to fog are not uncommon. The island is reached from Black's Harbour on the mainland. Call **Coastal Transport Grand Manan Ferries**, 662-3724, $47.95 for a vehicle with two people or $10 for a foot passenger, car w/ driver. Rsvs required, _www.coastaltransport.ca_. There are various guesthouses on the island, also **camping** at Seal Cove: **The Anchorage**, 662-7022/(888) 525-1655, $21.50, $24 w/hook-up. Check for current rates. _www.grandmanannb.com_ provides useful information.

FUNDY NATIONAL PARK Centrally located, the park is just over an hour from Moncton and within two hours of Fredericton and Saint John. It is only a few hours from the Maine/New Brunswick border and within a day's drive from Montréal or Boston. Fundy National Park has a spectacular setting, a vast area of rugged shore and inland forests, with unique ecosystems and rare birds. The Bay of Fundy has the world's highest tides (up to 16 metres). This allows visitors the rare experience of strolling along the ocean floor at low tide. For information, call the Park on 887-6000. $6 daily pass. _www.pc.gc.ca/pn-np/nb/fundy/index_e.asp_.

At **Hopewell Cape** on Rte 114, the Fundy tides have gouged four-storey sculptures out of the cliffs, May 20-June 10, Sept 6-Oct 10 daily 9am-5pm, June 11-June 24, Aug 20-Sept 5 daily 8am-7pm, June 25-Aug 19 daily 8am-8pm, $8 entrance. Call 734-3429 for details. _www.thehopewellrocks.ca_. The sculptures look like giant flower pots when the tide is low and you can explore them from the ocean floor. At high tide the flower pots disappear, leaving behind little tree-topped islands.

Accommodation
Camping: There are three front country campgrounds in the park – Headquarters, Chignecto North and Point Wolfe. $14/23, up to $30 w/hook-up. To reserve campsite, visit _www.pccamping.ca/parkscanada/en/park.cgi?p=14_ or call (877) 737-3783.

ST ANDREWS Just a short hop from Maine and the US border, St-Andrews-by-the-Sea, to give it its full name, was Canada's first seaside resort, designated a National Historic Site in 1998. The town was settled by Empire Loyalists in 1783 following the American Revolution, and contains original

Loyalist houses. Many of these were floated across the bay from Castine in Maine, now safe on dry land in King Street and Water Street. Try to visit **Saint Croix Island**, the site of Sieur de Monts and Samuel de Champlain's 1604 settlement. **Ministers Island** and the estate of the amazing Canadian Pacific Railway director, Sir William Van Horne, can be reached, at low tide, by driving across the ocean floor. Among other things, Van Horne was responsible for building the string of CPR hotel 'castles' across Canada, from the Chateau Frontenac to Chateau Lake Louise and beyond. The **Algonquin**, one of the CPR hotels, is St. Andrews' prominent landmark with a spectacular setting, overlooking the peninsula, a nice place to sip a beer or a coffee. *http://new-brunswick.net/new-brunswick/andrew.*

Whale watching is available, May-Sept from several companies along the seafront and pier. Try **Island Quest Marine,** King St, Market Wharf, 529-9885/(888) 252-9111: $49 pp. *www.townsearch.com/islandquest.* There is also **Quoddy Link Marine,** 6 King St, 529-2600/(877) 688-2600: $50 pp. *www.quoddylinkmarine.com.*

Accommodation
Salty Towers, 340 Water St, 529-4585. S-$55 (shared bath), D-$55 (shared bath), $75 (private bath). Access to kitchen. *www.salty-towers.com.*
Camping: Passamaquoddy Park Campground, 529-3439/(877) 393-7070, 1 km east of the town centre along Water St. Great sea views, showers and laundry. $20 basic, $24-$34 w/hook-up. *www.kok.ca.*

Information/Travel
Chamber of Commerce Welcome Center, 46 Reed Ave (next to the arena), 529-3555. Open daily 9am-6pm.
Acadian Lines, 199 Chesley St, 648-3500. Bus services throughout the Maritimes. *www.acadianbus.com.*

NOVA SCOTIA

Known as the Land of 10,000 Welcomes and the Festival Province, Canada's 'Ocean Playground' is famous for its attractive fishing villages, rocky, granite shores and historic spots like Louisbourg and Grand Pré. The early Scottish immigration to Nova Scotia is manifested in such events as the annual Highland Games in Antigonish and St Anne's Gaelic College. It is said that there is more Gaelic spoken in Nova Scotia than in Scotland.

Although the French were the first to attempt colonisation of the area, it was James I who first gave Nova Scotia (New Scotland) its own flag and coat-of-arms, when he granted the province to Sir William Alexander. The French, however, preferred the name Acadia, after explorer Verrazano's word for Peaceful Land, so the French thereafter became known as Acadians. By the Treaty of Utrecht in 1713, the province was finally ceded to the British. Cape Breton Island followed later after the siege of Louisbourg, in 1758. The 400th Anniversary of French exploration and settlement in Nova Scotia was in 2005.

Many Americans also emigrated to Nova Scotia in the late eighteenth and early nineteenth centuries, among them the Chesapeake Blacks and a group of 25,000 Loyalists—possibly the largest single emigration of cultured families in British history, since their numbers included over half of the living graduates of Harvard. They settled mostly around Sherbourne.

Driving is the best way to discover Nova Scotia. There are twelve specially designated tourist routes throughout the province. Among these, the Cabot Trail on Cape Breton Island is particularly recommended. Autumn is the most beautiful season; in summer, the ocean breeze always has a cooling effect. Although most people go to Halifax and the South Shore, Cape Breton Island is also worth a visit.

If you are at all keen on golf, Nova Scotia is the place to be. Ranked 2nd for Best Canadian Golf Destination in the 2001 Golfers' Choice Awards, Nova Scotia is undoubtedly a golfer's dream, with many of its courses offering spectacular seascapes! Visit *www.golfnovascotia.com*.

www.novascotia.com.

The telephone area code is 902.

HALIFAX Provincial capital and the largest city and economic hub of the Maritimes, the making of Halifax has been its ice-free harbour, so that not only does it deal with thousands of commercial vessels each year, but it is also Canada's chief naval base. Settled in 1749 by Govenor Edward Cornwallis, Halifax became Canada's first permanent British town, built as a response to the French fort at Louisbourg.

Although a thriving metropolis with the usual tall concrete buildings and expressways, the city does retain a certain charm with many constant reminders of its colourful past. The historic downtown areas of Halifax and its twin **Dartmouth** across the bay, are perfect for discovering by bicycle or on foot. Check with the Tourist Office for information on walking tours and the many festivals that go on in and around the town. **Citadel National Historic Site,** a hilltop fort in the middle of town, is a good place to start exploring and to get your bearings.

Connected to Halifax by two bridges and two ferries (said to be the oldest saltwater ferries in North America, $2 o/w), **Dartmouth** is known as the 'city of lakes', since there are some 22 lakes within the city boundaries. *www.halifaxinfo.com/fast-facts.php* 'Walk across Macdonald Bridge, free, for a very good view of both cities,' or take the #1 bus.

Accommodation
Dalhousie University residences, 6385 South St, 494-8840. S-$38.73 inc. tax, $25.28 w/student ID, D-$61.11, $46.56 w/student ID. Pool. May-Aug only. *www.dal.ca/confserv*.

Halifax Backpacker's Hostel, 2193 Gottingen St, 431-3170/(888) 430-3170. Dorm-$20, D-$57.50, Family Room-$65. 10 mins from downtown. Kitchen area, internet access ($5/hr). Open yr round. *www.halifaxbackpackers.com*.

HI-Halifax Heritage House Hostel, 1253 Barrington St, 422-3863. Dorm-$19 (6-8 beds), $20 (4 beds), $24 non-member (6-8 beds), $25 (4 beds), XP-$7. Kitchen, laundry, internet access ($1/10mins), TV lounge, no curfew. Check-in 2pm, out 11am. 'Very friendly.' *www.hostellingintl.ns.ca*.

Mount Saint Vincent University, 166 Bedford Hwy, 457-6286. About 15 mins from downtown. S-$38 inc. tax, $31 w/student ID, D-$53, $46 w/student ID. Gym. May-Aug only. Cheaper for weekly stays. Rsvs req. *www.msvu.ca*.

Camping: Laurie Park, 12 miles N of Halifax on Old Hwy 2, in Grand Lake, 861-1623. Sites $14-$50. June-Sept. 'Very basic.' *parks.gov.ns.ca*.

Food
Athens Restaurant, 6303 Quinpoll Rd, 422-1595. Greek and Canadian food. 'Good for breakfast.' Breakfast served till 4pm, about $4, entrées $10-$12. Licensed.

Midtown Tavern, 1684 Grafton St, 422-5213. Cheap pub-style food, nothing over $11. Mon-Sat 11am-11pm. Licensed

Satisfaction Feast, 1581 Grafton St, 422-3540. Breakfast from $4.50 to $6.50. Good vegetarian and vegan food. Lunch from $5, dinner from $10. People come from miles around for the homemade wholewheat bread and desserts ($4-5). Mon-Sat 11.30am-9pm, Wed 'til 4pm. *www.satisfactionfeast.com.*

Thirsty Duck, 5472 Spring Garden Rd, 422-1548. Pub menu, very reasonable prices, $5-15. Irish and English beer; good music. Mon-Wed 11am-11pm, Thur-Sat 'til 2am, Sun 'til 9pm. *www.thirstyduck.com.*

Of interest

Art Gallery of Nova Scotia, 1723 Hollis St, 424-7542. Regional, national and international art. Excellent exhibitions, including Inuit Art. Open daily 10am-5pm, Thur 'til 9pm. $15, $7 w/student ID. *www.agns.gov.ns.ca.*

The *Bluenose II* sails from Historic Properties for 2 hr am and pm cruises around the Harbour ($30). This is a replica of the schooner stamped on the back of the Canadian dime. Many other harbour cruises are also available. Call 634-4794/ (866) 579 4909, visit *www.fisheries.museum.gov.ns.ca* or check *www.bluenose2.ns.ca.*

Citadel National Historic Site, 426-5080. This star-shaped fortress surrounded by a moat (now a dry ditch) was built between 1828 and 1856 and is one of Canada's most visited and most important historic sites in Canada. The fortress was manned in both WWI and WWII, but it's been restored to the mid-Victorian period. There is a magnificent view of the harbour and the noon gun is fired daily. Free tours. 'Staff in uniform, friendly and well-informed.' There is an **Army Museum** recalling the military history of the fort. Grounds open year-round, Citadel mid June-mid Sept, daily 9am-6pm. $10, $5 w/student ID. *http://parkscanada.pch.gc.ca/lhn-nhs/ns/halifax/index_e.asp.*

Churches: St George's Round Church, Brunswick & Cornwallis Sts, 425-3658. An example of a very rare round church, built around 1800. Guided tours available, by donation. **St Mary's Basilica,** 423-4116 on Spring Garden Rd, has the highest granite spire in North America. Tours in summer Mon-Fri 10am & 2pm, free. **St Paul's Church,** Barrington & Duke Sts, 429-2240. Oldest Anglican church in Canada. Built in 1750, this is the oldest building in Halifax. *www.stpaulshalifax.org.* **Little Dutch Church,** Brunswick & Garrish Sts, built in 1756, was the first Lutheran church in Canada.

Dalhousie University, Coburg Rd, 494-2211. An attractive campus with the usual facilities and guided tours. *www.dal.ca.* The **Art Gallery,** 6101 University Ave, 494-2403, is worth a look. Open yr round, Tue-Sun 11am-5pm, suggested donation. *www.artgallery.dal.ca.*

Halifax Public Gardens, 423-9865, Spring Garden Rd & South Park St. 17 acres and 400 varieties of plants and flora. Fountains and floating flower-beds. Daily 8am-dusk. *www.halifaxpublicgardens.ca.*

Maritime Museum of the Atlantic, 1675 Lower Water St, 424-7490. Exhibits on the 1913 Halifax explosion (which killed 2000 people and flattened 300 acres of Halifax) and relics from the *Titanic*. Docked behind the museum is *CSS Acadia*, one of the earliest ships to chart the Arctic Ocean floor. Don't miss the stunning view of the harbour. Summer $8. Open daily 9:30am-5:30pm, Tue 'til 8pm. Winter $4: Closed Mon.Tue-Sun 9.30am-5pm,Tue 'til 8. *www.maritime.museum.gov.ns.ca.*

Nova Scotia Museum of Natural History, 1747 Summer St, 424-7353, 424-6099 for 24 hr recorded info. Featuring the province's natural and human history, the spectacular quillwork of the Micmac Indians and thousands of bees in glass enclosed hives. June 1-Oct. 15: Mon-Sat 9:30am-5:30pm, Wed 'til 8pm, Sun 1pm-5:30pm, Oct. 16-May 31 Tues 9:30am-5pm, 9:30-8pm, Thurs.-Sat. 9:30am-5pm, Sun. 1pm-5:30pm. $5 $2 w/ student ID, free Wed 5pm-8pm. *www.museum.gov.ns.ca/mnh.*

Pier 21, 1055 Marginal Rd, 425-7770. From 1928-1971, Pier 21 was Canada's 'Front

Door' for over a million immigrants, evacuees, refugees, troops and war brides. Several exhibits are on display, along with a 4-D multi-media presentation. Daily 9.30am-5.30pm in summer; Dec-Mar closed Sun & Mon. $8, $5.50 w/student ID. *www.pier21.ns.ca*.

Prince of Wales Martello Tower, 426-5080, located in Point Pleasant Park, the tower acted as part of the 'coastal defense network' set up by the British to protect against the French. Aug only, 10am-6pm daily. Free. *www.pc.gc.ca/lhn-nhs/ns/prince/visit/visit1_e.asp*.

Province House, 1726 Hollis St, 424-4661. Canada's oldest and smallest parliament house. Built in 1818 and called 'a gem of Georgian architecture' by Charles Dickens. 'The house has very detailed plasterwork and carving, very well kept.' Summer: Mon-Fri 9am-5pm, w/ends & hols 10am-4pm. $3. *www.pc.gc.ca/lhn-nhs/pe/provincehouse*.

Sir Sanford Fleming Park, overlooks the sailboat-dotted Northwest Arm. The land was donated in 1908 by Sir Sanford Fleming, the creator of Standard Time, designer of Canada's first postage stamp, and engineer of the Canadian-Pacific Railway. 'The Dingle' tower in the park commemorates the first elected assembly in the British Empire. Make the most of the walking trails and beaches.

York Redoubt, Purcell's Cove Rd, 15 miles W of Halifax on Rte 253, 426-5080. Site of historic fortification and magnificent harbour views. Picnicking facilities. Open daily dawn-dusk. Free. *www.pc.gc.ca/lhn-nhs/ns/york*.

Nearby: Peggy's Cove, Liverpool, Lunenberg, Bridgewater and the rest. Picturesque fishing villages but overrun by tourists. *www.peggyscove.ca*.

Shopping/Entertainment

Barrington St, Spring Garden Rd and the Historic Properties are all good places to shop. The **Scotia Square Complex** has the usual shopping mall attractions.

Halifax International Busker Festival, 429-3910. Annual August festival of street performers in downtown Halifax. *www.buskers.ca*.

The Nova Scotia International Tattoo, (800) 563-1114, at the beginning of July, is a popular extravaganza featuring both Canadian and international performers of all kinds. *www.nstattoo.ca*.

Shakespeare by the Sea, 422-0295, present the Bard's works outdoors in Point Pleasant Park, July-Sept. $10 suggested donation. www.shakespearebythesea.ca.

Internet access

Ceilidh Connection, 1672 Barrington St, 422-9800. $6/hr. Open Mon-Fri 10am-10pm, Sat-Sun noon-8pm. *www.ceilidhconnection.ca*.

Second Cup, 5425 Spring Garden Rd, 429-0883. Wi-fi for customers only, charge, and with any food or beverage purchase. Daily 7am-11pm. *www.secondcup.com*.

Spring Garden Road Library, 5381 Spring Garden Rd, 490-5700. Free access, with library card. 120 min a day time limit across any of 14 branches of the Halifax Library system. Tue-Thur 10am-9pm, Fri-Sat 'til 5pm. *www.halifaxpubliclibraries.ca*.

Information

Nova Scotia Tourism, 1 Maritime Pl, 425-5781/(800) 565-0000. Open daily in the summer 8am-11pm. *www.checkinnovascotia.com*.

Visitor Information Centre, 1595 Barrington St (cnr with Sackville St), 490-5946. Daily 8:30am-8pm.

Travel

For various ways of getting here, visit *www.halifaxinfo.com/getting-here.php*

Acadian Lines Bus station, 6040 Almon St (near the Forum, in the south end of peninsula Halifax), 454-9321. #7 connects with downtown. *www.acadianbus.com*.

DRL, (877) 450-2212, 1161 Hollis St, bus service to S. Shore and Yarmouth.

Metro Transit, 490-4000. Basic fare: $2, transfers available. Also runs the ferry, to

Dartmouth. Frequent departures from Upper Water St; $2 o/w. Bus transfers valid on ferry. *www.region.halifax.ns.ca/metrotransit/index.html*.

Share-A-Cab, arrangements should be made at least 24 hrs in advance of travel time. Call 429-5555/(800) 565-8669 for rates and schedules.

VIA Rail, 1161 Hollis St, (888) 842-7245. Trains are few and far between to Truro and Montreal. *www.viarail.ca*.

GRAND PRÉ NATIONAL HISTORIC PARK The restored site of an early Acadian settlement, from 1682 to 1755, and from where they were deported, from 1755 until 1762. The nearby dykeland (*grand pré* = great meadow) is where the French Acadians were deported to in 1755 after failing to take an oath of allegiance to the English king, preferring to remain neutral.

Longfellow immortalized the sad plight of the deported Acadians of Nova Scotia in his narrative poem *Evangeline* (see under *Louisiana* in USA section). There is a museum in the park with a section on Longfellow and a fine collection of Acadian relics, everything from farm tools to personal diaries. Nearby is the **Church of the Covenanters**. Built in 1790 by New England planters, this do-it-yourself church was constructed from hand-sawn boards, fastened together by square hand-made nails. The similarly homemade pulpit spirals halfway to the ceiling.

The gardens are nice for walking and the whole park is open daily May-Oct, 9am-6pm, $6.50. To get there from Halifax take Rte 101 N, the park is three miles east of Wolfville. Call 542-3631 for park info. *www.pc.gc.ca/lhn-nhs/ns/grandpre/index_e.asp www.grand-pre.com*.

ANNAPOLIS ROYAL Situated in the scenic Annapolis Valley, famous for its apples, this was the site of North America's oldest permanent settlement. Founded by de Monts and Champlain in 1604 and originally named Port Royal, it became Annapolis Royal in honour of Queen Anne, after its final capture by the British in 1710. The town then served as the Nova Scotian capital until the founding of Halifax in 1749. This tiny town has a **Visitor Centre** on Hwy 1, located in the Tidal Power Station on the Causeway, 532-5454; open daily 10am-7pm in summer. For lodgings and other visitor information, check *www.annapolisroyal.com*.

The site of the French fort of 1636 is now maintained as **Fort Anne National Historic Park** *www.pc.gc.ca/lhn-nhs/ns/fortanne* and seven miles away, on the north shore of the Annapolis River, is the **Port Royal National Historic Park**, 532-2898. This is a reconstruction of the 1605 settlement, based on the plan of a Normandy farm. Here, too, the oldest social club in North America was formed. *L'Ordre de Bon Temps* was organized by Champlain in 1606 and visitors to the province for more than three days can still become members. The park is open daily mid May-mid Oct, 9am-6pm, $4. *www.pc.gc.ca/lhn-nhs/ns/portroyal/index_e.asp.*

Thirty five miles south is **Kejimkujik National Park**, open 24 hours, year-round; the Visitors Centre is open daily during the summer 8:30am-9pm, 682-2772. The park entrance and information centre is at **Maitland Bridge**. Admission $5. The area was originally inhabited by the Micmac Indians. The park is good for canoeing, fishing, hiking and skiing in winter. Canoes can be rented for $8/hr, $25/day. You can also camp inside the park, $16-23.

Ask at info centre for details. *www.pc.gc.ca/pn-np/ns/kejimkujik.* 20 km away is the **Raven Haven HI-South Milford Hostel**, South Milford, 532-7320, on shore of Sandy Bottom Lake. Rooms $15. non-members $17; open June-Sept. 5 beds - res essential. On Sandy Bottom Lake, lots of activities. *www.hihostels.ca/hostels/NovaScotia/NovaScotiaRegion/RavenHavenHostel/Hostels.*

Kings Transit Authority operates bus services in the Annapolis Valley, between Bridgetown, Annapolis Royal and Greenwood, at $3 a trip. *www.kingstransit.ns.ca*

YARMOUTH The only place of any size on the western side of Nova Scotia, Yarmouth is the centre of a largely French-speaking area. During the days of sail this was an important shipbuilding centre, although today local industry is somewhat more diversified.

A good time to visit is at the end of July, when the **Western Nova Scotia Exhibition** is held here. The festival includes the usual agricultural and equestrian events plus local craft demonstrations and exhibits. *www.yarmouthexhibition.com* and *www.yarmouthonline.ca*.

Accommodation
El Rancho Motel, Rte 1, Hwy 1, 742-2408. S-$70, D-$80, overlooking Lake Milo. Kitchen facilities. Check-in anytime, out 11am.
Yarmouth Ice House Hostel, 44 Old Post Office Rd, 649-2818. Good for backpackers. S-$18, D-$14. Serves full bfast, $6, and all-you-can-eat seafood buffet, $15. Bike and canoe rentals: $5/day. Check-in after 2pm, out before 11am. *www.churchillmansion.com.* Associated with the 1890s **Churchill Mansion**, on a hill 9 miles north-east of Yarmouth on the Evangeline Trail. Doubles there are $69-89.

Travel
The Cat, 742-6800. North America's fastest catamaran serves Yarmouth and Bar Harbor, Maine (2 hr 45 mins); US$58 pp/$48 off season. US$99/89 vehicle. 'Luxury travel compared to 600 miles of hard driving.' *www.catferry.com.*

SYDNEY Situated on the Atlantic side of the province, Sydney is the chief town on Cape Breton Island and a good centre for exploring the rest of the island. It's a steel and coal town, a grim, but friendly, soot-blackened old place. Like the whole of Cape Breton Island, Sydney has a history of struggles against worker exploitation and bad social conditions. Since France ceded the island to Britain as part of the package-deal Treaty of Utrecht in 1713, hard times and social strife have frequently been the norm.

Sydney celebrates its heritage the first week of every August with a festival of music, sports and special events during **Action Week,** that actually lasts for 9 days. For info, call 563-5510, *www.actionweek.com.*

A ferry goes to Newfoundland from North Sydney across the bay. *http://sydney.capebretonisland.com.*

Accommodation
For lodgings, see *http://sydney.capebretonisland.com/lodging.html.*
Garden Court Cabins, 2518 Kings Rd, Sydney Forks, 564-6201 (14 miles W of Hwy 125 on Rte 4). Single rates $55-$85. On Portage Lake close to Blackett's Lake.

Of interest
Highland Games, Antigonish or St Anne's, in July. Kilts, pipes and drums, sword dancing, caber toss, etc. *www.gmhg.org.*

Nearby: In the picturesque, lakeside town of **Baddeck,** is the **Alexander Graham Bell National Historic Site of Canada,** Chebucto St, 295-2069. Displays, models, papers etc., relating to Bell's inventions. Edinburgh-born Bell first came to Baddeck in 1885 and returned the next year to establish a vacation home for his family, where he spent a substantial part of each year at Beinn Bhreagh. Aeronautical work was a large part of his life there, from early kite-flying experiments to the success of the Silver Dart in February 1909. The site includes a large collection of artifacts related to Bell's research, books, photographs and copies of material from his personal archives; and various personal items, furniture and awards received by Bell during his lifetime. June-Oct 8:30am-6pm, $6.50. *www.parkscanada.gc.ca.*

Glace Bay, 13 miles east, is the site of the **Miners Museum and Village**, 849-4522. Includes tour of underground mine and the village shows the life of a mining community 1850-1900s. Ask about Tue evening concerts by the Men of the Deeps, tkts $10, rsvs req. June-Sept, daily 10am-6pm, Tue 'til 7pm, otherwise 9am-4pm. $5, $10 w/mine tour. *www.minersmuseum.com.*

Information/Travel

Acadian Bus Lines, 99 Terminal Rd, 564-5533/(800) 567-5151, from Halifax and Baddeck. *www.acadianbus.com.*

Marine Atlantic Ferries to Argentia ($75.50/person o/w, $157/car, 14hrs) and Porte-aux-Basques, Newfoundland, ($27/person o/w, $76.50/car, 5-6hrs), (800) 341-7981. *www.marineatlantic.ca.*

Visitors Information, 74 Esplanade, Sydney, 539-9876. Daily in summer.

FORTRESS OF LOUISBOURG NATIONAL HISTORIC PARK
Built by the French between 1717 and 1740, this fortress was once the largest built in North America since the time of the Incas. Louisbourg played a crucial role in the French defense of the area and was finally won by Britain in 1760, but not before it had been blasted to rubble.

A faithful re-creation of a complete colonial town within the fortifications, with majestic gates, homes and formal gardens. There is a museum and tours by French uniformed guides are available. The park is open June-Sept; June and September: daily 9:30am-5pm, July and August: daily 9am-6pm, $15; call the Visitors Information Centre, 733-2280/733-3546, for details. *www.pc.gc.ca/lhn-nhs/ns/louisbourg.*

CAPE BRETON HIGHLANDS NATIONAL PARK
The park lies on the northern-most tip of Cape Breton (*www.capebretonisland.com*) sandwiched between the Gulf of St Lawrence and the Atlantic Ocean. It covers more than 360 square miles of rugged mountain country, beaches and quiet valleys. The whole is encircled by the 184 mile long **Cabot Trail**, an all-weather paved highway winding its way round the park, climbing four mountains en route and providing spectacular views of sea and mountains. In summer, however, it gets very crowded and the narrow, steep roads are jammed with cars. There are camping facilities in the park and good sea and freshwater swimming.

This is an area originally settled by Scots and many of the locals still speak Gaelic. There are park information centres at **Ingonish Beach** and **Cheticamp**, 224-2306. *http://cheticampns.com.* Admission to the park is $6. **Camping** is $18-$30 inside the park; call park info on 224-2306.

IONA The Nova Scotia **Highland Village**, 725-2272, includes a museum and other memorabilia of the early Scottish settlers. A highland festival is held here on the first Saturday in August. Open May-October, daily 9am-6pm, $8. The village is off Hwy 105, 15 miles east on Hwy 223 via Little Narrows, overlooking the Bras d'Or lakes. *highlandvillage.museum.gov.ns.ca*.

PRINCE EDWARD ISLAND

Prince Edward Island, known primarily as the home of *Anne of Green Gables* and as a great producer of spuds. It is Canada's smallest and thinnest province, being only 140 miles long, with an average width of just 20 miles and a population of a mere 136,500. Small as it is, the tiny province played a big role in the establishment of today's Canada: it played host to the first meeting of the Fathers of the Confederation, in 1864.

PEI was originally named 'Abegweit' by the local Micmac Indians, meaning 'land cradled on the waves'. The French colonised the island and baptized it Isle St Jean, but when it was ultimately ceded to Britain as a separate colony, the British renamed it after Prince Edward, Duke of Kent. Now known as the 'Garden of the Gulf', PEI is a popular spot for Canadian family vacations because of its great sandy beaches and warm waters, perfect for lazy summer sunning!

Note the colour of the soil on PEI: it's red because it contains iron, which rusts on exposure to the air. Limits are put on billboards here—you won't see any along the side of PEI's highways. The full effect of this constraint only hits you when you are bombarded with billboards back on the mainland.

In 1997, 124 years after the 1873 Terms of Union between Canada and PEI, a constitutional obligation was placed on the federal government to maintain 'continuous communication' between the island and the mainland. Consequently, PEI finally became linked to mainland Canada by the nine-mile long **Confederation Bridge**, which spans the Northumberland Strait. An engineering marvel, it is the longest bridge over icy waters in the world. It takes 10 minutes to cross the bridge by car, with a o/w toll of $40.50. For bicyclists, it's $8. *www.confederationbridge.com.*

Alternatively, you can reach this island paradise by ferry from Caribou, Nova Scotia, to Wood Islands, east of the capital (75 min, $12.50 r/t, $55 r/t car). Call **NFL Ferries**, (888) 249-7245, for more details or visit *www.nfl-bay.com*.

Go to *www.peiplay.com* for more general info about the island, including accommodation. The site lists 230 B&Bs for example. A note of caution: only camp in designated campgrounds—camping is prohibited everywhere else (including the beach).

The telephone area code is 902.

CHARLOTTETOWN The first meeting of the Fathers of the Confederation took place in Charlottetown in 1864. Out of this meeting came the future Dominion of Canada (hence the tag 'The Cradle of Confederation'). In the Confederation Chamber, Province House, where the meeting was held, a plaque proclaims: 'Providence Being Their Guide, They Builded Better Than They Knew'. The citizens of PEI were not so convinced however. They waited until 1873 before joining the Confederation. Even then, according to the then Governor General, Lord Dufferin, they came in 'under the impression that it is the Dominion that has been annexed to Prince Edward Island'. *www.visitcharlottetown.com.*

These days things are quieter hereabouts, only livening up in summer when Canadian families descend en masse to the town's waterfront and PEI's other tourist attraction, harness racing, gets going out at **Charlottetown Driving Park**, 892-6823, *www.charlottetowndrivingpark.com*. The restored waterfront section of town, Olde Charlottetown, offers the usual craft shops, eating places and boutiques. You can even tour the town in a London double-decker bus. *www.charlottetownpei.com*.

Accommodation

Charlottetown has dozens of hotels, motels, and bed & breakfasts including plenty of reasonably-priced tourist homes - rsvs are recommended during July and Aug. *www.visitcharlottetown.com/guide/accomm.cfm.*

University of PEI residences, University and Belvedere Ave, 566-0442. In **Blanchard Hall,** apartments sleep 4, w/kitchenette, lounge and private bath, $78.65 inc. tax; **Marion Hall,** S-$32.25 and **Bernardine Hall,** S-$51.45, D-$61.10. All rooms include bfast (Jul-Aug only and with the exception of Blanchard Hall). Rooms available May-Aug only. *www.upei.ca/housing*.

Blanchard Heritage Home, 163 Dorchester St, 894-9756, May-Oct, S-from $22, D-from $37.

Food

Cedar's Eatery, 81 University Ave, 892-7377. Large servings of Canadian and Lebanese food. Lunch specials from $5-7, dinner specials $7-$14. Bar upstairs and live music. Open Mon-Thur 11am-midnight, Fri-Sat 'til 1am, Sun 4-11pm. *www.cedarseatery.com.*

Olde Dublin Pub, 131 Sydney St, 892-6992. Serves pub food and seafood at moderate prices: entrées $8-10. Specials every day. Live Irish entertainment nightly in the summer. Daily 11am-2am. *www.oldedublinpub.com*.

Of interest

Abegweit Sightseeing Tours, 894-9966/(888) 461-9966, operate guided tours of both the south and north shores ($65), covering most points of interest including Fort Amherst National Historic Park and the Acadian Pioneer Village. Daily from Charlottetown Hotel at Kent & Pownal Sts. 1 hr guided tours ($9.50) of Charlottetown depart six times daily from the Confederation Centre, beginning at 10.30am. *www.peisland.com/abegweit/tours.htm*.

Confederation Centre of The Arts, Queen & Grafton Sts, 566-1267/(800) 565-0278. The focal point of the town's cultural life, it has an art gallery, museum, library and three theatres. In the main theatre a musical version of the story of PEI's favourite orphan, *Anne of Green Gables,* is staged every summer, June-Oct. Tkts $21-$62, call for performance dates. From May to October, a summer festival is held here annually. Museum/gallery open daily 9am-5pm June-Sept; rest of year Wed-Sat 11am-5pm, Sun 1-5pm. By donation. *www.confederationcentre.com*.

Province House, 165 Richmond St, 566-7626. The site of Confederation, Canada's founding fathers met here in 1864 to decide the fate of the Dominion. The provincial Legislature now meets here. Open year round, daily in summer 8:30am-6pm; winter weekdays only 9am-5pm. 45-min self-guided tours. Free. *http://parkscanada.pch.gc.ca/lhn-nhs/pe/provincehouse.*

Orwell Corner Historic Village, off Hwy 1, 25 kms east of Charlottetown, 651 8510. The life of a 1890s rural Acadian crossroad community with general store, blacksmith's shop, house, barns, church, school, community hall including the **PEI Agricultural Museum**. Open May-Oct.

Information/Travel
Charlottetown Visitor Centre, 178 Water St.
Acadian Bus Lines, 156 Belvedere Ave, 626 6432, operate from Halifax, Nova Scotia, and also to Summerside, 96 Water St, 436 2308. $50+tax o/w, $43 w/student ID. *www.acadianbus.com.* Be warned! There is no public transport on the island.
Shuttle Bus, 566-3243, operates 4 times a day between Charlottetown and Cavendish Visitor Centres, $13 o/w, $20 same day r/t. Call for times.
Yellow Cab, 892-6561. Offers pre-planned tours.

Internet access
Confederation Center Public Library, Queen & Richmond Sts, 368-4642. Free access, 1 hr time limit. Open Tue-Thur 10am-8pm, Fri-Sat 'til 5pm, Sun 1pm-5pm.

PRINCE EDWARD ISLAND NATIONAL PARK Situated north of Charlotte-town, the Park consists of 25 miles of sandy beaches backed by sandstone cliffs. Thanks to the Gulf Stream, the sea is beautifully warm. **Rustico** is one of the quieter beaches. Park entry $6. *www.pc.gc.ca/pn-np/pe/pei-ipe.*

Ask about good places for clamming. Assuming you pick the right spot, you can just wriggle your toes in the sand and dig up a good meal!

At **Cavendish Beach**, off Rte 6, is **Green Gables**, 672-6350. Built in the 1800s, the farmhouse inspired the setting of Lucy Maud Montgomery's famous novel, *Anne of Green Gables*. The house has been refurbished to portray the Victorian setting described in the novel. Daily in summer 9am-5pm, 'til 8pm July & Aug, $6.50. *www.pc.gc.ca/lhn-nhs/pe/greengables.* The beach here is very crowded during summer and probably best avoided. Camping sites and tourist homes abound on the island, call (888) PEI-PLAY.

NEWFOUNDLAND and LABRADOR

Newfoundland and Labrador are a bit off the beaten track, but it's worth taking a little time and trouble to get here. The island of Newfoundland is rich in historic associations. The Irish Saint Brendan was here as early as the 6th century and the Vikings from around 1000 AD. Newfoundland was 'discovered' by Prince Henry St Clair of Scotland in 1398 and more officially by John Cabot in 1497 and St John's was first placed on a world map in 1541. It was the first part of Canada to be settled by Europeans and the first overseas possession of the British Empire and is now a society neither wholly North American nor yet European.

Newfoundland's relative proximity to Europe has studded it with many firsts, including the first umbilical connection joining the two continents in 1858 when the first transatlantic telegraph cable was landed at Heart's Content in Trinity Bay, later more successfully in 1866 (the first attempt was disrupted by high voltages). The first message tapped out in Morse code on the finally successful cable was: "A treaty of peace has been signed between Austria and Prussia". In 1901, the first transatlantic wireless signal was received by Marconi near St John's at Signal Hill, now a National Historic Site. In 1956, another umbilical was hauled ashore at Clarenville, northwest of St John's on the Bonavista Peninsula - the first transatlantic telephone cable, with 30 direct telephone circuits from Europe to the US and six to Canada. *http://clarenville.newfoundland.ws*

The first non-stop transatlantic flight also took off from Newfoundland:

Capt. John Alcock and Lieut. A.W. Brown took off from St. John's in June 1919 in a converted Vickers Vimy bomber, flying 3,630 km to Clifden in Ireland in 16 hours, 12 minutes. In October 1945, the first regularly scheduled commercial flights across the North Atlantic (using DC-4s as opposed to seaplanes) were flown to England by American Export Airlines from New York via Gander in Newfoundland, the flights taking about 14 hours; Pan Am followed suit a few days later.

Fishing and related marine research are still the main industries, although mining is important and the oil industry has reached here too. **Labrador,** the serrated northeastern mainland of Canada, was added to Newfoundland in 1763. Until recent explorations and development of some of Labrador's natural resources (iron ore, timber), the area was virtually a virgin wilderness, with the small population scattered in rugged little fishing villages and centred around the airport at Goose Bay.

Strikingly beautiful, Newfoundland and Labrador offer spectacular seascapes (17,000 kilometres of coastline and an estimated two million seabirds), long beaches and picturesque fishing villages, some still with access only from the sea, vast forests, fjords (yes, there are fjords outside of Norway!), majestic mountains and hundreds of lakes—locally called 'ponds'—some of which are nearly 20 miles long!

Newfoundlanders' speech is unique: English interspersed with plenty of slang and colloquialisms. The hybrid nature of the province is also evident in the names of its towns, like Heart's Content, Come By Chance and Blow-Me-Down. The people here are very friendly and helpful, well prepared to take a visitor under a collective wing and known as 'Newfies' to the rest of Canada. Newfoundland is probably the only Canadian province to celebrate Guy Fawkes Day.

There is a daily car and passenger ferry service to Port-aux-Basques from North Sydney, Nova Scotia, (800) 341-7981, $27 pp plus $76.50 car o/w. A ferry also operates to Argentia, only 136 km from St John, $75.50 pp plus $157 car o/w. _www.marineatlantic.ca_. Once on the island, the Trans Canada Highway stretches from Port-aux-Basques to the capital, St John's, via Corner Brook and Terra Nova National Park. There is a bus service from the ferry to St John's. _www.gov.nf.ca/tourism_.

The telephone area code is 709.

ST JOHN'S A gentle though weather-beaten city, St John's overlooks a natural harbour situated on the island's east coast, 547 miles from Port-aux-Basques on the southwestern tip. As many as 22 species of whales, dolphins and porpoises live outside the harbour, making the waters prime for trips to view these beautiful creatures. Icebergs often float in the emerald-ocean outside the town, sometimes as late as July.

Nearby **Cape Spear** is just 1,640 miles from Cape Clair, Ireland and the city's strategic position has in the past made it the starting point for transatlantic contests and conflicts of one sort or another. The first successful transatlantic cable was landed nearby in 1866; the first transatlantic wireless signal was received by Marconi at St John's in 1901; and the first non-stop transatlantic flight took off from here in 1919.

Take a walk along Gower Street to see the rows of historical old houses.

Downtown Water Street has been the city's commercial centre for 400 years and is still the place to find interesting stores, restaurants and pubs. St John's has begun to develop more after the discovery of off-shore oil fields. The pastel-painted houses rising from the harbour look stunning from the water; however, most of the older buildings have been destroyed either by fire in the 19th century, or demolished in the 20th.

St.John's motto is *hanc primum sol illuminate* – 'Here the sun shines first!' meaning it's the first place in North America to see the sun rise each morning. Cape Spear is the perfect spot to experience this daily miracle of light. *www.city.st-johns.nf.ca*.

Accommodation
Check listings at *www.stjohns.ca/visitors/accommodation/index.jsp*.

Prescott Inn B&B, 21 Military Rd, 753-7733/(888) 263-3786. S-$60-$169 off season, $80-$199 high season. Central location. Original Newfoundland artwork on display. *www.prescottinn.nl.ca*.

The Roses, 9 Military Rd, 726-3336/(877) 767-3722. In season, S-$85, D-$95 w/private bath. Off-season rates lower. Bfast included. *www.therosesbandb.com*.

Youth Hostel, Hatcher House, Paton College, on the campus of Memorial University of Newfoundland, btwn Elizabeth Ave & Prince Phillip Dr, 737-7933 S-$25, $33 non-students, D-$19.50 pp, $27 pp non-students. Check-in after 2pm. Open early May-mid Aug only. *www.housing.mun.ca*.

Camping: CA Pippy Park, Alandale Rd, Nagles Place, 737-3669 or 3655/(877) 477 3655. $18 basic, $26 w/hook up. Open May-Oct. *www.pippypark.com*.

Food/Entertainment
There is a variety of reasonably priced places to eat on **Duckworth** and **Water Sts.**

Bianca's, 171 Water St, 726-9016, very elegant, rsvs req. Open for lunch Mon-Fri 12-2pm, dinner daily 6pm-9.30pm. *www.biancas.net*.

Ches's Snacks, 9 Freshwater Rd, 722-4083. Legendary fish & chips for over 50 years. Take-out fish $6-8. Daily 10am-2am, w/e til 3am. *www.chessfishandchips.ca*.

Classic Café East, 73 Duckworth, 726-4444. Open 8am-10pm. Traditional Newfoundland cuisine for smaller budget. Breakfast till 4pm, $3.99. Evening entrees $14 – 19. Specials every day. *www.classiccafeeast.com*.

The Ship Inn, 265 Duckworth St (on Solomon's Lane), 753-3870. One of many pubs and clubs that showcase local talent on the renowned folk music scene here. Also rock and sometimes classical in the afternoons. Open daily 11am-3am, except Mon & Tue 'til 2am.

Of interest
Anglican Cathedral, 16 Church Hill, 726-5677. Established in St. John's in 1699, this is the oldest Anglican parish in Canada. The cathedral is said to be one of the finest examples of ecclesiastical Gothic architecture in North America. Begun in 1847 and following the two fires, restored in 1905, it features sculptured arches and carved furnishings. It's a National Historic Site. Summer: daily 10am-5pm. Tours available by arrangement. *www.sji.ca/cathedral*. Also, **St John's Haunted Hike,** 70 Fleming St, 576-2087/685-3444, leaves from the west entrance of the cathedral and takes an hour or so. June-mid Sept: Sun-Thur 9:30pm. *www.hauntedhike.com*.

Memorial University Botanical Gardens, 306 Mt Scio Rd, 737-8590. Developed to display plants native to the province. Beautiful meandering walking trails, located within Pippy Park. May-Nov: daily 10am-4/5pm. June-Sep $5; low season $3. *www.mun.ca/botgarden*.

The Rooms Museum, 9 Bonaventure Ave, 757-8000. St John's is rich in history and folklore and this particular museum has the only relics in existence of the vanished Indian tribe, the Beothuks. Summer: Mon-Sat. 10am-5pm, Wed-Thu til 9pm. Closed

Sun. Low season closed Mon. $5, $4 w/student ID. *www.therooms.ca/archives*.

Quidi Vidi Battery (pronounced Kiddy Viddy), 729-2977. Just outside of St John's, the battery built to ward off American attacks in 1812 overlooks scenic Quidi Vidi village and is restored to its 1812 appearance. Five minutes from Signal Hill. Staffed by guides in period costume. Summer: daily 10am-5:30pm, $3. *www.tcr.gov.nl.ca/tcr/historicsites/Quidi%20Vidi.htm*.

Signal Hill National Historic Site, accessible from Duckworth St, 772-5367. So named because the arrival of ships was announced from here to the town below through a series of flag signals. It is also the site where Marconi received the first transatlantic wireless signal in 1901. Inside the park is **Cabot Tower**, built in 1897 to commemorate the 400th anniversary of John Cabot's discovery of Newfoundland and Queen Victoria's Diamond Jubilee. 'Million dollar view' of St. John's and the Atlantic and an interesting **Visitors Centre**: May 15-June 14 Daily 8:30am-4:30pm, Sept.-Oct. 15 Daily 8:30am-4:30pm, Oct. 16-May 14 Mon.-Fri. 8:30am-4:30pm. Admission $4. *www.pc.gc.ca/lhn-nhs/nl/signalhill/index_E.asp*.

Nearby: Trinity, on the Bonavista Peninsula, north of St John's. This town of 350 people has several national heritage sites and pretty streets lined with brightly coloured, saltbox-style homes. One highlight is the **Cape Bonavista Lighthouse**, 468-7444, $3, daily 10am-5:30pm, May-Sep. Thought to be the first land sighted by John Cabot in 1497. Restored to the 1870 appearance and with costumed guides. *www.historictrust.com/mockbeggar*.

Festivals: the annual **Royal St John's Regatta** on Quidi Vidi Lake takes place first Wed in August; the province's event of the year. Call 576-8921 for details. *www.stjohnsregatta.org*. The same week sees the **Newfoundland & Labrador Folk Festival**, 576-8508; folk music, dancing and storytelling. *www.sjfac.nf.net*.

Information/Travel

St John's Tourist Information, 348 Water St, on the waterfront, 576-8106. Daily 9am-5pm. *www.city.st-johns.nf.ca*.

Metro Bus, 245 Freshwater Rd, 722-9400, covers downtown St John's, $1.75 base fare. *www.metrobus.com*. For further afield you will have to take a tour. Try **Legend Tours**: 753-1497, **City & Outport Adventures**: 754-8687, *www.webpage.ca/tour* and **Discovery Tours**: 722-4533, *www.newfoundlandtours.com*.

Airport, *www.stjohnsairport.com* is situated north of town and is reached only by taxi: Call **Bugdens Taxi's**, 726-4400, $15-$20.

TERRA NOVA NATIONAL PARK In the central region of Newfoundland, around three hours away from St John's, this area was once covered by glaciers 750 feet thick, which left behind boulders, gravel, sand and grooved rock. The sea filled the valleys, leaving the hills as islands. The result is the incredibly beautiful **Bonavista Bay,** a picturesque wilderness with saltwater fjords, barrens and bogs. But it's certainly not swimming country. The cold Labrador Current bathes the shores and it's not unusual to see an iceberg.

Inland the park is thickly forested and hiking trails climb headland summits and follow the rugged coast. Moose are a common sight in the park and occasionally a fox or a bear may be spotted. Fishing, canoeing and camping are available inside the park, sites cost $13-$26 w/hook-up. Access to the park is easy since the Trans Canada Hwy passes right through it for 25 miles. Admission is $5. For Park info call 533-2801, for camping rsvs call (800) 414-6765. *www.pc.gc.ca/pn-np/nl/terranova/index_E.asp*.

DRL, 738-8088, also provides bus transportation from St John's. One bus daily (7:30am) to nearby Eastport Junction, approx. four hours, $44 o/w. *www.drlgroup.com/coachlines/coachlines.html*.

GROS MORNE NATIONAL PARK This is Newfoundland's second National Park, located on the island's west coast, eight hours away from St John's. This park, about 65 miles wide, is the more popular of the two because of the rugged beauty of its mountains. _www.grosmorne.com._ The landscape here is very different from that of the eastern coast of the province—colossal collisions of tectonic plates created formations as barren as the moon: 'fantastic'. Flora and fauna are abundant, orchids thrive, there are over 30 wild species in all and the park is home to giant Atlantic hares, woodland caribou and moose. Park entry fee, $8.

You can wade along the sandy beaches of **Shallow Bay,** or look for 'pillow rocks' that formed along the coast as lava cooled under water. You can travel by boat, winding up through the glaciated fjords of **Western Brook** or **Trout River Ponds** and a serious hike to the top of **Gros Morne Mountain** (16 kilometres, 7-8 hours) will reward you with a spectacular view of **Ten Mile Pond** and the **Long Range Mountains. Rocky Harbour** is the largest settlement in the park and the prettiest; take a walk along the coast to the **Lobster Cove Head Lighthouse. Western Brook Pond** is reminiscent of a Norwegian fjord. The easy three kilometer trail leads to the dock where you can take a boat tour, $38 pp, June-Oct, arranged through 458-2730, which will also have excursions to Seal Island in 2006 (458-2450). The **Lookout Trail**, 5 kilometres, is recommended as having some of the best views of the park, _www.parkscanada.gc.ca/grosmorne_. There are five **campsites** within the park, with sites from $14-$23/night. There is also **Woody Point Youth Hostel**, Bonne Bay, 453-7254/453-2470. Dorms and private rooms $20. Open year round. For groceries head for **Rocky Harbour.**

L'ANSE AUX MEADOWS NATIONAL HISTORIC SITE The oldest known European settlement in the New World. At the northern tip of Newfoundland and believed to be the site of the Viking settlement of 1000 AD, this is the only authenticated Viking settlement in North America. No standing ruins of their buildings have survived, but excavations have disclosed the size and location of structures and many everyday objects have been found, making this a UNESCO World Heritage Site. Guides on site daily. Open early June and September daily 9am-5pm, mid June-Labor day 'til 8pm; $9. Call 623-2608 for more info, _www.pc.gc.ca/lhn-nhs/nl/meadows._ From St John, L'Anse aux Meadows is a 12 hour drive.

ST PIÉRRE AND MIQUELON ISLANDS Off the southern coast of Newfoundland, these islands constitute the only remaining holdings of France in North America, retained by France under the Treaty of Paris in 1863 as a safe haven for French fisherman. Once called the 'Islands of 11,000 Virgins', these granite outcrops total only about 93 square miles, with a population of about seven thousand. French territory since the beginnings of _La Nouvelle France_, the natives _parlent français, mangent baguettes_ and pay for them in euros.

The main attraction of these wet and windy isles is the Gallic atmosphere rather than any particular sights. The treacherous waters surrounding the isles are said to have contributed to more than 650 wrecks. Just south of here is where 'the perfect storm' occurred. You can reach the islands by flying with **Air-Saint-Pierre** from St John's (NF, 726-9700), Halifax (902) 873-3566, and Sydney, Nova Scotia, Montréal and Moncton (New-Brunswick). In Canada, call (508) 410-0000 for info. *www.airsaintpierre.com.* There is also a **ferry,** the **SPM Express,** that runs daily at 2:45pm, $85 round trip, (800) 563-2006, from **Fortune**, NF, on Route 210. Canadians and Americans need to show proof of citizenship and all other nationalities must have a passport. *www.spmexpress.net,* **Tourist Information**: (800) 565-5118. *www.st-pierre-et-miquelon.com*.

LABRADOR This desolate land to the northeast of Québec is not the ideal travelling environment. Only 30,000 people live in Labrador, and the majority live in the few industrial communities, with the rest scattered along a heavily indented coastline that is icebound for most of the year. Much of the Province was, until recently, only accessible by air or sea and that is still true of the northern wilds. Separated from Newfoundland by the Belle Isle Straits, this part of Canada was first settled by Basque whalers, followed by Irish and west country English. The region has a dialect reminiscent of Shakespeare's era and a lot of other things here seem to have moved on just as slowly.

It is possible to explore the southernmost region on a day trip from **St Barbe** in Newfoundland. The sea crossing itself is reason to make the effort, often with views of whales and icebergs. The **ferry** runs daily, passengers $10.50, cars $21.50 one way. Call **Labrador Marine Inc.**, (866) 535-2567, for details. *www.gov.nl.ca/ferryservices*. This, the most accessible part of the region, probably has the most significant attractions, including the **Maritime Archaic Indian Burial Mound National Historic Site**, which at 7,500 years old marks the continent's earliest known burial site. The site is located at **L'Anse-Amour**, off Route 510, 920-2051. Also on Route 510 is **Red Bay National Historic Site**, 920-2142, detailing the town's whaling past. Open daily June-Oct, 9am-6pm, $7. *www.pc.gc.ca/lhn-hs/nl/redbay* .

Most of the coastal villages began as fur trading posts or are Indian settlements—the nomadic Inuit and Naskapi have managed to retain their culture and way of life unchanged for centuries. Labrador is just beginning to reap the many untapped resources of its harsh land - a new nickel mine at Voisey's Bay will begin production in a few years. **Happy Valley/Goose Bay** has an **airport** and a **Visitor's Centre**, 365 Hamilton River Rd, 896-3489, open daily in the summer: 8am-8pm, winter: Mon-Fri 8am-5pm. *www.tourismlabrador.com*. There is no public transport, so if you fly, be prepared to rent a car at the airport. Labrador is also a great spot for viewing the **Northern Lights** in the spring and autumn.

ONTARIO AND QUEBEC

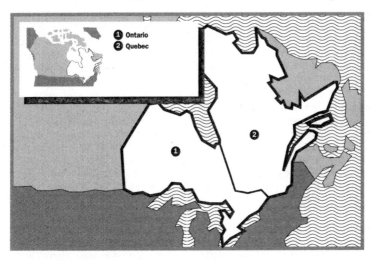

This section is devoted to those old enemies and still rivals, Ontario and Québec. Both provinces evolved out of vast wilderness areas first opened up by Indians and fur traders, only later to become the focus of a bitter rivalry as Québec was colonised by the French and Ontario by British and American Loyalists. In 1791 Québec became Lower Canada and Ontario became Upper Canada. In 1840 the Act of Union united the two and finally brought responsible and stable government to the area.

Cultural differences between the two provinces remain strong, but one thing that is pretty similar is the climate. Summers can be hot and humid and winters long, very cold and snowy. Both Québec and Ontario also offer progressive, modern cities, as well as vast regions of wilderness great for getting far away from whatever it is you're getting away from.

ONTARIO

This 'booming heartland' is Canada's fourth largest province but the most populous, with 40 percent of the nation's population and Canada's largest city. Ontario accounts for the largest share of the nation's income and more than half the nation's agricultural resources, including one of Canada's premier wine producing areas. In the last century, the province has leapt ahead of its neighbours, becoming highly industrialised while simultaneously reaping the benefits of the great forest and mineral wealth of the Canadian Shield that covers most of the northern regions. is second only to Michigan as North America's largest motor vehicle assembler - it exports more vehicles to the US than Japan or Mexico; and employment in manufacturing in the province is second only to that of California. But in recent years, service industries have come to dominate the province's economy, now accounting for three quarter's of its employment, led by business and financial services, professional and scientific technical services, arts and culture. _www.gov.on.ca_.

Ontario was first colonised not from Britain, but by Empire Loyalists from the USA. Previously there were only sporadic French settlements and trading posts in what was otherwise a vast wilderness. The ready transportation provided in the past by the Great Lakes (all of which lap Ontario's shores, with the exception of Michigan) and the St Lawrence Seaway, has linked the province to the industrial and consumer centres of the United States and has been a major factor behind Ontario's success story.

There is water virtually everywhere in Ontario and in addition to the Great Lakes, the province has a further 250,000 smaller lakes, numerous rivers and streams, a northern coastline on Hudson Bay and, of course, Niagara Falls. For more info call **Ontario Travel,** (905) 282-1721/(800) 668-2746, _www.ontariotravel.net_, or _www.soto.on.ca_ for areas south of Toronto.

National Parks: Bruce Peninsula, Georgian Bay Islands, Point Pelee, Pukaskwa, St Lawrence Islands, plus 23 National Historic Sites. _www.pc.gc.ca_.

OTTAWA Although the nation's capital with its million or so people has had the reputation of being a dull city, Ottawa has perked up considerably in the last few years. Dare we even say that Ottawa has become, well, almost a fun city to visit?! It has a lively student/youth emphasis and boasts a thriving cultural life, offering the visitor many excellent museums and art galleries, as well as top-notch theatrical performances. When the bars and restaurants start shutting down for the night, the popular solution is to cross the river into **Hull,** Québec, where everything is open until 3am.

The most colourful time of year to visit is during spring, when more than a million tulips bloom in the city and Ottawa celebrates its **Tulip Festival,** _www.tulipfestival.ca_. The tulip bulbs were a gift to Ottawa from the government of the Netherlands, as thanks for the refuge granted to the Dutch royal family during World War II. In summer the city is crowded with visitors and there are many festivals and activities.

Ottawa in the winter even has its charms. You can catch the **Winterlude Festival** in February, or just enjoy the spectacle of civil servants, with their suits and briefcases, skating to work on the 4½ mile-long Rideau Canal. The canal is known as the world's longest skating rink. _www.canadascapital.gc.ca/winterlude_.

Samuel de Champlain was here first in 1613, but didn't stay long and it took a further 200 years and the construction of the Rideau Canal before Ottawa was founded. Built between 1827 and 1831, the canal provided a waterway for British gunboats, allowing them to evade the international section of the St Lawrence, where they might be subject to American gun attacks. Queen Victoria chose Ottawa as the capital of Canada in 1857 because it was halfway between the main cities of Upper and Lower Canada—Toronto and Québec City—and therefore a neutral choice. _www.tourottawa.org_ is the official tourist site, _www.ottawakiosk.com_ is excellent for restaurants, and _www.canadascapital.gc.ca_ also has useful information.

The telephone area code is 613.

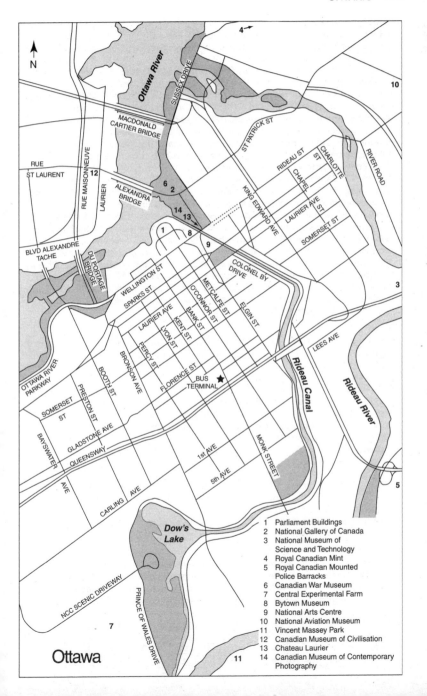

N

1   Parliament Buildings
2   National Gallery of Canada
3   National Museum of
    Science and Technology
4   Royal Canadian Mint
5   Royal Canadian Mounted
    Police Barracks
6   Canadian War Museum
7   Central Experimental Farm
8   Bytown Museum
9   National Arts Centre
10 National Aviation Museum
11 Vincent Massey Park
12 Canadian Museum of Civilisation
13 Chateau Laurier
14 Canadian Museum of Contemporary
    Photography

Ottawa

Accommodation

B&B places are abundant, except during May and early June when student groups and conventioneers arrive for summer residence. The site *www.ottawatourism.ca* has accommodation listings by type.

Ottawa B&B, 563-0161/(800) 461-7889, S-from $49, D-from $59, includes cooked bfast, shared bathroom and free parking. *www.bbcanada.com/8609.html*.

Ottawa International Hostel (HI-C), 75 Nicholas St, 235-2595. Heritage building, the former Carleton County Jail is the site of Canada's last public hanging. 'Sleep in the corridors of a former jail and take a shower in a cell.' Centrally located. Laundry, kitchen, large lounges and internet access ($1/10mins). 'Fantastic place; unique; friendly people.' On the #4 bus line. Many organised activities including biking, canoeing and tours. $22.05 members, $26.25 non-members. *www.hihostels.ca*.

University of Ottawa Residences, 90 University St, (613) 564-5400. Easy walk from downtown. Dorm rooms and shared showers. If you're passing through btw May 8 and August 25, reserve a room, known as Short Stay by contacting: *Reserve@uOttawa.ca. www.uottawa.ca/students/housing/shortstay.html*.

YWCA, 180 Argyle Ave, 237-1320. Close to bus station. 'Clean and bright.' Gym, TV, pool, kitchen with microwave. Cafeteria Mon-Sat 7am-2:30pm. S (shared bath)-$53, S (private bath)-$63, D (shared bath)-$63, Suite-$83. Weekly and group rates available. Rsvs req. Check-in 4pm, out 11am. *www.educomts.com/ymca-ywca*.

Camping: Gatineau Park, (819) 827-6055, has 3 campgrounds: **Lac Philippe Campground, Lac Taylor Campground** and **Lac la Peche**. All campgrounds are off Hwy 366 NW, Hull, within 45 mins-1 hr of Ottawa. Map available at Visitors Centre. Park has five beaches and boating facilities. Sites $25. *www.canadascapital.gc.ca/gatineau*.

Food

Ottawa claims to have more restaurants per capita than almost any other city in the country. Breakfast is cholesterol-rich here and a generous helping of eggs, potatoes, meat, toast and coffee is the norm! Good restaurants listing available on *www.ottawakiosk.com/restaur0.html*.

Byward Market, north of Rideau, 55 Byward Market Square, 562-3325. Local produce, cheese, meat, fish, fruit, clothing and arty bits and pieces; it's been here since 1826, one of Canada's oldest and largest public markets. 'Great.' 'Not to be missed.' The area around the market is good for eating places. Up to 175 stands. Daily. *www.byward-market.com*.

Father and Sons, 112 Osgoode St, 234-1173. Favoured by students, traditional tavern-style food and a variety of Lebanese specialities are served up; entrées $7-$9. Open Mon-Sat 7am-2am, Sun 8am-1am.

Theo's Greek Taverna, 911 Richmond Rd, 728-0909. Classic Greek food with a family atmosphere. Lunch $9-10; dinner entrées $14 on up. Open daily. *www.theosgreektaverna.com*.

Yesterdays, 152 Spark St Mall, 235-1424. 'An eclectic mix of everything', entrées $7-19. Open daily 11am-11pm.

Of interest

Canada Aviation Museum, Rockcliffe Airport, 11 Aviation Pkwy, 993-2010/(800) 463-2038. Offers special exhibitions in the summer and displays over 100 aircraft. Discover the role played by aeroplanes in the development of Canada. Summer: daily 9am-5pm, winter: Wed-Sun 10am-5pm. $6, $5 w/student ID. *www.aviation.nmstc.ca*.

Canadian Museum of Civilisation, 100 Laurier St, just across the river in Hull, Québec, (819) 776-7000/(800) 555-5621. This impressive museum explores the history of Canada's cultural heritage and has an IMAX Theatre. Open daily 9am-6pm, Thur 'til 9pm. $10, $6 w/student ID, half price Sun. *www.civilization.ca*.

Canadian Museum of Contemporary Photography, 1 Rideau Canal, 990-8257, for a glimpse of modern Canadian life. Summer: daily 10am-5pm, Thur 'til 8pm. $4, $3 w/ student ID, free Thur after 5pm Free. *www.cmcp.gallery.ca*.

Canadian War Museum, 330 Sussex Dr, (819) 776-8600/(800) 555-5621. Canada's military history from the early 1600s. Open daily 9:30am-5pm, Thur 'til 8pm. $10, $6 w/student ID, half price Sun, free Thur from 6-9pm and all day Canada Day (July 1st) and Nov 11th. *www.warmuseum.ca*.

Central Experimental Farm, Maple Dr, 991-3044/(866) 442-4416. Part of the Agriculture Museum, est. 1886 and HQ for the Canada Dept of Agriculture. Flowers, tropical greenhouse and animals. Great place for a picnic—beautiful site on the canal. Daily sunrise-sunset; greenhouse daily 9am-4pm. Horse-drawn wagon tours available. Exhibits $6, $5 w/ student ID, Independent visit $3. *www.agriculture.technomuses.ca/english/tour/farm.cfm*.

Parliament Hill. The Gothic-style, green copper-roofed buildings stand atop Parliament Hill overlooking the river. Completed in 1922, the three buildings replaced those destroyed by fire in 1916. Conducted tours daily every 30 mins, when Parliament is not in session, Mon-Fri 9:20am-7:20pm, weekends 9am-4:20pm; when Parliament is in session Mon-Fri 9am-12:50, 3:30-7:20, weekends 9am-4:20pm. Information 996-0896/(866) 599-4999. Free. During the summer there are son et lumière (sound and light) displays: Tue, Thur, Sat and Sun 9pm-9:30pm. When parliament is in session you can visit the House of Commons. The best view in the city is from the 302 ft-high **Peace Tower** in the square. The Tower has a carillon of 53 bells and during the summer the bells ring out hour-long concerts daily at 2pm in July/Aug, or shorter recitals at noon most weekdays Sept-June. In true Buckingham Palace tradition, the **Changing of the Guard**—complete with bearskins and red coats—takes place on Parliament Hill at 10am, weather permitting, from late June to late Aug. The flame located in front of the buildings burns eternally to represent Canada's unity. There is a white **Info Tent** by the Visitors Centre. *www.parl.gc.ca*.

National Arts Centre, Confederation Sq, 947-7000/(866) 850-ARTS. Completed in 1969, the complex includes theatres, concert halls, an opera house and an art gallery. Year round 9am-5pm, tours available. Box office: 755-1111. *www.nac-cna.ca*.

National Gallery of Canada, 380 Sussex Dr (opposite Notre Dame Basilica), 990-1985/(800) 319-2787. Canadian art of all periods in a modern glass building designed by Moshie Safdie. Worth visiting for insight into Canadian history. Summer: daily 10am-5pm, Thur 'til 8pm, winter: Wed-Sun 10am-5pm, Thur 'til 8pm. Free except for special exhibit, around $6, $5 w/student ID. 'Spectacular.' *www.national.gallery.ca*.

National Museum of Science and Technology, 1867 St Laurent Blvd, 991-3044/(866) 442-4416. 'a must for those who like to participate'. Allows visitors to explore the wonderful world of technology and transport with touchy-feely exhibits. Summer, daily 9am-5pm, winter, closed Mon. $6, $5 w/student ID. *www.science-tech.nmstc.ca*.

Rideau Canal. The 124-mile waterway that runs to Kingston on Lake Ontario. The 'Giant's Staircase', a series of 8 locks, lifts and drops boats some 80 ft between Ottawa River and Parliament Hill. In the winter the canal is turned into the world's biggest ice-skating rink and commuters skate to work! Cruises on the canal and river are available, $14 for 1 hr 15 mins, $12 w/student ID. They leave from the dock at the Conference Centre. Contact **Paul's Boat Lines**, 225-6781, *www.paulsboat-cruises.com*. You can also hire a bike at **Dows Lake**, 232-1001 and ride along the towpath. Near the locks is the **Bytown Museum**, 50 Canal Rd, 234-4570. An interesting look at old Ottawa. April-May 10am-2pm, May-Oct, Sat-Fri 10am-5pm, Sat and Sun 10am-4pm; $5, $3 w/student ID. *www.bytownmuseum.com*.

Royal Canadian Mint, 320 Sussex Dr, 993-8990/(800) 276-7714. Guided tours every half hour (rsvs req). Summer, Mon-Fri 9am-8:30pm, w/ends to 5:30pm; winter, 9am-5pm daily; $5 weekdays, $3.50 weekends. _www.mint.ca_.

Parks. There is a nice park at Somerset and Lyon and also the **Vincent Massey Park**. If you have transport, a trip to **Gatineau Park**, 5 miles beyond Hull, is worth a thought. Good swimming, cycling, hiking and fishing. 'The park gives an impression of the archetypal Canada; rugged country, timber floating down the Gatineau, etc.' **Dow's Lake Pavilion**, 101 Queen Elizabeth Dr, 232-1001, rents pedal boats, canoes and bikes. Open daily 11:30am-1am. Rentals by the hour with varying prices. _www.canadascapital.gc.ca_.

Entertainment
Read _What's On in Ottawa_, and check _www.ottawakiosk.com_ which lists events and festivals by date. For late entertainment, cross the river to **Hull** where the pubs are open longer. Ottawa has several English-style pubs. Try:

Barrymore's Music Hall, 323 Bank St (nr the Royal Oak), 233-0307, Ottawa's big venue for popular bands. _www.barrymores.on.ca_.

Byward Market, 55 Byward Market Sq, 562-3325, has cafes and nightclubs.

Elephant & Castle, 50 Rideau St, 234-5544, for fish 'n chips. Has patio overlooking the Rideau Canal. Part of chain. _www.elephantcastle.com_.

Earl of Sussex Pub, 431 Sussex Dr, 562-5544, open daily 11:30am-3am.

Festivals. Ottawa is full of festivals including Chamber Music, Dragon Boat, Fringe, Jazz, and Theatre. For a list, see _www.ottawaplus.ca/portal/feature/6024_.

Odyssey Theatre, 232-8407, hosts open-air comedy at Strathcona Park, end July-end Aug, based on the Italian Commedia dell' Arte—incorporating dance and drama. Call for tkt prices. _www.odysseytheatre.ca_.

Annual Central Canada Exhibition, 237-7222, end Aug in Lansdowne Park. Includes a fair, animals, crafts, concerts, etc, $9. _collections.ic.gc.ca/superex/english_.

Gatineau Hot Air Balloon Festival, if you are in town on Labor Day weekend in September, don't miss this festival, which launches itself from **La Baie Parc** in Gatineau and can be watched from Parliament Hill. _www.montgolfieresgatineau.com_.

Winterlude during the first 3 weekends of Feb, 239-5000, lines the Rideau Canal with ice sculptures, focusing on what it is like to be an Ottawan in winter! Free. _www.canadascapital.gc.ca/winterlude_.

Shopping
Rideau Centre, on Rideau, 5 min walk from the Arts Centre is Ottawa's primary shopping mall, 236-6565. Open Mon-Fri 9:30am-9pm, Sat 'til 6pm, Sun 11am-5pm. _www.rideaucentre.com_. Also check out **Sparks St Mall**, 230-0984, a 3-block traffic-free shopping section btwn Elgin and Bank. Fountains, sidewalk cafes, good shopping, etc. _www.ottawakiosk.com_. For Indian and Inuit stuff try Four Corners, 93 Sparks St, 233-2322, and **Snow Goose**, 83 Sparks St, 232-2213, open Mon-Fri 9:30am-5:30pm, Sat 'til 5pm. _www.snowgoose.ca_.

Internet access
Chapters, 47 Rideau St, in Byward Market, 241-0073. $2 per 20 mins.

Ottawa Public Library, 120 Metcalf St, 236-0301/580-2400, Mon-Thur 10am-8pm, Fri noon-6pm, Sat 10am-5pm. Free access. _www.library.ottawa.on.ca_.

Information
Read _Usually Reliable Source_ and _Penny Press_ for what's happening.

Capital InfoCentre, 90 Wellington St (across from Parliament Hill), 239-5000/(800) 465-1867. Open daily. Hi-tech, interactive tour planners and a 3D map of the city, as well as all the usual tourist info. _www.canadacapital.gc.ca_.

Travel
Bike One of the nicest ways to see Ottawa is by bike - an extensive system of bike-ways and routes is there to help you. Bicycles available for hire next to the Chateau

Laurier Hotel. For prices and info call **Rent-a-Bike**, 241-4140, $8/hr, $20/4hrs, $23/day. Daily 9am-6pm (credit card required). _www.cyberus.ca/~rentabike_.

OC Public Transport, 1500 St-Laurent, 741-4390 (for all bus info). Excellent system with buses congregating on either side of Rideau Centre. $2.75 basic fare, $6 all day pass. _www.octranspo.com_.

VIA Rail, 200 Tremblay Rd, (888) 842-7245. Passenger train service throughout Canada. _www.viarail.ca_. Rail station is 2 miles from city centre. To get there catch the #95 bus from the station, every 5 mins, $2.75.

Ottawa International Airport, 248-2000, (6 miles out of town). _www.ottawa-airport.com_. Bus #97 runs from outside the Rideau Centre, downtown, to the airport every 15 mins. A taxi ride, 523-1234, is around $20-$25 from downtown.

Greyhound, 265 Catherine St, 238-5900/(800) 668-4438 (ext.297). Bus terminal open 5:30am-2:30am. _www.greyhound.ca_.

MORRISBURG A small town on the St Lawrence whose main claim to fame is **Upper Canada Village,** a re-creation of a St Lawrence Valley community of the 19th century. The village is situated some 11 km east of Morrisburg on Hwy 2, in Crysler Farm Battlefield Park, 543-3704/(800) 437-2233. The park serves as a memorial to Canadians who died in the war of 1812 against the United States. The buildings here were all moved from their previous sites to save them from the path of the St Lawrence Seaway and include a tavern, mill, church, store, etc., all of which are fully operational. Vehicles are not allowed. Daily 9:30am-5pm mid May-mid Oct; $16.95, $10.50 w/student ID. _www.uppercanadavillage.com_.

KINGSTON A small, pleasant city situated at the meeting place of the St Lawrence and Lake Ontario. Early Kingston was built around the site of Fort Frontenac, then a French outpost, later to be replaced by the British Fort Henry, the principal British stronghold west of Québec. This was, ever so briefly, the capital of Canada (1841-44) and many of the distinctive limestone 19th century houses still survive.

The town is the home of **Queens University,** situated on the banks of the St Lawrence. _www.queensu.ca_. The **Kingston Fall Fair,** 542-6701, which in fact happens in late summer, is considered 'worth a stop'. Kingston is also a good centre for visiting the picturesque **Thousand Islands** in the St Lawrence. _www.tourism.kingstoncanada.com_.

Accommodation
Hilltop Motel, 2287 Princess St, 542-3846. A/C, TV. S-$32-$54, D-$69-$99. Check-in after 2pm, out 11am.

Queen's University Victoria Hall, 533-2223, has rooms May-Aug on the main campus. Rsvs pref. S-$54, D-$34 pp.. Bfast included. _www.queensu.ca/conference_.

Camping: Lake Ontario Park Campground, 542-6574, 2 miles W on King St. May-Sept. Sites for two $17, $20 w/hook-up, XP-$2.
_www.tourism.kingstoncanada.com/partners_accom.cfm?PartnerID=306_.

Rideau Acres, 546-2711, on Hwy 15 (north of exit 104/exit 623 on Hwy 401). Sites: $23 basic, $28-$31 for full service. _www.rideauacres.com_.

Food
The **Farmer's Market**, Market Sq, is open Tue, Thur & Sat from dawn-dusk.

Chez Piggy, 68 Rear Princess St (walk thru courtyard), 549-7673. Brunch dishes all under $11.25. Sun brunch served 11am-2:30pm. Rsvs recommended at w/ends.

Kingston Brewing Company, 34 Clarence St, 542-4978. The oldest brewing pub in Ontario, with true British ale served from a hand-pump. Produces own lager and Dragon's Breath Ale. Burgers, sandwiches and main courses under $10. Tours of brewery available during the week, call to arrange (free). Open daily 11am-2am.

Pilot House, 265 King St E, 542-0222. Beautifully fresh fish and chips and expensive English beer (12 kinds of draft). Daily 11:30am-11pm, bar 'til 1am.

Of interest

Bellevue House. John A. Macdonald, Canada's first Prime Minister, lived here at 35 Centre St, 545-8666. The century-old house has been restored and furnished in the style of the 1840s. Known locally as the 'Pekoe Pagoda' or 'Tea Caddy Castle' because of its comparatively frivolous appearance in contrast to the more solid limestone buildings of the city. The house is open daily in the summer 9am-6pm; call for winter hrs. $4. *www.pc.gc.ca/lhn-nhs/on/bellevue/index_e.asp*.

Fort Frederick, Royal Military College Museum, 541-6000. On RMS grounds (½ mile E of Hwy 2). Canada's West Point, founded in 1876. The museum, in a Martello Tower, features pictures and exhibits of old Kingston and Military College history and the Douglas collection of historic weapons. Open June-Labor Day, daily 10am-5pm. Free. *www.rmc.ca/other/museum/history_e.html#fort*.

Murney Tower Museum, Barrie St, 544-9925. Martello Tower used to serve as military housing, is now run by the Kingston Historical Society. Daily 10am-5pm, mid May-Labor Day. $3. *www.heritagekingston.org/murney.html*.

Old Fort Henry, E on Hwy 2 at junction Hwy 15. The fort has been restored and during the summer college students dressed in Victorian army uniforms give displays of drilling. Daily 10am-5pm, May 22-Sept 5, $11.25, Sept 6-25, $9.25. The fort is also a military museum. For info call 542-7388. *www.forthenry.com*.

Marine Museum of the Great Lakes, 55 Ontario St, 542-2261. 5 galleries with exhibits on Great Lakes history, local history and underwater archaeology. Also visit the coastguard ship. Open daily 10am-5pm. $5.25, $4.75 w/student ID. *www.marmus.ca*.

North of the city the **Rideau Lakes** extend for miles and miles. The **Rideau Hiking Trail** winds its way gently among them. You can take a free ferry to **Wolfe Island** in the St Lawrence. Ferries leave from City Hall. Once on the island it is possible to catch another boat ($3) to the US. *www.wolfeisland.com*.

Thousand Islands Boat Tours, 549-5544/(800) 848-0011. Departing from Crawford Dock at the foot of Brock St in downtown Kingston, there are additional tours of the harbour and Thousand Islands: $18.25-$42.20, lunch cruise (daily at 12:30pm), 3 hrs 15 min: $44. *www.ktic.ca*.

Gananoque Boat Tours. From Gananoque Quay, 20 miles from Kingston on Hwy 2, 382-2144. Trip lasts 3 hrs: $22, 1 hr: $15. Tours run mid May-mid Oct, July/Aug hrs: 3 hr tours, every 1½ hrs 9am-4:30pm, 1 hr tour: every 1½ hrs 10:30am-4:30pm. *www.ganboatline.com*.

Entertainment/Sport

Stages Niteclub, 390 Princess St, 547-3657. Bands and disco. Open Mon-Sat 9pm-2:30am. Also contact the Brass Pub for tickets. *www.stages.on.ca*.

Canadian Olympic-training Regatta Kingston (CORK). Annual event, held during the last/second-to-last week in Aug; one of the largest regattas in North America. Call 545-1322 for exact dates, or check *www.cork.org*.

Internet access / Information

Kingston Frontenac Public Library, 130 Johnson St, 549-8888. Free, 1 hr time limit. Open Mon-Thur 9am-9pm, Fri/Sat 9am-5pm and in winter only Sun 1pm-5pm.

Tourist Information Office, 209 Ontario St, 548-4415. Summer: daily 9am-8pm, otherwise 9am-5pm, Sun 10am-4pm. *tourism.kingstoncanada.com*,

John Deutsch University Centre Union, University St. Ride board, shops, post office, laundry, etc. *www.queensu.ca/jduc/const.html*.

Travel
VIA Rail Station, 800 Counter St, (888) 842-7245. *www.viarail.ca*. Take #4 bus.
Bus Terminal, 175 Counter St, 547-4916. Daily 6:30am-9pm. Take #2 bus.

ST LAWRENCE ISLANDS NATIONAL PARK The park is made up of 21 islands in the Thousand Islands area of the St Lawrence, between Kingston and Brockville and Mallorytown Landing on the mainland. The islands can be reached only by water taxi from Gananoque, Mallorytown Landing and Rockport, Ontario, or from Alexandria Bay and Clayton in New York State. The park is open daily, mid-May to mid-Oct. Free.

It's a peaceful, green-forested area, noted chiefly for its good fishing grounds. Camping facilities are available on the islands, $14. The **Visitors Centre** is located at 2 County Rd 5, **Mallorytown,** (613) 923-5261/(800) 839-8221. *www.pc.gc.ca/pn-np/on/lawren/index_E.asp*.

TORONTO In the past, they may have called it 'Toronto the Good' for its air of Victorian morals and prudishness, but today, Toronto is one of North America's liveliest and the most American of Canadian cities, with many of the characteristics of the metropolitan US but without the problems. It's a place of superlatives: the world's tallest building and longest street are here (Yonge Street at 1,896 km); Canada's major national newspaper, the *Globe & Mail*, is based here, with editions in each of Canada's regions; Canada's largest stock market and financial centre are here. And it's also **Silicon Valley North** with the Canadian HQs and research centres here of Apple, Hewlett-Packard and Sun Microsystems, among others.

Toronto is a cosmopolitan city, sprawling over 270 square miles, with many fine examples of skyscraper architecture, good shopping areas, excellent theatre, music and arts facilities (a new opera house is under construction on Richmond Street), a vibrant nightlife and fast highways. Yet it's a clean city, with markedly few poor areas, and the streets are fairly safe at night. *www.city.toronto.on.ca*.

Nearly half of Toronto's population was born somewhere else (the Caribbean, China and India to name just a few), about 20 percent of them arriving since 1990. Over a hundred ethnic groups are represented here, and there are 79 ethnic publications. Named for a Mohawk word meaning 'meeting place', Toronto today is a true meeting of cultures, languages and lifestyles. The annual **Caribana festival**, for example, held at the end of July, rivals London's Notting Hill festival in its offerings of West Indian music, food and ambiance. The city is home to one of North America's largest **Gay Pride** parades in June.

The city is laid out, for the most part, in an easy-to-navigate grid, with a good subway (underground) system, lots of buses, and streetcars along the major east-west streets: King, Queen, Dundas and College. It's very much a city of neighborhoods – **Chinatown**, **Greektown**, **Yorkville**, **Kensington Market** – each with its own distinctive character and, of course, dizzying choice of places to eat. For those who prefer the water to city streets, there's always a walk along the boardwalk at the **Toronto Beaches**, or a short ferry ride to **The Islands**.

Toronto is a great city for shopping and eating – the vast 27 km network

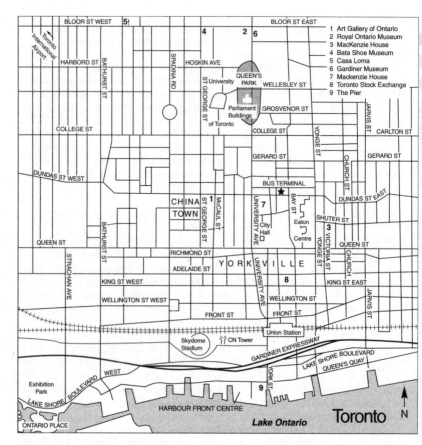

1 Art Gallery of Ontario
2 Royal Ontario Museum
3 MacKenzie House
4 Bata Shoe Museum
5 Casa Loma
6 Gardiner Museum
7 Mackenzie House
8 Toronto Stock Exchange
9 The Pier

Toronto N

of underground concourses linking all the major office buildings and hotels, designed to facilitate intracity walking during the cold winter months, is lined with 1,200 shops and food courts. According to the *Guinness Book of Records*, this network, called the PATH, is the world's largest underground shopping complex.

It's also worth taking a look at the windows of the **Royal Bank Building**. The golden glow emanating from them is real gold dust, mixed with the glass, proof of how rich Canada is and that most of the wealth and power, the envy of the other provinces, is situated right there on **Bay Street**. The corner of **King** and **Bay** is the financial hub of Toronto.

Toronto is also a starting point from which to visit other places in Ontario. **Niagara Falls** and **New York State** are 1½ hrs away down the Queen Elizabeth Way (QEW), to the north there is **Georgian Bay** and the vast **Algonquin Provincial Park**, while to the west there are **London** and **Stratford**. *www.torontotourism.com* and *www.toronto.com*.

The telephone area code is 416.

Accommodation

Canadiana Guest House and Backpackers, 42 Widmer St, 598-9090/(877) 215-1225. Dorms: for 4 people $25 ($27 in winter) w/student ID, otherwise $25; for 6-8 people $24 w/student ID, otherwise $26. Private rooms: S-$50-$60, D-$65-$70. A/C, kitchen, TV lounge, internet access. 'Good value.' *www.canadianalodging.com*.

Global Village Backpackers Hostel, 460 King St W, 703-8540, rsvs: (888) 844-7875. Dorms $25.99. Bar, laundry, kitchen, internet access. Discount for BUNAC members (to $24). Also in Vancouver and Banff. *www.globalbackpackers.com*.

Marigold International Travellers Hostel, 2011 Dundas St W, 536-8824. TV room, free morning coffee and donuts, free parking. $25 inc. tax. Mixed reports. 'No frills!' Check-in anytime, out 2pm.

Neill-Wycik College Hotel, 96 Gerrard St E, (800) 268-4358. Good facilities, baggage storage, central, 5 mins from subway. No A/C in rooms but A/C in lounges and TV room. Sauna and laundry. S-$42 inc. tax, D-$63. 20% student discount. 'Recommended.' May-Aug only. Airport shuttle. 'High rise hospitality.' *www.neill-wycik.com*.

HI-Toronto Hostel, 76 Church St S, 971-4440/(877) 848-8737. Ensuite bathrooms, private rooms available. 170 beds. Centrally located, a few minutes from the Eaton Centre. Rsvs essential in summer. Dorms $25 inc tax members, $29.28 non-members. Kitchen, laundry, internet access ($1/15 min), rooftop deck. 'Clean and friendly.' *www.hihostels.ca/toronto*.

University of Toronto, Scarborough Campus, 1263 Military Trail, 287-7367. 'Fantastic student residence.' $131 weekly (min 2 week stay). Mid May-mid Aug. 'Parties, sports facilities.' 'Basic uni accommodation, have to clean own rooms.' 'Full of other travellers/BUNACers in summer.' 30 mins from downtown. *www.utsc.utoronto.ca/residences*. For shorter stays the Uni Conference Services, 287-7369, can arrange group housing and have townhouses to sleep four (call for rates). For complete list of all summer residences, check "Summer Housing" at *http://link.library.utoronto.ca/studenthousing*. **University of Toronto Housing Service**, 214 College St, 978-8045. Has list of off-campus accommodation available and a contact sheet for student residences.

Camping: Indian Line Tourist Campground, 7625 Finch Ave W, (905) 678-1233/off-season 661-6600 ext. 203. This is the closest area to metropolitan Toronto. Sites $23 - $32 w/full hook-up. Showers, laundry. May-early Dec. Rsvs recommended July-Aug. *www.trcacamping.ca*.

Food

There are over 7,000 restaurants squeezed into this city! Favorite areas include **Bloor St W, Chinatown, Queen St** and **Village by the Grange**, the latter being home of super-cheap restaurants and vendors.

City View Café, located on the 8th floor of the historic Hudson's Bay Company department store (known as 'The Bay') at 176 Yonge Street, offers cafeteria-style meals for under $10, along with a great view of the city. Open Mon-Fri 10am-8 pm, Sat 9am-5pm and Sun 12 noon-5pm. The Yonge Street store also has two other restaurants, including **The Arcadian Court Restaurant**, offering a lunch buffet, and the pricier **Great Cooks on Eight** (closed on Sundays).

Elephant & Castle, on the corner of King and Simcoe. If you're feeling homesick, in addition to a wide variety of beers, this pub/restaurant will tempt you with steak and kidney or shepherd's pie or bangers and mash, all for under $10.

Fran's Restaurant, 20 College St, 923-9867. Breakfast. Spaghetti, fish and chips, burgers, etc. Entrées under $12. Open 24 hrs.

Java Joe's has 13 locations in Ontario inc. 70 Gerrard St W, 180 Dundas St W, and 310 Front St, 599-5282. Serves up bfast of bagel and coffee/tea. Sandwiches, wraps. Lunch specials for $6.50. 'Good value, pleasant surroundings.' Open Mon-Fri 7am-5pm. *www.javajoes.ca*.

Le Commensal, 655 Bay Street (entrance on Elm) serves fine vegetarian soups, salads, hot entrées and desserts, which you pay for by the pound. If you choose well you can eat well for under $10. There are other Commensals in Montreal, Quebec, Greenfield Park, Laval and Quebec. _www.toronto.com/lecommensal_.

Lick's Homeburgers and Ice Cream, 362-LICK, call for various locations (25 in total). For the messiest, yummiest burgers around in a fun atmosphere. Burgers from $4.49. _www.lickshomeburgers.com_.

Midtown Café, 552 College St W, 920-4533. Play pool or eat whilst listening to music. Large tapas menu, entrées $9-$11. Open Mon-Thur 5pm-3am, Fri-Sun 3pm-3am.

Sneaky Dees, 431 College St, 603-3090. Serves a bargain bfast for $4.95 (all day). Doubles as a night-time hot spot. 'Tuesday night half-price fajitas cannot go unmentioned!' Bottled beers are $2.50 on Wednesdays. Open Mon-Tues 11am-3am, We-Thu 11am-4am, Fri-Sat 9am-4:30am, Sun 9am-3am.

Toby's Goodeats, locations across the city (including Yonge & Bloor, Bloor & Bay, the Eaton Centre, Yonge & St Clair). Toby's serves up some of the best-value meals in the city for under $10.

The Whistling Oyster, 11 Duncan Street, has 'Dimsum Hours', 'Happy Oyster Hours' and 'Happy Little Pasta Hours' from 3 to 6pm and then 9 to 11pm Tues-Sat (til 12 am Thur to Sat), 12 noon to 11 pm on Mondays, and 3:30–11pm on Sundays, with prices ranging from $4.59 to $8.99.

Neighbourhoods

Among the many interesting neighbourhoods in the city are: **Chinatown** – although there are several smaller Chinatowns now, as the Chinese population continues to grow, for the main one follow Dundas Street E of University, just past the Art Gallery. Suddenly the street signs and storefronts are in Chinese. In addition to the Chinese restaurants, (and a smattering of Vietnamese), where you can eat for about $10-$15, you'll find traditional Chinese herb and medicine shops and street markets offering all sorts of exotic Oriental fruits (including the infamous durian), vegetables and spices. The **Chinese Gospel Church of Toronto**, at Dundas and Huron, holds Sunday services in English, Mandarin and Cantonese.

Distillery Historic District: on Mill St, once the heart of the Hiram Walker empire, this area of abandoned distilleries has been filled with top-class galleries, restaurants and shops. The easiest way to get there is to take the 504 King streetcar, get off at King and Parliament and walk two blocks S on Parliament.

The Docks, 11 Polson St, 461-3625. Restaurants, bars, clubs and golf! Strangely enough, all down by the waterfront. On the #510 streetcar route or take the 72A from Union Station. _www.thedocks.com_.

Front Street, along Lake Ontario just south of King, is home to **Union Station** as well as the **Royal York Hotel**, just across from it. The hotel, one of the Canadian Pacific Railway 'castles', opened in 1929 as the largest hotel and tallest building in the Commonwealth. Queen Elizabeth II stays here. The grandeur of this amazing place, which once had a 12-bed hospital, a 12,000-volume library and a concert hall that featured a mammoth pipe organ weighing 50 tons, is well worth a walk through the lobby and boutique halls. _www.fairmont.com/royalyork/_.

Greektown. Settled by Greek immigrants in the 1950s, this stretch of Danforth Ave (known to locals as simply **The Danforth**), with the largest Greek neighbourhood in North America, is the place to go for Greek food, buy a Greek newspaper or music, or hear Greek spoken in the street. Take the subway to Broadview or Chester and walk east. _www.greektowntoronto.com_.

Harbourfront, 235 Queen's Quay W, 973-4000 infoline. 92 acres of restaurants, antique markets, art shows, films, theatre, etc. on Lake Ontario. Free w/end concerts. Great place to spend a sunny summer afternoon, or free ice-skating in the winter (charge for skate rental). 'Amazing view of the city skyline'.

Kensington Market. From Chinatown, continue west along Dundas to Kensington Ave – a throwback to the sixties, with hippie-style 'vintage' clothing shops, and people to match – and turn right until you reach **Baldwin Street**, with its cheap restaurants and small markets, selling everything from food and veg to nuts and spices. Originally a Jewish neighbourhood, today West Indian music blares out of the shops, and the butchers are more likely to sell fresh goat for currying than kosher beef. **Reg**, at 200 Baldwin, will grind fresh peanut butter for you, as well as sell you dried fruits and Turkish delight. **Chocolate Addict**, at number 185, speaks for itself. There's even a 60's-style headshop (motto: 'Serving potheads since… I don't know when'), **Roach-a-Rama**, at 191A. The choices at **Global Cheese** (76 Kensington), would put a French fromager to shame.

King Street, west of John, is young, vibrant and trendy. It's also lined with restaurants and pubs in all price ranges. Check out **Fred's Not Here**, at 321 King, or its sister restaurant next door, the **Red Tomato**, where you can get a 2-course lunch for $10.99. **Hey Lucy**, at 295 King, has a rooftop patio open during the summer months. **Dhaba Indian Excellence**, 309 King, has an all-you-can-eat lunch, $10.95.

Nathan Philips Square, in front of City Hall, is host to a multitude of cultural events throughout the year, especially in summer – from weekend ethnic food and music festivals to Toronto's famous **Jazz Festival** (*www.tojazz.com*) in early summer. It's also the place to be if you find yourself in Toronto for New Year's Eve. The reflecting pool in the square becomes a skating rink in winter and is also home to various special events. Call the Events Hotline, 392-0458.

Ontario Place, 995 Lakeshore Blvd (on the lakefront), 314-9900/(866) ONE-4-FUN. A complex of manmade islands and lagoons, with marina and attractive parkland. Films at **Cinesphere** on what was once the 'largest screen in the world'; multimedia presentations of Ontario are shown in several unusual pavilions. Get lost in the **Megamaze** and lots of water-based activities. Fairly cheap food available in several different eating places. Well recommended by previous visitors. Open daily 'til 8pm in the summer, 5pm in winter. All day pass $32 includes rides, films, etc; grounds only $10—pay for activities as you go ($6 each). Take #511 Bathurst streetcar or #121 Front Esplanade bus from Union Station. Also served by GO Transit rail. *www.ontarioplace.com*. Opposite is the **Canadian National Exhibition**, 393-6000, *www.theex.com*. Otherwise known as CNE or 'The Ex', held annually next to Ontario Place during the 18 days before Labor Day and including Labor Day Mon. Admission around $10. Free admission to Ontario Place from the CNE during this time. A sort of glorified state fair, Canadian style and one of the largest annual exhibitions in the world.

St Lawrence Market, 95 Front St E, 392-7120, with its sidewalk cafes and restaurants. There are over 50 foodstalls in this historic 1844 building, Toronto's first city hall. Tue and Thur 8am-6pm, Fri 'til 7pm, Sat 5am-5pm. *www.stlawrencemarket.com*.

Westclair Italian Village (Little Italy) along St Clair Ave W btwn Dufferin and Lansdown, for fresh produce and a wide variety of food.

Yorkville North of Queens Park, east of Avenue Rd. Since this is where most of the **Toronto International Film Festival** action takes place, with an enormous new Cineplex, alongside the trendy restaurants, boutiques and galleries. Just around the corner from the intersection of Bloor and Yonge streets, it doesn't get much more chic in Toronto than this formerly run-down area. 'Lively, open 'til about 1am on Sat night—street theatre, music, etc.'

Of interest

Art Gallery of Ontario, 317 Dundas St W at McCaul, 977-0414. Rembrandt, Picasso, Impressionists, largest collection of Henry Moore sculptures in the world, plus Oldenburg's 'Hamburger' and collections by Canadian artists. 'Don't miss the Art Gallery shop!' Open Wed- Fri 10am-9pm, Sat & Sun 10:30am-5:30pm. Due to the construction currently going on at the AGO, some exhibits may be closed.

Admission has been reduced to $8 adults, $5 w/student ID, (free Wed eves 6pm-9pm) for the duration. *www.ago.net*.

Bata Shoe Museum, 327 Bloor St W, 979-7799. The only shoe museum in North America, with a collection of over 12,000 pairs from Elton's platforms to ancient Egyptian sandals. Open Tue, Wed, Fri and Sat 10am-pm, Thur 'til 8pm, Sun noon-5pm. Also open Mon in the summer 10am-5pm. $8, $6 w/student ID. *www.batashoemuseum.ca*.

Casa Loma, 1 Austin Terrace (Davenport at Spadina), 923-1171. An eccentric chateau-style mansion built by the late Sir Henry Pellatt between 1911 and 1914 at a reported cost of $3m. It was restored in 1967 and the proceeds from the daily tours go to charity. 'Fantastic.' Daily 9:30am-5pm, year round. $12. *www.casaloma.org*.

City Hall, 100 Queen St W at Bay St, 338-0338. The $30m creation of Finnish architect Viljo Revell, perhaps most impressive when lit at night. Brochure available for self-guided tour, Mon-Fri 8:30am-4:30pm.

CN Tower, 301 Front St, 360-8500. At 1,815 ft is the world's tallest building and one section has a glass floor you can walk across and look all the way down below! The Observation Deck is open in summer 9am-11pm. The 56-second elevator ride to the Observation Deck costs $25.99 inclusive to go to the Sky Pod. Classy 360 (revolving) restaurant and plenty of other eateries, tourist shops and simulator rides, as you would expect from one of Canada's premier tourist attractions. If you dine in the 360 Restaurant you don't pay for the elevator ride. 'Expect queues!' 'Great views over the city and up to 120 km away.' *www.cntower.ca*.

Gardiner Museum of Ceramic Art, 111 Queen's Park, 586-8080. The only museum of its kind in North America, with a vast collection of pottery and porcelain. Open Mon, Wed & Fri 10am-6pm, Tue & Thur 'til 8pm, Sat & Sun 'til 5pm. $10, $6 w/student ID. Free 1st Tue of the month. In early 2006, was undergoing an extensive renovation. *www.gardinermuseum.on.ca*.

Metro Toronto Zoo, off junction Hwy 401 and Meadowvale Rd, 392-5901. Featuring a 'gorilla rainforest' and polar bears. Year round daily from 9am; closing time varies with season, 6:30pm in the summer. $19. Take bus #86A from Kennedy Subway station. *www.torontozoo.com*.

Old Fort York, 392-6907. The birthplace of Toronto - on Garrison Rd, the Fort was built in 1793 and was the site of the 1812 Battle of York, when American forces attacked British defenders. In retaliation British forces later burnt down the White House in Washington DC. The fort now houses restored army quarters and a collection of antique weapons, tools, etc. Guided tours and demonstrations. In summer daily 10am-5pm, winter 'til 4pm. $6. *www.fortyork.ca*.

Ontario Science Centre, 770 Don Mills Rd and Eglinton Ave E, 696-1000/(888) 696-1110. A do-it-yourself-place that is 'part-museum, part fun fair'. 'Breathtaking.' 'An absolute must.' 'Definitely worth going to.' Open daily 10am-5pm. $14, $23 w/OMNIMAX film. *www.osc.ca*. Take Yonge Subway to Eglinton, then Eglinton East bus to Don Mills Rd.

Royal Ontario Museum, 100 Queen's Park, 586-8000. Has the largest Chinese art collection outside China and a fine natural history section. Sun-Sat 10am-6pm, Fri 'til 9:30pm, $15, $12 w/student ID. Free for last hr or after 4:30pm on Fri.

Sky Dome, 1 Blue Jays Way, 341-3034/341-3663. Located at the corner of Front & John Sts, this impressive structure boasts the world's first fully-retractable roof, which opens or closes in 20 mins and covers 8 acres. In 1992 Sky Dome set the World Record for the greatest number of inflated hot air balloons in an enclosed area – 46 in total! There are 7 bars and restaurants and you can catch a football or baseball game here starring Toronto's Argonauts, *www.argonauts.ca*, or the much-loved Blue Jays, (888) OK-GO-JAY, *www.bluejays.com*. Tours available, $12.50. If the roof is open, you can get a great view of a game from the top of the CN Tower. *www.rogerscentre.com*.

Toronto Stock Exchange, The Exchange Tower, 130 King St W, 947-4676. TSX Broadcast & Conference Centre has interactive exhibits, be a broker for a day! Free. Mon-Fri 10am-5pm. *www.tse.com*.

Parks. The best of the city's 1,500 parks and open spaces are **High Park** (free swimming), **Edwards Gardens, Don Mills, Forest Hill** and **Rosedale**. On a nice day you can take a day trip to the **Toronto Islands**, a four-mile long harbor paradise. Centre Island is the biggest and most visited. The car-free islands can be explored on foot or bike via the bridges. Call 392-1111 for more info, or visit *www.toronto.ca/parks/parks_gardens.htm*. The ferry ride to **Centre Island** in the harbour costs $6 rtn/$3.50 w/student ID, 203-0405, *www.centreisland.ca*. **Toronto Island Park**, a 15-minute ferry ride from the mainland, has a clothing-optional beach on its southern shore. Or take a stroll along the boardwalk in **The Beaches**, south of Queen St E, east from Woodbine. Nearby **Queen Street** is lined with funky restaurants, bars and shops of all kinds.

Festivals. Toronto has over a thousand festivals a year. **Toronto International Dragon Boat Race Festival**, 595-0313, held over 2 days in mid-June. Celebration includes traditional performances, foods and free outdoor lunchtime concerts. *www.dragonboats.com*. **Toronto International Film Festival**, early Sept, tkts available at the Festival Box Office, College Park, 444 Yonge St. Call 968-3456. *www.bell.ca/filmfest*. **Jazz Festival** (*www.tojazz.com*) in early summer.

Entertainment

Check the *Globe and Mail* and *Toronto Star* for daily entertainment listings, as well as the free weekly guides NOW and EYE. Also look for Key to *Toronto*, monthly. For free tkts to CBC TV shows and info on tours, call 205-3311, Mon-Fri 9am-5pm.

Carleton Cinemas, 20 Carleton St, 598-2309. Shows art and independent films. *www.cineplex.com*. There are many bars situated along Queen St W, some of which feature nightly live entertainment. Check out especially the **Rivoli**, 334 Queen St W, 596-1908, *www.rivoli.ca*. Also, **Lee's Palace**, 529 Bloor St W, just east of Bathurst for bands, 532-1598, and the **El Mocambo** at 464 Spadina Ave, 968-2001.

The Big Bop, 651 Queen St W, 504-6699. A multi-storey dance club with bands and different styles of music on each floor and a sofa-lounge upstairs, air-hockey tables/pool tables. Popular with students. Wed-Sat 8pm-3am. Cover $5-$10. Must be 19 or over. *www.thebigbop.com*.

Molson Indy, at the **Canadian National Exhibition**, 872-4639 for tkts. General admission 3-day pass: $59.50, seating: from $70 for 3 days. It varies every year, but is usually during July. *www.molsonindy.com*.

Hummingbird Centre, 1 Front St E, 393-7469. Opera, ballet, concerts, jazz and drama. Student rush seats available on night of performance. *www.hummingbirdcentre.com*.

St Lawrence Centre for the Arts, 27 Front St E, 366-1656. Drama, dance, opera, classical/contemporary music and musicals. *www.stlc.com*.

Yuk Yuk's, 224 Richmond St W, 967-6425. Offers a night of amateur stand-up comedians. Dinner available. Features excellent nightly shows. 'Canadian humour at its best.' Cover: $2 on Tue, $10-$17 rest of week. *www.yukyuks.com*.

Shopping

Queen St, west of University Ave, is renowned as the alternative student shopping area. 'Vibrant.' Also check out: **Eaton Centre Shopping Mall**, Yonge and Dundas, 598-8700. An impressive multi-levelled, glass-domed complex of stores, eating places and entertainment. 'Definitely worth a visit.' Open Mon-Fri 10am-9pm, Sat 9:30am-7pm, Sun noon-6pm. *www.torontoeatoncentre.com*.

Sam the Record Man, 347 Yonge and Dundas, 646-2775. Canada's largest music and store. Open Mon-Thur 9am-10pm, Fri-Sat 'til midnight, Sun 11am-7pm. *www.samscd.com*.

World's Biggest Bookstore, 20 Edward St at Yonge (1 block from the Eaton Centre),

977-7009. 17 miles of shelves with over 1 million books. Open daily 9am-10pm, Sun 11am-8pm. One of the Chapters chain. *www.indigo.ca*.

Internet access

The Cyberways Internet Café, 2340 Dundas St W, 539-9393. $2/15 mins, $5/one hr. Open daily 11am-10pm.

City Hall, Nathan Phillips Sq public libraries at, 100 Queen St W, 395-7390, or at 2161 Queen St E, 393-7703. You can book computer time at any of the city's 98 libraries, but you'll need a valid library card; book up to three days ahead. Sessions limited to two 30 mins a day. *www.tpl.toronto.on.ca*.

Information

Post Office at Front and Bay Sts. There is also a post office in **The Atrium**, a shopping mall on Bay Street.

Tourism Toronto, 207 Queen's Quay W, Harbourfront Centre, 203-2600/(800) 363-1990. More convenient office in the **Eaton Centre** on the lower floor. 2nd Kiosk at City Hall in the summer. Watch out for the roving visitor information van as well. Mon-Fri 8:30am-5pm, Sat 9am-6pm, Sun 10am-6pm. *www.torontotourism.com*.

Travel

Walking & Hiking. Toronto has a system of self guided, signed **Discovery Walks** that link city ravines, parks, gardens, beaches and neighbourhoods. *www.toronto.ca/parks/recreation facilities/discovery walks/discover index.htm*.

Biking. Toronto has lots of bikeways and a **Bicycle Plan** that aims to have about 1,000 kms of bikeways by 2011 including 495 kms of bike lanes, 249 kms of off-road paths, and 260 kms of signed routes. Currently the city has about 170 kms of bikeways throughout the city. For a free bikeway map, go to *www.toronto.ca/cycling*

Brown's Sport and Cycle Shop, 2447 Bloor St W, 763-4176. $24/day, $49.80 w/end, $99.80 weekly, $189 monthly, $500 deposit or credit card details! Mon-Wed 9:30am-6pm, Thur-Fri 'til 8pm, Sat 'til 5:30pm, Sun noon-4pm. *www.brownssports.com*.

Travel CUTS student travel office, 187 College St, 979-2406. Open Mon, Tue, Thur & Fri 9am-5pm, Wed 'til 7pm, Sat 10am-4pm. Smaller office at 74 Gerrard St E, 977-0441, open Mon-Fri 9am-6pm. *www.travelcuts.com*.

Local Transit Toronto Transit Commission (TTC) bus and subway, 393-4636. Subways, buses and "red rocket" streetcars form an integrated transport system. A single fare ($2.25) takes you anywhere in the city on a one way trip, and transfers between subway, streetcar and bus are free. Obtain the transfer when you pay your fare. On buses and streetcars, exact change is required. TTC day passes are also available. It's cheaper to buy tokens: five are $9.50, 10 tokens $19, monthly pass $98.75. Exact fare required for buses and streetcars. Day pass $7.75. Bus drivers do not give change. Some routes have night buses/streetcars that run from 1am-5:30am. Route maps available from ticket booths. *www.ttc.ca*.

Bus: Greyhound, 610 Bay St. Call 594-1010/(800) 661-8747 for info. Open 5am-1am daily, but call to check hours. *www.greyhound.ca*.

Magic Bus Tours, 16 Roncesvalles Ave, 516-7433. The cheap alternative!, 'Fun and psychedelic'...10-hr day trip to Niagara Falls leaves at 9am, 9:30am from 460 King St W. $40. Winery Tour day trip, $67+ exc taxes. *www.magicbuscompany.com*.

Ferries: Toronto Island Ferry, 392-8193. From mainland ferry dock, Harbourfront, at foot of Bay Street and Queens Quay, to Toronto Island Park: Hanlan's Point, Centre Island and Wards Island. Every 15/30 mins. $6 o/w, $3.50 w/student ID. *www.toronto.ca/parks/island*.

CAT: Toronto-Rochester. Toronto Terminal - 8 Unwin Ave, 462-2100/462-2103/ (877) 283-7327. New, Australian-built high-speed ferry across Lake Ontario to Rochester, NY, can reach up to 50 mph. Operated by Bay Ferries. Two sailings daily (exc Tues) in summer. $32 o/w summer, $29 rest of year. Res recommended. Passport required. *www.catfastferry.com*.

Rail: GO Trains, 869-3200, commuter trains and buses to Oshawa, Hamilton, etc. -

Ontario's inter-regional service. GO Trains and buses depart from Union Station. *www.gotransit.com*.

VIA Rail Canada, 65 Front St W, (888) 842-7245. From here you can catch trains to Vancouver three times a week (the Canadian), to Niagara Falls (1 hr 50 mins. Same day return $42.80 inc tax w/student ID), to Ottawa, Montreal, Sarnia, Windsor, and Sudbury/White River (Lake Superior). *www.viarail.ca*.

Car/Taxi: Toronto Driveaway Service, 5803 Yonge St, Suite #101, 225-7754/(800) 561-2658. Open Mon-Fri 9am-5pm, Sat 10am-1pm. *www.torontodriveaway.com*. Taxi fares are standard, metered and non-negotiable.

Air: Toronto, Pearson Airport (YYZ), (866) 207-1690, Canada's busiest airport. NB. The international terminal is long, and distant from the domestic terminals by shuttle bus. *www.gtaa.com*. Airport is 27 kms from downtown. City buses: the **192 Airport Rocket** route provides all-day service between Kipling Station on the Bloor-Danforth Subway and Terminal 3 (Departures), Terminal 2 (Arrivals) and Terminal 1. $2.25. **Airport Express Pacific Western** (905) 564-6333/ (800) 387-6787, buses between airport and downtown every 25 min and 55 min past the hr, from 4:55am-12:55am. $15.50 o/w, 10% student discount. *www.torontoairportexpress.com*. The **GO Transit** bus stop is at Terminal 2 Arrivals (post 20), and at Terminal 1 (column S2).

The Last Minute Club, 1300 Don Mills Rd, 441-2582. 'Best place to get really cheap flights.' Mon-Fri 8am-8pm, Sat/Sun 10am-4pm. $40 membership. *www.lastminute-club.com*.

HAMILTON Situated on the shores of Lake Ontario, roughly midway between Toronto and Niagara Falls, Hamilton was once Canada's King of Steel. The city is home to two of the principal steel companies in the nation, Stelco and Dofasco and like its US counterpart, Pittsburgh, is in the throes of an urban cleanup and renewal in the wake of the steel giants. The air and water are cleaner here these days and many new and interesting buildings have gone up around town. Hamilton is working hard to improve its image.

The city is also blessed with one of the largest landlocked harbours on the Great Lakes, as a result handling the third largest water tonnage in the country. Although primarily a shipping and industrial centre, Hamilton does offer a variety of non-steel related activities to the visitor. It is also within easy reach of Niagara, Brantford, Stratford and London. *www.myhamilton.ca*, *www.hamilton.ca* and *www.hamiltonundiscovered.com*.

The area code is 905.

Accommodation

McMaster University, 1280 Main St W, Sterling St entrance, 525-9140, 24 hr service desk. Shared bath, common room, kitchen facilities, access to indoor pool. From S-$52.64, Suite-$179.20 /night, weekly rates work out at $35.84/night and monthly $21.50. May-Aug only. *housing.mcmaster.ca/confs/sumguestrates.htm*.

Pines Motel, 395 Centennial Pkwy, 561-5652. Close to Confederation Park. S-$64 exc tax, D-$68. Check-in up to noon, out 11am.

YMCA, 79 James St S, 529-7102. S-$42 plus $20 key deposit, $95/week, $360/month. *www.ymcahb.on.ca*

YWCA, 75 MacNab St S, 522-9922. S-$27, $106/week. 'Reservations a good idea.' *www.ywcahamilton.org*.

Food

Barangas, 380 Van Wagner's Beach Rd, 544-7122. Food with an international flavour, dishes $9-$18. Open daily. *www.barangas.com*.

Black Forest Inn, 255 King St E, 528-3538. A festive atmosphere for good budget dining. Sandwiches $6-9 exc tax. Sample all kinds of schnitzels and sausages, all served with home fries and sauerkraut. Try the Black Forest cake for dessert. Main courses $9-$153. Closed Mons. *www.blackforestinn.ca*.

Farmers Market, Jackson Sq, 546-2096. The largest such market in Canada, founded in 1837. Tue & Thur 7am-6pm, Fri 8am-6pm, Sat 6am-6pm.

The Winking Judge, 25 Augusta St, 524-5626. Convivial crowd esp. at lunchtime and w/ends. 22 local microbeers on tap. Live, acoustic music, Tue, Fri & Sat. Pub fare items $8. Open daily. *www.winkingjudge.com*.

Of interest

African Lion Safari and Game Farm, W off Hwy 8, S of Cambridge, (519) 623-2620/(800) 461-9453. 1,500 exotic animals roam this drive-through wildlife park, inc. the white tiger. 'Look deep into the icy blue eyes of these rare large cats!' Open May-June: Mon-Fri 10am-4pm, Sat-Sun 'til 5pm, Jul-Aug: 10am-5:30pm daily, Sept-Oct 10am-4pm daily. Admission April 30-June 24 and Sept 6-Oct 10, $20.95, June 25-Sept 5, $24.95. *www.lionsafari.com*.

The Bruce Trail extends more than 700 km along the Niagara escarpment. Good for hiking, pleasant walks. 'Gorgeous.'

Canadian Football Hall of Fame, 58 Jackson St W, within City Hall Plaza area, 528-7566. Push button exhibits. Tue-Sat 9:30am-4:30pm. $3, $1.50 w/student ID. *www.footballhof.com*.

Canadian Warplane Heritage Museum, 280 Airport Rd, Hamilton Airport, Mt Hope, 679-4183. Museum houses the world's largest collection of planes remaining from WWII - Jet Age that are kept in flying condition. Watch the *'Flight of the Day'*, browse the archive exhibit gallery and memorabilia and experiment with video/audio interactives. Daily year-round 9am-5pm. $10. *www.warplane.com*.

Dundurn Castle, 610 York Blvd, 546-2872. Restored Victorian mansion of Sir Allen Napier MacNab, Prime Minister of United Canada, 1854-1856. In August be sure to hang around for the annual event *An Evening in Scotland – A Celebration of Scottish Heritage*, which features music and dance. Mansion open from Victoria Day-Labor Day 10am-4pm, otherwise noon-4pm, closed Mon. $10, $8 w/student ID. Includes tour and also Military Museum in Dundurn Park. *www.city.hamilton.on.ca*.

Hamilton Museum of Steam and Technology, 900 Woodward Ave, 546-4797. Housed in a 19th C. public works building. May-Sept daily 11am-4pm, otherwise noon-4pm. Closed Mon; $6, $4 w/ student ID. *www.city.hamilton.on.ca/culture-and-rec/museums/steam/default.asp*.

Hamilton Place, 50 Main St W. An impressive showcase for the performing arts and part of the downtown renewal project. Home of Hamilton Philharmonic, one of Canada's finest. Call 546-3100 for schedules. *www.hecfi.on.ca*.

Hess Village, 3 blocks btwn King & Main Sts. Restored Victorian mansions in a 19th century village. Stroll alongside the trendy shops, antiques, restaurants, etc. *www.hessvillage.com*.

McMaster University, 525-9140. Has one of Canada's first nuclear reactors and a planetarium. There is also an art gallery on campus. *www.mcmaster.ca*.

Royal Botanical Gardens, 680 Plains Rd W, 527-1158. Both natural and cultivated landscapes. Wildlife sanctuary called 'Cootes Paradise' where trails wind through some 1,200 acres of marsh and wooded ravines. Open 10am-dusk daily. $8, $6 w/student ID. *www.rbg.ca*.

Information/Travel

Hamilton Street Railway (local transit), 527-4441. Basic fare $2.10 (5 for $8.50). Ticket office at Hamilton GO Centre, 36 Hunter St E. *www.hamilton.ca/hsr*.

Tourist Information Centre, 34 James St S, 546-2666/(800) 263-8590. Mon-Sat 9am-5pm. 'Very helpful.' *www.hamiltonundiscovered.com*.

BRANTFORD Chief Joseph Brant brought the Mohawk Indians to settle here at the end of the American Revolution, the tribe having fought with the defeated Loyalist and British North American armies. Her Majesty's Chapel of the Mohawks was built in 1785 and ranks as the oldest church in Ontario and the only royal chapel outside the UK. King George III himself was pleased to donate money. Chief Brant's tomb adjoins the chapel.

The town's other claim to fame is **Tutela Heights,** the house overlooking the Grand River Valley where Alexander Graham Bell lived and to which he made the first long distance telephone call, all the way from Paris, Ontario, some 8 miles away. The call was made in August 1876, following Bell's first call in Boston. Also worth a visit is the **Six Nations Reserve,** 758-5444, where you can see how Native Indians really live. *www.sixnations.ca.*

The telephone area code is 519.

Of interest
Bell Homestead National Historic Site, 94 Tutela Heights Rd, 756-6220. Bell's birthplace and museum, furnished in the style of the 1870s. Open Tue-Sun 9:30am-4:30pm, $4, $3.50 w/student ID. *www.bellhomestead.on.ca.*
Brant Museum and Archives, 57 Charlotte St, 752-2483. Indian and pioneer displays. Wed-Fri 10am-4pm, Sat 1pm-4pm, July-Aug: Sun 1pm-4pm. $2, $1.50 w/student ID. Also, **Museum in the Square**, Market Sq Mall, 752-8578. Changing exhibitions, Mon-Fri 10am-4pm, July, Aug & Dec only: Sat 10am-4pm. Donations only. *brantmuseum.ca.*
Chiefswood, 8 miles E by Hwy 54, near Middleport, on Indian reservation, 752-5005. 1853 home of 'Mohawk Princess', well-known poetess Pauline Johnson, daughter of Indian Chief Johnson. Her works include *Flint and Feather* and *Legends of Vancouver*. Open May-Oct: Tue-Sun 10am-3pm. $5, $4 w/student ID, includes guided tour. *www.chiefswood.com.*

Information
Visitor and Tourism Centre, 399 Wayne Gretzky Pkwy, 751-9900/(800) 265-6299. Free welcome kits. *www.brantford.ca/tourism.*

NIAGARA FALLS The Rainbow Bridge, 50 cents, spans the Niagara River and connects the cities of Niagara Falls, NY, and Niagara Falls, Ontario. *www.niagarafallslive.com/rainbow_bridge.htm.* Whichever side of the river you stay on, the better view of the Horseshoe Falls is definitely from the Canadian vantage point. It's an awe-inspiring sight that somehow manages to remain so despite all the commercial junk and the jostling crowds you have to fight your way past to get there. Try going at dusk or dawn for a less impeded look and then again later in the evening when everything is floodlit. Snow and ice add a further grandeur to the scene in winter. Hydroelectric schemes, however, have reduced the flow and consequently slowed the erosion that moved the Falls 11 km in 12,000 years.

Since 1950 it has been possible to effectively 'turn down' the Falls at night with the water flow reduced to just 50 per cent. The environmental impact is still unknown. In the nineteenth century the Falls once stopped altogether, due to a build-up of ice up-river. The next-door town of **Niagara-on-the-Lake** is also worth a visit. The drive along the Niagara Pkwy from Niagara-on-the-Lake to the Falls is recommended. *www.discoverniagara.com* and *www.infoniagara.com. The area code is 905.*

Accommodation

Tourist homes are the best bet here. We suggest you call first, many tourist homes offer a free pick-up service from the bus depot. Beware of taxi drivers who try and take you to motels or the more expensive tourist homes. 'If arriving on the US side, be aware that it's a 45 min walk with bags and there are no buses.' For help, call the Visitors Centre (356-6061) and visit _www.infoniagara.com/lodging.html_ and _www.niagarafallstourism.com/accommodations.html_. NB: Rates increase at w/ends and during the summer.

Happiness Inn, 4181 Queen St (at River Rd), 354-1688. Outdoor heated pool, free bfast and coffee. May-June and Sept-Oct S-$55, D-$59-$95, July-Aug, S-$79-$129, D-$89-$139, Nov-April S-$39-$59, D-$45-$65. Will arrange student discounts (5%). Check-in after 2pm, out 11am. _www.happinessinn.com_.

Henri's Motel, 4671 River Rd, 358-6573. D-$50-$60. Family-owned, 1 mile from the Falls. 'Very friendly.' 'Decent rooms.' Check-out 11am.

Maple Leaf Motel, 6163 Falls View Blvd, 354-0841. Open Apr-Oct. 'Near Falls and very comfortable.' Low season: D-$54-$88; high season: $68-158. _www.ctdmotels.com/mapleleafmotel_.

Olympia Motel, 5099 Centre St, 356-2614. 'They gave us a student discount.' From D-$49, $79 for 4 people. 'Very friendly.' Three blocks to the Falls.

HI-Niagara Falls Hostel, 4549 Cataract Ave, 357-0770/(888) 749-0058. 2 blocks E of bus and train stations; 30 min walk to Falls. Amenities include a kitchen, common area, bike rentals, laundry facilities, lockers and internet access ($1/15 mins). Discounts available for the _Maid of the Mist_, the Whirlpool Jetboat and other locations. Diners, grocery stores and post offices in the vicinity. 'Very cosy and friendly.' From $18.90 members, $23.18 non-members. _www.hihostels.ca/niagarafalls_.

Niagara Falls Backpackers International Hostel, 4219 Huron St at Zimmerman, 357-4266/(800) 891-7022. Shared rm-$20, private rm $25, bed linens incl. Near bus and train station. Bfast incl., $15 bike rentals. 20 mins to the Falls. 'Friendly welcome.' _www.backpackers.ca_.

Camping: King Waldorf Tent & Trailer Park, 9015 Stanley Ave, near Marineland, 295-8191. 4 miles from the Falls. 'Very friendly, Scottish owner, 2 pools, laundry, free showers.' Campsites start at $34. May-Oct. _www.marinelandcanada.com_.

Riverside Park, 9 miles S on Niagara River Pkwy (on Niagara River banks), 382-2204. Laundry, pool, showers. Sites start at $26 for two w/hook-up, XP-$3. May-Oct. _www.riversidepark.net_.

Of interest

N.B: It is worth calling the **Niagara Parks Commission**, PO Box 150, Niagara Falls, Ontario, O2E 6T2, (877) NIA-PARK, if you are thinking about visiting more than one of the major attractions. Go to _www.niagaraparks.com_ to get updated info on which attractions are included in their packages. They have the best discounts in Niagara Falls (up to 30%).

Journey Behind the Falls, (877) 642-7275. Elevator and walk through tunnels from Table Rock House, 6650 Niagara Pkwy. Summer: Mon-Thur 9am-8:30pm, Fri-Sun 'til 9:30pm, shorter hours during winter. $10. 'Very amusing.' 'Worth it to hear and feel the force of the falls.' 'Amazing.' _www.niagaraparks.com/nfgg/behindthefalls.php_.

Maid of the Mist **boat trip**, 151 Buffalo Ave, 358-5781. The boats go to the base of the Falls. Waterproofs provided. $13. Definitely recommended. 'Most memorable thing I did in North America.' Boats run every 15 mins daily Mon-Fri 9:45am-4:45pm, Sat/Sun 9:45am-5:45pmt. _www.maidofthemist.com_.

Marineland, 8375 Stanley Ave, 356-8250. Dolphin and sealion shows, killer whales and rides. 'Rollercoaster, Dragon's Mountain, incredible.' $26.95. Summer: daily 9am-6pm. _www.marinelandcanada.com_.

Minolta Tower, 356-1501/(800) 461-2492. Rises 525 ft from brink of the Falls, with a restaurant near the top. $7. Open daily. _www.infoniagara.com/d-att-minolta.html_.

Nightmares Fear Factory, 5631 Victoria Ave, 357-FEAR. Elaborate haunted house, call for rates. Open Mar-Oct: Mon-Thur 6pm-10pm, Fri/Sat noon-1am, Sun noon-10pm. $9.19 'Scariest I've ever visited. Really does make you scream'.

Niagara Helicopters, 3731 Victoria Ave, 357-5672/(800) 281-8034. $100 for a 9 min tour. 9am-7:30pm during the summer. 'Expensive, but an amazing experience and impressive views.' _www.niagara-helicopters.com_ has a $10 discount voucher.

Skylon Tower, 5200 Robinson St, 356-2651. One of the tallest concrete structures in the world. See-through elevator; revolving restaurant at 500 ft. 'Arrive first around sunset and see the Falls floodlit by night and then by day.' 'Excellent view.' $10.50. Summer: daily 8am-midnight, winter: 10am-10pm. _www.skylontower.com_.

Whirlpool Aero Car, 354-8983/(877) 642-7275. Cable car crossing the Niagara River 3 miles from the Falls, views of the whirlpools below. Daily 9am-5pm $10 inc. tax. Weather permitting. _www.niagaraparks.com_.

The Whitewater Walk, 4330 River Rd, 374-1221/(877) NIA-PARK, scenic board-walk alongside the whitewater rapids, $7.50. Open daily 9am-5pm. 3 km from Horseshoe Falls. _www.niagaraparks.com_.

Nearby: Niagara-on-the-Lake. This is a very quaint, very clean, very English town, with a number of fine hotels and restaurants, and upscale shops along Queen Street, its main drag, as well as many affordable bed and breakfasts in private homes. Visit the **Tourist Office** at 26 Queen Street for information about lodging and things to do. _www.niagaraonthelake.com_. It's 15 miles, via car or along a lovely cycle/hiking path overlooking the Niagara River, to within walking distance of Niagara Falls.

The town is best known for its **Shaw Festival**. From Apr-Nov every year, three local theaters present a season of top-quality productions of plays by George Bernard Shaw and his contemporaries. Tkts from $42 to $82, but $20 w/student ID. Call the box office on 468-2172/(800) 511-7429 for more info _www.shawfest.com_.

Nearby is **Fort George**, 468-6600, a reconstructed 18th century military post. Apr 1st-Oct 31st: daily 10am-5pm, $8. _www.pc.gc.ca_.

The area around Niagara-on-the-Lake has numerous **wineries** – all offer tastings, though some might charge a few dollars for the privilege. _winesofontario.org_. Among the most well-known are Inniskillin, _www.inniskillin.com/index.asp_, Hernder Estate _www.hernder.com_, and Chateau des Charmes _www.chateaudescharmes.com_ For a good read about winegrowing throughout Canada, check _www.canadianvint-ners.com/woc/growingregions.html_.

Information/Travel

Niagara Falls Tourism, 5515 Stanley Ave, 356-6061/(800) 563-2557. 'Very helpful'. Summer: Mon-Fri 8am-7pm, w/ends 10am-6pm; shorter winter hrs. _www.discover-niagara.com_.

VIA Rail Canada, 4267 Bridge St, (888) 842-7245. From Toronto, you can catch trains to Niagara Falls that take an hour 50 mins. A same day return costs $42.80 inc tax w/student ID. 'A great day trip.' 'Don't catch the shuttle bus from the station to the Falls. It costs $3.75 and it's only a 10 min walk'. _www.viarail.ca_.

KITCHENER-WATERLOO A little bit of Germany lives exiled in Kitchener-Waterloo, a community delighting in beer halls and beer fests. The highlight of the year is the **Oktoberfest**, a week-long festival of German bands, beer, parades, dancing, sporting events and more beer.

Waterloo is often referred to as the 'Hartford of Canada' since the town is headquarters of a number of national insurance companies. The best days to visit K-W (a fairly easy 69 mile excursion from Toronto) are Wednesday and Saturday in time for the **Farmers' Market**, 741-2297, where black-bonneted and gowned Amish and Mennonite farming ladies and their menfolk sell their crafts and fresh-picked produce. Sixteen miles north at **Elmira,** there's the annual **Maple Syrup Festival,** (705) 924-2057, held in the spring. _www.kw-visitor.on.ca_.

The area code is 519.

Accommodation

There are plenty of reasonably priced motels on Victoria St in Kitchener. Rsvs req. during the Oktoberfest.

Kitchener Motel, 1485 Victoria St N, 745-1177/(800) 574 2156. TV, kitchenettes avail. D-from $55.70 +tax. Check-in after 11am. _www.kitchenermotel.ca_.

Camping: see **Bingemans** below. 744-1002 $29.95 basic, $32-$38 w/hook-up. 3 day packages available inc. waterpark entrance, from $120. _www.bingemans.com_.

Of interest

Kitchener is the site of **Woodside National Historic Park**, 528 Wellington St, 571-5684, boyhood home of William Lyon Mackenzie King, Prime Minister from 1921-1930 and 1935-1948. His former home and grounds are open to the public during the summer, 10am-5pm daily, May-Dec. $4, $2 w/student ID. _www.pc.gc.ca/lhn-nhs/on/woodside/index_e.asp_

Bingemans, 1380 Victoria St N, Kitchener., 744-1555/(800) 565-4631. Waterpark featuring wave pool, water slides, bumper boats etc. $15.95 or pay as you go for individual attractions. Open daily 8am-11pm. _www.bingemans.com_.

Doon Heritage Crossroads, Homer Watson Blvd, RR2, Kitchener, 748-1914. Recreation of rural Waterloo County Village of 1914. Daily May-Aug 10am-4:30pm, Sept-Dec: Mon-Fri only. $6, $4 w/student ID. _www.region.waterloo.on.ca_.

Oktoberfest, K-W Oktoberfest Inc., PO Box 1053, Kitchener, 570-4267/(888) 294-4267. Now attracts more than 700,000 people annually for 9 days of celebration in early Oct. Festival halls and tents serving frothy steins of beer and sauerkraut, oompah music, Miss Oktoberfest Pageant, archery tournament, ethnic dance performances, beer barrel races! All-you-can-eat-all-night Bavarian smorgasbord. _www.oktoberfest.ca_.

Information

Greater Kitchener-Waterloo Chamber of Commerce, 80 Queen St N, Kitchener, 576-5000/(888) 672-4282. _www.greaterkwchamber.com_.

GEORGIAN BAY ISLANDS NATIONAL PARK A good way north of Toronto on the way to Sudbury, this is one of Canada's smallest national parks. It consists of 59 islands or parts of islands in Georgian Bay. The largest of the islands, **Beausoleil,** is just five miles square, while all the rest combined add only two-fifths of a mile. Hiking (trails on Beausoleil Island), swimming, fishing and boating are the name of the game in this park. _www.pc.gc.ca/pn-np/on/georg_. The special feature of the park is the remarkable geological formations. The mainly Precambrian rock is more than 600 million years old and there are a few patches of sedimentary rock carved by glaciers into strange shapes.

Midland is the biggest nearby town for services and accommodation but boats to Beausoleil Island go from **Honey Harbour,** a popular summer resort off Rte 103. On Beausoleil, once the home of the Ojibway people, there are several campsites. Call the **Visitors Center,** 756-2415, for info and **camping** within the Park. One of the most popular is **Cedar Spring Campground,** near the Visitors Centre, on Beausoleil, $23; most other campgrounds, $14. _www.pc.gc.ca/pn-np/on/georg/visit/visit5a_e.asp_. You need to take a water taxi to the island and a number of companies will do this. Try **Honey Harbour Boat Club,** 756-2411, res req. Park entrance fee $5 from May-September.

The telephone area code is 705.

Accommodation
Chalet Motel, on Little Lake, 748 Yonge St W, Midland, 526-6571. Call for prices. *www.chaletmotelmidland.com.*

Park Villa Motel, 751 Yonge St W, adjoining Little Lake Pk, Midland, 526-2219/(888) 891-1190. D-from $89.95 in summer, $69.95 in winter; weekday-rates cheaper. Check-in after 2pm, out 11am. *www.parkvillamotel.com.*

Of interest
30,000 Island Cruise, at Midland Dock, 549-3388. 2½ hr trip among the islands of Georgian Bay at 10.45am, 1.45pm and Sat/Sun 4.30pm (from June-mid Sept) $21, $16 students. *www.midlandtours.com.*

Huronia Museum and Indian Village, 549 Little Lake Park Rd, Midland, 526-2844. Daily summer 9am-5.30pm, 'til 5pm winter. *www.huroniamuseum.com.*

Sainte-Marie Among the Hurons, 3 miles E of **Midland** on Hwy 12, 526-7838. Recreation of Jesuit mission that stood here 1639-1649, plus Huron longhouses, cookhouse, blacksmith, etc. Opening hours vary. *www.saintemarieamongthe-hurons.on.ca/english.*

Information
Georgian Bay Islands National Park, Box 28, Honey Harbour, ON, P0E 1E0, 756-2415. *www.pc.gc.ca.*

Southern Georgian Bay Chamber of Commerce, 208 King St, 526-7884. Mon- Fri 9am-5pm, Sat/Sun 9am-5pm during the summer. *www.southerngeorgianbay.on.ca.*

LONDON Not to be outdone by the other London, this one also has a River Thames flowing through the middle of the city. It also has its own **Covent Garden Market**. It's a town of comfortable size and a commercial and industrial centre. **Labatt's Brewery,** *www.labatt.com,* is perhaps the town's most famous industry.

London also offers the visitor a thriving cultural life. Physically it's a pleasant spot, also known as 'Forest City', situated midway between Toronto and Detroit. The University of Western Ontario is here and is said to have the most beautiful campus of any Canadian university. You will find it on the banks of the Thames, in the northern part of the city. *www.london.ca.*

The area code for London is 519.

Accommodation
For B&B accommodations priced from $45-$100 a night, contact the **London Area B&B Association,** whose own B&B is about 5 miles out of town but they also make reservations for others; 851-9988. *www.londonbb.ca.*

University of Western Ontario, Alumni House, University Drive, Housing Services, 661-3547. Essex Hall provides 4-bedroom suites with kitchens. Features include laundry and continental bfast. Rsvs required. Rooms: $35-$49 pp, $217-$331 weekly. May-Aug. *www.stayatwestern.ca.*

Food
Joe Kool's, 595 Richmond St, 663-5665. Tortillas, burgers, etc., entrées $7. 'Good live music'. Open daily 11am-2am.

Prince Albert's Diner, 565 Richmond St, 432-2835. 50s-style diner with great cheap meals. $4-8. Open daily 10am-3am.

Spageddy Eddy, 428 Richmond St, 645-3002. Seas of spaghetti with lashings of lasagna, salads. Entrées: lunch-$8, dinner-$12. Mon-Thur 11am-9pm, Fri/Sat 'til 10pm, Sun 4pm-8pm.

Of interest

Double Decker Bus Tour of London, 661-5000/(800) 265-2602. 2 hr city tours during the summer months, $12 inc. tax. *www.londontourism.ca*.

Eldon House, 481 Ridout St N, 661-5169. London's oldest house and now a historical museum, close by **Museum London**, 421 Ridout St N. Both Tue-Sun noon-5pm, donation only. *www.londonmuseum.on.ca/eldonhouse/eldon.html*.

Fanshawe Pioneer Village, 1424 Clarke Rd, 457-1296. Recreation of 19th century pre-railroad village. Log cabins, etc. May-Oct: Tue-Sun 10am-4:30pm, otherwise Tue-Fri 'til Dec. $5, $4 w/student ID. *www.fanshawepioneervillage.ca*

Museum of Indian Archaeology and Lawson Prehistoric Indian Village, 1600 Attawandaron Rd, 473-1360. Daily 10am-4:30pm. $3.50, $2.75 w/student ID. *www.uwo.ca/museum*.

Royal Canadian Regiment Museum, Wolseley, on Canadian Forces Base, London, 660-5102. History of Royal Canadian Regiment forces from 1883. Tue-Fri 10am-4pm, Sat/Sun from noon. Donations accepted. *www.rcrmuseum.ca*.

Entertainment

Barney's, 671 Richmond St, 432-1232. The local hangout, open since 1890, which attracts the young professional crowd. Cheap draught beer in the **Ceeps**. Arrive early to get a spot on the patio in the summer. Open daily 11am-2am, 'til 3am on the w/ends. *www.ceeps.com*.

Call the Office, 216 York St, 432-4433, east of Richmond. Live bands. Open from 9pm. *www.calltheoffice.com*.

Grand Theatre, 471 Richmond St, (800) 265-1593. Features drama, comedy and musicals from mid Oct-May. The theatre itself, built in 1901, is worth viewing. *www.grandtheatre.com*.

The Spoke Lounge, Room 105, UCC Building, University of Western Ontario, 661-3590. A popular campus pub. *www.usc.uwo.ca/spoke*.

Western Fairgrounds, home of the **Western Fair**, (800) 619-4629, an agricultural show with rides and games, Held annually in mid-Sept. *www.westernfair.com*.

Information

Visitors and Convention Services, 267 Dundas St, 661-5000/(800) 265-2602. Mon-Fri 8:30am-4:30pm. *www.londontourism.ca*.

Travel

Greyhound, 101 York St, 434-3245/(800) 661-8747. Open daily Monday-Sunday: 6.30 am-9.15 pm. *www.greyhound.ca*.

U-Need-A-Cab, 438-2121.

VIA Rail, 205 York St, (888) 842-7245. *www.viarail.ca*.

STRATFORD In 1953 this average-sized manufacturing town, on the banks of the River Avon, some 50 kilometers north of London, held its first Shakespearean festival. The now world-renowned season has since become an annual highlight on the Ontario calendar. The festival lasts for six months of the year, from May-Nov, attracting some of the best Shakespearean actors and actresses, as well as full houses every night.

Based in the **Festival Theatre**, but encompassing several other theatres too, the festival includes opera, original contemporary drama and music, as well as the best of the Bard. In September the town also hosts the **Walker Film Festival**, 90 Greenwood Dr, 273-2820, (tkts $9).

There's not much else of interest in Stratford except a walk along the riverside gardens and a look at the swans. Lake Victoria, (Avon River) at the middle of town, offers tranquility to take in the outstanding views and have a leisurely stroll. Heading west there is **Point Pelee National Park** *www.pc.gc.ca/pn-np/on/pelee/*, before going on to **Windsor** and crossing to the US. *www.city.stratford.on.ca*.

The telephone code is 519.

Accommodation

The **Festival Theatre** provides an accommodation service during the summer. You are advised to contact them first: call 271-4040/(800) 567-1600. Also the **Festival Accommodations Bureau**, 273-1600, can help you. *www.stratfordfestival.ca*.

Burnside Guest Home, 139 William St, 271-7076. Turn of the century home and member of 'Backpackers', this is the budget traveller's best bet and offers a great view of Lake Victoria. B&B rooms $50-$70, student rooms $25. Call ahead.

Camping: Wildwood Conservation Area, 7 miles W on Hwy 7, 284-2292/(866) 668-2267. Access to beach, pool and marina. $7 entrance, tent sites $23. Open May-Oct. *www.thamesriver.on.ca*.

Entertainment

Art in the Park, Lakeside & Front Sts. June-Sept, outdoor exhibitions of art and crafts for sale. Open Wed, Sat & Sun 10am-6pm.

Festival Theatre, (800) 567-1600. Tkts from $25-$29.90 for students at designated performances. Festival Theatre, Theatre (was Third Stage), Avon Theatre and Studio Theatre. The Festival Theatre is at 55 Queen St, Avon Theatre & Studio Theatre on Downie St and Tom Patterson on Lakeshore. Order from: Festival Box Office, PO Box 520, Stratford, ON, N5A 6V2. Various ticket discounts for students in Sept, Oct and Nov, often swamped by high school parties. Check the box office and website for student specials. 'Get there early on the day of the performance for returns.' *www.stratfordfestival.ca*.

Jazz on the River, Fri evenings 6:30pm-8pm, mid-June to early Sept.

Stratford Farmers' Market, Coliseum Fairground, 271-5130, Sat 7am-noon.

Information

Tourism Stratford, 30 York St, (800) 561-7926, open Tue-Sat 9am-8pm, Sun/Mon 'til 5pm during the festival season. At other times, there is another office at 47 Downie St, 271-5140. Mon-Fri 8am-4:30pm. Will send a free visitors guide if you call ahead. *www.city.stratford.on.ca*.

POINT PELEE NATIONAL PARK About 35 miles from Windsor, Point Pelee is a V-shaped sandpit that juts out into Lake Erie. On the same latitude as California, the park is the southernmost area of the Canadian mainland.

Only six square miles in area, Point Pelee is a unique remnant of the original deciduous forests of North America. Two thousand acres of the park are a freshwater swamp and the wildlife found here is unlike anything else to be seen in Canada. On the spring and fall bird migration routes, the park is a paradise for ornithologists. There are also several strange fish to be seen and lots of turtles and small water animals ambling around.

Point Pelee is quite developed as a tourist attraction and there are numerous nature trails, including a one-mile boardwalk trail. Canoes and bicycles can be rented during the summer months and the **Visitor Centre** has maps, exhibits, slide shows and other displays about the park. Entrance to the park is $6. There are two sites in the nearby town of **Leamington**. Park information: (519) 322-2365, *www.pc.gc.ca/pelee*.

SUDBURY Sudbury is some 247 miles northwest of Toronto and the centre of one of the richest mining areas in the world. The city is often referred to as the 'nickel capital of the world' due to the proliferation of the mineral to be found close to the surface. The local Chamber of Commerce will tell you that Sudbury enjoys more hours of sunshine per year than any other city in Ontario (and we have no reason to doubt them), but this is not a pretty area. Part of the empty landscape looks so like a moonscape that American astronauts came here to rehearse lunar rock collection techniques before embarking on the real thing. Be sure to see the lunar landscape of Sudbury Basin, a geological mystery that may have been caused by a gigantic meteor or volcanic eruption.

Away from the immediate vicinity of the town there are scores of lakes, rivers and untracked forests to refresh the soul after witnessing the ravages of civilisation. _www.city.greatersudbury.on.ca_ and _www.sudburytourism.ca_.
   The telephone area code is 705.

Accommodation
Cheapest is in the Ukrainian District, around **Kathleen St**. Your other best bets for lodgings are the chains, centered on **Regent St – Comfort Inn, Ramada Inn** and **Venture Inn**, but rates start at about D-$85.

Of interest/Information
There is really only one attraction: **Science North**, 100 Ramsey Lake Rd, 1 mile from Hwy 69 S, 522-3701. Has a number of exhibits, mainly located at this site. Inside the **Science Centre** you can conduct experiments such as simulating a hurricane, monitoring earthquakes on a seismograph, or observing the sun through a solar telescope. There are also a water playground, space exploration and weather command centres, and a fossil identification workshop. There is an **IMAX Theatre, Virtual Voyages** simulator ride, a cruise on **Lake Ramsey** and a 10 min drive away, **Dynamic Earth**, 122 Big Nickel Road, at Hwy 17. You can take a tour of the nickel mine and new surface exhibits. Summer hours are 9am-6pm, winter 10am-4pm daily. May change for individual exhibits and holidays. Single 'attractions' range from $6.50-$18 each, or an all day passport is $29.95. _www.sciencenorth.ca_.
Convention and Visitors Service, 200 Brady St, Tom Davies Sq, 673-4161/(800) 708-2505. Open Mon-Fri 8:30am-4:30pm. _www.city.greatersudbury.on.ca_.

SAULT STE MARIE First established in 1669 as a French Jesuit mission, Sault Ste Marie later became an important trading post in the heyday of the fur trade. Today 'The Soo', as locals call the town, oversees the great locks and canals that bypass St Mary's Rapids. **The Soo Locks,** connecting Lake Superior with St Mary's River and Lake Huron, allow enormous Atlantic ocean freighters to make the journey 1,748 miles inland. From special observation towers visitors can watch the ships rising and falling up to 40ft.

The town is connected to its US namesake across the river in Michigan by an auto toll bridge. Thunder Bay is 438 miles away to the northwest. _www.algomacentralrailway.com_. Visit _www.sault-canada.com_ for more info.
   Telephone area code is 705.

Accommodation/Food
Whatever you do, make your lodging reservations in advance.
Algonquin Hotel (HI-C), 864 Queen St E, 253-2311. A youth hostel, but all private rooms. 30 beds. Cooking facilities, linens and towels incl, parking, pub. S-$23/$26 non-members. _www.hihostels.ca/hostels/ontario/greatlakes/algonquinhostel/hostels/_.

Ambassador Motel, 1275 Great Northern Rd (Hwy 17), 759-6199. Low-season: from $59, high season: from $89 for 4 people. *www.ambassadormotel.com*.

Camping: KOA Sault Ste Marie, W on 5th line off Hwy 17, (5 ms north of town), 759-2344. Tent $24-$26, RV $26-$42. Cabins: $45-$66 (minimum of 4 people). *www.koakampgrounds.com/where/on/55150*.

Ernie's Coffee Shop, 13 Queen St, 253-9216. 'Big, cheap meals, excellent value.'

Of interest

Agawa Canyon Train, 946-7300/(800) 242-9287. Runs on the Algoma Central Railway. Central Railway Station, Bay St, next to Station Mall on the waterfront. Day trip north through spectacular scenery, or the entire line takes about 2 days, to the town of Hearst. Departs daily in summer at 8am, ret 5.30pm, $62 for the day trip, res req, esp. in the autumn when price rises to $81. *www.agawacanyontourtrain.com* or *www.algomacentralrailway.com*.

Ermantinger Old Stone House, 831 Queen St E, 759-5443. Completed in 1814 and a rare example of early Canadian architecture, costumed guides will tell you all about Ermantinger, a fur trader, who married an Indian Princess and lived in the house with their 13 children. April-Dec. Daily 9.30am-4.30pm in summer, weekdays otherwise. $5, $3 w/student ID.

Lake Superior Provincial Park. A fair ride north of here up Hwy 17—some 130 kms—but nonetheless worth the trip to this rugged wilderness park. Includes nature trails, moose hunting in season, Indian rock paintings, beaches, dozens of small lakes, canoeing and hiking. Three main campsites. Park can be accessed from **Agawa Canyon Train**. Call park info on 856-2284. 8am-4.30pm daily. *www.lakesuperiorprovincialpark.com*.

Lock Tours Canada Boat Cruises, 253-9850. Departs from the Roberta Bondar Park & Pavilion on the waterfront. Two hr cruises through the American (one of the world's busiest) and the Canadian locks. Also takes in St Mary's River. Runs daily May-Oct at 12.30pm and 3pm, plus 10am and 6pm in summer. $24.50 inc tax. *www.locktours.com*.

Waterfront Boardwalk, 759-5310, from the glamorous sounding Great Lakes Power Plant to the Roberta Bondar Park. The latter is the site of a huge tent-like pavilion. **Farmers Market**, 759-5310/(800) 361-1522, held here on Wed & Sat during the summer, 7am-dusk.

Information

Sault Ste Marie Chamber of Commerce, 334 Bay St, 949-7152. Open daily 9am-5pm. *www.ssmcoc.com*.

THUNDER BAY On the northern shore of Lake Superior and an amalgam of the towns of Port Arthur and Fort William, Thunder Bay is the western Canadian terminus of the Great Lakes/St Lawrence Seaway system and Canada's third largest port. Port Arthur is known as Thunder Bay North and Fort William is Thunder Bay South. The towns are the main outlet for Prairies grain and have a reputation for attracting swarms of huge (and hungry) black flies during the summer.

The city's new name was selected by plebiscite and is derived from the name of the bay and Thunder Cape, '**The Sleeping Giant**', a shoreline landmark. Lake Superior is renowned for its frequent thunderstorms and since in Indian legend the thunderbird was responsible for thunder, lightning and rain, that was how the bay got its name. It's 450 miles from Winnipeg to the west and about the same distance from Sault Ste Marie to the southeast. For listings and information on special events and activities, go to *www.visitthunderbay.com*.

The telephone area code is 807.

Accommodation

Confederation College (HI-C), Sibley Hall Residence, 960 William St, 475-6381. Mid May-mid Aug only. Res req. D-$15 w/ shared bath, $22 w/ private bath, S-$20 w/ shared bath, $25 w/ private bath. *www.confederationc.on.ca/residence/hostel.asp*.

Thunder Bay Backpackers Hostel, 1594 Lakeshore Dr & McKenzie Stn Rd, 983-2042. Hostel is a central point in the Backpackers Hostels Canada network. Run by world travellers and teachers, full of artefacts from around the world. 'World class skiing in season.' The owner is more than happy to provide information on places to stay all over the country. 'Friendly, warm hostel, baths, TV.' Internet access ($1/20 mins) and free bike rental. 'The best in Canada.' Close to Sleeping Giant. All private rooms $19. Tent sites $12, $19 for two. email: *info@thunderbayhostel.com*; website: *www.thunderbayhostel.com*. If coming from the east, ask the bus driver to let you off at the hostel.

Camping: Chippewa Park, south off Hwy 61, 623-3912. A wooded park on Lake Superior with a sandy beach, picnic grounds, a fun fair and wildlife exhibit. Daily, late June-Sept. $17.25 basic, $22 w/hook-up. Historical cabins $45, new cabins $60. *www.chippewapark.ca*.

Of interest

Amethyst Mine. Approx. 35 miles on Trans-Canada Hwy, then north on E Loon Rd, 622-6908. Self-guided or guided tour. Call for hrs. $3. *www.amethystmine.com*.

Centennial Park, Centennial Park Rd, east of Arundel St, 683-5762. Animal farm, a museum and a reproduction of a typical northern Ontario logging camp of the early 1900s. Summer: daily 11am-7pm, winter 'til 5pm. Free.

Fort William Historical Park, on the banks of the Kaministiquia River, 577-8461. Once a major trading post of the North West Company, it is now a 'living' reconstruction. Craft shops, farm, dairy, naval yard, Indian encampment, breadmaking, musket firing, etc. Daily, June 18-Sept 5 10am-6pm, May 21-June 17 & Sept 6-Oct 10 $12, $11 w/ student ID. *www.fwhp.ca*.

Hillcrest Park, High St. A lookout point with a panoramic view of Thunder Bay Harbour and the famous **Sleeping Giant**, he of the Indian folk legends from which the town derives its name. Impressively visible across the bay in Lake Superior.

Thunder Bay Museum, 425 E Donald St, 623-0801. Indian artefacts and general pioneering exhibits. Tue-Sat 1pm-5pm (winter), daily June-Aug 11am-5pm; $3. *www.thunderbaymuseum.com*.

Information/Travel

Tourism Thunder Bay, 500 E Donald St, (800) 667-8386. Open daily 8:30am-8:30pm. *www.visitthunderbay.com*.

Pagoda Info Centre, 170 Red River Rd, 345-6812. Wed-Sun 10am-6pm in summer.

Greyhound, 815 Fort William Rd, 345-2194/(800) 661-8747. Open daily 7:30am-11:30pm. $158.80 to Toronto o/w (7-day advance is $96.30). *www.greyhound.ca*.

ONTARIO'S NORTHLANDS Going north out of Toronto on the Trans-Canada Hwy, you can carry on round the lakes westwards to Sudbury, Sault Ste Marie and Thunder Bay, or else, at Orillia, you can get on to Rte 11, which will take you due north up to North Bay and from there to Ontario's little-explored north country. **North Bay** is 207 miles from Toronto and is a popular vacation spot, as well as the accepted jumping off point for the polar regions.

There's not much in North Bay itself, but there is ready access to the **Algonquin Provincial Park,** a vast area of woods and lakes good for hiking, canoeing and camping and also to **Lake Nipissing.** Pressing north, however, there is **Temagami,** a hunting, fishing, lumbering, mining and outfitting centre. The Temagami Provincial Forest was the province's pioneer forest, established in 1901 and providing mile upon mile of sparkling lakes and rugged forests. It's quiet country up here; even with modern communication systems, people are few. It's also mining country. **Cobalt** is the centre of a silver mining area and **Timmins** is the largest silver and zinc producing district in the world. You can visit mines and mining museums in both towns.

At **Cochrane**, 207 miles north of North Bay, the northbound highway runs out and the rest of the way is by rail. The **Polar Bear Express** runs daily during July and August, except Monday, up to **Moosonee** on **James Bay**, covering the 186 miles in 4½ hrs ($97.90, $83.20 w/ student ID). After September, the **Little Bear** does the same route (approx. $86.80 rtn incl. tax). It's a flag stop train so will stop anywhere; hail the train the way you would a taxi! It only runs three times a week, however: Monday, Wednesday and Friday northwards, southbound a day later. Rsvs req: call (800) 268-9281. It's a marvellous ride, the train packed with an odd assortment of people, everyone from tourists to miners, missionaries, geologists and adventurers. _www.polarbearexpress.ca_.

Moosonee counts as one of the last of the genuine frontier towns and is accessible only by rail or air. Since 1673 when the Hudson's Bay Company established a post on nearby Moose Factory Island, this has been an important rendezvous for fur traders and Indians. It's also a good place to see the full beauty of the **Aurora Borealis.** This is as far north as most people get, but there's still a lot of Ontario lapped by Arctic seas. Over 250 miles north of Moosonee and accessible only by air, is **Polar Bear Provincial Park.** This is a vast area of tundra and sub-arctic wilderness. The summer is short and the climate severe. The rewards of a visit here can be great however. There are polar bears, black bears, arctic foxes, wolves, otters, seals, moose and many other varieties of wildlife to see.

Accommodation

All the towns mentioned above have small hotels or motels, none of them especially cheap however. If planning to come this far off the beaten track, it is advisable to give yourself plenty of time to find places to stay. Remember that if everything is full in one town your next options may be several hours' driving further down the road. There are many campgrounds in this part of Ontario, but again the distances between them are often considerable.

Orillia Home Hostel (HI-C), 198 Borland St E, (705) 325-0970, $20 non-members, $16 members. Close to bus station; kitchen, laundry, etc. Organises canoe trips. _www.hihostels.ca/hostels/ontario/greatlakes/orilliahomehostel/hostels/index.html_.

South Algonquin Backpackers Hostel, 32990 Highway 62 North, **Maynooth**, (613) 338-2080/ (800) 595-8064. 17 beds. Dorms-from $17/ non-members $21. Always open. 'Clean and friendly. On Greyhound route.' Reservations receommended. _www.hihostels.ca/hostels/ontario/ontarioeast/maynooth/hostels_

The Portage Store, Box 10009, Algonquin Park, **Huntsville**, (705) 633-5622 (summer)/989-3645 (winter)/(888) 668-7275. Not a traditional hostel, but an outfitting company that serves as the gateway to the Algonquin interior. It regulates camping in the park, with a $9 pp fee per night. Tents are provided and so are the rest—canoeing, trekking and mosquitoes! Best park scenery in Ontario; moose and other wildlife. Has restaurant serving complete breakfasts from $6.50-10.50. _www.portagestore.com_.

Temagami Hostel, Smoothwater Outfitters, Box 40, Temagami, (705) 569-3539.
Located 14 kms N of the town, on Hwy 11. Canoe rentals, cross-country skiing.
B&B from $33, Dorms-$25, $82 private double,$92. _www.smoothwater.com_.

QUÉBEC

Québec is the largest province in Canada—its area is seven times that of the
UK—and it has a wonderful character all of its own, symbolized by the _Je me
souviens_ you see on the blue-and-white license plates of every car. The
phrase proclaims the distinct identity of today's Québecois – steeped in
their origins as descendants of _La Nouvelle France_, once the first cradle of
European civilization in North America, but now as removed from France
as today's New Englanders are from the English. Architect Eugène-Étienne
Taché selected the motto for inscription on l'Assemblée National du Québec
in 1883: _Je me souviens Que né sous le lys, Je croîs sous la rose_ - 'I remember that
while born under the fleur de lys (of France), I grow under the rose'(of
England). The result today is a charming, lively fusion of the new and old
worlds that no visitor to Canada should miss.

It was here in Québec in 1535, while looking for a route to China, that
explorer Jacques Cartier coined the word Canada, mistakenly thinking the
Iroquois word for village _kanata_ was the name of their territory. Cartier
called the famous river Sainte-Laurent after the saint whose day it was
when he named it, and a little later stood atop Mont Real near the Iroquois
village of Hochelaga, overlooking what would become today's Montréal. In
1608, at what is now the site of Québec City, Samuel de Champlain, the true
founder of the _Nouvelle France_, established the first permanent European
settlement in North America, named after the Algonkian word _kebec_ for
'where the river narrows'.

In Québec, under the aegis of Louis XIII and Cardinal Richelieu, and led
by Champlain, the French established the first fur trading monopoly in
North America, the _Compagnie de la Nouvelle-France_, pre-dating the _Hudson's
Bay Company_ (HBC) by more than forty years. It was those intrepid French
trappers and canoeists – the rugged _voyageurs_ – who forged intimate
relationships and inter-married with the native peoples and, ironically,
paved the way for the HBC.

And it was from Québec, under the royal instructions of Louis XIV from
1663 onwards, that the French extended their territories and trading posts
down the Mississippi to Louisville, St Louis, and to Louisiane (by la Salle in
1682 and formally by d'Iberville in 1699), stilting the westward aspirations
of American colonists. By the late 1600s, the archbishop of the Basilique
Notre-Dame-de-Québec in Montréal had a flock that stretched to the Gulf of
Mexico, an amazing diocese.

Today the old town of **Montréal** and the cobbled streets of **Québec City** –
the only walled town on the continent - are among the most historical,
fascinating and pleasant places to visit in all of North America, still very
much Nouvelle France, but coated with a relatively unobtrusive British
overlay. Britain entered the 'New France' in 1759, after General James Wolfe
ousted General Montcalm's men on the Plains of Abraham at Québec City
(both commanders dying during the half-hour engagement); a year later

French forces were overwhelmed by the British in Montréal, and Québec was formally handed to Britain under the Treaty of Paris in 1763.

In administering Québec, the British were careful to preserve the life and values there of the Canadiens, maintaining the province's seigneurial system, freedom of religion, property rights and French system of justice, and reviving the economy. Since then, despite attempts to separate, the Québecois have voted to remain in Canada's federation, and seemingly continue to grow, if not flourish, 'under the rose'.

Four-fifths of Québec lies within the area of the barren Canadian shield, with the lovely Laurentian mountains to the north and fertile prairies to the south of the river. The atmosphere in the smaller, unassuming rural towns, such as those along the historical **Chemin du Roy** (Hwy 138 along the north bank of the St Lawrence), contrasts sharply with the cosmopolitan sophistication of Montréal and the old world charm of Québec City. The official Québec website is at *www.bonjourquebec.com*. *Tourisme Québec* will send you a comprehensive catalogue of accommodation, (800) 266-5687.

National Parks: Forillon, La Mauricie, Minguan Archipelago. *www.bonjourquebec.com/anglais/attraits/parcs* and *www.pc.gc.ca/pn-np/list_e.asp*.

A Note on Language. Since nearly everything in Québec is in French, knowing the language is helpful here, even if it's basic. When you're driving, for example, it's certainly important to know what *Arrêt, Cédez, Ralentissez,* and *Travaux* mean: the provincial *Charte de la langue française - Charter of the French Language,* mandates the use of French on road signs. For these signs and what they signify, see *www.mtq.gouv.qc.ca/en/reseau/signalisation*.

Canada's Constitution provides, nevertheless, that English and French are both official languages throughout Canada so that most government institutions in the province include both on notices, descriptions and plaques, and most guides, commentaries, and wait staff in *restos* are bilingual. Most, though not all, tourist publications, museum catalogues and websites have English versions too.

A Note on Québec's Cuisine. The curious thing about Québec's multi-ethnic cuisine is that the best of the really indigenous *québecois* variety is found in unassuming, out-of-the-way bistros in which kitchens share the dining areas, such as **Le P'tit Plateau**, off Rue St Denis in Montréal or **Le Café du Cloche Penché** on St Joseph Est in Québec City. Here *tout est fait maison* and you're as likely to find the chef of the Chateau Frontenac at one table as a group of local students at the next, enjoying exquisite meals amidst *"atmosphère, bonne humeur, convivialité et bonne musique."*

You may also want to try Québec's unofficial national dish, *poutine*, a plate of *frites* and melted cheese curds drenched in gravy. Basically considered peasant food, *poutine* has been known to find its way to the menus of a few fine restaurants, served perhaps with a slice of *foie gras* instead of a pork sausage (eg. at **Au Pied de Cochon** in Montréal), though it's more often found in college cafeterias.

MONTRÉAL Canada's second largest metropolitan area spreads around the stubby knoll christened **Mont Réal** (Mount Royal) by Jacques Cartier in

1535; the steep, wooded *Mont* is a good spot to get your bearings of this pleasant city and start your visit there. At the time Cartier stood looking west from the *Mont*, he was certain he was peering towards China, but also saw, downstream, 'the most violent rapids it is possible to see, which we were unable to pass' that would prevent his passage to Cathay by ship. (Later these rapids were named **Lachine.**)

Cartier found a large Iroquois settlement, **Hochelaga** (Indian for 'beaver lake'), located close by the present **Lac de Castors** in the shadow of Mount Royal. But the Indians had gone by the time Samuel Champlain arrived on an exploratory mission 75 years later. At the place he landed in 1611, to be known as **Pointe-à-Callière**, Champlain found fowl and animals in abundance and butternuts, cherries, plums, strawberries and vines that were easily cultivated. Subsequently a group of French Jesuits, led by the Sieur de Maisonneuve, settled in 1642 near where Champlain had landed, holding their first mass there on May 17, Montréal's founders' day.

Besides being a huge commercial centre, home to Canada's first brewery and bank, one of the world's greatest inland ports, and one of Canada's liveliest communities, Montréal is a quilt of smaller, distinct neighbourhoods, all worth sampling and filled with activities and eateries of almost every kind. You can go from one district to another inexpensively via the city's rubber-tired Metro, and there are plenty of open-air walking trails through the city too. Montréalers consider their city to provide the best of everything in Canada—the best restaurants, shopping, nightclubs, the best bagels (ie. **St-Viateur Bagel and Café**) crêpes and the best smoked-meat sandwiches.

This is a cosmopolitan and vibrant city whose liveliness is epitomised in Vieux Montréal, on Crescent Street, or on Rue St Denis, where you can mingle with the Québecois and participate in Montréal's *joie de vivre*. The official tourism site is: *www.tourisme-montreal.org* and there are several helpful **InfoTouriste** offices in the city. Restaurants, lodgings, bars, nightlife, festivals and other insights can also be discovered at *www.moremontreal.com* and *www.toutmontreal.com*. For other pointers, try *www.montreal.com/info/faq.html* and the city's site *www.ville.montreal.qc.ca*.

The telephone area code is 514.

Accommodation

Alternative Backpackers of Old Montréal, 358 Rue St Piérre, 282-8069. 'The best hostel I've stayed in, right in the old town. Decor inside very arty. Spacious, clean, very friendly owners. Definitely recommended.' Dorms $18. Private rooms from $55. Linen may be rented, laundry, free internet access. *www.auberge-alternative.qc.ca*.

Auberge de Montréal (HI-C), 1030 Rue Mackay, 843-3317. Convenient location, great service and upbeat staff who will gladly assist with nightlife ideas and outings. Dorms each have private shower/toilet. Kitchen, internet access, A/C, ride board and twice weekly pub-crawl. 'Clean, safe, friendly.' Dorm from $24.75, private rooms from $65. 843-3317/ (866) 843-3317, *www.hostellingmontreal.com*.

B&B Le Matou 4420 Rue St Denis, 982-0030/ (866) 982-0030. Delicious home-made bfsts, close to parking and lively St Denis/Plateau Mont Royal area. Internet and TV. 'Very pleasant.' Doubles $89/99. *www.lematou.ca*.

Hotel de la Couronne, 1029 Rue St-Denis, 845-0901. From D-$45, ensuite-$120. Bfast and parking included. 'Friendly, clean, cheap. Ideally located close to Old Town.' *www.hoteldelacouronne.ca*.

Hotel de Paris, 901 Rue Sherbrooke Est, 522-6861. Renovated Victorian house, dorms $19, kitchen facilities, linen $3. 'Very cramped and no privacy.' from $50-$90 for non-hostel private rooms. Nr Old Montréal. *www.hotel-montreal.com*.

Hotel la Residence du Voyageur, 847 Rue Sherbourne Est, 527-9515. S/D-$50-$90, all rms have private bath, bfast inc. and free parking. *www.wworks.com/~resvoyager*.

Hotel le Breton, 1609 Rue St Hubert, 524-7273. 'A gem in the city's budget accommodation crown.' Clean and comfortable but rooms fill up quickly. 'French' bfast provided. S/D-$38-$85, weekly rates, TV and A/C, shared or private bath. (514) 524-7273, *www.lebreton.ca*.

Hotel St-Denis, 1254 Rue St-Denis, 849-4526/(800) 363-3364, in the heart of the Latin Quarter, prices incl. bfast, from S-$65, D-$139. *www.hotel-st-denis.com*.

Hotel Travelodge Montréal Centre, 50 Blvd Rene Levesque Ouest, 874-9090/(800) 578-7878. Next to Underground Montréal, rooms fit up to 4 people: $159. *www.the.travelodge.com*.

YWCA Hotel, 1355 Rue René Lévesque Blvd Ouest, 866-9941. Clean and safe, located downtown. Kitchen/TV on each floor, gym, laundry, lounge and computer room. High season with private bathroom S-$75, D-$85, low season S-$65, D-$75, high season with shared bathroom S-$60, D-$75, low season S-$50, D-$65. Rsvs accepted. *www.ydesfemmesmtl.org/*.

Collège Français (Vacances Canada 4 Saisons), 5155 Rue de Gaspé, 270-4459. 'Clean and simple.' Take Metro to Laurier. No laundry or kitchen. $14.50 dorm. Weekly rates available, open year round.

Concordia University, 7141 Sherbrooke Ouest, 848-2424 ext 4758. Shared common room and washroom. S-$35, D-$65. *residence.concordia.ca/*.

McGill University, Bishop Mountain Hall, 3935 University Street, 398-5200. Shared washroom, laundry, kitchenettes, common room with TV. Access to sports areas for a small fee. Garner Bldg has best views. Full bfast $8 daily. S-$45 exc tax, $40 w/student ID. $240-$270/week, $650-$700/month. Mid May-mid Aug only. *www.mcgill.ca/residences/summer/bmhrvc*.

Université de Montréal, 2350 Rue Edouard-Montpetit, 343-6531. Easy access by bus. Located on the edge of a beautiful campus; East Tower has best views. 'Highly recommended for value, location, ambience and comfort.' Inexpensive cafeteria on campus. Laundry, kitchen. Phone/sink in each room. Mid May-Aug. $35-$45, 10% discount w/ISIC. Weekly rates from $190. *www.resid.umontreal.ca*.

Camping: KOA Montréal-South, 130 Monette Blvd, St. Phillipe de Laprairie, 659-8626. 15 miles from city, take Autoroute 15 S over Pont Champlain. Pool, laundry, store, internet access, showers and daily shuttle available. $22-$28.

Food

For cheap eats, best to go to the Mont Royal metro stop and stroll within the **Rue Mont Royal/ Rue St-Denis** area where there are numerous clubs, bars, cafes and restaurants. A preppier crowd tends to gravitate towards **Rues Crescent** and **Peel** downtown. There are many Greek restaurants on **Prince Arthur Est** between St Laurent and Carré St Louis. Try perusing the free restaurant guide *Resto Montreal*, published by **Tourisme Montréal**, (877) 266-5687, and available at the info centers. NB. Always ask about the *Menu du jour*, which is usually the best value. Also note that many restos are 'bring your own wine' - *apportez votre vin*, which costs about $12-14 a bottle from SAQ government liquor stores but which works out cheaper by the glass than if you were charged per glass by the restaurant. Servers will cool and uncork any bottle you bring.

Amelio's, 3565 Ave Lorne, 845-8396. Italian-style pizza and pasta, average meal $6-$9. McGill 'ghetto', 'intimate atmosphere'. Open 11:30am-8:45pm, closed Sun. Mon & Sats open at 4pm.

Au Pain Doré, 1415 Rue Peel, 843 5151; 3611 Boul St-Laurent, 982 2520, and dozen others in Montréal area. Boulangerie artisanale: *Le vrai pain française!* Delicious breads, coffee, sandwiches, choc croissants, etc. *www.aupaindore.com*.

Au Pied de Cochon, 536 Duluth E, 281 1114, in Plateau Mont-Royal area. If you're ready to splurge, this is a packed and noisy bistro where you can find poutine served with game prepared in a wood oven. Open Tue-Sat.

Ben's, 990 Maisonneuve Ouest, 844-1000. Cheap deli, 7:30am-3am. Famous for its Montréal smoked meat. Breakfast till 11.30am. 'Cheerfully tacky deli that is packed at all hours.' Open daily.

Café Republique, 1429 Rue Crescent, 845-5999. Nice bistro in heart of McGill area, with deck where you can lounge as you watch the passers-by. Bfst $9.95, sandwiches $10.95, salads $6.95, burgers c$12. Interesting juices $4.75.

Carlos & Pepe's, 1420 Peel, 288-3090, near Peel Metro. Spicy assortment of Mexican delicacies—burritos, salsas, etc. Pub upstairs, dining room downstairs. Meals $4.95-$16.95. Daily11.30am 'til midnight. *www.carlosandpepes.com*.

L'Académie, 4051 Rue St-Denis, 849-2249 in Plateau Mont-Royal area. Fresh Italian and French cuisine, three floors packed with locals. Exquisite soups. Menu du jour $10.95-16.95. 'Delicious experience.' Bring your own wine from the SAQ next door.

La Paryse, 302 Ontario E, 842-2040. 'Best hamburgers in Montréal.' Hamburgers $5-7. Open 11am/noon-10.30/11pm. Closed Mons. A McGill favourite.

Le Bouringueur, 363 Rue St.Francois Xavier (coin St.Paul), 845-3646, in old town. Specializes in fish, *fruit de mer*, *choucroute*. Soup $4.95, *terrine de lapin* $6.25, seafood salad $9.95, *poisson de jour*, such as perch or turbot, $13.95.

Le Faubourg Food Hall, 1616 Ste Catherine Ouest, 939-3663, (Corner of Guy, Guy-Concordia Metro) shopping mall filled with various cafés, bistros, boulangeries, ethnic restaurants, shops selling fresh produce. *www.lefaubourg.com*.

Le P'tit Plateau, 330 Marie Anne Est (coin Drolet), 282-6342, off Rue St Denis, in Plateau Mont-Royal area, unassuming, out-of-the-way café bistro in which the kitchen shares the dining area, with delectable dishes from southwest France, and pleasant informal atmosphere. Everything made in-house. Tue-Sat. Sittings: 5.30/6.30pm, 8.30pm. Bring your own wine. 'Highly recommended.'

Mazurka, 64 Prince Arthur Est, 844-3539. 'Good, inexpensive Polish and continental style food.' $7.25 daily specials, inc soup and coffee ($8.75 weekends). Open seven days, noon-midnight.

Peel Pub, 1107 Ste Catherine Ouest, 844-6769. Old-fashioned tavern: fish and chips, dozens of beers. Big student hangout. Strongly recommended by past readers. 'The place to go if on a budget.' Bfast still only a meagre $1.99. Ask about daily specials $4.99-$7.99. Open daily, 7am-3am. *www.peelpub.com*.

St-Viateur Bagel and Café at 1127 Mont-Royal E, in Plateau Mont-Royal area, 528-6361/(866) 662-2435, and 5627 Monkland Ave, 487-8051, for hand-rolled, wood-fired, brick-oven bagels – the best. Open for bfst. Bagels range from $1.75-8.95. Also serve coffee, soups of the day, salads, and desserts. Open daily 6am-10/12pm.

Farmers Markets. Montréal has thirteen farmers markets, of which four are the largest: the 'luxurious' **Atwater Market** (Metro Lionel-Groulx, near the Lachine Canal bike path) that specializes in meats; the regionally famous **Marché Jean-Talon** in Little Italy (Metro Jean-Talon); **Marché Maisonneuve**, one of the oldest and largest farmers' markets in the city, renovated in the 90s, with Samedis Bio (organic Saturdays) during Aug-Oct (between Metros Pie-IX and Viau); and **Marché Lachine**, (Metro Agrignon, bus 195) the oldest market in the city. Open daily, usually 8am-5pm. For info on the markets, including their stalls and boutiques, check *www.marchespublics-mtl.com*, or call 937-7754.

Of Interest

Neighbourhoods. The four main districts of Montréal form quarters divided north-south by Boulevard Saint-Laurent and east-west by Rue Sherbrooke. Boul St Laurent is known locally as *The Main* because it splits the city east and west, with, generally, the English and immigrants to the west and Francophones to the east. The NW quadrant is the Mount Royal (Mont Royal) area; the NE quadrant the Plateau Mont-Royal; Downtown, including Chinatown, forms the SW quarter – and beyond that Lachine; and the SE quadrant is a mix of the Quartier Latin and The Village. South of downtown, between Rue Saint Antoine and the river is Vieux (old) Montréal and the Old Port; and south again is the Parc Jean-Drapeau.

Chinatown. This is a bustling area at the east end of downtown, of traditional Chinese stores selling herbs, medicines, food and crafts centered at Boul St. Laurent and the pedestrian section of Rue De La Gauchetière near the Place-D'Armes Metro. The district dates back to the 1860s when Chinese immigrants first came to Canada to work in mines and on the railroads. The first Chinese laundry here opened in 1877.

Downtown. This is the area south of Mount Royal flanked by Ave Greene to the west and McGill University and Chinatown to the east. Its main thoroughfare to the north is Rue Sherbrooke – Montréal's Fifth Avenue, and to the south, Rue St-Antoine. The far western section here, that flanks Mount Royal along fashionable Sherbrooke west and chic **Westmount Sq**, is somewhat British, with Victorian storefronts, bookshops, pubs, stately mansions, and some fine churches.

Closer in, around Rue Guy, you'll find **Concordia Uni**, with several streets further east crammed with good-value places to eat and for nightlife, especially Rue Ste-Catherine, Rue Crescent and Rue Peel. Along Rue Sherbrooke further east, past such stores as Hermes and Cartier, brings you to what's known as the **Quartier du Museé** – the museum quarter, which comprises the many buildings of the **Montréal Museé des Beaux-Arts (Museum of Fine Arts)**, 1379 Rue Sherbrooke Ouest; 285-2000. This oldest-established museum in Canada, founded in 1860, housed in a neo-classical edifice built in 1912, has a permanent collection of over 30,000 items. Besides an extensive collection of Canadian art, works held by the museum include those by Bruegel, Canaletto, Cézanne, Corot, Daubigny, Daumier, Gainsborough, Hogarth, Matisse, Monet, Picasso, Pissarro, Rembrandt, Renoir, Tiepolo, Sisley, Pellegrini and Tissot, among others. Open Tue-Sun 11am-5pm. The entire collection is free, but special exhibitions have fees ($15, $7.50 w/student ID). The Museum also has a full ongoing programme of special events including film matinees, lectures, symposia and workshops, and is where the **International Festival of Films on Art (FIFA)** _www.artfifa.com_ is held every September/October. _www.mmfa.qc.ca_.

To the south of the downtown area, there is the **Canadian Centre for Architecture (CCA)**, 1920 Rue Baile, 939-7026, that documents the changing concepts of world architecture, including those proposed for the future. Wed-Sun 10am-5pm, Thur 'til 9pm; $10, $5 w/student ID. Free after 5.30 pm on Thu. _www.cca.qc.ca_. Metros Atwater or Guy-Concordia.

NB. **Montréal Museum Pass** gives entry to 30 city museums. A pass for three con-secutive days is $39 inc tax, and includes a 3-day public transport tourist card (STM). Available from the **InfoTouriste Centres** (see below), at the museums them-selves, or by calling 873-2015. For use under Travel Tips – Once You are There: Visiting Museums at _www.tourisme-montreal.org_.

There are three churches worth a look in this area: the **Cathédrale Marie-Reine-Du-Monde**, (Mary, Queen of the World), 1085 Rue de la Cathedrale on Dominion Sq, 866-1661, is a scale reproduction of St Peter's in Rome, that covers about a quarter the area of St. Peters, opened for services in 1894 in an area that was by then dominated by Protestants. _www.cathedralecatholiquedemontreal.org._ Metro Bonaventure. The Anglican **St Georges Church**, 866-7113, built in 1870, is across the Place du Canada, at the corner of Peel and de la Gauchetière streets. A tapestry from Westminster Abbey, that was used during the coronation of Queen Elizabeth II, hangs in the church. _www.st-georges.org_ Metro Bonaventure. The **Anglican Christ**

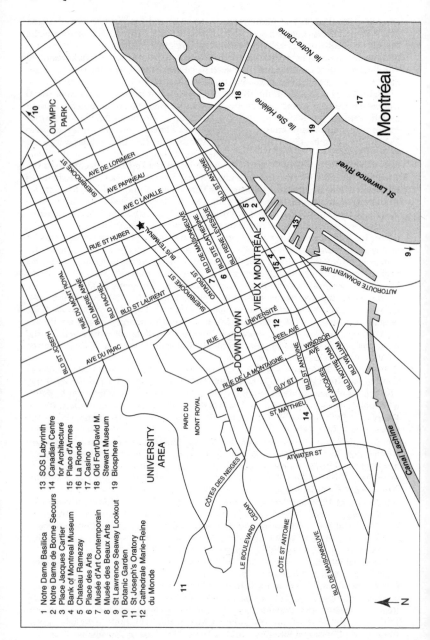

1 Notre Dame Basilica
2 Notre Dame de Bonne Secours
3 Place Jacques Cartier
4 Bank of Montreal Museum
5 Chateau Ramezay
6 Place des Arts
7 Musée d'Art Contemporain
8 Musée des Beaux Arts
9 St Lawrence Seaway Lookout
10 Botanic Garden
11 St Joseph's Oratory
12 Cathedrale Marie-Reine
du Monde
13 SOS Labyrinth
14 Canadian Centre
for Architecture
15 Place d'Armes
16 La Ronde
17 Casino
18 Old Fort/David M.
Stewart Museum
19 Biosphere

Church Cathedral, 1444 Union Avenue, 843-6577, dating to 1859, was modeled after a church in Norfolk and now sits on top of an underground mall known as La Place de La Cathédrale. _www.montreal.anglican.org/cathedral._ Metro McGill.

If you want to travel _en pieds_ downtown, you can do so for up to 33 kms (about 20 miles) in the city's **underground pedestrian network**, some of it beautifully tiled, all the way from McGill and Rue Sherbrooke to Rue Sainte-Antoine in the old city area, past more than a thousand stores, a nice way to go in the colder weather.

Hochelaga-Maisonneuve. This area to the east includes **Maisonneuve Park** at 4601 Rue Sherbrooke Est, 872-6555, a 25 acre park with a botanical garden, golf course, picnic areas and skating rink; and **Olympic Park** at 4141 Pierre-de-Coubertin Ave, 252-8687. After the 1976 Olympic Games, the Olympic Stadium became home to Montréal's baseball team, but then the **Expos** became the Washington, DC Nationals! Now an endless stream of exhibitions and events take place here. Daily 30 min tours in English and French include a brief history of the Olympics, a tour of the Sports Centre with its amazing Olympic pools, ending with a tour of the Olympic Stadium. $7.50, $6.75 w/student ID.

Next door is the **Montréal Tower**, offering spectacular views and a funicular with a breathtaking panorama of Montréal during a 2 min ascent to the top of the world's tallest inclined tower. It's the only one in the world on a curbed structure, a hydraulic system allowing the cabin to remain horizontal at all times. Open daily 9am-7pm; $13, $10 w/ student ID. 'Fantastic views across Montréal and deep into the Canadian countryside.' _www.rio.gouv.qc.ca._

Still within the Park is the **Montréal Biodôme**, 4777 Pierre-De-Coubertin Ave, 868-3056. Offers the chance to explore the wonders of Naturalia from remote corners of the planet: Tropical Rainforest, Laurentian Forest, St. Lawrence Marine ecosystem, Polar Worlds of the Arctic and Antarctic, all re-created under one dome - breathtakingly realistic and teeming with life. 'Great for all ages, plenty of animals to see from touching distance.' Daily 9am-5pm, 'til 6pm in summer. $11.75, $9 w/student ID. _www.biodome.qc.ca._

Across Rue Sherbrooke from the Olympic Complex are the **Montréal Botanical Garden and Insectarium**, 4581 Rue Cherbourg Est, 872-1400. One of the most significant (2nd largest) in the world: 30 specialised gardens spread out over 65 acres, a vast complex of greenhouses, the largest collection of Bonsai and Penjing trees in the western world, a 1,700 species orchid collection, and a Japanese and Chinese Garden. The **Insectarium** is unique in North America, combining science and entertainment and home to about 140,000 insect specimens. Daily 9am-6pm, shorter in winter. Nature Package (Insectarium, Botanical Garden, Biodôme) $19, $14.25 w/student ID. _www.ville.montreal.qc.ca/jardin._ Metros PIE-VX or Viau.

Little Italy & North. This area north of Mont-Royal is famous for the open-air **Jean-Talon Marché**, south of Rue Jean-Talon btwn Casgrain and Ave Henri-Julien, there since 1933. If you want to sample everything fresh that Quebec has to offer, as well as the people and atmosphere that go with it, this is one of the best places to visit in Montréal. The Market is hidden behind residential buildings, and small food shops and boutiques now surround it. But even as a best kept secret, it's swamped with shoppers from May through October, some even driving from as far as New England. Open daily from 8am. Metro Jean-Talon or De Castelnau on the blue line. _www.marchespublics-mtl.com_.

Mount Royal. At the top of the Mount, you can stand where Jacques Cartier stood in 1535, peering westward towards what he hoped was China, and, on a clear day, imagine the same spectacular views he had from the 234 m summit. From here, you can survey the St Lawrence and Ottawa Rivers, the Adirondacks and the Green Mountains of Vermont, and most of the city itself, so it's a good place to start your visit, just as Cartier realized. Not far from the top is a 30m high version of the cross originally erected by Maissoneuve, the founder of Montréal, in 1643, which, when lit at night, is widely visible. The park, est 1876, was originally landscaped by

Frederick Law Olmsted, the designer of New York's Central Park, although you may hardly recognize his work today. *www.lemontroyal.qc.ca*.

The best place to look over the city, close-up, by day or night is from the often-crowded lookout a few minutes from the cross, known as the **Belvédère Kondiaronk**, built in 1906. It's named for the Huron chief who signed the peace accord with the French Governor de Callière in 1701. The Belvédère fronts the **Chalet du Mont Royal**, whose inside murals portray the history of the city, but whose cruddy interior café seems strangely out of place. A few minutes stroll to the west, the **Maison Smith**, dating to 1858, displays aspects of the Park's history, environment and Aboriginal presence, and has a newly-opened **Café Smith** that's open all year round. Further west again is the **Lac de Castors**, named after the Iroquois settlement Cartier found, Hochelaga, Indian for "beaver lake."

There are 6.5 kms of walking and biking paths and almost 20 kms of cross-country ski trails in the park, but beware, many of the paths are poorly marked or not marked at all, perhaps because it's a favorite playground of Montréalers and they all known it so well. If you want, you can also walk to the two other "tops" in the park, at **Outremont** (211 m) and **Westmount** (201 m), both quite a distance from the actual summit. During the summer there are many open-air concerts, in winter skiing and skating. Check *www.lemontroyal.qc.ca/en_calendrier/index.html* for information on events. For info on the park, call 843-8240 or visit *www.montreal.com/parks/mtroyal.html*.

To get to the heights of the park from downtown, take Rue Simpson from the Guy-Concordia Metro stop and keep walking up the steps and paths. Or go to Mont-Royal Metro station, take the 11 bus, or walk, up the Ave du Mont-Royal. From the end of the Ave, or from the Cartier monument on the nearby Ave du Parc, a bunch of unmarked paths wind gradually toward the summit. NB. In summer, use sturdy shoes, and take bottled water and shades: the mountain is steep and the sun intense on clear days.

St Joseph's Oratory, 3800 Chemin Queen Mary, 733-8211/(877) 672-8647. West of Mont Royal, the Oratory is a marked feature of the Montréal skyline with a dome second only in height to that of St. Peters. It's the world's largest pilgrimage centre, with a remarkable 'way of the cross', the original chapel and two museums containing memorabilia of founder Brother André and religious art. Also famous for its cures said to have been effected through the prayers of the 'Miracle Man of Montréal'. Donations appreciated. St. Joseph is the patron saint of Canada. *www.saint-joseph.org*. Metro Snowdon.

Parc Jean-Drapeau is the name for the two smaller islands in the St Laurent River, connected to each other and the main island by bridges and the Metro yellow line (from UQAM) to Jean-Drapeau. The park stretches over both islands and has beaches, hiking and biking trails, swimming pools, and the **Floralies Gardens**. And you can sidle through the lagoons of **Île Notre-Dame** by canoe, kayak or pedal boat. Boat rentals: 872-0199. Three nights a week during the summer (Wed, Sat and Sun at 6.30 pm), there is free ballroom dancing next to the Jean-Drapeau Metro Station. 'Take picnic for a quiet day away from the city.' *www.parcjeandrapeau.com*. The larger island, **Île Sainte Hélène**, is home to a number of attractions:

The **Biosphere** (not to be confused with the Biodome), 283-5000, is concerned with the ecosystems of the St-Laurent River and Great Lakes and all things watery. Open daily, May-Labour Day, 10am-6pm, winter Noon-5pm, closed Tues. $9.78, $7.48 w/student ID. *www.biosphere.ec.gc.ca*.

The **Old Fort** and **David M Stewart Museum**. 861-6701. The Fort, the only one in Montreal, built by the British to defend the city against potential American attack, has bagpipe bands and French pageantry during the summer, and is a pleasant place to picnic. Open daily 10am-5pm; in winter closed Tues. $10, $7 w/student ID. $2 discount on river shuttle to island (call 281-8000). *www.stewart-museum.org*.

La Ronde, 397-2000, a Six Flags amusement park at the eastern end of the island with more than 40 rides and attractions, including 11 thrill rides – 'sensational waterskiing shows'. Rollercoaster, Le Monstre – 'very scary' – when built, it was the world's second-highest coaster and is the highest double-track wooden roller coaster ever made. Open May 14-Oct 30, daily June-Sept 10:00am-10:30pm, $30.42 daily admission plus taxes; parking $10.43. *www.laronde.com/en*.

The second island, the **Île Notre Dame**, was man-made for the '67 Expo and is home to the **Casino de Montréal**, 392-2746/ (800) 665-2274.

Plateau Mount Royal. This is one of Montréal's most pleasant, liveliest neighbour-hoods, extending from Mount Royal and Boul St Laurent to the West and Rue Sherbrooke to the South in a swathe of young professional residences north and east of the city. A good place to start is **Metro Mont-Royal**, whence you can wander down St Denis or along Mont-Royal Ave, past local bars, bistros, bookstores, gal-leries and sidewalk cafés whose tables bubble with conversations on warm summer evenings.

Pôle des Rapides (Lachine area) Following in Cartier's footsteps, the French explorer Sieur de La Salle was so certain China was just round the corner from Mont Royal, that acquaintances called his property to the south of it *La Petite Chine*, then *La Chine*, hence the famous **Lachine** and its Rapids were, as one account has it, 'ridiculously baptized'. As a key portage point, Lachine became the fur-trading hub of the North West Company, with forty of its warehouses housing thousands of pelts that had been paddled across the continent.

Attempts were made to build a canal here as early as 1689, but it was not until 1825 that the **Lachine Canal** was completed, that resulted in a transformation of Montréal's trade and industry. The Canal was evntually closed in 1970, eclipsed by the St Lawrence Seaway, but later revived and is now a national historical site with a 14 km trail and bike path, canoeing, and kayaking. The site's territory includes the canal, nearby park and part of the surrounding area. Free, but various boating charges. Open daily. Metro Charlevoix or Lionel-Groulx. *www.pc.gc.ca/lhn-nhs/qc/canallachine*. Historic and other guided cruises are available from the Atwater Market Quay from **Canal de Lachine Cruises**, 846-0428/ (866) 846-0448. Daily Jun-Oct, 1pm and 3:30pm. $16.75 exc taxes pp/$13.75 w/student ID. Metro Lionel Groulx. *www.croisierecanaldelachine.ca/fr*.

Quartier Est (East End). Directly south of UQAM, this is the cultural heart of the city, and some say, of the whole of Canada. The centrepiece of the Quartier is the **Place des Arts**, 175 Rue Sainte Catherine Ouest, 842-2112, Metro Place-des-Arts, that hosts Montréal's jazz and film festivals and ongoing programmes of ballet, opera and music, covering an extraordinary range of the arts, with some performances outdoors. On Thursdays at noon (12.10-12.50pm), there are lunchtime concerts. For performances, check *www.pda.qc.ca*.

The famous **Montréal International Jazz Festival**, 871-1881, has been held here for almost 30 years in late June/early July. The event has 500 concerts, the majority free, with 2,000 musicians from over 20 countries, with performances mostly in or around the block that houses the Place des Arts. 'An ecstatic jazz party that trans-forms the city into something so beautiful and bizarre that even the locals some-times feel like tourists.' Beyond the festival, jazz concerts are held at the Place des Arts all year round, with tickets ranging from $12 to $65. 871-1881/ (888) 515-0515 *www.montrealjazzfest.com*.

The **Montréal World Film Festival** is also held here, at the end of Aug/beginning Sept (office 1432 de Bleury St, 848-3883), mostly in the vicinity of the Place des Arts. It's the largest celebration of film in North America, with movies from over 70 countries, the festival ranked with those of Cannes, Berlin and Venice. Films are shown at Maisonneuve Theatre of the Place des Arts, 260 de Maisonneuve Blvd. West; Impérial Cinema, 1430 de Bleury St; Parisien Cinema Complex, 480 Ste-

Catherine St. West; Cinémathèque Québécoise, 335 de Maisonneuve Blvd East; and Cinéma ONF, 1564 St-Denis St. For details, check *www.ffm-montreal.org*.

Next door on the same block, the **Museé d'Art Contemporain**, at 185 Rue Ste Catherine Ouest, 847-6226, is the only institution of its type in Canada dedicated exclusively to all forms of contemporary art including paintings, sculpture, multimedia and performance art. Its collection has over 7,000 works. Tue-Sun 11am-6pm, Wed 'til 9pm, closed Mon. $8, $4 w/student ID. Free Wed from 6 to 9 p.m. *www.macm.org*.

South of this block is the huge **Complexe Desjardins**, 150 Rue Ste Catherine Ouest, 281-1870, the largest building in the metropolitan area, where dozens of stores surround a huge square on which entertainment is provided throughout the year. There's a large food court here. *www.complexedesjardins.com*.

Quartier Latin. This laid-back neighbourhood is at the lower end of the Rue St-Denis, from Rue Sherbrooke Est south to Boul de Maisonneuve Est where the **Université du Québec à Montréal** (UQAM) is located *www.uqam.ca*. It's named after the Latin Quarter in Paris (Latin was used at the Sorbonne), developing after the founding of Montréal's Laval University here in 1895 amidst the mid-19th C homes of the bourgeoisie. Laval U eventually became UQAM. There are dozens of bars, boutiques, bistros, cafés, dépanneurs (convenience stores), and restaurants along St-Denis and Rue Ontario Est; this is a nice route to amble along if you're on the way from downtown to the Plateau. Metro Berri-UQAM.

While you're in this Quartier, you may wish to visit: the **La Cinémathèque Québécoise**, 335 Boul de Maisonneuve Est, 842-9763, that preserves Canada's films and TV and screens 1,500 movies, programmes and videos a year. Check *www.cinematheque.qc.ca* for current showings and exhibits; The **Cinerobotheque**, 1564 Rue St, Denis, 496-6887, where you can see, in high tech, the National Film Board's trove of thousands of animated films, documentaries and features *www.nfb.ca/cinerobotheque*; and the **Bibliothèque Nationale du Québec**, 475 Boul de Maisonneuve Est, 873-1100, that preserves Québec's documentary heritage and disseminates it in a user-friendly way. Open daily, free. *www.bnquebec.ca*.

Vieux Montréal Situated on the Lower Terrace, this area includes business, finance, local government, some of the city's most interesting museums and sites, and cobbled streets. It's framed by Rue St Antoine to the north and Rue de la Commune along the river. *www.vieux.montreal.qc.ca/eng/accueila.htm*.

If you want to understand the real Vieux Montréal, the best place to start is at the ultra-modern museum **Pointe-à-Callière** (the **PàC**), 350 Place Royale, 872-9150, which dramatizes almost four centuries of the city's history on a five-storey screen for you as you sit, literally, right above the actual foundations of the original settlement there. And then it invites you to stroll through those same preserved catacombs, underground to another building! A truly memorable experience. Headphones provide bi-lingual commentaries. $11. The PàC has other, excellent exhibitions. Metro Place d'Armes. *http://www.pacmusee.qc.ca/indexan.html*.

Along Place d'Youville from the **PàC** at the corner of Rue St. Pierre is the **Centre d'histoire de Montréal**, 872-3207, with a living history of the city and its Amerindian heritage, and also free Jazz concerts on Sundays at 2pm and 4pm. Open Tue-Sun 10am-5pm. $4.50/$3 w/ student ID. *www.ville.montreal.qc.ca/chm*.

Or, for another taste of Montréal's past, try to find time to visit the **Château Ramezay Museum and Governor's Garden**, 280 Rue Notre-Dame Est, 861-3708, overlooking Place Jacques-Cartier. The excellent museum was built more than three hundred years ago, in 1705, by a governor of Montréal but occupied by the British after ousting Benjamin Franklin and Benedict Arnold who worked there when the Yanks took it over briefly, in 1776, to try to befriend Canadians. Franklin returned to the US convinced that 'it would be easier to buy Canada than to conquer it'. 'Fantastic museum!' 'Very interesting.' Open daily 10am-6pm; winter 'til 4:30pm. Closed Mon Sept-May. $7, $5 w/student ID. Metro Champ-de-Mars. *www.chateauramezay.qc.ca*.

Another way to track the city's history in this area is on foot, following the **Discovery Trail** of archaeological sites via a set of granite markers along the original path of the walls built during the 18th century, when Montréal was a fortified city. The 6 m walls were built under the aegis of King Louis XIV during 1717-1744, extending a total of 3,500 ms from the Porte de Québec in the eastern part of Old Town to just past where Rue McGill is to the west. The walls were dismantled by 1817 to free up city growth. A brochure about the Trail can be had from **Info Touriste** in Canada Square. *www.vieux.montreal.qc.ca/fortif/eng/decouva.htm*.

The **La Basilique Notre-Dame de Montréal - Notre-Dame Basilica**, 110 Rue Notre Dame Ouest, 842-2925, is the doyenne of churches in this area. Originally built in 1657, the Basilique was at the heart of the *Nouvelle France*, with an amazing parish that stretched, in the late 1600s, to the Gulf of Mexico. Built 1824-1829, the current, beautifully-proportioned basilica is usually packed during services. The gilded interior threatens to 'out-Pugin Pugin'. There are high-tech, multi-media *son et lumière* shows in the evenings. Tue-Sat at 6.30pm (Sat 7pm) and 8.30 pm, 842-2925/ (800) 361 4595, $10. *www.therewaslight.ca*. 'Interior decor is breathtaking'. June-Sept 8am-5pm. Tours available. Metro Place d'Armes. *www.basiliquenddm.org*.

The **Marguerite-Bourgeoys Museum and Chapelle de Notre Dame de Bonsecours**, 400 Rue St-Paul Est, 282-8670, overlooks the harbour. It's been dedicated to sailors since the original chapel was erected in 1658. The current chapel, built in 1771 and the oldest church still standing in the city, was once an important landmark for helmsmen navigating the river. There is a fine view of the river from the top of the tower. Marguerite Bourgeoys was Montréal's first teacher, who arrived in 1653 to found one of the first uncloistered communities of women in the Catholic Church. May-Oct 10am-5.30pm, 11am-3.30pm rest of year. $6, $4 w/student ID. *www.Marguerite-Bourgeoys.com*. Metros Champ-de-Mars.

In Vieux Montréal, **Nelson's Column**, erected in 1808, three years after the battle of Trafalgar, overlooks the **Place Jacques-Cartier**, the first monument to Nelson erected anywhere - more than 30 years before the one in Trafalgar Square! The sloping Place Jacques-Cartier is lined with restaurants with outdoor terraces that overlook beautiful floral landscaping in the centre of the Place; lower down is **Rue St. Paul** with its nightlife. **Rues Notre-Dame** and **De Bonsecours** make for pleasant strolls during the summer months – there's street activity in this area until all hours of the night, partly because over 3,000 people now live nearby.

The **Rue de la Commune** along the old port-side has many sidewalk restaurants and the restored **Bonsecours Market** building, 350 St Paul, 872-7730, once the Montréal Farmers' Market in the 19th C, has stores, cafés, exhibitions, Québec country cuisine restaurants, and craft galleries: You can buy food at the stalls or sit on its outdoor terraces and listen to a jazz band. 'Touristy.' *www.marchebonsecours.qc.ca*. Metro Champ-de-Mars.

A few blocks north, you'll find **St Jacques Street**, the Wall St of Montréal, with Canada's oldest Bank, the **Bank of Montréal**, est 1817, at #119 which has a Museum tracing its history as the country's financial centre. You'll also find the **Molson Bank**, est 1854, at #288, founded by the son of a Brit from Lincolnshire who, realizing that beer would be needed for the growing British population, founded the oldest brewery in North America (1786). In 1912, the Bank's owner at the time, Harry Molson, died on the *Titanic*.

To the east of the old town is the **Sir George-Étienne Cartier National Historic Site** at 458 Rue Notre-Dame Est, 283-2282, an inter-active museum of the 19th C celebrating the life and times of one of the fathers of the Canadian Confederation in 1867. $4. Open daily in summer. *www.pc.gc.ca/cartier*. Metro Champ-de-Mars.

Vieux Port. This park area stretches 2.5 kms along the harbour from Rue McGill to

Rue Berri to the east, filled with events, entertainment, exhibitions and cruises, with a walk/bike path along the way. *www.oldportofmontreal.com*. The **Montréal Science Centre** is here on the Quai King-Edward, 496-4629, with IMAX shows. *www.MontréalScienceCentre.com*. In the winter you can skate here on the **Bonsecours Basin**. The **Shed 16 Labyrinth**, Clock Tower pier, past Hangar 16, 499-0099, is a labyrinth that changes passageways weekly, to be explored by day or at night. 'Great fun; a really good way to spend an afternoon.' $12. May-Oct. *www.labyrintheduhangar16.com*.

The Village. This area to the east of downtown is the city's gay area, with some charming side streets such as Rue Lartigue, a wild nightlife and various festivals including the **Artfest** on Rue St Catherine Est in June/July, *www.festivaldesarts.org*. **Divers/Cité** in early August, its grand parade on Boul René-Lévesque, from De Lorimier to Berri, *www.diverscite.org*, and **Black & Blue** at different venues in October *www.bbcm.org/bb2005/enhome.htm*.

South of Montréal. Considering the critical importance of the railways in opening up and belting Canada together, you may like to take an interesting side trip, 28 km S from Montréal, to the **Canadian Railway Museum**, 120 St-Piérre (Rte 209) in St Constant, (450) 632-2410. This is largest railway museum in Canada, with 140 railway vehicles dating from 1863 onwards, and over 250,000 objects and documents. Daily 10am-6pm May-Labour Day, then weekends 10am-5pm. $12. *www.exporail.org*.

Entertainment

Read the free *Montréal Mirror* or *www.montrealmirror.com* under Music/Film/Arts, or *Voir www.voir.ca*, or check the Calendar of Events on *www.tourisme-montreal.org* catch up with what's going on. For some real night-time fun, hang out on St-Paul to see street performers, artists and the like.

Theatre is big here, so naturally there is a wide variety of theatrical groups, including the **Theatre du Nouveau Monde**, 866-8668 (French) *www.tnm.qc.ca*, or **Centaur Theatre**, 288-3161 (English) for tkt info; *www.centaurtheatre.com*. Montréal's main cultural complex is the **Place des Arts**, 175 Rue Ste Catherine Ouest, box office at 160 Maisonneuve Blvd, 842-2112, which features concert, dance and theatrical performances in five theatres and studios. See Quartier Est - East End, above.

Au Diable Vert, 4557 Rue St-Denis, 849-5888, in Plateau Mont-Royal area. Boho atmosphere, draught beers, free popcorn. Dancing bar, with DJ. Open daily. 9pm-3am. *www.audiablevert.net*.

Café Campus, 57 Rue Price Arthur Est, 844-1010. Drinking, dancing, French students. Three dance floors, shows every night that vary from jazz to rock and roll to folk. Cover ranges from $3-$7. Open daily till 3am. *www.cafecampus.com*.

Claddagh, 1443 Crescent St, 287-9354. Open 'til 3am daily, happy hour 4pm-8pm Mon-Fri. Live music Wed-Sat 10pm-2am, Sun 3-6pm jam sessions focused on Celtic and traditional Irish bands. *www.pubcladdagh.com*.

Jello Bar, 151 Rue Ontario Est, 285-2621. Over 50 martinis and lounge, live entertainment every evening. Retro-chic décor. RnB, Funk, House, Hip-Hop & Groove. 'Very cool.' Mon dance lessons 9-10pm. Open 'til 3am, *www.jellobar.com*.

Le Bifteck, 3702 Boul St-Laurent, 844-6211, studenty pub in Plateau Mont-Royal area. Pool tables. DJ music. St Laurent Metro.

Internet access

For access, check *www.montreal.com/tourism/intacc.html* and *www.toutmontreal.com/english/ieti/internet/cafes.html*.

Bibliothêque National de Québec, 475 Maissoneuve Est, 873 1100. Access available with student ID, proof of identity and student registration card. Tue-Fri 10 am-10 pm, Sat, Sun 10 am-5 pm. *www.bnquebec.ca*.

Information

All these centres are open daily in summer 8.30/9 am-7/7.30 pm, with more limited hours the rest of the year.

Infotouriste Centre, 1255 Rue Peel, corner of Ste-Catherine Ouest on Sq Dorchester, 873-2015. Metro Peel. This is a very helpful centre that will help you find anywhere in Montréal and in the whole of Québec - and how to get there, with maps and brochures about almost everything. *www.bonjourquebec.com*.

Tourist Welcome Office Old Montréal, 174 Notre-Dame Street Est, provides maps, museums pass, bicycle cards, etc. Very helpful. *www.tourism-montreal.org*.

Village Tourism Information Centre, 576 Ste-Catherine Street Est, Suite 200, 522 1885/(888) 595-8110. *www.infogayvillage.com*.

Tourisme Jeunesse, 4545 Ave Pierre-De Coubertin, 252-3117. Youth hostel membership, free maps, hostel info and advice. *www.tourismej.qc.ca*.

Travel

Biking. Montréal has over 300 km of bike paths, including the steep 6-km track to the top of Mont-Royal. There are four main bike trails in the vicinity: the **Lachine Canal**, with its 14.5-km tow-path; **Les Berges**, 21 km along the banks of the St. Lawrence, with a view of the **Lachine Rapids**; the **Parc Jean-Drapeau**, site of Formula One and Molson Indy car races, which transforms into a bike track in the off-race season. (Get there via the ferry from the Old Port); and the **West Island Heritage Bicycle Trail**, a 70-km stretch that includes 100 ancestral homes, parks and nature sites. The biggest non-competitive cycling event in the world is Montréal's **Tour de l'Île** with over 45,000 cyclists.

Public Transport. STM Metro and Bus public transport. The Société de Transport de Montréal (STM) metro is fully integrated with the bus system, whispering along on rubber tyres. 'A joy after New York.' Current fare: $2.50, $11.25 for 6 tkts. Tourist passes give unlimited travel, $8/day, $16 for 3 days. Ask for transfers (honoured on both buses and metro). Students aged 18 to 25 can travel with a reduced fare CAM (monthly pass) upon presentation of the *Carte Privilege* - for info call 288-6287. Daily 5:30am-1am. Free pocket maps of the Metro available at stations, and a set of maps can be downloaded from *www.stm.info.*

Car Allo Stop, 4317 Rue St Denis, 985-3032. Connects travellers with rides. Female drivers may be requested. 'More reliable than hitchhiking, cheaper than bus or train.' No longer goes to Ontario. *www.allostop.com*.

Bus & Tours. Greyhound: Centrale d'autobus de Montréal, 505 de Maisonneuve Est and Berri, 843-4231/ 800-661-8747. *www.greyhound.ca.* Metro: Berri-UQAM.

Orléans Express, Station Centrale d'autobus de Montréal, 505 de Maisonneuve Est 842-2281/ (888) 999-3977, is the main intercity bus carrier in Québec. (*www.smtbus.com*), *www.orleansexpress.com.*

Gray Line City Tours/Autocar Connaisseur, 1001 Dorchester Sq (in the InfoTouriste office), 398-9769/(800) 461-1223. May-Oct $34 for 1 hr 30 min hop-on/hop-off tours, $35/ $31.50 w/student ID, for 3 hrs, takes in over 200 points of interest. Nov-Apr two 3 hr tours a day only. **Departs from** 1255 Peel Street, nearby. Call for info. Metro Peel. *www.coachcanada.com/montrealsightseeing*

L'Aérobus. Free minibus service to the Central Bus Station is provided to/from all downtown Montréal hotels for Aérobus passengers.

Rail. VIA Rail. Central Station /Gare Centrale, 895 Rue de la Gauchetiére Ouest, under Queen Elizabeth Hotel. *www.viarail.ca*

Amtrak. Montréal (Central Station) is also served by Amtrak's *Adirondack* service to/from New York City (Penn.), three times daily, (800) 872-7245, *www.amtrak.com.* Metro Bonaventure.

Air. Montréal-Pierre Elliott Trudeau International Airport (YUL) – also known as **Montréal-Dorval**, 975 Roméo-Vachon Blvd North, 394-7377, 21 km from city centre, domestic, international and US flights. Flights by Air Canada Jazz to New

York take 1 hr 25 mins (88 departures weekly), Ottawa 40 mins (66 deps), and Toronto 1 hr 20 mins (196 deps). _www.admtl.com._ **L'Aérobus,** 843-4938, runs every 25 minutes from Trudeau International Airport, Post #8, Quai 6, to Montréal's Station Centrale d'autobus de Montréal, 505, de Maisonneuve Est, $14 o/w. _www.autobus.qc.ca._

Montréal–Mirabel International Airport 12300 Service A-4 Street, Mirabel, 394-7377/ (800) 465-1213, 55 km from city centre, is mainly for charter flights. When it opened in 1975, it was the largest airport in the world and many film makers have used its enormous hangars, immense terminals and massive airliners for productions. _www.admtl.com._

Taxi Diamond. 273-6331 _www.taxidiamond.com_, **Taxi Coop,** 725-2667, 725-9885; _www.taxi-coop.com._ **Pontiac,** 766-5522.

LES LAURENTIDES (THE LAURENTIAN MOUNTAINS)

This delightful region of a chain of mountains, lakes and forests, located just north and west of Montréal via Autoroute 15 and Hwy 117, is where urban Québecois and others from further afield come to get away from it all. A resort area in both winter and summer, it is known for camping, hiking and skiing. To obtain the _Tourism Guide to the Laurentians_, and for information on accommodation, call the Association Touristique des Laurentides (ATL) at (450) 436-8532. _www.laurentides.com._

Ste Agathe, built on the shore of Lac des Sables, is the major town of the Laurentians. Water sports and cruises are major pastimes here. For lodging and places to eat see _www.ste-agathe.com_. From the old railway station at Ste-Agathe, you can access one of the best-known trails in this part of Canada, the 200 kilometres **Linear Park** or Parc Linéaire known as **Le p'tit Train du Nord**, based on an old railway track that passes through dozens of villages. Here you can snowmobile, cross country ski, bike and hike. _www.laurentides.com/anglais/parc/Welcome.html_

Other towns of interest, most of them linked by the Linear Park, include: **St Donat,** the only village in Québec with two huge lakes side by side, Lake Archambault and Lake Ouareau. _www.st-donat.com;_ **St Sauveur des Monts,** 60 kilometres north of Montreal, is an arts and crafts centre with a bustling nightlife on its main street, _www.saint-sauveur.net;_ **Mont Laurier is** a farming area known as the capital of the Upper Laurentians, _www.mrc-antoine-labelle.qc.ca;_ and **Mont Tremblant,** at 935 metres, the highest peak in the Laurentians, is a year-round sports centre that caters to those interested in climbing, fishing, watersports and hiking in the summer. In winter, it's probably the most popular ski resort in the area. _www.mt-tremblant.com._

In the hills to the northeast of Montréal, north of **Trois Rivières** and accessible off Hwy 55, is the unspoiled **La Mauricie National Park,** (819) 538-3232, $6 entrance. The park's rolling hills and narrow valleys are dotted with lakes. Canoeing and cross-country skiing are extremely popular here. Moose, black bear, coyote and a great variety of birds are indigenous to the area. The park is open year-round. (819) 538-3232. Camping is available May-Oct, $23 unserviced, $25 serviced. Reservations strongly recommended in summer months. (877) 737-3783.

QUÉBEC CITY

Almost four hundred years ago, Samuel de Champlain founded the first permanent European settlement in North America here at

Cap Diamant in 1608, establishing the cradle of French civilization on the continent. Québec City, now the capital of the province, continues to be one of the most charming and historically interesting places to visit in all of North America. Named after the Algonkian word *kebec* for 'where the river narrows,' Québec City is the only walled city on the continent, one of the best examples of a fortified colonial town anywhere, complete with narrow, cobbled streets, a mighty fortress, a battlefield, a port hosting huge ocean liners and a commanding view of the St Lawrence River. Visually, it's stunning. In winter, it's a snowy Carnaval!

And 'cradle of civilization' is not an understatement: Even before Harvard was founded in Massachusetts, the French established a college here for both colonists and Indians. Four years later, they established a hospital that still operates, today as L'Hôtel-Dieu de Québec, the oldest hospital in North America. And after Québec City officially became the capital of *La Nouvelle France* in 1663, it became home to a church whose diocese would extend over the French crown's entire possessions in North America, at one point reaching to the Gulf of Mexico.

The British won Québec in 1759, when in pre-dawn darkness, General Wolfe and his men scaled the cliffs surrounding the French fortress via the Anse au Foulon and took General Montcalm and his troops by surprise. The site of this attack, the **Plains of Abraham** (named for the farmer who owned the land), is now a public park overlooked by the Citadel, a fortress completed by the British in 1831 as a deterrent to Americans.

From the early 19th Century onwards, travellers from Europe voyaged to see this mesmerising *Gibraltar of North America:* steamships shortened their Atlantic crossings, then completion of the Canadian Pacific Railway (CPR) in the 1880s reduced their travel-times to Asia by weeks. Thus Québec City, as Canada's foremost eastern portal, assumed huge new prominence, positioned as it is, neatly between the two continents to the West and East.

The town's geopolitical significance was embodied by the extraordinary **Château Frontenac,** a unique hotel built in 1893 as a 'stopover' by the CPR that dominates the city. It was soon mobbed by those headed for the Orient – or at least the Rockies, and by those who wished merely to participate in its grandeur. More than this, such was Québec City's critical geographical appeal, that here at the Frontenac Winston Churchill and Franklin D. Roosevelt chose to meet twice, secretly, first in 1943 to plan the final years of World War II in Europe and the Pacific, and then again in 1944 to plan the reconstruction of Europe and partition of Germany.

Now preparing to celebrate its 400th anniversary, this town of half-a-million people remains quintessentially French-speaking, with only a small proportion of its inhabitants speaking English as their first language. In some cases, their vocabulary is purer French than a Parisian's, yet North-Americanisms can't help but creep in. You'll feel at home here - the Québecois are friendly, easy-going, polite, cosmopolitan and readily willing to speak English.

Curiously, you'll find few ethnic restaurants here, though the numerous *crêperies* attest to some immigration from Brittany and the pubs may look British, but the food they serve is continental.

The town is best explored on foot. Stop by the excellent **Centre**

Infotouriste on Rue Ste-Anne, just across from the Chateau Frontenac and pick up a copy of *Québec City and Area Official Tourist Guide*, full of useful info as well as walking tours and trail routes. *www.ville.quebec.qc.ca; www.quebecregion.com*.

The telephone area code is 418.

Accommodation

There are several sources of info on lodgings in Québec City including: *www.quebecregion.com/e/hotels.asp* and *www.bbcanada.com/quebec*. A good place to start is on Rue St Ursule in the heart of Old Town, where all the B&B owners know each other, and will gladly find alternative lodging for you, if they're full. Try **B&B Chez Hubert** first, and go from there…

Au Petit Hotel, 3 Ruelle des Ursulines, 694-0965. Great location, in the heart of Vieux Québec. 'Small but clean rooms', private bath. S/D $65-110 plus tax May-Oct, $55-90 Nov-April, $10 for an additional person. Cont'l bfst $2.50.

Auberge De La Paix de Jeunesse, 31 Rue Couillard, 694-0735. Friendly staff, co-ed rooms. Kitchen facilities, $3 linens. Close by great bars/restaurants on Rue St Jean. Free bfast, all you can eat. $20. 'Central location, clean.' *www.aubergedelapaix.com*.

Auberge St Louis, 48 Rue St Louis, 692-2424/(888) 692-4105. In Vieux Québec. D:$89-$139. Cable TV. Full breakfast inc. *www.aubergestlouis.ca/id9.htm.*

B&B Chez Marie-Claire, 62 Rue Ste Ursule, 692-1556. From D-$95 plus taxes. Complete breakfast, parking, A/C incl. 'Central location, bright, clean rooms, friendly hostess.' *www.bbmarieclaire.com*.

Centre International de Séjour de Québec (HI-C), 19 Rue Ste Ursule, 694-0755. Laundry, internet access, microwave, TV, pool, ping-pong tables, living room, kitchen, café, limited street parking, linen provided. 'Very nice and well situated.' $25/$29 non-members breakfast inc; in larger rooms, $20/$24 non-members breakfast not inc. *www.cisq.org.*

Hôtel Manoir Charest, 448 Rue Dorchester Sud, 759-0228/ **(877) 868-5151**. High season S/D-$55-$99, off season S/D-$45-$65 . 'Clean and friendly.' Cont'l bfast and parking inc. *www.qbc.net/quebec/manoir-charest/english.htm.*

Laval University opens up its residence hall for short-term stays during the summer. Rates (breakfast not included) range from S-$28.76 (May-June), $34.51 (July-Aug) to D-$40.26 (May-June), $46.01 (July-Aug).). Check in after 2pm at the Pavillon Alphonse-Marie-Parent, room 1618. *www.sres.ulaval.ca*. The building also houses lots of cheap places to eat.

Hôtel Manoir LaSalle, 18 Rue Ste-Ursule, 692-9953. From S-$40, D-$55-75. Does not provide breakfast.

Maison Historique James Thompson (1793), 47 Rue Ste Ursule, 694-9042. Full breakfast. Free high speed internet. Thompson was the last surviving member of the battalion that fought in the battle of the Plains of Abraham. House is historic monument. S-D $65/100. *www.bbcanada.com/2055.html.*

Maison Ste Ursule, 40 Rue Ste Ursule, 694-9794. 15 private rooms. From S-$39, D-$119. *www.quebecweb.com/maisonste-ursule*.

YWCA, 855 Ave Holland, 683-2155. For women and couples only. Shared kitchen, access to pool and other physical activities. Internet access. S-$40 plus tax, D-$50 Apr-Oct; $35/45 Nov-Mar. *www.ywcaquebec.qc.ca*.

Camping: Camping de la Joie, 640 Rue Georges-Muir, Charlesbourg, 849-2264. 165 sites. $21-$30 for full service, plus tax. Showers, pool, laundry, trails, volleyball, internet, shuttle to Québec ($5). *www.campingdelajoie.com*.

Camping Piscine Turmel, 7000 Boul Ste-Anne (off Rte 138), Chateau-Richer, 824-4311. 155 sites, NW of Québec City. May-Sept. $22.61/26.08 night by services. Showers, laundry, restaurant, pool, shop, auto mechanics and ice cream parlour. 'Clean and well kept.' *www.quebecweb.com/campingturmel*.

Food

Bistro Frontenac, 1 Rue des Carrières, 692-3861, in mall under hotel. Small coffee shop that also has hot chocolate. Soup and sandwich $8.95.

Café Buade, 31 Rue Buade in Old Town, 692-3909. The oldest restaurant in Quebec. All day bfast, with cappuccino in large bowls. Complete breakfast $9.95-10.95. 'Bit touristy.' Open 7am-midnight. *www.cafebuade.com*.

Casse-Crèpe Bréton, 1136 Rue St Jean, 692-0438. Many choices of fillings for your 'make-your-own-crèpes'. Bfast specials $4-5, lunch specials, $9, 11am-2pm. Open daily 7am-11pm. 'Excellent crèpes.'

J A Moisan, 699 Rue St-Jean, 522-0685. *Épicerie Fine*: the oldest grocery store still in operation on the continent (1871). Buy groceries here for your own food concoctions. Daily 9am-10pm. *www.jamoisan.com.*

La Bouche-Bée ('open mouth'), 383 Rue St-Paul, 692 4680. Old port area. Small, inexpensive bistro.

La Fleur de Lotus, 38 Cte de la Fabrique, across from the Hôtel de Ville, 692-4286. 'A local favourite.' Cambodian, Thai, Vietnamese dishes. 11am-11pm daily.

Le Café du Cloche Penché, 203 St Joseph Est in downtown, 640-0597. At this bistro with the kitchen that's part of the dining area, *tout est fait maison,* and what's made is so exquisite and reasonable that you may find the chef of the Château Frontenac rubbing elbows with local students here. Lunch $13; evening *plats à la carte* $16–20, eg salad with duck leg confit $16.

Le Café du Monde, 84 Rue Dalhousie, in Vieux Port, 692 4455. Bistro Parisien with view of the St Lawrence, ocean liners and sailboats. Menu includes duck confit, salmon tartar, oat tatin apple pie, fish soups. Brunch Sat/Sun, 9.30am-2pm. *www.lecafedumonde.com.*

Le Commensal, 860 Rue St Jean, 647-3733. One of Canada's largest chains of vegetarian restaurants. Self-service hot and cold buffet, pay by weight (of the food!). Dinner $10-$18. 'Friendly.' 11am – 9.30pm.

Le Lapin Sauté, 52 Rue Petit-Champlain in Lower Town, 692-5325. *Resto champêtre* - rustic fare. "Picnic for Two" $18.95. Main dishes $8.95-13.95. Rabbit rillettes $5.95. Rabbit pie $15.95. Serves *Belle Gueule* beer. *www.lapinsaute.com.*

Le Petit Chateau, 5 Rue St-Louis, 694 1616. A block from the Frontenac. Crêpes, fondues, raclettes. Breakfast. Crepe forestiére (mushroom and eggs) $7.95. Crêpe bleuet with chocolate and hazelnut sauce, $3.84

Of interest

Neighbourhoods. Québec City is in fact two cities: Atop Cap Diamant (Diamond Rock) 102 metres above the St Lawrence River, is **Old (*Vieux*) Québec**, surrounded by the town walls, and the **Upper Town** to the west of the walls. This area is joined by a funicular railway (across from the Frontenac, fare $1.50) to **Lower Town (Basse Ville)**, the charming **Quartier Petit Champlain** and the **Old Port** area that spreads along the coastal part of Cap Diamant. Parading on the Terrasse Dufferin and the boardwalk, and around narrow, winding streets past grey-stone walls, sidewalk cafés and artists on the Rue du Trésor or Rue St-Pierre, it's easy to believe you've been transported to the alleys of a new Montmartre.

Vieux Québec - Inside the Walls. Terrasse Dufferin & Promenade des Gouverneurs-Begin your visit to Old Town here! There is a spectacular view of the St Lawrence from Terrasse Dufferin & the Promenade boardwalk that starts in front of the funicular and Chateau Frontenac and ends on the Plains of Abraham.

Basilique-Cathedrale Notre Dame de Québec, 20 Rue Buade, 692-2533/694-0665 for tours. Québec City is the oldest Episcopal see in North America, dating back to 1615 with the arrival of the Jesuits. Built on the site of the first chapel constructed by Champlain in 1633, the Notre-Dame de Québec Church was erected in 1647 and became the first parish church in North America in 1664. François de Laval was the first bishop. The church eventually served a diocese that stretched from Canada to

Mexico. Tours of the basilica and crypt are available, May-Oct Mon-Fri 9:30am-5:30pm, Sat-Sun till 4.30pm; Nov-Apr by res. $1. 'An atmospheric introduction to the history of the city.' Has six magical sound and light shows May-Oct weekdays 3.30pm, Sat-Sun starting 6.30pm. Info 694-4000. _www.patrimoinereligieux.com._

Fairmont le Château Frontenac, 1 Rue des Carrières, 692-3861. Named for Louis de Buade, Count of Frontenac, gouvernour of New France, 1672-1698, this hotel is one of Québec City's most prominent landmarks. Built in 1893 as a 'stopover' by the Canadian Pacific Railway, the Frontenac has hosted, among other distinguished luminaries, King George VI and Queen Elizabeth, Charles de Gaulle, Charles Lindberg, and Alfred Hitchcock. Tours are available from the lobby. _www.fairmont.com/frontenac._

La Citadelle, on Cap Diamant promontory, at the end of the Terrasse Dufferin & Promenade des Gouverneurs. The four-pointed Citadelle towers over the St. Lawrence, most of it built over the site of 17th C French defences by the British during the 1820s as a deterrent to the Yanks. It's still in active use and is second official home to every Governor General of Canada since 1872. Known as the _Gibraltar of America_, it is the largest fortification on the continent still garrisoned by regular troops. Changing of the Guard ceremony by the Royal 22nd Regiment, the 'Vandoos', takes place at 10am daily Jun-Sep and 'Beating the Retreat' at 7pm Fri-Sat-Sun in July/Aug. The **Royal 22nd Regimental Museum** includes three centuries of military objects such as firearms, decorations, and uniforms. The Museum and Citadelle are open daily for tours Jun-Sep 11am-4pm, shorter hrs toward season beginning and end; call for times, 694-2815. Tours last an hour, $8, $7 w/student ID. Tours of the GG's residence are available in summer 1-5pm, free, 648-3172. _www.gg.ca/visitus/citadelle/index_e.asp_ and _www.lacitadelle.qc.ca_.

The Fortifications de Québec are also worth a visit. This is the 4.6 km stone wall that encircles Vieux Québec, first constructed by Governor Frontenac, by 1690; the current wall, or enceinte, was finished in 1759. It was once over 75 m wide. There are great views of the city and port from the walkways. The ramparts (on Rue des Ramparts) are studded with old iron cannons. Tours are available, May-Oct daily 10am-5pm, restricted hrs the rest of the year. Entry $4. 90. Info 648-7016. _www.parcscanada.gc.ca/fortifications_.

Musée de l'Amérique Française, 2, Côte de la Fabrique, 692-2843/ (866) 710-8031. The multi-media _French America_ exhibition shows how French culture set its roots and expanded thoughout North America over more than 400 years. Most exhibitions are presented in both French and English. Jun-Sep, open daily, 9:30 am-5 pm, rest of year shorter hours. $5, $3 w/student ID. (Ask about the 3-site discovery package for one price. Save 20%.) _www.mcq.org/en/maf/index.html_

Museé du Fort, 10 Rue Ste-Anne, 692-1759. Diorama sound and light show that re-lives the six sieges of Québec, including the American attack on Québec led by Benedict Arnold during a snow storm on New Years Eve, 1775. Apr-Oct, daily 10am-5pm. Feb-Mar 11am-4pm. 25 min show $7.50 inc tax, $4.50 w/student ID. 'Interesting and enjoyable.' _www.museedufort.com_.

The Plains of Abraham The site, now known as **Battlefields Park**, was the scene of a pivotal clash between the French and British armies in 1759 that changed the course of North American history. Today it's a huge grassy historic meadow of a park that residents and tourists enjoy year-round. Reach it by walking along the Promenade or via Porte St-Louis. The **Discovery Pavilion of the Plains of Abraham** is at 835 Wilfrid-Laurier Avenue, 648-4071. Open daily in summer 8:30am-5:30pm, shorter hours in winter. There are a number of historic sites in the park, including the Wolfe Monument and the Jardin Jeanne D'Arc. The **Martello Towers**, completed in 1812 as defense against the Americans, are unique: Out of 196 such towers in the world, 16 were built in Canada, and four in Québec City, of which two survive on the Plains. Open daily in summer 10 am to 5 pm. Admission to all Park sites is available for $10/day from the **Interpretation Centre**, National Battlefields Commission, 390 Ave de Bernières, 648-4071. _www.ccbn-nbc.gc.ca/ en/index.php._

Museé National des Beaux-arts du Québec, Parc des Champs-de-Battaile, 643-2150/(888) 220-2150, displays Québec art (and the old city jail) in 12 galleries with 20,000+ works. In 2005, it made its largest acquisition of art works and objects, the Brousseau collection of Inuit art. Includes café-restaurant. Jun-Sep daily 10am-6pm, Wed 'til 9pm; winter, closed Mon. $10, $5 w/student ID. _www.mnba.qc.ca._

Basse Ville - Lower Town, Outside the Walls: Reached by the 100 m funicular from the Upper Town, this area is full of crowded, cobbled pedestrian streets, bistros and restos, arts and craft galleries, with colourful flower baskets and banners fluttering everywhere. In the historic **Place Royale** where Québec began - the site of Champlain's first settlement in 1608 that will soon celebrate its 400th anniversary, you may hear a musician playing the Beatles almost symphonically on brandy glasses or someone else playing the classics on a harp.

To the east of the Place is the **Quartier Petit Champlain,** the oldest commercial district in North America that spreads around Rue du Petit Champlain, with pleasant rues to amble down, browse along, sip coffee or wine on, or watch the rest of the world stroll by. For information, visit the Co-op at 61, Rue du Petit Champlain or call 692-2613/(877) 692-2613. At the east end of the Rue, you can see a _trompe-l'oeil_ work illustrating different scenes from the daily lives of the founders of the Quartier, a marvellous mural that looks uncannily real. _www.quartierpetit-champlain.com_, Close by, you can walk to the ferry and take a round trip across the mighty St. Lawrence, for $5, that will give you a full profile of this knoll of a city crowned by the Frontenac, pretty in the late afternoon.

Centre d'interprétation de Place-Royale, 27, rue Notre-Dame, 646-9072/ (866) 710-8031. Opened in 1999, the multi-media Centre is located where Champlain founded the first permanent French settlement in North America, part of the historic area recognized as a World Heritage Town by UNESCO in 1985. Jun-Sep, open daily, 9:30 am-5 pm, rest of year shorter hours. $4, $3 w/student ID. (Ask about the 3-site discovery package for one price.) _www.mcq.org/en/maf/index.html_.

Église Notre-Dame-des-Victoires, 32 Sous-le-Fort Street, Place Royale, 692-1650. One of the oldest churches in Québec, built partly on the foundations of the former _magasin du roy_ (the Kings's warehouse), part of Champlain's residence in 1624. Completed in 1688, its main altar resembles the city in that it is shaped like a fortress complete with turrets and battlements. Guided tours May-Oct. Free. Open daily 9am-5pm.

Museé de la Civilization, 85, Rue Dalhousie, 643-2158/ (866) 710-8031. Excellent permanent exhibition on the history of Québec, highlighting the distinct identity of the Québecois. Jun-Sep, open daily, 9:30 am-6.30 pm, rest of year shorter hours. $8, $5 w/student ID. (Ask about 3-site discovery package for one price. Save 20%.) _www.mcq.org/en/mcq/index.html_.

Upper Town, outside the walls to the west of Port St-Louis. This area is reached by continuing west from the walled city along Rue St-Louis and Grande Allee Est, which also brings you to the Battlefield Park area.

Assemblée Nationale du Québec - Parliament Buildings, on Grande Allée at Honore Mercier, 643-7239/(866) députés (337-8837). The main building, built in 1884, is in Second Empire style inspired by the Louvre. The bronze statues in front represent the historical figures of Québec. From the visitors gallery you can view debates in French. Guided tours are offered in English and French. Open Sep-June Mon-Fri 9am-4.30 pm; June-Sep, Daily 9am-4:30pm, weekends from 10 am. Free. Also Le Parlementaire restaurant and National Assembly Boutique. _www.assnat.qc.ca_.

L'Observatoire de la Capitale, Edifice Marie-Guyart, 1037, Rue de La Chevrotière. Ride to the top of Quebec's tallest building for a bird's eye view of the city.

Admission $5, $4 w/student ID. _www.observatoirecapitale.org_.

Beyond the City. Ile d'Orléans This large island in the St Lawrence is a slice of 17th century France. Wander around the old houses, mills, churches. Also known for its handicrafts, strawberries, home-made treats and **Chocolaterie**, 828-2250. Reached by the bridge from the mainland, with a 65 km round-island drive and bike path; various picturesque towns along the way. _www.iledorleans.com._

Chemin du Roy. Hwy 138 along the north bank of the St Lawrence southwest to Montréal, the Kings Highway is Canada's oldest road for vehicles, first completed in 1737 it runs mainly along the banks of the river from Saint-Augustin-de-Desmaures near Québec City, to Repentigny, in the Lanaudière region. _www.bonjourquebec.com/anglais/idees_vac/circuits/chemin_roy.html._ A useful brochure with a map is available from _www.bonjourquebec.com_.

Route de la Nouvelle France (Avenue Royale). If you take Hwy 138 east out of Québec City, you'll come to the **Chute de Montmorency** with its 83 m waterfall that's 30 m higher than Niagara, a footbridge 100 m above the falls, an ultra-modern cable car that whisks you to the top of the falls, and a 487-step panoramic stairway that clings to the side of the cliff. _www.sepaq.com/En/index.cfm._ After this, turn right on to Hwy 360 and you'll be on the **Avenue Royale,** also signposted with many historic points. There is a **Centre d'Interprétation de la Côte-de-Beaupré** well worth visiting at Château-Richer, 824-3677. _www.culture-quebec.qc.ca/cicb._ The route takes you to the Shrine of **Ste Anne-de-Beaupré**, the destination of millions of pilgrims yearly since 18th century ship-wrecked sailors believed Ste Anne was their saviour. Near **Beaupré,** venture to the 74 m **Canyon Ste-Anne** where you can cross three suspension bridges above a spectacular waterfall and rock walls. _www.canyonste-anne.qc.ca._ Continue along the river to picture-postcard **Baie St Paul** where there is an interesting collection of old-time French Canadiana. **The Centre d'Art de Baie St Paul** is at 4 Fafard and opposite is the **Centre d'Exposition**, well-known for showing local arts and crafts and contemporary art. _www.centredart-bsp.qc.ca._ Further on at **St Simeon** there is a ferry crossing to **Rivière du Loup**. There are lots of interesting and fun activities in and around the city in **winter** including: **Les Glissades de la Terrasse Dufferin Terrace - Ice Slides,** 829-9898, 694-9487, 933-5400, next to the Château Frontenac. Huge toboggans slide down at up to 90 km/h, the trip takes seconds. 11 am-11 pm. $2 pp for up to 4 slides.

 Québec and its region is packed with **festive events** from one end of the year to the other, including: **January/February - Carnaval - Winter Carnival**, 626-3716/(866) 422-7628, for 17 days, since 1894 the best-known of Québec's festivals and largest winter carnival in the world, held on the Plains of Abraham and Place d'Youville. Features slide runs, ice-sculptures, dog-sled races, night parades, ice soccer, horse-drawn sleigh rides (_en carriole_), music, skating, flapjack breakfasts and a snow-bath! _www.carnaval.qc.ca/en._ **July – Festival d'été de Québec,** 529-5200/(882) 992-5200. Ten days with over 500 performances from many countries at venues in Old Town. _www.infofestival.com._

Information/Internet

Centre Infotouriste, 12 Rue Ste-Anne, across from the Chateau Frontenac, (877) 266-5687 from elsewhere in Québec. Open daily Jun-Sep 8.30am-7.30pm; otherwise 9am-5pm. Québec Province tourist info. 'Most helpful.'

Bureau d'Information Touristique du Vieux Québec, 835 Ave Wilfrid-Laurier, a short walk outside the Porte St-Louis, 641-6290. Québec City & Area. Bilingual advice, lodging, tourist attractions, etc. 'Very helpful.' Open daily Jun-Sep 8.30am-7.30pm; otherwise 9am-5pm. _www.quebecregion.com_.

Tourisme Jeunesse, 94 Blvd Rene Levesque, 522-2552/ (866) 461-8585. Maps, travel guides, hostel membership and insurance sold. Make rsvs here for hostels. Open daily 10am-6pm, Thur/Fri 'til 9pm. _www.tourismej.qc.ca_.

CybarCafé, 359, St-Joseph Est, 529-5301, downtown. 24 hrs. _www.cybar-cafe.com._

Travel
The best way to travel in the city is to walk!

Public Transport: The Le Réseau de transport de la Capitale **(RTC)** provides extensive local bus services, 627-2511, with a few lines that criss-cross the city. The fare is $2.50 if you pay the driver ($2.20 if you buy your ticket at a *tabac*, $1.45 w/student ID); daily passes are available for $5.65. *www.stcuq.qc.ca.*

Intercity Bus: Terminus d'autobus de la Gare du Palais, 320 Rue Abraham-Martin. 525-3000/525-3030. **Intercar,** 5675 Rue de Tournelles, 627-9108/(888) 861-4592, *www.intercar.qc.ca. www.orleansexpress.com.* **Orléans Express,** 842-2281, mainly serves south and east of the river.

Car. If you're driving, note that the old city is full of one-way streets and off-street parking, if you don't have parking where you're staying, it's best in public lots or municipal parking garages ($8-11/day). Motor bikes are forbidden within the walls of the Old Town.

Allo Stop, 467 Rue St Jean, Québec, 522-0056. Ride share. *www.allostop.com.*

Ferries. Société des traversiers du Québec - Across the St Lawrence, 250, rue Saint-Paul (*Basse Ville*) 644-3704/837 2408/ (877) 787-7483. Daily departures from the wharf to Lévis, 6:30am-2.20am. Every half-hour. Trip takes 10 mins. Fare: Jun-Sep $2.50 o/w; low season $2, inc bicycle. Cars $5.60/$5.10. Nice views of Québec, especially at sunset. For details of this service and all other ferries across the St. Lawrence, including links to private ferries, check *www.traversiers.gouv.qc.ca.*

Rail. VIA Rail, Gare du Palais, 450 Rue de la Gare du Palais, 692-3940 (in Québec City) or (888) 842-7733. Also **Gare de St Foy**, 3255 Chemin de la Gare, 658-8798. From here to Montreal takes about three hours and costs $71. *www.viarail.ca.*

Air. Jean-Lesage International Airport (YQB), Ste Foy, Blvd Hamel to Blvd de l'Aéroport, 640-2600. 23 km from city centre. The only way to get into town from the airport is by taxi, at a fixed price of $27. **Coop Taxis Québec,** 525-5191. *www.taxicoop-quebec.com.*

LA GASPÉSIE (THE GASPÉ PENINSULA) This is the part of Québec Province jutting out above New Brunswick into the Gulf of St Lawrence. The word Gaspé derives from the Micmac Indian word meaning 'Lands End'. You'll appreciate this when standing on the shore at Gaspé, for there's nothing but sea between you and Europe. Picturesque fishing villages line the Peninsula; slow, pleasant places in summer, rugged in winter. Inland it's farming country, although a large area is taken up by the Gaspésian Provincial Park.

The route from Québec City to Gaspé runs along the mighty St Lawrence where the scenery closely resembles that of the Maritime Provinces. The North Shore is the more interesting ride, especially if you take the Ave Royale, but at some point you have to take a ferry to get to the South Shore. (The narrower the river at the point of crossing, the cheaper the ferry ride.)

The **Gaspésie Provincial Park** is called the 'sea of mountains' and includes the highest point in the province, 1,268 metre **Mont Jacques Cartier**. A great view of the scenery is almost guaranteed from the hike to the top and perhaps even a sight of the caribou who make this area their natural habitat. Mornings are the time you are most likely to see them. The park has 25 peaks over 1,000 metres high, including the well-known **Monts Chic-Chocs.** The park is open year round; for information call 763-7494. *www.sepaq.com/En/index.cfm.*

Round the top of the peninsula is **Gaspé** itself, where Jacques Cartier came ashore in 1533 and set up a cross to stake France's claim to Canada.

www.ville.gaspe.qc.ca/english/profile.html. The **Jacques-Cartier Heritage Walk** provides you with details of the long history and culture of the area: Get information about it and other local points of interest from the **Office du Tourisme**, 27 Blvd York East, 368-6335. *www.tourismegaspe.org/EN_H/*.

Nearby at the fvurthest reach of the peninsula is **Forillon National Park**, 122 Gaspé Blvd, 368-5505/(800) 463-6769, $6 entry. Forillon scenery is typified by jagged cliffs and fir-covered highlands. The park is criss-crossed by many hiking trails and on the way you may see deer, fox, bear or moose. Large colonies of seabirds such as cormorants, gannets and gulls nest on the cliff headlands and it is possible to see whales and seals basking offshore. Naturalists offer talks and slide presentations at the **Interpretation Centre** on Hwy 132 near **Cap des Rosiers**. There are also reception centres at Penouille and L'Anse-Au-Griffon.

The views all around the coast are fantastic but none better than a few kilometres south at **Percé**. The village takes its name from **Rocher Percé**, the pierced rock, which is just offshore. You can walk there on a sandbar at low tide, and it's also a good point for whale-spotting, April-December. *www.rocherperce.qc.ca.* From Percé boat trips go to nearby **Ile Bonaventure**, where there is a bird sanctuary. *www.rocherperce.ca/an/pat.asp*.

The telephone code is 418.

Accommodation

Auberge Le Balcon Vert Backpackers Hostel, 22 Cote du Balcon Vert, **Baie St-Paul**, 435-5587. Open June-Oct, Dorm $18/20, $42/47 for private cabin, $16.50/18.25 campsites. Breakfast $4.50. High up in the hills, has nice views. *www.balconvert.charlevoix.net.*

Auberge de Cap Aux Os Hostel (HI-C), 2095 Blvd Grande-Gréve, Gap-Aux-Os (actually within the Forillon National Park), 892-5153. $16/$20 non-members. Laundry, linen & bike rental. 'Very friendly, bilingual but mostly French.' Take coach or train from Québec City to Gaspé, 25 kms from hostel. Take taxi.' *www.hihostels.ca/hostels/Quebec/*.

Auberge du Château Bahia (HI-C), 152 Blvd Perron, Pointe à La Garde, Fax - 788-2048. On the shore of the **Baie des Chaleurs**. Castle with a hostel built by the owner, Jean. Laundry, linen rental, free bfast. Dinner served in castle, or afternoon tea on the terraces. 'Excellent atmosphere, excellent food, excellent host.' 'Phone before going to get exact location.' Dorms incl. bfast and linen. Bus stops in front of the hostel upon request. *www.hihostels.ca/hostels/Quebec.*

Auberge Internationale Ste-Anne-Des-Monts, 295 1st Ave Est, Ste-Anne-de-Monts, 763-7123, Shuttle runs into Gaspesian Parc during the summer. 80 beds in 20 rooms. Kitchen, baggage store, internet, laundry, parking. Dorm $24 and up, private room $54. Includes breakfast. Lots of outdoor activities. 'Staff helpful and always smiling.' *www.aubergesgaspesie.com/index.php.*

Camping at the park is available in the summer at **Cap-Bon-Ami**, **Des Rosiers** and **Petit Gaspé**. All three have good recreational facilities. Call (877) 737-3783 for reservations. $23, $25 w/services. *www.pc.gc.ca/pn-np/qc/forillon/index_e.asp.*

CANADIAN WINTER SPORTS

Canada is a winter wonderland of sports. The country's vast, untamed wilderness offers over 300 ski areas and some of the world's best snowboarding and downhill and cross-country skiing. Canadians are also mad keen on ice hockey. For general Canadian sports information go to _www.canadiansport.com_.

EAST—Canada's eastern resorts are a paradise for both downhill and cross-country enthusiasts and tend to be a good deal cheaper than those in the west.
Marble Mt, Steady Brook, Newfoundland, (709) 637-7600 or (888) 462-7253. Offers the best spring skiing east of the Rockies. Lots of trails and plenty of powder. Day pass $38, $28 w/student ID. _www.skimarble.com_.
Ontario and Québec are where the real action is:
Blue Mt, Collingwood, Ontario, (705) 445-0231. This is the biggest and highest ski area in S Ontario. Great diversity of runs with new ones being cleared regularly. Day pass $49. _www.bluemountain.ca_.
Horseshoe Resort, Barrie, Ontario, (705) 835-2790. This is the busiest resort in the Barrie area. Quieter times are during the week and at night. Good skiing for all levels. 'Helpful staff and well maintained runs.' Day pass $43 (8 hrs), 4 hr passes $38. _www.horseshoeresort.com_.
Loch Lomond, Thunder Bay, Ontario, (807) 475-7787. One of the best hills in Thunder Bay with a good cross-section of different skill level terrain. Day pass $37-$34, $32-29 w/student ID. _www.loch.on.ca_.
Mt St Louis Moonstone, Coldwater, Ontario, (705) 835-2112. Downhill and cross-country trails, good spot for beginners and intermediates. 'The hills are always groomed to perfection and lift lines are never too busy.' Day pass $45. _www.mslm.on.ca_.
Mt St Anne, Beaupré, Québec, (418) 827-4561. Great downhill, cross-country and 24 hr skiing with plenty of variety. 'A hidden treasure.' Day pass: $50.42, $39.99 (ages 14-22), ½ day: $39.12, $30.43 (ages 14-22). _www.mont-sainte-anne.com_.
Mt Tremblant, Québec, (819) 681-2000. Tremblant is the ultimate definition for tons of snow, countless number of trails and variety of terrain. 'Peaceful, scenic cross-country trails.' Good employment opportunities. Day pass $53. _www.tremblant.ca_.
Stoneham, Québec, (418) 848-2411. A medium sized resort with trails for every level. 'Great variety of terrain and great nightlife.' Day pass $41, $31 w/student ID. _www.ski-stoneham.com_.

WEST—The Rockies are _the_ place to ski in the west.
Fortress Mt, Kananaskis Country, Alberta, (403) 264-5825. Heaven for snowboarders, lots of natural half-pipes, powder, trees and no one to bug you. 'Love it.' Day pass: $33.65, $25.20 w/student ID, ½ day (after 12pm): $27, $21 w/student ID. _www.skifortress.com_.
Lake Louise, Alberta, (403) 522-3555. Plenty of snow and plenty of challenge, huge diversity of terrain, beautiful scenery and well groomed runs. Good employment opportunities in surrounding hotels and restaurants. 'An absolute treat for skiers and snowboarders, their bowls are the best!' Day pass $57, $47 w/student ID. _www.skilouise.com_.
Sunshine Village, Banff, Alberta, (403) 762-6500. Good powder and wide range of trails. Excellent for beginners. Good employment opportunities. Day pass $59, $47 w/student ID. _www.skibanff.com_.
Big White, Kelowna, BC, (250) 765-3101. Perfect for intermediates, one of the

best mountains for powder with wide groomed runs. Recently expanded with lots of new facilities and fast lifts. Day pass $56. _www.bigwhite.com_.

Red Mt, Rossland, BC, (250) 362-7384. One of Canada's oldest resorts, challenging to both skiers and snowboarders. Good powder, tree skiing, quiet lifts. 'Radical expert terrain but most of it is unmarked'. Day pass $48. _www.ski-red.com_.

Silver Star Mt, Vernon, BC, (250) 542-0224. Home of the Canadian National Cross Country Team, with over 45 km of groomed trails. Challenging downhill runs for all levels and, of course, outstanding cross-country conditions. Day pass $56. _www.skisilverstar.com_.

Whistler/Blackcomb, Whistler, BC, (800) 766-0449. Has been recognised as N America's best, most hard-core ski/snowboard resort. The most challenging peaks and the highest vertical rise in the north. Massive diversity of trails and outstanding facilities. 'Go to heaven and ski like hell.' 'Expensive but worth every penny.' Day pass $39 (students)-$47 (adults). _www.whistler-blackcomb.com_.

Information

For information on these resorts and others, visit _www.goski.com/resorts/rcan/canada.htm_ or _www.skinetcanada.com_.
Accommodation listings can be found at _www.canadianskihostels.com_.

ICE HOCKEY Hockey is Canada's most popular spectator sport by far and one of the country's most widely played recreational sports. The **National Hockey League** (NHL) is the professional league comprising 30 North American teams including 6 Canadian based teams. Although many teams are located in the US, the majority of NHL players are Canadian. The **Calgary Flames, Edmonton Oilers, Montreal Canadiens, Ottawa Senators, Toronto Maple Leafs** and the **Vancouver Canucks**, slug it out among the top teams for the Stanley Cup, a trophy symbolic of hockey supremacy in N America. The hockey season runs from October-June. _www.nhl.com_.

RINGETTE This is a relatively new sport that has attracted a large following in Canada. More than 50,000 ringette competitors play on approximately 2,500 teams. Played mostly by women, ringette is similar to ice hockey, but a rubber ring replaces the puck. Details can be obtained at _www.ringette.ca_.

SKATING Canada also excels at figure skating. A vast network of clubs throughout the country has produced a long line of medallists including Barbara Ann Scott and Kurt Browning in the Olympics and, more recently, Elvis Stojko in the World Championships. As a spectator sport, figure skating has steadily increased in popularity over the past several years. Although not as widely practised, speed skating has produced one of Canada's greatest Winter Olympians, Gaetan Boucher; the first Canadian ever to win two golds at the same Olympic Games in 1984.

CURLING It's a little like hockey, a little like chess, a little like shuffleboard, and a lot like mopping the floor. Canada is a forerunner in the world of curling, and won the first five World Curling Championships.

ICE-FISHING Exactly what you think it is-fishing through a hole you make in the ice-just be careful you don't fall in!

THE PRAIRIE PROVINCES

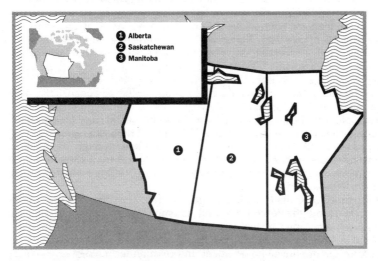

1. Alberta
2. Saskatchewan
3. Manitoba

The terrain in Alberta, Manitoba and Saskatchewan is primarily prairie, with countless sunflowers and endless acres of wheat. Even as western Alberta rises up to meet the glorious Canadian Rockies, you might hear locals sigh, 'the Rockies are nice, but they get in the way of the view'. Grain was once the foundation of the economy of these provinces, but today oil, information technology, cattle, and tourism are the leading industries.

Although the major cities of the prairie are fast-growing centres of commerce and culture, a rough frontier edge remains. Vast areas of virgin wilderness are still there for the intrepid to explore and conquer; it's even possible to travel for days in some places without ever seeing another human being.

ALBERTA

In 2005, when Alberta welcomed the Queen for its 100th birthday celebrations, the Province had plenty to celebrate. It's booming, debt free, growing fast, fully wired and festive amid some of the world's cleanest air and most stunning scenery. For more than twenty years, Alberta has enjoyed the highest rate of economic growth among Canada's provinces.

Alberta also arguably has the monopoly on Canada's natural beauty, in the heavily visited **Banff** and **Jasper National Parks**, and **Lake Louise** – Canada's largest ski area, and along the spectacular **Icefields Parkway**. You mustn't miss the grandeur of these amazing places, especially from the top of the Banff Gondola. Lake Louise – and Alberta itself, are named after Queen Victoria's fourth daughter, Princess Louise Caroline Alberta, wife of a Governor General of Canada, Sir John Campbell. Of all Canada's provinces, Alberta has the greatest variety of geographical features, from the towering Rockies to the west to the rolling agricultural land near the US border to flat, checkerboard farmlands to the northern boreal wilderness of lakes, rivers and millions of acres of forests. *www.abheritage.ca.*

There's plenty of white-watering and kayaking too, and thousands of kilometres of biking and hiking trails, including the many north-south highway "trails" reflecting aspects of Alberta, such as the **Boomtown, Buffalo** and **Cowboy Trails.** *www.albertatrailnet.com* or *www.trails-canada.com.* Once an economy dependent solely on wheat and cattle, Alberta is now reeling in the proceeds of a multi-billion dollar oil bonanza that will continue for at least the next twenty years. Texans call the Province 'Saudi-Alberta' and the 'Texas of Canada North', but the real oil story here is about Alberta's **oil sands**, first discovered in 1790 in the **Athabasca** region by Peter Pond of the North West Company. Now accessible with today's extraction technologies and profitable at today's prices, the oil from these bitumen sands represents 'resources beyond belief', among the largest hydrocarbon deposits in the world.

With most of Canada's oil and gas on tap, the three million or so Albertans enjoy the lowest tax and unemployment rates and highest investment per capita in the country, and continuing surpluses. In 2005, every man, woman and child in the Province received a $400 cheque in the mail from the provincial government! Information technology is also high on the list, producing about $9 billion a year, wired by Alberta's **Supernet** *www.albertasupernet.ca* that provides broadband access to almost every town in the Province. *www.alberta-canada.com.*

Although Alberta gets hot in summer, cold, snowy weather can linger into May before returning again as early as September. The driest place in Canada is Medicine Hat. *www.albertasource.ca.* Before going to Alberta, first visit the excellent websites *www.travelalberta.com* and *www.explorealberta.com* (which has over 900 places to stay and 600 campgrounds listed).

National Parks: Waterton Lakes, Banff, Jasper, Elk Island, Wood Buffalo (not developed, no accommodation). *www.pc.gc.ca/progs/np-pn/index_E.asp.* *The telephone area code is 780 for Edmonton and Jasper, 403 for Banff and Calgary.*

NORTH EAST ALBERTA This is where modern Alberta began, as a fur-trapping hub for the North West Company (NWC) and Hudson's Bay Company (HBC), and more recently revitalized as the undisputed center of one of the world's largest oil reserves, based on the Athabasca tar sands.

Fort Chipewyan at the western end of Lake Athabasca far in Alberta's north east was the earliest European settlement in the Province, named after the local Indians in 1788, one of the HBC's most important regional trading headquarters and the oldest continuously inhabited settlement in Alberta. To reach here in the 1700s, it was 75 days travel by canoe and portage from Lake Superior for the hardy, mostly French, *voyageurs* of the North West Company (NWC), a journey that began far to the east at Lachine on the St Lawrence River. Today, the only way to reach here in summer is a 50 minute flight from Fort McMurray via Air Mikisew, which has three services daily except Sunday, (800)-268-7112. *www.airmikisew.com.*

Fort Chipewyan is tiny, with a single general store and the **Peter Pond Hotel,** named after the old explorer and founding partner in the NWC who discovered the local tar sands. _www.peterpondsociety.com_. The **Bicentennial Museum**, with a history of the wood buffalo, is a replica of the Hudson's Bay Store, opened by the Fort Chipewyan Historical Society in 1990. Old fort sites, ancient trails, graveyards, trapper's cabins and other landmarks dot the nearby countryside. Places to stay include the **Fort Chipewyan Lodge** 697-3679, **Moose Crossing Lodge** 697-3521 _www.moosecrossing.ca_, and **Wah Pun B& B** 697-3030. _www.fortchipewyan.com._

North America's largest free-roaming buffalo herd is contained in the far NE of Alberta in **Wood Buffalo National Park,** Canada's largest national park and one of the largest in the world. This area is accessible only by water in summer and remains relatively undeveloped. It has World Heritage status from UNESCO. The Park is also a vast nesting area for migrant birds, including the only remaining natural nesting area for whooping cranes. In 1987, the local Cree Indians were given about $27 million and hunting rights on three million acres of the Park in settlement of long-standing land claims. All-weather road access to the Park is only via **Ft. Smith,** in the NW Territories, where there is another Visitor Centre, (867) 872-7960. For road conditions, check the Park Hotline at (867) 872-7962 or the Regional Municipality of Wood Buffalo at (780) 697-3600. The Park is open year round, free. _www.pc.gc.ca/buffalo._

Booming **Fort McMurray**, south of Fort Chipewyan and about five hours drive NW of Edmonton up Hwy 63, is the centre of Canada's incredible oil sands rush, sitting on the largest single known oil deposit in the world, estimated at the equivalent of 1.7-2.5 trillion barrels of heavy oil, thinly veiled by muskeg peat. As such, you can almost smell the money being mined here, some of it in open pits with lorries so enormous that smaller ones fly flags so they don't get run over.

The monster trucks, and an 850 tonne bucket-wheel excavator, are on display at the **Oil Sands Discovery Centre,** 515 MacKenzie Boulevard, 743-7167, sponsored by the Canadian Institute of Mining, Metallurgy and Petroleum. Open daily 9am-5pm in summer; rest of year 10am-4pm (closed Mondays). $6. _www.oilsandsdiscovery.com._ You can also 'experience the energy' on tours of **Syncrude Canada** or **Suncor Energy** mine sites, where huge shovels load 380 ton-payload trucks with black oil sands that you might mistake for molasses. The tours are arranged through **Fort McMurray Tourism**: Res req, recommended 7-10 days ahead, May-Oct, (800) 565-3947. Suncor's site, which handles about a million tons of rock a day, is the world's largest mining operation.

Places to stay in Fort McMurray, such as are available, are listed on _www.fortmcmurraytourism.com_. Be advised that almost 10,000 oil sand workers are living in camps, and another two thousand in hotels, so rooms may be scarce for the indefinite future. Be sure you line up a place to stay before you go.

EDMONTON   The Hudson's Bay Company had canny prescience when it established **Ft Edmonton** as a trading post in 1794: centrally located astride the North Saskatchewan River, the hexagonal fort would become HBC's most productive post in the territories, a key trading centre for Plains Indians, and eventually the provincial capital.

Now, Edmonton's proximity to the huge oil sands in north east Alberta and its role as air, rail and road transportation hub near the province's center of economic gravity have made it one of the fastest growing cities in Canada, with no end in sight. Most of Alberta's forests are north of Edmonton, so $6 billion a year forestry earnings (with annual caps on output) have also had a big impact on the city; northwestern Alberta, with its long summer daylight hours, is also one of the most productive northerly grain and cattle regions in North America.

Edmonton is the most northerly major city on the continent with a wealth of attractions, home to a progressive university, the first modern LRT/subway system in North America, the world's largest indoor shopping mall, **West Edmonton Mall** (in the only province with no local sales tax), and some of the finest sporting facilities anywhere. It's a good place to launch a trip up north or westward into the Rockies: Calgary is three hours drive south; Jasper four hours to the west; Dawson Creek, BC, on the way to Alaska, 8 hours to the north west; and Enterprise, the first stop in the Northwest Territories, 14 hours north. From Edmonton you can catch the famous VIA Rail *Canadian* west to Jasper and Vancouver or east to Winnipeg and Toronto. Before leaving, stop first and drive carefully at **Elk Island National Park**, home to herds of free roaming bison, moose, deer, and elk, less than an hour east of the city. *www.edmonton.com/tourism.*
The area code is 780.

Accommodation

Commercial Hotel, 10329 82nd Ave, 439-3981. S-$34, S-$45 w/ bath, D-$38, $56 w/bath, key deposit $10. Older hotel in Old Strathcona. Coffee shop. Live entertainment daily at Blues on Whyte pub. 439-5058. *www.spirit-of-canada.com.*

Downtown YMCA, 10030 102 A Ave, 421-9622. Nr Greyhound. Dorm rooms $25 (5 night max); student rates $115 weekly (6th Fl); S-$38-$50, D-$46-$56, $10 key deposit. Free internet, TV common room, indoor pool. *www.edmonton.ymca.ca.*

Edmonton HI-Hostel, 10647 81st Ave, 988-6836/(877) 467-8336. 88 beds. Common room, snack bar, showers, kitchen/laundry, BBQs in summer. $21-24 IYH members, $26-29 non, June-Sept; less rest of year. Cycling in river valley, summer festivals. Discounts for members at local cafes, museums. 'Easy walk from downtown. Comfortable.' *www.hihostels.ca/hostels/Alberta.*

Grand Hotel, 10266 103 St, 422-6365/(888) 422-6365. S-$42-58, D-$55-65t. 75 rooms. Character and charm. Handy location-across from Greyhound. Breakfast included.

St Joseph's College, 89th Ave at 114 St on Uni of Alberta campus, 492-7681 x 222. A better alternative to the more institutionalised and expensive uni accom nearby. S /w breakfast -#$25, weekly $140. Full board S-$35, weekly $210. Rsvs in summer. *www.ualberta.ca/~stjoseph.*

University of Alberta Residence, Lister Hall, 87th Ave & 116th St, 492-4281/(800) 615-4807. Open to non-students May-Aug, dorm S-$30, semi-private S-$39 D-$40-$49. *www.uofaweb.ualberta.ca/residences. See Guest Accom.*

Camping: Shoreline Camping and Fishing Resort, 6 km off Boyle on Hwy 663 E. 2 hrs from Edmonton, 689-4363. Sites $17, $25 w/full-hook up, outdoor pool, volleyball courts and boat launch. *www.northgate.ab.ca/northgat/shoreline*

FOOD

Downtown along 104 St is **Restaurant Row** with an array of eateries within walking distance of each other and abundance of coffee shops. On **Whyte**, from 99 St to 109 St, there are lots of eateries and coffee shops in Old Strathcona.

Chianti's, 10501 82 Ave, 439-9829. Inexpensive Italian dishes, ranging from pasta to seafood, and daily speciality wines. Sun-Thur 11am-11pm, Fri/Sat 'til 12am. Mon-Tues all day pasta dishes, $5.95.

David's, 8407 Argyll Rd, 468-1167. Come dine here for the true taste of Alberta beef. Inc dry ribs, mud pies. Mon-Wed 7am-9pm, Thu-Sat 7am-10pm.

Earl's, five locations, one on Uni of Alberta campus, an Oiltown institution. Generous servings. Ask for a pint of Albino Rino.

King & I, 8208 107 St, 433-2222. Thai/Viet on the cheap, with good vegetarian dishes. Dinner from $13, Mon-Thu 11.30am-10.30pm, Sat 4.30pm-11.30pm. The Stones eat here when in town - the menu was take-out fare during their rehearsals.

Sidetrack Café, 10333 112 St, 421-1326. Cozy, with live music nightly, cover varies. Inc 889 railroad dining car. $1 off draft pints 4-7pm. Pasta, burgers, pizza and steaks, $8-15. Mon-Fri 4pm-1am, Sat-Sun from 9am. _www.sidetrackcafe.com._

Of Interest

Alberta Government House, 12845 102 Ave, 427-2281. Built in 1913 as a residence of the Lt. Governors, the sandstone building has also seen service as a WWII Veterans hospital. In 1985, it was designated a Provincial Historic Resource. It's open to the public on Sat, Sun and hols 11am-4.30pm. Free guided tours. _www.assembly.ab.ca/lao/library/lt-gov/house.htm._

Chinatown, 102 Ave & 97 St, E of downtown. See the Harbin Gate that opens into the heart of Edmonton's Chinese community, named after Edmonton's sister city far north in Heilongjiang province in China, with similar short summers and long winters. Be sure to roll a ball in the lion's mouth for good luck. Chinatown centres on 95th St, btw 102nd and Jasper. _www.ecmcc.ca._

Edmonton Art Gallery (99th St & 102A Ave) 2 Sir Winston Churchill Sq, 422-6223. More than 30 exhibitions each year include contemporary and historical art from Canada and around the world. Has 5,000 items in collection.Tue-Wed and Fri 10.30am-5pm, Thu 10.30-8pm Sat-Sun 11am-5pm. $9, $6 w/student ID. Thurs 4pm-8pm, free _www.edmontonartgallery.com._

Edmonton Queen **Riverboat,** 9734 98th Ave, 424-2628, (888) 855-2628, paddlewheeler cruises from Rafter's Landing on the North Saskatchewan, three times daily, 11am, 2pm, 6 pm (w dinner), Thu-Sun. One hour or so. $15.95, dinner cruise extra. Sun noon is brunch cruise. Rsvs required. _www.edmontonqueen.com._

Fort Edmonton Historical Park, corner of Whitemud and Fox Dr, 496-8787. Canada's largest living history museum, on 158 acres, is a reconstruction of 75+ buildings on a Hudson's Bay Co Trading Post of 1846. 'Worth a visit.' Summer daily 10am-6pm, $9.25. _www.edmonton.ca/fort_ Nearby is the **John Janzen Nature Centre** with 3.5 kilometres of self-guided nature trails. $1.75.

Odyssium, 11211 142nd St, 451-3344. Over $2 million worth of exhibits, IMAX film theatre, computer labs, exhibit gallery, observatory with the largest planetarium dome in Canada, and science stage. In 2005, AB-TELUS and the Odyssium announced a 20-year partnership to expand and enhance exhibits and programming at the facility, to be re-named 'TELUS World of Science Edmonton'. $9.95 museum day pass, $9.95 IMAX tkt/$8.95 students; combo admission $15.95/$13.50. Daily 10am-9pm. _www.odyssium.com._

Old Strathcona Historic Distric. In August about half-a-million people come to here south of Edmonton's downtown, to Edmonton's **Fringe Theatre Festival,** _www.fringetheatreadventures.ca,_ the largest in North America, second in size only to Edinburgh's. This trendy district, with buildings dating to 1891, houses scores of cafes and restaurants, a Saturday farmer's market with 130 stalls (10310 83 Avenue), eight theatre companies and dozens of antique stores (at the **Antique Mall** on 103rd St), - Edmonton's version of Greenwich Village.

The main drag, **Whyte Ave** (82nd Ave), has been the centre of things since the 1890s when the railway reached here and the Klondike Gold Rush spurred its development. The **Strathcona Visitors Centre** has maps available for walking tours; open Mon-Fri 8:30am-4:30pm., at Suite 401, 10324 Whyte Ave, 433-5866, *www.osf.strathcona.org.* In July, here you'll find the **Whyte Ave Street Sale, Silly Summer Parade**, and the **Art Walk Parade** *www.oldstrathcona.ca, www.osba.ab.ca.* Then there's the **Historic Edmonton Week Festival** and **Doors Open** in late July, celebrating people, history and architecture of the city *www.historicedmonton.ca*, and the **International Film Festival** in October *www.edmontonfilmfest.com*.

Old Strathcona buzzes with over thirty pubs and nightspots on or close to Whyte. From 104 St at 85 Ave in Old Strathcona, the **Edmonton Radial Railway Society** takes you on a scenic 20 minute streetcar ride 48 metres above the N Saskatchewan, the highest river crossing by a streetcar in the world, to Edmonton's Legislature (Grandin LRT Station) and Jasper Ave, downtown. Fare $3 r/t. Daily May-late Aug. Every ½ hr, 11am-3pm. 437 7721. *www.edmonton-radial-railway.ab.ca.*

Legislature Building 97th Ave & 108th St, 427-7362. Near the site of the original Fort Edmonton. Built in Beaux-arts style in granite and sandstone at the beginning of this century (1907-12). On the Fifth floor is an acoustic curiosity called the Magic Spot and paintings of Alberta's 'Famous Five' - women who were instrumental, in 1925, in changing Canadian law to include women as persons in matters of rights and privileges. Free tours every hr or $^1/_2$ hr. Summer Mon-Fri 8.30am-5pm, Sat-Sun 9am-5pm; winter slightly shorter hours. *www.assembly.ab.ca.*

Royal Alberta Museum, 12845 102nd Ave, 453-9100, W of downtown. Has three major galleries: **Wild Alberta** – beneath the prairies, inside a stream, below the snow-pack: how ecosystems work; **Natural History** - cross section of 381 year-old Douglas fir, exquisite gems and minerals 'whose shape and colour almost defy belief,' 3-dimensional guide to the birds of Alberta, dinosaurs and giants of the Ice Age, etc. and **Syncrude Gallery of Aboriginal Culture** - First Peoples' history spanning 11,000 years. Daily 9am-5pm. $10, $7 w/student ID. Sat & Sun 9am-11am half price. *www.pma.edmonton.ab.ca.*

Muttart Conservatory 9626-96A St, 496-8755. Four glass pyramids nestled in the city centre feature more than 700 species of plants from jungles to deserts to cool and misty temperate climates. Mon-Fri 9am-5.30pm, Sat-Sun 11am-5.30pm, $7.50. *www.edmonton.ca/muttart.*

Ukrainian Canadian Archives and Museum of Alberta 9543 110 Ave and, in future, 9662 Jasper Avenue, 424-7580. Traces history of Ukranian pioneers in Alberta, one of the largest ethnic groups on the Canadian prairies. Includes costumes, paintings, folk art. Tues-Fri 10am-5pm, Sat from noon. Hours subject to change, phone prior to visit. Donations appreciated. *www.ucama.ca.*

Valley Zoo, 13315 Buena Vista Road at 87th Ave, W of Edmonton, nr N Saskatchewan River, 496-8787/6912. 70-acre home to over 100 exotic and endangered species and around 300 animals. Daily 9.30am-8pm, $7.50. *www.edmonton.ca/attractions.*

West Edmonton Mall (WEM) 170th St & 87th Ave, 444-5380, (800) 661-8890. Listed by *Guinness* as the largest shopping centre in the world and largest parking lot (20,000 cars, free). Covers 48 city blocks, with over 800 stores, markets, cafes and eateries. Eight theme areas including **Galaxyland Amusement Park**, world's largest indoor amusement park, with 25 rides and attractions, **World Water Park,** world's largest indoor wave pool, **Deep Sea Adventure** with Santa Maria, exact replica of Columbus' ship, in world's largest indoor lake; **Sea Life Caverns** with over 200 species of fish, sharks, penguins, and Giant Pacific Octopus; 21 movie theatres, dolphin tank, bungee jumping, casinos, skating rink where the Oilers practice, petting zoo, 10 aviaries—you name it! 'Mind boggling.' 'A must see.' Daily Mon-Sat 10am-9pm, Sun noon-6pm. *www.westedmontonmall.com.*

Entertainment

Check *www.edmontonplus.ca* for all current and planned entertainment in the city, by date, type, and neighbourhood. Edmonton has a talented opera company and symphony orchestra. For performance information, call the **Edmonton Opera** (_www.edmontonopera.com_) at Winspear Centre, 9720 102 Avenue NW, 424-4040 or the **Edmonton Symphony** (_www.edmontonsymphony.com_), also at the Winspear Centre, box office #4 Sir Winston Churchill Square, in the Arts District, downtown Edmonton, 428-1414.

Festivals. Edmonton is packed with festivals, especially in July, and especially in Old Strathcona (see above). There are over 20 major festivals throughout the year. Among the events: **Edmonton Folk Music Festival,** four days in mid-Aug, Gallagher Park (Cloverdale, E of downtown), 429-1899. Features traditional and bluegrass music, country, blues and Celtic music—all under the bright Alberta sun. Tickets go fast. _www.edmontonfolkfest.org._

Edmonton Street Performers Festival, Sir Winston Churchill Sq, 99 Street and 102 Ave in downtown Arts District, 425-5162, ten days in mid-July. Downtown streets come alive with magicians, jugglers, clowns, mime artists, musicians and comics. _www.edmontonstreetfest.com._

Fringe Theatre Festival, 10330 84 Ave, 448-9000. For 10 days in mid-Aug. Main festival is located in and around the TransAlta Arts Barns btw 103 St (Gateway Boulevard) and 104 St (Calgary Trail) and btw Whyte Ave and 86th Ave. Tickets max $13, $10 at door. _www.fringetheatreadventures.ca._

Jazz City International Festival, 202-10518 82 Ave NW, 432-7166, 10 days late June. Will celebrate 25th birthday in 2006 after hiatus in 2005. Canadian and overseas jazz musicians. Venues inc Abbey Glen Park, McIntyre Park, TransAlta Art Barns, Winspear Centre etc. Running simultaneously is **The Works,** a celebration of the visual arts. _www.jazzcity.ca._

Klondike Days, 423-2822/472 7210, (888) 800-7275. Edmonton returns to the 1890s for Klondike Days, 10 days at end-July, a whirlwind of street festivities at a dozen venues, capped off with the great **Klondike Days Exposition** at **Northlands Park**. 'Excellent entertainment.' Immense, cheap, 'Klondike pancake breakfasts' are served in the open air, massed marching bands compete in the streets, and down the North Saskatchewan River float more than 100 of the weirdest-looking home-built rafts ever seen. _www.klondikedays.com._

Information/Internet Access

Edmonton Tourism, Visitor Information Centre (VIC) World Trade Centre, 9990 Jasper Ave., main floor, 426-4715, (800) 463-4667, weekdays summer and winter 6am-9pm, weekends 9am-5pm; also the main Gateway Park Information Centre, at 2404 Gateway Blvd, SW (Hw 2 S), 496-8400, has longer hours: daily 8am-8pm; after Labor Day, daily 8.30am-4.30pm. _www.tourism.ede.org._

Wi-Fi Spots, Holiday Inn Edmonton-Convention Center, all Earls restaurants, Fairmont Hotel, West Edmonton Mall, and Westin Hotel, among others. _www.jiwire.com_, _www.hotpepper.ca/wifi._

Internet at Cyber One, 13222 118th Ave, 413-9982. Open daily noon-midnight; $6/hr. _www.cyber-one.ca_ and **Cyber Cafe Planet Inc,** 10442 82 Ave in Old Strathcona, above the Greek restaurant, 433-9730 and 10354 Jasper Ave, 425-9730. Open daily, 24 hours, $5/hr. Serve coffee and snacks.

Stanley A Milner Public Library, 7 Sir Winston Churchill Square, 496-7000. Free access, rsvs rec. Mon-Fri 9am-9pm, Sat 9am-6pm, Sun 1pm-5pm. _www.epl.ca_ and _www.publib.edmonton.ab.ca._ Alberta's SuperNet connects all Alberta libraries with new broadband applications being developed by Alberta Education, Alberta Health & Wellness, the Government of Alberta and municipal governments. _www.albertasupernet.ca._

Travel

City Transit. Edmonton Transit System (ETS), 496-1611 for info. Operates city buses as well as the silent, streamlined and comfortable LRT (Light Rail Transit).

For schedules and maps, see _www.edmonton.ca/transit_ Edmonton is considered the 'birthplace of modern LRT in North America,' built over 25 years ago. Goes 12.3 km from the NE (Clareview), tunneling via six underground stops under Churchill and Jasper Ave downtown, crossing the N Saskatchewan River to the campus of Alberta Uni. Basic fare: $2 o/w, day pass $6. Note: ETS does not provide service to the International Airport as it is outside the city.

Greyhound, 10324 103 St, 420-2400/413-8747/(800)661-8747. _www.greyhound.ca._

Red Arrow Express 425-0820/(800) 232-1958. Three-hour coach service between Edmonton and Calgary via Red Deer, weekdays, five-hour service to Ft McMurray and to Banff and Lake Louise. Tkts and pick up at Holiday Inn Express Plaza, Plaza Level, 10014 104th Street. _www.redarrow.pwt.ca._

CN/VIA Rail Station, 12360 121st St, off the Yellowhead Trail, approx. 8-10 km from downtown; taxi $8-$9, no transit bus, (888) 842-7245. The cross-country _Canadian_, three times a week from Toronto to Vancouver stops at Edmonton.

Edmonton International Airport (EIA), 890-8382/(800) 268-7134, 18 miles S of the city near Leduc on Hwy 2, 35 minutes from d/town. _www.edmontonairports.com_. Airport Express, within the VIC at downtown World Trade Centre, provides check-in and transportation services, with self-serve Air Canada and WestJet check-in kiosks and flight information screens. **Sky Shuttle,** 465-8515, runs from airport to the VIC and other stops downtown, inc Greyhound terminal, nine hotels, every 20 minutes to and from the airport, weekdays, 6 am-9 pm, every 30 minutes on weekends, trip takes about 40-55 minutes; also has West End (WEM) and University runs every 45 minutes. Check website for schedules. $10/13 o/w. _www.edmontonskyshuttle.com_

Co-op Taxi, 425-2525. _www.co-optaxi.com_, **Yellow Cab** 462-3456,   _ww.edmonton-skyshuttle.com/YellowCab.html._

NEARBY EDMONTON All round Edmonton in every direction, there are

trails. Nearby Edmonton, 20 minutes to the north west on the 34 km **St Albert Trail** (Hwy 2), is **St Albert**, the oldest non-fortified community in Alberta, first settled by the Metis and the French. Its river-lot system is styled after those of rural Québec, along the Sturgeon River. For information, go to the Visitor's Centre on the trail at the entrance to the city, 459-1724. The farmer's market in downtown St. Albert, is Western's Canada's largest; every Saturday July-Sept.

The **Alberta Buffalo Trail** is a loose-knit cluster of communities in East Central Alberta (_www.albertabuffalotrail.org_) including **Stettler**, two hours or so south of Edmonton, via Hwy 2 and east on Hwy 12, where you can ride the **Alberta Prairie Railway** on day-long excursions pulled by vintage locos, with meals, entertainment and perhaps a train robbery! Year-round, 4611 - 47 Avenue, (403) 742-2811/ (800) 282-3994. _www.absteamtrain.com_.

Less than an hour east of Edmonton on Hwy 16, **Elk Island National Park** is an aspen wilderness full of herds of bison (known more commonly as buffalo), 1,600 wapiti deer, 900 elk and 400 moose; over 250 species of birds plus over 2,000 beavers and countless tiny critters. The 194 sq km park is Canada's only national park completely surrounded by a fence, 2.2 metres high, designed to keep out predators such as wolves and bears to protect the park's herds of 450 plains and 350 wood bison. Though these herds are impressive to behold, these are trifling numbers compared to the millions of buffalo that once roamed the North American continent from Florida to Oregon. The buffalo were hunted almost to extinction by the end of the 19th century. At Elk Island, it's possible to observe them at close range, but only on the other side of a strong fence. Walking on the buffalo range itself is discouraged!

Elk Island is open throughout the year. The **Visitor Centre** is located north of Hwy 16, 992-5790. Entrance fee: $6, $15 for up to 7 persons. The Park has over 100 kilometres of trails - walks, hikes, campfire talks and theatre programmes are offered by the park rangers. Recreation facilities, including golf, are available on the east shore of Astotin Lake. Camping facilities cost $23 for basic site. _www.parkscanada.gc.ca/elk._

Ukrainian Cultural Heritage Village, on Hwy 16, 25 minutes east of Edmonton, 662-3640. Ukrainian immigrants, played an important role in taming Canada, especially in the west. There are over 1.2 million Canadians of Ukrainian background, making them one of the largest ethnic groups in the country. _www.ucc.ca (go to links)._ This village portrays farmsteads, zemlianka, shops and churches in living-history, with costumed interpreters as real-life Ukrainian settlers who came to the Bloc Settlement in east central Alberta from 1892 to 1933.0. Stroll or go by horse-drawn wagon; authentic Ukrainian fare. Daily 10am-6pm, $8. After Labor Day, open weekends only.

THE ROCKIES Directly west and south west of Edmonton are one of the grandest natural wonders of North America, the Canadian Rockies, straddled to the north by the **Jasper National Park,** four hours drive west from Edmonton and to the south by the **Banff National Park,** an hour or so west of Calgary. The two are linked by a great scenic north-south route, the 230 kilometres **Icefields Parkway**, from Jasper to Lake Louise that takes about three hours, and the **Trans-Canada Highway.** There are ten HI-Hostels in the Park area. The _Mountain Guide_, that covers Banff, Jasper, Kootenay, Yoho, Mount Revelstoke and Glacier National Parks is available from National Park Information Centres, park gates and campgrounds.

The area code in the Jasper region is 780; in the Banff area it's 403.

JASPER NATIONAL PARK In 1817, when factor Jasper Hawes took command of the North West Company's provision post at Brûlé Lake for brigades crossing the **Athabasca Pass** headed for the Pacific, the post became known as 'Jasper's House' and the park and town were named after him. This is the wildest of Canada's mountain parks: 10,878 sq kilometres of lofty, green-forested, snow-capped mountains, canyons, dazzling lakes, glaciers and hot mineral springs, with 1,200 kilometres of back-country trails and some spectacular drives. The vast complex of national parkland here is very popular, with three million people visiting each year. Entry is $8. Camping from $19/night. _www.explorejasper.com_, _www.parkscanada.ca_, _www.pc.gc.ca/pn-np/ab/jasper_ and _www.jaspernationalpark.com_.

Among the animals in the Park are grizzly bears, beavers, caribou, cougars, coyotes, deer, elk, goats, snowshoe hares, lynx, marmots, pine martens, moose, porcupines, sheep, wolves and wolverines. The park includes the highest peak in Alberta - **Mt. Columbia**, 3,747 m; the hydrographic apex of North America, the **Columbia Icefield**, the **Maligne Valley karst**; and the only sand-dune ecosystem in the four mountain parks - **Jasper Lake dunes**. The four park system is a designated UNESCO World Heritage Site.

Spring arrives in mid-April, reaching the mountains by mid-June; summer brings long days in a short season. In July temperatures average 22.5 C. Fall colours burst out in September and October, with lovely clear skies and cooler temperatures. Winter is long and varied, with cold stormy weather that can change quickly to mild chinook winds.

The **Jasper National Park Information Centre** is at 500 Connaught Dr in Jasper, open 365 days, (780) 852-6176. There is also a Parks Canada information desk at the Icefield Centre, 103 km south of Jasper, open daily May-Oct, (780) 852-6288.

One of Jasper Park's biggest attractions is the 22 km long **Maligne Lake**, the second largest glacier-fed lake in the world and one of the most beautiful, surrounded by spectacular peaks heaped with glaciers. The name *La Rivière Maligne* was given by Father P.J. de Smet, a Jesuit missionary, in 1845. The lake is about 48 kilometres south east of Jasper - an hour or so by car along Hwy 16, then take Maligne Road.

Canoes, kayaks and other boats are available at Maligne Lodge, at $25 per hour or $75 per day. The Lodge has home-baked bread, sandwiches, coffee, chili, beer, etc. Before you arrive at the Lake, be sure to visit **Maligne Canyon,** 11 kilometres from Jasper, which has self-guided trails and six footbridges, and a tea-house open in summer. The canyon is a 55 km deep karst incision, one of the best in the Rockies. The Rock Gardens and Boulder Gardens along the way are one of Jasper's best rock climbing areas. There are canyon trips in winter literally on the fantastic frozen river of ice. **Maligne Canyon Restaurant,** 852-3583, is fully licenced, overlooks the Canyon, has fresh salads, pastries and sandwiches made to order. Outside patio barbeque. Apr-Oct, 7am-9pm.

Further along, from the Lodge on the lake, 90-minute cruises on glass-bottomed boats take you to the famous **Spirit Island** with trained guides. Daily, May-Oct. Every hour on the hour 10am-5pm. $35. 850-3370, (866) 625-4463. _www.malignelake.com._ The tour to the lake from Jasper comes highly recommended by previous visitors. You can get tickets at the **Maligne Lake Ticket Office** in the Jasper Marketplace, 627 Patricia St. There are four shuttle buses to the lake daily in summer, starting 8.30am from Jasper.

Within the park it is possible to drive through some of the west's most spectacular mountain scenery. **Whistlers Mountain** is one of the more accessible points: The longest and highest guided aerial tramway in Canada, fifteen minutes south of Jasper off Hwy 93, has put the mountain within reach of even the most nervous would-be mountaineers. In seven minutes, the **Jasper Tramway** whisks you to near the top of the towering peak, to the Upper Station at 2,277 metres. Once you've hiked to the exposed, tree-less summit – about 45 minutes more, the view over the rooftops of the Rockies is breathtaking, including the Rockies highest peak, **Mt Robson** (3,954 ms), on clear days. (**The Whistlers** is named after the high-pitched whistle a hoary marmot makes when it senses danger.) _www.explorejasper.com/sights/tramway.htm._

At the top of the tramway, the buffet-style **Treeline Restaurant** provides a 260° vista of surrounding mountain ranges. 8.30am-10pm in summer, 10am-5pm shoulder periods. $22 inc tax. (780) 852-3093, (866) 850-8726. Close to Whistler Hostel and Campground. Bus connections from RR station, hotels and hostel. _www.jaspertramway.com._ Close to Whistler's, about 20 minutes from downtown Jasper, the **Ski Marmot Basin** overlooks the town with a basket of 84 uncrowded trails for skiing and snowboarding on dry powder. 852-3816, (866) 952-3816. _www.skimarmot.com._

Mt Edith Cavell (3,363 m) is accessible June-October off the old Hwy 93A, 29 kilometres south of Jasper by the narrow, winding 14 kilometres Cavell Road close to the mountain's north face. The mountain, famous for moraines, the Cavell Meadows, and alpine flowers, is named after a British nurse executed during WWII for her part in helping Allied prisoners escape occupied Brussels.

Also in the park are the **Miette Hot Springs,** 60 km east of Jasper along Hwy 16 and off near Pocahontas in the Fiddle Valley; they're the hottest springs in the Canadian Rockies, cooled from 54° C to a soothing 39°C . Miette includes two hot pools, a cool pool and poolside cafe. Open daily May–Oct., $6.25 or $8.75 for the day. 866-3939, (800) 767-1611.

In contrast, there's the huge **Columbia Icefield,** 2 hours north of Banff, whose melting waters empty into the Atlantic, Pacific and Arctic Oceans. Sixty-five miles south from Jasper on Hwy 93, the Icefield is 389 sq kilometres , the largest body of ice south of Alaska, at the peak of which lies the point of **Triple Divide**, where water can flow to either the Atlantic, the Pacific or the Arctic Oceans. Tours are available from the **Icefields Interpretive Centre**, part of the **Icefield Centre**, 103 km south of Jasper, 130 km north of Lake Louise. **Brewster's Ice Age Adventure** provides tours onto the slopes of the **Athabasca Glacier** facing the Centre on vehicles. Apr-Oct, peak Jul-Aug. 90 minutes, dep every 15/30 minutes 9/10am-5pm. _www.columbiaicefield.com._

The recommended way to the glacier in summer is on **Brewster's,** _www.brewster.ca,_ huge 6-wheeled glacier-travel **Snocoach Ice Explorers**, that take 56 passengers from the Centre up the 32% grade to the glacier parking lot over ice 300 ms thick. Heavy jackets must be worn, even in the height of summer and sunblock is advisable. Includes slopes of the **Athabasca Glacier** facing the centre. 90-minutes. $31.95 inc tax. 9am-5pm, Apr-Oct, Sep. peak Jul-Aug. Res not req. Busiest period 10:30am-3pm. (877) 423-7433/(403) 762-6735. _www.columbiaicefield.com_ and _www.brewster.ca._

Icewalks, led by certified guides, leave daily from the Toe-of-the-Glacier parking lot; reserve at the Icefield Chalet Hotel front desk, (780) 852-5595, (800) 565-7547. You can walk across parts of the glacier, but hidden crevasses have killed people and can be dangerous: Don't go beyond the barriers! Better arrange to see the glacier by snowmobile - trips are available on **Athabasca Glacier**, just a mile from the road.

JASPER Jasper is a town of 4,500 people, spread on the banks of the Athabasca River on the eastern slope of the Rockies, accessible from Edmonton - four hours drive along Hwy 16 (**The Yellowhead Highway**), and four-and-a-half hours north west from Calgary along Hwy 93, the **Icelands Parkway**. It's about three hours south of here to Lake Louise. Should you arrive by train, take note of the 70-ft **Raven Totem Pole** at the railway depot, carved by Simeon Stiltae, a master carver of the Haida Indians of the Queen Charlotte Islands.

The first recorded visit here was by a surveyor, David Thompson, in 1810, after which the North West Company built a supply post at Brûlé Lake for its traders crossing the Athabasca Pass, in 1813. The factor at the post was Jasper Hawes. Seven years later, Pierre Bostonnais led a group from the Hudson's Bay Company through the northern Rockies from here. Jasper's history is told at the **Jasper-Yellowhead Museum and Archives**, 400 Pyramid Lake Rd, across from the Jasper Aquatic Centre, (780) 852-3013. Open 10am-9pm daily in summer, 10am-5pm rest of year. $4/$3 student.

At Jasper is the Park headquarters, the municipality is unique in sharing governance with the Parks Canada Agency. _www.jaspercanadianrockies.com_ and _www.jasper-alberta.com_.

Accommodation

Past visitors have recommended contacting the tourist homes/B&Bs for very reasonable rates. **The Jasper Tourism and Commerce Bureau,** 623 Patricia St, 852-3858, has a list of camping grounds, hostels, and hotels in the area, including a vacancy report, see _www.jaspercanadianrockies.com/accommodations.html_ and **Parks Canada Information Office**, 500 Connaught Dr, 852-6176, provides a list of approved tourist homes. **Rocky Mountain Reservations** provides free booking service for accommodation for Banff, Jasper, Lake Louise, Canmore and Kananaskis, inc B&Bs and private homes. _www.rockymountainreservations.com._ Also _www.explorejasper.com/lodging.htm._

Bear Hill Lodge, 100 Bonhomme Street, Box 700, Jasper. (780) 852-3209. Forest cottage/standard rooms w/ one double and one single bed, full bath. Room rates for two guests inc breakfast -$160/night June-Aug, $89 rest of year. _www.bearhilllodge.com._

Jasper House Bungalows, Box 817, 3 km south of Jasper on Hwy 93, (780) 852-4535. 56 cedar log units, inc standard motel rooms, Athabasca River running behind the property. Standard rooms: 2 doubles, full bath, max 4 persons, $150 summer, $105 rest of year. _www.jasperhouse.com._

Sunwapta Falls Resort, Icefield Parkway, 52 km from Jasper on Hwy 93, (780) 852-4852, (888) 828-5777. Cabins in wilderness setting: Rocky Mountain double: room with private bath, two double beds, fridge, and sun deck, for 2 to 4 persons. Price based on double occupancy: Spring/Fall - $99, Summer $179. _www.sunwapta.com._

Hostels: All **HI** hostels in the Jasper area can be contacted on one number 852-3215/(877) 852-0781. Call to make rsvs or email: _jasper@hihostels.ca_ or check out the website at _www.hihostels.ca/hostels/Alberta_ for more information. In summer, reservations recommended or essential.

Athabasca Falls HI-Hostel, 2 km S from Jasper on Hwy 93; E side of Hwy 93. 40 beds. Rustic - no running water, showers, or flush toilets. Purified water for cooking, propane stoves and electric fridges and lights. Cannot make same day arrival res, walk in basis only. Hiking, mountain biking and cross-country ski trails throughout valley, Athabasca Falls nearby. $15+tax members/ $20 non-members.

Beauty Creek Basic HI-Hostel, 87 km S of Jasper; W side of Hwy 93. 22 beds. Rustic - no running water, showers use state-of-the art, man-powered wash house, no flush toilets. Purified water for cooking; propane refrigerator, stoves and lights. Cannot make same day arrival res, walk in only. Cycling destination, close to Stanley Falls, 17 km to Columbia Icefield. Partial closure Oct-Apr; $15/ $20.

Jasper HI-Hostel, 7 km SW of Jasper on Whistler's Mountain Rd, off Hwy 93. Year-round. Res 'essential.' Hiking, biking, skiing, barbecue. Summer: $22/$27. Shuttle service to/from bus and train depots available mid-Apr to mid-Oct.

Maligne Canyon HI-Hostel, 11 km E of Jasper on Maligne Lake Road. 24 beds. Just above Maligne Canyon, open all year. Rustic - no running water, showers, or flush toilets. Purified water for cooking; refrigerator, propane stoves and lights. Hiking, cycling, and cross-country skiing trails, nearby Skyline Trail offers one of the park's most scenic hikes. $15/$20.

Mt Edith Cavell HI-Hostel, 26 km S of Jasper; 13 km off Hwy 93A. 32 beds. 10.5 km straight uphill, not accessible by car in winter or spring - mid-Oct - mid-June accessible only by skiing/snowshoeing. Walk in basis only. Rustic hostel - no running water, showers, or flush toilets. Purified water for cooking; propane refrigerator, stoves and lights. 'Superb area for hiking/skiing.' Partial closure Oct-June. $15/$20.

Camping: There are ten campgrounds in the Park area with 1772 sites available during the peak season. The nearest ones to Jasper are at **Whistler's** on Icefield Pkwy S 4 km from Jasper and nr Jasper HI-Hostel, 852-3963, and **Wapiti,** also on Icefield Pkwy S, 5 km from Jasper, 852-3992. Both have shower facilities and cost $24/site. Firewood permit, $7. Gets very cold at night. May-Sep/Oct. Reservations, 852-6176 or _www.pccamping.ca._ Reservations rec July,August, inc Skyline, Tonquin, Brazeau Loop and Maligne Lake and Pass areas. Res up to 3 mos ahead: Contact Jasper Townsite Trail Office

Food

Earls, 600 Patricia St, 2nd Floor, 852-2393. Edmonton-based, Canadian menu. $6-$15 and incredible views. Summer: daily, 11.30am-midnight; winter daily, 4pm-10pm.Chinook salmon, delicious 10" thin pizzas. Wings half-price 3-6pm, all Wed.

The Jasper Pizza Place, 402 Connaught Dr, 852-3225. Popular with locals, licensed and very reasonable. Under $10 for pizza, burgers, salads and tacos. Entrees $7-15. Pizzas cooked in wood-burning oven. Roof deck. Open 11am-11pm/midnight.

Jasper Brewing Company, 624 Connaught Dr, 852 4111. Jasper's first brew-pub, pure Rocky brews plus sandwiches, pasta, steak: 'local fusion with southern twist.' _www.jasperbrewingco.ca._

Mountain Foods Café, 606 Connaught Dr, 852-4050. Extensive breakfast selection and deli sandwiches perfect for bfast or lunch. $5-10. Daily, summer: 8am-8pm.

Scoops and Loops, 504 Patricia St, 852-4333. Ice cream store with sandwiches ($4/5) and pastries in summer; sushi ($5), udon noodles and ice cream all year. Mon-Sat summer 10.30am-midnight 11pm, winter 11am- 8Sun 10am-10pm.

Of interest

Jasper Adventure Centre, 604 Connaught Dr (summer), 306 Connaught Drive (winter), 852-5595/(800) 565-7547, are a useful contact as they organize tours and act as a booking agent for other activity companies, in and around Jasper. Visit _www.jasperadventurecentre.com_ for more info.

Jasper Heritage Folk Festival, 852-3615. Annual weekend event in late July/early Aug, the folk festival is set amid the grandeur of the Rockies; includes blues, jazz, bluegrass and country. _www.jasper.ca/folkfestival._

Water Tours – There are several available of different kinds: **Jasper Raft Tours,** 852-2665/(888) 553-5628. Tkt office is in the Chaba Movie Theatre, departure point is the Totem Pole in front of the train station. Also picks up at Jasper Park Lodge. 3 hr trips on Athabasca River running through June-Sept at 9am, 12.30pm, 7pm; $47. Produce student ID and request a discount! _www.jasperrafttours.com._ The sister company, **White Water Rafting,** the oldest outfitter in Canada, has a wide variety of trips, 852-7238, (800) 557-7238. _www.whitewaterraftingjasper.com_ Also, **Rocky Mountain River Guides,** 626 Connaught Dr, 852-3777, offer three different trips: 3-4 hr river trip-$70, 3 hr canyon trip-$60 and the 2 hr trip-$45. _www.rmriverguides.com._ **Maligne Rafting Adventures,** 852-3370/ (866) 625-4463. Offer rafting, boat and canoe rentals and 2-3 hr trips down the Athabasca River, 9am,11.30am, 3pm and 5pm, $47 & $60. _www.mra.ab.ca._

Information/Travel

Brewster Transportation and Tours, based in Banff, 100 Gopher Street, (403) 762-

6700/(877) 791-5500. Provides local transport and sightseeing. June-Sept. 'Quite pricey.' 'Predictable.' 'A last resort.' *www.brewster.ca.*

Jasper National Park Townsite Information Centre/ Parks Canada Trail Office, 500 Connaught Dr, 852-6176/77. Trail maps, many pamphlets and helpful staff full of visitor info. Courtesy phone available to aid accommodation searches. Place to register for backcountry rsvs (852-6177), camping, guided tours, historic walks, trail rsvs and information, safety registrations and wilderness passes. Daily 8.30am-7pm in summer; winter 9am-4/5pm. *www.parkscanada.gc.ca/jasper.*

Jasper Tourism & Commerce, 409 Patricia St, 852-3858. Mon-Fri 9am-5pm. Look under *Activities* and other headings at *www.jaspercanadianrockies.com.*

Heritage Taxi, 611 Patricia, 852-5558.

Maligne Lake Shuttle Service, 627 Patricia St, 852-3370.

Rocky Mountaineer Railtours, (800) 665-7245, *www.rockymountaineer.com.*

Sun Dog Shuttle Service and Tours, 414 Connaught Drive, 852-4056/(888) 786-3641, run services from Calgary Airport to various hotels in Jasper/Banff; and shared transportation between Jasper, Lake Louise, Banff, and Calgary. Fares vary according to distance. They also operate many day trips and tours, from horse riding to white water in the area. Check *www.sundogtours.com.* Also check **The Rocky Express** under Banff *Travel* section.

VIA Rail Canada Station at 607 Connaught Drive, (888) VIA-RAIL.

LAKE LOUISE-BANFF-CANMORE South of Jasper along the **Icefields Parkway** (Hwy 93) and Hwy 1, the **Trans-Canada Highway**, are three of Canada's most scenic and popular destinations – **Lake Louise**, the *Jewel of the Rockies*, three hours south of Jasper where the Icefields Parkway ends, **Banff** less than an hour further south and **Canmore** a short distance south of Banff, all embraced by spectacular Rocky Mountain highs and packed with some four million visitors year-round.

Yoho National Park and nearby **Emerald Lake** are also 'recommended, with fantastic scenery', reachable down Trans-Canada Hwy 1 from Lake Louise, or from Banff, but 'unless you have a car, forget trying to see both parks'.

NB. Be especially **wary of bears and other animals** on the highways through the National Parks in this area: because of them, speed limits within the Parks are reduced from 110 to 90 km/hr or from 70 to 50 kilometres/hr, fences set away from the road are designed to prevent animals crossing and 'Texas Grates' (ie. like cattle grids) hinder animals from straying on highways. You'll notice grassy 'animal bridges' straddling Hwy 1 north of Banff, built to allow and encourage bears and other animals to migrate on their traditional routes. In the wild, bears may threaten you, if they are surprised: keep food smells away from them, stock garbage in the special animal-proof bins arrayed in the Parks, let bears know you are there by talking loudly etc, and travel in groups if possible. If you do encounter a bear or cougar, stay calm, talk calmly and back away slowly. Don't try to feed them: it's illegal - and dangerous - to feed wild animals here. (It's also forbidden to pick wild flowers in the Parks.)

Must do experiences in this area: the **Bow Lake/ Peyto Lake overlook** on the Icefield Parkway, **Lake Louise**, the **Johnston Canyon** off the Bow Valley Parkway between Lake Louise and Banff, **Banff Gondola**, and the **Banff Hot Springs**. *The area code is 403.*

LAKE LOUISE Lake Louise lies 1,731 metres up in a hanging valley formed during the Ice Age. Don't let the invitingly placid turquoise waters of this exquisite jewel fool you: the water is a chilly 10 degrees C, and the most swimming done here is during the **Polar Dip** in July. Tiny **Lake Louise Village** (pop 500) well below the Lake, at 1,540m, is in the Banff National Park, 55 kms north of Banff township on the Jasper highroad, and named after Queen Victoria's fourth daughter, Princess Louise Caroline Alberta. It's the heart of Canada's largest single ski area, with over 200 kms of trails. The inspiring scenery around Lake Louise has awed many artists including the English-born Canadian Frederic Bell-Smith (1846-1923) who visited here in 1889 with fellow artist Albert Bierstadt (1830–1902), famous for his huge canvasses on Yosemite. Bierstadt's dramatic oil painting of Lake Louise can be seen at the New York Met. *Above Lake Louise*, by Bell-Smith, is at the Edmonton Art Gallery.

From the village, journey to **Moraine Lake** (once pictured on the back of the Canadian $20 bill) 12 kms east, 20 mins from the village, the **Valley of the Ten Peaks** and back through **Larth Valley** over **Sentinel Peak**, or walk out to the **Plain of the Six Glaciers** via **Lake Agnes**. You will need lots of time and a pair of sturdy shoes (or snow shoes in the winter—several feet of snow is the norm). Also worth a mention is the **Great Divide**, located near the picnic area at the park, accessed via Hwy 1 west of town. From this geographic point all waters flow either west to the Pacific or east to the Atlantic. You can actually see where the split occurs.

The other jewel at Lake Louise is the elegant **Fairmont Hotels Chateau Lake Louise**, 111 Lake Louise Drive, 522-3511, an almost legendary Victorian pile with a stunning presence over the Lake, where Queen Elizabeth II and Prince Phillip have stayed, as well as such legends as John Barrymore, Douglas Fairbanks, Alfred Hitchcock, and Marilyn Monroe. You can reach it via a $5 **Lake Louise Shuttle Bus** from the Village. (522-2700/763-9898).

The must-do **Lakeshore Stroll** from the Chateau is about 4 kms, takes about two hours r/t, and is sometimes crowded. Everyone does the Stroll and most everyone will be happy to take your picture for you. It's high and dry so go slow and take water. There are two **Tea Houses** accessible by trails from the Chateau: the one at **Lake Agnes** is a 3-hour steep tromp on a stony trail 'not for the weak-kneed'. It's the oldest and highest (2,135 m) tea room in Canada, originally built in 1905 by CPR surveyors. Nearby is the **Big Beehive**, a stark rocky knoll (2,270 m), reached via the trail along the shimmering glacial Lake Agnes up a challenging path. The **Plain of Six Glaciers Tea House,** also built by CPR surveyors, is a longer walk from the Chateau (about 4 hrs) past the end of the lake towards Victoria Glacier, which you can also reach via Lake Agnes. Both tea houses, open daily June-Oct, provide soup, sandwiches, home-baked bread, scones, cold drinks and desserts, tea and even coffee, all trekked up by sure-footed horses, as you'll see as you hike up the paths. By mid-Oct these paths are usually snow-bound. Use sturdy shoes. Other trails from the Chateau go to **Fairview Lookout** (1 hr) and **Saddleback Pass** (4 hrs). Ask for a trail map from the hotel concierge.

Lake Louise Gondola and Interpretive Centre, 522-3555/ **(**800) 258-7669, is 3.7 kms north of town, off Trans-Canada Hwy. The gondola takes 14 minutes to transport you to 2,088 m where amazing views await of the town, Victoria Glacier and the Great Divide. Many free nature programmes, including why grizzly bears are 90 percent vegetarian, and 45 minute interpretive walks that cost $5 pp. Daily 8.30am-6pm June-Sept. $22. Bfast, lunch available at **Lodge of the Ten Peaks** at base of gondola – Ride & Dine: $24 breakfast/$28 lunch. Skiing Nov-May. Free shuttle from Lake Louise Village hotels available. *www.lakelouisegondola.com* and *www.skilouise.com.*

The **Lake Louise Visitor Centre** is in the village, next to Samson Mall, 522-3833. Open 9am-7pm in summer, rest of year 9am-4/5pm. **Lake Louise Backcountry Trails Office** is at 522-1264. *www.bannflakelouise.com.*

Note that close by the village, along with the CPR railway line, the Trans-Canada Hwy 1 swings east to British Columbia (BC) over the **Kicking Horse Pass**, with a timber arch marking the Continental divide. You should continue a few minutes down the highway to the amazing **Spiral Tunnels** railway exhibit and stop-off, on the right going down. If you can, wait for and watch a train going through – of which there are many, and all of them long. For details, see the BC chapter.

Accommodation

Lake Louise Inn, 210 Village Road, (403) 522-3791, (800) 661-9237, has a night's lodging plus summer gondola ride from $114+ tax per person based on double occupancy, with B&B summer specials as low as $90.50. *www.lakelouiseinn.com.*

HI-Hostels There are several in the Lake Louise vicinity, all with tel (403) 670-7580/(866) 762-4122. *www.hihostels.ca/hostels/Alberta.*

Castle Mountain HI-Hostel, Hwy 1A and 93 S. 1.5 km E of junction of Trans-Canada and 93 S. 25 km E of Lake Louise. 28 beds. Access to Norquay, Sunshine, Lake Louise, trails, springs and falls. Common room with wood-burning fireplace. Open year-round. Prices subject to change, linen included (no sleeping bags). $23 member, $27 non-member (taxes inc).

Lake Louise HI-Hostel (Canadian Alpine Centre), Village Rd, Box 115, 522-2202. 150 beds. Modernized, clean hostel minutes from centre of Lake Louise Village with kitchen, /laundry, licensed cafe, mountaineering resource library, guided hikes, fireplace, sauna, live music. **Bill Peyto's Café**, named after one of the earliest local mountain guides, has breakfasts ($4.75-9.75), soups, chili and salads ($5.25-9.25), burger, sandwiches ($8.75-10.25) up to entrees ($8.50-17.50), beer & wine. Book early in high season. 'A palace!' $34/$37 in summer; private rooms $78/ $86. Book early in high season: Res essential. Open year round.

Mosquito Creek HI-Hostel, on Hwy 93, 26 km N of Lake Louise next to Mosquito Campground. 32 beds. Wilderness hostel - no running water, shower or flush toilet. Purified water avail for cooking. 'Great Sauna!' Hiking, mountaineering, cross-country skiing. $23/$27. Includes linen.

Rampart Creek HI-Hostel, 12 km N of Saskatchewan River crossing on the Icefields Pkwy, 762-4122. 24 beds. World-class rock and ice climbing. Rustic - no running water, showers or flush toilets. Purified water for cooking. 'Loads of atmosphere but no common area. Handy for ice climbing and saunas followed by a dip in the creek!!' Partial closure Oct-Apr. $23/$27.

Whiskey Jack HI-Hostel 670-7580/(866) 762-4122. Is 27 km W of Lake Louise on Hwy 1. 27 beds. The hostel is actually in the nearby Yoho National Park in BC, a short walk from Takakkaw Falls, one of Canada's highest waterfalls. Great views and relaxing campfire at the end of the day. $23, $27 non-members. Closed Oct thru mid-June. Basic facilities. *www.hihostels.ca/hostels/Alberta.*

Food

Samson Mall at Lake Louise Village has several reasonably-priced places to eat including **Laggans,** the cheapest for food, sandwiches, and coffee; bakery/deli cafeteria style. 522-2017; **Trailhead Café,** breakfasts, pitas, wraps, 522-2006; **Village Grill** Breakfast (all-day), Chinese food, pasta, burgers, sandwiches, 522-3897; **Station Restaurant,** at nearby 1909 old station, 200 Sentinel Rd, 522-2600. Beef, burgers, salmon; and **Bill Peyto's Café** at the HI-Hostel (see above).

Travel
Greyhound/Brewster at Lake Louise Investments, Samson Mall, 522-3870. Open Mon-Fri 7am-6pm, Sat-Sun till 5pm. Services to Banff, Jasper, Calgary, etc.
Lake Louise Shuttle Service/Taxi 522-2700, 763-9898. Also goes to Banff, Calgary.

BANFF NATIONAL PARK   Banff National Park, the birthplace of Canada's national parks and the third oldest in the world, is also Canada's number one tourist draw and a UNESCO World Heritage Site. The Park was established in 1885, three years after three Canadian Pacific Railway (CPR) workers stumbled upon a cave on the side of **Sulphur Mountain** that overlooks Banff. It wasn't just your run-of-the-mill cave; it was, and still is, dispatching a steady stream of piping hot, sulphurous mineral water out of the hillside: the resulting outdoor spa is: a wonderfully soothing experience - another of the meanings of Springtime in the Rockies!

Taking in 6,641 sq kms, the Park radiates a sense of alpine-style grandeur, but it's the dry, equable climate and hot mineral springs that have brought Banff fame and fortune. The Park stretches from Athabasca/Columbia Icefield in the north to Kananaskis County south of Banff and includes over a thousand glaciers. The **Castleguard Caves** in the north west of the Park are Canada's longest cave system.

The Park and town of Banff are named after Banffshire in Scotland, the name picked by CPR Land Commissioner, John MacTavish as one of many Scottish tags for planned CPR stations. It also happened to be the birthplace of Lord Strathcona, a founding president of the CPR, who drove in its last spike in 1885.

During the summer months, hiking is popular on the 1,600 kilometres of trails that encircle the mountains. It can be tough going, though, and the inexperienced shouldn't tackle the trails without a guide. After the first mountaineering death in North America of Philip Stanley Abbot in 1896, the CPR even brought Swiss guides to the Rockies to lead tourists safely through the mountains. The first royal visit to Banff was in 1901 by the Duke of York and his wife, Mary, later King George V and Queen Mary. *www.banffheritagetourism.com* and *www.digitalbanff.com.*

Glacial lakes are one of the most compelling features of the park. **Peyto Lake** (named after Bill Peyto, famous explorer and guide of the 1890s) changes from being a deep blue colour in the early summer to an 'unbelievably beautiful turquoise' later in the year as the glacier melts into it. Tourists have been known to ask the locals whether the highly photogenic lake is drained each year to paint the bottom blue! The glacier that feeds the lake is receding at 70 ft a year. At 44 kilometres north of Lake Louise on the Icefield Parkway, there is a turnoff and short, signed subalpine walk to the spectacular **Peyto Lake Lookout** at about 7,000 ft, often snowy, even in summer. To the north are the lake, Peyto glacier and Mistaya Valley; the **Timberline Trail** starts from the lookout, which is near the Bow Valley watershed summit (2,078 m).

South from Lake Louise to Banff, the **Bow Valley Parkway** (Hwy 1A) is a recommended scenic, alternative drive to Banff on the east side of the river. It's slower than Hwy 1 (60 km/hr limit) but is marked by many lay-bys with interpretive exhibits, and in particular has a turn off parking lot at the trail to the spell-binding **Johnston Canyon**, 25 kilometres north west of Banff. Catwalks clinging to the canyon sides take you through firs, pines and spruce to the Lower (1.1 km) and Upper (2.7 km) falls and beyond, a wonderful experience you won't forget! The Lower Falls includes a cave you can walk through to view them from another angle.

If you don't have much time in Banff, there is a beautiful trail walk along the glacial green **Bow River** that flows through town to **Bow Falls** near the **Banff Springs Hotel**. The scenery really is spectacular and tourists do not overrun the area, especially in winter. Although the cold temperatures cause the Bow Falls to freeze, they are still breathtaking. You may also see herds of elk tiptoeing on the ice further down the valley. An alternative short walk is the trail up nearaby **Tunnel Mountain**, which takes an hour or so from the bus station to the summit.

It is possible to walk up **Mt Rundle** or **Cascade Mountain** during the summer, but it's wise to let people know when you're going and when you plan to return, for safety's sake. If you're on Mt Rundle, make sure that you're on the **Sulphur Mountain Trail**. It's easy to mistakenly take the less scenic path, which runs along the river valley; the Banff Info Center has free, very detailed maps, to help avoid picking the wrong path! The Bow Valley Parkway (Hwy 1A), the alternative drive up to Lake Louise on the east side of the river is slow (60 km/hr limit) but pleasant and marked by interpretive exhibits.

In the Park, July has average highs of 22°C and the sun rises at 5:30am and sets at 10pm. At the other end of the scale, January is coldest with only 8 hrs of daylight and lows averaging -15°C plus wind chill that may make -20° on the thermometer feel like -30°. Temperatures also fall about 1° every 200 m you go up. Extremes here are more bearable due to the relative dryness of the air.

As noted above, be careful of the black and grizzly bears who live in the park. They are out and about in full force in summer, but are occasionally seen in winter as well. You may also see caribou, cougars, coyotes, Rocky Mountain goats, moose, big-horn sheep, and lots of wapiti elk—beware the mean-spirited elk! The park is home of the southern-most herd of the endangered woodland caribou. Entry to the Park is $8 for individuals. 13 campgrounds with 2,468 sites range from $19 up (a few "primitive" sites are $14). Call 762-1550 for details or visit _www.pc.gc.ca/pn-np/ab/banff._

The area code is 403.

BANFF At 1,384 m, Banff is 'Canada's Highest Town'. Situated 128 kilometres west of Calgary – an hour or so's drive, and 284 kilometres south of Jasper – almost four hours' drive, the town is always buzzing with activity. It's within striking distance of the most exciting things to do in this region: excellent downhill skiing in the winter—a choice of three ski areas within easy reach—and canoeing, cycling, golfing, hiking, and climbing in the summer. The several million visitors each year to this little town (pop 7,100) astride the Bow River are rarely at a loss for something to do. Banff is a lively centre, home of the **Banff School of Fine Arts** and a variety of festivals in summer and at Christmas. Aside from the various places worth visiting in downtown Banff along and around Banff Avenue, the main drag, there are two experiences here you shouldn't miss: the Banff cable car gondola and Upper Hot Springs, both close to town, and open year round

The **Banff Gondola,** the first in Canada, is at the end of Mountain Ave, 762-5483, 2.5 kilometres from downtown (take the #3 local bus). In only 8 minutes, you fly up in Swiss-made egg-shaped bubbles from 1,583 m to near the top of the **Sulphur Mountain** at 2,281 m. From there you can walk up a series of boardwalks to the roof of the Rockies where perches the historic **Cosmic Ray Station** observatory preserved just as it was, with bunks, stove and old newspaper. When it's clear and the skies are blue, you'll have a mesmerizing view of the Bow River Valley towards Lake Louise, Banff town, and dozens of Rocky peaks. It's a really breathtaking panorama, in more ways than one!

At the **Upper Hot Springs**, on Mountain Avenue, just round the corner from the foot of the gondola, 4 kms S of Banff,. 762-1515/(800) 767-1611, is the famous pool with spectacular views in a 1932 heritage restored bathhouse, fed by natural sulphur springs that bubble down the mountain near the front entrance, with water usually around 40°C: Heated, pressurized, loaded with minerals, but great for relaxing actually not smelling much of sulphur. Take your own swimsuit; you can stow your belongings visibly on a shelf next to pool. 'Highly recommended. Great Rockies experience.' although it will cost you $7.50. Operated by Parks Canada. Daily 9am-11pm in summer, 10am-10/11pm in winter. Take #3 local bus from town. _www.pc.gc.ca/regional/sourcesthermales-hotsprings/visit/banff E.asp._

The historic **Fairmont Banff Springs Hotel**, 405 Spray Ave, 762-2211, built in 1888, was another one of the string of grand hotels lining the railway like castles designed by the CPR to promote Banff as a popular, spectacular stopover on a direct route bridging the Atlantic with the Pacific. Today the Hotel is a historic site, call for info on guided tours.

In winter, the ski areas of Ski Banff at Norquay, Sunshine Village and Lake Louise have over 250 runs and 30 lifts - the **Mt Norquay Chair Lift** offers fantastic views, but to ride it, you have to plan on skiing down. _www.skibig3.com._ **Sunshine Village**, 8 km W of Banff, is the highest ski resort in the Canadian Rockies at 2,729 m, with 107 trails, the longest 8.1 kms. It's known for wide-open bowl skiing: the Continental Divide creates a vast bowl of deep snow here.

In recent years, the Banff area has become the favourite playground of Japanese tourists; many of the town's signs are printed in both Japanese and English. This sudden interest in Banff partly stems from a Japanese soap opera that uses the famous Banff Springs Hotel as its backdrop. As a result, the hotel is constantly full of honeymooners from the Pacific Rim. 'Really touristy but a very attractive town with spectacular surroundings.' In 2006, a _"Banff Refreshing"_ project is sprucing up downtown. _www.pc.gc.ca/docs/v-g/guidem-mguide/sec8/gm-mg3a E.asp_, _www.banff.com_, _www.bannflakelouise.com_, _www.banff.ca._ and _www.discoverbanff.com._

The telephone area code is 403.

Accommodation

Accommodation options in and around the town are generally expensive, but there are many hostels in the Park area, undoubtedly the best bet for the budget traveller. B&Bs start at $60 + tax per room based on double occupancy. Listings with rates and websites of B&Bs are at _www.discoverbanff.com/WheretoStay_ and in the _Bed & Breakfast Directory (Inspected Premises)_ issued by Alberta B&B Association available from _www.bbalberta.com_. NB. Not advisable to arrive in Banff on Sun eve without rsvs, especially in summer.

HI-Banff Alpine Centre, 801 Coyote Drive (on Tunnel Mountain Road), Res 670-7580/(866) 762-4122, 403-762-4123 (hostel) 3 km from downtown, 45 min walk from train or bus station. 216 beds. Kitchen and game room. 'Excellent hostel. Comfortable, friendly and near some great hikes.' Close to Whyte Museum and Banff Hot Springs, plenty of outdoor sports. Laundry and kitchen facilities, sauna and restaurant. In 'Top 10' HI hostels worldwide. Includes 'The Storm Cellar, Banff's Pub and Gamehouse.' Stay here and get 15% discounts at Banff sites. $28.50 member/ $32.50 non-member in summer, less in winter. _www.hihostels.ca/hostels/Alberta/SouthernAlbertaRegion/HI-BanffAlpineCentre/Hostels._

YWCA/Y Mountain Lodge, 102 Spray Ave, 762-3560 and 3200/ (800) 813-4138. Next to Bow River, close to downtown. Common kitchen, email kiosk, public telephones and laundry. On-site licensed bistro serves meals 7am-10pm. Dorms, $31. Private rooms available for budget rates (although higher in summer), from $75. _www.ywcabanff.ab.ca, www.ymountainlodge.com._

Tan-Y-Bryn B&B, Mrs Cowan, 118 Otter St, 762-3696. Since 1926. 7/8 rooms have shared bathrooms and some rooms have washbasins. Continental bfast included. 'Super guest house.' $40-$75+ summer. _http://tan-y-bryn.zip411.net._

Food

Aardvark Pizza, 304a Caribou at Banff Ave. 762-5500. 'Cheap, tasty and handy for post pub munchies!' Open daily, 11am-4am.

Athena Pizza, 110 Banff Ave, 2nd Fl, 762-4022. 'Large deep pan, $22.50 feeds 4.' Open daily, noon-1am.

Bruno's Bar & Grill, 304 Caribou, 762-8115, named after nature photographer Bruno Engler. Burgers, pizza, seafood. 8am-2am. Bkft till 5pm. Happy hr 4-7 pm.

Cascade Plaza Food Court, 317 Banff Ave (lower level), 762-8484. 'Great Chinese/Japanese food. $5.50 for a big plateful.'

Earls, 229 Banff Ave, upstairs, 762-4414. Burgers, sandwiches, soups, curry, individual pizzas, steaks, fish (cedar planked Chinook salmon). Cheese bacon burger $12.99, 10" Sicilian pizza $12.99, local Albino beer.

Evelyn's, Evelyn's Too and **Evelyn's Again,** 119 and 201 Banff Ave, 229 Bear St, 762-0352/0330/2907 are local favourites; serve great coffee, fresh baked goodies and famous for their sandwiches. Daily 7am-11pm. _www.taximike.com/evelyns.html._

Guido's, 116 Banff Ave above McDonalds, 762-4002. Italian. 'Generous 3-course meal. One of the best eating places in Canada.' Daily 5pm-11pm.

Joe's Diner, 221 Banff Ave, 762-5529. 50's style decor & music. Home-cooked meals. Chili, milkshakes, burgers, etc. 'Good and cheap.' Open daily, 8am-9pm.

Johnny Ray's, 201 Wolf, 762-5955, 'Louisiana Boat Docks'. Cajun food – poboy sandwiches from $7. 11 pm to 2 am.

Tommy's Neighbourhood Pub, 120 Banff Ave, 762-8888. Good value food, friendly staff. BBQ burgers. Open daily 11am-2am. _www.taximike.com/tommy.html._

Of interest

Banff Centre, 107 Tunnel Mountain Drive, 762-6100/(800) 422-6233. Arts, cultural, and educational institution and conference facility. Dance, drama, exhibitions, art shows, movies, music, creative experiences etc. Hosts **Banff Arts Festival** throughout the summer (May-Aug) - in 2005, a thousand different performers! Plus the **Banff Int'l Writers Festival** (Oct), **Banff Mountain Film Festival** (Oct/Nov) and **Book Festival** (Nov). Details of programme schedules and tickets from (800) 413-8368 or 762-6301. *www.banffcentre.ca.*

Banff Park Museum, 91-93 Banff Ave, 762-1558. Opened in 1895, and in this cross-log building since 1903, this is one of Canada's oldest museums and a National Historic Site. 10am-6pm daily in summer; rest of year 1-5pm. $4. *www.pc.gc.ca/lhn-nhs/ab/banff/index_E.asp.*

Indian Trading Post, at Birch and Cave, 762-2456. Over a century old Stoney Indian store sells local and national Indian crafts and 'furs direct from trappers'.

Buffalo Nations Luxton Museum, 1 Birch Ave, 762-2388. Chronicles the history of the region's original inhabitants, the Sioux and Blackfoot. Twenty interactive sections. Associated with Banff's Buffalo Nations Tribal Days. Daily 10am-6pm, $6, $4 w/ student ID. *http://collections.ic.gc.ca/luxton.*

Natural History Museum, 108 Banff Ave, 762-4652. Archaeology, evolution, geology, and plant life of the Rockies plus films. Shows local cave system, including Castlegar Cave under the Columbia Icefield. Sept-May 11am-5pm, 11am-7pm rest of year; free.

Whyte Museum of the Canadian Rockies, 111 Bear St, 762-2291. Named after locally-based landscape painters Catherine and Peter Whyte whose dramatic works feature here. Daily, summer 10am-5pm, $6, $3.50 w /student ID.

Entertainment

Banff Avenue, is the centre of the local universe, and shops here are consequently overpriced and a little tacky. A plan was afoot in 2005 to widen the Avenue sidewalks, add more greenery and places to sit along its main blocks. (Try **Calgary** for cheaper prices or **Canmore** for a more relaxed shopping experience.) The local rag, *The Crag & Canyon*, has info on local events. *www.banffcragandcanyon.com'.* Locals nights and happy hours should keep you going from Sun-Thur! On Tues it's only $6.50 for the **Lux Cinema** on 229 Bear St, 762-8595.

Aurora, 110 Banff Ave, Lower Fl, 760-5300. Lounge and nightclub open 5 nights a week: Tues, Thur, Sun 75 cent draft, 25 cent wings before midnight! *www.aurorabanff.com.*

Melissa's Bar, 218 Lynx St (upstairs), 762-5511. Since 1928, a log cathedral. Stuff yourself with free popcorn while drinks get cheaper by the hour, Tue, Thurs and Sat. Happy Hour 4.30-7pm. Daily 7am-2am.

Rose and Crown Pub, 202 Banff Ave (upstairs), 762-2121. Banff's oldest pub. Live music nightly, foosball, video games, pool and great food. Home away from home! Rooftop patio. Open 11am-2am. Also in Calgary. *www.banffroseandcrown.com.*

Wild Bill's, 201 Banff Ave, 762-0333. Named after Wild Bill Peyto, a legendary old local cowboy. 'Best value in town and live music nightly.' Try your hand at line dancing, Wed! Open 11am-2am. *www.wbsaloon.com.*

Information

Banff Information Centre, Banff Lake Louise Tourism, 224 Banff Ave, 762-8421. Open daily, in summer 8am-8pm. *www.banfflakelouise.com/generalinfo.*

National Parks Info Center is also here. 762-1550. *www.pc.gc.ca/pn-np/ab/banff/visit/visit5_E.asp.*

Lake Louise Info Centre, next to Samson Mall, 522-3833. Open daily, summer 9am-7pm. *www.pc.gc.ca/pn-np/ab/banff/visit/visit5_E.asp.*

Travel

Air. There are several scheduled shuttle bus services to/ from Calgary Int'l Airport and Banff (2 hrs, $48 o/w inc GST in 2006) and Lake Louise (3hrs, $56) by **Brewster Airporter** (762-3330/ (800) 760-6934) *www.brewster.ca/Day Trips/Airport_Shuttles.asp;* Banff ($47 o/w +GST) and Canmore by **Banff Airporter** (762-3330 in Banff or (888) 449-2901) *www.banffairporter.com;* and Banff ($51 o/w inc GST) and Lake Louise ($60) by **Rocky Mountain Sky Shuttle** (762- 5200 in Banff or (888) 762-8754) _www.rockymountainskyshuttle.com,_ **Brewster** also goes through to Jasper.

Bus & Coach. In season, buses to the ski areas can be expensive, so if you're staying for the winter season, a pass is the best option.

Banff Transit (aka the Happy Bus) Transit shuttle services within Banff, 762-1207. Three daily bus services run the length of Banff Ave between Fairmont Banff Springs Hotel, town centre, Tunnel Mountain hotels, and to the RV campground in summer. Hours vary seasonally, cost $1. Every half hour on both routes. The Happy Bus also takes skiers to nightspots around Banff until midnight. In 2005, Sulphur Mountain bus route was added, and service doubled on Banff Avenue.

Brewster Transportation, 100 Gopher Street, 762-6700 or 760-6934/(877) 791- 5500. Banff to Jasper, Columbia Icefield, Lake Louise, Samson Mall and Chateau Lake Louise, Canmore, Calgary, Airport - Quality Inn Airport, 4804 Edmonton Trail NE, and downtown hotels ($48), and **Red Arrow** service to Red Deer ($79) and Edmonton ($93).

Greyhound, 100 Gopher Street, c/o Brewster, 762-6751, open daily 7.45am-9pm.

Canoes/Rowing boats are on hire at Banff and Lake Louise; and at Lake Minnewanka and Bow River motor boats are available. Motor boats are not allowed on Lake Louise. Hostels and the Y run/organise rafting trips, $60-$110.

Bactrax, 225 Bear St, 762-8177. **Mountain bikes** available from $8-$12p/hr, $30-42 p/day depending on style. Open 8am-8pm. _www.snowtips-bactrax.com_.

Car Rentals: Avis (762-3222), **Hertz** (762-2027), and **Tilden** (762- 2688) car rentals are available in town. **Taxis** are available at stands.

Horses, Saddle horses from **Martins Stables, Banff Springs Hotel,** 762-4551. Have various guided tours, call or visit _www.horseback.com_. Also try **Fairmont Chateau Lake Louise,** 522-3511/(800) 441-1414. _www.fairmont.com._

Tours & Excursions: Brewster, 100 Gopher Street, 762-6700/(800) 760-6934. Has operated tours here for over a century. Has several excursions inc Beautiful Banff, Mountain Lakes and Waterfalls, Columbia Icefield, and Jasper.

Discover Banff Tours 215 Banff Ave, 760-5007/(877) 565-9372. Inc Discover Lake Louise and Moraine Lake, Discover Banff, Glacial Trail, and Hoodoo Float Tour; whitewater trips on Kananaskis, Bow and Kicking Horse Rivers; and horse rides on the Spray River, Sundance Loop and Sulphur Mountain _www.bannfftours.com._

Moose Travel (604) 777-9905/ (888) 244-6673) has many Banff-based two-day jump on/jump off round-trips, inc the _Rockies_ $115 r/t tax inc w/student ID, Banff/Jasper/Banff via Lake Louise - and variety of other trips in W Canada.

Rocky Express, 934-5972/(888) 464-4842. Fun, flexible tours for small groups covering Banff and Jasper National Parks in assoc with HI. Various tour packages from Banff & Calgary hostels: 3-10 day tours, $199-699 inc accommodation, taxes and most meals.

CANMORE/ KANANASKIS COUNTRY Canmore, an old pioneer town named after Malcolm of Canmore, King of Scotland from 1057 to 1093, is twenty minutes south of Banff at the north-western tip of Kananaskis Country, about an hour west of Calgary. _www.canmorealberta.com._ and _www.tourismcanmore.com._ Its history has been bound to coal mining until 1979, still witnessed by a Miner's Union Hall built in 1913. While retaining the haunting presence of the early settlers, Canmore displays a more modern side with the **Canmore Nordic Centre**, built for the XVth Olympic Winter Games and used for the Alberta Centennial World Cup in December 2005. _www.canmore2005.com._ The centre is open year-round, drawing flocks of mountain bikers, roller bladers and hikers in the summer; it has 60 kms of world-class cross-country and biathlon trail systems for the winter. The town also has access to the Banff/Lake Louise ski areas up the road, and is a centre for **heli-skiing**. _www.rkheliski.com._

The **Canmore Heritage Day Folk Festival** is held the first weekend in August. It's Alberta's longest-running folk music festival, _www.canmore-folkfestival.com_. Every September, the **Canmore Highland Games** celebrates the town's Scottish heritage, _www.CanmoreHighlandGames.ca._

Try the **Canmore HI-Hostel** for a good, cheap place to stay. Hiking, skiing, golfing, rafting. $20 member, $27 non-member. Private rooms available. _www.hihostels.ca_.

Tucked away between Banff and Calgary, **Kananaskis Country** is a recreation area that contains sections of three provincial parks (Bow Valley, Peter Lougheed and Bragg Creek). This 4,000 sq km back country area offers skiing, snowmobiling and windsurfing. There are excellent hiking trails and plenty of unpaved roads and trails for mountain biking. Visit _www.discoverkananaskis.com_ for more details.

CALGARY Despite bursting its cowboy breeches, gushing with oil and gas wealth, and spinning into the 21st Century with the highest average personal income in Canada and youngest population (average age 34), dynamic Calgary still retains much charm among and around its mountain of offices that gleam over Alberta's prairies. This fast growing city of almost 900,000 enjoys a friendly rivalry with Edmonton, 186 miles to the north.

The energy capital of Canada, Calgary, like Edmonton, went through a massive urban growth explosion during the late seventies. Calgary's growth has stabilised in recent years with the rapid growth in Alberta's wealth from oil sands and natural gas. The gleaming office towers that went up in the lee of the Rockies during these boom years now house the HQs of over 80 Canadian companies headquarters, including some of the world's largest oil and gas exploration and distribution firms.

Fort Calgary, named after Calgary Bay in Scotland, was erected in 1875 at the fork of the Bow and Elbow Rivers by the North West Mounted Police – later the RCMP, the Mounties, whose hallmark was, and remains today, a profoundly polite etiquette. The highly-respected NWMP were charged with providing law and order for the thousands of settlers making the long march west to create a formal, newly-emerging Canadian presence on the plains north of the 49th parallel. Perhaps more important, the Mounties were there to establish peaceful relations with First Nations who feared the changes the new railway and its "iron horse" might bring. The **Museum of the NWMP** is located in Fort Macleod, south of Calgary nearer the border with the US, well worth visiting. _www.nwmpmuseum.com._

Ten years later, in 1885, the **Canadian Pacific Railway** (CPR) completed its link to Vancouver over Kicking Horse Pass to the west, spurring trade and passengers destined for the Pacific, substantially reducing journey times to Asia from Europe. Calgary, no longer a tent city, was now on the route of the transcontinental CPR, and gradually became a huge rail centre enabling the shipment of grain, cattle and ore across the Rockies; it was formally incorporated in 1894. Later, the **Trans-Canada Highway**, Hwy 1, driven through the north part of Calgary, also linked with the west coast, channelling tourists and trucks into the awesome arms of the Rockies, just an hour or so distant.

Despite its clean, corporate air, Calgary is a festive place. At one time, the city's main claim to fame was the internationally known **Stampede**, ten days of annual revelry every July devoted to the city's cowboy, past. But in 1988 Calgary busted out of its cowboy breeches and became a city of international standing by hosting the **Winter Olympic Games.** The legacy of the games lives on at various winter sports facilities, including 70 and 90 metre ski jumps, bobsleigh and luge tracks, and an impressive indoor speed skating oval.

Despite its northerly location, Calgary's million people seldom see a rain cloud and get less snow than New York City. The city has over 2,000 hours of sunshine a year. Local weather is determined by the **Chinook**, a mass of warm air rushing in from the Pacific that can instantly send the temperature from minus 10°C to plus 15°C. Calgary's ice hockey team is named after it. _www.tourismcalgary.com_ and _www.calgary.ca_.

The area code is 403.

Accommodation
Contact the **B&B Association of Calgary,** on 277-0023 for info; it is never too early to make rsvs, especially for stays in July. _www.bbcalgary.com_. Also listings by type and price on _www.tourismcalgary.com_ - best buys are D-$99 listings such as for Best Westerns and Quality Inns.

Calgary HI-Hostel, 520 7th Ave SE, 269-8239/(866) 762-4122. Dorm: members, $30 non ($34 during Stampede). Private: $60 member, $68 non. Has 4-night stay special (4th night 50% off) and 7-night special (7th night free). Lower in winter. Located downtown, resembles a ski lodge. 'Excellent facilities.' _www.hihostels.ca_.

St Louis Hotel, 430 8th Ave, 262-6341. S-$28, D-$40. Restaurant on site.

YWCA, 320 5th Ave SE, 263-1550. From $45; key deposit. Includes use (at limited times) of gym and pool. _www.ywcaofcalgary.com_.

University of Calgary, Kananaskis Hall and Rundle Hall, 220-3203. S-$35, D-$50. Monthly rates available. 'Good facilities, gym, cheap meals.' _www.ucalgary.ca/residence/conference_and_casual/index.html_ _www.ucalgary.ca_.

Food
Downtown's food offerings are mostly concentrated in the **Stephen Avenue Mall,** 8th Ave S btwn 1st St SE and 3rd St SW and 17th Ave SW, btwn 1st and 14th Sts. Lots of places 'sandwiched' among interesting shops. _www.downtowncalgary.com_. Also try the **Kensington—Louise Crossing area,** Memorial Dr. and 10th St NW.

Buzzards Restaurant 140-10 Ave SW, at 1st St SW, 264-6959. Cowboy cuisine in downtown, inc steaks, burgers, and Stampede specialities such as prairie oysters, mixed nuts, and great balls of fire that you may not wish to know about. Open 11am-10pm Mon-Sat, 4-10pm Sun. _http://cowboycuisine.com._

Cheesecake Café, 3 locations; try 7600 MacLeod Trail, 255-7443. Pasta, burgers, sandwiches and a seemingly never-ending choice of cheesecakes-try the white choc & raspberry! Mon-Thu 11am-11pm, Fri-Sat 'til 1am, Sun 10am-11pm. _www.cheesecakecafe.ca_.

Earl's, various locations. 'Delicious 10" pizzas and local beers on tap.' 'Great burgers, great prices.' _www.earls.ca_.

Joey's Only, fish & chips and seafood. All-U-can-eat chips. Inexpensive, good food. For locations call 243-4584/(800) 661-2123. _www.joeys-only.com_.

Nick's Steak House and Pizza, 2430 Crowchild Trail NW, 282-9278. Close to Uni of Calgary, across from McMahon Stadium. Open daily 11.30am-11.30pm.

North Hill Diner, 802 16th Ave NW, 282-5848. Open daily 7am-midnight.

Ranchman's, 9615 Macleod Trail S (Hwy 2), 15 mins from downtown, between Heritage and Southland LRT stations, 253-1100. Huge bar/restaurant with boot stompin' live country music and dance hall. Cowboy fare, with Texas-style barbeque starring Grade AAA Alberta beef, ribs & chicken. "Canada's Greatest Honky Tonk! Calgary's favourite Stampede hotspot!" Complimentary country dance lessons when you buy food and/or drinks worth $5 or more. 10.30am-2am Mon-Sat. *www.ranchmans.com.*

Smitty's Pancake House, for locations call 229-3838—big b/fasts. *www.smittys.ca.*

Soma Café, 2040 42nd Ave SW, 243-4483. Live bands on w/ends. Internet. *http://somacafe.reveal.ca.*

Of interest

Calgary Tower, 101 9th Ave at Centre St South, 266-7171. Offers fantastic views of the city and the Rockies. You can step out, literally, into space on a glass floor, 525 ft up and look straight down and out, as if suspended in mid-air. There's an optical illusion as the shaft on the Tower appears to bend away from you. Summer, daily 76.30am-10.30pm; winter 9am-9pm., $11.95. Grill, dining room open in summer. *www.calgarytower.com.*

Calgary Zoo, Botanical Garden and Prehistoric Park, 1300 Zoo Rd NE, Memorial Dr & 12th St E on George's Island, 232-9300/(800) 588-9993. Home to over 1000 animals, an aviary, a large display of cement reptiles and prehistoric monsters. Daily 9am-5pm, $15. *www.calgaryzoo.ab.ca.*

Calgary Science Centre, Mewata Park, 701 11th St & 7th Ave SW, 268-8300. Museum has vintage aircraft, model rockets and a weather station, exhibits on space and electricity; the Discovery Dome has various shows about space and earth. $12 access to all exhibits and 1 Discovery Dome show. Summer: daily 9.30am-5.30pm. *www.calgaryscience.ca.*

Fort Calgary Historic Park, 750 9th Ave SE, 290-1875. Calgary's birthplace. Traces early Northwest Mounted Police life and prairie natural history. Daily May-Oct 9am-5pm, off-season Mon-Fri, 9am-5pm. $10, $8 w/student ID. *www.fortcalgary.com.*

Glenbow Museum, 130 9th Ave SE, across from Palliser Sq, 268-4100. One of Canada's largest museums with over a million artifacts and 28,000 works of art in vast collections and artefacts of Western Canada. 'Very worthwhile.' with a large collection of Canadian art and native artefacts. Has excellent exhibitions. Daily 9am-5pm, Sun from noon, Thurs 'til 9pm. $12, $8 w/student ID inc GST. $14/9 on weekends. *www.glenbow.org.*

Canada Olympic Park, 88 Canada Olympic Rd, Hwy 1 W, 247-5452. The legacy of the **Winter Olympic Games** held in 1988 in Calgary lives on at various winter sports facilities on the outskirts of town. Take an **Olympic Odyssey Bus tour** to visit the **Olympic Hall Of Fame and Museum**, explore Canada's only Olympic bobsleigh/luge/skeleton track, and the world's only indoor refrigerated push facility, **The Ice House - CODA's National Sliding Centre.** Then you'll discover the highest point in Calgary from the observation deck of the 90 metre **Ski Jump Tower.** In the winter, the public can try bobsleigh, luge, skeleton, skiing and snowboarding. In the summer it's a mountain bike park. Daily 8am-9pm, $10. Visit *www.coda.ca* and *www.canadaolympicpark.ca.*

Heritage Park Historical Village, 1900 Heritage Dr, 259-1900. Calgary was once the Northwest Mountie outpost A; this and other aspects of the city's past are dealt with in the park. The reconstructed frontier village includes a Hudson's's Bay Co. trading post, an Indian village, trapper's cabin, ranch, school, and blacksmiths, $13, $22 w/ rides included. Daily 9am-5pm. *www.heritagepark.ca.*

Prince's Island Park, on the northern edge of downtown, has special events and is just nice for sunbathing, walking and biking. and the location of the **Eau Claire** market, 264-6450. *www.eauclairemarket.com.*

Nearby: Bar U Ranch, 395-2331/(800) 568-4996, 13 km south of Longview on Hwy 22, near the Rockies. A National Historic Site, featuring displays and demonstrations about the history of ranching in Canada. Self-guided tours with various interpreters on site and authentic cowboy grub available. Open May-Oct daily 10am-6pm, $6.50. *www.parkscanada.ca*.

Entertainment

Epcor Theatre, Performing Arts Center of Calgary, 205 8th Ave. Calgary Symphony Orchestra and live theatre. Call the 24 hr show info line, 294-7455. *www.epcorcenter.org*.

Festivals: Afrikadey, 234-9110, held annually, the 2nd week Aug. Featuring the music and cutlture of the entire African diaspora: Africa, the Caribbean, and the North and South Americas. *www.afrikadey.com.*

Calgary Dragon Boat Race & Cultural Festival, 216-0145, big splash with over 70 teams held in August before the Stampede. *www.calgarydragonboat.com.*

Calgary Folk Music Festival, 233-0904, held annually, last w/ end of July. This 4-day festival, set on the river in Prince's Park; traditional Canadian folk music with acoustic and electric folk, Celtic, world beat and country. *www.calgaryfolkfest.com*.

Calgary International Jazz Festival, (780) 432-7166. Held around the last week of June annually. Venues: clubs, theatres and open-air stages, throughout the city. $5-$35, with a few free out-door concerts and workshops too. *www.jazzcity.ca*.

Calgary Stampede, 1410 Olympic Way SE. For info & tkts, 269-9822; tkts only call (800) 661-1767. Held around the second week in July in **Stampede Park** at end of 17th Ave. Calgary returns to its wild wild cowboy past with today's working cattle folk: Steer wrestling, bull dogging, bronco riding, mutton busters, amazing rodeo events, chuckwagon races with four horses just as they used to be on the prairies, free pancake breakfasts (but must stand in line), bands, parades, parties and tons of Texas two-steppin'. A tradition since 1912, the star of 37 rodeos held in Alberta. For info & tkts, call 261-0101; for tkts only call (800) 661-1767. '10 days of fun and enjoyment.' *www.calgarystampede.com*.

Information/Internet Access

Tourism Calgary: Calgary Convention and Visitors Bureau, 200-238 11th Ave SE, 2nd floor, 2632-85102766/. The office has accommodation rsvs: (800) 661-1678. 8am-5pm. Mon-Fri, *www.tourismcalgary.com*.

Calgary International Airport, 735-1372. Information Center located on first level in Arrivals, adjacent to Carousel 4. Daily 6am-11pm. *www.calgaryairport.com*.

Cinescape, Eau Claire Mkt, 200 Barclay Parade, 265-4511. Features a full service restaurant & bar. 3 station iCafe. $5/hour, $3/half hour.

WR Castell Central Public Library, 616 MacLeod, 260-2600, and all 17 public libraries in Calgary. *http://calgarypubliclibrary.com/library/public_pcs.htm.* Summer: Mon-Thu 10am-9pm, Fri-Sat 10am-5pm. $2 donation/hr.

Travel

Walking, Biking. There are 580 km of multi-use paths that span the length and width of the city, suitable for joggers, roller-skating and biking, plus 260 km of marked bicycle routes, the most extensive urban pathway and bikeway network in North America. Along the banks of the Bow and Elbow Rivers are long, pleasant promenades. NB. Hitchhiking is illegal within city limits.

Calgary Transit, 224 7 Ave SW, downtown, 262-1000. Includes bus and three light rail routes, to Dalhousie, Whitehorn and Somerset/Bridlewood; more are planned. Fares $2 cash, exact amount required. Book of 10, $17.50. Free bus transfers within 90 mins, ask operator for transfer ticket. Fares free in 7th Ave corridor on C-Train and three LRT lines. *www.calgarytransit.com*.

Air.Calgary International Airport (YYC), 735-1372, is located 12 miles N of downtown, serviced. by 27 national and international airlines. From the airport to/from downtown Calgary: **Airporter Shuttle Express,** 509-4799, counter in Arrivals, will take you anywhere to and from downtown for $12 per person, on the half hour (eg.

to downtown Marriott), $27 for 3 or 4. Also has service to downtown Greyhound Station, $15. *www.airportshuttleexpress.com*. Metered taxi from rank will cost about $28-30. For bus to town take #57 city bus, $2, which runs every ½ hr 6am-8pm, and every hr 'til 11pm to. Takes you to Whitehorn LRT station, which will take you quickly in to downtown Calgary and beyond.

www.calgarytransit.com.*www.airportshuttleexpress.com* *www.calgaryairport.com*.

Buses to the Rockies and Elsewhere. Check the counters at Arrivals Hall. There are several scheduled services to/ from Calgary Int'l Airport and Banff, Lake Louise (3 hrs, $56), Jasper and Edmonton by **Brewster Airporter** (800) 760-6934) *www.brewster.ca/Day Trips/Airport Shuttles.asp*; Banff ($47 o/w + GST) and Canmore by **Banff Airporter** (888) 449-2901 *www.banffairporter.com*; and Banff and Lake Louise ($60) by **Rocky Mountain Sky Shuttle**, (888) 762-8754, *www.rockymountainskyshuttle.com*.

Greyhound, 877 Greyhound Way SW, 260-0877/(800) 661-8747. (Leave terminal by 9th Ave exit and take #104, 108, 101, 112 bus to town, $2.) *www.greyhound.com*.

DRUMHELLER Located 146 kms east of Calgary in the heart of the Badlands, Drumheller Valley has an interesting history that spans back some 70 million years to a time when the land was flat, the climate tropical, and plants and animals flourished. These vast plains, crossed by many rivers originating in the Rocky Mountains and spilling into the **Bear Paw Sea,** were the home of what we today know as the dinosaur and **Dinosaur Trail**.

As these giants died, their bodies were covered with sediment from the rivers, which is now an excavation site where more than 30 skeletons of prehistoric beasts have been found. Everything from yard-long bipeds to the 40-ft-long Tyrannosaurus Rex has been found in this mile-wide valley. The area also has petrified forests and weird geological formations such as hoodoos, dolomites and buttes. The yucca plant, another survivor of prehistory, is found here, also in fossil form. *www.dinosaurvalley.com* and *www.traveldrumheller.com.*

Driving into Drumheller, in the heart of the Badlands of the Red Deer River Valley, layer upon layer of the earth's history are revealed. The world's largest dinosaur was unveiled here in 2000, approx four times larger than a life-sized Tyrannosaurus Rex, which you can climb 106 steps inside to reach its mouth, from where you can gaze upon Drumheller and its surroundings. The town and its area has been the stage for many movies, including *Superman, Shanghai Noon, The Virginian*, and *Bye Bye Blues*.

East of Drumheller, on Hwy 10, are hoodoos, mushroom-like sandstone formations formed by water and wind erosion and topped by protective capstones. The **Drumheller Tourist Information Centre** is at 60 - 1st Avenue West beneath the dinosaur: 823-8100/ (866) 823-8100. *www.virtuallydrumheller.com*.

Accommodation

Travelodge, 101 Grove Place, off Hwy 9, 823-5302. AC, TV, from $90. *www.travelodge.com*.

The Pines B&B and RV Resort, Drumheller, 823-8281. Spacious rooms, D-$80 per night. Full breakfast included. *www.thepopeleasepines.com*.

Rivergrove Campground and Cabins, Red Deer River, Drumheller, 4 km from the Tyrrell Museum, 823-6655. Camping, $20, cabins, $69-$130 including all mod cons. Laundry, large playground, basketball and volleyball courts and an arcade, 'excellent shaded tenting'. *www.virtuallydrumheller.com/rivergrove*.

Of interest
The **Royal Tyrrell Museum**, 823-7707/(888) 440-4240 in **Midland Provincial Park** on Hwy 838 a few minutes from town, is one of the largest palaeontology museums in the world, opened in 1985. It houses over 300 complete dinosaur skeletons. In the *Dinosaur Hall*, almost 40 mounted dinosaur skeletons are displayed. In the *Extreme Theropods Gallery*, you can see everything from the smallest chicken-sized *Compsognathus* to the tallest *Giganotosaurus* over 13 metres tall. Daily 9am-9pm, $10. *www.tyrrellmuseum.com*.

MEDICINE HAT   To the south east of Calgary, 293 kms drive on Hwy 1, is a town whose best claim to fame is its unusual name. Legend has it that this was the site of a great battle between Cree and Blackfeet Indians. The Cree fought bravely until their medicine man deserted them, losing his head-dress in the middle of the nearby river. The Cree warriors believed this to be a bad omen, laid down their weapons and were immediately annihilated by the Blackfeet.

The spot became known as 'Saamis,' meaning 'medicine man's hat'. Now its nickname is *Gas City*. Discover the Pure Energy of the largest natural gas reserve in the world, set in arid, almost desert-like terrain. According to Environment Canada, Medicine Hat receives 2,512 hours of sunshine a year, making it the sunniest spot in Canada! Its 100th birthday is 2006, *www.tourismmedicinehat.com* and *www.city.medicine-hat.ab.ca.* The **Visitor Centre** at 8 Gehring Rd SE, 527-6422, hosts historical walking tours.

Accommodation
Best Western Inn, 722 Redcliff Dr. SW, 527-3700. $79 up. Jacuzzi, pool and fitness centre. *www.bestwestern.com*.
Comfort Inn & Suites, 2317 Trans Cdn Way SE, 504-1700. From $60. Free continental bfast. Indoor pool. *www.comfortinn.com*.

Of interest
Medicine Hat Clay Products Historic District, 713 Medalta Avenue SE, 529-1070. Medalta Potteries is a heritage site with the Hycroft China operation, recently renovated, three blocks away. The Great Wall of China display shows pieces produced in the Medicine Hat Potteries from 1912 to 1988. Open daily during the summer, 10am-6pm, $6. *www.medalta.org/index.html.*
Medicine Hat Museum and Art Gallery, 1302 Bomford Cr, 502-8580. Houses artifacts of the Plains peoples and first European settlers, with local art works as well as human history and natural science exhibitions. Daily 9am-5pm, w/ends 10/12am-5pm. *www.medicinehat.ca.*
Saamis Teepee, along the TransCanada Hwy, 527-6773. The world's tallest tepee, built for the Calgary Winter Olympics in 1988, overlooks an archaeological dig where Indian artifacts have been discovered. Made entirely of steel and stands 20 storeys high. Ten large, circular storyboards ring the tepee, bearing paintings by noted native artists. Interpretive Centre open May 15 to Sept, 9 am-9 pm daily.

WRITING-ON-STONE PROVINCIAL PARK   South west of Medicine Hat and 350 kms south east of Calgary, nearly on the US border, 40 km from the small town of **Milk River** on Hwy 501, is this park of great biological, geo-logical and cultural interest. The site, overlooking the Milk River, contains one of North America's largest concentrations of pictographs and petro-glyphs. Inscribed on massive sandstone outcrops, these examples of plains rock art were carved by nomadic Shoshone and Blackfoot tribes. There is also has a reconstructed North West Mounted Police outpost depicting the area's role in bringing law and order to the Canadian west.

This site is open year round but access is only on the one and a half hour guided tours, daily from May through beginning of Sept. Call for info on special events, 647-2364/(877) 877-3515. 64 camping sites $17-$20 per night; $12 off-season.

HEAD-SMASHED-IN BUFFALO JUMP   If the name isn't enough to pique your curiosity, then the fact that this historical interpretative centre is a UNESCO World Heritage site may. The centre is located 18 km north west of **Fort Macleod** on secondary Hwy 875, 175 km south of Calgary, 553-2731.

The Plains Indians who once inhabited this area hunted buffalo by driving herds of the massive beasts over the huge sandstone cliffs to certain death below. According to legend, a young Indian brave tried to watch one of the hunts from a sheltered ledge below (somewhat like standing underneath a waterfall). So many animals were driven over the cliff that, after the hunt, his people found him with his skull crushed by the weight of the buffalo. The startlingly illogical name makes perfect sense.

WATERTON LAKES NATIONAL PARK   The other part of the Waterton/ Glacier International Peace Park and Biosphere Reserve (see also under Montana), 266 kilometres, about two hours or so south of Calgary. Mountains rise abruptly from the prairie in the south-western corner of the province, giving way to magnificent jagged alpine scenery.

Between the Park and Glacier Park to the south, there are over 1400 kilometres (850 miles) of maintained World Class hiking trails. There are more with 255 kilometres (overthan 1900 miles) of trails within the Waterton Lakes Park for walking and riding. The Park, which is a UNESCO World Heritage Site, iIt's also a good spot for fishing and canoeing. The park also features three campsites, along with several cabins and hotels for a not-quite-so-rustic experience. The high elevation and frigid glacial water conspire to make Waterton's lakes too cold for swimming.

A drive north on Rte 6 will take you close to a herd of plains buffalo. Go south on the same road and you cross the border on the way to Browning, Montana. You can also reach the US by boat. The *IMV International* sails daily between **Waterton Park** townsite and Goathaunt Landing in Glacier National Park, Apr-Oct, four times daily, $27 r/t.

Park admission $5 per person or $12.50 per carload. The park headquarters is located in Waterton Park townsite on the west shore of Upper Waterton Lake. The park information office is open daily during the summer. Park rangers arrange guided hikes and the interpreted theatre programme daily 8:30pm at both Falls Theatre and Crandell Theatre. **Visitors Centre**, 859-2252/ 859-5133, daily 8am-7pm. Camping $193-$30 per night. *www.watertonpark.com*.

MANITOBA

Situated in the heart of the continent, the province extends 760 miles from the 49th to the 60th parallel, from the US border to the Northwest Territories. But despite its centrality, the province has both a 400-mile-long coastline on Hudson Bay, where the port of **Churchill** can be found and hundreds more miles of shorelines round an astonishing 100,000 lakes, the largest of which is Lake Winnipeg, making the province one of the greatest aquatic places on earth! Manitoba was thus ideal for the waterborne cargoes that made **York Factory** on the Hudson Bay the first trading post, then hub for almost 250 years of the *Hudson's Bay Company's* (HBC) fur-trading activities. York, called a Factory because it was the residence of the Factor (chief trader), was closed down by the HBC only as recently as 1957. It's now a National Historic Site that still can be reached only by water. *www.pc.gc.ca/lhn-nhs/mb/yorkfactory.*

The present population of Manitoba includes a large percentage of German and Ukrainian immigrants, although the English, Scots and French still predominate. After the rail link to the east reached Manitoba in 1881, settlers flocked to the new province to clear the land and grow wheat and Winnipeg became the metropolis of the Canadian west.

Though classified as a Prairie Province, three-fifths of Manitoba is rocky forest land. Even this area, however, is rather flat. If you're travelling across the province, the landscape can get pretty tedious. Infinite prairies stretch out to the west and endless forests and lakes abound in the east. *www.travelmanitoba.com.*

National Parks: Riding Mountain, Wapusk. *www.pc.gc.ca.*
The telephone area code is 204.

WINNIPEG   A stop here is almost a necessity if you're travelling across Canada. Canada's sixth largest city, this provincial capital has plenty to offer, especially if you can time a visit to coincide with one of the festivals happening in and around Winnipeg in the summer months. Among these are the **Winnipeg Folk Festival,** held annually at Birds Hill Park in July and **Folklorama,** Winnipeg's cultural celebration, held early August.

Winnipeg (from the Cree word 'Winnipee' meaning 'muddy waters') is very 'culture-conscious', with good theatre, a symphony orchestra, the world-renowned Royal Winnipeg Ballet, plus an ample supply of museums and art galleries. It's also a major financial and distribution centre for western Canada, hence the vast grain elevators, railway yards, stockyards, flour mills and meat packaging plants.

The Red River divides the city roughly north to south. Across the river from downtown Winnipeg is the French-Canadian suburb, St Boniface. This community retains its own culture while mixing well with the Anglophones in Winnipeg. Many services are, therefore, offered in both languages. Winnipeg is known for its long and brutally cold winters, but summer daytime temperatures are comfortably in the high 70s and 80s before cooling off in the evenings. An indoor pedestrian system in town means you can go almost anywhere without being bothered by the weather. *www.destinationwinnipeg.ca* and *www.winnipeg.ca/interhom/.*

Accommodation
Backpackers Guest House Int'l, 168 Maryland St, 772-1272, (800) 743-4423. $20-$24 dorm, private rooms $44. Kitchen, laundry and access to downtown. Mixed reports. *backpackerswinnipeg.com.*
Ivey House Int'l Hostel, 210 Maryland St (Broadway & Sherbrooke), 772-3022. $20-

member, $24 non. Bike rentals avail. Check-in 8am-midnight. Furnished kitchen. Rsvs recommended summer and fall. 'Very friendly.' Central.

Massons B&B, 181 Masson, St Boniface, 237-9230, $45-55. Shared bathroom, breakfast included. Central downtown location.

McLaren Hotel, 554 Main St (across from the Centennial Centre), 943-8518. $30-55. Very central. Restaurant in hotel. Bike rentals nearby.

University of Manitoba Residence, 26 MacLean Cr, 474-9942. Check in at Room 110, Pembina Hall. May-Aug, co-ed, single occupancy only. Week or less $23.37/day; week or more $13.28/day; month $315. Extra fee gives access to pool and sports facilities on campus.

Camping: Travellers RV Resort, Murdoch Road, 256-2186, $16 per couple per night. May–Sept. Showers, playground, mini golf, pool and internet access. _www.travellersresort.com_.

Food

Alycia's, 559 Cathedral Ave, 586-9697. Ukrainian home cuisine, 'try the pirogies, pan fried pasta stuffed with potato and cheese, delicious'. Dishes come separately or in combinations, $5-9. Mon-Fri 8am-8pm, Sat from 9am.

Fat Angel, 220 Main St, 944-0396. 'Funky, colourful dining spot.' Entrees, light meals, vegetarian food and pizza, $9-$18. Lunch Mon-Fri 11.30am-2.00pm, dinner Mon-Thu 5:00pm-9:30pm, Fri/Sat 5pm-midnight.

Kelekis, 1100 Main St N, 582-1786. Renowned restaurant, since 1931. Hot dogs and fifty year old batter recipe for traditional English fish and chips. Burgers, shoestring fries. Good and cheap. Mon-Thur 8am-7:30pm, Fri-Sat 'til 9:45pm.

Nikos Restaurant, 740 Corydon Ave, 478-1144. Bistro style setting for home-style Greek and Canadian fare. Everything from moussaka to subs. Entrees $9-$15. Daily 10am-10pm, Thur-Sat 'til 11pm summer.

Old Market Cafe, Old Market Square. Numerous speciality kiosks feature a variety of foods. Good in summer. Outdoor patio. Next door is **King's Head**, a British style pub.

Sweet Palace, 1425 Pembina Hwy, S of downtown, 475-7867. Indian specialities including over 35 desserts. Lunch buffet $9, dinner buffet $13. Tue-Thur 11am-9pm, Fri-Sat 'til 10pm.

Of interest

Walking tours of Historic Winnipeg begin in the renewal zone of the 1960s and wind through the streets and around the buildings of the Exchange District, where the city's commercial and wholesale history began. Tours depart on the hour, 11am-2pm, Tue-Sun, from Old Market Square, and last approx $1^1/2$ hours, $5. Call 942-6716 for more information.

Assiniboine Park, Corydon Ave W at Shaftsbury, 986-7275. On the Assiniboine River with miniature railway and an English garden. The lush foliage makes this park very popular in the summer. There is always some sort of production here, be it Shakespeare, the symphony, or the ballet. In winter, activities shift to skating, sleigh rides and tobogganing. Also located within the park is a sculpture garden dedicated to the works of local artist Leo Mol. Free.

Assiniboine Park Conservatory, 986-5537, houses the tropical 'Palm House' and a gallery featuring works by local artists. Daily 9am-8pm, summer, free.

Assiniboine Park Zoo, 986-6921, one of the world's most northerly zoos housing native wildlife. There's also a statue in honour of Winnie the Pooh, who was named after Winnipeg. 9am-8pm daily, summer only, $4.25. _www.zoosociety.com/_.

Centre Culturel Franco-Manitobian, 340 Blvd Provencher, 233-8972. Its resident cultural groups, promote French culture through live musical entertainment, art exhibitions, theatre and art courses. Taste French-Canadian cuisine in **Le Café Jardin** or on the garden terrace, Mon-Fri 11.30am-2pm. The centre is open Mon-Fri 9am-5pm, Sat-Sun, free. _www.ccfm.mb.ca/_.

The Forks This development at the confluence of the Red and Assiniboine Rivers celebrates the transformation of the Canadian west. Attractions include **Johnston Terminal**, formerly a 4-storey warehouse, now home to a variety of shops and restaurants. **Forks Market**, 942-6302, a vast array of ethnic cuisine, local and national arts and crafts. 9.30am-9pm daily. *www.theforks.com/*.

The Forks National Historic Site, 983-6757. A traditional aboriginal stopping place, the Forks was the site of Fort Rouge, Fort Gibraltar and the two Forts Garry. Nine acres on the west bank of the Red River offers festivals and heritage entertainment from May 'til Labour Day. $4. *www.pc.gc.ca/lhn-nhs/mb/forks/index_e.asp*.

Legislative Building, Broadway and Osborne, 945-5813. Completed in 1919 and built from native Tyndal stone, this neo-classical style building houses, as well as the legislative chambers, an art gallery, a museum and a tourist office. It is set in a 30-acre landscaped park and the grounds contain statues of Queen Victoria, statesmen and poets. The Golden Boy perched atop the dome of the building, sheathed in 23.5 karat gold, symbolises 'Equality for All and Freedom Forever'. Created in a Paris foundry that was bombed during WWI, the Golden Boy spent $2^1/_2$ yrs in the hold of a troop ship before making his way to Winnipeg. 8am-6pm daily, guided tours on the hr, free.

Living Prairie Museum and Nature Preservation Park, 2795 Ness Ave, 832-0167. See what the prairie looked like before the settlers came. Daily July-Aug, 10am-5pm. Free. The prairie is open daylight hours. 'Take insect repellent!'

Lower Fort Garry, on the banks of the Red River 19 mi N of Winnipeg on Hwy 9, 785-6050, *www.pc.gc.ca*. This National Historic Park is the only stone fort of the fur-trading days in North America still intact. The park is open daily from, 9am-5pm, tours available, $6.50. There is also a museum with nice displays of pioneer and Indian goods, maps and clothes. To reach the fort take the Selkirk bus from downtown Winnipeg, $5.75 o/w, **Beaver Bus Lines**, 989-7007. *www.beaverbus.com*.

The Museum of Man and Nature, 190 Rupert Ave, 956-2830, next to the Centennial Centre concert hall, 956-1360. Features provincial history and natural history of the Manitoba grasslands, a science center and planetarium. Daily in summer, 10am-5pm, Thurs 'til 8pm. $8 just the museum, $18 for a value pass. *www.manitobamuseum.mb.ca*.

Oseredok—Ukrainian Cultural and Education Centre, 184 Alexander Ave E, 942-0218. Folk art, documents, costumes, and history. 10am-4pm Mon-Sat, donation appreciated. *www.oseredok.org*.

Riel House National Historic Park, 330 River Rd, 257-1783. Built in 1880-81, the Riel home has been restored to reflect its appearance in the spring of 1886. Louis Riel was the founding father of Manitoba and led the Metis revolt of 1869/70. Although he never lived in the house, it was here his body was laid in state following his execution in 1885. Daily 10am-6pm, May-Aug only; $4. *www.pc.gc.ca/lhn-nhs/mb/riel/index_e.asp*.

River Interpretive Tours, 986-5663, boat tours exploring the city's waterways. The cruise follows the beginnings of the fur trade, the early forts and shows the importance water transportation played in developing Winnipeg. Tours depart from Forks Historic Docks Site Tue-Fri 10am-7pm departures about every 2 hours. $1^1/_2$ hours, $8. *www.winnipeg.ca/cms/leisure*.

Royal Canadian Mint, 520 Lagimodiere Blvd, 983-6429. One of the largest and most modern mints in the world, strikes all Canadian coins as well as coins for several other countries. Tours every $^1/_2$ hr. May-Aug Mon-Fri 9am-5pm, last tour 4pm. Call to make a reservation. *www.mint.ca*.

St Boniface. Across the Red River, the city's French Quarter and is the site of the largest stockyards in the British Commonwealth. A historic and cultural cornerstone of the city, it is the birthplace and final resting place of Louis Riel and original site of the Red River Colony.

St Boniface Cathedral, 190 Ave de la Cathédrale, 233-7304. The oldest basilica in western Canada, originally built in 1818, destroyed twice by fire. The latest structure was built in 1972 and still has the facade of the 1908 basilica that survived the fire. Open Mon-Fri 8.30am-4.30pm. *www.members.shaw.ca/cathedrale.*

Upper Fort Garry Gate, the only bit remaining of the original Fort stands in a small park S of Broadway off Fort St. This stone structure was Manitoba's own 'Gateway to the Golden West'. Free.

Winnipeg Art Gallery, 300, Memorial Boulevard, 786-6641. One of Canada's eminnent public art galleries. Tours run Tue-Sun 11am-5pm, Wed 'til 9pm, $6, $4 w/student ID. *www.wag.mb.ca/.*

Shopping/Events

Osborne Village, between River and Corydon Junction. Boutiques, craft and speciality shops and eating places. Look for the **Medea**, a co-op art gallery found in the Village. The **Exchange District** and **Old Market Square** are also interesting places to shop. Portage Ave is the main downtown shopping area. Portage Place has shops, restaurants, and **IMAX Theatre**, 393 Portage Run Ave, 956-4629, with a gigantic 55ft x 70ft screen. Tkts $8.50. *www.imaxwinnipeg.com.*

The Winnipeg Folk Festival takes place annually at the beginning of July in **Birds Hill Provincial Park**. This internationally renowned festival features the best in bluegrass, jazz, and gospel music. The park is accessible from Hwy 59 N of Winnipeg or through Winnipeg Transit. *www.winnipegfolkfestival.ca.*

Folklorama, 982-6210, (800) 665-0234, is Winnipeg's multi-cultural celebration held in early August. *www.folklorama.ca.*

Jazz Winnipeg Festival, 989-4656. Features the best in international, national and local jazz performers on free outdoor stages at locations throughout downtown and the Exchange District. Takes place mid-June. *www.jazzwinnipeg.com.*

Information/ Internet access

Manitoba Visitors Reception Centre, Room 101, Legislative Building, 450 Broadway at Osborne, 945-3777, (800) 665 0040. Maps and literature. Pick up a copy of *Passport to Winnipeg* for up-to-date information.

The **Explore Manitoba Centre**, 21 Fort Market Rd, 945-3777. Provides general tourist information. Free internet. 10am-6pm daily.

Tourism Winnipeg, 279 Portage Ave, 943-1970, (800)-665-0204.

Public Libraries. Most of Winnipeg's 20 public libraries have internet access. For branch details, check *http://wpl.winnipeg.ca/library/contact/branches/branches.asp.*

Travel

Bike hire: several locations in Assiniboine Park; ask at Visitors Centre.

Transit. Bus $1.85, transfers valid for 60 minutes. 68 fixed routes throughout the city. *www.winnipegtransit.com.*

Greyhound, 487 Portage Ave, 783-8857, (800) 661-8747. *www.greyhound.com.*

Splash Dash Water Bus, 783-6633. 30 min water taxi tours along the Red and Assiniboine Rivers depart from the Forks Historical Harbour every 15 minutes from May-Oct, 10am-9pm; $7.

VIA Rail. the transcontinental *Canadian* from Vancouver to Toronto stops here three times a week in both directions. The *Hudson Bay* (#693) travels to Churchill, leaving Winnipeg on Tuesday, Thursday and Sunday evenings, a two night trip to Churchill. $144 o/w. *www.viarail.ca.*

Winnipeg International Airport, (YWG) 20 minutes W of downtown, is served by the local transit buses, 986-5700. A taxi will cost around $20 o/w, call 925-3131.

RIDING MOUNTAIN NATIONAL PARK
The park occupies the vast plateau of western Manitoba's Riding Mountain. As it rises to 2200 ft, breathtaking views of the distant prairie lands unfold.

The total area of Riding Mountain Park is about 1200 square miles. Although parts of it are flagrantly commercialised, there are still large tracts of untamed wilderness to be explored by boat or by taking one of the hiking and horse trails. You'll see a fair amount of wildlife here; deer, elk, moose and bears abound and at **Lake Audy** there's also a herd of bison. It's a good spot for fishing too. **Clear Lake** is the part most exploited for and by tourists. The township of **Wasagaming** (an Indian term meaning 'clear water'), on the south shore of the lake has campsites, lodges, motels and cabins as well as many other resort-type facilities, right down to a movie theatre built like a rustic log cabin.

The park is reached from Winnipeg via Rte 4 to Minnedosa, and then on Rte 10. Daily admission $6 per person. Camping $22-30 per night. Call the Visitors Center, 848-7275, (800) 707-8480. _www.parkscanada.gc.ca/riding_.

CHURCHILL   Known as the 'Polar Bear Capital of the World', Churchill is the only human settlement where polar bears can be observed in the wild. It's known for more than just its great white inhabitants, though. Churchill has been a trading port since 1689 and served as the launching point for the first settlers to Manitoba. Today it's still the easiest part of the 'frozen north' to see. During the short July-October shipping season, this sub-arctic seaport handles vast amounts of grain and other goods for export.

The partially-restored **Prince of Wales Fort**, the northernmost fort in North America, was built by the British in 1732. It took 11 years to build and has 42-ft-thick walls. Despite this insurance against all-comers, the garrison surrendered to the French without firing a single shot in 1782.

Churchill is a great place to view some of the wonders of nature. From September to April, the beautiful **Aurora Borealis** (Northern Lights) are visible and good for picture-taking. Churchill has made it even easier for you to watch its sky explode with colour; the **Tundra Domes** offer clear, comfortable viewing from plexi-glass seating areas. Perhaps it isn't as authentic, but it beats sitting out in the cold. The summer daylight ruins the viewing conditions.

To make up for it, whale watching is best in the summer months, from July-early September. The beluga whales come in and out with the tides. Polar bears are most frequently seen roaming around the city in September and October and are periodically airlifted to other regions. The large numbers of polar bears sparked the decision to grant National Park status to **Wapusk National Park**, one of the world's largest polar bear maternity denning sites. On the tundra, lichens and miniature shrubs and flowers bloom each spring and autumn and a short distance inland there are patches of _Taiga_, sub-Arctic forest. _www.hudsonbaypost.com._

Note that Churchill is only accessible by plane or train. Look into the package deals put together by VIA Rail (see Winnipeg).

Accommodation
Northern Lights Lodge, 101 Kelsey Blvd, 675-2403. Hot tub, sauna, $80-100, much more in Nov for bear season. TV, bar. _www.northernlightslodge.com_.
Polar Inn, 153 Kelsey Bvld, 675-8878, S-$98, D-$135 includes breakfast, more during bear season.

Of interest/Information
The Eskimo Museum, next to the Catholic Church on LaVerendrye St, 675-2030.

Fur trade memorabilia, kayaks and Canadian Inuit art and carvings dating from about 1700 BC, that are among the oldest in the world. Tues-Sat 9am-noon, 1pm-5pm, Mon-Sat. Free. 'Worth visiting.' *http://flash.lakeheadu.ca/~smboyce.*

Fort Prince of Wales National Historic Site, 675-8863, at W bank of mouth of Churchill River. Now partially restored. Open daily. The fort is only accessible by boat, $8 per person. *www.pc.gc.ca/lhn-nhs/mb/prince.*

Parks Canada, Manitoba North Historic Sites, Bayport Plaza, 675-8863. Daily 1pm-9pm.

SASKATCHEWAN

It's no wonder Saskatchewan is known as the 'Wheat Province'. It's responsible for over half of the wheat grown in Canada and the country's leading cereal producer. Wedged between Alberta and Manitoba, Saskatchewan is the keystone of the Canadian prairies. Although the Trans Canada Highway winds through seemingly endless, flat expanses of wheat fields in southern Saskatchewan, the province does have a more diverse geography. From the scenic hills of the Qu'Appelle Valley to the Cypress Hills in the Southwest and the badlands in the Southeast, Saskatchewan is anything but wholly flat. The province is also Canada's second highest oil producer after neighbouring Alberta.

Given the flatness of the terrain and the purity of the atmosphere, visibility in the south can be up to 20 miles. Watch the sky—sunrises and sunsets are beautiful, and cloud formations during wild prairie storms can be spectacular. As you travel north of the prairies past Hwy 16, the yellow landscape gives way to green rolling hills, and, still further north, to rugged parkland—lakes, rivers and evergreen forests.

Saskatchewan derives its name from 'Kisiskatchewan', a Cree word meaning 'the river that flows swiftly'. The river in question was, no doubt, the South Saskatchewan, where generations of Northern Plains Indians gathered to hunt and fish. The earliest written records of what is now Saskatchewan date to 1690, when Henry Kelsey of the Hudson's Bay Company became the first European to explore the region. Other explorers soon followed, opening the area to fur trade. More recently, oil exploration in the south has led to the discovery of helium and potash, as well as large quantities of 'bubbling crude'. In the summer, the weather is hot and dry, while the winters are long, cold and snowy. *www.sasktourism.com*.

National Parks: Prince Albert, Grasslands. *www.pc.gc.ca.*

The telephone area code is 306.

REGINA Nestled in the heart of the wheatlands, Regina is the universally-accepted stopping place between Winnipeg and Calgary. The present-day capital of Saskatchewan, Regina served a brief stint as capital of the entire Northwest Territories in 1883, just one year after it was established. Situated along the railroad, the town was a government outpost and headquarters for the North West Mounted Police until the province of Saskatchewan was created in 1905.

The town was christened Regina for Queen Victoria in 1882 after the Canadian Pacific Railway completed its track across the Pacific. Prior to Regina, the town had a more poetic moniker, Pile O'Bones (a reference to the

Indian buffalo killing mound at the site), a name considered inappropriate for a capital city. Thanks to the addition of a manmade lake and 350,000 hand-planted trees, the Regina landscape is more picturesque than one might perhaps expect. _www.tourismregina.com_, _www.inregina.com._

Accommodation
B & J'S B & B, 2066 Ottawa St, 522-4575. Shared bathrooms $35-55. Weekly rates available. Free coffee and pastries in the morning.
Turgeon Hostel (HI-C), 2310 McIntyre St (at the College), 791-8165. $20-member, $25-non. Near downtown, ¹/₂ blk from Wascana Park. Cooking facilities, laundry, common room, library. 'Great place—clean, convenient.' Closed Jan. _www.hihostels.ca_.
YMCA, 2400 13th Ave, 757-9622. $23 with student ID, $17, $85/$65/week, $288/208/month $5 key deposit. Shared bathrooms. Men only. _http://regina.ymca.ca_.
YWCA, 1940 McIntyre St, 525-2141. $35p/night, $2 key deposit. $168 wk, $285 month. Some rooms have basin, fridge; shared kitchen, showers, laundry. Internet access. _www.ywcaregina.com_.
Camping: Comfort Plus Campground, 12 km E on Hwy 1, 781-2810. 'Clean, quiet and quaint' 1 km off the hwy. Recreation hall, internet access, heated pool, laundry, showers, store. Sites, $18-$24, May-Oct. _www.geocities.com/comfortplus2003_.
Kings' Acres Campground, 1 km E of Regina on Hwy 1, N service road behind Tourism Regina, 522-1619. Sites $16-$26. Indoor recreation facility, city water supply, showers, store. April-Nov.

Food
Boston Pizza, 545, Albert St N at Ring Rd and Gordon Rd at Rae St, 949-5455. Inexpensive Italian. Open Sun-Thur 11am-2am, Fri-Sat 'til 3am. _www.bostonpizza.com_.
The Novia Cafe, 2158 12th Ave, 522-6465. A trendy Regina tradition. 'Don't miss the cream pie.' Open 7am-5pm Mon-Fri. Open since 1900s.

Of interest
Government House, corner of Dewdney Ave and Connaught St, 787-5717 official residence of the Lieutenant Governors from 1891-1945. Explore rooms restored to Victorian elegance. Tue-Sun 10am-4pm, free. _www.gr.gov.sk.ca/govhouse_.
RCMP Centennial Museum, 60500, Dewdney Ave W, 780-5838. The official museum of the Royal Canadian Mounted Police portrays the history of the force in relation to the development of Canada. Daily Jun-Sep 8am-6.45pm, Sep-May 10am-4.45pm. Tours in summer only. Donations appreciated. **The Sergeant Major's Parade**, is held on the Parade Square at the Training Academy, 780-5900, Mon-Fri at 12.45pm.
St Paul's Cathedral, 12th Ave and McIntyre St, 522-6439. The oldest house of worship in Regina, dating back to 1894. Open daily 9am-4pm, call ahead for tours. The area around the cathedral swells with quaint shops, restaurants and coffee houses— 'a lovely place to pass the afternoon.'
Wascana Centre, in the heart of the city, this 2300 acre park built around Wascana Lake, is home to many of the province's top attractions. A place of government, recreation, education and culture. _www.wascana.sk.ca_. Home to the provincial **Legislative Building**, 787-5357, built between 1908 and 1912 and designed to reflect the architecture of English Renaissance. Daily May 19th-Sep 2nd, 8am-9pm, tours every 30 minutes, free. **The MacKenzie Art Gallery** celebrated its 50th anniversary in 2003, 3475 Albert St, in the SW corner of Wascana Centre, 584-4250. Historical and contemporary works by Canadian and American and international artists. Daily 10am-5:30pm, Thu and Fri 'til 10pm, free. _www.mackenzieartgallery.sk.ca_.
Royal Saskatchewan Museum: 787-2815. First Nations Gallery traces 10,000 yrs of Aboriginal culture, the Earth Sciences Gallery depicts over 2 billion yrs of geological evolution. Features traditional and contemporary Aboriginal art, books

and crafts. Daily May-Sep 9am-5.30pm, daily Sep-Apr 'til 4.30pm. $2, $1 w/student ID. _www.royalsaskmuseum.ca_.

Saskatchewan Science Centre, (800) 667-6300, is located inside the old Regina powerhouse building, a landmark on the north shore of Wascana lake since 1914. Mon-Fri 9am-6pm, Sat/Sun from 10am. $7. Next door is the **Kramer IMAX Theatre**, 522-4629, watch breathtaking films and special effects on the huge screen. $7. _www.sasksciencecentre.com_.

Willow Island, at the N end of Wascana Lake, is accessible only by a ferry that departs from the dock off Wascana Dr, 347-1810. The island is a popular picnic and BBQ site. Nature walks are popular. Part of the University of Regina campus is also located in the park. Multiple activities may be arranged from the **Wascana Centre.**

Buffalo Days are held in Regina Exhibition Park, Dewdney Ave W, 781-9300, late Jul-early Aug. Kicked off by 'Pile-of-Bones Sunday', a celebration of Saskatchewan traditions such as chuckwagon races, a logging contest, an agricultural fair and exhibition. One of Saskatchewan's biggest attractions is the **Kinsmen Rock-n the Valley**, 352-2300, in Craven, 26 mi N of Regina. In mid-July, the population of this small town swells nearly one hundred-fold as thousands congregate for the local rock 'n roll festival. Following the festival is Saskatchewan's largest **rodeo**, the last weekend in July, 565-0565.

Information/Travel

Tourism Regina Visitor Information Center, Hwy 1E, (800) 661-5099. **Saskatchewan Transportation Company**, 2041 Hamilton St, 787-3340, (800) 661-8747. Bus to Saskatoon, 3 daily, One way $30.90 with student ID. _www.stcbus.com_. **Regina Airport** is reachable by cab only. Call 586-6555, $10-$15. _www.yqr.ca_.

Internet access

Cafe Ultimate, 1852 Scarth St, 584-2112. Open Mon-Thur 8am-11pm, Sat from 9am, Sun 1pm-11pm; $7/hr.

SASKATOON Saskatoon started in 1883 as the proposed capital of a temperance colony. An Ontario organisation acquired 100,000 acres of land and settlement began at nearby Moose Jaw. Something about the prospects of living on the Canadian prairie without alcohol didn't quite catch on. The population of Saskatoon failed to increase, and plans for the temperance colony were essentially scrapped. Nevertheless, the city continued to develop as a trading centre. However, there are still a few dry establishments to be found here today

The scenic South Saskatchewan River cuts right through the middle of the town; the parklands along its bank make Saskatoon a really pretty place, especially in the summer. It's an easy-going town with friendly residents. _www.city.saskatoon.sk.ca/_.

Accommodation/Food

The Senator, 3rd Ave S at 21 St E, 244-6141. $65-100. TV, bath. Rsvs recommended. Very central. _www.hotelsenator.ca_.

YWCA, 510 25th St E, 244-0944. $38, $120 weekly, $285 monthly. $10 key deposit. Includes use of pool. Women only. Call to reserve. _www.ywcasaskatoon.com_.

David's Lounge and Restaurant, 294 Venture Cr off Circle Drive North, 664-1133. Good for big hearty breakfasts. Open Mon-Sat 7am-10pm, Sun 9am-9pm.

Louis' Campus Pub, on the University of Saskatchewan campus, 966-7000. Named after the rebellious Louis Riel. A favourite summertime haunt. Lunch on the patio. Open Mon-Thur 11an-8pm, Fri. _www.ussu.ca/louis_.

Of interest

Stretching 19 km along both sides of the South Saskatchewan River, near Spadina

Cres, the **Meewasin Valley Trail**, cuts right through the heart of Saskatoon. Picnic areas, BBQ sites, lookouts and interpretative signs along the way. The trail head is at **Meewasin Valley Centre and Gift Shop**, 402 3rd Ave, 665-6888. Mon-Fri 9am-5pm, 10:30am-5:00pm w/end and hols. _www.meewasin.com_. Also in the park is the **Mendel Art Gallery**, 950 Spadina Cres, 975-7610, _www.mendel.ca_. 9am-9pm. Free. For a change from the ordinary, try Shakespeare prairie-style at the **Shakespeare on the Saskatchewan Festival**, 653-2300, early Jul-mid-Aug, in the park. Buy tkts in advance. _www.shakespeareonthesaskatchewan.com_.

The **University of Saskatchewan**, 966-4343, is home to many attractions including the **University Observatory**, 966-6429, the **Gordon Snelgrove Art Gallery**, 996-4208, **Museum of Antiquities**, 966-7818, **The Diefenbaker Canada Centre**, 966-8384 offering a major display relating to Canadian politics, and the **Museum of Natural Sciences and Geology**, 996-4399. Call for individual opening times, donations appreciated. _www.usask.ca_.

Ukrainian Museum of Canada, 910 Spadina Cres E, 244-3800. Folk art, costumes, photographs and exhibits depicting the history of Ukrainian immigrants in Saskatchewan. Summer, Tue-Sat 10am-5pm, Sun 1pm-5pm. $3. _www.umc.sk.ca_.

The **Western Development Museum**, 2610 Lorne Ave, 931-1910. Turn of the century 'Pioneer Street'—family life, transportation, industry, agriculture, etc. The museum's collection is 'said to be the best of its kind in North America'. 'Good.' Daily 9am-5pm, $7.25, $5.25 w/student ID. _www.wdm.ca_.

SaskTel-Saskatchewan Jazz Festival, 652-1421, held in downtown Saskatoon. Emphasis on mainstream jazz and a wide variety of other styles from Dixieland and blues to contemporary fusion and gospel. Dates change annually, call for details. _www.saskjazz.com_.

Information/Travel
Visitors and Convention Bureau, 305 Idylwyld Dr N #6, 242-1206, (800) 567-2444.
Saskatchewan Transportation, 50 23rd St E, 933-8000, (800) 661-8747. Bus to Regina, 3 daily, $30.90 one way.
Saskatoon airport is reachable by taxi only. $13-16. Call 653-3333.

PRINCE ALBERT NATIONAL PARK This 1496-square mile park, 140 miles north of Saskatoon, typifies the lake and woodland wilderness country lying to the north of the prairies. It's an excellent area for canoeing with many connecting rivers between the lakes. From 1931-8 it was home to Grey Owl, one of the world's most famous park naturalists and impostors. Born Archibald Belaney, old Grey was an Englishman who came to Canada to fulfil a boyhood dream of living in the wilderness. Donning traditional clothing, he presented himself as the son of an Apache woman and carried out valuable research work for the park. Visit the cabin he lived in for 7 yrs. Accessible by boat or canoe across the lake or on foot in summer. Entrance to the park is $6.

Accommodation in the park includes campsites, hotels and cabins. **Waskesiu** is the main service centre where most hotels and motels can be found at some expense. For **Park info: Prince Albert National Park**, 663-4522; or **Prince Albert Tourism and Convention Bureau**, 3700 2nd Ave W, 953-4386. In the park **camping: Beaver Glen**, $20, $25 w/hook-up. You can also brave it and camp in the back country for $8. **Sandy Lake** and **Namekus**, $14. Campers must register, 663-4513. _www.parkscanada.pch.gc.ca_.

THE PACIFIC

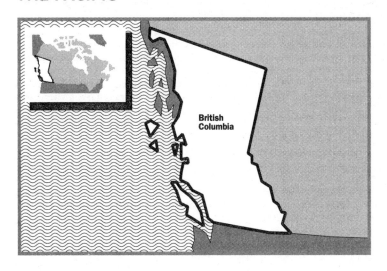

British
Columbia

BRITISH COLUMBIA

Arguably Canada's most scenic province, British Columbia lies sandwiched between the Pacific Ocean and the Rocky Mountains. This is an almost storybook land of towering snow-topped mountains, timbered foothills, fertile valleys, pristine, unspoiled lakes and mightier rivers, speckled with dozens of provincial and national parks. The spectacular coastline has deep fjords dotted with islands, long surfing beaches, old-growth Douglas firs, and ranges of craggy mountain peaks.

Inland there is a large plateau that provides British Columbia's bounteous fruit and wine country, focused on the sunny **Okanagan Valley;** the gold and silver mining towns, **Barkerville** and **Sandon,** whose fortunes in the 1890s helped propel the Province's economy into the 20th century; and the ranching, oil and gas of **Peace River** in the north east. The plateau is bounded to the east by a series of mountain ranges, extending to the Rocky Mountain Trench, flanked by bubbling natural spas in the "Springdom" of **East Kootenay** and the **Selkirk Mountains**. From here flow the Fraser, Columbia and Peace Rivers. The south west corner of British Columbia is considered one of the world's best climatic regions with mild winters and sunny, temperate summers reminiscent of the Mediterranean. Consequently, this area is popular with immigrants. BC's melting pot of cultures and customs is reflected in the languages spoken here: Cantonese, Punjabi, Spanish, German and French, after English. Samples of the world's best Chinese food may be had in Vancouver, known once as 'Hong Kouver,' and dramatic dragon boat races have long been part of the local scene.

No doubt the climate, plentiful lands, and abundance of fish and wild animals also attracted Canada's 'First Nations' from Asia over a landbridge known as **Beringia**, _www.beringia.com_, peoples whose cultures can be traced in some 20,000 sites in the province dating back over 10,000 years. At least half of Canada's native peoples lived in BC prior to the coming of the Europeans, some, such as the Haida and Tlingit, with unique languages unrelated to any other. Today, almost two hundred bands of First Nations live in BC: Their history of art, music, cuisine, architecture and lifestyles can still be explored, portrayed by aboriginal elders, guides and artisans.

This vast and beautiful province, four times the size of Great Britain, was a late developer in colonial terms. Although Sir Francis Drake came this way, searching for the mythical Northwest Passage, and Captain Cook landed here, and a war was almost fought between Britain and Spain over domination of the area, it was years before the region was fully explored. In July 1793, Stornoway-born Alexander Mackenzie ('Big Mack') arrived at King Island, west of **Bella Coola**, on behalf of the North West Company, becoming the first European to cross the continent overland north of Mexico, a dozen years before Lewis and Clark. To the south, the seething 850-mile **Fraser River** is named after a grumpy, Vermont-born Scot, Simon Fraser, who first voyaged down it in 1808 in a hair-raising expedition.

Vancouver Island was not designated a colony until 1849, when it was first administered for the Crown by the Hudson's Bay Company and the mainland not until 1866. British Columbia became a formal province in 1871. As recently as the 1880s there were no real communications and no railroad link with the east – the last spike of the Canadian Pacific Railroad was hammered in near **Revelstoke** only in 1885, by a Scot, Donald Smith (aka Lord Strathcona). Until then, the Rockies formed a natural, almost impassable barrier between BC and the rest of the Confederation. _http://victoria.tc.ca/Resources/bchistory.html._

Today, the whole province still only has a population of about four million, but in recent years has enjoyed one of the highest standards of living in Canada thanks to its abundance of natural resources and Vancouver's trade role as Canada's Pacific Gateway. In 2005, laid-back **Vancouver** was judged third among all major world cities for its quality of life and **Victoria**, BC's old-time capital, continues to seduce visitors with its old-time charm.   _www.britishcolumbia.com_,   _www.vacationsbc.com_, and _www.HelloBC.com_.

National Parks: Glacier, Gwaii Haanas Reserve, Kootenay, Mount Revelstoke, Pacific Rim and Yoho. Visit _www.parkscanada.pch.gc.ca_ or _www.canadianparks.com._

The telephone area codes are 604 and 778 around the Vancouver metro area. Elsewhere it's 250.

VANCOUVER This port metropolis rivals Cape Town, Hong Kong, and San Francisco for the sheer physical beauty of its setting. Behind the city sit the snow-capped Blue Mountains of the Coast Range, rising more than 1,500 metres. Lapping its shores are the clear blue waters of Georgia Strait and English Bay. Across the Strait, snuggled with smaller islands, is 500+ kilometres long **Vancouver Island** _www.vancouverisland.com_, and _www.victoriabc.com._ To the south is the estuary carved out by the Fraser River. The city was named after Captain George Vancouver who first visited the region in

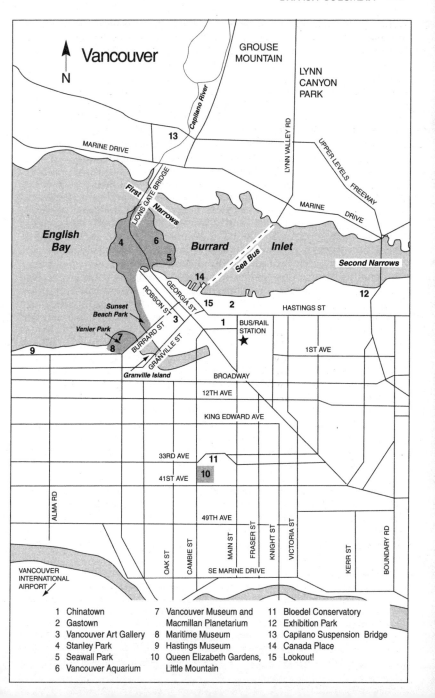

1 Chinatown
2 Gastown
3 Vancouver Art Gallery
4 Stanley Park
5 Seawall Park
6 Vancouver Aquarium

7 Vancouver Museum and
  Macmillan Planetarium
8 Maritime Museum
9 Hastings Museum
10 Queen Elizabeth Gardens,
  Little Mountain

11 Bloedel Conservatory
12 Exhibition Park
13 Capilano Suspension Bridge
14 Canada Place
15 Lookout!

the 1790s on behalf of George III, sent by the King to disabuse the Spanish at Nootka and explore the Columbia River, Oregon and inner coast.

Easy-going 'Van City' now covers the peninsula between the Fraser River and Burrard Inlet and the areas way beyond. **Lion's Gate** and other bridges link the various suburbs to the city centre via streets that are rarely congested. Once downtown in 'Van', as the city is affectionately known by locals, you are within easy reach of sandy beaches or ski slopes and lots of greenery: within city limits, there are over 200 parks, most notable of which are the thickly wooded **Stanley Park,** which *National Geographic* calls 'one of the world's great open spaces', and **Queen Elizabeth Park,** the literal highpoint of the city. *www.city.vancouver.bc.ca/parks/parks.*

Vancouver's colourful **Chinatown** (Pender and Keefer E) is North America's second largest, with Cantonese spoken in almost a third of city homes. The Chinese have long had a presence here: well before the city was incorporated (in 1886), Chinese labourers worked in canneries, coalmines, gold fields, and timber mills in BC. Between 1881 and 1885, thousands of Chinese were contracted to build the Canadian Pacific Railway (CPR). When the railway was finished, many of them came back here to live; and more came back after the Klondike Gold Rush of 1897.

Canada's **Pacific Gateway** has a harbour frontage of 98 miles, marked with piles of bright yellow sulphur and brown potash brought in from the interior, and containers from the prairies filled with wheat, barley and canola, ready to be shipped out on freighters that ply Burrard Inlet day and night. The railroads too have always had an important part to play in Vancouver's communications system; one of the most spectacular rides is that up into **Fraser Canyon,** once the final heartbreak of the men pushing their way north to the **Barkerville** gold fields with only mules and camels to help them. If you're heading back east from here, this is the route to take. *www.fraservalleyguide.com.*

Vancouver hosted Expo '86, the last World's Fair in North America and will host the **2010 Olympic Winter Games,** *www.winter2010.com,* along with nearby Whistler, Grouse and other resorts. Vancouver has also long been 'Hollywood North', the location of choice for many American filmmakers, providing a diverse backdrop for all types of movie sets.

Vancouver's climate is mild – it's the warmest year-round city in Canada, but it does rain a fair amount, especially in winter. Always have an umbrella handy (every store has a brolly bin). January is the coldest month with temperatures averaging 3° C; in July temperatures average 20° C. Snow is rare and roses frequently bloom at Christmas.

www.tourismvancouver.com   *www.bcpassport.com,*   *www.city.vancouver.bc.ca*
www.vancouvercitytourist.com.

Accommodation

NB: Finding accommodation in Vancouver can be difficult: book ahead! If you have a car, be sure to ask about parking. Parking garages here are called 'Parkades.' **British Columbia Tourism,** (800) HELLO-BC, makes hotel rsvs in Vancouver and throughout the province. It sometimes has discounted rates. A credit card is needed to secure the reservation. *www.hellobc.com.* All Canadian Hostels can be found on the web at *www.hihostels.ca,* where local discounts are offered at cafes, clubs and more: check the site for info. Another site for hostels, cheap hotels, places to eat and a general 'insider's' guide on Vancouver can be found at *www.bcpassport.com*, or call (800) 438-9970.

Roomies, 1542 W 8th Ave, 904-4295. Roommate referral service with furnished apartments and sublets for a \$15 basic fee. *info@roomies.com* & *www.roomies.com*.

The Cambie Hostel, 300 Cambie St, 684-6466. Centrally located, 'basic and cheap'. Dorm \$20, semi-private room, \$22.50; linens incl. Internet \$1/15 mins. Free muffin and coffee for b/fast. Has a pub and restaurant. *www.cambiehostels.com*.

C & N Backpackers Hostel; 2 locations; 927 Main St and Central Station Hostel, 1038 Main St. Call 682-2441/(888) 434-6060 for both. Nr Main St and the Science World/SkyTrain stop. Take bus #3 or #16 that stops outside the hostel to/from downtown. Free pick-up can be arranged for stays over 3 nights; call for info. Dorm \$16, private room S/D-\$40 (Central Station location, XP-\$5). No curfew, internet \$1/10 mins and reasonably priced restaurant on site at Central Station Hostel. 'Clean, fun, centrally located, super atmosphere, kitchen, parking and laundry.' 'Renovated, clean kitchen, internet, groups welcome, friendly and helpful staff, restaurant and pub on site.' *www.cnnbackpackers.com*.

Hazelwood Hotel, 344 E Hastings St, 688-7467, in Chinatown. Monthly rentals only, \$400, \$450 w/bath.

Hostelling International Downtown (HI-C), 1114 Burnaby St, 684-4565/(888) 203-4302. Located in Vancouver's W/end, close to metropolitan neighbourhood: shops; attractions; Sunset Beach and nightlife. Open 24 hrs, 'excellent'. June-Sept: member \$24, non-member \$28. Rsvs recommended. *www.hihostels.ca*.

HI-Vancouver Central, 1025 Granville Street, 685-5335/(888) 203-8333. The newest hostel in Vancouver is set in the entertainment district, with its own bar, The Royal. Offers comfy mattresses, individual toilets, free linens and bar w/great specials and live music. Dorm: members \$20, non-members \$24, private rooms vary. *www.hihostels.ca*.

HI-Jericho Beach Hostel, 1515 Discovery St, 224-3208/(888) 203-4303. At the foot of Jericho Beach: take #4 bus from Granville St to 4th & NW Marine Drive, then walk 5 mins downhill to Discovery St or call for free shuttle bus info. This service runs daily 8am-4pm. Largest Canadian hostel with excellent facilities. Book ahead in summer. 'A great place but arrive early' (before 11am). 'Beautiful area.' Members \$20, non-members \$24. Private rooms, D-\$51-\$61. Bike rental \$20/day. *www.hihostels.ca*.

Kingston Hotel, 757 Richards St, 684-9024/(888) 731-3304. Very European with a Swedish sauna and a cafe, TV lounge and laundry. 'Nice place.' 'Good people.' S-\$48-\$98, D-\$58-\$135, XP-\$10. Bfast incl. *www.kingstonhotelvancouver.com*.

Patricia Hotel, 403 E Hastings, 255-4301/(800) 359-6279. S/D-\$90, 'Close to downtown.' 'A dangerous area.' *www.canadianhotelguide.com*.

Same Sun Backpacker Lodge, 1018 Granville Street, 682-8226, (877) 562-2783. Largest hostel in downtown (was **Global Village**). 150+ dorm beds. Private rooms, quad rooms, laundry, internet, games area, lockers. \$28 (w Stud ID) in summer, June 1–Oct 1)/\$21.40 winter. Doubles \$49/52 summer. *www.samesun.com/vancouver.html*.

Sylvia Hotel, 1154 Gilford Street, 681-9321. On English Bay near Stanley Park, minutes from downtown. Has bar, restaurant, and parking. Free internet. 'Highly recommended.' S-D-\$95+ in summer, \$75-100, Oct 1-Apr 30. *www.sylviahotel.com*.

YMCA, 955 Burrard St, 681-0221/(888) 595-9622. Private rooms: S-\$48, D-\$62, (rooms w/TV \$2 extra). Co-ed. 'Conveniently situated, friendly staff.' *www.vanymca.org*.

YWCA, 733 Beatty St, 895-5830 (800) 663-1424. Downtown. In summer S-\$57, semi-private doubles from \$86, private-\$113, triple \$97. Coffee shop on-site, co-ed, TV lounge, laundry, walking distance to YWCA pool and fitness centre with wkly and mthly rates available. *www.ywcahotel.com*.

University residence: Simon Fraser University, McTaggart and **Gage Halls,** Burnaby, 291-4503. Shared kitchen, washroom, recreational facilities, 45 min drive to downtown. S-$20 no linen, S-$26 w/linen, limited number of double rooms available, $45 w/linen. May-end Aug only. Call for info about long-term accommodation and monthly rates. *www.sfu.ca/conference-accommodation/.*

Camping: Surrey Timberland Campsite, 3418 King George Hwy, 531-1033. $16 incl tax, $22 w/full hook-up. 40 mins from Vancouver. *brayentltd@aol.com.*

Porteau Cove Campground, 689-9025/(800) 689-9025. 38 km north of Vancouver, on Hwy 99 toward Whistler. Tent site $22/night.

Food

There are many neighbourhoods filled with ethnic restaurants inc Chinatown (see below), Indian/Punjabi restaurants on five blocks on Main near 49th, and sushi restaurants are everywhere. In the West End, try Denman btwn Davie and Georgia, Davie btwn Broughton and Burrard, Yaletown area, etc. for scads of multi-ethnic restaurants, inc many pizzerias. For a variety of interesting, self-service eateries, visit **Granville Island,** *www.granvilleisland.com,* The **Café at Vancouver Art Gallery** is a pleasant downtown bistro. **Earls,** based in Edmonton, has four nice restaurants here, including one on Robson downtown. Also see: *www.vaneats.com* and *www.discovervancouver.com/restaurants.asp.*

Burger Heaven, 77 10th St, 522-8339. 'Good atmosphere, reasonable prices.' Sun-Thu 11.30am-9pm and 'til 10pm Fri-Sat.

Cambie Bar and Grill, 300 Cambie St, 684-6466 Est. 1887. 'Low price tavern, student hangout.' Cheap beer and food specials for only $5. Daily 11am-1am, Sun 'til midnight. **Bakery Cafe** at 312 Cambie St – also a must! *www.cambiehostels.com.*

Enthuze, 871 Denman, 669-6266. Variety of fusion foods, inc Mediterranean, Kowloon Barbeque ($7.95), Kho Phi Phi (Thai, $8.95), Sake Salmon ($12.95) etc.

Heavenly Muffins, 601 W Hastings, 681-9104. Mon-Fri 6am-7pm. Endless selection of muffins, sandwiches, juices, coffees and more.

Keg Restaurants, est 1971, now over 80 locations. Try the original! Keg Caesars, 595 Hornby St. 687-4044. Also on Granville Island. Inexpensive; salad bar, seafood, burgers. 'Keg-sized drinks.' Mon-Wed 11.30am-midnight, Thu-Sat 'til 1am, Sun 'til 11pm. *www.kegsteakhouse.com.*

La Luna Café, 117-131 Water Street, Gastown 687-5862, Specialty coffee house and eatery. Nice coffee, light food, non-touristy.

Maria's Taverna, 2324 W 4th Ave in Kitsilano (731-4722) and 1037 Denman in West End (681-8500), Greek dishes inc for take out and delivery.

Milestones All Star Cafe, 11 locations in Vancouver including 1210 Denman, 662-3431, where it began in the West End, and 2966 W 4th Ave, 734-8616. in Kits. Pizza, burgers, salad, subs. Plenty of food, good prices. Lunch and Dinner $11-$19. Mon-Thu 11am-11pm, Fri 'til midnight, Sat 9.30am-midnight, Sun 'til 10pm. *www.milestonerestaurants.com.*

Old Spaghetti Factory, 53 Water St, Gastown, 684-1288. Large portions at reasonable prices. Daily 11.30am-11pm, Sun 'til 10pm. Est 1970. *www.oldspaghetti-factory.ca.*

Seasons Hill Top Bistro, Queen Elizabeth Park, 874-8008/ 800 632-9422. Glass gazebo with great vistas on highest point of the city. West Coast cuisine. Expensive, but worth having carrot & ginger soup ($7) or more to experience the view. This is where Boris Yeltsin and Bill Clinton dined in 1993, and Sarah MacLaughlin had her wedding reception. Menus at *www.vancouverdine.com/seasons/home.html.*

Sophie's Cosmic Café, 2095 W 4th Ave in Kitsilano, since 1988. 732-6810. Classic 50s-style diner with outdoor terrace. Serves many and bountiful b/fasts ('til 5pm), lunch, tasty desserts and shakes, and casual dinner. Not to be missed! 'Best chocolate shake in town.' Daily 8am-9.30pm. *www.sophiescosmiccafe.com.*

Taf's Cafe, 829 Granville St, 684-8900. 'Arty atmosphere cafe. Reasonably priced.

You can leave messages and luggage here.' Sun-Thu 11am-Midnight, Fri-Sat 'til 1am. Lunch specials, 11am-3pm. *www.tafs-cafe.com.*

The Only Cafe, 20 E Hastings, 681-6546. Seafood - fish & oysters, since 1912. Friendly, counter-service. The fish with chips is sock-eye salmon, among others. 'Basic but tasty meal. A Gastown institution.' 'Queues, popular with locals.' Price: $7.50-$13. Daily specials $9.50. 'Fantastic clam chowder', $3.50. Daily 11am-8pm.

Sequoia Grill at the Teahouse 7501 Stanley Park Dr, NW side of Stanley Park overlooking English Bay. 669-3281/(800) 280-9893. Patio. West Coast cuisine. 'Only when you want to splurge, expensive but really lovely.' 'Exquisite sunsets.' Lunch $7-28. "Small plates" 2.30-5.30pm. Dinner 5.30-9.45pm. Brunch Sat & Sun. *www.vancouverdine.com.*

Vancouver Art Gallery Café, 750 Hornby, 662-4719. Five kinds of salmon quiche; delicious pies and soups. Outdoor, oasis-like terrace. 'Good value, unhurried atmosphere.' Daily 10am-5:30pm, Thu till 9 pm. *www.vanartgallery.bc.ca.*

White Spot Restaurants, since 1938, many locations, original at Granville and 67th. Try 2518 W Broadway (at Larch), 731-2434. Good and cheap. Triple O Sunny Starts. Daily 6.30am-11pm. *www.whitespot.ca.*

University of BC, Students' Union Bldg, 6138 Student Union Blvd, 822-3461, cafeteria style; from $4. Mon-Fri 7.30am-2pm. *www.foodserv.ubc.ca/locations.htm.*

Vancouver food blog: *www.evevancouver.ca/food/hamilton.htm.*

Of interest

Stanley Park. This is the largest and oldest of Vancouver's parks – the third largest urban park in North America at 1000 acres, just a few minutes from downtown, occupying the peninsula at the mouth of Burrard Inlet. It's criss-crossed by quiet trails in evergreen woods filled with towering Red Cedars, Douglas Firs and Western Hemlocks, surrounded by a waters-edge 9 km walk, bike trail and one-way drive, and joined to N Vancouver by the **Lion's Gate** suspension bridge. From **Prospect Point** on the Stanley Park Drive near the bridge, you can gaze across the sea to Vancouver Island, a serene experience at sunset (669-2737), *www.prospectpoint.ca.* Lord Stanley, Governor General of Canada, dedicated the Park in 1888: "To the use and enjoyment of people of all colours, creeds and customs for all time." Close by Stanley's statue is one of **Robert Burns.**

Biking in and round this large Park is recommended: Hire bikes outside the park entrance on Denman in the nearby **West End,** eg., **Bayshore Bike Rental,** 745 Denman, 688-2453; **Bikes and Blades,** 718 Denman, 602-9899; **Denman Bike Shop,** 710 Denman, 685-9755; **Spokes Bicycle Rental and Espresso Bar,** 1798 W. Georgia, 688-5141 *www.vancouverbikerental.com*; **Stanley Park Cycle Rentals,** 768 Denman, 688-0087.) *www.seethewestend.com/denport/denport.htm* and *http://englishbay.com/recreation, http://www.seethewestend.com/denport/denport.htm.* Rollerblading is another option— 'the best thing I did in North America'!

The 8.7 km **Seawall Promenade,** from which you can see float planes buzz skywards from downtown, passes a cluster of the multi-coloured **Brockton Totem Poles,** where a Visitors Centre can tell you about the poles (ie. not idols nor religious objects) and the people who carved them. Beyond is the **Nine O'clock Gun,** originally fired to warn fisherman to stop fishing at 6 pm on Sundays, later changed to 9pm as a time signal for the general population. It still booms nightly.

In summer (mid-June to end-Sept), you can get on and off a **free shuttle bus** at most points along the Promenade. Horse-drawn carriage rides are also available at $18.65 w/student ID, 681-5115, *www.stanleyparktours.com.* If you like trains, a **Miniature Railway** reproduces CPR's first trans-Canada trip in 1886, on an eight minute ride through towering rainforest (257-8531).

The **Vancouver Aquarium Marine Science Centre** in the east of the Park, called 'Canada's best Aquarium', is open all year, housing 33,700 fishes of 300 species; nearly 30,000 invertebrates, including sea stars, jellyfish and octopi, plus mammals. June-Sept: daily 9.30am-7pm. $17.50, $12.95 w/student ID. 'Brilliant. Could have watched the whales for hours.' 659-3474. *www.vanaqua.org.*

The Park, which shelters over 200 species of waterfowl, seabirds and songbirds on the **Pacific Flyway**, also includes a bird sanctuary, **Lost Lagoon**, named after *Ode to the Lost Lagoon* written by Canada's famed West End poet, Pauline Johnson.

The Park also has an 18-hole golf course, rugby ground and cricket pitch, 17 free tennis courts, and theatre under the stars. You can cool off at Second or Third Beaches on English Bay and at Lumberman's Arch Water Park and a fresh water pool at Second Beach. And at **Ceperley Playground** near Second Beach, a **free dance programme** is offered Mon-Thu evenings (7.30-9.30pm) during the summer. *www.city.vancouver.bc.ca/parks/arts/danceatdusk.htm.*

There are four restaurants in the Park: Sequoia Grill, 669-3281 *www.sequoiagrill.com,* Fish House, 681-7275 *www.fishhousestanleypark.com,* Prospect Point Café, 669-2737 *www.prospectpoint.ca,* and, in summer, the Pavilion Rose Garden Tea House, 602-3088. *www.city.vancouver.bc.ca/parks/parks/stanley* and *www.seestanleypark.com.*

Downtown

Canada Place, at the foot of Burrard St. on Burrard Inlet is an unusual building resembling a cruise ship. The Canadian Pavilion during Expo '86, it's now Vancouver's **Trade and Convention Centre**. The 5-storey **CN IMAX theatre** is also housed here, 682-IMAX, 1-800-582-4629. *www.imax.com/vancouver/.* Standard price $11.50. At the **Waterfront** here, you catch the SeaBus to N Vancouver, the SkyTrain, Translink buses, and float planes to Victoria.

Chinatown, reached by the **Silk Road Trail** from downtown, colourfully focussed on Main, E Keefer and E Pender Sts. Gift shops, Asian imports, night clubs and lots of Chinese restaurants and stores featuring such delicacies as fun see, longan, mangosteen, ping gwoal, rambutan, and santol – all identified only in Chinese. Medicinal markets offer dried snakeskins, among others. Many locals speak only Cantonese. The **Sam Kee Building** here at 8 W Pender, built about 5 ft wide in 1913, is listed by the *Guinness Book of Records* as the narrowest building in the world. SkyTrain: Stadium or Main Street stations. *www.vancouverchinatown.ca.*

Gastown, on **Water St** a few minutes E from the Waterfront Centre, was the original heart of Vancouver, named after garrulous 'Gassy Jack' Deighton who arrived in 1867 with a barrel of whiskey on the South Shore of Burrard Inlet. His saloon was built within 24 hours after the non-stop talker promised his barrel free to all who helped, and became so popular that the whole town was dubbed 'Gastown'. Later, in 1886, Gastown was incorporated as the City of Vancouver, but the same year, a brush-clearing fire turned all but two of the city's 400 original buildings to ashes. Now brick-lined Gastown is a pleasant area full of trendy boutiques, cafés and restaurants, antique shops and pubs. Horse-and- carriages ply Water St in the evenings, providing Victorian ambience. The major event here is the **Storyeum** (see below). Don't miss the 'World's First Steam Powered Clock' (1977) at Water and Cambie – every quarter hour it plays tunes like an organ, on the hour chiming like a little Big Ben and letting off steam. Thing is, it works on electricity. *www.gastown.org* and visual *www.seegastown.com.*

HSBC Building Atrium, 885 W Georgia, 879-7714. Has an amazing 90 ft buffed aluminium, 3,500 lb pendulum, seemingly in perpetual motion, that is hypnotic to watch. When you stand beneath it, you feel as if you're on a ship. *www.pendulumgallery.bc.ca.*

Lookout! Harbour Centre Tower, 555 W Hastings St, 689-0421. Ride a glass elevator 166 m in 50 seconds to the observation deck of the tallest tower in BC for a 360 degree view of city, harbour and surroundings. All day tkt $10, $7 w/student ID. Summer: daily 8.30am-10.30pm. Free if you dine at the revolving restaurant! *www.vancouverlookout.com.*

Robson St, between Howe and Broughton. European import stores, continental restaurants. Once nicknamed 'Robsonstrasse', after European immigrants opened small delicatessens, patisseries, and chic boutiques on the street. Now compared to Rodeo Drive with such stores as La Senza, bebe, La Vie En Rose, etc. Packed! 'Vibrant. Great at weekends.' _www.robsonstreet.ca/shops_ Burrard Street Station.

Science World, 1455 Quebec St, 443-7443. For the domed IMAX experience. A short SkyTrain ride from Canada Place. Science World, $13.75, $9.50 w/student ID, has a combo ticket with CN IMAX, $18.75, $14.50 w/student ID. Otherwise the CN IMAX is $11.25, $9 w/student ID. Summer: Daily 10am-6pm. _www.scienceworld.bc.ca._ False Creek Ferries dep to Granville Island and Vanier Park every 30 mins, 9.55am-5.25pm daily; $8.50 o/w _www.granvilleislandferries.bc.ca_ And via _Aquabus_ to Granville Island every 30 mins $6 o/w. _www.aquabus.bc.ca._

Storyeum, 142 Water St in Gastown, few mins from Waterfront Station, 687-8142/(800) 687-8142, offers a live tour of BC in an hour-or-so dramatized musical history trip through a series of inter-active subterranean theatres. NB. If you have coffee at La Luna Café at 117 Water St, opposite, you can get coupons that save $2 for each of up to five people. On the hour and half-hour, daily. $21.95, 13-18 $18.95, _www.storyeum.com._

Vancouver Art Gallery, 750 Hornby St, 662-4719. Est 1931, the largest art gallery in western Canada. Innovative collection of over 8,000 classic and contemporary pieces of art and photography, including one of the most comprehensive photo-based collections in North America. Excellent ongoing exhibit of paintings by west coast modernist Emily Carr (1871-1945). Daily 10am-5.30pm, Thu 'til 9pm; $15, $10 w/student ID. Has excellent, oasis-like café. _www.vanartgallery.bc.ca._

Granville Island

On the south shore of False Creek, beneath the Granville St Bridge, reachable by small ferries or, from the south, via road since the island is really an isthmus, with a pleasant public park and local community at back. The lively, crowded 'Island' has a public market, maritime section, craftworks, galleries and studios, cafes and restaurants, institutes and theatres, and even industry. This is where Vancouver's writers, storytellers are, and fringe festivals are held, among others. Fishing boats deliver fresh fish nearby; and you can hire runabouts here to cruise False Creek.

Granville Public Market is open daily 9am-7pm with dozens of places to eat and stalls with fresh produce, fish, bread and other local edibles: A delightful place to stop, lunch and be entertained indoors or on the quay. Browse the market, galleries, theatres, and craft stores: Enjoy your sushi under $3, Indian Candy (smoked salmon, about $2), fresh fruit, chocolate and ice cream, or other rainbows of choice as you watch sailboats, scullers, seagulls, city high-rises, with snow-capped heights at back.

While here, you should visit the **Crafthouse Shop** of the Crafts Association of BC (687-6511) _www.cabc.com_ to see local crafts, the prestigious **Emily Carr Institute of Art & Design,** _www.eciad.ca_ and nearby **Pacific Institute of Culinary Arts,** _www.picachef.com,_ which add distinctive creative (and first nations') touches to the island community. _www.granvilleisland.com._ You can also go whale watching daily, Apr-Oct, at **Wild Whales Vancouver,** 1806 Mast Tower Rd, 699 2011 _www.whalesvancouver.com._

Reach Granville Island via **False Creek Ferries** from the Aquatic Centre near Burrard Bridge ($2.50 o/w every 5 mins, 7am-10.30pm in summer, daily, $4 r/t, pay on board), and from Science World & OmniMax Theatre at the end of False Creek, via Yaletown ($6 o/w every 15 mins, 10am-8pm, daily). _www.granvilleislandferries.bc.ca._ Or via **Aquabus** from Hornby St on the other side of Burrard Bridge every five mins ($2.0 o/w), or from Science World where there's a SkyTrain stop, every 30 mins ($6 o/w). _www.aquabus.bc.ca._

Vancouver South & West

Beaches and Swimming Pools: Some 18 km of beaches surround Vancouver. Info at 738-8535. Recommended spots include **English Bay** where the Vancouver Polar Bear Swim (info 665-3418) has taken place since 1920. It's at 2:30pm on New Year's Day. In 2005, there were 1,600 participants - the water temp (9C) was warmer than the air temp (3C). *www.city.vancouver.bc.ca/parks/events/polarbear.* Near UBC (see below) is 7.8 kms long **Wreck Beach** at the tip of Burrard Inlet, Canada's first and largest, legal, clothing-optional (CO) beach, ie., sun your buns for free. *www.wreckbeach.org.* There is a breathtaking view of Vancouver Island. **Tower Beach,** also CO, named after searchlight towers built during WWII, is round the corner from Wreck Beach, near UBC's Museum of Anthropology. *www.members.shaw.ca/co-bc/co-vancouver.html.* Other notable Vancouver beaches include **Jericho, Kitsilano** (locally known as Kits), **Locarno,** the **Stanley Park Beaches,** and **Spanish Banks.** Designated *Quiet Beaches* are Locarno, Spanish Bank W, and Sunset. *www.city.vancouver.bc.ca/parks/rec/beaches.* The city operates 15 swimming pools, including heated **Kitsilano Beach Pool,** the only salt water pool in Vancouver and one of few in the world. **Second Beach Pool** in Stanley Park is heated, beach-entry style.

Queen Elizabeth Park, 30 E 30th Ave, S of False Creek at 27th Ave and Cambie. 257-8584. The highest point in the city - 167 m, with 360 deg view of Vancouver skyline, a riot of colour in summer, it's dominated by the **Bloedel Conservatory and Floral Conservatory**, the world's second-largest domed conservatory, a triodetic dome filled with over 500 species of plants. Self-guided tours through tropical rain-forest, subtropical and desert climates with 27 stops, 10am-5pm daily. $4.25. When you enter the park, keep left for the side with the views overlooking the **North Shore Mountains** and harbour. Near the Conservatory is a **Japanese Garden**, and there is a rose garden and arboretum. From the **Lookout** above the sunken gardens, there is a good view, and intriguing sculptures by Henry Moore – *Knife Edge* - and J. Seward Johnson – *The Photographer* - at the top near the **Seasons Hill Top Bistro,** site of the 1993 Vancouver Summit dinner for Boris Yeltsin and Bill Clinton. The Park has lawn bowls and many tennis courts. To reach the park, take a #15 Cambie southbound bus from Burrard station to 33rd and Cambie. *www.city.vancouver.bc.ca/parks/parks/queenelizabeth.*

University of British Columbia (UBC) *www.ubc.ca* at Point Grey, adjacent to miles of forested trails in the **Pacific Spirit Regional Park** and with a population of some 40,000 students, has a good swimming pool, cafeteria, bookshop and world class **Museum of Anthropology,** 6393 N.W. Marine Drive, 822-5087. The Museum has one of the finest collections of West Coast Native Art. *www.moa.ubc.ca,* Wed-Sun 10am-5pm, Tue til 9pm. Free Tue after 5pm. $9, $7 w/student ID. In UBC grounds behind the museum is the **Nitobe Japanese Garden,** considered to be the 'best traditional, authentic Japanese Tea and Stroll Garden in North America'. Open daily 10am-5/6pm. $4, $2.50 w/student ID. *www.nitobe.org.* There is also a **Totem Park** with carvings and buildings representing a segment of a Haida Indian village. To reach the mammoth UBC campus, from Granville Station, take #4 bus or #17 UBC bus southbound on Granville Mall. Also #9, 25, and 99.

Vanier Park on the south of English Bay is home to the **Vancouver Museum,** the **Vancouver Maritime Museum,** and the **H.R. MacMillan Space Centre**. *www.greatervancouverparks.com/Vanier01.html.* Reach the park (Maritime Museum) by False Creek Ferries from Aquatic Centre ($2.50 o/w every 15 mins, 10am-8pm, daily), and from Science World via Granville Island ($8.50 o/w every 30 mins, 10am-8pm, daily). *www.granvilleislandferries.bc.ca* or take #22 or 2 bus, from Burrard Station and visit: **Hastings Mill Museum,** 1575 Alma Rd, 734-1212. The Mill was the area's first sawmill, and one of the few buildings surviving the Great Fire of June, 1886 - it's the oldest building in Vancouver. Eventually, the settlement known as Granville developed round it. Now a museum with Indian artefacts, mementoes of pioneer days and pictures of the city's development. Tue-Sun 11am-4pm. Sept 16-May 31: Sat and Sun only, 1pm-4pm. Donations.

H.R. Macmillan Space Centre, 1100 Chestnut St, 738-7827. Housed in same building as Vancouver Museum. Numerous hands-on exhibits: in the Cosmic Courtyard, design a spacecraft or morph into an alien; travel to Mars on the Virtual Voyages Simulator and watch a show at the Ground Station Canada or Star theatres. Show times vary; call ahead. Rsvs recommended. Price includes unlimited shows at the planetarium, theatres and a ride on virtual simulator: $13.50, $10.50 w/student ID. *www.hrmacmillanspacecenter.com.*

Maritime Museum, 1905 Ogden Ave, foot of Cypress St, 257-8300. The fortunes of Vancouver have been inexorably linked to the sea and the Fraser River: this Museum, established almost 50 years ago, brings every aspect of that dynamic history to life. Its exhibits focus on the complete 1920s RCMP ship *St Roch*, the first ship to navigate the Northwest Passage in both directions and to circumnavigate the continent of North America. Museum events cover everything from Canada's maritime Arctica to the Mongol fleet that invaded Japan in 1281. Daily:10am-5pm, $8, $5.50 w/student ID. *www.vmm.bc.ca.*

Vancouver Museum, 1100 Chestnut St, 736-4431. Large circular building fronted by an amazing abstract fountain. Permanent exhibit traces the development of the Northwest Coast from the Ice Age through pioneer days to the present. Exhibits change regularly. Tues-Sun 10am-5pm, Thu 'til 9pm. $10, $6 w/student ID. *www.vanmuseum.bc.ca.*

Vancouver East, Burnaby

Exhibition Park, 2901 East Hastings Street (bounded by Renfrew, Hastings and Cassiar Sts) off Rte 1 is the 115-acre home of the 94,000 sq.ft **Pacific Coliseum** and site of the annual **Pacific National Exhibition (PNE),** which will be 96 years old in 2006. 253-2311. The PNE takes place for 2 wks mid Aug-Labour Day. $15 p/day. 'Fantastic. Includes lumberjack competition, rodeo, Demolition Derby, exhibitions, fair, etc.' The **PlayLand,** BC's newest amusement attraction within the Park, has 30 rides, games and special events. Unlimited ride one-day pass, $26.95 from 7-11s, $29.95 at gate. Summer: daily 11am-9pm. *www.pne.bc.ca.*

Simon Fraser University, on 430-acres atop 400 m-high Burnaby Mountain, 291-3111, the giant module design of this ultra-modern seat of learning makes it possible to move around the 25,000 student university totally under cover. The views from up here are superb. To reach the campus catch a #10 bus on Hastings East, change at Kootenay Loop to the #135-SFU. *www.sfu.ca.*

Vancouver North

The area is reached in 12 mins across Burrard Inlet by **Seabus -** two catamaran ferries, seating up to 400 passengers, from **Waterfront** in downtown Vancouver to **Lonsdale Quay** on the North Shore. Deps every 15 min, every 30 min evenings and Sundays. $2.25. Seabus is part of the Translink system allowing transfers to Skytrain and buses at both terminals. *www.translink.bc.ca/Transportation Services/-SeaBus.*

Capilano Suspension Bridge, 3735 Capilano Rd N, 985-7474. Exit 14 on Hwy 1. Literally one of the most breathtaking local sights, since 1889 the swinging 137-metre long suspension bridge has been visited by everyone from Bob Hope to Marilyn Monroe to the Rolling Stones. The park is named after the Indian chief Ki-ap-a-la-no, who the explorer Simon Fraser met in 1808. The bridge spans a spectacular 70 m-deep gorge, but is only prelude to the fantastic **Treetops Walkway** strung high up in the towering rainforest, the first of its kind in North America. The bridge gives you sea legs - a slight sway, but the aerial Walkway leaves you breathless, along with Peter Pan, transcending from one giant Douglas fir to the next high above the ground. Then take the **Cliffhanger Walk**! Uncommercialized trading post. Salish totems. $24.95, $18.50 w/student ID. 9am-7.30pm. 'Experience of a lifetime!' _www.capbridge.com._

Grouse Mountain, 6400 Nancy Greene Way, 984-0661. The **Skyride,** North America's largest aerial tramway, starts at the top of Capilano Rd. In winter services a 25-run ski area that will be an Olympic venue in 2010. Ride huge gondolas to the 1250 m 'Peak of Vancouver' for incredible views, a cup of coffee or a quick hike (every 15 mins, 9 am-10 pm daily). Restaurants, open-air BBQ and a café are rewards once up there. Complimentary 45 min Lumberjack Show (12 pm, 2:30 pm, 4:30 pm, May-mid-Oct), refuge centre for endangered wildlife-with two orphan grizzlies, and 'Born to Fly' eagle's eye show (on the hour, 10am-9pm) make great entertainment. 'Take food with you and make a day of it'. 'Spectacular. Not to be missed. Best thing I did in North America.' 'We went on a cloudy day and had an amazing time walking in the clouds.' You can hike the **Grouse Grind Trail** up the mountain, although it's steep and you're advised not to walk back down. _www.gvrd.bc.ca/services/grouse-grind.asp._ You should be physically fit, wear the proper gear and prepare for changing climates. $29.95. Highway #1 W to Capilano Road N. _www.grousemountain.com._

Lynn Canyon Park, 3663 Park Road, North Vancouver, 981-3103. The bridge (free) swings high above Lynn Canyon Creek. Swimming in the creek is nice too and there is an 'excellent' ecology centre by the park entrance. To get there: Seabus to Lonsdale Quay, take 229 bus to Peters Rd, then walk. By car, take the Upper Levels Hwy to Lynn Valley Rd. 'Peaceful and uncrowded.' Park open daily 7am-9pm summer; the ecology centre is open in the summer 10am-5pm, rest of year noon-4pm. _www.dnv.org/ecology._

Entertainment

Check _www.vancouverplus.ca_ for, among other things, brew pubs, micro-breweries and pubs, as well as restaurants of all kinds. Granville St is the city's entertainment hotspot. Gastown has many pubs with live entertainment: **Alibi Room,** 157 Alexander St, 623-3383. Soups $4-6 (inc chilled cucumber and avocado), Sandwiches $6-9 (inc chicken ciabatta club). Beer on tap $3.25-5.25. Great martini list, $7. Owner Rick Stevenson is a film producer whose first film made at Oxford included fellow-student, Hugh Grant. Snazzy website _www.alibiroom.com._

 Jolly Taxpayer Pub, 828 W Hastings St, 681-3550, close to Stanley Park. Traditional British-style pub. Show all the major sports events, including soccer, AKA football! Daily10am-midnight, Sun 11am-9pm. _www.jollytaxpayerhotel.com._

Downtown also has some great clubs and bars. Try: **Caprice**, 965-967 Granville St, 681-2114, 685-3288. Converted 10,000 sq ft cinema. Two separate environments: bar/grill lounge and a nightclub. Modern designs and classy atmosphere. 'Favourite haunt of visiting celebrities.' Retro night on Tue really draws the crowds.' Fri & Sat: dress to impress! Tues-Sun, 9pm-2am. Cover $4-$10. _www.capricenightclub.com._

Commodore Ballroom, 868 Granville, 739-4550. For over 75 years, the heart of Vancouver's nightlife, with sprung dance-floor. 'Premiere concert hall in Canada.' Among the acts that have played here: Talking Heads, Tina Turner, Dizzy Gillespie, Beastie Boys, Kiss, Nirvana, The Police, Snoop Dogg & Dr. Dre, Clash, etc. Must be 19+. _www.hob.com/venues/concerts/commodore_

Roxy, 932 Granville St, 331-7999. 'Good atmosphere, extremely popular with locals.' 'Great in-house bands.' Two house bands with live music nightly. Cover $7. Daily 7pm-2am, Fri/Sat 'til 3am. _www.roxyvan.com._

Festivals Vancouver loves to party. Throughout the year, the city is host to numerous festivals and celebrations for every imaginable group and cause. Some of the best follow with their websites, but for more info and tickets to other events contact the **Tourism Bureau,** _www.tourismvancouver.com/things to do/festivals.cfm._

and visit **Touristinfo Centre** for half-price tickets of the day at Plaza Level, 200 Burrard St, 684-2787. Tue-Sat, 10am-5pm. *www.ticketstonight.ca.*
Bard on the Beach Shakespeare Festival June-Sept, four productions in tents in Vanier Park. 301 - 601 Cambie Street, 737-0625. Toll free (877) 739-0559. Tickets 739-0559 or online. Regular \$28.50, Previews \$18. 1 pm Tue-Fri \$16. *www.bardonthebeach.org.*
Festival Vancouver, first two weeks in August. 400 - 873 Beatty Street, 688-1152. Celebration of music, over 50 classical, jazz and world concerts at ten venues. *www.festivalvancouver.bc.ca.*
International Dragon Boat Festival, third wk/end in June on Falls Creek. Performing and culinary arts, boat racing, nightly entertainment. \$6 advance tkts and \$9 at the gate. *www.adbf.com.*
Sea Vancouver Festival held in July. 302 - 788 Beatty Street, 872-0928. Celebrates life by the sea: inc Tall Ships Challenge from all over the world, regattas, beach bacci, boat cruises, fireworks grand finale. July. *www.seavancouver.ca.*
Vancouver Folk Music Festival, Mid-July at Jericho Beach Park, 602-9798/(800) 883-3655. Dozens of acts from across Canada and the world. Tkts: Fri \$40, Sat & Sun \$55, to see it all \$120. Student discounts (apply in person with ID), Fri \$24, Sat & Sun \$30 and weekend \$65. *www.thefestival.bc.ca.*
Vancouver Fringe Festival, September, Granville Island. 1402 Anderson Street, 257-0350. Over 500 performances. Tickets \$10 or \$8 at door of venues (10% of house is held for the door). *www.vancouverfringe.com.*
Vancouver International Jazz Festival, late June-early July. Hotline: 872-5200. Nearly 400 citywide outdoor and club events from Gastown to Granville Island. Many free. Festival 3-pack \$27. *www.coastaljazz.ca.*

Information

Pick up free copies of *Georgia Straight, West Ender* and *Vancouver Courier* for what's on where. Lots of good websites: *www.vancouvercitytourist.com, www.tourismvancouver.com, www.eyeseavancouver.com, www.city.vancouver.bc.ca, www.discovervancouver.com, www.bcpassport.com.*
Tourism British Columbia, (800) HELLO-BC. Daily 7am-9pm, wk/ends 8am-6pm. *www.hellobc.com/en-CA/RegionsCities/Vancouver.htm?S=N.*
Tourism Vancouver, Waterfront Centre, 200 Burrard St, 683-2000. Info kiosks at airport and in Gastown. Open daily 8.30am-6pm. *www.tourismvancouver.com.*
WI-FI. Check *www.wififreespot.com/can.html* Include **Blenz,** 1201 Robson at Bute 681-8092; **Interactive Café,** 107–12 Water Street, Gastown, 687-2284; **Jewel Café**, 52 Alexander, 688-8075; **La Solace Café,** 4883 Mackenzie, 266-4029; **La Vieille France Café,** 380 Robson; **Mega Wraps Pita Bread**, 878 West Broadway, 874-3734; **Melting Point Gallery**, 1111 Commercial Drive, 254-3338; **Our Town Café,** 245 E. Broadway; **Penny Farthing Inn,** 2855 West 6th Avenue 739-9002; **Take 5 Café**, 429 Granville, 697-9090; **Trees Organic Coffee**, 450 Granville. 684-5060.

Internet Access

There are cyber cafes all over town, esp along Robson and Denman Sts. **Central Branch Public Library**, 350 W Georgia St, 331-3600, has free internet access, ½ hr time limit, first come first served. Mon-Thu 10am-8pm, Fri-Sat 'til 5pm, Sun 1pm-5pm. *www.vpl.ca.* **Coffee Coast**, 101-1595 W Broadway, 731-1011; Cybercafe, 779 Denman, 633-9389; **Cyberia Circuit Lounge**, 1284 Robson , 633-1477; Cyber Space Internet Café, 1741 Robson, 684-6004; **Dakoda's Internet Café,** 1602 Yew in Kitsilano, 731-5616; **Downtown Computer Centre**, 1035 Davie, 682-5240; **E-Hotwired Computer,** 1072 Davie, 682-5272; **Internet Coffee**, 1104 Davie, 682-6668; **Kitsilano Cyber Café**, 3514 4th Avenue, 737-0595; **PC Link** 871 Denman, 605-0406; **Star Internet Café**, 1690 Robson; **Websters Internet Café 3**, 40 Robson, 915-9327; and **Wicked Gastown Internet Café,** 330 West Cordova, 684-0825.

Travel

Hitching is legal and common in Vancouver but no safer than anywhere else in North America and BUNAC does not advocate it. **Taxis** are metered; cost from airport is about $20-30, depending on your destination.

Walking. Vancouver is pedestrian-friendly. There are trails all over town, round the bays, at waters edge in Stanley Park and French Creek and through the many green areas. At crosswalks, beepers twitter kindly for the blind when lights go green. In residential areas downtown, there are 'traffic-calmed' streets. And most neighbourhood stores place dog water bowls at the door. Four of the best known walking trails are Chinatown, Gastown, Shaughnessy, and Yaletown - See: *www.city.vancouver.bc.ca/commsvcs/planning/heritage/walks/.*

Biking. Vancouver has a ubiquitous 129 kms of bicycle routes all round the bays, parks and through town: for a free map, call the Bike Hotline at 871-6070 or visit the info desk at City Hall. Routes include the **Mosaic Bikeway** that connects with the 15,000 km **Trans Canada Trail** for walkers, bikers, horse riders and skiers. For bike maps also check *www.city.vancouver.bc.ca/cycling, www.translink.bc.ca,* and *www.vancouver.ca/engsvcs/transport/cycling/routes.htm#getmap.*

Bus. Vancouver has an integrated transportation system run by the **TransLink** authority that operates Coast Mountain Bus Company, the automated SkyTrain, SeaBus to N Vancouver, TransLink buses, and West Coast Express, which all meet at Waterfront Station on W. Cordova St. For all transit information call 953-3333 or visit *www.translink.bc.ca.* Service is provided 18-20 hours daily on most bus routes, operating every 10 min or less. **Fares** in the zonal transit system (exc West Coast Express) are the same for bus, SkyTrain, and SeaBus - $2.25 for 1 zone, $3.25 for 2 zones and $4.50 for 3, with concession fares of $1.50-3 for student 14-19 yrs. All routes are $1.50 after 6.30 pm, on weekends, and holidays. Free transfers between buses and other systems are valid for 90 mins of travel—ask the operator for one when you board. A Translink **DayPass** costs $8, is valid for unlimited, all-day travel and available at stores and SkyTrain stops. For stunning views, take bus #19 from Granville Station to Stanley Park, or the SeaBus from Waterfront and bus #236 to Grouse Mountain.

Coast Mountain Bus Company provides 75 percent of all transit trips in the Vancouver region with buses, one of North America's largest electric trolley fleets, three B-Line rapid bus services, highway Express Coaches, and Community Shuttle minibuses. B-Lines are now using GPS and signal priority technologies. 953-3333. For schedules, check *www.translink.bc.ca.*

Greyhound Canada. Pacific Central Station, 1150 Station St, 683-8133, (800) 661-8747. Services to all major BC destinations and beyond.

Gray Line Tours, 879-3363/(800) 667-0882. Double Decker Attractions Loop Tour 2 hrs in hop-on, hop-off double deckers/trolleys with 21 stops, every 30 mins starting 8.30 am. *www.grayline.ca.*

Pacific Coach Lines 'Downtown to Downtown' Vancouver to Victoria, Pacific Central Station, 1150 Station St. 662-7575/8074, (800) 661-1725. Eight daily deps (via ferry). About 3.5 hrs, $37.50 o/w, $73 r/t. *www.pacificcoach.com.* However, although slower, it is much cheaper to use public transport, using the ferry services. Skytrain, buses #s 601, 620 (two transfers) from Pacific Central Station to Tsawwassen ferry terminal (1hr 15 min), $4.50 w/days and $3 w/end and evenings. Ferry, individuals $10 o/w, 386-3431/(888) 223-3779, (Vehicles from $33). *www.bcferries.com.* From Swartz Bay, Victoria take #70 bus to Victoria.

Light Rail. SkyTrain, part of TransLink, operates the Expo and Millennium lines, the world's longest automated light rapid transit system (49 km), every 2 mins or more connecting downtown with Burnaby, New Westminster and Surrey. Service connects to buses and **SeaBus.** For amazing route map – touch stations you want for connections. *www.translink.bc.ca/Transportation Services/SkyTrain.*

Coquitlam Light Rail Transit Line will link Coquitlam, Port Moody and Lougheed city centres via new 11 km LRT in 2009, connecting with buses, SkyTrain, West Coast Express, and points beyond.

Ferries. Albion Ferry, a free service for vehicles and walk-on passengers across the Fraser River, between Maple Ridge on the north bank and Fort Langley on the south. Two ferries operate daily, 5am-1.30am, at 15 min intervals during the day.

Aquabus, Zip to and from **Granville Island** across **False Creek** to downtown stops and Science World on the rainbow bright **Aquabus,** $2-$5. Call 689-5858 or *www.aquabus.bc.ca.*

BC Ferries, (250) 386-3431/(888) 724-5223 in BC. Regular service from the mainland to Vancouver Island (takes about an hour-and-a-half) and surrounding islands. Schedules and prices vary depending on destination, call for details. Take SeaBus and #250 or #257 (express) to Horseshoe Bay for services to Victoria. Victoria $10 o/w, vehicle-$32.75. *www.bcferries.com.* NB. HQ at 1112 Fort, Victoria.

False Creek Ferries, 684-7781. In blue cockleshells daily to Granville Island (GI) and Maritime Museum (MM) from Aquatic Centre ($2.50 o/w, $4 r/t) every 5 mins, 7am-10.30pm (GI), every 15 min 10am-8pm (MM) daily), and from Science World to GI, via Stamps Landing ($6 o/w every 15 mins, 10am-8pm), Jun-Sept. Book of 10 tickets $17. For Oct-May see   *www.granvilleislandferries.bc.ca.*

SeaBus. Double-ended catamarans, seating up to 400 passengers, whisk you across Burrard Inlet in 15 mins from Waterfront Station downtown to Lonsdale Quay on North Shore. $2.25. SeaBus is part of the Translink system allowing transfers to SkyTrain and buses. *www.translink.bc.ca/Transportation Services/SeaBus.*

Air. Vancouver International Airport (YVR), south of town. *www.yvr.ca.* By car, it can be reached via Granville, Hwy 99, following Grant McConachie Way, 207-7077. Or take bus #98B or #496 from Burrard Station/downtown to Airport Station Bus Terminal, then transfer to #424 to Domestic Terminal. About 60 mins.   From Airport, #620 connects to BC Ferries in Tsawwassen, #100 to Vancouver and points east, #491 to Richmond and Steveston. Taxis are metered, to downtown is about $25 (inc taxes). **YVR Airporter,** 946-8866/(800) 668-3141, runs 25 min services every 30 mins to and from downtown hotels, SkyTrain and SeaBus stations, Granville Island, and other locations. $12 o/w, $18 return. *www.yvrairporter.com.*

Air Canada & Air Canada Jazz Airline Up to 18 daily 25 min flights to Victoria International Airport. Reservations (888) 247-2262 Flight info (888) 422-7533. *www.aircanada.com* and *www.flyjazz.ca* For timetables, see *www.actimetable.com.*

Craig Air, 266-0267 (Tofino) or (877) 886-3466 Scheduled daily flights at from Vancouver to Victoria (40 mins), thence to Tofino/Ucluelet (30 mins), using 10 seat turbo-prop. $145+tax *www.craigair.com.*

Pacific Coastal Airlines, South Terminal YVR, (800) 663-2872, or (604) 273-8666. Local regional airline for over 40 years, flies to/from Victoria (YYR) upto 7 times daily. Seven of 18 aircraft are float planes. *www.pacific-coastal.com.*

West Jet. Low-cost fun flights, Calgary-based. Reservations (888) 937-8538) or (800) 538-5696. *www.westjet.com* and *www.westjet.ca.*

Float Planes to and from Victoria and Vancouver Island Check all for standby fares. Some fly from the airport YVR, some from the waterfront downtown.

Amigo Airways. 1956 Zorkin Road, Nanaimo (866) 692-6440 toll free, (250) 753-1115. Daily flights between Vancouver and Nanaimo Harbour & Airport, $49 Seat Confirmed, $25* Standby 'Fiesta Fare'. *www.amigoairways.ca.* Also to Gulf Islands.

Baxter Aviation. 1075 West Waterfront Rd. 683-6525. Scheduled 25 min services to Nanaimo from Vancouver. **Harbour Air.** Downtown at 1075 West Waterfront Road, Place. 274-1277. Daily flights to Victoria, Nanaimo and Gulf Islands. *www.harbourair.com.* **Seair Seaplanes,** 4640 Inglis Dr. Richmond. 273-8900, 1-800-447-3247. Daily services from YVR to Gulf Islands. **West Coast Air.** 1075 W Waterfront Rd, W of

Canada Place, 606-6888, (800) 347-2222. Up to 16 flights daily to Victoria (1000 Wharf St at Broughton, Inner Harbour). *www.westcoastair.com.*

Rail. Amtrak Pacific Central Station, 1150 Station St. (800) 872-7245. *Amtrak Cascades* Vancouver to Eugene, Oregon, via Seattle and Portland, past Mount St. Helens, across Columbia River Gorge. Regional cuisine, microbrews, and Seattle coffees avail. Five trains daily, dep 5.45am, 8.45am, 12.30pm, 5pm, and 6pm. 3 hrs 45 mins/4 hrs to Seattle; 11 hrs to Eugene, Oregon. US$57 to Eugene. *www.amtrak.com.*

Downtown Historic Railway 873-7742, w/es, holidays between Science World Station and Granville Island Station, every 30 mins, 1-5 pm, May-Oct. $2 r/t., *www.trams.ca/dhr.html* and *www.vancouver.ca/engsvcs/transport/railway.*

VIA Rail (888) 842-7245. The *Canadian* travels three times a week between Vancouver and Toronto, taking about three whole days. Dep Vancouver 5.30 pm every Tues, Fri, Sun (arr Toronto 8pm three days later). *www.viarail.ca.*

West Coast Express, Waterfront Station, 488-8906/(800) 570-7245. Five commuter services, weekdays only, to/from waterfront up the Fraser Valley to Mission City. Incoming in morning; outgoing at night. On-board cappuccino bar. $10.25 o/w. Part of TransLink system. *www.westcoastexpress.com.*

West Coast Rail Tours, Pacific Central Station, 1150 Station St. 524-1011, (800) 722-1233. Variety of dramatic 1-7 day rail tours throughout BC. Some of the tours are steam-hauled: Ask about the 4-6-4 *Royal Hudson's!* Check *www.wcra.org.*

WHISTLER Vancouver's main local partner in the 2010 Winter Olympics, Whistler lies two hours north of Vancouver and is easily accessible from the city by bus and car up Hwy 99. Canada's National Ski Team uses Whistler Mountain (lift-serviced height 1,530 metres) as its official training area. Nearby **Blackcomb**, the 'Mile-High Mountain', has the longest lift-serviced vertical (1,609 metres) and longest uninterrupted fall line skiing in North America. Runs there stretch up to 11 kilometres.

The two mountains have the largest combined ski area on the North American continent, with 7,000 acres of ski-able terrain, over 200 trails, 12 massive alpine bowls and three glaciers, and ski conditions here rank among the world's best. Even in summer, it's possible to ski/snowboard on the **Horstman Glacier.** Also in summer, this area of great natural beauty is ideal for mountain biking (over 200 kilometres of trails), hiking, horse-riding, jet-boating, and white-water rafting - and bungee jumping. (Call 938-9333 for bungee shuttle to and from Whistler Village.)
www.tourismwhistler.com; www.whistler.net www.whistlerblackcomb.com.

Accommodation/Travel
Whistler Hostel (HI-C), 5678 Alta Lake Rd, Whistler, 932-5492. Timber cabin on picturesque Alta Lake, good base to explore the area. Great facilities and only 10 mins from the main resort. Internet $1/10 mins. Prices, low season: members-$20, non-$24. *www.hihostels.ca/hostels/BC/BCRegion/Whistler/Hostels.*
Also check *www.whistlerretreats.com.*
Greyhound, 482-8747, runs a 2-2.5 hr bus 7/8 times/day to and from Vancouver Depot, 1150 Station St. $16.59 o/w/$14.93 students. *www.greyhound.ca.*
Whistler Express Bus 8695 Barnard Street, Vancouver. 266-5386 or toll free (877) 317-7788. Operates to Vancouver Int'l Airport and Hotels to/from Whistler via Lion's Gate Bridge and Squamish, 11 services daily in winter, seven in summer (April-Dec). $65 o/w. Operated by Perimeter Bus. *www.perimeterbus.com.*
Whistler & Valley Express (WAVE) Local buses. *www.busonline.ca/regions/whi-/schedules/map.cfm?region=0&.*

VANCOUVER ISLAND The Island, and the Gulf Islands that shelter it to leeward, are invaded annually by thousands of tourists attracted by the temperate climate, spectacular beaches and coastline, old-growth forests, mountain resorts, and history. In the 18th century, **Nootka**, on the Island's west coast, was almost the source of war between Britain and Spain, which colonized it following Captain Cook's landing at Yuquot in 1778. Vancouver Island was later granted as a "colony" to the Hudson's Bay Company in 1849 by the British government to stem a possible American invasion from Oregon – and an offer to colonize it by the Mormons. The huge island – almost a sub-continent by itself - bounded from the mainland of BC by the Strait of Georgia, is an outdoor paradise, with mining, fishing, logging and manufacturing the chief breadwinners and a growing number of wineries in Cowichan Valley.

It's also home to two thirds of Canada's artists, no doubt inspired by Canada's favourite impressionist, Emily Carr. There are good ferry and air connections with the mainland (See Vancouver and Victoria sections.) and with Prince Rupert via Port Hardy to the north. _www.islands.bc.ca._ Also check the excellent and helpful site _www.vancouverisland.com/Regions/._ **Victoria,** the capital of the Island, is situated on the southern tip.

NORTH VANCOUVER ISLAND About 1000 Nuu-chah-nulth people are scattered throughout this area with Band villages on Espinoza Inlet (Ocluje), and near Zeballos (Ehatis) and Gold River (Tsaxana). _www.north-island.ca_ and _www.vancouverisland.com/Regions/#1._

Port Hardy, the largest community in the North and gateway to the inside coast passage and Prince Rupert, is named for the Sir Thomas Hardy who held the dying Lord Nelson in his arms at Trafalgar. Today Port Hardy is the terminus for BC Ferries to Prince Rupert ('one of the world's most awe-inspiring voyages',) and Bella Coola. _www.bcferries.bc.ca._ You can also watch here for grey, humpback, killer, and minke whales. The area offers fishing, scuba diving, caving, kayaking and boating, and is a jumping off spot for hikers, including an 8-hour trek to the tip of **Cape Scott Provincial Park**, "one of the wildest, windiest, most woebegone locales", and **Tex Lyon Trail**, a rugged 5-hour coastal trail to Dillon Point.

Accommodation
For B & Bs, cottages and campgrounds, see _www.ph-chamber.bc.ca/accomo.html._
Betty Hamilton's B&B, 9415 Mayors Way, 949-6638. S-$50, D-$65-70. B/fast included. 'Really nice after all my hostels and Betty certainly looked after me.' Rsvs recommended. _http://bbcanada.com/hamiltonbb._

Travel
Island Coach Lines, run by Grayline/ Laidlaw Coach Lines. Connects to Victoria and Pt. Alberni/Tofino, via Nanaimo (6 hrs). Stops at all local communities. _www.grayline.ca/victoria._
BC Ferries, 1112 Fort Street, Victoria, BC V8V 4V2 1 (888) 223-3779 from anywhere in British Columbia; (250) 386-3431 from outside BC. **Inside Coast Passage Ferry** to Prince Rupert, 15 hrs. $86; $75.75 in shoulder (Spring and Autumn) and $59 in low (winter) seasons. **Discovery Coast Passage Ferry** to Bella Coola, 33 hours. _www.bcferries.bc.ca._
Pacific Coastal Airlines, the local regional airline, flies from Vancouver to Pt Hardy. Tel: (800) 663-2872 _www.pacific-coastal.com._

Nearby is **Port Alice**, one of the few places in Canada with an orchid named after it, officially listed in the Royal Horticultural Society's *Book of Registered Orchid Hybrids*. **Port McNeill** is the centre of logging in the North Island. **Telegraph Cove,** half-an-hour south of Port McNeill, was the end of a pre-WW I telegraph line and relay station in WW II. It's one of the last boardwalk communities in BC, with all buildings above water on stilts. Further south, is **Woss**, in the Nimpkish Valley, which has boating, caving, camping, fishing, hiking, and an old 113 steam locomotive, used for many years for logging.

NOOTKA, up on the Pacific Coast, was where Captain James Cook's ships *H.M.S. Resolution* and *H.M.S. Discovery* landed, at Resolution Cove, in March 1778, claiming the area for Britain. Coincidentally, John Ledyard, a Connecticut Yankee who was a marine on Cook's crew, became the first American to walk on the west coast of the continent. Ledyard bartered with local Mowachaht people for sea otter pelts, starting a gainful trade that put Nootka firmly on the European map by the end of the century.

At **Yuquot (Friendly Cove)** on Nootka's southern tip, Cook met Chief Maquinna, of the Nootka people *www.yuquot.ca*. Subsequently, the island was visited by hundreds of British fur traders, including those from the East India Company (chartered by Elizabeth I in 1600). These visitors and the arrival of Russian traders greatly upset the Spaniards based in Mexico, who decided to build a fort and full settlement at **San Lorenzo** at Yuquot in June,1789, in an attempt to establish Spanish sovereignty over the area. Yuquot remained Spain's main port north of Mexico for many years.

Today Nootka and its environs are wonderful for caving, diving, fishing, kite-boarding, hiking, kayaking, and wind-surfing. The nearest access point is **Gold River,** an hour's scenic drive from Campbell River, nestled in the area where Chinese immigrants extracted gold in the 1860s. *www.village.goldriver.bc.ca* The town was built in 1965 round a pulp mill. Take a waterproof: it has plenty of rain - 104" a year. From here you can fly or go by boat to Nootka. For pubs, restaurants and coffee shops in Gold River see *www.village.goldriver.bc.ca/pages/dining.html.*

Accommodation
Gold River Chalet, 390 Nimpkish Drive, Gold River, BC V0P1G0 (866) 450-2688 or (250) 283-2688 Email: *goldriverchalet@cablerocket.com*. Rates from $49-$79. Free wifi, high-speed internet. *www.goldriverchalet.com.*
The Glass Haus B&B, Maquinna Cres, Gold River, BC V0P1G0, PO Box 1018. (250) 283-7505 Double $55, single $45. *www.glasshausbandb.com.*
Nootka Island - Nootka Island Wilderness Retreat (250) 283-7528 'Hike Nootka Island Trail. Hear ravens, cry of the wolf…see spouts of whales. Smell the fragrance of deep musky mosses in the ancient forest. Observe a black bear…' Includes full breakfast. $65 night. *www.nootkaisland.ca.*
Yuquot/Friendly Cove -Yuquot Cabins & Campground. Tel: (250) 283-2054. Wake to the sound of Pacific Ocean waves! Beachfront rustic cabins, $100 per night per cabin mid June-mid Sept. $75 off-season. Bring food, drinking water, bedding, towels, torch…and rain gear. (800) 238-2933 or (250) 283-2015 ext-113. Email: *mjames@yuquot.ca.*

Travel
Yuquot/Friendly Cove can be reached only by boat or by aircraft:

Nootka Sound Service PO Box 57, Gold River, BC V0P 1G0 Info/Reserv year-round - (250) 283-2515; *Uchuck III:* (250) 283-2325. e-mail: *info@mvuchuck.com*.The *Uchuck III* makes regularly scheduled day trips through Nootka Sound, with overnight trip to Yuquot on Thursdays. Departs from Government Dock in **Gold River**. Reservations required. *www.mvuchuck.com/historic.htm.*

Maxi's Water Taxi is also available from Gold River to Friendly Cove. PO Box 1122, Gold River, BC, V0P 1G0. Tel: (604) 283-2282. Left at BC Info Centre in Gold River, 14 km to Government Wharf where 12-passenger *First Citizen* is docked. Bring sweater, rain jacket and sturdy shoes. 'Breathtaking scenic views of Nootka Sound.' *www.yuquot.ca/maxiswatertaxi.htm.*

Air Nootka float-plane service, Gold River to Yuquot. *www.airnootka.com.*

Pacific Coastal Airlines, local regional airline, flies from Vancouver to Campbell River, the closest regional airport to the Gold River/Nootka area. (800) 663-2872 *www.pacific-coastal.com.*

Information
Campbell River Tourist Info Centre (250) 287-4636.
Gold River Tourist Info Centre, (250) 283-2202 or 283-2418. *www.village.goldriver.bc.ca*

WEST COAST - PACIFIC RIM
This is a wild coastal region, with seemingly endless **surfing beaches** and range of spectacular weather, much of it under the aegis of the **Pacific Rim National Park**. There are two ways to get here by road – via Hwy 4, the Pacific Rim Highway, across the mountains west of **Parksville** and **Port Alberni** towards **Tofino,** the western terminus of the Trans Canada Highway; and north along the coast up Hwy 14 from **Jordan River** (near Victoria). You can also get to the west coast by packet steamer from Port Alberni. Not for nothing is the Pacific Rim also known as the 'Raincoast' - precipitation here is amongst the world's heaviest, raining down about 3 metres (120 inches) a year, fortunately mostly in winter when storm watching is a popular pastime. Booking ahead is recommended.

Port Alberni, on Hwy 4 up from Parksville, known as the *Gateway to the Pacific Rim,* is at the head of the Island's longest inlet (Alberni Inlet) - a saltwater port inland 40 kilometres from the west coast. It has several attractions, chief among which is its other moniker: *Salmon Capital of the World!* The harbour has boat rentals, fishing charters, tackle shops, restaurants and galleries. In summer, a steam loco chugs for a tour along the waterfront. At nearby **McLean Mill National Historic Site** period characters relive the pioneers of the logging industry, May to September.

Pacific Rim National Park Reserve, Box 280, Ucluelet, BC, V0R 3A0, Tel: (250) 726-7721 is open mid-March through mid-Oct. The Pacific Rim Visitor Centre is at the Tofino-Ucluelet junction on Highway 4. For details see *www.pc.gc.ca/pn-np/bc/pacificrim/index_e.asp.* and *www.bcadventure.com-/adventure/explore/island/trails/pacrim2.htm.* The park's **Wickaninnish Interpretive Centre,** near **Combers Beach** in Wickaninnish Bay, adjacent to Hwy 4 at the end of Long Beach Road, displays the geographical and natural history of the Pacific Northwest, focussing on the influence of the Pacific on nature and man, illustrated by artifacts used by Nuu-chah-nulth Indians, the traditional local inhabitants. Open daily, late spring to fall. The area's great for watching grey, humpback and killer whales making their way along the coast, plus porpoises, seals, sea lions and elephant seals. Whale observation tours are led by naturalists.

Tofino, 130 kms west of Port Alberni at the tip of **Esowista Peninsula** was named in 1792 after Spanish hydrographer Vicente Tofino de San Miguel; the first trading post and hotel was established here in 1875. 'Unbelievably georgeous.' Now it's a fishing and resort village with renowned local beaches., _www.tofino-bc.com_ and _www.my-tofino.com_. Nearby **Cox Bay**, midway between Tofino and Pacific Rim National Park, is called Canada's Surfer's Paradise or Malibu. Perhaps not coincidentally, the ocean temperatures here are the warmest in Canada but the Pacific Ocean is still too cold for swimming. Some surfers live along the beach, others come from Vancouver just for the rides - for true afficionadoes the winter storm season produces the best peeling waves. **Long Beach**, with a 12-mile strand between Tofino and **Ucluelet** to the south, has the only surf camp in Canada, for adults and youths, and the country's only all-women surfing school. _www.surfingvancouverisland.com/surf/._

Ucluelet, named from a Nuu-chah-nulth phrase 'Yu-clutl-ahts,' meaning 'the people with a good landing place for canoes', was a First Nation village to the east of the inlet, where the main settlement remains. Now it's a logging, fishing and tourist port, also reached by water from Port Alberni by the Stavanger-built packet _Frances Barkley_ (named after golden-haired Frances and hubby Captain William Charles Barkley who reached Nootka in June, 1787, a few years after Captain Cook) and Glasgow-built _Lady Rose_ of the **Lady Rose Marine Services** which has been plying the Alberni Inlet via Barkley Sound and Bamfield year-round for the last 60 years or so, carrying cargo, mail and up to 100/200 passengers daily.

Hot Springs Cove reputedly has the best hot springs in Canada. The least known too, for you can only reach the springs by canoe or water-taxi from Tofino (or aqua plane) and easy 2 kilometre boardwalk trail from the dock. The springs bubble up at more than 47°C/117°F, flowing down a gully via several pools into the ocean. High tide flushes and cools the water in the two lower pools twice daily. The highest pool is so hot that you can only bathe in winter when cooler run-off waters mix with the springs, which are surrounded by old-growth rain forest. Sneakers (as protection against possible jagged rocks underfoot) are the only dress needed while bathing, but most wear something. Box 2000, Tofino, BC V0R 2Z0, Tel: (888) 781-9977. There is a nearby lodge operated by the Hesquiat First Nations.

Accommodation

There are two hotels on the beach:

Paddler's Inn B&B, 320 Main St, Tofino, (250) 725-4222, email: _paddlers@island.net._ Five rooms. Continental breakfast Water-side: $80/dbl occupancy, $70/sgl. Street-side: $70/dbl occupancy, $60/sgl.

Cedar Street Guest House, 290 Cedar St, Tofino. Breakfast self-serve. $105/dbl occupancy 3 nights or less; $95/night 4 nights or more.

There are **campsites** in the Long Beach area and on the Ucluelet access road, as well as at Tofino. Try the **Green Point Campsite,** (604) 689-9025, on Hwy 4, the only site in the park; nearly all campsites here must be reserved: rsvs fee, $6 and campsite, $20/night. _www.discovercamping.ca._

Travel
Island Coach Lines, run by Grayline/Laidlaw Coach Lines.. Connects to Victoria via Nanaimo, *www.grayline.ca/victoria.*
Tofino Bus, 564 Campbell Street, Tofino, BC Tel: (250) 725-2871 and 1 (866) 986-3466. Express to Tofino/Ucluelet from Victoria, *www.tofinobus.com.*
Craig Air, 266-0267 (Tofino) or (877) 886-3466. Scheduled daily flights in summer, *www.craigair.com.*
Tofino Air, #50, 1st St, Tofino (866) 486-3247. Scheduled and scenic flights from Tofino, Sechelt, Nanaimo, Vancouver and Gulf Islands. *www.tofinoair.ca.*
Sonicblue Airways. Three flights daily Tofino/Vancouver. O/W $142. 303-5360 Airport Rd S. Richmond BC V7B 1B4. (604) 278-1608, *www.sonicblueair.com.*

SOUTH ISLAND & GREATER VICTORIA Back over on the southeastern side of the island there is a superb drive from Victoria north to **Duncan,** where the Forest Museum offers a long steam train ride and a large open forestry museum. *www.bcforestmuseum.com.*

Nanaimo, further north up Hwy 1, is the island's fastest growing town, a ferry ride from Vancouver, with a pleasant, Mediterranean-like micro-climate unique to North America - moderate rain in winter, dry and sunny in summer, good at any time of year for scuba, rock-climbing, kayaking, sailing, biking and bungee-jumping, all within sight of majestic mountains. And full of cricket pitches. *www.tourism.nanaimo.bc.ca.*

 The town is famous, among other things, for its **International Bathtub Race** held (since 1967) on the fourth Sunday every July, as part of a week long Marine Festival. A Canadian Scottish pancake breakfast starts the day at 7, then, at 11 am, a souped-up 'bathtubs' race 36 miles fom Nanaimo harbour to Departure Bay. For details see: *www.bathtub.island.net.*

In late August, the **Vancouver Island Exhibition** has been held for over 100 years at **Beban Park**: agriculture and horticultural displays, livestock competitions, petting zoo, midway and show featuring Canada's country stars. *www.viex.ca.*

Visit **Petroglyph Park** 4 kilometres south of Nanaimo with its preserved Indian sandstone carvings thousands of years old. **Newcastle Island Marine Park** is reached by passenger ferry from Maffeo Sutton Park (R/T $7), a sanctuary for wildlife. It has 15 kilometres of interpretive trails, forests, historic sites, and inland lakes. Nanaimo is also an easy base from which to explore the surrounding towns, such as **Chemainus** (city of murals), **Courtenay** and **Campbell River** (noted for whale watching). There are 'mini hostels' in both Duncan and Nanaimo.

The area code for this region is 250.

Accommodation
Nichol St Hostel, 65 Nichol St, 753-1188/(800) 861-1366. Communal kitchen, laundry facilities, showers. Picturesque with outdoor patio. Registration from 12pm-11pm with dorms for $17-$20, private rooms, family rooms and cottages from $40 for two. *www.nanaimohostel.com.*
Cambie Hostel, 63 Victoria Cres, Old quarter of downtown, 754-5323. Home to a bar, grill and bakery, with live entertainment Fri and Sat. Free b/fast, linens, laundry facilities and shuttle pick-ups. TV and internet, $5/hr. Dorm beds: July-Sept $22.50, thereafter $20, linen incl. *www.cambiehostels.com.*

Travel

Bus. BC Transit - Nanaimo Regional Transit System, 6300 Hammond Bay Road, Nanaimo, V9T 6N2, 390-4531, Toll free in BC: 1-877-607-4111. Local services to Parksville, Qualicum Beach, ferry terminal and Malaspina. $2 o/w. www.busonline.ca/regions/nan.

Island Coach Lines, run by Grayline/ Laidlaw Coach Lines. Connects to Victoria, Pt. Alberni/Tofino, and Port Hardy. www.grayline.ca/victoria.

Ferry. BC Ferries, 1112 Fort Street, Victoria, BC V8V 4V2 1 (888) 223-3779 from anywhere in British Columbia; (250) 386-3431 from outside BC. Variety of routes to southern Vancouver Island. See www.bcferries.com/schedules/mainland/.

Harbour Lynx Express, 80 min catamaran ferry to/from Vancouver. Nanaimo: Unit #5 - Pioneer Waterfront Plaza on Front St. Tel: (250)754-5969. Vancouver: 609 Waterfront Rd. (South SeaBus Terminal Waterfront Station in downtown Vancouver.) Tel: (604) 688-2114. www.harbourlynx.com.

Rail. VIA Rail, (888) 842-0744. The *Malahat*, named after a First Nation, stops here (station at 321 Selby St) once daily in each direction on its trips from Victoria to Courtenay. Stops over Nanaimo's bridge so you can watch bungee-jumpers. No meals served. www.viarail.com.

Air (*See also Vancouver.*) **Baxter Aviation** Scheduled 25 min seaplane services to/from Vancouver. www.baxterair.com.

Harbour Air. Scheduled 25 min seaplane services to/from Vancouver. www.harbour-air.com.

Amigo Airways. Four daily seaplane flights between Nanaimo Harbour & Vancouver Airport.' www.amigoairways.ca.

VICTORIA, the former fort and trading post of the Hudson's's Bay Company (HBC) and now provincial capital, is noted for having Canada's mildest climate, an unhurried atmosphere, and dozens of beautiful English gardens. Each spring, horticultural-minded residents count the blossoms in the city, usually about four mind-boggling billion. Perhaps even more colourful is Victoria's amazing kaleidoscope of historical characters, which spring from every page of the engaging *More English than the English, A Very Social History of Victoria* by Terry Reksten. Rudyard Kipling called the city: 'Brighton Pavilion with the Himalayas for a backdrop'.

HBC, chartered in London by Charles II in 1670 and known locally for the influence it exerted as 'Here Before Christ', established Fort Victoria in 1843 at the southern tip of Vancouver Island to maintain a British fur-trapping edge north of the 49th parallel.

By far the most famous native of Victoria is the painter and writer **Emily Carr,** (1871-1945). For years Carr painted totem poles all over BC: 'Indian Art broadened my seeing, loosened the formal tightness I had learned in England's schools.' After studying in Paris at an art academy at which Gauguin, Matisse, and Whistler had been students, Carr returned to BC, her art gradually transformed into whirling, spellbinding impressions reminiscent of Van Gogh and early Picasso.

The charming garden city, curled round a harbour overlooked by the dowager Empress Hotel and Parliament Buildings, has the largest number of British-born residents and the highest number of drivers over 90 in Canada. As such, it likes to preserve its touch of Olde England for the benefit of a year-round tourist industry. Afternoon tea, fish n' chips, British souvenir shops, tweed, china and double-decker buses all have their place, but if you can get beyond all that, you will find Victoria a pleasant place to be for a time, with plenty to do and see in and around the town, including whale watching, sailing, sea kayaking, and trail-riding.

With over 7,000 daily bikers, Victoria is also North America's most bicycle-friendly city, proclaimed the Cycling Capital of Canada by the Queen in 2000 (see _www.gvcc.bc.ca_). It's many bike paths include the **Galloping Goose Trail**, a 55 kilometres former railway starting in town, that reaches out west of the city past old-growth Douglas Firs, slender canyons, marshlands, round Sooke Basin, and by Sooke Potholes Provincial Park to an old goldmining centre Leechtown. The 29 kilometres **Lochside Trail** leads from Victoria north to Sidney and Swartz Bay.

Visit _www.tourismvictoria.com_, _www.city.victoria.bc.ca_   and _www.victoria-bcguide.com_.

Accommodation
Lodging is difficult to find in summer. Book ahead if possible. **Victoria Visitors Bureau,** 812 Wharf St, 953-2033/(800) 663-3883, can help find accommodation.The _www.tourismvictoria.com_ site has an extensive list of different types of lodgings, including their websites; _www.bctravel.com_ also has many listings.
Cherry Bank Hotel, 825 Burdett Ave, 385-5380/(800) 998-6688. S/D-$69, $99 w/ private bathroom; bfast incl. 'Comfortable, central, recommended by locals.' _www.bctravel.com/cherrybank.html._
Craigmyle Guest Home, 1037 Craigdarrock Rd, 1 km east of Inner Harbour, 595-5411/(888) 595-5411. S-$65, D-$90, Q-$140. All rms have private bath/shower, full English bfast incl. _www.bctravel.com/craigmyle.html._
Hotel Douglas, 1450 Douglas St, 383-4157/(800) 332-9981. S/D-$50 (winter)-$80 (summer), w shared bath to S/D-$70/$110 triple queen, XP-$15. Located in city centre, 1015 mins to harbour, close to City Hall. _www.hoteldouglas.com._
Ocean Island Backpackers Inn, 791 Pandora Ave, 385-1788/(888) 888-4180. $18-23 dorm, $25-59 private double. All linen incl. No curfew, open 24 hrs, in central downtown. Kitchen facs, bar and café on site; daily 7am-1am. Clean, friendly hostel, w/internet access and planned events. _www.oceanisland.com._
Selkirk Guest House, 934 Selkirk Ave, 389-1213/(800) 974-6638. Located on the waterfront. 4 bed dorm rooms: $25/night, linen incl. Private rms available, D/S-$90, some w/kitchen and private baths. Kitchen/laundry facilities, rowboat and canoes avail. Waterside hot-tub. Full breakfast $7. _www.selkirkguesthouse.com._
University of Victoria Residence, 721-8395. May-Aug, both students and non-students. S-$44, D-$55 incl linens, full bfast. Stays over 14 days, $33.50 incl. meals. Over 30 days $27.75/night, also includes meals. _http://housing.uvic.ca._
Victoria Backpackers International Hostel, 1608 Quadra St, 386-4471. Dorm $15 incl. linen. Private rm w/shared bath $30/40. 'Very spacious rooms,' 'A great place to stay. Really friendly and run by a complete lunatic!' _www.turtlerefuge.com._
Victoria International Hostel, 516 Yates St, 385-4511/(888) 883-0099. Dorms $17-$24; depends on season and member status. Kitchen, laundry, linens, lockers, hostel-based programmes. Rsvs highly recommended. Close to bus station and the train station. _www.hihostels.ca._
YWCA, corner of Broughton and Quadra Sts, 386-7511. Females only. S-$35, D-$70. 'Upgraded with coffee shop', Mon-Fri 7am-2pm. _www.ymywca.victoria.bc.ca._

Food
Chinatown, Fisgard and Government Sts, inexpensive Chinese eateries.
Fisherman's Wharf, St Lawrence and Erie Sts, great place to buy seafood.
Ferris' Oyster Bar & Grill, 536 Yates St, 360-1824, has airy back garden, features

oyster burgers, curried chicken pita, sobe, diablos and local beers such as Hermans's, Nelson Paddywack and Shaftesbury. 'Like a local pub. Very pleasant.' *www.ferrisoysterbar.com.*

James Bay Cyber Café and Bookstore (also a Laundromat next door), 143 Menzies St, 386-4700. 'Instead of watching clothes go round in the laundromat, hang out in the cafe next door—fabulous idea!' Internet 10¢/min, serves coffee, b/fast, and lunch. Daily 7.30am-9pm.

Scotts Restaurant, 650 Yates St, 382-1289. Daily 6am-9pm. Meals from $6.

Smitty's, 850 Douglas, 383-5612. In business over 30 years. Value prices: cowpoke breakfast $6, lifestyle breakfast $6.55, skillet $8.79, waffles, and pancakes, also lunches and dinner, plus local beers. Daily 6.30am-10pm. *www.smittys.ca*.

Tomoe Japanese Restaurant, 726 Johnson St, 381-0223. 'Delicious, cheap food.' Lunches: Mon-Fri 11.30am-2pm, dinner: Mon-Thu 5.30-10pm, Fri-Sat 'til 10.30pm.

Of interest

Art Gallery of Greater Victoria, 1040 Moss St, 384-4101. Includes contemporary and Asian – Chinese, Indian, and Japanese sections and collections of the paintings and drawings by Emily Carr. Permanent collection of 15,000 objets d'art.. Mon-Sun 10am-5pm, Thu 'til 9pm. $8, $6 students w/ID. *http://aggv.bc.ca.*

Beacon Hill Park. Since 1882, 200 acres of afternoon concerts, wooded trails, bird sanctuaries, horse-drawn carriages, peacocks, and pleasant picnic spots. 'Nice for walking and having a peaceful time by the lake.' *www.beaconhillpark.ca* and *www.beaconhillpark.com.* Hosts the annual Luminaria light and magic festival in later July *www.luminaravictoria.com.* In 1956, the World's tallest totem pole created by First Nation's artist Mungo Martin was raised here, by public subscription (subscribers included Bing Crosby, Gracie Fields and Sir Winston Churchill). In 2001, the 160 ft cedar pole, from nearby Sooke, was fully restored. An old Indian village once stood where the Park is now.

Butchart Gardens, 14 miles north of the city off Hwy 17 in **Brentwood Bay,** 652-4422. A Rose garden, Sunken garden, Japanese garden and formal Italian garden are among the features of Victoria's most spectacular, 55-acre park - started in a limestone quarry by the Butcharts over 100-years ago, now transformed by thousands of tiny multi-coloured lights on magical summer evenings. The Aeolian pipe organ of the Butcharts still plays on **Fireworks Saturdays** after the show (every Saturday night, July 2 – Sept 3). 'Definitely worthwhile.' 'Don't take the special tour bus.' *www.butchartgardens.com.*

Carr House, 207 Government St, 383 5843, not far from Inner Harbour. Birthplace and home of eccentric Emily Carr, perhaps Canada's greatest painter and writer; her family's 1864 house restored to original lived-in state. Highly recommended. Tue-Sat, free, 11am-4pm. *www.emilycarr.ca , www.emilycarr.com.*

Christ Church Cathedral, Quadra and Rockland Sts, 383-2714. Mother Church of the Diocese of BC covering Vancouver Island and the Gulf Islands. *www.christchurchcathedral.bc.ca.*

Craigdarroch Castle, 1050 Joan Crescent, 592-5323. Sandstone castle built in late 1880s by Scottish immigrant Robert Dunsmuir and his wife, Joan. Now a museum with stained glass windows, Victorian furnishings, original mosaics and paintings, and 87 stairs. Tower has panoramic view of Olympic mountains. Daily, 10am-4.30pm, $10, $6.50 w/student ID. *www.craigdarrochcastle.com.*

Market Square, 560 Johnson St, nr Johnson Bridge. Attractive pedestrian mall with shops, restaurants and bars.

Maritime Museum of British Columbia, 28 Bastion Square, 385-4222. Daily, summer, 9.30am-4.30pm (5pm in summer), $8, $5 w/student ID. Programmes on Capt Cook, piracy, and the HBC. and Also a number of renovated 19th-century buildings housing curio shops and boutiques. 'Nice place for just sitting, sometimes there is free entertainment around noon.' *www.mmbc.bc.ca.*

Parliament Buildings, Government and Belleville Sts, 387-3046; 387-8669. James Douglas, Governor of the colony of Vancouver Island for HBC in 1849, on also becoming governor of the mainland colony, est. 1858, commissioned the first public buildings in Victoria the following year. The current seat of British Columbia's government is a palatial, turreted Victorian building first opened in 1898 (added to in 1915 and restored in 1973), topped by a gilded seven-foot figure of Captain George Vancouver, the first British navigator to circle Vancouver Island. Guided tours available daily throughout summer months. Call or visit _www.legis.gov.bc.ca_.
Royal British Columbia Museum, 675 Belleville St, 356-7226/(888) 447-7977, anchors a complex that includes the **National Geographic IMAX Theatre, BC Archives, Helmcken House, St. Ann's Schoolhouse, the Netherlands Carillon, Thunderbird Park** and **Mungo Martin House - Wawadit'la.** The **Museum** has a mesmerizing, realistic turn-of-the-20th century frontier town, including a theatre with silent movies and steam train, a coastal rain forest exhibit with live ocean animals, the First Peoples Gallery, with Haida Argillite carvings and Kwakwaka'wakw ceremonial masks, a Living Land/Living Sea gallery that transports you back 90 million years in BC climatically – and forward to 2050, and a display of plants native to BC. Museum and IMAX open daily. Museum, 9am-5pm: $12.50, $8.70 w/student ID. IMAX, 10am-8pm: $10.50/$9.50. _www.royalbcmuseum.bc.ca_ and _www.imaxvictoria.com_ The **Helmcken House,** the oldest house in BC, was built in 1852 by Dr. John Sebastian Helmcken, when he married the daughter of James Douglas, the first governor of BC. Still on its original site, the good doctor's original 19th century medical kit is among the items on display. Daily 10am-5pm, $7, $6 w/student ID. **St Ann's Schoolhouse,** built by Jacques Lequechier in 1844. Free. The **Netherlands Carillon** was a gift of the Dutch community of British Columbia to the people of BC in honour of Canada's Centennial. Queen Juliana of the Netherlands laid the cornerstone on May 23, 1967 and the tower housing 62 bells opened a year later. Recitals held Sundays at 3 pm May through Oct. Free, 356-7226. **Thunderbird Park** was set up in 1940 to display BC's finest totem pole art: the late Chief Mungo Martin was Head Carver of the Totem Restoration Programme. Aside from Martin's house front pole, all current poles are replicas, although a new Kwakwaka'wakw pole was raised in 2000. Free. **Mungo Martin House** - Wawadit'la, a traditional "big house", was entrusted to the museum by Chief Martin's family. Not open to the public.
Undersea Gardens, 490 Belleville St, Inner Harbour, 382-5717. View a large collection of sea plants, octopus, crabs, and other sea life in a special vessel – over 5,000 animals inhabit aquaria round the vessel in a natural, protected environment. Also scuba diving shows with Armstrong the giant Pacific octopus. Daily 9am-8.30pm May-Sept; rest of year 9.30am-5/6pm. $8.50. _www.pacificunderseagardens.com._
Whale Watching: _www.ecotoursvictoria.com/page03/group3.htm_ has listings of good tours in the area. Try: **Sea Quest,** in Sydney (N of Victoria), 9801 Sea Port Place, (888) 656-7599; and **Ocean Explorations,** 602 Broughton St, Victoria, 383-6722/(888) 442-6722, offer three hour tours, first starting 9am ($85-student rate $64, standby $59), small number groups and zodiac boats. _www.oceanexplorations.com._

Information
Tourism Victoria Info Centre, 812 Wharf St, Inner Harbour, 953-2033; toll free (800) 663-3883, open daily in summer 8.30am-6.30pm, 9am-5pm rest of year. _www.tourismvictoria.com._

Internet and WiFi Access
Central Library, 735 Broughton St, 382-7241, and all Greater Victoria Public Library (GVPL) locations: Free, 2 half-hour internet sessions/day with passport or drivers licence for proof of residency. Mon-Sat 9am-6pm, Tues-Thurs 'til 9pm, Sun 1pm-

5pm. *www.gvpl.ca* GVPL and Victoria Free-Net Association provide free WiFi access at all branches, as part of South Island Community Access Network (SICAN) supported by Industry Canada's Community Access Program. Library card and password are required, available on request at libraries. Visitors can register to obtain access. *www.gvpl.ca/whatshappening/wireless_factsheet.htm.*

Travel

Many ferries, including high-speed catamarans, and air services connect Victoria to mainland BC and Washington State each day, arriving and departing the Inner Harbour, Sidney and Swartz Bay Ferry Terminal, half-an-hour from downtown Victoria, and from the airport. (*See also under Vancouver.*)

Ferries. BC Ferries, 1112 Fort Street, Victoria, BC V8V 4V2 1 (888) 223-3779) in BC; (250) 386-3431 outside BC. Vancouver $10 o/w. Public bus approx. 1 hr to ferry which takes 1 hr 35 mins, smooth, cool ride with melting pot of passengers, lovely, breezy crossings in summer. 'Like sailing across a lake in New England.' To southern Vancouver Island – Tsawwassen from Swartz Bay. Plan to be at terminal at least 30 mins before dep. $10 o/w ($10.50 holidays). Lines, or BC Transit (Rte 70) to Swartz Bay from downtown Victoria. For details, see *www.bcferries.com/schedules/mainland/tssw-current.html.*

Black Ball Transport, 430 Belleville St., Victoria, BC V8V-1W9. 386-2202. Coho Ferry to Port Angeles, Washington State. 95 minutes. No advance res. Four sailings daily May-Sep. US$9.50. In Port Angeles,101 E. Railroad Ave, Port Angeles, WA, 98362 (360) 457-4491. *www.cohoferry.com.*

Victoria Clipper, 254 Belleville Street, Victoria, BC V8V 1W9 in Inner Harbour (Belleville Terminal). 382-8100/(800) 888-2535, catamaran service to Seattle takes approx. 2.75 hrs. US $72 o/w, $120 r/t. In summer, 2-hr **Victoria Express** service available (Tel 361-9144) dep 5.30pm, cost US$81/$133. Seattle terminal 2701 Alaskan Way, Pier 69, Seattle, WA 98121. (206) 448-5000 *www.victoriaclipper.com.*

Victoria-San Juan Cruises (800) 443-4552. Dep Victoria Inner Harbour daily at 5pm, arr Bellingham, Washington State, 8 pm. "See whales 70% of the time." US$79/$89 r/t ."All you can eat BBQ" on board. In US, Bellingham Cruise Terminal, 355 Harris Avenue Suite #104, Bellingham, WA 98225.(360) 738-8099 *www.whales.com/daycruise.html.*

Washington State Ferries Terminal 2499 Ocean Avenue, Sidney BC V8L1T3, 17 miles north of Victoria, B.C. on Highway 17. Sidney to Anacortes, one ferry a day at 11.40am, arr 2.45pm. US$13.80 o/w. *www.wsdot.wa.gov/Ferries/.*

Bus. Grayline Tours, Victoria (800) 663-8390. All buses depart opposite Empress Hotel. Schedules, prices subject to change. *www.grayline.ca/victoria.*

Island Coach Lines, run by Grayline/Laidlaw Coach. 27th St, 334-2475/(800) 318-0818. Scheduled services from Victoria to Nanaimo, Tofino, and Port Hardy. Stops at all local communities, including Courtenay and Pt Alberni. **BC Ferries,** (888) 223-3779 in BC. *www.grayline.ca/victoria.*

Pacific Coach Lines, 700 Douglas St, 385-4411/(800) 661-1725. Buses and connections between Victoria and Vancouver. Dep Victoria bus terminal for Vancouver on the hour, 6am through 8pm (9pm in summer). Vancouver $32 o/w, $62 r/t, includes ferry fare. *www.pacificcoach.com.*

Tofino Bus – Long Beach Link, 564 Campbell Street, Tofino, 725-2871, (866) 986-3466 and (866) 726-7790. Dep Victoria daily at Hostelling International, 516 Yates St. at 8.15am/2.30pm (summer) and Ocean Island Backpackers Inn, 791 Pandora at 8.30 am/2.45pm (summer), arr Ucluluet 1.45pm/7.45pm (summer), Tofino 1.50pm/8pm (summer). $50 o/w/$95 r/t plus tax. Surfboards and bikes carried free. For schedules, see *www.tofinobus.com.*

Victoria Regional Transit, local bus, 382-6161. Use #70 from downtown Victoria to Swartz Bay (BC Ferries) and to Victoria Int'l Airport. $2.00 one zone, $2.75 two zones. *www.transitbc.com.*

Rail. VIA Rail. Tickets at Victoria station, 450 Pandora Avenue 953-9000 ext. 5800, (888) 842-0744, (800) 561-8630. The *Malahat* - E & N Railiner, runs once daily running in each direction, dep noon, approx 4.5 hrs from Victoria to Courtenay (station at 899, Cumberland Rd), via Nanaimo (station at 321 Selby St): The journey is beautiful— in a small-one car including engine steam train. Train stops over Nanaimo's bridge so you can watch the bungee-jumpers.

Air and Float Planes (*See Vancouver*). **Air Canada & Air Canada Jazz Airline** Upto 18 daily 25 min flights from Victoria International Airport to Vancouver (YVR). Reservations (888) 247-2262 Flight info (888) 422-7533. *www.aircanada.com* and *www.flyjazz.ca* For AC timetables, see *www.actimetable.com.*

Craig Air, 266 0267 (Tofino) or (877) 886-3466; **Harbour Air,** 1075 West Waterfront Road, 3 blocks west of Canada Place. 384-2215. During week, 23 half-hr seaplane flights to Vancouver daily. *www.harbour-air.com*; **Pacific Coastal Airlines,** flies from Victoria Vancouver. (800) 663-2872, or (604) 273-8666.

Victoria International Airport (YYR), #201 - 1640 Electra Boulevard, Sidney, BC, V8L 5V4. 953-7500. 18 km N of Victoria. Accessible by Rte 70 bus from downtown ($2 o/w Victoria Regional Transit, 382-6161). *www.cyyj.ca, www.victoriaairport.com.*

SOOKE is 40-minutes west of Victoria along Highway 14 reachable by BC Transit. A further 45 miles north up the highway is **Port Renfrew**, the start of the **West Coast Trail**, a spectacular drive through rain forests, up a jagged coast and past some amazing beaches, especially at **Jordan River**. Sooke derives its name from T'sou-ke, a local stickleback fish. West of Sooke there is a "phantom point" - Point No Point - that can be seen from certain angles but not others. A little old teahouse sits at the point. *www.sookenet.com/sooke.html, www.sookeharbour.com, www.sooke.org* and *www.westshore.bc.ca/booksmusic.*

Sooke is a an arts and music centre, and home to the Island's largest juried art show and other events including a **Bluegrass Festival** in June *www.sookebluegrass.com*; **All Sooke Day** in July, with the longest running Canadian logging championships and sports *www.allsookeday.com* (Note: the future of the 70-year old festival has been uncertain, call 642-5486 for status); the **Sooke Festival of Performing Arts** for two weeks in late July and early August, with theatre, dance, and musical companies; and the **Sooke River Music Festival** in mid-August. There's a country market on Saturdays in summer. The **Sooke Regional Museum and Visitor Info Centre**, 2070 Phillips Rd. at Hwy 14, Tel: 642-6351, displays logging and salmon fishing history and First Nations culture. *www.insooke.com/museum*

Outdoors, the **Sooke Potholes Provincial Park,** three miles off Hwy 14, has deep, polished sandstone rock pools and potholes carved by glaciers, wonderful for clear water swimming and picnicking. The **Galloping Goose Trail** runs for about 20 kms from Roche Cove Regional Park to the Sooke Potholes and Leechtown. The **Juan de Fuca Marine Trail** begins at China Beach and continues a tough but accessible 47-km hike north.

OKANAGAN VALLEY/SIMILKAMEEN & KELOWNA For over a century, this has been the hub of BC's expanding **wine and fruit production**. East on Hwy 1 out of Vancouver, Hwy 3 takes you over the **Cascade Mountains** and down into the **Okanagan Valley/Similkameen** area to near the US border. From there, starting at **Osoyoos**, literally hundreds of orchards and vineyards straddle Hwy 97 northwards up Okanagan Valley and a series of lakes past Penticton, Summerland, Kelowna, and Vernon up to Salmon Arm. Or you can take Hwys 5 and 97C directly to **Kelowna** (395 kilometres, about 4 hours drive from Vancouver), capital of the Okanagan fruit region on the long Okanagan Lake, and use "K-Town" as your base.

Here you can go boating, camping, hiking, mountain biking (on the KVR - **Kettle Valley Trail**), ski-ing, swimming, wind and wake-surfing, and sunbathing on miles of lake-side beaches. With its long, sunny growing period, one third of Canada's grapes are also produced here, in 350 vineyards, with most grapes (85%) harvested by hand. Good therefore for summer jobs, or if you're taking it slow, for a nice holiday just lying by the lake in the sun. _www.tourismkelowna.org_ and _www.thompsonokanagan.com._

Some of the 59 wineries in the Okanagan Valley from Osoyoos to Vernon have tasting rooms; most are open summers and through the wine crush in September. Here you can sample, among others, Cabernet Sauvignon, Chardonnay Musque, Gamay Noir, Gewurztraminer, Merlot, Pinot Auxerrois, Pinot Blanc, Pinot Grigio, Pinot Gris, and Pinot Noir, Late Harvest Rieslings, Siegerrebe, Syrah, and Zweigelt. Independent vineyards have more than doubled in number in the past five years.

There are four **Okanagan Wine Festivals** annually: **Spring,** during the first four days in May year during bud-break (100+ events); **Summer,** held at Silver Star Mountain Resort, Vernon, second weekend in August; **Fall,** ten days in early October at the peak of the grape harvest (165+ events throughout the valley); and **Winter Icewine Festival** third week every January at Sun Peaks Resort, (800) 807-3257, celebrating Okanagan's exquisite Icewines. Past awards and dates for future events are listed on their website, which also lists 61 wineries, inc visiting hours. _www.owfs.com._ The site lists almost 300 wine-related events in the Spring and Fall.

Kelowna tourism website has an excellent month-by-month calendar of events _www.tourismkelowna.org_. Also try the **Downtown Kelowna** site at _www.downtownkelowna.com_, which includes dining and shopping guides.

In the town's cultural district are: **Kelowna Museum,** 470 Queensway Avenue, (250) 763-2417. Includes First Nations Gallery representing Inuit, Northwest Coast, Plateau and Eastern First Nations; Ethnography Gallery. _www.kelownamuseum.ca_   **Wine Museum** - Close by in historic Laurel Packinghouse, 1304 Ellis St, 868-0441. Self-guided tour with tasting of currently available wines. **Orchard Industry Museum** - Also at 1304 Ellis Street, 763-0433.

Accommodation

Kelowna Accommodation – Good site is _www.okaccommodations.com/kelowna._

Kelowna International Hostel, 2343 Pandosy St, 763-6024. Recently renovated 30 bed hostel. Private or semi-private rooms starting at $13/night. Internet, laundry facilities, TV lounge, lockers, free parking. Pick-up from bus station or airport available (call ahead). _www.kelowna-hostel.bc.ca._

Same Sun Backpacker Lodge, (250) 763-9814, (877) 562-2783. Same Sun Lodges of Western Canada began here in 1995. New, a/c, custom-designed building downtown across from beach, sleeps 118. Dorms and private rooms with semi-private bathrooms. TV, laundry, internet, lockers. $24.40 (w stud ID) in summer, June 1 – Oct 1)/$21.40 winter. Doubles $59/49. _www.samesun.com/kelowna.html._

Willow Inn, 235 Queensway, 762-2122/(800) 268-1055. Close to lake and park downtown. Rates are based on number of guests: $65-120.

Hiawatha Park Campground, 3795 Lakeshore Rd, (888) 784-7275. 3 miles S of Kelowna. Campsites $37 for 2 persons, $39 w/hook up. Laundry, store, pool, hot tub, free showers. *www.hiawatharvpark.com.*

Information/Travel
Tourism Kelowna Visitor Info Centre, 544 Harvey Avenue, 861-1515/(800) 663-4345. Open Mon-Fri 8am-7pm, Sat-Sun 9am-7pm in summer; shorter hours in winter. *www.tourismkelowna.com.*
Thompson Okanagan Tourism Association, 1332 Water Street, Kelowna, 860-5999, (800) 567-2275. Regional info, from Valemount to Osoyoos. Free local, regional and wine region maps *www.thompsonokanagan.com* or *www.totabc.com.*
Greyhound, 2366 Leckie Rd, 860-3835/860-1468/(800) 661-8747. 7am-7pm and 11pm-Midnight. *www.greyhound.ca/en/locations.*
Kelowna City Bus Transit, 860-8121. $1.75 one zone, $2 multi-zone. *www.busonline.ca/regions/kel.*
Kelowna International Airport (YLW), 5533 Airport Way, (250) 765-5125.

KAMLOOPS, sunny 'hub city' and old cowtown. Going north east from Vancouver, the **Trans Canada Highway** (Hwy 1) takes the Fraser Canyon route to Kamloops. More direct is via the **Coquihalla Highway** (Hwy 5), turning off Hwy 1 at Hope, then directly north east to Kamloops, which, this way, is 3-4 hours drive from Vancouver. Going north, Hwy 5 becomes the **Yellowhead Highway,** bound for Jasper. The original Canadian Pacific and Canadian Northern rail lines also cross in Kamloops, making it a major crossroads. These different routes make Kamloops a useful stopover between Vancouver and Banff or a jumping-off point for visits to the **Revelstoke, Yoho, Glacier,** and **Kootenay National Parks.**

The city is famous for its climate, with the hottest summers in Canada and over 2,000 hours of sunshine, according to *Statistics Canada*. But although it's Canada's second driest city, Kamloops also gets 34 inches of snow in winter, and nearby, at Canada's 3rd largest ski resort, **Sun Peaks,** an amazing 17 ft every year!

Kamloops has a **Cowboy Festival** in early March featuring cowboy musicians, poets, singers, songwriters, and others, at Calvary Temple Church, 1205 Rogers Way, and Cactus Jack's Dance Hall at 400 Seymour St. Sponsor: BC Cowboy Heritage Society, Box 137, V2C 5K3 (250) 579-5667, (888) 763-2224. *www.bcchs.com, www.cowboy-museum.com.*

The **Kamloops Museum,** 207 Seymour St, 828-3576, displays the region's history and culture, agricultural and Indian history, Tues-Sat 9.30am-4.30pm, free. *www.adventurekamloops.com.*

Accommodation/Food
Check *www.kamloopshotelsmotels.com* and *www.kamloopschamber.bc.ca.*
Kamloops Old Courthouse Hostel, 7 W Seymour St, 828-7991/(866) STAY-KAM. Dorm $16 members, $20 non. Discounts for longer stays. Renovated 1904 courthouse: dine in original courtroom, sleep in old judges' chambers, shower in jail cells. Downtown location. Kitchen, laundry, TV. *www.hihostels.ca.*
Thrift Lodge, 2459 E Trans Canada Hwy, 374-2488/(800) 661-7769. Summer: S-$54, D-$57, $3-XP; facs incl outdoor pool, AC, cable TV, free b/fast. *www.thrift-lodge.kamloops.com.*
Check out the bars in town for cheap meals. Try **Duffy's,** 1797 Pacific Way, 372-5453, huge beer collection. *www.duffys.kamloops.com;* **Kelly O'Bryan's,** 244 Victoria St, 828-1559. *www.kellyobryans.com* **Mr Mike's Steakhouse,** 23-750 Fortune Dr, 376-

6834. 'A place for a pig-out. Don't be put off by the exterior.' Mon-Sat 11am-9pm, Sun from 10am (two other locations); **Ricky's All-Day Grill**   90B 1967 E.Trans Canada Hwy, 851-9845 Breakfasts inc Santa Fe-style potato pancakes.

Information/Travel

Kamloops Visitor Centre, 1290 W Trans Canada Hwy, 374-3377/(800) 662-1994. Summer daily, 9am-7pm. _www.adventurekamloops.com._

Greyhound, 725 Notre Dame, 374-1212/(800) 661-8747. Open daily 6.30am-1.30am. _www.greyhound.ca._

Kamloops City Bus Transit, 376-1216. $2 basic fare, free transfers available. _www.busonline.ca/regions/kam._

VIA Rail. (888) 845-7245 for info, reservations. _Canadian_ stops here three times a week, from Jasper and Vancouver. 7 hrs 35 mins to Jasper, $79 _www.viarail.com._

Kamloops Heritage Rail has steam-powered trips on weekends. Restored 1912 steam train _Spirit of Kamloops_ tour is 7 mile/11 km r/t, 1 hr 10 min. _Armstrong Express_ 3 hrs in Fall, Thompson River to Salmon River Valley. _www.kamrail.com._

Kamloops Airport 3035 Airport Rd, (250) 376-3613. BC Transit bus to airport. 376-1216. _www.kamloopsairport.com._

CARIBOO/ BARKERVILLE & WILLIAMS LAKE North of Kamloops, fur traders

first settled the Cariboo/Chilcotin area of north-east BC. The **Great Cariboo Gold Rush** of 1862 in **Barkerville,** 55 miles east of **Quesnel**, then paved the way for cattle ranchers, via the amazing 365-mile **Cariboo Wagon Road** (now Hwys 1 and 97) built by the Royal Engineers in 1862-65 under the direction of Governor James Douglas, from Yale near Vancouver all the way north to Barkerville. Among other things, two dozen camels were imported from Manchuria as beasts of burden for the road, causing a stink among horses, fancying smelly socks as fodder, and eventually being set loose – some may still be out there!

The **Barkerville** settlement really started on August 17, 1862 when Billy Barker, an Englishman from Cambridgeshire, struck pay dirt that would earn him and his company $500,000, from a strip of land only 600 ft long. By the end of 1863, 3,000 claims had been staked round the area; the total gold removed that year was worth about $4 million, a fortune – some consider the town and its gold to be the catalyst responsible for the creation of BC Province. Consequently, Barkerville became a boom town, with as many as twenty swinging saloons at one time, and, not surprisingly, the largest population north of San Francisco.

The shaft that started it all is now a part of the restored gold rush town with 120+ historic buildings at **Barkerville Historic Park.** You will need a car to get there. In the town you can pan for gold, call at the Gold Commissioner's office, visit Trapper Dan's cabin in Chinatown, have your photograph taken in period clothes, and visit the same type of variety shows miners once enjoyed at the Theatre Royal. A museum tells the saga of the settlement with photos, exhibits and artefacts. Visitor Reception Centre has maps. Call (250) 994-3302 for info. Daily 8.30am-8pm, $12.50. May to Sept. _www.barkerville.ca_ , _www.heritage.gov.bc.ca_, and _www.barkerville.com._

There is a campground near the park and fairly inexpensive motel accommodation in nearby **Wells.** The park is open year-round with reduced opening hours and no guided tours after Labor Day.

MOUNT REVELSTOKE NATIONAL PARK   The park, midway between Kamloops and Banff, is situated in the **Selkirk Range,** more jagged and spiky than the Rockies and especially famous for its excellent skiing. Revelstoke is famous for having had the most snow in a single season of anywhere in Canada. The summit drive to the top of **Mount Revelstoke** is the 26 kilometres **Meadows-in-the-Sky Parkway** with scenic views - the upper sub-alpine zone of the peak is famous for wildflowers, which blossom in brilliant colours in August. At the summit there is the 9 kilometres **Jade Lakes Trail** winding through forests and meadows with fantastic views of distant peaks, glaciers and mountain lakes.

The Trans Canada Hwy 1 runs along the southern edge of the park following the scenic **Illecillewaet River.** There are two self-guided tours available. One is a tour of the rain forest, the **Giant Cedars Nature Trail**, the other of the rare skunk cabbage plants, the **Skunk Cabbage Trail**. Park services are provided in the town of **Revelstoke,** a quiet, pretty place set amidst the Selkirk and Monashee mountains, with a summer jazz festival and railway museum. Just a few kilometres to the west of Revelstoke is the village of **Craigellachie** where the last spike of the Canadian Pacific Railroad was driven in on November 7th, 1885, by Donald Smith, Governor of the HBC, thus completing the longest railway line in the world at the time. *www.railwaymuseum.com, www.revelstokecc.bc.ca.* Entrance to the park is $5. Call 837-7500 or visit *www.pc.gc.ca/pn-np/bc/revelstoke* for info.

Accommodation
Revelstoke *www.kootenays-bc.com/Accommodations/Revelstoke/RoomRatesUnder$100.*
Frontier Motel, at jct of Hwys 1 & 23 N, 837-5119/(800) 382-7763. Summer S-$52, D-$58, incl full b/fast.
Mountain View Motel, 1017 First St W, 837-4900. Summer: $52-60, XP-$10. Kitchens available in some rooms. AC, cable TV. Central location.
R Motel, 1500 1st St W, 837-2164. S-$55, D-$60, XP-$5. Twin $63, 4 persons $75. Free b/fast, TV, AC.
SameSun Backpacker Lodge, 400 2nd W, 837-4050/(877) 562-2783. Dorm $21.40, free linens; private rooms $43 summer/$39 winter. Boasts one of the world's best ski deals: $29 pp. gets you a place to stay and a lift ticket (normally $34). Internet access, games room, lounges and TV area. Off-season rates available for long stays; call for info. *www.samesun.com/revelstoke_hostel.html.*
Camping: Canada West Campground, 3069 Trans Canada Highway, 2½ miles west of Revelstoke, 837-4420. $19 for 2, $22-25 w/hook up, XP-$2; laundry, showers, outdoor heated pool, waterslide. *www.canadawest.revelstoke.com.*
Canyon Hot Springs Campground, 35 km east of Revelstoke, 35 km west of Rogers Pass, 837-2420. Campsite $25 for 2, $33 w/hook up, XP-$3. Showers, laundry, mineral pools. *www.canyonhotsprings.com.*

Information
Chamber of Commerce, 204 Campbell Ave, 837-5345, (800) 487-1493. Daily 8.30am-4.30pm. *www.seerevelstoke.com.*
Seasonal Visitor Info, 837-3522/(800) 487-1493. Summer, daily 9am-10pm.
Mount Revelstoke National Park, 837-7500. Mon-Fri 8am-noon, 1pm-4.30pm.

SELKIRK/EAST KOOTENAY 'SPRINGDOM'   The Selkirk Mountains and East Kootenay areas bubble with mineral springs to bask and relax in along BC Rockies' section of the Pacific 'Ring of Fire'. A useful Guide is *Hot Springs of Western Canada: A Complete Guide* by Glenn Woodsworth. For maps and

more details, check _www.kootenayrockies.com/hotspringsmap2.html_   and
_www.bchotsprings.com_1

The main hot and cool springs are the following:

Ainsworth, 229-4212. Round and down from Sandon, on Hwy 31, 17 km north of
Balfour, 20 km south of Kaslo. Take 2-hr r/t Balfour ferry across Kootenay Lake -
the longest free ferry ride in the world. $7 single swim, daypass $11. 10am- 9:30pm,
daily. _www.hotnaturally.com_ and _www.britishcolumbia.com/hotsprings/?id=11._

Canyon , 837-2420, 35 km east of Revelstoke on Hwy 1. Immerse in 39°C mineral
waters or swim in a 26°C pool. $6.50 single swim, daypass $8.50. _www.canyon-
hotsprings.com._

Fairmont, 345-6311, (800) 663-4979. Between Kimberley and Radium on Hwy.
93/95 Canada's largest all natural hot mineral spring water pool complex. $6.54
single swim, daypass $9.35. 8am-10pm daily. _www.fairmonthotsprings.com._

Halcyon, 265-3554, (888) 689-4699. On Hwy 23, 68 km S of Revelstoke, 32 km north
of Nakusp, along Upper Arrow Lake. Hot pool 40°C, warm pool 38°C, large
mineral pool 30°C, and cold plunger 13°C. $7.95 single swim, daypass $12.50. 8am-
10/11pm daily. Free ferry across lake. _www.halcyon-hotsprings.com._

Lussier, 422-3003, Kootenay Park Services. south of Fairmont on Hwy 93/95, near
entrance to Whiteswan Lake Provincial Park, 17.5 kms on Whiteswan Forestry
Road, 5-minute hike to Lussier River. Non-commercial. First pool max temp 43°C;
bottom pool alongside river is coolest, about 34°C in summer. Pools can
accommodate several people at a time. Must wear bathing suits.

Nakusp, 265-4528, (800) 909-8819. 101 km south of Revelstoke down Hwy 23,12 km
NE of Nakusp. Naturally heated mineral springs, kept at 38°C and 41°C in winter
and 36° and 40°C in summer. $6.25 single swim, daypass $9.25. 9.30/10am-
9.30/10pm daily. _www.nakusphotsprings.com._

Radium, 347-9485, (800) 767-1611. Operated by **Parks Canada**. At junction of Hwys
93 and 95 in Kootenay River Valley, 19 km north of Invermere, 105 km south of
Golden. Largest hot spring pool in Canada. $6.50 single swim, daypass $9.75.
Noon-9/10pm daily. _www.radiumhotsprings.com/pools.htm._

GLACIER NATIONAL PARK From Revelstoke, continue 72 kilometres
eastwards along the Trans Canada Hwy 1, and you quickly come to this
park, established 1886 in the heart of the Selkirk Mountains. As its name
tells you, **Glacier** is an area of ice fields with deep, awesome canyons and
caverns, alpine meadows and silent forests. There are many trails within it
and, like Revelstoke, this too is a skier's paradise. The Alpine Club of
Canada holds summer and winter camps here. The Park is said to be the
birthplace of mountaineering in North America: in 1888, the Rev. William
Spotswood Green and Rev. Henry Swanzy, two Brits, completed the first
recreational technical climbs in the Selkirks.

In the centre of Glacier is **Rogers Pass**, named for discoverer Major A.B.
Rogers, Engineer-in-Chief for the CP railway, and designated a National
Historic Site for its role as an essential link in the building of the CPR. At the
Pass, annual snowfall sometimes reaches 23 metres, so that special protection is necessary for the railway and Trans Canada Highway running
through it. Concrete snow sheds and manmade hillocks at the bottom of
avalanche chutes slow the cascading snow, while artillery fire is used to
bring down the snow before it accumulates to critical depths. Travellers
through Rogers Pass in winter may feel more secure in the knowledge that

they are passing through one of the longest controlled avalanche areas in the world.

Eight hiking trails begin at **Illecillewaet Campground,** 3 kilometres west of Rogers Pass, up the Illecillewaet and Asulkan valleys. The **Meeting of the Waters** trail is short (1 kilometres) and easy, leading to the dramatic confluence of the two rivers. The longer **Avalanche Crest** trail offers magnificent views of Rogers Pass, the Hermit Range, and the Illecillewaet River Valley.

Admission to the park is $5 for one and $12.50 for 2-7 persons, daily. Climbers and overnight walkers must register with the wardens at **Rogers Pass Discovery Centre,** 837-7500. Park services and accommodation are available at Rogers Pass. The Centre is open year-round, except for Christmas Day and all November. Hours vary by season, June-Sept, daily 8am-7pm. *www.pc.gc.ca/pn-np/bc/glacier.*

Accommodation
See also under Revelstoke.

Golden Municipal Campground, 1407 S 9th St, Golden, on banks of Kicking Horse River, 344-5412. $15, $17 w/hook up, hot showers and an outdoor pool.

National Park Campsites: try Illecillewaet River (60 sites), 3 km W of Rogers pass summit or **Loop Brook** (20 sites), 5 km W of Rogers Pass summit. Both campgrounds cost $17/camp/night and have firewood (fire permit, $6), toilets and shelters. Open Jun-Oct. Back country camping is available at various locations. You do need to be registered and have a permit, $8 overnight, available from the Rogers Pass Discovery Centre.

Information
At **Kimberley** (S of Golden on Hwy 93/95), **Kootenay Rockies Tourism**, 905 Warren Avenue, V1A 2Y5, 427-4838. Brochure hotline: (800) 661-6603. Lists places to see, dining, accommodation, events, etc. *www.kootenayrockies.com.*

At **Golden,** the centre of **Kicking Horse Country** and six national parks:
Golden Tourism Association, Box 20181, Golden. Includes calendar of events; accommodation; avalanche reports, etc. *www.tourismgolden.com/events.*

Golden Chamber of Commerce, 500 10th Ave N, 344-7125/(800) 622-GOLD.

YOHO NATIONAL PARK Going 55 kilometres further east from Golden along Hwy 1, **Yoho** National Park is 'in the shadow of the Great Divide' on the BC flank of the Rockies, adjoining Banff National Park on the Alberta side and close to Lake Louise (27 kilometres). Yoho is named from the Cree word meaning 'how wonderful'. This awesome park has 28 peaks over 3,000 metres and is traversed by the spectacular **Kicking Horse River** from east to west (over which erosion has created a natural flat-rock bridge, 3 kilometres west of Field). The river was first explored by Europeans in 1857.

In 1881, the Canadian Pacific Railway (CPR) decided to use **Kicking Horse Pass** for its trans-continental line, requiring an original grade of 4.5%, the steepest of any in North America, and taking five engines to pull trains up it. Later the CPR's amazing **Spiral Tunnels**, completed in 1909, reduced the grade to a safer 2.2%. The tunnels can be seen 8 kilometres east of **Field** on a pull-off with explanations of the tunnels on the Trans-Canada Hwy 1, or 2 kilometres north of Kicking Horse Campground on Yoho Valley Road. They're best seen when one of CPR's mile long freight trains is snaking through the figure eight curves at different levels, which is often. Then you can see the same train at several different levels at once, a truly amazing sight! NB. Easiest visited from Lake Louise, less than half-an-hour away.

Yoho is a mountaineer's park with 400+ kilometres of trails leading the walker across the roof of the Rockies. Worth looking at are the beuatiful turquoise alpine **Emerald** and **O'Hara Lakes**, the curtain of mist at **Laughing Falls**, the strangely shaped pillars of **Hoodoo Valley,** and **Takakkaw** ('magnificent') **Falls**, at 254 metres, the third highest in Canada. The **Burgess Shale Formation,** a UNESCO World Heritage Site, contains fossilized remains of 120+ marine animal species dating back 515 million years. The **Yoho National Park Visitor Centre** is in **Field,** 343-6783. Open 9am-7pm daily in summer; 9am-4/5pm rest of year. Entrance to the park is $7, $14 for 2-7 persons, daily. NB: Yoho is on Mountain Time, 1 hour ahead of Pacific Time (most of BC). *www.pc.gc.ca/pn-np/bc/yoho.*

Accommodation
See Golden above, and Banff, Alberta.

There are four developed campgrounds in Yoho with 279 sites, and various cabins within the park. The campgrounds are at **Hoodoo Creek,** Jun-Sep (106 sites); **Kicking Horse,** June-Sep (92, boiling water required); **Takakkaw Falls,** (walk-in, 'unbeatable views') June-Sep (35); and **Monarch,** May-Sep (46). First-come, first served; rsvs system being developed. $17-$22 per night. Extra $6 for firewood. **Yoho** also operates 5 backcountry campgrounds, 4 in the **Yoho Valley** and 1 in the **Ottertail Valley,** $8 pp. Call 343-6783 for rsvs on backcountry camping.

There are **campgrounds and** motels within the park and accommodation is available in the town of **Radium Hot Springs**. **Redstreak Campground,** 2.5 kilometres from Radium Hot Springs, $22, $26/30 w/hook-up, 242 sites. May-Oct. Reservations at Redstreak can be made via *www.pccamping.ca* or toll free 1-877-737-3783; **McLeod Meadows,** 27 kilometres north from W Gate entrance, $17. **Marble Canyon,** 86 kilometresnorth of W Gate entrance, $17. 61 sites. Jun-Sep; and winter camping at **Dolly Varden,** Sept-May, is free. Back-country camping $8.

KOOTENAY NATIONAL PARK South of Yoho, lying along the Vermilion-Sinclair section of the Banff-Windermere Parkway (Hwy 93), **Kootenay** is rich in canyons, glaciers and ice fields as well as wildlife. Bears, moose, elk, deer and Rocky Mountain goats all live here. The Park, established 1920, has many attractions. The striking **Marble Canyon,** one of several canyons in Kootenay, is formed of grey limestone and quartzite laced with white and grey dolomite and lies just off the highway. Other sites are the rust-coloured mineral pools and ochre beds of the **Paint Pots** - considered a sacred site by First Nations, **Olive Lake** nestled in the Sinclair Pass and the iron-rich cliffs of the **Redwall Fault** greeeting visitors from the south.

The southern entrance to the park is near **Radium Hot Springs** where the **Kootenay National Park Visitor Centre** is located at 7556 Main Street East, 347-9505. Open 9am-7pm daily in summer; 9am-4/5pm rest of year.

Accommodation
There are campgrounds and motels within the park and accommodation is available in the town of Radium Hot Springs. Within the Park there are 431 campsites available: **Redstreak Campground,** 2.5 kilometres from Radium Hot Springs, $22, $26/30 w/hook-up, 242 sites. May-Oct. Reservations at Redstreak can be made via *www.pccamping.ca* or toll free 1-877-737-3783; **McLeod Meadows,** 27 kilometres north from W Gate entrance, $17. 98 sites. May-Sep: and **Marble**

Canyon, 86 kilometresnorth of W Gate entrance, $17. 61 sites. Jun-Sep; and winter camping at **Dolly Varden,** Sept-May, is free. Back-country camping $8. *www.pc.gc.ca/pn-np/bc/kootenay/.*

PRINCE GEORGE Crossroads and 'Capital' of Northern BC. This fairly uninteresting town has become the take-off point for the Yukon and North West Territories. It's about four hours by car from Jasper and about seven hours from Kamloops. Travellers en route to Alaska from Jasper use the Yellowhead Hwy (Hwy 16). At Prince George go north on to Hwy 97 to Dawson Creek and the Alaska Hwy, or NW on Hwys 16 and 37 for Alaska. Or you can continue on Hwy 16 winding over the Hazelton Mountains to Prince Rupert on the coast (about 10 hrs). If you are travelling north from Kamloops, Hwy 5 picks up the 16 at Tete Jaune Cache.

Originally a fur trading post established by Simon Fraser in 1807, today's Prince George was born of a railway - the Grand Trunk Pacific Railway (later CN Rail), which arrived in 1914. Today timber drives the local economy, with forestry, plywood manufacture,12 sawmills and three pulp mills. Prince George is the fourth largest city in BC, pop 77,000, with cafés, art galleries, boutiques and museums. *www.city.pg.bc.ca.*

There is a **Railway & Forestry Museum**, 850 River Road, 563-7351, which has 60 pieces of rolling stock dating from 1899 to the 1960s and oral histories of the Grand Trunk Pacific / CN Railroads. Entrance $5. *www.pgrfm.bc.ca.* Also the **Exploration Place Science Centre and Museum** with seven galleries, including one covering the much parodied Pacific Great Eastern (PGE) railway, at 333 Becott Place, 562-1612, (866) 562-1612. *www.the-explorationplace.com.* The **PG Airport (YXS)** is at 4141 Airport Rd, 963-2400. Prince George is about an hour's non-stop flight from Vancouver by Air Canada Jazz, Flightlink, or Westjet.

Prince George is also the main overnight stopping point for the VIARail *Skeena* service from Jasper to Prince Rupert, with hotel stays required. The *Skeena* leaves Jasper and Prince Rupert three times a week, on Wed, Fri and Sun. *www.viarail.ca.* The **Northern BC Tourism Association** has places to stay, maps and local info at #303-1268 5th Avenue, 561-0432, (800) 663-8843 *www.nbctourism.com.*

Accommodation
Prince George Hotel, 487 George St, 564-7211, $50-65, above this English pub.
Blue Spruce Campground, 4433 Kimball Rd, 964-7272/(877) 964-7272. 128 sites. $18, $23.50 full-hook, for two people, XP-$2. Internet, outdoor pool.

DAWSON CREEK. A small, but rapidly growing boom-town about six hours north east of Prince George on Hwy 97, Dawson Creek marks the start of the 1,500 mile WWII Alaska Highway. The Mile Zero Cairn is the centre of town. *www.alaskayukontravel.com.* **Northern Alberta Railway Park** includes the Cairn, Dawson Creek Station Museum, Dawson Creek Art Gallery and, on Saturdays, the Farmer's Market. *www.hellonorth.com.* Dawson Creek was first settled in 1912 when the railroad was extended here to ship grain from the area, including wheat, oats, barley, and rye.

Tourism Dawson Creek Visitor Info Centre is at 900 Alaska Avenue, 782-9595. **Central Mountain Air** (888) 865-8585 *www.flycma.com* and

HawkAir _www.hawkair.net_   provide scheduled flights. For accommodations and camping in Dawson's Creek, check _www.tourismdawsoncreek.com/-accommodations._ **Mile 0 Campground**, 1 mile west of Alaska Hwy next to golf course, 782-2590. 47 sites with hook-ups, 26 without. $12.50, $18.25 w/hook-up, inc hot showers and laundry. Outdoor pool.

FORT ST JAMES NATIONAL HISTORIC SITE On the way from Prince George to Prince Rupert on Hwy 16 heading west. Worth a 45 minute detour at **Vanderhoof** up Hwy 27 to the shores of **Stuart Lake** to visit this restored fur trading post established by Simon Fraser for the North West Company (NWC) in 1806. The fort became the centre of the northern fur trade district, christened by Fraser as New Caledonia. At the site, you can step back in time to the 19th century old post and visit gardens and historic buildings, restored to a single year in time, 1896. Watch Carrier people practising traditional arts such as canoe building, hide tanning and the drying and smoking of salmon. The Hudson's Bay Company, which absorbed the NWC in 1821, closed this post as recently as 1952. Daily, 9am-5pm, May-Sep, $5.75. Info: 996-7191. _www.pc.gc.ca/lhn-nhs/bc/stjames._

PRINCE RUPERT Marvelously situated on Kaien Island among the fjords of **Hecate Strait** at the mouth of the beautiful **Skeena River,** Prince Rupert is BC's 'City of Rainbows,' with multiple bows sometimes appearing every misty day. There are plenty of those: this is Canada's wettest city, so take an umbrella! It's about 10 hours driving west from Prince George. Also known as the 'Halibut Capital of the World', Prince Rupert is the fishing centre of north west BC. The season's peak is in early August, the best time to visit the canneries, one of which is the **North Pacific Historic Fishing Village** south of town, BC's oldest surviving salmon cannery, built in 1889. _www.tourismprincerupert.com_ and _www.rupert.bc.ca._

Sometimes called BC's 'forgotten port', Prince Rupert has always been a transportation hub. With a deep, ice-free harbour, it's the southernmost port of the Alaska Ferry System, the northern terminus of BC Ferries, a cruise ship stopping point, and the western terminus of VIA Rail's scenic *Skeena* train from Jasper and long CN Rail coal, grain and lumber freightliners from across Canada.

Soon it will be even more of a hub: The town is undergoing a huge railway upgrading with new container terminal and port facilities that will eventually place it above Vancouver's capacity, sped by expanding trade with Asia, gridlock on other transcontinental lines, and sailing time to Asia, via Great Circle routes, 19 hours less than that from LA. There are also plans afoot for construction to begin in 2008 on a 1,200 kilometres oil pipeline over the Rockies to Edmonton in Alberta (the Enbridge Gateway), possibly even two, if Terasen's Trans Mountain line gets built.

In earlier days, this area was a stronghold of the Haida and Tsimpsian Indians. The **Museum of Northern British Columbia,** 100 1st Ave W, 624-3207, contains a rare collection of Indian treasures. In front stands a superb totem pole. Inside, there are more totems, masks, carvings and beadwork. Open the Treasure Box of the Ancient Ones! Sept-May: Mon-Sat 9am-5pm, June-Aug: Mon-Sat 9am-8pm, Sun 9am-5pm, $5, $2 w/student ID.

www.museumofnorthernbc.com. The associated **Kwinitsa Railway Museum** on the waterfront, tells the dramatic tale of the GTPR.

Accommodation

Accommodation tends to be expensive. A good listing of different types is at *www.tourismprincerupert.com,* at **Visitors Information Bureau,** and at **Prince Rupert Library** *www.princerupertlibrary.ca.*

Aleeda Motel, 900 3rd Ave, 627-1367/(888) 460-2023. May-Sep S-$60, D-$70, Twin $80, XP-$10. Oct-May S-$45, D or Twin-$50, XP-$10. *http://aleedamotel.bc.ca/.*

Pioneer Hostel, 167 3rd Ave E, 624-2334(888) 794-9998. Dorm-$16, private S-$35, D-$42.80, all incl. linens. 'Small, clean and cosy.' Best to book early.

Raffles Inn, 1080 3rd Ave W, 624-9161/(800) 663-3207. Rooms $40-$60/night S-$50, D-$56, T-$72. 'Comfortable and clean.' Overlooks harbour, near ferries & bus station. $2.99 b/fast available. Cable TV in all rooms. *www.tkp-biz.com/rafflesinn.*

Park Ave Campground, 1750 Park Ave, 624-5861, (800) 667-1994. 77 sites. Close to ferry terminal. Hot showers. Covered areas for cooking and eating. $12.84 open tents. *www.princerupertlibrary.ca/parkavecampgrounds.*

Of interest

Butze Rapids. You get a good view from Hwy 16, en route from Prince George. Has a reversing tidal stream that rivals the falls at Saint John, New Brunswick.

Cow Bay. Trendy district where everything is painted black and white; one of the oldest sections with historic buildings, many built on pilings overlooking the harbor. Dairy cattle first unloaded in 1906 had to swim ashore here. Try **Cowpuccino's Coffee House,** 25 Cow Bay Road, with its outdoor seating and home-made everything, **Cow Bay Café,** 205 Cow Bay Road, and **Java-dot-Cup** 516 3rd Ave. W, 622-2822: Less than $2 for 30 mins.

North Pacific Historic Fishing Village, 1889 Skeena Dr, Port Edward, 628-3538. Approx 20 kms S of Prince Rupert, take Port Edward turnoff on Hwy 16, 6 kms past Port Edward on Skeena Drive. National Historic Site. Original 1989 cannery buildings, wooden fishing boats, fishing exhibits. 9am-6pm daily, $12, $10 w/student ID. *www.district.portedward.bc.ca/northpacific*

Queen Charlotte Islands, west of Prince George. Miles of sandy beaches. A place for taking it easy. Graham Island in the north, and Moresby Island in the south are the main islands, separated by the very narrow Skidegate Channel (pronounced "Skid-eh-Gate"). July is driest. Cape Saint James at the southern tip has had some of the highest wind velocities ever recorded in Canada. Accessible from Prince Rupert by plane; or BC Ferry. 8 hours. $25.25 o/w. *www.bctravel.com/queencharlotteislands.*

Bella Coola. South of Prince Rupert in the Central Coast area is **Bella Coola,** at the end of Hwy 20, 456 kilometres west from Williams Lake, a five hour drive. This is where, in 1793, Sir Alexander Mackenzie of the North West Company became the first white man to travel overland on the 'grease trails' from the Fraser River to the Bella Coola Valley, thus becoming the first European to traverse the entire North American Continent north of Mexico. There is a **Heritage Trail** that retraces Big Mack's footsteps. A century later, a hundred or so Norwegians from the Midwest settled here at the end of the fjord-like Burke Channel, soon followed by many more, descendents of whom still reside here. The **Norwegian Heritage House** was built by one of the settlers around 1900 - visits by prior arrangement, 982-2270. The **Bella Coola Museum** is open June-Sept, 10 am-5 pm, Sun-Fri.

This scenic, but isolated spot is accessible by two daily flights from Vancouver via Pacific Coast Airlines *www.pacific-coastal.com;* and by BC Ferry's Discovery Coast route. *www.bcferries.bc.ca* Accommodation and restaurants are listed on *www.bellacoola.ca.*

Information

Visitors Information Bureau, 100-215 Cow Bay Road, 624-5637/(800) 667-1994. *www.tourismprincerupert.com.*
Prince Rupert Library, 101 6th Ave W, 627 1345, has internet room and accommodation listings. *www.princerupertlibrary.ca.*

Travel

Ferries: BC Ferries, 386-3431, (888) 223-3779. The nicest way to approach Prince Rupert is undoubtedly by sea. BC Ferries voyages from here to **Port Hardy** on Vancouver Island, making the trip during June, July and Sept on even-numbered days and during August on odd days. *www.bcferries.com.*
Alaska Marine Highway Ferries, (800) 642-0066 (Juneau), several boats a week leave Prince Rupert for Juneau (US$138) and Haines (US$156), Alaska, 1½ days,. If you want a shorter trip, take the one to Ketchikan, passing through glaciers and fjords en route, 6½ hours, US$52. 'Very beautiful.' *www.ferryalaska.com.*
Rail & Bus. VIA Rail. The *Skeena* leaves for a 31-hr highly-scenic trip via Skeen Valley, Terrace and Prince George to Jasper every Sun, Wed, Fri at 8 am, arr 4 pm next day. Station in Prince Rupert is at 2000 Park Ave. *www.viarail.ca/pdf/guides/-en_skeena.pdf.*
Prince Rupert/Port Edward Transit. For rides around the city. $1.25/$1 with student ID. Port Edward $1.75/$1.25. $2.50/$2 to North Pacific Historic Fishing Village. *www.busonline.ca/regions/prr/schedules/map.cfm?*.
Greyhound Bus Linard Holdings, 112 6 St, 624-5090. Office open 8:30am-12:30pm and 4pm-8:45pm. *www.greyhound.ca/en.*
Air: Prince Rupert Airport, 624-6274, cell 624-1024. 30 mins from downtown; bus deps from Highliner Plaza Hotel downtown to meet each arrival and departure, via ferry to and from the hotel, 622-2222. *www.ypr.ca.*

THE TERRITORIES

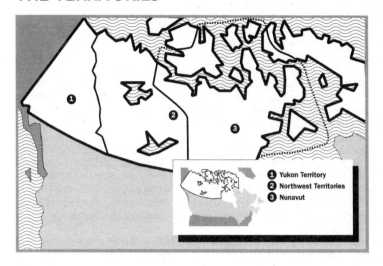

*It's the great, big, broad land way up yonder, It's the forest where silence has lease,
It's the beauty that thrills me with wonder, It's the stillness that fills me with peace.
The Spell of the Yukon, Robert Service*

The Greatest Outdoors! Canada's three territories above the 60th parallel are the land of the midnight sun, the aurora borealis, of diamonds in tundra, of sub-arctic wildlife and flowers, bison, buffalo and caribou, wide blue summer skies, and hundreds of emerald-blue lakes. The heart of this vast region is the 1,800 km **Mackenzie River,** whose north-flowing watery veins form the third largest river basin in the Americas after the Amazon and Mississippi. In the far west of the area is Canada's highest mountain, **Mt Logan,** 5,959 ms, surrounded by deep ice fields.

Here recorded history is relatively short. The exploration of the Mackenzie for a passage to China, just over two centuries ago, in 1789, in four birch-bark canoes from Lake Athabasca to the icy Beaufort Sea by the intrepid Nor'Wester, Alexander Mackenzie, was the first such incursion by Europeans into a region where the Deh Cho, Dene, Inuit, Metis and other First Nations have existed for thousands of years. In the Territories, there are today more than a dozen official languages and an institution devoted to the **Beringia** land-bridge heritage of the region that brought DNA from Central Asia to North America.

In this huge arena criss-crossed by hardy bush pilots, distances are great and vistas sometimes barren, but long trips to historic sights, fun events such as the **Solstice Festival** in Yellowknife in July when you can golf at midnight, superb outdoor activities such as white-watering the **Slave River Rapids** and the **Yukon River Quest Canoe and Kayak Race** – the world's longest, and scenic wonders such as the **Virginia Falls** on the Nahanni River

- twice as high as Niagara, are worthwhile, if you're interested and willing to take a deep plunge into nature.

Driving tips in this region: always check where the next nearest fuel supplies will be – they may be hundreds of kilometres away; always carry extra petrol, food, first aid, a usable spare and insect repellent; keep your headlights on at all times (it's the law), especially on dusty roads in summer - preferably fitted with mesh protection; be ever watchful for bison and other roamers; and take plenty of breaks; when planning the trip, always consider the daylight available – it varies from less than five hours in December to 21 hours in June, so don't wait for dark before you stop.

Fur trading defined this region, as indeed it once defined all of Canada. Two hundred years ago, the as-yet unnamed Yukon and Northwest Territories were fur-trading areas of the North West Company (NWC) and Nunavut the domain of the Hudson's Bay Company (HBC) - Nunavut originally known as 'Rupert's Land' after the first governor of the HBC. The vast territory of the North West Company, which merged with the HBC in 1821, and Rupert's Land, were purchased in their entirety from the HBC by the Canadian government in 1869 for $1.5 million, to become a single administrative entity.

In 1898, following the **Klondike** and **Yukon River** gold rushes that brought 30,000 prospectors and their hangers-on to the area around **Dawson City**, the Yukon was designated a separate territory by the Canadian government to fend off possible annexation by Alaska. The boundaries of Northwest Territories were further delineated in 1905 when Alberta and Saskatchewan became provinces below the 60th parallel; and in 1999 Nunavut separated from the Northwest Territories, when the Inuit assumed control over their homeland. Much of the more recent development has been spurred by gas and oil field production.

If you are planning a trip to Nunavut, Northwest Territories, or Yukon, be sure to contact the provincial tourist offices in advance. They have excellent and detailed information, including road and campground guides, package tours, accommodation, water sports, festivals and events. Check with Nunavut Tourism at (867) 979-6551/(866) 686-2888, *www.nunavuttourism.com*. Northwest Territories Tourism: (867) 873-7200/(800) 661-0788, *www.explorenwt.com*, and Yukon Tourism (867) 667-3084/(800) 661-0494.

The telephone area code for the entire region and this section is 867.

NUNAVUT

A separate Canadian territory since only April 1999, Nunavut is much closer geographically and culturally to the Arctic environment of Greenland than to anywhere else in North America. Even the far reaches of Alaska seem tame in comparison to the northern isles of Nunavut. Formed from the eastern portion of the Northwest Territories, Nunavut, which means 'our land' in Inuit, has achieved an elective government for its people.

The landscape is typically Arctic, and most of the territory lies above the tree line. It can be both stark and beautiful at the same time, and varies from dramatic mountains and fjords on the shores of **Baffin** and **Ellesmere Islands**, to lakes and tundra further west. In Nunavut, polar bears roam, walruses bask on shorelines, caribou, grizzly bears, and muskox wander the tundra, narwhals cruise the ocean. In winter, the Northern Lights sparkle in the night sky.

The climate ranges from -40C in the far north during winter, to between the much more bearable temperatures of 2-10C (and almost 24 hours of sunshine) during the summer. Snow flurries are a possibility year round; in summer, so are bugs, and some form of insect repellent is advisable. April is a good month for snow sports -and daylight, in July water activities – kayaking, canoeing, rafting are possible.

The territory covers one-fifth of Canada's landmass, spans four times zones geographically (but only uses three—from 5-7 hours behind GMT), and has a population of approx 29,000, for its two million square kilometres. The mean age of the population is only 22 years, the youngest in Canada, as well as being the fastest growing. The Inuit native people make up 85% of the population and there are four official languages: Inuktitut, Inuinnaqtun, English and French.

European explorers looking for a passage to China came here as early as the 16th century. Sponsored by Elizabeth I and the Cathay Company, Sir Martin Frobisher founded the first settlement on what is now called **Iqaluit** on **Frobisher Bay** in 1578. His fifteen ships sailed deep into what would later be called the **Hudson's Strait.** Europeans began influencing the Inuits following establishment of the Hudson's Bay Company (HBC) in 1670. In Nunavut, whose southern border splits the Hudson's Bay in half, the Inuits supplied the ubiquitous HBC with furs, gradually abandoning seasonal migrations and culture based on hunting for a livelihood dependent on trade. In 1914, the HBC began establishing trading posts on Baffin Island, but the fur market collapsed twenty years later and the Inuits were relocated to permanent, more centralized settlements by the Canadian government. _www.collectionscanada.ca._

Today there is an emphasis on harmony and compromise between the natives and later settlers of Nunavut. Education and training are creating a workforce representative of the population. Local aboriginal arts and crafts are highly regarded and have provided a good income for many years, but now the Inuit are able to enter all sectors of employment.

Nunavut boasts only 21 lonely kilometres of roads, from Nanisivik to Arctic Bay. Small plane services and bush pilots are your main connections.

National Parks: Auyuittuq, Quttinirpaaq, Sirmilik. _www.pc.gc.ca._

IQALUIT. Canada's northernmost capital (previously known as Frobisher Bay), is by far the largest community in Nunavut with about 6,500 residents, located amid rugged tundra landscapes on the southern coast of Baffin Island, with Nunavut's best airport, opened in WWII (and also a back-up landing site for NASA's Space Shuttle). Other travellers include a Baffin Island caribou herd that sometimes comes through town, which is close to the herd's migration route. Near here, by boat, dog team or snowmobile, is the historic Thule site at nearby **Qaummaarviit**.

In Iqaluit, **St. Jude's Cathedral** was hand-built in the shape of an igloo with pulpit and altar rails shaped like a qamutik (sled) and cross of two mounted narwhal tusks. The **Nunavut Legislative Assembly Building** has carvings, paintings and tapestries, including a diamond-tipped sceptre carved from a 7-foot long narwhal tusk. In town, there's the **Nunavut Arts and Crafts Centre and** the **Nunatta Sunakkutaangit Museum.** The local **Unikkaarvik Visitors Centre**, 979-4636, gives information on day hikes and local wildlife and displays the so-called 'David of the North,' a life-sized stone carving of an Inuit drum dancer. 979-5617/979-0386. _www.city.iqaluit.nu.ca._

Elsewhere in Nunavut: If you have the inclination and means to make the trip, Nunavut's diverse geography will help you commune with nature in ways you'll probably never forget: ice, mountain and big wall rock climbs (**Mts Thor** and **Asgard**), challenging hikes (**Akshayuk Pass** and **Sirmilik National Park**), kite-skiing, canoeing and rafting sub-arctic rivers (**Coppermine, Hood, Thelon, Soper,** and **Kazan**) kayaking icy oceans, bird watching, viewing arctic flora – long summer days and hardy wildlife. Getting there is an adventure in itself.

The first place to contact before any visit is _www.nunavutparks.com_ which has details of regional parks and the ten Visitors Centres in Nunavut. For national parks, before going, check with the National Parks of Canada office in Iqaluit, 975-4643, _www.pc.gc.ca._

For the more adventurous, **Auyuittuq National Park**, 473-8828/2500, is nearest to the Inuit settlement of **Pangnirtung** on Baffin Island, and is renowned for its spectacular fjords, active glaciers including the massive Penny Ice Cap, mountains and archaeological sites. It is possible to arrive either by boat or snowmobile from **Broughton Island** and Pangnirtung, after flights from Iqaluit. You must register your entry at one of the parks visitor's office, and park entry costs $15 p/day, $40 for 3 nights or $100 for an annual pass. _www.pc.gc.ca/pn-np/nu/auyuittuq._

Even less accessible is the remote northern park of **Ellesmere Island - Quttinirpaaq National Park**, 975-4643 /473-8828. This is the site of deep glacial valleys and mountains and remnants of the last glaciation that covered most of North America ten thousand years ago. The Park has no trees, and no darkness in summer. Several nunataks (peaks protruding through the icecap) are over 2,500 m above sea level. Again you must register for this park and the same fees apply as at Auyuittuq Park. (866) 686-2888. _www.nunavuttourism.com._

Accommodation

Inns North is a chain run by the native people, with 20 locations throughout Nunavut and the Northwest Territories, including as far north as Pond Inlet and Resolute Bay. (888) 866-6784. _www.innsnorth.com._

Iqaluit - Crazy Caribou B&B, House #490 (Happy Valley), 979-2449, (866) 341-4441. Five guest rooms, sauna, whirlpool. Deck with BBQ, view of Koojesse Inlet, Frobisher Bay. Continental b'fast. $120 per night per person (inc GST), add person in room $20/person (includes GST). Free shuttle to/from airport. _www.leelieenterprises.ca._

Qikiqtarjuaq, 'Iceberg Capital of Nunavut', near **Auyuittuq National Park - Leelie Lodge**. (866) 341-4441. $100 per night, meals ranging from $15-$45 for breakfast, lunch or dinner. _www.leelieenterprises.ca._

Tour Operators

This is an area where a specialised tour company might be a good idea, although they are expensive! There are over forty tour operators and outfitters listed by

Nunavut Tourism, with activities ranging from arctic kayaking to Nordic trekking to wildlife photography. From Kimminit, south of Iqaluit, **Mayukalik HTO**, 939-2355, has a range of half and fall-day. For tours and accommodation in Auyuittuq National Park, Qikiqtarjuaq, **Leelie Enterprises**, 927-8002, (866) 341-4441, offers eco-adventure cultural and wildlife tours at $250/person/day+ GST, inc meals. *www.leelieenterprises.ca*

Getting there and back
Passenger transport to Nunavut is by air. Direct Scheduled Flights to Iqaluit, Rankin Bay Inlet and Cambridge Bay are available from, Quebec, Montreal, Ottawa, Winnipeg, and Edmonton (via Yellowknife). A direct jet flight from Ottawa to Iqaluit takes just under three hours. Carriers include: Ontario-based **First Air**, (867) 979-8302 (Iqaluit), (613) 839-3340 (Montreal), (800) 267-1247 *www.firstair.ca*; Indian-owned **Canadian North**, (800) 661-1505, *www.cdn-north.com* , **Calm Air**, (204) 778-6471/(800) 839-2256, *www.calmair.com*; and Winnipeg-based **Kivalliq Air**. (204) 888-5619, (877) 855-1500. *www.kivalliqair.com*.

Flights Within Nunavut Travel between communities is mostly by air: **First Air** has secheduled services to most communities in Nunavut; **Calm Air** and **Kivalliq Air** service Hudson's Bay destinations. Iqaluit-based **Air Nunavut**, 979-4018, provides charter services. *http://inuit.pail.ca/air-nunavut.htm.*

NORTHWEST TERRITORIES

The Northwest Territories (NWT) take in an area of 1.2 million sq ms, larger than France and Spain combined, and is a vast, mostly unexplored, lonesome wilderness. Its sparse population of 42,000, about half of whom are aboriginal, is scattered in 32 communities located on historic fur trade routes, the Mackenzie, Liard and Coppermine Rivers, and along the Arctic coast. About half the population—20,000 people—make their home in lively **Yellowknife**, the 'Diamond Capital,' that is slowly being transformed by the rising economic fortunes of the NWT.

The Territories are not, however, entirely perpetual ice and snow. Although half the mainland and all the islands lie within the Arctic zone, the land varies from flat, forested valleys to never-melting ice peaks; from blossom-packed meadows to steep, bleak cliffs, and from warm, sandy shores to frigid, glacial banks. Temperatures range from highs of 35°C in summer to minus 45°C in winter.

In Canada's political system, the NWT is technically in the 'federal electoral riding of Western Arctic', with one MP and one Senator. It's one of two jurisdictions in Canada operating under a consensus system of government rather than party politics: all members of the NWT Legislative Assembly in Yellowknife are elected as independents in their constituencies, then elect the Speaker of the Assembly by secret ballot. The legislative building features Canada's only round assembly chamber, shaped like a traditional snowhouse, symbolic of NW's style of government. *www.assembly.gov.nt.ca.*

In this region, such was the pre-eminence of the fur trade – including bear, beaver, deer, elk, fisher, fox, lynx, marten, muskrat, otter, wolf, and wolverine, that for 150 years, beaver skins were literally the local currency With the more recent discoveries of diamonds, rich mineral deposits and exploitation of oil and gas fields, life in the NWT is starting to change, and will continue to do so.

National Parks: Aulavik, Nahanni, Tuktut Nogait, Wood Buffalo.

YELLOWKNIFE. Less than 500 kilometres from the Arctic Circle on Great Slave Lake, Yellowknife takes its name from the Copper Indians – or Yellowknives – who used copper blades for hunting; the lake is named after the local Slave Indians. If you fancy a two-day drive or 23-hour trip by Greyhound from Edmonton, Yellowknife is one of the best spots in the world for viewing the **Aurora Borealis** (Northern Lights) November through April, with Aurora tours available by dog sled along the frozen shores of Slave Lake. Summers in Yellowknife are the sunniest in Canada and this is the most festive city in the region (eg. the **Raven Mad Daze** at the summer solstice in June), crowned with wide, blue, everlasting skies. _www.northernfrontier.com_, _www.looknorth.ca_ and _www.yellowknife.ca_.

Until the mid 1990s, it was said the gold in Yellowknife was paved with streets, with mining tunnels running literally under city roadways. With the gold now mostly gone, diamonds have injected new life, money and zest into the region. At **Ekati,** 300 kilometres north east of the city, North America's first diamond mine began production in 1998, yielding about 7 million carats in 2003 alone. Its life expectancy is at least 25 years. More diamonds have been discovered in nearby **Lac de Gras.**

Yellowknife, where all Ekati's diamonds are sorted and valued prior to shipment, is now assuredly and fondly known as the Diamond Capital of North America, along with all the accoutrements of the role, as noted by Clifford Krauss in the _New York Times_ in 2005: 'Yellowknife restaurants have the longest and most expensive wine lists in the Arctic.'

The one resource Yellowknifers can depend on, however, notes Krauss, is the town's garbage dump, where almost anything can be found, from electric guitars to outboard motors, left by transients unwilling to pay expensive shipping costs. So well-known is the dump in Canada's media (the local paper has a weekly column about it) and so much part of local life, that when the city began levying dumping fees in mid-2005, one of the townsfolk told Krauss: 'I say, if they close this down to the public, what's the reason to live here anymore?'

Although you won't find any kryptonite here, the town is also the hometown of Margot Kidder, daughter of a mining engineer, famous for playing the role of Lois Lane in the _Superman_ movies. You can even take a stroll down '**Lois Lane**' in Old Town, named in honor of Kidder.

Accommodation, Food, Transit, Information

Since this is the most highly developed region in the Territory and the hub for travel to remoter areas, it is also quite expensive. Discover North has B&B, hotels, and other **accommodation** listings at _www.northernfrontier.com._

Information - Northern Frontier Visitor's Centre, #4 4807-49th St. Downtown Yellowknife. Maps and other useful information. Summer 8:30am–6pm Mon-Sun, Winter 8:30am – 5:30pm Mon-Fri. Noon to 4pm Sat, Sun, Holidays. Also at Yellowknife Airport: 8:30am-5:30pm. Mon-Fri. 873-4262, (877) 881-4262. _www.northernfrontier.com._ Tourist information is also available from **Northwest Arctic Tourism,** 4916 47th St, 873-7200/(800) 661-0788. _www.explorenwt.com._

Bus. There are three routes in the **Yellowknife Transit** system run by **Cardinal Coach**, 873-4693, one of which (#1) goes to the airport every half hour. 6:30am-7:30pm, Mon- Fri. $2.50/students $1.50.

Internet. Yellowknife Public Library, Centre Square Mall (49th St at 49th Ave) has free internet and WiFi availability. PC reservations recommended at 920-5642.

Of Interest
Bush Pilot's Monument. Top of the Rock in Old Town, 360 degree view, six stories up, good place to see the fall and winter aurora.
Diavik Diamond Display, 5007 50th Avenue, 669-6500. Diavik's downtown office has interesting displays of the search for diamonds and development of diamond mines in the treeless tundra far to the north of the city. _www.diavik.ca._
Frame Lake Walking Trail. 9 km. Skirts picturesque Frame Lake for walking and biking, with interpretive plaques.
Old Town and Wildcat Café. Native crafts, smoked Arctic char, water views, original town buildings, bush planes on floats…Wildcat Café's log-cabin has old-time ambiance, with pilots and musicians dropping in for dinner or jamming.
Prince of Wales Northern Heritage Centre, 873-7551. Summer: June-Aug. Daily:10:30am-5:30pm _www.pwnhc.ca._
Snow King Winter Festival. Early March for 30 days at Snow King's Castle near Old Town on Great Slave Lake. Many events including snow and ice carving, Royal Ball with Old Time Fiddle Dance and Aurora Photography Workshop.
Midnight Golf Classic. Mid-June. Yellowknife Golf Club two-day annual event. 873-4326. First flight is at 6pm; includes midnight buffet. Then contend with thieving ravens, sand fairways and astroturf greens. _www.ykgolf.com._
Celebrate Canada! Ten days in late June including: **Raven Mad Daze** Four days end-June: With 24 sunlit hours, Yellowknifers go raven mad: street sales on Franklin Avenue, live bands, and plenty of finger food till well past midnight. Just when you think the sun has disappeared, it pops up again and its time to go boating… _www.solsticefestival.ca._

Other places worth visiting in NWT. The Territories are a place of vast natural beauty, with half a million square miles of unspoilt wilderness, wild rivers, mountain forests and sweeping tundra in which you can bike, canoe, hike, kayak, raft and swim, or just spot birds and animals.

Fort Smith, just across from the Albertan frontier and once the territorial capital, is a sprawling mixture of shacks, log cabins and modern, government-built establishments. The Hudson's's Bay Company established a trading post here in 1874, and the town later became a stopping place for gold-seekers on their way to the Yukon. _www.town.fort-smith.nt.ca._ The **Northern Life Museum**, 110 King St, 872-2859, relates the human history of the area, has over 10,000 artifacts, including a collection of dinosaur bones and mammoth tusks. Daily 1-5pm, free. _http://collections.ic.gc.ca/canoe/aboutnlm.htm._

Fort Smith is also the headquarters of **Wood Buffalo**, 872-7960, Canada's largest National Park and the second-largest national park in the world, established to protect the world's largest free roaming herd of bison and the summer nesting grounds of the rare whooping crane. The Park is boreal forest with streams, lakes and towering cliffs, perfect for hiking, cross-country skiing or snow-shoeing. Salt plains here are unique remains of a long-gone ocean. It's a UNESCO World Heritage Site. _www.pc.gc.ca/pn-np/nt/woodbuffalo._

Between Fort Smith and Fort Fitzgerald are the renowned 25 km **Slave River Rapids** – the Rapids of the Drowned, Mountain Rapids, Pelican Rapids and Class VI Cassette Rapids, each also accessible by trails as well as by kayaking and white-watering. To the west, the **Mackenzie Highway** (Hwy 1) follows along Canada's longest river, where during the ice-free months, June to October, tugs and barges ply up and down, and hardy canoeists and trailer-boaters can join them for one of the loneliest, loveliest trips in the world.

Further west, **Nahanni National Park**, 695-3151, is north west of **Fort Simpson** up Hwy 7, the **Liard Trail**. This wilderness area of hot springs, waterfalls, canyons and river rapids was the first UNESCO World Heritage Site, in 1978. Here you will find 90 metres high **Virginia Falls,** more than twice the height of Niagara Falls, with a series of Class III rapids. The park is inaccessible by road; die-hards can hike into the park then canoe down the S Nahanni River, through one of the deepest river canyons in the world - up to 1,200 ms high. At 'The Gate', a narrow gap is flanked by a vertical wall 460 metres high. Unless you have a death wish, flightsee there by floatplane. _www.chrs.ca/Rivers/SouthNahanni/SouthNahanni-F e.htm._ Park excursion/camping fee, $10 daily. The **National Park Visitor Centre** in **Fort Simpson**, 695-3151 features extensive displays on the history, culture and geography of the area. _www.pc.gc.ca/pn-np/nt/nahanni._ Air connections are available from various points, including Fort Simpson, _www.fortsimpson.com._

To the north, up the Mackenzie Hwy, to **Norman Wells**, the 372 km **Canol H**To the far north is **Inuvik** (pop 3,500), supplied by local natural gas from Ikhil and reachable via the **Dempster Hwy** from near Dawson City in the Yukon, from where you can go even further north, to **Tuktoyaktuk (Tuk)** to dip toes in the Arctic Ocean and see beluga and bowhead whales. The **Mackenzie Gas Project** plans a $7 billion, 1,220 km, 30 inch diameter natural gas pipeline from three points in the delta (Taglu, Parsons Lake, and Niglintgak) north of Inuvik that will go south east down the river via Norman Wells and Fort Simpson, to north west Alberta. Construction of the pipeline, that could move 1.2 billion cu m/day, its gathering system in the delta, and a separate gas liquids pipeline, will revitalize the Inuvik area. _www.mackenziegasproject.com._

On the way up from the Yukon, the **Dempster Highway** engineering feat traverses the Continental Divide three times, Canada's only road going above the Arctic Circle (at the 66th parallel, where there's a marker you can be photographed at). From Inuvik, outfitters can arrange bird watching, boat tours, cross-country ski-ing, hiking, rafting, and flight-seeing of various kinds. In December and January there is 24 hour darkness in this remote Inuit region, compensated by the spectacular Aurora Borealis, when temperatures can drop to minus 45C. There is a Sunrise Festival in Inuvik when the sun returns. The **Western Arctic Regional Visitor Centre** on Mackenzie Road as you enter town, open June-Sept, 777-4727, issues Arctic Circle Certificates. **Air North, First Air and NorthWright Airways** service Inuvik (see below). For hotels, B&Bs, tour operators, and events, check _www.inuvik.ca_, **Parks Canada Visitor's Centre,** 580-3233.

Getting there and back. By **road you have three options: From Alberta** - the nearest major Canadian city to southern NWT is Edmonton, Alberta, about 1,100 kilometres to Enterprise (about 13 hours or so) and 1,500 kilometres to Yellowknife. The **Mackenzie Highway** (Hwy 1) starts at the Alberta boundary, then saunters north and west to Ft Simpson, Norman Wells and Ft Good Hope. **From British Columbia**, you can take the **Alaska Highway** and turn off north on Hwy 77 to Fort

Liard, just over the NWT border. From Dawson Creek, it's about 10 hours to Ft Liard. **From the Yukon,** there is a third, remoter option, via the 734 km **Dempster Highway,** about 14 hours from Dawson City to Inuvik.

Greyhound. Buses from Edmonton, Alberta leave several times a week for Hays River (LE Holdings, 16 – 102nd St, 874-6966) and Yellowknife (13 Kamlake Rd, 873-4892), with two transfers. Within NWT, Greyhound has limited services to Enterprise, Ft Liard, Ft Providence, Ft Simpson, Ft Smith, and Rae. *www.greyhound.ca.*

By air. Flights by smaller airlines depart regularly from Ottawa to Yellowknife, and Calgary and Edmonton to Hay River, Inuvik, Norman Wells, and Yellowknife, via Indian-owned **Canadian North** (800) 661-1505, 669-4010 (HQ Yellowknife) *www.canadiannorth.com;* from Edmonton, Whitehorse, and Winnipeg to Yellowknife, via Ontario-based **First Air** (which also has connections within NWT to Hay River, Inuvik, and Ft Simpson, and to numerous destinations in Nunavut) (800) 267-1247 *www.firstair.ca;* from Edmonton and Grande Prairie in Alberta to Yellowknife, via Ft Smith, by **Northwestern Air,** based in Ft Smith (877) 872-2216 *www.nwal.ca;* and from Dawson City and Whitehorse to Inuvik via **Air North** (Yukon's airline) 668-2228, (800) 661-0407 *www.flyairnorth.com.* Always check on dates and times of schedules. **Yellowknife Airport (YZF/CYZF)** is 5 km from town reached by Yellowknife Transit every half hour, Rte 1. 873-4680.

Within NWT. Once in Yellowknife, scheduled flights are available to and within the remoter parts of the NWT, Nunavut and the Arctic lands via **NorthWright Airways** based in Norman Wells, 587-2333 *www.north-wrightairways.com;* and via Yellowknife-based **Air Tindi,** 669-8260, (888) 545-6794 *www.airtindi.com.*

THE YUKON TERRITORY

The Yukon Territory boasts Canada's highest peak, **Mt Logan** (5,959 m), over 200 species of birds and wildflowers, five times more caribou than people, the largest cluster of grizzly bears in Canada and as romantic a history as you could find anywhere. Its past and future are tied to Asia, from the Beringia land bridge, crossed by people from Siberia before the last Ice Age, to today's talk of an Alaska-Canada rail link that would transport minerals and coal from the Yukon to China.

Fur-trading brought the Hudson's Bay Company (HBC) into the Yukon in the mid-1800s but it was the **Klondike Gold Rush** of 1898 that really put the area on the map (and led to its creation as a territory that year). Armed with hope, thirty thousand gold-seekers climbed the forbidding **Chilkoot** and **White Passes** and pressed on down the Yukon River north to **Dawson City.** The **White Pass and Yukon** railway was built over the top from Skagway to Whitehorse by 1900 and dozens of paddle-wheeler steamboats soon plied their trade on Yukon's rivers. In two years Dawson City, at the junction of the Klondike and Yukon Rivers, grew from a tiny hamlet to a settlement of 40,000 and became known as the Paris of the North.

It's still very much the Wild West in the Yukon, where, as someone told the *New York Times* in 2005, 'you check your past at the door.' According to the *Times,* no less than the premier of the Yukon, Dennis Fentie, elected in 2002, served 17 months in a federal penitentiary.

If you're planning to visit the Yukon and want to relive the atmosphere of the Klondike days, try reading aloud the mesmerizing verses of **Robert Service** in *The Spell of the Yukon* and *Ballads of a Cheechako.* Especially recommended are *The Shooting of Dan McGrew* and *The Cremation of Sam McGee*. Just who was that lady who pinched Dan's poke in the Malamute saloon? *www.robertwservice.com.*

Following the Gold Rush, the Yukon settled back into its trapping days, once again becoming a remote spot on a map in northwestern Canada – even though its size is greater than that of Texas. Then, when the Japanese occupied the Aleutian Islands in WWII, another rush to the Yukon was on: army engineers built the **Alaska Highway** as a troop route in 1942, the 2,400 kilometre road beginning at Dawson Creek, BC, and winding its way via Yukon's capital of **Whitehorse** to Fairbanks. At **Watson Lake,** contribute to the famous **Sign Post Forest**, over 10,000 signs welcoming you to the Yukon, started in 1942 by a homesick GI.

About a quarter of Yukon's 30,000 current population are aboriginals of 14 Nations whose existence dates back tens of thousands of years, including the Aishihik, Champagne Gwich'in, Han, Kaska, Kluane, Tagish, Tanana, Tlingit, Tutchone, and Vuntut. Tools and bones from twenty centuries ago have been found in caves in the north of the Territory.

Today, there's not much gold found in the Yukon anymore, mineral production has fallen, and timber production is down too, but fur remains important and natural gas is growing in significance. The proposed **Alaska-Canada Rail Link** that could carry Yukon's mineral and coal exports to Asia will, if it comes to pass, have a profound effect on the Yukon economy.

For a comprehensive guide to the many canoeing, hiking, kayaking, rafting, ski-ing, sledding, trekking, and other outdoor opportunities in the Yukon, check *www.yukonadventure.com* and *www.yukonwild.com.*
National Parks: Kluane, Ivvavik and Vuntut. *www.pc.gc.ca.*

WHITEHORSE Sixty percent of the Yukon's population lives in **Whitehorse,** about 23,000, which makes it the largest place north of the 60th Parallel. Born of the Gold Rush in 1898, it's now the leading shipping, transportation, tourism and mining centre of the region. It sits close to the Alaska Hwy, has the Territory's main airport and provides access to the White Pass and Yukon railway from Skagway. Whitehorse is also the headquarters of the **Territory Mounties – the RCMP**. One part of its past is preserved at the **Frantic Follies**, 2nd Ave & Wood St, 668-2042, a turn of the century vaudeville revue, May-Sept, $20 (37 years old in 2006). *www.franticfollies.com.* There's plenty to do and see in Whitehorse. *www.visitwhitehorse.com.*

Accommodation
Beez Kneez Bakpakers, 408 Hoge, downtown, 456-2333. Free high speed internet. Wi-fi. Free bicycles. Deck to bask in 24 hr sunlight. $20 pp. Year-round. *www.bzkneez.com.*
Hostel Hide, 410 Jeckell, downtown, 633-4933. 6 hostel rooms. Wi-fi, outdoor Jacuzzi. $2 off first night if you give family recipe. $20 pp. *www.hide-on-jeckell.com.*
Yukon Inn, 4220 4th Ave, 667-2527/ (800) 681-0454. 95 rooms. Cable TV, restaurant. S/D-$89-$99 in summer.Year-round. *www.yukoninn.com.*
98 Hotel, 110 Wood St, 667-2641. $35-50. 16 units (w/out private bath). $10 refundable key deposit. Basic, clean rooms. 24 hr, rsvs advisable.
Robert Service Campground, 1 km from town on South Access Rd, 120 Robert Service Way, 668-3721. Beside Yukon River and **Millennium Trail** (from **Miles Canyon** to town, then to **Grey Mountains**). Mostly walk-in sites: $14, $2 all-you-

can-burn firewood. Hot showers and plumbing, café on site: coffee and baked goods. 15 min walk from downtown.

Of Interest
Yukon Beringia Interpretive Centre. Km 1473 on the Alaska Hwy, S of airport. 667-8855. Interactive presentation on the land bridge between Siberia and North America that was part of huge area called Beringia, across which native peoples migrated. Daily June-Aug 8.30am-7pm, May & Sep 9am-6pm. $6/$4 w/student ID. *www.beringia.com.*

SS Klondike II **Sternwheeler** National Historic Site. 300 Main St, (800) 661-0486. With the Gold Rush, the upper Yukon River became the major riverboat route into the interior: Altogether 250 sternwheelers were built to ply the river and its tributaries between 1866 and 1936. From 1937 to 1952, the *SS Klondike II,* with general merchandise and passengers, could make the downstream run from Whitehorse to Dawson, 741 kilometres, in about 36 hours. Dry-docked on W bank of river, downtown Whitehorse. $5. May to mid-Sept. *www.pc.gc.ca/lhn-nhs/yt/ssklondike.*

WD McBride Museum, 1st Ave and Wood St, 667-2709, Gold Rush, native and Indian mementoes including Sam McGee's actual cabin, steam locomotive, sleigh wagon, guns, geology, natural history and Mounted Police exhibits, plus gold panning, and daily audio-visual and live presentations on Yukon history. May-Sep Mon-Fri 10am-9pm, Sat-Sun 10am-7pm, $5, $4 w/student ID. Limited hours winter. *www.macbridemuseum.com.*

Also Of Interest: Old Log Church Museum, 668-2555. Hear about the bishop who ate his boots. **Miles Canyon/Canyon City,** 9 km from town, where stampeders lived in 1898. **Takhini Hot Springs,** 633-2706, 30 km N of town. *www.takhinihot-springs.yk.ca.* **Waterfront Trolley,** daily in summer, from Visitor Centre and Whitehorse Station, 667-8401, operated by Miles Canyon Historic Railway Society, 1093 First Avenue, 667-6355, which also operates the **Copper Belt Railway.** *www.yukonalaska.com/railway* **Yukon Brewing Company,** 102a Copper Road, 668-4183, since 1997, free tour and samples – the only brewery north of the 60th. *www.yukonbeer.com* **Yukon Transportation Museum,** 668-4792, on Alaska Hwy near Airport. *www.yukontransportmuseum.homestead.com.*

Yukon River Quest Canoe and Kayak Race, 668-4630/ 333-5628, at end-July, is the longest canoe and kayak paddling marathon in the world, from Whitehorse to Dawson City, some 700 km in 3-5 days under the midnight sun, launched with a Le Mans-style run to boats from Main Street in Whitehorse. *www.yukonriverquest.com.*

Yukon River Bathtub Race, 668-3662, in mid-August, is also some race: the longest & toughest bath-tub race in the world for high-tech tubs, on the Yukon River, also from Whitehorse north to Dawson City in 13-16 hours , arriving in the middle of Dawson City's Discovery days Festival. *www.tubrace.com.*

Klondyke Harvest Fair, 668-6864, 2-days late August, huge country fair of everything grown and crafted in the Yukon. *www.yukonaa.com.*

In February 2007, the **Canada Winter Games** will be held for the first time ever in Canada's North, in Whitehorse. *www.city.whitehorse.yk.ca.*

Information/Internet/Bus
Visitor Centre, 100 Hanson St, 667 3084. *www.yukoninfo.com.*

Internet Access; Whitehorse Public Library, 2nd Avenue, open daily, next to the Yukon Government administration building. 667-5239, and all fourteen libraries in Yukon. *www.community.gov.yk.ca/libraries*

Transit. Within Whitehorse, bus fares are $2.

Getting there and back
You can fly directly to **Whitehorse** from Edmonton/Calgary, Frankfurt, Alaska, and Vancouver, drive (or take the bus) to Whitehorse for several days from British

Columbia and Alberta, or else travel by BC Ferries/Alaska Marine Highway or cruise ships to **Skagway**, Alaska, and from there drive 3 hours to Whitehorse.
Road. From Edmonton, it's 2,012 kilometres by road to Whitehorse, from Calgary 2,310 kilometres, and from Vancouver 2,675 kilometres. From Prince George in BC, the driving time is about 19 hours to Watson Lake, either via Dawson Creek or Kitwanga.
Greyhound Canada, (800) 661-8747 services Whitehorse (18078 Yukon Ltd., 2191 2nd Ave, 667-2223) from Dawson Creek in BC three days a week (Mon, Wed, Fri), *www.greyhound.ca.*
Air. There are daily flights by **Air Canada Jazz** from Vancouver to Whitehorse that take about two-and-a-half hours, non-stop. (888) 247-2262. *www.aircanada.com.* **Air North,** Yukon's airline, 668-2228, (800) 661-0407, flies from Calgary, Edmonton, Fairbanks, Juneau (in summer), Inuvik (NWT) and Vancouver to Whitehorse, *www.flyairnorth.com*. **First Air** has services to Ft Simpson and Yellowknife in the NWT, and thence on to Nunavut. *www.firstair.ca.* **Whitehorse Airport (YXY)** 667-8440, (800) 661-0408, is home of the world's largest weathervane—a DC3 aircraft that rotates on a pedestal. The famous plane belonged to the Yukon Airlines fleet from 1946 to 1970. **Whitehorse Transit** has services every 35-40 mins to the airport from downtown.
Rail. Skagway – Whitehorse. Built 1898-1900, the scenic **White Pass and Yukon** narrow gauge railway, now restored, brought prospectors from Skagway to Whitehorse and back via grades of up to 3.9 percent. Whitehorse Station, 667-8401. (907) 983-2217/(800) 343-7373. Excursions on the railway, which is an International Historic Civil Engineering Landmark, along with the Eiffel Tower and Statue of Liberty, start from Skagway. *www.wpyr.com.*

KLUANE NATIONAL PARK In the southwestern corner of the Yukon, 160 kilometres west of Whitehorse, is the mountainous **Kluane National Park**, 634-7250. The park has the world's largest non-polar ice field and Canada's highest peak, **Mt Logan** (5,959 ms), as well as a great variety of wildlife, including Canada's largest grizzly bear population. The rugged, snowy mountains of Kluane typify the storybook picture one has of the Yukon. But even though Canada's lowest ever recorded temperature of -63C was at Snag, just up the Alaska Hwy from here, Kluane is not a perpetual winter wonderland. Summers here are warm with almost total daylight during June and although winters are cold, they are generally no more so than in many Canadian provinces.

In summer, you can do the 1-day, 10 kilometres hike - the King's Throne Trail, climbing to a cirque and rock glacier with great lake and mountain views, then a steep main ridge to the summit. Beware high winds and mosquitoes! **Visitor Centres** with trail maps are at **Haines Junction**, open daily mid-May-mid-Sept. and **Tachal Dhal** (Sheep Mountain) in the Slim's River Valley, an hour's drive north of Haines Junction. *www.onedayhikes.com/Hikes.asp?HikesID=163.*

The **Alaska Hwy**, near the park's north east boundary, provides an easy way to view the eastern edge of the park and glimpse the spectacular peaks beyond. 'This is Big Country that beats Montana.' **Camping** is available within the park at **Kathleen Lake**, 27 kilometres south of Haines Junction off Haines Rd, call park, no rsvs. 39 sites. Good hiking and fishing area, $6 firewood. Open Jun-Sept 21st, sites $10. *www.parkscanada.gc.ca/kluane.*

If foraging for provisions doesn't appeal to you, you're in bread nirvana.

Located next to the visitor centre is **Haines Junction Village Bakery**, 634-2867, with 22 types of breads, pastries, pies, and cakes. Has salmon bake, local music series on Friday nights. Internet available.

DAWSON CITY   In **Dawson City**, 300 kilometres south of the Arctic Circle, some of the buildings hurriedly thrown up in 1898 still stand. At the height of the Gold Rush more than 40,000 people lived here, at the meeting point of the Yukon and Klondike Rivers. Gold dredging concluded in the 1960s, the population plummeted and is now just 1,200, capitalizing on the tourist trade with gold panning and an old time music hall - **Diamond Tooth Gerties Gambling Hall** is Canada's first casino: can-can girls, food and beverages in Klondike style. May-September, three shows nightly. $6 cover. There is an artist's colony here too. And at the **Downtown Hotel** you can try Sourtoe Cocktails, drinks mixed with human toes - actual toes that have been dehydrated and preserved in salt. 'You can drink it fast, you can drink it slow— But the lips have gotta touch the toe.' Then join the Sourtoe Cocktail Club! _www.sourtoecocktailclub.com_.

Accommodation
Dawson City River Hostel, 993-6823, across the river from town, just go left off the free ferry. Mid-May-Sept. HI affiliated hostel, with dorm, $16 members, $20 non, private rooms, S/D-$41 and a tent sites, $13 for 1, $8.50 each over 1 person. All have free use of the kitchen and bathroom facilities. Wood-fired sauna. Tours available, of Arctic Circle, etc. _www.yukonhostels.com_.
Dawson City Bunkhouse, Front and Princess St, 993-6164. 32 shared rooms. Built in 2000 as an authentic wood sturn of the century style. Central location, ave. $83, with shared shower and bath.
Yukon River Campground W Dawson, nr ferry landing, May-Sep. Camp sites $7.
Gold Rush Campground, 5th Ave and York St, 993-5247, (866) 330-5006. In centre of city. 83 campsites. Showers, laundromat, TV, store. Sites $19, $31.50-$38.50 w/hook-up. May-Sep. _www.goldrushcampground.com_.

Of interest/Information
Dänojà Zho Cultural Centre, 993-6768/5385, celebrates traditional and contemporary experience of the Tr'ondëk Hwëch'in. **Hammerstone Gallery** displays archaeological artifacts, reproductions of tools, costumes, and life sized photographs. Daily May-Sept. _www.trondek.com_.
Dawson Historic Complex, 5th Ave and Church St, 993 7200/993-7237. Consists of many buildings within the townsite of Dawson City, including the Yukon's first museum, built in 1901, **Dawson City Museum.** Daily, 10am-6pm, May- Labor Day; by appointment in winter. $5.
Jack London Cabin, 8th Ave, 993-5575. Photos, documents, newspaper articles and other London memorabilia. Relocation of the Cabin from 120 kilometres S of Dawson City was subject of award-winning documentary. Daily. May-Sept. $2.
Getting There. The drive from Whitehorse is about 6 hours; **Air North**, 668-2228, (800) 661-0407, flies to Dawson City from Whitehorse in 1 hr 10 mins. **Alkan Air** 993-5440/ 668 2107, also has services. _www.alkanair.com_. **Airport (YDA)** is about 20 kilometres SE of town on Klondike Hwy.
Visitors Centre, Front and King Sts, 993-5566. 8am-8pm May-Sep. _www.yukoninfo.com_.
Internet access free at community library in Robert Service School, 993-5571.

3. Mexico

BACKGROUND - MEXICO

This guide is intended primarily for 'on the road' travel in North America and so this chapter concentrates on selected areas of Mexico deemed likely to be of greatest interest for visitors primarily spending time in the USA and Canada. For longer stays, further reading is recommended and necessary, but for a brief visit this chapter gives you valuable general background information and highlights selected areas to visit from the USA.

Before you go

Mexico is anxious to keep formalities to a minimum for tourists. Anyone content with a visit of three days or less to a border town, or to within 20 to 30 miles of the border with the US, need only present a passport.

For trips further afield, a tourist card (FM-T) is needed and costs approximately $25. If you try to leave the border area without one, you may be stopped and sent back at customs posts 20 miles into Mexico. Cards are issued by Mexican embassies, consulates and tourist offices, by certain travel agencies and at the border itself. If you are flying in, the fee for the tourist card is generally included. All you need is a valid passport, or for US and Canadian nationals, other proof of citizenship. Travellers under 18 also require an authorization signed by both parents and witnessed by a Commissioner for Oaths or Notary Public. The tourist card suffices for citizens of the UK, most other European countries, the US and Canada, but nationals of Australia and New Zealand are required to obtain full visas. Those in doubt should refer to the nearest Mexican consulate. At the port of entry, both card and passport must be shown, together with a cholera certificate if you have been in an infected area during the preceding five days. No other vaccinations are required, but vaccinations for Hepatitis B and tetanus are recommended.

European visitors receive a card valid for 90 days from the date of entry. US citizens are given 180 days, but in both cases *Migración* officials can vary the duration at whim, often stamping the card with a 30 day limit, as well as charging for the privilege on occasion. The card must be used to enter Mexico within 90 days of the issuing date. So if planning to spend several months in the US first you should obtain the card there at the end of your stay, rather than from the home country. There are Mexican Consulates in most major US cities and border towns.

If you are likely to need an extension, request a longer validation when first applying; doing it within Mexico is time-consuming and may involve a trip back to the border to get a new card. In Mexico City you can try your luck at the **Visa Renewal Office**, located at Ave. Ejército Nacional # 862, Colonia Polanco, Mexico, City, (55) 2581-0118. Open Mon-Fri. 9am-1:30pm. Be prepared for a long wait. The card is issued in duplicate: one part is taken from you on entry, the other as you leave. Once in Mexico you are obliged by law to carry it with you at all times, and you can be fined quite heavily for overstaying the expiry date, particularly if you have a car.

If you are on an Exchange Program visa, do not let US officials take your DS-2019, or any other visa documentation when you cross into Mexico. You need it to get back into the US! In London, the Mexican Embassy is at: 42 Hertford Street, Mayfair, W1Y 7TF, 0870 162 0853. Fax (020) 7495-4035. You can visit their website at *www.embamex.co.uk*. In the US the Mexican Embassy is at 1911 Pennsylvania Ave NW, Washington DC 20006, (202) 728-1600. You can visit their website at *www.embassyofmexico.org/english*.

Getting there

Most travellers (and probably the overwhelming majority using this guide) will be visiting Mexico via the US. Major American, Mexican or international carriers fly from Los Angeles, Chicago, New York, Miami, San Antonio and other US and Canadian cities to Mexico City and elsewhere in Mexico. British Airways fly direct from London to Mexico City but it may be cheaper to fly to the US and shop around there for a flight to Mexico, rather than fly direct from Europe.

Trips originating from major US cities to Mexico City cost around $550 but you may be able to find better fares if you do some research. For brief round-trips from the US, it is also worth checking with the various airline websites and major US booking engines as they all offer competitive on-line only fares. Students under 26 can often get big discounts if booking their tickets with student travel organisations like STA Travel, *www.statravel.com*.

Majors carriers flying to Mexico include Aeromexico (*www.aeromexico.com*), American (*www.aa.com*), America West (*www.americawest.com*), Continental (*www.continental.com*), Delta (*www.delta.com*), Mexicana (*www.mexicana.com*), and United (*www.united.com*). Major US booking engines include Expedia (*www.expedia.com*), Priceline (*www.priceline.com*), Orbitz (*www.orbitz.com*), and Travelocity (*www.travelocity.com*). There is a nominal departure tax on passengers leaving Mexico which is generally included in the ticket price.

There are 12 major, and a number of minor, crossing points along the US-Mexico border. The most important are **Tijuana** (12 miles south of San Diego), **Calexico-Mexicali**, **Nogales** (south of Tucson), **Douglas/Agua Prieta**, **El Paso/Ciudad Juárez**, **Eagle Pass/Piedras Negras**, **Laredo/Nuevo Laredo**, **Hidalgo/Reynosa** and **Brownsville/Matamoros**. If you have a car, the smaller border crossings (such as **Tecate**, 40 miles east of San Diego) are often less bureaucratic. Car travellers should avoid Tijuana, especially on weekends. There are generally long delays caused by extensive searches for drugs and aliens. El Paso/Ciudad Juárez border is often mentioned by readers as the easiest crossing. Matamoros is the crossing point closest to Mexico City (622 miles/996 kms); after you pass the border you will encounter further checkpoints.

Amtrak goes to the border at El Paso and Laredo from where you make your own arrangements by bus or plane.

Car rentals

Reservations for car rentals in Mexico can be made in the US with the major companies (Hertz, Avis, Budget, Dollar, Thrifty and National). The major international car-hire companies, plus of course many Mexican companies, have offices throughout the country. In theory all the companies in Mexico charge the same rates for any given car type, as rates are set by the Government, but shopping around, especially among smaller local companies, can often get you significant savings. You can also try to take advantage of special offers if you book the car via the major international car hire companies' websites. The official rates are based on time plus kilometres at inland towns and daily rates including 200 km/day on the coast. Be sure to check on extra costs for insurance, and to determine whether you are dealing in miles or kilometres. Car hire is not especially inexpensive in Mexico. Expect to pay at least around US$47-92 per day.

When you drive in Mexico you need to carry proof of Mexican auto liability insurance which is usually provided by the car rental company. An international driver's license should be used, available from AAA in the US and Canada or in the United Kingdom from the RAC or AA.

GENERAL INFORMATION

Geography and climate

Running from north to south, the two chains of the **Sierra Madre** dominate and dictate the country's geography and climate. The vast central plateau lies between the mountain ranges and drops to the **Rió Grande** valley in the north. Around the area of the capital, just south of the Tropic of Cancer, there is a further jumble of mountains, finally petering out in the narrow and comparatively flat Isthmus of **Tehuantepec**. From **Tijuana** in the northwest to **Mérida** in the **Yucatán**, Mexico stretches for 2750 miles.

Between the altitudes of 5,000 and 8,000 feet the climate is mild. The descent to sea level corresponds to an increase in temperature, so that the lowlands are very hot in summer as well as being very warm in winter. The Central Plateau, where **Mexico City** is located (altitude 7,350 feet), enjoys a pleasant, spring-like climate. It is warm and sunny throughout the year, although regular afternoon showers or storms can be expected from June to October, the rainy season.

In the deserts of northern Mexico and throughout **Baja California**, temperatures of over 100°F are to be expected during the summer months. It is similarly hot on the coast, although the sea breezes are cooling. But in the lush tropical jungle lands to the south of the Tropic of Cancer, humidity is high and the annual rainfall is nearly as great as anywhere else in the world. On the northern side of the Isthmus of **Tehuantepec**, rainfall reaches a staggering 10 feet a year. The large numbers of rivers and the frequency with which they become rushing, swollen torrents make the land impassable by permanent rail or road systems.

What to wear

Light clothing made of natural fibers (cotton, etc.) is recommended. Bring a jacket or something warmer for Mexico City and the Central Plateau's cool evenings, plus raingear for the rainy season. Shoes, rather than sandals, are a necessity for uneven streets and climbing up pyramids.

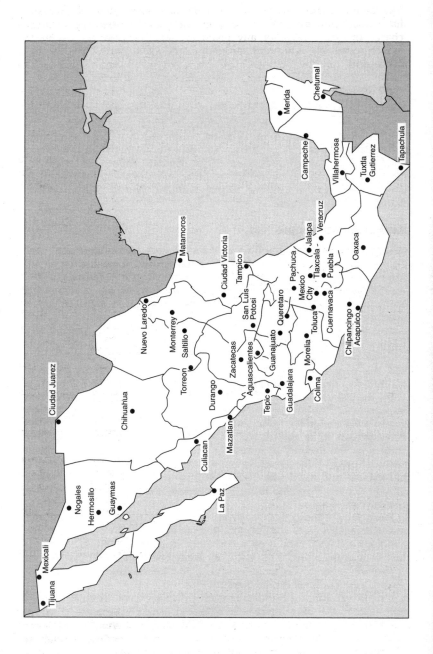

Lavenderías automáticas (laundromats) and **tintorerías** (dry cleaners) can be found in larger towns and cities. Many hotels also offer their own laundry service. In smaller places you'll have to rely on two stones and the washing powder you have remembered to pack, along with the spare plug for the sink.

Time zones

Virtually all of Mexico, from the Yucatán to the Pacific due west of Mexico City, falls within the zone corresponding to Central Standard Time in the US. The west coast from **Tepic** up to the border and including the southern half of Baja California, is an hour earlier, while the northern half of Baja is an hour earlier still and corresponds to Pacific Standard Time in the US. During the winter months the central and southern parts of Mexico are one hour later than the northern portion. During summer, they are two hours later than the northern portion.

Mexico and its people

Modern Mexico is the product of three distinct historical phases: pre-Columbian (or pre-Cortés) Indian, three centuries of Spanish colonial rule and since 1821, independent Mexican government. The Revolution of 1910 was followed by ten years of near-anarchy during which one in every eight Mexicans was killed, and although the peasants played a crucial role in overthrowing the corrupt aristocracy, in the end it was (and is) the middle classes who benefited from the uninterrupted tenure of the **Institutional Revolutionary Party** (PRI) for 71 years from 1929 to 2000. There is at present a higher percentage of landless peasants than when the Revolution began, and the poor live in overcrowded slums where illiteracy is common, malnutrition rampant and basic services often non-existent.

For the last ten years, however, there have been some indications of slow improvement. The country is not as desperately poor as it was and the new government under the leadership of President Vicente Fox and the **PAN Party** appears to be making real efforts to root out some of the social ills. Until now the benefits of industrial and agricultural development have been defeated by the explosive population growth. Although the area of harvestable land has doubled since 1940, the population has risen from 20 million to over 97 million in the same period, and half of them are under fifteen years of age.

Financially, Mexico is in a strong position in terms of external debt management. In early 2005, its total foreign debt was $79.6 billion, which, although still high, has been a considerable improvement, especially as Mexico was able to retire the last of its **Brady bonds** in 2003. In addition to comfortable foreign exchange coverage, Mexico continues to enjoy easy access to international capital markets.

Despite gestures of independence, Mexico keeps seeking foreign investment and to a great extent is economically dependent on its neighbours to the north. For ten years, **NAFTA**—the North American Free Trade Agreement—has given Mexican business direct access to the US and Canada, and vice versa. The relationship, however, remains epitomized by the ceaseless flow of undocumented immigrants across the US border, and by the remaining existence of *maquiladora* (in-bond manufacturing) industries on the Mexican side. This allows US companies to take advantage of cheap Mexican labour to produce products for sale in the USA.

Politics

At first glance, Mexican politics appears to be an alphabet soup of letters with the parties known as **PAN, PRD, PT, PVEM,** and of course, **PRI**. PRI is the Partido Revolucionario Institucional. The party is not very revolutionary but was certainly institutional since it was the most popular and largest party in Mexico and ruled the country from 1929 until 2000. PAN stands for Partido Accion Nacional and is a conservative-catholic coalition.

It still remains to be seen if Vicente Fox can stamp out the corruption and crime at high levels of Mexican political life while having to deal with continued unrest in the province of Chiapas, relationships with the USA and poor conditions at home.

Culture

Mexico is a fascinating and colourful country, physically and culturally, bridging the gap between America North and South. It is a feast of art and history, with more than 11,000 archaeological sites, temples, pyramids and palaces of bygone civilizations, and many museums that are generally regarded as being among the best in the world. (See box). Although Mexico City and resort towns like Acapulco have their share of tall buildings, expensive hotels and general North American glitter, rural Mexico is something else again and the whole pace of life visibly alters the moment you cross the border from the United States.

Three centuries of Spanish rule have left their mark not only on the lifestyle of the country but also on its appearance. The fusion of Spanish baroque with the intricate decorative style of the Indians produced the distinctive and dramatic style called Mexican Colonial. A number of towns rich in Mexican Colonial buildings are preserved as national monuments and new building is forbidden. The most important colonial towns are: **Guadalajara, León, Guanajuato, San Miguel de Allende, Morelia, Taxco, Cholula, Puebla, Mérida** and **San Luis Potosi**.

Despite its Spanish architectural and linguistic overtones, Mexico has a distinctly Indian soul: fatalistic, taciturn, reflective and strong on tradition and folklore. You will notice this most sharply in the villages, where it is easy to misinterpret the dignified shyness of the villagers as coldness. Various towns stand out as being Indian in character: **Querétaro** (where the Mexican constitution was drafted in 1917), **Pátzcuaro, Oaxaca, Tehuantepec** and **San Cristobal de las Casas**. Not to be missed are Indian market days and festivals. **Toluca**, an hour's drive from Mexico City, has an outstanding Indian market.

Money

The exchange rate with the US dollar is (at press time) about $1 to N$10.50. Due to its variable rate it is a good idea to check the latest exchange rates just before you travel. The prices given in this section use the above exchange rate.

Mexico uses the $ sign for the peso, unfortunately the same as the US dollar sign; where necessary the two are distinguished by the addition of the suffixes MN (Moneda Nacional) for pesos and US or 'dls' for dollars. Important note: all peso prices in this section are written as—pesos. US dollar prices are given as US$.

Shop around for the best exchange rates, especially in the large cities and resort areas. Generally the best rates can be obtained at the **casas de cambio** (money exchanges). Try to avoid the hotels for changing money if possible. Many larger stores and some market vendors will accept dollars but check carefully on the rates they are using.

Banks: Banking hours are 9am-4pm Monday-Friday and some larger banks will be open on Saturday. (The casas de cambio are usually open till around 5pm.) The larger banks (**Bánamex, Bancomer, Bital**) are the best for changing money if there are no casas de cambio around in the provinces. Major credit cards are accepted in most places but the cheaper hotels and restaurants may not take them. Don't take it for granted—always ask first.

Tipping and Tax: Ten-15 percent is the standard tip. Service charges are very rarely added to the bill when you receive it so they must be determined by the total before tax. Almost everything you have to buy or pay for, including hotels and restaurant food, has **IVA** (Impuesto al valor agregado)—value added tax—on it, which may be included or shown separately.

Health

Medical services are good and in Mexico City it's easy to find an English-speaking doctor. Fees are reasonable compared to the US, and some hospitals will examine you and give prescriptions free. Nevertheless, where a fee is likely, you should ask for a quote beforehand, and insurance is advisable. 'If you travel in the US before Mexico, you'll hear many ghastly tales of internal infections and uncontrollable bacteria, even though the water is so chlorinated that you're more likely to kill off your own bacteria than find any new ones.'

For the long-term traveller, acclimatization is the best policy, but it can take from three days to four weeks. If needed, you can stop **turista** spoiling a brief trip by using **Lomotil** (which delays the symptoms but will not remove the cause), or **Pepto-Bismol**, the antibiotic **Bactrim**, or **Kaomycin**. **Entero-Vioform** may still sometimes be on sale, despite being banned everywhere else. It makes you go blind.

If you have decided just to 'get used to it', then be cautious. Drink only bottled water. If you are not sure about the water, boil it for 30 minutes or use purification tablets. Be careful when buying food from street vendors: is the fat rancid? Beware of ice cream, salads, unpeeled fruit and vegetables washed in impure water. Eating plenty of garlic, onions and lime juice (which act as natural purifiers and preventatives) may help, but need to be taken in large quantities. **Té de Perro** (dog tea), fresh coconut juice and plain boiled white rice are the native Mexican recommendations.

Anti-malarial drugs are advisable in tropical and southern coastal areas—but as Mexico denies (perhaps rightly) that it has malaria, it's difficult to get any drugs for it there, so bring them with you. It wouldn't hurt to have inoculations against **yellow fever**, **cholera**, **typhoid** and **polio**, especially if you travel to coastal areas in the south. To protect yourself against **dengue fever** bring mosquito repellent and 'Afterbite' – it's worth it!

'It helps to warn people but hopefully they won't be frightened off.' It is recommended that you definitely travel with health insurance.

Language

The more alert among you will have guessed by now that it's Spanish, although in some areas Indian languages are still spoken—e.g. Mayan in the Yucatán. The point is, you should learn some Spanish, especially the words for numbers, food and directions. 'Well worth learning some Spanish if you can: don't expect too many Mexicans to know English.' Your efforts in Spanish will normally be encouraged and appreciated by the local people.

Public Holidays

Mexico's religious and political calendar supplies many excuses for public holidays. Expect everything to close down on the following dates:

January 1	**New Year's Day**	October 12	**Dia de la Raza**
February 5	**Constitution Day**	November 1**	**All Saints' Day**
March 21	**Juárez Birthday**	November 2	**All Souls' Day**
March-April*	**Holy Thursday**		(or Day of the Dead)
March-April*	**Good Friday**	November 20	**Revolution Day**
May 1	**Labor Day**	December 12**	**Our Lady of**
May 5	**Battle of Puebla Day**		**Guadalupe Day**
September 15**	**Declaration of**	December 24**	**Christmas Eve**
	Independence	December 25	**Christmas Day**
September 16	**Independence Day**	December 31**	**New Year's Eve**

* Date varies with year.   **Usually working half a day.

On top of these, every town has its own festival and fiesta days, with processions, fireworks, and dancing in the streets. Local tourist authorities will fill you in on the details.

Communications

Mail: Do not have mail sent **Lista de Correos** (Poste Restante) unless you are sure of being able to collect it within 10 days. After that time it is likely to be 'lost'. Letters or postcards to North America are a minimum of US$0.50; to Europe, US$0.65; to Australia and New Zealand, US$0.70. Important mail should be sent as registered mail from a post office and never put in an letter box. 'Send mail only from post offices—letter boxes not reliable.'

Chances are that packages sent in or out of the country will not make it to their destination via regular mail. You can use Mexico's most reliable express mail service, **MexPost**, located in post offices. International package services like **Fedex**, **UPS** or **DHL** are also available.

WEBSITES ABOUT MEXICO

www.visitmexico.com: Mexican Tourism Board official website.
www.mexicodesconocido.com.mx: information about Mexico's natural and cultural wealth.
www.maps-of-mexico.com: Maps of Mexico.
www.travel.yahoo.com: Yahoo's travel guide for Mexico. Click on the travel guides link and then click on the Mexico link.
www.expedia.com: Expedia's Mexican guide includes general information about Mexico as well as maps and accurate descriptions on accommodations throughout Mexico. Search for destinations/Country/Mexico.
www.isic.org: Student travel website. Search for the destinations links and then click on the Mexican travel guide link.
travel.roughguides.com : Complete travel guide of Mexico.
www.diegorivera.com: Official website about Diego Rivera, his wife Frieda Kahlo, and their works.
www.hostelmexico.com: Hostel network in Mexico.
www.mundojoven.com: Information about airfares, buses, hotels, tours, and student identification cards.

E-mail offers an easy alternative to calls or mail. Mexico is filled with cybercafes where you can rent a computer for as little as $2 per hour. To find a list of Mexican cybercafes visit: *www.netcafeguide.com/countries/mexico.htm*.
Telephones. Public phone booths are found in most cities and larger towns. Public phones do not accept coins, only prepaid calling cards (ladatel) available from grocery stores, drug stores, etc. Elsewhere make use of telephones in stores, tobacco stands, hotels, etc.

To make a call from one city to another in Mexico, dial 01 + the city code + and the number. Numbers in Mexico are seven digits except in Monterrey, Guadalajara and Mexico City. To make a direct international call, dial 00 + country code + and the number. From other public phones, dial 020 for the long distance operator for calls within Mexico or 090 for the international operator. In smaller towns look for the **'Larga distancia'** sign outside a store or cafe in the centre of town. Collect calls (reverse charges) are called **llamadas por cobrar**.

Some important phone numbers used throughout Mexico are: **emergency assistance**—(55) 5250-0123 & (55) 5250-0151; **local information** 040. For calls to the UK the code is: 44 for Australia the code is: 61. For the US or Canada the code is: 1.

Electricity

All Mexico is on 110V, 60 cycles AC—in common with the rest of North America. It's a good idea to take a small torch as electricity can be uncertain, especially in small towns.

Mexico uses the **metric system**. See Appendix.

Shopping

The favorable rate of exchange and colorful markets will tempt even those who hate to shop. Mexico is famous for its arts and crafts and the markets guarantee some of the best entertainment anywhere. Look for woven goods, baskets, pottery, jewelry, leather goods, woodcarving, metalwork and lacquerware. Some of towns or states specialize in a particular craft or style.

The government-run **FONART** shops feature some of the best local works and will give a general idea of price variations. FONART shops are generally a bit higher and will not bargain, but sometimes the quality is superior to what is available in the market. Prices and quality vary. Be sure to look over everything carefully. The vendor may guarantee that the sarape you're holding is 'pura lana', pure wool, but you know acrylic when you see and touch it. Bargaining is a fine art and expected.

'The cheapest market by far for sarapes, ponchos and embroidery is Mitla, near Oaxaca. Knock them down to one-third the asking price, and make rapid decisions in order to keep the price down.'

Information

There are Mexican Government tourist offices in most US cities and border towns. Here are the main addresses:

New York: 375 Park Avenue Floor 19, Suite 1905, New York, NY 10152, (212) 308-2110, Fax (212) 308-9060; **Houston**: 1010 Fomdren St, Houston, TX 77096, (713) 772-2581, Fax (713) 772-6058; **Los Angeles**: 2401 W 6th St, 5th Floor, Los Angeles CA 90057, (213) 351-2075, Fax (213) 351-2074; **Washington, DC**: 1911 Pennsylvania Ave NW, Washington, DC 20006, (202) 728-1600, Fax (202) 728-1758; **Toronto**: 199 Bay St, Suite 4440, Commerce Court West between King and Wellington , Toronto, Ontario M5L1A9 3E2, (416) 368-2875; **Miami**: 5975 Sunset Drive, South Miami, FL 33143 (786) 621-2909, Fax (786) 621-2907; **Chicago**: 300 North Michigan Ave, 4th Fl, Chicago IL 60601, (312) 606-9252, Fax (312) 606-9012.

For information 24 hrs a day, call 1-800-482-9832.

In **London,** the Mexican Ministry of Tourism is at Wakefield House, 41 Trinity Square, London EC3N 4DJ, (20) 7488-9392, fax (20) 7265-0704. You can visit their website at: _www.mexicotravel.co.uk_.

Once in Mexico itself, tourist information is provided at federal, state and local levels and most towns on the tourist track have at least one information office. Bear in mind that the level of service provided is extremely variable, and in particular do not presume that English will be spoken. You might also find maps and directories available for free at airports or at the border Look for the booth: **Modulos Paisanos**.

National parks

'Both Mexican and foreign visitors are admitted from 8am-5pm throughout the year' according to the official tourism handbook, but most National Parks are without visible regulation and either merge imperceptibly with the surrounding farmland or are undeveloped and inaccessible wilderness. Don't expect the services of Yosemite or Yellowstone. NB: all beaches in Mexico are federally owned and free. For more information on National Parks visit: _www.mexonline.com/natlpark.htm_.

ON THE ROAD

Accommodation

The range of **hotel accommodation** in Mexico is wide, from ultra-modern marble skyscrapers and US-style motels along the major highways, to colonial inns and **haciendas** to modest guesthouses, called **pensiones** or **casas de huespedes**. There is also a marked difference between north and south Mexico. In the north of the country, hotels tend to be older, often none too clean with bad plumbing and large noisy ceiling fans to hum you to sleep. In southern Mexico, hotels 'are a joy'. They are rarely full and often offer a high standard of comfort and cleanliness at low rates. It is fairly common to find hotels that are converted old aristocratic residences built around a central courtyard. Hoteliers will probably offer you their most expensive room first.

A useful phrase in the circumstances is: *Quisiera algo más barato, por favor* (I'd like something cheaper, please). Ask to see the room first: *Quiero ver el cuarto, por favor*. Of course a double room always works out cheaper per person than two singles, but also one double bed—**cama matrimonial**—is cheaper than two beds in a room. On the other hand, cheaper hotels often don't mind how many people take a room. 'Travelling in a group of four, considerable savings are possible. Most hotel beds are big enough for two people; therefore a double-bedded room can accommodate four.'

Prices are fixed, and should be prominently displayed by law. In general you should expect to pay about US$20-$30 per person per night in a basic but tolerable hotel a few blocks from the centre of town. An intermediate standard hotel should cost US$45-$65. It should rarely be necessary to pay more than this, though if you want to pay US$140 and up for a US-style resort hotel, that's possible too.

Hotel rates may vary between high and low season. High season extends from mid-December to Easter or the beginning of May, the remaining months being low season. Seasonal variations will be more marked at coastal resorts. As most travellers using this Guide tour North America, including Mexico, in the summer months, low season rates are quoted.

'We notice that cockroaches are mentioned by people assessing places to stay. Even the best hotels are full of them—they are part of the scene and should not be regarded as unusual.'

'As it is rare indeed for Mexican wash basins to have plugs, I would recommend travellers to be equipped with this useful item.'

Hostels: visit *www.hostelmexico.com* to see locations and fees.

Camping: Hotels are so cheap that it is difficult to justify taking a tent. Where campsites exist, they tend to double as trailer parks and be some distance from areas of interest. Camping independently in the middle of nowhere is definitely pushing your luck, though in some of the beach resorts, nights under the stars are a feasible option. Those who insist on doing things the hard way should get *Traveler's Guide to Camping in Mexico*, by Mike & Terry Church, US$20. The Secretaría de Turismo publishes a useful brochure: go to Ave. Presidente Mazarik # 172, Col. Polanco (55) 5250-0151, Mon.-Fri. 8am-6pm Sat. 10am-3 pm.

Food and drink

High altitude slows digestion, so it's customary to eat a large, late, lingering lunch and a light supper. (You may be wise to eat less than usual until your stomach adjusts.) Do not eat unpeeled fruit and avoid drinking tap water, unprocessed milk products and ice cubes.

Stick to bottled water, bottled juices, soft drinks or the excellent Mexican beer. Mexican milkshakes or **licuados** are made with various fruits and are delicious; probably best to avoid licuados con leche (those made with milk). Go to a jugos and licuados shop for watershake, and home-made fruit ice creams.' 'The most important thing is to eat plenty of limes, garlic and onions—all natural disinfectants—we didn't have any stomach troubles.'

Mexican cuisine is much more than tacos and beans but the basic menu revolves around ground maize (first discovered by the Mayans), cheese, tomatoes, beans, rice and a handful of flavourings: garlic, onion, cumin and chilies of varying temperatures. The ground maize flour is made into pancake-shaped tortillas, which appear in a variety of dishes and also on their own to be eaten like bread. Tortillas are also made with wheat flour: restaurants will customarily ask, '*De maíz o de harina?*' (Do you want corn or flour tortillas?). **Enchiladas** are tortillas rolled and filled with cheese, beef, etc., baked and lightly sauced. **Tacos**, **tostadas**, **flautas** and **chalupas** all use fried tortillas, which are either stacked or filled with cheese, beans, meat, chicken, sauce, etc. **Tamales** use softer corn dough, filled with spicy meat and sauce and wrapped in corn husks to steam through.

Other dishes to sample: **pollo con mole** (chicken in a sauce containing chocolate, garlic and other spices), fresh shrimp and fish (often served Veracruz style with green peppers, tomatoes, etc). Beans and rice accompany every meal, even breakfast. A good breakfast dish is **huevos rancheros**, eggs in a spicy tomato-based sauce. Mexico is also noted for its pastries, honey and chocolate drinks.

breakfast: *desayuno*	beer: *cerveza*
coffee and a roll: *café con panes*	soft drink: *refresco*
lunch: *almuerzo* (lighter) or *comida*	mineral water: *agua mineral*
dinner/supper: *cena*	bread: *pan*
fixed-price meal: *comida corrida*	potatoes: *papas*
eggs: *huevos*	vegetables (greens): *verduras*
fish: *pescado*	bacon: *tocino*
meat: *carne*	ham: *jamón*
salad: *ensalada*	cheese: *queso*
fruit: *fruta*	

There are over 80 types of chilies in Mexico ranging in taste from sweet to steamroller hot. The different sauces are served from little containers found on tabletops so the diner can determine how mild or hot the dish will be. Best bargain for lunch is **comida corrida** or **menu de hoy**. This can be a filling four-course meal and cost as little as US$4.50. 'I want something not too spicy, please': *Quiero algo no muy picante, por favor*.

The best-known hard liquor is **tequila**, a potent clear drink made from the maguey plant tasting 'similar to kerosene'. The sharp-spiked maguey is also the source for other highly-intoxicating liquors such as **aguamiel**, **pulque**, and **mezcal**. Look for the fat worm at the bottom of mezcal. It guarantees that you have the real thing. If you don't drink it (and by the time you reach the bottom of the bottle you won't know or care), some people like to fry them for snacks. Margarita cocktails are made with tequila but are primarily popular with turistas. The Mexicans prefer to take their tequila neat with a little salt and lime on the back of the hand. Mexico produces some decent wines but is famous for its beer; don't pass up **Dos Equis** dark.

Travel

Now for your basic Spanish travel vocabulary: please—*por favor*; thank you—*gracias*; bus—*autobús*; train—*tren* or *ferrocarril*; plane—*avión*; auto—*carro*; ticket—*boleto*; second class—*segunda clase*; first class—*primera clase*; first class reserved seat (on trains)—*primera especial*; sleeping car—*coche dormitorio*; which platform?—*cuál andén*? which departure door/gate?—*cuál sala*? What time?—*A qué hora*? And inevitably: How many hours late are we?—*Cuántas horas de retraso tenemos*? Street—*calle*; arrival—*llegada*; departure—*salida*; detour—*desviación*; north—*norte*; south—*sur*; east—*este* or *oriente* (and abbreviated Ote); west—*oeste* or *poniente* (abbreviated Pte). Junction—*empalme*; indicates a route where one must change buses/trains; avoid empalmes at all costs. Also, these will be useful : I need your help—*Necesito que me ayude, por favor*; Where is the bathroom, please—*Dónde está el baño, por favor*?

Bus: Bus travel is the most popular means of transportation for Mexicans. Buses are absurdly inexpensive by American or European standards: Tijuana to Mexico City (1871 miles/2995 kms) costs about US$220 round trip for the cheapest seats on Estrella Blanca ('White Star') lines. For timetables and on-line reservations visit their website at <u>www.estrellablanca.com.mx</u>. All seats are reserved on first class (primera) buses, but 'beware of boarding a bus where there are no seats left—you may be standing for several hours for first class fare'. Sometimes it's advisable to book for second class also, although in southern Mexico a reader advises: 'Normally there are no standby passengers on first class and you get a reserved seat; on second class buses this is rarely the case'.

Standards of comfort, speed, newness of buses, etc., vary more between bus lines than between first and second class, although second class will invariably be slower (sometimes days slower with attendant expenses) and cheaper on longer runs. 'Mexico City to Mazatlán, on a second class bus, took 24 hours. Scenery superb, driving horrifying. Great journey.' Travelers generally recommend deluxe or first class buses: 'By far the best—quite exciting, cheap, fast'. Most towns have separate terminals for first and second class buses. Always take along food, a sweater (for over-air-conditioned vehicle) and toilet paper.

When making reservations you are always allotted a particular seat on a particular bus so if you want a front seat book a couple of days ahead. No refunds are made if you miss the bus; and be careful of buying a ticket for a bus that is just pulling out of the bus station! No single carrier covers the whole country and in some areas as many as 20 companies may be in competition, and while this doesn't mean much variation in fares, it can mean a big difference in service. Greyhound passes are not valid in Mexico, though by waving a student card you can sometimes get a substantial discount. Greyhound do sell Estrella Blanca bus tickets from some locations in Texas, thus guaranteeing an onward seat from gateway cities.

Though you shouldn't have too much faith in the precision of its contents, ask for **un horario**—a timetable—showing all bus lines and issued free. Bus Information from Mexico City: Central del Norte: (55) 5587-1552 (*www.centraldelnorte.com*); Central del Sur: (55) 5689-9745; Central del Oriente (TAPO): (55) 5762-5977; Central del Poniente: (55) 5271-0149.

Rail: Train travel is now virtually nonexistent in Mexico. The only two lines operating are the route from Chihuahua to Los Mochis through the **Copper** (Tarahumara) **Canyon** and the **Tequila Express** route from Guadalajara to Amatitan. The Copper Canyon is four times wider than the Grand Canyon. Enroute the train passes through 87 tunnels, crosses over 36 bridges, crosses the Continental Divide three times, and climbs to 8071 feet at the track's highest point. The Canyon is the home of the semi-nomadic Tarahumara Indians. Stop off at Créel if you want to visit them (See Copper Canyon box.) The Tequila Express route takes passengers to a Mexican tequila distillery for a day trip. Prices range from US$20 to US$100. Call (614) 439-7212, or visit their websites at *www.ferromex.com.mx* or *www.chepe.com.mx*.

Air: If time is short you may well want to consider city hopping by air. Although obviously more expensive than bus, the plane wins hands down for comfort and will give you more time in the places you really want to visit. Mexican domestic airlines include, Mexicana (see the '*Getting There*' section), Aeromexico, AeroCalifornia, Aeromar or Azteca. Check the Mexicana website, *www.mexicana.com*, for various passes and other offers for domestic travel and travel into Mexico from Miami and Los Angeles.

Car: Taking a car to Mexico offers the prospect of unlimited freedom of movement, but 'also of unlimited hassles if you fall foul of Mexican bureaucracy'. First, you need a car permit, which is issued with your tourist card, and the card itself is specially stamped. (The permit is not strictly necessary for Baja-only trips.) You cannot then leave Mexico without your car. If called away in an emergency, you must pay Mexican customs to look after it until your return and in theory, if the vehicle is written off in an accident, it must be hauled back to the border at your expense. Airlines are not allowed to sell international tickets to visitors with the special card without proof that the vehicle has been lodged with the authorities.

At the border you must produce a valid license and registration certificate. A UK license is likely to produce incomprehension in the average Mexican traffic cop; an international one is recommended. Only Mexican insurance is valid in Mexico. You can get it at the border where 24-hour insurance brokers exist for the purpose. It is advisable to increase public liability and property damage coverage beyond the minimum.

Some practical concerns: do not try to drive your Cadillac or BMW autodrive car from Los Angeles to Oaxaca. Choose a rugged vehicle and take plenty of spares: basic VWs, Dodges and Fords are manufactured in Mexico and are most easily repairable. All main roads are patrolled by the **Green Angels fleet**, radio-coordinated patrol cars with English speaking two man crews (*Angeles Verdes*). If you have a problem, contact Direccion de Turismo (Tourist Safety) 01800-90392 and they will connect you. They are equipped to handle minor repairs, give first aid and supply information: a raised hood will convey your need of assistance.

Garage repairs are reported as 'often incredibly cheap, particularly if you avoid 'authorized dealers', where you should expect to pay through the nose. Get a quote first!' Although you are not permitted to sell your car in Mexico, in theory you can do so in Guatemala and Belize, though these days purchasers are hard to find.

Pemex, the nationalized gasoline supplier, produces two grades of petrol. 'Don't buy cheap gas. Pemex Nova caused our car to shudder and stall. A mixture of Nova and the (better quality) Extra was a vast improvement.' Extra is, however, hard to find outside the larger towns, and some travelers modify their vehicles to take low-grade fuel.

It's important to note that all US cars manufactured after 1975 require unleaded gasoline. Outside the big cities unleaded petrol is undependable or not to be found and the use of anything else may damage the catalytic converter and ruin the entire engine. Garage attendants are notorious for swindling tourists: watch the dial carefully. Fuel itself is very cheap, at about US$0.60 per litre. 'Never let the gas level go low, and fill up at every opportunity. Gas stations are few and far between in remoter areas.'

Mexico has good main highways. Petrol stations (Pemex) are infrequent on the road, but most villages will have a 'vendedor de gasolina', who will sell you a can-full and syphon it into your tank. Ask: *Dónde se vende gasolina aquí, por favor*? Once off major highways, be on the alert. Branches or rocks strewn across the road are an indication of a hazard ahead. Watch for potholes, rocks and narrow bridges (puente angosto), and slow down in advance of the sometimes vicious 'speed bumps' (topes) near roadside communities. Unless absolutely necessary, do not drive at night: many Mexican drivers rarely use headlights, and wandering cattle, donkeys, hens and pedestrians never do.

Car theft is a frequent occurrence: it is worth paying extra for a hotel with a secure car park. And US plates tend to attract the meticulous attention of traffic police. 'You are considered fair game for police along the road, who will stop you and fine you for 'speeding'. Haggle with them—they always come down to five to ten dollars. One man was asleep in his car in Nuevo Laredo when he was arrested for speeding: the car was parked at the time.'

'Drivers should be warned that after entering the country there is a 'free zone' of about 100 miles, with three or four customs stations along the road. You will have to bribe at least one official in order not to have your car ripped apart. But once you leave the 'free zone' you will have no more problems with customs and hardly see any police.'

Mexico's principal highways lead from **Nogales**, **Juárez**, **Piedras Negras**, **Nuevo Laredo**, **Reynosa** and **Matamoros**, all on the border, to Mexico City. The most expensive road in the world is the new toll highway from Mexico City to the Pacific coast resorts, including Acapulco. It costs US$58 to drive the full length.

The most scenic road in Mexico is the well-maintained 150D which sweeps through the Puebla Valley past the volcanic peaks of Popocatépetl and Orizaba, climbs into lush rain forests and down through foothills covered with flowers and coffee plantations, to end up in the flat sugarcane country around Veracruz. Note, however, a pretty sturdy vehicle is often needed: this is particularly true in Baja, where a four-wheel drive is a major asset.

Some signs: *Alto*—Stop; *No se estacione*—no parking; *bajada frene con motor*—steep hill, use low gear; *vado a 70 metros*—ford 70 metres; *cruce de peatones*—pedestrian crossing; *peligro*—danger; *camino sinuoso*—winding road; (*tramo de) curvas peligrosas*—(series of) dangerous curves; *topes a 150 metros*—speed bumps 150 metres; *Ote* (abbr.)—east; *Pte* (abbr.)—west.

Urban Travel: Most cities of any size have a good public transport service on buses, minibuses or converted vans. The flat fare is usually about US$0.65. When choosing a destination note that Centro is the centre of town and Central is the bus station.

Hitching: Can be hazardous with long waits (not just for a lift but for a car to come along) in high temperatures. Hitching is definitely **not** recommended especially for women or anyone travelling alone.

For Women Alone: For better or worse, machismo is still alive and well in Mexico. The causes and results of machismo are frequently discussed and written about but it still doesn't make things any easier for women. Males from 8 to 80 feel compelled to remark on a woman's (and especially a foreigner's) legs, arms, breasts, hair, eyes, etc. In a country of dark-haired people, light or blonde hair has come to symbolize sexiness or higher status. Bare arms and legs, no bra and a casual manner signify that a woman is free and easy. Use common sense—don't hitchhike or enter cantinas.

The best way to deal with hassles is to say nothing and continue walking. If possible, travel with a male friend (although machos will still try to pick you up) or a couple of women friends. 'I travelled alone and despite many warnings (mostly from US citizens!) I felt very safe. Mexicans seem more curious and friendly than anything else.'

MEXICO - FURTHER READING

For anyone planning more than a brief trip to Mexico, the following are recommended for additional information.

Traveler's Guide to Mexican Camping by Mike & Terry Church.

Let's Go: Mexico is an annually updated, group-researched 617 page guide, full of detailed background and essential practical information.

The Hungry Traveler: Menu Translator and Food Guide to Mexico, by Marita Adair.

Eat Smart in Mexico describes how to decipher the menu, know the market foods and embark on a tasting adventure, by Joan & David Peterson.

Access Mexico by Harper Perennial, contains 43 detailed maps to help you get around.

Insider's Guide to Mexico by Peggy Bond.

Other useful guides - *Get Upclose* by Stephen Wolf. *Mexico (The Rough Guide)* by John Fisher. *Fodor's (Exploring Mexico)* by Fiona Dunlop. *Lonely Planet Mexico* by John Noble. *AAA Mexico Travel Book*.

NORTHWEST MEXICO

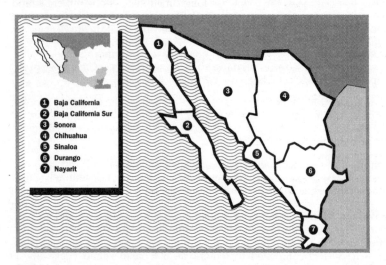

1 Baja California
2 Baja California Sur
3 Sonora
4 Chihuahua
5 Sinaloa
6 Durango
7 Nayarit

This vast arid region of stark desert, sharp mountains, deep valleys and canyons contains the states of Baja California, Sonora, Chihuahua, Durango, Nayarit and Sinaloa.

The nearness of Mexico to the US is deceptive once you learn that one way or another, you must cross many miles of thinly populated and largely dull terrain in this northern sector in order to get anywhere more interesting. The coastline offers some relief, especially from Hermosillo, Sonora, southward as it gradually becomes greener, until you reach the lush and humid jungle around Tepic and San Blás in Nayarit.

Baja California has its own peninsula to the west; poorest of Mexican states, beautiful in a bare-bones sort of way, especially on its eastern coast on the warm Sea of Cortéz (also called the Gulf of California).

BAJA CALIFORNIA

TIJUANA Previous editions of this guide have dismissed Tijuana and the other border towns; yet more readers visit 'TJ' than anywhere else in Mexico, numbering themselves among the millions of day trippers passing through the city each year. You will do Mexico an injustice if you judge it by the border towns, but you will do yourself an injustice if you fail to take the opportunity provided by a free day in San Diego, El Paso or Laredo to experience an abrupt cultural discontinuity available in few other places on the planet. The most cursory trip across puts into sudden perspective everything the traveler has taken for granted in the course of a trip round the US.

Tourist trap, home of cheap assembly plants, staging post for illegal immigrants en route to *El Norte*, Tijuana's every aspect depends on its proximity to the border. Possessing few Mexican virtues but pandering to most American vices, the town has long functioned as a commercial and sexual bargain basement for southern California, and although a municipal clean-up campaign has edged the more blatant prostitution and sex shows to the outskirts, hustle is still the name of the game for the storekeepers, street traders and taxi drivers competing for your attention.

There are bargains to be had if you bargain ruthlessly: good deals likely for leather goods, blankets and non-Mexican items such as cameras and name brand clothing. 'You can knock all goods down to a third of the asking price. Take US dollars.' 'Some great buys if you enjoy haggling.' 'If you go in a spirit of sociological inquiry, remember to have fun. Well worth a day visit.' 'I enjoyed every minute of it.'

Accommodation
Tijuana has over a hundred hotels: Those in the southeast section of the city are reputedly the quietest and most salubrious. Expect to pay US$24-$42, and be prepared to haggle. 'Lower prices possible if you don't mind sleaze.' There are several small, inexpensive hotels on **Avenida Madero**, to the left as you leave the old Tres Estrellas De Oro bus station.

Hotel Cesar, (Birthplace of Ceasar Salad!) Revolución & Calle 5, (664) 685-16-06, US$40-UD$50.

Hotel Nelson, Revolución 721, (664) 685-4302. 'Clean, decent bathrooms, relatively inexpensive. S/D-US$45. Also has a good restaurant.'

Food
Carnitas Uruapan, Blvd. Aguascalientes #1650, (664) 681-6181. Deep-fried pork (carnitas) in various combinations. Popular with locals and tourists. One order US$9. Open 8am-3am.

Nelson (see Hotel Nelson). Reasonable prices for full-scale Mexican meals.

La Especial, Revolución #18 in between 3& 4, 664) 685-6654. Open 9am-11pm.

La Placita, Revolución in between 3 & 4, (664) 688-2704. Open 8am-12pm.

Of interest
Centro Cultural Tijuana (CECUT), Paseo de los Heroes & Calle Mina, Zona Río, (666) 687-9600. New cultural museum of striking modern design with archaeological, historical and handicrafts displays. Auditorium with multimedia show in English (afternoons) and Spanish (evenings), also theatre, art shops, and restaurant. Daily 10am-9pm. Show admission includes free pass to museaum. _www.cecut.gob.mx_.

The Museo De las Californias, in the Centro Cultural Tijuana, contains an art gallery and natural history museum. Be sure to look for the gray whale cranium as well as paintings by various noted Mexican artists. The museum also has a restaurant, gift shop, and theatre.

It you are interested in **shopping**, check out the **Mercado Hidalgo** in the Zona Rio, which is frequented more by locals than tourists. The main tourist shopping area is on Revolucion between Calle Juarez and Calle Zapata, though many interesting shops are located in the _Bazar de México_.

Entertainment
Jai Alai. Fronton Palacio Revolución and Calle 7, (664) 686-3958. Fast and furious version of squash using arm baskets to hurl hard rubber ball against court walls. Exhibitions only Fri-Sat. Open 7pm-10pm. Admission US$4.50-US$10.

Bullfighting. Toreo de Tijuana. The season changes every year, but is usually from May-Oct. In one of two rings. Call for ticket prices (52) 686-1470. 'Amazing and disgusting.' _www.bullfights.org_.

Racetrack (*Hipódrome*), Boulevard Agua Caliente. In front of Calimax, (664) 633-7309. Moorish-influenced building containing enclosed and open-air stands. Races Tues, Sat. and Sun matinee 1:15pm and from 7:15pm-11pm. Free admission.

Information
State Tourism Office, Paseo de los Heroes #10289, (526) 634-6330.

Travel
To Tijuana: see section on San Diego, California. From San Diego Amtrak terminal, the **San Diego Trolley** will take you to US border suburb of San Ysidro (approx. US$7); then its a 20 minute walk to centre, or the local bus from the border to Avenida Revolución (Tijuana) costs no more than US$4.50. Some local buses are: Volante, Diamante & ABC. 'Taxi from border should cost no more than UF$10.'

If passing straight through, get either the **shuttle bus** from Amtrak or the Greyhound service from LA and San Diego: these both take you to the new so-called 'central' bus station on the eastern edge of town. The old Tres Estrellas terminal near the border has poor connecting service and a $4 taxi ride is the only other option. **Mexicoach** offers an excessively expensive centre-to-centre service from San Diego.

Onward: frequent bus services to Ensenada (2 hrs), Mexicali (3 hrs), Santa Ana (11 hrs), Los Mochis (22 hrs), Mazatlán (28 hrs), Guadalajara (40 hrs), Mexico City and points between. Six buses daily to La Paz (22 hrs).

BAJA BEYOND TIJUANA After Tijuana the paved but narrow and variable quality Transpeninsular Highway (Mexico 1) leads the bus traveller to the tip of Baja at the resort center of **Cabo San Lucas**, 1,000 dusty miles and 20 hours further on. Known for its sport fishing and beautiful beaches, this is where the Gulf of California and the Pacific Ocean meet. To explore most areas of interest en route you need a car, and often a four-wheel drive vehicle. Buses do not prolong their rest stops at the roadside towns, which in most cases is no great loss. Expect visions of desolate beauty and long passages of tedium, expecially when the road loses sight of the coast.

Of interest
The mountains, forest and trout streams of **San Pedro Mártir National Park** lie two hours away from **Colonet**, 74 miles from Ensenada. Superb hiking and climbing but check at the turn off that the dirt road is open all the way. Further down the highway, the agricultural town of **San Quintín** offers good markets and restaurants. **Bahia San Quintín**, five miles away by dirt road, has fine beaches, expensive motels and excellent seafood.

The next 250 miles or so consist of bleak inland desert. Those with an interest in salt evaporation plants will enjoy **Guerrero Negro**, at the border of Baja California Sur: otherwise its only virtue lies in its proximity to **Scammon's Lagoon**, breeding ground for gray whales and an incredible spectacle during the breeding period of late December-February. Four wheel drive needed for the 20 mile trek.

San Ignacio, is a delightful oasis village with date palms imported by its Jesuit founders in the eighteenth century, a reconstructed mission, and its own wine. But more and cheaper accommodations will be found 50 miles further on at **Santa Rosalía**, a copper mining town on interest for its friendly inhabitants, ugly galvanized steel church, and thrice-weekly ferry to **Guaymas** on the mainland, the shortest and cheapest crossing. Boats depart (subject to change): Tue & Fri at 10pm, arrives 7am. The trip costs (o/w) US$55 saloon class, shared cabin US$75, first class US$65, and US258 for cars. For more information contact **Sematur Office** (615) 152-0014 or (615) 152-0013. *www.ferrysantarosalia.com*.

The desert oasis of **Mulegé** has hotels and restaurants and, two hours away by four wheel drive, Baja's best cave paintings. Loreto itself was founded in 1697, but most in evidence now is work-in-progress on the government-sponsored resort.

La Paz follows after another 200 miles of boring inland desert. For years an isolated pearl-fishing centre, the ferry service and completion of Hwy 1 have turned La Paz into a major tourist town, but the centre at least preserved a relaxed charm. Not much to see except the famous sunsets, some good beaches and snorkelling, but many good restaurants and hotels, and the Zócalo (main plaza) is spectacularly lit at night.

Also now available in La Paz, as well as in **Cabo San Lucas** and **Loreto**, is **kayaking**. Care should be taken in choosing an outfitter before you go. Most outfitters run trips from November to May. You can expect more wind and waves in the winter, but the weather will always be hot and dry. Get more information about kayaking in Mexico from the following: **GORP** (_www.gorp.com_, (877) 440-4677); **REI Adventures** (_www.reiadventures.com_, 800-622-2236); **iExplore** (_www.iexplore.com_, 800-I-EXPLORE); **SeaTrek** (_www.sealtrekkayak.com_, 415-488-1000); **Tofino Expeditions** (_www.tofino.com_, (800) 677-0877); and the **Mexico Tourism Board** (_www.visitmexico.com_, 1-800-44-MEXICO). **Tourist Information Office**, km 5.5 North Highway, in the Fidepaz Building. (612) 124-0100 or (612) 124-0103. Daily 9 am-8 pm.

Ferries: From **La Paz to Mazatlán**, Thurs-Tues, departure time is 3pm, arrival time is 9am. 65 pesos salon class, 129 pesos tourist class, cabin 194 pesos, special 258 pesos. For more information contact (800) 969 6900. **From La Paz to Topolobampo (Los Mochis),** 43 pesos salon class, 86 pesos tourist class, cabin 120 pesos, special 172 pesos. Mon, Wed and Fri departs at 9pm, arrives 8am.

Cabo San Lucas lies 120 miles further south at the tip of the peninsula, and is a purpose-built tourist town with little time for the budget-conscious, who will have better luck at **San José del Cabo**. _www.allaboutcabo.com_. The whole southern tip has beautiful and-so far-unspoiled beaches, a couple of which, on Rte 9 out of San Lucas, are accessible to campers. **Sierra de la Laguna National Part**, reached by dirt road from **Pescadero**, offers pine forests and the occasional puma. The La Paz-Mazatlán ferry route, followed by the bus, are the best ways to get there.

Ferries: the Baja-mainland routes make few concessions to tourist convenience or comfort. You must queue for tickets several hours before they go on sale, and be prepared for long waits and customs hassles. Salon class is incredibly cheap, but inbolves a long and rowdy voyage with two hundred or so others crowded together on bus seats. Tourist class cabins are still a bargain, but frequent air conditioning breakdowns often make them unendurable. Taking a car across demands a willingness to wait several _days_ (commercial vehicles always get priority) and pay substantial bribes. As if all this wasn't enough, the food is awful too. The ferry service has recently been privatized and hopefully will improve. Flights duplicate most ferry routes and are definitely less exhausting, albeit more expensive.

OTHER NORTHWESTERN TOWNS

MEXICALI The inland border town located 136 kilometres east of Tijuana and departure point for bus and rail routes to West Coast destinations. One of the hottest places in Mexico, with few concessions to tourists or to anyone else: accommodation choice is between a few hotels priced at US levels or Zona Rosa sleaze. However, for even the short stay border-hopper, the trip from Tijuana (the new terminal) is recommended: the three hour ride gives an acceptably brief taste of the starkness of Northern Mexico, and the descent on the eastern side of the mountains towards Mexicali is both hair-raising and dramatic. _www.mexicali.gob.mx_.

San Felipe, a 2 hour, 125 mile drive from Mexicali, through desert and beautifully harsh mountains, is a likeable, ramshackle fishing village with miles of white sand beaches and superb fishing. After this an unpaved road continues south to join route 1 from Ensenada. *www.sanfelipe.com.mx*.

Ensenada is a slightly hipper version of Tijuana, 70 miles south via a new toll road. A thriving fishing industry fails to impart authenticity to anything but the cheap and tasty seafood. The town is full of Californians, especially at weekends, and is one of the few towns where you will get better value from US dollars than from pesos. But 'the drive to Ensenada along the coast is beautiful - well worth crossing the border just to experience the complete change of environment'. *www.ensenada.com*.

CIUDAD JUAREZ. Over the bridge from El Paso, and seemingly part of the same urban sprawl. This is the city about which Bob Dylan wrote his most depressing song ever (*Just Like Tom Thumb's Blues*). Souvenirs, gambling, racetracks and brothels, and it's easy to get lost in the rain. But still worth a quick visit (the market is recommended), rather than cowering on the other side of the border: 'it's easy to make the crossing for a much, much cheaper hotel room than you'll find in El Paso.' *www.juarez.info*.

From Ciudad Juárez you can take a bus to Chihuahua, Mexico City or most other destinations. Instead of the direct route of the Chihuahua it is possible to go via **Nuevo Casas Grandes** to visit **Paquime,** the most important prehispanic archaeological site in Northern Mexico. 'Get up early to squeeze this trip into a day.' 'Beware of low flying taxi drivers.' NB: Mexican buses to Chihuahua and Mexico City also depart from El Paso Greyhound terminal. By air, **Gonzalez Airport** to Mexico City, about US$485 r/t. Call Aeromexico, inside Mexico 01-800-021-4050, in the US 1-800-237-6639.

CHIHUAHUA. The first major town on the route down from El Paso. A prosperous industrial and cattle-shipping centre, once famous for breeding tiny, hairless and bad-tempered dogs of the same name.

The Chihuahua Cathedral is one of the most beautiful churches in Northern Mexico. Construction began in 1727, funded by wealth from the silver mines in Santa Eulalia, and, due in part to intervening Indian wars, was not completed until almost 100 years later. Built in colonial style, the cathedral overlooks the Plaza Principal.

The Placio de Govierno, where Miguel Hidalgo, the 'Father of Mexico', was executed at 7am July 30th 1811, is decorated with 'lovely lurid murals'.

Quinta Luz, the Museum of Pancho Villa, is a fortresslike 50 room mansion, Villa's home and hideout, at Calle 10, #3010 Col. Santa Rosa, (614) 416-2958. Now state-run, after being in the hands of Villa's 'official' widow for many years: see Villa emorabilia including weapons and the bullet-scarred car in which he was assassinated in 1923.

Chihuahua is also the starting point for the dramatic **Al Pacífico** train ride through the Barranca del Cobre (**Copper Canyon**). This is one of the world's most spectacular train rides and is a perfect trip for those who love hiking. For information about travel to the Copper Canyon, see separate box. For more information on Chihuahua call the **State Tourist Office** located at Calle Libertad #1300, Col. Centro, (614) 410-1077.

LOS MOCHIS. Once you are in Chihuahua, you may want to consider going to Los Mochis on the coast of Sinaloa, of interest only as the southern terminus for the ferry connections with **La Paz** in nearby **Tropolobampo.** For more information on Los Mochis call the tourist office: (668) 815-1090. _www.losmochis.com_.

Travel from Los Mochis is available by bus, train or ferry. Although the city has many bus carriers, **Elite Bus Station** (668) 981-3811 is the most obvious and modern one.

The **Al Pacifico Train** (also known as "Chepe") leaves Los Mochis at 6 am. Tickets are about US$55, 2nd Class, and US$105, 1st Class (only for the Copper Canyon tour). For information call Viajes Flamingos, (668) 812-1613. Starting from Los Mochis end reportedly gives best views; sit on the right. Station is 3 miles out of town - allow plenty of time for local bus or taxi. Los Mochis station uses Chihuahua time, one hour earlier than local time.

Ferry for La Paz, if operating (see Baja section), leaves from Topolobampo for the 8 hour trip, Mon-Sat at 10 pm. Often sold out 24 hrs ahead. Nowhere to stay in Topolobampo, but 'a night out under the stars is fun. Fishermen cook freshly caught fish and shrimp over wood fires and invite you to partake. But buying even basics is difficult - don't count on it for food for the ferry'. Going straight from the ferry to the Al Pacifico, or vice versa, is difficult and an exhausting trip: a stopover in Los Mochis is recommended.

MAZATLAN. A big, boisterous and a major gringo tourist town, offers a ten mile strip of international hotels and some superb game fishing. The old section of the town has more affordable hotels, local colour and an element of risk. The El Cid Hotel rents out windsurfers, sailboats, catamarans and snorkel gear. _www.mazatlan.com.mx_.

Piedra Isla, a tiny island just offshore, has good beaches, diving and camping possibilities: very congenial after the last boat leaves at 4:30 pm. Also of interest, 'the route (Mexico 40) from Mazatlán to Durango is absolutely breathtaking. Although it's just over 300 miles, it took us a long time to cover as the road twists and turns up to 7000 ft where it crosses the Continental Divide. A part of Mexico that should not be missed.' Take Transportes Monterrey-Saltillo bus for the 6 hour trip.

Coming down the coast and an hour's trive off the highway just north of **Tepic** takes you through increasingly lush tropical country to **San Blás,** once a sleepy seaside village, but no longer. 'Signs advertising granola and yogurt, expensive hotels and food, dirty beaches and medium surfing.' 'Very hippified but nice with a good swimming beach.' 'bring lots of insect repellent - famous for its gnats.' 'We really liked it here. The beach is lovely and the town is pretty with nice places to sit and eat.' _www.visitsanblas.com_.

Buses from Tepic to San Blás run fairly regularly. 'Interesting jungle scenery enroute.' The bus station is on Calle Sinaloa in the Zócalo, (323) 285-0043. Take a small boat trip into the jungle lagoons and creeks behind the town. Dawm is the best time for you to catch the animals (or vice versa). For more information contact **Oficina de Turismo de Tepic** (311) 216-5661.

THE COPPER CANYON

Copper Canyon (Los Mochis and Chihuahua) The spectacular Copper Canyon was formed some 20-30 million years ago, when intense volcanic activity raised the Sierra Madre mountain range. Copper Canyon is 300 feet deeper and four times wider than the Grand Canyon. In the high parts of the canyon there is an impressive variety of vegetation and wildlife. During the summer the climate is cool, and during the winter the temperature can drop below freezing. The temperature at the base of the canyon is hot, and the plant and animal life markedly different.

The descent to the bottom of the canyon can take two days, and those who make the trek should be in good physical condition. It is recommended to make the descent in winter or spring, to avoid the summer heat of the canyon floor.

The canyon is populated by Tarahumara Indians. Despite the tourism, they live in largely traditional ways and are known for their basketry and long distance running abilities. For more information visit *www.mexicoscoppercanyon.com*, *www.coppercanyon-mexico.com*.

How To Get There: The best way to reach and experience the canyon is by train. There is an incredible trip from Chihuahua to Los Mochis, which takes 14 hrs one way. The train passes through 86 tunnels, over 37 bridges and covers more than 400 miles. The train stops at many different points along the way, allowing passengers to see and photograph the spectacular views. "Chepe" as this train is familiarly known, has renovated its First Express and Economic Class Fleet.

First Express Class leaves from Chihuahua to Los Mochis and vice versa at 6:00 am daily. Train tickets cost US$1080. The train stops in the main tourist points: Cuauhtemoc, Creel, Divisadero, Posada Barrancas, Bahuichivo/Cerocahui, in the state of Chihuahua and, Temoris, El Fuerte and Los Mochis in the state of Sinaloa. Arrival time at each destination is approximately 79:30 p.m.

Economic Class costs US$530 and leaves from Chihuahua to Los Mochis and vice versa at 7:00 am daily. Arrival time at each destination is approximately 101:2500 p.m. The train performs 15 official stops but may make as many as 50 stops at any "flagged station" at passengers' request. Sales and reservations (614)-439-7212, e-mail: chepe@ferromex.com.mx, or visit *www.chepe.com.mmx*. For more information you can also contact the **Tourism Administration Office** (614) 436-7210.

Where To Stop Off And Why. Créel Station: this is the doorway to the Sierra Tarahumara. From here you can get to the Tarahumaras Caves, Arareko Lake, rock formations in the Valley of the Mushrooms, the Elephant Stone, and the Valley of the Frogs. Four km from the nearby town of Cusarare are the Cusarare waterfalls. Local tours offer horseback rides and trips to the waterfalls. Tours run between US$2015 and US$350. Camping is also possible but bring a tent (summer is rainy season).

Batopilas: one of the more beautiful parts of the Copper Canyon, Batopilas has a descent from 2,200 metres to 460 metres above sea level. From the vantage point of Bufa you can appreciate the splendor of this magnificent canyon.

Divisadero Station: an impressive view of the canyon is located at an altitude of 1300 meters, at the Urique River. There is a path to the bottom of the canyon, and an excellent opportunity to experience the variety of vegetation from pine forest to tropical.

Basaseachic National Park: this park has two of the highest waterfalls in Mexico. Basaseachic Falls is 254 metres high and Piedra Volada is 456 metres high. The **Candamena Canyon** is located here, and excursions to the bottom are offered.

NORTHEAST MEXICO

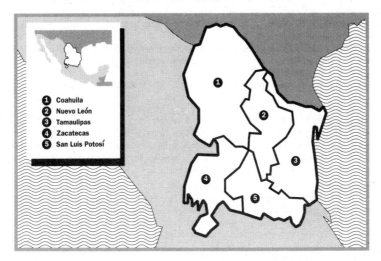

1 Coahuila
2 Nuevo León
3 Tamaulipas
4 Zacatecas
5 San Luis Potosí

The northeast states offer little worth tarrying for. The border towns east of Juárez-Nuevo Laredo, Reynosa and Matamoros provide similar experiences to the others, and are worth a quick visit but no more. 'Nuevo Laredo is a corrupt dump and an insult to Mexico'; Matamoros has either 'exceptionally friendly people' or 'unbelievably officious and venal immigration officers', depending on whom you listen to. All three cities offer flights to Mexico City and a bus route via Monterrey.

Another route south is the Pan American Highway, Mexico 85, taking you from Nuevo Laredo to Monterrey, Nuevo Leon.

MONTERREY

NUEVO LEÓN This state is an important economic centre of Mexico. In addition to its modern capital city of Monterrey, one of the three largest cities in Mexico, Nuevo León also has interesting deserts, vegetation, waterfalls, caverns, and museums.

In **Monterrey** you can find the famous **Macro Plaza** also known as the Gran Plaza, comprising 100 acres in the heart of the city. Completed in 1985, it is one of the world's largest squares. Nearby are shops, restaurants, important government buildings, museums, and downtown hotels. In the centre of the Macro Plaza is the large Fountain of Life (*La Fuente de la Vida*), one of several fountains in the plaza.

Of interest
Museum of Contemporary Art (Marcos Museum). This amazing museum is located in the heart of the Macro Plaza in the old town at Zuazua and Padre Raymundo Jordon, (818) 342-4820. The Museum was designed in contemporary Mexican style by the famous Mexican architect Ricardo Legorreta. It has 11 galleries that display the art of Mexico, Latin America, and other parts of the world. Tue-Sun 11am-7pm. Small charge, free on Wednesdays. *www.mytol.com/marco*.

Obispado Museum, 8333-9588. The Obispado was built by the Catholic Church in 1788. Sitting on a hilltop overlooking the city, it was used as a fort during the Mexican-American war in 1847, the French intervention in 1862, and the Mexican Revolution in 1915. Today the building is used primarily as a museum. Tue-Sun 10am-5pm, small charge.

Planetarium Museum of Science, Art, and Technology, complete with an IMAX theatre, as well as Plaza Sesamo, an amusement part inspired by the children's TV programme, Sesame Street. 8303-0002.

Parque Nacional Cumbres, where the famous 75 ft **Horsetail Falls** (*'Cascada de Cola de Caballo'*) is located. The falls can be reached by foot, horseback, or carriage. From Monterrey, take Hwy 85 NW for 145 km. Daily 8am-7pm, nominal fee.

South of the city of Monterrey you will find the interesting **Grutas De Garcia Caves** that are some 500,000 years old. These caves were once submerged by an ancient sea, and marine fossils can be seen in the walls. To reach the caves, take Hwy 40 west from Monterrey for 40 km to Saltillo, then 9 kilometres on marked road to the caves. Daily 9am-5pm, US$5.50.

Information

State Tourism Office, (818) 345-0902 or (818) 345-0870, Cinco de Mayo #525, between Zaragoza & Escobedo (Elizondo Paez Building, third Floor).

Tours: around the city contact **Osetur** (818) 347-1533 or 347-1599, Calle Lomas Grandes #2700 San Francisco Building, 5th floor, Col. Lomas Largas.

OTHER NORTHEASTERN TOWNS

Saltillo, 50 miles up in the hills to the west, is preferable if you need to break your journey. Saltillo is in a fertile valley surrounded by mountains. The architecture of this city illustrates different periods of Mexico's history. The **Santiago Cathedral** is famous worldwide for its altarpieces and its baroque-churrigueresque style. The **Recinto Juárez** was a home of the Juárez government and has become a museum that keeps documents and objects from the 1800's. Also famous for those colorful hand-woven sarapes (symbols of Mexico), abundant silver, pan de pulque and delicious beef meats, Saltillo is a calming oasis in the middle of the desert, where in Mexico, deserts cover between 50 and 60 percent of the territory. *www.saltillo.gob.mx*.

The recently built **Museo del Desierto** highlights the largest desert in North America (comprising seven Mexican states) and puts Saltillo on a par with some of the top museums of its kind in the world. This 'living' museum includes exhibits on geology, ecology, palaeontology, and the desert. It is located on Prolongación Pérez Treviño 3745, Parque Las maravillas, *www.museodelesierto.org*, (844) 410-6632. 52 pesos. For more information contact the **Saltillo Tourism Office,** Blvd. Francisco Coss y M. Acuñ s/n, Zona Centro, (844) 412-5122.

Zacatecas, south of Saltillo on Hwy 54, is the capital city of the state of the same name and is built on the side of a 7000 ft mountain. It's still a silver mining centre and is famous for its baroque cathedral and the **Quemada Ruins.** For 'marvellous views' of the area, take a ride on the cablecar (*teleférico*) north of the Plaza. Small fee. The **Teleférico** will take you from the old town to the **Cerro de la Bufa** (great view). Open daily 10am-6pm. (492)922-56-94. The **Rafael Coronel Museum,** also known as ex-convent of San Francisco. Open Thu-Tue 10am-2pm. Admission US$2, (492) 922-81-16.

Zacatecas Museum, Explanada del Cerro de la Bufadora next to the Patrocinio Sanctuary. Open daily 10am-4:30pm, (492) 922-8066.

Don't leave without seeing **Hotel Quinta Real,** which used to be a Plaza de Toros (bullfighting ring) and is built in old colonial style. Also worth visiting, **Jerez de Zacatecas** where Zacatecas' high society used to live. For more information contact the **Zacatecas Tourism Office,** Av. Hidalgo #403, Second floor, Col. Centro, (492) 924-0552. _www.zacatecas.gob.mx_.

South from Saltillo on Hwy 57 is the state of **San Luis Potosi** filled with magnificent landscapes - forests, springs, waterfalls, and spas. There are artisans' villages where you can experience local traditions, fiestas and customs. Several towns date from pre-hispanic times, such as **Real de Catorce,** an extraordinary place once considered the most thriving mining centre of the New Spain. Reached by a 1.5 kilometre long tunnel, this site is considered almost a ghost town with only a couple of hundred inhabitants, worth visiting because of its stunning architectural remains and incredible natural scenery. Huichol Indians travel miles from the north to Real de Catorce in springtime to gather peyote, a woolly cactus considered sacred with hallucinogen effects. _www.sanluispotosi.gov.mx_. _www.realdecatorce.net_.

Further south towards Mexico City is **San Luis Potosí City,** a gold and silver mining town of considerable historical interest and with a distinctive regional cuisine. The **Plaza de Armas** or main square has four town squares. It is the site of the **Cathedral,** the **City Hall** and the **Palacio de Gobierno,** all these erected between the 16th and 18th centuries. The city is full of museums such as the **Museo Nacional de las Máscaras,** (444) 812-3025. Open Tue-Fri. 10am-2pm & 4pm-6pm, Sat-Sun 10am-2pm. Admission $.50; **Museo Taurino** (Bullfighting Museum), (444) 822-15-01. Open Tue-Sat. 11am-2pm & 5pm-8pm. Free admission

DISCOVERING MEXICO'S ANCIENT CIVILIZATIONS

Aztecs, Mayas, Mixtecs, Olmecs, Toltecs, Zapotecs—great civilizations have flourished in Mexico for at least 4000 years. To discover their fascinating remains and share their drama, you'll have to journey to the south of the country, where each state's tourism secretariat can provide you with maps, information on tours, brochures and other assistance about the main sites and how to get to them.

Highly recommended, before going to the field, is a first stop in Mexico City at the excellent **Museo Nacional de Antropologia**, located at Paseo de la Reforma, Colonia Chapultepec, Polanco. Tue-Sun 9am-7pm. Admission $38 pesos. For information, call (55) 5553-6266. Metro Stations: Auditorio and Chapultepec. For information on current exhibits visit the museum's website _www.mna.inah.gob.mx_. Also look in at the **Museo Nacional de Culturas Populares**, located at Calle Hidalgo #289, Colonia Coyoacan, also in Mexico City. Tue-Thu, 10 am-6pm, Fri-Sun, 10am-8 pm. Free Admission. For information, call (55) 658-1265. _www.cnca.gob.mx/cnca/popul/mncp.htm_.

Mexico's pre-Columbian heritage is often divided into three distinct periods: pre-classic (2000 BC to 200 AD); classic (200 AD to 900 AD); and post-classic (900 AD to the Spanish conquest in 1521 AD).

PRE-CLASSIC—2000 BC to 200 AD The **Olmecs** founded one of the earliest great civilizations of Mesoamerica, which is often considered the 'mother culture' of the region. Early advances in agriculture led to the rise of Olmec towns and ceremonial centers in what are now the states of **Veracruz** and **Tabasco**. Staple crops of the Olmecs included beans, corn, and squash, though the Olmec diet may have at times included other humans. The Olmecs domesticated dogs and turkeys, had elaborate religious ceremonies and structures, and are famous for their stone carvings, including monumental stone heads between 1.5 and 3 meters tall weighing up to 20 tons.

The primary Olmec cities were Tres Zapotes and La Venta. **La Venta**, 84 miles west of Villahermosa in Tabasco, is still an interesting site to visit, even though the archaeological finds were transferred in toto to escape destruction from oil drilling in the 1950s. Many colossal Olmec heads of basalt can be seen at the archaeological museum in Mexico City, the Tabasco Museum in Villahermosa, and at Parque Museo La Venta, located at Boulevard Adolfo Ruiz Cortines s/n, near the airport. Apart from three large stone heads, La Venta has stelae, altars, mosaics, a model of the original city and a Zoo. Self-guided tour map, US$2, daily 8am-5pm. For tourist information in Villahermosa, call the Centro de Turismo de Tabasco (993) 316-3633, or go to Ave. Los Rios #113. Tourist information can also be found at tourist information booths in the Museo La Venta, bus stations, airport, and around town.

The **Zapotecs** inhabited what is now **Oaxaca** in southern Mexico. Their primary city was **Monte Albán** (the 'White City'), the elaborate ruins of which can still be explored today. The region was later conquered by the Mixtecs, who were craftsmen skilled in precious metals, ceramics, and mosaics. For information and maps in Oaxaca, call the tourism office (951) 516-0717 or go to Ave. Murguia 206 Zona Centro.

CLASSIC —200 AD-900 AD The dominant influence of the classic period is the **Mayan** civilization. The Maya were the largest homogenous group of Indians north of Peru, and their society stretched from present-day Honduras throughout the Yucatán peninsula. Approximately 6 million Mayans inhabit the area today. The Mayan civilization built massive pyramids throughout Central America, including the impressive sites at **Uxmal** and **Chichén Itzá** at the tip of the Yucatán and at the ancient partially excavated city of **Palenque**. For maps and information on reaching these sites visit their website _www.mayayucatan.com.mx_, call the tourism office (999) 930-3760 or go to Calle 59# 514, Central Zone, Mérida, Yucatan.

UXMAL and CHICHEN ITZA. Along with Palenque, **Uxmal** was one of the chief Mayan cities and the showpiece of that civilization's finest architectural accomplishments. **Chichén Itzá**, on the other hand, was first a Mayan city and later occupied and built on by the belligerent Toltecs, becoming in the process the most stupendous city in the Yucatán.

Fifty miles of good road lead from **Mérida** to Uxmal, where the clean, open lines of the ancient city create an impression of serenity and brilliant organization on a par with the greatest cities of either Eastern or Western civilization at that time. As white as marble and gilded by the sunshine, the limestone complex of the **Nunnery Quadrangle**, the Palace of the Governor and the Pyramid of the Soothsayer has a fascinating and almost modern beauty. The friezes of the palaces are decorated with stone mosaics in intricate geometric designs. Open daily 8am-5pm, free on Sundays and holidays, otherwise a nominal fee is charged.

In the 10th century the peaceful Mayan world was disturbed by the war-like Toltecs, who came down from their northern plateau capital of **Tula** to conquer the Yucatán cities and make **Chichén Itzá** their southern capital. The monumental constructions you see there are both Mayan (eg. El Caracol, the circular observatory) and Toltec (eg. the Court of a Thousand Columns). The city is dominated by the Great Pyramid, the Temple of Kukulcán, with its stairways of 91 steps on each of four sides, making a total of 364. That figure plus one step round the top totals the days in the year. Other points of interest include the Ball Court and its inscriptions and the Sacred Well into which human sacrifices were hurled. Daily 8 am-6 pm, free on Sundays and holidays, otherwise a nominal fee is charged.

PALENQUE About 130 kilometres inland from **Villahermosa** are the jungle ruins of the classic Mayan sacred city of **Palenque**, which flourished AD 300-700. Built on the first spurs of the Usumacinta Mountains, the gleaming white palaces, temples and pyramids rise from the high virgin jungle. Its visually-compelling site, compact size (the excavated portion is about three-quarters of a mile by half a mile, out of the 20-square-mile extent of the city) and its dramatic burial chamber make Palenque, to many minds, more outstanding than Chichén Itzá. The 1950 discovery of an ornate crypt containing fantastically jade-bedecked remains of a Mayan priest-king revised archaeologists' theories about Mayan pyramids, which were earlier believed to be mere supports for the temples on top. Although it's a hot, steep and slippery journey, you should climb the Temple of the Inscriptions, descend the 80 feet into its crypt to view the bas-reliefs: chilling and wonderful. Maps and site information are available in Palenque or Chiapas, call (961) 613-9396. Museum opens daily 9 am-4 pm. Site is open daily from 8 am-5 pm. Admission US$4, free on Sundays.

The Mayans developed advanced mathematics, astronomy, and writing systems. Religious ceremony was central to Maya culture, which at times included human sacrifice. Losers of sporting events might also expect to be beheaded, or tied into a ball and rolled down the steep steps of a pyramid. Although the ancient Maya shared a common culture, like the ancient Greeks they were politically divided into as many as 20 sovereign states, rather than ruled by a unified empire.

Such division may ultimately have led to constant warfare and the eventual downfall of their civilization. In addition to the main Mayan sites mentioned here, there are many smaller ruins scattered throughout the Yucatán, such as those at **Tulum** on the Caribbean coast. For tour information, call **Chiapas Tour** (961) 614-2068 or visit their website *www.chiapastour.com.mx*.

POST-CLASSIC—900 AD-1521 AD The **Toltecs** were mighty warriors who occupied the northern section of the Valley of Mexico. Their primary city was **Tula**, approximately 80 km north of Mexico City, where the Temple of Tlahuizcalpantecuhtli was built (yes, Tlahuizcalpantecuhtli). Giant stone warriors, standing nearly 5 meters high, guard the temple.

The Toltecs conquered the city of **Teotihuacán**, near present-day Mexico City. Teotihuacán is one of the most important ceremonial centers in ancient Mesoamerica, and includes the massive Pyramid of the Sun, 63 meters high, and the Pyramid of the Moon, 42 meters high. The Toltecs spread the cultural influence of the Teotihuacanos, including the cult of Quetzálcoatl (the 'Sovereign Plumed Serpent'), throughout their empire. The rise of the Toltecs, however, transformed much of Mesoamerica from a theocracy to a warrior aristocracy.

The **Aztecs**, who sometimes referred to themselves as the Mexicas, created the most complex culture in all of Mesoamerica. Their primary city was **Tenochtitlán**, built in 1325 on small islands in Lake Texcoco where modern-day Mexico City is located. According to legend, the site was chosen when the wandering Aztecs came upon an eagle perched upon a cactus eating a snake, fulfilling a prophecy. Today, the Mexican flag incorporates this scene.

Influenced by the Toltecs, the focus of Aztec life was war and conquest. Only the Incas in Peru had a larger empire in the Americas. However, the Aztecs also built great cities, developed a sophisticated calendar, devised a system of imperial administration and tribute, and made great advances in agriculture. Among their many gods, the Aztecs continued to worship Quetzálcoatl. When the Spanish arrived in Mexico in 1519, with their light skin and hair, horses, muskets and armour, they were mistaken as gods.

Cortés, aided by Indian tribes who had been mistreated by the Aztecs, was able to conquer Tenochtitlán and overthrow the mighty Aztec empire.

Unfortunately, the Spaniards did a thorough job in eliminating much of the Aztec civilization. Virtually nothing remains of the giant pyramids dedicated to Tlaloc the rain god and Huitzilpochtli the sun god. Some minor remains of the ancient city of Tenochtitlán are located in the suburbs of Mexico City, and some smaller pyramids can be found at Santa Cecilia, Calixtlahuaca, and particularly Malinalco, some 48 km from **Toluca**, where there are temples dedicated to two Aztec military orders, the Knights of the Jaguar and the Knights of the Eagle. Other Aztec artifacts can be viewed in the **Museo Nacional de Antropologia** in Mexico City.

WHAT TO SEE NEAR MEXICO CITY The Pyramids of **Teotihuacan** and Temple of **Quetzálcoatl** are part of the ruins of the once-great city built by the mysterious Teotihuacanos, about whom little is known other than that they were a militaristic, highly regimented society. At its peak in about 300 A.D., **Teotihuacan** was the world's sixth largest city, bigger than Rome, and only 10% of the city has been excavated.

For reasons yet to be uncovered, the Teotihuacan civilization disappeared between 600 and 700 A.D., and it was not until hundreds of years later that the Aztecs assumed control of the site, naming it Teotihuacan, 'The Place of the Gods.' The Pyramid of the Sun is 216 ft high (248 steps to the top where the sacrifices were made) and the older Pyramid of the Moon, one half km away, although less vast, is just as impressive. The **Temple of Quetzálcoatl** is about ine kilometre from the pyramids and has some superb Toltec carvings. When climbing pyramids, take care—they're very steep. And traders are everywhere—even at the top of the pyramids selling fake artifacts that 'they made at home'.

To get there, take Metro to Indios Verdes (last station on north end of line 3), then cross the street to the bus station (Central Camionera del Norte) and take bus marked 'Piramides' (NB: no backpacks on Metro.) Frequent buses from Terminal del Norte direct to site every 15 minutes. The last bus from the pyramids to Mexico City leaves at 6pm. For more information, call Autobuses Teotihuacan (55) 5587-0501. Free guided tours available in English, Italian, and French for groups of 5 or more. Daily 8am-5pm, US$4. Free on holidays and Sundays.

CENTRAL MEXICO

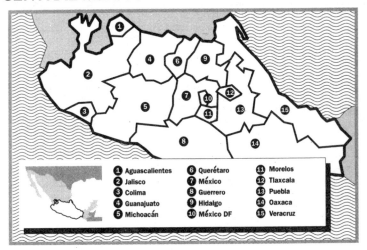

1 Aguascalientes	6 Querétaro	11 Morelos
2 Jalisco	7 México	12 Tlaxcala
3 Colima	8 Guerrero	13 Puebla
4 Guanajuato	9 Hidalgo	14 Oaxaca
5 Michoacán	10 México DF	15 Veracruz

Mexico seems to save itself scenically, culturally and every other way, in order to burst upon you in central Mexico in a rich outpouring of volcanic mountains, pre-Columbian monuments, luxuriant flowers, exuberant people and picturesque architecture. This is the region where the Mexican love of colour manifests itself and the air is cool and fresh on the high Central Plateau. Be prepared for mugginess on either coast around Acapulco and Veracruz, however.

Mexico City lies in the centre of this region, surrounded by a dozen tiny states from Tlaxcala to Guanajuato. Northwest of Mexico City is the orbit of Guadalajara, second largest city and home to the largest colony of American expatriates. That fact makes its outlying satellite towns of Tlaquepaque, Chapala, Ajijic and so on, quite expensive.

MEXICO CITY   The Aztec city of Tenochtitlán had a population of 300,000 by 1521, when stout Cortés demolished it to build Mexico City from the remains. Today that figure represents the number of new residents the city acquires *each year*, making it likely that total population will reach 23 million during the lifetime of this guide.

México D.F. (pronounced 'day effy', for Distrito Féderal) is the nation's cultural, economic and transportation hub, with most of the country's people living on the surrounding plateau. As well as being the largest city in the world, it is probably the most polluted, with a smog level to make LA seem positively bracing and a crime level to make New York City seem like the Garden of Eden on a Sunday afternoon: be alert, especially away from the centre. The altitude—7400 ft—together with the crowds, suicidal traffic and incessant din, can quickly exhaust the unacclimatised traveller.

Visit the city for its striking architecture, from Aztec through Spanish

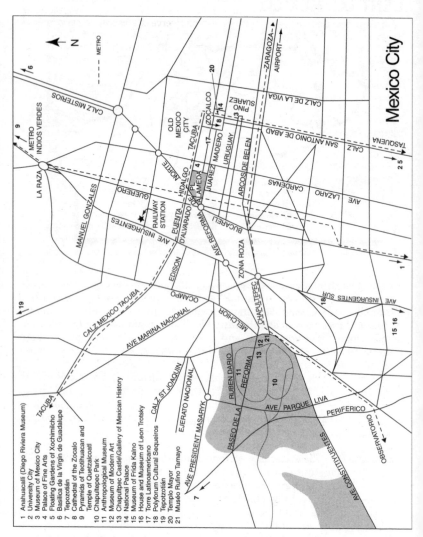

← N --- METRO

Mexico City

1 Anahuacalli (Diego Riviera Museum)
2 University City
3 Museum of Mexico City
4 Palace of Fine Arts
5 Floating Gardens of Xochimilcho
6 Basilica de la Virgin de Guadalupe
7 Tepozotlán
8 Cathedral of the Zócalo
9 Pyramids of Teotihuacan and
  Temple of Quetzalcoatl
10 Chapultepec Park
11 Anthropological Museum
12 Museum of Modern Art
13 Chapultepec Castle/Gallery of Mexican History
14 National Palace
15 Museum of Frida Kalno
16 House and Museum of Leon Trotsky
17 Torre Latinoamericano
18 Polyforum Cultural Sequeiros
19 Tepotzotlán
20 Templo Mayor
21 Muséo Rufino Tamayo

Colonial to modern, from pyramids to enamelled skyscrapers, from modern
subways to archaeological finds preserved *in situ* at Metro stops. Great
wealth and poverty exist side by side but residents at all economic levels
tend to be the most hospitable of Mexicans. 'North America is incomplete
without a visit to this vast and fascinating city.'

Accommodation

Best area for low price accommodation is around Alameda Park, especially
Revillagigedo Street, Plaza San Fernando, Zarazoga, and (further west just before

Insurgentes) Bernal Díaz and Bernadino de Sahagun. Also try the area immediately surrounding the Zócalo. Be prepared to add 25% to these prices during summer: during this period, pressure on a diminishing reserve of low cost hotels is intense, and a room in Cuernavaca, about an hour away by bus, may be a viable option.

Del Angel, Rio Lerma 154, from US$60, (55) 5533-1032. Rstrnt, downtown.

Hotel San Francisco, Luis Moya N 11 Col Centro, from US$36. TV, bar, restaurant. (55) 5521-8960.

Hotel Prim, Versalles 46, from US$44. Laundry, TV. (55) 5592-4600.

Parque Ensenada, Av Alvaro Obregon, from US$46, (55) 5208-0694. Rstrnt, 20 mins from airport, in 'Cultural Corridor'.

Hostal Las Dos Fridas, Hamburgo #301, (55) 5286-3849. US$14-US$24. Cable TV, internet service.

Food

Mexico City is a good place to taste frothy **Mexican hot chocolate**, a drink once so prized that only the Aztec and Mayan nobility drank it, to the tune of 50 tiny cups a day. A dish invented locally and now popular all over Mexico is *carne asada a la tampiqueña* (grilled beef Tampico style). Due to reports of rude waiters and rapacious mariachis, Plaza Garibaldi is no longer recommended as 'best and cheapest'. 'Good cheap eating at small restaurants around Glorieta Insurgentes situated where Insurgentes crosses Avenida Chapultepec. Fewer mariachis than Garibaldi but you can sit in greater comfort to hear them.'

Cafeterias Sanborns are all over Mexico City and they are excellent for breakfast, lunch or dinner. Some of the locations are: Insurgentes Norte #70 Colonia Santa Maria la Rivera, (55) 5566-1320. Ave. Insurgentes #1605 Col San José Insurgentes, (55) 5662-5077. Parroquia #179 Col del Valle, (5) 534-7626. Ave Fco. I. Madero #4, (55) 5512-1334. Salamanca #74 Col Roma, (55) 5533-3242.

'Zona Rosa' is a pleasant place to go strolling and there are some cheap restaurants among the plush sidewalk cafes.

For real Mexican tacos (not to be confused with the Tex-Mex variety found in most parts of the US), try **El Fogoncito**, with more than nine establishments in Mexico City, El Fogoncito has been serving Mexican tacos since 1968. Some locations include: Ave. Revolucion #1221, Col. Los Alpes (55) 5660-4025, Campeche #171A, Col. Roma (55) 8596-4632, Leibnitz #54, Col. Anzures, (55) 5531-6469. *www.fogoncito.com/*.

Visit **Los Bisquets de Obregon** if you want to experience an affordable and authentic Mexican meal. This family-style restaurant has the best *café con leche* in town and offers biscuits prepared a number of ways. You can also order their great *enchiladas.* Alvaro Obregon #60 with more than 15 branches throughout the city

Of interest

Museo Anahuacalli. Diego Rivera-designed black lava building housing his large collection of Aztec, Pre-Columbian artifacts. Ave. del Museo #150 Col. San Pablo de Tepetlapa, (55) 5617-4310. Open Tue-Sun 10am-6pm. 30 pesos, 20 w/student ID, closed Mondays.

Polyforum Cultural Siqueiros, a monument designed by and in honor of the artist. 'The march of humanity mural is indescribably wonderful like being inside an opium dream.' Ave. Insurgentes Sur #701, Col. Napoles, (55) 5536-4520 in the Hotel de Mexico. Open 9am-7pm. Sound and light show in the evening. *www.polyforumsiqueiros.com*.

Ciudad Universitaria, home of UNAM, the Universidad Nacional Autonoma de México. 11 miles south, located at Insurgentes Sur # 3000 is the Centro Cultural Universitario (cultural center), reached by buses from downtown or trolley bus from Eje Central Lázaro Cárdenas. Famous for its modern design and colourful murals, mosaics and bas-reliefs by Rivera, Juan O'Gorman, Siqueiros and others. *www.ciudad-universitaria.com*.

Torre Latinoamericana, miniature empire state building that floats, with a magnificent view (smog and weather permitting) from its 44th floor observatory. Corner of Cárdenas and Madero #2 Col. Centro. Open 9:30am-11pm. Small charge to go to top floor. An aquarium in basement.

Museo de la Cuidad de Mexico, built and rebuilt on site of a razed Aztec temple (only cornerstone remains), it provides an excellent introduction to the city's history, with models, murals, photographs. Good background for the start of your visit. Pino Suárez 30, three blocks south of Zócalo, (55) 5542-0083. Tues-Sun 10am-6pm. Closed Mon. Free.

Palacio de Bellas Artes, this heavy white opera house contains Mexico's finest art collection. Upstairs are some of the best murals by Orozco, Siqueiros, Rivera and Tamayo. 'Worth every centavo.' (55) 5512-2593. Open Tues-Sun, 10am-6pm.

Basílica de la Virgen de Guadalupe, the holiest of Mexican shrines, it honours the nation's patron saint, the Virgin of Guadalupe. Legend has it that she appeared to an Indian, Juan Diego, in 1531. Devout visitors show their faith by walking on their knees across the vast, cement courtyard. Indians, dressed in national costume, dance and parade by on her feast day, December 12. The old cathedral leans in all directions and is slowly sinking into the soft lakebed soil. The new basilica was designed by Pedro Ramirez Vasquez, architect of the national museum of anthropology. Take bus to la Villa, on Reforma, or metro to Basílica. *www.virgendeguadalupe.org.mx*.

Tepotzotlán, has a magnificent 18th century church, possibly Mexico's finest, with a monastery and an interesting collection of colonial religious art. 25 miles north by *auto-pista* (expressway). From Mexico City, buses to Tepoztlán run regularly from the Terminal del Sur and the Terminal Poniente. Open Tue-Sun 9am-6pm.

Alameda, a park since 1592, lies west of the Palacio de Bellas Artes between Juárez and Hidalgo Avenues. Originally the site of executions for those found guilty by the Spanish inquisition, it is now the scene of popular Sunday concerts and family outings. On June 13, Mexico's single women line up at the church of San Juan de Dios and plead with St. Anthony to find a husband for them.

Zócalo, or **Plaza de la Constitución**, has been the centre of the country from Aztec times. Second only in size to Red Square, vehicular traffic is restricted. The Cathedral, National Palace, Templo Mayor, and much more, are all within five minutes of each other.

The Cathedral at the Zócalo is the oldest church edifice on the North American continent, built on the ruins of the Aztec temple. Has plumb-line showing how the cathedral has shifted. On the east side of the Zócalo is the **National Palace**, begun in 1692, and for its enormous and impressive murals by Diego Rivera.

Templo Mayor, just off the corner of the Zócalo, between the cathedral and the National Palace, is the excavated site of the Aztec Templo Mayor—really twin temples and several associated buildings. Although only the lower and internal parts remain, the ruins are extremely impressive. At the rear of the site is the **Muséo del Templo Mayor** which houses many of the artifacts recovered during the excavations, (55) 5542-0606. Open Tues-Sun 9am-5pm. Admission 16 pesos. Free on Sundays. Guided tours available in English Mon-Fri mornings only. Not to be missed.

Pyramids of Teotihuacán and **Temple of Quetzalcoatl,** for details see '*Ancient Civilixations*' box.

Chapultepec Park, most of the city's important museums are around the park, but it is also an attraction in its own right, especially on Sundays when all the families in the city seem to parade there. 'Should be a compulsory visit—very colourful.' Free zoo includes the first captive pandas born outside China. Open daily.

Anthropological Museum. The claim that this is the finest museum in the world is well-founded: 'certainly one of the world's top ten'. Contains Mexico's past and present. The museum has recovered some of its most prized treasures that were stolen in December, 1985, but they are not displayed yet. 'Deserves every accolade thrown at it. Worth going here before you visit the pyramids at Teotihuacán.' cameras but no tripods allowed, so bring fast film or flash. 'Worth taking your own photos, since postcards of exhibits are very poor and few (as in all Mexican museums I've visited).' Open Tue-Sun 9am-7pm. Small charge, free on Sun.

Gallery of Mexican History, a cleverly designed building within Chapultepec Castle, with a first-rate presentation of Mexican history since 1500. Open 9am-5:30pm daily. Small charge, free on Sundays.

Museum of Modern Art, has Mexico's more recent masterpieces. 'Excellent collection, not only of Orozco, Rivera, etc., but some charming primitive paintings.' be sure to see La Revolución by Lozano. Open Tue-Sun 10am-5.30pm. Small charge, free on Sundays. Located at the entrance of Chapultepec Park, corner of Reforma and Ghandhi Street.

Chapultepec Castle, inside Chapultepec Park, an old castle with original furnishings and objects d'art that found fame in 1848 when young Mexican cadets fought off invading Americans here. Rather than surrender, the final six wrapped themselves in Mexican flags and jumped from the parapets to their death. Unless you want to copy them 'beware stone parapets and banisters, both very unsafe. Castle not impressive but worth visiting for the murals'.

Muséo Rufino Tamayo, exhibitions of modern art and sculpture, including the personal collection of Mexico's best known living artist, Rufino Tamayo. The building itself is worth a visit. Located opposite the Museum of Modern Art, east of the Anthropological Museum. (55) 5286-6529. Open Tue-Sun 10am-6 pm, free guided tours Sat-Sun 10am-2pm. Small charge, free admission on Sundays. www.museotamayo.org.

House and Museum of Leon Trotsky, Rio Churubusco #410, Col. del Carmen Coyoacan, (55) 5658-8732. Ring door buzzer to be let in. This is where Trotsky was pick-axed to death in 1940; his tomb is in the garden. The house is preserved as he left it. Open Tue-Sun 10am-5 pm, closed Mon. US$1.50. 'Really interesting'.

Muséo Frida Kahlo, Frida was Diego Rivera's wife and a prominent artist in her own right. Their colonial style house is filled with their effects and many of Frida's works. Five min. walk from Trotsky House, corner of Allende and Londres #247, (55) 5554-5999. Open Tues-Sun 10am-6pm. Closed Mon. US$3.

The Volcanoes of Popocatépetl and Iztaccihuatl can be seen on a clear day in the east, although 'for good views take bus to Amecameca from ADO terminal'. The peaks are some 3000 ft higher than Mounts Rainier or Whitney in the USA. 'Mind-blowing view when sitting on the side of bus from Mexico City to Puebla.'

Mexican Independence Day Celebrations, on September 15 at 11pm, the Mexican President gives the traditional cry of liberty to crowd in the Zócalo amid churchbells ringing, fireworks firing, confetti floating, much rejoicing.

Entertainment

Bullfight season runs Nov to March; other times of year, you can see *novilladas* (younger bullfighters, younger bulls) which are cheaper and may please you just as well if you know nothing of bullfighting. Fights Sun at 4 pm; booking in advance recommended. Take 17 bus down Insurgentes Sur to Plaza California, 1 block from the Plaza. Monumental (also known as Plaza México) is at 42,000 seats the biggest in the world; buy '*sol*' seats in *barrera* or *tendido* sections to have the best views, (555) 611-44-13. Open daily 9am-6pm. Tickets from 15-180 pesos. For more information visit www.lamexico.com.

Ballet Folklorico at the Palacio de Bellas Artes, Ave. Juarez y Eje Central Lazaro

Cárdenas, Sun at 9.30 am and 8.30 pm; Wed at 8.30 pm. 'A real must—not classical ballet but a series of short dances representing Spanish, Indian and Mexican cultures.' Incredible costumes! Reserve in advance, (55) 5521-9251. Tickets from 300-500 pesos.

Soccer matches take place all year-round. You have various options to experience the great enthusiasm for the most popular sport in Mexico. Five teams have their home ground in historic *World Cup* stadiums around this city: **Club América**, Azteca Stadium (Mexico's largest stadium, seats 100,000 people), Calzada de Tlalpan #3465 *www.esmas.com/clubamerica*; **Cruz-Azul**, Azul Stadium located right next to Plaza Mexico (see bullfight) *www.cuz-azul.com.mx*; **Pumas-UNAM**, Olimpic Stadium located inside UNAM (University City) West Insurgentes Avenue *www.pumas.unam.mx*; **Atlante**, Neza Stadium, Avenida Lázaro Cárdenas s/n, Ciudad Nezahualcóyotl *www.club-atlante.com*; and **Diablos Rojos de Toluca** *(Red Devils)*, Nemesio Diez Stadium or *Bombonera*, Ave. Morelos in Toluca, an hour west of Mexico City *www.diablos.com.mx*. Matches are usually played on Saturdays and Sundays. Tickets US$5-US$20 can be purchased at the ticket window of each stadium or through Ticketmaster (55) 5325-9000.

Plaza Garibaldi, nightly after 9pm, mariachi music, sometimes free, sometimes not. Can be dangerous—be careful.

Plaza Hidalgo, located at the heart of Coyoacan, a place surrounded by majestic mansions, art galleries, restaurants and bohemian life. Was an important Pre-Hispanic Centre and seat of the Franciscan Foundation of the XVI century.

El Hijo del Cuervo a much frequented bar featuring live rock and bohemian Latin music. Open daily 1pm-2am. (55) 5658-7824. *www.elhijodelcuervo.com.mx*.

Shopping

Many good markets including the Saturday market at **Plaza San Jacinto** in the suburb of San Angel. **San Juan Market** on Ayuntamiento is a city-run market with many Mexican handicrafts and a good place to practice haggling. The **Handicrafts Museum** is on the **Plaza de la Cuidadela** at Avenida Balderas and has lots of trash and treasures. The **Thieves Market** (adjoining the Mercado La Lagunilla on Rayon between Allende and Commonfort) is open on Sundays. **La Lagunilla** is also especially interesting on Sundays when vendors come from all over the city to set up booths. You can find books, guidebooks and American magazines at **American Bookstore,** Madero 25.

If you are looking for modern style malls, check out **Santa Fe, Plaza Satelite**, or **Perisur.**

Information

Post Office on Lázaro Cárdenas and **Tacuba,** has a *poste-restante* section where letters are held up to 10 days. (55) 5521-7394. Open Mon-Fri 8am-10pm, Sat 8.30am-8pm, Sun 8am-4pm.

Mexico City News is an all-English newspaper with a good travel section.

Mexican Government Tourist Bureau, Presidente Masaryk #172, 01-800-903-9200, north of Chapultepec Park—rather out of the way. Otherwise (55) 5250-0123 for English-language tourist information. 'Go there in the morning.' *www.visitmexico.com*.

Mexico City travel and tourist information from **D.F. Tourist Office**, Amberes and Londres in the Zona Rosa, (55) 5525-9380 or (55) 5525-9381. Open 9am-7pm. *www.mexicocity.gob.mx*.

Tourist Police, (Green Angels) located at Florencia St. #20 Col. Juarez, Zona Rosa for more information (55) 5250-8221 also available in Acapulco and Puerto Vallarta.

American-British Cowdray Hospital, Observatorio and Calle Sur # 136. Call (55) 5230-8000 or in emergencies, (55) 5230-8161 or (55) 5230-8163. Open 24 hours. *www.abchospital.com*.

British Embassy: Calle Río Lerma #71 Col. Cuahutemoc. (55) 5242-8500 or (55) 5207-2089. *www.embajadabritanica.com.mx*. **US**: Paseo de la Reforma # 305 Col. Cuahutemoc. (55) 5080-2000. *www.usembassy-mexico.gov*.

Travel

Taxis. 4 types, drivers described as '99.9% cheats—best to find out roughly how much the journey should cost before taking it. Wherever possible, fight to the death!' Regular taxis **(yellow)** have meters, and you pay 10% more at night. Jitney or '*pesero*' taxis **(green)** cruise the main streets: convenient but be careful with these cabs since they are famous for hijackings and robberies. Although it's better to avoid riding alone, don't let the driver allow a stranger to get in the cab with you. Sitio taxis **(red)** operate from ranks on street corners - agree on the fare beforehand if possible. You can also call Servi-Taxis (55) 5271-2560. Outside hotels, etc., you'll find unmetered taxis; always agree on fare beforehand. These cabs are usually expensive but the safest around. 'Taxi meter or not, arrange price beforehand.'

Buses. Municipal buses cost US$0.60, *Peseros* (white and green mini buses) US$0.45. If time is short, take 'this incredible tour' by **Gray Line Tours (Turibus)**: (55) 5208-1163, contact Mr. Maldonado. Full day **City Tour** costs US$55 per person, one-half day $35 per person. If staying any length of time it is suggested that you get a street map and a Metro guide.

The Mexico City Metro, opened in September 1969, now carries some 5 million passengers daily at a ridiculously low price. 'The world's best transport bargain.' 'Use wherever possible, the streets are choked with traffic.' But avoid during rush hours (7-10am, 5-8pm) and be prepared to jostle with the rest of them at other times. Work out connections in advance—no overall plans inside stations. Backpacks, suitcases and large packages are *banned* during rush hours —this can be strictly applied. Women and children should take advantage of separate queues and cars provided at worst times, and everyone should beware endemic bag-snatching and slashing. Some stops have artifacts uncovered during excavation: **Aztec Pyramid Foundation at Pino Suarez**, more artifacts at **Bellas Artes** and **Zocalo**. 'Clean, fast and incredibly simple to use.' When leaving the city, it is best to consult the Tourist Office for information.

Air: Aeropuerto Internacional de la Ciudad de Mexico, International Airport, (55) 5571-3600 or 5784-4811. Flights to all Mexican destinations. From the airport take the official yellow taxis, buying a fixed price ticket to your destination from desks at the end of the Arrivals Building. You can also call this service for transport to the airport, but it costs the same or more than a regular taxi. Or, take the Metro to 'Terminal Aerea line 5'—but transfers involved and remember baggage limitations.

For buses getting into or out of Mexico City: 4 terminals, each located near a Metro stop. North arrivals/departures at **Terminal Central del Norte**, (55) 587-1552. Open 24 hours. Take Metro to La Raza and go to Autobuses del Norte, line 5. (Also get there by bus, Insurgentes Norte then Cien Metros.) South: **Terminal Sur**, at the Taxquena Metro stop, southern end of line 2, (55) 5689-9745. West: **Terminal Poniente**, Avenida Rio Tacubaya Sur #122, Col. Real del Monte, (55) 5271-4519 at Observatorio Metro station, west end of line 1. East: **Terminal Central del Oriente** (also known as ADO or TAPO), (55) 5762-5977, at the San Lázaro Metro station, to the east on line 1. (See Introduction to Mexico).

OTHER CENTRAL TOWNS
All the places mentioned below can be easily reached from Mexico City by bus or car.

Queretaro, a lovely, lively town, loaded with history, lies about 140 miles to the north west of the capital. It's a bit off the usual beaten tourist track and is recommended for its freshness, friendly townsfolk and the numerous hidden plazas and cobblestoned by-ways tucked off the main streets. The Treaty of Guadalupe Hidalgo ending the US-Mexican War was signed here and the present Mexican Constitution was drafted here in 1916. **Tourism Office** (442) 238-5000 _www.queretaro.gob.mx/turismo_.

To the west of Mexico City is the State of **Michoacan**, famous as the meeting place for millions of monarch butterflies. The state is dotted with craftsmen's villages with Tarascan traditions and an amazing variety of natural attractions, such as thermal waters, grottoes, rivers, and lagoons. **Morelia, Pátzcuaro, Ucareo, Charo** and **Cuitzeo** are known for their colonial architecture and fine sweets! **Tourism Office** (443) 312-8081 _www.michoacan-travel.com_.

Also west of Mexico City is **San Miguel de Allende**, in the State of Guanajuato, a big draw for American students, writers and artists, is a treasure house of art, past and present, put together on the backs of the fortunes made from silver. The town's mountainside setting adds to the charm. _www.sanmiguelguide.com_.

To the west is **Guanajuato**, the state capital and another Spanish colonial town. As one of the finest cities in Mexico, it was declared a World Heritage Site by UNESCO in 1988, and is known for its festive spirit and events. The International Cervantes Arts and Music Festival takes place here in October and November. **Tourism Office** (473) 732-82-75. _www.guanajuato-travel.com_.

About an hour's drive west of Mexico City, and with some magnificent scenery in between, is **Toluca**. Sitting at 8760 ft, Toluca is the highest city in Mexico and is famous for its main attraction, the **Friday Market**. Local Indian stall-keepers come from miles around to sell local specialties like straw goods, papier mache figures and sweaters. Bargain without mercy but first check out the prices at the government store next to the **Museum of Popular Arts and Crafts**, east of the bus station. You can often do better here than at the market. **Tourism Office** 01-800-849-1333. _www.toluca.gob.mx_.

The centre of modern Mexico's silver industry is **Taxco** in the State of Guerrero, about 130 miles south from Mexico City, sitting high in the Sierra Madre. The views around here are marvellous and the city is preserved as a national monument, preventing construction of modern buildings.

For a more typical resort-type experience, hop on a bus (or drive the expensive toll road) and head south to **Acapulco,** the largest and still most famous resort of the Pacific. **Tourism Office** (744) 484-4583. _www.sectur.guerrero.gob.mx_. Other Pacific resort towns of interest are **Ixtapa** in Guerrero, **Manzanillo** in Colima, or **Vallarta** in Jalisco. _www.ixtapa-zihuatanejo.com_, _www.gomanzanillo.com_, _www.puertovallarta.net_.

Also in Jalisco is **Guadalajara,** Mexico's second largest city, modern and contemporary, representing the essence of _being a Mexican_ due to its traditions (home of Tequila and Mariachi music) and conservative ideas imbued with the spirit of its nearly 500 years of history. _http://guadalajaramx.ags.myareaguide.com_.

To the east of Mexico's capital is **Puebla**. Situated amidst wild and mountainous scenery, Puebla is renowned for its ceramics as well as the snow-capped volcanoes of **Popocatépetl** (dormant) and **Ixtacoihuatl** (extinct) and nearby **Cholula**, a pre-Columbian religious centre. Puebla is also the home of _mole_, an unusual sauce made up of the odd combination of chocolate and chilli—usually served over turkey or chicken—and, against all odds, absolutely delicious. *www.turismopuebla.com.mx*.

BEYOND CENTRAL MEXICO

When the sea beckons, head east to Mexico's chief port since the days of the Spanish invasion, **Veracruz**. Cortes landed here in 1519 and with the advent of the gold and silver trade to Europe, Veracruz became a frequent point of attack by British and French forces. These days, it's a sometimes calm and bohemian port city with influences split between old Spain and the Caribbean. Veracruz offers the carefree attitude of its people, its delicious cuisine and its music. *www.veracruz.gob.mx*.

Start with a traditional *lechero* (coffee with milk) at **La Parroquia**, continue with a trip to the **Veracruz Aquarium** (the largest in Latin America), the legendary fortress of **San Juan de Ulúa** or try different diving, kayaking or sport fishing. At night music takes over the plazas where the people of Veracruz gather to dance Danzón. You can also hear the sound of harps, violins, guitars and pianos in **Los Portales** or experience the endless nights of Veracruz at a bar or a nightclub like **La Casona de la Condesa**, Callejón de la Lagunilla No.17. (229) 933-5451.

Heading south from Mexico City, there's **Oaxaca,** a city preserved for centuries where the Colonial style still radiates through the altarpieces and green stone of its buildings. The legacy of different Pre-Hispanic cultures lives on in its goldsmiths, handicrafts, cuisines, music and colourful fiestas, streets and markets. *www.oaxaca-travel.com*. Near Oaxaca you will find the Zapotec centre of **Monte Albán** and the Mixtec site at **Mitla** to explore (see *Ancient Civilisations*).

The state of Oaxaca has wonderful beaches such as **Huatulco, Puerto Escondido, Zipolite**, and **Puerto Angel. Tourism Office** (951) 516-0123. *www.oaxaca.gob.mx/sedetur*.

Moving further southeast into the beautiful, lush and untouched territory in the **Yucatan**, you are in the land of the Maya. The astounding Mayan ruins at **Palenque, Chichén Itzá** and **Uxmal** (see *Ancient Civilisations Box*) contrast sharply with the modern Caribbean resort towns of **Cancun** and **Cozumel.** *www.cancun.com*. *www.cozumel.net*. NB. This area sustained considerable hurricane damage in October 2005. It is advisable to check carefully on the pace of the recovery from the devastation before going here.

Prices in **Cancun** are at New York levels, the hotel strip is as gaudy as anywhere in Florida, but the beaches are beautiful and free and the sea is deep blue, warm and inviting. A perfect end to a trip to Mexico? Perhaps, especially if you can combine soaking up the sun on the beach with a visit to **Isla Mujeres** for snorkeling in turquoise waters *www.isla-mujeres.net/home.htm*, an excursion to **Tulum** on the coast, or to **Chichén Itzá** inland. **Tourism Office** (998) 881-9000.

Appendix   TABLE OF WEIGHTS AND MEASURES

Conversion to and from the metric system

Mexico employs the metric system. **Canada** has almost completed the changeover to metric, and the **United States** as yet uses it only sporadically and within its National Parks.

Temperature

°C	°F
50°C	120°F
45°C	110°F
40°C	100°F
35°C	90°F
30°C	80°F
25°C	70°F
20°C	60°F
15°C	50°F
10°C	40°F
5°C	30°F
0°C	20°F
-5°C	10°F
-10°C	0°F
-15°C	

Fahrenheit into Centigrade/Celsius: subtract 32 from Fahrenheit temperature, then multiply by 5, then divide by 9. *Centigrade/Celsius into Fahrenheit:* multiply Centigrade/Celsius by 9, then divide by 5 then add 32.

Linear Measure

0.3937 inches	1 centimetre
1 inch	2.54 centimetres
1 foot (12 in)	0.3048 metres
1 yard (3 ft)	0.9144 metres
39.37 inches	1 metre
0.621 miles	1 kilometre
1 mile (5280 ft)	1.6093 kilometres
3 miles	4.8 kilometres
10 miles	16 kilometres
60 miles	98.6 kilometres
100 miles	160.9 kilometres

Weight

0.0353 ounces	1 gram
1 ounce	28.3495 grams
1 pound (16 oz)	453.59 grams
2.2046 pounds	1 kilogram
1 ton (2000 lbs)	907.18 kilograms

Liquid Measure

1 US fluid ounce	0.0296 litres
1 US pint (16 US fl oz)	0.4732 litres
1 US quart (2 US pints)	0.9464 litres
1.0567 US quarts	1 litre
1 US gallon (4 US quarts)	3.7854 litres
3 US gallons	11.3 litres
4 US gallons	15.1 litres
10 US gallons	37.8 litres
15 US gallons	56.8 litres

The British imperial gallon (used in Canada) has 20 fluid ounces and 4 imperial quarts and is equal to 4.546 litres.

Speed

25 km/h	equals (approx.)	15 m.p.h.
40 km/h	equals (approx.)	25 m.p.h.
50 km/h	equals (approx.)	30 m.p.h.
60 km/h	equals (approx.)	37 m.p.h.
80 km/h	equals (approx.)	50 m.p.h.
100 km/h	equals (approx.)	60 m.p.h.
112 km/h	equals (approx.)	70 m.p.h.

INDEX

AMENDMENTS TO THIS GUIDE

The detail, accuracy and usefulness of future editions of this Guide depend greatly on your help. Share the benefit of your experiences with other travellers by sending us as much information as you can on events, accommodation, eating places, places of interest, entertainment, travel and general tips on things to see and do.

Amendments and suggestions can be emailed to: _Moneywiseguide@bunacusa.org_. Or you can use the printed forms below and on the next page. Additional information can be sent on separate sheets of paper. If you are suggesting new hotels, eating places, places to see, etc., please give **full** information: ie. **correct name, address, phone numbers, price, website** and so on. **This is very important**. Without complete information your special 'hot' tip may not get published. Thank you! We welcome your feedback

Please use these slips _only_ for this guidebook information and not for any other BUNAC publications. Completed slips and other information should be sent to: General Editor, _The Moneywise Guide to North America_, BUNAC, 16 Bowling Green Lane, London EC1R 0QH, England.
Or to:
Moneywise Guide, BUNAC, PO Box 430, Southbury, CT 06488, USA.

The deadline for information to be included in the 2007 edition of the Guide is 16th October, 2006.

Place: Date:

Subject: Page no:

Correction/Addition   Comments
